TREATMENT DEVELOPMENT STRATEGIES FOR ALZHEIMER'S DISEASE

edited by
Thomas Crook, PhD
Raymond T. Bartus, PhD
Steven Ferris, PhD
Samuel Gershon, MD

Published by Mark Powley Associates, Inc.

Published by Mark Powley Associates, Inc.
Copyright© 1986 by Mark Powley Associates, Inc.
15 Meigs Avenue, Madison, Connecticut 06443

Printed in the United States of America 🏴

ISBN: 0-943378-05-2

DEDICATED
in memory of
G. Harold and Leila Y. Mathers

CONTRIBUTORS

Harvey Altman, PhD
Department of Psychiatry
Lafayette Clinic
951 East Lafayette
Detroit, Michigan 48207

Roberto Amador, MD
Rockefeller University
1230 York Avenue
New York, New York 10021

Curtis A. Bagne, PhD
Lafayette Clinic and
Wayne State University School of Medicine
Detroit, Michigan 48207

William A. Banks, MD
Veterans Administration Medical Center
1601 Perdido Street
New Orleans, Louisiana 70146

Raymond T. Bartus, PhD
Department of Central Nervous
System Research
Medical Research Division of
American Cyanamid Company
Pearl River, New York 10965

Michel Baudry, PhD
Department of Psychobiology and Center for
Neurobiology of Learning and Memory
University of California at Irvine
Irvine, California 92717

Jan K. Blusztajn, PhD
Department of Applied Biological Sciences
Massachusetts Institute of Technology
Cambridge, Massachusetts 02139

David M. Bowen, MD
Institute of Neurology
University of London
The National Hospital
Queens Square
London WC1 3BG England

Gösta Bucht, MD
Umeå Dementia Research Group
Department of Geriatric and
Long-Term Care Medicine
University of Umeå
S-901 87 Umeå, Sweden

Gabriella Calderini, PhD
Department of Pharmacology
University of Florida Medical School
Gainesville, Florida 32610

S. Calzolari, PhD
Fidia Neurobiological Research Laboratories
Via Ponte della Fabbrica 3/a
Abano Terme, Italy

Joy Cavagnaro, PhD
Genetic and Immunotoxicology Laboratory
Hazelton Biotechnology Corporation
9200 Leesburg Turnpike
Vienna, Virginia 22180

L. Cavicchioli, PhD
Fidia Neurobiological Research Laboratory
Via Ponte della Fabbrica 3/a
Abano Terme, Italy

Ina Cholst, MD
Department of Obstetrics and Gynecology
New York Hospital - Cornell Medical Center
525 E. 68th Street
New York, New York 10021

Gene D. Cohen, MD, PhD
Director, Program on Aging
National Institute of Mental Health
Rockville, Maryland 20857

Carl Cotman, PhD
Department of Psychobiology
University of California at Irvine
Irvine, California 92717

Fulton T. Crews, PhD
Department of Pharmacology
University of Florida Medical School
Gainesville, Florida 32610

Thomas Crook, PhD
Memory Assessment Clinics, Inc.
8311 Wisconsin Avenue
Bethesda, Maryland 20814

R. Dal Toso, PhD
Fidia Neurobiological Research Laboratories
Via Ponte della Fabbrica 3/a
Abano Terme, Italy

Peter Davies, PhD
Departments of Pathology and Neuroscience
Albert Einstein College of Medicine
1300 Morris Park Avenue
Bronx, New York 10461

Alan N. Davison, DSc, FRC Path
Institute of Neurology
University of London
The National Hospital
Queens Square
London WC1 3BG England

Reginald L. Dean, MS
Department of Central Nervous
System Research
Medical Research Division of
American Cyanamid Company
Pearl River, New York 10965

Howard Fillit, MD
Rockefeller University
1230 York Avenue
New York, New York 10021

Stephen K. Fisher, PhD
Department of Central Nervous
System Research
Medical Research Division of
American Cyanamid Company
Pearl River, New York 10965

Christopher J. Fowler, PhD
Umeå Dementia Research Group
Department of Geriatric and
Long-Term Care Medicine
University of Umeå
S-901 87 Umeå, Sweden

Don Marshall Gash, PhD
Department of Anatomy
University of Rochester
School of Medicine and Dentistry
Rochester, New York 14642

Samuel Gershon, MD
Lafayette Clinic and
Wayne State University School of Medicine
Detroit, Michigan 48207

Gary E. Gibson, PhD
Burke Rehabilitation Center
Cornell Medical Center
White Plains, New York 10605

Rueben A. Gonzales, PhD
Department of Pharmacology
University of Florida Medical School
Gainesville, Florida 32610

Robert E. Harbaugh, MD
Section of Neurosurgery
Dartmouth-Hitchcock Medical Center
Hanover, New Hampshire 03756

Pamela G. Holbrook, MS
Department of Applied Biological Sciences
Massachusetts Institute of Technology
Cambridge, Massachusetts 02139

Leo Hollister, MD
Veterans Administration Medical Center
3081 Miranda Avenue
Palo Alto, California 94304

Abba J. Kastin, MD
Veterans Administration Medical Center
1601 Perdido Street
New Orleans, Louisiana 70146

Jeffrey H. Kordower, PhD
Department of Anatomy
University of Rochester
School of Medicine and Dentistry
Rochester, New York 14642

Neil M. Kurtz, MD
Clinical CNS Research
Bristol Myers Company
Wallingford, Connecticut 06492

Philip Landfield, PhD
Departments of Physiology
and Pharmacology
Bowman Gray School of Medicine
Wake Forest University
300 South Hawthorne Road
Winston-Salem, North Carolina 27103

Karin Larsen
Department of Pharmacology
University of Florida Medical School
Gainesville, Florida 32610

John Larson, PhD
Department of Psychobiology
Center for Neurobiology of
Learning and Memory
University of California at Irvine
Irvine, California 92717

Paul Leber, MD
Office of New Drug Evaluation
National Center for Drugs and Biologics
Food and Drug Administration
Rockville, Maryland 20857

A. Leon, PhD
Fidia Neurobiological Research Laboratories
Via Ponte della Fabbrica 3/a
Abano Terme, Italy

Mordechai Liscovitch, PhD
Department of Applied Biological Sciences
Massachusetts Institute of Technology
Cambridge, Massachusetts 02139

Victoria Luine, PhD
Rockefeller University
1230 York Avenue
New York, New York 10021

Gary Lynch, PhD
Department of Psychobiology
Center for Neurobiology of
Learning and Memory
University of California at Irvine
Irvine, California 92717

Jean-Claude Maire, PhD
Department de Pharmacologia
Centre Medical Universitaire
Geneva, Switzerland

Charlotte Mauron
Department of Applied Biological Sciences
Massachusetts Institute of Technology
Cambridge, Massachusetts 02139

Bruce S. McEwen, PhD
Rockefeller University
1230 York Avenue
New York, New York 10021

Edwin M. Meyer, PhD
Department of Pharmacology
University of Florida Medical School
Gainesville, Florida 32610

Howard J. Normile, PhD
Department of Psychiatry
Lafayette Clinic
951 East Lafayette
Detroit, Michigan 48207

Mary F.D. Notter, PhD
Department of Anatomy
University of Rochester
School of Medicine and Dentistry
Rochester, New York 14642

Debbie Otero
Department of Pharmacology
University of Florida Medical School
Gainesville, Florida 32610

Christine Peterson, PhD
Burke Rehabilitation Center
Cornell Medical Center
White Plains, New York 10605

William M. Petrie, MD
Department of Psychiatry
Vanderbilt University School of Medicine
Nashville, Tennessee 37232

Nunzio Pomaro, MD
The Nathan S. Kline Institute
for Psychiatric Research
Orangeburg, New York 10962

Robert Raulli
Department of Pharmacology
University of Florida Medical School
Gainesville, Florida 32610

U. Ingrid Richardson, PhD
Department of Applied Biological Sciences
Massachusetts Institute of Technology
Cambridge, Massachusetts 02139

Donald S. Robinson, MD
Clinical CNS Research
Bristol Myers Company
Wallingford, Connecticut 06492

Eugene Roberts, PhD
Department of Neurobiochemistry
Beckman Research Institute
of the City of Hope
Duarte, California 91010

John Rotrosen, MD
Psychiatry Service
New York Veterans Administration
Medical Center
408 First Avenue
New York, New York 10010

Robert M. Sapolsky, MD, PhD
Mather Fellows of the Life Sciences
Research Foundation
The Clayton Foundation Laboratories
for Peptide Biology
The Salk Institute
San Diego, California 92138

Michael Stanley, PhD
Department of Psychiatry
Columbia University and
New York State Psychiatric Institute
New York, New York 10032

Mariateresa Tacconi, PhD
Instituto di Ricerche Farmacologiche
Mario Negri
Milan, Italy

Cynthia Theiss
Department of Pharmacology
University of Florida Medical School
Gainesville, Florida 32610

G. Toffano, PhD
Fidia Neurobiological Research Laboratories
Via Ponte della Fabbrica 3/a
Abano Terme, Italy

William Wallace, PhD
Umeå Dementia Research Group
Department of Geriatric and
Long-Term Care Medicine
University of Umeå
S-901 87 Umeå, Sweden

Herman Weinreb, MD
Rockefeller University
1230 York Avenue
New York, New York 10021

Peter J. Whitehouse, MD, PhD
Departments of Neurology and Neuroscience
Neuropathology Laboratory
The Johns Hopkins University
School of Medicine
Baltimore, Maryland 21205

Bengt Winblad, MD
Umeå Dementia Research Group
Department of Geriatric and Long-Term
Care Medicine
University of Umeå
S-901 87 Umeå, Sweden

Richard Wurtman, MD
Department of Applied Biological Sciences
Massachusetts Institute of Technology
Cambridge, Massachusetts 02139

John B. Zabriskie, MD
Rockefeller University
1230 York Avenue
New York, New York 10021

Steven F. Zornetzer, PhD
Office of Naval Research
800 North Quincy Street
Arlington, Virginia 22217

Foreword

Gene D. Cohen, MD, PhD

At the beginning of the 20th century, only 4% of the United States' population was 65 years of age or older. Today that figure exceeds 11% and, if present trends continue, it will reach 20% within 50 years. In absolute numbers, the over-65 American population has grown from 3 million persons in 1900 to more than 27 million by the mid-1980's and will grow to fully 50 million persons by the year 2030. Similar demographic changes are occurring in many industrialized nations.

While progress in treating illness and in promoting health has played an important role in extending longevity and improving the quality of later life for more and more Americans, certain disorders have loomed larger among the aged. Alzheimer's disease, in particular, stands out because of its devastating impact on individuals, families, and society, in general.

Alzheimer's disease is a brain disorder of unknown etiology that is characterized by a progressive loss of memory and intellectual function. It is estimated that approximately 6% of people over 65 suffer from this dread illness, while over half of the residents of nursing homes are diagnosed as having Alzheimer's disease or a related disorder. Nursing home costs associated with this disorder alone have been calculated to exceed $15 billion a year in the United States. The prevalence of Alzheimer's disease increases with advancing age, causing great public health concern with the age group 85 and older expected to grow seven-fold in numbers between the years 1980 and 2050—from 2.2 million to 16 million during this period.

National and federal attention to the enormity of the problem has been growing significantly over the past few years. Several national institutes have formed an important partnership in expanding research efforts focused on Alzheimer's disease, while a Secretarial Task Force chaired by the assistant secretary for health has been formed to further coordinate this process in the Department of Health and Human Services. The concern and involvement of families has similarly become dramatically apparent with the remarkable growth and contributions of the Alzheimer's Disease and Related Disorders Association.

Still, the cause of and cure for Alzheimer's disease remain elusive. Scientifically, Alzheimer's disease has emerged as one of the great mysteries in modern day science — a disorder with increasing but diverse clues that are taking us down different pathways in the fashion of a veritable "whodunnit" mystery saga. The search for its cause has taken us from the corners of the globe to the depths of the brain. The corners of the globe route led investigators to the highlands of New Guinea, where one of the early hypotheses as to etiology emerged out of the study of a related disorder. The trip to the depths of the brain has been enabled by new brain imaging technology such as the PET Scan, through which we have also entered a new frontier of research on the brain and on relationships between brain and behavior. The clues for cracking the mystery of Alzheimer's disease continue to mount, and in the process a host of new ideas are emerging with regard to new strategies for treating this disorder.

The National Institute of Mental Health (NIMH), working very closely with other federal research programs and private industry, has been particularly active in helping to generate ideas and to support studies in this area. In 1981, NIMH coordinated a government/industry/academia collaboration that resulted in a publication entitled *Strategies for the Development of an Effective Treatment for Senile Dementia* (Crook & Gershon). This publication led to a number of creative and extremely interesting drug trials. The very encouraging response to this book on the part of investigators in many laboratories in America and in other countries as well has resulted in numerous requests for a follow-up publication with the same goal. This is the purpose of the present book, whose contributors reflect the extraordinary scientific energy and creative thinking that we hope will soon lead to new treatment breakthroughs for Alzheimer's disease.

REFERENCES

Crook, T., & Gershon, S. (1981). *Strategies for the development of an effective treatment for senile dementia.* New Canaan, Conn: Mark Powley Associates.

Preface

The objective of this book is to explore innovative approaches to the development of an effective treatment for Alzheimer's disease (AD) and related disorders. We were privileged to have an outstanding group of senior neuroscientists approach this task from a number of different perspectives. Each of these investigators was asked to develop a chapter providing a rationale to guide drug development in AD and to conclude the chapter with specific recommendations for future clinical trials. Chapter authors were asked to be as specific as possible in describing the pharmacologic characteristics of an "ideal" therapeutic agent for AD and asked to consider whether any existing compounds approximate these characteristics and, thus, merit consideration for clinical trials.

We believe that chapter authors were remarkably successful in introducing creative, new ideas that will substantially broaden the search for an effective treatment for AD. Throughout the book the reader will find recommendations for specific strategies, and often specific compounds, to be evaluated in clinical research.

This volume is the third in a series by the same publisher aimed at the development of an effective treatment for AD and related disorders. The first volume, *Strategies for the Development of an Effective Treatment for Senile Dementia,* was published in 1981 and the second, *Assessment in Geriatric Psychopharmacology,* was published late in 1983. The objective of the first book was much the same as the present volume and the objective of the second was to present a straightforward guide to assessing drug effects in clinical trials. The readers of both the first book and this book will be struck by advances made in neuroscience research during the past five years that are relevant to AD. This progress provides a basis for hope that a treatment for this tragic disorder will be developed in the near future.

Financial support for this publication and for a meeting of chapter authors during 1985 was provided by the foundation formed by the persons in whose memory this book is dedicated, the G. Harold and Leila Y. Mathers Charitable Foundation, and by the following companies: Ciba-Geigy Corporation; Fidia Pharmaceutical Corporation; Miles Pharmaceuticals; Sandoz, Inc.; Schering-Plough Corporation; UCB s.a.; American Cyanamid Corporation; Johnson and Johnson; McNeil Pharmaceuticals; Intermedics Infusaid, Inc.; Hoechst-Roussel, Inc.; Berlex Laboratories, Inc.; Hoffman-La Roche, Inc.; Warner Lambert, Parke-Davis, Inc.; A. H. Robins Company; Merck and Company; Bristol-Myers Company; E. I. Dupont De Nemours and Company; G. D. Searle and Company; and the Pennwalt Corporation. Without the very generous support and the deep commitment to AD research of the Mathers Foundation and the individual companies listed, this project would not have been possible.

In addition to the chapter authors and the organizations that made this publication possible, we wish to thank Ms. Lillian Altman, Ms. Ellen Lyon, Ms. Linda Martin, and Ms. Joan Reynolds of Memory Assessment Clinics, Inc., and Ms. Janice Chillemi and her staff at Mark Powley Associates, Inc., for their excellent and tireless editorial and production efforts. Finally, we sincerely thank Dr. Albert A. Manian, the Fund for Medical Research and Education, and the Brain Research Fund of Michigan, Inc. for their invaluable contributions to this project.

The development of an effective treatment for AD is likely to require a major collaborative effort on the part of talented and dedicated individuals from academia, industry, and government. We believe that this publication provides evidence that such an effort is underway and that victims of AD and members of their families now have reason for hope.

The Editors

TABLE OF CONTENTS

Foreword . . . . Gene D. Cohen, MD, PhD
Preface . . . . The Editors

Chapter   **Page**

1 Establishing the Efficacy of Drugs With
Psychogeriatric Indications
Paul Leber, MD **1**

2 Drugs to Treat Age-Related Cognitive Disorders:
On the Threshold of a New Era in the
Pharmaceutical Industry
Raymond T. Bartus, PhD **15**

3 Can the Pathophysiology of Dementia Lead to
Rational Therapy?
David M. Bowen, PhD, and
Alan N. Davison, DSc, FRC Path **35**

4 Beyond the Transmitter-Based Approach to
Alzheimer's Disease
Bengt Winblad, MD, Gosta Bucht, MD,
Christopher J. Fowler, PhD and
William Wallace, PhD **67**

5 Synaptic Plasticity in the Hippocampus: Implications
for Alzheimer's Disease
Carl W. Cotman, PhD,
Manuel Nieto-Sampedro, PhD, and
James W. Geddes, PhD **99**

6 Proteases, Neuronal Stability, and Brain Aging:
An Hypothesis
Gary Lynch, PhD, John Larson, PhD, and
Michel Baudry, PhD **119**

Chapter		Page

7 Stress, Glucocorticoids, and Their Role in Degenerative Changes in the Aging Hippocampus
Robert M. Sapolsky, MD, PhD, and
Bruce S. McEwen, PhD **151**

8 Guides Through the Labyrinth of AD: Dehydroepiandrosterone, Potassium Channels, and the C4 Component of Complement
Eugene Roberts, PhD **173**

9 Preventive Approaches to Normal Brain Aging and Alzheimer's Disease
Philip W. Landfield, PhD **221**

10 Aging, Peptides, and the Blood-Brain Barrier: Implications and Speculations
William A. Banks, MD, and
Abba J. Kastin, MD **245**

11 Possible Immunological Treatments for Alzheimer's Disease
Joy Cavagnaro, PhD **267**

12 Are Gangliosides a Rational Pharmacological Tool for the Treatment of Chronic Neurodegenerative Diseases?
R. Dal Taso, PhD, L. Cavicchioli, PhD,
S. Calzolari, PhD, A. Leon, PhD, and
G. Toffano, PhD **293**

13 Hormonal Therapy for Alzheimer's Disease
Howard Fillit, MD, Herman Weinreb, MD,
Ina Cholst, MD, Victoria Luine, PhD,
Roberto Amador, MD, John B. Zabriskie, MD, and
Bruce S. McEwen, PhD **311**

14 The Noradrenergic Locus Coeruleus and Senescent Memory Dysfunction
Steven F. Zornetzer, PhD **337**

15 Sertonin, Learning, and Memory: Implications for the Treatment of Dementia
Harvey Altman, PhD, and
Howard J. Normile, PhD **361**

Chapter	Page

16 Presynaptic and Postsynaptic Approaches to Enhancing Central Cholinergic Neurotransmission
Fulton T. Crews, PhD, Edwin M. Meyer, PhD, Rueben A. Gonzales, PhD, Cynthia Theiss, Debbie Otero, Karin Larsen, Robert Raulli, and Gabriella Calderini, PhD **385**

17 Cholinergic Treatment for Age-Related Memory Disturbances
Raymond T. Bartus, PhD, Reginald L. Dean, MS, and Stephen K. Fisher, PhD **421**

18 The Functional Status of Central Muscarinic Receptors in Alzheimer's Disease: Assessment and Therapeutic Implications
Nunzio Pomara, MD, and Michael Stanley, PhD .. **451**

19 Cholinergic and Somatostatin Deficits in the Alzheimer Brain
Peter Davies, PhD **473**

20 Development of Neurotransmitter-Specific Therapeutic Approaches in Alzheimer's Disease
Peter J. Whitehouse, MD, PhD **483**

21 Consideration of Neurotransmitters and Calcium Metabolism in Therapeutic Design
Gary E. Gibson, PhD, and Christine Peterson, PhD **499**

22 Membrane Lipids: Can Modification Reduce Symptoms or Halt Progression of Alzheimer's Disease?
John Rotrosen, MD **519**

23 Pathogenesis: Possible Role of Choline Phospholipids
Jan K. Blusztajn, PhD, Pamela G. Holbrook, MS, Mordechai Liscovitch, PhD, Jean-Claude Maire, PhD, Charlotte Mauron, BS, U. Ingrid Richardson, PhD, Mariateresa Tacconi, PhD, and Richard J. Wurtman, MD **539**

Chapter   Page

24 Drug Delivery to the Brain by Central Infusion:
Clinical Application of a Chemical Paradigm of
Brain Function
Robert E. Harbaugh, MD **553**

25 Cognitive Dysfunctions and Neural Implants
Don Marshall Gash, PhD, Mary F.D. Noter, PhD, and
Jeffrey H. Kordower, PhD **567**

26 Alzheimer's Disease: Strategies for
Treatment and Research
Curtis A. Bagne, PhD, Nunzio Pomara, MD,
Thomas Crook, PhD, and Samuel Gershon, MD . **585**

27 Pharmacologic Treatment — From the Viewpoint of
the Clinical Investigator
William M. Petrie, MD **639**

28 A Scientific and Pharmaceutical
Industry Perspective
Donald S. Robinson, MD, and Neil M. Kurtz, MD **655**

29 Summary and Conclusions
Leo Hollister, MD **671**

Index **678**

1

Establishing the Efficacy of Drugs With Psychogeriatric Indications

Paul Leber, MD

In 1981, the editors of this volume asked that I write a chapter for a book they were compiling entitled *Assessment in Geriatric Psychopharmacology* (Leber, 1983a). They asked that I address the question, "On the basis of what evidence is a drug considered to be efficacious for use in geriatric patients?"

Although the last 4 years have seen an enormous increase in the amount of basic and clinical research in the fields of aging and dementia, the problems confronting those who seek to market drugs for so-called "psychogeriatric" indications have remained essentially unchanged. Consequently, I have agreed to the republication of the original chapter virtually unaltered. (I have, however, included occasional comments within brackets in cases where hindsight now suggests that further discussion of a point is warranted.)

While many of the clinically vexing issues identified in the original chapter remain unresolved, they have not been ignored by workers in the field. To the contrary, over the past 4 years, several investigators, including the editors of this volume, have developed various strategies and procedural methods intended to improve the reliability and validity of measures and techniques used for evaluating drug effects in dementia and aging; and these efforts are to be applauded. Indeed, even a set of clinical anchor points for the Sandoz Clinical Assessment Geriatric Scale (SCAG) has been published for the first time, potentially repairing one major weakness of the scale (Venn, 1983). Of course, the utility, sensitivity, reliability, and validity of the newer techniques have yet to be fully examined, but the very existence of multiple devices intended to evaluate dementia and cognitive impairment makes it possible to assess issues of concurrent and external validity in a way not possible a few years ago.

It is still too soon to tell whether advances in psychometric instrumentation (e.g., electronic devices for assessing motor and cognitive performance) and medical diagnostic techniques including brain imaging (e.g., NMR, PET) and brain function/state assessment devices (e.g., EEG power analysis, etc.) will have a substantive effect upon the field of psychogeriatric drug development. However, it is clear that strides are being made toward developing better means to diagnose and classify impaired patients, a result that can only increase the chances for successful development of any drug with an action restricted to a specific type of cognitive impairment (i.e., the use of precise and biologically meaningful diagnostic criteria for subject selection can increase the prevalence of patients admitted to a study who have the potential to respond to drug treatment).

In any case, my apology for republication given, I return to the original chapter and the question asked.

The strictly legal regulatory response to the question is straightforward. The standards of evidence that are applied to "psychogeriatric" drugs are, by force of law, identical to those applied to any other class of drug product. Although correct, I believe this reply fails to respond to the actual concerns underlying the editors' question. What investigators in the field of clinical geriatric psychopharmacology really want to discover is what sort of evidence and argument is likely to convince the Food and Drug Administration (FDA) and its advisors that a given drug with a claimed psychogeriatric indication is worthy of approval.

CONTROVERSIES IN GERIATRIC PSYCHOPHARMACOLOGY

As the prescient reader well knows, there is little likelihood that I, or anyone, can offer any guaranteed recipe for successful psychogeriatric drug development. The field of geriatric psychopharmacology is a controversial one. Consequently, there is no widely accepted set of rules, as there is in other fields, for dealing with the usual sort of issues that arise in the course of the development and study of a new drug treatment. Indeed, even the most fundamental issues are unsettled.

There is, to start, no general understanding of the term psychogeriatric drug, and even my definition of the term may be a potential source of controversy. In this chapter, I use the term to refer to drug products of two types: (a) those intended to treat any cognitive, emotional, or behavioral deficit alleged to be caused by "normal" aging, and (b) those intended as a treatment of a disease or condition (or some epiphenomena of the disease or condition) that is found solely, or at least most frequently, among the elderly. Admittedly, this distinction is largely heuristic and is made mainly to draw attention to the conceptual origin of the important regulatory issue of "pseudospecificity" in labeling claims discussed later in this chapter.

The distinction between age-caused and age-associated pathology can itself be a controversial matter. First, an attempt to make the distinction presents somewhat of a conundrum. Is there truly a meaningful difference between phenomena due to "aging" and those due to the effects of any number of diseases and injuries that have assaulted the body and soul of the older subject? Moreover, as a practical matter, given the current state of knowledge, how would one demonstrate that a specific entity was age- rather than disease-related?

The problem of defining "age-related impairment" should become moot if one can select a specific disease or condition as a goal of treatment (e.g., Alzheimer's disease [AD]). However, a worker in the field will not escape controversy this easily. Not all diseases or syndromes alleged to occur in the elderly are as widely accepted as is AD. A syndrome may be challenged as an invalid construct, or it may be so inadequately characterized as to be of little practical use. Some syndromes may be merely posing as diseases and represent little more than age-attributed phenomena. One may reasonably inquire, for example, whether "benign senescent forgetfulness" is a disease or even a meaningful syndrome. Some older individuals complain of memory deficits, but one may wonder if their forgetfulness has anything to do with their "senescence"; certainly similar complaints are seen in the middle-aged.

Controversies in the field are not restricted to issues of nomenclature and diagnosis. A debate over ethics plagues psychiatry, especially geropsychiatry and, in turn, the developer of psychogeriatric drugs. Even if a behavior seen in the elderly is considered to be a sign of psychopathology, not everyone will agree that the behavior is an appropriate target of drug treatment. It is a matter of controversy, often a bitter one, whether drugs should be used to control what can be seen merely as obnoxious behaviors in a population of disadvantaged individuals who lack a practical ability to defend themselves and their civil rights.

Beyond disputes about the construct validity of specific age-related impairments and the legitimacy of treatment goals lies a cluster of problems that arise because there is no widely accepted set of operational criteria to identify appropriate elderly subjects for participation in clinical drug trials.

As a means for selecting subjects for clinical studies, arbitrary age requirements and ad hoc investigator judgments have proven to be poor substitutes for the fully developed and generally accepted diagnostic algorithms that are available in other fields of clinical pharmacology. If experts can argue about the identifying characteristics or diagnosis of subjects in a clinical investigation, the study must be considered seriously flawed. For example, if the data collected fail to establish that the patients entered in a study have dementia, no amount of post hoc effort and analysis will make the study a source of evidence on the product's efficacy as an antidementia agent. [Unless, perhaps, independent records exist that can be used to establish the diagnoses of the patients entered.]

Lack of agreement on the rules for diagnosis in geropsychiatry is both a consequence and a reflection of a more fundamental problem in the field. The various phenomena that are the objects of treatment — pathologic signs, symptoms, behaviors — are not precisely defined. There is, therefore, an understandable lack of consensus among experts about which phenomena should be expected to respond to drug treatment and what to call any response that occurs. Thus, there is no clear definition for an antidementia agent. In the absence of general agreement about the phenomena that make up these various constructs, it is not too surprising that there are few, generally accepted, quantitative measures of the constructs. Thus, there is no single, standard battery of tests to measure drug-induced global improvement in "cognition," "judgment," or "dementia."

As if all these problems were not enough, the lack of a "benchmark" drug product for the treatment of dementia, or for any of the putative age-related impairments, creates uncertainty about the type and magnitude of drug response that experts will accept as clinically meaningful. Although the Federal Food, Drug, and Cosmetic Act does not specify a minimum degree of efficacy for drug approval, the agency's advisors are obviously influenced by the magnitude of a drug's effect in their assessment of its relative benefits and risks. Thus, the finding of a small drug placebo difference on a rating scale of arguable clinical validity may fail to convince experts that the drug ought to be approved for use.

[It seems important to elaborate on this point. Generally, if the results of a prospectively randomized, concurrently controlled, trial reveal that an experimental drug is superior to either placebo, an active control treatment, or a lower fixed dose of the experimental drug, the agency must accept the finding as evidence of efficacy. Taken on its own, the size of the difference between treatments is irrelevant as long as 1) it is *not* explained by fraud, bias, or chance, and 2) the study design in which the difference was detected allows the difference to be unambiguously attributed to drug effect. Of course, the observed superiority must be demonstrated on some outcome assessment measure validly linked to the product's claimed indication.]

Nonetheless, the prudent sponsor must still consider a product's therapeutic potency in his plans for its development because the therapeutic effect may simply be too insubstantial to justify the risks associated with the product's use.

Obviously, these are but a few of the many difficult and complex issues that must be addressed and at least partially resolved before any specific set of recommendations on psychogeriatric drug development is possible. Indeed, in view of the unsettled state of geriatric psychopharmacology, the FDA has so far elected not to issue guidelines on the development of drugs for the cognitively and emotionally impaired elderly. The agency remains committed to developing guidelines, but believes that there is an inadequate consensus in the field at the moment. Furthermore, Drug Product Class Guidelines are inherently practical documents that generally reflect an extensive experience gained during the successful development of drugs belonging to the particular class. Clearly, we have had minimal experience developing successful psychogeriatric drugs, and it is difficult to draft guidelines based purely on theoretical speculations.

FDA is considering the issuance of general guidelines for the assessment of drugs in the elderly. The aim of these guidelines, however, is not to specify particular procedures, but to assure that sufficient, relevant data are amassed to develop adequate directions for the use of new products in the elderly (Temple, 1985).

Concern has been voiced that the absence of an official set of rules makes the development of drugs for the cognitively and emotionally impaired elderly a risky enterprise and discourages drug development in the field. In my view, this concern is unwarranted. If a drug can exert a measurable, consistent beneficial effect on a legitimate symptom or sign truly related to a geriatric disease or condition, and if it is relatively safe, I have no doubt that the product can be successfully developed and marketed. It would be disingenuous to pretend that the undertaking would be without difficulty; however, the rewards (moral, medical, and financial) would, in my opinion, be commensurate with the effort. With this in mind, in the remainder of the chapter I offer specific suggestions and exhortations about preferred approaches to the development and study of new psychogeriatric drugs.

CRITICAL SECTIONS OF THE CODE OF FEDERAL REGULATIONS

The Federal Food, Drug, and Cosmetic Act sets out the basic requirements for drug approval. These requirements are developed in detail in Title 21 of the Code of Federal Regulation (CFR). It is useful, before discussing specific issues in the development of psychogeriatric drugs, to review three important sections of the Code.

One critical section [21 CFR 314.126]; formerly [21 CFR 314.111(a)(1)(5)(i)] describes the kind and quality of evidence that is necessary to demonstrate drug safety and efficacy. The Code reflects the wisdom of the scientific method and demands that the safety and effectiveness of a new drug be established by "substantial evidence," derived from "adequate and well-controlled investigations, including clinical investigations [conducted] by experts qualified by scientific training and experience." The evidence must be of such quality that it can "fairly and responsibly be concluded by such experts that the drug will have the effect" claimed for it by the sponsor.

A second important section of the Code [21 CFR 314.9(a)(1)] deals with an aspect of drug development that is often neglected until it is too late to do anything but regret the oversight. This section details the kind of information that must be included in the official labeling of a new prescription drug product. If the need to acquire this information is not considered early in the planning of a drug development program, valuable resources may be wasted.

The proposed labeling for a product must provide adequate directions for the prescribing practitioner to use the drug for the purposes for which the drug is approved. The labeling must identify which patients will benefit from using the product, how they will benefit, and how they might be harmed. Indeed, the labeling requirements can be used as an aid in the planning of New Drug Applications submissions. If one can draft a complete label as specified in the Code

[21 CFR 201.57], and provide evidence to support each statement in the draft, the chances are good that the drug product is approvable. On the other hand, if one has difficulty satisfying the labeling requirements or justifying statements in the draft, the product is probably in trouble. For example, in the case of psychogeriatric drugs, the ease with which one can reliably identify the patient population for whom the drug is intended is probably a good guide to how meaningful the clinical trial entry criteria were. Clearly, the need for adequate labeling presents a barrier to the approval of drugs studied in ambiguously defined samples of geriatric subjects.

MAJOR ISSUES IN DRUG DEVELOPMENT

Given the lack of consensus in geropsychiatry and the requirements of our domestic drug law, what matters deserve special attention in the development of a drug product with psychogeriatric indications?

Selecting a Treatment Indication

Because all New Drug Applications are evaluated in light of their claimed indications, the design of a clinical drug development program must consider what claim will be made for the product. Indeed, an inappropriate choice for a product's claimed indication may doom the sponsor's chances for approval before the first patient is studied.

Above all, I would advise the sponsor to avoid claims for diseases or conditions that are not generally recognized as entities sui generis. It is far less risky to develop a drug for "senile dementia" than for some inadequately defined and poorly characterized entity such as "age-related cognitive impairment" or "benign senescent forgetfulness." If a sponsor is tempted to ignore this advice, I suggest that he or she poll the experts! It is better to learn before the start rather than after the completion of a multicenter trial whether most experts reject the diagnostic construct used to select patients for study.

In a similar vein, a sponsor is wise to shun the development of putative remedies designed solely to control obnoxious behaviors (e.g., hostility, uncooperativeness). The specter of a drug product being used to control the cantankerous behavior of a harmless unfortunate who is warehoused in a substandard nursing home is of palpable moral and ethical concern. Responsible experts may reject as inappropriate and illegitimate a sponsor's claim for such a product. Of course, if obnoxious behavior is a reflection of an underlying disease process, some may argue that its treatment is justified. Perhaps so, but the solution then is to develop a treatment for the underlying disease process. To be clear, the Federal Food, Drug, and Cosmetic Act does not speak to this specific issue, but there are very practical reasons for following this advice. Why make the difficult process of psychogeriatric drug development even more difficult by injecting a substantive ethical question into the drug approval process?

Subject Selection

Picking an appropriate indication — that is, a disease, syndrome, or recognized age-related impairment — is only the first step. Careful consideration must be given also to how subjects who suffer from the condition named in the product's indication are selected for participation in clinical trials. There must be assurance that the process used to pit and cull candidates for clinical trials is thorough and reliable. The advice here is the following: Select subjects for entry only if they meet specific eligibility criteria and fail to meet specific exclusion criteria. In turn, describe these criteria in explicit operational terms. In my experience, clinical trials that capture subjects in vague, idiosyncratic, and arbitrary ways are lodestones for criticism. Remember, even if a clinical trial produces positive evidence of a drug effect, it will be of little value if it is not obvious to what patient population the trial results apply. Beware of incomplete diagnostic workups! Even if it is not the usual clinical practice to do a particular test because it is too "academic," do it anyway as long as it does not injure the patient. In short, err in the direction of an exhaustive workup. An "unnecessary" Computerized Axial Tomography (CT) scan may reveal a meningioma, or a "needless" lumbar puncture may reveal neurosyphilis. Again my advice is based on the reasoning given earlier: Confirmation of a result by two or more independent techniques will lend validity to a claim; thoroughness will impress the skeptical. I make no claim that specific definitions, diagnostic algorithms, and thoroughness will preclude diagnostic error, but this approach should ensure that what is done will be unambiguous, potentially repeatable, and favorably received.

Adequate characterization of trial participants does not end with the assignment of a diagnosis. The severity of each patient's illness should be described using a well-known rating or staging instrument if possible. Drug response may well be a function of disease severity. When a disease is characterized by a chronic and progressive course, it can be important to identify the stage of progression of the disease in each subject. In the example of AD, it would be valuable to know whether a drug's effect is observable at all points in the course of the disease or only at some. For example, a drug that acts by stimulating residual, intact brain tissue to compensate for injury to other brain regions might lose effectiveness as the degenerative process progresses. In contrast, a drug that successfully suppresses hallucinations of organic origin may have no reasonable use in the mild, prodromal phases of AD.

"Pseudospecificity"

A well-designed drug development program should lead to an unambiguous conclusion about the efficacy and uses of a drug product. A major hazard for the developer of psychogeriatric drugs is the failure to recognize that certain investigational strategies do not properly evaluate a product's claimed age-related use. Because the agency has rejected and will continue to reject "pseudospecific" labeling claims for drug products — they are not only misleading but inequitable — it is worthwhile to discuss this problem in some detail.

A claim for a drug product is pseudospecific when its apparent specificity arises solely as a consequence of a sponsor's decision to limit the study of the drug to subjects with the specific characteristics or traits cited in the claim. For example, if a drug were selectively evaluated in the elderly (defined as a group whose members exceed some arbitrary age) and were found to have a moderate antidepressant effect, a claim that the product is indicated for depression in the elderly would be pseudospecific. Why? Because the specificity of the drug's effect is not demonstrated; it is merely asserted on specious grounds. To demonstrate that age and drug response are linked requires an evaluation of the drug in not one but all age groups. The issue is, beyond one of reason and logic, one of equity to other sponsors. Why should an incompletely evaluated drug enjoy an unearned and possibly advantageous labeling claim while a fully tested drug product is denied one?

It is important to emphasize that pseudospecificity usually arises when symptoms and not diseases become the indication for a drug's use. If a drug were to be approved for use in a disease (e.g., AD), patient age would be irrelevant and age would not appear in the claimed indication for the product. This point is important to keep in mind, as it is the sponsor's obligation to demonstrate that a labeling claim for a symptomatic treatment is not a pseudospecific claim.

Selecting Measures of Treatment Outcome

Having carefully selected and characterized a patient sample and chosen an appropriate goal of therapy, the sponsor of a psychogeriatric drug product still has many difficult problems to face in the assessment of clinical changes that may be induced by drug effects. Instruments that are used to diagnose a specific pathological condition are not necessarily capable of detecting changes in the condition induced by drug treatment. For example, what should be used to assess drug-induced improvement in AD? Which signs and symptoms of the disease should be followed and with what methods? The concept of dementia is not as clearly defined or as well characterized as one might hope. One speaks, for example, of cognitive impairment as the sine qua non for the diagnosis of AD, and each expert can enumerate the specific deficits that he or she personally believes constitute the construct of cognitive impairment (e.g., decreased ability to attend to tasks, defective short-term memory, inability to abstract). However, it is not at all evident that each expert will generate an identical list. It is prudent, therefore, to be certain that the phenomena selected to represent cognitive impairment in a protocol are broadly accepted by the community.

Agreement on which specific deficits represent the construct of cognitive impairment is critical but insufficient if the protocol also fails to specify how these deficits are detected and how their severity is measured. Even more important, evidence to support the reliability and validity of each measure must be adduced. It is not enough to assert that a given test is an appropriate measure. For example, the validity of word-list recall as a measure of clinically significant memory function can be challenged easily if it is used as a general measure of memory. (However, word-list recall is a good measure of short-term memory, trace consolidation, and some degree of recall from some form of storage.) The more clearly a test or scale is tied to meaningful change in patient behavior or performance, the more acceptable it will be.

One approach to the problem of unvalidated measures is to employ several independent measures of the same phenomena. In contrast to the strategy used in fields with well-established instruments, using redundant rating scales may be helpful in geriatric psychopharmacology. If each of several independent, but unvalidated, instruments gives the same result, a case is made for the validity of the construct measured.

[This recommendation must *not* be misconstrued as a call to evaluate multiple outcomes in the hope of finding one or two among many on which drug and placebo can be discriminated. To the contrary, the suggestion is intended solely to present a strategy for validating clinical measures; it requires that all tests show confirmatory results. "Multiplicity" of outcomes is a major problem in psychopharmacology assessment and is to be avoided (Tukey, 1977).

Obviously, concerns that apply to measures of cognition also apply to measures of all other clinical constructs, including mood, self-care, motivation, and so on. As mentioned earlier, an attempt to develop treatments for abstractions or vague constructs, whether symptoms or syndromes, is quite risky. Unless an established, well-characterized, operational test system exists to detect and measure the construct, challenge is possible no matter how carefully data are collected. Accuracy and precision of measurement do not prove validity. It is worth considering this warning when contemplating the use of a new device or test methodology that is endorsed as valid only by its creator.

Trial Design

One other issue in the demonstration of drug efficacy requires comment: the choice of experimental trial design. In my view, the only acceptable approach is a clinical trial that employs randomized, prospective, concurrent assignment of patients—under totally blind conditions—to the new drug and placebo. An "active" control may be included as well so long as it is clearly understood that proof of efficacy will depend on the demonstration of superiority of the experimental drug to placebo and not on the demonstration of its equivalence to the "active" drug (Leber, 1983b). [One alternative approach to the demonstration of efficacy that has yet to be evaluated fully is the fixed dose, dose-response design. In this design, different fixed doses of the experimental drug are compared. Efficacy is demonstrated by showing that a linear relationship exists between dose and clinical outcome.]

Experts may disagree on the choice between parallel and crossover designs. In my personal view, the parallel design is clearly best for the evaluation of any long-term treatment of a progressive illness. Counterbalanced crossover designs may have some utility in the evaluation of relatively short-term treatments of stable pathologies but, in general, outcomes are often difficult to assess because of treatment order and carryover effects.

Safety Assessment

So far this chapter has focused on matters related to the demonstration of the efficacy of psychogeriatric drugs. The reader must remember, however, that proof of a drug's efficacy is only one of several requirements that must be met before a drug can be approved. As I mentioned earlier, neither the efficacy nor safety of a drug is evaluated in isolation. A regulatory decision to approve a drug reflects, among other things, a judgment (albeit one based on evidence) that the potential benefits of the product, under the conditions of use proposed in the labeling, are worth its risks. Logically, the more beneficial a drug, the more acceptable the risks associated with its use. The converse is also true, however, and this factor must be considered in the design of any psychogeriatric drug development program. If a drug product is expected to produce only modest changes in the condition for which its use is recommended, it must be shown to have a very minimal potential for harm. A careful, thorough, and systematic evaluation of a drug's potential to cause injury is, therefore, critical to the sponsor's case for approval. A drug evaluation program that focuses on efficacy and pays mere lip service to safety will be self-defeating.

The safety assessment should include extensive data about the absorption, distribution, metabolism, and routes of elimination (ADME) of the product. This information is critical for any drug, but is especially important in a population in which disease, concomitant medications, and age itself may have dramatic effects on these ADME parameters.

Because most treatments developed expressly for the elderly are likely to be applied over extended periods of time, the drug assessment program should provide evidence that the product is safe in chronic use. In a population with a large number of risk factors, this may prove to be a difficult task. Indeed, a comment about the design of such studies in the elderly is appropriate.

Demonstration of safety depends, among other things, on the absolute number of patients evaluated. Evidence of relative safety is commonly sought by following a large cohort of drug-treated patients using appropriate tests and examinations. The larger the cohort, the more precisely the risks of drug use can be estimated (Leber, 1982). Consequently, it is common practice to follow the largest drug cohort possible, often without a control cohort, on the assumption that spontaneous adverse events are unlikely to occur. This uncontrolled approach is risky in the elderly because they are at higher risk than other groups for any number and kind of spontaneous untoward events. Indeed, in my opinion, exposure of elderly patients to a new drug without an appropriate control group is a mistake; it can only damage a drug's reputation if something goes wrong spontaneously. The prudent sponsor will, therefore, elect to employ a placebo or active drug control in all safety studies. Although not an absolute protection, this design provides at least a potential opportunity to discriminate between untoward events caused by a drug and those arising by chance.

SUMMARY

Undoubtedly, many of the current difficulties encountered in the development of psychogeriatric drugs are a direct consequence of the relatively modest potency of the current generation of drug products. Although there is considerable interest in the study of aging and its related diseases, the problems of psychogeriatric drug assessment are likely to persist, in my view, until a potent benchmark drug is developed. The past history of psychopharmacology, I believe, supports this prediction. Until the development of phenothiazines, in particular chlorpromazine, was there really any standard system for assessing antipsychotic drugs?

In this chapter, I have attempted to delineate some of the vexing problems that may confront the developer of psychogeriatric drugs. I have offered some comments and advice about possible ways to deal with, or at least minimize, the effect of these problems. There are no insurmountable barriers to the approval of psychogeriatric drugs, but their development and evaluation is likely to remain one of the more trying, and potentially most rewarding, endeavors in clinical pharmacology.

REFERENCES

Leber, P. (1982). Safe passage (how good a guarantee?). *Psychopharmacology Bulletin, 18,* 6-10.

Leber, P. (1983a). Establishing the efficacy of drugs with psychogeriatric indications. In T. Crook, S. Ferris, & R. Bartus (Eds.), *Assessment in geriatric psychopharmacology* (pp. 1-12). New Canaan, CT: Mark Powley Associates, Inc.

Leber, P. (1983b). *The implicit assumptions of active control trials.* Paper presented at the Annual Meeting of the Society for Clinical Trials, St. Louis, MO.

Temple, R. (1985, April). *FDA guidelines for clinical testing of drugs in the elderly.* Paper presented at the DIA Workshop on Geriatric Drug Testing and Development - Practical Applications, Bethesda, MD.

Tukey, J.W. (1977). Some thoughts on clinical trials, especially problems of multiplicity. *Science, 198,* 679-684.

Venn, R.D. (1983). The Sandoz Clinical Assessment-Geriatric (SCAG) Scale. *Gerontology, 29,* 185-198.

2

Drugs to Treat Age-Related Cognitive Disorders: On the Threshold of a New Era in the Pharmaceutical Industry

Raymond T. Bartus, PhD

This chapter is dedicated to the memory and free spirit of Dr. Duncan A. McCarthy, who had the vision to see what might be possible and the courage to campaign to get it started.

During the last 5 to 10 years a number of institutions have exhibited a marked increase in attention toward cognitive problems associated with Alzheimer's disease (AD) and other age-related disturbances. This interest is, in part, related to a growing awareness of the scope of this dehumanizing problem, its potential impact on the economies and social fabric of developed countries, and the projected exacerbation of these problems as unprecedented demographic shifts continue to increase the number and proportion of elderly people in the Western countries and Japan.

There is little question that most authorities concerned with the problem consider pharmacological treatment to be a potentially valuable component of an effective solution. Yet, as with any new area of scientific inquiry, a certain degree of confusion and controversy is associated with the accelerated interest and research activity. Presumably, varying interpretations of these issues are, at least partly, responsible for why a number of pharmaceutical companies have initiated research and development (R & D) programs in this emerging area, while many others continue to take a more cautious, and sometimes skeptical, position. This paper will attempt to identify a number of the more salient or controversial issues related to the concept of developing and using drugs to treat age-related cognitive impairments. These issues will be discussed in terms of the current needs and expectations of the medical community, the impact of changing demographic patterns on these needs, the role the pharmaceutical industry can play in meeting these needs, and the effect that recent advances in the neurobiology of aging may have on achieving success.

THE IMPACT OF UNPRECEDENTED DEMOGRAPHIC SHIFTS ON THE PHARMACEUTICAL INDUSTRY

As a society, we are becoming increasingly older. Already there are more than 25 million people in the United States 65 years and older (U.S. Department of Health and Human Services [USDHHS], 1984), and the number of people in this age bracket is growing more than three times faster than the population as a whole (Lamy, 1980). Additionally, a new demographic class is emerging in Western society — the older old. People in this classification (i.e., around 85 years and older) represent the single, fastest growing segment in the United States and Europe. Indeed, the U.S. Census Bureau projects that people who reached age 65 in 1983 will, on average, live an additional 12 years.

The importance of these numbers to the pharmaceutical industry becomes apparent when the medical condition and treatment approaches related to the elderly are considered. People in this age bracket suffer an average of five different diseases or maladies concurrently (Gryfe, C.I. & Gryfe, B.M., 1984; Lowenstein & Schrier, 1982), and are, in turn, treated with a large and varied array of prescription drugs (Lamy, 1980, 1981; Thompson, Moran, & Nies, 1983a). The annual prescription demand for the aged in 1980 was 11.2 and 14.3 prescriptions per male and female, respectively (i.e., three times that for people under 65) (Lamy, 1980). The amount spent for prescription drugs for the elderly exceeds $3 billion annually in the United States alone (Schmucker, 1984; Vestal, 1982), and is increasing at a rate in excess of 15% annually (Office of Technology Assessment [OTA], 1985).

Moreover, the elderly have idiosyncratic medical needs that differ from those of other age segments in at least two important ways. First, certain diseases become much more prevalent after age 65 (Fuller, 1983), and as the number of people in this age bracket increases, so will the magnitude of the problems associated with these age-related diseases. Secondly, there is a growing awareness that serious complications often occur when conventional pharmaceuticals are used to treat elderly patients, regardless of the medical problem (Thompson, Moran, & Nies, 1983b). Dramatic and unpredictable shifts in the therapeutic window, increased incidence and severity of side effects, and complications due to multiple drug use are just some of the recognized problems faced when drugs are given to elderly patients (Greenblatt, Sellers, & Shader, 1982; Lamy, 1981; Levenson, 1979; Ouslander, 1981; Salzman, 1979; Segal, Thompson, & Floyd, 1979; Siegel, 1982). Thus, problems associated with drug treatment in the elderly population are greater and more specialized, and the market size considerably larger, and growing more rapidly, than seems to be commonly recognized by the pharmaceutical industry. To date, only a handful of companies in the United States have formal programs that directly address geriatric health problems, and these notable exceptions have primarily focused on the same area — Geriatric Cognitive Disturbances. Although the geriatric marketing and sales efforts of European pharmaceutical companies have traditionally been more aggressive, the focus has been similarly narrow, and the R & D approaches certainly no more sophisticated or innovative than those of American laboratories (e.g., see Giurgea & Mourvieff-Lesuisse, 1976; Meier-Ruge et al., 1975; Nandy & Lal, 1976; Nicolaus, 1982; Schindler, Rush, & Fielding, 1984).

COGNITIVE DISTURBANCES IN THE ELDERLY: AN EMERGING AREA IN THERAPEUTICS

Although one might legitimately argue that the industry has thus far been too narrow in its focus toward geriatric pharmaceutical needs, an objective consideration of alternative age-related maladies reveals compelling arguments for giving high priority to programs for treating geriatric cognition, as shown in Table 1.

Over the 10 to 15 years since the earliest programs were first launched in the United States, the points outlined in Table 1 have become even more compelling. This is especially true in light of the increased scientific, government, and media attention and to issues involving the increased numbers of elderly in our society, in general, and to problems associated with senile dementia, in particular.

TABLE 1

Factors Encouraging the Development of Drug Discovery Programs for Geriatric Cognition

1. Number of clinical incidents is high

2. Patient and family concern and complaints are high

3. Problem is closely associated with a medically-recognized disease state (i.e., Alzheimer's disease), facilitating acceptance of eventual treatment

4. Scientific state-of-the-art is sufficiently advanced to allow in-house screening program

5. Competitive situation is excellent

Memory Loss as an Early Symptom of Senile Dementia

Senile dementia (especially AD) is considered to be the number one health problem by the National Institute on Aging (NIA) (Goldsmith, 1984) and is considered by organizations within both the executive (USDHHS, 1984) and legislative branches of the federal government to be reaching epidemic proportions in the United States (OTA, 1985). It is currently listed as the fourth leading medical cause of death (behind heart disease, cancer, and stroke) (Bond, 1983), and accounts for one half of all long-term institutionalization of people over 60 (OTA, 1985). The incidence at age 65 is one in ten, and increases to approximately one in three by age 85 (USDHHS, 1984). Because this latter segment of our population is experiencing the most dramatic increases in absolute and relative numbers, problems associated with dementia are complicated even further and will undoubtedly worsen during the next decade.

The effects of AD on families (Rabins, Mace, & Lucas, 1982) and society (Plum, 1979) are staggering. The disease progresses insidiously, eventually destroying the functional capacity of the brain. This is first manifested in loss of memory and in other cognitive disturbances. Eventually it progresses to the point where its victims are unable to perform even the simplest tasks and can no longer care for themselves (Reisberg, Ferris, & Crook, 1982). Most often this leads to institutionalization or a similar radical solution, at tremendous emotional and financial burdens to families and society (Anderson, 1981; Cowell, 1983; Gwyther & Blazer, 1984). Once Alzheimer's disease begins to progress, the projected life span of the individual is reduced substantially and death usually occurs within 4 to 8 years, either from direct symptoms or secondary complications of the disease.

It is estimated that the federal government currently spends well over $20 billion annually on care, rehabilitation, and treatment for Alzheimer patients, with costs projected to escalate to $35 billion by 1990 (Butler, 1982; OTA, 1985). Although the financial and emotional costs to family members are not easily calculable, the financial burden to family members for direct care is most likely at least as great and is escalating as rapidly as that of the federal government (i.e., $35 billion annually by 1990, or nearly $10,000 per family per year) (OTA, 1985; USDHHS, 1983).

Because of these considerations, treatment of the primary symptoms of early stage AD might be considered to be one of the more formidable and humanitarian challenges currently facing the pharmaceutical industry. Additionally, the size and scope of the problem suggests that drugs for this indication also potentially represent one of the largest and most lucrative geriatric market areas for the pharmaceutical industry. Even if such treatment could cure the victims of AD or halt the disease's insidious progression, significant relief of the major cognitive symptoms would greatly increase the quality of life of all involved and markedly reduce the financial and emotional consequences (Bond, 1983; OTA, 1985; USDHHS, 1980;). In fact, partial improvement (rather than total elimination) of symptoms is often considered a realistic endpoint for many diseases in the elderly (Bond, 1983).

Memory Loss in Non-Diseased Elderly

Despite the tremendous attention directed toward the memory loss and related cognitive disturbances of AD, the need for effective treatment for age-related cognitive disturbances is hardly restricted to Alzheimer's patients. For example, it is now becoming recognized that even normal aging is associated with a selective loss of certain mental abilities, especially those requiring or involving memory. In fact, impairments in memory for recent events appear to be the price paid by members of all mammalian species that are successful in surviving into the postreproductive, senescent years (Bartus & Dean, 1985). In humans, non-diseased age-related loss of memory (referred to by some as benign senescent forgetfulness) is sometimes considered to be one of the most consistent and dehumanizing consequences of aging (Kral, 1978; Weinberg, 1980). The number of patient-to-physician complaints is also high, with approximately 90% of people over age 65 expressing concern (Zelinsky, in press).

Although the decline in memory ability in non-diseased aging in no way approaches the more severe and broader loss of mental capacity seen in AD, the effects on the individual and family can be dramatic, nevertheless. Performance on the job is often compromised, while the quality of life can be significantly affected, particularly when the induction of secondary psychiatric symptoms, such as depression occurs (Cohen & Faulkner, 1984; Weinberg, 1980; Zelinsky, in press). Thus, effective treatment of age-related memory disturbances in non-demented elderly represents a legitimate and noble medical goal that would benefit millions. Given the sheer numbers alone, the market size would be considerably larger than that of AD, and the likelihood of developing effective treatment in the near future is arguably greater (Bartus, Dean, Flicker, & Beer, 1983; Bartus, Flicker, & Dean, 1983; Crook, Ferris, & Bartus, 1983).

Additional Indications of Age-Related Memory Loss

In addition to the cognitive disturbances found in advanced age and AD, a number of other age-correlated conditions exist that also decrease cognitive ability. For example, in the United States alone, approximately three-quarters of a million people suffer partial to total mental incapacitation due to a condition defined as "multi-infarct dementia" [National Institutes of Health (NIH), 1981; Rathmann & Conner, 1984]. Multi-infarct dementia is caused by the cumulative effects of a series of small, sometimes undetected strokes, which over a period of time result in a significant reduction in mental ability (Hackinski, Lassen, & Marshall, 1974). Additionally, another one-half million people suffer loss of neurologic function due to larger, more serious strokes (USDHHS, 1983); 80% of these patients are over the age of 60 (Evans, Prudham, & Wandless, 1980; Sahs, Hartman, & Aronson, 1976). Another 900,000 people are hospitalized each year in the United States for head injuries (USDHHS, 1983).

Even in the milder cases (i.e., unconsciousness for less than 20 minutes), measurable cognitive loss persists beyond 6 months (Rimel, Giordani, & Barth, 1981). Interestingly, recent epidemiological studies indicate that the probability of developing AD later in life increases markedly in these patients (Heyman et al., 1984; Rudelli, Strom, Welch, & Ambler, 1982).

Finally, cognitive impairments associated with prescription drug use in the elderly (especially related to widespread use of polypharmacy) have become a serious problem (Cape, 1979; Richelson, 1984; Salzman, 1979). Over 85% of all people over 65 years take regular prescription medicine (the majority, several drugs) (Lamy, 1980; Law & Chalmers, 1976), and many of these drugs are now known to induce or exacerbate loss of memory and other cognitive problems (Jarvik, Gritz, & Schneider, 1972).

Clearly, the consequences of many of these conditions could be substantially reduced if a drug were available that could effectively improve or partially restore the cognitive capacity of the elderly patient. Because of the medical, economic, and psychosocial enormity of the problem, and the fact that little in the way of effective treatment yet exists, the development of efficacious drugs to treat age-related cognitive problems could represent the next significant medical contribution that the pharmaceutical industry will provide. As discussed later in this chapter, in many ways the stage appears to be set to begin to accomplish this task.

LIMITATIONS IN THE CURRENT STATE-OF-THE-ART: MAJOR OBSTACLES OR REASONABLE CHALLENGES?

Despite the fact that there exist many good reasons for establishing research programs to develop drugs for treating age-related cognitive loss, the majority of companies in the United States still are not engaged in this area of research. Moreover, when one considers those companies involved, some are now well into their second decade of research in this area, and apparently no new New Drug Applications (NDAs) have been approved (United States Food and Drug Administration Report, 1984). During this same period, a number of companies initiated programs, invested time, money, and other resources and eventually terminated formal efforts, without success.

The crucial questions are: Why haven't more companies initiated programs, and why haven't those programs that have been initiated been more successful to date? Although it would be presumptuous to claim to know the answers to questions of this type for any individual case, one can nevertheless identify certain general problems or concerns in this emerging area of pharmacology from a drug development perspective. Certainly, some of the same factors that presumably caused problems for the early leaders in this field seem to be at least partly responsible for discouraging others from entering the field. These are listed in Table 2.

To be sure, these problems offer significant challenges to greater progress in this area. Indeed many might argue that they represent currently insurmountable obstacles. But regardless of whether they may have impeded progress in the past, the question is how formidable they continue to be today.

There is little question that, compared to other more traditional areas of pharmaceutical drug development, one faces many problems when establishing a research program for the treatment of age-related

TABLE 2

Arguments Cited Against Establishing
Geriatric Cognition Programs

1. Scientific state of art remains weak
   a. no pharmacological standards
   b. no recognized animal models
   c. no genuine insight regarding cause-effect relationships

2. Clinical assessment methodology is confused
   a. no conventional assessment method
   b. existing tools insensitive to degrees of clinical severity, subtle effects of drug treatment, or both
   c. measurements lack face validity and construct validity (i.e., meaningful utility)

3. Leading companies are already too advanced and have monopoly on expertise, impeding ability of latecomers to compete effectively

4. Miracle drug would be required to gain FDA approval, penetrate market, or provide adequate return of investment

cognitive disturbances. For example, no drug marketed for this purpose yet demonstrates clear evidence of efficacy (Albert, 1983; Goodnick & Gershon, 1984). The only currently FDA-approved drug is Hydergine®, gaining approval in 1973 under now-obsolete guidelines for proving efficacy, established by the Food, Drug & Cosmetic Act of 1962. Most authorities now agree that its degree of efficacy is marginal, nonspecific, and that it is of limited clinical utility (Gaitz & Hartford, 1980; Hollister & Yesavage, 1984; Hughes, Williams, & Currier, 1976; Loveren-Huyben et al., 1984; McDonald, 1979; Yesavage, 1983; Yesavage, Westphal, & Rush, 1981). Thus, little or no direction exists for developing analogue chemical structures of existing efficacious drugs. Additionally, no reasonably complete explanation of the neurochemical factors responsible for age-related cognitive loss has yet been formulated (Bartus, Dean, Beer, & Lippa, 1982; Bartus, Flicker, & Dean, 1983) making directed synthesis of novel compounds a difficult task, to say the least. Finally, no commonly accepted animal models have yet been developed to provide concretely valid screening information, or for improving predictions of clinical effects from secondary and tertiary testing. In summary, one could argue that none of the traditional means of discovering or developing new drugs is readily available to researchers in this relatively new pharmaceutical area. Although these arguments continue to be valid, the deficiencies they describe are not obsolete. In fact, research of the last decade (stimulated in part by the early interest, support, and information generated by the pioneer programs in the industry) has made considerable progress (see Crook et al., 1983, and relevant chapters in this volume). Consequently, there exists considerably less risk now than 10 years ago, although the medical / humanitarian size and scope of the problem has continued to increase, and the opportunity for substantial marketing success has, therefore, not diminished significantly (Bond, 1983). Although work in this area is just beginning to attract widespread attention, clear progress has been made in developing better animal models, and in identifying neurochemical variables contributing to the memory loss. This progress undoubtedly makes the task of developing rational screening programs more feasible now than ever before. Several of the chapters in this volume, and in the two previous sister volumes (*Assessment in Geriatric Psychopharmacology* and *Strategies for the Development of an Effective Treatment for Senile Dementia*) (Crook, Ferris, & Bartus, 1983; Crook & Gershon, 1981) attest to this progress.

Perhaps, most promising in this regard is that laboratory studies have convincingly demonstrated that memory loss occurs with advanced age in many mammals, including numerous species of mice (Bartus, Dean, Goas, & Lippa, 1980; Dean et al., 1981; Kubanis, Gobbel, & Zornetzer, 1981; Strong, Hicks, Hsu, Bartus, & Enna, 1980), rats (Gold & McGaugh, 1975; Lippa et al., 1980) and monkeys (Bartus, Dean, & Beer, 1980; Bartus, Fleming, & Johnson, 1978; Davis, 1978; Medin, 1969). Moreover, this impairment is conceptually and operationally similar to that suffered, to varying degrees, by advanced aged and early demented humans (Flicker, Bartus, Crook, & Ferris, 1984). This cross-species similarity supports the idea that the memory loss associated with advanced age and dementia share similar biological underpinnings, and that aged animals might be useful as model systems for studying age-associated memory loss and potential treatment approaches (Bartus, Flicker, & Dean, 1983). Indeed, recent studies with reference drugs suggest that pharmacological data from logically derived animal models can be used to verify weak clinical observations, as well as provide a rationale to help direct future clinical trials in the area of geriatric psychopharmacology (Bartus, Dean, Flicker, & Beer, 1983; Bartus, Flicker, & Dean, 1983). Thus, the use of aged animals and appropriate behavioral paradigms to measure loss of memory provides an additional empirical tool for screening and developing drugs intended to reduce the memory losses associated with old age, as well as AD.

Thus, although we are barely beginning to unravel the variables responsible for the loss of cognitive capacity in old age or dementia (USDHHS, 1984), a number of empirical findings can be applied to help develop an effective, rational drug discovery and development program for this indication (Bartus, Flicker, & Dean, 1983).

Further, several drugs currently marketed in Europe, as well as newer compounds developed in the United States, Europe, and Japan, which are currently in various phases of clinical testing, give some indication of providing marginal relief of the cognitive symptoms (Albert, 1983; Bond, 1983; Goodnick & Gershon, 1984). Many believe that with more sensitive and sophisticated clinical assessment tools, and closer attention to individual differences in effective dose and possible subpopulations of patients, more accurate quantification of these rather subtle effects should be possible, at least for some of the better drugs (Albert, 1983; Crook et al., 1983; Flicker et al., 1984; Goodnick & Gershon, 1984). Information of this type would be invaluable in helping to develop newer and superior drugs.

More recent efforts to develop valid and reliable animal models in conjunction with sensitive and valid clinical assessment procedures present a unique opportunity in central nervous system (CNS) pharmacology to use animal tests to gain accurate, predictive information about a drug's efficacy, independent of the chemical class or entity (Bartus, Dean, Flicker, & Beer, 1983; Bartus, Flicker, & Dean, 1983). As animal models and human assessment techniques in this area continue to improve, and especially as information from one is used to help the other evolve, one should expect the task of identifying potentially interesting compounds and of selecting those most likely to be efficacious to become progressively easier. Certainly, the development of corresponding animal and human test procedures should offer significant advantages over those methods used to discover, select, and develop the generation of drugs currently undergoing clinical tests for this indication. Preliminary clinical data for these compounds have begun to accumulate, and although notable drugs may possess significant efficacy for modestly reducing the degree of cognitive disturbance, it appears unlikely that a dramatic therapeutic advance will occur in the near future (Albert, 1983; OTA, 1985). In fact, most claims for superior activity of the newer compounds are based primarily on differences in potency, and not increases in the efficacy, especially on any objective, clinically meaningful measure of age-related memory loss. Thus, despite growing interest and competition, the opportunity for making a significant impact in this area appears to be as good (or better) today, as it was a decade ago when many companies began their pioneering programs.

WHAT'S NEXT: SPECULATION BASED ON THE CURRENT ZEITGEIST

It is important to recognize that few authoritative investigators expect any drug developed in the near future to completely reverse the cognitive dysfunction of AD, let alone halt its insidious attack on the mind (Albert, 1983; Editorial, 1984; OTA, 1985). Yet, epidemiological and sociological studies suggest that much human suffering could be reduced and tens of billions of dollars saved annually by patients and their families simply by increasing the intellectual capacity of Alzheimer's patients to the point where self-care is possible and the need for expensive and dehumanizing institutionalization is, therefore, eliminated (Bond, 1983; OTA, 1985). In fact, according to a recent study by Blue Cross and Blue Shield of Massachusetts and Harvard University Medical School, more than 60% of all single elderly people would become terminally impoverished after only 3 months in a nursing home (*Aldrich*, 1985). One might expect certain positive consequences (e.g., improved self-esteem, increased quality of life, and continued productivity) to occur by simply reducing the degree of age-related memory loss in non-diseased elderly, as well. In fact, it is recognized that adequate mental function of many elderly is maintained only through a delicate balance of compensatory mechanisms (USDHHS, 1980) and that once a critical threshold is passed, cognitive function often deteriorates very dramatically (OTA, 1985). Thus, significant benefits to a large number of patients could be gained, and substantial inroads into this important market could be achieved with a drug that produces modest, but reliable improvement in a meaningful proportion of the patients tested. It is from this perspective that all current generation drugs should be developed, evaluated, and marketed.

The real question that must be asked is how good must a drug be to be successful? Obviously, this question is impossible to answer with any degree of certainty and is better considered in a rhetorical context. It seems quite clear that the next drug approved and marketed for some indication involving age-related cognitive disturbances need not be the miracle drug that certain sensation-seeking segments of the lay press expects, or that a number of industry executives often assume is necessary for gaining Food and Drug Administration approval. Medical progress rarely, if ever, occurs with such giant steps (Margotta, 1968; Thomas 1984), and certainly should not be expected to in a scientific-medical area as complex as geriatric memory loss. To set the standards for approval too high would deprive a proportion of responsive patients of needed symptomatic relief and could eventually suffocate future efforts to find even more effective treatment. Thus, to expect currently developed drugs to completely restore lost cognitive function would be impractical and illogical.

On the other hand, it seems perfectly reasonable to expect the next drug approved for use in treating cognitive disturbances in the elderly to be perfectly safe, have predictably measurable effects in at least a subpopulation of patients in the clinic, and produce positive changes in behavior that are noted and welcomed in the home environment by the patient or the immediate family. One can be certain that once such a drug is approved and marketed, it will be tremendously successful by all standards. The market size will certainly expand beyond any projections based on current sales or surveys. Moreover, the nature and scope of the medical problem will require and encourage the introduction of additional, similar drugs. Although some may initially be disappointed that these first-generation drugs do not possess overwhelming efficacy, most government regulatory officials may be as pleased as the medical community and family members that even modest relief of such dehumanizing symptoms is safely available to a proportion of sufferers. But, perhaps most importantly, the interest stimulated, information gained, and momentum established by the introduction of such drugs should serve as a catalyst responsible for developing newer and far superior generations of future drugs. In time, truly remarkable treatment is a reasonable goal and should be expected.

One need only look at the work done in this area over the last 10 years, and the growing problems and pressures created by an aging society, to see that the circumstances required to make these events happen already exist and are currently in place. The cycle of events has begun to turn and is accelerating. The rest is, primarily, a matter of time.

REFERENCES

Albert, M. (1983). Treating memory disorders in the elderly — Outlook for the future. *Drug Therapy, 13,* 61-71.

Aldrich, N. (Ed.), *Aging Services News* (1985). Silver Spring, Maryland: Business Publisher, Inc., 9 (15) 113.

Anderson, O.W. (1981). The social strategy of disease control: The case of senile dementia. In N.E. Miller & G.D. Cohen (Eds.), *Clinical aspects of Alzheimer's disease and senile dementia* (pp. 333-341). New York: Raven Press.

Bartus, R.T., & Dean, R.L. (1985). Developing and utilizing animal models in the search for an effective treatment for age-related memory disturbances. In C. Gottfries (Ed.), *Physiological aging and dementia* (pp. 231-267). Basle: S. Karger Press.

Bartus, R.T., Dean, R.L., & Beer, B. (1980). Memory deficits in aged Cebus monkeys and facilitation with central cholinomimetics. *Neurobiology of Aging, 1,* 145-152.

Bartus, R.T., Dean, R.L., Beer, B., & Lippa, A.S. (1982). The cholinergic hypothesis of geriatric memory dysfunction. *Science, 217,* 408-417.

Bartus, R.T., Dean, R.L., Flicker, C., & Beer, B. (1983). Behavioral and pharmacological studies using animal models of aging: Implications for studying and treating dementia of Alzheimer's type. In R. Katzman (Ed.), *Banbury Report 15: Biological aspects of Alzheimer's disease* (pp. 207-218). Cold Spring Harbor, NY: Cold Spring Harbor Laboratory.

Bartus, R.T., Dean, R.L., Goas, J.A., & Lippa, A.S. (1980). Age-related changes in passive avoidance retention: Modulation with dietary choline. *Science, 209,* 301-303.

Bartus, R.T., Fleming, D., & Johnson, H.R. (1978). Aging in the rhesus monkey: Debilitating effects on short-term memory. *Journal of Gerontology, 33,* 858-871.

Bartus, R.T., Flicker, C., & Dean, R.L. (1983). Logical principles for the development of animal models of age-related memory impairments. In T. Crook, S. Ferris, & R.T. Bartus (Eds.), *Assessment for geriatric psychopharmacology* (pp. 263-299). New Canaan, CT: Mark Powley Associates, Inc.

Bond, W.S. (1983). Dementia, Alzheimer's disease and drugs for memory enhancement. *Drug Newsletter, 2,* 65-72.

Butler, R.N. (1982). Charting the conquest of senility. *Bulletin of the New York Academy of Medicine, 58,* 362-381.

Cape, R.D.T. (1979). Drugs and confusional states. In J. Crooks & I.H. Stevenson (Eds.), *Drugs and the elderly* (pp. 267-277). Baltimore: University Park Press.

Cohen, G., & Faulkner, D. (1984). Memory in old age: "Good in parts." *New Scientist, 11,* 49-51.

Cowell, D.D. (1983). Senile dementia of the Alzheimer's type: A costly problem. *Journal of the American Geriatrics Society, 31,* 61.

Crook, T., Ferris, S., & Bartus, R.T. (Eds.). (1983). *Assessment in geriatric psychopharmacology.* New Canaan, CT: Mark Powley Associates, Inc.

Crook, T., & Gershon, S. (Eds.). (1981). *Strategies for the development of an effective treatment for senile dementia.* New Canaan, CT: Mark Powley Associates, Inc.

Davis, R.T. (1978). Old monkey behavior. *Experimental Gerontology, 13,* 237-250.

Dean, R.L., Scozzafava, J., Goas, J.A., Regan, B., Beer, B., & Bartus, R.T. (1981). Age-related differences in behavior across the life span of the C57BL/6J mouse. *Experimental Aging Research, 7,* 427-451.

Editorial. (1984). Ergot for dementia? *The Lancet, 2,* 1313-1314.

Evans, J.G., Prudham, D., & Wandless, I. (1980). Risk factors for stroke in the elderly. In G. Barbagallo-Sangiorgi, & A.N. Exton-Smith (Eds.), *The aging brain, neurological and mental disturbances* (pp. 113-126). New York: Plenum Press.

Flicker, C., Bartus, R.T., Crook, T., & Ferris, S.H. (1984). Effects of aging and dementia upon recent visuospatial memory. *Neurobiology of Aging, 5,* 275-282.

Fuller, E. (1983). Aging: How does it affect health? *Patient Care, 17,* 71-72.

Gaitz, C.M., & Hartford, J.T. (1980). Ergots in the treatment of mental disorders of old age. In M. Goldstein, D.P. Caine, A. Lieberman, & M.O. Thorner (Eds.), *Advances in biochemical psychopharmacology: Vol. 23. Ergot compounds and brain function: Neuroendocrine and neuropsychiatric aspects* (pp. 349-356). New York: Raven Press.

Giurgea, C., & Mouravieff-Lesuisse, F. (1976). Central hypoxic models and correlations with aging brain. In *Proceedings of the International Congress of the Collegium Internationale Neuro-Psycho-Pharmacologicum,* 1623-1631.

Gold, P.E., & McGaugh, J.L. (1975). Changes in learning and memory during aging. In J.M. Ordy, & K.R. Brizzee (Eds.), *Advances in behavioral biology: Vol. 16. Neurobiology of aging* (pp. 145-158). New York: Plenum Press.

Goldsmith, M.F. (1984). Youngest institute addresses aging problems. *Journal of the American Medical Association, 252,* 2315-2317.

Goodnick, P., & Gershon, S. (1984). Chemotherapy of cognitive disorders in geriatric subjects. *Journal of Clinical Psychiatry, 45,* 196-209.

Greenblatt, D.J., Sellers, E.M., & Shader, R.I. (1982). Drug disposition in old age. *New England Journal of Medicine, 306,* 1081-1086.

Gryfe, C.I., & Gryfe, B.M. (1984). Drug therapy of the aged: The problem of compliance and the roles of physicians and pharmacists. *Journal of the American Geriatrics Society, 32,* 301-307.

Gwyther, L.P., & Blazer, D.G. (1984). Family therapy and the dementia patient. *American Family Physician, 29,* 149-156.

Hachinski, V.C., Lassen, N.A., & Marshall, J.C. (1974). Multi-Infarct dementia: A cause of mental deterioration in the elderly. *The Lancet, 2,* 207-210.

Heyman, A., Wilkinson, W.E., Stafford, J.A., Helms, M.J., Sigmon, A.H., & Weinberg, T. (1984). Alzheimer's disease: A study of epidemiological aspects. Annals of Neurology, 15, 335-341.

Hollister, L.E., & Yesavage, J. (1984). Ergoloid mesylates for senile dementias: Unanswered questions. Annals of Internal Medicine, 100, 894-898.

Hughes, J.J., Williams, J.G., & Currier, R.D. (1976). An ergot alkaloid preparation (hydergine) in the treatment of dementia: Critical review of the clinical literature. Journal of the American Geriatrics Society, 24, 490-497.

Jarvik, M.E., Gritz, E.R., & Schneider, N.G. (1972). Drugs and memory disorders in human aging. Behavioral Biology, 7, 643-668.

Kral, V.A. (1978). Benign senescent forgetfulness. In R. Katzman, R.D. Terry, & K.L. Bick (Eds.), Alzheimer's disease: Senile dementia and related disorders (pp. 47-51). New York: Raven Press.

Kubanis, P., Gobbel, G., & Zornetzer, S.F. (1981). Age-related memory deficits in Swiss mice. Behavioral and Neural Biology, 32, 242-247.

Lamy, P.P. (1980). Prescribing for the elderly. Boston: John Wright.

Lamy, P.P. (1981). Special features of geriatric prescribing. Geriatrics, 36, 42-52.

Law, R., & Chalmers, C. (1976). Medicines and elderly people: A general practice survey. British Medical Journal, 1, 565-568.

Levenson, A.J. (Ed.). (1979). Neuropsychiatric side-effects of drugs in the elderly. New York: Raven Press.

Lippa, A.S., Pelham, R.W., Beer, B., Critchett, D.J., Dean, R.L., & Bartus, R.T. (1980). Brain cholinergic function and memory in aged rats. Neurobiology of Aging, 1, 10-16.

Loveren-Huyben, C.M.S., Engelaar, H.F.W.J., Hermans, M.B.M., van der Bom, J.A., Leering, C., & Munnichs, J.M.A. (1984). Double-blind clinical and psychologic study of ergoloid mesylates (Hydergin®) in subjects with senile mental deterioration. Journal of the American Geriatrics Society, 32, 584-588.

Lowenstein, S.R., & Schrier, R.W. (1982). Social and political aspects of aging. In R.W. Schrier (Ed.), Clinical internal medicine in the aged (pp. 1-23). Philadelphia: W.B. Saunders Company.

Margotta, R. (1968). The story of medicine. New York: Golden Press.

McDonald, R.J. (1979). Hydergine: A review of 26 clinical studies.

Pharmakopsychiatric Neuro-Psychopharmakologie, 12, 407-422.

Medin, D.L. (1969). Form perception and pattern reproduction by monkeys. *Journal of Comparative and Physiological Psychology, 68,* 412-419.

Meier-Ruge, W., Enz, A., Gygax, P., Hunziker, O., Iwangoff, P., & Reichlmeier, K. (1975). Experimental pathology in basic research of the aging brain. In S. Gershon & A. Raskin (Eds.), *Geneses and treatment of psychotic disorders in the elderly* (pp. 55-126). New York: Raven Press.

Nandy, K., & Lal, H. (1976). Neuronal lipofuscin and learning deficits in aging mammals. *Proceedings of the 11th International Congress of the Collegium Internationale Neuro-Psychopharmacologicum,* 1633-1645.

National Institutes of Health. (1981). *The dementias* (NIH Publication No. 81-2252). Bethesda, MD: U.S. Government Printing Office.

Nicolaus, B.J.R. (1982). Chemistry and pharmacology of nootropics. *Drug Development Research, 2,* 463-474.

Office of Technology Assessment, United States Congress (1985). *Technology and aging in America.* Washington, D.C.

Ouslander, J. (1981). Drug therapy in the elderly. *Annals of Internal Medicine, 95,* 711-722.

Plum, F. (1979). Dementia: An approaching epidemic. *Nature, 279,* 372-373.

Rabins, P.V., Mace, N.L., & Lucas, M.J. (1982). The impact of dementia on the family. *Journal of the American Medical Association, 248,* 333-335.

Rathmann, K.L., & Conner, C.S. (1984). Alzheimer's disease: Clinical features, pathogenesis, and treatment. *Drug Intelligence and Clinical Pharmacy, 18,* 684-691.

Reisberg, B., Ferris, S.H., & Crook, T. (1982). Signs, symptoms and course of age-associated cognitive decline. In S. Corkin, K.L. Davis, J.H. Growdon, E. Usdin, & R.J. Wurtman (Eds.), *Alzheimer's disease: A report of progress in research* (pp. 177-182). New York: Raven Press.

Richelson, E. (1984). Psychotropics and the elderly: Interactions to watch for. *Geriatrics, 30,* 30-42.

Rimel, R., Giordani, M., & Barth, J. (1981). Disability caused by minor head injury. *Neurosurgery, 9,* 221-228.

Rudelli, R., Strom, J.O., Welch, P.T., & Ambler, M.W. (1982). Post-traumatic premature Alzheimer's disease. *Archives of Neurology, 39,* 570-575.

Sahs, A.L., Hartman, E.C., & Aronson, S.M. (1976). *Guidelines for stroke care* (DHEW Publication No. 76-14017). Washington, D.C.: U.S. Government Printing Office.

Salzman, C. (1979). Polypharmacy and drug-drug interactions in the elderly. In K. Nandy (Ed.), *Geriatric psychopharmacology* (pp. 117-126). New York: Elsevier.

Schlinder, U., Rush, D.K., & Fielding, S. (1984). Nootropic drugs: Animal models for studying effects on cognition. *Drug Development Research, 4,* 567-576.

Schmucker, D.L. (1984). Drug disposition in the elderly: A review of the critical factors. *Journal of the American Geriatrics Society, 32,* 144-149.

Segal, J.L., Thompson, J.F., & Floyd, R.A. (1979). Drug utilization and prescribing patterns in a skilled nursing facility: The need for a rational approach to therapeutics. *Journal of the American Geriatrics Society, 27,* 117-122.

Siegel, E.B. (1982). Drugs and the aging. *Regulatory Toxicology and Pharmacology, 2,* 287-295.

Strong, R., Hicks, P., Hsu, L., Bartus, R.T., & Enna, S.J. (1980). Age-related alterations in the brain cholinergic system and behavior. *Neurobiology of Aging, 1,* 59-63.

Thomas, L. (1984). *The lives of a cell: Notes of a biology watcher.* New York: Viking Press.

Thompson, T.L., Moran, M.G. & Nies, A.S. (1983a). Psychotropic drug use in the elderly, Part 1. *New England Journal of Medicine, 308,* 134-138.

Thompson, T.L., Moran, M.G., & Nies, A.S. (1983b). Psychotropic drug use in the elderly, Part 2. *New England Journal of Medicine, 308,* 194-199.

U.S. Department of Health and Human Services. (1980). *Alzheimer's disease: A scientific guide for health practitioners* (NIH Publication No. 81-2251). Bethesda, MD: National Institute of Health.

U.S. Department of Health and Human Services. (1983). *National Institute of Neurological and Communicative Disorders and Stroke fact book: September, 1983* (NIH Publication No. 83-1683). Bethesda, MD: National Institute of Health.

U.S. Department of Health and Human Services. (1984). *Alzheimer's disease: Report of the Secretary's Task Force on Alzheimer's disease* (DHHS Publication No. [ADM] 84-1323). Washington, D.C.: U.S. Government Printing Office.

U.S. Food and Drug Administration (1984). *New drug introductions, discontinuations and safety issues:* A UK/USA comparison, 1960-1982. Richmond, Surrey: PJB Publications Ltd.

Vestal, R.F. (1982). Pharmacology and aging. *Journal of the American Geriatrics Society, 30,* 191-200.

Weinberg, J. (1980). Geriatric psychiatry. In H.I. Kaplan, A.M. Freedman, & B.J. Sadock (Eds.), *Comprehensive textbook of psychiatry/III* (3rd ed., Vol. III, pp. 3024-3042). Baltimore: Williams & Williams.

Yesavage, J.A. (1983). Opportunities for and obstacles to treatments for dementias. *Journal of the American Geriatrics Society, 31,* 59-60.

Yesavage, J.A., Westphal, J., & Rush, L. (1981). Senile dementia: Combined pharmacological and psychologic treatment. *Journal of the American Geriatrics Society, 29,* 164-171.

Zelinsky, D. (In press). Complaints of memory loss in community dwelling elderly. In L. Poon (Ed.), *The handbook of clinical memory assessment in older adults.* Washington, D.C.: American Psychological Association.

ACKNOWLEDGMENT

The author gratefully acknowledges the assistance of Barbara Hovsepian, Carmela Nardella, Reginald Dean, and Sara Ellen Smith, and comments from Drs. Charles Flicker and Bernard Dubnick in the course of preparing this manuscript. Also, sincere gratitude is extended to Drs. B. Dubnick, A. Oronsky, G. Sutherland, and especially B. Beer (Lederle Laboratories of American Cyanamid Co.) and Drs. E. Elslager, D. Maxwell, R. Hodges, and especially D. McCarthy (Parke-Davis Research Laboratories of Warner-Lambert/Parke-Davis Co., during the author's tenure until 1978). Each individual played a significant role in creating the climate, supporting the work, and encouraging the thinking responsible for the ideas expressed, and much of the author's work referred to in this manuscript.

3

Can the Pathophysiology of Dementia Lead to Rational Therapy?

David M. Bowen, PhD, and Alan N. Davison, DSc, FRC Path

Although the etiology of Alzheimer's disease (AD) is unknown, there are conditions in which the cause of dementia is recognized. Study of the pathophysiology of these examples of dementing illness may help us understand common mechanisms leading to cognitive and behavioral changes, as well as providing clues to other possible etiological factors. Alternatively, it may be that a number of separate defects (in neurotransmitter imbalance or selective neuronal dysfunction) result in a single broad functional expression of disease (e.g., loss of short-term memory).

CLINICAL CLASSIFICATION

The range of neurological, general medical, and psychiatric conditions that can lead to a suspicion of a primary dementing illness is wide. The DSM-III (American Psychiatric Association, 1980) classification indicates that dementia is only one of seven organic brain syndromes. The most common example of dementia is AD. This condition is typified by an acquired progressive decline in memory and global cognitive impairment with ultimate diagnosis depending on neuropathological assessment of a defined density (McKhann et al., 1984) of plaques and tangles. Clinical and pathological criteria have led to identification of groups in which diffuse or focal degenerative changes occur (e.g., Pick's disease and dementia accompanying Huntington's chorea or multiple sclerosis).

In the case of multi-infarct dementia, the step-wise decline in cognitive ability is associated with multiple areas of ischemia. The cause of the disease is vascular and the potential for therapeutic interven-

TABLE 1

Diseases Causing Dementia

Diffuse parenchymatous diseases
of the central nervous system

Presenile dementias
  Alzheimer's disease
  Creutzfeldt-Jakob disease
  Parkinson-dementia complex
    of Guam
  Huntington's chorea

Senile dementia

Other degenerative diseases
  Progressive myoclonus epilepsy
  Progressive supranuclear palsy
  Parkinson's disease
  Multiple sclerosis

Metabolic disorders
  Myxedema
  Parathyroid disease
  Wilson's disease, etc.

Vascular disorders
  Arteriosclerosis

Hypoxia and anoxia
Tension hydrocephalus
Deficiency diseases
  Wernicke-Korsakoff
    syndrome
  Pellagra

Vitamin B_{12} deficiency

Toxins and drugs
Brain tumors
Trauma
  Head injuries
  Punch-drunk syndrome

Subdural hematoma
Heat stroke

(After Hasse, 1977)

tion therefore depends on treatment of the basic vascular disease. In young or middle-aged subjects the search for remedial conditions is normally comprehensive, including various imaging procedures. In one report of intensive neurological investigation of presenile patients referred with presumptive dementia, 15% were found to be suffering from diseases not primarily affecting learning and memory (Marsden & Harrison, 1972). Possible cause was ascribed to 36 patients, and 15% of the whole series were thought to be amenable to treatment.

A serious problem arises with the large group of dementias occurring in the elderly. Many are not referred for specialist opinion; and, it is often judged unwarranted to press investigations to the limit. It is in this group particularly that the precise indications for investigation and the range to be employed stand in need of clarification. The value of screening procedures, including computerized axial tomography, in terms of useful yield and potential treatment, remains to be established.

Special problem areas include "normal pressure (communicating) hydrocephalus" and subcortical dementia. Typical examples of "normal pressure hydrocephalus" of the type often responsive to shunting can be detected only by radiographic procedures that are not routinely employed in the elderly. It is not known how often the syndrome is missed or whether partial and intermediate forms may contribute to disability. The literature on clinical response to shunting operations in the primary dementias is small and generally of poor quality but there have been some reports of success (Lishman, 1977).

In the subcortical dementias the brain stem bears the brunt of pathological damage while the cerebral cortex is thought to be relatively intact. In such disorders, such as progressive supranuclear palsy, the mental changes are probably due to loss of afferent inputs into the intact cortex. Identification of the neurotransmitter containing pathways could lead to the possibility that replacement therapy may ultimately be available to allow restoration of function. There is also an element of subcortical failure, potentially remedial, in some of the primary dementias (Whitehouse et al., 1982). However, the clinical associations of subcortical failure are imperfectly understood. Whether the manifestations contain elements decisive enough to allow a differentiation from cortical dementia (Mayeux, Stern, Rosen, & Benson, 1983) remains uncertain.

TABLE 2

Final Diagnosis of Dementia in Patients* Referred for Specialist Investigation at the National Hospital, Queen's Square, London (1968-69) Presumed to be Suffering from Dementia

Demented:	No. of patients	Not demented:	No. patients
Intracranial space-occupying mass	8	Psychiatric depression	8
Arteriosclerotic dementia	8	hysteria	1
Dementia in alcoholics	6	mania	1
Possible normal pressure	5	Drug toxicity	2
Communicating hydrocephalus		Epilepsy	1
Creutzfeldt-Jakob disease	3	Unknown	2
Huntington's chorea	3		15
Posttraumatic cerebral atrophy	1		
Postsubarachnoid hemorrhage	1	Dementia uncertain	7
Limbic encephalitis	1		
Cerebral atrophy of unknown cause	48		
	84	*Total number of patients referred	106

(After Marsden & Harrison, 1972)

SLOW VIRUSES

There are some clinical features of Creutzfeldt-Jakob disease that resemble those of AD. In both diseases, progressive dementia predominates in the middle-aged. AD is usually a slower process but on occasion may be rapid and accompanied by myoclonus and even typical electroencephalogram (EEG) changes (Matthews, 1982). Creutzfeldt-Jakob, but not AD, can be transmitted to primates.

Pathological examination in Creutzfeldt-Jakob disease shows a characteristic spongiform subacute encephalopathy. Plaque-like masses with amyloid and tangles have only been seen occasionally. Vacuolation affecting neuronal cell bodies, axons, dendrites, and synapses occurs and astrocytes are affected. A 45% loss of neurons from the nucleus basalis has been reported in one case of Creutzfeldt-Jakob disease (Arendt, T., Bigl, & Arendt, A., 1984). There is also neuronal loss from the middle and deeper cortical layers (large pyramidal cells are particularly affected) with marked astrocytic proliferation (Tomlinson & Corsellis, 1984), some microglial reaction, and the frequent, but not constant, development of a spongy state. The vasculature is not appreciably affected; myelin loss is minor.

The Creutzfeldt-Jakob agent can be transmitted to animals when similar abnormalities are seen as those described in kuru and in some respects to experimental scrapie. Protease-resistant proteins have been isolated from the brain of patients with Creutzfeldt-Jakob disease (Bockman, Kingsbury, McKinley, Bendheim, & Prusiner, 1985). The proteins react with antibodies raised against the scrapie prion protein. However, although neuronal loss and gliosis occurs in scrapie, the neuropathology is not identical to that of Creutzfeldt-Jakob disease.

Neurotransmitters

In one case of Creutzfeldt-Jakob disease, monoamine metabolism was found to be disturbed (Brun, Gottfries, & Roos, 1971). Concentrations of dopamine in the striatum and noradrenaline in the pons and hypothalamus were markedly reduced compared to control. Reductions were also found in the concentration of 5-hydroxytryptamine (5-HT) and its metabolites. Loading tests with probenecid and cerebrospinal fluid (CSF) analysis suggested a low turnover of dopamine. There are two reports (Bowen, Benton, Spillane, Smith, & Allen, 1982; Sorbi, Antuono, & Amaducci, 1980) of reduction in choline acetyltransferase (CAT) activity in Creutzfeldt-Jakob disease, and some data suggests that the enzyme is affected in certain strains of mice infected with the scrapie agent (McDermott, Fraser, & Dickinson, 1978). However, in hamsters inoculated intracerebrally with scrapie (263K strain) no alteration was found in CAT activity in the cortex, hippocampus, basal ganglia, brain stem, thalamus, or cerebellum (Masullo, Pocchiari, Gibbs, & Gajdusek, 1984). Binding of quinuclidinyl benzilate to muscarinic receptors was significantly decreased by 25%. No changes in brain glutamate decarboxylase or cholinergic enzyme activities were found in experimental murine scrapie by Iqbal, Somerville, Thompson, and Wisniewski (1985).

DEMENTIA ASSOCIATED WITH ALCOHOLISM

Brain damage may result as the subacute or chronic effects of alcoholism. Wernicke's encephalopathy and its clinical associations, Korsakoff's psychosis, is the best known of these syndromes and may present with acute, subacute, or chronic manifestations. It is induced by nutritional (especially thiamine) deficiency (Perry, R.H., 1984). Brain atrophy develops at an enhanced rate and there are significant reductions in cerebral blood flow in patients with Wernicke-Korsakoff dementia (Meyer, Largen, Shaw, Mortel, & Rogers, 1984). It has been proposed that neuronal aging is exaggerated by chronic alcoholism (Carlsson et al., 1980).

Neurotransmitters

Neurotransmitter changes are found similar to those in AD. Thus CAT activity was found to be reduced in the cingulate gyrus by Carlsson et al. (1980). In a study of the brain of three alcoholics with dementia, Antuono, Sorbi, Bracco, Fusco, and Amaducci (1980) found CAT activity to be about a third that of controls. Various regions of the neocortex, hippocampus, and cerebellum were examined. Little loss of muscarinic receptor activity was noted. Significant loss of 5-HT was found in the hypothalamus and caudate nucleus compared to AD where levels of this biogenic amine were lower in the

TABLE 3

Neurotransmitter Concentrations and Enzyme Activity in the Brain of Patients with Chronic Alcoholism

	Caudate nucleus	Hypothalamus	Hippocampus	Cingulate gyrus
	(Percent of controls)			
Dopamine	45	0	—	—
Homovanillic acid	86	85	53	—
Norepinephrine	65	66	70	49
3-Methoxy-4-hydroxy-phenylglycol (MHPG)	164	103	111	127
5-Hydroxytryptamine	30	11	47	57
5-Hydroxyindoleacetic acid (5-HIAA)	60	34	59	91
Choline acetyltransferase (CAT)	90	113	81	76

(After Carlsson et al., 1980)

lower in the hippocampus compared to alcoholic dementia. The loss of CAT activity is consistent with the reduction of nerve cell populations reported in the basal forebrain nuclei.

HUNTINGTON'S CHOREA

Huntington's chorea is thought to be due to a single autosomal dominant gene (Gusella et al., 1983). Usually behavioral changes appear early followed by chorea and, finally, dementia. A general behavioral inefficiency is more in evidence than the memory disability of AD. Relative preservation of memory is found as opposed to personality and intellectual disorientation (Mahendra, 1984). This conforms to the criteria of a subcortical dementia in which prominent pathological changes are seen in subcortical nuclear structures (e.g., progressive supranuclear palsy, Parkinson's disease). Clinically this syndrome manifests itself by:
1. emotional or personality changes;
2. memory disorder;
3. defective ability to manipulate acquired knowledge; and
4. marked slowness in the rate of information processing.
Criteria for dementia, necessarily present in all Alzheimer patients, are found in only half those with Huntington's disease (Mayeux et al., 1983). Mayeux and his colleages argue that the concept of subcortical dementia is misleading for the pattern of neuropsychological impairment is not distinct and neuropathology indicates a possible combination of cortical and subcortical degeneration.

In nine cases of Huntington's disease examined (Arendt, T., Bigl, Arendt, A., & Tennstedt, 1983) no loss was found in the neuronal population of the nucleus basalis although there was about 40% loss of cells in the globus pallidus, which did not occur in Parkinson's, Alzheimer's or in Korsakoff's disease. However, diffuse loss of cortical grey matter has been described (Bird & Spokes, 1982) though not as extensive as in the striatum. Cortical cell loss occurs in layers 3, 4, and 6.

Neurotransmitters

There is substantial loss of glutamate decarboxylase and CAT activity in the basal ganglia. No significant loss of CAT or glutamate

TABLE 4

Changes in the Neuronal Population of the Basal Forebrain Nuclei in Korsakoff's Disease

Mean Neuronal Loss %

Total neuronal loss	Medial septal nucleus	Diagonal band of Broca	Nucleus basalis
47	40	57	47

There was a mean loss of 20% brain weight in Korsakoff's disease but no significant loss in wet brain weight or neuronal density in alcoholics without dementia.

(Arendt, T., Bigl, Arendt, A., & Tennstedt, 1983)

decarboxylase activity has been noted in the cortex. It was proposed that the cortical nerve cell loss may be those (possibly glutamatergic) neurons subserving the corticostriatal pathway. The striatum has a high concentration of glutamate receptors so that deafferentation of descending fibers could result in degenerative changes in the striatum (see Pearce et al., 1984).

In model experiments following striatal injection of the rigid-glutamate analogue kainate into rat brain there is neuronal loss (particularly Golgi-11 striatal neurons) with reduction in glutamate decarboxylase, and CAT activities (Coyle, 1983). Intrinsic neurons (especially acetylcholine [ACh] and γ-aminobutyric acid [GABA] containing neurons) are destroyed and alterations in postsynaptic receptor densities parallel those found in Huntington's chorea. Importantly, hippocampal CA 3-4 pyramidal cells distant from the striatal lesion are degenerated. There was extensive and uneven damage in the deeper layers of the cerebral cortex and pyriform cortex-amygdaloid nuclei (Friedle, Kelly, & Moore, 1978). Impairments in learning and memory have been reported by Divac, Markowitsch, and Pritzel (1978).

PARKINSON'S DISEASE

Parkinson's disease is an extrapyramidal condition in which there is degeneration of the nigro-striatal dopaminergic system. This sys-

TABLE 5

Transmitter and Enzyme Changes in Huntington's Chorea

	Dopamine	Noradrenaline	CAT activity	Glutamate decarboxylase
Putamen	+69%	N.S.	-34%	-54%
Caudate nucleus	+32	+63	-43	-50
Nucleus accumbens	+87	+46	-17	N.S.
Septal nuclei	N.S.	N.S.	—	—
Temporal cortex	—	—	N.S.	—
Motor cortex	—	—	N.S.	N.S.
Hippocampus	—	—	N.S.	N.S.

N.S. = not significant

(After Bird & Spokes, 1982; Bird, Stranahan, Sumi, & Raskind, 1983) tem is responsible for some of the motor disorders associated with the disease. However, the syndrome is also frequently accompanied by depression, cognitive defects, and frontal type symptoms, the origins of which are unknown, although a deficiency of the mesocorticolimbic dopaminergic pathways may be involved (Ruberg, Ploska, Javoy-Agid, & Agid, 1982).

Etiology

The cause of the loss in nigral neurons in idiopathic Parkinson's disease is unknown. But the possible association of viral infection was suggested following the outbreak of encephalitis lethargica. The virus responsible has not been identified. Results of extensive serological studies comparing viral antibodies in the serum and CSF of parkinsonian patients and controls have not demonstrated any clearly defined, biologically significant relationship between antibodies to specific viruses and the occurrences of postencephalitic and idiopathic Parkinson's disease (Elizan et al., 1979; Elizan, Schwartz, Yahr, & Casals, 1978; Elizan, Yahr, & Casals, 1979). No evidence suggestive of viral persistence was noted by this group in their studies of rapid postmortem brain tissue material (substantia nigra, caudate nucleus, hypothalamus) from nine patients with idiopathic Parkinson's disease. Viral isolation techniques, electron microscopy, and indirect immunofluorescence (with serological probes for herpes simplex virus type 1, influenza A / NWS, and Edmonston strain of measles virus) were used (Schwartz & Elizan, 1979). Within the limits of detection of nucleic acid reassociation experiments, no evidence of herpes simplex virus (HSV) type 1 or influenza A / NWS virus-coded nucleic acids in any of the 40 defined loci from nine parkinsonian brains (Wetmur, Schwartz, & Elizan, 1979) was found.

Loss of neurons in the substantia nigra has been ascribed to intracellular generation of reactive forms of reduced oxygen (hydrogen peroxide, superoxide, and hydroxyl radicals) damaging dopaminergic neurons (Cohen, 1983). One mechanism for this toxic effect may be mediated by monoamine oxidase leading to neuromelanin formation (see Mann & Yates, 1982; Marsden, 1983).

Another interesting and topical possibility is the action of endogenous neurotoxins. An illustration of the possible selective action of a neurotoxin is provided by 1-methyl-4-phenyl-1, 2, 3, 6-tetrahydropyridine, (MPTP) which has a selective cumulative action on the

TABLE 6

Accumulation of the MPTP Metabolite (MPP⁺) in Monkey Brain

1-methyl-4-phenylpyridinium (MPP⁺)
Concentration (μg/g) After:

	24 hours	72 hours
Cerebellum	2.7	0.7
Frontoparietal cortex	2.5	1.2
Temporo-occipital cortex	2.0	1.0
Substantia nigra	9.0	11.0
Basal ganglia	8.2	5.7

Treatment with 2 mg/kg 1-methyl-4-phenyl-1,2,3,6-tetrahydropyridine (MPTP) was continued four times two hourly.

(After Irwin & Langston, 1985)

basal ganglia. It is possible that free radicals or peroxides are generated in the process of conversion of MPTP to MPP⁺ (Langston, 1985).

Intellectual impairment is prevalent among parkinsonian subjects. The incidence of dementia is estimated to be five times higher in parkinsonian subjects than in the general population, and the suggestion has been made on the basis of neuropathological similarities (presence of neurofibrillary tangles and senile plaques) that parkinsonism and AD are related degenerative diseases. Nevertheless, the majority of individuals with Parkinson disease do not have extensive AD pathology, tangles are absent, and neuritic plaques are little more in number than in aged controls (Perry, E.K. et al., 1985).

Neurotransmitters

It is of interest that both Ruberg et al., (1982) and Perry, R.H. et al., (1983) have reported a reduction in CAT activity in parkinsoni-

TABLE 7

Mean Biochemical and Neuropathological Correlates in Parkinson's Disease and Alzheimer's Disease Compared to Controls

	Normal	Parkinson's disease Mentally normal	Parkinson's disease Impaired	Alzheimer's disease
Age (mean in years) number of cases in parentheses	79 (8)	74 (4)	72 (7)	83 (8)
Neocortical plaque count	6	8	6	22
Neurofibrillary tangles	absent	absent	absent	present
Nucleus basalis neuron count	162	134	45	150
CAT activity frontal cortex	8.6	5.4	2.7	3.5

(Data from Perry et al.. 1985)

an patients with dementia in the absence of Alzheimer pathology. These changes may relate to the extensive loss of neurons from the nucleus basalis without the concomitant formation of neuritic plaques. A decrease in CAT activity has been reported in the striatum, cortex, and hippocampus of parkinsonian subjects with no apparent intellectual impairment. (Perry, E.K. et al., 1985). Increased muscarinic receptor density has been observed in the frontal cortex and basal ganglia—possibly as the result of drug induction or, more plausibly, due to loss of presynaptic cholinergic terminals.

ALZHEIMER'S DISEASE

The dominant change in neurotransmitter metabolism is in markers of presynaptic cholinergic neuronal activity (Bowen, 1981). With the exception of the putamen, this loss occurs widely in the brain, especially in the hippocampus, amygdala, and neocortex. In this respect, the hippocampus (Ball et al., 1985), and the amygdala may turn out to be particularly critical brain regions. This points to a need to know more about septal-hippocampal pathways as well as the distribution of descending projections from large cortical neurons. Loss of activity of the ACh synthesizing enzyme, CAT is accompanied by an increase in the density of neuritic plaques in the neocortex although the relationship is not linear (Perry, E.K. et al., 1978). Subjects with early-onset AD are particularly severely affected histologically and CAT activity is proportionately lower than in elderly patients (Bowen et al., 1979). There is good evidence that loss (Whitehouse et al., 1982) or shrinkage (Pearson et al., 1983) of neurons from the nuclei of the basal forebrain leads to neuritic plaque formation (somatostatin immunoreactivity has been detected in neuritic plaques [Morrison, Rogers, Scherr, Benoit, & Bloom, 1985]). The cholinergic system is particularly affected since ascending projections from the nucleus basalis utilize ACh as neurotransmitter. However, not all plaques are thought to be derived from degenerating cholinergic neurites. Muscarinic cholinergic receptor concentration does not alter except possibly in M_2-receptors in the frontal cortex (Mash, Sevush, Flynn, Norenberg, & Potter, 1984). Since CAT activity is not rate-limiting in ACh synthesis, it was necessary to show that formation and stimulated release of the amine were impaired in AD. Fresh surgical tissue samples were cut into prisms to produce crude synaptosomes, and these were incubated with ^{14}C-glucose (Sims, Bowen,

TABLE 8

Clinical and Pathological Findings in Biopsied Patients with Suspected Alzheimer's Disease

Presence of plaques and tangles in biopsy sample	Present		Rare	Absent
	nonfamiliar	familiar		
Number of patients	8	3	3	6
Amnesia	7	2/2	2	3/5
Aphasia	5/7	2/2	0	2/5
Visuospatial impairment	5/6	1/1	0/2	2/5
CAT act. % control	38%	31%	42%	80%

(After Bowen et al., 1982)

& Davison, 1981). Significant reduction was observed in ACh synthesis under resting and stimulated conditions in AD patients with histological evidence of the disease (Bowen et al., 1983). Choline uptake into biopsy samples was similarly reduced (Sims et al., 1983). However, despite the clinical appearance of AD, examination of biopsy tissue in some presenile patients showed unexpectedly low plaque and tangle count with no significant impairment of ACh synthesis (Bowen et al., 1982; Sims et al., 1983). Other work points to the dysfunction or loss of cortical neurons and the correlation of tangle formation to cognitive defect (Wilcock, Esiri, Bowen, & Smith, 1982). In AD there is an unexplained reduction in the amount of deep grey matter, including the area containing the caudate nucleus, which is innervated by neocortical nerve cells from all lobes of the brain. Some studies relate certain "cortical" cognitive symptoms to a probable dysfunction of the corticostriatal pathway, which is thought to use L-glutamate as its neurotransmitter. Unfortunately, the techniques used for studying excitatory amino acid-releasing nerve terminals in animals are difficult to apply to the subcortex of human brain. Thus, the binding of [³H]L-glutamate to postsynaptic receptor sites on membranes prepared from the caudate nucleus has been

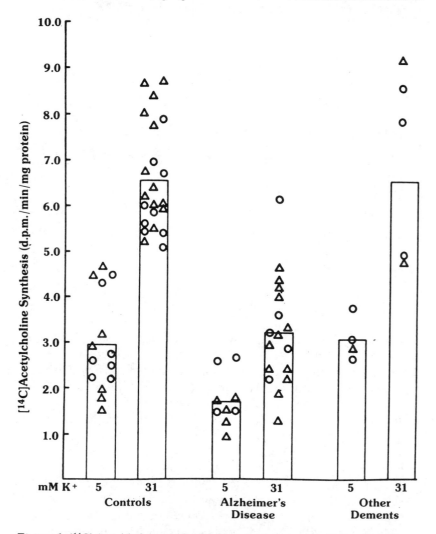

Figure 1. [¹⁴C] Acetylcholine synthesis measured in the presence of either 5 mM K⁺ or 31 mM K⁺ in samples of temporal neocortex (Δ) and frontal neocortex (O) from neurosurgical controls, patients with histologically confirmed Alzheimer's disease, and other demented patients. Samples from patients with Alzheimer's disease were significantly different (p<0.01; Wilcoxon rank test) from control samples measured under the same conditions.

(After Sims et al., 1983)

(With permission of the authors and the *Journal of Neurochemistry*)

TABLE 9

Biochemical Parameters in Alzheimer's Disease and Control Caudate Nucleus Samples

Variable measured	Control	Alzheimer
Caudate nucleus weight, g	3.06 ± 0.43	2.67 ± 0.43***
Total protein, mg/caudate	380 ± 94	281 ± 42***
CAT activity, nmol/mg/min	297 ± 119	118 ± 77***
"Total dopamine," pmol/mg	150.0 ± 44.0	99.9 ± 47.9***
"Total serotonin," pmol/mg	25.0 ± 11.0	20.9 ± 12.0
Norepinephrine, pmol/mg	2.4 ± 1.2	2.3 ± 1.1
^{3}H-Glutamate binding		
0.3 μM, pmol/mg membrane protein	10.3 ± 6.5	16.8 ± 6.8**
1.0 μM, pmol/mg	22.0 ± 8.4	28.6 ± 11.8

The results are the means $\pm$SD (per mg total protein, except where stated otherwise) for 12-13 control and 13-15 Alzheimer's samples. Asterisks identify significant differences from control **$p<0.02$; ***$p<$at least 0.01.
(After Pearce et al., 1984)

examined (Pearce et al., 1984). Whereas the Alzheimer brains with high tangle counts had remarkable increases in specific binding of [^{3}H]L-glutamate at both concentration of ligand tested, those with lower counts showed smaller increases in binding. This provides some evidence of a change in excitatory amino acid neurotransmission in AD for hemidecortication of rats results in an elevated binding of [^{3}H]L-glutamate to striatal membranes (Roberts et al., 1982). This is possibly indicative of a change in AD in glutamate receptors, secondary to dysfunction of descending excitatory amino acid-releasing pathways from neurons in the neocortex (Bowen, Davison, Francis, Palmer, & Pearce, 1985). Recently, Roberts, Crow, and Polak (1985) have localized somatostatin-immunoreactivity in tangle-bearing neuron cell bodies in the temporal cortex. These authors suggest that somatostatin neurons in the temporal cortex are a primary focus for the disease process, and that the loss of somatostatin content is an early event in the production of symptoms and the subsequent (or concomitant) cortical atrophy. The cholinergic deficit and atrophy of the basal nucleus of Meynert may then be a secondary consequence of the loss of cortical somatostatin neurons from a region that provides the major input to the basal nucleus.

PATHOGENESIS OF DEMENTIA AND THERAPY

Consideration of the pathophysiology of the various conditions leading to dementia (reviewed in this article) suggests that selective loss of neurons (including large neurons in the cortex) and a defect in the cholinergic system emerge as the most common features. It has been argued (Perry, R.H. et al., 1982) that this loss is due to a "dying back" of cholinergic afferents probably resulting from primary cortical pathology. Indeed, loss or damage to cortical neurons seems to be frequently associated with dementia. It may therefore be speculated that the early and primary change in AD is that affecting cortical neurons. Thus experimental cortical lesions result in retrograde degeneration of cholinergic cells in the nucleus basalis (Sofroniew, Pearson, Eckenstein, Cuello, & Powell, 1983).

Nerve Cell Loss

Although large nerve cells are obviously easy to identify, it is noteworthy that they seem to be preferentially affected in degenerative disease of the central nervous system (CNS). An example is the large cholinergic motor neuron so devastatingly affected in motor neuron disease (amyotrophic lateral sclerosis). In AD it is the magnocellular population of the basal forebrain nuclei and the large cortical pyramidal cells that appear to be at risk (Terry, Peck, DeTeresa, Schechter, & Horoupian, 1981). Similarly, large nerve cells are affected in the locus coeruleus in Parkinson's disease.

The reason for the premature death of nerve cells is unknown. One of the most widely held concepts is that of the free radical hypothesis. Cells with high metabolic rate (such as large neurons) can, through excess formation of superoxide radical, lead to cell death and damage to membrane lipid and fragmentation of deoxy-

TABLE 10

Summary of Pathophysiology in Dementias of Different Cause

	Plaques and tangles	Cortical neuronal defect	Cortical metabolic defect	Cortical CAT	Nucleus basalis loss of cells
Creutzfeldt-Jakob disease	absent	present	—	reduced	lost
Alcoholic dementia	absent[1]	some	present	reduced	lost
Huntington's chorea	absent	present	normal[3]	normal	no loss
Parkinson's disease	insignificant	some[2]	present	reduced	some loss
Alzheimer's disease	present	present	present	reduced	lost

[1]Duchen & Jacobs, 1984
[2]Oppenheimer, 1984
[3]Kuhl et al., 1982

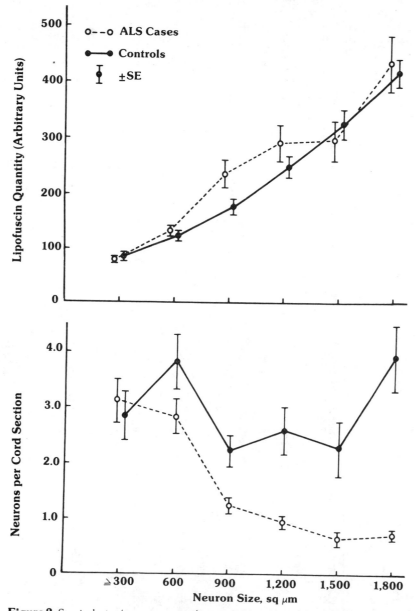

Figure 2. Survival rates (neurons per cord section), (b) and lipofuscin quantities (a) of ventral horn neurons segregated by neuronal size. Vertical bars for each point indicate SEM. Neurons from ALS cases are compared with neurons from controls.

(With kind permission of Dr. G.B. McHolm and the American Medical Association; McHolm, Aguilar, & Norris, 1984) ribonucleic acid (DNA) (Halliwell & Gutteridge, 1985). Lipid peroxide formation occurs with the formation of malonaldehyde (Horrocks, Van Rollins, & Yates, 1981; Tappel, 1973), leading to lipofuscin and possibly cross-linked neurofilament polymers (Selkoe, 1982).

RECOMMENDATIONS

Prophylaxis: Strategies to Prevent Neuronal Loss

So far there is little hard evidence that oxygen radicals may serve as mediators of neurotoxic reactions leading to degenerative disease. Further work on the complex interaction of superoxide and hydroxyl radicals in the aging brain with antioxidative systems (e.g., iron complexes, vitamins E and C, coenzyme Q, and glutathione) may provide a nutritional basis for the preventive therapy of aging and dementia (see Roberts, 1982). Scavengers of hydroxyl radicals such as 1-phenyl-3-(2 thiazolyl)-2 thiourea (PTTU) protect against neurodegeneration induced by 6-hydroxydopamine and 6-aminodopa-

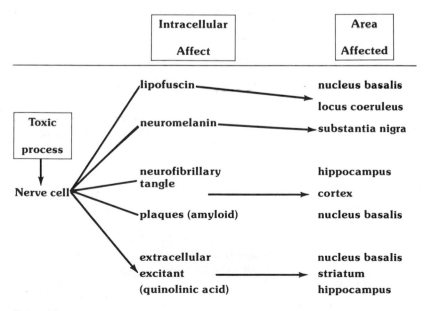

Figure 3. Neurotoxic pathology

mine (Cohen et al., 1976). Increased monoamine oxidase (type B) activity in AD has been reported in the cingulate gyrus, caudate nucleus, and especially in the hippocampus (Carlsson, 1983). Since Cohen (1983) suggested treatment of patients with Parkinson's disease with specific monoamine oxidase inhibitors increases cellular dopamine concentration (protecting against superoxide), and limits hydrogen peroxide formation, drugs such as deprenyl may be worth assessment. In addition to free radical formation, other neurotoxic mechanisms may be responsible for selective loss of neurons. One such possibility is the tryptophan metabolite, quinolinic acid whose concentration in the rat brain increases with age. This excitotoxin is known to act preferentially on neurons of the nucleus accumbens, striatum, and hippocampus (Schwarcz & Kohler, 1983). Quinolinic acid phosphoribosyltransferase catalyzes the conversion to nicotine mononucleotide mainly in synaptic endings (Foster, Zinkand, & Schwarcz, 1985). The enzyme's activity is low in regions susceptible to the neurotoxic action of quinolinic acid (e.g., hippocampus, striatum, retina, and frontal cortex). Further work is required to establish whether quinolinic acid has any neurotoxic role in AD.

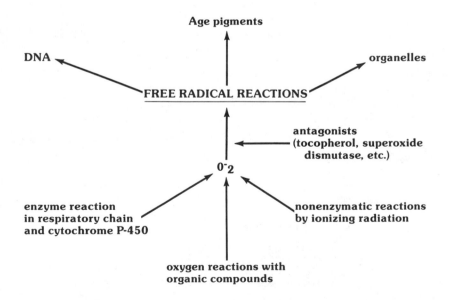

Figure 4. Free radical formation

Therapy: Neurotransmitter Replacement

Memory loss and intellectual deterioration can occur in the absence of Alzheimer-type pathology in the neocortex, but changes in the cholinergic system still emerge as the dominant neurotransmitter system affected in the dementias. Changes in noradrenergic nerve cells, intrinsic cortical neurons, postsynaptic cortical receptors, and possibly serotonergic nerve cells may not be closely associated with AD (Francis et al., 1985).

Clinical Trials

Several factors need to be taken into account. First, the question of diagnosis is important particularly in relatively younger patients. Ideally, selection of patients should be confirmed by biopsy or finally at postmortem. Design of a clinical trial needs to take account of the possibility that (a) 10 to 20% of demented patients may not have a cholinergic defect, that (b) other neurotransmitter defects also need a remedy (e.g., 5-HT), and that (c) brain atrophy and neuronal loss are so severe that effective therapy is not possible. Simplifying the search for suitably active drugs may mean treating patients with "pure" cholinergic defects unaccompanied by cortical plaques and tangles. Thus patients with parkinsonian dementia or alcoholic dementia may be particularly suitable for initial assessment.

The Cholinergic Hypothesis

As we have emphasized, the major neurotransmitter defect in dementia is in the cholinergic system. The confirmation of the "cholinergic hypothesis" of geriatric memory dysfunction has led to considerable interest in the prospects for therapy (Bartus, Dean, Beer, & Lippa, 1982). There is a need to find a cholinergic agonist that penetrates into the brain and interacts with remaining postsynaptic receptors (see DeKosky, 1984). Preferably, such drugs should be tested on fresh human nervous tissue from cases of AD shown to have postsynaptic functional activity. The use of rapid postmortem samples may be of value in demonstrating effective strategies. The recent demonstration of some improvement in general cognitive functions

TABLE 11

Strategies in Treatment of Alzheimer's Disease

1. Prophylaxis

a. Discovery of etiological factors.

b. Prevention of nerve cell loss.

c. Prevention of tangle formation.

d. Amelioration of disease progress—choline?

2. Therapy

a. Stimulation of intact muscarinic receptors.

b. Interaction with autoreceptors on presynaptic cholinergic terminals.

c. Amplification of acetylcholine action (e.g., by anticholinesterases).

d. Use of nootropics.

e. Use of other transmitter-related drugs (e.g., inhibition of 5-hydroxytryptamine reuptake).

in a minority of AD patients treated with a muscarinic agonist is encouraging (Wettstein & Spiegel, 1984), as are the results of intracranial infusion of bethanechol in a small group of patients (Harbaugh, Roberts, Coombs, Saunders, & Reeder, 1984). These trials underline the importance of definitive diagnosis and treatment at an early stage for effective therapy.

CONCLUSION

Comparison of the pathophysiology of several different examples of dementing disease indicates some common features probably linking with functional change. In most cases (except Huntington's chorea) there are changes in the cholinergic system. Loss of neurons in the basal forebrain leads to reduction in CAT activity in the neocortex and parts of the limbic system. Since postsynaptic cholinergic receptors are generally intact, this deficiency is potentially treatable. This conclusion is supported by the work of Fine, Dunnett, Björklund, and Iversen (1985) who have succeeded in restoring cholinergic and inhibitory avoidance memory in rats with ibotenic acid lesions in the nucleus basalis. Transplantation of dissociated cells from the embryonic ventral forebrain to the neocortex, ipsilateral to the nucleus basalis lesions, was effective but grafts of noncholinergic cells were not. A second important pathological change is in the large cortical neurons — some of these are lost or impaired in all cases of dementia and some contain tangles. It is postulated that these are glutamate-containing nerve cells with projections to the striatum, amygdala, and brain stem. It may be speculated that drugs stimulating glutamate receptors may have a role in therapy. Effort should concentrate on discovering likely mechanisms leading to such cell loss and tangle formation so that rational prophylactic treatment can be started to prevent progressive degenerative change from occurring.

REFERENCES

American Psychiatric Association. (1980). *Diagnostic and statistical manual of mental disorders*, 3rd ed. Washington, D.C.: American Psychiatric Association.

Antuono, P., Sorbi, S., Bracco, L., Fusco, T., & Amaducci, L. (1980). A discrete sampling technique in senile dementia of the Alzheimer type and alcoholic dementia: Study of the cholinergic system. In L. Amaducci, A.N. Davison, & P. Antuono (Eds.), *Aging of the brain and dementia* (pp. 151-158). New York: Raven Press.

Arendt, T., Bigl, V., & Arendt, A. (1984). Neurone loss in the nucleus basalis of Meynert in Creutzfeldt-Jakob disease. *Acta Neuropathologica, 65*, 85-88.

Arendt, T., Bigl, V., Arendt, A., & Tennstedt, A. (1983). Loss of neurons in the nucleus basalis of Meynert in Alzheimer's disease, paralysis agitans, and Korsakoff's disease. *Acta Neuropathologica, 61*, 101-108.

Ball, M.J., Fisman, M., Hachinski, V., Blume, W., Fox, A., Kral, V.A., Kirshen, A.J., Fox, H., & Merskey, H. (1985). A new definition of Alzheimer's disease: A hippocampal dementia. Lancet, 1, 14-16.

Bartus, R.T., Dean, R.L., Beer, B., & Lippa, A.S. (1982). The cholinergic hypothesis of geriatric memory dysfunction. Science, 217, 408-417.

Bird, E.D., & Spokes, E.G.S. (1982). Huntington's chorea. In T.J. Crow (Ed.), Disorders of neurohumoural transmission (pp. 144-182). London: Academic Press.

Bird, T.D., Stranahan, S., Sumi, S.M., & Raskind, M. (1983). Alzheimer's disease: Choline acetyltransferase activity in brain tissue from clinical and pathological subgroups. Annals of Neurology, 14, 284-293.

Bockman, J.M., Kingsbury, D.T., McKinley, M.P., Bendheim, P.E., & Prusiner, S.B. (1985). Creutzfeldt-Jakob disease prion proteins in human brains. New England Journal of Medicine, 312, 73-78.

Bowen, D.M. (1981). Alzheimer's disease. In A.N. Davison & R.H.S. Thompson (Eds.), The molecular basis of neuropathology (pg. 649). London: Edward Arnold.

Bowen, D.M., Allen, S.J., Benton, J.S., Goodhardt, M.J., Haan, E.A., Palmer, A.M., Sims, N.R., Smith, C.C.T., Spillane, J.A., Esiri, M.M., Neary, D., Snowdon, J.S., Wilcock, G.K., & Davison, A.N. (1983). Biochemical assessment of serotonergic and cholinergic dysfunction and cerebral atrophy in Alzheimer's disease. Journal of Neurochemistry, 41, 266-272.

Bowen, D.M., Benton, J.S., Spillane, J.A., Smith, C.C.T., & Allen, S.J. (1982). Choline acetyltransferase activity and histopathology of frontal neocortex from biopsies of demented patients. Journal of Neurological Sciences, 57, 191-202.

Bowen, D.M., Davison, A.N., Francis, P.T., Palmer, A.M., & Pearce, B.R. (1985). Neurotransmitter and metabolic dysfunction in Alzheimer's dementia: Relationship to histopathological features. In F.C. Rose (Ed.), Research progress in dementia. Basel: S. Karger.

Bowen, D.M., White, P., Spillane, J.A., Goodhardt, M.J., Curzon, G., Iwangoff, P., Meier-Ruge, W., & Davison, A.N. (1979). Accelerated ageing or selective neuronal loss as an important cause of dementia? Lancet, 1, 11-14.

Brun, A., Gottfries, C.G., & Roos, B.E. (1971). Studies of the monoamine metabolism in the central nervous system in Jakob-Creutzfeldt disease. *Acta Neurologica Scandinavica, 47,* 642-645.

Carlsson, A. (1983). Changes in neurotransmitter systems in the aging brain and in Alzheimer's disease. In B. Reisberg (Ed.), *Alzheimer's disease. The standard reference* (pp. 100-107). New York: The Free Press.

Carlsson, A., Adolfsson, R., Aquilonius, S.M., Gottfries, C.G., Oreland, L., Svennerholm, L., & Winblad, B. (1980). Biogenic amines in human brain in normal aging, senile dementia, and chronic alcoholism. In M. Goldstein, A. Lieberman, D.B. Calne, & M.O. Thorner (Eds.), *Ergot compounds and brain function (advances in biochemical psychopharmacology)* (pp. 295-304). New York: Raven Press.

Cohen, G. (1983). The pathobiology of Parkinson's disease: Biochemical aspects of dopamine neuron senescence. *Journal of Neural Transmission,* (Suppl. 19) 89-103.

Cohen, G., Heikkila, R.E., Allis, B., Cabbat, E., Dembiec, D., MacNamee, D., Mytilineou, C., & Winston, B. (1976). Destruction of sympathetic nerve terminals by 6-hydroxydopamine: Protection by 1-phenyl-3(2-thiazolyl)-2-thiourea, diethyldithiocarbamate, methimazole, cysteamine, ethanol and n-butanol. *The Journal of Pharmacology and Experimental Therapeutics, 199,* 336-352.

Coyle, J.T. (1983). Short review — Neurotoxic action of kainic acid. *Journal of Neurochemistry, 41,* 1-11.

DeKosky, S.T. (1984). Recovery of function in senile dementia of the Alzheimer type. In S.W. Scheff (Ed.), *Aging and recovery of function in the central nervous system* (pp. 207-217). New York: Plenum Press.

Divac, I., Markowitsch, H.J., & Pritzel, M. (1978). Behavioral and anatomic consequences of small intra-striatal injections of kainic acid in the rat. *Brain Research, 151,* 523-532.

Duchen, L.W., & Jacobs, J.M. (1984). Nutritional deficiencies and metabolic disorders. In J. Hume Adams, J.A.N. Corsellis, & L.W. Duchen (Eds.), *Greenfield's neuropathology* (4th ed., pp. 573-627). London: Edward Arnold.

Elizan, T.S., Madden, D.L., Noble, G.R., Herrmann, K.L., Gardner, J., Schwartz, J., Smith, H., Jr., Sever, J.L., & Yahr, M.D. (1979). Viral antibodies in serum and CSF of parkinsonian patients and controls. *Archives of Neurology, 36,* 529-534.

Elizan, T.S., Schwartz, J., Yahr, M.D., & Casals, J. (1978). Antibodies against arboviruses in postencephalitic and idiopathic Parkinson's disease. *Archives of Neurology, 35,* 257-260.

Elizan, T.S., Yahr, M.D., & Casals, J. (1979). Indirect immunofluorescence test against lymphocytic choriomeningitis (LCM) virus in Parkinson's disease. *Mount Sinai Journal of Medicine, 46,* 597-598.

Fine, A., Dunnett, S.B., Bjorklund, A., & Iversen, S.D. (1985). Cholinergic ventral forebrain grafts to neocortex improve inhibitory avoidance memory in a rat model of Alzheimer's disease. *Neuroscience Letters,* (Suppl.) 21, S80.

Foster, A.C., Zinkand, W.C., & Schwarcz, R. (1985). Quinolinic acid phosphoribosyltransferase in rat brain. *Journal of Neurochemistry, 44,* 446-455.

Francis, P.T., Palmer, A.M., Sims, N.R., Bowen, D.M., Davison, A.N., Esiri, M.M., Neary, D., Snowden, J.S., & Wilcock, G.K. (1985). Neurochemical studies suggest treatment strategies for early-onset Alzheimer's disease. *New England Journal of Medicine, 313,* 7-11.

Friedle, N.M., Kelly, P.H., & Moore, K.E. (1978). Regional brain atrophy and reductions in glutamate release and uptake after intrastriatal kainic acid. *British Journal of Pharmacology, 63,* 151-178.

Gusella, J.F., Wexler, N.S., Conneally, P.M., Naylor, S.L., Anderson, M.A., Tanzi, R.E., Watkins, P.C., Ottina, K., Wallace, M.R., Sakaguchi, A.Y., Yound, A.B., & Shoulson, I. (1983). A polymorphic DNA marker genetically linked to Huntington's disease. *Nature, 306,* 234-238.

Halliwell, B., & Gutterridge, J.M.C. (1985). Oxygen radicals and the nervous system. *Trends in Neurosciences, 8,* 22-26.

Harbaugh, R.E., Roberts, D.W., Coombs, D.W., Saunders, R.L., & Reeder, T.M. (1984). Preliminary report: Intracranial cholinergic drug infusion in patients with Alzheimer's disease. *Neurosurgery, 15,* 514-518.

Hasse, G.R. (1977). Diseases presenting as dementia. In C.E. Wells (Ed.), *Dementia* (2nd ed., pp. 27-68). Philadelphia: F.A. Davis Co.

Horrocks, L.A., Van Rollins, M., & Yates, A.J. (1981). Lipid changes in the ageing brain. In A.N. Davison & R.H.S. Thompson (Eds.), *The molecular basis of neuropathology* (pp. 601-630). London: Edward Arnold.

Iqbal, K., Somerville, R.A., Thompson, C.H., & Wisniewski, H.M.

(1985). Brain glutamate decarboxylase and cholinergic enzyme activities in scrapie. *Journal of the Neurological Sciences, 67,* 345-350.

Irwin, I., & Langston, J.W. (1985). Selective accumulation of MPP+ in the substantia nigra: A key to neurotoxicity? *Life Sciences, 36,* 207-213.

Kuhl, D.E., Phelps, M.E., Markham, C.H., Metter, E.J., Riege, W.H., & Winter, J. (1982). Cerebral metabolism and atrophy in Huntington's disease determined by 18 FDG and computed tomographic scan. *Annals of Neurology, 12,* 425-434.

Langston, J.W. (1985). MPTP and Parkinson's disease. *Trends in Neurosciences, 8,* 79-83.

Lishman, W.A. (1977). *Senile and presenile dementias: A report of the MRC subcommittee.* London: MRC.

Mahendra, B. (1984). *Dementia. A survey of the syndrome of dementia.* Lancaster, England: MTP Press Ltd.

Mann, D.M., & Yates, P.O. (1982). Pathogenesis of Parkinson's disease. *Archives of Neurology, 39,* 545-549.

Marsden, C.D. (1983). Neuromelanin and Parkinson's disease. *Journal of Neural Transmission, 19,* 121-141.

Marsden, C.D., & Harrison, M.J. (1972). Outcome of investigation of patients with presenile dementia. *British Medical Journal, 2,* 249-252.

Mash, D.C., Sevush, S., Flynn, D.D., Norenberg, M.D., & Potter, L.T. (1984). Loss of M2-receptors in Alzheimer's disease. *Neurology, 34,* 120.

Masullo, C., Pocchiari, M., Gibbs, C.J., Jr., & Gajdusek, D.C. (1984). Choline acetyltransferase activity and ^{3}H-quinuclidinylbenzilate binding in brains of scrapie-infected hamsters. *Neuroscience Letters, 51,* 87-93.

Matthews, W.B. (1982). Spongiform virus encephalopathy. In W.B. Matthews & G.H. Glaser (Eds.), *Recent advances in clinical neurology,* No. 3 (pp. 229-238). New York: Churchill Livingstone.

Mayeux, R., Stern, Y., Rosen, J., & Benson, D.F. (1983). Is "subcortical dementia" a recognizable clinical entity? *Annals of Neurology, 14,* 278-283.

McDermott, F.R., Fraser, H., & Dickinson, A.G. (1978). Reduced choline-acetyltransferase activity in scrapie mouse brain. *Lancet, II,* 318-319.

McHolm, G.B., Aguilar, M.J., & Norris, F.H. (1984). Lipofuscin in amyotrophic lateral sclerosis. *Archives of Neurology, 41,* 1187-1188.

McKhann, G., Drachman, D., Folstein, M., Katzman, R., Price, D., & Stadlan, E.M. (1984). Clinical diagnosis of Alzheimer's disease: Report of the NINCDS-ADRDA Work Group under the auspices of Department of Health and Human Services Task Force on Alzheimer's Disease. *Neurology, 34,* 939-944.

Meyer, J.S., Largen, J.W., Jr., Shaw, T., Mortel, K.F., & Rogers, R. (1984). Interactions of normal aging, senile dementia, multi-infarct dementia and alcoholism in the elderly. In J.T. Hartford & T. Samorajski (Eds.), *Alcoholism in the elderly. Social and biomedical issues* (pp. 227-253). New York: Raven Press Books Ltd.

Morrison, J.H., Rogers, J., Scherr, S., Benoit, R., & Bloom, F.E. (1985). Somatostatin immunoreactivity in neuritic plaques of Alzheimer's patients. *Nature, 314,* 90-92.

Oppenheimer, D.R. (1984). Diseases of the basal ganglia, cerebellum and motor neurons. In J. H. Adams, J.A.N. Corsellis, & L.W. Duchen (Eds.), *Greenfield's neuropathology* (2nd ed., pp. 699-748). London: Edward Arnold.

Pearce, B.R., Palmer, A.M., Bowen, D.M., Wilcock, G.K., Esiri, M.M., & Davison, A.N. (1984). Neurotransmitter dysfunction and atrophy of the caudate nucleus in Alzheimer's disease. *Neurochemical Pathology, 2,* 221-233.

Pearson, R.C.A., Sofroniew, M.V., Cuello, A.C., Powell, T.P.S., Eckenstein, R., Esiri, M.M., & Wilcock, G.K. (1983). Persistence of cholinergic neurons in the basal nucleus in a brain with senile dementia of the Alzheimer's type demonstrated by immunohistochemical staining for choline acetyltransferase. *Brain Research, 289,* 375-379.

Perry, E.K., Curtis, M., Dick, D.J., Candy, J.M., Atack, J.R., Bloxham, C.A., Blessed, G., Fairbairn, A., Tomlinson, B.E., & Perry, R.H. (1985). Cholinergic correlates of cognitive impairment in Parkinson's disease: Comparisons with Alzheimer's disease. *Journal of Neurology, Neurosurgery and Psychiatry, 48,* 413-421.

Perry, E.K., Tomlinson, B.E., Blessed, G., Bergmann, K., Gibson, P.H., & Perry, R.H. (1978). Correlation of cholinergic abnormalities with senile plaques and mental test scores in senile dementia.

British Medical Journal, ii, 1457-1459.

Perry, R.H. (1984). Neuropathology of dementia. In J.M.S. Pearce (Ed.), *Dementia, A clinical approach* (pp. 89-116). London: Blackwell Scientific.

Perry, R.H., Candy, J.M., Perry, E.K., Irving, D., Blessed, G., Fairbairn, A.F., & Tomlinson, B.E. (1982). Extensive loss of choline acetyltransferase activity is not reflected by neuronal loss in the nucleus of Meynert in Alzheimer's disease. *Neuroscience Letters, 33,* 311-315.

Perry, R.H., Tomlinson, B.E., Candy, J.M., Blessed, G., Foster, J.F., Bloxham, C.A., & Perry, E.K. (1983). Cortical cholinergic deficit in mentally impaired Parkinsonian patients. *Lancet, II,* 789-790.

Roberts, E. (1982). Potential therapies in aging and senile dementias. *Annals of the New York Academy of Sciences, 396,* 165-178.

Roberts, G.W., Crow, T.J., & Polak, J.M. (1985). Location of neuronal tangles in somatostatin neurones in Alzheimer's disease. *Nature, 314,* 92-94.

Roberts, P.J., McBean, G.J., Sharif, N.A., & Thomas, E.M. (1982). Striatal glutamergic functions: Modifications following specific lesions. *Brain Research, 235,* 83-91.

Ruberg, M., Ploska, A., Javoy-Agid, F., & Agid, Y. (1982). Muscarinic binding with choline acetyltransferase activity in Parkinsonian subjects with reference to dementia. *Brain Research, 235,* 83-91.

Schwarcz, R., & Kohler, C. (1983). Differential vulnerability of central neurons of the rat to quinolinic acid. *Neuroscience Letters, 38,* 85-90.

Schwartz, J., & Elizan, T.S. (1979). Search for viral particles and virus-specific products in idiopathic Parkinson's disease brain material. *Annals of Neurology, 6,* 261-263.

Selkoe, D.J. (1982). Molecular pathology of the aging human brain. *Trends in Neurosciences, 5,* 332-336.

Sims, N.R., Bowen, D.M., Allen, S.J., Smith, C.C.T., Neary, D., Thomas, D.J., & Davison, A.N. (1983). Presynaptic cholinergic dysfunction in patients with dementia. *Journal of Neurochemistry, 40,* 503-509.

Sims, N.R., Bowen, D.M., & Davison, A.N. (1981). [14C]-acetylcholine synthesis and 14 C-carbon dioxide production from U-[14C]-glucose by tissue prisms from human neocortex. *Biochemical Journal, 196,* 867-876.

Sofroniew, M.V., Pearson, R.C.A., Eckenstein, F., Cuello, A.C., & Powell, T.P.S. (1983). Retrograde changes in cholinergic neurons in the basal forebrain of the rat following cortical damage. *Brain Research, 289,* 370-374.

Sorbi, S., Antuono, P., & Amaducci, L. (1980). Choline acetyltransferase (CAT) and acetylcholinesterase (AChE) abnormalities in senile dementia: Importance of biochemical measures in human postmortem brain specimen. *Italian Journal of the Neurological Sciences, 1,* 75-83.

Tappel, A.L. (1973). Lipid peroxidation damage to cell components. *Federal Proceedings, 32,* 1870-1874.

Terry, R.D., Peck, A., DeTeresa, R., Schechter, R., & Horoupian, D.S., (1981). Some morphometric aspects of the brain in senile dementia of the Alzheimer's type. *Annals of Neurology, 10,* 184-192.

Tomlinson, B.E., & Corsellis, J.A.N. (1984). Aging and the dementias. In J.H. Adams, J.A.N. Corsellis, & L.W. Duchen (Eds.), *Greenfield's neuropathology* (4th ed., pp. 951-1025). London: Edward Arnold.

Wetmur, J.G., Schwartz, J., & Elizan, T.S. (1979). Nucleic acid homology studies of viral nucleic acids in idiopathic Parkinson's disease. *Archives of Neurology, 36,* 462-464.

Wettstein, A., & Spiegel, R. (1984). Clinical trials with the cholinergic drug RS 86 in Alzheimer's disease (AD) and senile dementia of the Alzheimer type (SDAT). *Psychopharmacology, 84,* 572-573.

Whitehouse, P.J., Price, D.L., Struble, R.G., Clark, A.W., Coyle, J.T., & Delong, M.R. (1982). Alzheimer's disease and senile dementia: Loss of neurons in the basal forebrain. *Science, 215,* 1237-1239.

Wilcock, G.K., Esiri, M.M., Bowen, D.M., & Smith, C.C.T. (1982). Alzheimer's disease. Correlation of cortical choline acetyltransferase activity with the severity of dementia and histological abnormalities. *Journal of the Neurological Sciences, 57,* 407-417.

4

Beyond the Transmitter-Based Approach To Alzheimer's Disease

Bengt Winblad, MD, Gösta Bucht, MD,
Christopher J. Fowler, PhD, and William Wallace, PhD

The intention of this article is to speculate about research approaches to Alzheimer's disease (AD) with a view to illuminate the pathogenesis and possible diagnostic aids of the disease which might lead to more appropriate treatments than those presently available.

The first part of this chapter presents some limitations of the current experimental approaches to AD. The pathogenesis of the disease, a suggestion for a novel means of diagnosis, and various treatments will also be presented. The article will be concluded by the proposal of a more precise classification of the disease for research purposes that differentiates AD into subgroups according to age of onset and symptomatology.

LIMITATIONS OF CURRENT EXPERIMENTAL APPROACHES TO ALZHEIMER'S DISEASE

Although theories abound, the cause of AD is not known (for review, see Wurtman, 1985). One approach has been to determine whether there is a "primary lesion" responsible for the symptoms of AD. This line of research was inspired by the neurochemistry of Parkinson's disease where a dopaminergic lesion was apparent and where replacement therapy with L-DOPA has proved to be an effective treatment.

The most emphasized "primary lesion" for AD has been that of the cortical cholinergic neurons. In particular, a loss of cholinergic cell bodies in the basal nucleus of Meynert leading to considerable cortical cholinergic depletion has been implicated (Coyle, Price, & DeLong, 1983; Greenwald, Mohs, & Davis, 1983). Such observations have led to extensive clinical trials of cholinergic precursors such as choline and lecithin and of cholinesterase inhibitors such as physostigmine, with variable degrees of success (Davis & Mohs, 1982; Levy, Little, Chuaqui, & Reith, 1983; Wettstein, 1983). There are a number of criticisms that can be levelled at the "primary lesion" approach, for the presenile form of the disease, in general, and to the cholinergic hypothesis, in particular. These are considered briefly below.

1. *Lesion Selectivity.*   In Parkinson's disease, there is a fairly selective lesion of the nigrostriatal dopaminergic innervation. Lesions in other transmitter systems only appear at more advanced stages of the illness, where, interestingly, dementia comes into the picture. In AD (i.e., both presenile and senile forms taken together) the cholinergic lesion is by no means the only transmitter deficit being found. Reductions in noradrenaline (Table 2), serotonin (Table 3) and neuropeptides such as somatostatin (Davies, Katzman, & Terry, 1980; Rossor, Iversen, Reynolds, Mountjoy, & Roth, 1984) have also been reported. Furthermore, as pointed out by Bowen et al. (1983), the degree of atrophy of the cortex is greater than would be expected if a selective degeneration of cholinergic neurons had occurred.

2. *Animal Models.*   If a lesion in the basal nucleus of Meynert is the primary lesion in AD, then it would be expected that many of the symptoms of this disease could be produced in rats with lesions of the nucleus basalis magnocellularis (which is the rodent equivalent of the basal nucleus of Meynert). Flicker, Dean, Watkins, Fisher, and Bartus (1983) have demonstrated that performance of rats in a passive avoidance test was reduced after ibotenic acid lesion of the nucleus basalis magnocellularis. It is, however, difficult to draw conclusions concerning learning and memory based on passive avoidance tests alone (see Bammer, 1982), unless the test is used in conjunction with other tests for both "working" and "reference" memory (for discussion, see Archer & Fowler, 1985). It should also be stressed that memory impairment is but one symptom of AD. In many ways it is not the most distressing one for both the patient and those responsible for the care of the patient.

3. *Treatment.*   Analagous to the situation in Parkinson's disease and if it is assumed that the primary lesion is cholinergic, it might be expected that replacement therapy with cholinergic precursors or cholinergic agents should prove useful for the treatment of AD (particularly the senile form). While inserting the caveat that many of the studies on the effects of choline, physostigmine, and lecithin have been undertaken on patients with severe dementia, the ther-

apeutic potential of these agents seems to be rather small. The efficacy, if any, of choline and lecithin might also be due to their effects on cell membrane function rather than to their properties as cholinergic precursors.

From the above discussion, it can be concluded that while the cholinergic deficit in AD perhaps is the most pronounced neurotransmitter deficit and perhaps the only one that can "meet the criteria for significance" (Greenwald et al., 1983), the transmitter-deficit approach may not be the most useful approach, particularly for the presenile form of the disease. It seems to the present authors that the various neurotransmitter deficits, while undoubtedly providing the explanations for the symptomatology of the disease, are essentially a secondary event resulting from the neuron loss produced by the disease process. Thus, therapy based on neurotransmitter "cocktails" may alleviate some of the symptoms of the disease but will not attack the root of the disease or its final incapacitating stages. However, the transmitter deficits that have been demonstrated may lead to useful early diagnostic tests for AD (Lamb, Bradshaw, & Szabadi, 1983).

MODEL FOR THE DEVELOPMENT OF ALZHEIMER'S DISEASE: ALTERNATIVE PATHOGENESIS

The neurochemical studies so far performed have indicated that a number of neurotransmitters and neuromodulators are severely depleted in AD; however, several others are not affected to any significant extent. These include, for example, GABA, substance P, and met-enkephalin (Rossor, Emson, Mountjoy, Roth, & Iverson, 1982; Yates et al., 1982).

A hypothesis for the pathogenesis of the disease giving an explanation of why three particular transmitter systems (serotonergic, noradrenergic, and cholinergic) should be affected has been put forward (Hardy et al., 1985). This hypothesis emphasizes the concept that subcortical degeneration may be a consequence of retrograde axonal degeneration which, in turn, results from primary cortical abnormalities. The hypothesis rests upon the discovery of an altered blood-brain barrier in AD, (Alafuzoff, Adolfsson, Bucht, & Winblad, 1983; Mann et al., 1982a; Wisniewski & Koslowski, 1982).

Cerebral blood vessels are known to be innervated both seroto-ninergically (Edvinsson, Deguerce, Duverger, MacKenzie, & Scatton, 1983) and cholinergically (Eckenstein & Baughman, 1983; Estrada, Hamel, & Krause, 1983), and there is evidence to support a noradrenergic innervation from the locus coeruleus of cerebral blood vessels as well (for review, see Mann, 1983). This raises the possibility that in AD the nerve terminals located on the cerebral microvessels are no longer protected by the blood-brain barrier from neurotoxic effects of agents present in the blood, such as perhaps heavy metals or viruses. Alternatively, exposure of the nerve terminals as a result of a deficiency in the blood-brain barrier results in the production of antibodies which degenerate the nerve terminals and produce the senile plaques.

EXCITOTOXINS AND PROTECTING FACTORS

While neurofibrillary tangles are seen in the basal nucleus of Meynert, the raphe nuclei, and the locus coeruleus (Ishii, 1966), very few tangles are seen in the substantia nigra. Thus, the degenera-tive processes associated with AD seem to spare a number of neurons associated with certain transmitters but not others. This raises the question of whether the neurons that are spared contain some sort of protecting factor against degeneration, while the other neurons do not, or, alternatively, whether the neurons that degenerate con-tain some sort of endogenous toxin, while the resistant neurons do not. These two possibilities are considered below.

1. Protecting factors. In a recent study by Bowen et al. (1983) the entire temporal lobe of control and late-onset dementia patients indicated that while the lobe weight of the dementia patients was 80% of control, the content of the ganglioside NeuNAc was only 65% of control. In experimental animals, treatment with the gangli-oside GM_1 has been shown to promote neuritogenesis in mono-layer cultures of mouse neuroblastoma cells (Facci et al., 1984), to reduce dopamine cell body degeneration in the rat substantia nigra after hemitransection (Agnati et al., 1983; Toffano et al., 1984), to reduce the depletion of serotonin in the frontal and occipital cortices of rats pretreated with 5,7-dihydroxytryptamine (Jonsson, Kojima, & Gorio, 1983), and to enhance regrowth of rat cerebral cortical noradrenaline nerve terminals after 6-hydroxydopamine lesion (Kojima, Gorio, Janigro, & Jonsson, 1984). These findings raise the possibility that gangliosides protect neurons from degenerative processes and that the content of the critical ganglioside(s) is low in neuron populations susceptible to degeneration. If this speculation is correct, it would be expected that the ganglioside concentration is lower in cholinergic neurons originating in the basal nucleus of Meynert and terminating in the cerebral cortex (or in the serotonergic neurons from the raphe nuclei to the cortex) than for the cortical GABAergic interneurons. It may be that the levels become lower with age and reach a critical level where the susceptible neurons are no longer protected and become particularly sensitive to degeneration induced by some precipitating factor (a toxin, a virus, etc.). Such a speculation may be possible to test by histochemical techniques in both human postmortem and animal brain tissue of different ages.

2. *Excitotoxins.*   An alternative is that rather than having too little protecting factor(s), the susceptible neurons are in contact with endogenous compounds that are damaging to the nerve. The endogenous excitotoxin quinolinic acid is, for example, unevenly distributed across the brain, with the highest concentrations being found in the cortex and the lowest in the striatum (Moroni, Lombardi, Carla, & Moneti, 1984). Quinolinic acid, however, does not seem to be a suitable candidate toxin for AD, since it produces lesions of the cell bodies while sparing the axons to a large extent (for review, see Foster, French, Whetsell, & Kohler, 1983; Schwarcz, Collins, & Schwarcz, 1984). On the other hand, other endogenous compounds may be present in the brain that are toxic to nerve terminals. The excitatory amino acids aspartate and glutamate, for example, may have excitotoxic properties. Glutamate and aspartate release from unstimulated and potassium-stimulated human cortical miniprisms is the same, however, in control and AD biopsy samples (Bowen, Smith, & Davison, 1983). These findings would at first argue against the notion that these amino acids are responsible for the neuronal degeneration seen in AD. It is, however, possible that certain neuron populations in the AD brains are more sensitive to the excitotoxic effects of aspartate and glutamate than either the same neuron populations in normal brains or neuron populations that are spared in AD. The finding that the potassium-stimulated (but not basal) release of glutamate from human cortical biopsy samples increases with age (Bowen, Smith, & Davison, 1983) is consistent with the notion whereby the susceptible neurons are spared until older ages when a toxic level of glutamate is reached. It may be possible to test this notion *in vitro* by studying the effect of aspartate and glutamate on

control and AD brains, if such explants can be preserved in culture. Thus a combination of 1 and 2 above, while still in the realm of wild speculation, may provide an explanation for the neurochemical changes found in AD.

DIAGNOSTIC AIDS—
MOLECULAR BIOLOGICAL ASPECTS

One of the main criteria for an effective treatment of AD is that suitable diagnostic aids be developed so that the disease can be diagnosed with reliability at an early stage. At present, as concluded by Dahl (1983), "in the absence of a specific and simple diagnosis for Alzheimer's disease, the diagnosis is one of exclusion." A number of techniques, such as computerized tomography and proton NMR imaging, have been tried as possible diagnostic tests (Besson et al., 1983; Brinkman, Sarwar, Levin, & Morris, 1981; Bucht, Adolfsson, & Winblad, 1984) with rather disappointing results. Thus, with no current viable way of diagnosing the disease with a single test even after it has begun to develop, other means of diagnosis are badly needed. One such possibility is the use of genetic analysis as a means to diagnose the likelihood of an individual developing AD.

Diagnosis of AD would be greatly facilitated by the discovery of a genetic abnormality associated with the disease. The identification of a gene whose modification is associated with AD will allow the characterization of the primary cellular events involved in the disease (through the characterization of the gene product) and the detection of those individuals at risk to develop the disease later in life (since it may be possible to use peripheral tissue). The search for such a modified gene does not necessarily require the use of post-mortem tissue, although the use of such tissue could greatly facilitate the search by presenting a starting point for the examination of the genome for the "Alzheimer gene."

To identify an "Alzheimer gene," such a gene or genes must exist. There is evidence of a genetic component to at least one form of the disease, familial Alzheimer's disease (FAD). In addition, such a molecular genetic approach has been successfully applied to Huntington's disease, another neurological disease that has presented some similar research problems as AD (Gusella et al., 1984). However, the genetic component of AD is considerably less well-characterized than in Huntington's disease, making the experimental approaches much more complicated. Again, these complications may be overcome by the combination of molecular genetic analysis and neurochemical characterization of the afflicted tissue.

GENETIC COMPONENT OF ALZHEIMER'S DISEASE

It has been difficult to determine whether AD is an inherited condition for numerous reasons. The epidemiological analysis of families in which a member manifests this disease has been hindered by such problems as the selective use of histopathological examination of autopsy tissue definitely to diagnose AD, the lack of definitive diagnosis in living patients, the expression of the disease late in life, and the possibility that the current definition of the disease may be the result of various etiologies.

The evidence implicating a genetic component to this disease has come from studies of families exhibiting the disease, epidemiological examinations of the general population, and relating Down's syndrome to AD. Breitner and Folstein (1984) have examined living demented patients for development of AD, using language disorder and apraxia to define the disease. They found an age-specific risk of dementia among the siblings and children of these probands, and termed this genetically-induced form of the disease FAD. They have suggested that FAD is a dominant genetic disorder with an age-dependent penetrance. Heston, Mastri, Andersson, and White (1981) and Heston, (1983), after analyzing 125 probands and their primary and secondary relatives, reported that those related to someone with AD are more likely to develop the disease earlier in life, thereby suggesting that the inherited form of AD accelerates the disease in those who would develop it anyway. It has also been reported that relatives of those probands with a later onset of the disease are less likely to develop AD (Jarvik, 1978). Thus, the familial form of the disease (which is estimated to be one-third of all AD cases) is represented by an earlier onset, a greater severity of symptoms, and a greater risk to relatives. These observations have led Wright and Whalley (1984) and others to suggest that the differences observed in the age of onset may define two different forms of the disease, with the early onset form representing an inheritable disease and the late onset form more compatable with an acceleration of the aging process.

The final type of evidence implicating a genetic component is the observed relationship between Down's syndrome (trisomy 21) and AD (Heston & Mastri, 1977). Down's syndrome, a condition attributable to chromosomal aberrations, induces neuropathological changes similar to AD in the brains of those suffering from this condition and who have lived past 40 years, an advanced age for Down's syndrome cases. However, whether such cases also suffer from AD has been questioned (Epstein, 1983), particularly since clinical diagnosis of dementia is difficult in these patients.

In conclusion, the genetic component of AD may be responsible for FAD, which is believed to involve an early onset of dementia, an increased severity of the symptoms, a shortened survival time, and greater risk to primary relatives. Whether this form of the disease actually has a distinct etiology or simply represents a different form of reaction of the individual brain to the common etiology of AD has not been examined.

THE IDENTIFICATION OF THE "ALZHEIMER GENE"

Gusella et al. (1984) have investigated another inherited neuropathological condition, Huntington's disease, by combining genetic linkage analysis with recombinant DNA technology. They have used DNA markers of the human genome to identify fragments of the human genome that have alterations of their base sequence in certain individuals producing genomic polymorphisms. These DNA markers, which are small portions of the human genome that are derived from known chromosomal locations, have been cloned. A genomic polymorphism can be identified when these DNA markers detect a change in the base pattern of the genes as unique genomic fragments that are produced by digestion with restriction endonucleases. Such unique genomic patterns are called restriction fragment length polymorphisms (RFLP). They represent altered DNA base sequences that are present within only a few individuals. Since the DNA markers correlate to known chromosomal locations, these polymorphisms can be similarly localized.

Gusella and associates found that a particular RFLP, localized to the short arm of chromosome 4, is genetically related to Huntington's disease. However, this RFLP does not represent "the Huntington's gene."

The identification of an "Alzheimer gene" would require an appropriate probe of the genome and a means of confirming the identity of such a gene. Three different approaches may be used to obtain a probe to identify responsible genes. First, analogous to the search for the Huntington's disease, random DNA markers of the human genome may be used to detect RFLP's which may then be tested for co-inheritance with AD. Studies such as these have in fact been initiated (Nee et al., 1983). However, a major obstacle is the lack of well-characterized Alzheimer families that can be used to analyze for co-inheritance with suspected RFLP's. A second approach would be the use of recombinant complementary DNA (cDNA) probes to known gene products. Such cDNA probes already exist for many of the neurotransmitter systems, neuropeptides, and neuronal markers that have been shown to be affected in Alzheimer postmortem tissue. These probes may be used to examine the structure of the corresponding genes within the afflicted tissue and control tissue to determine whether alterations in these particular genes correlate with the disease. The advantages of this approach over that using DNA markers is that a specific gene (and one whose identity is known) is being examined. In addition, the determination does not rely solely on the test of co-inheritance. However, a distinct disadvantage would be the limited number of genes that could be examined. A third approach would combine the advantages of using DNA markers, which make no initial assumptions about the identity of the gene with those of using specific cDNA probes, which identify specific genes and do not rely upon a co-inheritance determination. Probes may be constructed from messenger RNA, which is either present only within the Alzheimer brain or specifically absent from the afflicted tissue. Such messenger RNA may be enriched from postmortem brain tissue using standard molecular biological techniques. Most likely there will be numerous messenger RNA species whose levels will be altered in such tissue, the great majority of which will be due to secondary effects of the disease. The construction of cDNA from all of these affected RNA's will allow the examination of the corresponding genes using RFLP analysis. Thus, similar to DNA markers, such unidentified cDNA probes can detect change in the gene structure and, similar to other specific cDNA probes, Alzheimer cDNA probes will directly identify the responsible gene. With a preliminary identification, the association of the gene with the disease could be determined with co-inheritance tests. In addition, the gene product could be characterized (with the cDNA already in hand) to investigate the neuronal events responsible for AD.

PROPOSED TREATMENTS

1. Treatment of the disease process itself

At present, there is no obvious treatment that will arrest the progression of the disease although there is conflicting evidence concerning the efficacy of the "metabolic enhancers," such as Hydergine® (see Branconnier, 1983). Two recent approaches in animal models, however, have been found either to protect against neuronal loss after lesion, or even to produce reinnervation of nervous tissue, namely ganglioside GM_1 treatment (Agnati et al., 1983; Jonsson et al., 1983; Toffano et al., 1984) and grafts with fetal tissue (Gage, Stenevi, Björklund, Dunnett, & Kelly, 1985; Schmidt, Ingvar, Lindvall, Stenevi, & Björklund, 1982), respectively. The usefulness of these approaches in senile dementia, needless to say, is rather difficult to gauge, because of the considerable neuronal plasticity found in some rat brain regions. Wenk and Olton (1984), for example, have shown that while a unilateral lesion by ibotenic acid of the nucleus basalis magnocellularis in the rat leads within a week to a 60% decrease in neocortical choline acetyltransferase (CAT) activity (with respect to the unlesioned side), there was a recovery of activity with time so that 12 weeks after lesion the neocortical CAT activities on the unlesioned and lesioned sides were the same (Wenk & Olton, 1984). The rat is also able to recover lost locomotor activity 4 weeks after unilateral ablation of the motor cortex, the recovery being accelerated by a single dose of amphetamine 24 hours after surgery (Feeney, Gonzalez, & Law, 1982).

In the cat, on the other hand, the loss of motor ability after cortical ablation is prolonged and is only temporarily reversed by amphetamine treatment (Feeney & Hovda, 1983). Many of the reported experiments with the ganglioside GM_1 have been undertaken with young rats (150-200g body weight), and the ganglioside treatment started relatively soon after the lesion had been produced (Toffano et al., 1984). Without wishing to detract in any way from the impressive results produced by ganglioside GM_1 treatment in lesioned rats, it is arguable whether this lesion/treatment paradigm is a useful predictor for the outcome of treatment of an elderly patient with a progressive degenerating disorder, especially when treatment does not start until a long time after the degenerative processes have begun. A more predictive value might, on the other hand, come from studies in animals where there is less neuronal plasticity. The simplest model for this is the aged rat where fetal grafts into the hippocampal and septal regions have been shown to increase memory and learning performance to an impressive extent (Gage, Björklund, Stenevi, Dunnett, & Kelly, 1984; Gage, Dunnett, Stenevi, & Björklund, 1983).

The next stage is to use animal models where the histopathological changes mirror more closely those found in AD (for review see Brizzee, Ordy, Hofer, & Kaack, 1978).

Because of the presumably small degree of neuronal plasticity in the aged human brain, it is likely that compounds that have been shown to protect against the effects of lesions in animal studies will have less dramatic effects in the senile patient. Such compounds, however, might have useful prophylactic value. Clinical testing of a compound for prophylactic properties is always very difficult and expensive unless there is an obvious target group of individuals who have a high vulnerability for the disease under study.

2. Treatment of the secondary symptoms

The neurotransmitter deficits found in the demented patient lead to a multitude of symptoms that are distressing both for the patient and those involved with the patient's care. Many of the drugs presently available for the treatment of the secondary symptoms, such as antidepressants and neuroleptics, have anticholinergic side effects that further disorientate the patient. It is thus important to develop effective antidepressant and antipsychotic drugs without anticholinergic side effects that can be used in the treatment of the secondary symptoms associated with AD.

One word of caution, based on animal model studies, should be mentioned. In a study where the locomotor performance of rats was determined at different times after unilateral ablation of the motor cortex, Feeney et al. (1982) found that haloperidol treatment delayed the recovery of performance. This result, though subject to the constraints discussed earlier when transposing data from young rats to man, raises the specter that treatment of the secondary symptoms of dementia might, in fact, hinder recovery induced by treatment with a drug (or a surgical procedure such as cell grafts) that cures the patient of the disease. In all probability, that problem is a long way into the future.

DIFFERENTIATING DEMENTIA SUBGROUPS

Throughout the previous discussion it has become evident that dementia should be divided into various subgroups. It should be stressed that there is a need for differentiating the demented patients to select the appropriate treatment strategies. This approach has recently been considered in detail (Lauter, 1985; Roth, 1985). Initially, a distinction must be made between senile dementia (SD) and multi-infarct dementia. They are undoubtedly two different conditions with different neuropathological bases (Alafuzoff, Adolfsson, Grundke-Iqbal, & Winblad, 1985) and with different characteristic clinical criteria (Bucht et al., 1984; Hachinski et al., 1975; Roth, 1971).

The early onset form (which we term AD) may be considered to represent a separate, small, rather homogeneous group different from the late onset form of SD, which is a large rather heterogeneous group (Gottfries, 1985). This distinction is based on the following criteria.

A) Clinical data.   From a clinical point of view, AD represents a rather homogeneous group who suffered an early onset (sixth or seventh decade in most cases) and a malignant progression and commonly exhibit neurological signs indicating focal lesions in the parietal and temporal lobes. On the other hand, SD exhibits a less uniform progression with varying symptoms. The progression of SD is commonly not so severe as in AD (Seltzer & Sherwin, 1983; Gottfries, 1985; Roth, 1985). A further classification of progressive dementia in a prospective study with postmortem histopathology has shown that a combination of clinical data might indicate a further subgrouping of dementia patients as compared to the DSM-III classification (American Psychiatric Association, 1980) (Adolfsson et al., 1985).

B) Genetic data.   The genetic evidence for a distinction between the early and late onset forms of the disease includes epidemiological and family studies, as has been presented earlier in this article.

C) Neuropathological data.   The morphological changes (senile plaques and neurofibrillary tangles) found in SD are identical to those described by Alzheimer in AD. However, there are quantitative differences with more severe changes in AD (Corsellis, 1962; Rothschild & Kasansin, 1936). Gellerstedt (1933) also found plaques and tangles in the normal aged brain. However, the number of plaques and tangles is considerably less than in the demented tissue. These structural changes are found in Parkinson's disease and Down's syndrome. Therefore the disease specificity of the plaques and tangles has been questioned (Gottfries, 1985). Another reason to differentiate AD and SD is the finding (Bondareff et al., 1981) that the neurons of locus coeruleus, which constitute the cells of origin for the active adrenergic projections to the whole AD brain, exhibit a 60% to 80% loss but only about a 20% loss in SD. Furthermore, in SD the neuronal loss is not significantly greater than that found for normal age-matched individuals (Mountjoy, Roth, Evans, N.J.R., & Evans, H.M., 1983).

Whereas AD has been described as a grey matter disorder (specifically neuron loss), alterations of the white matter such as incomplete infarctions have been described in SD by Brun and Englund (1981). Those white matter components that have been found to be changed in SD include characteristic myelin lipids, phospholipids, cholesterol, cerebrosides, and sulfatides (Gottfries, Karlsson, & Svennerholm, 1985).

D) Neurochemical differences. Distinctions between cases of early and late onset forms of the disease also arise from differences in the concentrations of different catecholaminergic and cholinergic transmitters and their markers in many brain regions (Gottfries et al., 1983; Winblad et al., 1982). Rossor et al. (1984) pointed out that older patients (SD) had a relatively pure cholinergic deficit confined to hippocampus and the temporal lobe together with reduced concentration of somatostatin, whereas younger patients (AD) had a wide-spread and severe cholinergic deficit together with abnormalities of noradrenaline and other transmitters. Rossor et al. (1984) concluded that their data did not support the concept of AD representing an acceleration of the normal aging process and that AD may represent a distinct form of pre-SD which differs in important respects from dementia of old age.

In addition, when analyzing different transmitters in one and the same brain area, the correlation among different neurotransmitters was found to be considerably lower in AD than in age-matched controls (Winblad et al., 1982). This suggests that an imbalance among different neurotransmitter system may be characteristic of AD and that subgroups might exist of patients in whom different types of transmitters are insufficient.

FINAL REMARKS

A rational pharmacological treatment to AD will have to await a more precise mapping of losses of neurons and neurotransmitters. In theory, substitution therapy would appear possible, provided that the biochemical deficiencies can be identified for each individual by methods such as, for example, CSF investigations, and that suitable agonists substituting for the missing neurotransmitters are available.

Based on clinical, genetic, biochemical and morphological grounds, there is evidence to suggest that early onset Alzheimer patients, later onset SD patients, and patients with vascular dementias represent separate disease groups. For research purposes further subgroups should be considered in SD on the basis on a genetic component and different clinical signs, such as, progression of disease and focal neurological signs.

The therapeutic advantages of characterizing the pathogenesis and identifying an "Alzheimer gene" would be great. The ability to identify those at risk to develop the disease will allow those individuals to begin any therapies very early in the course of the disease (or indeed even before), enhancing the potential of the therapy. The identification of the gene product will give us a more complete characterization of the pathogenesis, allowing the most intelligent design of drug therapies.

REFERENCES

Adolfsson, R., Alafuzoff, I., & Winblad, B. (1985). *Histopathological validation of the DSM-III criteria in Alzheimer's disease and multi-infarct dementia.* (Manuscript in preparation.)

Adolfsson, R., Gottfries, C.G., Roos, B.E., & Winblad, B. (1979). Changes in brain catecholamines in patients with dementia of Alzheimer type. *British Journal of Psychiatry, 135,* 216-223.

Agnati, L.F., Fuxe, K., Calza, L., Benefenati, F., Cavicchioli, L., Toffano, G., & Goldstein, M. (1983). Gangliosides increase the survival of lesioned nigral dopamine neurons and favour the recovery of dopaminergic synaptic function in striatum of rats by collateral sprouting. *Acta Physiologica Scandinavica, 119,* 347-364.

Alafuzoff, I., Adolfsson, R., Bucht, G., & Winblad, B. (1983). Albumin and immunoglobulin in plasma and cerebrospinal fluid and blood-cerebrospinal fluid barrier function in patients with dementia of Alzheimer type and multi-infarct dementia. *Journal of the Neurological Sciences, 60,* 465-472.

Alafuzoff, I., Adolfsson, R., Grundke-Iqbal, I., & Winblad, B. (1985). Perivascular deposition of serum proteins in cerebral cortex in multiinfarct dementia. *Acta Neuropathologica, 66,* 292-298.

American Psychiatric Association. (1980). *Diagnostic and statistical manual,* 3rd ed. Washington, D.C.: American Psychiatric Association.

Arai, H., Kosaka, K., & Iizuka, T. (1984). Changes in biogenic amines and their metabolites in postmortem brains from patients with Alzheimer's type dementia. *Journal of Neurochemistry, 43,* 388-393.

Archer, T., & Fowler, C.J. (1985). Towards an animal model for the cholinergic lesion in Alzheimer's disease. *Trends in Pharmacological Sciences, 5,* 61.

Argentiero, V., & Tavolato, B. (1980). Dopamine and serotonin metabolite levels in the cerebrospinal fluid in Alzheimer's presenile dementia under basic conditions and after stimulation with cerebral cortex phospholipids. *Journal of Neurology, 224,* 53-58.

Atack, J.R., Perry, E.K., Bonham,, J.R., Perry, R.H., Tomlinson, B.E., Blessed, G., & Fairbairn, A. (1983). Molecular forms of acetylcholinesterase in senile dementia of Alzheimer type: Selective loss of the intermediate (10S) form. *Neuroscience Letters, 40,* 199-205.

Bammer, G. (1982). Pharmacological investigations of neurotransmitter involvement in passive avoidance responding: A review and some new results. *Neuroscience and Biobehavioral Reviews, 6,* 247-296.

Bareggi, S., Franceschi, M., Bonini, L., Zecca, L., & Smirne, S. (1982). Decreased CSF concentration of homovanillic acid and GABA in Alzheimer's disease. *Archives of Neurology, 39,* 709-712.

Benton, J.S., Bowen, D.M., Allen, S.J., Haan, E.A., Davison, A.N., Neary, D., Murphy, R.P., & Snowdon, J.S. (1982). Alzheimer's disease as a disorder of the isodendritic core [Letter to the editor]. *Lancet, I,* 456.

Berger, B., & Alvarez, C. (1983). Pathologie de l'innervation catecholaminergique du cortex cerebral dars le demence de type Alzheimer. *La Presse Medicale, 12,* 3109-3114.

Berger, B., Escourolle, R., & Moyne, M.A. (1976). Axones catecholaminergiques du cortex cerebral humain. *Revue Neurologique, 132,* 183-194.

Besson, J.A.O., Corrigan, F.M., Foreman, E.I., Ashcroft, G.W., Eastwood, L.M., & Smith, F.W. (1983). Differentiating senile dementia of Alzheimer type and multi-infarct dementia by proton NMR imaging [Letter to the editor]. *Lancet, II,* 789.

Björklund, A., Gage, F.H., Stenevi, U., Dunnett, S.B., & Kelly, P.A. (1985). Intracerebral neural grafting in animal models of aging brain: Strategies, rationale and preliminary results. *Danish Medical Bulletin, 32,* 35-39.

Bondareff, W., Mountjoy, C.Q., & Roth, M. (1981). Selective loss of neurons of origin of adrenergic projection to cerebral cortex (nucleus locus coeruleus) in senile dementia [Letter to the editor]. *Lancet, 4,* 783-784.

Bondareff, W., Mountjoy, C.Q., & Roth, M. (1982). Loss of neurons of origins of the adrenergic projection to cerebral cortex (nucleus locus coeruleus) in senile dementia. *Neurology, 32,* 164-168.

Bowen, D.M., Allen, S.J., Benton, J.S., Goodhardt, M.J., Haan, E.A., Palmer, A.M., Sims, N.R., Smith, C.C.T., Spillane, J.A., Esiri, M.M., Neary D., Snowden, J.S., Wilcock, G.K., & Davison, A.N. (1983). Biochemical assessment of serotonergic and cholinergic dysfunction and cerebral atrophy in Alzheimer's disease. *Journal of Neurochemistry, 41,* 266-272.

Bowen, D.M., Smith, C.C.T., & Davison, A.N. (1983). Excitotoxicity in aging and dementia. In K. Fuxe, P. Roberts, & R. Schwarcz (Eds.), *Excitotoxins* (pp. 354-362). London: MacMillan.

Bowen, D.M., Smith, C.B., White, P., & Davison, A.N. (1976). Neurotransmitter-Related enzymes and indices of hypoxia in senile dementia and other abiotrophies. *Brain, 99,* 459-496.

Branconnier, R.J. (1983). The efficacy of the cerebral metabolic enhancers in the treatment of senile dementia. *Psychopharmacology Bulletin, 19,* 212-219.

Breitner, J.C.S., & Folstein, M.F. (1984). Familial Alzheimer dementia: A prevalent disorder with specific clinical features. *Psychological Medicine, 14,* 63-80.

Brinkman, S.D., Sarwar, M., Levin, H.S., & Morris, H.H. (1981). Quantitative indexes of computed tomography in dementia and normal aging. *Radiology, 138,* 89-92.

Brizzee, K.R., Ordy, J.M., Hofer, H., & Kaack, B. (1978). Animal models for the study of senile brain disease and aging changes in the brain. In R. Katzman, R.D. Terry, & K.L. Bick (Eds.), *Alzheimer's disease: Senile dementia and related disorders* (pp. 515-553). New York: Raven Press.

Brun, A., & Englund, E. (1981). Regional pattern of degeneration in Alzheimer's disease: Neuronal loss and histopathological grading. *Histopathology, 5,* 549-564.

Bucht, G., Adolfsson, R., & Winblad, B. (1984). Senile dementia of Alzheimer type and multi-infarct dementia - A clinical description and diagnostic problems. *Journal of the American Geriatrics Society, 32,* 491-498.

Carlsson, A., Adofsson, R., Aquilonius, S.M., Gottfries, C.G., Oreland, L., Svennerholm, L., & Winblad, B. (1980). Biogenic amines in human brain in normal aging, senile dementia, and chronic alcoholism. In M. Goldstein, D.B. Calne, A. Lieberman, & M.O. Thorner (Eds.), *Ergot compounds and brain function: Neuroendocrine and neuropsychiatric aspects* (pp. 295-304). New York: Raven Press.

Corsellis, J.A.N. (1962). *Mental illness and the aging brain.* Oxford: Oxford University Press.

Coyle, J.T., Price, D.L., & DeLong, M.R. (1983). Alzheimer's disease: A disorder of cortical cholinergic innervation. *Science, 219,* 1184-1190.

Cross, A.J., Crow, T.J., Johnson, J.A., Joseph, M.H., Perry, E.K., Perry, R.H., Blessed, G., & Tomlinson, B.E. (1983). Monoamine metabolism in senile dementia of Alzheimer type. *Journal of the Neurological Sciences, 60,* 383-392.

Cross, A.J., Crow, T.J., Perry, E.K., Perry, R.H., Blessed, G., & Tomlinson, B.E. (1981). Reduced dopamine-beta-hydroxylase activity in Alzheimer's disease. *British Medical Journal, 282,* 93-94.

Dahl, D.S. (1983). Diagnosis of Alzheimer's disease. *Postgraduate Medicine, 73,* 217-221.

Davies, P. (1979). Neurotransmitter-related enzymes in senile demetia of the Alzheimer type. *Brain Research, 171,* 319-327.

Davies, P., Katzman, R., & Terry, R.D. (1980). Reduced somatostatin-like immunoreactivity in cerebral cortex from cases of Alzheimer's disease and Alzheimer senile dementia. *Nature, 288,* 279-280.

Davies, P., & Maloney, A.F.J. (1976). Selective loss of central cholinergic neurons in Alzheimer's disease [Letter to the editor]. *Lancet, II,* 1403.

Davis, K.L., & Mohs, R.C. (1982). Enhancement of memory processes in Alzheimer's disease with multiple-dose intravenous physostigmine. *American Journal of Psychiatry, 139,* 1421-1424.

Eckenstein, F., & Baughman, R.W. (1984). Two types of cholinergic innervation in cortex, one co-localized with vasoactive intestinal polypeptide. *Nature, 309,* 153-155.

Edvinsson, L., Deguerce, A., Duverger, D., Mackenzie, E.T., & Scatton, B. (1983). Central serotonergic nerves project to the pial vessels of the brain. *Nature, 306,* 85-87.

Epstein, C.J. (1983). Down's syndrome and Alzheimer's disease: Implications and approaches. In R. Katzman (Ed.), *Banbury report 15. Biological aspects of Alzheimer's disease* (pp. 169-182). Cold Spring Harbor, N.Y.: Cold Spring Harbor Laboratory.

Estrada, C., Hamel, E., & Krause, D.N. (1983). Biochemical evidence for cholinergic innervation of intracerebral blood vessels. *Brain Research, 256,* 261-270.

Facci, L., Leon, A., Toffano, G., Sonnino, S., Ghidoni, R.G., & Tattamanti, W.C. (1984). Promotion of neuritogenesis in mouse neuroblastoma cells by exogenous gangliosides. Relationship between the effect and the cell association of ganglioside GM_1. *Journal of Neurochemistry, 42,* 299-305.

Feeney, D.M., Gonzalez, A., & Law, W.A. (1982). Amphetamine, haloperidol and experience interact to affect rate of recovery after motor cortex injury. *Science, 217,* 855-857.

Feeney, D.M., & Hovda, D.A. (1983). Amphetamine and apomorphine restore tactile placing after motor cortex injury in the cat. *Psychopharmacology, 79,* 67-71.

Flicker, C., Dean, R.L., Watkins, D.L., Fisher, S.K., & Bartus, R.T. (1983). Behavioral and neurochemical effects following neurotoxic lesions of a major cholinergic input to the cerebral cortex in the rat. *Pharmacology, Biochemistry and Behavior, 18,* 973-981.

Forno, L.S. (1966). Pathology of Parkinsonism. *Journal of Neurosurgery, 24* (suppl.), 266-271.

Forno, L.S. (1978). The locus coeruleus in Alzheimer's disease. *Jour-*

nal of Neuropathology and Experimental Neurology, 37, 614.

Foster, A.C., Collins, J.F., & Schwarcz, R. (1983). On the excitotoxic properties of quinolinic acid, 2,3-piperidine dicarboxylic acids and structurally related compounds. Neuropharmacology, 22, 1331-1342.

Gage, F.H., Björklund, A., Stenevi, U., Dunnett, S.B., & Kelly, P.A.T. (1984). Intrahippocampal septal grafts ameliorate learning impairments in aged rats. Science, 225, 533-536.

Gage, F.H., Dunnett, S.B., Stenevi, U., & Björklund, A. (1983). Aged rats: Recovery of motor impairments by intrastriatal nigral grafts. Science, 221, 966-969.

Gellerstedt, N. (1933). Zur Kenntnis der Hirnveranderungen bei der normalen Altersinvolution. Uppsala Lakarforenings Forhandlinger, 38, 193.

Gottfries, C.G. (1985). Definition of normal aging, senile dementia and Alzheimer's disease. In C.G. Gottfries (Ed.), Normal aging, Alzheimer's disease and senile dementia. Aspects on etiology, pathogenesis, diagnosis and treatment (pp. 11-18). Belgium: Editions de l'Universite de Belgium.

Gottfries, C.G., Adolfsson, R., Aquilonius, S.M., Carlsson, A., Eckernas, S.A., Nordberg, A., Oreland, L., Svennerholm, L., Wiberg, A., & Winblad, B. (1983). Biochemical changes in dementia disorders of Alzheimer type (AD/SDAT). Neurobiology of Aging, 3, 261-271.

Gottfries, C.G., Gottfries, I., & Roos, B.E. (1969). Homovanillic acid and 5-hydroxyindoleacetic acid in the cerebrospinal fluid of patients with senile dementia, presenile dementia and parkinsonism. Journal of Neurochemistry, 16, 1341-1345.

Gottfries, C.G., Karlsson, I., & Svennerholm, L. (1985). Senile dementia - A "white matter" disease. In C.G. Gottfries (Ed.), Normal aging, Alzheimer's disease and senile dementia. Aspects on etiology, pathogenesis, diagnosis and treatment (pp. 111-120). Belgium: Editions de l'Universite de Belgium.

Gottfries, C.G., Kjallquist, A., Ponten, U., Roos, B.E., & Sundberg, G. (1974). Cerebrospinal fluid pH and monoamine and glucolytic metabolites in Alzheimer's disease. British Journal of Psychiatry, 124, 280-287.

Gottfries, C.G., & Roos, B.E. (1973). Acid monoamine metabolites in cerebrospinal fluid from patients with presenile dementia (Alzheimer's disease). *Acta Psychiatrica Scandinavica, 49,* 257-263.

Gottfries, C.G., Roos, B.E., & Winblad, B. (1976). Monoamine and monoamine metabolites in the human brain post mortem in senile dementia. *Aktuelle Gerontologie, 6,* 429-435.

Greenwald, B.S., Mohs, R.C., & Davis, K.L. (1983). Neurotransmitter deficits in Alzheimer's disease: Criteria for significance. *Journal of the American Geriatrics Society, 31,* 310-316.

Gusella, J.F., Tanzi, R.E., Andersson, M.A., Mobbs, W., Gibbons, K., Raschtchian, R., Gilliam, T.G., Wallace, M.R., Wexler, N.S., & Conneally, P.M. (1984). DNA markers for nervous system diseases. *Science, 225,* 1320-1326.

Hachinski, V.C., Iliff, L.D., Zilhka, E., Du Boulay, G.H., McAlister, V.L., Marshall, J., Ross Russel, R.W., & Symon, L. (1975). Cerebral blood flow in dementia. *Archives of Neurology, 32,* 632-637.

Hardy, J., Adolfsson, R., Alafuzoff, I., Bucht, G., Marcusson, J., Nyberg, P., Perdahl, E., Wester, P., & Winblad, B. (1985). Transmitter deficits in Alzheimer's disease. *Neurochemistry International, 7,* 545-563.

Heston, L.L. (1983). Dementia of the Alzheimer type: A perspective from family studies. In R. Katzman (Ed.), *Banbury report 15. Biological aspects of Alzheimer's disease* (pp. 183-190). Cold Spring Harbor, N.Y.: Cold Spring Harbor Laboratory.

Heston, L.L., & Mastri, A.R. (1977). The genetics of Alzheimer's disease: Associations with hematologic malignancy and Down's syndrome. *Archives of General Psychiatry, 34,* 976-981.

Heston, L.L., Mastri, A.R., Andersson, V.E., & White, J. (1981). Dementia of the Alzheimer type: Clinical genetics, natural history, and associated conditions. *Archives of General Psychiatry, 38,* 1085-1090.

Ishii, T. (1966). Distribution of Alzheimer's neurofibrillary changes in the brain stem and the hypothalamus of senile dementia. *Acta Neuropathologica, 6,* 181-187.

Iversen, L.L., Rossor, M.N., Reynolds, G.P., Hills, R., Roth, M., Mountjoy, C.Q., Foote, S.L., Morrison, J.H., & Bloom, F.E. (1983). Loss of pigmented dopamine beta-hydroxylase positive cells from locus coeruleus in senile dementia of Alzheimer type. *Neuroscience Letters, 39,* 95-100.

Jarvik, L.F. (1978). Genetic factors and chromosomal aberrations in Alzheimer's disease, senile dementia and related disorders. In R. Katzman, R.D. Terry, & K.L. Bick (Eds.), *Senile dementia and related disorders* (pp. 273-277). Raven Press: New York.

Johnsson, S., & Domino, E.F. (1971). Cholinergic enzymatic activity of cerebrospinal fluid of patients with various neurological diseases. *Clinica Chemica Acta, 35,* 421-428.

Jonsson, G., Kojima, H., & Gorio, A. (1983). GM_1 Ganglioside has a counteracting effect on neurotoxin induced alteration of the postnatal development of central serotonin (5-HT) neurons. *Neuroscience Letters,* (Suppl.) 14, 185.

Kay, A.D., Milstein, S., Kaufman, S., Rapoport, S.I., & Cutler, N.R. (1984). 5-HIAA and HVA in the CSF of patients with Alzheimer's disease. *Neurology, 34* (Suppl 1), 161.

Kojima, H., Gorio, A., Janigro, D., & Jonsson, G. (1984). GM_1 ganglioside enhances regrowth of noradrenaline nerve terminals in rat cerebral cortex lesioned by the neurotoxin 6-hydroxydopamine. *Neuroscience, 13,* 1011-1022.

Lamb, K., Bradshaw, C.M., & Szabadi, E. (1983). The responsiveness of human eccrine sweat glands to choline and carbachol. Application to the study of peripheral cholinergic functioning in Alzheimer-Type dementia. *European Journal of Clinical Pharmacology, 24,* 55-62.

Lauter, H. (1985). What do we know about Alzheimer's disease today? *Danish Medical Bulletin, 32,* 1-21.

Levy, R., Little, A., Chuaqui, P., & Reith, M. (1983). Early results from double-blind, placebo-controlled trial of high dose phosphatidylcholine in Alzheimer's disease [Letter to the editor]. *Lancet, I,* 987-988.

Mann, D.M.A. (1983). The locus coeruelus and its possible role in aging and degenerative disease of the human central nervous system. *Mechanisms of Ageing and Development, 23,* 73-94.

Mann, D.M.A., Lincoln, J., Yates, P.O., & Brennan, C.M. (1980). Monoamine metabolism in Down's syndrome [Letter to the editor]. *Lancet, II,* 1366-1367.

Mann, D.M.A., Lincoln, J., Yates, P.O., Stamp, J.E., & Toper, S. (1980). Changes in the monoamine containing neurons of the human CNS in senile dementia. *British Journal of Psychiatry, 136,* 533-541.

Mann, D.M.A., Yates, P.O., & Hawkes, J. (1982a). Plaques and tangles and transmitter deficiencies in dementia. *Journal of Neurology, Neurosurgery, and Psychiatry, 45*, 563-564.

Mann, D.M.A., Yates, P.O., & Hawkes, J. (1982b). The noradrenergic system in Alzheimer's and multi-infarct dementias. *Journal of Neurology, Neurosurgery and Psychiatry, 45*, 113-119.

Mann, D.M.A., Yates, P.O., & Marcyniuk, B. (1984). Alzheimer's presenile dementia, senile dementia of Alzheimer type and Down's syndrome in middle age form an age-related continuum of pathological changes. *Neuropathology and Applied Neurobiology, 10*, 185-207.

Moroni, F., Lombardi, G., Carla, V., & Moneti, G. (1984). The excitotoxin quinolinic acid is present and unevenly distributed in the rat brain. *Brain Research, 295*, 352-355.

Mountjoy, C.Q., Roth, M., Evans, N.J.R., & Evans, H.M. (1983). Cortical neuronal counts in normal elderly controls and demented patients. *Neurobiology of Aging, 4*, 1-11.

Nagai, T., McGeer, P.L., Peng, J.H., McGeer, E.G., & Dolman, C.E. (1983). Choline acetyltransferase immunohistochemistry in brains of Alzheimer's disease patients and controls. *Neuroscience Letters, 36*, 195-199.

Nee, L.E., Polinsky, R.J., Roswell, E., Weingartner, H., Smallberg, S., & Ebert, M. (1983). A family with histologically confirmed Alzheimer's disease. *Archives of Neurology, 40*, 203-208.

Nyberg, P., Adolfsson, R., Hardy, J.A., Nordberg, A., Wester, P., & Winblad, B. (1985). Catecholamine topochemistry in human basal ganglia. Comparison between normal and Alzheimer brains. *Brain Research, 333*, 139-142.

Palmer, A.M., Sims, N.S., Bowen, D.M., Neary, D., Palo, J., Wikstrom, J., & Davison, A.N. (1984). Monoamine metabolite concentrations in lumbar cerebrospinal fluid of patients with histologically verified Alzheimer's dementia. *Journal of Neurology, Neurosurgery and Psychiatry, 47*, 481-484.

Perry, E.K., Blessed, G., Tomlinson, B.E., Perry, R.H., Crow, T.J., Cross, A.J., Dockray, G.J., Dimaline, R., & Arregui, A. (1981). Neurochemical activities in human temporal lobe related to aging and Alzheimer type changes. *Neurobiology of Aging, 2*, 251-256.

Perry, E.K., Gibson, P.H., Blessed, G., Perry, R.H., & Tomlinson,

B.E. (1977). Neurotransmitter enzyme abnormalities in senile dementia.. *Journal of the Neurological Sciences, 34,* 247-265.

Perry, E.K., Perry, R.H., Tomlinson, B.E., Blessed, G., & Gibson, P.H. (1980). Coenzyme A acetylating enzymes in Alzheimer's disease: Possible cholinergic compartments of pyruvate dehydrogenase. *Neuroscience Letters, 18,* 105-110.

Perry, E.K., Tomlinson, B.E., Blessed, G., Perry, R.H., Cross, A.J., & Crow, T.J. (1981). Neuropathological and biochemical observations on the noradrenergic system in Alzheimer disease. *Journal of the Neurological Sciences, 51,* 279-287.

Perry, R.H., Candy, J.M., Perry, E.K., Irving, D., Blessed, G., Fairbairn, A.F., & Tomlinson, B.E. (1982). Extensive loss of choline acetyltransferase activity is not reflected by neuronal loss in the nucleus of Meynert in Alzheimer's disease. *Neuroscience Letters, 33,* 311-315.

Pilleri, G. (1966). The Kluver-Bucy syndrome in man. A clinicoanatomical contribution to the function of the medial temporal lobe structures. *Psychiatria et Neurologia, 152,* 65-103.

Pope, A., Hess, H.H., & Levin, E. (1965). Neurochemical pathology of the cerebral cortex in presenile dementias. *Transactions of the American Neurological Association, 89,* 15-16.

Richter, J.A., Perry, E.K., & Tomlinson, B.E. (1980). Acetylcholine and choline levels in postmortem human brain tissue; preliminary observations in Alzheimer's disease. *Life Sciences, 26,* 1683-1689.

Rossor, M.N., Emson, P.C., Mountjoy, C.Q., Roth, M., & Iversen, L.L. (1982). Neurotransmitters of the cerebral cortex in senile dementia of Alzheimer type. *Experimental Brain Research, Suppl. 5,* 153-157.

Rossor, M.N., Iversen, L.L., Reynolds, G.P., Mountjoy, C.Q., & Roth, M. (1984). Neurochemical characteristics of early and late onset types of Alzheimer's disease. *Clinical Research, 288,* 961-964.

Rossor, M.N., Svendsen, C., Hunt, S.P., Mountjoy, C.Q., Roth, M., & Iversen, L.L. (1982). The substantia innominata in Alzheimer's disease; an histochemical and biochemical study of cholinergic marker enzymes. *Neuroscience Letters, 28,* 217-222.

Roth, M. (1971). Classification and aetiology in mental disorders of old age: Some recent developments. In D.W.K. Kay & A. Walk (Eds.), *Recent developments in psychogeriatrics* (pp. 1-18). Ashford: Headley Bros.

Roth, M. (1985). Some strategies for tackling the problems of senile dementia and related disorders within the next decade. *Danish Medical Bulletin, 32,* 92-111.

Rothschild, D., & Kasansin, J. (1936). Clinicopathologic study of Alzheimer's disease: Relationship to senile condition. *Archives of Neurology and Psychiatry, 36,* 293-321.

Rylett, R.T., Ball, M.J., & Colhoun, E.H. (1983). Evidence for high affinity choline transport in synaptosomes prepared from hippocampus and neocortex of patients with Alzheimer's disease. *Brain Research, 289,* 169-175.

Schmidt, R.H., Ingvar, M., Lindvall, O., Stenevi, U., & Björklund, A. (1982). Functional activity of substantia nigra grafts reinnervating the striatum: Neurotransmitter metabolism and (14C) 2-deoxyglucose autoradiography. *Journal of Neurochemistry, 38,* 737-748.

Schwarcz, R., Foster, A.C., French, E.D., Whetsell, W.O., & Kohler, C. (1984). Current topics. II. Excitotoxic models for neurodegenerative disorders. *Life Sciences, 35,* 19-32.

Seltzer, B., & Sherwin, I. (1983). A comparison of clinical features in early and late onset primary degenerative dementia. *Archives of Neurology, 40,* 143-146.

Sims, N.R., Bowen, D.M., Allen, S.J., Smith, C.C.T., Neary, D., Thomas, D.J., & Davison, A.N. (1983). Presynaptic cholinergic dysfunctions in patients with dementia. *Journal of Neurochemistry, 40,* 503-509.

Soininen, H., Jolkkonen, J.T., Reinikainen, K.J., Halonen, T.O., & Riekkinen, P.J. (1984). Reduced cholinesterase activity and somatostatin like immunoreactivity in the cerebrospinal fluid of patients with dementia of the Alzheimer type. *Journal of the Neurological Sciences, 63,* 167-172.

Soininen, H., MacDonald, E., Rekonen, M., & Riekkinen, P.J. (1981). Homovanillic acid and 5-hydroxyindoleacetic acid levels in cerebrospinal fluid of patients with senile dementia of Alzheimer type. *Acta Neurologica Scandinavica, 64,* 101-107.

Soininen, H., Pitkanen, A., Halonen, T., & Riekkinen, P.J. (1984). Dopamine-beta-hydroxylase and acetylcholinesterase activities of cerebrospinal fluid in Alzheimer's disease. *Acta Neurologica Scandinavica, 69,* 29-34.

Toffano, G., Savoini, G.E., Moroni, F., Lombardi, G., Calza, L., &

Agnati, L.F. (1984). Chronic GM_1 ganglioside treatment reduces dopamine cell body degeneration in the substantia nigra after unilateral hemitransection in the rat. *Brain Research, 296,* 233-239.

Tomlinson, B.E., Irving, D., & Blessed, G. (1981). Cell loss in the locus coeruleus in senile dementia of Alzheimer type. *Journal of the Neurological Sciences, 49,* 419-428.

Wenk, G.L., & Olton, D.S. (1984). Recovery of neocortical choline acetyltransferase activity following ibotenic acid injection into the nucleus basalis of Meynert in rats. *Brain Research, 293,* 184-186.

Wettstein, A. (1983). No effect from double-blind trial of physostigmine and lecithin in Alzheimer's disease. *Annals of Neurology, 13,* 210-212.

Whitehouse, P.J., Price, D.L., Clark, A.W., Coyle, J.T., & DeLong, M.K. (1981). Alzheimer's disease: Evidence for selective loss of cholinergic neurons in the nucleus basalis. *Annals of Neurology, 10,* 122-126.

Whitehouse, P.J., Price, D.L., Struble, R.G., Coyle, J.T., & DeLong, M.A. (1982). Alzheimer's disease and senile dementia - Loss of neurons in the basal forebrain. *Science, 215,* 1237-1239.

Winblad, B., Adolfsson, R., Carlsson, A., & Gottfries, C.G. (1982). Biogenic amines in brains of patients with Alzheimer's disease. In S. Corkin, K.L. Davis, J.H. Growdon, E. Usdin, & R.J. Wurtman (Eds.), *Alzheimer's disease* (pp. 25-33). New York: Raven Press.

Wisniewski, H.M., & Kozlowski, P.B. (1982). Evidence for blood-brain barrier changes in senile dementia of Alzheimer's type (AD/SDAT). Alzheimer's disease, Down's syndrome and aging. *Annals of the New York Academy of Sciences, 386,* 119-129.

Wood, P.L., Etienne, P., Gauthier, L.S., Cajal, S., & Nair, N.P.V. (1982). Reduced lumbar CSF somatostatin in Alzheimer's disease. *Life Sciences, 31,* 2073-2079.

Wright, A.F., & Whalley, L.J. (1984). Genetics, aging and dementia. *British Journal of Psychiatry, 145,* 20-38.

Wurtman, R.J. (1985). Alzheimer's disease. *Scientific American, 252(1),* 62-74.

Yamada, M., & Mehraein, P. (1977). Verteilungsmuster der senilen Veranderungen in den Hirnstammkernen. *Psychiatrica et Neurologica Japanica, 31,* 219-224.

Yates, C.M., Harmar, A.J., Rosie, R., Sheward, J., Sanchez de Levy,

G., Simpson, J., Maloney, A.F.J., Gordon, A., & Fink, G. (1982). Thyrotropin-releasing hormone, luteinizing hormone - releasing hormone and substance P immunoreactivity in postmortem brain from cases of Alzheimer-type dementia and Down's syndrome. *Brain Research, 258,* 45-52.

Yates, C.M., Ritchie, I.M., Simpson, J., Maloney, A.F.J., & Gordon, A. (1981). Noradrenaline in Alzheimer-Type dementia and Down's syndrome [Letter to the editor]. *Lancet, II,* 39-40.

Yates, C.M., Simpson, J., Gordon, A., Maloney, A.F.J., Allison, Y., Ritchie, I.M., & Urquhart, A. (1983). Catecholamines and cholinergic enzymes in presenile and senile Alzheimer type dementia and Down's syndrome. *Brain Research, 280,* 119-126.

ACKNOWLEDGEMENT

We would like to thank Karin Gladh for her editorial assistance. Original work cited in this discussion document was funded by the Swedish Medical Research Council, King Gustav V and Queen Victoria's Foundation, Loo and Hans Ostermans, Gun och Bertil Stohne's, and Fred and Ingrid Thuring's Foundations.

TABLE 1

The Cholinergic System in Alzheimer's Disease

Cell loss in nucleus basalis
Mann, Yates, & Marcyniuk, 1984
Nagai, McGeer, Peng, McGeer, & Dolman, 1983
Perry, R.H. et al., 1982
Pilleri, 1966
Rossor et al., 1982
Whitehouse, Price, Clark, Coyle, & DeLong, 1981
Whitehouse, Price, Struble, Coyle, & DeLong, 1982
and many others

Reduced nucleolar volume in nucleus basalis neurons
Mann et al., 1984

TABLE 1 Continued

Tangles in nucleus basalis
Ishii, 1966

Decrease of acetylcholine
Richter, Perry, & Tomlinson, 1980   Temporal cortex

Decrease of choline acetyltransferase

Bowen, Smith, White, & Davison, 1976	Cortex
Davies, 1979	Many brain regions
Davies & Maloney, 1976	Many brain regions
Perry, E.K., Gibson, Blessed, Perry, R.H., Roth, & Tomlinson, 1977	Many brain regions
and many others	

Decrease of acetylcholinesterase

Pope, Hess, & Levin, 1965	A preliminary report
Davies, 1979	Many brain regions
Atack et al., 1983	Loss specific to one molecular form
Soininen, MacDonald, Rekonen, & Riekkinen, 1981*	CSF
Soininen, Pitkanen, Halonen, & Riekkinen, 1984*	CSF

No decrease of acetylcholinesterase

Davies, 1979*	CSF
Johnson & Domino, 1971*	CSF
Wood, Etienne, Gauthier, Cajal, & Nair, 1982*	CSF

Decrease of pyruvate dehydrogenase

Perry, E.K., Perry, R.H., Tomlinson, Blessed, & Gibson, 1980	Possible cholinergic compartment of this enzyme

Reduction of synaptosomal choline uptake

Rylett, Ball, & Colhoun, 1983	PM synaptosomes: greater loss in hippocampus than frontal cortex

*Clinically diagnosed only

TABLE 2

The Noradrenergic System in Alzheimer's Disease

Cell loss in locus coeruleus
Bondareff, Mountjoy, & Roth, 1981
Bondareff, Mountjoy, & Roth, 1982
Forno, 1966
Forno, 1978
Iversen et al., 1983
Mann, Lincoln, Yates, Stamp, & Toper, 1980
Mann, Yates, & Hawkes, 1982b
Mann et al., 1984
Perry, E.K., Tomlinson, et al., 1981
Tomlinson, Irving, & Blessed, 1981
Yamada & Mehraein, 1977

Reduced nucleolar volume in locus coeruleus neurons
Mann et al., 1982b
Mann et al., 1984

Tangles in locus coeruleus
Ishii, 1966

Decrease of noradrenaline

Gottfries, Roos, & Winblad, 1976[*]	Hypothalamus, caudate, and putamen
Berger, Escourolle, & Moyne, 1976	Histofluorescence study of cortical biopsies
Adolfsson, Gottfries, Roos, & Winblad, 1979[*]	Putamen and cortex
Carlsson et al., 1980[*]	Caudate, hypo-thalamus, hippo-campus and cingulate cortex
Yates et al., 1981	Hypothalamus
Gottfries et al., 1983	Hypothalamus, caudate nucleus, hippocampus and cingulate cortex

TABLE 2 Continued

Berger & Alvarez, 1983	Histofluorescence study of cortical biopsies
Yates et al., 1983	Hypothalamus
Arai, Kosaka, & Iizuka, 1984	Many brain regions
Nyberg et al., 1984	Caudate, putamen and globus pallidus
No decrease of tyrosine hydroxylase	
Davies & Maloney, 1976	Cerebral cortex. No data given. Small number of cases
Decrease of dopamine-beta-hydroxylase	
Cross et al., 1981	Cerebral cortex and hippocampus
Perry, E.K., Blessed, et al., 1981	Temporal cortex
Davies & Maloney, 1976	Cerebral cortex, No data given. Small number of cases
Soininen, Jolkkonen, Reinikainen, Halonen & Riekkinen, 1984*	CSF
Increase in 3-methoxy-4-hydroxyphenylglycol	
Carlsson et al., 1980*	Caudate and cingulate cortex
Gottfries et al., 1983	Significant in caudate nucleus hippocampus and cingulate cortex
No change in 3-methoxy-4-hydroxyphenylglycol	
Palmer et al., 1984	CSF
Decrease of 3-methoxy-4-hydroxyphenylglycol	
Mann, Lincoln, Yates, & Brennan, 1980	Urine excretion
Cross et al., 1983	Hippocampus and cortical regions
Reduced noradrenaline uptake	
Benton et al., 1982	Temporal cortex biopsy specimens

*Clinically diagnosed only

TABLE 3

The Serotoninergic System in Alzheimer's Disease

Cell loss in the raphe (dorsal tegmental) nucleus
Mann et al., 1984

Reduced nucleolar volume in raphe neurons
Mann & Yates, 1983

Tangles in the raphe
Ishii, 1966
Yamada & Mehraein, 1977

Decrease of serotonin

Carlsson et al., 1980*	Caudate, hippocampus, cingulate cortex and hypothalamus
Winblad, Adolfsson, Carlsson, & Gottfries, 1982	Several brain regions
Gottfries et al., 1983	Hypothalamus, caudate hippocampus and cingulate cortex

Loss of 5-hydroxyindoleacetic acid

Gottfries, Gottfries, & Roos, 1969	CSF
Gottfries & Roos, 1973*	CSF. Impaired increase after probenecid loading
Gottfries, Kjallquist, Ponten, Roos, & Sundberg, 1974	CSF
Adolfsson et al., 1979	Cingulate cortex and hippocampus
Argentiero & Tavolato, 1980*	CSF
Carlsson et al., 1980*	Hypothalamus and hippocampus
Soininen et al., 1981*	CSF. Reduced in severe cases

TABLE 3 Continued

Winblad et al., 1982	Several brain regions
Cross et al., 1983	Hippocampus and cortical regions
Palmer et al., 1984	CSF
Arai et al., 1984	Many brain regions

No decrease of 5-hydroxyindoleacetic acid

Wood et al., 1982*	CSF
Bareggi, Franceschi, Bonini, Zecca, & Smirne, 1982*	CSF
Kay, Milstein, Kaugman, Rapoport, & Cutler, 1984*	CSF

Decrease of imipramine binding

Bowen et al., 1983b	Temporal cortex

Reduced serotonin uptake

Benton et al., 1982	Temporal cortex biopsy specimens

*Clinically diagnosed only

5

Synaptic Plasticity in the Hippocampus: Implications for Alzheimer's Disease

Carl W. Cotman, PhD, Manuel Nieto-Sampedro, PhD, and James W. Geddes, PhD

A major goal in the development of successful treatments for Alzheimer's disease (AD) lies in the discovery of interventions able to prevent or compensate for neuronal loss. This information must come from basic studies on the properties of susceptible neurons and their response to injury. The mature and aged central nervous system (CNS) possesses natural compensatory mechanisms, which aid in its healing after injury. In AD, some of these activities are intact and operative and perhaps compensate for neuronal loss. Ultimately, however, it is clear that cellular degeneration predominates, perhaps due to failure of the processes responsible for compensation. By studying these mechanisms, we can evaluate the success or failure of the natural adaptive properties of the human brain in offsetting neurodegenerative disorders. Rebuilding of neural circuits after cell loss could alleviate the functional decay of the diseased brain.

It is well-known that growth factors play a key role in the development of the nervous system. In this chapter, we will argue further that neuron-survival and neurite-promoting factors also play a role in the rebuilding of CNS circuits after injury. Polypeptide growth factors encompass at least three general groups: Those that affect survival; those that affect morphological or neurite-promoting activities; and those that underly the differentiation and specification of properties such as neurotransmitters. We postulate that a subgroup of polypeptide growth factors, which increase in response to injury, are fundamental to the normal operation and repair of the CNS (Cotman & Nieto-Sampedro, 1983; Nieto-Sampedro & Cotman, 1985). By analogy, polypeptide growth factors may also be involved in dysfunctions of the aged brain and of the brain of Alzheimer's patients. Over the past several years we have been involved in an extensive series of studies to examine the consequences of loss of neuronal cells on the growth of new synapses and on the production of the growth factors that respond to injury and participate in the repair and stabilization of neuronal circuits.

Our studies have been carried out primarily on the entorhinal cortex and its projections to the hippocampus (Figure 1), structures that have recently been shown to be compromised in AD. Hyman, Van Hoesen, Damasio, and Barnes (1984) reported that AD is accompanied by a severe loss of layer II stellate neurons in the entorhinal cortex as well as the pyramidal cells of the subiculum. Layer II stellate cells of the entorhinal cortex provide the exclusive cortical input

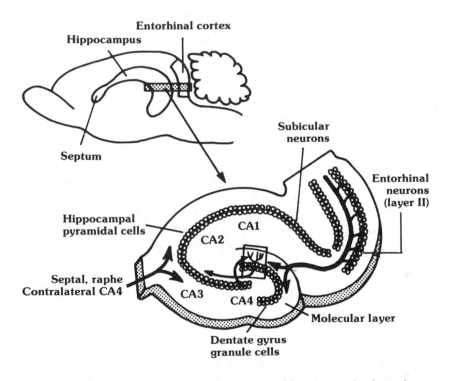

Figure 1. The main structural features of the hippocampal formation can be observed in a horizontal section through the rat brain. Granule cells are the predominant neuronal type in the dentate gyrus, whereas pyramidal cells are the majority in subfields CA1 to CA4 of the hippocampus proper. The major extrinsic afferent to the dentate gyrus originates in the entorhinal cortex and projects to the outer two thirds of the dentate molecular layer. CA1 neurons project to the subiculum, which provides output from the hippocampal formation to various cortical and subcortical systems.

to the dentate gyrus of the hippocampal formation, so that their loss isolates the hippocampus from its cortical input. Loss of subicular neurons, moreover, deprives the hippocampal formation of its major output. These pathological lesions are further compounded by direct neuronal loss in the hippocampus itself (Ball et al., 1985). This pattern of cell loss functionally isolates the hippocampus and may underly the severe memory loss seen in AD, since it is well-known that damage to the hippocampus or its circuitry can produce severe memory deficits. Thus, this type of lesion may be fundamental to understanding the basis of behavioral impairment in AD. It is important to note that the loss of entorhinal-hippocampal-subicular cells has been described in patients with the characteristics of AD where there is no corresponding loss of forebrain cholinergic neurons (Ball et al., 1985).

We shall discuss the effect that injury of the entorhinal cortex has on neuron-survival and neurite-promoting factors. The nature of the potential source of these factors and their overall regulation in relationship to hippocampal plasticity will be discussed. Finally, it will be shown that some of these mechanisms appear operative in the human brain.

INJURY-INDUCED NEURONAL SURVIVAL AND GROWTH FACTORS

In the course of a series of studies on the survival and integration of brain transplants, it was observed that the survival of certain types of transplanted neurons improves if the cells are placed into an area of damage several days after the injury (see Cotman & Nieto-Sampedro, 1984, for review). Striatal neurons benefit particularly from the delay procedure, but the survival and integration of transplanted entorhinal, septal, and raphe neurons is also considerably enhanced.

It was hypothesized that injury to the CNS is accompanied by an increase of neurotrophic factors and that their appearance is a major cause of the enhanced survival of delayed implants (Lewis & Cotman, 1982). Factors that promote neuron survival are known to appear following peripheral nerve injury (Ebendal, Olson, Seiger, & Hedlund, 1980; Lundborg, Longo, & Varon, 1982), but the possibility that brain injury induces the release of trophic factors had not been tested previously.

A wound was made in the entorhinal cortex of neonatal, adult, or aged rats, and the lesion cavity was filled with a fragment of saline-moistened Gelfoam. At various times postlesion the animals were sacrificed, and both the Gelfoam fragment and the tissue surrounding the wound cavity were separately analyzed for their content of neurotrophic activity using cell culture assays (see Figure 2A). Dissociated cultures of neurons from embryonic rat brain corpus striatum, hippocampus, and septum, as well as various peripheral neurons were used (Manthorpe et al., 1983; Needels, Nieto-Sampedro, Whittemore, & Cotman, 1985; Nieto-Sampedro et al., 1982; Nieto-Sampedro, Manthorpe, Barbin, Varon, & Cotman, 1983; Whittemore, Nieto-Sampedro, Needels, & Cotman, 1985).

The results clearly demonstrate that injury to the CNS causes a time-dependent increase in the activity of neurotrophic factors both

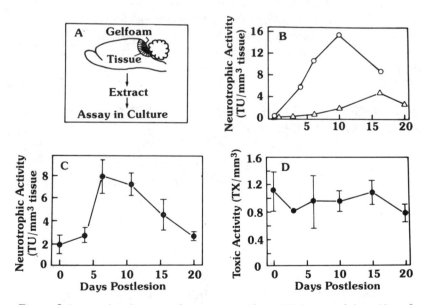

Figure 2. Injury-induced neurotrophic activity in rat brain. (A) A cavity of about 40 mm³is vacuum-aspirated in the rat's occipital-entorhinal cortex and the cavity filled with a fragment of Gelfoam soaked in saline. At various times postlesion the animals are sacrificed and the Gelfoam fragment and the tissue around the cavity removed and extracted with dilute buffer. The extracts of tissue (O) and Gelfoam (△) are tested for neurotrophic activity on cultured neurons from (B) chick embryo ciliary ganglion, and (C) rat striatal neurons. (D) Brain extracts also contain components that are neurotoxic for cultured striatal neurons. Neurotoxic activity does not change significantly after a lesion. Data adapted from Needels, Nieto-Sampedro, Whittemore, & Cotman, 1985; Nieto-Sampedro et al., 1983; & Whittemore et al., 1985.

in the tissue surrounding the injury and in the wound cavity (Gelfoam) (see Figures 2B & 2C). The trophic response to injury occurs in the developing, mature, or aged rodent brain. The maximal levels of trophic activity for peripheral neurons increase progressively in neonatal, adult, and aged animals, and they are reached at 3, 10, and 15 days postlesion, respectively (Needels et al., 1985). The activity was highest on sympathetic ganglion neurons and one order of magnitude lower on dorsal root and ciliary ganglion cells. Injury-induced enhancement of neurotrophic activity occurs after damage to any region of the CNS parenchyma but not in the corpus callosum. Accumulation of neurotrophic activity in the Gelfoam placed into the wound cavities in neonatal and adult animals lags behind the levels in tissue by 4 to 5 days suggesting that either neurotrophic factors or the cells that produce them are transferred from the tissue into the Gelfoam.

Injury-induced neurotrophic activities appear in response to several types of trauma including cytotoxic lesions produced by kainic acid (KA) (Nieto-Sampedro et al., 1983), infarcts produced by middle cerebral artery occlusion (Needels, Young, & Cotman, 1985, unpublished observations), and spinal cord injury (Millaruelo, Nieto-Sampedro, Yu, & Cotman, in press). These data indicate that the response to CNS injury is relatively general. We expect that highly specific factors are involved and correlated to the particular cell type affected, but direct data are not available at present.

Are neurotrophic factors also present in the human brain? Recently both biopsy and autopsy tissues have been examined for the presence of trophic activities. Neurotrophic activity is measurable in normal human brain using cell culture assays (Cotman, Nieto-Sampedro, & Gibbs, 1984). Cerebrospinal fluids also have low but significant levels of neurotrophic activity (Longo et al., 1984). Thus, it should be possible to evaluate the activities of neurotrophic factors in the brain after injury and in various neurodegenerative diseases.

The induction of trophic factors is important with respect to the occurrence and extent of secondary neuronal degeneration following injury. The time course for the induction of neurotrophic factors closely corresponds to termination of secondary cell death (see Nieto-Sampedro & Cotman, 1985). However, considering that extensive secondary neuronal degeneration occurs in the first few days postlesion, it seems that injury induction of trophic activity is not sufficiently rapid to provide adequate support to a large proportion of injured neurons. Many injured neurons, particularly those with very short axon stumps, die in the interim. The above hypothesis predicts that if provided sufficiently early, neurotrophic factors should prevent secondary cell death. A direct test of this hypothesis has not been carried out. However, we have used transplanted neurons to evaluate the *in vivo* action of neurotrophic factors on neuronal survival.

THE SURVIVAL OF BRAIN TRANSPLANTS IS ENHANCED BY EXOGENOUSLY ADDED EXTRACTS FROM INJURED BRAIN

Our hypothesis predicts that exogenously added neuron-survival factors should enhance the survival of CNS tissue transplanted into freshly made wound cavities. Accordingly, fresh cavities were filled with transplanted tissue and covered with either Gelfoam soaked in wound fluid or with a Gelfoam transferred directly from an animal that had received a lesion 8 days earlier. Survival of transplanted striatal neurons was improved in animals supplied with extracts from injured brain (Nieto-Sampedro et al., 1984). It is likely that neurotrophic factors are, at least in part, responsible for the enhanced survival. Clearly, however, neuronal survival is also dependent on vascularization and on substances such as angiogenesis factors that may be present in the extracts and contribute to their effect. The molecular properties of the neurotrophic activities that support brain neurons need to be studied in more detail.

PRESENCE OF NEUROTOXIC FACTORS IN THE CNS

It has long been suspected that the CNS has inhibitory factors that may be partially responsible for the neuronal loss and the failure of complete regeneration. The control of innervation territories and the absence of hyperinnervation (Cotman, Lewis, & Hand, 1981; Cotman, Nieto-Sampedro, & Harris, 1981; Diamond, Cooper, Turner, & MacIntyre, 1976; Goldowitz & Cotman, 1980) may involve inhibitory factors carried by either afferent fibers or target cells. Hyperinnervation can indeed be caused in the central or peripheral nervous system (PNS) by blocking axonal transport (Diamond et al., 1976; Goldowitz & Cotman, 1980). Inhibitors of neuronal survival and sprouting have been recently described (Manthorpe, Varon, &

Adler, 1981; Manthorpe et al., 1983; Nieto-Sampedro et al., 1983). We found that activity inhibitory to neuronal survival was present in noninjured brain tissue at all ages and was four-fold greater in adult and aged brain than in neonatal tissue (see Figure 2D). The activity does not change in either tissue or Gelfoam following injury. At present, the molecular identity of this activity is unknown.

INJURY-INDUCED NEURITE-PROMOTING FACTORS AND REACTIVE SYNAPTOGENESIS

The spontaneous response of the CNS to neuronal damage includes replacement of lost synapses and reorganization of the circuitry. Synapse formation that occurs in response to perturbations, such as neuronal loss, that are not part of the developmental program is referred to as reactive synaptogenesis. Lynch, Matthews, Mosko, Parks, and Cotman (1972) first reported that entorhinal lesions trigger reactive synaptogenesis in the denervated dentate gyrus. This process has now been extensively studied and recently reviewed (Cotman & Nieto-Sampedro, 1984).

We have recently examined the effect of bilateral entorhinal ablation on the appearance in the deafferented hippocampi of factors capable of promoting neurite extension from cultured neurons (Needels, Nieto-Sampedro, & Cotman, in press). The animals were sacrificed at various times postlesion and extracts of tissue prepared and tested for neurite-promoting activity. Test cells were primary cultures of ciliary ganglion neurons that were freed of nonneuronal elements and plated at low density to avoid indirect interfering effects. Neurons were kept alive either by supplying them with survival factors that lacked neurite promoting activity or by increasing the $K+$ concentration of the culture medium. In the absence of brain extract, the neurons assume a rounded morphology that they maintain for prolonged periods.

Compared to the basal level in noninjured brain, the neurite promoting activity of extracts of deafferented hippocampus or cortex increases four- to five-fold beginning 5 days postlesion and reaching a maximum at 10 days (see Figure 3). The time course of neurite-promoting activity parallels that of sprouting in the hippocampus (see Figure 3), and slighty precedes reactive synaptogenesis (Mathews, Cotman, & Lynch, 1976; Nadler, Cotman, & Lynch, 1977; Scheff, Benardo, & Cotman, 1978). Thus, growth factors have potential role as reagents capable of promoting recovery of function after injury.

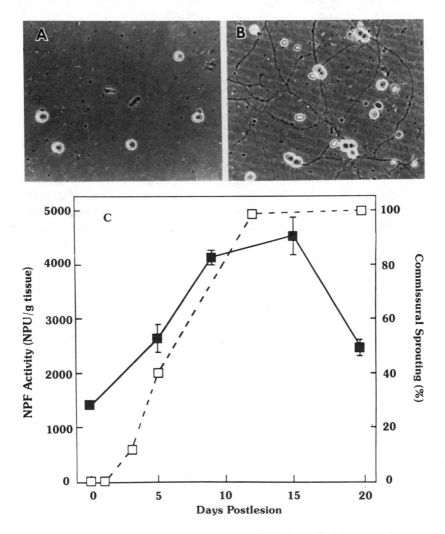

Figure 3. Injury-induced neurite-promoting activity. (A) Ciliary ganglion neurons can be separated from nonneuronal cells and maintained in tissue culture as healthy spherical cells with no neurites. (B) Neurites can be promoted by the addition of injured-brain extracts. (C) Injury-induction of neurite-promoting activity (■) closely correlates with sprouting of commissural/associational fibers after entorhinal ablation (□). Data adapted from Nadler et al., 1977; Scheff et al., 1978, and Needels, Nieto-Sampedro, & Cotman, 1985.

The Role of Glial Cells in Facilitating Recovery From Brain Injury

Growth factors, as indicated from the above evidence, enhance the survival of transplanted neurons, reduce secondary cell death and axonal degeneration, and promote neurite sprouting. The increased cell survival and axon sprouting make it conceivable that these factors could accelerate behavioral recovery. Recently we have undertaken experiments to evaluate the possible role of supplying additional trophic activities to the injured brain to see if they would facilitate behavioral recovery.

Frontal cortex ablation produces a learning deficit in a reinforced alternation task that can be alleviated by transplantation of embryonic frontal cortex (Labbe, Firl, Mufson, & Stein, 1983). However, it appears that the onset of behavioral recovery is so rapid that new synaptic connections between the transplant and host are unlikely to mediate the restitution of function, suggesting the possible involvement of other factors. We hypothesized that growth factors induced by injury might facilitate recovery.

To evaluate this notion, we transplanted Gelfoam fragments from a 5-day-postlesion wound cavity in neonatal rats to adult hosts immediately after frontal cortex ablation. We reasoned that the Gelfoam might contain sufficient trophic factors that could be released into the injured brain, thereby ameliorating the effects of the trauma. Ten days after surgery animals began T-maze acclimation and testing on a reinforced alternation task. In brief, water-deprived rats were placed in a T-maze and allowed to choose either right or left arms for the first water reinforcement. After the first run, only a choice opposite to the previously correct choice was rewarded. Rats were tested in this task 5 days a week on 10 trials per day either until they reached a criterion or for a maximum of 30 testing days.

Performance on this learning task was examined at two levels of criterion, 1) the first day that a rat made 9 out of 10 correct choices, and 2) the first day that the animal made 19 out of 20 correct choices on two consecutive days. Control rats, with sham operations, made 9/10 correct choices in approximately 5 days, and 19/20 choices in approximately 9 days (see Figure 4). Animals with frontal cortex lesions reached criteria much more slowly, in 10 days for 9/10 choices or in 20 days for 19/20 choices.

In contrast, animals with wound-Gelfoam learned the task at a rate indistinguishable from that of sham-operated animals. Thus, the Gelfoam contains some activities that facilitate recovery. Gelfoam soaked in wound-fluid extracts was also examined. These extracts fail to accelerate recovery, perhaps because the activity is lost in preparation or because it is not supplied continuously. It was observed that the wound-Gelfoam fragments contain a population of nonneuronal cells. We hypothesized that these nonneuronal cells, many of which were astroglia, may have been providing a source of factors to the injured brain (Kesslak, Nieto-Sampedro, Globus, & Cotman, 1986). It is well-known that astrocytes produce neurotrophic factors *in vitro* (Seifert & Muller, 1984). By analogy, glial cells present in the Gelfoam might provide a continuous source of trophic factors and thereby accelerate behavioral recovery. Acute administration of the trophic factors (that is, Gelfoam soaked in the extracts) may be insufficient to produce this recovery.

Therefore, we attempted to determine if the glial cells might be responsible for the increased rate of recovery by using purified glial cells grown in culture on Gelfoam fragments. These astrocytes were transplanted into the wound cavity after frontal cortex ablation. The

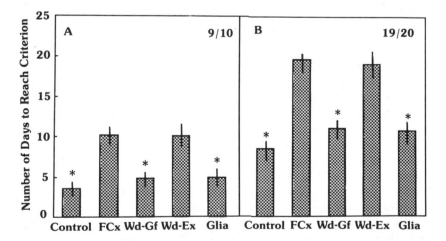

Figure 4. Time to reach criterion after frontal cortex ablation in a reinforced alternation task. Means and SEMs for groups at two performance criteria (see text). The groups are: Control = sham-operated controls (n=8); FCx = frontal cortex lesion (n=9); Wd-GF = wound-Gelfoam fragment from wound cavity (n=7); Wd-Ex = wound-fluid extract, cell free extracts from injured tissue or Gelfoam fragments (n=10); and Glia = glial-Gelfoam, purified astrocytes grown on Gelfoam fragments and subsequently transplanted into the adult host lesion (n=7). Post-hoc analysis indicated significant differences between FCx and all other groups (*p<.05; from Kesslak et al., 1986).

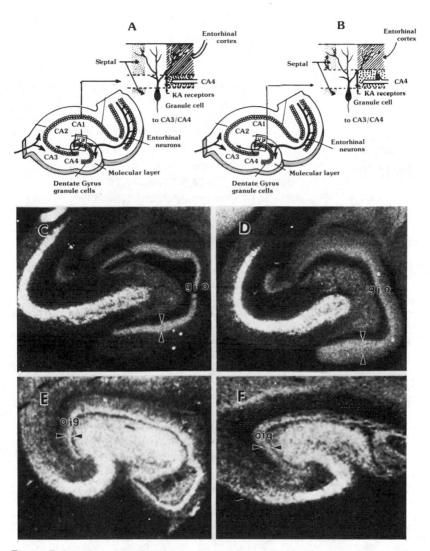

Figure 5. Schematic view of the hippocampus in a normal individual (A) and in a patient with AD (B). Autoradiograms of ³H-kainate binding to rodent (C,D) and human (E,F) hippocampal sections. (C) Control Sprague-Dawley rat hippocampus. (D) Rat hippocampus following a unilateral entorhinal cortex lesion. (E) Human hippocampus from a 73-year-old male nondemented patient. (F) Human hippocampus from a 70-year-old female patient with AD. Arrows indicate the region of high KA binding site density corresponding to the C / A terminal zone. Expansion of this region can be observed in (D) and (F). Abbreviations: g, granule cell layer of the dentate gyrus; i, inner portion of the dentate gyrus molecular layer corresponding to the commissural / associational (C / A) system terminal zone; o, outer portion of the molecular layer corresponding to the perforant path terminal zone.

groups that received glial cells did not differ significantly from sham-operated controls or wound-Gelfoam transplants (see Figure 5). Thus, these studies clearly demonstrate that behavioral recovery after frontal cortex lesions does not require replacement of lost neurons. Within the time frame of recovery this therapy may provide growth and maintenance factors to the injured brain area and thereby minimize the severity of the injury. Clearly, further work is needed, but it appears that nonneural structures, such as glial cells, acting in response to injury may enhance functional recovery and provide a new direction for investigating disease and trauma. In this context, it is interesting to speculate that a malfunction of glial cells, such as their inability to provide proper growth factors, may represent the primary deficit in AD.

Possible Relationship Between Animal Studies and the Human Brain

In view of the abundant background studies in animal models, an important future goal lies in extending this work to the human brain. At present, little has been done, particularly at the molecular level.

We have begun to study the consequences of entorhinal cell loss on axon sprouting or reactive synaptogenesis. In this process, residual axons from undamaged neurons will sprout new endings that replace the lost connections. While this process cannot replace the lost cells, it can often produce additional input from homologous cells, thereby restoring some of the lost input (Cotman, Nieto-Sampedro, & Harris, 1981). In the case of entorhinal cell loss, it has been reported that the sprouting reactions can serve some partial restoration of function (Loesche & Steward, 1977; Scheff & Cotman, 1977).

We have used two markers of axon sprouting to compare the response of the human brain to neuronal loss in the entorhinal cortex of AD patients with the rodent response to lesions of the entorhinal cortex (Geddes et al., 1985). In rodents, an entorhinal lesion causes sprouting of commissural-associational fibers (originating from CA4 cells in the hippocampus) into the denervated molecular layer, thereby enhancing their synaptic inputs (see Figure 5A & 5B). This particular response is paralleled by a spread in the distribution of the postsynaptic receptor sites for the neurotransmitter related to these fibers. Specifically, the termination of the commissural-associational

fibers contains a high density of the KA subtype of glutamate binding sites that are not present in the layer where entorhinal afferents
end. However, after entorhinal ablation, there is a spread of kainate
binding sites into the denervated entorhinal zone (see Figure 5B &
5C) associated with sprouting of the commissural-associational fibers.
Thus, axon sprouting of the commissural-associational fibers in the
denervated molecular layer of the dentate gyrus was paralleled by
an expanded distribution of kainate binding sites.

At present, it is not possible to follow fiber growth of the commissural-associational system in the human brain because it requires
the use of orthograde or retrograde tracing methods. However, the
distribution of kainate sites can be readily studied in postmortem tissues, thereby giving an indication of possible plasticity in this system. In the hippocampus obtained postmortem from AD patients,
we found an expansion of a kainate receptor field (see Figure 5E
& 5F) similar to that observed in the deafferentated rodent. This
demonstrates that synaptic plasticity occurs within at least one of
the neural systems affected by AD.

To determine if plasticity extends to other systems, we have studied
the septal system. Sprouting of the cholinergic septal input has been
studied extensively in the rodent hippocampus and can be readily
measured by the distribution and intensity of the stain for acetylcholinesterase (AChE) activity. The use of this response as a marker
for sprouting in AD is often precluded by the loss of cholinergic input to the hippocampus (Coyle, Price, & DeLong, 1983). In older-
onset AD patients in whom significant cholinergic input to the hippocampus is present (see Ball et al., 1985; Mann, Yates, & Marcynink, 1984), intensification of AChE activity is observed in the
denervated zone of the dentate molecular layer (see Figure 6). These
results indicate that cholinergic neurons in AD patients are also capable of a sprouting response. Furthermore, in AD patients in whom
there is severe cholinergic loss, there are numerous AChE-positive
plaques in the denervated outer molecular layer (see Figure 6). The
distribution of AChE-positive plaques in this region is in accord with
a sprouting of the septal input to the hippocampus. It is therefore
possible that the AChE-positive plaques in this zone may represent
an aberrant sprouting response rather than a degenerative event.

The observed expansion of a neurotransmitter receptor field and
the increase in activity of a transmitter metabolizing enzyme are in
marked contrast to the numerous reports of reduction in transmitter-
related parameters in AD (Bowen & Davison, 1984; Coyle, Singer,

McKinney, & Price, 1984; Morrison, Rogers, Scherr, Benoit, & Bloom, 1985; Rossor, Iverson, Reynolds, Mountjoy, & Roth, 1984; Selkoe & Kosik, 1984; Terry & Davies, 1980), including previous work on acidic amino acid receptors (Greenamyre et al., 1985). It appears that the brain of an AD patient is capable of compensatory growth responses along with the degenerative events. This implies that some of the underlying molecular events responsive to trauma are operative and, in fact, may be attempting to offset the severity of cell loss associated with the disease. It is apparent that the loss of neurons, whether occurring slowly in the course of a disease, as in AD, or rapidly, as when caused by injury, produces a similar end result. This striking resemblance between the human CNS response

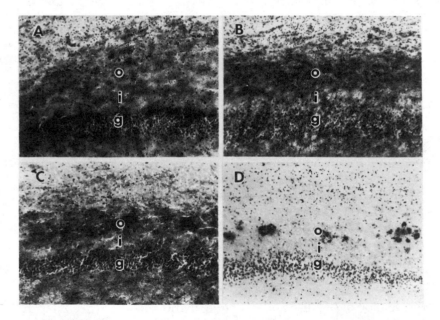

Figure 6. Acetylcholinesterase staining of the dentate gyrus molecular layer in human hippocampal sections. (A) Hippocampus from a 73-year-old male patient with no history of dementia. (B-D) Hippocampal sections from 71-, 79-, and 67-year-old male patients with AD, respectively. Intensification of AChE activity in the outer molecular layer, indicative of sprouting of the cholinergic septal input, can be observed in (B). AChE positive-plaques are apparent in the outer molecular layer in (D). (C) may represent an intermediate condition in which AChE positive-plaques are beginning to become visible. Abbreviations: g, granule cell layer of the dentate gyrus; i, inner portion of the dentate gyrus molecular layer; o, outer portion of the dentate gyrus molecular layer.

to disease-induced denervation and the rodent CNS response to a lesion-induced denervation suggests that entorhinal cortex lesions in rodents present a viable model for some aspects of AD.

CONCLUSION AND RECOMMENDATIONS

What are the implications of this work for the development of treatments of AD? While it is clear that most CNS growth occurs during development, the adult CNS retains mechanisms that provide for its maintenance and repair. As our data show, many of the cellular mechanisms that operate in development are also operative in the mature nervous system and become actualized when necessary. In aging and age-related neurodegenerative diseases such as AD, these mechanisms may fail in part. This would result in a weakening of the cells. It could result in cellular degeneration or perhaps render these cells more susceptible to other neuropathogens that ultimately cause degeneration. Neurotrophic factor production and utilization may be fundamental mechanisms providing for enhanced neuronal maintenance and viability in the course of aging, just as they play a role in the formation of the nervous system. We suspect that the regulation of glial-neuronal interactions may be fundamental to long-term CNS maintenance and the proper control of neurotrophic factor activities.

Our results on synaptic plasticity indicate that some plasticity mechanisms are intact in the Alzheimer's brain. In particular, it would seem that neurite-promoting activities are operative. It still remains to be determined, however, whether neuron-survival activities exist at normal levels or more appropriately, if they are induced and working to counteract neural degeneration. We would predict that one or more such factors are in fact compromised in AD, and that this is a fundamental mechanism responsible for the severity of degeneration. Neuron loss may be aided by degenerative enzymes such as calpain (see Chapter 6, this volume). We know, though, that in the normal adult or aged brain such degradative enzymes are regulated and do not prevail. For reasons as yet not understood, the balance of maintenance and growth responses shifts towards degeneration in the disease. In attempting to understand the fundamental basis of neural degeneration in AD, a profitable strategy will be to probe the function of the basic repair mechanisms at a molecular and cellular level, and seek intervention methods to counteract cellular degeneration. By probing these mechanisms, it may be possible to build on and augment the natural responses that the brain uses to maintain and repair itself. The similarity between the response in rodents to entorhinal cell loss and that in AD patients indicates that studies using the rodent model may be directly applicable to AD. This would greatly facilitate the application of basic research to AD and encourage the simultaneous pursuit of basic and clinical studies.

REFERENCES

Ball, M.J., Hachinski, V., Fox, A., Kirshen, A.J., Fishman, M., Blume, W., Kral, V.A., Fox, H., & Mersky, H. (1985). A new definition of Alzheimer's disease: A hippocampal dementia. *Lancet, 1* (8419), 14-16.

Bowen, D.M., & Davison, A.N. (1984). Dementia in the elderly: Biochemical aspects. *Journal of the Royal College of Physicians of London, 18,* 25-27.

Cotman, C.W., Lewis, E.R., & Hand, D. (1981). The critical afferent theory: A mechanism to account for septohippocampal development and plasticity. In H. Flohr & W. Precht (Eds.), *Proceedings in the life sciences* (pp. 13-26). Heidelberg: Springer-Verlag.

Cotman, C.W., & Nieto-Sampedro, M. (1983). Trophic influences on the *in vivo* survival of transplanted cholinergic neurons: A model system for the study of neuron loss in Alzheimer's disease. In R. Katzman (Ed.), *Branbury Report 15: Biological aspects of Alzheimer's disease* (pp. 275-284). Cold Spring Harbor, N.Y.: Cold Spring Harbor Laboratory.

Cotman, C.W., & Nieto-Sampedro, M. (1984). Cell biology of synaptic plasticity. *Science, 225,* 1287-1294.

Cotman, C.W., Nieto-Sampedro, M., & Gibbs, R. (1984). Enhancing the self-repairing potential of the central nervous system after injury. *Central Nervous System Trauma, 1,* 3-14.

Cotman, C.W., Nieto-Sampedro, M., & Harris, E. (1981). Synapse replacement in the nervous system of adult vertebrates. *Physiological Reviews, 61,* 684-784.

Coyle, J.T., Price, D.L., & DeLong, M.R. (1983). Alzheimer's disease: A disorder of cortical cholinergic innervation. *Science, 219,* 1184-1190.

Coyle, J.T., Singer, H., McKinney, M., & Price, D. (1984). Neurotransmitter specific alterations in dementing disorders: Insights from animal models. *Journal of Psychiatric Research, 18*, 501-512.

Diamond, J.E., Cooper, E., Turner, C., & MacIntyre, L. (1976). Trophic regulation of nerve sprouting. *Science, 198*, 371-377.

Ebendal, T., Olson, L., Seiger, A., & Hedlund, K.-O. (1980). Nerve growth factors in the rat iris. *Nature, 286*, 25-28.

Geddes, J., Monaghan, D.T., Cotman, C.W., Lott, I.T., Kim, R.C., & Chui, H.C. (1985). Plasticity of hippocampal circuitry in Alzheimer's disease. *Science, 230*, 1179-1181.

Goldowitz, D., & Cotman, C.W. (1980). Axonal transport and axon sprouting in the adult dentate gyrus; an autoradiographic study. *Neuroscience, 5*, 2163-2174.

Greenamyre, J.T., Penney, J.B., Young, A.B., D'Amato, C.J., Hicks, S.P., & Shoulson, I. (1985). Alterations in L-glutamate binding in Alzheimer's and Huntington's diseases. *Science, 227*, 1496-1499.

Hyman, B.I., Van Hoesen, G.W., Damasio, A.R., & Barnes, C.L. (1984). Alzheimer's disease: Cell-Specific pathology isolates the hippocampal formation. *Science, 225*, 1168-1170.

Kesslak, J.P., Nieto-Sampedro, M., Globus, J., & Cotman, C.W. (1986). *Glial cell transplants promote behavioral recovery after frontal cortex lesion.* (Manuscript submitted for publication.)

Labbe, R., Firl, A., Jr., Mufson, E.J., & Stein, D.G. (1983). Fetal brain transplants: Reduction of cognitive deficits in rats with frontal cortex lesions. *Science, 221*, 470-472.

Lewis, E.R., & Cotman, C.W. (1982). Mechanisms of septal lamination in the developing hippocampus analyzed by outgrowth of fibers from septal implants. II. Absence of guidance by degenerating debris. *Journal of Neuroscience, 2*, 66-77.

Loesche, J., & Steward, O. (1977). Behavioral correlates of denervation and reinnervation of the hippocampal formation of the rat: Recovery of alternation performance following unilateral entorhinal cortex lesions. *Brain Research Bulletin, 2*, 31-39.

Longo, F.M., Selak, I., Zovickian, J., Manthorpe, M., Varon, S., & U, H.S. (1984). Neuronotrophic activities in cerebrospinal fluid of head trauma patients. *Experimental Neurology, 84*, 207-218.

Lundborg, G., Longo, F.M., & Varon, S. (1982). Nerve regeneration model and trophic factors in vivo. *Brain Research, 232*, 157-161.

Lynch, G.S., Matthews, D.A., Mosko, S., Parks, T., & Cotman, C.W. (1972). Induced acetylcholinesterase-rich layer in rat dentate gyrus following entorhinal lesions. Brain Research, 42, 311-318.

Mann, D., Yates, P.O., & Marcynink, B. (1984). Changes in nerve cells of the Nucleus Basalis of Meynert in Alzheimer's disease and their relationship to aging and to the accumulation of lipofuscin pigment. Mechanisms of Ageing and Development, 25, 189-204.

Manthorpe, M., Nieto-Sampedro, M., Skaper, S.D., Lewis, E.R., Barbin, G., Longo, F.M., Cotman, C.W., & Varon, S. (1983). Neuronotrophic activity in brain wounds of the developing rat. Correlation with implant survival in the wound cavity. Brain Research, 267, 47-56.

Manthorpe, M., Varon, S., & Adler, R. (1981). Neurite-Promoting factor in conditioned medium from RN22 schwannoma cultures: Bioassay, fractionation, and properties. Journal of Neurochemistry, 37, 759-767.

Matthews, D.A., Cotman, C.W., & Lynch, G.S. (1976). An electron microscopic study of lesion-induced synaptogenesis in the dentate gyrus of the adult rat. I. Magnitude and time course of degeneration. Brain Research, 115, 1-21.

Millaruelo, A.I., Nieto-Sampedro, M., Yu, J., & Cotman, C.W. (in press). Neurotrophic activity in the central and peripheral nervous systems of the cat. Effects of injury. Brain Research.

Morrison, J.H., Rogers, J., Scherr, S., Benoit, R., & Bloom, F.E., (1985). Somatostatin immunoreactivity in neuritic plaques of Alzheimer's patients. Nature, 314, 90-92.

Nadler, J.V., Cotman, C.W., & Lynch, G.S. (1977). Histochemical evidence of altered development of cholinergic fibers in the rat dentate gyrus following lesions. I. Time course after complete unilateral entorhinal lesion at various ages. Journal of Comparative Neurology, 171, 561-587.

Needels, D.L., Nieto-Sampedro, M., & Cotman, C.W. (in press). Induction of a novel neurite-promoting activity in rat brain following injury. Neuroscience.

Needels, D.L., Nieto-Sampedro, M., Whittemore, S.R., & Cotman, C.W. (1985). Neuronotrophic activity for ciliary ganglion neurons. Induction following injury to the brain of neonatal, adult and aged rats. Development Brain Research, 18, 275-284.

Nieto-Sampedro, M., & Cotman, C.W. (1985). Growth factor induction and temporal order in CNS repair. In C.W. Cotman (Ed.), *Synaptic plasticity* (pp. 407-455). New York: Guilford Press.

Nieto-Sampedro, M., Lewis, E.R., Cotman, C.W., Manthorpe, M., Skaper, S.D., Barbin, G., Longo, F.M., & Varon, S. (1982). Brain injury causes a time-dependent increase in neuronotrophic activity at the lesion site. *Science, 217,* 860-861.

Nieto-Sampedro, M., Manthorpe, M., Barbin, G., Varon, S., & Cotman, C.W. (1983). Injury-induced neuronotrophic activity in adult brain. Correlation with survival of delayed implants in the wound cavity. *Journal of Neuroscience, 3,* 2219-2229.

Nieto-Sampedro, M., Whittemore, S.R., Needels, D.L., Larsen, J., & Cotman, C.W. (1984). The survival of brain transplants is enhanced by extracts of injured brain. *Proceedings of the National Academy of Sciences, USA, 81,* 6250-6254.

Rossor, M.N., Iverson, L.L., Reynolds, G.P., Mountjoy, C.Q., & Roth, M. (1984). Neurochemical characteristics of early and late onset types of Alzheimer's disease. *British Medical Journal, 288,* 961-964.

Scheff, S.W., Bernardo, L.S., & Cotman, C.W. (1978). Effect of serial lesion on sprouting in the dentate gyrus: Onset and decline of catalytic effect. *Brain Research, 150,* 45-53.

Scheff, S.W., & Cotman, C.W. (1977). Recovery of spontaneous alternation following lesions of the entorhinal cortex in adult rats: Possible correlation to axon sprouting. *Behavioral Biology, 21,* 286-293.

Seifert, W., & Muller, H.W. (1984). Neuron-Glia interaction in mammalian brain: Preparation and quantitative bioassay of a neurotrophic factor (NTF) from primary astrocytes. In D.W. Barnes, D.A. Sirbasku, & G.H. Sato (Eds.), *Cell culture methods for molecular and cell biology* (Vol. 4, pp. 67-77). New York: Alan R. Liss, Inc.

Selkoe, D., & Kosik, K. (1984). Neurochemical changes with aging. In M. Albert (Ed.), *Clinical neurology of aging* (pp. 53-75). New York: Oxford University Press.

Terry, R.D., & Davies, P. (1980). Dementia of the Alzheimer type. *Annual Review of Neuroscience, 3,* 77-95.

Whittemore, S.R., Nieto-Sampedro, M., Needels, D.L., & Cotman, C.W. (1985). Neuronotrophic factors for mammalian neurons: Injury induction in neonatal, adult and aged rat brain. *Developmental Brain Research, 20* 169-178.

6

Proteases, Neuronal Stability, and Brain Aging: An Hypothesis

Gary Lynch, PhD, John Larson, PhD, and Michel Baudry, PhD

Aging produces progressive and extensive atrophy and degeneration in the brain. The agents responsible for these age-related effects are unknown, but enough has been established at a phenomenological level to allow some deductions about their natures. First, the underlying mechanisms must be capable of producing the atrophy of dendrites and axons; this rather obvious point suggests that a search might usefully begin with those few cell biochemical reactions that have been linked to degeneration in contexts other than aging. Second, age-related neuropathologies are not manifested to the same degree in different brain structures. Cell loss, for example, approaches 50% of the total population in some regions and cannot be detected in others; neurofibrillary tangles in the forebrain of normal aged brains are also quite restricted in their distribution (Kemper, 1984). Thus, it is unlikely that the cellular processes that produce brain atrophy and degeneration are operating at the same pace or with the same intensity in all parts of the brain. Third, animals age at different rates. Maximum life span, presumably a reflection of aging rate, varies by two orders of magnitude across the mammals. Although data on this point are scarce, we can reasonably assume that the time of appearance of age-related neuropathologies depends on the life span of a given species and therefore that the kinetics of the cellular process(es) producing neuropathology vary greatly in different species.

It appears then that we are looking for cellular mechanisms that produce atrophy and degeneration of neurons and, in some fundamental way, vary greatly between cell types, brain regions, and animal species. In this chapter, we will employ this list of criteria to develop the hypothesis that calcium-dependent proteases are involved in brain aging. The discussion will be divided into four sections.

First, we will consider several lines of evidence that implicate this class of enzymes in the production of cytoskeletal breakdown and pathology.

Second, the literature relating brain size to maximum life span (and hence to rate of aging) in mammals will be reviewed and data presented showing that variations in calcium-dependent proteolytic activity can account for this relationship.

Third, immunocytochemical data showing that at least one variant of calcium-sensitive protease varies greatly in concentration across brain regions and cell types will be described.

Finally, we will advance the suggestion that the rate at which the constituents of brain cells are broken down and replaced dictates the rate at which the brain ages and at which pathology develops.

CALCIUM-ACTIVATED PROTEASES AND CELL DEGENERATION

Calcium-activated neutral thiol (cysteine) proteases are found throughout the body and in virtually all types of cells (Murachi, Hatanaka, Yasumoto, Nakayama, & Tanaka, 1981). Two forms of the enzymes have been distinguished on the basis of the concentration of calcium needed for half-maximal activation (5 μM vs 200 μM) (De Martino, 1981; Klein, Lehotay, & Godek, 1981; Malik, Fenko, Iqbal, & Wisniewski, 1983; Siman, Baudry, & Lynch, 1983; Zimmerman & Schlaepfer, 1982). Both enzymes are composed of two subunits, a catalytic polypeptide of 80,000 daltons and a second smaller protein of 30,000 daltons with unknown function. Despite their similarities, the low- and high-threshold variants (for which the names calpain I and II have been proposed [Murachi, Tanaka, Hatanaka, & Murakami, 1981]) are antigenically distinct and have significant differences in amino acid composition (Yoshimura, Hatanaka, Kitahara, Kawaguchi, & Murachi, 1984; Yumoto, Kikuchi, Sasaki, & Murachi, 1984). The gene for calpain II has been sequenced and may represent a merger of genes for papain and calmodulin (Ohno et al., 1984). The known substrates of both calpains are for the most part proteins that form the cell cytoskeleton or that serve to cross-link its elements with each other or with the cell membrane. These include microtubule-associated proteins, neurofilament proteins, tubulin, spectrin, and fodrin (or brain spectrin) (Baudry, Bundman, Smith, & Lynch, 1981; Klein et al., 1981; Siman,

Baudry, & Lynch, 1984; Zimmerman & Schlaepfer, 1982). With regard to cellular localization, calpain is found in both soluble and membrane fractions (Siman et al., 1983).

Although the nature of the known substrates of calpains provides clues, the functions of these enzymes are still poorly understood. The calcium concentrations needed to activate the low-threshold enzyme are about an order of magnitude higher than resting intracellular levels suggesting that calpain is activated by discrete and unusual events. Activation of calpain II requires calcium concentrations a thousand times higher than resting levels, and it is not clear under what kind of conditions this might occur. However, calpain II can undergo autoproteolysis to generate a third calpain form (calpain IIb according to the terminology of Hathaway, Werth, and Haeberle [1982]) with a calcium requirement similar to that for calpain I. Thus pools of inactive and potentially active enzyme might exist *in situ*. Recent work has provided strong evidence that calpain I participates in the shape changes in both red blood cells (Siman, Baudry, & Lynch, 1986) and platelets (Fox, Goll, Reynolds, & Phillips, 1985) that occur under various physiological conditions. This points to a role for the protease in production of structural reorganization. We have also shown that the membrane-associated variant of calpain produces irreversible changes in the binding of glutamate, a probable neurotransmitter at a majority of excitatory synapses in mammalian central nervous system (CNS) (Fagg & Foster, 1983), to synaptic membranes isolated from forebrain structures (Baudry & Lynch, 1984; Baudry et al., 1981; Siman, Baudry, & Lynch, 1985), and have advanced the hypothesis that this enzyme produces long-lasting alterations in synaptic morphology and function (Lynch & Baudry, 1984). Calpain has also been implicated in the processing of membrane-bound coated vesicles in muscle fibers (Libby, Bursztajn, & Goldberg, 1980) and in the regulation of the amount of one form of brain spectrin (Siman et al., 1986).

Most of the interest in calpain, however, has focused on the possibility that it is responsible for certain forms of muscle and nerve pathology. Evidence has steadily accumulated that muscle deterioration associated with disease or various experimental manipulations, particularly denervation, is due to elevated levels of intracellular calcium (Fleckenstein, 1977; Leonard & Salpeter, 1979). Calcium has also been implicated in degeneration in a host of other cell types (Schanne, Kane, Young, & Farber, 1979). These findings led to a search for a calcium-sensitive process that produces cytoskeletal breakdown, membrane deterioration, and other events that precede and accompany pathology. The discovery of calpain and the identification of its substrates as cytoskeletal elements offered one possibility, and recent work from several laboratories has now provided experimental evidence linking the enzyme to atrophy and degeneration. Thus calpain activity is increased in denervated muscle (Elce, Hasspieler, & Boegman, 1983), and the pathological effects of both denervation as well as prolonged application of cholinergic agonists to muscle are retarded by inhibitors of calpain (Libby & Goldberg, 1978; Salpeter, Leonard, & Kasprzak, 1981; Sher, Stracher, Shafiq, & Hardystashin, 1981; Stracher, McGowan, & Shafiq, 1978). Moreover, dystrophic muscles in animals and humans have been found to contain abnormally high calpain activity (Dayton, Schollmeyer, Chan, & Allen, 1979; Kar & Pearson, 1976; Neerunjun & Dubowitz, 1979), and the phases of muscle atrophy accompanying molting in crabs are associated with increased calpain activity (Mykles & Skinner, 1983). The connection between calpain and pathology is probably not unique to muscles, since the cytoskeletal breakdown found in cut axons is significantly slowed by maintaining nerves in calcium-free solutions as well as by application of inhibitors of calpain (Ishizaki, Tashiro, & Kurokawa, 1983; Pant & Gainer, 1980; Schlaepfer & Micko, 1978). Calpain is also found in purified myelin and the suggestion has been made that it is responsible for the early stages of demyelination found in multiple sclerosis (Singh, I. & Singh, A.K., 1983).

The evidence that calpain is involved in a variety of pathological conditions in various cell types raises the possibility that it might also play a role in the age-related atrophy and degeneration found in brain. In the following sections we will explore this idea by asking first if comparative differences in the rate of aging are correlated with differences in calpain activity and if the enzyme exhibits regional differences that might account for the differential effects of aging on brain cell populations.

BRAIN CALPAIN AND RATE OF AGING IN DIFFERENT GROUPS OF ANIMALS: BODY SIZE, BRAIN SIZE, AND LONGEVITY

Big animals live longer than smaller ones. This critical observation was first noted for domestic animals in the early part of this century (Friedenthal, 1910) and, although often ignored by neurogerontologists, has played an important role in the development of theories of aging.

Sacher (1959) first showed that mammalian life span, like other physiological variables, scales to body size according to an allometric power function of the form: $L = KP^{0.20}$ (where L = maximum life span for the species, P = body weight, and K is a constant). Figure 1a is a plot of log maximum life span against log body weight for 255 species of eutherian mammals. Linear regression gives a slope of 0.19 (corresponding to the exponent of the power function) and a correlation coefficient of 0.77. As noted by Sacher (1959), the excellence of the correlation is particularly impressive when one considers the error that must be contained in many of the maximum life span estimates. However, the analysis as shown here incorporates a potentially serious flaw: the graph describes a relationship for the mammals as a class, but most of the species represented are from four orders (56 rodents, 52 carnivores, 41 artiodactyls, and 56 primates). Figure 1b provides what might be called an "orders" curve in which each order of mammal (for which data are available) is represented by a single point. This value is derived by calculating a geometric mean for all the families represented in the data base; the family points in turn are calculated from their constituent genera, which are themselves the geometric means of the species contained within them. The "orders" curve reveals the most interesting point that Chiroptera (bats) and Insectivora are the only orders to deviate greatly from the longevity: Body weight equation ($L = KP^{0.20}$; $r = 0.95$) for mammals. It should be noted that almost all of the longevity estimates used here are from zoo records since these are usually much greater than estimates from studies of wild animals; bats, however, do not survive well in captivity, and the majority of data points for this order are from banding studies. It is very likely, therefore, that the values of maximum life span for the bats are underestimated, making the divergence of this group all the more striking.

Understandably enough, most of the work on the longevity: Body size relationship has been directed at the mammals; however, analysis of bird data provides critically important perspective to the results described above. Figure 2 shows maximum life span and body weight for 15 orders of birds (calculated from 51 species values). It is clear that most birds live much longer than mammals and that maximum life span scales at a lower power of body weight in birds ($L = KP^{0.14}$

A

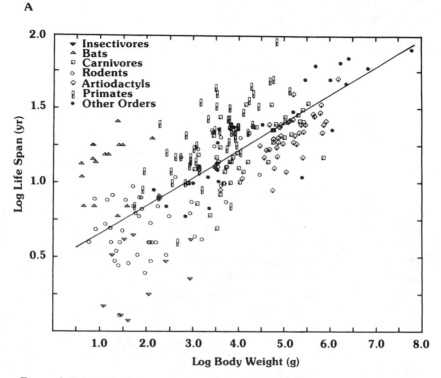

Figure 1. Relationship between body weight and maximum life span in eutherian mammals.

A. Plot of log life span (L) and log body weight (P) for 255 species. The line of best fit was found by linear regression (excluding bat and insectivore species) and is described by the equation: log L = 0.19 log P + 0.47 (r= 0.77).

vs. L = KP[0.20] in mammals) (see Lindstedt & Calder, 1976; Mallouk, 1975). On the average, a bird will live about four times as long as a mammal — excepting always the bats — of equivalent body weight (e.g., pigeons, 30 years; guinea pig, 8 years) and even the shortest-lived bird (hummingbird, 8 years) lives as long or longer than 20% of the mammals. These points raise the question of whether it is the birds or the mammals that have exceptional life spans or if, in fact, there is anything like a pattern for the vertebrate phylum. There are not nearly enough data in the literature for the other classes of vertebrates to answer these questions, but life spans have been reported for various fish, amphibians, and reptiles that would be most unusual for mammals.

B

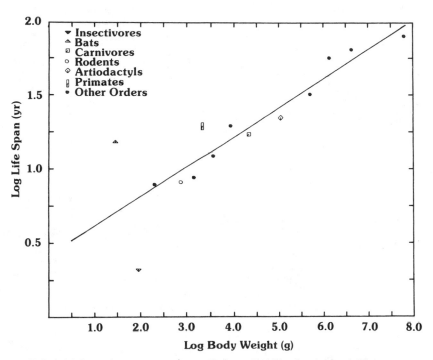

B. As in (a), but with one average data point for each of 14 orders (see text). The equation describing the regression line (excluding bats and insectivores) is: log L = 0.20 log P + 0.42 (r = 0.95).

These results provide us with several points that need to be addressed by hypotheses about causes of aging:

1. Maximum life span in mammals is related to body size by a power equation with an exponent of 0.20.

2. Bats have life spans greatly in excess of that predicted by the longevity: body size equation for mammals.

3. Birds live much longer than mammals and have a different longevity: body size equation.

The question now arises as to what feature(s) of body size explains its relationship to life span.

The correlate of body size most often associated with rate of aging is basal metabolic rate. These two variables are usually thought to

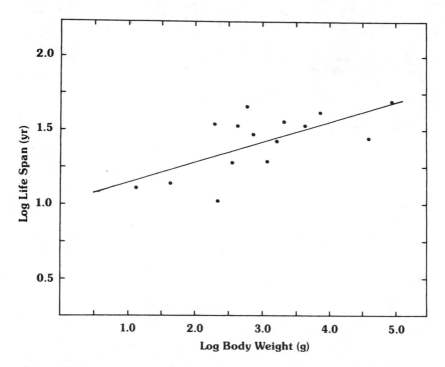

Figure 2. Relationship between body weight and maximum life span in birds. Log life span (L) is plotted against log body weight (P) for an average data point for each of 15 orders (derived from a sample of 51 species). The regression equation is: $\log L = 0.14 \log P + 1.01$ ($r = 0.67$).

be related by the equation $M = KP^{0.75}$ (M = basal metabolic rate; P = body size) (Kleiber, 1947) indicating that metabolic rate *per unit body mass* declines with increasing body size. Associated with this, a number of variables related to metabolism (heart and breathing rate, for instance) decrease with increases in body size. These observations prompted the idea that bigger animals live longer because their cellular metabolism is slower and leads to a slow-down of all long-term processes including aging. Metabolic rate is an intuitively attractive candidate for a major determinant of rate of aging but there are several problems in using it to explain the phenomenology described above. For one, basal metabolic rate scales at the same power of body weight in both mammals and birds (Kleiber, 1947; Lasiewski & Dawson, 1967), whereas life span scales at a different power of body weight in these two classes. It might also be noted that the relationship between metabolic rate and body size is remarkably constant within different species and that the within-species exponent of the power function only is slightly less than that obtained when calculating across species [i.e., $M = KP^{0.67}$ *within species* vs. $M = KP^{0.75}$ for all mammals (Heusner, 1982)]. This is potentially a very significant point because there is reason to suspect that the relationship between longevity and body size is not nearly so constant in different groups of mammals as is that between metabolic rate and body size. The slope of the maximum life span to body size curve for primates, for instance, is steeper than that for mammals, as a group (slope of 0.28 vs. 0.20; $P<.05$) (unpublished observations), yet the primate metabolic rate to body size curve cannot be distinguished from that for mammals as a whole (Armstrong, 1983). At the other extreme, life span actually *decreases* with body size across breeds of dogs (Comfort, 1979) (correlation between the two variables, $r = -0.92$), yet bigger dogs exhibit the expected decrease in weight-specific basal metabolic rate (Heusner, 1982). Thus, the allometric relationship between longevity and body size may vary considerably within different groupings of mammals; to the extent this is a general phenomenon, we would have to question the idea that relatively invariant relationships such as that for metabolic rate to body size can, by themselves, explain longevity.

Probably the best known of all allometric relationships is that for brain to body size, and indeed the recognition of allometry as a determinant of body form began with the efforts of Julian Huxley to find an appropriate means for expressing relative brain size (Huxley, 1932). It was widely believed for years that the correct exponent of the brain to body size equation was 0.67 ($E = KP^{0.67}$, where $E =$ brain weight and $P =$ body weight) (Jerison, 1973), and given that this is also the geometric formula relating the surface area to the volume of a sphere, much discussion ensued on the possibility that brain volume was scaled to body surface area; however, more recent work, using a larger sample of mammal species, has convincingly shown that in actuality the exponent of the power equation is about 0.75 (Eisenberg & Wilson, 1978; Hofman, 1982; Martin, 1981). The similarity of this exponent to that for the equation relating basal metabolism to body size led to the suggestion that metabolism dictates brain size (Armstrong, 1983; Martin, 1981). It is ironic that at about the time researchers realized that the exponent of brain to body size was 0.75 rather than 0.67, Heusner (1982) argued that the exponent of the metabolism to body size equation should be changed from 0.75 to 0.67.

Brain size correlates quite well with maximum life span, as expected from its excellent correlation with body size (Figure 3). In fact, as first documented by Sacher (1959), brain size is actually a better predictor of longevity than body size. This led Sacher and others after him (Hofman, 1983) to raise the possibility that life span is to some degree determined by brain size, a suggestion that is intuitively reasonable given the critical role of brain in regulating body homeostasis. Calder (1976), however, has argued that the better correlation for longevity to brain size simply reflects the fact that measurements of brain are much less variable than are those for body size. He suggests that brain weight or volume is a better index of the "true" size of an adult animal than is body weight, influenced as this latter variable is by health, feeding conditions, and so forth. This argument implies that relative brain size ("encephalization") would be a poorer predictor of life span than brain size alone since it combines a good (brain) and a not-as-good (body size) estimate of body size; but, as

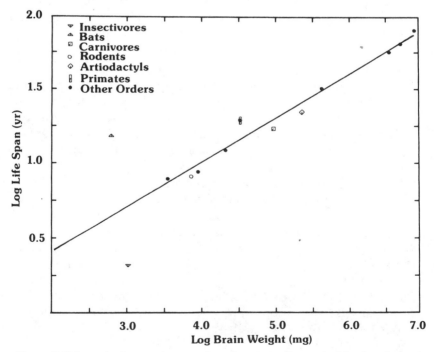

Figure 3. Relationship between brain weight and maximum life span for 14 orders of mammals. Excluding the bats and insectivores, log life span = 0.30 log brain weight − 0.19 (r = 0.98).

shown by Sacher (1959) and Hofman (1983), relative brain size provides an even more reliable predictor of longevity than brain size alone. The scaling exponent for brain weight to body weight varies considerably among various subgroups of mammals, as well as for mammals versus other classes of vertebrates (Martin, 1981), and thus cannot be excluded as a possible explanation for variations in the longevity to body size scaling exponent. As noted above, life span does not increase with body size in the birds to the same degree that it does for mammals, and this is also the case for brain size ($E = KP^{0.56}$ vs. $E = KP^{0.75}$ for birds and mammals, respectively). Primates as an order have a steeper longevity to body size curve than does the mammalian class and this is also true for their brain to body curve ($E = KP^{0.85}$ vs. $E = KP^{0.75}$). Finally, it is well-established that the exponents for the within-species brain to body size equations are much lower than those derived across all groups of mammals and, as described, dogs have a negative life span to body size relationship. Perhaps it is the case that the amount of added brain accompanying increases in body size must reach a certain value in order for life span to be extended. This would in turn suggest that body and brain size, and the relationship between them, determine longevity rather than the absolute values of either. Sacher (1959) and others (Hofman, 1983; Mallouk, 1975) reached this conclusion from the observation that brain and body size together are better predictors of maximum life span than either alone. In any event, these arguments support the idea that the effect of body size on aging is mediated to an important degree by its influence on brain size. However, relative brain size cannot account for the surprising longevity of the bats, as is evident from Figure 3.

The above arguments can be summarized as follows:

1. The equation describing the relationship of life span to body size for the mammals as a class does not hold for birds or all orders and species of mammals; primates have a steeper longevity to body curve and at least one species of mammals exhibits a negative power function.

2. Differences in the metabolism to body size equations cannot explain these variations.

3. The relationship of brain size to body size does vary across mammalian groups and taxonomic levels as would be expected for a variable involved in determining rate of aging.

4. However, the brain to body size relationship will not account for the unusual longevity of bats.

COMPARATIVE STUDIES OF CALPAIN ACTIVITY

Brain size is determined by a variety of factors and any link it might have with rate of aging presumably must be expressed through, or be a reflection of, a cellular process that is tightly correlated with it. The comparative data provide us with important guidelines for identifying that process.

1. It should co-vary with mammalian brain size — ideally, the equation should have an exponent that would account for the slope of the longevity to brain size curve.

2. The process should in some important way be different in bat brains.

3. It should also be distinctly different in avian versus mammalian brains.

Because of the possible role of calcium-dependent proteases in inducing age-related pathologies, we investigated the relationships among calpain activity, brain size, and rate of aging, reflected by maximal life span.

Figure 4 describes soluble (cytoplasmic) calcium-dependent proteolytic activity in cerebral cortex as a function of brain size in mammals. Calpain I, the low-threshold enzyme, while clearly present in brain, exhibited activities too low to allow for reliable comparisons — accordingly, the results shown here were determined with concentrations of calcium adequate to trigger both calpain I and calpain II. It is clear that total calcium-dependent proteolytic activity is strongly and negatively correlated with brain size. Equally evident is the fact that the bats are strikingly divergent from other orders of mammals (Baudry, DuBrin, Beasley, Leon, & Lynch, in press). It should be noted that several specimens obtained from two families of bats were assayed, and all gave comparable results. Thus it seems that bats have uniquely low levels of total calpain activity in the soluble fractions of their brains.

The exponent of the power function relating calpain activity to brain size was found to be about -0.38. This point, combined with the fact that the extreme longevity of bats is accompanied by a comparably unusually low level of calpain activity, means that total enzyme activity should be almost linearly related to life span. This is indeed the case as shown in Figure 5, which indicates that the exponent of the power function relating life span to calpain activity is close to unity. The relationship of calpain activity to brain size and

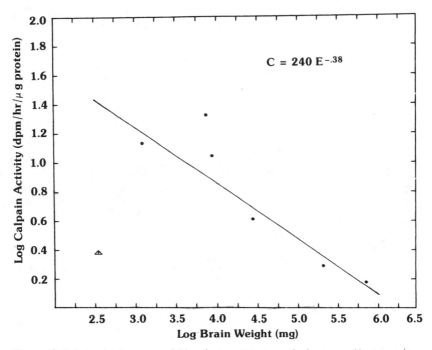

Figure 4. Relationship between soluble calpain activity in cerebral cortex and brain weight in mammals. Each data point represents an average value for one order. Excluding bats and the opossum, log calpain activity = − 0.38 log brain weight + 2.38 (r = 0.91).

life span is by no means typical. Oxidative metabolism per unit tissue, for example, scales to brain size with an exponent of about −0.13 (Mink, Blumenschine, & Adams, 1981), which is too low to account for the longevity to brain size equation. Various indices of glial cell metabolism suggest that this variable does not change with brain size (Tower & Young, 1973).

What of birds and other vertebrate classes? We have data for the telencephalon of only five species (from different orders) of birds and for these we find that total calpain activity is high and does not appear to vary with brain size (Baudry, Simonson, DuBrin, & Lynch, 1986). Although this finding indicates that calcium-dependent proteolysis is different in birds and mammals, it does not provide any obvious explanation for the greater longevity of the birds. We will return to this point later.

The results for the other classes of vertebrates are surprising. Several specimens of lizards were assayed to provide information on the rep-

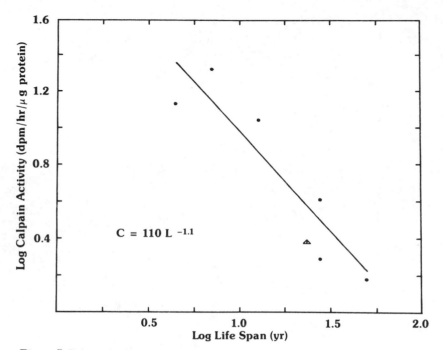

Figure 5. Relationship between calpain activity and life span in 7 orders of mammals. Linear regression gives the equation: log calpain activity = −1.1 log life span + 2.04 (r = 0.91).

tiles; these animals had low calpain activity but also had significant amounts of calcium-independent neutral proteolytic activity. This stands in marked contrast to mammals and birds in which virtually all proteolytic activity in brain soluble fractions at physiological pH is calcium-dependent. Amphibians (frogs and newts) had very high levels of this unidentified calcium-independent enzyme and very little calpain activity. Fish provided the strangest results of all: their brains had virtually no detectable proteolytic activity (calcium-dependent or -independent) at neutral pH although the acidic proteases could be readily measured. This finding was so unexpected that assays were repeated on the three great subgroups of fish (jawless, cartilaginous, and bony); in none of the samples could we find reliable evidence of neutral proteolytic activity (Baudry et al., 1986).

These findings suggest a number of possible evolutionary scenarios, but more immediately they indicate that proteolysis in brain varies greatly across the classes of vertebrates. Against this background, we can only conclude that the relationship of brain calpain to rate of aging is probably unique to the mammals.

To summarize, calpain activity exhibits the following relationships:

1. a strong negative correlation with brain size,
2. very low activity in the bat brain,
3. near linearity with rate of aging, and
4. dramatic differences across the classes of vertebrates.

REGIONAL DISTRIBUTION OF CALPAIN IN BRAIN

One of the striking features of brain aging, in mammals at least, is that its manifestations are unequally distributed. Neurofibrillary tangles found in normal aged human brains are localized in very discrete subdivisions. In forebrain, for example, they are restricted to specific layers of the entorhinal cortex and to the subiculum, a major component of the hippocampal formation. Cell loss also occurs to very different degrees in the human brain. Thus about 50% of the large pyramidal cells in neocortex disappear between ages 20 to 70 while other regions show virtually no losses with age (Kemper, 1984). Age-related diseases also affect different brain regions with varying degrees of severity. Van Hoesen and his associates (Hyman, Van Hoesen, Damasion, & Barnes, 1984) have recently demonstrated severe pathology in layers II and IV-V of the entorhinal cortex and in subiculum in the brains of Alzheimer's disease (AD) patients in which adjacent sections of hippocampus appear more or less normal. They argue that these regions may be among the first to be affected by the disease and point out that pathology in these areas would severely disrupt hippocampal function and thus, perhaps, account for the anterograde amnesia so characteristic of AD patients. It has also been suggested that cholinergic cell populations in the basal forebrain are particularly at risk in AD (Perry, 1980). The question of whether AD is simply an exaggeration of normal brain aging or indeed is a distinct disease entity is still unresolved (Bowen et al., 1979).

The causes of age-related cell pathology, why it takes the forms it does, and why it should be so unevenly distributed across brain are fundamental problems for neurogerontology. If the calcium-dependent proteases are involved in these pathologies, we might expect to find that they vary in concentrations across brain regions and cell types. In a first study we simply measured total calpain activity in eight brain subdivisions and found that brain stem and cerebellum had somewhat higher levels of activity than the forebrain; the olfactory bulbs were unique among telencephalic derivatives in that they exhibited calpain values comparable to those found in the lower brain regions (Simonson, Baudry, Siman, & Lynch, 1985). To obtain a much more detailed picture, we developed monoclonal and polyclonal antibodies against rat calpain I and used immuno-histochemical procedures to map the distribution of the enzyme. These experiments demonstrated that calpain concentrations vary considerably not only between brain regions but within given structures and across cell types (Siman et al., 1985). High levels of the enzyme were found in the olfactory nerves and the alpha-motoneurons of the spinal cord, a point that is potentially interest-ing since the axons of the first (Graziadei & Monti-Graziadei, 1977) and the terminals of the second (Barker & Ip, 1966; Smith & Rosen-heimer, 1982) are known to undergo continuous degeneration and regeneration in normal adult mammals. In the neocortex, calpain levels were highest in the large pyramidal cells of the deeper cortical layers, whereas in the hippocampal formation, the subiculum was the most prominently stained structure, with the granule cells and pyramidal neurons of hippocampus itself showing much lower con-centrations. Other neurons containing high calpain levels were found in the basal forebrain, including the cholinergic cell groups, the pars compacta of substantia nigra, the Purkinje's cells (but not the gran-ule cells) of the cerebellum, and the motor nuclei of the brain stem. Only preliminary comparative data are available, but it appears that the distribution found in the rat is typical of the mammals, including primates.

These experiments demonstrate that calpain is differentially dis-tributed in the brain and does appear to be present in high concen-tration in those cells that are at risk in aging. In cerebral cortex, for example, cell losses with aging are much more pronounced for the larger neurons (see Kemper, 1984, for a review) and these contain the highest levels of calpain in isocortex. As mentioned, the subicu-lum exhibits prominent pathologies in normal aging and in AD, and neurons in this region stand out from the remainder of the hippocam-pus and retrohippocampal area in terms of calpain concentration. Decreases in dopamine levels and losses of dopamine-containing cell bodies are prominent in aging (Finch, Marshall, & Randall, 1981), and the relevant neurons possess unusually high calpain concen-trations. Similarly, aging in the rat causes severe pathology of the cerebellar Purkinje's cells, and again calpain is highly concentrated in these neurons compared to the adjacent granule cells. Finally, the basal forebrain cholinergic neurons, which are thought to be severely affected by aging (Perry, 1980), are conspicuously stained with calpain antibodies.

Clearly, it would be useful to test the correlation between calpain concentration and the occurrence of age-related neuropathology directly, especially for humans. But judging from these preliminary data, calpain clearly satisfies the third criterion — unequal distribution between brain regions and cells — for a mechanism involved in the production of brain aging.

NEURONAL STABILITY AND AGING

We have argued that the calpains satisfy several criteria for an agent involved in brain aging and in particular in the development of pathology. These enzymes have been linked to cellular degeneration in several circumstances, their activity co-varies with rate of aging, and they differ in concentration and activity between cell types and brain regions. The following section will address the questions of why these variations exist and how, in a mechanistic sense, they might produce the pathology of brain aging. We will discuss the idea that calpain activity paces the rate of structural turnover in neurons and then argue that there are reasons to suspect that turnover should vary across brains of different sizes and neurons of different types. Possible linkages between rate of turnover (or relative stability) and the development of neuropathology will then be considered.

TURNOVER AND STABILITY IN BRAINS OF DIFFERENT SIZES

There is reasonably convincing evidence that degeneration and replacement ("turnover") of cell processes is an ongoing phenomenon in neurons (Cotman, Nieto-Sampedro, & Harris, 1981). It has been established that a measurable percentage of motoneuron terminals is in an advanced stage of degeneration in healthy adult animals and that this population is continuously balanced by axonal sprouting (Barker & Ip, 1966; Smith & Rosenheimer, 1982). Evidence for the turnover of axonal and dendritic processes has also been obtained in the lateral vestibular nucleus of the brain stem (Sotelo

& Palay, 1971), and a still more dramatic example is found in the olfactory nerve (Graziadei & Monti-Graziadei, 1978). Based on these findings it appears that degeneration and regeneration of neuronal processes are common features of many types of neurons. Studies on cultured muscle cells indicate that synaptic specializations are periodically budded off from the membrane to form coated vesicles, which are then degraded by lysosomes, suggesting that turnover of synapses is a continuous process in these preparations (Libby et al., 1980). Similar coated vesicles are also found in brain cells and show marked fluctuations in numbers during periods of experimentally-induced synaptic loss and replacement (McWilliams & Lynch, 1981); breakdown and replacement of postsynaptic specializations may thus be a feature of brain as well.

The calpains are well-suited to participate in the turnover process. They degrade proteins that form the cytoskeleton or cross-link its elements with the membrane or each other — highly localized activation of the enzymes could thus serve to eliminate the supportive network underlying and maintaining spines, terminals, and fine branches of the axonal and dendritic ramifications. There is also evidence that calpain is necessary for the merger of membrane-derived vesicles with the lysosomes (Libby et al., 1980). The enzymes could thus serve to promote local breakdown and the further processing of the membrane-enclosed elements that result from it. It is therefore reasonable to propose that the amount and / or activity of calpain determines the rate at which structural turnover proceeds in axonal and dendritic branches. In this regard the expansion of brain size across mammals of different body sizes presents an interesting problem, since it is accompanied by a very substantial extension of the dendritic arborizations and presumably of the axonal branches that provide innervation. This is evident from the fact that the density of neurons (number of cells per unit volume) in cerebral cortex is strongly and negatively correlated with brain size; that is, density scales to about the negative cube root of brain size ($D = kE^{-0.3}$, where D is the number of cells per mm^3 and E is the brain weight, on a mouse-to-whale dimension) (Tower, 1954). The decreasing density of neurons with increasing brain size is not accompanied by an increase of glial cells, since all available evidence indicates that the density of these elements as well as the relative volume they occupy is constant across mammals (see Tower & Young, 1973, for a discussion). This points to a positive relationship between brain size and volume occupied by dendritic/axonal branches. Indeed dendritic length in cortical neurons has been found to correlate positively with brain size with an exponent of about 0.3 (Bok, 1959; see Jerison, 1973, for a summary of the data). Over the orders of magnitude in mammalian brain size, these allometric relationships produce great differences in the size and complexity of dendritic trees. Assuming that turnover of synapses, dendritic spines, and axon terminals is occurring continuously, the great expansion of the neuron's processes must place an ever increasing demand on the protein and lipid synthesis machinery. Yet an increase in dendritic size (with greater brain size) is not accompanied by anything like a comparable increase in the size of the cell body of neurons (Shariff, 1953). Thus, the marked elaboration of the neuron that accompanies increasing brain size in mammals is probably not matched by an equivalent increment in the Golgi apparatus, rough endoplasmic reticulum, and other elements needed to produce macromolecules and constituents of the cell cytoskeleton and membrane.

Accordingly, the possibility must be considered that the expansion of the afferent and efferent processes of the neuron is not coupled to increases in the synthetic capacity needed to maintain a constant rate of turnover. A solution to this problem would be to decrease the rate at which cell processes are broken down and thus must be replaced as brain size increases — in this way the synthetic and degenerative aspects of the turnover equation could be aligned. One means of accomplishing this would be to dilute a relatively constant amount of degradative enzymes in the ever increasing volume of axonal and dendritic processes. The suggestion being made here is that the strong negative correlation between calpain activity and brain size found in mammalian brain is linked to a negative relationship between brain size and rate of neuronal turnover or, in essence, that neurons in larger brains possess relatively greater stability.

The above argument should not be taken to imply that calpain levels within the same brain will vary inversely with the size of a neuron or the extent of its processes; presumably, concentrations of the enzyme will reflect the conditions and demands associated with various categories of cells. The proposed hypothesis is that homologous groups of neurons in different species will have different degrees of dendritic and axonal ramifications (depending on absolute brain size) and this will be accompanied by systematic variations in calpain concentration and turnover rate of cytoskeletal elements. The question of how these latter variables might affect the rate at which pathology and aging develop will be discussed below.

It might be noted that the concept of neuronal stability as outlined above assumes that neurons and large axonal and dendritic arborizations cannot be replaced. It is well-established that there is virtually no postdevelopmental neurogenesis in mammalian brain and that the cells lost with aging are not replaced; moreover, axonal sprouting and regeneration in mammalian brain are abortive (Gall, Ivy, & Lynch, in press, for a review). Recent studies by Nottebohm and his collaborators have suggested that this constancy does not hold for all vertebrates, and specifically that birds (several unrelated species were tested) add thousands of new neurons per day to the telencephalon (Nottebohm, 1984). Moreover, at least some of the new cells become integrated into existing circuitries as functional units. It has been shown that certain telencephalic nuclei gain and lose neurons on a seasonal basis, probably in response to variations in the levels of specific hormones (Goldman & Nottebohm, 1983). Comparable studies have not been conducted for fish, amphibians, and reptiles, but it is known that fish and amphibian brains have growth capacities that are far greater than those found in the mammals. Fish, for example, are able to regenerate entire neuronal pathways (Guth & Windle, 1970). Any deleterious effects resulting from the continual turnover of terminals, spines, and so forth, may thus have more drastic consequences in mammalian brain, which lacks the ability to reproduce neurons and has more limited axonal and dendritic growth capacity than is the case for the brains of birds, reptiles, and other vertebrates.

POSSIBLE VARIATIONS IN TURNOVER WITHIN THE MAMMALIAN BRAIN

In the context of the hypothesis discussed above, the observed variability of calpain amount or activity among cells and regions of mammalian brain implies that fundamental aspects of turnover must also differ among neuron types. There is reason to suspect that this is true. While degeneration and growth profiles are found with some frequency at several sites in the nervous system (see above), they were virtually never encountered during the course of intensive quantitative analysis of hippocampal dentate gyrus (McWilliams & Lynch, 1978, 1979, 1983) of rats from young adulthood to early old age. We cannot extrapolate from this to breakdown and replacement of smaller components of the neuron (synapses, patches of membrane and underlying cytoskeleton, etc.), but the ultrastructural work does encourage the idea that turnover, at least of whole anatomical units, does vary among neurons. Why should this be? Recent work from several laboratories has shown that degeneration, both of whole cells and of particular groups of axonal projections, plays a vital role in the sculpting of circuitries throughout the brain during the developmental period (Cowan, Fawcett, O'Leary, & Stanfield, 1984; Ivy & Killackey, 1981). The picture emerging from these studies is one of "exuberant" growth that must be selectively "pruned" (Schneider, 1970) to achieve the organization that persists throughout adult life. It is possible that degenerative activities are much more vital in some projections, and hence cell types, than in others. If this is so, then the enzymes responsible for breakdown are synthesized at different rates across neurons and brain regions. There is no necessary reason for assuming that these early differences are not maintained into adulthood. According to this idea, the high concentrations of calpain found in some cells and regions in the mature brain might reflect developmental histories; possibly relevant to this point, preliminary immunocytochemical data indicate that an unequal distribution of calpain is also present in the brains of newborn rats (unpublished data).

Another reason to suspect that calpain concentrations and the breakdown of cellular elements might differ between cell types concerns the amount of material that must be processed. Lysosomes are concentrated in the somata and primary processes of neurons where they break down and digest membrane-bound organelles that, in part at least, are delivered to those regions by retrograde transport from the distal branches of axons and dendrites. As noted, Libby et al. (1980) have made the interesting suggestion that calpain acts on these organelles to prepare them for merger with each other and the lysosomes. Large cells with very elaborate dendrites and axons would presumably have large quantities of retrogradely transported material to process and thus higher concentrations of calpain in the perinuclear regions and primary dendrites. Immunocytochemical studies of rat and monkey brains indicate that this is generally true in that calpain is clearly more prominent in large than small neurons; it must be emphasized, however, that very obvious differences are found between groups of large cells (Siman et al., 1985).

TURNOVER AND BRAIN AGING

Finally, there is the issue of how calpain activity with its postulated links to turnover might be related to the rate of brain aging and the pace at which pathology appears during aging. By way of analogy with earlier arguments concerning limits on the number of heart beats, cell divisions, and so forth, that can occur over the course of life (see Hayflick, 1984; Sacher, 1982, for reviews), we might imagine that the number of times that synapses, spines, and so forth, are broken down and replaced is relatively constant for all neurons and therefore that neurons with rapid turnover have shorter life spans. While reasonable, ideas of this type provide few suggestions about the nature of the hypothetical limits. For purposes of discussion, we will describe two possible linkages between calpain concentrations and rate of aging and occurrence of neuropathology.

It will be recalled that calpain has a threshold for calcium that is well above the resting levels found inside neurons. Fluctuations in internal calcium levels are used by neurons to accomplish a variety of functions, including transmitter release and the control of postsynaptic after potentials (Rasmussen, 1970). Lasek and Black (1977) suggested that calcium fluxes serve to regulate cytoskeletal turnover in axon terminals, a role for which calpain is ideally suited. We have proposed that intense depolarization of spines produces calcium concentrations adequate for localized activation of membrane-associated calpain and that this mechanism is used to produce quasi-permanent changes in the structure, transmitter receptor distribution, and numbers of synaptic connections (see Lynch & Baudry, 1984, for a review). Discrete activation of calpain presumably requires precise control of calcium influxes as well as of the intracellular devices that buffer the cation's concentration. Alterations in either of these processes would produce prolonged and more widely distributed activation of calpain. The consequences of this would depend upon the concentrations of the enzymes associated with various dendritic and axonal compartments. Thus, the cytoskeleton of cells with high levels of enzymes would be at greater risk during those occasions on which mistakes in calcium regulation occur.

There is evidence that disturbances in the calcium regulatory machinery occur over the course of aging (see Khachaturian, 1984, for a review); for example, it has been reported that mitochondrial calcium transport deteriorates with aging in brain as well as in other tissues (Hansford & Castro, 1982; Leslie, Chandler, Barr, & Farrar,

1985). Effects such as these could have a major effect on the regulation of calpain. Alterations in calcium buffering occurring during physiological activity would have a greater chance of producing cytoskeletal breakdown in cells with higher levels of cytosolic calpain. Thus if widespread deterioration of calcium buffering does occur during aging, its pathological effects would be detected first in neurons with high concentrations of calpain.

The possibility that aging directly affects calpain and its interactions with its substrates or with the lysosomal degradative system also deserves consideration. Turnover, as discussed, probably involves local degradation of cytoskeletal and structural elements by calpain followed by lysosomal digestion; if the balance between calpain and lysosomal protease activities were to become disturbed, then incomplete breakdown could occur, possibly resulting in the accumulation of membrane-bound and cytoskeletal elements in the cytoplasm. One might imagine, for example, that an active calpain system operating in conjunction with an impaired lysosomal system could produce a gradual buildup of incompletely digested material. Conversely, disturbances in calpain's activities might produce elements that are inappropriate substrates for the lysosomes. In either scenario, cells with high levels of calpain and turnover would be the most severely affected. It is of interest in this regard that pharmacological treatments that interfere with calpain or lysosomal proteases produce a rapid and dramatic accumulation of ceroid-lipofuscin in the brains of young rats and that these effects are much more severe in some cell types than others (Ivy, Schottler, Wenzel, Baudry, & Lynch, 1984).

The above discussed factors are not exclusive. For example, prolonged activation of calpain in one part of the dendritic field could produce local pathology as well as material inappropriate for normal lysosomal processing.

SUMMARY AND CONCLUSION

It is our hypothesis that calcium-activated proteases are causal agents in brain aging and, in particular, in the gradual development of pathology and degeneration. This review has presented three lines of argument in support of this idea:

1. The calpains have been implicated in experimentally-induced and disease-related degeneration; it is not implausible that they are

similarly involved in other cases of pathology, including those that occur in brain during aging. It should be noted that calpain degrades cytoskeletal elements and possibly membrane-associated material destined for further proteolysis by lysosomes; the lipofuscin that steadily accumulates during aging typically contains membranes and is associated with the lysosomes while at least some age-related pathologies involve cytoskeletal disturbances (e.g., neurofibrillary tangles).

2. Variations in brain calpain activity provide a reasonable explanation for one of the most striking aspects of aging—namely, that longevity is highly correlated with brain size across the mammals. Moreover, the one order of mammals with exceptional life spans (from the perspective of brain or body size) was found to have exceptionally low levels of calpain. Thus, the activity of a potentially destructive enzyme has been found to correlate almost linearly with the rate of brain aging.

3. Calpain concentrations vary considerably across brain regions and cell types in mammalian brain; moreover, there appears to be some degree of correspondence between cells that are severely affected by aging and cells with high levels of calpain. The possibility thus exists that differences in calpain concentrations can account for the variations in pathology that are characteristic of mammalian brain aging.

To explain why calpain levels should exhibit the variations they do we postulated that, among other functions, the enzyme is involved in the turnover of cytoskeletal and structural elements, and that turnover rate varies as a function of brain size and cell types. According to this idea, relatively stable neurons (i.e., cells with low rates of turnover) contain lower concentrations of cytosolic calpain, and are therefore less prone to the degenerative effects that can result from the prolonged or widespread activation of the enzyme.

REFERENCES

Armstrong, E. (1983). Relative brain size and metabolism in mammals. *Science, 220,* 1302-1304.

Barker, D., & Ip, M.C. (1966). Sprouting and degeneration of mammalian motor axons in normal and deafferented skeletal muscle. *Proceedings of the Royal Society London Ser. Biol., 163,* 538-556.

Baudry, M., Bundman, M., Smith, E., & Lynch, G. (1981). Micromolar levels of calcium stimulate proteolytic activity and glutamate receptor binding in rat brain synaptic membranes. *Science, 212,* 937-938.

Baudry, M., DuBrin, R., Beasley, L., Leon, M., & Lynch, G. (in press). Bat's brain contains low levels of calcium-dependent protease activity: Implications for the cellular mechanisms of aging. *Neurobiology of Aging.*

Baudry, M., & Lynch, G. (1981). Hippocampal glutamate receptors. *Molecular Cellular Biochemistry, 38,* 5-18.

Baudry, M., & Lynch, G. (1984). Glutamate receptor regulation and the substrates of memory. In G. Lynch, J. McGaugh, & N. Weinberger (Eds.), *Neurobiology of learning and memory* (pp. 431-447). New York: The Guilford Press.

Baudry, M., Simonson, L., Dubrin, R., & Lynch, G. (1986). A comparative study of soluble calcium-dependent proteolytic activity in brain. *Journal of Neurobiology, 17,* 15-28.

Bok, S.T. (1959). *Histonomy of the cerebral cortex.* Amsterdam: Elsevier.

Bowen, D.M., White, P., Spillane, J.A., Goodhardt, M.J., Curzon, G., Iwangoff, P., Meier-Ruge, W., & Davison, A.N. (1979). Accelerated aging or selective neuronal loss as an important cause of dementia. *Lancet, 1,* 11-14.

Calder, W.A. (1976). Aging in vertebrates: Allometric considerations of spleen size and life-span. *Federation Proceedings, 35,* 96-97.

Comfort, A. (1979). *The biology of senescence.* New York: Elsevier.

Cotman, C.W., Nieto-Sampedro, M., & Harris, E.W. (1981). Synapse replacement in the nervous system of adult vertebrates. *Physiological Reviews, 61,* 684-784.

Cowan, W.M., Fawcett, J.W., O'Leary, D.D.M., & Stanfield, B.B. (1984). Regressive events in neurogenesis. *Science, 225,* 1258-1265.

Dayton, W.R., Schollmeyer, J.V., Chan, A.C., & Allen, C.E. (1979). Elevated levels of a calcium-activated muscle protease in rapidly atrophying muscles from vitamin E-deficient rabbits. *Biochemica Biophysica Acta, 584,* 216-230.

DeMartino, G.N. (1981). Calcium-Dependent proteolytic activity in rat liver: Identification of two proteases with different calcium requirements. *Archives of Biochemistry and Biophysics, 211,* 253-257.

Eisenberg, J.F., & Wilson, D.E. (1978). Relative brain size and feeding strategies in the chiroptera. *Evolution, 32,* 740-751.

Elce, J.S., Hasspieler, R., & Boegman, R.J. (1983). Ca^{2+}-Activated protease in denervated rat skeletal muscle measured by an immunoassay. *Experimental Neurology, 81,* 320-329.

Fagg, G.E., & Foster, A.C. (1983). Amino acid neurotransmitters and their pathways in the mammalian central nervous system. *Neuroscience, 9,* 701-719.

Finch, C.W., Marshall, J.F., & Randall, P.K. (1981). Aging and basal ganglion function. *Annual Review of Gerontology and Geriatrics, 2,* 49-87.

Fleckenstein, A. (1977). Specific pharmacology of calcium in myocardium, cardiac pacemakers and vascular smooth muscle. *Annual Review of Pharmacology and Toxicology, 17,* 149-166.

Fox, J.E.B., Goll, D.E., Reynolds, C.C., & Phillips, D.R. (1985). Identification of two proteins (actin-binding protein and P235) that are hydrolyzed by Ca^{2+}-dependent protease during platelet aggregation. *Journal of Biological Chemistry, 260,* 1060-1066.

Friedenthal, H. (1910). Ueber die giltigkeit des massenwirkung fur den lebendigen substanz. *Zentralbl. Physiol., 24,* 321-327.

Gall, C., Ivy, G., & Lynch, G. (1986). Neuroanatomical plasticity: Its role in the organization and re-organization of the central nervous system. In J.M. Tanner & F. Falkner (Eds.), *Human growth, a comprehensive treatise* (2nd ed.) (pp. 411-436.) New York: Plenum Press.

Goldman, S.A., & Nottebohm, F. (1983). Neuronal production, migration and differentiation in a vocal control nucleus of the adult female canary brain. *Proceedings of the National Academy of Sciences, USA, 80,* 2390-2394.

Graziadei, P.P.C., & Monti-Graziadei, G.A. (1978). Continuous nerve cell renewal in the olfactory system. In H. Autrum (Ed.) *Handbook of sensory physiology IX* (pp. 55-83). New York: Springer-Verlag.

Guth, L., & Windle, W.F. (1970). The enigma of central nervous regeneration. *Experimental Neurology, 28,* 1-43.

Hansford, R.G., & Castro, F. (1982). Effect of senescence on Ca^{2+} transport by heart mitochondria, *Mechanisms of Ageing and Development, 19,* 5-13.

Hathaway, D.R., Werth, D.K., & Haeberle, J.R. (1982). Limited autolysis reduces the Ca^{2+} requirement of a smooth muscle

Ca^{2+}-activated protease. *Journal of Biological Chemistry, 257,* 9072-9077.

Hayflick, L. (1984). Intracellular determinants of cell aging. *Mechanisms of Ageing and Development, 28,* 177-187.

Heusner, A.A. (1982). Energy metabolism and body size: I. Is the 0.75 mass exponent of Kleiber's equation a statistical artifact? *Respiration Physiology, 48,* 1-12.

Hofman, M.A. (1982). Encephalization in mammals in relation to the size of the cerebral cortex. *Brain, Behavior, and Evolution, 20,* 84-96.

Hofman, M.A. (1983). Energy metabolism, brain size and longevity in mammals. *Quarterly Review of Biology, 58,* 495-512.

Huxley, J.S. (1932). *Problems of relative growth.* London: Methuen.

Hyman, B.T., Van Hoesen, G.W., Damasion, A.R., & Barnes, C.L. (1984). Alzheimer's disease: Cell specific pathology isolates the hippocampal formation. *Science, 225,* 1168-1170.

Ishizaki, Y., Tashiro, T., & Kurokawa, M. (1983). A calcium-activated protease which preferentially degrades the 160-kDa component of the neurofilament triplet. *European Journal of Biochemistry, 131,* 41-45.

Ivy, G.O., & Killackey, H.P. (1981). Ontogeny of the distribution of callosal projection neurons in the rat parietal cortex. *Journal of Comparative Neurology, 195,* 367-389.

Ivy, G., Schottler, F., Wenzel, J., Baudry, M., & Lynch, G. (1984). Inhibition of lysosomal enzymes: Accumulation of lipofuscin-like dense bodies in the brain. *Science, 226,* 985-987.

Jerison, H.J. (1973). *Evolution of the brain and intelligence.* New York: Academic Press.

Kar, N.C., & Pearson, C.M., (1976). Hydrolytic enzymes and human muscular dystrophy. In L.P. Rowland (Ed.), *Pathogenesis of human muscular dystrophy* (pp. 387-393). Amsterdam: Excerpta Medica.

Kemper, T. (1984). Neuroanatomical and neuropathological changes in normal aging and in dementia. In M.L. Albert (Ed.), *Clinical neurology of aging* (pp. 9-52). Oxford: Oxford University Press.

Khachaturian, Z.S. (1984). Toward theories of brain aging. In I. Kaye & E. Burrows (Eds.), *Handbook of studies on psychiatry and old age* (pp. 157-194). Amsterdam: Elsevier Biomedical Press.

Kleiber, M. (1947). Body size and metabolic rate. *Physiological Reviews, 27,* 511-541.

Klein, I., Lehotay, D., & Godek, M. (1981). Characterization of a calcium-activated protease that hydrolyzes a microtubule-associated protein. *Archives of Biochemistry and Biophysics, 208,* 520-527.

Lasek, R.J., & Black, M.M. (1977). How do axons stop growing? Some clues from the metabolism of proteins in the slow component of axonal transport. In S. Roberts, A. Lajtha, & W.H. Gispen (Eds.), *Mechanisms, regulation and special function of protein synthesis in the brain (pp. 161-170).* Amsterdam: Elsevier Biomedical Press.

Lasiewski, R.C., & Dawson, W.R. (1967). A reexamination of the relation between standard metabolic rate and body weight in birds. *Condor, 69,* 13-23.

Leonard, J.P., & Salpeter, M.M. (1979). Agonist-induced myopathy at the neuromuscular junction is mediated by calcium. *Journal of Cell Biology, 82,* 811-819.

Leslie, S.W., Chandler, J., Barr, E.M., & Farrar, R.P. (1985). Reduced calcium uptake by rat brain mitochondria and synaptosomes in response to aging. *Brain Research, 329,* 177-183.

Libby, P., Bursztajn, S., & Goldberg, A.L. (1980). Degradation of the acetylcholine receptor in cultured muscle cells: Selective inhibition and the fate of undegraded receptors. *Cell, 19,* 481-491.

Libby, P., & Goldbert, A.L. (1978). Leupeptin, a protease inhibitor, decreases protein degradation in normal and diseased muscles. *Science, 199,* 534-536.

Lynch, G., & Baudry, M. (1984). The biochemistry of memory: A new and specific hypothesis. *Science, 224,* 1057-1063.

Malik, M.N., Fenko, M.D., Igbal, K., & Wisniewski, H.M. (1983). Purification and characterization of two forms of Ca^{2+}-activated neutral protease from calf brain. *Journal of Biological Chemistry, 258,* 8955-8962.

Mallouk, R.S. (1975). Longevity in vertebrates is proportional to relative brain weight. *Federation Proceedings, 34,* 2102-2103.

Martin, R.D. (1981). Relative brain size and basal metabolic rate in terrestrial vertebrates. *Nature, 293,* 57-60.

McWilliams, J.R., & Lynch, G.S. (1978). Terminal proliferation and synaptogenesis following partial deafferentation. *Journal of Comparative Neurology, 180,* 581-615.

McWilliams, J.R., & Lynch, G.S. (1979). Terminal proliferation in the partially deafferented dentate gyrus. Time courses for the appearance and removal of degeneration and the replacement of lost terminals. *Journal of Comparative Neurology, 187,* 191-198.

McWilliams, J.R., & Lynch, G.S. (1981). Sprouting in the hippocampus is accompanied by an increase in coated vesicles. *Brain Research, 211,* 158-164.

McWilliams, J.R., & Lynch, G.S. (1983). Rate of synaptic replacement in denervated rat hippocampus declines precipitously from the juvenile period to adulthood. *Science, 221,* 572-574.

Mink, J.W., Blumenschine, R.J., & Adams, D.B. (1981). Ratio of central nervous system to body metabolism in vertebrates: Its constancy and functional basis. *American Journal of Physiology, 241,* 203-212.

Murachi, T., Hatanaka, M., Yasumoto, Y., Nakayama, N., & Tanaka, K. (1981). A quantitative distribution study on calpain and calpastatin in rat tissues and cells. *Biochemistry International, 2,* 651-656.

Murachi, T., Tanaka, U., Hatanaka, M., & Murakami, T. (1981). Intracellular Ca^{2+}-dependent protease (calpain) and its high-molecular weight endogenous inhibitor (calpastatin). *Advances in Enzyme Regulation, 19,* 407-424.

Mykles, D.L., & Skinner, D.M. (1983). Ca^{2+}-Dependent proteolytic activity in crab claw muscle. *Journal of Biological Chemistry, 258,* 10474-10480.

Neerunjun, J.S., & Dubowitz, V. (1979). Increased calcium-activated neutral protease activity in muscles of dystrophic hamsters and mice. *Journal of Neurological Science, 40,* 105-111.

Nottebohm, F. (1984). Birdsong as a model in which to study brain processes related to learning. *Condor, 86,* 227-236.

Ohno, S., Emori, Y., Imajoh, S., Kawasaki, H., Kisaragi, M., & Suzuki, U. (1984). Evolutionary origin of a calcium-dependent protease by fusion of genes for a thiol protease and a calcium binding protein? *Nature, 312,* 566-570.

Perry, E.K. (1980). The cholinergic system in old age and Alzheimer's disease. *Age/Aging, 9,* 1-8.

Rasmussen, H. (1970). Cell communication, calcium ion and cyclicadenosine monophosphate. *Science, 170,* 404-412.

Sacher, G.A. (1959). Relation of life-span to brain weight and body weight in mammals. In G.E.W. Wolstenholme & M. O'Connor (Eds.),

The life-span of animals. Boston: Little, Brown Co.

Sacher, G.A. (1982). Evolutionary theory in gerontology. *Perspectives in Biology and Medicine, 25,* 339-353.

Salpeter, M., Leonard, J.P., & Kasprzak, E. (1982). Agonist-Induced postsynaptic myopathy. *Neuroscience Commentaries, 1,* 73-83.

Schanne, F.A.X., Kane, A.B., Young, E.E., & Farber, J.L. (1979). Calcium dependence of toxic cell death: A final common pathway. *Science, 206,* 700-702.

Schlaepfer, W.W., & Micko, S. (1978). Chemical and structural changes of neurofilaments in transected rat sciatic nerve. *Journal of Cell Biology, 78,* 369-378.

Schneider, G.E. (1970). Mechanisms of functional recovery following lesion of visual cortex or superior colliculus in neonate and adult hamsters. *Brain, Behavior, and Evolution, 3,* 285-323.

Shariff, G.A. (1953). Cell counts in the primate cerebral cortex. *Journal of Comparative Neurology, 98,* 381-400.

Sher, J.M., Stracher, A., Shafiq, S.A., & Hardystashin, J. (1981). Successful treatment of murine muscular dystrophy with the proteinase inhibitor leupeptin. *Proceedings of the National Academy of Sciences, USA, 78,* 7794-7798.

Siman, R., Baudry, M., & Lynch, G. (1983). Purification from synaptosomal plasma membranes of calpain I, a thiol-protease activated by micromolar calcium concentrations. *Journal of Neurochemistry, 41,* 950-956.

Siman, R., Baudry, M., & Lynch, G. (1984). Brain fodrin: Substrate for the endogenous calcium-activated protease calpain I. *Proceedings of the National Academy of Sciences (USA), 81,* 3276-3280.

Siman, R., Baudry, M., & Lynch, G. (1984). Brain fodrin: Substrate for the endogenous calcium-activated protease calpain I. *Proceedings of the National Academy of Sciences, USA, 81,* 3276-3280.

Siman, R., Baudry, M., & Lynch, G. (1986). Calcium-Activated proteases as possible mediators of synaptic plasticity. In G.M. Edelman, W.E. Goll, & W.M. Cowan (Eds.), *New insights into synaptic function.* New York: John Wiley & Sons.

Siman, R., Gall, C., Perlmutter, L., Christian, C., Baudry, M., & Lynch, G. (1985). Distribution of calpain I, an enzyme associated with degenerative activity, in rat brain. *Brain Research, 347,* 399-403.

Simonson, L., Baudry, M., Siman, R., & Lynch, G. (1985). Regional distribution of soluble calcium-activated proteinase activity in neonatal and adult rat brain. *Brain Research, 327,* 153-159.

Singh, I., & Singh, A.K. (1983). Degradation of myelin proteins by brain endogenous neutral protease. *Neuroscience Letters, 39,* 77-82.

Smith, D.O., & Rosenheimer, J.L. (1982). Decreased sprouting and degeneration of nerve terminals of active muscles in aged rats. *Journal of Neurophysiology, 48,* 100-109.

Sotelo, C., & Palay, S.L. (1971). Altered axons and axon terminals in the lateral vestibular nucleus of the rat: Possible example of axonal remodeling. *Laboratory Investigation, 25,* 653-671.

Stracher, A., McGowan, E.B., & Shafiq, S.A. (1978). Muscular dystrophy: Inhibition of degeneration *in vivo* with protease inhibitors. *Science, 200,* 50-52.

Tower, D.B. (1954). Structural and functional organization of mammalian cerebral cortex: The correlation of neurone density with brain size. *Journal of Comparative Neurology, 101,* 19-51.

Tower, D.B., & Young, O.M. (1973). The activities of butyrylcholinesterase and carbonic anhydrase, the rate of anaerobic glycolysis, and the question of a constant density of glial cells in cerebral cortices of various mammalian species from mouse to whale. *Journal of Neurochemistry, 20,* 269-278.

Yoshimura, N., Hatanaka, M., Kitahara, A., Kawaguchi, N., & Murachi, T. (1984). Intracellular localization of two distinct Ca^{2+} proteases (calpain I and calpain II) as demonstrated by using discriminative antibodies. *Journal of Biological Chemistry, 259,* 9847-9852.

Yoshimura, N., Kikuchi, T., Sasaki, T., Kitahara, A., Hatanaka, M., & Murachi, T. (1983). Two distinct Ca^{2+} proteases (calpain I and calpain II) purified concurrently by the same method from rat kidney. *Journal of Biological Chemistry, 258,* 8883-8889.

Yumoto, N., Kikuchi, T., Sasaki, T., & Murachi, T. (1984). Comparison of tryptic peptides from the heavy and light subunits of calpain I and calpain II by high-performance liquid chromatography. *Journal of Biochemistry, 96,* 1531-1537.

Zimmerman, V.J.P., & Schlaepfer, W.W. (1982). Characterization of a brain calcium-activated protease that degrades neurofilament proteins. *Biochemistry, 21,* 3977-3983.

7

Stress, Glucocorticoids, and Their Role in Degenerative Changes in the Aging Hippocampus

Robert M. Sapolsky, MD, PhD, and Bruce S. McEwen, PhD

The purpose of this volume is to assemble innovative recommendations regarding the management of Alzheimer's disease (AD). That such a collection could have been contemplated reflects the relative optimism that permeates current work in this field. Tremendous progress has been made in understanding the disorder in recent years, and this volume represents one of the first times that the question, "What is AD?" has been replaced by, "What can be done about it?" In our view, a central feature of this progress has been the focusing on the neuron damage typical of AD — its anatomical and neurochemical specificity and its functional consequences. Understandably, numerous researchers are now investigating the causes of the specificity of neuron loss. However, separate from the specifics of AD, the pathophysiology of neurotoxicity remains poorly understood. Whether one examines the loss of hippocampal and cortical neurons in AD, dopaminergic neurons in Parkinson's disease, hippocampal damage following hypoxia-ischemia, or the loss of neurons during aging, there is still very little understanding as to why a neuron dies.

Our work has indirectly brought us to consider this issue, both with respect to neuron loss during aging and in neuropathological states. We have studied neuronal loss in the hippocampus of the aging rodent and the functional consequences of such loss. Furthermore, we have identified one of the causes of the neuron loss. What is of considerable interest to us is that it is not an external insult, a toxin, an unconventional virus, or autoimmune attack. Rather, it appears as if cumulative exposure to glucocorticoids — the adrenal steroids released during stress, which are, in fact, essential for life — is a prime cause of loss of hippocampal neurons during senescence. Our work shows that glucocorticoids induce a generalized state of metabolic vulnerability in hippocampal neurons such that a variety of metabolic or neuropathologic insults are more potent in the presence of high titers of glucocorticoids. In this chapter, we review our work demonstrating the role of and one possible mechanism accounting for glucocorticoid-induced neurotoxicity in the aging hippocampus. These studies have a number of implications for the understanding of AD. First, some of the neuroendocrine abnormalities observed in the aged rat are strikingly similar to those of the AD patient. We present evidence that the hippocampal damage typical of both groups plays a role in these impairments. Next, the mechanisms of glucocorticoid neurotoxicity suggest that glucocorticoid milieu might play a role in the severity of the neuropathological insult in AD. Finally, we speculate that glucocorticoid milieu might also influence the likelihood of the onset of the disorder.

We began our work with an interest in stress and aging. Senescence has been frequently characterized as a state of decreased adaptiveness to environmental challenges and a decreased capacity to reequilibrate following disruptions of homeostasis. Thus, we initially examined whether an aged rodent can appropriately respond to stress. As neuroendocrinologists, our attention naturally turned to the adrenocortical hormones released during stress — the glucocorticoids. These steroids are released as the final step in a neuroendocrine cascade beginning with stress-induced release of corticotropin-releasing factor (CRF) by the hypothalamus, which triggers the release of adrenocorticotrophic hormone (ACTH) by the pituitary, which, in turn, stimulates adrenocortical secretion of glucocorticoids. Glucocorticoids shift the balance of metabolism away from storage of energy substrates in adipose and liver and thus increase levels of readily utilizable energy substrates in the circulation. Furthermore, they increase cardiovascular tone. Finally, they suppress numerous costly anabolic processes such as growth and tissue repair, the immune response, and reproduction for more auspicious times (Krieger, 1982; Yates, Marsh, & Maran, 1980). Activation of the adrenocortical axis during stress is central to the physiological adaptations of the organism that allow it to survive the stressor. The notorious fragility of adrenalectomized experimental animals or humans with adrenocortical insufficiencies in the face of stressors testifies to the role of the steroids. Thus, we initially examined whether the aged male rat secretes corticosterone, its species-typical glucocorticoid, in response to stress.

As shown with a variety of stressors by ourselves and others, aged rats are abundantly capable of mobilizing an adrenocortical stress response, and most features of the response do not change with age (reviewed in Sapolsky, Krey, & McEwen, 1983a). The speed and plateau of corticosterone secretion, the reserve capacity of the adrenal for secreting the hormone following chronic stress, the circadian rhythm of its secretion, the binding of the steroid in the blood by its transport globulin, and its clearance from the circulation are all similar in young and aged animals (Sapolsky et al., 1983a).

What is impaired with age, however, is the capacity to terminate corticosterone secretion when the stressor abates (Sapolsky et al., 1983a, Sapolsky, Krey, & McEwen, 1984). Figure 1 demonstrates the similar rise in corticosterone titer in young and aged Fischer 344 rats in response to an hour of the stress of immobilization. Upon the abatement of the stressor, young subjects present titers in the basal range within 1 hour, whereas aged subjects maintain elevated levels of the hormone for up to 24 hours (Ida et al., 1984). Factoring of the clearance rate of the hormone out of these data demonstrates that the dysfunction is one of secretion; aged subjects fail to terminate secretion of corticosterone at the end of stress (Sapolsky et al., 1983a).

Before pursuing this hypersecretion further, we wanted to assure ourselves that this defect was physiologically meaningful (i.e., that these excessive titers of corticosterone in the aged rat during the post-stress recovery period are deleterious in some manner). We expected this to be the case. Just as much of the critical adaptations of the body to acute physical stress are mediated by glucocorticoids, much of what is pathogenic about chronic stress is due to excessive exposure to the steroids. When done in excess, the short-term actions of glucocorticoids in increasing levels of circulating energy substrates, at the cost of energy storage, can eventuate in myopathy, fatigue, or steroid diabetes. Likewise, the prolonged inhibition of reproduction produces the amenorrhea or impotency typical of severe stress. As another example, chronic stress, at least partially via elevated glucocorticoid levels, promotes establishment and accelerates the growth of tumors (cf Riley, 1981). This glucocorticoid effect may be related to the immunosuppressive actions of the steroid (including thymic involution, lymphocytopenia, suppression of lymphokine, and interferon release and suppression of Natural Killer cell activity [Munck, Guyre, & Holbrook, 1984]) or to its ability to promote angiogenesis (Folkman, Langer, Linhardt, Howdenschild, & Taylor, 1983).

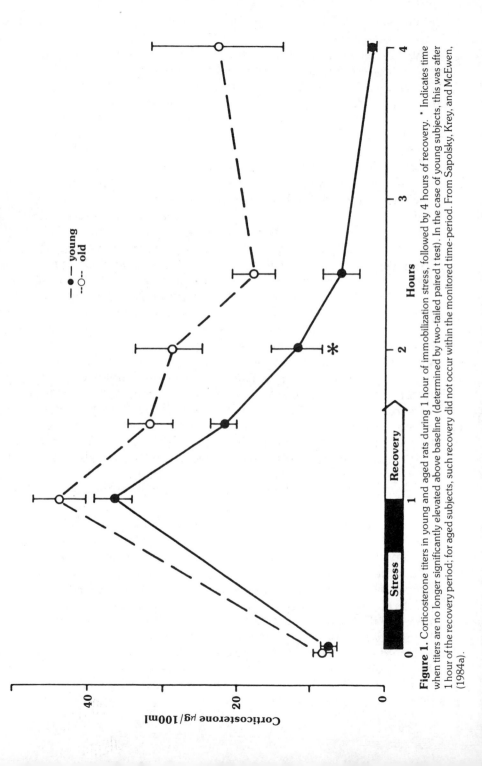

Figure 1. Corticosterone titers in young and aged rats during 1 hour of immobilization stress, followed by 4 hours of recovery. * Indicates time when titers are no longer significantly elevated above baseline (determined by two-tailed paired t test). In the case of young subjects, this was after 1 hour of the recovery period; for aged subjects, such recovery did not occur within the monitored time-period. From Sapolsky, Krey, and McEwen, (1984a).

We examined whether the corticosterone hypersecretion in the aged rat during the poststress period was deleterious within this framework. We asked, "If excessive glucocorticoid exposure can be tumorigenic, and if aged rats hypersecrete corticosterone following the end of stress, will chronic stress perferentially accelerate tumor growth in aged rats?" This is indeed what we observed after inoculating controls or chronically stressed rats of various ages with fetal rat cells transformed with Fujinami sarcoma virus. The vast potentiation of tumor weight in aged, stressed rats appears due to the excessive corticosterone; infusion of young rats with additional corticosterone at the end of each stressor to mimic the defect of the aged similarly potentiates tumor weight (Sapolsky & Donnelly, 1985).

Satisfied that we were looking at a defect of physiological importance, we examined the corticosterone hypersecretion in further detail. It soon became clear that this defect is but one of a number of cases of hyperadrenocorticism observed in the aged rat. Relative to young controls, corticosterone titers are elevated for prolonged periods during habituation to mild stressors (Sapolsky et al., 1983a). Furthermore, basal titers of corticosterone and ACTH rise with age (reviewed in Sapolsky et al., 1983a). (Levels of the recently characterized CRF in the pituitary portal blood of the aged rat have not yet been measured.) These indices of hyperadrenocorticism in the aged rat appear due to a progressive loss of sensitivity of the adrenocortical axis to feedback inhibition by circulating glucocorticoids. The adrenocortical axis is a closed-loop feedback system where circulating titers of glucocorticoids are sensed in steroid-sensitive sites in the brain and pituitary that inhibit subsequent CRF and ACTH release. The parameters of such feedback and the interactions between a stimulatory stress signal and an inhibitory glucocorticoid signal are impressively complex (Keller-Wood & Dallman, 1984) and beyond the scope of this chapter. One fact that is pertinent, however, is that sensitivity of one or more of these sites to the inhibitory effects of glucocorticoids appears to decline with age. Rats are resistant to the suppressive effects of both the synthetic glucocorticoid dexamethasone and of corticosterone itself upon subsequent corticosterone secretion (Oxenkrug, McIntyre, Stanley, & Gershon, 1984; Sapolsky, Krey, & McEwen, unpublished data).

As students of the steroid receptor, we have been well-schooled in the notion that target tissue sensitivity to a hormone can change in parallel with alterations in the concentrations of receptors for that hormone. Thus, we next examined whether the impaired feedback sensitivity of the aged adrenocortical axis is associated with a loss of corticosterone receptors somewhere in the brain. We uncovered a very specific loss in the hippocampus, the principal target tissue for glucocorticoids (with approximately three-fold higher concentrations of receptors for the steroid than in any other brain region). Receptor concentrations decline progressively with age with approximately a 40% loss by 28 months of age (Sapolsky, Krey, & McEwen, 1983b). This loss is anatomically selective as small declines occur in the amygdala but in no other region of the brain. Subsequent studies have clarified this receptor defect in considerable anatomical and cellular detail. The receptor loss is entirely attributable to loss of cytosolic corticosterone receptors and with no loss of affinity of the receptor for the steroid or in its capacity to subsequently translocate to cell nuclei (Sapolsky et al., 1983b). Furthermore, the loss is confined to the population of receptors found in hippocampal neurons. In contract, there is a small *increase* in the number of corticosterone receptors in hippocampal glia, which appears to parallel the glial proliferation typical of the aged brain (discussed in Sapolsky, Krey, & McEwen, 1985). Autoradiographic analysis of the aged brain revealed that the receptor loss does not occur uniformly throughout the hippocampus but is concentrated in the pyramidal cells of Ammon's horn (Sapolsky, Krey, McEwen, & Rainbow, 1984). Finally, and most importantly, high-resolution autoradiography revealed that there is not only a loss of average numbers of corticosterone receptors per neuron but, in addition, a loss of receptor-containing neurons themselves (Sapolsky et al., 1984). Prior studies have demonstrated loss of neurons in these regions of the aged rodent hippocampus (Brizzee & Ordy, 1979; Landfield, Braun, & Pitler, 1981; Landfield, Rose, Sandles, Wohlstadter, & Lynch, 1977). Our findings demonstrate that it is corticosterone-sensitive neurons (i.e., those bearing corticosterone receptors) that are lost.

Could this loss of hippocampal neurons and of the corticosterone receptors that they contain dampen feedback sensitivity of the adrenocortical axis and produce corticosterone hypersecretion? This appears to be so. The pituitary and the hypothalamus are the principal sites that mediate inhibition of adrenocortical function by circulating glucocorticoids. However, the hippocampus can have a small inhibitory influence on the axis. As evidence, lesioning of the structure or of its efferent projections produces elevated basal and stressed titers of corticosterone whereas stimulation of most regions of the structure leads to inhibition of adrenocortical secretion. Furthermore, destruction of the structure attenuates the capacity of glucocorticoids to inhibit the adrenocortical axis (reviewed in McEwen, 1982). Thus, the hippocampus mediates some of the inhibitory effects of glucocorticoids on CRF release. Such an action can be via direct inhibition of hypothalamic release of CRF or via sensitization of the hypothalamus to the inhibitory effects of glucocorticoids. In either case, replication of the hippocampal damage in the aged rat produces the syndrome of corticosterone hypersecretion observed in the same subjects. We demonstrated this by showing that lesions of the hippocampus, grossly replicating the neuron loss of the aged structure, eventuate in hypersecretion of corticosterone during the poststress recovery period (Sapolsky, Krey, & McEwen, 1984). We next investigated a more subtle question: does loss of the corticosterone receptors, separate from the loss of their hippocampal neurons, also contribute to the dampened sensitivity of the adrenocortical axis? This appears to be the case. To demonstrate this, we developed two models in which we could reversibly deplete the hippocampus of approximately 40% of its corticosterone receptors without altering the numbers of neurons themselves. Consistently, such receptor depletions are accompanied by hypersecretion of corticosterone during the poststress recovery period (Sapolsky, Krey, & McEwen, 1984). As the first model, we exploited the autoregulation of hormone receptor concentrations by their ligand, specifically the decrease in the concentration of receptors that typically follows sustained exposure to elevated titers of their hormone. Within the brain, the hippocampal corticosterone receptors are more sensitive than any other brain region to such "down regulation" by sustained stress or elevated corticosterone levels (Sapolsky, Krey, & McEwen, 1983c). This preferential sensitivity is perhaps due to the markedly high levels of receptors in the structure. After carefully characterizing the parameters of such down regulation, we were able to select a regimen of corticosterone administration that selectively decreases the concentration of corticosterone receptors only in the hippocampus. Following such treatment, corticosterone hypersecretion during the poststress recovery period is observed that is of a similar magnitude as that in the aged rat. Furthermore, rats exposed to prolonged elevations of glucocorticoids are also less sensitive to the inhibitory feedback effects of glucocorticoids (Vernikos, Dallman, Bonnar, Katzen, & Shinsako, 1982). Finally, the down regulation of hippocampal corticosterone receptors is reversible in that within a week after the cessation of the particular treatment regimen utilized in these studies receptor concentrations normalized. Such normalization is accompanied by a capacity to terminate corticosterone secretion after the end of stress (Sapolsky, Krey, & McEwen, 1984).

As our second model, we studied the Brattleboro rat, which has diminished concentrations of hippocampal corticosterone receptors but without losses elsewhere within the brain (Veldhuis & de Kloet, 1982). This defect appears related to the congenital absence of vasopressin in these animals, specifically the intralimbic vasopressin, which serves a neurotransmitter or neuromodulatory role, since replenishment of the absent peptide transiently normalizes the steroid receptor deficit (Felt, Sapolsky, & McEwen, 1984; Sapolsky et al., 1984; Veldhuis & de Kloet, 1982). We found that the untreated Brattleboro rat has the similar poststress hypersecretion of corticosterone as observed in the aged and down regulated rats, and that the hypersecretion is eliminated by normalization of hippocampal corticosterone receptor number. Finally, suspension of vasopressin replacement results in a progressive decline in corticosterone receptor number in the hippocampus and a progressive reemergence of the corticosterone hypersecretion (Sapolsky, Krey, & McEwen, 1984). Thus, the attenuated sensitivity of the adrenocortical axis to feedback inhibition in the aged rat appears to result from the hippocampal damage typical of the senescent. Both the loss of the receptors (and with them the capacity to accurately assess a corticosterone signal in the circulation) and the loss of the neurons (and with them the means to transduce this signal to inhibitory inputs to the hypothalamus), contribute to this dysfunction.

Our attention thus turned to the cause of the hippocampal damage in the aged brain. We investigated a number of published reports of neurochemical manipulations that altered hippocampal corticosterone receptor number and examined whether such manipulations mimicked the features of the aged hippocampus — the cellular and anatomical selectivity of the receptor loss, and most importantly, the loss of the host neurons themselves. Such approaches, including manipulating the vasopressinergic, catecholaminergic, and indolaminergic inputs into the hippocampus, were disappointing as effects involved *only* changes in the numbers of receptors per neuron without alterations in neuron number (Sapolsky et al., 1984).

At this stage, we considered the possibility that exposure to corticosterone itself is the critical feature in hippocampal aging. This notion did not seem excessively fanciful. First, we had observed that it is neurons bearing corticosterone receptors that are preferentially lost (Sapolsky et al., 1984). Furthermore, work in the 1960s demonstrated that pharmacologically-elevated titers of glucocorticoids preferentially damage neurons in the hippocampus (Muhlen & Ockenfels, 1969). Finally, adrenalectomy of middle-aged rats (i.e., 12 months of age) prevents the progressive damage typical of the aged hippocampus (Landfield, Baskin, & Pitler, 1981). We thus examined the effects of chronic exposure to stress or to titers of corticosterone in the high physiological range on the hippocampus. We found that merely a week of stress or corticosterone exposure potently down regulates hippocampal corticosterone receptors. Such a regimen is of limited relevance to aging because, as already described, the receptor loss reverses rapidly after the end of such treatment, seen in Figure 2, and this down regulation involves changes in the number of receptors per neuron only (Sapolsky et al., 1985). Exposure to elevated corticosterone titers for 3 months, however, produced extremely persistent receptor loss (Figure 2). Furthermore, this loss was accompanied by a decrease in the absolute numbers of cells in Ammon's horn in the hippocampus. High-resolution autoradiography with tritiated corticosterone indicated that, as in the aged rat, it is corticosterone-sensitive cells that are lost. Finally, morphological and size analysis of the hippocampus suggested that the cells lost are neurons. The cells lost are the same size class as the neurons lost in the aged hippocampus, and, importantly, as in the aged structure and this loss is accompanied by a proliferation of darkly staining glia, markers of neuronal damage (Sapolsky et al., 1985).

When coupled with the previously cited reports concerning adrenalectomy of middle-aged rats, our studies suggest that cumulative exposure to basal titers of corticosterone over the life span plays a role in the degenerative changes in the aging hippocampus and that excessive stress, via corticosterone secretion, can accelerate this hippocampal aging. That physiological levels of an endogenous hormone play such a destructive role was surprising but not without precedent, since cumulative exposure to estrogen appears to be responsible for the neuronal damage that progressively occurs in the hypothalamus of the female rodent and that underlies aspects of reproductive failure (Finch, Felicio, Mobbs, & Nelson, 1984). Furthermore, the deleterious effects of hyperadrenocorticism including lymphocytopenia, myopathy, and involution of the thymus,

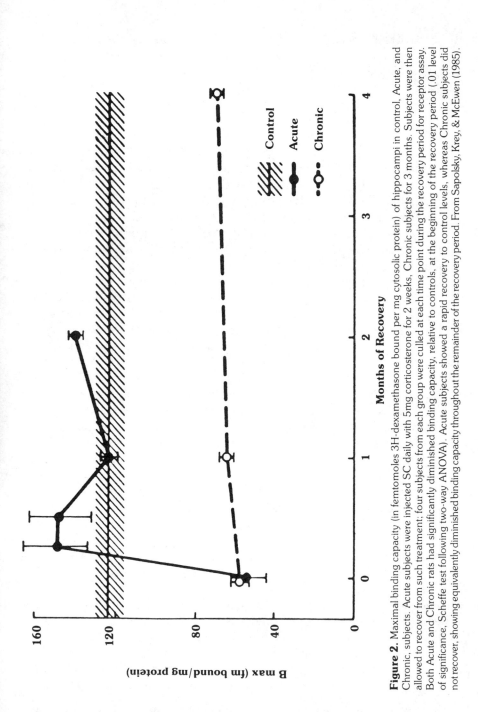

Figure 2. Maximal binding capacity (in femtomoles 3H-dexamethasone bound per mg cytosolic protein) of hippocampi in control, Acute, and Chronic, subjects. Acute subjects were injected SC daily with 5mg corticosterone for 2 weeks, Chronic subjects for 3 months. Subjects were then allowed to recover from such treatment; four subjects from each group were culled at each time point during the recovery period for receptor assay. Both Acute and Chronic rats had significantly diminished binding capacity, relative to controls, at the beginning of the recovery period (.01 level of significance, Scheffe test following two-way ANOVA). Acute subjects showed a rapid recovery to control levels, whereas Chronic subjects did not recover, showing equivalently diminished binding capacity throughout the remainder of the recovery period. From Sapolsky, Krey, & McEwen (1985).

suggest that glucocorticoid-induced neurotoxicity in the hippocampus falls within the overall framework of the catabolic actions of the hormone.

In beginning to study the mechanisms of such neurotoxicity, we reasoned that glucocorticoids need not be directly toxic to hippocampal neurons. Instead, they may induce a sufficiently catabolic state in the neurons as to endanger them without irreversibly damaging them. As such, when exposure to the steroid abated and in the absence of concomitant perturbations, neurons would be capable of recovering from the transient catabolic state in which glucose uptake, protein synthesis, and so on were inhibited. However, should a metabolic insult occur during the period of postglucocorticoid vulnerability in these neurons, their capacity to survive such a challenge would be compromised. Such a model predicts that a wide range of neurotoxic insults to the hippocampus would be more potent in animals with elevated titers of glucocorticoids and less so in adrenalectomized subjects. We have collected considerable evidence for such a model as seen in Table 1. Hypoxic-ischemic injury or microinfusion of the excitotoxin kainic acid or the antimetabolite 3-acetylpyridine (3-AP) are all more potently destructive to the hippocampus in rats maintained with high corticosterone titers (Sapolsky, 1985a,b; Sapolsky & Pulsinelli, 1985). Conversely, damage is attenuated by adrenalectomy. These three insults damage different cellfields of the hippocampus with differing mechanisms of action (for example, kainic acid appears to interact with the excitatory amino acid neurotransmitter system, while 3-AP inhibits adenosine triphosphate synthesis). Furthermore, corticosterone does not appear to synergize with them by modulating the specific mechanism of action of the toxic insult. For example, corticosterone fails to alter the diffusion or binding of kainic acid in the hippocampus, and the synergy between the two only occurs in corticosterone-sensitive regions of the brain (Sapolsky, 1985a). These findings suggest that it is a *generalized* metabolic state of vulnerability that is induced in these neurons such that their capacity to survive any of a variety of insults is impaired. We have studied the parameters of this vulnerability further. Both a history of exposure to elevated corticosterone titers (i.e., prior to the insult) as well as elevated titers in the immediate aftermath of the insult can potentiate damage (although the exact parameters appear to vary with the insult and the hippocampal cell fields involved) (Sapolsky, 1985a,b; Sapolsky & Pulsinelli, 1985). Furthermore, relatively brief periods of corticosterone exposure significantly potentiate damage — as lit-

TABLE 1

Modulation of the Severity of Neurotoxin- or Ischemia-Induced Hippocampal Damage by Glucocorticoid Milieu

Neuropathologic Insult	Adrenalectomized	Intact	Corticost
Kainic acid microinfusion:			
CA$_3$ cell field	55 ± 10	107 ± 24	119 ± 19
Total hippocampus	122 ± 31	199 ± 34	227 ± 43
3-Acetylpyridine microinfusion:			
Dentate gyrus (dorsal)	9 ± 5	23 ± 10	94 ± 25
Total hippocampus	10 ± 5	27 ± 17	133 ± 30
Hypoxia-ischemia, CA$_1$ cell field			
% of rats with no damage	50	20	15
% with moderate damage	30	25	0
% with severe damage	20	55	85

Note: Demonstration that three different neuropathologic insults to the hippocampus are more toxic in the presence of corticosterone titers elevated to the high physiologic range (CORTICOST rats) and are attenuated in their toxicity in adrenalectomized subjects. Kainic acid and 3-acetylpyridine data are from Sapolsky, 1985a, 1985b, respectively. In both cases, the volume of damage is presented for the whole hippocampus and for the cell field most sensitive to the particular neurotoxin; damage is expressed as cubic microns x 10^5. Hypoxia-ischemia data are from Sapolsky and Pulsinelli (1985) and submitted. Data from CA$_1$, the hippocampal cell field most vulnerable to hypoxia-ischemia, are presented as percentage of rats in each group with either no damage, moderate (1-50% of neurons damaged), or severe damage (greater than 50%).

tle as 48 hours bracketing the infusion of 3-AP, for example (Sapolsky, 1985b). Finally, the catabolic effects of glucocorticoids on neuronal metabolism appear to be critical to this endangerment. Glucocorticoids inhibit the uptake of glucose (Landgraf, Mitro, & Hess, 1978) on which neurons are vitally dependent (having little storage capacity for glycogen, and a nearly complete reliance on glucose, among the saccharides). All of the toxic insults utilized either directly impair the capacity of the neuron to generate adequate energy substrates or place undue demands on the neurons for such limited substrates. We reasoned that the blockade of glucose uptake by glucocorticoids is central to synergy between glucocorticoids and these varied insults. We have evidence that supplementation of rats with additional energy substrates that can be utilized by hippocampal neurons (e.g., high levels of glucose, mannose, or ketones such as hydroxbutyrate) can prevent the synergizing of hippocampal damage (Sapolsky, in press).

These findings suggest that the rate of hippocampal aging in the normal, nonpathologic state is influenced by interactions between extrinsic metabolic insults and intrinsic aging processes. The frequency and severity of minor metabolic challenges — transient periods of hypoglycemia, hypoxia, acidosis, hyperexcitation, and so on — will alter the extent to which the adrenocortical axis can damage the hippocampus. The fact that many external stressors besides stimulating corticosterone secretion also directly challenge cerebral metabolism, which further implicates "external hit frequency" as one factor in hippocampal degeneration with age. This way of framing these data reflects our interest in the neuroendocrinology of *normal* aging, in which we ask, "Will extrinsic insults to the brain alter the severity of glucocorticoid-induced damage to the hippocampus?" In considering AD, however, the emphasis of the interaction should be reversed. Will glucocorticoid milieu alter the severity of hippocampal damage in the AD patient? In this light, we now summarize the model of hippocampal aging that our data suggest and speculate on its relationship to AD.

CONCLUSIONS AND SPECIFIC RECOMMENDATIONS

The regulation of corticosterone secretion by the hippocampus and the acute and cumulative effects of corticosterone, in turn, on the hippocampus combine to form a feed-forward cascade which emerges with aging. Transient periods of sustained stress via elevated corticosterone titers lead to down regulation of corticosterone receptor number in the hippocampus. When sufficiently pronounced, such down regulation dampens the hippocampus inhibitory role in the adrenocortical axis leading to more pronounced secretion of corticosterone with subsequent stress. This in turn leads to further down regulation, further hyperadrenocorticism until, at some point (and perhaps contingent on coincident metabolic challenges to the brain), hippocampal neurons are damaged by the corticosterone and irreversible commitment to this degenerative circle has occurred. We have written previously about the constraints and implications of this model, focusing on the parameters and reversibility of various steps. For the present the most important point is the critical permissive role of excessive stress, especially stress that challenges cerebral metabolism, in initiating and accelerating this cycle. There are three broad areas of relevance to the understanding and, possibly, the management of AD. We list them from least to most speculative.

1. The role of hippocampal damage in the cognitive and endocrine features of AD

Animals with experimentally-induced damage to the hippocampus, aged rats, and AD patients share a number of pathologies: destruction of hippocampal neurons, impaired cognition, and glucocorticoid hypersecretion secondary to impaired adrenocortical feedback sensitivity. An extensive literature with both human and nonhuman subjects implicates the hippocampus as central to memory consolidation and retrieval and the hippocampal damage as powerfully disruptive of cognition (O'Keefe & Nadel, 1978). The role of the hippocampal damage in the cognitive impairments typical of senescence is nicely demonstrated in the previously discussed study in which middle-aged rats were adrenalectomized and maintained until old age. As described the degenerative markers of typical hippocampal aging (decreased neuronal density, glial reactivity, and infiltration) are diminished or eliminated in such glucocorticoid-free rats. Importantly, such rats also are free of some of the cognitive impairments found in age-matched controls (Landfield et al., 1981). These studies suggest that the hippocampal damage in the aged rat and the AD sufferer eventuate in impaired cognition (at the same time one must fully recognize the at least equal importance of the cortical damage in AD). Attribution of cognitive dysfunction in AD to the hippocampal damage is hardly a new idea and the present data merely lend further support to the notion. What has not been suggested, to our knowledge, is the similar role of the hippocampal damage in the adrenocortical hyperactivity of the AD patient. The adrenocortical axis of the normal, aged human does not show the abnormalities of the aged rat; the basal, stressed, and post-stress titers of cortisol are not elevated, and sensitivity to dexamethasone is relatively intact (Blichert-Toft et al., 1976; Grad, Rosenberg, & Liberman, 1971; Tourigny-Rivard, Raskind, & Rivard, 1981). However, approximately 50% of individuals with AD present elevated cortisol titers and dexamethasone resistance, and there is a dramatic interaction between age and this adrenocortical hyperactivity. Late-onset AD patients are more likely to be dexamethasone-resistant than are early-onset patients, and the latter group becomes more resistant with passing age (Davis et al., in press). While hyperadrenocorticism is not a defining feature of either the aged human or the AD patient, the trait is nearly penetrant in both populations, such that the interaction of the two produces a dramatic emergence of the adrenocortical hyperactivity. The human hippocampus appears to play an inhibitory role in adrenocortical function much as in other species examined (Mandell, Chapman, Rand, & Walter, 1963). Our data implicate hippocampal damage as a causative agent when the adrenocortical hyperactivity is observed in AD. Once the interaction of the pathologic state with the age of the patient is recognized and accounted for, the severity of adrenocortical hyperactivity in AD might be a useful marker for the extent of hippocampal damage. It is of interest to note that major depressive illnesses are associated in approximately 50% of cases with elevated cortisol titers and dexamethasone resistance. As with AD there is an interaction with age of the subject such that by the time elderly individuals are considered, fully 90% of depressives are dexamethasone-resistant (Georgotas, Stokes, Krakowski, Fanelli, & Cooper, 1984; Jacobs, Mason, Kosten, Brown, & Ostfeld, 1984; Rubinow, Post, Savard, & Gold, 1984; Stokes et al., 1984). We speculate rather tentatively that the stressors that often precede and predispose toward depressive episodes may produce down regulation of cortisol receptors in the hippocampus, sufficiently so in older sufferers to dampen feedback regulation of the axis.

2. Glucocorticoids as an exacerbating factor in AD after the disease has been established

As described above, glucocorticoid milieu consistently modulates the severity of hippocampal damage induced by kainic acid, 3-acetylpyridine, or hypoxia-ischemia. The final case is the most relevant from a clinical standpoint. Rats subjected to transient four-vessel occlusion, which most closely resembles the forebrain ischemia associated with cardiac arrest, present extensive hippocampal damage a few days following the hypoxic-ischemic insult. Elevation of corticosterone to the high physiological range at the time of reperfusion and throughout the postinsult period exacerbates damage. More important is the observation that adrenalectomy immediately following reperfusion reduces the extent of hippocampal damage to below that observed in control subjects (Sapolsky & Pulsinelli, 1985). This indicates that the extent of corticosterone secretion in the aftermath of hypoxia-ischemia (which turns out to be considerable) is sufficient to potentiate hippocampal damage. Thus, what is regarded as "normative" poststroke damage to the hippocampus is, in fact, normative damage exacerbated by the excessive glucocorticoid secretion at that time. As such, it is not only critical to prevent the hippocampus from being exposed to excessive levels of corticosterone in the aftermath of the insult, but attenuation of "normal" adrenocortical function might be therapeutically useful (Sapolsky & Pulsinelli, 1985).

A similar strategy might prove therapeutic for AD. Once damage to the hippocampus has been detected, excessive secretion of cortisol and possibly even basal titers of the hormone may accelerate the course of subsequent hippocampal damage. Given the assumptions (remaining to be proved) that the general features of our model apply to the human, that the as yet unidentified insult to the hippocampus in AD synergizes with glucocorticoids, and that the full extent of hippocampal degeneration has not occurred by the time AD becomes clinically penetrant, we recommend that:

— Considerable effort be made to minimize stressors in the life of the AD patient.

— Use of corticosteroids for ancillary medical problems be avoided.

— Basal adrenocortical activity be inhibited with glucocorticoid-synthesis inhibitors such as metyrapone, or that glucocorticoid receptor antagonists be utilized to block glucocorticoid action in the brain.

We recognize the management problem involved in such long-

term treatment in addition to the considerable metabolic consequences of a pharmacological "adrenalectomy." Nonetheless, in the
spirit of this volume's speculative approach, we offer these recommendations as a first therapeutic approximation should the assumptions listed above be met.

3. Glucocorticoids as promoters of the establishment of AD

The neuropathological markers that are hallmarks of AD include
senile plaques, neurofibrillary tangles, and dense accumulations of
lipofuscin. However, all of these occur, albeit with a lesser intensity,
in non-AD human brains. This has led to the suggestion that AD
is a threshold disease rather than a qualitatively distinct entity (discussed in Wisniewski & Iqbal, 1980). If this is the case, and if the
assumptions outlined above prove true, excessive glucocorticoid exposure over the life span might increase the likelihood of sufficient
hippocampal damage to make the disease clinically expressed. If
such were the case, individuals with histories of excessive stress, with
Cushing's syndrome, or with prolonged administration of glucocorticoids to control, for example, an autoimmune disorder, might be
at risk for AD. Untreated cushingoid syndromes and autoimmune
disorders of sufficient severity to warrant sustained glucocorticoid
therapy are generally incompatible with long life span and sufficient
cumulative damage for emergence of AD-like symptoms, which
makes the testing of this hypothesis difficult. However, one tantalizing, if tragic, group of studies suggests that chronic stress in humans
is associated with neurological disorders, cerebral atrophy, and high
rates of dementia. Study subjects in these reports are either recent
torture victims or survivors of Nazi concentration or internment camps
(Jensen et al., 1982; Thygesen, Hermann, & Willanger, 1970). If
less profound stress can induce hippocampal damage and if AD is
indeed on a qualitative continuum with lesser amounts of hippocampal damage in some manner, then a history of excessive adrenocortical activity might predispose towards AD. Were this the case,
were newly developed radiological imaging techniques capable of
identifying early-stage AD and, most importantly, were it then possible to therapeutically intervene with such early cases, we make the
following highly speculative recommendations:

— Individuals with histories of excessive stress or, for medical reasons, of excessive exposure to exogenous glucocorticoids be con-

sidered to be at risk for AD and be monitored accordingly.

— Family members of victims of AD, which appears to have a familial component, should be considered to be at risk for AD themselves;
thus, stress and pharmacologic administration of glucocorticoids
should be minimized.

A decade ago, to write a chapter such as this filled with recommendations about the management and even the retardation of the
onset of AD would have been considered floridly delusional. At
present, it is merely speculative and extrapolative to an extreme. We
hope that progress will continue unabated in the study of AD, such
that these ideas will ultimately be testable.

REFERENCES

Blichert-Toft, M., & Hummer, L. (1976). Immunoreactive corticotro-
phin reserve in old age in man during and after surgical stress. *Journal of Gerontology, 31,* 539-545.

Brizzee, K., & Ordy, J. (1979). Age pigments, cell loss and hippocampal function. *Mechanisms of Ageing and Development, 9,* 143-162.

Davis, K., Davis, B., Greenwald, B., Mohs, R., Mathe, A., Johns,
C., & Horvath, T. (In press). Cortisol and Alzheimer disease. I: Basal
studies. *Archives of General Psychiatry.*

Felt, B., Sapolsky, R., & McEwen, B. (1984). Regulation of hippocampal corticosterone receptors by a vasopressin analogue. *Peptides,
5,* 1225-1227.

Finch, C., Felicio, L., Mobb, C., & Nelson, J. (1984). Ovarian and
steroidal influences on neuroendocrine aging processes in female
rodents. *Endocrine Reviews, 5,* 467-497.

Folkman, J., Langer, R., Linhardt, R., Haudenschild, C., & Taylor,
S. (1983). Angiogenesis inhibition and tumor regression caused by
heparin or a heparin fragment in the presence of cortisone. *Science,
221,* 719-723.

Georgotas, A., Stokes, P., Krakowski, M., Fanelli, C., & Cooper, T.
(1984). Hypothalamic-pituitary-adrenocortical function in geriatric
depression: Diagnostic and treatment implications. *Biological Psychiatry, 19,* 685-693.

Grad, B., Rosenberg, G., & Liberman, H. (1971). Diurnal variation of serum cortisol level of geriatric subjects. *Journal of Gerontology, 26*, 351-352.

Ida, Y., Tanaka, M., Tsuda, A., Kohno, Y., Hoaki, Y., Nakasawa, R., Iimori, K., & Nagasaki, N. (1984). Recovery of stress-induced increases in noradrenaline turnover is delayed in specific brain regions of old rats. *Life Sciences, 34*, 2357-2363.

Jacobs, S., Mason, J., Kosten, T., Brown, S., & Ostfeld, A. (1984). Urinary-Free cortisol excretion in relation to age in acutely stressed persons with depressive symptoms. *Psychosomatic Medicine, 46*, 213-221.

Jensen, T.S., Genefke, I.K., Hyldebrandt, N., Pedersen, H., Petersen, H., & Weile, B. (1982). Cerebral atrophy in young torture victims [Letter to the editor]. *New England Journal of Medicine, 307*, 1341.

Keller-Wood, M., & Dallman, M. (1984). Corticosteroid inhibition of ACTH secretion. *Endocrine Reviews, 5*, 1-24.

Krieger, D.T. (1982). Cushing's syndrome. *Monographs on Endocrinology, 22*, 1-142.

Landfield, P., Braun, L., & Pitler, T. (1981). Brain aging correlates: Retardation by hormonal-pharmacological treatments. *Science, 214*, 581-584.

Landfield, P., Rose, G., Sandles, L., Wohlstadter, T., & Lynch, G. (1977). Patterns of astroglial hypertrophy and neuronal degeneration in the hippocampus of aged, memory-deficient rats. *Journal of Gerontology, 32*, 3-12.

Landgraf, R., Mitro, A., & Hess, J. (1978). Regional net uptake of 14C-glucose by rat brain under the influence of corticosterone. *Endocrine Experimentalis, 12*, 119-128.

Mandell, A., Chapman, L., Rand, R., & Walter, R. (1963). Plasma corticosteroids: Changes in concentration after stimulation of hippocampus and amygdala. *Science, 139*, 1212-1213.

McEwen, B. (1982). Glucocorticoids and hippocampus: Receptors in search of a function. In P. Ganten & D. Pfaff (Eds.), *Current topics in neuroendocrinology 2* (pp. 23-46). Berlin: Springer-Verlag.

Muhlen, K., & Ockenfels, H. (1969). Morphologische veranderungen im diencephalon und telencephalon nach storungen des regelkreises adenohypophyse-nebennierenrinde. 3. Ergebnisse beim meerschweinchen nach verabreichung von cortison und hydrocortison. *Zeitschrift fur Zellforschung und Mikroskopische Anatomie*, *93*, 126-141.

Munck, A., Guyre, P., & Holbrook, N. (1984). Physiological functions of glucocorticoids in stress and their relation to pharmacological actions. *Endocrine Reviews, 5*, 25-44.

O'Keefe, J., & Nadel, L. (1978). *The hippocampus as a cognitive map*. Oxford: The Clarendon Press.

Oxenkrug, G., McIntyre, I., Stanley, M., & Gershon, S. (1984). Dexamethasone suppression test: Experimental model in rats, and effect of age. *Biological Psychiatry, 19*, 413-416.

Riley, V. (1981). Psychoneuroendocrine influences on immunocompetence and neoplasia. *Science, 212*, 1100-1108.

Rubinow, D., Post, R., Savard, R., & Gold, P. (1984). Cortison hypersecretion and cognitive impairment in depression. *Archives of General Psychiatry, 41*, 279-283.

Sapolsky, R. (1985a). Glucocorticoid toxicity in the hippocampus: Temporal aspects of neuronal vulnerability. *Brain Research, 359*, 300-306.

Sapolsky, R. (1985b). A mechanism for glucocorticoid toxicity in the hippocampus: Increased neuronal vulnerability to metabolic insults. *Journal of Neuroscience, 5*, 1228-1233.

Sapolsky, R. (in press). C_1 glucocorticoids in the hippocampus: Reversal by supplementation with brain fuels. *Journal of Neuroscience*.

Sapolsky, R., & Donnelly, T. (1985). Vulnerability to stress-induced tumor growth increases with age: Role of glucocorticoids. *Endocrinology, 117*, 662-665.

Sapolsky, R., Krey, L., & McEwen, B. (1983a). The adrenocortical stress-response in the aged male rat: Impairment of recovery from stress. *Experimental Gerontology, 18*, 55-64.

Sapolsky, R., Krey, L., & McEwen, B. (1983b). Corticosterone receptors decline in a site-specific manner in the aged rat brain. *Brain Research, 289*, 235-240.

Sapolsky, R., Krey, L., & McEwen, B. (1983c). Stress down-regulates corticosterone receptors in a site-specific manner in the brain. *Endocrinology, 114*, 287-292.

Sapolsky, R., Krey, L., & McEwen, B. (1984). Glucocorticoid-Sensitive hippocampal neurons are involved in terminating the adrenocortical stress response. *Proceedings of the National Academy of Sciences, USA, 81*, 6174-6177.

Sapolsky, R., Krey, L., & McEwen, B. (1985). Prolonged glucocorticoid exposure reduces hippocampal neuron number: Implications for aging. *Journal of Neuroscience, 5*, 1221-1227.

Sapolsky, R., Krey, L., McEwen, B., & Rainbow, T. (1984). Do vasopressin-related peptides induce hippocampal corticosterone receptors? Implications for aging. *Journal of Neuroscience, 4*, 1479-1485.

Sapolsky, R., & Pulsinelli, W. (1985). Glucocorticoids potentiate ischemic injury to neurons: Therapeutic implications. *Science, 229*, 1397-1400.

Stokes, P., Stoll, P., Koslow, S., Maas, J., Davis, J., Swann, A., & Robins, E. (1984). Pretreatment DST and hypothalamic-pituitary-adrenocortical function in depressed patients and comparison groups. *Archives of General Psychiatry, 41*, 257-267.

Thygesen, P., Hermann, K., & Willanger, R. (1970). Concentration camp survivors in Denmark: Persecution, disease, disability, compensation. *Danish Medical Bulletin, 17*, 65-108.

Tourigny-Rivard, M., Raskind, M., & Rivard, D. (1981). The dexamethasone suppression test in an elderly population. *Biological Psychiatry, 16*, 1177-1184.

Veldhuis, H.D., & de Kloet, E.R. (1982). Vasopressin-related peptides increase the hippocampal corticosterone receptor capacity of diabetes insipidus (Brattleboro) rats. *Endocrinology, 110*, 153-157.

Vernikos, J., Dallman, M., Bonner, C., Katzen, A., & Shinsako, J. (1982). Pituitary-adrenal function in rats chronically exposed to cold. *Endocrinology, 110*, 413-417.

Wisniewski, H.M., & Iqbal, K. (1980). Ageing of the brain and dementia. *Trends in Neurosciences, 3*, 226-228.

Yates, F., Marsh, D., & Maran, J. (1980). The adrenal cortex. In V. Mountcastle (Ed.), *Medical physiology* (pp. 1558-1602). St. Louis: Mosby.

8

Guides Through the Labyrinth of AD: Dehydroepiandrosterone, Potassium Channels, and the C4 Component of Complement

Eugene Roberts, PhD

The purpose of this effort is to attempt to identify rate limiting processes leading to age-related deterioration of nervous system function and/or to senile dementia of the Alzheimer's type (SDAT) which might be amenable to manipulation by available therapeutic modalities. A neurobehavioral model is presented in which an important role is assigned to the cholinergic system of the brain stem and basal forebrain core, which is of decisive importance in maintaining the waking state, consciousness, and the ability to learn, and which is known to deteriorate functionally and structurally in Alzheimer's disease (AD). Links to incoordinations in a number of bodily systems with age are correlated with decrements in sex hormone levels, generally, and most specifically with uniquely monotonic decreases after puberty in both males and females in serum levels of dehydroepiandrosterone (DHEA) and dehydroepiandrosterone sulfate (DHEAS), substances that serve as precursors for both androgens and estrogens in tissues of the body. A review of the literature reveals that administration of DHEA and DHEAS may exert ameliorative effects in such different conditions as diabetes, obesity, autoimmune disease, cancer, and connective tissue disorder, possibly by releasing diverse aspects of metabolic machinery necessary for effective intracellular and extracellular communication to take place.

A consideration of the role of K^+ channels in membranes suggests that their coordinated production, activation, and inactivation is required for maintenance of adaptive responsivities to external signals by cells, be they ova, lymphocytes, or neurons. K^+ channels play singularly important roles in the sequences of membrane events involved in all neural activities from impulse generation and conduction to neurotransmitter release. In AD, there is defective release of acetylcholine (ACh), which by its actions on muscarinic receptors in the central nervous system (CNS) blocks K^+ channels. K^+ channel blockers can substitute for ACh and restore neural activity. Recent data on T lymphocytes reveals that opening of K^+ channels is required for them to respond to antigenic stimuli. Since maladaptive underactivity in CNS function in AD and incoordinated overactivity of immune cells often coexist in aging and AD, and since both may be in part attributable to failure to close K^+ channels appropriately, the administration of K^+ channel blockers may correct both defects at once.

Because there are many metabolic crossroads at which DHEA and DHEAS meet with K^+ channels, it is suggested that coadministration of the above hormonal substances with appropriate quantities of K^+ channel blockers might exert remarkable recyberneticizing effects on both nervous and immune systems and on their relations to each other in aging and in AD. It would be wise to ensure an adequate dietary supply of choline that might be necessary for supporting increased (ACh) turnover.

INTRODUCTION

Once again, as in 1980, I have been asked by the brave editors of this volume to speculate with regard to strategies for treatment and prevention of SDAT. In previous papers I attempted to lay a theoretical foundation for a series of therapeutic suggestions (Roberts, 1976, 1981, 1982). With a few modifications (Roberts, 1984) I still hold to it; but, in retrospect, it appears to have been too limited in scope. Much scientific water has flowed under the bridge since that time, but no truly effective therapies are in sight, the causes of the disease still are unknown, and prophylactic measures have not been devised. This is not attributable to a lack of effort, which has increased enormously worldwide and for which there now is much expanded financial support. Perhaps what is needed is the encouragement the present opportunity offers to break out of the orthodoxies that tended to develop so quickly and to become fixed in the scientific firmament.

Three major areas are worthy of concern: genetics, aging, and ubiquitous environmental factors to which some individuals may react idiosyncratically. Unquestionably there are inherited factors associated with at least some forms of AD (Breitner & Folstein, 1984; Cook, Schneck, & Clark, 1981; Goudsmit et al., 1981; Heston & Mastri, 1977; Heyman et al., 1983; Nee et al., 1983; Weitkamp, Nee, Keats, Polinsky, & Guttormsen, 1983). A number of efforts are under way to determine whether or not there are DNA restriction fragment length polymorphisms that correlate with the segregation of AD in family members of sufficiently extensive pedigrees, with the eventual hope of cloning the gene for the disorder. By this means it may be possible to approach the identification of the abnormal gene product and, therefore, the cause of this disorder, at least in the case of the affected families. Those not engaged in the latter type of effort concern themselves with aspects of the other two areas in the belief that in the near future their results may converge with the genetic findings at the level of the molecular defect, whether or not the origin of AD always has an identifiable genetic basis.

Failure in optimal nervous system function under primitive conditions would lead rapidly to the demise of an organism. Manifestations of aging of the nervous system — whether one looks at neuropathologic, physiologic, neurochemical, or behavioral aspects — appear to reflect a final common path taken by organisms when behavioral options ordinarily available to achieve adaptive responses are precluded by degeneration of the neural machinery. Even during the early "normal" adult period, degenerative changes probably are taking place to some extent but are being compensated for by activities of redundant neural elements and by adjustments in neural feedback and modulator systems. However, eventually pathologic changes may become sufficiently extensive so that the latter activities are inadequate and the social behavior and physiological responses of the severely affected individual become maladaptive and, in the case of humans, survival becomes dependent upon extensive use of artificial social and medical support systems. The endstage pathologies observed are characterized by degenerative changes in cells in many brain regions and are associated with losses of neuronal cells, decreases in neuronal processes in surviving cells, and increases in glial elements. Viral and bacterial infections; dietary deficiencies and imbalances; cardiovascular, metabolic, and endocrine disorders; anoxia, various types of space-occupying lesions and traumata, and toxins may cause degenerative changes or may predispose to such changes in response to subsequent cerebral insult or injury. Accelerated degeneration of neural, endothelial, neuroendocrine, and endocrine elements, together with incoordination in the networks of relations among the cellular components of the immune system and coincident disruption of neurovascular relations and breakdown of the blood-brain barrier in the affected regions, could predispose to the development of both circulating and cellular autoantibodies to various polymeric components of cellular and extracellular components in the disrupted regions. This may lead to enhanced cellular destruction and deposition of the relatively indigestible debris of immune complexes in capillaries and extracellular sites. Another consequence of perturbation of the immune system might be immunosuppression with resultant activation of latent viruses destructive to the nervous system.

Cells, like organisms, are integrated organizations of a highly heterogeneous nature. They contain thousands of different chemical substances of varying degrees of complexity in physical and chemical interactions with each other in various subcellular organelles and compartments, many of which are morphologically distinguishable by light or electron microscopy. The structures of cell membranes and of membranes of the intracellular organelles have varying stabilities. The membranes have differing degrees of exchangeability with their immediate environment, and the enzyme systems associated with them catalyze some of the chemical reactions by which the internal needs of the individual cells are subserved as well as by which the relations with the extracellular environment are maintained. When ligands attach to their specific receptors on particular membranes, cascades of biochemical reactions are set in motion in a coordinated way so that in a brief period the cells of which they are a part react appropriately in a manner compatible with their individual behavioral repertoire. Any havoc wrought by the messages the ligands bring is repaired, and the cellular machinery may be altered in such a way as to integrate the messages that the ligands bring. Manifestations of aging—pathologic, physiologic, or biochemical— appear to reflect a common path taken by cells when the mechanisms ordinarily available to achieve adaptive responses, such as those alluded to above, are precluded by degenerative changes in the cellular machinery. Degenerative changes always must be taking place to some extent in any given cell, but are being compensated for by redundant cellular elements and by cybernetic adjustments among the varieties of degradative and synthetic mechanisms. As in the case of the whole organism, when this is no longer possible, aging is said to take place and cell death eventually occurs. Let us conclude, then, that aging phenomena, at all levels from social to molecular, result in decyberneticization, i.e., disruption of meaningful communication channels between components of relevant members of interlocking systems, so that eventually overtly observable adaptive behaviors are not possible and the organism literally crumbles, like a biological Tower of Babel.

Because sporadic AD almost always occurs coextensively with aging, many pathological features of decyberneticization are shared. However, AD should not be considered entirely in the same category as normal attritional types of aging because, in addition to the above general types of aging changes, important genetic components exist in familial AD (there are pedigrees showing what appears to be an autosomal dominant transmission of the disorder) and idiosyncratic reactions to ubiquitously present environmental factors also may play an important role. Behavioral, pathologic, and biochemical data are consistent with the possibility that in AD the degenerative changes observed in several brain regions are correlated with initial malfunction and subsequent degeneration of terminals of neurons whose somata lie in regions of the brain stem core and whose fibers project to many structures both above and below their location. In AD there often is a specific loss of neurons in the basal nucleus of Meynert (Whitehouse, Price, Clark, Coyle, & DeLong, 1981) and sometimes in the locus coeruleus (Bondareff, Mountjoy, & Roth, 1982), which are the major sources of extrinsic cholinergic and noradrenergic inputs, respectively, projecting widely and diffusely upon all telencephalic structures. There is evidence that the hippocampus, a region of the brain known to play a key role in memory formation, essentially may be removed from brain circuitry by lesions at its input and output sites (Hyman, Van Hoesen, Damasio, & Barnes, 1984).

Both in AD and in "normal" aging, changes in membranes of capillary endothelial cells may influence the rate of entry of substances into the CNS by diffusion, pinocytosis, or carrier-mediated transport; or the rate of pumping of K^+ ions out of the brain extracellular compartment may be changed. Indeed, it has been suggested from detailed electron microscopic observations that capillary degeneration with the formation of amyloid fibrils may be the primary change in the genesis of senile plaques in AD (Miyakawa, Shimoji, Kuramoto, & Higuchi, 1982). Effects on neural membranes may produce decreases in their conductile properties, changes in release characteristics from terminals of neurotransmitters and modulators, alterations in the sensitivity of pre- and postsynaptic receptors to the action of the latter, and changes in degrees of electrotonic communication between neurons via gap junctions. At the onset of the disease, a whole host of cybernetic adjustments would be expected to be taking place, structural and enzymatic, so that metabolic steady states different from those found before would exist at cellular and tissue levels, and new transactional states would be found at the systems level in the CNS. This process may continue as the disease progresses, until breakdowns occur in one or another rate-limiting process, leading to progressive deterioration and finally fatal loss of adaptive function.

In view of the great complexity of the biological situation touched upon above and the ripple-like, radiating effects of a disease process at any of the levels mentioned, one would not be surprised eventually to find changes in a myriad of measured parameters in an organism affected by AD. *But, limited as our knowledge may be, our task is to attempt to identify those events that are rate-limiting at each of the levels and to develop a scenario of events which seems reasonable in terms of available data and which points to testable hypotheses and to new ways of dealing with the problems of AD.*

NEUROBEHAVIORAL FRAMEWORK—EMPHASIS ON THE ROLE OF THE CHOLINERGIC SYSTEM

My working model is a "homing" model, the primary assumption being that the behavior of a healthy waking organism is aimed at attaining a hedonic state, i.e., the organism is a hedonic optimizer (Roberts & Matthysse, 1970). The waking organism seeks the optimal state of well being which is associated with comfort, pleasure, ease, satisfaction, absence of anxiety and boredom, and so forth. Displacement from such a state may result in human beings (and possibly in other organisms) in feelings of anxiety, discomfort, boredom, or pain. Continual changes in the external environment and in the internal metabolism of the organism generally act counter to the maintenance or achievement of an hedonic state and tend to displace the organism from it. At all times, an awake organism finds itself in a multi-sensory environment, which it scans internally and externally for physical and chemical changes with specialized receptors. It responds to the patterning of the relative values of the effective sensory cues, an abstraction of the environmental realities. At any particular time, the changing pattern in the perceived environment, external and internal, is the stimulus for the organism.

When an organism is presented with a novel effective stimulus setting, receptors are activated in a unique fashion, i.e., the types and numbers of receptors activated and their sequence and intensity of activation result in a receptor and neural activation pattern different from any experienced previously by the organism. Through-put and coordinating command circuits as well as auxiliary modulatory neural circuits are released simultaneously. These circuits may be considered to consist of cascades of serially aligned neuronal assemblies in which coded patterns of information entering originally from sensory transducers are progressively refined by the reduction of redundancy and the selection of particular features. The transformations of coded patterns in different neural sectors are achieved to a considerable extent by negative feedback loops that exist between and within the sectors; and their temporal and spatial integration is achieved by activity of neural command centers, such as the cerebellar cortex, hippocampus, basal ganglia, reticular nucleus of the thalamus, and association cortex. The "hard-wired" neuronal elements of the through-put and command neuronal circuits, the blueprints for the construction of whose framework largely are inherited by the organism, are surrounded by local circuit neurons whose specific commitments may be made during development, as well as later in life, and which not only participate in virtually all phases of information processing but also may undergo plastic changes that may be involved in long-term retention of experience. Communication between the neural elements in these circuits largely takes place through synaptic and gap junctions on a millisecond or submillisecond time scale. I would like to suggest that, in many instances in which they act in the CNS, ACh, the catecholamines, serotonin, neuroactive peptides, steroids, and prostaglandins, as well as probably a host of still unknown substances, may serve to optimize regional nervous system activity in relation to functional demands without themselves necessarily being involved in specific information transmittal. Upon release from nerve terminals or vesicle-containing varicosities, they exert chemical actions that influence the efficacy of the information-transmitting junctions in the mainline and command circuits.

Since it is not possible *a priori* to predict which neural circuits will be necessary to solve the problems posed by novel situations, it is necessary at the outset to have all of the neural machinery available. I propose that this is achieved largely through activation of cholinergic neurons in the brain stem and basal forebrain, which receive multisensory inputs and, through their widely ramifying terminals, excite or disinhibit activity throughout the brain in a coordinated fashion. In this manner all relevant neural units are brought to a level of activity at which they are readily available for whatever roles in information processing may subsequently be required of them. A schematic summary is shown in Figure 1 of the direct monosynaptic cholinergic pathways from magnocellular nuclei of the basal forebrain of the rat to the cortex. These neurons, whose branches fan out in a manner very similar to that observed for the noradrenergic neurons of the locus coeruleus, terminate in various cortical and subcortical loci, often after long traverses away from their cell bodies. Simultaneously, through terminals on the blood vessels in the activated regions, the cholinergic neurons produce a vasodilation, making it possible for the currently enhanced activity and future demands to be fueled with sufficient supplies of glucose and oxygen (Brayden & Bevan, 1985; Scremin, Rovere, Raynald, & Giardini, 1973).

One particularly important role of the cholinergic system may be the facilitation of exchange of information between the thalamus and the cortex. The reticular nucleus of the thalamus, which consists of

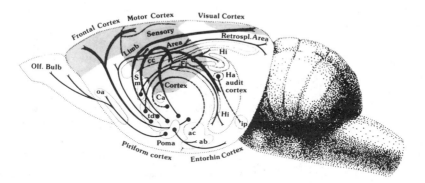

Figure 1. Schematic drawing summarizing the direct monosynaptic cholinergic pathways from magnocellular nuclei of the basal forebrain of the rat to the cortex. Neocortical fields receive their cholinergic innervation from scattered cell groups situated in the substantia innominata (dark neurons not designated lying outside and between the nuclei of origin innervating paleo- and archicortical fields). Olfactory bulb and entorhinal cortex are innervated by cholinergic neurons of the nuc. preopticus magnocellularis (poma); the hippocampal formation and the limbic cortex from cholinergic cells of the medial septum (sm) and Broca's diagnoal tract nucleus (td). Abbreviations: ab, nuc. amygdaloideus basalis; ac, nuc. amygdaloideus centralis; Ca, commissura anterior; CC, corpus callosum; Ha, nuc. habenulae lateralis; Hi, hippocampus; ip, nuc. interpeduncularis; oa, nuc. olfactorius anterior; Fi, fimbria hippocampi; Sm, stria medullaris thalami; td, nuc. tractus diagnoalis (Broca). (Figure 11 of Wenk, Bigl, & Meyer, 1980; reprinted with permission of the authors.)

GABA neurons that fit like a glove over the rostral pole and ventro-lateral faces of the thalamus and which send inhibitory projections into the thalamus (Houser, Vaughn, Barber, & Roberts, 1980), receive a large extrinsic projection of cholinergic terminals (Ben-Ari, Dingledine, Kanazawa, & Kelly, 1976; Dingledine & Kelly, 1977; Steriade, Ropert, Kitsikis, & Oakson, 1980). The latter input probably activates the GABA-ergic neurons of the thalamic reticular nucleus, which together with activation of other types of neurons facilitates and coordinates thalamo-cortical communication. Obviously, a pathological disturbance in the function of the cholinergic system would lead to aberrations of perception and behavior. An adequate and coordinated input of ACh acting to decrease K^+ conductance via muscarinic receptors probably is necessary for achieving optimal opening and adjustment of thalamic gates (Scheibel, 1980), as well as possibly other such gates in the CNS. Failure of this to occur would lead to an insufficient flow of processed sensory information to the cortex or distortions in it so that the organism would be unable to make realistic assessment of its environment and to develop adaptive behavioral strategies or, possibly, even to remain conscious. The latter may be the situation in AD, when general anesthetics are used, or when the brain stem core is transected at the appropriate level. Gross disturbances produced in the function of the reticular nucleus of the thalamus by too potently inhibiting its GABAergic neurons could lead to aberrations of perception and behavior. Even seizures could occur because of a greatly increased and chaotic input into the cortex, as may be the case when high levels of cholinomimetic drugs, cholinesterase inhibitors, 4-aminopyridine, or phencyclidine (PCP) are administered.

Cholinergic neurons probably generate the ascending activating influences that help maintain tonic patterns in thalamocortical systems during waking and desynchronized sleep states and generate the neural activities leading to EEG desynchronization (Steriade et al., 1980). From much work it is certain that the noradrenergic system emanating from the locus coeruleus is not important for neocortical and allocortical activation. But the latter system probably is importantly involved in reducing the signal to noise ratio at successive stages of problem solving by the organism and, like italicized words in a sentence or an exclamation mark at the end of it, serves to indicate the main lesson to be learned from an experience and when it should be learned. It seems as though the cholinergic and noradrenergic systems have a Yin and Yang relationship. The cholinergic system opens up neural circuits and the noradrenergic closes them down in an orderly fashion, all the way up and down the neuraxis, from cortex to dorsal horn in the spinal cord, while helping guide the system to an optimal solution. The noradrenergic locus coeruleus system (see Foote, Bloom, & Aston-Jones, 1983, for review), which is insensitive to direct sensory input, probably is activated, as are other brain regions, by signals from the cholinergic system. It then is in free-flowing bidirectional contact with each of the other activated neural systems, as well as with the cholinergic system. It exerts largely inhibitory neuronal effects and, when it releases norepinephrine in regions near blood vessels, can cause vasoconstriction, thereby facilitating functional shutdown in the neural regions where this occurs.

During an early stage of response to a novel situation, I propose that elements of the cholinergic system are activated by combinations of excitation and disinhibition, but largely by the latter, i.e., release from inhibition exerted by tonically active GABAergic and glycinergic neurons (Roberts, 1976). Inhibition of such inhibitory neurons may be facilitated by the action of neurally released endogenous opioids, the enkephalins, which are known to markedly decrease the efficacy of a number of GABAergic pathways in the vertebrate nervous system and have been shown specifically to depress inhibitory interneurons in the hippocampus, thereby increasing the firing rates of the pyramidal cells through disinhibition (Nicoll, Alger, & Jahr, 1980).

During early stages of response to displacement from the hedonic state, there would be maximal desynchronization of firing within and between other neural regions in the CNS. The behavior observed initially would generally be of the "alarm" type indigenous to the species studied. For a period after the first experience with the stimulus, more primary sensory neural circuits would be active than when, subsequently, the stimulus intensity is being reduced by effective behavior. I presume that by blocking K^+ channels of both excitatory and inhibitory nerves (North & Egan, 1984), ACh generally increases release of neurotransmitters from all activated neural elements, thereby facilitating coordinated activity of perseverating circuits, which may consist of neural combinations never used before. At this time, the extent of increases in connectivities in the circuits in use, which probably reflects plastic changes (long-term potentiation?) in rate-limiting synapses, will be largely a function of time of use and frequency of firing. As the problem solving process continues, activity in the cholinergic system is decreased in intensity by combinations of decreased environmental inputs and feedbacks from the activated neural activity in other brain regions. Activity in the largely inhibitory noradrenergic system progressively accelerates as that of the cholinergic one becomes restricted. As the problem approaches solution, there is a continuum of increases and decreases in activity of the noradrenergic and cholinergic systems, respectively. Eventually, neural activity in brain regions irrelevant to solution of the problem at hand will have been reduced essentially to basal levels.

I now postulate that the synchronous firing of specific phase-locked neuronal oscillators in both the noradrenergic centers (reward centers?) and the still active neurons in the cholinergic centers begins to occur and becomes a signal to the organism that appropriate behavior options which will solve or ameliorate the problem that has given rise to feelings of dysphoria or anxiety are about to be released and that achievement of the hedonic state is in sight. The closer the approach to the latter, the greater will be the synchrony of firing in the participating neuronal groups, indicating that the consummatory goals are imminently attainable and that the hedonic state is achievable, perhaps reaching maximal degrees of synchrony just before the beginning of consummation, as, for example, just prior to attainment of food or achievement of sex. In a highly coupled system, such as ordinarily exists in an organism facing real problems of existence and achieving realistic solutions to them, I posit that the system operates in the manner described above. However, the oscillators can be made to operate independently of the usual environmental signals by electrical stimulation or by drugs. Whether produced by approach to solutions of existential problems, by drugs, by artificial brain stimulation, or by ideas which are symbolic equivalents for biological realities, I propose that these oscillations, at least in human beings, are accompanied by a temporary euphorigenic rush of feeling or a "high." This may be the basis for the poetic vision of Paradise. However, once achieved, the neural and chemical inhibitory feedbacks cause the reversion of activity within and between the latter oscillators to a nonoscillatory type, and this might be associated with the despair of Paradise lost. The substances or conditions giving rise to the oscillations that become associated with the feeling of a "high" may become relentlessly sought after. The latter may be considered to be a basic characteristic of most human beings and, perhaps, is related to addictability (see Roberts, 1983, for relevant discussion and references).

The enhanced release of norepinephrine during the proposed synchronization serves as the "motivation" for the behavior, while activity of cholinergic neurons releases the neural circuits selected for the adaptive behavior like rockets from a launching pad, with minimal interference. I also propose that at the peak firing frequencies there is liberation of a substance, possibly a peptide, from the terminals of the cholinergic nerves that essentially serves as a "now-print" signal, viz., it helps release at the activated synapses rate-limiting biochemical reactions which can enhance connectivities of the connections in regions to which the terminals project.

Upon experience of an organism with a particular new stimulus set, the net effect of the maximal development of connectivities, would be the establishment of a cybernetic system, different at least in some respects from any present in the organism before. With continued experience in a given situation, after the first moment of stimulation, the activation of the minimal number of neural circuits and the minimal release of hormones would be accompanied by behavior that would approach the maximal efficiency attainable by the organism under the circumstances. Herein would be the essence of a system with a defined structure that has remarkable self-organizing and plastic properties and that lays down memories. In man, at least, it is known that a continuum of states of memory exists, from knowledge that is easily verbalized to knowledge the existence of which can only be inferred by indirect techniques, such as showing a small economy in the relearning of a response that was ostensibly completely forgotten.

COMMUNICATION BETWEEN NEURAL UNITS

Much of the communication that takes place between receptor and neuron, between neuron and neuron, and between neuron and effector cell is believed to occur via the extracellular liberation of a substance or combinations of substances which interact with specialized regions of membranes of neurons or membranes of muscle or gland cells to produce either excitatory or inhibitory effects. The key to the action of transmitter substances lies in the nature of the changes they cause in conformations of receptive membrane regions on neurons. A transmitter is neither excitatory nor inhibitory in itself, but only in relation to a particular membrane with which it interacts. Thus, a given neuron may liberate a particular transmitter from its axonal terminals onto the membranes of many other neurons. In some instances, the transmitter may exert excitatory effects and in others, inhibitory effects. The demonstration that at a given synapse GABA or ACh is released, for example, is not sufficient evidence to identify it as an inhibitory or excitatory synapse, respectively. Supporting physiological evidence always is necessary for such a functional assignment to be made. ACh is always excitatory when it interacts with nicotinic receptors at neuromuscular junctions and inhibitory when it acts on muscarinic receptors of cells in the reticular nucleus of the thalamus. Although not yet thoroughly analyzed at the physiologic and ultrastructural levels in most regions of the vertebrate nervous system, there is reason to believe that electrotonic interactions through gap junctions and field effects also may be of key importance in complex information processing (Bennett & Goodenough, 1978; Taylor & Dudek, 1984).

Excitatory effects upon a neuron occur most frequently on dendrites. The action of an excitatory transmitter is believed to result in a configurational change in the membrane upon which it impinges which increases its permeability to cations and, in turn, decreases the potential across the membrane (depolarization). The sodium current usually is believed to be responsible for most of the observed depolarization of postsynaptic membrances, although calcium flows into the cell as well. The changes in membrane potential and increases of free intracellular calcium that may occur from inward flow and/or from release from mitochondria during nerve activity cause the opening of potassium channels. Outward potassium currents then repolarize the cell and, in many instances, produce a hyperpolarization before the calcium balance is restored via the action of Ca^{2+}-Mg^{2+} ATPase and mitochondrial reuptake. The potassium channels then are closed, and the action of Na^+-K^+ ATPase restores the monocation balance.

The time-sequence coordination of the latter events is such that there is, in effect, a pulsatile increase of free intraterminal Ca^{2+} that reflects accurately the amount of depolarization to which the membrane of the nerve terminal has been subjected. The increase in free Ca^{2+} either directly or via its interaction with special Ca^{2+} binding proteins, calmodulin, troponin C, and S-100 are examples, releases many intracellular and intramembraneous processes which continue until free Ca^{2+} is reduced to the resting level either by pumping mechanisms or by intracellular binding or sequestration, viz., binding of Ca^{2+} by mitochondria. One of the processes triggered by increase in free intraterminal Ca^{2+} is the fusion of transmitter-containing membranous vesicles clustered at surfaces apposing postsynaptic receptive sites with the external membrane of the nerve terminal and the consequent release therefrom of neurotransmitters and probably other neuroactive substances into the subsynaptic cleft. Increase in free intracellular calcium, brief as it may be, also is believed to trigger the sequence of events that releases the metabolic reactions required for recovery from nerve activity and for the possible retention at pre- and postsynaptic sites of a biochemical "memory" of the experience. During this period, various enzymes related to cyclic nucleotide metabolism are activated as well as phosphoprotein phosphatases, phosphokinases, phospholipases, proteases, transglutaminases, etc. There are alterations in degrees of phosphorylation of membrane components and enzymes, with resulting release of metabolic recovery reactions, alteration of membrane affinities for anions and cations, and, in general, occurrence of cascades of interdependent reactions throughout the cellular machinery. Actual physical restructuring also may take place. There may result short-term or long-term changes in the activities of neurons and in their relations to each other.

Inhibitory transmitters, which most often are liberated on dendrites close to the cell body or on the cell body itself, increase the permeability of membranes to anions (particularly chloride) and enhance resistance to depolarization. Inhibitory mechanisms accelerate the rate of return of the resting potential of all depolarized membrane segments which the transmitter contacts, and stabilize (decrease sensitivity to stimulation) undepolarized membrane segments. GABA, the major inhibitory neurotransmitter in the CNS of vertebrate organisms, typically produces an increase in membrane permeability to chloride ions that is measured as an increase in membrane conductance.

There is constant interaction among all of the excitatory and inhibitory influences that impinge on the membrane of a neuron. Many factors determine, at a particular time, whether or not the spatially and temporally summated effects of directly excitatory and disinhibitory inputs are sufficient to reduce the membrane potential to the critical level at which the all-or-none propagation of a spike discharge takes place along the axon or, in nonspiking neurons, to reduce the potential to an extent that would result in an increase in transmitter release from its terminals. In the past, neuronal circuits were considered almost entirely in terms of excitatory events. The first neurons in the circuits were presumed to be excited by some input and to pass on excitatory or depolarizing messages synaptically in such a way that there would result a progressive excitation passed from neuron to neuron, until the final neuron in the circuit would depolarize an effector cell, muscle, or gland. Inhibition was considered to play, at most, a vague modulatory role. Only within the last 30 years, since the discovery of GABA, have the major and essential roles of neural inhibition and disinhibition in nervous system function become fully recognized (Roberts, 1976, 1984).

A LEAD FROM SHAKESPEARE

Armed with the preceding highly oversimplified and impressionistic view of nervous system function, with thorough descriptions at various levels of the phenomenology of AD (Reisberg, 1983), and with the knowledge that whatever currently available theoretical or practical knowledge might be required would be available from the literature or by inquiry from colleagues worldwide, I have spent many hours searching for the threads from which to begin to weave some sort of meaningful tapestry into which would fit many of the still unconnected observations. Being chemically trained and molecularly oriented, it was not possible at an early point in the process for me to relate meaningfully to the relatively inchoate neuroarcheological findings concerning the shards found in the brains of those dying of the disease, the neurofibrillary tangles, the neuritic (senile) and amyloid plaques, and the granulovacuolar degenerations. Even the more precise observation about the essentially complete pathological interruption of the afferent and efferent pathways of the hippocampal formation (Hyman et al., 1984), a structure crucial to memory, did not afford me a suitable handle. Although major molecular insights eventually may come from work with amyloid proteins and observations on prions (Prusiner et al., 1983), one must await further developments before postulating causal relations of the latter with AD. Many have been laboring under the light cast by the findings of the relatively specific, and often severe, presynaptic cholinergic deficits that were observed early in the chemical work on AD and the subsequent tracing of this deficit to malfunction and destruction of cholinergic neurons in the basal nucleus of Meynert and the medial septum (Bartus, Dean, Pontecorvo, & Flicker, 1985). The latter, together with the minor obligatto furnished by findings of changes in some peptidic components in several brain regions in AD (Appel, 1984; Beal & Martin, 1984; Hughes, 1984), have given rise to many suggestions for clinical trials. Many preliminary trials and some relatively extensive controlled clinical studies have been performed or are in the planning stages. Together with even more empirically based clinical trials of "stimulants," the mechanisms of whose action largely are unknown, these have furnished the bulk of therapeutic endeavor to date.

However, in the end it was most useful for me to locate my "thread" by perusing repeatedly descriptions of the clinical progression of AD.

They seemed to read like an expansion of Shakespeare's concise characterization of what happens to a man from the sixth of his seven ages on to his final demise.
(from *As You Like It*):
. . .The sixth age shifts
Into the lean and slippered pantaloon,
With spectacles on nose and pouch on side,
His youthful hose well saved, a world too wide
For his shrunk shank: and his big manly voice,
Turning again toward childish treble, pipes
And whistles in his sound. Last scene of all,
That ends this strange eventful history,
Is second childishness, and mere oblivion,
Sans teeth, sans eyes, sans taste, sans everything.
Shakespeare, unparalleled genius of an observer that he was, had seen clearly that in male aging and/or AD a loss in muscle mass and other androgen-related characteristics preceded frank signs of mental deterioration.

SOME THOUGHTS ABOUT AD AND SEX HORMONES

There is a large literature on sex hormone levels as they relate to aging in human beings as well as in a number of subhuman species. For as long as they have been known, androgens and estrogens have been administered to males and females, respectively, to retard one or another feature of aging. The literature on the subject is replete with less than satisfactory measurements and experimental designs. In those instances in which documentation was adequate, problems often arose that precluded prolonged use of the hormones. Endometrial bleeding, prostatic hypertrophy, and danger of carcinogenesis have been among the several danger signs along the road. Obviously, cybernetic control mechanisms of the organism were being overwhelmed by the exogenously imposed hormonal thrusts. Recently it was reported that administration of estradiol produced some beneficial effects in selected female AD patients. However, the utility of the approach was limited by some of the above-mentioned dangers (see Fillit, this volume). It occurred to me that a better approach than to administer the sex hormones, themselves, might be to give DHEA or its sulfate DHEAS. The latter are normally occurring precursors of androgens, which in turn are precursors for estrogens. If the DHEA and DHEAS could penetrate to androgen- or estrogen-synthetic sites in the various tissues, conditions existing at such sites would determine quantities and rates of androgen and estrogen synthesis. Such hormone synthesis would be more likely to be subject to meaningful cybernetic controls. Administration of DHEA and DHEAS might not be nearly as intrusive physiologically as the administration of arbitrarily selected amounts of the hormones, themselves. The possibility exists that DHEA and DHEAS and/or intermediate metabolites on the way to androgens and estrogens also might react with special cytosolic receptors for them and exert important cellular functions. A computer search did not reveal a single reference mentioning DHEA or DHEAS and AD in the same context.

DHEA and DHEAS fit into the steroid metabolic scheme in the following fashion. The biosynthesis of steroid hormones begins with cholesterol and cholesterol sulfate, from which androgens, estrogens, progesterone, and adrenal cortical steroids all eventually derive. Pregnenolone, a key cholesterol metabolite, is a major precursor of all of the steroid hormones. Its formation is rate-limiting and is regulated by pituitary hormones, such as leutinizing hormone (LH) and follicle-stimulating hormone (FSH) in ovaries and testes and ACTH and possibly a non-ACTH pituitary hormone (Parker, Lifrak, & Odell, 1983) in the adrenals. In the human, pregnenolone goes via 17α-hydroxypregnenolone to DHEA, from which is formed the androgen, testosterone, in the testes, ovaries, adrenal cortex, and placenta. Testosterone is a precursor of the equally potent androgen, dihydrotestosterone, in the prostate, skin, hair follicles, and brain. Testosterone also is the precursor for estrogen formation by aromatization. In the female, the latter takes place largely in the ovaries, but estrogens also are formed from androgenic precursors in both males and females in other tissues, including muscle, adipose tissues, liver, and brain. The rate of estrogen formation from circulating androgens is increased in hyperthyroidism, certain forms of liver disease, and obesity; it may be decreased in some other pathological states.

DHEA and DHEAS are the most abundant steroids in blood, levels of DHEAS being far higher than those of DHEA. Serum levels of the above substances largely are determined by synthesis and secretion from the adrenal cortex, but also to a small extent from other tissues (Parker & Odell, 1980). Low serum values of DHEA and DHEAS found at birth persist through the sixth year of life and then rise abruptly at the seventh year (de Peretti & Forest, 1978). Increases continue until approximately the 16th year in both sexes, but only in males do they increase thereafter, maximal levels being attained between 20 and 24 years of age (Orentreich, Brind, Rizer, & Vogelman, 1984). From puberty on, the blood levels of men are significantly higher than those of women (at all ages from 20-69 years, $P<0.001$, by Student's t test) probably reflecting a testicular contribution to the serum pool (Orentreich et al., 1984). Perhaps most important for present consideration is the observation that progressive declines in serum concentrations in these steroids take place in both sexes at all subsequent ages, values at 70 years of age being approximately only 20% of those found at the peak (Figure 2). This appears to be unique among the classes of steroid hormones.

It is interesting to note from Figure 2 that DHEAS and DHEA levels are close to minimal at ages when the incidence of AD (sporadic form) begins to increase significantly. To my knowledge, no study comparable to the above with normal individuals has been made in patients with AD or other age-related disorders in which there is impairment of cognitive function. Onset of motoneuron disease peaks at 60-65 years (McComas, Upton, & Sica, 1973).

The fact that there is a relative lack of significant circadian, monthly, seasonal, or annual rhythmicity in serum levels of DHEA and DHEAS (Orentreich et al., 1984) suggests that their release into the blood may serve to buffer the organism against the vicissitudes of large fluctuations of these substances, which may be necessary for many important ongoing tissue functions (see below). In this light, the decreases in their serum levels with age could presage changes in metabolism in many tissues that might have far-reaching consequences. Age-related progressive decreases in serum levels of DHEA and DHEAS may reflect gradual decrements in output of pituitary hormones which control the production of pregnenolone, their precursor. The release of pituitary hormones may, in turn, be controlled by hypothalamic hormones and also by feedback inhibition by serum levels of DHEA and DHEAS and other steroids. A decreased release of LHRH from the hypothalamus, for example, could result in decreased pituitary release of LH which, in turn, could lead to a tendency to decreased formation of DHEA and DHEAS in gonadal tissue, as a result of which there might be decreased rates of formation of androgens and estrogens. However, the latter tendency might be counteracted by increases in secretion of chorionic gonadotropin.

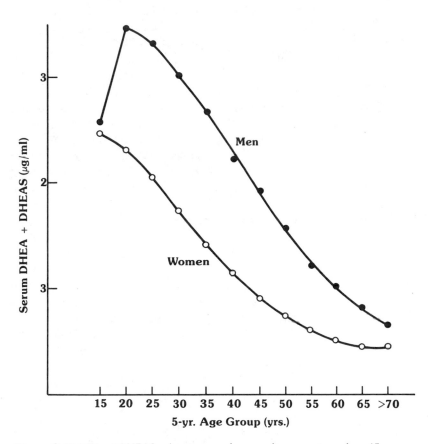

Figure 2. DHEA and DHEAS values in sera of men and women at ages from 15 years. Data replotted from values given in Table 1 of Orentreich et al., 1984.

Probably all of the above hormones act on tissues by binding to specific membrane receptors, whose activation leads, often through effects on cyclic nucleotide mechanisms, to the release of rate-limiting reactions at consequent steps of relevant cascades. Even if normal levels of hypothalamic and pituitary hormones were to be maintained with aging, the receptor sensitivity or metabolic aspects of the ensuing reaction cascade of the responding tissues might be decreased. For example, a study with aging humans showed there to be no impairment of the ability of the adrenals to respond to acute ACTH stimulation with production and secretion of Δ^4-steroids (cortisol, androstenedione, 17-hydroxyprogesterone, and pregnenolone), but there was a significant decrease in stimulatability of secretion of Δ^5-steroids (DHEA, DHEAS, 17-hydroxypregnenolone, and progesterone) (Vermeulen, Deslypere, Schelfhout, Verdonck, & Rubens, 1982). Another study showed that in older individuals (72-102 years old, average 85 years) basal levels of cortisol and aldosterone and the ACTH-stimulatability of their formation and release were essentially the same as in younger individuals (35-62 years old, average 51 years); but the basal levels of DHEA and DHEAS were significantly higher in the younger group than in the older one and no stimulation at all by ACTH of increase in serum levels of these substances was observed in the older group (Parker, Gral, Perrigo, & Skowsky, 1981). A decrease was found with aging in circulating levels of the Δ^5-androgens, DHEA and DHEAS, in postmenopausal women, while the concentrations of the Δ^4-steroids (progestins, cortisol, and estrogens) remained constant (Meldrum, Davidson, Tataryn, & Judd, 1981). The fact that in the latter instance a decrease of Δ^5- androgens was found while levels of their precursors were normal, led to the suggestion that there might be an age-related decrement in activity of 17,20 desmolase, the enzyme that converts 17β-hydroxypregnenolone to DHEA and its 3-hydroxysulfate ester to DHEAS. Thus, the data cited above show clearly that not only do the serum levels of DHEA and DHEAS fall with age similarly in both sexes, but also that the stimulatability of the release of these substances by ACTH from the adrenal cortex, their chief serum source, is markedly reduced in the aging human organism.

A definitive molecular function cannot yet be assigned to DHEA or DHEAS at the cellular level in any tissue. Only recently pregnenolone (P), its sulfate ester (PS), and DHEA and DHEAS were shown to be present in rat brain at levels much higher than those found in plasma; but experiments to date have failed to demonstrate in brain the formation of P from cholesterol or of DHEA from P (Corpechot, Robel, Axelson, Sjovall, & Baulieu, 1981; Corpechot et al., 1983; Robel et al., 1984). All of the enzymes necessary to convert PS and DHEAS to androgens and estrogens are present in brain. ^{3}H-DHEA and ^{3}H-P enter the brain after subcutaneous injection in oil, but they appear to enter into a compartment which does not equilibrate readily with most of the endogenously contained steriods. It appears that brain metabolism of DHEA and DHEAS occurs largely independently of hormonal control mechanisms of the type to which the adrenals and other peripheral tissues may be subject, since in comparison with sham-operated controls, brain levels of P, PS, DHEA, and DHEAS were not altered significantly by adrenalectomy plus orchiectomy, and levels of DHEA and DHEAS were not affected significantly by administration of ACTH or dexamethasone (Robel et al., 1984). The finding of higher levels of P and DHEA in hypothalamus and olfactory bulb than in other brain structures, the demonstration that DHEA injection inhibits aggressive behavior of castrated male mice toward lactating female intruders, and the occurrence of significant changes in content of P + PS and DHEA + DHEAS in olfactory bulb, amygdala, and hypothalamus after exposure of male rats to female siblings suggest that these substances, at the least, are related to aggressive and/or sexual behavior. Remarkable increases in DHEAS observed in the hypothalamus of males upon exposure to females suggest the possibility that the hypothalamus might liberate DHEAS into the adenohypophysis where it might serve as precursor for androgen and estrogen synthesis or as a releaser of other hormones into the circulation (Robel et al., 1984). The above substances also may have some important direct neural actions of their own. P, DHEA, and DHEAS applied directly to neurons in the septo-preoptic area of adult female guinea pigs generally exerted excitatory effects, DHEAS being effective in 39 percent of the neurons tested (Carette & Poulain, 1984). The pattern of responsivity suggested a common neural mechanism for the substances tested. Much work remains to be done to elucidate the details of membrane action of these substances, particularly the identification of ionic and/or cyclic nucleotide mechanisms that might be operative. Similarly, such studies with various types of lymphocytes may be crucial in elucidating effects of DHEA and DHEAS on immune and other mechanisms, to be discussed below.

RECYBERNETICIZING ROLES FOR DHEA AND DHEAS AND/OR THEIR METABOLITES

In pathological conditions, abnormalities arise or are induced in patterns of communication among various components within cells or among cell types that comprise the particular system being observed. Conversion of closed loop systems (cybernetically effective) to open loop ones (cybernetically ineffective) can lead to growth or to pathological manifestations at intracellular, cellular, and organismic levels. Disease is failed cybernetics. It seems to me that ideal therapy for any pathological state would be that which would alleviate inadequate intra- and intercellular communication by affecting the system in such a manner that rate-limiting chemical reactions and/or physical relationships would be returned to within an operational range which would make possible recyberneticization of the system.

DHEA and its metabolites may play such roles in diabetes, obesity, autoimmune diseases, and cancer. In the present sketchy state of affairs, in most instances it is not possible to invoke specific molecular sites of action, since they may range all the way from effects on DNS transcription to local regulation of membrane permeabilities to ions. Rather I will content myself with recounting some of the phenomenology.

DHEA and DHEAS were shown to have remarkable therapeutic effects when fed to mice with genetic or chemically induced diabetes and, under some conditions, prevented excessive weight gains in genetically obese mice (Coleman, Leiter, & Applezweig, 1984; Coleman, Leiter, & Schwizer, 1982; Coleman, Schwizer, & Leiter, 1984). Effectiveness of DHEA was modulated by the genetic background of the host. DHEA, DHEAS, and metabolites which arise from them via testosterone, α- and β-hydroxyetiocholanone and 17β-estradiol, all were found to prevent in a strain of genetically susceptible mice the development of a severe diabetes characterized by obesity, chronic hyperglycemia, relative insulinopenia coupled with severe insulin resistance, and severe necrosis of the β-cells. Since DHEA and the hydroxyetiocholanones were effective only when fed, but β-estradiol was effective on injection, and the metabolites of DHEA were effective in much smaller doses than DHEA, itself, it is possible that the beneficial effects of DHEA may be mediated by its metabolites and that metabolic conversion of DHEA to active metabolites may occur by intestinal processing. Since there appear to be synergic actions among the metabolites, it is likely that the members of the metabolic cascade arising from DHEA may exert their effects at several different rate-limiting loci in carbohydrate utilization. A particularly impressive finding was that treatment with DHEA for 4 weeks improved glucose tolerance of aged normal mice in comparison with untreated aged controls (Coleman et al., 1984).

Feeding of DHEA to rats produced remarkable reductions in body weight, in content of carcass lipid and cholesterol, and in the cellularity of adipose tissue, in comparison with controls eating similar amounts of the same diet without DHEA (Cleary, Hood, Chando, Hansen, & Billheimer, 1984; Cleary, Seidenstat, Tannen, &

Schwartz, 1982; Shepherd & Cleary, 1984; Yen, Allan, Pearson, Acton, & Greenberg, 1977). In addition to its well-known inhibition of glucose-6-phosphate dehydrogenase (G6PD), administration of DHEA has been found to increase liver activity of long chain fatty acyl-CoA hydrolase (Cleary et al., 1984). The decrease in G6PD appears to occur in instances when the activity is elevated above some basal level and suggests that the primary antiobesity effect of DHEA may be attributable to an energy wasting process, a futile cycle, such as may result when there is an increased rate of hydrolysis of long chain fatty acyl-CoA. Removal of CoA by the above hydrolase from the activated fatty acid after its formation by the energy requiring step catalyzed by fatty acyl CoA synthase wastes energy while preventing the fatty acid from entering its various metabolic pathways, among which are the syntheses of triglycerides and phospholipids. Actually, the antiobesity effects of DHEA may be a result of combinations of both of the effects mentioned above.

Both in mice (NZB/NZWF$_1$), an animal model of autoimmune disease, and humans with systemic lupus erythematosus (SLE), which is an autoimmune disorder, the nervous system is severely affected and behavioral abnormalities are observed. Although immunologically normal C57BL/6 mice exhibited increased serum levels of brain-reactive antibodies with age and eventual decreases in their ability to learn a conditioned avoidance response, NZB mice showed higher levels of such antibodies than C57BL/6 mice at all ages tested and were unable to learn the avoidance task even at 2 to 4 months of age. The above data led to the suggestion that the NZB mouse might serve as an animal model of AD (Nandy, Lal, Bennett, M., & Bennett, D., 1983). Elegant observations of a number of relevant parameters in NZB/NZWF$_1$ mice led to the suggestion "that sex hormones modulate immunologic regulation and that androgenic hormones are protective in murine lupus" (Roubinian, Papoian, & Talal, 1977). It is, therefore, of the greatest interest in the context of the present discussion that long-term administration of DHEA to NZB mice retarded the development of manifestations of the autoimmune disorder and that androgen administration seemed to be protective against the murine SLE (Schwartz, Nyce, & Tannen, 1984).

Random crosslinking of extracellular and intracellular macromolecules, making them nonfunctional and resistant to the degradation necessary for turnover and renewal long has been believed to be an important factor in the aging process (Nagy, I. & Nagy, K.,

1980). Rigidification of structural proteins could lead to a decyberneticization of intracellular and extracellular chemical communication patterns among all components of living systems. The wrinkled skin and stringy, inelastic tissues of an aging individual are overt reflections of such processes, which probably are pervasive throughout the whole organism. The insoluble debris observed in brains of aged individuals also may be an example. Collagen, the most abundant protein, makes up about 30 percent of the body protein or 6 percent of the body mass. Together with several other types of proteins and proteoglycans, it serves to make up the extracellular matrices of the body that maintain all basic structural supports. Polymers of high molecular weight and variable structures abound throughout these matrices; and many hereditary and environmentally induced disorders are known to occur as a result of one or another abnormality in these connective tissue components or in their relations to each other. Although turnover of collagen in adult organisms undoubtedly is slow, it still must occur to remove denatured debris, particularly subsequent to injury, so that regeneration can take place. Although in principle it is known that such degradation may be initiated by specific collagenases and brought to completion by a variety of extracellular and intracellular (lysosomal) proteases, virtually nothing is known of the details of the degradative processes for collagen in any particular instance. It is, therefore, of some interest that it has been found that DHEAS stimulated production of collagenase when added to culture medium containing gravid rabbit uterine cervices, but not by direct action on the uterus (Ito et al., 1984). On the other hand, DHEA and 17β-estradiol, major metabolites of DHEAS *in vivo*, depressed collagenase production. Increases in cytoplasmic DHEAS-binding protein in uterine cervices paralleled the progress of pregnancy, indicating an important role for DHEAS in cervical ripening. The latter results suggest the possibility that DHEA and DHEAS also may play coordinating roles in collagen metabolism, in general, and that they may help regulate collagen deposition and removal when it is appropriate to do so. Much is known and much more remains to be learned about the hormonal control of metabolism of proteoglycans and mucopolysaccharides. This information will not be dealt with here, except to indicate that the synthesis, degradation, polymerization, and depolymerization of these important tissue constituents are under complex sets of hormonal controls. The synthesis of hyaluronic acid in the cock's comb is increased by administration of testosterone. There is decreased ability to synthesize glucosaminoglycans in uncontrolled diabetes, which can be corrected to some extent by administration of insulin. No specific studies dealing with the effects of DHEA or DHEAS on the metabolism of the latter types of substances came to my attention.

Finally, long-term administration of DHEA to female mice of a strain susceptible to spontaneous occurrence of breast cancer not only reduced their weight gain by comparison with controls but also markedly decreased tumor formation (Schwartz, 1979). Likewise, chemical induction of lung (Schwartz & Tannen, 1981), skin (Pashko, Rovito, Williams, Sobel, & Schwartz, 1984; Pashko & Schwartz, 1983), and colon (Nyce, Magee, Hard, & Schwartz, 1984) tumors was retarded by including DHEA in the diet. The mechanisms of these effects still are not clear, although one suspects that enhanced efficacy of immunological defenses may be involved.

SOME REMARKABLE RELEVANT CLINICAL FINDINGS

The C1 inhibitor is a key protein of the extraordinarily beautifully coordinated and remarkably complex complement system of proteins in the serum. It helps regulate the assembly of the recognition unit of the classical complement pathway by preventing two constituents of this unit from proteolytically splitting the third component, C4, in an inadvertent manner and thus incoordinating the smooth functioning of the complement system in its defensive role against foreign antigens. In the course of events, C4 is split into two components, C4a and C4b. The latter (C4b) can attach covalently to cell surface structures and acts as an opsonin, increasing the phagocytic activity; the former (C4a) is an anaphylotoxin, releasing histamine from mast cells, thereby causing vasodilation and increasing vascular permeability, i.e., producing a local inflammatory response. Hereditary angioedema (HAE) is a disorder in which, among other effects, are found edema of the lungs with airway obstruction, urticaria, and intestinal swelling. In this disease there is a deficiency of the C1 inhibitor; and abnormally low levels of C1 and C4 are found in the serum of patients with this disease. The low value of C4 possibly is attributable to an accelerated rate of cleavage to C4a and C4b because of the deficiency of C1 inhibitor or to a subnormal rate of formation and/or secretion of C4. For some time it had been known that androgens improved the symptoms in individuals with this disorder; but, as might be expected, long term treatment with these substances led to many undesirable side effects. Recently, (Koo, Feher, K.G., Feher, T., & Fust, 1983) it was found that oral administration of DHEAS over a long period of time greatly improved the symptoms of all patients with HAE studied, without producing toxic side effects. DHEA, DHEAS, and C1 serum levels were not significantly altered by the treatment, but the C4 levels in the serum showed remarkable elevations, in some instances increasing 10- to 20-fold over the pretreatment levels. Although the mechanism of the effects observed still is not known, the latter is a beautiful example of the rebalancing by DHEAS of a complex malfunctioning system related to immune defenses that had been thrown out of kilter, in this instance by a genetic defect.

In searching for a marker for AD, a study was made in sera of significant numbers of patients with sporadic AD, Parkinson's disease, and in normal age-matched controls of the distribution of several proteins, all of which are controlled by genes in the histocompatibility complex (MHC) on chromosome 6 (Nerl, Mayeux, & O'Neill, 1984). The only significant difference in gene frequencies among the three groups studied was a remarkable increase in patients with sporadic AD of a rare variant of the C4 component of complement, the C4*B2 allele, and a corresponding decrease in the C4*B1 allele. The C4 system is highly polymorphic (Belt, Carroll, & Porter, 1984). This might be attributable to genetic variation in glycosylation of C4, which may be related to its cell lytic properties (Karp, Atkinson, & Shreffler, 1982). In previous studies the C4*B2 allele was associated with C4*A4 and C4*A2 alleles; but in the present one it was independent of an increase in any allele at the C4A locus, leading to the statement, "This finding suggests an involvement of the C4*B2 product itself in the etiology of AD." Although the properties of the C4*B2 variant have not yet been fully explored, it was shown to be active in erythrocyte lysis. Because of the critical role of complement in host defenses against foreign antigens and in the destruction of virus-infected or otherwise injured cells, one could speculate that, when the C4*B2 variant is present, there is enhanced destruction of such injured cells. In those instances when this variant is not present, particular combinations of variants of the several complement components in association with cell surfaces with special features might lead to a similar result. One wonders, therefore, whether in such an instance, DHEAS might be effective in interrupting the pathological progression, as in the case of HAE, no matter what the antigen, complement, and membrane relations might be. All of the pathological sequelae found in the brains of AD patients could be consequential to an exaggerated attack by components of complement on neural, glial, or endothelial cellular elements in particular regions of the brain.

CLINICAL TRIALS OF DHEA AND DHEAS IN AD ARE WARRANTED

I believe that there was no natural selection for longevity. Time's arrow always has pointed in the direction of selection of those characteristics that adapted a species to survival in its particular environment until it could at least reproduce its numbers. There may even have been selection of self-destruct mechanisms that come into play at the cessation of the reproductive period which would serve to remove such organisms from competition for limiting resources with the breeding population. It is from this perspective that the preceding discussion about the cyberneticizing roles of DHEA and DHEAS and their progressive decrements in aging makes so much sense and recommend these apparently nontoxic substances for testing as potentially prophylactic and therapeutic agents in aging and AD. They are beyond the metabolic branch point of pregnenolone, at which decisions are made as to how the subsequent metabolic flow should be fractionated between the mineralocorticoid, androgen → estrogen, and glucocorticoid pathways. In the presence of tightly coupled cybernetic control mechanisms, each of the above pathways might get all the precursor that it needs to produce sufficient quantities of the relevant substances to facilitate key processes at all levels of existence. This is what one generally would expect to see in the vigor of youth. However, under conditions of stress, real or perceived, in young or old organisms, priorities would have to be established which would first maintain essential functions for survival of an individual organism and only then for its reproductive activites. Without generation of sufficient metabolic energy and its appropriate coupling to all cellular functions, death would ensue rapidly, the nervous system being especially sensitive to such deprivation. In stress related to serious illness there is a shift in pregnenolone metabolism away from DHEA and DHEAS production to that of glucocorticoids (Parker, Levin, & Lifrak, 1985), which are acutely necessary for survival by virtue of their roles in the control of energetics. Determination made before and after surgical removal of adrenocortical adenomas in patients in whom ACTH secretion presumably was suppressed by feedback inhibition by excess serum cortisol during the presence in them of the tumors suggested that a deficiency of ACTH may result in a longer-lasting loss of the ability to secrete DHEAS than of the ability to secrete cortisol (Yamaji, Ishibashi, Sekihara, Itabashi, & Yanaihara, 1984). Although there are as yet few relevant comparative data, one might expect the mineralocorticoids to be second to the glucocorticoids in line of priority because of their role in the maintenance of the delicate ionic balances between the cellular and extracellular environments which, after detachment from the placenta, are so essential for mammalian life either on the ionically unfriendly surfaces of the earth or in the depths of the sea. Survival in states of ionic imbalance may be longer than when energy supplies become limiting. The last in the line of priorities would be the androgen → estrogen pathway, since reproductive activities tend to be much more attenuated, being crucial for the survival of the species, but not at all for any particular individual. Although many mechanisms for establishment of priorities are conceivable, the simplest would be if the enzyme which converts pregnenolone to 17α-hydroxypregnenolone, the first substance on the pathways to cortisol and DHEA, were to have a higher affinity for pregnenolone than the enzyme that converts the latter to progesterone, the first substance on the path to aldosterone, and if, similarly, the conversion of 17α-hydroxypregnenolone to cortisol were more facile than conversion to DHEA. Although, to my knowledge, data for making such direct comparisons still are not available for any particular tissue, evidence suggests that the 17,20-desmolase, the enzyme catalyzing the formation of DHEA from 17α-hydroxypregnenolone, may become rate-limiting under some circumstances. When chemical and neural signals are broadcast within an organism, and to it from its environment, that its reproductive period is coming to an end, there may be initiated the sequence of events that leads to decreases in levels of DHEA and DHEAS in serum and tissues. The consequently progressive incoordination in metabolism and in communication patterns among the cellular elements of the immune networks may hasten the final demise of the organism.

Even though there are vast lacunae in our knowledge of the functions of DHEA and DHEAS, it is apparent that these substances and the substances for which they serve as precursors can affect many processes that are known to go awry in normal aging and in AD.

It will be important to determine whether or not returning DHEA and DHEAS serum levels toward those observed at younger ages, and, therefore, increasing their availability for many tissues, will reverse some of the symptoms observed in AD and/or prevent their progression. In the successful clinical study of the effects of DHEAS in hereditary angioneurotic edema cited above (Koo et al., 1983), oral doses up to 74 mg were given every other day or every 3 days for 3-29 months with no ill effects reported. In the latter instance, significant elevations of the levels of DHEA and DHEAS in serum were not achieved, even when clinical improvement was noted.

POTASSIUM CHANNELS IN MEMBRANES AND AD

My attention first was directed to the role of K^+ channels in AD because it occurred to me that there are behavioral parallels, albeit with a vastly different time course, between the sequences of events in the progression of AD and those observed at successive stages of general anesthesia. In both instances it is likely that decreases in the release of neurotransmitters and possibly changes in the responsivities of receptive sites to their effects result in progressive incoordinations in nervous system function, which eventually could lead to total loss of capacity of the nervous system to process information and to the demise of the organism, viz., communication between cells falls to a meaningless level.

Intracellular recordings from motoneurons and hippocampal pyramidal cells indicated that general anesthetics hyperpolarize vertebrate central neurons by increasing K^+ channels in open configurations, with potencies and in concentrations that correspond to those producing anesthesia in intact organisms (Nicoll & Madison, 1982). The roles of K^+ channels and their importance in the sequences of membrane events involved in all neural activities, from conduction of the nerve impulse to controlling transmitter release, have been briefly alluded to before and cannot be discussed in detail here (see Hille, 1984, for discussion). Suffice it to say that the ability of the membrane of a particular cell, neural or non-neural, to integrate metabolically the chemical and physical signals which it receives and to respond in manner reflecting their nature and intensity, be it by release of transmitter, enzyme, hormone, or antibody or by contraction or mitosis, minimally requires a critically orchestrated interaction of K^+ channels with the other membrane events that occur. Some K^+

channels are voltage-gated, others are sensitive to intracellular Ca^{2+} concentrations, and others may be regulated by still other means. Not only do changes in the distributions of numbers and types of channels in membranes of cells take place during development (Baud & Barish, 1984), but they differ in cells of different tissues and probably from cell to cell within a tissue. Changes in K^+ channels may be involved in plastic changes that occur at synapses in learning (Kandel, 1979) and in the "tuning" of neural elements to each other when particular combinations of nerve circuits must participate together in solving problems. K^+ channels may be important targets for hormones and neuromodulators. The rates of production and degradation of K^+ channel components must be integrated with the extent and types of ongoing cellular activities, and the rate of transcription of the appropriate genes must be adjusted accordingly. Mutations in K^+ channels already have been described in *Drosophila* (Jan, Y.N., & Jan, L.Y., 1977; Jan, L.Y. et al., 1983; Salkoff, 1983), and there is no reason to doubt that multiple alleles and mutations will be found for different K^+ channel proteins in higher organisms. The suggestion that the latter might, indeed, be the case comes from recent experiments in which the K^+ channels in T lymphocytes of two congenic strains of mice are being characterized, differing from each other at a single genetic locus which develop a lymphoproliferative disorder resembling SLE. Lymphocytes from mice of these two strains were found to differ markedly from each other with regard to their expression of K^+ channel properties under several test conditions (deCoursey et al., 1985).

In view of the above, if I were a saboteur with the assignment of producing an initially subtle and subsequently progressive debilitation of individuals, such as one sees in aging and in AD, I would choose to devise agents or conditions which gradually would attack irreversibly a key aspect of K^+ channel function. The surest way would be to gradually decrease the capability for genetic transcription of major K^+ channel components, so that the ability of cells to adjust to changing conditions progressively would be lost. From this all else could flow, so that eventually cells in the organism and, thus, the organism, itself, would collapse like Oliver Wendell Holmes' "one-hoss shay." Two major paths, or combinations of them, to wreak the required damage would be possible. One would be to inactivate the pertinent genes by virus-like agents, by chemical means, or by irradiation; and another would be to gradually decrease the availability or efficacy of substances, such as DHEA and DHEAS or some of the adrenal steriods that derive from them which may be necessary for achieving optimally coordinated rates of transcription of pertinent genes. The latter road may be the one to "normal" aging, while a combination of both may be what happens in AD. In this way normal aging processes and AD generally would be coextensive, but AD would have some special characteristics.

There is evidence that steroid-receptor complexes may modulate gene expression by binding to DNA sites near promoter regions (Groner et al., 1984; Bourgeois, Pfahl, & Baulieu, 1984; Pfahl, McGinnis, Hendricks, Groner, & Hynes, 1983). Let us then suppose that ligand-receptor complexes formed by naturally occurring androgen-related steriods with appropriate receptors might be competing with toxic entities (free radicals, alkylating agents, viruses, etc.) for attachment to DNA sites relevant to the transcription of genes for K^+ channel components and that affinities of the DNA for the steroid-receptor complexes would be decreased or destroyed if the toxic entities were to attack the DNA sites first. The probability of inactivation of such DNA sites by the toxic entities would be less in the presence of a plethora of the pertinent steroids and their receptors in the environment than when their levels would be lower or absent, as in aging. Following successful attack on such loci by the toxic materials, there could be a loss of hormone-inducible transcription, i.e., there would be a loss of hormonal responsivity and, therefore, control. In most instances, with the exception of malignant cells, this would be expected to lead to decreased adaptability and viability of the affected cells. But in a tissue with regenerative capacity such as liver, the situation might be mitigated by enhanced division of unaffected cells so that eventually the aboriginal state of a tissue prior to the genetic injury might be reestablished. In the case of the nervous system, this would be possible for non-neural elements in it, such as glial and endothelial cells and fibroblasts, but not for neurons because the latter usually do not undergo mitosis in mature organisms. For the nervous system, and therefore for the organism as a whole, the course would be downhill all of the way, only the rate of decline varying from one circumstance to another. For neurons whose role is to receive, integrate, and transmit signals on a millisecond time scale and to adapt to changing circumstances with plastic changes, e.g., glutamatergic or GABAergic neurons, it would be of little use to regenerate lost cell processes, reestablish synapses, etc. if they no longer could produce the array of K^+ channel proteins (or other ion channel proteins) necessary to perform their highly demanding roles. It would not help the performance of an opera singer with a failed voice to be in otherwise fine physical condition. The best defense in the latter circumstance would be to remove such neurons from the circuits of which they are members and to replace them with healthy redundant ones, in which young nervous systems seem to abound. However, in the case of neurons and neuronal systems whose functions are less subtle and critical with regard to timing and amounts of transmitter liberated, such as the noradrenergic and cholinergic ones may be, there might be great utility in fostering regeneration and even in attempting replacement by transplantation, as long as the new neurons would retain some degree of excitability and could release their respective messengers tonically in a continuous fashion as a result of passive inward depolarizing ionic currents which are followed automatically by repolarization, even in the absence of reestablishment of informational connections. Because of the latter possibility, currently there is more hope of achieving some meaningful therapies in conditions in which release of neural modulators, viz., dopamine in Parkinson's disease or ACh in AD, becomes rate-limiting than when mainline transmitters such as GABA and glutamate are affected (Daniloff, Wells, & Ellis, 1984; Dravid & Van Deusen, 1984; Freed et al., 1980; Gahwiler & Brown, 1985; Kromer, Bjorklund, & Stenevi, 1980, 1981). Strategies are difficult to conceive for effectively substituting for GABA-ergic cells such as the Purkinje cells of the cerebellar cortex, the hippocampal basket cells, or neurons of the reticular nucleus of the thalamus or for the glutamatergic cells that project from the entorhinal cortex to the hippocampus.

PHARMACOLOGICAL SUPPORT FOR THE K^+ CHANNEL IDEA

In view of my original conjectures about the similarity between AD and general anesthesia and their possible convergence at effects on K^+ channels, it was of great interest for me to discover that there already exists a large literature dealing with a K^+ channel blocker, 4-aminopyridine (4AP) (Soni & Kam, 1982), the administration of which rapidly overcomes the effects of general anesthesia (Booth,

Hatch, & Crawford, 1982; Hatch, Booth, Kitzman, Wallner, & Clark, 1983; Martinez-Aguirre & Crul, 1979; Wallner et al., 1982) and which may improve symptoms in some patients with AD (Wesseling et al., 1984). Tetrahydroaminoacridine (THA) a structurally related substance that has shown ameliorative effects in AD (Summers, Kaufman, Altman, & Fischer, 1980; Summers, Viesselman, March, & Candelora, 1981), possesses anticholinesterase activity (Albin, Bunegin, Massopust, Jr., & Jannetta, 1974) but probably exerts its main effects by blocking K^+ channels (Roberts, unpublished). 4AP and THA may be prototypic of a class of drugs that block voltage-gated K^+ channels in cells in many regions of the body, from brain to lymphocyte. What is fascinating about substances that block voltage-gated K^+ channels is that they may heighten potentialities for meaningful communication in a debilitated CNS, while at the same time decreasing proliferative (Chandy, deCoursey, Cahalan, McLaughlin, & Gupta, 1984) and cytotoxic (Fukushima, Hagiwara, & Henkart, 1984) activities of T lymphocytes. These are precisely the directions in which one would wish to move if one were to attempt to reverse some of the effects observed in aging or AD, provided one could restore the balance in the optimal fashion without pushing the CNS toward the seizure state and the immune system into a state of such ineffectiveness that it could lead to increased liability to infection, malignancy, or autoimmune reactions. As in most pharmacological studies, one has to contend with the inverted U phenomenon, the desired effect reaching a maximum at a given dose and then declining at some higher doses. Since the dose-response curves for the neural and immunological effects of K^+ channel blockers are not likely to be the same, a more sophisticated balancing of dose might be required than if only one effect was being considered.

Results from experiments ranging from those with intact animals to isolated nerve terminals and from receptors to the cortex and thence to the neuromuscular junction, only some of which can be cited here, are consistent with the interpretation that 4AP can enhance the release of all neurotransmitters and neuromodulators as a result of blocking K^+ channels at all levels of the CNS (Agoston, Hargittai, & Nagy, 1983; Buckle & Haas, 1982; Casamenti, Corradetti, Loffelhoz, Mantovani, & Pepeu, 1982; Dolezal & Tucek, 1983; Edvinsson, Hardebo, & Lundh, 1981; Jankowska, Lundberg, Rudomin, & Sykova, 1982; Laskey, Schondorf, & Polosa, 1984; Murray, N.M.F., & Newsom-Davis, 1981; Saade, Banna, Khoury, Jabbur,

& Wall, 1982; Tapia & Sitges, 1982; Thomson & Wilson, 1983). 4AP partially reversed the behavioral deficit produced by anoxia in mice (Gibson, Pelmas, & Peterson, 1983). I would like to suggest that it would be worthwhile to study similarly a number of the "stimulants" already being examined for efficacy in AD, such as Hydergine, centrophenoxine, and piracetam and related nootropic agents. The data in the literature are consistent with the idea that the latter substances, and possibly others such as quinine and quinacrine, may exert K^+ channel blocking effects. If such studies are to be performed, I would like to suggest that the most direct and quantitative methods possible be employed, preferably at the membrane level, so that efficacies can be compared rapidly and structure-activity relations optimized.

It has been known for some time that soon after stimulation by phytohemagglutinin there is stimulation of the uptake of K^+, and recently it has been demonstrated that voltage-gated K^+ channels must be opened for the activation of human T lymphocytes to take place in the presence of phytohemagglutinins or alloantigens (Cahalan, Chandy, deCoursey, & Gupta, 1985; Chandy et al., 1984). Metabolic events consequent to activation, such as DNA and protein synthesis, including interleukin-2 production, were inhibited by 4AP, quinine, and other K^+ channel blockers (Chandy et al., 1984). Attachment of mitogenic monoclonal antibodies to unstimulated cells increased the K^+ current almost twofold (Matteson & Deutsch, 1984). Interestingly, verapamil, a substance employed clinically because of its Ca^{2+} channel blocking action, was the most potent of the substances tested both with regard to blockade of voltage-gated K^+ currents and inhibition of mitogenesis (Chandy et al., 1984). Congruent with the latter was the finding that acute verapamil poisoning in cats, characterized by profound cardiovascular depression and neuromuscular blockade, was completely reversed by administration of 4AP at a time when extremely high concentrations of verapamil still were present in the blood (Agoston et al., 1984). Arecoline, a cholinomimetic stimulant present in the much-used betel preparations in India and other countries of the East, which probably inhibits K^+ channels in the same manner as does ACh, inhibits both humoral and cell-mediated responses in mice (Shahabuddin & Rao, 1980). It is possible that such immunosuppressive effects may work hand-in-glove with some carcinogenic components of betelquid to contribute to the high incidence of oral and oropharyngeal cancers that occur in India.

PCP, originally proposed as an anesthetic, is a potent psychotomimetic drug in man, the abuse of which has attained epidemic proportions. It has a number of effects on the CNS and on behavior. Administration of PCP to monkeys increased the neuronal activity as well as responsivity to sensory stimuli in the posterior parietal association cortex. In the rat it produced increased turnover of ACh in the frontal and parietal cortices in the diencephalon, but not in the striatum or hippocampus (Murray, T.F., & Cheney, 1981). The latter suggests that PCP activates the cholinergic system of the brain stem and basal forebrain but not the indigenous cholinergic circuitry of the striatum nor the medial septal neurons that give rise to the septohippocampal cholinergic inputs. Physiological experiments suggest that PCP is a K^+ channel blocker, whatever other effects it may have (Albuquerque, Aguayo, Warnick, Ickowicz, & Blaustein, 1983). PCP also has been found to be an immunodepressant in several *in vitro* tests with B and T lymphocytes and to inhibit production of interleukin 1 by activated monocytes (Khansari, Whitten, & Fudenberg, in press). The latter defect was corrected by the *in vitro* addition of piracetam, which in separate studies had been shown to improve memory and learning ability, to accelerate hippocampal release of ACh (Wurtman, Magil, & Reinstein, 1981), to facilitate cortical activation (Nikolova, Tsikalova, Nikolov, & Taskov, 1979), and to increase cerebral blood flow (Nikolova et al., 1979), among other effects. All of the latter could be consequential to activation of the brain stem cholinergic system or could be exerted independently by K^+ channel blockade at relevant sites. Finally, it has been reported that some defects were found in T cell function in *in vitro* tests in approximately one third of a group of AD patients and that only in those patients with the *in vitro* defects was marked clinical improvement noted upon administration of piracetam (Fudenberg et al., 1984).

THERAPEUTIC IMPLICATIONS

The empirical conclusions from the foregoing considerations are straightforward. If the ideas are correct, administration of DHEA and/or DHEAS alone or in suitable combinations with 4AP, THA, or other K^+ channel blockers should help reestablish communications within and between bodily systems that are cybernetically subnormally effective or completely ineffective in aging individuals with and without AD. Restoration of function could be expected to take place to the extent that there are sufficient numbers of potentially operational units remaining in rate-limiting systems (neural, endocrine, immunological, circulatory, etc.). Further deterioration of critical aspects of the system might be halted if grossly pathological relationships could be corrected by the treatment, e.g., rebalancing the adjustment between the nature and extent of cellular injury and the destructive potential of the immunological defense systems. It is unlikely that specific therapies for familial and sporadic forms of AD will be devised until the causes, genetic or environmental, are known. However, the currently suggested approaches might yield therapies of some value and are worthy of testing.

The problems with which we are dealing are particularly difficult because they relate not only to molecular and cellular properties but also to emergent properties of the whole system, such as memory, cognition, and the like. Since we do not possess the Rosetta Stones for the languages of intracellular, intercellular, and intersystem communication networks in the human organism, it behooves us to recognize the improbability of finding a magic bullet. It is not likely that a penicillin-like cure for AD will be found, unless AD turns out to be an infectious process or is found to be caused by a specific toxic substance.

REFERENCES

Agoston, D., Hargittai, P., & Nagy, A. (1983). Effects of a 4-aminopyridine in calcium movements and changes of membrane potential in pinched-off nerve terminals from rat cerebral cortex. *Journal of Neurochemistry, 41,* 745-751.

Agoston, S., Maestrone, E., van Hezik, E.J., Ket, J.M., Houwertjes, M.C., & Uges, D.R.A. (1984). Effective treatment of verapamil intoxication with 4-aminopyridine in the cat. *Journal of Clinical Investigation, 73,* 1291-1296.

Albin, M.S., Bunegin, L., Massopust, L.C., Jr., & Jannetta, P.J. (1974). Ketamine-Induced postanesthetic delirium attenuated by tetrahydroaminoacridine. *Experimental Neurology, 44,* 126-129.

Albuquerque, E.X., Aguayo, L.G., Warnick, J.E., Ickowicz, R.K., & Blaustein, M.P. (1983). Interactions of phencyclidine with ion channels of nerve and muscle: Behavioral implications. *Federation Proceedings, 42,* 2584-2589.

Appel, S.H. (1984). Neuropeptides and Alzheimer's disease: Potential role of neurotrophic factors. In R.J. Wurtman, S.H. Corkin, & J.H. Growdon (Eds.), *Alzheimer's disease: advances in basic research and therapies* (pp. 275-291). London: Center for Brain Sciences and Metabolism Charitable Trust.

Bartus, R.T., Dean, R.L., Pontecorvo, M.J., & Flicker, C. (1985). The cholinergic hypothesis: A historical overview, current perspective and future directions. *Annals of the New York Academy of Sciences, 444,* 332-358.

Baud, C., & Barish, M.E. (1984). Changes in membrane hydrogen and sodium conductances during progesterone-induced maturation of ambystoma oocytes. *Developmental Biology, 105,* 423-434.

Beal, M.F., & Martin, J.B. (1984). Somatostatin: Normal and abnormal observations in the central nervous system. In R.J. Wurtman, S.H. Corkin, & J.H. Growdon (Eds.), *Alzheimer's disease: Advances in basic research and therapies* (pp. 229-257). London: Center for Brain Sciences and Metabolism Charitable Trust.

Belt, K.T., Carroll, M.C., & Porter, R.R. (1984). The structural basis of the multiple forms of human complement component C4. *Cell, 36,* 907-914.

Ben-Ari, Y., Dingledine, R., Kanazawa, I., & Kelly, J.S. (1976). Inhibitory effects of acetylcholine on neurones in the feline nucleus reticularis thalami. *Journal of Physiology, 261,* 647-671.

Bennett, M.V.L., & Goodenough, D.A. (1978). Gap junctions, electrotonic coupling, and intercellular communication. *Neurosciences Research Program Bulletin, 16,* 373-486.

Bondareff, W., Mountjoy, C.Q., & Roth, M. (1982). Loss of neurons of origin of the adrenergic projection to cerebral cortex (nucleus locus ceruleus) in senile dementia. *Neurology, 32,* 164-168.

Booth, N.H., Hatch, R.C., & Crawford, L.M. (1982). Reversal of the neuroleptanalgesic effect of droperidolfentanyl in the dog by 4-aminopyridine and naloxone. *American Journal of Veterinary Research, 43,* 1227-1231.

Bourgeois, S., Pfahl, M., & Baulieu, E.-E. (1984). DNA binding properties of glucocorticosteroid receptors bound to the steroid antagonist RU-486. *EMBO Journal, 3,* 751-755.

Brayden, J.E., & Bevan, J.A. (1985). Neurogenic muscarinic vasodilation in the cat. An example of endothelial cell-independent cholinergic relaxation. *Circulation Research, 56,* 205-211.

Breitner, J.C.S., & Folstein, M.F. (1984). Familial Alzheimer dementia: A prevalent disorder with specific clinical features. *Psychological Medicine, 14,* 63-80.

Buckle, P.J., & Haas, H.L. (1982). Enhancement of synaptic transmission by 4-aminopyridine in hippocampal slices of the rat. *Journal of Physiology, 326,* 109-122.

Cahalan, M.D., Chandy, K.G., DeCoursey, T.E., & Gupta, S. (1985). A voltage-gated potassium channel in human T lymphocytes. *Journal of Physiology, 358,* 197-237.

Carette, B., & Poulain, P. (1984). Excitatory effect of dehydroepiandrosterone, its sulphate ester and pregnenolone sulphate, applied by iontophoresis and pressure, on single neurones in the septopreoptic area of the guinea pig. *Neuroscience Letters, 45,* 205-210.

Casamenti, F., Corradetti, R., Loffelhoz, K., Mantovani, P., & Pepeu, G. (1982). Effects of 4-aminopyridine on acetylcholine output from the cerebral cortex of the rat *in vivo. British Journal of Pharmacology, 76,* 439-445.

Chandy, K.G., DeCoursey, T.E., Cahalan, M.D., McLaughlin, C., & Gupta, S. (1984). Voltage-Gated potassium channels are required for human T lymphocyte activation. *Journal of Experimental Medicine, 160,* 369-385.

Cleary, M.P., Hood, S.S., Chando, C., Hansen, C.T., & Billheimer, J.T. (1984). Response of sucrose-fed BHE rats to dehydroepiandrosterone. *Nutrition Research, 4,* 485-494.

Cleary, M.P., Seidenstat, R., Tannen, R.H., & Schwartz, A.G. (1982). The effect of dehydroepiandrosterone on adipose tissue cellularity in mice (41511). *Proceedings of the Society for Experimental Biology and Medicine, 171,* 276-284.

Coleman, D.L., Leiter, E.H., & Applezweig, N. (1984). Therapeutic effects of dehydroepiandrosterone metabolites in diabetes mutant mice (C57BL/KsJ-db/db). *Endocrinology, 115,* 239-243.

Coleman, D.L., Leiter, E.H., & Schwizer, R.W. (1982). Therapeutic effects of dehydroepiandrosterone (DHEA) in diabetic mice. *Diabetes, 31,* 830-833.

Coleman, D.L., Schwizer, R.W., & Leiter, E.H. (1984). Effect of genetic background on the therapeutic effects of dehydroepiandrosterone (DHEA) in diabetes-obesity mutants and in aged normal mice. *Diabetes, 33,* 26-32.

Cook, R.H., Schneck, S.A., & Clark, D.B. (1981). Twins with Alzheimer's disease. *Archives of Neurology, 38,* 300-301.

Corpechot, C., Robel, P., Axelson, M., Sjovall, J., & Baulieu, E.-E. (1981). Characterization and measurement of dehydroepiandrosterone sulfate in rat brain. *Proceedings of the National Academy of Sciences, USA, 78,* 4704-4707.

Corpechot, C., Synguelakis, M., Talha, S., Axelson, M., Sjovall, J., Vihko, R., Baulieu, E.-E., & Robel, P. (1983). Pregnenolone and its sulfate ester in the rat brain. *Brain Research, 270,* 119-125.

Daniloff, J.K., Wells, J., & Ellis, J. (1984). Cross-species septal transplants: Recovery of choline acetyltransferase activity. *Brain Research, 324,* 151-154.

deCoursey, T.E., Chandy, K.G., Fischbach, M., Talal, N., Gupta, S., & Cahalan, M.D. (1985). Two types of K channels in T lymphocytes from MRL mice. *Biophysical Journal, 47,* 387a.

dePeretti, E., & Forest, M.G. (1978). Pattern of plasma dehydroepiandrosterone sulfate levels in humans from birth to adulthood: Evidence for testicular production. *Journal of Clinical Endocrinology and Metabolism, 47,* 572-577.

Dingledine, R., & Kelly, J.S. (1977). Brain stem stimulation and the acetylcholine-evoked inhibition of neurones in the feline nucleus reticularis thalami. *Journal of Physiology, 271,* 135-154.

Dolezal, V., & Tucek, S. (1983). The effects of 4-aminopyridine and tetrodotoxin on the release of acetylcholine from rat striatal slices. *Naunyn-Schmiedebergs Archives of Pharmacology, 323,* 90-95.

Dravid, A.R., & Van Deusen, E.B. (1984). Recovery of enzyme markers for cholinergic terminals in septo-temporal regions of the hippocampus following selective fimbrial lesions in adult rats. *Brain Research, 324,* 119-128.

Edvinsson, L., Hardebo, J.E., & Lundh, H. (1981). Action of 4-aminopyridine on the cerebral circulation. *Acta Neurologica Scandinavica, 63,* 122-130.

Foote, S.L., Bloom, F.E., & Aston-Jones, G. (1983). Nucleus locus ceruleus: New evidence of anatomical and physiological specificity. *Physiological Reviews, 63,* 844-914.

Freed, W.J., Perlow, M.J., Karoum, F., Seiger, A., Olson, L., Hoffer, B.J., & Wyatt, R.J. (1980). Restoration of dopaminergic function by grafting of fetal rat substantia nigra to the caudate nucleus: Long-term behavioral, biochemical, and histochemical studies. *Annals of Neurology, 8,* 510-519.

Fudenberg, H.H., Whitten, H.D., Arnaud, P., Khansari, N., Tsang, K.Y., & Hames, C.G. (1984). Immune diagnosis of a subset of Alzheimer's disease with preliminary implications for immunotherapy. *Biomedicine and Pharmacotherapy, 38,* 290-297.

Fukushima, Y., Hagiwara, S., & Henkart, M. (1984). Potassium current in clonal cytotoxic T lymphocytes from the mouse. *Journal of Physiology, 351,* 645-656.

Gahwiler, B.H., & Brown, D.A. (1985). Functional innervation of cultured hippocampal neurones by cholinergic afferents from co-cultured septal explants. *Nature, 313,* 577-579.

Gibson, G.E., Pelmas, C.J., & Peterson, C. (1983). Cholinergic drugs and 4-aminopyridine alter hypoxic-induced behavioral deficits. *Pharmacology, Biochemistry and Behavior, 18,* 909-916.

Goudsmit, J., White, B.J., Weitkamp, L.R., Keats, B.J.B., Morrow, C.H., & Gajdusek, D.C. (1981). Familial Alzheimer's disease in two kindreds of the same geographic and ethnic origin. *Journal of the Neurological Sciences, 49,* 79-89.

Groner, B., Ponta, H., Rahmsdorf, U., Herrlich, P., Pfahl, M., & Hynes, N.E. (1984). Glucocorticoid hormone interactions with cloned proviral DNA of mouse mammary tumor virus. *Journal of Steroid Biochemistry, 20,* 95-98.

Hatch, R.C., Booth, N.H., Kitzman, J.V., Wallner, B.M., & Clark, J.D. (1983). Antagonism of ketamine anesthesia in cats by 4-aminopyridine and yohimbine. *American Journal of Veterinary Research, 44,* 417-423.

Heston, L.L., & Mastri, A.R. (1977). The genetics of Alzheimer's disease. Associations with hematologic malignancy and Down's syndrome. *Archives of General Psychiatry, 34,* 976-981.

Heyman, A., Wilkinson, W.E., Hurwitz, B.J., Schmechel, D., Sigmon, A.H., Weinberg, T., Helms, M.J., & Swift, M. (1983). Alzheimer's disease: Genetic aspects and associated clinical disorders. *Annals of Neurology, 14,* 507-515.

Hille, B. (1984). *Ionic channels of excitable membranes.* Sunderland, MA: Sinauer Associates, Inc.

Houser, C.R., Vaughn, J.E., Barber, R.P., & Roberts, E. (1980). GABA neurons are the major cell type of the nucleus reticularis thalami. *Brain Research, 200,* 341-354.

Hughes, J. (1984). Strategies for manipulating peptidergic transmission. In R.J. Wurtman, S.H. Corkin, & J.H. Growdon (Eds.),

Alzheimer's disease: Advances in basic research and therapies (pp. 259-273). London: Center for Brain Sciences and Metabolism Charitable Trust.

Hyman, B.T., Van Hoesen, G.W., Damasio, A.R., & Barnes, C.L. (1984). Alzheimer's disease: Cell-specific pathology isolates the hippocampal formation. *Science, 225,* 1168-1170.

Ito, A., Sano, H., Ikeuchi, T., Sakyo, K., Hirakawa, S., & Mori, Y. (1984). Effect of dehydroepiandrosterone sulfate on collagenase production in rabbit uterine cervix culture. *Biochemical Medicine, 31,* 257-266.

Jan, L.Y., Barbel, S., Timpe, L., Laffer, C., Salkoff, L., O'Farrell, P., & Jan, Y.N. (1983). Mutating a gene for a potassium channel by hybrid dysgenesis: An approach to the cloning of the *Shaker* locus in *Drosophila.* In *Cold Springs Harbor Symposia on Quantitative Biology, 48* (Pt. 2), 233-245.

Jan, Y.N., & Jan, L.Y. (1977). Two mutations of synaptic transmission in *Drosophila. Proceedings of the Royal Society of London:* (Series B. Biological Sciences), *198,* 87-108.

Jankowska, E., Lundberg, A., Rudomin, P., & Sykova, E. (1982). Effects of 4-aminopyridine on synaptic transmission in the cat spinal cord. *Brain Research, 240,* 117-129.

Kandel, E.R. (1979). Cellular insights into behavior and learning. *Harvey Lectures Series, 73,* 19-92.

Karp, D.R., Atkinson, J.P., & Shreffler, D.C. (1982). Genetic variation in glycosylation of the fourth component of murine complement. Association with hemolytic activity. *Journal of Biological Chemistry, 257,* 7330-7335.

Khansari, N., Whitten, H.D., & Fudenberg, H.H. (1984). Phencyclidine induced immunodepression. *Science, 225,* 76-78.

Koo, E., Feher, K.G., Feher, T., & Fust, G. (1983). Effect of dehydroepiandrosterone on hereditary angioedema. *Klinische Woch, 61,* 715-717.

Kromer, L.F., Bjorklund, A., & Stenevi, U. (1980). Innervation of embryonic hippocampal implants by regenerating axons of cholinergic septal neurons in the adult rat. *Brain Research, 210,* 153-171.

Kromer, L.F., Bjorklund, A., & Stenevi, U. (1981). Regeneration of the septohippocampal pathways in adult rats is promoted by utilizing embryonic hippocampal implants as bridges. *Brain Research, 210,* 173-200.

Laskey, W., Schondorf, R., & Polosa, C. (1984). Effects of 4-aminopyridine on sympathetic preganglionic neuron activity. *Journal of the Autonomic Nervous System, 11,* 201-206.

Martinez-Aguirre, E., & Crul, J.F. (1979). Effect of tetrahydroaminoacridine and 4-aminopyridine on recovery from ketamine-diazepam anesthesia in the maccacus rhesus monkey. *Acta Anaesthesiologica Belgica, 30,* 231-238.

Matteson, D.R., & Deutsch, C. (1984). K channels in T lymphocytes: A patch clamp study using monoclonal antibody adhesion. *Nature, 307,* 468-471.

McComas, A.J., Upton, A.R.M., & Sica, R.E.P. (1973). Motoneurone disease and ageing. *Lancet, 2,* 1477-1480.

Meldrum, D.R., Davidson, B.J., Tataryn, I.V., & Judd, H.L. (1981). Changes in circulating steroids with aging in postmenopausal women. *Obstetrics and Gynecology, 57,* 624-628.

Miyakawa, T., Shimoji, A., Kuramoto, R., & Higuchi, Y. (1982). The relationship between senile plaques and cerebral blood vessels in Alzheimer's disease and senile dementia. *Virchows Archiv. B. Cell Pathology, 40,* 121-129.

Murray, N.M.F., & Newsom-Davis, J. (1981). Treatment with oral 4-aminopyridine in disorders of neuromuscular transmission. *Neurology, 31,* 265-271.

Murray, T.F., & Cheney, D. L. (1981). The effect of phencycldine on the turnover rate of acetylcholine in various regions of rat brain. *Journal of Pharmacology and Experimental Therapeutics, 217,* 733-737.

Nagy, I.ZS., & Nagy, K. (1980). On the role of cross-linking of cellular proteins in aging. *Mechanisms of Ageing and Development, 14,* 245-251.

Nandy, K., Lal, H., Bennett, M., & Bennett, D. (1983). Correlation between a learning disorder and elevated brain-reactive antibodies in aged C57BL/6 and young NZB mice. *Life Sciences, 33,* 1499-1503.

Nee, L.E., Polinsky, R.J., Eldridge, R., Weingartner, H., Smallberg, S., & Ebert, M. (1983). A family with histologically confirmed Alzheimer's disease. *Archives of Neurology, 40,* 203-208.

Nerl, C., Mayeux, R., & O'Neill, G.J. (1984). HLA-Linked complement markers in Alzheimer's and Parkinson's disease: C4 variant

(C4B2) a possible marker for senile dementia of the Alzheimer type. *Neurology, 34,* 310-314.

Nicoll, R.A., Alger, B.E., & Jahr, C.E. (1980). Enkephalin blocks inhibitory pathways in the vertebrate CNS. *Nature, 287,* 22-25.

Nicoll, R.A., & Madison, D.V. (1982). General anesthetics hyperpolarize neurons in the vertebrate central nervous system. *Science, 217,* 1055-1057.

Nikolova, M., Tsikalova, R., Nikolov, R., & Taskov, M. (1979). Simultaneous investigation of the cerebral circulation and cortical bioelectrical activity in dogs under the influence of piracetam. *Methods and Findings in Experimental and Clinical Pharmacology, 1,* 97-104.

North, R.A., & Egan, T.M. (1984). Actions of acetylcholine on the membrane of single brain neurones. In R.J. Wurtman, S.H. Corkin, & J.H. Growdon (Eds.), *Alzheimer's disease: Advances in basic research and therapies* (pp. 145-159). London: Center for Brain Sciences and Metabolism Charitable Trust.

Nyce, J.W., Magee, P.N., Hard, G.C., & Schwartz, A.G. (1984). Inhibition of 1,2-dimethylhydrazine-induced colon tumorigenesis in Balb/c mice by dehydroepiandrosterone. *Carcinogenesis, 5,* 57-62.

Orentreich, N., Brind, J.L., Rizer, R.L., & Vogelman, J.H. (1984). Age changes and sex differences in serum dehydroepiandrosterone sulfate concentrations throughout adulthood. *Journal of Clinical Endocrinology and Metabolism, 59,* 551-555.

Parker, L., Gral, T., Perrigo, V., & Skowsky, R. (1981). Decreased adrenal androgen sensitivity to ACTH during aging. *Metabolism, 30,* 601-604.

Parker, L.N., Levin, E.R., & Lifrak, E.T. (1985). Evidence for adrenocortical adaptation to severe illness. *Journal of Clinical Endocrinology and Metabolism, 60,* 947-953.

Parker, L.N., Lifrak, E.T., & Odell, W.D. (1983). A 60,000 molecular weight human pituitary glycopeptide stimulates adrenal androgen secretion. *Endocrinology, 113,* 2092-2096.

Parker, L.N., & Odell, W.D. (1980). Control of adrenal androgen secretion. *Endocrine Reviews, 1,* 392-410.

Pashko, L.L., Rovito, R.J., Williams, J.R., Sobel, E.L., & Schwartz, A.G. (1984). Dehydroepiandrosterone (DHEA) and 3β-methylandrost-5-en-17-one: Inhibitors of 7,12-dimethylbenz[a]anthracene (DMBA)-initiated and 12-0-tetradecanoylphorbol-13-acetate (TPA)-

promoted skin papilloma formation in mice. *Carcinogenesis, 5,* 463-466.

Pashko, L.L., & Schwartz, A.G. (1983). Effect of food restriction, dehydroepiandrosterone, or obesity on the binding of ^{3}H-7,12-dimethylbenz(a)anthracene to mouse skin in DNA. *Journal of Gerontology, 38,* 8-12.

Pfahl, M., McGinnis, D., Hendricks, M., Groner, B., & Hynes, N.E. (1983). Correlation of glucocorticoid receptor binding sites on MMTV proviral DNA with hormone inducible transcription. *Science, 222,* 1341-1343.

Prusiner, S.B., McKinley, M.P., Bowman, K.A., Bolton, D.C., Bendheim, P.E., Groth, D.F., & Glenner, G.G. (1983). Scrapie prions aggregate to form amyloid-like birefringent rods. *Cell, 35,* 349-358.

Reisberg, B. (Ed.). (1983). *Alzheimer's disease. The standard reference.* New York: The Free Press.

Robel, P., Corpechot, C., Synguelakis, M., Groyer, A., Clarke, C., Schlegel, M.L., Brazeau, P., & Baulieu, E.E. (1984). Pregnenolone, dehydroepiandrosterone, and their sulfate esters in rat brain. In F. Celotti et al. (Eds.). *Metabolism of hormonal steroids in the neuroendocrine structures* (pp. 185-194). New York: Raven Press.

Roberts, E. (1976). Disinhibition as an organizing principle in the nervous system — The role of the GABA system. Application to neurologic and psychiatric disorders. In E. Roberts, T.N. Chase, & D.B. Tower (Eds.), *GABA in nervous system function* (pp. 515-539). New York: Raven Press.

Roberts, E. (1981). A speculative consideration on the neurobiology and treatment of senile dementia. In T. Crook & S. Gershon (Eds.), *Strategies for the development of an effective treatment for senile dementia* (pp. 247-320). New Canaan, CT: Mark Powley Associates, Inc.

Roberts, E. (1982). Potential therapies in aging and senile dementias. In F. Marott Sinex & C.R. Merril (Eds.), *Alzheimer's disease, Down's syndrome, and aging* (pp. 165-178). New York: New York Academy of Sciences.

Roberts, E. (1983). Alcoholism — A speculative view from the bridge. In *Alcohol and Protein Synthesis: Ethanol, Nucleic Acid, and Protein Synthesis in the Brain and Other Organs* (pp. 221-295). Proceedings of a Workshop October 24-25, 1980, Long Beach, CA sponsored by National Institute on Alcohol Abuse and Alcoholism College of Medicine, University of California at Irvine. Res. Monograph No. 10. DHHS Publication No. (ADM) 83-1198.

Roberts, E. (1984). GABA-Related phenomena, models of nervous system function, and seizures. *Annals of Neurology, 16* (Suppl), S77-S89.

Roberts, E., & Matthysse, S. (1970). Neurochemistry: At the cross-roads of neurobiology. *Annual Review of Biochemistry, 39,* 777-820.

Roubinian, J.R., Papoian, R., & Talal, N. (1977). Androgenic hormones modulate autoantibody responses and improve survival in murine lupus. *Journal of Clinical Investigation, 59,* 1066-1070.

Saade, N.E., Banna, N.R., Khoury, A., Jabbur, S.J., & Wall, P.D. (1982). Cutaneous receptive field alterations induced by 4-amino-pyridine. *Brain Research, 232,* 177-180.

Salkoff, L. (1983). Genetic and voltage-clamp analysis of a *Droso-phila* potassium channel. *Cold Spring Harbor Symposia on Quan-titative Biology, 48* (Pt. 2), 221-231.

Scheibel, A.B. (1980). Anatomical and physiological substrates of arousal: A view from the bridge. In J.A. Hobson & M.A.B. Brazier (Eds.), *The reticular formation revisited* (pp. 55-66). New York: Raven Press.

Schwartz, A.G. (1979). Inhibition of spontaneous breast cancer for-mation in female C3H (A^{vy}/a) mice by long-term treatment with dehydroepiandrosterone. *Cancer Research, 39,* 1129-1132.

Schwartz, A.G., Nyce, J.W., & Tannen, R.H. (1984). Inhibition of tumorigenesis and autoimmune development in mice by dehydroepi-androsterone. *Modern Aging Research, 6,* 177-184.

Schwartz, A.G., & Tannen, R.H. (1981). Inhibition of 7,12-dimethyl-benz[a]anthracene- and urethan-induced lung tumor formation in A/J mice by long-term treatment with dehydroepiandrosterone. *Car-cinogenesis, 2,* 1335-1337.

Scremin, O.U., Rovere, A.A., Raynald, A.C., & Giardini, A. (1973). Cholinergic control of blood flow in the cerebral cortex of the rat. *Stroke, 4,* 232-239.

Shahabuddin, S., & Rao, A.R. (1980). Effect of arecoline on the humoral and cell mediated immune responses in mice. *Indian Journal of Experimental Biology, 18,* 1493-1494.

Shepherd, A., & Cleary, M.P. (1984). Metabolic alterations after de-hydroepiandrosterone treatment in Zucker rats. *American Journal* of Physiology, 246 (2 Part 1), E123-E128.

Soni, N., & Kam, P. (1982). 4-Aminopyridine — A review. Anaesthesia and Intensive Care, 10, 120-126.

Steriade, M., Ropert, N., Kitsikis, A., & Oakson, G. (1980). Ascending activating neuronal networks in midbrain reticular core and related rostral systems. In J.A. Hobson & M.A.B. Brazier (Eds.), The reticular formation revisited (pp. 125-167). New York: Raven Press.

Summers, W.K., Kaufman, K.R., Altman, F., Jr., & Fischer, J.M. (1980). THA — A review of the literature and its use in treatment of five overdose patients. Clinical Toxicology, 16, 269-281.

Summers, W.K., Viesselman, J.O., Marsh, G.M., & Candelora, K. (1981). Use of THA in treatment of Alzheimer-like dementia: Pilot study in twelve patients. Biological Psychiatry, 16, 145-153.

Tapia, R., & Sitges, M. (1982). Effect of 4-aminopyridine on transmitter release in synaptosomes. Brain Research, 250, 291-299.

Taylor, C.P., & Dudek, F.E. (1984). Excitation of hippocampal pyramidal cells by an electrical field effect. Journal of Neurophysiology, 52, 126-142.

Thomsen, R.H., & Wilson, D.F. (1983). Effects of 4-aminopyridine and 3,4-diaminopyridine on transmitter release at the neuromuscular junction. Journal of Pharmacology and Experimental Therapeutics, 227, 260-265.

Vermeulen, A., Deslypere, J.P., Schelfhout, W., Verdonck, L., & Rubens, R. (1982). Adrenocortical function in old age: Response to acute adrenocorticotropin stimulation. Journal of Clinical Endocrinology and Metabolism, 54, 187-191.

Wallner, B.M., Hatch, R.C., Booth, N.H., Kitzman, J.V., Clark, J.D., & Brown, J. (1982). Complete immobility produced in dogs by xylazine-atropine: Antagonism by 4-aminopyridine and yohimbine. American Journal of Veterinary Research, 43, 2259-2265.

Weitkamp, L.R., Nee, L., Keats, B., Polinsky, R.J., & Guttormsen, S. (1983). Alzheimer disease: Evidence for susceptibility loci on chromosomes 6 and 14. American Journal of Human Genetics, 35, 443-453.

Wenk, H., Bigl, V., & Meyer, U. (1980). Cholinergic projections from magnocellular nuclei of the basal forebrain to cortical areas in rats. Brain Research Reviews, 2, 295-316.

Wesseling, H., Agoston, S., Van Dam, G.B.P., Pasma, J., DeWitt,

D.J., & Havinga, H. (1984). Effects of 4-aminopyridine in elderly patients with Alzheimer's disease. *New England Journal of Medicine, 310,* 988-989.

Whitehouse, P.J., Price, D.L., Clark, A.W., Coyle, J.T., & DeLong, M.R. (1981). Alzheimer disease: Evidence for selective loss of cholinergic neurons in the nucleus basalis. *Annals of Neurology, 10,* 122-126.

Wurtman, R.J., Magil, S.G., & Reinstein, D.K. (1981). Piracetam diminishes hippocampal acetylcholine levels in rats. *Life Sciences, 28,* 1091-1093.

Yamaji, T., Ishibashi, M., Sekihara, H., Itabashi, A., & Yanaihara, T. (1984). Serum dehydroepiandrosterone sulfate in Cushing's syndrome. *Journal of Clinical Endocrinology and Metabolism, 59,* 1164-1168.

Yen, T.T., Allan, J.A., Pearson, D.V., Acton, J.M., & Greenberg, M.M. (1977). Prevention of obesity in A^{vy}/a mice by dehydroepiandrosterone. *Lipids, 12,* 409-413.

Preventive Approaches to Normal Brain Aging and Alzheimer's Disease

Philip W. Landfield, PhD

The general charge to chapter authors was to consider current research directions that might lead to the development of new treatment strategies for Alzheimer's disease (AD). This chapter briefly reviews long-term animal experiments from our laboratory, since the chronic treatment paradigms employed in such experiments seem potentially relevant to the development of preventive therapies against brain decline. That is, in these studies pharmacological or physiological treatments are maintained in aging rats for prolonged periods (e.g., 6 to 10 months), and it is then determined whether the rate of brain aging (as assessed on a multi-variable index) has been retarded. The experiments are designed to test a critical prediction of any causal hypotheses of brain aging, namely, that altering a putative etiological process of brain aging for prolonged periods should be able to reduce neurobiological correlates of brain aging (cf. Landfield, 1978, 1981a). The treatments must be maintained for extended durations since evidence of an effect on etiological factors depends upon the delayed appearance of a gradual biological process (brain aging).

As described below, our studies in rodents have indicated that the rate of mammalian brain aging is not immutable and it, therefore, seems feasible that chronic treatment paradigms could have therapeutic as well as basic science implications. However, such therapeutic implications clearly depend on whether the processes of rodent brain aging share some mechanisms in common with those of human brain aging and/or AD. Because of this fundamental consideration, the complex issue of the relationship of brain aging in animal models to human age-related brain decline is also briefly considered here.

There are at least three broad categories of therapeutic approaches to major neuropathological syndromes, including a) replacement therapies (e.g., pharmacologic administration of deficient chemical substances, transplantation of tissues with the capacity to synthesize deficient substances, compensatory activation of impaired or alternate systems, etc.); b) regrowth or regenerative therapies; and c) preventive therapies in which the onset or the progression of pathology is prevented or retarded.

The possibility of developing a replacement therapy for AD has attracted considerable attention in recent years and is currently the focus of intense research activity. This interest has, of course, been given an important impetus by recent advances in the study of cholinergic deficits in AD (e.g., see reviews in the present volume and in Bartus, Dean, Beer, & Lippa, 1982; Corkin, Davis, Growdon, Usdin, & Wurtman, 1982; Coyle, Price, & DeLong, 1983; Davies, 1981) and in neural transplantation research (cf. review in Gash, Collier, & Sladek, 1985). Although increasing evidence indicates that at least several transmitter systems are severely affected in AD (cf. Corkin et al., 1982; and chapters by Whitehouse or Winblad, this volume), cholinergic systems appear to be among the most susceptible and may be affected particularly early in the course of AD. Thus, a therapeutic approach in which cholinergic activity and the activity of other transmitter systems is increased pharmacologically or by transplant seems to hold considerable promise. Such strategies have, of course, been successful in the treatment of some of the manifestations of Parkinson's disease or, in a nonneural context, of diabetes.

Regenerative approaches (e.g., in which the affected systems are trophically stimulated to exhibit at least partial recovery) are also stimulating substantial current interest although further basic advances in the understanding of factors that govern development or regeneration in specific systems, and selective cell-cell recognition, are still necessary before these approaches yield treatment strategies (cf. Appel, 1984; Cotman, this volume).

Preventive and retardant approaches to the treatment of AD or brain aging have, as yet, received little consideration. However, the concomitant application of some preventive/retardant therapy may prove to be a requisite for the effective application of replacement treatments. That is, the pathological course of AD is so rapid and inexorable (cf. reviews in Corkin et al., 1982; Katzman, Terry, & Bick, 1978) that it may only be possible to successfully exploit replacement therapies if progression of the disease can be concurrently slowed. The limited success of precursor replacement therapy to date has been generally attributed to the rapid course of cholinergic neuron deterioration and the inability of these neurons to utilize transmitter precursors (e.g. Corkin et al., 1982). Thus, while the continued development of replacement therapies will obviously be necessary, retardant therapy may also be of particular value in a pathological condition such as AD, in which the rate of disease progression appears to overwhelm attempts to remediate.

While few would dispute the virtues of prevention, such approaches generally depend upon an understanding of the underlying etiology and the etiology of AD is, of course, not yet understood. As noted earlier, clear evidence of an etiological contribution of a process to a disease generally requires evidence that the disease can be blocked by experimental alteration of that process. AD has, as yet, been found only in humans and, considering ethical and health concerns, extensive intervention studies in normal humans or incipient AD subjects will be difficult.

NORMAL BRAIN AGING IN ANIMAL MODELS: IMPLICATIONS FOR ALZHEIMER'S DISEASE

Clearly an animal model of AD would be highly valuable for studies on the development of preventive therapies. However, other species are not known to spontaneously develop AD. Experimentally induced animal models seem likely to prove of value in the development of replacement therapies although an animal model of etiological factors in AD cannot, by definition, be one in which the investigator induces an analogous deficit with an electrolytic, chemical, or surgical lesion. More relevant to the development of preventive strategies, perhaps, are animal models of AD that are induced by the administration of suspected etiological factors (e.g., aluminum, viruses, etc.) (e.g., Merz et al., 1984; Perl, Gajdusek, Garruto, Yanagihara, & Gibbs, 1982; Wisniewski, Morentz, & Lossinsky, 1981) although conclusive evidence on the etiological basis of AD has, of course, not yet been found.

Another major potential source of animal models for the development of therapies in AD, which is widely overlooked, is the population of normally aging animals. Whether there is a relationship of normal brain aging to AD is a question that may well be critical to the development of preventive therapies in AD; however, it is also one that is highly controversial. Views on this issue range from those that maintain that AD is simply the quantitative extreme of normal brain aging to those that completely discount any influence of brain aging on AD and maintain that the two conditions are completely separate entities.

The main evidence in support of the view that AD and brain aging are related arises from observations that the topographical and cellular patterns of pathology seen in normal brain aging in humans are qualitatively very similar to those seen in AD (cf. Katzman et al., 1978; Tomlinson & Henderson, 1976; Wisniewski & Terry, 1973) and that AD is more frequent in the elderly. Conversely, the extreme quantitative (and a few qualitative) differences in pathology found between AD and brain aging, and the lack of universality of AD among the elderly, provide the main arguments against an association of the two phenomena.

Nevertheless, it seems highly unlikely that the patterns of cellular pathology (e.g., plaques, tangles, granulovacuolar degeneration, etc.) and topographical pathology (e.g., major pathology in neocortex and hippocampus, some subcortical pathology, etc.) could be so similar in the two conditions without the existence of some common underlying factor. If one were to calculate the probability of two unrelated pathological entities sharing six or seven major pathological symptoms out of a presumed universe of many dozens of possible neuropathological symptoms, the likelihood of such overlap occurring solely by chance would clearly be extremely small and well below the level at which we would generally accept a statistically significant rejection of a chance event.

Thus, it seems likely that there is some association, if only in the sense that separate etiological factors may act on a common final pathway of degeneration in the two conditions. We have suggested elsewhere (Landfield, Pitler, & Applegate, 1984) that the basis for the qualitative similarities may lie in the induction of a form of "runaway" brain aging by the genetic, physiological, or exogenous factors that underlie the etiology of AD. That is, in this view, the manifestations of AD reflects the activation and acceleration of the normal "machinery" of brain aging but the underlying cause depends upon the intervention of an etiological factor beyond those seen in normal aging. Moreover, as normal brain aging progresses, it appears to increase its own susceptibility to the intervention of this additional etiological process.

Other hypotheses can no doubt explain the qualitative similarity and vast quantitative disparity between normal brain aging and AD, as well as the increased probability of developing AD with age. At this point, however, the above view appears able to account for most observations and thus may serve as a useful framework for a consideration of whether animal models of normal brain aging might prove relevant in the development of preventive strategies for AD.

It may appear paradoxical that normal brain aging is proposed here as a model for studying the prevention of AD, while at the same time it is proposed that AD results in part from an etiological mechanism not found in normal brain aging. However, if AD results from acceleration of the causal chain that normally drives brain aging, then it might be possible to interrupt this causal sequence of deterioration by retarding brain aging processes, regardless of the factors that have induced these processes. Moreover, knowing the causal sequence of events in brain aging should provide important clues to the site of action and the nature of the Alzheimer's etiological factor. Furthermore, if brain aging does in fact increase susceptibility to this factor, then retarding brain aging should retard the development of susceptibility and thereby, perhaps, interrupt an accelerating positive feedback loop between increasing susceptibility and increasing pathology.

In sum, if the above views are approximately correct, then developing the means to retard normal brain aging might well also provide a method for inhibiting the processes through which the AD etiological factors induce their effects and might reduce the aspects of brain aging that apparently increase the brain's susceptibility to AD.

Of course, the etiological mechanisms of a complex biological process such as brain aging are likely to prove substantially more intricate than those that are specific to AD. Nevertheless, the availability of animal models of normal brain aging at least enables us to conduct the long-term experimental intervention studies that seem critical to studies of etiology and, therefore, to the development of preventive or retardant therapies. Thus, such animal models present an opportunity to define the effects of potentially relevant agents before attempting to apply them in humans.

In addition to the question of whether normal human brain aging is related to AD, the issue of whether animal models of normal brain aging are relevant to normal human brain aging is also not a simple one. That is, the overt patterns of age-related brain decline both differ in a number of respects and exhibit some common properties across mammalian species. However, this question has been discussed extensively elsewhere (Landfield, 1981a, 1982; National Academy of Sciences, 1981) and only a few basic conclusions are briefly summarized here. The similarity of general, nonneural aging patterns across mammalian species (e.g., development, sexual maturity, declining reproductive and physiological capacity, onset of pathology, etc.) suggests that common mechanisms of nonneural aging are shared by essentially all mammalian species. With specific regard to brain aging, however, those manifestations of brain aging that are similar across species may reflect common underlying processes, whereas those that differ may reflect species-specific adaptations or the interactions of such adaptations with common underlying mechanisms of brain aging.

Thus, if at least some common mechanisms of brain aging are shared by mammalian species and if AD does in some way depend upon the acceleration of normal brain aging processes in humans (both of which possibilities are certainly consistent with present evidence), then the study of animal models of normal brain aging should prove extremely valuable to the eventual treatment of AD.

Finally, it should be noted that although AD is obviously a catastrophic illness and a major social health problem, the subtle influences of normal brain aging affect many more individuals than do the extreme consequences of AD. These subtle but deleterious effects in our most experienced individuals (e.g., the elderly) may also represent a major loss to both the individual and society. Therefore, therapies that can influence normal brain aging as well as AD may have an impact well beyond that of treating AD alone.

CONCEPTUAL ISSUES IN LONG-TERM ETIOLOGICAL STUDIES

In our studies of the complex causal factors that modulate normal brain aging, my laboratory has, as noted, focused on the development of long-term intervention paradigms and quantitative indices of brain aging. These approaches enable us to determine whether a chronic treatment can retard the course of age-dependent brain alteration thereby enabling us to test critical predictions deriving from specific etiological hypotheses. As noted, such long-term treatments are essential in studies of factors that cumulatively modulate a gradual process such as brain aging.

In studies of the rat we operationally define long-term as chronic intervention studies of longer than 6 months (e.g., comprising more than 20% of the animal's life span). However, studies involving this large a fraction of the life span are impractical in humans, and longer-term human studies will most likely have to utilize compromise durations (e.g., 1-5 years).

Despite the ability of chronic treatment paradigms to answer questions that cannot be addressed in shorter studies, several conceptual problems arise in such experiments. Among these are (a) systemic administration of an agent (which is generally the only feasible approach in long-term studies) provides little information on the site or mechanism of action of the agent and therefore makes interpretation of the agent's effect somewhat difficult; and (b) apparent retardation of brain aging by a treatment may not be specific to aging processes and the effect may instead be mediated by inhibition of general pathology or by stimulation of non-age-related trophic processes (cf. Landfield, 1981b; 1982).

Of course, the above mentioned issues address basic science problems rather than the therapeutic concerns of primary interest to the present symposium. From the standpoint of human health, it is not essential to know precisely how or where a treatment acts if that treatment is able to retard age-related brain decline (and, of course, does not induce other major pathology). In any case, some of the above problems can be substantially reduced by using an index of multiple measures of brain aging such that a relatively unique profile of age-related change can be assessed (i.e., that is unlikely to be associated with a general pathology not related to age) (cf. Landfield, 1982).

MEASUREMENT OF BRAIN AGING IN LONG-TERM PARADIGMS

Among the key elements in any attempt to study methods of altering the course of age-related brain decline is the development of sensitive measures of neurobiological age. Obviously, we will be unable to assess the effectiveness of any agent or treatment unless we can detect subtle alterations in the degree of brain aging. The term "subtle" should be emphasized since it is clear that the normally aged brain is not massively deteriorated. Average young-aged differences on many variables may only range from 20% to 30% and there is considerable variability among aged animals in the degree of age-related change they exhibit. In fact, a substantial percentage of aged animals overlap with the young groups on any given index of brain aging.

Thus, because brain aging changes are subtle and variable and since all quantitative neurobiological measures of course contribute additional error variance, the systematic measurement of brain aging presents considerable problems. Beyond this, however, the measurement of experimentally induced changes (which may well be only partial) in these modest age-related differences presents still more formidable problems.

These issues have been discussed elsewhere in more detail (Landfield, 1982) and in this section our approaches to these problems are only briefly described. There is a long history of anatomical and behavioral studies of brain aging changes and many of the indices we use to assess brain aging in chronic studies derive from these disciplines. For a number of reasons, however, not the least of which was a lack of standardized, healthy aged animals, much of the early reported work on brain morphologic correlates of aging has become controversial.

Therefore, to systematically assess brain aging in a well-defined and restricted brain system we have undertaken extensive morphometric studies of field CA1 of the hippocampus in large numbers of barrier-reared, infection-free Fischer rats (see Figure 1). The hippocampus appears to be a useful model structure for these studies because of its extensive involvement in normal brain aging and AD and because of its association with complex information processing and memory storage functions. Moreover, it has been widely used as a neurobiological model system because of the distinct lamination of its cellular and fiber systems.

Quantitative electron and light microscopic studies are extremely time-consuming and a single ultrastructural study may require the quantitative assessment of 5 to 8 variables on up to 1,500 separate electron micrographs to reliably detect the subtle and variable changes that occur in brain aging. Thus, group sizes must be sufficient for detecting both age and treatment effects and numerous micrographs must be analyzed from each animal. In addition, since ultrastructural or even light microscopic variables differ considerably across very small distances in the brain, it is critical that micrographs be shot from as precisely the same region in each animal as possible and that extremely careful trimming and sectioning procedures be employed. Similarly, age-dependent behavioral differences are also subtle and can only be detected on certain tasks and with careful measurement approaches.

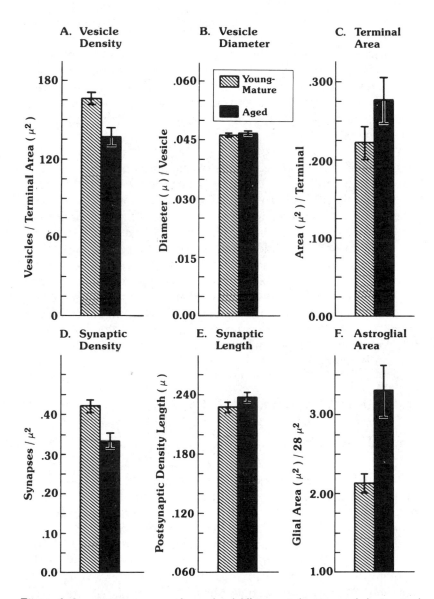

Figure 1. Quantitative measures of age-related differences in hippocampal ultrastructural variables. Data were obtained from a highly restricted region of CA1 pyramidal cell apical dendrites, in the zone of greatest density of Schaffer-commissural afferent terminals. Among the most consistent age changes seen in three replications of such analyses is the decrease in synaptic density (D). Since the size of axon terminals (C) and of postsynaptic density length (E) tends to increase with age, smaller synapses cannot account for the age-related decrease in synaptic density. Data from Applegate, Campbell, and Landfield (1984).

To date, we have primarily employed electrophysiological methods only for studies of underlying mechanisms of functional brain changes; however, some of the observed neurophysiological alterations have now been found with sufficient consistency to apparently permit their use as standard measures of the degree of brain aging. As with morphological and behavioral changes, however, neurophysiological age changes are subtle and require careful, quantitative analyses for their detection.

In sum, it can be noted that measurements of brain aging and of the effects of long-term treatments on brain aging require the systematic quantitative analysis of brain tissue from relatively large numbers of animals, preferably using multidisciplinary indices. Moreover, because the normal aged brain does not exhibit massive deterioration, the procedures must be sensitive and reliable enough to allow the detection of subtle differences.

Finally, it should be noted that long-term studies with aging animals require that substantial precautions be taken to prevent infection since it is well-established that disease can alter measures of brain aging and the aged animals are, of course, highly susceptible to infection. Animals in these studies are therefore maintained behind air barrier systems, only handled under very clean conditions and only treated with sterile needles.

STUDIES ON ETIOLOGICAL FACTORS

Adrenal Steroids

The possibility that adrenal steroids participate in the aging process was suggested by early studies of the accelerated aging and death of Pacific salmon, who die on first spawning from massive hyperadrenocorticism. Further, elevated glucocorticoids appear to accelerate age-like pathology in the cardiovascular system (Wexler, 1976).

With regard to the brain, the hippocampus contains essentially the highest concentration of corticosterone receptors among brain structures (McEwen, Gerlach, & Micco, 1975) and, as noted earlier, is severely affected by age-related pathology.

Thus, it seemed possible that corticosteroids might contribute to aging of the brain by exerting a gradual, cumulative effect on brain aging, even at normal steroid levels (e.g., brain aging could be a byproduct of the normal physiological effects of corticosteroids).

Moreover, if this were the case, then brain aging should be accelerated by prolonged elevation of glucocorticoid activity and retarded by prolonged reduction of such activity (cf. Landfield, 1978).

Correlational studies can provide an initial test of the likelihood that a process participates in brain aging. We conducted such studies and found that plasma corticosterone, or adrenal weight, were correlated with a quantitative index of hippocampal morphological aging (reactivity of astrocytes) (Landfield, Waymire, & Lynch, 1978). Further, at least in this strain of rats, plasma corticosteroids were found to increase with age.

With these initial results, we undertook several long-term studies of the effects of chronically altering plasma glucocorticoids on light microscopic indices of brain aging (e.g., Landfield, Baskin, & Pitler, 1981; Landfield, Wurtz, Lindsey, & Lynch, 1979). These studies yielded further evidence consistent with the hypothesis that glucocorticoids modulate some aspects of brain aging.

In particular, the evidence that prolonged adrenalectomy (e.g., 7 to 9 months) in mid-aged rats retarded the development of several (but not all) indices of brain aging indicated that even normal levels of plasma corticosteroids contribute to some aspects of brain aging. Conceptually analogous studies have also been conducted in ovariectomized rats by other investigators, and the results suggest that aging of the arcuate nucleus can be reduced by reducing estrogenic stimulation of that region (cf. Schipper, Brawer, Nelson, Felicio, & Finch, 1981).

We have, in addition, carried out electron microscopic studies (Landfield, Applegate, & Pitler, 1982) that indicate long-term adrenalectomy can also alter ultrastructural correlates of brain aging, although this treatment does not apparently influence all electron microscopic correlates of aging.

Thus, these results indicate that altering circulating steroid activity influences some aspects of brain aging in rats. As noted above, however, such data do not provide direct information on the pathway and site of the effects. That is, altering glucocorticoids in turn alters many other physiological systems and, of course, also leads to an elevation in adrenocorticotrophic hormone (ACTH). Since ACTH-related peptides exert direct influences on behavior and brain neurochemistry (Gispen, van Ree, & deWied, 1977) and have been examined for efficacy in treating Alzheimer's patients (see below), the elevation of ACTH could be one indirect route through which glucocorticoid alterations might affect brain aging.

However, recent studies by Sapolsky, Krey, and McEwen (1985) have shed important light on this subject since they indicate that the hippocampal cells lost with aging appear to be those that contain significant concentrations of corticosterone receptors. These latter studies, therefore, provide evidence of a direct effect of steroids on hippocampal neuronal aging.

Neuropeptides and Neural Stimulants

To examine the possibility that the elevation in ACTH might be partly responsible for effects on brain aging, we conducted long-term studies in which ORG 2766, an analog of $ACTH_{4-9}$, was administered to mid-aged rats five times weekly for approximately 9 months. Two weeks after the cessation of ORG 2766 administration we assessed reversal maze learning performance and a number of light microscopic variables.

In addition, ACTH-related peptides had been found to have some neural stimulant activity and neural activation alone has been reported to exert some trophic activity. We therefore administered subconvulsive doses of the well-established neural stimulant pentylenetetrazol (PTZ) to a parallel group of aging rats in order to determine whether PTZ-induced effects might be similar to those of ORG 2766.

As shown in Figure 2, ORG 2766 and PTZ both retarded development of several light microscopic indices of brain aging in rats, as did chronic adrenalectomy. Moreover, the drugs retarded the age-related decline in maze reversal learning. However, the profiles of the peptide and stimulant effects were different from those of the adrenalectomy effect, suggesting that peptides (perhaps through stimulant actions) and steroids may each exert an independent and somewhat opposite effect on brain aging correlates.

Both ORG 2766 and PTZ have been previously studied in relatively short-term experiments for efficacy in AD but only modest effects have been seen (cf. reviews in Berger & Tinklenberg, 1981; Ferris, 1981). However, as noted earlier, severely affected Alzheimer's subjects may be highly refractory to any therapy and chronic treatments may act by different mechanisms than do acute treatments.

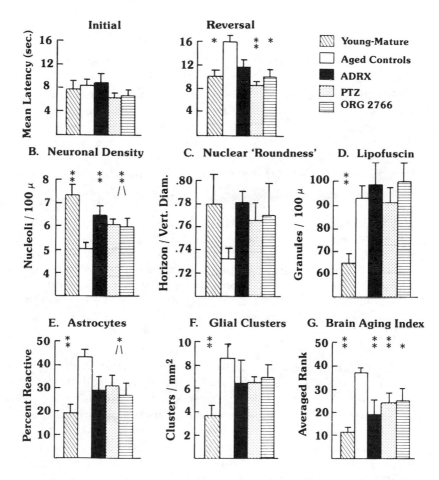

A. Maze Learning

Figure 2. Means (± S.E.M.) of behavioral and morphologic variables following 9 months of chronic treatment. A: The age-dependent behavioral impairment, indicated by elevated latency, is confined to the reversal phase of the maze learning task. Both the ORG 2766 and the PTZ groups, but not the adrenalectomized animals, performed significantly better than aged controls. G: Composite index incorporating variables shown individually (in B, C, E and F). The PTZ and ORG 2766 groups exhibited similar profiles and the two drugs may act by related mechanisms. Therefore, these two groups were combined for statistical analyses on the individual morphologic variables (but not on behavioral measures or on the composite index). Significance level of difference from aged controls: **p .01, *p .05 (two-tailed). From Landfield, Baskin, and Pitler (1981); with permission of the A.A.A.S.

The Role of Calcium in Brain Aging

One of the more consistent functional deficits we have seen in neurophysiological studies is an age-related impairment in hippocampal frequency potentiation (the growth in neural potentials during repetitive synaptic stimulation) (Landfield, McGaugh, & Lynch, 1978; Landfield & Morgan, 1984; Landfield, Pitler, Applegate, & Robinson, 1983). Frequency potentiation is a fundamental form of neural plasticity, and we have also found evidence that its impairment is relevant to impaired behavioral plasticity in aged animals (Landfield & Morgan, 1984).

In addition, we found that the deficit in frequency potentiation can be counteracted in aged animals by raising extracellular magnesium, either in vitro (Landfield, 1981b) or in vivo (Landfield & Morgan, 1984) (Figure 3). Moreover, the latter treatment improves maze reversal learning in aged rats (Figure 4).

Since Mg^{2+} is a well-established competitive inhibitor of the synaptic actions of Ca^{2+}, these results suggested that Ca^{2+} might be relatively elevated in hippocampal neurons of aged rats. In addition, this view was consistent with a growing interest in the hypothesis that elevated Ca^{2+} is important in brain aging (cf. Khachaturian, 1984).

In a more direct test of this possibility, we utilized intracellular recording in hippocampal slices to examine the afterhyperpolarizations (AHPs) that follow an intracellularly induced burst of action potentials. These AHPs are known to result from an increase in Ca^{2+}-dependent K^+ conductance and to be uncontaminated by other conductances.

As shown in Figure 5, we found that the AHPs and associated conductance increases were substantially prolonged in aged rat slices (Landfield & Pitler, 1984). Moreover, the AHPs were similarly prolonged in high Ca^{2+} and greatly reduced in high Mg^{2+}. Thus, these and other neurophysiological data (e.g., Landfield et al., 1983) as well as data from other laboratories (Khachaturian, 1984; Michaelis, Johe, & Kitos, 1984; Peterson & Gibson, 1983) are consistent with the view that Ca^{2+} homeostasis is altered in aged rat brain, and that such alteration may impair neurophysiological and behavioral functions. Further, it has also been found that elevated Ca^{2+} can accelerate the disintegration of intracellular structure and the nerve cells themselves (cf. Schlaepfer & Hasler, 1979).

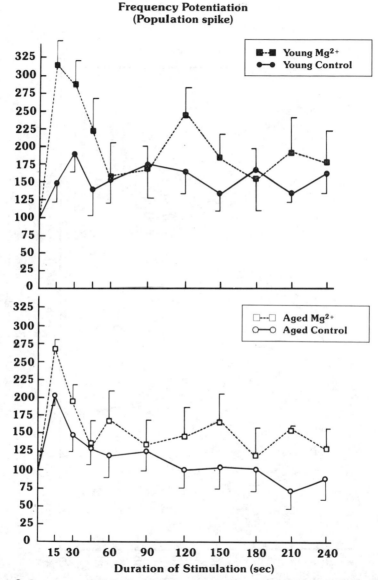

Figure 3. Group mean (± S.E.M.) of CA1 population spike amplitude (percent of control) during a 4 min train of 7 Hz Schaffer-commissural stimulation, in urethane-anesthetized rats. Upper graph shows the effect of high plasma Mg^{2+} on frequency potentiation of the spike in young animals and the lower graph shows a similar effect in aged animals. The major action of Mg^{2+} was on maximal spike amplitude during 7 Hz, although spike maintenance during prolonged stimulation was also enhanced by Mg^{2+} in aged animals. From Landfield and Morgan (1984); with permission of Elsevier.

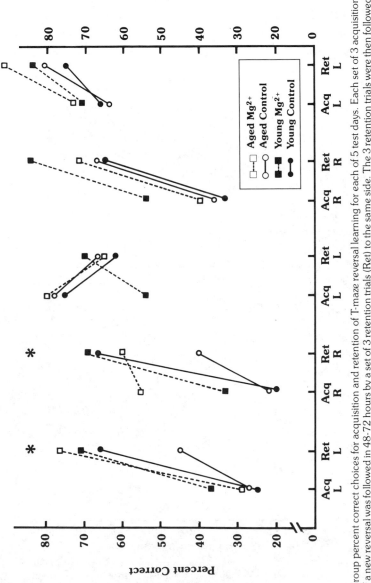

Figure 4. Group percent correct choices for acquisition and retention of T-maze reversal learning for each of 5 test days. Each set of 3 acquisition (Acq) trials of a new reversal was followed in 48–72 hours by a set of 3 retention trials (Ret) to the same side. The 3 retention trials were then followed in 5 minutes by 3 acquisition trials of a new reversal to the opposite side (L and R: left and right). On the first two retention tests the aged Mg^{2+}-treated group performed significantly better than the aged control group and comparably to the two young groups (asterisks). Data on running latencies showed similar results. From Landfield and Morgan (1984); with permission of Elsevier.

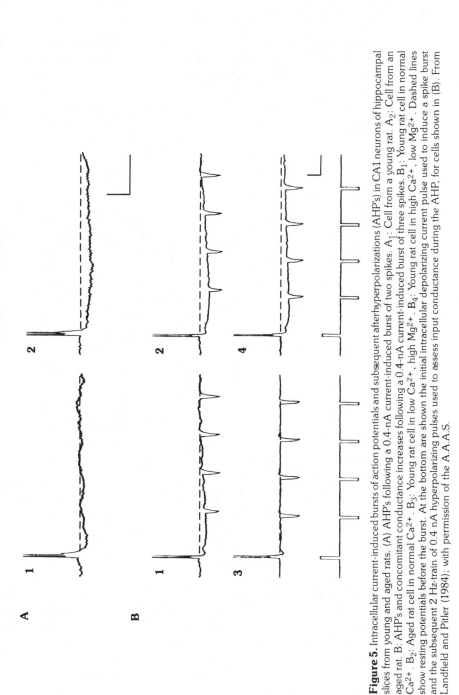

Figure 5. Intracellular current-induced bursts of action potentials and subsequent afterhyperpolarizations (AHP's) in CA1 neurons of hippocampal slices from young and aged rats. (A) AHP's following a 0.4-nA current-induced burst of two spikes. A_1: Cell from a young rat. A_2: Cell from an aged rat. B: AHP's and concomitant conductance increases following a 0.4-nA current-induced burst of three spikes. B_1: Young rat cell in normal Ca^{2+}. B_2: Aged rat cell in normal Ca^{2+}. B_3: Young rat cell in low Ca^{2+}, high Mg^{2+}. B_4: Young rat cell in high Ca^{2+}, low Mg^{2+}. Dashed lines show resting potentials before the burst. At the bottom are shown the initial intracellular depolarizing current pulse used to induce a spike burst and the subsequent 2 Hz-train of 0.4 nA hyperpolarizing pulses used to assess input conductance during the AHP, for cells shown in (B). From Landfield and Pitler (1984); with permission of the A.A.A.S.

Clearly these various results suggest that long-term treatments with Mg^{2+} or with other Ca^{2+}-blocking agents would be of particular interest in the context of possible preventive therapies in brain aging. Furthermore, with regard to AD, it should be noted that neurofibrillary, tangle-bearing neurons from subjects with extensive neuropathology have been found to contain elevated Ca^{2+} as well as elevated aluminum (Pearl et al., 1982).

CONCLUSIONS

1. The severity and rapidity of progressive degeneration in AD indicate that it may well be necessary to develop a concurrent preventive or retardant therapy before replacement therapies can be fully exploited.
2. Preventive therapies generally require knowledge of etiology and, in the present context, must be tested in chronic, relatively long-term paradigms (since the effectiveness of such chronic treatments can only be gauged by the delayed appearance of gradual, cumulative changes associated with aging). Thus, without the availability of animal models, preventive therapies for age-related brain decline are unlikely to be developed in the near future.
3. Animal models of normal brain aging may prove to be useful in studies of preventive, chronic treatments for AD since normal brain aging and AD appear to be related at some basic levels. Moreover, normal brain aging processes appear to share some common factors across all mammalian species. Therefore, studies of rodents seem likely to be relevant to humans.
4. The etiological factors in AD may act through the acceleration of normal brain aging processes and normal aging may in turn increase susceptibility to the effects of these etiological factors. Thus, if treatments are found that slow normal brain aging such treatments may also slow the progression of AD, both by interfering with the AD-induced acceleration of brain aging phenomena and by postponing the onset of susceptibility to AD.
5. Since normal brain aging is not associated with massive neural deterioration, the study of long-term treatment effects requires a highly quantitative and rigorous approach to permit the detection of subtle alterations in the course of brain aging. In addition, aging animals must be carefully maintained for prolonged periods to prevent infection and premature pathology.

6. Studies to date indicate that the rate of brain aging is not immutable, and that glucocorticoids may "drive" some aspects of brain aging, whereas neuropeptides and neural stimulants may retard some aspects of brain aging. In addition, some correlates of brain aging may be accelerated by the accumulation of intracellular Ca^{2+}. Thus, brain aging may be influenced by a variety of physio-chemical mechanisms.

RECOMMENDATIONS

1. A series of treatments with potential value in the preventive therapy of normal and abnormal age-related brain decline should be defined in long-term studies using animal models of normal brain aging. Defining such treatments will require intensive basic science research on etiological mechanisms of brain aging and a highly systematic and comprehensive approach to measurement.
2. The difficult task of establishing the necessary procedures for longer-term clinical trials in Alzheimer's subjects and in normal human subjects at greater risk of developing AD must also begin.
3. Because the procedures for carrying out systematic long-term studies in both animals and humans are extremely demanding and require rigorous evaluation and diagnostic techniques, it seems quite possible that partnerships among academia, industry and government will be necessary for establishing successful programs.
4. Based upon animal data already available, chronic studies in early AD patients should be initiated with neuropeptides and some of the safer neural stimulants. Previous tests with these agents have, perhaps, been too brief to detect gradual retardant or trophic effects. Extensive studies with chronic animals should also be conducted with a series of Ca^{2+} blocking agents (including magnesium) and with other neuropeptides and stimulants not yet examined in animal experiments.
5. Pharmaceutical research should also concentrate on developing a glucocorticoid blocking agent that is effective in chronic studies. The acute effects of current antiglucocorticoid agents are generally counteracted over longer periods by compensatory increases in ACTH.

REFERENCES

Appel, S.H. (1984). Neurotrophic factors and diseases of aging: An approach to ALS, Parkinsonism and Alzheimer's disease. In D.G. Scarpelli & G. Migaki (Eds.), *Comparative pathobiology of major age-related diseases: Current status and research frontiers* (pp. 411-424). New York: Alan R. Liss.

Applegate, M.D., Campbell G., & Landfield, P.W. (1984). Reorganization of ultrastructure in aging rat hippocampus: A stereological analysis. *Society for Neurosciences Abstracts, 10,* 450.

Bartus, R.T., Dean, R.L., Beer, B., & Lippa, A.S. (1982). The cholinergic hypothesis of geriatric memory dysfunction. *Science, 217,* 408-417.

Berger, P.A., & Tinklenberg, J.R. (1981). Neuropeptides and senile dementia. In T. Crook & S. Gershon (Eds.), *Strategies for the development of an effective treatment for senile dementia* (pp. 151-172). New Canaan, CT: Mark Powley Associates, Inc.

Corkin, S., Davis, K.L., Growdon, J.H., Usdin, E., & Wurtman, R.J. (Eds.). (1982). *Alzheimer's disease: A report of progress in research.* New York: Raven Press.

Coyle, J.T., Price, D.L., & DeLong, M.R. (1983). Alzheimer's disease: A disorder of cortical cholinergic innervation. *Science, 219,* 1184-1190.

Davies, P. (1981). Theoretical treatment possibilities for dementia of the Alzheimer type: The cholinergic hypothesis. In T. Crook & S. Gershon (Eds.), *Strategies for the development of an effective treatment for senile dementia* (pp. 19-34). New Canaan, CT: Mark Powley Associates, Inc.

Ferris, S.H. (1981). Empirical studies in senile dementia with central nervous system stimulants and metabolic enhancers. In T. Crook & S. Gershon (Eds.), *Strategies for the development of an effective treatment for senile dementia* (pp. 173-188). New Canaan, CT: Mark Powley Associates, Inc.

Gash, D.M., Collier, T.J., & Sladek, J.R., Jr. (1985). Neural transplantation: A review of recent developments and potential applications to the aged brain. *Neurobiology of Aging, 6,* 131-150.

Gispen, W.H., van Ree, J.M., & de Wied, D. (1977). Lipotropin and the central nervous system. *International Review of Neurobiology, 20,* 209-250.

Katzman, R., Terry, R.D., & Bick, K.L. (Eds.). (1978). *Alzheimer's disease: Senile dementia and related disorders.* New York: Raven Press.

Khachaturian, Z.S. (1984). Towards theories of brain aging. In D. Kay & G.D. Burrows (Eds.), *Handbook of studies on psychiatry and old age* (pp. 7-30). Amsterdam: Elsevier, B.V.

Landfield, P.W. (1978). An endocrine hypothesis of brain aging and studies on brain-endocrine correlations and monosynaptic neurophysiology during aging. In C. Finch, D. Potter, & A. Kenny (Eds.), *Parkinson's disease II: Aging and neuroendocrine relationships* (pp. 179-200). New York: Plenum Press.

Landfield, P.W. (1981a). Adrenocortical hypotheses of brain and somatic aging. In R. Schimke (Ed.), *Biological mechanisms in aging: Conference proceedings* (pp. 658-672). Bethesda, MD: U.S. Department of Health and Human Services (NIH Publication No. 81-2194).

Landfield, P.W. (1981b). Age-Related impairment of hippocampal frequency potentiation: Evidence of an underlying deficit in transmitter release from studies of magnesium-bathed hippocampal slices. *Society for Neuroscience Abstracts, 7,* 371.

Landfield, P.W. (1982). Measurement of brain aging: Conceptual issues and neurobiological indices. In R. Adelman & G. Roth (Eds.), *Endocrine and neuroendocrine mechanisms of aging* (pp. 183-208). Boca Raton, FL: CRC Press.

Landfield, P.W., Applegate, M.D., & Pitler, T.A. (1982). Increased synaptic density in hippocampus of aging rats chronically treated with a neural stimulant. *Society for Neuroscience Abstracts, 8,* 439.

Landfield, P.W., Baskin, R.K., & Pitler, T.A. (1981). Brain aging correlates: Retardation by hormonal-pharmacological treatments. *Science, 214,* 581-584.

Landfield, P.W., McGaugh, J.L., & Lynch, G.S. (1978). Impaired synaptic potentiation processes in the hippocampus of aged, memory-deficient rats. *Brain Research, 150,* 85-101.

Landfield, P.W., & Morgan G. (1984). Chronically elevating plasma Mg^{2+} improves hippocampal frequency potentiation and reversal learning in aged and young rats. *Brain Research, 322,* 167-171.

Landfield, P.W., & Pitler, T.A. (1984). Prolonged Ca^{2+}-dependent after hyperpolarizations in hippocampal neurons of aged rats. *Science, 226,* 1089-1092.

Landfield, P.W., Pitler, T.A., & Applegate, M.D. (1984). Nerve cell and synaptic decline in brain aging: Implications for animal models and for an hypothesis of Alzheimer's disease. In D.G. Scarpelli & G. Migaki (Eds.), Comparative pathobiology of major age-related diseases: Current status and research frontiers (pp. 333-356). New York: Alan R. Liss.

Landfield, P.W., Pitler, T.A., Applegate, M.D., & Robinson, J.H. (1983). Intracellular studies of the age-related deficit in hippocampal frequency potentiation: Apparent calcium saturation in synapses of aged rats. Society for Neuroscience Abstracts, 9, 923.

Landfield, P.W., Waymire, J.L., & Lynch, G.S. (1978). Hippocampal aging and adrenocorticoids: Quantitative correlations. Science, 202, 1098-1102.

Landfield, P.W., Wurtz, C., Lindsey, J.D., & Lynch, G. (1979). Long-Term adrenalectomy reduces some morphological correlates of brain aging. Society for Neuroscience Abstracts, 5, 7.

McEwen, B.S., Gerlach, J.L., & Micco, D.J. (1975). Putative glucocorticoid receptors in hippocampus and other regions of the rat brain. In R.L. Isaacson & K.H. Pribram (Eds.), The hippocampus (pp. 285-322). New York: Plenum Press.

Merz, P.A., Rohwer, R.G., Kascak, R., Wisniewski, H.M., Somerville, R.A., Gibbs, C.J., & Gajdusek, D.C. (1984). Infection-specific particle from the unconventional slow virus diseases. Science, 225, 437-440.

Michaelis, M.L., Johe, K., & Kitos, T.E. (1984). Age-dependent alterations in synaptic membrane systems for Ca^{2+} regulation. Mechanisms of Ageing and Development, 25, 215-225.

National Academy of Sciences (1981). Mammalian models for research on aging. Washington, D.C.: National Academy Press.

Perl, D.P., Gajdusek, D.C., Garruto, R.M., Yanagihara, R.T., & Gibbs, C.J. (1982). Intraneuronal aluminum accumulation in amyotrophic lateral sclerosis and Parkinsonism-Dementia of Guam. Science, 217, 1053-1055.

Peterson, C., & Gibson, G.E. (1983). Aging and 3-4 diaminopyridine alter synaptosomal calcium uptake. Journal of Biological Chemistry, 19, 11482-11486.

Sapolsky, R.M., Krey, L.C., & McEwen, B.S. (1985). Prolonged glucocorticoid exposure reduces hippocampal neuron number: Implications for aging. *Journal of Neuroscience, 5,* 1479-1485.

Schipper, H., Brawer, J.R., Nelson, J.F., Felicio, L.S., & Finch, C.E. (1981). Role of the gonads in the histologic aging of the hypothalamic arcuate nucleus. *Biology of Reproduction, 25,* 413-419.

Schlaepfer, W.W., & Hasler, M.B. (1979). Characterization of the calcium-induced disruption of neurofilaments in rat peripheral nerve. *Brain Research, 168,* 299-309.

Tomlinson, B.E., & Henderson, G. (1976). Some quantitative cerebral findings in normal and demented old people. In R.D. Terry & S. Gershon (Eds.), *Neurobiology of aging* (pp. 183-204). New York: Raven Press.

Wexler, B.C. (1976). Comparative aspects of hyperadrenocorticism and aging. In A.F. Everitt & J.A. Burgess (Eds.), *Hypothalamus pituitary and aging* (pp. 333-361). Springfield, Ill: Charles C Thomas.

Wisniewski, H.M., Morentz, R.C., & Lossinsky, M.S. (1981). Evidence for induction of localized amyloid deposits and neuritic plaques by an infectious agent. *Annals of Neurology, 10,* 517-522.

Wisniewski, H.M., & Terry, R.D. (1973). Morphology of the aging brain, human and animal. In D.M. Ford (Ed.), *Progress in brain research: Vol. 40. Neurobiological aspects of maturation and aging* (pp. 167-186). New York: Elsevier Scientific Publishing Company.

ACKNOWLEDGMENTS

Aspects of the research described in this paper were supported by grants AG04207 and AGO4542 from the NIH. The excellent assistance of Robin Howell and T.J. Pope in preparing the manuscript is greatly appreciated.

10

Aging, Peptides, and the Blood-Brain Barrier: Implications and Speculations

William A. Banks, MD, and Abba J. Kastin, MD

Biochemical, behavioral, and morphological studies suggest that peptides and the blood-brain barrier (BBB) are involved in normal aging and in Alzheimer's disease (AD). This review will examine the relevance of these interactions to drug treatment strategies for AD.

RELEVANCE OF PEPTIDES, THE BBB, AND AGING

Many peptides have significant effects on behavior and other manifestations of central nervous system (CNS) function including learning, attention, and memory. It is easy to imagine, then, how alterations in levels of these peptides could lead to the manifestations of AD. Furthermore, since peptides administered systemically can exert many CNS effects (Kastin, Banks, Zadina, & Graf, 1983; Kastin, Olson, Schally, & Coy, 1979), therapeutic roles have been sought for them with some preliminary success (Ehrensing & Kastin, 1978; Kastin & Barbeau, 1972).

Peptides, the BBB, and the effects of aging can also interact with each other in ways that are relevant to AD research. The BBB is a relevant subject in the study of AD because the efficacy of any therapeutic agent administered systemically will be defined mainly by its ability to cross the BBB and thus penetrate into the brain. The BBB is also important in regulating the brain's exposure to nutrients, modulators, and toxins so that any changes in its function could lead to CNS dysfunction. The relationship of the BBB to peptide physiology is, however, particularly important. Most of the centrally active peptides are found in the blood and the CNS (Hökfelt, Johansson, Ljungdahl, Lundberg, & Schultzberg, 1980; Krieger & Martin, 1981), so that the question of penetration of these peptides from one side of the BBB to the other must be considered both for the physiologically "normal" state as well as for those states in which the BBB is altered. Many of the central effects seen with peripheral administration of peptides are probably due to the small amounts of peptides that cross the BBB.

Likewise, it is necessary to consider the role that aging plays in BBB/peptide interactions. A distinction should be made between changes due to aging and changes due to AD itself. Furthermore, normal aging and AD may be separate but synergistic processes, in which case it may be easier to improve symptoms by addressing the changes of aging rather than the possibly irreversible changes of AD. Peptides can also influence the penetration of nonpeptide substances across the BBB. Changes in peptide levels with aging or in AD could influence the ability of these substances to penetrate the BBB. Thus, BBB/peptide/aging interactions are important considerations in understanding and devising treatments for AD.

CHANGES IN PEPTIDE LEVELS

Studies indicate that peptide levels in the brain are altered in the aging process. Substance P, neurotensin, luteinizing hormone-releasing hormone (LHRH), somatostatin, methionine-enkephalin, leucine-enkephalin, adrenocorticotropic hormone (ACTH), α-melanocyte-stimulating hormone (α-MSH), γ-lipotropin (γ-LPH), thyrotropin-releasing hormone (TRH), and β-endorphin have all been shown to decrease in various brain regions with increasing age (Barden et al., 1981; Barnea, Cho, & Porter, 1982; Buck, Burks, & Yamamura, 1982; Dupont, Savard, Merand, Labrie, & Boissier, 1981; Gambert, Garthwaite, Pontzer, & Hagen, 1980; Hoffman, G.E., & Sladek, 1980; Landfield, Sundberg, Smith, Eldridge, & Morris, 1980). The subject is less well studied in AD. Somatostatin, but not vasoactive intestinal peptide (VIP) or cholecystokinin, is decreased in the brain of patients with AD (Davies, Katzman, & Terry, 1980; Rossor et al., 1980a,b, 1981). Arginine vasopressin (AVP) levels were found to be unchanged throughout the brains of Alzheimer's patients in comparison to age-matched controls except for lower levels in the globus pallidus (Rossor et al., 1980c). Levels of β-endorphin in the cerebrospinal fluid (CSF) were reduced in Alzheimer's patients and correlated with reduced psychological function (Kaiya et al., 1983). Decreased AVP levels in the CSF have been found in patients with primary dementia and parkinsonism, but not in patients with cerebrovascular disease, multiple sclerosis, or dementia due to normal pressure hydrocephalus (Sorensen, Hammer, Vorstrup, & Gjerris, 1983; Sundquist, Forsling, Olsson, & Akerlund, 1983). CSF levels of VIP were no different between controls and patients with AD (Sharpless et al., 1984). Apparently, opiate receptor levels may also be reduced in the brains of aging animals (Messing et al., 1980). Not surprisingly, the response of aged animals to peptides and their nonpeptide agonists and antagonists can also be reduced (Gosnell, Levine, & Morley, 1983).

In general, it appears that when peptide levels are altered in aging, they tend to be reduced. To some degree, this reflects a general decrease in brain mass and biochemical activity. This does not mean that aging or AD should only be considered a problem of peptide deficiencies. It appears that some peptides are affected more than others, so that it is more likely that peptide "imbalances" occur. For instance, although β-endorphin and enkephalin levels are reduced in the brain as a result of aging, arguments have been advanced that an excess of opiate activity might be responsible for some of the problems of learning and memory associated with dementia syndromes (Kastin, Olson, Sandman, & Ehrensing, 1981; Roberts, 1981). Since then, preliminary results have shown that the opiate antagonist naloxone has some therapeutic benefit in such cases (Reisberg et al., 1983). Thus, although opiate levels are low in absolute terms, they may be elevated relative to naturally occurring opiate antagonists.

Many of the changes seen in the CNS of aged rats begin early, during "middle age" (14 months), rather than during senescence (Landfield et al., 1980). These changes have been associated with decreasing function of the hypothalamic-pituitary axis (Meites, 1982) that could, in turn, result in decreased function of the endocrine system and alterations in circadian rhythyms. This could then lead to generalized deterioration or "aging" of the target organ systems. Changes in brain peptide levels could result in peripheral, as well as central, manifestations of aging. Within the brain, ACTH, TRH, and AVP (De Wied & Versteeg, 1979; Van Ree, Bohus, Versteeg, & De Wied, 1978; Wood, Mathe-Sorenssen, Cheney, & Costa, 1978; Yarbrough, 1983) have been shown to be important in maintaining acetylcholine (ACh) and catecholamine activity. Alterations in the levels of these peptides may thus be responsible for the lowered levels of ACh and catecholamines seen in dementia. The extent to which altered peptide levels are themselves a manifestation of aging or dementia (rather than a cause) is, of course, unknown. However, administration of some of these peptides or their analogues has been shown to improve (MSH/ACTH 4-10, AVP) or impair (oxytocin) memory in senescent monkeys (Bartus, Dean, & Beer, 1982). ACTH or its structural analogue, ORG-2766, can retard age-related changes in the hippocampus (Landfield, Baskin, & Pitler, 1981). AVP and its analogues have also been shown to improve memory, concentration, or attention in young and aged persons and AD patients (De Wied & Van Ree, 1982), although negative results have also been reported (Carey & Miller, 1982; Fehm-Wolfsdorf, Born, Elbert, Voigt, & Fehm, 1985; Hostetter, Jubb, & Kozlowski, 1980; Williams, A.R., Carey, & Miller, 1983). This suggests that once the aging process is set in motion, peptides (or lack of them) can, at the least, enhance or reverse age-related changes.

ALTERATIONS IN THE BBB

As with any capillary bed, substances penetrate the BBB in one of several ways. Substances may "leak" between adjacent endothelial cells or move through a cell via channels, fenestrations, or pinocytotic vesicles. Fusion of adjacent cell membranes and a reduction in the number of fenestrations and pinocytotic vesicles combine to account for the relative impermeability of the BBB. Substances may also cross by diffusion through the membrane. The ability of a substance to cross by this mechanism is dependent on its physicochemical properties such as charge, molecular weight, and, most importantly, lipophilicity. Selected substances may also cross by virtue of specific carrier-mediated transport systems. Thus, changes in BBB permeability could represent alterations in any of these mechanisms of penetration.

Histological studies show definite changes in the capillary bed of the brain with aging. Bar (1978) has shown a decrease in the number and an increase in the length of brain endothelial cells that make up the BBB in the rat. He also noted a decrease in the mean diameter of the capillary lumen. Aged macaque monkeys also have a decrease in lumen size (although there is an increase in size until middle age) with thinning of the capillary wall and a decrease in the number of endothelial mitochondria (Burns, Buschmann, Kruckeberg, Gaetano, & Meyer, 1981). Morphometric changes appear to demonstrate some regional variation (Hicks, Rolsten, Brizzee, & Samorajski, 1983). These changes are probably related to aging itself rather than to the hypertension that often accompanies aging (Hunziker, Abdel' Al, Schulz, & Schweizer, 1978).

Despite such alterations, it appears that the BBB is not disrupted. Rapoport, Ohno, and Pettigrew (1979) found that the permeability of the BBB in rats to sucrose (a substance that penetrates into the brain primarily by virtue of the BBB's "leakiness") was unchanged throughout the brain of aged rats, except possibly in the white matter. The cerebral distribution space for sucrose was reduced, however, suggesting a reduced extracellular brain space in aged rats. Similarly, neither albumin (Sankar, Blossom, Clemons, & Charles, 1983) nor horseradish peroxidase (Rudick & Buell, 1983) seems to leak through more measurably in older animals. A single study of postmortem material found increased immunostaining of serum proteins in the brains from patients with AD suggesting that the BBB may be disrupted in this disease (Wisniewski & Kozlowski, 1982). In humans, capillary bed changes increase with age, and it has been postulated that these changes directly alter transport mechanisms, leading to abnormal neuronal function (Ravens, 1978) and mental deterioration (Pickworth, 1937). These proposals are consistent with the observation that carrier-mediated transport, but not lipid-mediated permeability, changes with maturation (Cornford, Braun, Oldendorf, & Hill, 1982). Samuels, Fish, Schwartz, and Hochgeschwender (1983) were unable to demonstrate any effect on the carrier-mediated transport of amino acids from the blood into the brain's astrocytes with age. There was, however, a decline in the rate of a second, slower transport process that probably represents transport of the amino acids out of the astrocytes and into neurons. It may be relevant that many therapies for the depression and mood disorders that increase in incidence and prevalence with aging alter the lipophilic and carrier-mediated properties of the BBB (Preskorn et al., 1981).

Only about 20-30% of the CSF is produced by the brain endothelial cells (Rapoport, 1976, pp. 45-46). The majority of CSF is produced by the choroid plexus. The vessels that supply the choroid plexus do not have the morphologic features typical of other blood vessels responsible for the decreased permeability of BBB, but the ependymal lining or tanycytes that interface between the vessels and the CSF do have these features. Thus, the blood-CSF barrier is located at anatomically different site but has a similar ultrastructure and functions that are complementary to the BBB. Changes occur with age at the blood-CSF barrier. CSF albumin levels and CSF/serum albumin ratios in man increase steadily from 6 months to 30 years (Eeg-Ologsson, Link, & Wigertz, 1981). Lactate, which is restricted by the blood-CSF/brain barrier, also increases in the CSF of humans as a function of age (Yesavage & Berger, 1980). These studies suggest an increased permeability in the blood-CSF barrier, although altered metabolic processes such as increased lactate production or decreased turnover of CSF with age could also explain such results. Morphological studies have shown that aged rats develop significant intracellular separations between the tanycytes responsible for the integrity of the blood-CSF barrier at the circumventricular organs (Scott & Sladek, 1981).

Again, the situation is less clear in AD. Lactate has been reported to be increased in CSF from patients with AD (Gottfries, Kjallquist, & Ponten, 1974). One report indicates that proteins are increased in CSF of AD patients compared to aged, matched controls (Alafuzoff, Adolfsson, Bucht, & Winblad, 1983), while a second study found no such elevation beyond that accounted for by age (Deutsch et al., 1983). A third study found no difference in protein CSF levels between patients with dementia and Down's syndrome and aged, matched controls (Elovaara, 1984).

It is clear that morphological changes occur in the BBB and blood-CSF barrier with age. The functional significance of such changes is unclear, although it appears that the BBB is not actually disrupted. It is even less clear if changes occur in AD beyond those expected with normal aging. Nevertheless, those changes related to aging (and any eventually found for AD) could be responsible for the deterioration of central functions by impairing BBB function.

For substances that are highly lipophilic or have blood-to-brain carrier-mediated transport systems that are not normally saturated, the rate of blood flow through the brain is important in determining the amount of material that enters the brain. The regional blood volume is not changed in aged rats except in the pons and medulla (Rapoport et al., 1979). The cerebral blood flow as measured by [133]xenon is reduced, however, in healthy aged patients with or without significant atherosclerotic cardiovascular disease (Zemcov, Barclay, & Blass, 1984) and in AD patients (Risberg & Gustafson, 1983). In both aged and AD patients, the main areas with decreased flow rate are the parietal, occipital, and temporal regions, while Pick's disease and multi-infarct dementia have different patterns. Cerebral vascular constriction in response to 100% oxygen is reduced with aging. No further reduction has been found in patients with AD although the decrease in basal flow rate has been confirmed (Amano, Meyer, Okabe, Shaw, & Mortel, 1983). These studies suggest a significant change in cerebral blood flow with aging, with similar, more extensive changes occurring in AD.

BBB-PEPTIDE INTERACTIONS

Interactions between the BBB and peptides occur in at least two ways. First, peptides may influence brain permeability to other substances. For example, insulin increases glucose transfer across the BBB (Hertz, Paulson, Barry, Christiansen, & Svendsen, 1981). This peptide-facilitated BBB permeability can be very selective as illustrated by the finding that α-MSH, but not MIF-1 (MSH-release inhibiting factor, Pro-Leu-Gly-NH$_2$), can increase the permeability of the BBB in the rat to ^{99m}Tc-pertechnetate, but not to radioiodinated serum albumin (RISA) (Kastin & Fabre, 1982; Sankar, Domer, & Kastin, 1981). Other studies have shown that the ACTH/MSH analogue ORG-2766 can reduce BBB permeability to antipyrine without altering cerebral blood flow (Goldman & Murphy, 1981), and that melanotropic peptides administered centrally increase permeability of the blood-CSF barrier to albumin, mannitol, inulin, and sucrose but not to glucose, d-aminoisobutyric acid or valine (Rudman & Kutner, 1978). It has been shown that behavioral changes induced by aluminum, which crosses the BBB and has been implicated as a neurotoxin in dialysis dementia (Sideman & Manor, 1982) and senile dementia (Bjorksten, 1982; De Boni & Crapper McLachlan, 1980), can be altered by parathyroid hormone (PTH) (Commissaris et al., 1982). This suggests that PTH may alter BBB transport or the central actions of aluminum. Peptides can also exert hemodynamic effects. For example, vasoactive intestinal peptide (Heistad, Marcus, Said, & Gross, 1980) increases cerebral blood flow, while substance P (Mroz & Leeman, 1977) and neurotensin (Bissette, Manberge, Nemeroff, & Prange, 1978) can induce hypotension.

Peptides may also cross the BBB. This has been a controversial subject, and is reviewed more extensively elsewhere (Banks & Kastin, 1985c). Perhaps the best studied peptide in this respect is delta sleep-inducing peptide (DSIP). DSIP lent itself uniquely well to the study of the problem of peptide membrane penetration because of the existence of an antibody that requires at least eight of its nine amino acids for cross-reactivity. Detection of immunoactivity followed by separation chromatography can, therefore, confirm passage of intact peptide. Our group has shown that DSIP crosses the BBB of the rat and the blood-CSF barrier of the dog in intact form (Banks, Kastin, & Coy, 1982; Kastin, Banks, Castellanos, Nissen, & Coy, 1982). Other peptides shown to cross include β-endorphin (Houghten, Swann, & Li, 1980; Merin, Hollt, Przewlocki, & Herz, 1980), α-MSH (Kastin et al., 1976), and cyclo Leu-Gly (Hoffman P.L., Walter, & Bulat, 1977). DSIP circulates largely in bound (Kastin, Castellanos, Banks, & Coy, 1981) or aggregated (Kastin, Castellanos, Fischman, Proffitt, & Graf, 1984a) form, and it appears that the unbound form is the principal constituent that crosses. In addition, the degree of penetration varies among the analogues of a given peptide (Banks et al., 1982; Kastin et al., 1982; Rapoport, Klee, Pettigrew, & Ohno, 1980). These characteristics suggest that peptides do not cross by virtue of the BBB's "leakiness." The penetration of DSIP across the BBB does not appear to be saturable (Banks, Kastin, & Coy, 1984). Further studies indicate that most peptides cross the BBB to a low degree and that the octanol coefficient, a measure of lipophilicity, is a good predictor of the degree of penetration (Banks & Kastin, 1984b). This suggests that most peptides permeate the BBB via membrane diffusion.

Studies with aluminum chloride support the supposition that most peptides penetrate the BBB by membrane diffusion. Aluminum increases the permeability of the BBB to nonpeptide substances without disrupting the BBB (Banks & Kastin, 1985a). It appears to do this possibly by combining with the membrane, but not the penetrating substance, to increase the membrane's lipophilic properties (Banks & Kastin, 1985b). A study using a membrane model suggests that aluminum does this by forming the $Al(OH)_4{}^-$ ion and combining with the membrane's carboxylated headgroups (Tracey & Boivin, 1983). Aluminum increases the permeability of the BBB to peptides and increases the strength of the correlation between lipophilicity and peptide penetration (Banks & Kastin, 1985c). We have postulated that this increase in BBB permeability to peptides and centrally active nonpeptides may be the mechanism by which aluminum induces dialysis dementia (Banks & Kastin, 1983a). Aluminum has also been postulated as a causal agent in AD (Bjorksten, 1982; De Boni & Crapper McLachlan, 1980) as well as in the parkinsonism dementia syndrome of Guam (Perl, Gajdusek, Garruto, Vanagihara, & Gibbs, 1982).

One of the most exciting developments in the pathophysiology of AD is the discovery that the levels of many peptides and neurotransmitters in the brain are greatly reduced. The most impressive reduction occurs in the cholinergic system. It is not clear what environmental/genetic milieu triggers the deterioration of this system. Aluminum is a noncompetitive inhibitor of acetylcholinesterase (AChE) (Marquis, 1983). In some species, it can also induce neurofibrillary tangles that have decreased choline acetyltransferase activity (Kosik, Bradley, Good, Rasool, & Selkoe, 1983) and decreases uptake of gamma-aminobutyric acid and glycine (Sturman, Wisniewski, & Shek, 1983). Interestingly, aluminum can also reduce CSF production by inhibiting carbonic anhydrase activity (Vogh & Maren, 1984). The aluminum-induced change in BBB permeability, however, appears to precede changes in cholinergic tone as measured by AChE activity (Banks & Kastin, 1985b).

It is possible that any effect that increases BBB permeability could result in a decrease in cholinergic tone. ACh increases the permeability of the BBB (Domer, Boerthe, Bing, & Reddix, 1983). Therefore, assuming a negative feedback loop between cholinergic tone and BBB permeability, an increase in permeability could result in suppression of cholinergic tone. To the extent that AD is a lesion of increased BBB permeability, treatment with cholinergic agonists might be limited since such treatment would tend to further increase BBB permeability.

It should be noted that even an acute, traumatic disruption of the blood-CSF barrier has different effects on the CSF/plasma ratio of different peptides (Banks & Kastin, 1983b). This again suggests difficulties for therapeutic attacks that attempt to treat abnormalities in peptide levels as isolated problems. Treatments that tend to reduce BBB permeability, used either alone or in conjunction with cholinergics, might be useful in the treatment of AD. Two modalities that reduce lipophilic BBB permeability are lithium and electroconvulsive shock therapy (Preskorn et al., 1981). We have found in preliminary studies (with H. Ladson) that lithium can cause a small decrease in the permeation of DSIP across the BBB. Lithium can also affect the BBB's carrier-mediated transport systems and decrease CSF production (Barkai, 1985; Ehrlich, Diamond, Braun, Cornford, & Oldendorf, 1980; Ehrlich & Wright, 1982). Interestingly, both these modalities can be effective in the treatment of depression, which shares many clinical symptoms with AD. Preliminary trials with lithium suggest that it may indeed improve dementia (Havens & Cole, 1982; Williams, K.H., & Goldstein, 1979), although lithium toxicity can also cause dementia. This suggests that if lithium is useful in dementia, its therapeutic range may be narrow as it is for the treatment of mania. We have also found in preliminary studies that streptozotocin-induced diabetic rats may have a reduced permeation of DSIP across the BBB. Interestingly, diabetes mellitus seems to confer a protective effect against AD (Bucht, Adolfsson, Lithner, & Winblad, 1983). This may be due to changes in the permeability of the BBB in this disease.

An electric light helps orient the AD patient awakening in the middle of the night. It may be possible to use light as another form of therapy for AD by stimulating pineal function. Melatonin production by the pineal can be either inhibited or stimulated by specific alterations in lighting conditions. Peptides in the pineal may act similarly. Melatonin levels, which decrease with age (Brown, Young, Gauthier, Tsui, & Grota, 1979), can attenuate age-related changes in responses to morphine, while lighting conditions that inhibit pineal function exacerbate such changes (Kavaliers, Hirst, & Teskey, 1983). We have found that alterations in lighting can increase BBB permeability to DSIP, presumably by inhibiting pineal function (Banks, Kastin, & Selznick, 1985). Perhaps lighting conditions designed to stimulate the pineal indolamines or peptides can be useful therapeutically in AD.

CARRIER-MEDIATED TRANSPORT OF PEPTIDES

Although it appears that most peptides cross the BBB by direct membrane permeation, there are significant exceptions. In the study mentioned above, it was noted that a few peptides had a much lower penetration across the BBB than would have been predicted by their octanol coefficient. These peptides had several features in common, including low molecular weight (MW = < 1000) and an N-terminal tyrosine. Further investigation showed a saturable, carrier-mediated system capable of transport of these substances from the brain to the blood (Banks & Kastin, 1984a). Transport of ^{125}I-N-Tyr-MIF-1 out of the brain is inhibited by unlabeled N-Tyr-MIF-1 and methionine enkephalin, but not by MIF-1, tyrosine, or several other substances tested. Studies currently under way show that an N-terminal tyrosine is critical for transport, and that the system works best for small peptides of four or five amino acids. Thus, this intriguing system seems to be highly specific for compounds such as the enkephalins (opiates) and Tyr-MIF-1 (Tyr-Pro-Leu-Gly-NH$_2$), a compound with anti-opiate activity (Kastin, Stephens, Ehrensing, & Fischman, 1984b). Although it may at first seem paradoxical that a system would transport both an opiate and an opiate antagonist, it may be that such a system can work as a regulatory mechanism. If, for example, the brain level of methionine enkephalin were suddenly increased, it would competitively inhibit the transport of N-Tyr-MIF-1, thus concomitantly increasing antiopiate activity in a compensatory mechanism.

Such a situation, unfortunately, also complicates any possible attempts to modulate the system. It appears that high doses of leucine, but not tyrosine, alanine, Gly-Gly, or glutamic acid inhibit the system. This raises the possibility of using a nonpeptide as a therapeutic agent. Inhibition of the system, however, could result in an increase of both opiate and antiopiate activity. Likewise, any treatment that would raise brain levels of methionine enkephalin would also raise N-Tyr-MIF-1 levels by inhibiting its transport out of the brain. It may be necessary, then, to approach the idea of "peptide therapeutics" as an exercise in the restoration of balance rather than simply as a problem of excesses or deficiencies.

This peptide transport system also undergoes changes with aging. Results show that inhibition of the transport system of the uncompetitive type occurs with aging (Banks & Kastin, 1985d). The cause of this inhibition is unclear, but it appears that the levels of enkephalins are reduced with aging (Dupont et al., 1981).

RECOMMENDATIONS

From the foregoing, it can be seen that the areas of BBB-peptide interactions in aging and dementia are poorly studied and complex. This makes it difficult to suggest specific therapeutic agents to be tried in AD. Nevertheless, certain strategies seem to present themselves. We will attempt to summarize these.

1. Treatment of the aging process as an underlying, predisposing condition in AD. Changes in BBB morphology and, apparently, permeability begin to occur well before senescence. It may be easier to counter these changes than the perhaps less reversible pathology of AD. Effects on BBB permeability may complicate treatment with cholinergics.

2. Treatment with peptides can reverse age-related changes and may be effective in AD. AVP, ACTH, MIF-1, and some of their structural analogues have all been used with some success. A more effective approach may be to consider the problem one of relative peptide imbalances rather than to look for problems of absolute deficiencies or excesses.

3. Manipulation of the BBB. In addition to treatment with peptides, several nonpeptide substances look promising. These include lithium, electroconvulsive shock therapy, manipulations in lighting, and, possibly, melatonin. Leucine may be a useful inhibitor of the carrier-mediated transport system for small, N-tyrosinated peptides.

REFERENCES

Alafuzoff, I., Adolfsson, R., Bucht, G., & Winblad, B. (1983). Albumin and immunoglobulin in plasma and cerebrospinal fluid, and blood-cerebrospinal fluid barrier function in patients with dementia of Alzheimer-type and multi-infarct dementia. *Journal of the Neurological Sciences, 60,* 456-472.

Amano, T., Meyer, J.S., Okabe, T., Shaw, T., & Mortel, K.F. (1983). Cerebral vasomotor responses during oxygen inhalation: Results in normal aging and dementia. *Archives of Neurology, 40,* 277-282.

Banks, W.A., & Kastin, A.J. (1983a). Aluminium increases permeability of the blood-brain barrier to labelled DSIP and β-endorphin: Possible implications for senile and dialysis dementia. *The Lancet, ii,* 1227-1229.

Banks, W.A., & Kastin, A.J. (1983b). CSF-plasma relationships for DSIP and some other neuropeptides. *Pharmacology, Biochemistry and Behavior, 19,* 1037-1040.

Banks, W.A., & Kastin, A.J. (1984a). A brain-to-blood carrier-mediated transport for small, N-tyrosinated peptides. *Pharmacology, Biochemistry and Behavior, 21,* 943-946.

Banks, W.A., & Kastin, A.J. (1984b). Physicochemical factors as predictors of blood-brain barrier penetrance of iodinated peptides. *Clinical Research, 32,* 873A.

Banks, W.A., & Kastin, A.J. (1985a). Aluminum alters the permeability of the blood-brain barrier to some nonpeptides. *Neuropharmacology, 24,* 407-412.

Banks, W.A., & Kastin, A.J. (1985b). The aluminum-induced increase in blood-brain barrier permeability to delta sleep-inducing peptide occurs throughout the brain and is independent of phosphorus and acetylcholinesterase levels. *Psychopharmacology, 86,* 84-89.

Banks, W.A., & Kastin, A.J. (1985c). Peptides and the blood-brain barrier: Lipophilicity as a predictor of permeability. *Brain Research Bulletin 15:* 287-292.

Banks, W.A., & Kastin, A.S. (1985d). Aging and the blood-brain barrier. Changes in the carrier-mediated transport of peptides in rats. *Neuroscience Letters, 61,* 171-175.

Banks, W.A., & Kastin, A.J. (1985e). Permeability of the blood-brain barrier to neuropeptides: The case for penetration. *Psychoneuroendocrinology 10:* 385-399.

Banks, W.A., Kastin, A.J., & Coy, D.H. (1982). Delta sleep-inducing peptide crosses the blood-brain barrier in dogs: Some correlations with protein binding. *Pharmacology, Biochemistry and Behavior, 17,* 1009-1014.

Banks, W.A., Kastin, A.J., & Coy, D.H. (1984). Evidence that ^{125}I-N-Tyr-delta sleep-inducing peptide crosses the blood-brain barrier by a non-competitive mechanism. *Brain Research, 301,* 201-207.

Banks, W.A., Kastin, A.J., & Selznick, J.K. (1985). Modulation of immunoactive levels of DSIP and blood-brain barrier permeability by lighting and diurnal rhythm. *Journal of Neuroscience Research, 14,* 347-355.

Bar, T. (1978). Morphometric evaluation of capillaries in different laminae of rat cerebral cortex by automatic image analysis: Changes during development and aging. *Advances in Neurology, 20,* 1-9.

Barden, N., Dupont, A., Labrie, F., Merand, Y., Rouleau, D., Vaudry, H., & Boissier, J.R. (1981). Age-dependent changes in the β-endorphin content of discrete rat brain nuclei. *Brain Research, 208,* 209-212.

Barkai, A.J. (1985). Antidepressants, CSF formation and calcium removal in the intact rat brain. *Federation Proceedings, 44,* 2785A.

Barnea, A., Cho, G., & Porter, J.C. (1982). A reduction in the concentration of immunoreactive corticotropin, melanotropin and lipotropin in the brain of the aging rat. *Brain Research, 232,* 345-353.

Bartus, R.T., Dean, R.L., & Beer, B. (1982). Neuropeptide effects on memory in aged monkeys. *Neurobiology of Aging, 3,* 61-68.

Bissette, G., Manberg, P., Nemeroff, C.B., & Prange, A.J., Jr. (1978).

Neurotensin, a biologically active peptide. *Life Sciences, 23,* 2173-2182.

Bjorksten, J.A. (1982). Aluminum as a cause of senile dementia. *Comprehensive Therapy, 8,* 73-76.

Brown, G.M., Young, S.N., Gauthier, S., Tsui, H., & Grota, L.J. (1979). Melatonin in cerebrospinal fluid in daytime: Its origin and variation with age. *Life Sciences, 25,* 929-936.

Bucht, G., Adolfsson, R., Lithner, F., & Winblad, B. (1983). Changes in blood glucose and insulin secretion in patients with senile dementia of Alzheimer type. *Acta Medica Scandinavica, 213,* 387-392.

Buck, S.H., Burks, T.F., & Yamamura, H.I. (1982). Neuropeptide alterations in the central nervous system in aging. *Gerontology, 28,* 25-34.

Burns, E.M., Buschmann, M.B.T., Kruckeberg, T.W., Gaetano, P.K., & Meyer, J.M. (1981). Blood-brain barrier, aging, brain blood flow, and sleep. *Advances in Neurology, 30,* 301-306.

Carey, R.J., & Miller, M. (1982). Absences of learning and memory deficits in the vasopressin-deficient rat (Brattleboro Strain). *Behavioral Brain Research, 6,* 1-13.

Commissaris, R.L., Cordon, J.J., Sprague, S., Keiser, J., Mayor, G.H., & Rech, R.H. (1982). Behavioral changes in rats after chronic aluminum and parathyroid hormone administration. *Neurobehavioral Toxicology and Teratology, 4,* 403-410.

Cornford, E.M., Braun, L.D., Oldendorf, W.H., & Hill, M.A. (1982). Comparison of lipid-mediated blood-brain barrier penetrability in neonates and adults. *American Journal of Physiology, 243,* C161-C168.

Davies, P., Katzman, R., & Terry, R.D. (1980). Reduced somatostatin-like immunoreactivity in cerebral cortex from cases of Alzheimer's disease and Alzheimer senile dementia. *Nature, 288,* 279-280.

DeBoni, U., & Crapper McLachlan, D.R. (1980). Senile dementia and Alzheimer's disease: A current view. *Life Sciences, 27,* 1-14.

Deutsch, S.I., Mohs, R.C., Levy, M.I., Rothpearl, A.B., Stockton, D., Horvath, T., Coco, A., & Davis, K.L. (1983). Acetylcholinesterase activity in CSF in schizophrenia, depression, Alzheimer's disease, and normals. *Biological Psychiatry, 18,* 1363-1373.

DeWied, D., & Van Ree, J.N. (1982). Neuropeptides, mental performance and aging. *Life Sciences, 31,* 709-719.

DeWied, D., & Versteeg, D.H.G. (1979). Neurohypophyseal principles and memory. *Federation Proceeding, 38,* 2348-2354.

Domer, F.R., Boerthe, S.B., Bing, E.G., & Reddix, I. (1983). Histamine- and acetylcholine-induced changes in the permeability of the blood-brain barrier of normotensive and spontaneously hypertensive rats. *Neuropharmacology, 22,* 615-619.

Dupont, A., Savard, P., Merand, Y., Labrie, F., & Boissier, J.R. (1981). Age-related changes in central nervous system enkephalins and substance P. *Life Sciences, 29,* 2317-2322.

Eeg-Ologsson, O., Link, H., & Wigertz, A. (1981). Concentrations of CSF proteins as a measure of blood-brain barrier function and synthesis of Ig G within the CNS in "normal" subjects from the age 6 months to 30 years. *Acta Paediatrica Scandinavica, 70,* 167-170.

Ehrensing, R.H., & Kastin, A.J. (1978). Dose-related biphasic effect of Prolyl-Leucyl-Glycinamide (MIF-1) in depression. *American Journal of Psychiatry, 135,* 562-566.

Ehrlich, B.E., Diamond, J.M., Braun, L.D., Cornford, E.M., & Oldendorf, W.H. (1980). Effects of lithium on blood-brain barrier transport of the neurotransmitter precursors choline, tyrosine and tryptophan. *Brain Research, 193,* 604-607.

Ehrlich, B.E., & Wright, E.M. (1982). Choline and PAH transport across blood-CSF barriers: The effect of lithium. *Brain Research, 250,* 245-249.

Elovaara, I. (1984). Proteins in serum and cerebrospinal fluid in demented patients with Down's syndrome. *Acta Neurologica Scandinavica, 69,* 302-305.

Fehm-Wolfsdorf, G., Born, J., Elbert, T., Voigt, K., & Fehm, H.F. (1985). Vasopressin does not enhance memory processes: A study in human twins. *Peptides, 6,* 297-300.

Gambert, S.R., Garthwaite, T.L., Pontzer, C.H., & Hagen, T.C. (1980). Age-related changes in central nervous system beta-endorphin and ACTH. *Neuroendocrinology, 31,* 252-255.

Goldman, H., & Murphy, S. (1981). An analogue of ACTH/MSH$_{4-9}$, ORG-2766, reduces permeability of the blood-brain barrier. *Pharmacology, Biochemistry and Behavior, 14,* 845-848.

Gosnell, B.A., Levine, A.S., & Morley, J.E. (1983). The effects of aging on opioid modulation of feeding in rats. *Life Sciences, 32,* 2793-2799.

Gottfries, C.G., Kjallquist, A., Ponten, U., Roos, B.E., & Sundborg, G. (1974). Cerebrospinal fluid pH and monoamine and glycolytic metabolites in Alzheimer's disease. British Journal of Psychiatry, 124, 280-287.

Havens, W.W., & Cole, J. (1982). Successful treatment of dementia with lithium [Letter to the editor]. Journal of Clinical Psychopharmacology, 2, 71-72.

Hertz, M.M., Paulson, O.B., Barry, D.I., Christiansen, J.S., & Svendsen, P.A. (1981). Insulin increases glucose transfer across the blood-brain barrier in man. Journal of Clinical Investigation, 67, 597-604.

Hicks, P., Rolsten, C., Brizzee, D., & Samorajski, T. (1983). Age-related changes in rat brain capillaries. Neurobiology of Aging, 4, 69-75.

Hiestad, D.D., Marcus, M.L., Said, S.I., & Gross, P.M. (1980). Effect of acetylcholine and vasoactive intestinal peptide on cerebral blood flow. American Journal of Physiology, 239, H73-H80.

Hoffman, G.E., & Sladek, J.R., Jr. (1980). Age-related changes in dopamine, LHRH and somatostatin in the rat hypothalamus. Neurobiology of Aging, 1, 27-37.

Hoffman, P.L., Walter, R., & Bulat, M. (1977). An enzymatically stable peptide with activity in the central nervous system: Its penetration through the blood-CSF barrier. Brain Research, 122, 87-94.

Hökfelt, T., Johansson, O., Ljungdahl, A., Lundberg, J.M., & Schultzberg, M. (1980). Peptidergic neurons. Nature, 284, 515-521.

Hostetter, G., Jubb, S.L., & Kozlowski, G.P. (1980). An inability of subcutaneous vasopressin to affect passive avoidance behavior. Neuroendocrinology, 30, 174-177.

Houghten, R.A., Swann, R.W., & Li, C.H. (1980). β-Endorphin: Stability, clearance, behavior, and entry into the central nervous system after intravenous injection of the tritiated peptide in rats and rabbits. Proceedings of the National Academy of Sciences, USA, 77, 4588-4591.

Hunziker, O., Abdel' Al, S., Schulz, U., & Schweizer, A. (1978). Architecture of cerebral capillaries in aged human subjects with hypertension. Advances in Neurology, 20, 471-477.

Kaiya, H., Tanaka, T., Takeuchi, K., Morita, K., Adachi, S., Shirakawa, H., Ueki, H., & Namba, M. (1983). Decreased levels of β-endorphin-like immunoreactivity in cerebrospinal fluid of patients with senile dementia of Alzheimer type. *Life Sciences, 33,* 1039-1043.

Kastin, A.J., & Barbeau, A. (1972). Preliminary clinical studies with L-prolyl-L-leucyl-glycine amide in Parkinson's disease. *Canadian Medical Association Journal, 107,* 1079-1081.

Kastin, A.J., Banks, W.A., Castellanos, P.F., Nissen, C., & Coy, D.H. (1982). Differential penetration of DSIP peptides into rat brain. *Pharmacology, Biochemistry and Behavior, 17,* 1187-1191.

Kastin, A.J., Banks, W.A., Zadina, J.E., & Graf, M. (1983). Brain peptides: The dangers of constricted nomenclatures. *Life Sciences, 32,* 295-301.

Kastin, A.J., & Fabre, L.A. (1982). Limitations to effect of α-MSH on permeability of blood-brain barrier to IV^{99m}Tc-pertechnetate. *Pharmacology, Biochemistry and Behavior, 17,* 1199-1201.

Kastin, A.J., Castellanos, P.F., Banks, W.A., & Coy, D.H. (1981). Radioimmunoassay of DSIP-like material in human blood: Possible protein binding. *Pharmacology, Biochemistry and Behavior, 15,* 969-974.

Kastin, A.J., Castellanos, P.F., Fischman, A.J., Proffitt, J.K., & Graf, M.V. (1984a). Evidence for peptide aggregation. *Pharmacology, Biochemistry and Behavior, 21,* 969-973.

Kastin, A.J., Nissen, C., Nikolics, K., Medzihradszky, K., Coy, D.H., Teplan, I., & Schally, A.V. (1976). Distribution of ^{3}H- α-MSH in rat brain. *Brain Research Bulletin, 1,* 19-26.

Kastin, A.J., Olson, G.A., Sandman, C.A., & Ehrensing, R.H. (1981). Possible role of peptides in senile dementia. In T. Crook and S. Gershon (Eds.), *Strategies for the development of an effective treatment for senile dementia* (pp. 139-152). New Canaan, CT: Mark Powley Associates.

Kastin, A.J., Olson, R.D., Schally, A.V., & Coy, D.H. (1979). CNS effects of peripherally administered brain peptides. *Life Sciences, 25,* 401-414.

Kastin, A.J., Stephens, E., Ehrensing, R.H., & Fischman, A.J. (1984b). Tyr-MIF-1 acts as an opiate antagonist in the tail-flick test. *Pharmacology, Biochemistry and Behavior, 21,* 937-941.

Kavaliers, M., Hirst, M., & Campbell Teskey, G. (1983). Aging, opioid analgesia and the pineal gland. *Life Sciences, 32,* 2279-2287.

Kosik, K.S., Bradley, W.G., Good, P.F., Rasool, C.G., & Selkoe, D.J.

(1983). Cholinergic function in lumbar aluminum myelopathy. *Journal of Neuropathology and Experimental Neurology, 42,* 365-375.

Krieger, D.T., & Martin, J.B. (1981). Brain peptides. *New England Journal of Medicine, 304,* 876-885, 944-951.

Landfield, P.W., Baskin, R.K., & Pitler, T.A. (1981). Brain aging correlates: Retardation by hormonal-pharmacological treatments. *Science, 214,* 581-585.

Landfield, P.W., Sundberg, D.K., Smith, M.S., Eldridge, J.C., & Morris, M. (1980). Mammalian aging: Theoretical implications of changes in brain and endocrine systems during mid- and late-life in rats. *Peptides, 1* (Suppl.), 185-196.

Marquis, J.K. (1983). Aluminum inhibition of human serum cholinesterase. *Bulletin of Environmental Contamination and Toxicology, 31,* 164-169.

Meites, J. (1982). Changes in neuroendocrine control of anterior pituitary function during aging. *Neuroendocrinology, 34,* 151-156.

Merin, M., Hollt, V., Przewlocki, R., & Herz, A. (1980). Low permeation of systematically administered human β-endorphin into rabbit brain measured by radio-immunoassays differentiating human and rabbit β-endorphin. *Life Sciences, 27,* 281-289.

Messing, R.B., Vasques, B.J., Spiehler, V.R., Martinez, J.L., Jr., Jensen, R.A., Rigter, H., & McGaugh, J.L. (1980). ^{3}H-Dihydromorphine binding in brain regions of young and aged rats. *Life Sciences, 26,* 921-927.

Mroz, E.A., & Leeman, S.E. (1977). Substance P. *Vitamin and Hormone, 35,* 209-281.

Perl, D.P., Gajdusek, C., Garruto, R.M., Vanagihara, R.T., & Gibbs, C.J. (1982). Intraneuronal aluminium in amyotrophic lateral sclerosis and Parkinsonism — Dementia of Guam. *Science, 217,* 1053-1055.

Pickworth, F.A. (1937). Cerebral ischemia and mental disorder. *Journal of Mental Science, 83,* 512-533.

Preskorn, S.H., Irwin, G.H., Simpson, S., Friesen, D., Rinne, J., & Jerkovich, G. (1981). Medical therapies for mood disorders alter the blood-brain barrier. *Science, 213,* 469-471.

Rapoport, S.I. (1976). *Blood-brain barrier in physiology and medicine.* New York: Raven Press.

Rapoport, S.I., Klee, W.A., Pettigrew, K.D., & Ohno, K. (1980). Entry of opioid peptides into the central nervous system. *Science, 207,* 84-86.

Rapoport, S.I., Ohno, K., & Pettigrew, K.D. (1979). Blood-brain barrier permeability in senescent rats. *Journal of Gerontology, 34,* 162-169.

Ravens, J.R. (1978). Vascular changes in the human senile brain. *Advances in Neurology, 20,* 487-499.

Reisberg, B., Ferris, S.H., Anand, R., Mir, P., Geibel, V., De Leon, M.J., & Roberts, E. (1983). Effects of naloxone in senile dementia: A double-blind trial. *New England Journal of Medicine, 308,* 721-722.

Risberg, J., & Gustafson, L. (1983). [133]Xe cerebral blood flow in dementia and in neuropsychiatry research. In P.L. Magistretti (Ed.), *Functional radionuclide imaging of the brain* (pp. 151-159). New York: Raven Press.

Roberts, E. (1981). A speculative consideration on the neurobiology and treatment of senile dementia. In T. Crook & S. Gershon (Eds.), *Strategies for the development of an effective treatment for senile dementia* (pp. 247-320). New Canaan, CT: Mark Powley Associates, Inc.

Rossor, M.N., Emson, P.C., Mountjoy, C.Q., Roth, Sir M., & Iversen, L.L. (1980a). Reduced amounts of immunoreactive somatostatin in the temporal cortex in senile dementia of Alzheimer's type. *Neuroscience Letters, 20,* 373-377.

Rossor, M.N., Fahrenkrug, J., Emson, P., Mountjoy, C.Q., Iversen, L.L., & Roth, M. (1980b). Reduced cortical choline acetyltransferase in senile dementia of Alzheimer's type is not accompanied by changes in vasoactive intestinal peptide. *Brain Research, 20,* 249-253.

Rossor, M.N., Iversen, L.L., Mountjoy, C.Q., Roth, M., Hawthorn, J., Ang, V.Y., & Jenkins, J.S. (1980c). Arginine vasopressin and choline acetyltransferase in brains of patients with Alzheimer's type senile dementia. *The Lancet, II,* 1367-1368.

Rossor, M.N., Rehfeld, J.F., Emson, P.C., Mountjoy, C.Q., Roth, M., & Iversen, L.L. (1981). Normal cortical concentration of cholecystokinin with reduced choline acetyltransferase activity in senile dementia of Alzheimer's type. *Life Sciences, 29,* 405-410.

Rudick, R.A., & Buell, S.J. (1983). Integrity of blood-brain barrier to peroxidase in senescent mice. *Neurobiology of Aging, 4,* 283-287.

Rudman, D., & Kutner, M.H. (1978). Melanotropic peptides increase permeability of plasma/cerebrospinal fluid barrier. *American Journal of Physiology, 234*(3), E327-332.

Samuels, S., Fish, I., Schwartz, S.A., & Hochgeschwender, U. (1983). Age-related changes in blood-to-brain amino acid transport and incorporation into brain protein. *Neurochemical Research, 8,* 167-177.

Sankar, R., Blossom, E., Clemons, K., & Charles, P. (1983). Age-associated changes in the effects of amphetamine on the blood-brain barrier of rats. *Neurobiology of Aging, 4,* 65-68.

Sankar, R., Domer, F.R., & Kastin, A.J. (1981). Selective effects of α-MSH and MIF-1 on the blood-brain barrier. *Peptides, 2,* 345-347.

Scott, D.E., & Sladek, J.R., Jr. (1981). Age-related changes in the endocrine hypothalamus: I. Tanycytes and the blood-brain-cerebrospinal fluid barrier. *Neurobiology of Aging, 2,* 89-94.

Sharpless, N.S., Thal, L.J., Perlow, M.J., Tabaddor, K., Waltz, J.M., Shapiro, K.N., Amin, I.M., Engel, J., Jr., & Crandall, P.H. (1984). Vasoactive intestinal peptide in cerebrospinal fluid. *Peptides, 5,* 429-433.

Sideman, S., & Manor, D. (1982). The dialysis dementia syndrome and aluminum intoxication. *Nephron, 31,* 1-10.

Sorensen, P.S., Hammer, M., Vorstrup, S., & Gjerris, F. (1983). CSF and plasma vasopressin concentrations in dementia. *Journal of Neurology, Neurosurgery, and Psychiatry, 46,* 911-916.

Sturman, J.A., Wisniewski, H.M., & Shek, J.W. (1983). High affinity uptake of GABA and glycine by rabbits with aluminum-induced neurofibrillary changes. *Neurochemical Research, 8,* 1097-1109.

Sundquist, J., Forsling, M.L., Olsson, J.E., & Akerlund, M. (1983). Cerebrospinal fluid arginine vasopressin in degenerative disorders and other neurological diseases. *Journal of Neurology, Neurosurgery, and Psychiatry, 46,* 14-17.

Tracey, A.S., & Boivin, T.L. (1983). Interactions of the aluminum (III) ion in a model membrane system. *Journal of the American Chemical Society, 105,* 4901-4905.

Van Ree, J.M., Bohus, B., Versteeg, D.H.G., & De Wied, D. (1978). Neurohypophyseal principles and memory processes. *Biochemical Pharmacology, 27,* 1793-1800.

Vogh, B.P., & Maren, T.H. (1984). Importance of carbonic anhydrase in the production of cerebrospinal fluid. *Annals of the New*

York Academy of Sciences, 429, 607-608.

Williams, A.R., Carey, R.J., & Miller, M. (1983). Behavioral differences between vasopressin-deficient (Brattleboro) and normal Long-Evans rats. Peptides, 4, 711-716.

Williams, K.H., & Goldstein, G. (1979). Cognitive and affective response to lithium in patients with organic brain syndrome. American Journal of Psychiatry, 136, 800-803.

Wisniewski, H.M., & Kozlowski, P.B. (1982). Evidence for blood-brain barrier changes in senile dementia of the Alzheimer type (SDAT). Annals of the New York Academy of Sciences, 396, 119-129.

Wood, P.L., Malthe-Sorenssen, D., Cheney, D.L., & Costa, E. (1978). Increase of hippocampal acetylcholine turnover rate and the stretching-yawning syndrome elicited by alpha-MSH and ACTH. Life Sciences, 22, 673-678.

Yarbrough, G.G. (1983). Thyrotropin releasing hormone and CNS cholinergic neurons. Life Sciences, 33, 111-118.

Yesavage, J., & Berger, P.A. (1980). Correlation of cerebrospinal fluid lactate with age. American Journal of Psychiatry, 137, 8-9.

Zemcov, A., Barclay, L., & Blass, J.P. (1984). Regional decline of cerebral blood flow with age in cognitively intact subjects. Neurobiology of Aging, 5, 1-6.

11

Possible Immunological Treatments for Alzheimer's Disease

Joy Cavagnaro, PhD

Systemic age changes in the immune system suggest an age-related decline in the regulatory control of immune reactivity. The involution of the thymus gland and decreased levels of thymic hormones seem to play an essential role in the imbalance of hormonal- and cell-mediated immune responses. However, the influence of other homeostatic mechanisms, such as the central nervous system (CNS) and endocrine system have also been implicated.

There is still some debate as to whether Alzheimer's disease (AD) represents an exaggeration or acceleration of normal cerebral aging or an independent disease whose susceptibility is increased by the process of aging (Walford, 1982). In any event, it appears as though a multi-factorial approach must be used in designing effective therapeutic regimens to correct the primary neuroendocrine lesions and coincident impaired immune function that define AD.

BASIC CONCEPTS IN IMMUNOLOGY

The immune system, not unlike the neuroendocrine system, is a complex network of regulatory interactions. Normal immunologic homeostasis requires an appropriate interaction between effector, helper, and suppressor mechanisms. Thymus-derived lymphocytes, T cells, function as regulatory cells or cytotoxic effector cells. Bursal equivalent lymphocytes, B cells, are the cells responsible for immunoglobulin production. The major population of phagocytic cells that participate in the immune response is the monocyte. Monocytes circulate briefly in the blood before migrating into tissue where they transform into macrophages.

Immune system cells produce numerous humoral substances

including lymphokines, monokines, vasoactive compounds, immunoglobulins, and some complement components. Immunoglobulins and complement often act at sites that are distinct from the cells that produce them and are traditionally discussed as humoral immunity.

Immune recognition generally proceeds through a well-defined sequence of events. An antigen is recognized by macrophages, processed, and then presented to T cells. Lymphokines may then direct the mobilization of additional T cells, macrophages, and other effector cells. B cells will be recruited if an immunoglobulin response is called for. B cells proliferate and transform into plasma cells and produce IgM followed by IgG antibodies. T-independent antigens (e.g., bacterial polysaccharide [LPS], and polyvinylpyrrolidone [PVP]), on the other hand, are capable of eliciting an antibody response without the involvement of T cells (Cohn, 1983).

The means by which immune response cells recognize normal host cells from foreign antigens is via the genetically determined histocompatibility antigen system (HLA). The HLA complex is also important in the cell-to-cell interaction that occurs as part of the immune response.

Congenital defects of most of the components of the immune response and acquired abnormalities have been described. Some diseases may also result from improper regulation of the immune response or may be associated with drug therapy, infection, or neoplasia. At a cellular level, dysfunction may be caused by abnormal helper or suppressor activity, blocking antibodies, circulating immune complexes, or primary effector cell abnormalities. All of the above mechanisms have been implicated in playing a role in the immunological dysfunction of the elderly (Bonomo, Antonaci, & Jirillo, 1983; Cavagnaro, 1983; Kay, 1979).

ALZHEIMER'S DISEASE: AN IMMUNOLOGIC DISORDER

Alterations in indices of immunological function might be expected in either persistent viral infections of the brain or in the presence of an altered brain autoimmunity (Miller, Neighbour, Katzman, Aronson, & Lipkowitz, 1981). Infections or immunologic factors (or both) have been implicated in the pathogenesis or course of AD (Blass

& Weksler, 1983; MacDonald, Goldstone, Morris, Exton-Smith, & Callard, 1982; Schmidt, 1983).

The immune and neuroendocrine systems are characterized by complex interactions between cells that depend on both direct cell contact and humoral mediators. Each of the major classes of immune cells (i.e., helper and supressor T cells, natural killer cells, B cells, and macrophages) appears to have an antigenic counterpart in cells of the CNS. Antigens shared by cell types within the immune system and the nervous system include: Fc receptors and Ia antigens on B cells, macrophages and glial cells; T3 antigen on T helper cells and synaptosome membranes; antigens recognized by OKT8 monoclonal antibody are present on T suppressor cells and oligodendrocytes; anti-human T-cell monoclonal antibodies bind to T cells and Purkinje cells and anti-Leu 7 antibody bind to both natural killer cells and central and peripheral nervous tissues (Fundenberg, Whitten, Arnaud, & Khansari, 1984).

In addition, messages are transmitted to other cells by soluble humoral factors: lymphokines and lymphotoxins in the immune system and neurotransmitters and neurotoxins in the CNS. Moreover, various immune cell subsets have been shown to have receptors for endogenous neurotransmitters (e.g., endorphins, dopamine, serotonin, and substance P) that appear identical to those present on brain cells (Payan, Brewster, & Goetzl, 1983).

The concept of memory is a component of both systems as well. A distinction in the two exists, however, in that memory or the anamnestic immune response tends to be less affected by aging; that is, aging itself is generally associated with an impaired primary immune response but an intact secondary response. The classic histopathologic lesions of AD are concentrated in the hippocampus and frontal cortex areas of the brain believed to be associated with memory.

Supporting evidence suggesting that the disease may be associated with the immune system relies on the findings that senile plaques contain amyloid deposits, which are also frequently found in patients with myeloma, rheumatoid arthritis, and other immunologic disorders (Glenner, 1982, 1983). Eikelenboom and Stam (1982) showed that plaques also contain the complement factors C_1q, C_3b, C_3c, C_3d, and C_4. An increase in complement hemolytic activity in AD patients and an increase in the complement factors with respect to control groups have also been reported in AD patients (Ricchieri, Ongaro, Argentiero, & Tavolato, 1983). Nandy (1978) has shown that antibrain antibodies are also increased in the sera of patients with senile dementia (SD) Pentland, Christie, Watson, and Yap, (1982), have reported that the levels of serum immunoglobulins, IgA, IgG, and IgM are reduced in AD patients. However, no significant abnormality has been found to indicate an autoimmune disorder.

While the evidence is inconclusive, studies have shown an association of HLA with AD. Transmission of HLA haplotypes and immunoglobulin (Gm) allotypes, on chromosomes 6 and 14, respectively, has been reported in 97 members of a single kindred, containing 257 individuals, 45 of whom were determined by clinical examination, autopsy, or historical data to have had AD (Walford, 1982; Weitkamp, Nee, Keats, Polinsky, & Guttormsen, 1983). If the evidence for an association of AD with chromosome 14 is supported, then the recent reports that the genes encoding the α-chain of the human T-cell receptor are present on chromosome 14 (Jones, Morse, Kao, Carbone, & Palmer, 1985) and that rearrangements in a particular region of the chromosome 14 may affect the growth of T cells and be involved in the development of T cell malignancies (Hecht, Morgan, Kaiser-McCaw Hecht, & Smith, 1984), may become more significant.

A variety of clinical conditions, including acute graft-versus-host (GVH) disease, multiple sclerosis, and several other autoimmune diseases such as systemic lupus erythematosus, hemolytic anemia, severe atopic eczema, and inflammatory bowel disease, have shown a loss in suppressor T cells. Conditions characterized by enhanced suppressor activity include a rare patient with acquired agammaglobulinemia and several patients with chronic GVH disease. The excessive numbers of suppressor cells exclusive of any change in interferon (IFN) production may cause prolonged immunological unresponsiveness (Miller et al., 1981).

The hypothalamus is frequently affected in AD, and recent studies have shown immunological abnormalities including decreased lymphocyte proliferation in rats with experimental lesions in the anterior hypothalamus. Patients with AD show significantly enhanced suppressor activity when compared with either young or aged controls. There is no significant difference between IFN levels in AD patients and aged controls which may indicate that factors other than IFN are at least partially involved in mediating the suppressor effect in diseased individuals. The finding of enhanced suppressor cell activity in SD patients raises the possibility that this active impairment of the immune response may allow an infectious agent to gain a foothold resulting in CNS damage (Miller et al., 1981). Patients in the acute phase of infectious mononucleosis have both activation and increase of suppressor T cells, but during convalescence the proportions of T-cell subsets and immune function return to normal (Reinherz, O'Brien, & Rosenthal, 1980).

NEUROENDOCRINE CORRELATES
OF THE IMMUNE RESPONSE

Embryonically, the CNS is comprised of the spinal cord and brain, which are derived from folds of the embryonic ectodermal sheet of cells. Adjacent embryonic tissue forms the neural crest. Neural crest cells migrate throughout the body to form the elements of the autonomic or peripheral nervous system (PNS) (Barnstable, 1982). Thymus development depends on a direct interaction of the neural crest, specifically mesenchymal derivatives, with pharyngeal epithelium. Thymic aplasia or dysplasia in Di George's syndrome has been shown to result from an incomplete contribution by the neural crest during embryonic development (Bockman & Kirby, 1984). Functionally, an interrelationship between the two systems continues in the mature organism.

The possibility that neurophysiologic factors influence immunity was demonstrated initially by the finding of altered lymphocytes and antibody responses in animals with experimentally induced lesions of the CNS (Pierpaoli & Sorkin, 1969). It was later demonstrated that the immune response was significantly comprised in hypothalamus-lesioned and reticular formation-lesioned animals. The most pronounced changes of the cellular makeup of the thymus was observed in rats with lesions in hypothalamic, reticular formation, and superior collicular areas (Isakovic & Jankovic, 1973). However, only hypothalamus-lesioned rats exhibited significant alterations in the spleen and lymph nodes, which correlated with the reports showing a decreased capacity for antibody production, Arthus sensitivity, and delayed-type hypersensitivity. More recently it has been shown that these alterations are due to the loss of corticotropin (ACTH). ACTH secretion is mediated by corticotropin-releasing factor (CRF) acting in concert with vasopressin and possibly other substances such as oxytocin, epinephrine, and angiotensin II (Ono, Samson,

McDonald, Lumpkin, Bedran de Castro, & McCann, 1985).
It has been claimed that stimulation of both sympathetic and parasympathetic zones of the hypothalamus leads to involution of the thymus, most probably because of changes in the neurosecretory system, which results in hyperaction of the adrenal cortex. Adrenal cortical secretion and administration of corticosteroids have a negative influence on lymphatic organs (Everitt, 1980).

Steroids interfere mainly with short-lived lymphocytes, which are the great majority of lymphocytes found in the thymus, spleen, and lymph nodes. The thymus medulla contains corticosteroid-resistant, GVH-producing and mitogen reactive cells. Studies of local production of hormones by various endocrine tissues and steroid hormone implants have revealed that cortisone, cortisol, and testosterone produce zonal involution and that estradiol, estriol, and estrone cause diffuse involution of the thymus (Friedman, Bomze, Rothman, & Drutz, 1964).

The capacities of physiologically relevant concentrations of the sensory neuropeptides, somatostatin, and substance P to enhance or inhibit the activities of diverse immunocompetent leukocytes and to elicit or suppress humoral components of inflammation, support the possibility of involvement of these neuropeptides in the modulation of local immune function (Payan et al., 1983).

Much effort has gone into the investigation of the pathogenesis of a T-cell immunodeficiency state observed in patients with glioblastoma. Impaired T cell-mediated immunity is evidenced by cutaneous anergy, diminished numbers of T cells and marked depression of lymphocyte blastogenic responsiveness. Schwyzer and Fontana (1985) reported on a human glioblastoma cell line, which constitutively secretes a soluble factor with biologic and biochemical characteristics of the human macrophage-derived monokine, interleukin 1 (IL 1). The cell line also produces a factor that inhibits the effects of IL 1 and IL 2 on T cells. If the inhibitory factors that are produced by the B cell line and the glioblastoma line are also produced by the corresponding nontransformed cells, the B cells and astrocytes, the authors suggest that these factors could also represent negative feedback circuits that regulate the extent of T cell activation.

ENDOGENOUS NEUROTRANSMITTERS

The observation that in AD there is a marked loss of cholinergic activity led to the theory that the associated dementia is the result of a cholinergic deficiency (Bartus, Dean, Beer, & Lippa, 1980). Reports of a selective loss of cholinergic neurons in the basal forebrain lent morphological support to this view. However, it has also become evident that the topography of the AD lesions involves the neocortex, hippocampal formation, and amygdala, as well as the basal forebrain nuclei (Davies, 1983). Clearly, more than one transmitter system must be affected with such a distribution of lesions. This view is supported by recent studies showing that alterations in somatostatin-mediated and noradrenergic systems are also apparent in AD (Morrison, Rogers, Scherr, Benoit, & Bloom, 1985).

Among various potential causes of the cholinergic derangement and the existence of a primary lesion in the cortex is the hypothesis that a key abnormality in AD involves the production or processing of specific trophic factors normally supplied by the cortex for the maintenance of afferent processes of subcortical origin (Perry, R.H., Candy, & Perry, E.K., 1983).

The three neuropeptides that appear to be present in large numbers of cortical and hippocampal neurons are cholecystokinin octapeptide, vasointestinal peptide (VIP) and somatostatin (SOM). Both cholecystokinin and VIP are found in 2% to 5% of distinct populations of cortical neurons. VIP and substance P have been proposed as potential transmitters for cerebral vasodilation (Lee, Saito, & Berezin, 1984). In contrast, acetylcholine (ACh) acts more like a transmitter for constriction of cerebral blood vessels. Both cholecystokinin and VIP seem to be present in normal concentrations in the Alzheimer brain. Somatostatin concentrations, on the other hand, have been reported to be reduced in those cases of AD that have very large numbers of neuritic plaques and neurofibrillary tangles (Roberts, Crow, & Polak, 1985). Moreover, Morrison et al., (1985) have suggested that somatostatin neurons in the temporal cortex are a primary focus for the disease process and that the loss of somatostatin content is an early event in the production of symptoms and the subsequent or concomitant cortical atrophy.

Neuronotrophic factors such as nerve growth factors (NGF) are thought to be produced by astroglia. NGF, when injected into the hippocampus, is detected in areas of cholinergic cell bodies. In addition, distinct growth factors have been detected in vivo in this region of the brain. Assuming that a cholinoneuronotrophic factor is produced in certain astroglia for the maintenance of cholinergic axons arising from the nucleus basalis, it has been proposed that in parallel with other trophic hormones its release may be modulated by one or more smaller peptides (Perry, R.H. et al., 1983).

NGF can display biological effects on cells of nonneuronal origin and function, specifically stimulation of polymorphonuclear leukocyte chemotaxis *in vitro*, and it may play a role in the early inflammatory response to injury (Gee, Boyle, Munger, Lawman, & Young, 1983). The concentration of NGF required for this effect is similar to that which stimulates ganglionic neurite outgrowth.

The cholinergic deficit and atrophy of the basal nucleus of Meynert may be a secondary consequence of the loss of cortical somatostatin neurons from a region that provides the major input to the basal nucleus. The reason for the selectivity of the AD process is unknown but presumably is related to the physiological properties of susceptible somatostatin neurons in the cortex.

The most likely modulators for CNS control of immunologic responses are the endorphins and met-enkephalins. These neuropeptides can express both direct stimulating or suppressive activities for lymphocytes in *in vitro* models. Studies of the *in vivo* infusion of β-endorphin into the cerebral ventricle of the rat results in the migration of macrophage-like cells and are consistent with the *in vitro* evidence for a chemotactic effect of β-endorphin (VanEpps & Saland, 1984). The finding that human lymphocytes secrete endorphin-like substances implies that endogenous neuropeptides may mediate some aspects of lymphocyte autoregulation.

Behavioral effects involving memory and learning have been demonstrated for the neuropeptide vasopressin. Comparison of the distribution of vasopressin with that of the enkephalins in the neurohypophyseal hormone release (Choy, 1983). In humans, aging enhances the vasopressin release response to osmotic stimuli (Helderman et al., 1978). That is, for any given increase in plasma osmolality, plasma vasopressin rises more in old compared with young adults. In many elderly individuals, however, a hypotensive stimulus produces little or no change in the hormone concentrations. The only other neuropeptide system reportedly shown to change in AD is substance P (SP), but this evidence is unconfirmed (Davis, 1983).

Substance P has been identified in the CNS, PNS, and the intestinal tract, and has been implicated in the mediation of hypersensitivity. Elevated levels of SP are detected in sensory nerves supplying localized sites of chronic inflammation. SP has also been shown to elicit specific mast cells and polymorphonuclear leukocyte functional responses (Levine et al., 1984; Payan, Levine, & Goetzl, 1984).

Neuropeptide Y (NPY) appears to be located in certain brain stem noradrenergic and adrenergic nuclei that project to the hypothalamus and also in intrinsic hypothalamic neurons. NPY receptors have been measured in the rat brain with high concentrations in the hypothalamus. NPY acts on structures adjacent to the third ventricle to inhibit the secretion of leutinizing hormone (LH) and growth hormone (GH), but not follicle-stimulating hormone (FSH). However, it can directly stimulate the secretion of all three hormones from the cells of the anterior pituitary *in vitro* (McDonald, Lumpkin, Samson, & McCann, 1985). In the aged rat hypothalamus, significant reductions have been reported in the content of GH-releasing factors, LH-releasing factors; and prolactin-inhibiting factor, and increases in FSH-releasing factor (for review, see Everitt, 1980). It is likely that NPY may play a physiologically significant role at both hypothalamic and pituitary sites and influence the secretion of pituitary hormones.

CHROMOSOME CHANGES IN AD

Cytogenetic studies of AD patients are inconclusive with respect to both the incidence of aneuploidy and the occurrence of breaks and fragments (Buckton, Whalley, Lee, & Christie, 1983; Moorhead and Heyman, 1983; Smith, Broe, & Williamson, 1983). Increased chromosome aneuploidy has been found in females but not males with AD (Moorhead & Heyman, 1983). Chromosome abnormalities observed in female patients were similar to those observed in elderly controls, though in the latter group there was an increase in the frequency of cells that had lost an X chromosome. In the female AD patients and the aged controls, while there was an increase in the frequency of autosomal aneuploid cells, no single chromosome was preferentially affected. Because chromosome abnormalities found in AD are similar in nature, but not as extensive as those observed in senescence in the absence of dementia, it is argued that chromosome aneuploidy is more likely to be related to processes concerned with aging rather than specifically linked to the dementia of AD.

If there is a significant gain or loss in the number of chromosomes in the circulating lymphocytes *in vivo*, then one would expect to see a corresponding increase or decrease in the DNA/cell ratio in individual cells. This does occur, for example, as a concomitant of aging. Cook-Deegan and Austin (1983) were unable to show a correlation between the variation in DNA content and the presence of AD, even of AD, even in individuals whose cultured lymphocytes had earlier shown high degrees of aneuploidy (10%). Their interpretation was that DNA content in circulating lymphocytes is indeed normal, and previous reports of high aneuploidy reflect some reproducible artifacts induced during the lengthy process of altering lymphocytes *in vitro* and then preparing them for chromosome study. This carries the implication that the primary defect in such cases lies not in chromosome structure, but rather in the processes that govern cell division. Lymphocytes of some patients with AD, particularly of the familial type may, by virtue of an intrinsic defect, be more sensitive to certain concentrations and/or durations of exogenous factors known to disrupt mitosis *in vitro*.

Hypersensitivity to DNA-damaging agents occurs in several inherited neurodegenerations. Alzheimer cell lines are significantly more sensitive to ionizing radiation-type DNA damaging agents (i.e., x-rays), as well as to the x-ray mimetic, DNA-damaging chemical, N-methyl-N-nitro-N-nitrosoguanidine (MNNG) (Robbins et al., 1983). The normal sensitivity of the AD lines to UV radiation indicates that they are not hypersensitive to all types of DNA-damaging agents. While the basis for the hypersensitivity is not known, the hypersensitivity may be a specific defect in the repairs of x-ray-type DNA damage. Moreover, the authors propose that the death of neurons *in vivo* in AD results from the accumulation of unrepaired neural DNA that has received radiomimetic damage from intracellular metabolites and/or from spontaneous hydrolytic reactions.

The mechanism of alteration of immune function by ionizing radiation is complex. It is dependent on the quality of radiation, dose, route, number of exposures, interval between exposures, and time after exposure. This underscores the complexity of the mechanisms of action of ionizing radiation in immune functions. That immunoenhancement sometimes can be seen after a single exposure to radiation and immunosuppression after multiple exposures suggests that the regulatory control of the immune system is susceptible to radiation.

CHROMATIN ALTERATIONS

Many degenerative diseases of the nervous system are associated with increased condensation of the chromatin. (Feit, 1983). Studies by Crapper and DeBoni (1978) and Lewis, Lukew, and DeBoni, (1981) have provided physical and biochemical evidence of an almatin structure in AD. Crapper and DeBoni first showed that when nuclei were isolated from the brain and subjected to sonication, a large fraction of the total nuclei chromatin was in the more highly condensed heterochromatin form in patients with AD than in aged matched controls. The heterochromatin fraction could not be transcribed by RNA polymerase. This larger fraction of heterochromatin in the brains of patients with AD correlates with the previous biochemical evidence of reduced brain protein synthesis in that condition. Subsequent studies employing the enzyme micrococcal nuclease to digest chromatin confirms the alteration in chromatin structure in AD. The change in chromatin structure affected both neuronal and glial nuclei. In addition, these studies suggested that the more condensed chromatin in AD may be related to the presence of H1 histones with unique electrophilic properties rather than to a change in DNA.

There is evidence that the level of an endogenous chromosomal protease in the thymus gland correlates with the age of the animal (Cavagnaro, 1979). A sharp increase in the level of the thymus chromosomal protease of the aged animal may result from either activation of the protease in the residual T cells in aged animals or to the increase in specific activity due to increases in the nonlymphoid mass, which may have a higher level of the chromosomal protease than the T cells. It is assumed that the protease is involved in the continuous turnover of chromosomal proteins throughout the cell cycle and in the limited turnover of histone H1 in the G1 phase of the cell cycle. Of the tissues tested (kidney, liver, and thymus) the age-related increase was observed only in the thymus. Further studies of the nuclear protease of the brain may help to explain a biochemical influence on the chromatin structure of AD.

AGE-RELATED CHANGES IN THE IMMUNE SYSTEM

The thymic lymphocytic mass decreases with age primarily as a result of atrophy of the cortex. The onset of this decrease in coincident with attainment of sexual maturity. Subsequently, atrophy of the epithelial cells and decreased levels of thymic hormones have been observed.

Histologically, the cortex of an involuted thymus is sparsely populated with lymphocytes that are replaced by numerous macrophages filled with lipoid granules. In addition, infiltration of plasma and mast cells can be observed in the medulla as well as in the cortex. Although the size of lymph nodes and spleen remains about the same after adulthood in individuals without lymphatic neoplasia, the cellular corpuscle of these tissues shifts so that there are diminished numbers of germinal centers and increased numbers of plasma cells and macrophages, as well as increased amounts of connective tissue.

Basically, all immune potential is depressed by aging: Delayed cutaneous hypersensitivity responses, proliferation induced by mitogens or antigens, and lymphokine production have all been found to be impaired (Bonomo et al., 1983; Kay, 1979). Aging promotes a decline in maturation and immune reactivity of T cells, but the relative percent of peripheral T cells remains normal. There is an age-associated increase in the number of suppressor T cells. Concomitant with the suppressor cell changes with age, which include a failure in the mechanism of regulation of these cells, is the decline of the helper function of T cells with age. Humoral immune response is impaired in the elderly, even if B-cell percentage and serum immunoglobulin levels are unaffected. These findings suggest a suppressive mechanism mediated by T cells themselves or by their soluble products. In addition, the role of monocyte/macrophage cell lineage in the suppression of B cell responses is also considered an age-related change (Cavagnaro, 1983).

AGE-RELATED CHANGES IN THE NEUROENDOCRINE SYSTEM

The brains of aged individuals can be characterized by atrophy and loss of neuronal elements. Significant decreases occur with age in the activity of enzymes associated with catecholamine metabolism, especially dopaminergic enzymes, which are highly vulnerable to age change. In the human hypothalamus significant decreases occur with age in the activity of enzymes associated with the metabolism of catecholamines, γ-aminobutyric acid (GABA) and ACh (Everitt, 1980).

Many of the regulatory actions of the hypothalamus are mediated by the autonomic nervous system. Unfortunately, little is known about aging in this system. Only in the area of the hypothalamic control of endocrine function is it possible to relate defects in the hypothalamus to the determination of peripheral functions with age. There is considerable literature suggesting that age changes in the hypothalamic-hypophyseal area may lead to secondary age changes in the endocrine system (for review see Everitt, 1980). In fact, changes in hypothalamic catecholamine metabolism have been implicated in triggering a cascade of age-related changes.

Apart from the increase with age in FSH and LH, there appear to be no major changes in the basal plasma levels. Basal plasma GH levels show little or no change with age. There is no change in the plasma prolactin level. Basal plasma glucocorticoid levels show no significant change with age between maturity and old age. Removal of cortisol, however, is much slower in old age and, therefore, a lower cortisol secretion rate can maintain a normal plasma cortisol level in aged individuals. There is no significant difference in basal plasma ACTH. Plasma total testosterone levels decline progressively in males. Compensatory increases occur in serum FSH and LH, but these are not as marked as in postmenopausal women.

Several hypotheses have been advanced to explain peripheral aging on the basis of various deficiencies or excesses of neurotransmitter and hormones, and include: (a) hypothalamic disregulation, (b) hypothalamic elevation, (c) neuroendocrine deficiency, (d) neurotransmitter, (e) hypopituitary, (f) hypothyroid, (g) neuroendocrine overstimulation, (h) pituitary, and (g) stress theory. Normal aging is clearly under genetic control, and it seems highly probable that at least part of this control is exercised through a regulatory center in the brain that is the direct cause of aging. Deficiencies of a vital component at any state in the neuroendocrine pathway (e.g., neurotransmitter, hypothalamic-releasing hormone, pituitary trophic hormone, or target hormone) can lead to age changes that may be reversed with appropriate replacement therapy.

IMMUNOPHARMACOLOGY

All cells involved in immunologic responses, with the possible exception of lymphocytes, have the capacity to synthesize prostaglandins (PGs). Every cell type in this category, including stimulated but not unstimulated lymphocytes, has the capacity to respond to exogeneous PGs. As such, PGs may be a target (e.g., by decreasing their synthesis) for chemical intervention (Coffey & Middleton, 1977).

There have been studies suggesting that corticosteroids may regulate PG transport and inhibit cyclooxygenase. PGs of the E type may elicit immunosuppressive responses by increasing intracellular cAMP levels. In *in vitro* studies, PGEs have been shown to inhibit lysosome enzyme release from human leukocytes exposed to immune complexes, inhibit release of IgE-dependent immunoglobulin, inhibit transformation of human lymphocytes after mitogen exposure, inhibit lymphocyte secretion from sensitized human lymphocytes, and reduce granulocyte adhesion. The *in vitro* effects of PGEs in causing immunosuppression suggest that PGEs may play a similar role *in vivo*.

There is a large body of evidence to support the belief that the unabated cell proliferation associated with cancer is due to a suppression of the immunologic response. High levels of PGEs have been found in many cancerous conditions including neurogenic tumors, pheochromocytomas, and carcinoid and pancreatic tumors.

The function of all leukocytes in inflammation is not well understood and, in fact, there is little agreement on the chemotactic mechanism by which they accumulate at the inflammed site. There is a consensus, however, that neutrophils (PMN) represent the first cell type to arrive at the site of inflammation. Lysomal enzymes are released as a function of PMN activation and concurrently PGs and leukotrienes (e.g., LTB_4.) are also released. With time and inflammation of a more chronic nature, macrophages play a more dominant role. Their ability to release PGs led to the concept that migration inhibitory factor (MIF), derived from activated T cells, stimulates formation in macrophage of PGs, which act on the lymphocytes as negative-feedback inhibitors to prevent MIF release. Under conditions in which the lymphocytes are unresponsive to this negative-feedback action, the macrophages produce excessive amounts of PGs, which produce the symptoms of inflammation. In addition to release of MIF, lymphocytes also have the capacity to destroy target cells and release chemotactic, cytotoxic, and mitogenic agents.

An interesting model of modulation of the immunologic response by sensory neuropeptides has been proposed by Payan et al. (1984). They have proposed that following a noxious or injurious exposure, impulses are stimulated in neuropeptide-containing C-fibers to release SP and SOM from the peripheral terminals by an axon reflex. The immediate effects of SP include vasodilatation and increased permeability of regional microcirculation as well as activation of mast cells to release histamine, leukotactic peptides, and leukotrienes. The mast cell-derived mediators could amplify the initial inflammatory response, whereas histamine may enhance release of SP by activating the terminals of the C-fibers directly. Histamine increases vascular permeability. Increased vascular permeability promotes the local delivery of both the protein and cellular elements of adaptive immunity so that SP could augment the activity of T cells that accumulate at the site of the reaction. The principal direct effects of SOM released from peripheral terminals include prevention of recruitment of basophils, enhancement of monocyte/macrophage function, and suppression of T-lymphocyte activation.

BLOOD-BRAIN BARRIER

The complex interactions between sensory neuropeptides and effector pathways or the immune system could achieve optimal expression in hypersensitivity reactions and inflammation in the absence of specifically immunocompetent cells. Although neuronal active compounds are numerous, their entry into the sequestered regions of the brain are strictly regulated. Hormone-receptor contact may thus be controlled not only by hormone levels but also by receptor accessibility.

Most neuropeptides are known to occur both in the CNS and in blood. For many peptides, such as enkephalins and somatostatin, poor penetration of the blood-brain barrier is shown. In other cases, β-endorphin and angiotensin peptides are rapidly degraded during or just after their entry into brain cerebrospinal fluid (CSF). Some peptides, such as insulin and the lipotropin-derived peptides, enter the CSF to a slight or moderate extent in the intact form. Many peptide hormones, such as insulin, calcitonin, and angiotensin, act directly on receptors in the circumventricular organs where the blood-brain barrier is absent (Meisenberg & Simmons, 1983).

Oxytocin and vasopressin alter the properties of the blood-brain barrier, which may result in altered nutrient supply to the brain. Changes in the level of vasopressin with age or in AD may thus have a marked influence on the transcellular transport of neuropeptides through the endothelium to the brain.

Of potential interest is the recent study by Broadwell, Balin, Salcman, and Kaplan (1983), suggesting that a brain-blood barrier exists at the level of capillaries and arterioles in the brain but not in the median eminence of the hypothalamus. Open junctions observed between some median eminence ependymal cells permit the bidirectional exchange of substances between the median eminence capillaries and the third ventricle.

HISTAMINE-CONTAINING NEURONS

Histamine may also function as a neurotransmitter in the mammalian CNS. In the brain, the highest histamine content is found in the hypothalamus and in certain areas of the mesencephalon (Panula, Yang, & Costa, 1984). Biochemical measurements of histamine and its synthesizing enzyme, histidine decarboxylase, in various regions of intact and lesioned brains suggest that brains contain long axon histamine-containing neurons. Adenylate cyclase activity has been shown to be stimulated by histamine in brain structures.

Realizing the potential importance of histamine, it is of interest to speculate on the following feedback mechanism. It has been suggested that histamine may enhance the release of SP from sensory afferent neurons and, in turn, may augment the activity of T cells. Somatostatin is also released from sensory afferent neurons and may suppress T-cell activation (Panula et al., 1984).

Histamine also has a direct effect on T cells (Beer, Osband, McCaffrey, Suter, & Rocklin, 1982). At low concentrations histamine binds to the higher-affinity H_1 receptors on T cells, augmenting the immune response. At higher concentrations of histamine, the lesser-affinity H_2 receptors are occupied and result in immunosuppression (Cavagnaro, Cohen, Cathcart, & Osband, 1982). The availability of pharmacologically relevant levels of histamine near the responding brain cells may create a similar dual-feedback mechanism and at high histamine concentrations serve to promote a general immunosuppressive effect as is seen in AD.

TREATMENTS THAT RETARD OR REVERSE THE IMMUNOLOGICAL CONSEQUENCES OF AGING

Various experimental approaches have been implemented to delay the onset of age involution of the thymus and/or its resulting sequalae of effects, as well as restore the decline in immune functions (Cavagnaro, 1983).

With respect to neuroendocrine balance, hypophysectomy and thyroid hormone administration have been performed in old mice. Sex steriods have been shown to inhibit thymus growth, either by inhibiting cellular proliferation or by accelerating cellular loss. There is, in fact, a receptor on thymic epithelial cells that binds estradiol, diethylstilbesterol, and high concentrations of dihydrotestorsterone.

On T cells, there are receptors present that bind testosterone and cortisol. Orchidectomy but not ovariectomy causes hypertrophy of the thymus and, hence, a delay in its involution.

Another approach to intervention has been the use of existing normal stem cells to replace the defective long-lived peripheral lymphocyte pool. Ikehara et al. (1985) have recently reported that the T-cell dysfunction in autoimmune-prone mice, previously attributed to involutionary changes that occur in the thymus, may be attributed to abnormalities that result in the stem cells. They suggest that bone marrow transplantation may be a strategy to be considered as an approach to the treatment of autoimmune diseases in humans.

In terms of dietary manipulations, dietary restrictions in early life have been reported to prolong proper immunological responsiveness by delaying the age-dependent changes in the growth and structure of the thymus. A relationship between dietary protein and carbohydrate intake has also been reported concerning the metabolism of serotonin and catecholamines. Addition of specific nutrients to the diet has markedly improved the percentage of T-cell subpopulations and the immune response.

Immunological capacity has been restored by chemical therapy in both young and aged immunologically insufficient animals using polynucleotide adjuvants and immunostimulatory agents, such as bestatin and penicillamine. Thyroxine has been shown to increase thymic weights and histological development of the thymic cortex. Adrenocortical steroids have been shown to increase the life span of hypophysectomized rats and a strain of short-lived mice, thereby relating adrenocortical function to life duration. An excess of corticosteroids, as previously suggested, however, may also accelerate the aging phenomenon.

The sulfhydryl compound mercaptoethanol has proved to be effective in enhancing various responses of young and old lymphocytes. To date, however, the most encouraging results of immunorestoration by chemical intervention have been the use of the various thymic hormones.

TOWARD AN EFFECTIVE IMMUNOLOGICAL TREATMENT OF AD

If the hypothesis that neurotransmitters are the counterpart of lymphokines proves viable, then it may be prudent to consider the therapeutic strategies that have recently been initiated using lympho-kines and other biological response modifiers.

The circadian rhythms of the humoral- and cell-mediated immune response might also be considered when designing an optimal treatment regimen. Since many physiological functions, including the endocrine system, exhibit circadian rhythms, it may be of interest, for example, to take advantage of alteration of corticosterone secretion during therapy (Christie, Whalley, Dick, & Fink, 1983; Hayashi & Kikuchi, 1985).

Specific high-affinity receptors for biologically active phorbol esters have been detected in the cytosol and membrane fractions of several cell types including lymphoid cells and more recently hippocampal pyramidal neurons (Baraban, Snyder, & Alger, 1985). Phorbol esters, compounds with inflammatory and tumor-promoting properties, bind to and activate protein kinase C. Protein kinase C is a calcium- and phospholipid-stimulated phosphorylating enzyme that occurs ubiquitously in the body but is most concentrated in the brain. In peripheral tissues, protein kinase C mediates cellular responses to membrane receptor stimulation. Protein kinase C has been implicated in synaptic transmission and in mediating the modulator actions of neurotransmitters (e.g., inhibition of calcium dependent potassium conductance) (Baraban et al., 1985). Protein kinase C may play a role in neuronal function by regulating membrane ionic conductance.

Grinstein, Cohen, Goetz, Rothstein, and Gelfarb (1985) have recently reported that Na^+/H^+ exchange is mediated by the stimulation of protein kinase C. Activation of the Na^+ exchanger in T cells is brought about by a change in cytoplasm pH. Increased Na^+/H^+ exchange also produces cell swelling, which may be one of the earlier manifestations in the growth-promoting properties of the phorbol esters.

The ionic components of the mitogenic pathways in eukaryotic cells are highly conserved. Agents that cause a Ca^{2+} signal in thymocytes (e.g., concanavalin A) and fibroblasts (e.g., A23187) also generate a pH signal. The same relationship holds for the cell-specific mitogens that cause a Ca^{2+} signal in fibroblasts (EGF, epidermal growth factor, vasopressin and prostaglandin F_2). Somatostatin occurs in the synaptosomal fraction of axon terminals and is released in vitro upon electrical depolarization in the presence of calcium (Payan et al., 1984).

The implication that the pH and Ca^{2+} signals can be generated independently in response to receptor-mitogen interaction is consistent with the suggestion that both Ca^{2+} and pH signals can be generated from phosphatidylinositol 4,5-bisphophate breakdown to inositol 1,4,5-triphosphate and diacylglycerol. The former can release intracellular Ca^{2+} and the latter activate protein kinase C to cause the pH increase (Hesketh et al., 1985). Thus, it appears that intervention at the level of protein kinase C may prove potentially therapeutic to both neuronal and immune lesions in AD.

Based upon the analogies between the CNS and immune system, Fudenberg et al. (1984) have suggested using 1-acetamide-2-pyrrolidone (1a,2p) as a prophalytic treatment for AD. This compound, an analogue of PVP, previously described as a T-independent antigen, and polyclonal B-cell mitogen, has been shown to enhance learning in dyslexia. The authors have reported that 1a,2p significantly improves the production of IL 1 both *in vitro* and *in vivo*. They propose that the benefits of 1a,2p be realized by one of at least four ways: (a) increasing the number and/or function of ACh receptors on undestroyed neurons, (b) acting as a CNS mitogen and thus actually replace destroyed neurons, (c) restore homeostatic control exerted by GABA-ergic neurons or ACh neurons, and (d) increase the production of cytokines by macrophage-like glial cells.

SUMMARY

Since the etiology of AD may reveal that it is a syndrome comprised of several different diseases, optimum therapy will be dictated by a correct diagnosis of the disease. Multiple approaches and therapies may then be indicated to include intervention at the level of prostaglandin synthesis; histamine, protein kinase C and calcium concentrations and/or the ACh receptor. In addition increases in the production of endogenous immune-derived or neuroendocrine-derived cytokines may have a prophylatic or therapeutic effect. Special attention to the immune system defects and correlates with the neuroendocrine system presented in this chapter should be at the least considered in any comprehensive approach to treatment.

REFERENCES

Baraban, J.M., Snyder, S.H., & Alger, B.E. (1985). Protein kinase C regulates ionic conductance in hippocampal pyramidal neurons: Electrophysiological effects of phorbol esters. *Proceedings of the*

National Academy of Sciences, USA, 82, 2538-2542.

Barnstable, C.J. (1982). Monoclonal antibodies - Tools to dissect the nervous system. Immunology Today, 3, 157-168.

Bartus, R.T., Dean, R.L., Beer, B., & Lippa, A. (1980). The cholinergic hypothesis of geriatric memory dysfunction. Science, 217, 408-417.

Beer, D.J., Osband, M.E., McCaffrey, R.P., Suter, N.A., & Rocklin, R.E. (1982). Abnormal histamine-induced suppressor-cell function in atopic subjects. New England Journal of Medicine, 306, 454-458.

Blass, J.P., & Weksler, M.E. (1983). Toward an effective treatment of Alzheimer's disease. Annals of Internal Medicine, 98, 251-252.

Bockman, D.E., & Kirby, M.L. (1984). Dependence of thymus development on derivatives of the neural crest. Science, 223, 498-500.

Bonomo, L., Antonaci, S., & Jirillo, E. (1983). Cell-mediated immune response in the elderly: Experimental and clinical approaches. Bulletin De L'Institut Pasteur, 81, 347-365.

Broadwell, R.D., Balin, B.J., Salcman, M., & Kaplan, R.S. (1983). Brain-blood barrier? Yes and no. Proceedings of the National Academy of Sciences, USA, 80, 7352-7356.

Buckton, K.E., Whalley, L.J., Lee, M., & Christie, J.E. (1983). Chromosome changes in Alzheimer's presenile dementia. Journal of Medical Genetics, 20, 46-51.

Cavagnaro, J. (1979). Localization and future characterization of an endogenous chromosomal protease. Unpublished doctoral dissertation, University of North Carolina at Chapel Hill.

Cavagnaro, J. (1983). Treatments that retard or reverse the immunological losses of age. In R.F. Walker & R.L. Cooper (Eds.), Experimental and clinical interventions in aging (pp. 133-162). New York: Marcel Dekker.

Cavagnaro, J., Cohen, E., Cathcart, E., & Osband, M. (1982). Susceptibility to Azocasein induced amyloidosis may result from abnormal histamine receptors of lymphocytes. Federation Proceedings, 41, 813.

Choy, V.J. (1983). Structure and function of the aged hypothalamo-neurohypophysial system. In R.F. Walker & R.L. Cooper (Eds.), Experimental and clinical interventions in aging (pp. 215-238). New York: Marcel Dekker.

Christie, J.E., Whalley, L.J., Dick, H., & Fink, G. (1983). Plasma cortisol concentrations in the functional psychoses and Alzheimer type dementia: A neuroendocrine day approach in drug-free patients. *Journal of Steroid Biochemistry, 19,* 247-250.

Coffey, R.G., & Middleton, E., Jr. (1977). Antiallergy therapy. In J.W. Hadden, R.G. Coffey, & F. Spreafico (Eds.), *Immunopharmacology* (pp. 203-226). New York: Plenum Medical Book Company.

Cohn, J.R. (1983). Basic considerations in immunology. In R.F. Walker & R.L. Cooper (Eds.), *Experimental and clinical interventions in aging* (pp. 121-132). New York: Marcel Dekker.

Cook-Deegan, R.M., & Austin, J.H. (1983). Implications of normal lymphocyte DNA content in familial Alzheimer's disease [Letter to the editor]. *American Journal of Medical Genetics, 15,* 511-513.

Crapper, D.R., & DeBoni, U. (1978). Brain aging and Alzheimer's disease. *Canadian Psychiatric Association Journal, 23,* 229-233.

Davies, P. (1983). Neurotransmitters and neuropeptides in Alzheimer's disease. In R. Katzman (Ed.), *Banbury report 15: Biological aspects of Alzheimer's disease* (pp. 255-265). Cold Spring Harbor, N.Y.: Cold Spring Harbor Laboratory.

Eikelenboom, P., & Stam, F.C. (1982). Immunoglobulins and complement factors in senile plaques. An immunoperoxidase study. *Acta Neuropathologica, 57,* 239-242.

Everitt, A.V. (1980). The neuroendocrine system and aging. *Gerontology, 26,* 108-119.

Feit, H. (1983). Chromatin alterations in neurologic disease. *Archives of Neurology, 40,* 528.

Friedman, N.B., Bomze, E.J., Rothman, S., & Drutz, E. (1964). The effects of local hormonal organ transplants and steroid hormone implants upon the thymus gland. *Annals of the New York Academy of Science, 113,* 918-932.

Fudenberg, H.H., Whitten, H.D., Arnaud, P., & Khansari, N. (1984). Hypothesis: Is Alzheimer's disease an immunological disorder? Observations and speculations. *Clinical Immunology and Immunopathology, 32,* 127-131.

Gee, A.P., Boyle, M.D.P., Munger, K.L., Lawman, M.F.P., & Young, M. (1983). Nerve growth factor: Stimulation of polymorphonuclear leukocyte chemotaxis in vitro. *Proceedings of the National Academy of Sciences, USA, 80,* 7215-7218.

Glenner, G.G. (1982). Alzheimer's disease (senile dementia): A research update and critique with recommendations. *Journal of the American Geriatrics Society, 30,* 59-62.

Glenner, G.G. (1983). Alzheimer's disease: Multiple cerebral amyloidosis. In R. Katzman (Ed.), *Banbury report 15: Biological aspects of Alzheimer's disease* (pp. 139-144). Cold Spring Harbor, N.Y.: Cold Spring Harbor Laboratory.

Goedert, M., Otten, U., Hunt, S.P., Bond, A., Chapman, D., Schlumpf, M., & Lichtensteiger, W. (1984). Biochemical and anatomical effects of antibodies against nerve growth factor on developing rat sensory ganglia. *Proceedings of the National Academy of Science, USA, 81,* 1580-1584.

Grinstein, S., Cohen, S., Goetz, J.D., Rothstein, A., & Gelfarb, E.W. (1985). Characterization of the activation of the Na^+/H^+ exchange in lymphocytes by phorbal esters: Change in cytoplasmic pH dependence of the antiport. *Proceedings of the National Academy of Science, USA, 82,* 1429-1433.

Hayashi, O., & Kikuchi, M. (1985). The influence of phase shift in the light-dark cycle on humoral immune responses of mice to sheep red blood cells and polyvinylpyrrolidone. *Journal of Immunology, 34,* 1455-1461.

Hecht, F., Morgan, R., Kaiser-McCaw Hecht, B., & Smith, S.D. (1984). Common region on chromosome 14 in T-cell leukemia and lymphoma. *Science, 226,* 1445-1447.

Heldermen, J.H., Vestal, R.E., Rowe, J.W., Tobin, J.D., Andres, R., & Robertson, G.L. (1978). The response of arginine vasopressin to intravenous ethanol and hypertonic saline in man. The impact of aging. *Journal of Gerontology, 33,* 39-47.

Hesketh, T.R., Moore, J.P., Morris, J.D.H., Taylor, M.V., Rogers, J., Smith, G.A., & Metcalfe, J.C. (1985). A common sequence of calcium and pH signals in the mitogenic stimulation of eukaryotic cells. *Nature, 313,* 481-484.

Ikehara, S., Good, R.A., Nakamura, T., Sekita, K., Inoue, S., Oo, M.M., Muso, E., Ogawa, K., & Hamashima, Y. (1985). Rationale for bone marrow transplantation in the treatment of autoimmune diseases. *Proceedings of the National Academy of Sciences, USA, 82,* 2483-2487.

Isakovic, K., & Jankovic, B.D. (1973). Neuro-endocrine correlates of immune response. II. Changes in the lymphatic organs of brain-lesioned rats. *International Archives of Allergy and Applied Immunology, 45, 373-384.*

Jones, C., Morse, H.G., Kao, F., Carbone, A., & Palmer, E. (1985). Human T-cell receptor-γ-chain genes: Location on chromosome 14. *Science, 228,* 83-85.

Kay, M.M.B. (1979). The thymus: Clock for immunologic aging. *The Journal of Investigative Dermatology, 73,* 29-38.

Lee, T.J.F., Saito, A., & Berezin, I. (1984). Vasoactive intestinal polypeptide-like substance: The potential transmitter for cerebral vasodilation. *Science, 224,* 898-900.

Levine, J.D., Clark, R., Devor, M., Helms, C., Moskowitz, M.A., & Basbaum, A.I. (1984). Intraneuronal substance P contributes to the severity of experimental arthritis. *Science, 226,* 547-549.

Lewis, P.N., Lukiw, U.J., & DeBoni, U. (1981). Changes in chromatin structures associated with Alzheimer's disease. *Journal of Neurochemistry, 37(5),* 1193-1202.

MacDonald, S.M., Goldstone, A.H., Morris, J.E., Exton-Smith, A.N., & Callard, R.E. (1982). Immunological parameters in the aged and in Alzheimer's disease. *Clinical Experimental Immunology, 49,* 123-128.

McDonald, J.K., Lumpkin, M.D., Samson, W.K., & McCann, S.M. (1985). Neuropeptide Y affects secretion of luteinizing hormone and growth hormone on ovariectomized rats. *Proceedings of the National Academy of Sciences, USA, 82,* 561-564.

Meisenberg, G., & Simmons, W.H. (1983). Peptides and the blood-barrier. *Life Sciences, 32,* 2611-2623.

Miller, A.E., Neighbour, P.A., Katzman, R., Aronson, M., & Lipkowitz, R. (1981). Immunological studies in senile dementia of the Alzheimer type: Evidence for enhanced suppressor cell activity. *Annals of Neurology, 10,* 506-510.

Moorhead, P.S., & Heyman, A. (1983). Chromosome studies of patients with Alzheimer's disease. *American Journal of Medical Genetics, 14,* 545-556.

Morrison, J.H., Rogers, J., Scherr, S., Benoit, R., & Bloom, F.E. (1985). Somatostatin immunoreactivity in neuritic plaques of Alzheimer's patients. *Nature, 314,* 90-92.

Nandy, K. (1978). Brain-reactive antibodies in aging and senile dementia. In R. Katzman, R.D. Terry, & K.L. Bick (Eds.), *Alzheimer's* disease: Senile dementia and related disorders (pp. 503-512). New York: Raven Press.

Ono, N., Samson, W.K., McDonald, J.K., Lumpkin, M.D., Bedran de Castro, J.C., & McCann, S.M. (1985). Effects of intravenous and intraventricular injection of antisera directed against corticotropin-releasing factor on the secretion of anterior pituitary hormones *Proceedings of the National Academy of Sciences, USA, 82,* 7787-7790.

Panula, P., Yang, H.-Y.T., & Costa, E. (1984). Histamine-containing neurons in the rat hypothalamus. *Proceedings of the National Academy of Sciences, USA, 81,* 2572-2576.

Payan, D.G., Brewster, D.R., & Goetzl, E.J. (1983). Specific stimulation of human T lymphocytes by substance P. *Journal of Immunology,* 131(4), 1613-1615.

Payan, D.G., Levine, J.D., & Goetzl, E.J. (1984). Modulation of immunity and hypersensitivity by sensory neuropeptides. *Journal of Immunology,* 4, 1601-1604.

Pentland, B., Christie, J.E., Watson, K.C., & Yap, P.L. (1982). Immunological parameters in Alzheimer's pre-senile dementia. *Acta Psychiatrica Scandinavica,* 65, 375-379.

Perry, R.H., Candy, J.M., & Perry, E.K. (1983). Some observations and speculations concerning the cholinergic system and neuropeptides in Alzheimer's disease. In R. Katzman (Ed.), *Banbury report 15: Biological aspects of Alzheimer's disease* (pp. 351-361). Cold Spring Harbor, N.Y.: Cold Spring Harbor Laboratory.

Pierpaoli, W., & Sorkin, E. (1969). Relationship between developmental hormones, the thymus, and immunological capacity. In L. Fine-Donati & M. Hanna (Eds.), *Lymphatic tissue and germinal centers in immune response* (pp. 397-401). New York: Plenum Press.

Reinherz, E.L., O'Brien, C., & Rosenthal, P. (1980). The cellular basis for viral-induced immunodeficiency: Analysis by monoclonal antibodies. *Journal of Immunology, 126,* 1269-1274.

Ricchieri, G.L., Ongaro, G., Argentiero, V., & Tavolato, B. (1983). The complement system and plasma protein levels in Alzheimer's disease. *Acta Neurologica, 5,* 103-108.

Robbins, J.H., Otsuka, F., Tarone, R.E., Polinsky, R.J., Brumback, R.A., Moshell, A.N., Nee, L.E., Ganges, M.B., & Cayeux, S.J. (1983). Radiosensitivity in Alzheimer's disease and Parkinson's disease. *Lancet, 1,* 468-469.

Roberts, G.W., Crow, T.J., & Polak, J.M. (1985). Location of neuronal tangles in somatostatin neurones in Alzheimer's disease. *Nature, 314,* 92-94.

Schmidt, G. (1983). Mechanisms and possible causes of Alzheimer's disease. *Postgraduate Medicine, 73,* 206-211.

Schwyzer, M., & Fontana, A. (1985). Partial purification and biochemical characterization of a T-Cell suppressor factor produced by human glioblastoma cells. *Journal of Immunology, 134,* 1003-1009.

Smith, A., Broe, G.A., & Williamson, M. (1983). Chromosome aneuploidy in Alzheimer's disease. *Clinical Genetics, 24,* 54-57.

Van Epps, D.E., & Saland, L. (1984). B-Endorphin and met-enkephalin stimulate human peripheral blood mononuclear cell chemotaxis. *Journal of Immunology, 132,* 3046-3053.

Walford, R.L. (1982). Immunological studies of Down's syndrome and Alzheimer's disease. *Annals of the New York Academy of Sciences, 396,* 95-106.

Weitkamp, L.R., Nee, L., Keats, B., Polinsky, R.J., & Guttormsen, S. (1983). Alzheimer's disease: Evidence for susceptibility loci on chromosomes 6 and 14. *American Journal of Human Genetics, 35,* 443-453.

ACKNOWLEDGEMENT

I thank Sara, A.J., and Dr. Richard M. Lewis for their ageless support.

12

Are Gangliosides a Rational Pharmacological Tool for the Treatment of Chronic Neurodegenerative Diseases?

R. Dal Toso, PhD, L. Cavicchioli, PhD, S. Calzolari, PhD, A. Leon, PhD, and G. Toffano, PhD

Knowledge of the biochemical and neuroanatomical correlates of the most common neurodegenerative diseases, namely Parkinson's and Alzheimer's diseases (AD) and amyotrophic lateral sclerosis (ALS), has greatly increased in the last two decades (Calne, Kebanian, Silbergeld, & Evarts, 1979; Davies & Maloney, 1976; Munsat & Bradley, 1979). These disorders are now known to be characterized by functional abnormalities of defined neuronal pathways (e.g., depletion of related neurotransmitters and loss of physiological control of the innervated areas) due to selective vulnerability or death of specific neuronal cell types. Nevertheless, the prognosis in patients affected by these disorders is still condemning today. Lost neuronal cells are not replaceable in adult mammals, and effective pharmacological treatments aiming at reducing or halting the progression of these diseases have yet to be developed. With regard to the latter aspect, current therapies primarily consist of attempts to replace the reduced neurotransmitter levels. As far as Parkinson's disease is concerned, dopaminergic agonist administration (Hefti & Melamed, 1980; Hornykiewicz, 1970) has proven useful in providing some beneficial relief from the clinical symptoms but unable to prevent the progressive destruction of the remaining nigrostriatal connectivity. In addition, application of similar substitutive therapies for other neurodegenerative diseases (i.e., cholinomimetic agents for AD) has not yet even symptomatically proven consistently useful (Rossor, 1982).

Obviously the above therapeutical gap is due to lack of comprehension of both the etiology and the pathogenetic mechanisms involved in these disorders. Such information is a fundamental prerequisite for any possible future development of therapies; no longer empirical or symptomatic but rationally based on the underlying pathology at the cellular and molecular levels.

Attempts to understand the etiology and pathogenetic mechanisms of neurodegenerative disease have been fruitless until now (Crapper, Quittar, Krishnau, Dalton, & DeBon, 1980; Graham, 1979; Marttila, Kalimo, Ziola, Halonen, & Rinne, 1978; Vella, 1984). However, after years of pessimism, the tremendous advance in basic and applied neuroscience research in the last decade has perhaps finally offered significant clues. One important clue could come from the suggestion that target-derived neuronotrophic factors can play a major role in repair, and possibly maintenance of, neuronal survival and correct functional intracerebral connections in adulthood. Should this be the case, as already hypothesized by Appel (1981), one might suppose, *a priori*, that independent of the etiological cause, progressive neuronal failure and cell death will occur following the depletion or inhibition of the neuronotrophic factors *in vivo*.

Along these lines, the following topics will be examined: (a) evidence and role of neuronotrophic factors in the adult mammalian central nervous system (CNS); (b) evidence for the implication of neuronotrophic factors in neurodegenerative diseases; and (c) new therapeutical possibilities in neurodegenerative diseases (i.e., GM_1 monosialoganglioside).

EVIDENCE AND ROLE OF NEURONOTROPHIC FACTORS IN ADULT CNS

One relevant outcome of the study of developing neurons has been an emphasis on the importance of target-derived "neuronotrophic" factors capable of regulating neuronal cell survival, growth of neurites, and formation of selective synaptic contacts during ontogenesis. Their determinant role is exemplified by the phenomena of developmental neuronal death, generally assumed to be due to competition between growing innervating axons for target-derived trophic support. This has lead to the idea that similar or functionally equivalent influences regulate neuronal survival in the adult state. Support for this hypothesis mainly derives from the nerve growth factor (NGF) paradigm.

NGF is now known to be a target-produced neuronotrophic agent essential for survival and neurite growth during development of sympathetic and sensory neurons (Thoenen & Barde, 1980). Sympathetic neurons maintain their responsiveness to NGF throughout the life span (Nja & Purves, 1978). After target disconnection in the adult, NGF synthesis and release increases (Ebendal, Olson, Seiger, & Hedlund, 1980) suggesting that the same agent involved in neuronal development and maintenance is probably a component of the repair mechanisms operating *in vivo* after neuronal injury. In addition decreased beta-NGF biological activity has been suggested to cause familial dysautonomia (Siggers et al., 1976), a neurological disease involving extensive neuronal loss in sympathetic ganglia. Together these results suggest that (a) NGF may be only one of a large class of specific target-derived neuronotrophic factors, each affecting defined neuronal populations; (b) these factors presumably regulate neuronal survival not only during development but also in the adult state; (c) in the adult, the synthesis of the neuronotrophic factors is presumably regulated by the degree of target innervation; and (d) absence of neuronotrophic activity in humans may lead to neurological deficits associated with neuronal cell death.

Aware of these issues, many laboratories have begun to search for neuronotrophic factors in the adult mammalian CNS, and the attempts, though still preliminary, have been successful. In fact, using neuronal cell cultures as bioassay systems, normal adult brain extracts have been shown to contain trypsin-labile agents capable of increasing survival of various neuronal cells *in vitro*. In addition, particularly interesting is the observation that injury increases the titer of the trophic agents at the lesion site (Nieto-Sampedro, Manthorpe, Barbin, Varon, & Cotman, 1983). This increase parallels the occurrence of successful grafting of embryonic explants into adult host CNS. In this context, Gage, Björklund, and Stenevi (1984) have reported that the fimbria-fornix lesion is a necessary prerequisite for a successful implantation of embryonic superior cervical ganglia into the adult rat CNS. The authors suggested that a specific hippocampal-derived trophic factor becomes available for the embryonic grafts only after hippocampal denervation.

As one might have hoped, the above suggests that neuronotrophic factors are present and operative in the adult brain where they may be involved in regulating neuronal cell survival in both a normal and lesioned state. However, it must nevertheless be recalled that evidence favoring this aspect is still only indirect. Thus one major future task is the identification and characterization of the putative neuronotrophic factors. In this context, successful purification of at least one of the neuronotrophic factors has been achieved by Barde, Edgar, and Thoenen (1982) and Turner, Barde, Schwab, and Thoenen

(1983). Further work along this line will certainly provide valid information as to the nature, number, specificity, and role of the neuronotrophic factors in adult normal and injured CNS. It most probably will have major consequences with regard to neurodegenerative diseases.

EVIDENCE FOR THE IMPLICATION OF NEURONOTROPHIC FACTORS IN NEURODEGENERATIVE DISEASES

The working hypothesis regarding the involvement of neuronotrophic factors in neurodegenerative diseases fundamentally relies on the concept that neuronal survival in the adult depends on the presence of specific target-derived neuronotrophic factors. The implication is that in each disease the degeneration of the neuronal pathway involves a decreased availability of a specific neuronotrophic signal. Impairment of trophic interactions may be due to altered postsynaptic cell synthesis and release, insufficient or incorrect presynaptic cell responsiveness or, the presence of agents negatively interfering with the trophic signal transmission. With regard to the last concept, it is possible that neurodegenerative diseases may be associated with the appearance of neuronotoxic agents. If so, destruction of the neurons may be the result of an altered equilibrium between neuronotrophic and neurotoxic activity, whereby the latter is prevalent.

Although there is as yet no direct evidence that decreased trophic activity is implicated in neurodegenerative diseases, circumstantial evidence favoring this hypothesis is available. Sera of patients suffering from ALS contain immunoglobulins that specifically show a sprouting and growth-promoting (for the spinal neurons) 56-Kd muscle-derived protein (Gurney, 1984; Gurney, Belton, Cashman, & Antel, 1984). In addition, we have obtained evidence that sera from patients with idiopathic Parkinson's disease specifically impair the expression of dopaminergic characteristics in primary mesencephalic-striatal co-cultures. The inhibitory activity appears to correlate with the presence of complement components. In fact, heat-inactivated sera (56° for 30') of parkinsonian patients have no effect on dopaminergic features, whereas addition of heat-inactivated parkinsonian sera supplemented with noninactivated control sera decreased the expression of the dopaminergic features *in vitro*. Although identification, biological characterization, and mechanisms of action of the responsi-

TABLE 1

Effect of Sera of Patients with Idiopathic Parkinson's Disease on Dopamine and GABA Uptake in Mesencephalic-Striatal Co-Cultures

	% DA Uptake	% GABA Uptake
Control sera	100 ± 8	100 ± 6
Parkinsonian sera	$53 \pm 12^*$	103 ± 10

Note. Rostral mesencephalic tegmentum and corpus striatum were dissected from 13- and 15-day-old mouse embryos, respectively, and plated in chemically defined medium. Four hours after plating, 50 μl of sera from control or parkinsonian subjects were added to co-cultures. ^{3}H-DA and ^{14}C-GABA uptake were performed after 4 days in culture, as previously described (Prochiantz, Daquet, Hebert, & Glowinski, 1981). Data are mean $\pm$ S.E.M. of three independent determinations done in triplicate.

*p<0.01 vs. control sera (Student's t test).

ble agents are currently under investigation, the working hypothesis is that parkinsonian sera contain antibodies capable of inhibiting trophic influences, perhaps of the target striatal cells, occurring in the culture system. Nevertheless, it is not clear whether these antibodies play a role in the pathogenesis of ALS and Parkinson's disease or if they represent a secondary response to neuromuscular and neuronal destruction.

Even though it is appealing, this hypothesis does not uncover the etiology of these disorders since the primary cause for the inadequate supply or inhibition of the target-derived trophic activity remains obscure. However, if validated, it offers the opportunity for the development of new therapeutical strategies aiming at avoiding progressive degeneration of neuronal pathways. In this respect, the use of pharmacological agents capable of either directly replacing the missing trophic factors, improving and modulating the trophic signal transmission, or inhibiting neuronotoxic agents may be useful.

Although serious consideration of replacement therapy must await purification of the neuronotrophic factors, today corrective therapy appears to be immediately available. Indeed, as exemplified below, GM$_1$ monosialoganglioside (nomenclature according to

Svennerholm, 1963) may constitute an alternative therapeutical approach in neurodegenerative disease.

THERAPEUTIC POTENTIAL OF MONOSIALOGANGLIOSIDE IN NEURODEGENERATIVE DISEASES: A POSSIBLE UNIFYING THERAPY

Studies from our own and other laboratories have recently documented the capability of GM_1 monosialoganglioside to enhance functional recovery following specific lesions of adult mammalian brain. Approaches for investigating such a prospective effect of chronic ganglioside administration essentially derive from evidence indicating that such molecules may play a prominent role in the regulation of morphological and biochemical neuronal behaviors during development and in adulthood (for recent reviews, see Haber & Gorio, 1984; Ledeen, Yu, Rapport, & Suzuki, 1984).

Of particular relevance is that administration of GM_1 antibodies to neonatal rodents induces in the adult behavioral deficits associated with morphological abnormalities of the neuronal cells (Kasarskis, Karpiak, Rapport, Yu, & Bass, 1981) and inhibits regeneration (Sparrow, McGuiness, Schwartz, & Grafstein, 1984). Conversely GM_1 treatment accelerates neuronal maturation in rats and facilitates biochemical and behavioral recovery after some types of injury in the adult mammalian CNS as shown in Table 2.

Although the molecular mechanisms involved in the above mentioned GM_1 effects are still unknown, studies utilizing neuronal cell cultures suggest that the GM_1 action on neuronal survival and neurite outgrowth *in vitro* necessitates the presence of neuronotrophic molecules and occurs via potentiation of their activity. GM_1 is not a growth-promoting agent by itself. In this regard, GM_1 has been shown to amplify the NGF-induced neurite outgrowth in pheochromocytoma cells (Ferrari, Fabris, & Gorio, 1983) and in dorsal root ganglionic (DRG) neuronal cells in culture (Leon et al., 1984) seen in Figure 1, while antibodies to GM_1 have been reported to inhibit NGF-induced neurite outgrowth in DRG explants (Schwartz & Spirman, 1982). Lastly, GM_1 has been reported to be capable even of affecting development and survival of nonNGF responsive neurons *in vitro* (e.g., fetal mesencephalic neurons in culture) (Dal Toso et al., 1985). Therefore, GM_1 is capable of potentiating the ef-

TABLE 2

Lesions and Parameters Used to Monitor GM$_1$ Effects on CNS Neuronal Recovery

Lesion	Parameters	References
Partial unilateral hemitransection	Striatal: TH activity, TH immunofluorescence. Nigral: TH immunofluorescence. Apomorphine-induced rotational behavior.	Toffano et al. (1983) Toffano, Savoini, Aporti, et al. (1984b) Agnati et al. (1983) Toffano, Savoini, Moroni, et al. (1984c)
Medioventral septal lesion	Hippocampal choline acetyltransferase and acetycholine esterase activity	Oderfeld-Nowak et al. (1984)
Entorhinal cortex ablation	Alternation behavior	Karpiak (1983)
Bilateral electro-thermic lesions of the caudate nuclei	Two-choice footshock learning maze	Sabel, Slavin, and Stein (1984)

TABLE 2 Continued

Lesion	Parameters	References
Cortical 6-OH-DA infusion to newborn rat	Endogenous sodium content	Kojima, Gorio, Janigro, and Jensson (1984)
Electrolytic lesion of nucleus basalis magnocellularis	High-affinity choline uptake in frontal and parietal cortex	Pedata, Giovanelli, and Pepeu (1984)
Monocular deprivation in newborn kitten	Functional binocular reorganization of the visual cortex	Carmignoto, Canella, and Bisti (1984)
5, 7-Dihydroxy-tryptamine, s.c. to newborn rat	Serotonin levels in the CNS	Jonsson et al. (1984)

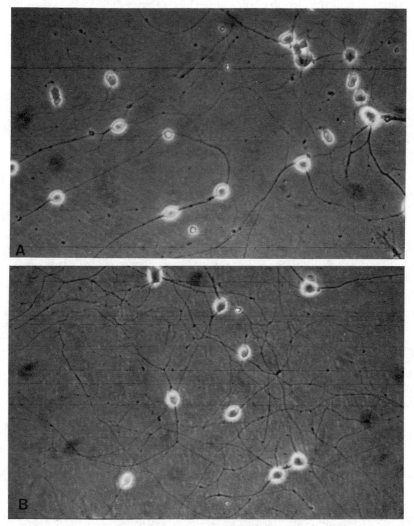

Figure 1. Photomicrographs of fetal chick dissociated dorsal root ganglionic cells after 10 days in culture. Dorsal root ganglia were dissected from 8-day-old embryos (Leon et al., 1984). Enriched dissociated neuronal cell cultures were prepared according to Barde, Edgar, and Thoenen (1980) and plated at a density of 5 ganglia/30 mm Falcon dishes. Culture media consisted of DMEM-medium 199 (3:1 v/v) containing 5% fetal calf serum, 5% horse serum, and 10 μg/ml NGF (2.5S subunit). Monosialoganglioside GM_1 was added (on plating day at a concentration of $10^{-7}M$).

a) Control cells.
b) Ganglioside-treated cells. Note increased neurite branching and complexity.

ficacy of different trophic agents acting on specific cellular populations. This possibility has recently been further substantiated by the
studies of Hakomori and associates concerning the interaction between GM_1 and the platelet-derived growth factor (PDGF) receptors of 3T3 fibroblasts (Bremer et al., 1984).

Available data obtained *in vivo* also tend to favor the possibility
that GM_1 effects occur via modulation of lesion-induced neuronotrophic activity occurring *in situ*. In a follow-up study, which we conducted in adult rats following injury of the nigrostriatal pathway, we
observed that the GM_1 capability to facilitate recovery depends on
the type of injury. In fact, in contrast to mechanical hemitransection, no GM_1-induced recovery in striatal tyrosine hydroxylase (TH)
activity was evident when the pathway was lesioned by injection of
6-hydroxydopamine (6-OH-DA) into the substantia nigra (Toffano
et al., 1984a). To clarify this discrepancy, extracts of striatum and
substantia nigra of lesioned animals were tested for the presence of
neuronotrophic activity. Whereas increased titers of neuronotrophic
activity occurred following mechanical injury both in striatum and
substantia nigra, no increase of neuronotrophic activity was found
in the substantia nigra injected with neurotoxin. This is in accord with
the idea that neuronotrophic factors are involved in CNS repair
processes, and that the occurrence of GM_1 beneficial effects after
brain injury requires increased titers of trophic activities at the lesion
sites. Furthermore, the simultaneous addition of GM_1 and the
trophic extracts to mesencephalic cell cultures resulted in a synergistic effect on dopaminergic and GABAergic parameters *in vitro*,
indicating that GM_1 is capable of potentiating the trophic activity
contained in the brain extracts. Further experimental support for the
involvement of neuronotrophic factors in the GM_1 effects *in vivo* is
derived from the observation that the GM_1 treatment protocol
necessary to obtain beneficial effects in transected nigro-striatal pathways is dependent on the age of the rats. In 2-, 12-, and 18-month-
old hemitransected rats, the GM_1-induced increase of striatal TH
activity was significantly apparent after 2, 4, and 8 weeks of treatment,
respectively. In addition, we observed that in 12- and 18-month-
old saline-treated lesioned rats there occurred a more pronounced
decrease of striatal TH activity 30 days after the hemitransection when
compared to 2-month-old rats.

With regard to the age dependency of GM_1 effect in unilaterally
hemitransected rats, Needels, Wittemore, Nieto-Sampedro, and
Cotman (1983) reported that induction of neuronotrophic activity

TABLE 3

Time Course of the Effect of GM₁ Ganglioside on the Recovery of Striatal Tyrosine Hydroxylase (TH) Activity of Differently Aged Rats with Partial Unilateral Hemitransection

Treatment		Striatal TH activity (Les./Unles. %)		
		2 months	12 months	18 months
Saline	8[a]	51 ± 4	56 ± 4	— —
GM₁	8	47 ± 3	58 ± 5	— —
Saline	15	55 ± 4	60 ± 6	— —
GM₁	15	75 ± 8*	55 ± 7	— —
Saline	30	59 ± 5	30 ± 3**	40 ± 7
GM₁	30	88 ± 10*	75 ± 8*	36 ± 8
Saline	42	61 ± 4	— —	18 ± 3**
GM₁	42	92 ± 7*	— —	49 ± 6
Saline	56	65 ± 6	— —	25 ± 4**
GM₁	56	95 ± 10*	— —	70 ± 8*

Note. Treatment with GM₁ (30 mg/kg IP) started on the second day after surgery (Toffano et al., 1983). Values are the mean ± S.E.M. of the apparent Vmax of TH (lesioned/unlesioned %). The Vmax of TH determined in the striatum (18.93 ± 1.01 nmol $CO_2.h^{-1}.mg^{-1}$ protein) of the unlesioned side of the groups treated with saline was not significantly different from that of the GM₁-treated 8 days after surgery and remained in the same range when measured at day 15 or 30.

a = days of treatment.
*$p<0.01$ vs. the respective saline-treated groups.
**$p<0.02$ vs. the respective 2-month-old group.

following CNS injury is slower in aged brain than in young adult or neonate rat. Should this be the case, the results obtained in rats of

various ages suggest that the increasing age-dependent delay of neuronotrophic induction is responsible for more prominent retrograde
degeneration and increased latency in the appearance of significant
GM_1-induced repair process.

Although we have only begun to explore the phenomena of CNS
target-derived neuronotrophic factors and the association with neuronal cell survival and neurodegenerative disease in the adult, it is
nevertheless feasible to postulate that therapy with GM_1 ganglioside
can modulate neuronal cell (i.e., presynaptic cell) responsiveness
to the factor. In principal, this may provide a rationale for the use
of GM_1 as pharmacological agent in neurodegenerative diseases.
If a partial deficit or inhibition of the neuronotrophic activity occurs
in these diseases, GM_1, by acting synergistically with the neuronotrophic factor, may decrease progressive presynaptic neuronal cell
death and favor beneficial adaptive responses. In this context, it must
be recalled that GM_1 can affect the efficacy of different neuronotrophic agents acting on specific neuronal subpopulations. This
peculiar characteristic permits the therapeutical utilization of GM_1
in various neurodegenerative diseases (concept of unifying hypothesis and unifying therapy) and ideally overcomes problems inherent
to substitutive therapy. The latter will necessarily require specific and
purified neuronotrophic factors for each neurodegenerative disorder,
whereas therapy with GM_1 relies on the fact that each denervated
target area produces its own specific trophic agent *in situ*. Alternatively, should neurodegenerative diseases be associated with complete absence of target-derived neuronotrophic factors, one may
consider the combination of substitutive therapy with the missing
neuronotrophic factor together with GM_1. This association will most
probably permit reduction of the therapeutical dose of the neuronotrophic agent limiting its side effects such as maladaptive neuronal
behavior.

FUTURE PROSPECTS

A successful therapeutic approach to chronic neurodegenerative
diseases largely depends on the knowledge of the pathogenetic
mechanisms involved in the neuroanatomical and biochemical alterations together with a deeper understanding of the etiological
causes.

The possibility that insufficient target-derived survival and growth-
promoting factors may be involved in neurodegenerative mechan-

isms is of great interest. Future progress in the identification and purification of target-derived CNS neuronotrophic factors together with sophisticated technology, such as gene cloning and molecular biology, should lead to increased comprehension of the role of the trophic agents in adult CNS and, hopefully, substantiate their involvement in neurodegenerative diseases. Nevertheless, research in the trophic field, even though still preliminary, has already opened a window that offers novel opportunities for therapeutical developments in these diseases. In this context, agents capable of modulating trophic signal transmission, such as GM_1 monosialoganglioside, are now available and deserve clinical investigation.

REFERENCES

Agnati, L.F., Fuxe, K., Calza, L., Benfenati, F., Cavicchioli, L., Toffano, G., & Goldstein, M. (1983).Gangliosides increase the survival of lesioned nigral dopamine neurons and favor the recovery of dopaminergic synaptic function in striatum of rats by collateral sprouting. *Acta Physiologica Scandinavica, 119,* 347-363.

Appel, S.H. (1981). A unifying hypothesis for the cause of amyotrophic lateral sclerosis, parkinsonism and Alzheimer's disease. *Annals of Neurology, 10,* 499-505.

Barde, Y.A., Edgar, D., & Thoenen, H. (1980). Sensory neurons in culture: Changing requirements for survival factors during embryonic development. *Proceedings of the National Academy of Sciences, USA, 77,* 1199-1203.

Barde, Y.A., Edgar, D., & Thoenen, H. (1982). Purification of a new neuronotrophic factor from mammalian brain. *EMBO Journal, 1,* 549-553.

Bremer, E.C., Hakomori, S.I., Bowen-Pope, D.F., Raines, E., & Ross, R. (1984). Ganglioside-mediated modulation of cell growth, growth factor binding, and receptor phosphorylation. *Journal of Biological Chemistry, 259,* 6818-6825.

Calne, D.B., Kebanian, J., Silbergeld, E., & Evarts, E. (1979). Advances in the neuropharmacology of parkinsonism. *Annals of Internal Medicine, 90,* 219-229.

Carmignoto, G., Canella, R., & Bisti, S. (1984). Can functional reorganization of area 17 following monocular deprivation be modified by GM_1 internal ester treatment? *Journal of Neuroscience Research, 12,* 477-483.

Crapper, D.R., Quittar, S., Krishnau, S.S., Dalton, A.J., & DeBon, V. (1980). Intranuclear aluminium content in Alzheimer's disease, dialysis encephalopathy and experimental aluminum encephalopathy. *Acta Neuropathologica, 50,* 19-24.

Dal Toso, R., Presti, D., Giorgi, O., Favaron, M., Soronco, C., Vicini, S., Toffano, G., Azzone, G.F., and Leon, A. (1985). Development of phenotypic traits and survival of neurons in dissociated fetal mesencephalic serum-free cell cultures. I: Selective effects of cell density and stimulation by adult mammalian brain extraction. (Manuscript submitted for publication.)

Davies, P., & Maloney, A.J.F. (1976). Selective loss of central cholinergic neurons in Alzheimer's disease [Letter to the editor]. *Lancet, 2,* 1403.

Ebendal, T., Olson, L., Seiger, A., & Hedlund, K.O. (1980). Nerve growth factors in the rat iris. *Nature, 286,* 25-28.

Ferrari, G., Fabris, M., & Gorio, A. (1983). Ganglioside enhance neurite outgrowth in PC12 cells. *Developmental Brain Research, 8,* 215-221.

Gage, F.H., Björklund, A., & Stenevi, U. (1984). Denervation releases a neuronal survival factor in adult rat hippocampus. *Nature, 308,* 637-639.

Graham, D.G. (1979). On the origin and significance of neuromelanin. *Archives of Pathology and Laboratory Medicine, 103,* 359-362.

Gurney, M.E. (1984). Suppression of sprouting at the neuromuscular junction by immune sera. *Nature, 307,* 546-548.

Gurney, M.E., Belton, A.C., Cashman, N., & Antel, J.P. (1984). Inhibition of terminal axonal sprouting by serum from patients with amyotrophic lateral sclerosis. *New England Journal of Medicine, 311,* 933-939.

Haber, B., & Gorio, A. (1984). Special issue on neurobiology of gangliosides. *Journal of Neuroscience Research, 12,* 2-3.

Hefti, F., & Melamed, E. (1980). L-DOPA's mechanisms of action in Parkinson's disease. *Trends in Neurosciences, 3,* 229-231.

Hornykiewicz, O. (1970). How does L-DOPA work in Parkinsonism? In A. Barbeau & F. McDowell (Eds.), *L-DOPA and Parkinsonism.* Philadelphia: F.A. Davis.

Jonsson, G., Gorio, A., Hallman, H., Janigro, D., Kojima, H., Luthman, S., & Zanoni, R. (1984). Effects of GM_1 ganglioside on developing and mature serotonin and noradrenaline neurons lesioned by selective neurotoxins. *Journal of Neuroscience Research,* *12,* 459-475.

Karpiak, S.E. (1983). Ganglioside treatment improves recovery of alteration behavior after unilateral cortex lesion. *Experimental Neurology,* *81,* 330-339.

Kasarskis, E.J., Karpiak, S.E., Rapport, M.M., Yu, R.K., & Bass, N.H. (1981). Abnormal maturation of cerebral cortex and behavioral deficit in adult rats after neonatal administration of antibodies to ganglioside. *Development Brain Research,* *1,* 25-35.

Kojima, M., Gorio, A., Janigro, D., & Jonsson, G. (1984). GM_1 ganglioside enhances regrowth of noradrenaline nerve terminals in rat cerebral cortex lesioned by the neurotoxin 6-hydroxydopamine. *Neuroscience.*

Ledeen, R.W., Yu, R.K., Rapport, M.M., & Suzuki, K. (1984). *Ganglioside structure, function and biomedical potential.* New York: Plenum Press.

Leon, A., Benvegnu, D., Dal Toso, R., Presti, D., Facci, L., Giorgi, O., & Toffano, G. (1984). Dorsal root ganglia and nerve growth factor: A model for understanding the mechanism of GM_1 effects of neuronal repair. *Journal of Neuroscience Research,* *12,* 277-287.

Marttila, R.J., Kalimo, K., Ziola, B.R., Halonen, P.E., & Rinne, U.K. (1978). Herpes simplex virus subunit antibodies in patients with Parkinson's disease. *Acta Neurologica,* *35,* 668-671.

Munsat, T.L., & Bradley, W.G. (1979). Amyotrophic lateral sclerosis. In H.R. Tyler & D.M. Dawson (Eds.), *Current neurology* (Vol. 2). Boston: Houghton Mifflin.

Needels, D.L., Wittemore, S.R., Nieto-Sampedro, M., & Cotman, C.W. (1983). Characterization of injury-induced neuronotrophic activity in neonate, mature and aged rat brain. *American Neuroscience Meeting,* Abstract No. 243.14.

Nieto-Sampedro, M., Manthorpe, M., Barbin, G., Varon, S., & Cotman, C.W. (1983). Injury-induced neuronotrophic activity in adult rat brain. Correlation with survival of delayed implants in a wound cavity. *Journal of Neuroscience,* *3,* 2219-2229.

Nja, A., & Purves, D. (1978). The effects of nerve growth factor and its antiserum of synapses in the superior cervical ganglion of the Guinea pig. *Journal of Physiology,* *277,* 53-75.

Oderfeld-Nowak, B., Skup, M., Ulas, J., Jezierska, M., Gradkowska,

M., & Zaremba, M. (1984). Effect of GM_1 ganglioside treatment on postlesion responses of cholinergic enzymes in rat hippocampus after various partial deafferentation. Journal of Neuroscience Research, 122, 409-420.

Pedata, F., Giovanelli, L., & Pepeu, G. (1984). GM_1 ganglioside facilitates the recovery of high-affinity choline uptake in the cerebral cortex of rats with a lesion of the nucleus basalis magnocellularis. Journal of Neuroscience Research, 12, 421-427.

Prochiantz, A., Daguet, M.C., Hebert, A., & Glowinski, J. (1981). Specific stimulation of in vitro maturation of mesencephalic dopaminergic neurons by striatal membranes. Nature, 293, 570-572.

Rossor, M.N. (1982). Neurotransmitters and CNS diseases dementia. Lancet, 2, 1200-1204.

Sabel, B.A., Slavin, M.D., & Stein, D.G. (1984). GM_1 ganglioside treatment facilitates behavioral recovery from bilateral brain damage. Science, 225, 340-342.

Schwartz, M., & Spirman, N. (1982). Sprouting from chicken embryo dorsal root ganglia induced by nerve growth factor is specifically inhibited by affinity-purified antiganglioside antibodies. Proceedings of the National Academy of Sciences, USA, 79, 6080-6083.

Siggers, D.C., Rogers, J.C., Boyer, S.H., Margolet, L., Dorkin, H., Banerjee, S.P., & Shooter, E.M. (1976). Increased nerve growth factor beta-chain cross reacting material in familial dysautonomia. New England Journal of Medicine, 295, 629-634.

Sparrow, J.R., McGuinnes, C., Schwartz, M., & Grafstein, B. (1984). Antibodies to gangliosides inhibit goldfish optic nerve regeneration in vivo. Journal of Neuroscience Research, 12, 233-243.

Svennerholm, L. (1963). Chromatographic separation of human brain gangliosides. Journal of Neurochemistry, 10, 613-623.

Thoenen, H., & Barde, Y.A. (1980). Physiology of nerve growth factor. Physiological Reviews, 60, 1284-1335.

Toffano, G., Agnati, L.F., Fuxe, K., Aldinio, C., Consolazione, A., Valenti, G., & Savoini, G. (1984a). Effect of GM_1 ganglioside treatment on the recovery of dopaminergic nigro-striatal neurons after different types of lesion. Acta Physiologica Scandinavica, 122, 313-321.

Toffano, G., Savoini, G., Aporti, F., Calzolari, S., Consolazione, A.,

Maura, G., Marchi, M., Raiteri, M., & Agnati, L.F. (1984b). The functional recovery of damaged brain: The effect of GM_1 ganglioside. *Journal of Neuroscience Research, 12,* 297-340.

Toffano, G., Savoini, G., Moroni, F., Lombardi, G., Calza, L., & Agnati, L.F. (1983). GM_1 ganglioside stimulates the regeneration of dopaminergic neurons in the central nervous system. *Brain Research, 261,* 163-166.

Toffano, G., Savoini, G., Moroni, F., Lombardi, G., Calza, L., & Agnati, L.F. (1984c). Chronic GM_1 ganglioside treatment reduces dopamine cell body degeneration in the substantia nigra after unilateral hemitransection in rat. *Brain Research, 296,* 233-239.

Turner, J.E., Barde, Y.A., Schwab, M.E., & Thoenen, H. (1983). Extract from brain stimulates neurite outgrowth from fetal rat retinal explants. *Developmental Brain Research, 6,* 77-83.

Vella, V. (1984). A review of the etiology of multiple sclerosis. *Italian Journal of the Neurological Sciences, 5,* 347-356.

13

Hormonal Therapy for Alzheimer's Disease

Howard Fillit, MD, Herman Weinreb, MD,
Ina Cholst, MD, Victoria Luine, PhD,
Roberto Amador, MD, John B. Zabriskie, MD,
and Bruce S. McEwen, PhD

Hormones such as estrogen may represent a new and potentially effective treatment strategy for Alzheimer's disease (AD). Hormonal therapy may affect multiple neurotransmitter systems via genomic and nongenomic mechanisms. Estrogens may be effective therapy for the emotional disorders often associated with AD, may improve cognitive function by affecting emotional modulating factors that influence cognitive function, and could have possible primary benefits on higher cognitive function. The use of estrogen for AD in elderly postmenopausal women may also have a role in prevention of the disease, in that postmenopausal estrogen deficiency may contribute to the development of neuronal dysfunction and death which occurs in AD. In this chapter, we will review the biologic basis for the clinical effects of estrogen on brain function, previous clinical studies employing estrogen for cognitive and emotional disorders in women, and our own studies employing estradiol for AD in women.

NEUROBIOLOGICAL ASPECTS OF ESTROGEN EFFECTS ON BRAIN FUNCTION

The essential perspectives to be reviewed in this section are that (1) a clear biologic basis exists for the concept that estrogen may influence brain development and function; (2) that gonadal hormones influence brain development according to gender; and (3) that gonadal hormones have effects on postnatal brain function and adult behavior. These concepts provide the scientific basis for the hypothesis that estrogen may have an effect on emotional and cognitive function in humans.

The cellular mechanisms of steroid hormone action in general have been the subject of intense investigation recently (Pfaff & McEwen, 1983). Inductive and direct effects of hormones such as estrogen on neurons have been demonstrated. Inductive effects involve the induction of ribonucleic acid (RNA) and protein synthesis via genomic mechanisms, resulting in changes in the levels of specific gene products such as neurotransmitter synthesizing enzymes. Inductive effects of estrogens also include the expression of gonadal hormone receptors in specific regions of brain. These inductive effects are delayed and prolonged regulatory effects. Direct effects of steroid hormones on neurons do not require protein synthesis and appear to take place rapidly. For example, estrogens have been shown to be capable of altering the electrical activity of neurons, particularly in the hypothalamus (Kelly, Moss, Dudley, & Fawcett, 1977). Estrogen-sensitive neurons are also capable of aromatizing testosterone to estradiol and may respond to progestins, indicating further complexities in the action of estrogens on neuronal cells.

Receptors for all five classes of steroid hormones have been demonstrated on specific cell types in brain, including estrogens, progestins, androgens, glucocorticoids, and mineralocorticoids (McEwen, Davis, Parsons, & Pfaff, 1979). Estrogen-sensitive neurons have been shown to possess specific cytosolic receptors for estrogens. These estrogen-sensitive neurons have been noted in both male and female brain and are found in specific loci, including the pituitary, hypothalamus, limbic forebrain (including amygdala and lateral septum), and cerebral cortex. Receptors for circulating estradiol have been identified in nuclei of the basal forebrain, which is the major source of cholinergic innervation to the cerebral cortex, limbic system, hippocampus, and hypothalamus (Luine, Khylchevskaya, & McEwen, 1975). This region is also the suspected locus of cholinergic pathology in AD (Coyle, Price, & DeLong, 1983; Whitehouse et al., 1982). Recent studies have indicated that tyrosine hydroxylase-containing neurons contain receptors for estradiol (Sar, 1984), and that estradiol may have modulating effects on the levels of tyrosine hydroxylase in specific regions of brain. These studies have indicated possible effects of estradiol on central dopaminergic systems and have been substantiated by clinical studies suggesting that estrogens may influence movement disorders, such as tardive dyskinesias, particularly in postmenopausal women (Bedard, Boucher, DiPaolo, &

Labrie, 1984; Chiodo, & Caggiula, 1983). Indeed, a number of neurotransmitter systems have been suggested to be responsive to estrogen, including cholinergic, dopaminergic, serotonergic, GABAergic, adrenergic and opioid systems, although not all of these effects have been demonstrated *in vivo* or at physiologic concentrations (McEwen et al., 1984). Although estrogen-sensitive neurons account for only a small number of neurons in the brain, the actions of estradiol can have widespread effects on brain function as a result of changes in the neurochemistry of estrophilic neurons and their interaction with other neurons.

Gonadal hormones have been demonstrated to have effects on brain development and adult function. Such effects have been distinguished into two categories; "organizational" and "activational" effects (McEwen et al., 1984; Rubin, Reinisch, & Haskett, 1981). "Organizational" effects are trophic effects, which occur primarily during development and result in permanent modifications of morphology and neuronal function. During development, sex steroid hormones play a crucial role in the differentiation of the brain according to gender, such that the resulting adult brain is capable of either male or female behavior and responsiveness. The mechanism of such organizational effects is not entirely understood but may involve the stimulation of growth of nerve processes, the stabilization of neurons against cell death, and the promotion of differentiation (Toran-Allerand, 1981). From a therapeutic view, it is interesting to note that there appear to be gender differences in the response of neurons to injury. Male sprouting of neurons in the hippocampus after deafferentiation is less than in females (Loy & Milner, 1980). Whether these trophic effects of gonadal hormones on neurons could play a therapeutic role is not known. Significant gender differences have been demonstrated in the innervation of specific regions of brain (DeVries, Buijs, & Van Leeuwen, 1984). The induction and differentiation of specific vasopressin-containing neurons by sex steroids during development illustrates organizational differences in gender-related brain development. With regard to postnatal organizational effects of gonadal hormones on brain function and behavior, the studies of bird song by Nottebohm (1980) have demonstrated that gonadal hormones are capable of both trophic effects on neuronal growth and the periodic development of specific neuronal groups that are responsible for gender-related language production and reception during the mating season. Thus, hormone-stimulated growth of groups of neurons may be induced by sex steroids, while hormone-induced differentiation may result in the expression of specific neurochemicals or neurochemical receptors by specific cell types.

Reversible effects, called "activational" effects, occur after development, primarily result in relative alterations in cell function, may be genomic or nongenomic, and often demonstrate gender-related differences (McEwen et al., 1984). Sex steroids can regulate the structural components of cells, their enzyme proteins, and the degree to which receptor molecules for neurotransmitters and other hormones are expressed. For example, ACh regulation appears to differ between the genders. Studies in the rat brain have shown that the activities of choline acetyltransferase and acetylcholinesterase, which synthesize and degrade ACh, are responsive to the levels of circulating estrogenic hormones (Luine et al., 1975). In ovariectomized rats, estrogen administration increases the activity of choline acetyltransferase by inducing de novo enzyme synthesis (Luine & McEwen, 1983; Luine, Park, Joh, Reis, & McEwen, 1980). These studies have suggested a sex difference in the effects of estrogen on the rat basal forebrain: Estradiol increases cholinergic enzyme activity in certain forebrain nuclei of ovariectomized females but has no effect or a decremental effect in these same nuclei in castrated males. Serotonin-receptor regulation may also be different between the two genders (McEwen et al., 1984). In summary, gonadal hormones have profound influences on brain development and postnatal function, via either trophic effects derived from their organizational properties or via activational effects on neuronal function.

CLINICAL STUDIES OF THE EFFECTS OF GONADAL HORMONES ON BRAIN FUNCTION IN HUMANS

In humans, gonadal hormone effects on adult behavior may be phylogenetically related to reproductive behavior in animals, such as aggression in males and the ability to attract a male during ovulation in females. However, these gonadal hormonal influences on human behavior include aspects of human cognitive and emotional function that probably have become integrated into human personality and are difficult to discern. Nevertheless, recent studies have suggested gonadal hormone-dependent gender differences in human behavior (Ehrhardt & Meyer-Bahlburg, 1979; Rubin et al., 1981). For example, a relationship has been suggested between violent behavior in male prisoners and elevated circulating testosterone. In addition, reduction in circulating testosterone with antiandrogenic agents may diminish aggressive antisocial behavior, aberrant sexual behavior, and aberrant erotic mental imagery in men who are genetically prone to such behavior. Supplementation of testosterone to hypogonadal men increases not only their aggressiveness, but also has an effect on sexual fantasy and mental imagery, clearly indicating an effect of testosterone on higher cognitive functioning in humans. In addition, patients with prostatic carcinoma treated with high-dose estrogen routinely demonstrate mood changes and other changes in personality. In women, the relationship of gonadal hormones to brain function is suggested by the cognitive and emotional changes accompanying the premenstrual syndrome (Reid & Yen, 1981; Vaitukaitis, 1984), which may be treatable with hormonal therapy (Muse, Cetel, Futterman, & Yen, 1984). Kerr (1976) has made the interesting argument that the emotional changes in some women that are associated with low estrogen levels during menstruation and the menopause, such as irritability and depression, may be the human counterparts of female animal reproductive behavior during nonovulatory periods that give the male appropriate behavioral signals that the female is unreceptive. Indeed, we do recognize typical gender-related behavior in humans much as we recognize such behavior in animals, even though there are strong societal influences on human behavior. As we accept that gender-related behavior in animals is hormonally determined, we may consider that human behavior may also have a hormonal component, and that hormones such as estrogen may have an effect on cognition, emotion, and behavior even in humans.

Hormone replacement therapy for the treatment of menopausal and postmenopausal symptoms has been used since the nineteenth century (Utian, 1980). Indeed, the menopause and postmenopausal periods of life are modern problems without an evolutionary counterpart. Even in 1900, the average life expectancy was only 40 years, so that the average woman throughout most of history did not live beyond the reproductive years. During the 1940's and 1950's, estrogen replacement therapy for menopausal and postmenopausal disorders was common until it was recognized in the 1960's that such therapy could be associated with serious side effects (Gambrell, 1982). Since then, clinical investigations have determined that estrogen replacement therapy may be safely administered with the appropriate precautions and regimens (such as cyclic therapy), and may be justified for specific menopausal and postmenopausal estrogen deficiency diseases in which the risk-to-benefit ratio justifies their use, such as vasomotor instability, atrophic vaginitis, and osteoporosis.

Psychological symptoms accompany menstruation and the menopause, including difficulties in attention, concentration, and memory, as well as emotional disorders such as irritability and depression (Furuhjelm & Fedor-Freybergh, 1976). These changes in cognitive and emotional behavior may be secondary to hormonal changes occurring during these periods of life. While the primary effect of estrogen deficiency appears to be on emotion, hormonally dependent emotional changes could result in secondary cognitive difficulties in humans. For example, emotional modulating factors play an important role in learning and memory (Lynch, McGaugh, & Weinberger, 1984). However, there are many confounding factors that influence cognitive and emotional function in humans, such as personality and life history, as well as psychological adaptation to the physical symptoms of the menopause. In some women, higher cognition may be capable of suppressing or controlling such emotional disturbances. However, when such hormonally induced emotional disturbances are severe or when cognitive processes are unable to control such emotional disturbances because of stress or neurotic problems, then the hormonally induced emotional disturbances may become clinically prominent.

These confounding factors make it difficult to determine the actual role of changes in gonadal hormone levels on the cognitive and emotional disorders that may accompany menstruation and the menopausal and postmenopausal periods. It seems likely that not all menopausal and postmenopausal cognitive and emotional disorders are due to estrogen deficiency and would be estrogen responsive. Although several controlled studies have suggested a benefit of estrogen on cognitive and emotional function in menopausal and postmenopausal women, estrogens are currently not recommended for cognitive and emotional disorders of the menopause and postmenopausal period because the risk-to-benefit ratio is perceived to be high. Nevertheless, a role for hormone replacement therapy in the treatment of psychological symptoms in menopausal and postmenopausal women may be developed in the future, particularly when one considers that safer, more effective methods of providing hormone replacement therapy with newer synthetic compounds may be possible.

Studies utilizing estrogen for cognitive and emotional disorders in menopausal and postmenopausal women have varied in a number of important aspects. Such variables have included: the patient populations studied (menstrual, castrated, menopausal, postmenopausal); the target symptoms being treated (e.g., depression, memory disturbances, or irritability); the psychometric assessment scales used to measure cognitive and emotional status; the type of estrogen used (conjugated estrogens also containing progestins, synthetic estrogens, or various estradiol preparations), and the dosages and length of time of estrogen administration; and the study design (open trials, double-blind studies, placebo controlled, etc.). In particular, differences may exist with regard to the psychotropic effects of various synthetic and naturally occurring estrogens. Since oral contraceptives contain multiple metabolites of estrogens as well as progestins, it is difficult to evaluate the actual role of estradiol, other estrogens, and progestins in their efficacy. In the following discussion, a few representative studies will be reviewed in some detail to give the reader a perspective regarding the possible beneficial effects of estrogen therapy for cognitive and emotional disorders in susceptible women that have been suggested by several investigations.

Rauramo, Lagerspetz, Engblom, and Punnonen (1975) studied the role of estrogen replacement therapy for psychological symptoms appearing after castration in three groups of women. Group 1 was a castrated group, having undergone recent bilateral oophorectomy; Group 2 was a similar castrated group that was given estradiol valerate, 2 mg/day, initiated 1 month after surgery; and Group 3 was a control group who had undergone only hysterectomy, and received no estrogen. On subjective evaluations of mood, the estrogen-treated group showed mood reports close to the normal state while the untreated castrated group differed significantly from the other two groups in being emotionally more disordered, with greater reports of anxiety and neurovegetative symptoms, as well as memory dysfunction and lack of ability to concentrate.

In a randomized double-blind prospective trial of estrogen-progesterone on psychological function in 38 women with menopausal symptoms, Gerdes, Sonnendecker, and Polakow (1982) reported significant improvement with estrogen therapy. The patients were divided into three groups; one group was given Premarin (1.25 mg/day) for 3 weeks, followed by no therapy for 1 week; a second group was given Premarin plus medrogesterone 5 mg from day 16 to 21; and a third group was given clonidine for 28 days.

Placebo controls were used in each group during crossover periods. The results showed that estrogen therapy resulted in a significant improvement in depressive symptoms as measured by a number of different psychometric scales. No effect of placebo or clonidine was noted on any psychometric parameters.

In studies of emotional and cognitive disorders of postmenopausal women, De Lignieres and Vincens (1982) studied 56 postmenopausal women who were carefully monitored according to hormonal status (with estradiol and gonadotrophin levels) before and during estrogen therapy. Estradiol-17 beta (1.5 mg/day, percutaneously) was given for 3 months. At the end of 3 months, 300 mg/day of progesterone for 10 days was given. Psychological tests included measures of depression, anxiety, and aggressiveness. Prior to therapy, all women had plasma estradiol levels below 50 pg/ml. During estrogen therapy, persistently low blood estrogen levels in one subgroup of women were associated with no significant change in the incidence of depression, anxiety, and aggressiveness. In a second subgroup, therapeutic blood levels of estradiol consistent with premenopausal physiologic levels were associated with highly significant improvement in symptoms of depression, aggressiveness, and anxiety. In a third subgroup with elevated estrogen levels during therapy, significant improvements were noted in depression while aggressiveness and anxiety were increased. The addition of progesterone to this latter group markedly reduced the symptoms of anxiety and aggressiveness, with loss of irritability. This study emphasizes the variable responses of individuals to estrogen therapy and suggests that some of the controversy about whether estrogen is beneficial may be due to variations in blood levels in individual patients. The study also suggests that low plasma estrogen is associated with depression in some postmenopausal women.

Klaiber, Broverman, Vogel, and Kobayashi (1979) have suggested that depressive symptoms in estrogen-deficient postmenopausal women may be due to an impairment of central adrenergic function. Evidence has been presented that estrogen may enhance central adrenergic function directly (Grenngrass & Tonge, 1974). It has also been postulated that catechol estrogens may competitively inhibit the enzymatic methylation and biologic inactivation of norepinephrine by catechol-0-methyltransferase, and thus estrogen might also potentiate the action of norepinephrine (Ball, Knuppen, & Haupt, 1972). Estrogens were also shown to inhibit human plasma monoamine oxidase (MAO) activity (Klaiber, Broverman, Vogel, &

Kobayashi, 1972) and thus might have an antidepressant activity by making more norepinephrine available for synaptic transmission in adrenergic neurons.

Klaiber et al., (1979) studied 40 women with primary, recurrent, unipolar, major depressive disorders who had had extended histories of at least 2 years' duration of unsuccessful treatment by a variety of conventional therapies including electroshock, antidepressants, and psychotherapy. The patients were divided into pre- and post-menopausal groups, based on history and their hormonal state (i.e., serum luteinizing hormone [LH]). The study was placebo controlled and conducted in a blind fashion. The women were treated through three menstrual cycles and received Premarin, in doses from 5 to 25 mg, and cyclical therapy with Provera. Mean Hamilton scores for both groups were around 30 at outset. In the estrogen-treated group, the mean score dropped 9 points, while in the placebo group, the mean score dropped by only 0.1 point. Group analysis revealed a subgroup of responders among the estrogen-treated group. Six estrogen-treated women showed improvements of more than 15 points and were noted to have almost complete remissions of their long-standing pathological depression. None of the patients in the placebo group showed improvements of more than 10 points, and the condition of 8/17 became worse. This study appears to show marked effects of estrogen in improving postmenopausal depression in some women who are unresponsive to conventional antidepressant therapy, suggesting that estrogen may have a unique clinical antidepressant effect in postmenopausal women.

Other clinical studies of estrogen therapy in postmenopausal women have demonstrated an effect of estrogen on memory and other cognitive functions. Hackman and Galbraith (1976) tested the effect on memory of piperazine estrone sulphate (1.5 mg twice daily for 3 weeks followed by a 1 week interval of no drug) in menopausal women in a 6 month double-blind, placebo-controlled study. Ten patients had clinical signs of menopausal estrogen deficiency, and eight had undergone bilateral oophorectomy in the 6 months prior to study. The Guild memory test was used to assess memory, which evaluated six different memory functions: (1) initial recall of meaningful verbal material; (2) delayed recall or retention of same; (3) initial associative memory; (4) retention of newly formed associations; (5) initial concentration or immediate rote memory; and (6) nonverbal memory recall (numbers or designs). The results showed a statistical ($p < 0.02\%$) improvement in memory in the estrogen-treated group, with a subgroup of patients showing much more dramatic improvement than others. Analysis of the data suggested that the mechanisms of improvement in memory may have been related to improvements in emotional function such as mood.

Furuhjelm and Fedor-Freybergh (1976) studied three groups of women with psychological symptoms. Group 1 consisted of 27 menopausal women with new onset of menstrual irregularities and psychological symptoms, including nervousness, anxiety, depression, and sleep disturbances. They were treated with 1 mg/day of estradiol valerate for 12 days, followed by 1 mg estradiol valerate and 30 mg of L-norgestrel for 10 days, followed by 0.5 mg estradiol valerate for 6 days. Group 2 was 26 postmenopausal women treated with the same regimen, except that the doses of estradiol were doubled. Group 3 was 25 postmenopausal women, 12 received placebo, and 13 were treated with 2 mg of estradiol valerate for 3 months. Hormonal balance was studied by measuring serum LH and follicle-stimulating hormone (FSH), as well as serum low polar estrogens (including estrone and estradiol-17 beta) before and during estrogen therapy. After therapy with estradiol (1 mg/day), the serum estrogen level increased by approximately 50 pg/ml to a level consistent with the follicular phase of menstruation; on 2 mg/day, the serum levels increased by 100 pg/ml. A number of psychometric studies were performed. All groups had evidence of depressive symptoms, as evidenced by the Hamilton Depression Scale and the Sabbatsberg Depression Self-Rating Scale. By these tests, a significant improvement was noted after 1 month of estrogen therapy, and progressive improvement was noted after 3 and 6 months of therapy in both pre- and postmenopausal women. Improvement was also noted on tests of choice reaction time, attention, short-term memory, and concentration. A tendency to reverse cognition decline was also noted when the treatment group was compared to controls. Greater improvement was noted on more complicated tasks compared to simple tasks. The authors concluded that estrogen therapy for menopausal and postmenopausal symptoms may actually prevent decline in mental performance, in addition to reversing cognitive and emotional disturbances that have already appeared.

Campbell (1976) conducted two placebo-controlled, double-blind trial studies of estrogen therapy in postmenopausal women with psychological symptoms. In the first study, 64 postmenopausal women with severe menopausal symptoms, including 44 with severe vasomotor symptoms, were given 3 months of Premarin (1.25 mg/day) for 3 weekly courses followed by one treatment-free week between courses. The patients were also given placebo for similar periods, in a crossover design. A second study lasting 12 months, involved women with less severe symptoms. Various psychometric scales were employed to measure emotional status including, depression, neuroticism and extroversion, and general health. In both studies, significant improvements were noted in memory, irritability, anxiety, and optimism, as well as physiologic symptoms such as vasomotor symptoms and urinary frequency. Of interest, in 20 women with severe menopausal symptoms, improvements were noted only for memory, anxiety, and vaginal dryness and no improvement was seen in vasomotor symptoms, suggesting that improvements in cognitive and emotional function were independent of the effects on vasomotor symptoms.

Finally, Collins et al. (1982) studied the psychophysiological stress responses of postmenopausal women. Seventeen females with a history of vasomotor symptoms and amenorrhea of at least 6 months' duration, with serum FSH levels greater than 40 IU / 1 confirming the postmenopausal state were studied. The patients were given cyclic therapy with beta-estradiol and estriol combined with norethindrone. The study was conducted in a blind fashion and the effects of practice and habituation to the tests were included in the study design. Stress was induced by mental performance tests, including mental arithmetic, visual search tasks, and cognitive conflict tasks. A scale of self-reports was also used to determine the emotional, pyschological, and psychosomatic state of each subject during the test period. Statistically significant improvement was noted in self-reported relief of tension, anxiety and memory. In two memory-loaded tasks, arithmetic and visual search, greater improvements were noted after treatment with estrogen. Thus, the subjects self-reported improvement in memory function was substantiated by their performance. No change in blood pressure or heart rate, cortisol, testosterone and androstenedione was demonstrated in response to mental stress during therapy with estrogen, but adrenaline and noradrenaline responses to stress were reduced during estrogen therapy suggesting a possible adrenergic-related mechanism of action of estrogen in these tasks.

In sum, these studies illustrate the improvements in cognitive and emotional function that may be seen with estrogen-replacement therapy in menopausal and postmenopausal women. The actual mechanisms by which estrogen exerts its clinical effects on cognitive and emotional function have been investigated but are not really known. Further clinical studies are needed to elucidate the role of estrogen deficiency in disorders such as memory dysfunction and depression in postmenopausal women and the role of estrogen replacement therapy in treating these disorders.

CLINICAL STUDIES OF ESTROGEN THERAPY IN POSTMENOPAUSAL WOMEN WITH DEMENTIA

In view of the possibility that postmenopausal estrogen deficiency may cause cognitive and emotional disorders, it is interesting to note a study in which estrogen was given to elderly postmenopausal nursing home residents with organic brain syndrome (Kantor, Michael, Shore, & Ludvigson, 1968; Michael, Kantor, & Shore, 1970). These investigators employed Premarin (0.625 mg/day) and measured psychological function and behavior using the Hospital Adjustment Scale. The test measured communication and interpersonal relationships; self-care and social responsibility; and measures related to work, activities, and recreation. The study was a double-blind study over 3 years, conducted by nurses who applied the scale. Initially, there were no significant cognitive or functional differences between the groups. However, with time a gradual decline in score was noted in the placebo group, while the estrogen group maintained its cognitive, emotional, and social behavioral function. At every interval tested, the placebo group was below the estrogen-treated group beginning at 3 months after therapy, and these differences were statistically significant. The results were even more marked when dropouts from both groups were considered. No harmful side effects were noted. The results suggested that estrogen administration to elderly nursing home residents with organic brain syndrome may prevent the progression of cognitive dysfunction.

Considering that estrogen may affect multiple neurotransmitter systems and might have effects on cognitive and emotional function in estrogen-deficient postmenopausal women, we conducted a preliminary open trial to assess the safety and potential efficacy of low-dose estrogen therapy in postmenopausal women with AD. Informed consent was obtained from all participants and, in all cases, from their spouses or guardians as well. Seven women were recruited from the Alzheimer's Disease and Related Disorders Clinic at The

Rockefeller University Hospital. All women fulfilled research criteria for the clinical diagnosis of probable AD (McKhann et al., 1984). All patients underwent a complete gynecological examination. Assessments consisted of the following: Global Deterioration Scale (Reisberg, Ferris, DeLeon, & Crook, 1982), Blessed Dementia Scale (Blessed, Tomlinson, & Roth, 1968), Hamilton Depression Scale (Hamilton, 1976), Wechsler Adult Intelligence Scale (selected verbal and performance subtests) (Matarazzo, 1972), Mini-Mental Status Exam (Folstein, Folstein, & McHugh, 1975), Hachinski Ischemic Score (Hachinski et al., 1975), Randt Memory Test (Brown, Randt, & Osborne, 1983), and the Mattis Dementia Rating Scale (Mattis, 1976). No patient had an Hachinski score above 4.

Following the initial assessment, patients were given micronized estradiol (Estrace, Mead Johnson Laboratories) orally, 2 mg/day in divided dosages, for 6 weeks. Medical, neurological, gynecologic, and selected psychometric tests were repeated at 3 weeks and 6 weeks after beginning treatment, and 3 weeks after completion of the trial. Three of seven women demonstrated emotional and cognitive improvements during estrogen therapy. On the Mini-Mental Status Exam, the median baseline score in this responding group was 14; after 3 and 6 weeks of estrogen therapy, this score improved to 20. On the Hamilton Depression Scale, the median baseline score was 21; during therapy, the score improved to 10 at 3 weeks, and 11 at 6 weeks. Improvements were also noted on specific items of the Randt Memory Test (general information, five items, repeating numbers). These clinically observable improvements approached but did not achieve statistical significance by the t-test for repeated measures (Zar, 1975), probably due to the small sample size and the variance in initial baseline scores between the estradiol responsive and nonresponsive groups. An analysis of the psychometric testing revealed that the improvements in the estrogen-responsive group were primarily related to attention, orientation, mood, social interaction, and memory (in one patient). Daily psychometric evaluations performed in two responders following discontinuation of estradiol demonstrated that a mean period of 9 days elapsed before their psychometric parameters returned to the initial baseline value. Their decline in performance correlated with falling estradiol levels.

A further analysis of the psychometric data revealed that the response to estradiol therapy was dependent on initial baseline cognitive and emotional status. Patients with higher Hamilton scores, lower Mini-Mental Status scores, and higher Randt general information

TABLE 1

Low-Dose Estrogen Therapy in Alzheimer's Disease: Longitudinal Studies

	Baseline	3 Weeks	6 Weeks
Nonresponders (n = 4)			
Hamilton Depression Scale	9.0	9.0	9.0
Mini-Mental Status	3.5	3.0	3.5
Randt Memory Test			
General Information	2.0	2.0	2.0
Five Items	0	0	0
Repeating Numbers (forward / backward)	5/0	4/0	5/0
Responders (n = 3)			
Hamilton Depression Scale	21	10	11
Mini-Mental Status	14	20	20
Randt Memory Test			
General Information	8	10	10
Five Items	0	0	3
Repeating Numbers (forward / backward)	6/0	6/3	6/3

Note: Results are expressed as the median for each group.

and repeating numbers scores, were the patients who showed improvements with therapy. Fisher's exact test (Zar, 1975) confirmed a statistically significant ($P = 0.03$) relationship between the baseline scores and improvements in scores in 3 and 6 weeks for all tests in which improvement was noted. The estradiol responsive group had an older age of onset of dementia (median 72 years vs. 61 years in nonresponders), with less advanced disease as manifested by lower baseline Global Deterioration scores (median 4.5 vs. 5.5 in nonresponders). The responding group also had less severe cognitive decline as manifested by higher baseline Mini-Mental Status scores (median 14) vs. nonresponders (median 3.5) and a lower prevalence of moderate to severe aphasia, agnosia, or apraxia in responders (0 of 3 patients) versus nonresponders (4 of 4 patients). The responding group had more severe emotional dysfunction as evidenced by their higher baseline Hamilton depression score (median 21) versus

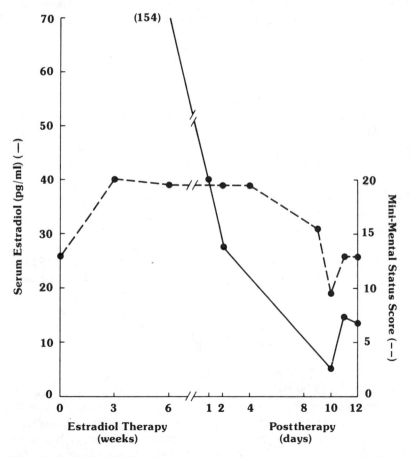

Figure Legend: Correlation of changes in cognitive function as assessed by the Mini-Mental Status exam with changes in serum estradiol during estradiol therapy and during the "washout" period posttherapy.

nonresponders (median 9). Laboratory data indicated that responders were more likely to have radiologic evidence of osteoporosis (2 of 3 patients) than nonresponders (0 of 4 patients).

Complications of therapy were observed in two patients. One patient developed vaginal bleeding on withdrawal of estrogen. An endometrial biopsy disclosed hyperplastic changes. Following treatment with a progestational agent, a follow-up biopsy at 3 months revealed only aplasia characteristic of the normal postmenopausal endometrium. Another patient developed transient breast tenderness, which did not interfere with continued treatment. Thus, no unexpected side effects were noted related to the use of estrogen in postmenopausal women with dementia.

DISCUSSION

In this preliminary open trial, low dosages of estradiol appeared to benefit brain function in a subgroup of postmenopausal women with AD. The estradiol-responsive women evidenced the presence of a systemic estrogen-deficiency state as manifested by osteoporosis. The primary therapeutic benefit of estrogen appeared to be clinically related to its effects on the emotional disorders associated with AD in some patients, but an effect on memory was noted in one patient in this short-term study.

Cognition and emotion are complicated functions of the human organism that are just beginning to be understood. Although cognitive disturbances are typically the most prominent feature of AD in its early stages, emotional disturbances, such as disorders of mood (anxiety, agitation, dysphoria, or depression), arousal, motivation and affect, are also common in dementia and may represent a biologic component of the disease (Gurland & Toner, 1982; Marco & Tandels, 1984; Miller, 1980; Reifler, Larson, & Hanley, 1982). In AD, the relationship of primary disorders of emotion to the cognitive deficits may be significant. From a neuropsychological point of view, emotional factors can have important modulating effects on memory and learning in both animals and man (Lynch et al., 1984). Depression, agitation, and other emotional disorders in patients with AD may have a biologic basis in the pathology and neurochemistry of the disease (Marco & Randels, 1984). Disease involving the "isodendritic core" of the subcortical brain may have widespread effects on emotional function, in addition to effects on cognitive function (Rosser, 1982). It is clear that AD involves subcortical structures of brain in addition to cortical structures (McDuff & Sumi, 1985). Loss of cells from the locus coeruleus have been demonstrated that appear to parallel the loss of cells from the nucleus basalis in some patients (Tomlinson, Irving, & Blessed, 1981). Recent neurochemical studies have demonstrated that other neurotransmitter systems in addition to the cholinergic system (Bartus, Dean, Beer, & Lippa, 1982) may be involved in AD, particularly deficits in catecholamine neurotransmitters such as norepinephrine (Bondareff, Mountjoy, & Roth, 1982; Bowen et al., 1983; Cross et al., 1981). Alexopoulos, Lieberman, Young, & Shamoian (1983) demonstrated a correlation between depressive symptomatology and abnormal monoamine function in patients with AD. Thus, in addition to the cognitive disorders and cholinergic dysfunction that occurs in AD, the clinical observations of emotional disorders in patients in AD may have a basis in the neurochemical and neuroanatomical pathology of AD.

The estradiol-responsive patients in our study had emotional disorders associated with their dementia that were unresponsive to conventional antidepressant therapy. Although the responding patients had moderately high Hamilton scores, in view of their prior nonresponse to conventional antidepressant therapy, their significant cognitive impairments, and their progressive clinical course, a primary diagnosis of pseudodementia secondary to a major depression was very unlikely. Miller (1980) has also emphasized the high ratings on the Hamilton Psychiatric Rating Scale for depression that may be noted in demented patients. Indeed, scoring on the Hamilton Scale is not specific for depression. For example, neurovegetative symptoms and sleep disorders may be due to depression or dementia.

However, estrogen may have an effect on emotional disorders that is unique. Klaiber et al. (1979) demonstrated that severely depressed postmenopausal women unresponsive to conventional antidepressant therapy may have complete remissions of long-standing pathologic depression with estrogen-replacement therapy. Indeed, a biologic basis for an effect of estrogens in affective illness has been suggested (Grenngrass & Tonge, 1974; Kendall, Stancel, & Enna, 1982; Klaiber et al., 1972). Thus, estrogen may have a unique effect on emotional disorders in estrogen-deficient postmenopausal women, which is not shared by conventional antidepressants, and could be particularly relevant in postmenopausal patients with AD.

Other studies have indicated that improvement of depressive emotional symptoms in demented patients may result in improved cognitive function (Raskind, 1983). Although cortical dysfunction in dementia, such as memory loss, is generally unresponsive to treatment, an effect of estradiol in enhancing memory was noted in one patient in our study. Whether prolonged estrogen therapy would have a therapeutic effect on memory was not investigated but remains a possibility, particularly in view of other clinical studies suggesting that beneficial effects on memory in postmenopausal women may require estrogen therapy over a period of months (Furuhjeim & Fedor-Freybergh, 1976; Hackman & Galbraith, 1976).

We have also treated one women with Parkinson's disease, dementia, and depression who had become refractory to dopaminergic agents during the preceding 5 years and had not responded to a course of antidepressant and electroconvulsive therapy for depression. During estradiol therapy, she demonstrated improvements in attention, orientation, mood, and activities of daily living, while neurological exam revealed less hypomimia, but other features of her Parkinson's disease were unchanged. Dementia is frequent in Parkinson's disease and may be related to a loss of core neurons, including cholinergic neurons, in the basal forebrain as in AD (Whitehouse, Hedreen, White, & Price, 1983). We may speculate that the response to estradiol in this postmenopausal woman with degenerative dementia accompanying Parkinson's disease and the response to estradiol in AD may have a common basis.

The clinical improvements in cognition and emotion seen in response to estradiol in our demented patients may have been due to a number of effects of estradiol on brain function, including direct (membrane) and indirect (genomic) activational effects. Estrogen may directly influence cortical functions such as memory, perhaps by enhancing neurotransmitter function in pertinent cortical systems, either by increasing the production of neurotransmitter protein (Luine et al., 1975), or by influences on neurotransmitter receptors (for example, see Kendall et al., 1982). Estrogen-replacement therapy in AD may also act via trophic mechanisms on neurons susceptible to estrogen deficiency (Arai, Matsumoto, & Nishizuka, 1978; Toran-Allerand, 1981).

Although long-term estrogen therapy in postmenopausal women appears safe when given properly for specific indications, such therapy is not without risks (Gambrell, 1982). In view of the possible side effects of estrogen therapy in elderly women, we must caution against the general clinical use of estrogens in patients with AD until further controled clinical research trials are undertaken and the risk-to-benefit ratio for the use of estrogen in AD is carefully assessed.

SUMMARY AND RECOMMENDATIONS

Hormones such as estrogen have been shown to have important biologic effects on neurons. Both organizational and activational effects have been demonstrated. Gonadal hormones have been demonstrated to have significant effects on behavior in animals. Although their effects on human behavior are less clear, it seems reasonable to suspect that estrogen has an important effect on human brain function and behavior as well. Thus, during states of estrogen deficiency, such as the postmenopausal period of life, the lack of estrogen could have serious psychological implications for susceptible women.

From the point of view of pathogenesis, prolonged post-menopausal estrogen deficiency could result in the loss of estrogen effects on susceptible neurons and could be related to the development of cognitive and emotional deficits in postmenopausal women with AD. Estrogen deficiency in postmenopausal women is known to involve a number of organs, including the endometrium, the vaginal epithelium, and bone (Gambrell, 1982), and may be a more significant factor in postmenopausal diseases such as osteoporosis than aging itself (Richelson, Wahner, Melton, & Riggs, 1984). Prolonged postmenopausal estrogen deficiency could result in the loss of trophic estrogenic influences necessary for specific neuronal cell survival (Toran-Allerand, 1981) or the loss of normal reparative neuronal response to injury (Arai et al., 1978). We may speculate that estrogen therapy could prevent or retard the development of AD in susceptible postmenopausal women. Estrogen deficiency could also result in the abnormal regulation of brain neurochemical receptors (Kendall et al., 1982) or the deficient expression of various neurotransmitters (Luine et al., 1975). Thus, estrogen therapy may also have potential benefits for the treatment of cognitive and emotional disorders of AD by physiologically or pharmacologically correcting dysregulated neurotransmitter systems. Indeed, a number of controlled studies have demonstrated that estrogen may be therapeutic for some of the emotional and cognitive problems that occur in some menopausal and postmenopausal women.

In conclusion, estrogen therapy for AD has a rational scientific basis. The data from this preliminary open trial indicate that estradiol may be of value in the symptomatic treatment of a subgroup of post-menopausal women with AD. Since a variety of estrogen compounds exist with differing properties in regard to their psychotropic effects, steroidal effects, estrogenic activity, mode of delivery, and side effects, testing of naturally occurring and synthetic estrogens should be done to determine which estrogen derivatives may be most useful as trophic agents that may prevent neuronal cell loss; as psychotropic agents for improving cognitive and emotional function; and which estrogens are most brain specific with the fewest peripheral side effects. Controlled clinical research trials are needed to establish and to further define a potential therapeutic role for estrogens and other hormones in AD and related dementias.

REFERENCES

Alexopoulos, G.S., Lieberman, K.W., Young, R.C., & Shamoian, C.A. (1983). Monoamines and monoamine oxidase in primary degenerative dementia. In C.A. Shamoian (Ed.), *Biology and treatment of dementia in the elderly* (pp. 59-71). Washington, D.C.: American Psychiatric Press.

Arai, Y., Matsumoto, A., & Nishizuka, M. (1978). Synaptogenic action of estrogen on the hypothalamic arcuate nucleus (ARCN) of the developing rat brain and of the deafferented adult brain in female rats. In G. Dorner & M. Kawakami (Eds.), *Hormones and brain development* (pp. 43-48). Amsterdam: Elsevier/North-Holland Biomedical Press.

Ball, P., Knuppen, R., & Haupt, M. (1972). Interactions between estrogens and catechol amines. III. Studies on the methylation of catechol estrogens, catechol amines and other catechols by the catechol-0-methyltransferase of human liver. *Journal of Clinical Endocrinology and Metabolism, 34,* 736-746.

Bartus, R.T., Dean, R.L., Beer, B., & Lippa, A.S. (1982). The cholinergic hypothesis of geriatric memory dysfunction. *Science, 217,* 408-417.

Bedard, P., Boucher, R., DiPaolo, T., & Labrie, F. (1984). Interaction between estradiol, prolactin, and striatal dopaminergic mechanisms. *Advances in Neurology, 40,* 489-495.

Blessed, G., Tomlinson, B.E., & Roth, M. (1968). The association between quantitative measures of dementia and of senile change in the cerebral gray matter of elderly subjects. *British Journal of Psychiatry, 114,* 797-811.

Bondareff, W., Mountjoy, C.Q., & Roth, M. (1982). Loss of neurons of origin of the adrenergic projection to cerebral cortex (nucleus locus ceruleus) in senile dementia. *Neurology, 32,* 164-168.

Bowen, D.M., Allen, S.J., Benton, J.S., Goodhardt, M.J., Haan, E.A., Palmer, A.M., Sims, N.R., Smith, C.C.T., Spillane, J.A., Esiri, M.M., Neary, D., Snowdon, J.S., Wilcock, G.K., & Davison, A.N. (1983). Biochemical assessment of serotonergic and cholinergic dysfunction and cerebral atrophy in Alzheimer's disease. *Journal of Neurochemistry, 41,* 266-272.

Brown, E.R., Randt, C.T., & Osborne, D.P., Jr. (1983). Assessment of memory disturbance in aging. In A. Agnoli, G. Crepaldi, P.F. Spano, & M. Trabucchi (Eds.), *Aging brain and ergot alkaloids* (pp. 131-137). New York: Raven Press.

Campbell, S. (1976). Double-blind psychometric studies on the effect of natural estrogens on post-menopausal women. In S. Campbell (Ed.), *The management of the menopause and postmenopausal years* (pp. 149-169). Baltimore: University Park Press.

Chiodo, A., & Caggiula, A.R. (1983). Substantia nigra dopamine neurons: Alterations in basal discharge rates and autoreceptor sensitivity induced by estrogen. *Neuropharmacology, 22,* 593-599.

Collins, A., Hanson, U., Eneroth, P., Hagenfeldt, K., Lundberg, U., & Frankenhaeuser, M. (1982). Psychophysiological stress responses in postmenopausal women before and after hormonal replacement therapy. *Human Neurobiology, 1,* 153-159.

Coyle, J.T., Price, D.L., & DeLong, M.R. (1983). Alzheimer's disease: A disorder of cortical cholinergic innervation. *Science, 219,* 1184-1190.

Cross, A.J., Crow, T.J., Perry, E.K., Perry, R.H., Blessed, G., & Tomlinson, B.E. (1981). Reduced dopamine beta-hydroxylase activity in Alzheimer's disease. *British Medical Journal, 282,* 93-94.

de Lignieres, B., & Vincens, M. (1982). Differential effects of exogenous oestradiol and progesterone on mood in postmenopausal women; individual dose effect relationship. *Maturitas, 4,* 67-72.

DeVries, G.J., Buijis, R.M., & Van Leeuwen, F.W. (1984). Sex differences in vasopressin and other neurotransmitter systems in the brain. In G.J. DeVries, (Ed.), *Progress in brain research* (pp. 185-204). Amsterdam: Elsevier Science Publishers.

Ehrhardt, A., & Meyer-Bahlburg, H.F. (1979). Prenatal sex hormones and the developing brain: Effects on psychosocial differentiation and cognitive function. *Annual Review of Medicine: Selected Topics in the Clinical Sciences, 30,* 417-430.

Folstein, M., Folstein, S., & McHugh, P.R. (1975). Mini-Mental State: A practical method for grading the cognitive state of patients for the clinician. *Journal of Psychiatric Research, 12,* 189-198.

Furuhjelm, M., & Fedor-Freybergh, P. (1976). The influence of estrogens on the psyche in climacteric and post-menopausal women. In P.A. Van Keep, R.B. Greenblatt, & M.M. Albeaux-Fernet (Eds.), *Consensus on menopause research* (pp. 84-93). Baltimore: University Park Press.

Gambrell, D.R. (1982). The menopause: Benefits and risks of estrogen-progestogen replacement therapy. *Fertility and Sterility, 37,* 457-474.

Gerdes, L.C., Sonnendecker, E.W., & Polakow, E.S. (1982). Psychological changes effected by estrogen-progestogen and clonidine treatment in climacteric women. *American Journal of Obstetrics and Gynecology, 142,* 98-103.

Grenngrass, P.M., & Tonge, S.R. (1974). The accumulation of noradrenaline and 5-hydroxytryptamine in three regions of mouse brain after tetrabenzine and iproniazid; effects of ethinylestradiol and progesterone. *Psychopharmacology, 39,* 187-191.

Gurland, B.J., & Toner, J.A. (1982). Depression in the elderly: A review of recently published studies. *Annual Review of Gerontology and Geriatrics, 3,* 229-265.

Hachinski, V.C., Iliff, L.D., Zilhka, E., Du Boulay, G.H., McAllister, V.L., Marshall, J., Ross Russell, R.W., & Lindsay, S. (1975). Cerebral blood flow in dementia. *Archives of Neurology, 32,* 632-637.

Hackman, B.W., & Galbraith, D. (1976). Replacement therapy with piperazine oestrone sulphate ("Harmogen") and its effect on memory. *Current Medical Research and Opinion, 4,* 303-306.

Hamilton, M. (1976). Development of a rating scale for primary depressive illness. *British Journal of Social and Clinical Psychology, 6,* 278-296.

Kantor, H.I., Michael, C.M., Shore, H., & Ludvigson, H.W. (1968). Administration of estrogens to older women, a psychometric evaluation. *American Journal of Obstetrics & Gynecology, 101,* 58-61.

Kelly, M.J., Moss, R.L., Dudley, C.A. & Fawcett, C.P. (1977). The specificity of the response of preoptic-septal area neurons to estrogen: 17-beta-estradiol vs. 17-alpha estradiol and the response of extrahypothalamic neurons. *Experimental Brain Research, 30,* 43-52.

Kendall, D.A., Stancel, G.M., & Enna, S.J. (1982). The influence of sex hormones on antidepressant induced alterations in neurotransmitter receptor binding. *Journal of Neuroscience, 2,* 354-360.

Kerr, M.D. (1976). Psychological changes following hormonal therapy. In S. Campbell (Ed.), *The management of the menopause and postmenopausal years* (pp. 127-133). Baltimore: University Park Press.

Klaiber, E.L., Broverman, D.M., Vogel, W., & Kobayashi, Y. (1979). Estrogen therapy for severe persistent depressions in women. *Archives of General Psychiatry, 36,* 550-554.

Klaiber, E.L., Broverman, D.M., Vogel, W., Kobayashi, Y., & Moriarty, D. (1972). Effects of estrogen therapy on plasma MAO activity and EEG driving responses of depressed women. *American Journal of Psychiatry, 128,* 1492-1498.

Loy, R., & Milner, T.A. (1980). Sexual dimorphism in extent of axonal sprouting in rat hippocampus. *Science, 208,* 1282-1283.

Luine, V.N., Khylchevskaya, R.I., & McEwen, B.S. (1975). Effect of gonadal steroids on activities of monoamine oxidase and choline acetylase in rat brain. *Brain Research, 86,* 293-306.

Luine, V.N., & McEwen, B.S. (1983). Sex differences in cholinergic enzymes of diagonal band nuclei in the rat preoptic area. *Neuroendocrinology, 36,* 475-482.

Luine, V.N., Park, D., Joh, T., Reis, D., & McEwen, B.S. (1980). Immunochemical demonstration of increased choline acetyltransferase concentration in rat preoptic area after estradiol administration. *Brain Research, 191,* 273-277.

Lynch, G., McGaugh, J., & Weinberger, N.M. (Eds.). (1984). *Neurobiology of learning and memory.* New York: The Guilford Press.

Marco, L.A., & Randels, P.M. (1984). Neurobiology of cognitive deterioration. In W.E. Kelly (Ed.), *Alzheimer's disease and related* disorders; research and management (pp. 44-79). Springfield: Charles C Thomas.

Matarazzo, J.D. (1972). Wechsler's measurement of adult intelligence (5th ed.). Baltimore: Williams & Wilkins.

Mattis, S. (1976). Mental status examination for organic mental syndrome in the elderly patient. In L. Bellak & T.B. Karasu (Eds.), Geriatric psychiatry (pp. 77-121). New York: Grune & Stratton.

McDuff, T., & Sumi, S.M. (1985). Subcortical degeneration in Alzheimer's disease. Neurology, 35, 123-126.

McEwen, B.S., Biegon, A., Fischette, C.T., Luine, V.N., Parsons, B., & Rainbow, T.C. (1984). Towards a neurochemical basis of steroid hormone action. In L. Martini & W. Ganong (Eds.), Frontiers in neuroendocrinology (pp. 1153-1176). New York: Raven Press.

McEwen, B.S., Davis, P.G., Parsons, B., & Pfaff, D. (1979). The brain target for steroid hormone action. Annual Review of Neuroscience, 2, 65-112.

McKhann, G., Drachman, D., Folstein, M., Katzman, R., Price, D., & Stadlan, E.M. (1984). Clinical diagnosis of Alzheimer's disease: Report of the NINCDS-ADRDA work group under the auspices of the Department of Health and Human Services Task Force on Alzheimer's Disease. Neurology, 34, 939-944.

Michael, C.M., Kantor, H.I., & Shore, H. (1970). Further psychometric evaluation of older women — The effect of estrogen administration. Journal of Gerontology, 25, 337-341.

Miller, N.E. (1980). The measurement of mood in senile brain disease: Exam ratings and self reports. In J.O. Cole & J.E. Barret (Eds.), Psychopathology of the aged (pp. 97-118). New York: Raven Press.

Muse, K.N., Cetel, N.S., Futterman, L.A., & Yen, S.S.C. (1984). The Premenstrual Syndrome, "effects of medical ovariectomy." New England Journal of Medicine, 311, 1345-1349.

Nottebohm, F. (1980). Testosterone triggers growth of brain vocal control nuclei in adult female canaries. Brain Research, 189, 429-436.

Pfaff, D.W., & McEwen, B.S. (1983). Actions of estrogens and progestins on nerve cells. Science, 219, 808-814.

Raskind, M. (1983). Biologic parameters in the differential diagnosis of dementia and depression. In C.A. Shamoian (Ed.), Biology and treatment of dementia in the elderly (pp. 92-106). Washington, D.C.: American Psychiatric Press.

Rauramo, L., Lagerspetz, K., Engblom, P., & Punnonen, R. (1975). The effect of castration and peroral estrogen therapy on some psychological functions. In P.A. van Keep & C. Lauritzem (Eds.), *Estrogens in the post-menopause: Vol. 3. Frontiers of hormone research* (pp. 94-104). Basel, Switzerland: S. Karger.

Reid, C.T., & Ye, S.S.C. (1981). Premenstrual syndrome. *American Journal of Obstetrics and Gynecology, 139,* 85-104.

Reifler, B.V., Larson, E., & Hanley, R. (1982). Coexistence of cognitive impairment and depression in geriatric outpatients. *American Journal of Psychiatry, 139,* 623-629.

Reisberg, B., Ferris, S.H., DeLeon, M.J., & Crook, T. (1982). The Global Deterioration Scale for assessment of primary degenerative dementia. *American Journal of Psychiatry, 139,* 1136-1139.

Richelson, L.S., Wahner, B.W., Melton, L.J., & Riggs, B.L. (1984). Relative contributions of aging and estrogen deficiency to postmenopausal bone loss. *New England Journal of Medicine, 31,* 1273-1275.

Rossor, M.N. (1982). Dementia. *Lancet, ii,* 1200-1204.

Rubin, R.T., Reinisch, J.M., & Haskett, R.F. (1981). Postnatal gonadal steroid effects on human behavior. *Science, 211,* 1318-1324.

Sar, M. (1984). Estradiol is concentrated in tyrosine hydroxylase-containing neurons of the hypothalamus. *Science, 223,* 938-940.

Tomlinson, B.E., Irving, D., & Blessed, G. (1981). Cell loss in the locus coeruleus in senile dementia of the Alzheimer's type. *Journal of the Neurological Sciences, 49,* 419-428.

Toran-Allerand, C.D. (1981). Cellular aspects of sexual differentiation of the brain. In G. Jagiello & H.J. Vogel (Eds.), *Bioregulation of reproduction* (pp. 43-57). New York: Academic Press.

Utian, W.H. (1980). *Menopause in modern perspective: A guide to clinical practice.* New York: Appleton-Century-Crofts.

Vaitukaitis, J.L. (1984). Premenstrual syndrome. *New England Journal of Medicine, 311,* 1371-1373.

Whitehouse, P.J., Hedreen, J.C., White, C.L., & Price, D.L. (1983). Basal forebrain neurons in the dementia of Parkinson's disease. *Annals of Neurology, 13,* 243-248.

Whitehouse, P.J., Price, D.L., Struble, R.G., Clark, A.W., Coyle, J.T., & DeLong, M.R. (1982). Alzheimer's disease and senile dementia:

Loss of neurons in the basal forebrain. *Science, 215,* 1237-1239.

Zar, J.H. (1974). *Biostatistical analysis.* Englewood Cliffs, NJ: Prentice-Hall.

14

The Noradrenergic Locus Coeruleus and Senescent Memory Dysfunction

Steven F. Zornetzer, PhD

There is a large and growing literature describing the many age-related psychobiological changes associated with memory decline in normal aging (c.f., Bartus, Dean, Beer, & Lippa, 1982; Dean et al., 1981; Jensen et al., 1981; Kubanis & Zornetzer, 1981). The reader interested in delving further into these topics should additionally consider these excellent reviews.

Pioneering studies by Ruch (1934) and Gilbert (1941) demonstrated clearly that, relative to young adults, the aged exhibit a decline in performance on tests of learning and memory capabilities. Once age-related performance deficits were established, experimental attention focused on identifying the particular aspects of cognitive functioning that are impaired with aging. There has been, and continues to be, a decided lack of agreement on this matter. In particular, changes in both nonspecific processes and in memory-specific processes have been invoked to account for the same behavioral performance deficits (see Gold & McGaugh, 1975). The complicated task of localizing the sources of cognitive impairment associated with normal aging is an important goal. This goal is additionally complicated when age-related pathological processes such as Alzheimer's-associated cognitive and behavioral dysfunctions are juxtaposed on the substrate of normally occurring brain and behavioral changes. Scientists and clinicians need to address specifically both the conceptual and empirical linkages and disparities between normal age-produced and pathologically associated memory and cognitive deficits. The degree of overlap versus discontinuity in these two approaches needs to be better understood.

NEUROBIOLOGICAL STUDIES

The Search for a Neurobiological Substrate

There is an important caveat that needs to be mentioned from the outset. The study of neurobiological and associated behavioral changes occurring with normal aging is often blurred by the study of these same phenomena in age-related "pathological" conditions. This is best illustrated by the recent proliferation of interest in and new data pertaining to Alzheimer's disease (AD). If, as some have suggested (see below), AD is nothing more than an acceleration of normal aging processes, then data obtained from normal aging animals (which do not develop AD) may indeed be a valid model for studying some aspects of human AD. Conversely, clinical-pathological correlates of human AD may provide important insights into normal aging. Of course, we should keep in mind that this need not be the case at all, and that the basic assumption may be faulty (i.e., data obtained from normal aged organisms might have little or no relationship to AD and vice versa).

AD as a Research Focal Point

A common deficit in both normal aging and AD is a decline in memory. The dramatic loss of cholinergic neurons observed in AD has led to the hypothesis that degeneration of cholinergic systems may be responsible for the loss of higher order function in these individuals. Recent data suggest that there is a relation between the severity of the clinical expression of AD and transmitter-specific changes in cholinergic neurons located in the basal forebrain (Bowen et al., 1977; Davies & Maloney, 1976; Perry, E.K., Blessed, & Tomlinson, 1977). These cholinergic neuron changes are believed to occur specifically in magnocellular cholinergic basal forebrain systems located in the medial septum, diagonal band of Broca, and nucleus basalis of Meynert. These data, coupled with the hypothesis (Price et al., 1982) that degenerating cholinergic neurons and terminals originating in basal forebrain give rise to neuritic plaques, support the growing conventional wisdom that pathogenetic processes primary to the basal forebrain cholinergic system are closely associated with AD.

Since AD is thought to represent an acceleration of normal aging processes, it has been proposed that cholinergic dysfunction may underlie normal age-related memory deficits (Drachman & Leavitt, 1974; Drachman & Sahakian, 1980). The finding that, in young subjects, blockage of cholinergic systems results in interruption of normal memory processes (Drachman, 1977) has strengthened this hypothesis. Disturbingly, however, interventive strategies designed to stimulate cholinergic systems have not resulted in significant generalized improvement in age-related memory loss (Ferris, Sathananthan, Reisberg, & Gershon, 1979; Mohs et al., 1979, 1980; Vroulis & Smith, 1981).

Multiple Neurotransmitter Involvement

Although basal forebrain cholinergic activity has taken "center stage" with respect to its pathogenetic importance in age-related memory loss, it is very unlikely, given our current knowledge of brain complexity, that any single neurotransmitter would selectively and exclusively be involved in disorders of cognitive function and memory (c.f., Zornetzer, 1978; Gold & Zornetzer, 1983). Other neurotransmitter systems have been implicated in normal memory processes, particularly catecholamines and opioids (Gallagher & Kapp, 1978; Messing et al., 1979; Stein, Belluzzi, & Wise, 1975; Zornetzer, Abraham, & Appleton, 1978). A growing literature has also described multiple neurochemical, (Finch, 1978; Ponzio, Brunello, & Algeri, 1978; Simpkins, Mueller, Huang, & Meites, 1977), neuroanatomical, (Landfield, Rose, Sandles, Wohlstadter, & Lynch, 1977; Rogers, Silver, Shoemaker, & Bloom, 1980) and behavioral (Bartus, 1979; Bartus, Dean, & Fleming, 1979; Barnes, 1979; Gold & McGaugh, 1975; Kubanis, Gobbel, & Zornetzer, 1981; Zornetzer, Thompson, & Rogers, 1982) changes in aged animals. It is therefore possible that age-related memory deficits may result from concurrent changes in several neurotransmitter systems. This point can be made even more strongly in the case of AD, in which there is widespread degeneration and cell loss seen in postmortem tissue (c.f., Brody, 1970, 1976). Rather than review the entire morphologic and neurotransmitter literature on age-related brain changes, let us focus upon available data for noncholinergic neuronal systems. For purposes of both example and personal interest, the paragraphs below will focus on the noradrenergic nucleus locus coeruleus (LC).

Vijayashankar and Brody (1979) were the first to report significant cell loss of LC neurons in presumably normal senescent human brain. These data were extended by Bondareff, Mountjoy, and Roth (1982), who reported that in patients with AD, cell loss in LC was significantly greater than occurred with normal aging. Further, two subclasses of Alzheimer's patients could be identified: a group having severe cognitive impairment and 80% cell loss in LC, and a less impaired group with correspondingly less LC cell loss. Recently, Mann, Yates, and Marcynuik (1984) directly compared cell loss and nucleus volume changes in both nucleus basalis and the LC from brains of AD patients. Their findings indicated that in AD individuals under 80 years, the extent of cellular loss and damage in the LC exceeded that in nucleus basalis. Interestingly, there is conflicting evidence regarding age-related loss of neurons in nucleus basalis of normal senescent humans. Chui, Bondareff, Zarow, and Slager (1984) report no loss of basalis neurons over the age range of 20 to 90 years. Similar results have been reported by Whitehouse et al. (1983). At variance with these findings are those of McGeer, P.L., McGeer, E.G., Suzuki, Dolman, and Nagai (1984), who do report significant neuronal loss in nucleus basalis over the range from 38 weeks to 95 years. Collectively, these morphological data are of interest for a number of reasons. First, the LC system, like the basal forebrain cholinergic system, constitutes a neurotransmitter dominant (norepinephrine [NE] in the case of the LC and acetylcholine [ACh] in the case of the basalis) brain region showing significant cell loss with *both* normal aging and AD. Second, and importantly, data suggest the extent of cell loss in LC appears directly correlated with the degree of impaired cognitive function. This second point is significant in that it parallels the observations and speculations that the four major pathognomonic findings in AD (neurofibrillary tangles, senile plaques, granulovascular degeneration, and Hirano bodies) are similarly related in prevalence to the severity of impaired cognitive function. Accordingly, all these changes are also found in normal-aged brains but they are quantitatively more frequent in brains from AD patients (Appel, 1981). These data from the noradrenergic LC suggest that age-related cognitive decline may be quantitatively related to transmitter-specific dysfunction(s).

Other, more functional data support these morphological findings regarding catecholamine-specific cell loss in normal aging and AD. Several investigations have reported reduced activity of catecholamine systems in aged rat brain (Algeri, 1978; Finch, 1973, 1976).

Further, a reduced activity with age of tyrosine hydroxylase, the rate limiting enzyme in the synthesis of catecholamines, has been reported for humans (Cote & Kremzner, 1974; McGeer, E.G., & McGeer, P.L., 1973) and rodents (Algeri, 1978). Postmortem studies in humans have reported reduced levels of dopamine (DA) and NE related to age (Adolfsson, Gottfries, Roos, & Winblad, 1979; Carlsson & Winblad, 1976).

Clearly, from this brief discussion of the data describing age-related changes in catecholamine systems, there is good reason to consider the possibility that these systems, particularly the noradrenergic nucleus LC, may be at least as important as the changes occurring in basal forebrain in cholinergic systems, which have received greater attention. Further, there is considerable additional support for the idea that the LC system plays an essential modulatory role in metabolic (Abraham, Delanoy, Dunn, & Zornetzer, 1979), sensorimotor (Aston-Jones & Bloom, 1981), attentional (Mason, 1981), and higher order (memory) functions (Zornetzer et al., 1978) in normal-aged subjects. These data, coupled with both published and new data (see below) from my own laboratory, strongly reinforce the hypothesis that functional decline of the noradrenergic LC system may be directly implicated in normal age-related cognitive decline and possibly in the more precipitous functional decline observed in AD.

Recent anatomical studies have suggested that there are several brain loci where functional interactions could occur between the locus coeruleus, nucleus basalis, and other neurotransmitter-defined systems of interest (e.g., the DA cells of the substantia nigra-ventral tegmental area and the widespread opiate-containing systems). Of particular interest here are the interactions between noradrenergic neurons of the LC and cholinergic neurons of the nucleus basalis. Although it is known that LC axons traverse the basal forebrain regions that contain nucleus basalis neurons (Fallon & Moore, 1978; Fallon, Koziell, & Moore, 1978), there has not been convincing evidence that LC innervates these neurons. Based on the density of the LC fibers in these regions, such a projection would be sparse as best. Likewise, a projection from nucleus basalis neurons to the LC has not been demonstrated. The presence of moderately dense acetyl-choline esterase (AChE)-positive neuropil in and around the LC could be the dendrites of the AChE-positive cells (cholinoceptive but not cholinergic) or another cholinergic input. A more likely site of noradrenergic-cholinergic interaction is in the cerebral cortex where dense noradrenergic (Morrison, Grzanna, Molliver, & Coyle, 1978) and cholinergic (Jacobowitz & Palkovitz, 1974) innervation overlap, especially in layers I and II. A more isolated but nonetheless dense catecholamine innervation on layer II of supragenual cortex arises in the central tegmental area (Lindvall, Bjorkland, Moore, & Stenevi, 1974; Moore & Bloom, 1978). Connections between the two major catecholamine cell groups could provide a second level of interaction. These include the innervation of the LC by the ventral tegmental area and a possible reciprocal innervation of the ventral tegmental area by the LC (Jones & Moore, 1977).

Another important consideration is the role of opiate interactions with the catecholamine and cholinergic systems. In this regard, there is some evidence for anatomical projections of opiate-containing neurons to cholinergic neurons of the basal forebrain (Fallon, personal communication) and LC (Herkenham & Pert, 1982). Reciprocal projections of the cell groups to opiate-containing cells are unknown but based on the widespread localization of opiate cell bodies and terminals, such connections are likely to exist and could be involved in the widespread neuronal dysfunction accompanying AD.

As an interim summary, it can be concluded that a number of projections could account for interactions among cholinergic, catecholaminergic, and opiate systems as they relate to AD. The regions of greatest potential for interaction of cholinergic and catecholaminergic systems are the superficial layers of the cerebral cortex.

LOCUS COERULEUS AND MEMORY

In 1976, studies were begun in young adult rodents implicating an important role of the nucleus LC in memory processes (Zornetzer & Gold, 1976; Zornetzer et al., 1978). These studies were amplified and further supported by others (see Gold & Zornetzer, 1983; Zornetzer, 1978, for reviews). One particularly interesting study (Stein et al., 1975) reported that pharmacological inhibition of brain NE synthesis resulted in impaired memory. Administration of NE directly into forebrain ventricular systems, thereby bypassing synthesis inhibition, restored normal memory function.

As discussed above, aged organisms, ranging from man to mice, develop memory dysfunction. Recently, my laboratory has begun studying these age-related memory impairments in rats and mice (Kubanis et al., 1981; Kubanis, Zornetzer, & Freund, 1982; Zornetzer et al., 1982). One conclusion from the data obtained to date is that, generally, aged rodents do not have severe acquisition or learning deficits. Rather, they have an accelerated loss of recently acquired information (i.e., they forget faster then do young rodents). This accelerated loss of recently acquired information appears quite general to a variety of learning-memory situations (i.e., short-term, intermediate-term, and long-term memory) (Zornetzer et al., 1982).

Considerable interest and effort have been (and are being) devoted to developing effective interventive, usually pharmacologic, strategies to ameliorate these age-related memorial and cognitive deficits (Etienne et al., 1978; Hier & Caplan, 1980; Hughes, Williams, & Currier, 1976; Loew, 1980; Scott, 1979).

In general, two main thrusts are being used. The first involves administration of agents that increase the efficacy of the cholinergic system in the brain. Such treatments include precursor loading with lecithin and/or choline (Boyd, Graham-White, Blackwood, Glen, & McQueen, 1977; Mohs, Davis, Tinklenberg, & Hollister, 1980) or administration of cholinesterase inhibitors (Drachman & Sahakian, 1980). The second thrust has led to the development of a new class of pharmacologic agents, the nootropics, believed to improve cognitive function in the aged. Accordingly, agents such as piracetam, Hydergine®, vincamine, centrophenoxine, and soon, which have varied actions on brain blood flow and/or metabolism (see Ban, 1978), are being tested. To date, their efficacy in improving cognitive function in the edlerly is not convincing.

A careful evaluation of each of these research thrusts leads to two observations: (1) There has been an excessively narrow and exclusive focus on the cholinergic system and memory impairment, and (2) The data reported thus far are collectively neither convincing nor impressive (with occasional exception) (c.f., Bartus & Dean, 1980). Perhaps the latter observation is derived from the former observation!

Manipulation of central catecholamines in aging brain represents an additional strategy to supplement the two research strategies described briefly above. The NE-containing LC is certainly another candidate transmitter-dominant system likely to be involved in cognitive function or its regulation. The fact that LC neurons and their terminal field receptors show widespread age-related changes make LC an ideal system to study. Accordingly, the hypothesis tested in the study reported below was, "Can experimental manipulation of the LC alter normally expected age-related memory decline?" The results provide exciting new data suggesting that age-related memory failure in senescent rodents can be significantly retarded as a result of direct LC modulation. A brief description of these experiments follows.

The initial phase of the experiment simply documented, using the male C57BL/6J mouse, that aged (24 months) animals remember more poorly than young (5 months) controls. To demonstrate this, we used a single-trial step-down inhibitory avoidance apparatus (see Kubanis et al., 1981, for details). The results are shown in Figure 1.

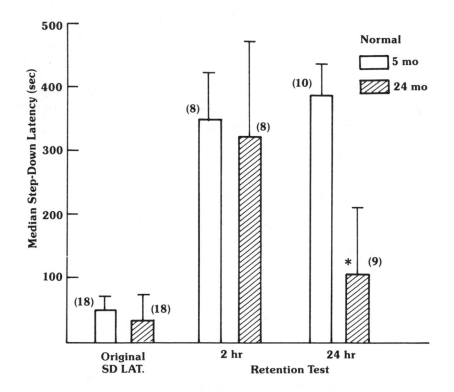

Figure 1. Median step-down latency (sec) of aged and young C57BL/6J male mice. The figure indicates that original step-down latencies in naive mice did not differ between young and aged groups. When tested two hours after training, both young and aged mice had a long step-down latency suggesting good memory of the inhibitory avoidance response. Independent groups of mice tested 24 hours after training indicated that aged, but not young, mice now had a significant (p<.02) performance deficit suggesting memory loss.

The second phase of the experiment was designed to test directly the hypothesis stated above. Groups of mice, either 5 months or 18 months at the start of the experiment, were surgically prepared, using stereotaxic procedures, with chronic indwelling electrodes targeted bilaterally for the LC. This is a well-established procedure in my laboratory (c.f., Prado de Carvalho & Zornetzer, 1981).

Following a 10-day postsurgical recovery period, mice began an electrical stimulation regimen consisting of regular stimulation of the LC at 48-hour intervals for 6 months. Thus, at the termination of this prolonged intermittent electric stimulation period, mice were either 11 months or 24 months old. Stimulation parameters for independent groups of mice were either 100 μA or 50 μA current delivered at 60 Hz using 0.1ms biphasic pulses. Each stimulation session lasted 10 minutes, with actual stimulation administered intermittently during this period.

The third phase of the experiment began 1 week after the last electrical stimulation was administered. All mice were trained in the step-down inhibitory avoidance task. Mice were then tested 24 hours later for retention of the shock avoidance response. Following the behavioral experiments all mice were sacrificed and the electrode tip location was histologically verified. As the results in Figure 2 indicate, 24-month old sham-stimulated mice typically forget (i.e., have a shorter step-down latency) the inhibitory avoidance response when tested 24 hours after learning. The data from the 24-month old mice having received chronic and repeated LC electrical stimulation are shown in Figure 2.

As these data indicate, regular repeated prior electrical stimulation of the LC resulted in improved performance compared to aged controls when tested 24 hours after learning. In fact, performance of the LC-stimulated (50 μA) aged mice was indistinguishable from that of young controls.

Surgical intervention and electrode implantation of the brain represent a rather extreme procedure for ameliorating age-related memory decline. In an attempt to circumvent this problem, a pharmacological approach seemed more desirable. Accordingly, our first pharmacological approach to LC activation involved the use of piperoxan, an α_2-noradrenergic receptor blocking agent shown to have an excitatory action upon LC neurons (Cedarbaum & Aghajanian, 1976) when administered systemically. Piperoxan is believed to activate LC neurons by directly blocking auto- and collateral inhibition in the LC. These intranuclear inhibitory projections utilize the α_2-receptor. Thus, α_2-blockade results in release from inhibition and greater LC cell firing (Cedarbaum & Aghajanian, 1976). Presumably, elevated LC cell firing would result in correspondingly greater synaptic release of NE at the many terminal fields of the LC in the forebrain and other brain regions.

The experimental protocol was designed to parallel the electrical stimulation experiment just described. Mice, 5 months and 18 months of age at the start of the experiment, were divided into independent groups. Animals received either 0.5 or 1.5 mg/kg piperoxan or saline intraperitoneally (IP). Injections were given once every 48 hours for 6 months. Injection sites were systematically varied to avoid producing peritoneal irritation or infection.

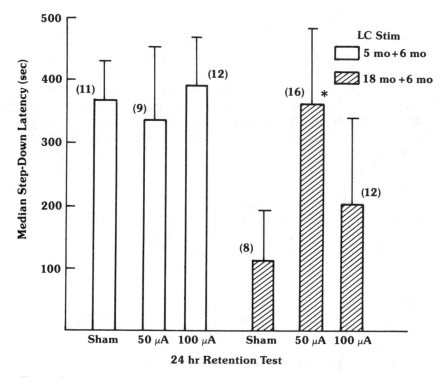

Figure 2. The effects of prior 6-month intermittent electrical stimulation of the LC upon memory of the inhibitory avoidance response. All stimulation was ended one week prior to training. The data indicate that stimulation at 50 μA current resulted in significant facilitation in performance in aged mice. Young mice, curiously, were not affected by the treatment. The higher current level (150 μA) did not result in significant facilitation of performance.

At the end of the 6-month drug administration period, all mice had a one-week drug-free period prior to behavioral training and memory testing. At the end of this week, mice were trained and tested on the step-down inhibitory avoidance task, as described previously.

The results of this experiment are shown in Figure 3. Twenty-four-month-old mice who had received repeated administration of piperoxan showed no performance deficit compared to young controls. Aged saline control mice performed as expected (i.e., these mice had a significant age-related performance deficit when tested 24 hours after training). It should be noted that prior long-term piperoxan treatment did not appear to alter initial step-down latencies in the mice. This observation would argue against the possibility that the piperoxan effect was due merely to altered activity or anxiety

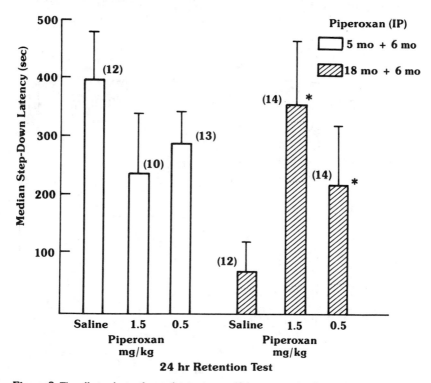

Figure 3. The effects of prior 6-month injection, at 48-hour intervals, of piperoxan on memory of the inhibitory avoidance response. Drug administration was ended 1 week prior to training. The data indicate that both doses of piperoxan (0.5 and 1.5 mg/kg, IP) resulted in significant improvement of aged, but not young, mice.

levels. These data are interpreted to suggest that piperoxan, a pharmacological agent capable of increasing LC cell activity, is also capable of significantly reducing age-related memory impairment.

A final experiment in this series evaluated forgetting in a normal young control population compared to normal aged and experimentally-treated aged mice from the above described experiments. The rationale for this experiment was to evaluate the dynamics of forgetting in young and aged groups to determine whether the experimentally treated aged mice who demonstrated "youthful" 24-hour retention also demonstrated "youthful" memory decay over longer periods. Such forgetting would suggest that the memory storage processes in the LC-stimulated and/or piperoxan-injected aged animals were similar to those processes normally occurring in young animals. Dissimilar forgetting curves between treated aged mice and young controls might suggest that the "youthful" 24-hour retention

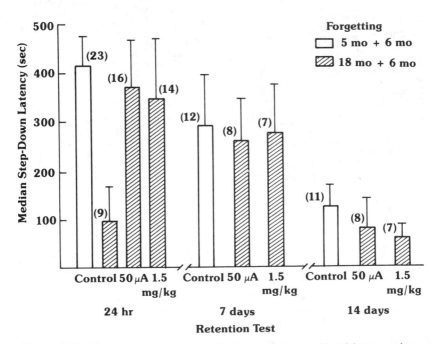

Figure 4. The effects of prior treatment in aged mice upon forgetting of the inhibitory avoidance step-down response over a 14-day period. The data indicate that both direct electrical stimulation of the LC (50 μA) and IP piperoxan administration (1.5 mg/kg) resulted in forgetting in aged mice indistinguishable from that of young mice.

in aged mice was not an accurate predictor of memory trace strength in the aged mice. In this experiment mice were tested for retention of step-down inhibitory avoidance 7 days and again at 14 days after original 24-hour testing. In this design all mice were tested on three separate occasions. Ideally, independent groups of animals would be used in such a paradigm to avoid potential confounding problems associated with different rates of extinction, and soon, which might occur among different groups of subjects. Due to limited numbers of aged mice, this was not possible in the present experiment.

The results of this experiment are shown in Figure 4. Normal aged control mice show rapid forgetting of the inhibitory avoidance response, with significant loss of performance at 24 hours and essentially naive behavior by 7 days. Normal young controls evidence significant retention performance at 24 hours, 7 days, and 14 days. As Figure 4 indicates, there is a decline in retention performance throughout this 14-day posttraining period. Both groups of previously treated (either 50 μA electrical stimulation delivered to the LC or IP injections of 1.5 mg/kg piperoxan) aged mice evidenced forgetting that was not statistically different. Interventive strategies administered during a period of life preceding senescence can serve to protect memory from normally occurring age-related decline.

If the LC plays an important role in sustaining youthful memory, then aged animals with good memory, might be expected to show differences in the LC. Experiments were performed in collaboration with Drs. Frances Leslie and Sandra Laughlin at University of California, Irvine, to investigate this. For this study, aged CFW mice (24 to 26 months) were used. Mice were first trained and tested for 24-hour retention in a step-through inhibitory avoidance apparatus. Following testing, mice were coded and sacrificed. Complete serial sections through the LC were obtained for each animal. Sections were thionine-stained. Two independent raters counted each section using as an identification criterion the presence of a nucleolus within the soma of LC neurons. Counts were compared and averaged between the two observers. Interobserver variability ($<5\%$) was not statistically significant. After all tissue was analyzed, the code was broken and the data analyzed according to behavioral performance. The results are shown in Figure 5. As the data show, a significant correlation was found between good retention performance 24 hours after training and the total LC cell count. Those mice with poor retention performance generally had fewer cells in LC than those mice with good retention performance. Studies are in progress to enlarge this data base and further explore these exciting results.

As a summary statement for this experiment, the data do support the hypothesis that loss of noradrenergic function emanating from the LC contributes to age-related memory impairment.

CONCLUSIONS

The implications taken from these new findings are very important. First, the data suggest that age-related memory loss need not be inevitable. Appropriate intervention strategies can at least delay their onset. The extent to which this delay can be maintained relative to life span is not understood at present. Many more careful experiments need to be conducted. Second, activation of LC electrical

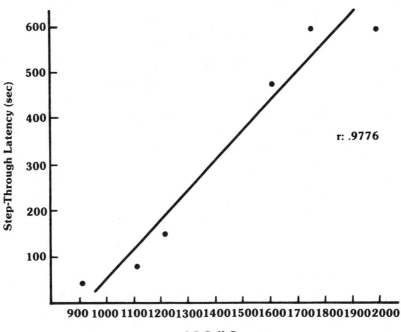

Figure 5. The relationship between LC cell number and 24-hour retention performance in aged CFW mice. The data indicate a significant relationship between LC cell number and retention performance.

activity appears to be an important condition leading to the persistence of youthful memory function into senescence. The result of both the electrical stimulation and the piperoxan treatments would suggest the LC is a common target for the site of action of the two treatments. The question of what is necessary versus sufficient LC activation, *vis a vis* memory function, is not presently understood. The 6-month protocol used in the two experiments described above was chosen based on the assumption that if LC cell function was normally diminished during aging, the point of onset for such diminished function would likely be during middle age, which for the C57BL/6 mouse is about 18 months (Finch, 1978). Accordingly, long-term artificial activation of LC was provided in an attempt to sustain and/or mimic greater LC functional output.

At this juncture it is important to determine (1) the mechanism through which LC activation serves to sustain youthful memory function in aged rodents, and (2) the optimal parameters for obtaining improved memory function. Presumably the effect is in some way related to cellular changes occurring, or perhaps not occurring, at distant terminal projection fields receiving LC synaptic endings. One very interesting possibility is that NE-containing LC terminals and/or postsynaptic receptors modulate basal forebrain cholinergic activity directly. Alternatively, LC terminals may interact at common cortical postsynaptic target sites with cholinergic terminals. In either case, loss of normal LC function with aging might result in diminished cholinergic efficacy. This testable hypothesis awaits further study.

RECOMMENDATIONS

Certain caveats must preface any specific recommendations for new directions in pharmacological interventive (or preventive) strategies for senile dementia(s). The first of these caveats is that an extension in logic or fact from normal aged rodents to humans with significant neuropathology is risky at best and foolish at worse. Second, the assumption used throughout this paper that LC is neurotransmitter specific for NE is clearly an oversimplification used for heuristic purposes. As with most, if not all, complex mammalian brain regions, neurons within those regions do not represent pure and homogeneous cellular factories manufacturing one and only one neurotransmitter. There is widespread agreement today that most central nervous system neurons co-localize multiple neurotransmitters or putative neurotransmitters. Accordingly, it is not clear that modification of neural activity in the LC, for example using either electrical or pharmacologic tools, results in exclusively NE-associated postsynaptic changes. It is possible, if not probable, that other co-localized neuroactive substances within LC neurons are also altered by the treatment. Quite possibly it is one of these neuroactive substances, rather than NE, that is associated with the preservation of youthful memory in senescent animals.

The recommendations emerging from the data reported here are: (1) Future pharmacological research seeking to ameliorate age-related (normal or pathological) memory dysfunction should place greater emphasis on the nucleus LC as a candidate target neural substrate; (2) pharmacological interventive strategies should consider a preventive approach with intervention begun *prior* to the onset of significant age-related neural and behavioral dysfunction. It may be too late to intervene meaningfully after clinically detectable symptomology is manifested; (3) pharmacological agents highly specific to the central α_2-noradrenergic system should be more actively explored with regard to possible nootropic properties; (4) greater attention to multiple neurotransmitter interactions must be vigorously explored. The notion that a single neurotransmitter system is either responsible for causing or capable of reversing extensive and varied manifestations of age-related neuropathologies is simply unrealistic. Such a notion reflects the ignorance of early day phrenologists. An enlightened approach, albeit considerably more complex, must incorporate multiple system strategies.

REFERENCES

Abraham, W.C., Delanoy, R.L., Dunn, A.J., & Zornetzer, S.F. (1979). Locus coeruleus stimulation decreases deoxyglucose uptake in mouse cerebral cortex. *Brain Research, 172,* 387-392.

Adolfsson, R., Gottfries, C.G., Roos, B.E., & Winblad, B. (1979). Post mortem distribution of dopamine and homovanillic acid in human brain, variations related to age and a review of the literature. *Journal of Neurological Transmission, 45,* 81-105.

Algeri, S., Bonati, M., Brunello, N., & Ponzio, F. (1978). Biochemical changes in central catecholaminergic neurons of the senescent rat. In P. Deniker, C. Radouco-Thomas, A. Villeneuve, D. Baronet-

LaCroix, & F. Garcin (Eds.), *Neuro-Psychopharmacology. Proceedings of the Tenth Congress of the Collequim International Neuro-Psychopharmacologicum, Quebec, July 4-9, 1976: Vol II. Workshop 6. Models in geriatric neuro-psychopharmacology* (pp. 1647-1654). Oxford: Pergamon Press.

Appel, S.H. (1981). Alzheimer's disease. In S.J. Enna, T. Samorajski, & B. Beer (Eds.), *Brain neurotransmitters and receptors in aging and age-related disorders, 17* (pp. 183-189). New York: Raven Press.

Aston-Jones, G., & Bloom, F.E. (1981). Norepinephrine-containing locus coeruleus neurons in behaving rats exhibit pronounced responses to non-noxious environmental stimuli. *Journal of Neuroscience, 1,* 887-900.

Ban, T.A. (1978). Vasodilators, stimulants and anobolic agents in the treatment of geropsychiatric patients. In M.A. Lipton, A. DiMascio, & K.F. Killam (Eds.), *Psychopharmacology: A generation of progress* (pp. 1525-1533). New York: Raven Press.

Barnes, C.A. (1979). Memory deficits associated with senescence: A neurophysiological and behavioral study in the rat. *Journal of Comparative and Physiological Psychology, 93,* 74-101.

Bartus, R.T. (1979). Physostigmine and recent memory: Effects in young and aged non-human primates. *Science, 206,* 1087-1089.

Bartus, R.T., & Dean, R.L. (1980). Facilitation of aged primate memory via pharmacological manipulation of central cholinergic activity. *Neurobiology of Aging, 1,* 145-152.

Bartus, R.T., Dean, R.L., Beer, B., & Lippa, A.S. (1982). The cholinergic hypothesis of geriatric memory dysfunction. *Science, 217,* 408-417.

Bartus, R.T., Dean, R.L., & Fleming, D.L. (1979). Aging in the rhesus monkey: Effects on visual discrimination learning and reversal learning. *Journal of Gerontology, 34,* 209-219.

Bondareff, W., Mountjoy, C.Q., & Roth, M. (1982). Loss of neurons of origin of the adrenergic projection to cerebral cortex (nucleus locus coeruleus) in senile dementia. *Neurology, 32,* 164-168.

Bowen, D.M., Smith, C.B., White, P., Goodhart, M.J., Spillane, J.A., Flack, R.H., & Davison, A.N. (1977). Chemical pathology of the organic dementias. *Brain, 100,* 397-426.

Boyd, W.D., Graham-White, J., Blackwood, G., Glen, I., & McQueen, J. (1977). Clinical effects of choline in Alzheimer senile dementia [Letter to the editor]. *Lancet, 2,* 711.

Brody, H. (1970). Structural changes in the aging nervous system. In H.T. Blumenthal (Ed.), *Interdisciplinary topics in gerontology* (Vol. 7, pp. 9-21). New York: S. Karger.

Brody, H. (1976). An examination of cerebral cortex and brain stem aging. In R.D. Terry & S. Gershon (Eds.), *Neurobiology of aging* (pp. 177-182). New York: Raven Press.

Carlsson, A., & Winblad, B. (1976). Influence of age and time interval between death and autopsy on dopamine and 3-methoxytyramine levels in human basal ganglia. *Journal of Neural Transmission, 38,* 271-276.

Cedarbaum, J.M., & Aghajanian, G.K. (1976). Noradrenergic neurons of the locus coeruleus: Inhibitation by epinephrine and activation by the alpha-antagonist piperoxan. *Brain Research, 112,* 413-419.

Chui, H.C., Bondareff, W., Zarrow, C., & Slager, U. (1984). Stability of neuronal number in the human nucleus basalis of Meynert with age. *Neurobiology of Aging, 5,* 83-88.

Cote, L.J., & Kremzner, L.T. (1974). Changes in neurotransmitter systems with increasing age in human brain. In *Transactions of the American Society for Neurochemistry.* 5th Annual Meeting, (pg. 83). New Orleans, LA: Society for Neurochemistry.

Davies, P., & Maloney, A. (1976). Selective loss of central cholinergic neurons in Alzheimer's disease [Letter to the editor]. *Lancet, 11,* 1403.

Dean, R.L., Scozzafava, J., Goas, J.A., Regan, B., Beer, B., & Bartus, R.T. (1981). Age-related differences in behavior across the life-span of the C57BL/6J mouse. *Experimental Aging Research, 7,* 427-451.

Drachman, D.A. (1977). Memory and cognitive function in man: Does the cholinergic system have a specific role? *Neurology, 27,* 783-790.

Drachman, D.A., & Leavitt, J. (1974). Human memory and the cholinergic system: A relationship to aging? *Archives of Neurology, 30,* 113-121.

Drachman, D.A., & Sahakian, B.J. (1980). Memory and cognitive function in the elderly. A preliminary trial of physostigmine. *Archives of Neurology, 37,* 674-675.

Etienne, P., Gauthier, S., Johnson, G., Collier, B., Mendis, T., Dastorr,

D., Cole, M., & Muller, H.F. (1978). Clinical effects of choline in Alzheimer's disease [Letter to the editor]. *Lancet, 1,* 508-509.

Fallon, J.H., Kozrell, D.A., & Moore, R.Y. (1978). Catecholamine innervation of the basal forebrain: II. Amygdala, suprarhinal cortex and entorhinal cortex. *Journal of Comparative Neurology, 180,* 509-532.

Fallon, J.H., & Moore, R.Y. (1978). Catecholamine innervation of the basal forebrain: II. Olfactory tubercle, and piriform cortex. *Journal of Comparative Neurology, 180,* 533-544.

Ferris, S.H., Sathananthan, G., Reisberg, B., & Gershon, S. (1979). Long-term choline treatment of memory-impaired elderly patients. *Science, 205,* 1039-1040.

Finch, C.E. (1973). Catecholamine metabolism in the brains of aging male mice. *Brain Research, 52,* 267-276.

Finch, C.E. (1976). The regulation of physiological changes during mammalian aging. *The Quarterly Review of Biology, 51,* 49-83.

Finch, C.E. (1978). Age-related changes in brain catecholamines: A synopsis of findings in C57BL/6J mice and other rodent models. In C.E. Finch, D.E. Potter, & A.D. Kenny (Eds.), *Advances in experimental medicine and biology: Vol. 113. Parkinson's disease II* (pp. 15-39). New York: Plenum Press.

Gallagher, M., & Kapp, B.S. (1978). Manipulation of opiate activity in the amygdala alters memory processes. *Life Sciences, 23,* 1973-1978.

Gilbert, J.G. (1941). Memory loss in senescence. *Journal of Abnormal and Social Psychology, 36,* 73-86.

Gold, P.E., & McGaugh, J.L. (1975). Changes in learning and memory during aging. In I.M. Ordy & K.R. Brizzee (Eds.), *Neurobiology of aging* (pp. 145-158). New York: Plenum Press.

Gold, P.E., & Zornetzer, S.F. (1983). The mnemon and its juices: Neuromodulation of memory process. *Behavioral and Neural Biology, 38,* 151-189.

Herkenham, M., & Pert, C.G. (1982). Light microscopic localization of brain opiate receptors: A general autoradiographic method which preserves tissue quality. *Journal of Neuroscience, 2,* 1129-1149.

Hier, D.B., & Caplan, L.R. (1980). Drugs for senile dementia. *Drugs, 20,* 74-80.

Hughes, J.R., Williams, J.G., & Currier, R.D. (1976). An ergot alkaloid preparation (Hydergine) in the treatment of dementia: Critical review of the clinical literature. *Journal of the American Geriatric Society, 24,* 490-497.

Jacobowitz, D.M., & Palkovitz, M. (1974). Topographic atlas of catecholamine and acetylcholinesterase-containing neurons in the rat brain: I. Forebrain (telencephalon, diencephalon). *Journal of Comparative Neurology, 157,* 13-28.

Jensen, R.A., Messing, R.B., Martinez, J.L., Jr., Vasquez, B.J., Spiehler, V.R., & McGaugh, J.L. (1981). Changes in brain peptide systems and altered learning and memory processes in aged animals. In J.L. Martinez, Jr., R.A. Jensen, R.B. Messing, H. Rigter, & J.L. McGaugh (Eds.), *Endogenous peptides and learning and memory processes* (pp. 463-477). New York: Academic Press.

Jones, B.E., & Moore, R.Y. (1977). Ascending projections of the locus coeruleus in the rat: II. Autoradiographic study. *Brain Research, 127,* 23-53.

Kubanis, P., Gobbel, G., & Zornetzer, S.F. (1981). Age-related memory deficits in Swiss mice. *Behavioral and Neural Biology, 32,* 241-247.

Kubanis, P., & Zornetzer, S.F. (1981). Age-related behavioral and neurobiological changes: A review with an emphasis on memory. *Behavioral and Neural Biology, 31,* 115-172.

Kubanis, P., Zornetzer, S.F., & Freund, G. (1982). Memory and postsynaptic cholinergic receptors in aging mice. *Pharmacology, Biochemistry and Behavior, 17,* 313-322.

Landfield, P.W., Rose, G., Sandles, L., Wohlstadter, T., & Lynch, G. (1977). Patterns of astroglial hypertrophy and neuronal degeneration in the hippocampus of aged, memory-deficient rats. *Journal of Gerontology, 32,* 3-12.

Lindvall, O., Bjorkland, A., Moore, R.Y., & Stenevi, J. (1974). Mesencephalic dopamine neurons projecting to neocortex. *Brain Research, 81,* 325-331.

Loew, D.M. (1980). Pharmacologic approaches to the treatment of senile dementia. In L. Amaducci, A.N. Davison, & P. Antuono (Eds.), *Aging of the brain and dementia* (Vol. 13, pp. 287-294). New York: Raven Press.

Mann, D.M., Yates, P.O., & Marcynvik, B. (1984). A comparison of changes in the nucleus basalis and locus coeruleus in Alzheimer's disease. *Journal of Neurology, Neurosurgery, and Psychiatry, 47,* 201-203.

Mason, S.T. (1981). Noradrenaline in the brain: Progress in theories of behavioral function. *Progress in Neurobiology, 16,* 263-303.

McGeer, E.G., & McGeer, P.L. (1973). Some characteristics of brain tyrosine hydroxylase. In A.J. Mandell (Ed.), *New concepts in neurotransmitter regulation* (pp. 53-68). New York: Plenum Press.

McGeer, P.L., McGeer, E.G., Suzuki, J., Dolman, C.E., & Nagai, T. (1984). Aging, Alzheimer's disease and the cholinergic system of the basal forebrain. *Neurology, 34,* 741-745.

Messing, R.B., Jensen, R.A., Martinez, J.L., Jr., Spiehler, V.R., Vasquez, B.J., Soumireu-Mourat, B., Liang, K.C., & McGaugh, J.L. (1979). Naloxone enhancement of memory. *Behavioral and Neural Biology, 27,* 266-275.

Mohs, R.C., Davis, K.L., & Tinklenberg, J.R., (1980). Choline chloride effects on memory in the elderly. *Neurobiology of Aging, 1,* 21-25.

Mohs, R.C., Davis, K.L., Tinklenberg, J.R., Hollister, L., Yesavage, J.A., & Kopell, B.S. (1979). Choline chloride treatment of memory deficits in the elderly. *American Journal of Psychiatry, 136,* 1275-1277.

Moore, R.Y., & Bloom, F.E. (1978). Central catecholamine neurone systems: Anatomy and physiology of the dopamine systems. *Annual Review of Neuroscience, 1,* 129-169.

Morrison, J., Grzanna, R., Molliver, M., & Coyle, J. (1978). The distribution and orientation of noradrenergic fibers in neocortex of the rat: An immunofluorescence study. *Journal of Comparative Neurology, 181,* 17-40.

Perry, E.K., Perry, R.H., Blessed, G., & Tomlinson, B. (1977). Necropsy evidence of central cholinergic deficits in senile dementia [Letter to the editor]. *Lancet, 1,* 189.

Ponzio, F., Brunello, N., & Algeri, S. (1978). Catecholamine synthesis in brain of aging rats. *Journal of Neurochemistry, 30,* 1617-1620.

Prado de Carvalho, L., & Zornetzer, S.F. (1981). The involvement of the locus coeruleus in memory. *Behavioral and Neural Biology, 31,* 173-186.

Price, D.L., Whitehouse, P.J., Struble, R.G., Clark, A.W., Coyle, J.T., Delong, M.R., & Hedrenn, J.C. (1982). Basal forebrain cholinergic systems in Alzheimer's disease and related dementias. *Neuroscience Comment, 1,* 84-92.

Rogers, J., Silver, M.A., Shoemaker, W.J., & Bloom, F.E. (1980). Senescent changes in a neurobiological model system: Cerebellar Purkinje cell electrophysiology and correlative anatomy. *Neurobiology of Aging, 1,* 3-11.

Ruch, F.L. (1934). The differentiative effects of age upon human learning. *Journal of Genetic Psychiatry, 11,* 261-286.

Scott, F.L. (1979). A review of some current drugs in the pharmacotherapy of organic brain syndrome. In A. Cherkin, C.E. Finch, N. Kharasch, T. Makinodon, F.L. Scott, & B.S. Strehler (Eds.), *Physiology and cell biology of aging* (pp. 164-183). New York: Raven Press.

Simpkins, J.W., Mueller, G.P., Huang, H.H., & Meites, J. (1977). Evidence for depressed catecholamine and enhanced serotonin metabolism in aging male rats: Possible relation to gonadotrophin secretion. *Endocrinology, 100,* 1672-1678.

Stein, L., Belluzzi, J.D., & Wise, C.D. (1975). Memory enhancement by central administrations of norepinephine. *Brain Research, 84,* 329-335.

Vijayashankar, N., & Brody, H. (1979). A quantitative study of the pigmental neurons in the nuclei locus coeruleus and subcoeruleus in man as related to aging. *Journal of Neuropathology and Experimental Neurology, 38,* 490-497.

Vroulis, G.A., & Smith, R.C. (1981). Cholinergic drugs and memory disorders in Alzheimer's type dementia. In S.J. Enna, T. Samorajski, & B. Beer (Eds.), *Brain neurotransmitter and receptors in aging and age-related disorders* (Vol. 17, pp. 143-161). New York: Raven Press.

Whitehouse, P.J., Parhad, I.M., Hedrenn, J.C., Clark, A.W., White, C.L., Struble, R.G., & Price, D.L. (1983). Integrity of the nucleus basalis in normal aging. *Neurology, 33*(Suppl. 2), 159.

Zornetzer, S.F. (1978). Neurotransmitter modulation and memory: A new neuropharmacological phrenology? In M.A. Lipton, A. Dimascio, & K.F. Killam (Eds.), *Psychopharmacology: A generation of progress* (pp. 637-649). New York: Raven Press.

Zornetzer, S.F., Abraham, W.C., & Appleton, R. (1978). Locus coeruleus and labile memory. *Pharmacology, Biochemistry and Behavior, 9,* 227-234.

Zornetzer, S.F., & Gold, M. (1976). The locus coeruleus: Its possible role in memory consolidation. *Physiology and Behavior, 16,* 331-336.

Zornetzer, S.F., Thompson, R., & Rogers, J. (1982). Rapid forgetting in aged rats. *Behavioral and Neural Biology, 36,* 49-60.

15

Serotonin, Learning, and Memory: Implications for the Treatment of Dementia

Harvey J. Altman, PhD, and Howard J. Normile, PhD

One of the primary behavioral manifestations of Alzheimer's disease (AD) is a progressive deterioration of memory. Much attention has, therefore, focused on elucidating those factors that may be responsible for this deterioration. In recent years, this research has been directed mainly at the cholinergic (AChergic) nervous system because (1) a number of significant changes appear to occur within the AChergic nervous system as a result of AD (Altman, Nordy, & Ögren, 1984); Bowen, Davison, Francis, Neary, & Palmer, 1984; Perry, E.K., & Perry, R.H., 1980; Rosser et al., 1982; Rylett, Ball, & Colhoun, 1983; Sims et al., 1980; Whitehouse, Price, Struble, Coyle, & DeLong, 1982), and (2) treatments that interfere with normal AChergic functioning disrupt learning and memory (Davis et al., 1978; Drachman & Leavitt, 1974; Sitaram, Weingartner, & Gillin, 1978), whereas treatments that augment this system's functioning appear to have the opposite effect (Sitaram et al., 1978). However, the AChergic nervous system is not the only neurotransmitter system of the brain to be affected by AD. It is also not the only neurotransmitter system suspected of playing a significant role in learning and memory. There is an accumulating body of evidence suggesting that significant changes occur in the functional and/or structural integrity of the serotonergic (5-HTergic) nervous system in AD (Benton et al., 1982; Bowen et al., 1983; Curcio & Kemper, in press; Gottfries et al., 1983; Mann, Yates, & Marcyniuk, 1984). In addition, there is a significant body of data suggesting that serotonin (5-HT) plays a role in the processes underlying learning and memory (Altman et al., 1984; Archer, Ögren, & Johensson, 1981; Ögren, 1982a,b).

For the past several years our laboratory has been examining the role of 5-HT in the processing of information by the brain. In general, we find that interference with this system's activity facilitates learning and memory in animals. The purpose of this chapter is to review the results of some of these experiments and to discuss their possible implications in the development of effective treatment strategies for AD.

THE EFFECT OF SEROTONERGIC REUPTAKE INHIBITION ON MEMORY

We initially became interested in the role of 5-HT in learning and memory following the somewhat surprising outcome of an experiment that examined the effects of pretest administration of two selective 5-HT reuptake blockers, alaproclate (ALAP) and zimeldine (ZIM), on memory retrieval in Swiss Webster mice (Altman et al., 1984). It has been shown by numerous investigators that stimulation of 5-HTergic neurotransmission results in a disruption of learning and memory (Archer et al., 1981; Essman, 1973; Fibiger, Lepiane, & Phillips, 1978; Joyce & Hurwitz, 1964; Ögren, 1982a); whereas, lesions of the 5-HTergic nervous system generally produce the opposite effect (Brady, 1970; Lorens, 1978; Lorens & Yunger, 1974; Schlessinger & Schreiber, 1968; Srebro & Lorens, 1975; Steranka & Barrett, 1974; Tenen, 1967). It was, therefore, expected that potentiation of 5-HTergic activity following inhibition of uptake should also interfere with the performance of animals in our study. However, this did not turn out to be the case.

Briefly, mice were trained to avoid the darker chamber of a standard two-chamber shuttle box by pairing entrance into the darker chamber with mild (0.13 mA) foot shock. Twenty-four hours later the animals were tested for retention of the original avoidance habit. Pretest administration of ALAP and ZIM resulted in a highly significant dose-dependent and time-dependent suppression of responding, as shown in Figures 1 and 2, that could not be explained in terms of nonspecific effects of the drugs on behavior in general (i.e., illness, reduced activity, or thirst). That is, a group of noncontingently trained animals, injected with the highest dose of each compound examined, did not exhibit a significant elevation in test latencies. Several attempts were then made to block the effects of the reuptake inhibitors. Pretreatment with quipazine, a putative 5-HTergic agonist, completely blocked the enhancement of memory induced by ALAP and ZIM. On the other hand, cyproheptadine, a highly selective and potent 5-HTergic receptor antagonist, appeared to potentiate the effects of

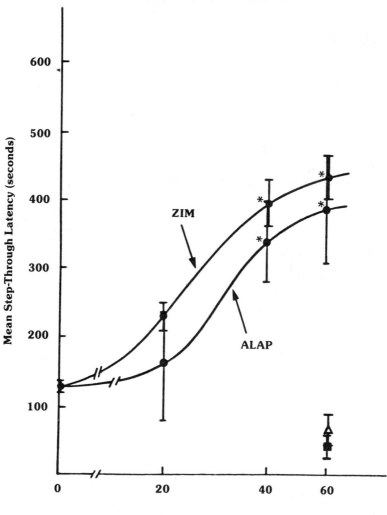

Dose Response: Pre-Test ALAP and ZIM

Figure 1. Mean latencies of individual groups of mice injected with one of several doses of ALAP or ZIM, 30 minutes prior to the retention test. Two groups of noncontingently shocked mice were administered the 60 mg/kg dose of either ALAP (△) or ZIM (■).
*p < 0.05 vs the zero dose (saline).

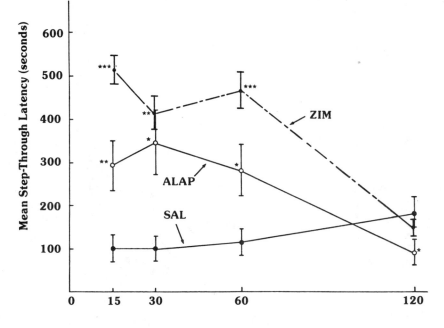

Figure 2. Mean latencies of individual groups of mice injected with either SAL, ALAP, or ZIM (40 mg/kg), at various times prior to the retention test.
*$p < 0.05$, **$p < 0.002$ vs SAL.

the two reuptake inhibitors. This effect failed, however, to reach statistical significance (essentially because of ceiling effects). These results suggest that inhibition of 5-HTergic reuptake may be an effective way of enhancing memory retrieval. In addition, the potentiation of the reuptake inhibitor's effects on memory by cyproheptadine suggests that the action of these two drugs may be similar. For example, it could be hypothesized that the increased amount of neurotransmitter within the synapse would not only be expected to stimulate post-synaptic receptors, but presynaptic receptors as well. Stimulation of presynaptic autoreceptors would be expected to reduce 5-HT release (Farnebo & Hamberger, 1974). Quipazine, which has also been shown to block autoreceptors (Martin & Sanders-Bush, 1982), might, therefore, be attenuating the effects of the 5-HT reuptake inhibitors by blocking autoreceptors. The increased latencies exhibited by the animals injected with ALAP and ZIM preceded by cyproheptadine may have resulted from the dual effect of reducing release and blocking postsynaptic receptors.

THE EFFECT OF SEROTONERGIC ANTAGONISTS ON MEMORY

The results of the previous study suggested that the effects following blockade of 5-HT reuptake and blockade of postsynaptic 5-HT receptors on the processes underlying memory retrieval may be similar. We, therefore, began to examine the effects of 5-HT receptor antagonists on memory (Altman & Normile, in press).

Briefly, thirsty male Swiss Webster mice were trained in a modification of the standard inhibitory avoidance paradigm (i.e., Lick-Suppression Task) to avoid drinking from a water tube by pairing tube contact with a weak shock (0.75 mA). Retention was measured as the duration of suppression of drinking 48 hours later under extinction conditions. In the first part of the study the effects of pretest administration of a number of 5-HTergic receptor antagonists (ketanserin, pirenperone, methysergide, metergoline and mianserin) on memory retrieval were assessed. As seen in Table 1, a dose-dependent increase in the latency to complete 5 seconds of drinking was demonstrated. This increase in response latencies could not be attributed to a generalized lack of motivation, illness, or sedation as noncontingently trained animals, injected with the highest dose of each compound examined, did not exhibit similarly elevated latencies.

To further assess the effects of acute 5-HTergic receptor blockade on memory, an additional group of mice was administered pirenperone immediately following training (Normile & Altman, 1985). Again, blockade of 5-HTergic receptors resulted in a dose-dependent increase in the latency to complete 5 seconds of drinking during the retention test (Figure 3).

The results of this study suggest for the first time that acute blockade of 5-HTergic receptors either prior to testing or immediately after training can enhance memory of a weakly learned avoidance habit.

TABLE 1

The Effects of Pretest Administration of Serotonergic Receptor Antagonists on Memory Retrieval

Drug Condition		Dose (mg/kg)	N	Median Latency	Interquartile Range Q_1 - Q_3
Saline		-	20	135.9	77.1 - 356.6
Pirenperone		0.42	11	82.0	55.5 - 623.9
		0.56	11	87.0	35.0 - 450.5
		0.75	14	495.7	149.2 - 1305.0[a]
		1.0	17	960.2	347.0 - 2000.0[c]
		1.8	12	759.6	101.9 - 2000.0[b]
		2.4	12	1066.3	737.6 - 2000.0[d]
	(NCS)*	2.4	13	27.1	19.5 - 64.3[e]
Ketanserin		1.8	12	73.4	45.5 - 254.7
		2.4	12	179.0	24.6 - 434.4
		4.2	17	115.7	34.7 - 1107.1
		5.6	16	486.6	169.9 - 2000.0[b]
		7.5	12	1604.6	472.4 - 2000.0[c]
		10.0	15	1602.7	198.8 - 2000.0[c]
	(NCS)*	10.0	10	51.0	35.8 - 68.7[e]
Methysergide		2.4	10	310.4	209.2 - 753.3
		4.2	10	584.4	74.5 - 2000.0
		5.6	11	876.3	178.2 - 2000.0[b]
		10.0	17	707.9	221.5 - 2000.0[c]
		18.0	7	1174.8	826.2 - 2000.0[d]
	(NCS)*	18.0	9	49.2	36.9 - 98.0[e]
Metergoline		0.42	12	171.2	130.0 - 281.9
		1.0	12	64.6	38.9 - 149.5
		2.4	12	79.9	30.8 - 411.0
		4.2	12	833.9	265.7 - 1327.9[b]
		5.6	11	955.9	343.4 - 2000.0[c]
		7.5	12	2000.0	703.5 - 2000.0[c]
	(NCS)*	7.5	8	62.3	42.9 - 380.8[e]
Mianserin		3.2	12	276.6	160.8 - 537.3
		5.6	16	481.6	330.8 - 1188.5
		7.5	12	614.1	90.0 - 1694.4
		10.0	11	739.4	200.4 - 2000.0[c]
		13.0	11	1215.6	445.2 - 2000.0[d]
	(NCS)*	13.0	8	36.6	30.9 - 71.2[e]

[a] $p < 0.05$; [b] $p < 0.02$; [c] $p < 0.002$; [d] $p < 0.001$ Compared to saline

[e] $p < 0.001$ Compared to the same dose contingently shocked.

*Noncontingently shocked animals.

THE EFFECTS OF REUPTAKE INHIBITION AND RECEPTOR BLOCKADE ON LONG-TERM FORGETTING.

The purpose of the next series of experiments was to determine whether receptor blockade and/or inhibition of uptake would affect how long a particular habit was retained or restore the memory once it had been forgotten (Altman, 1985).

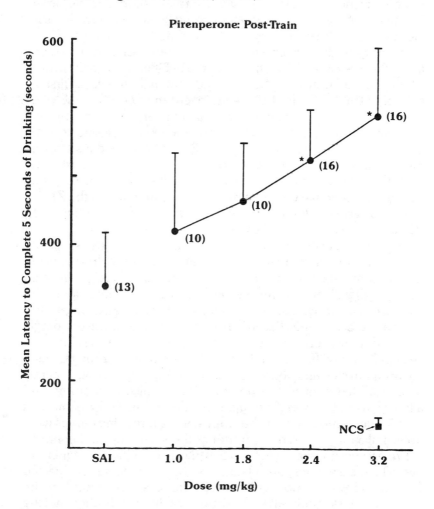

Pirenperone: Post-Train

Figure 3. Effects of immediate posttrain pirenperone injections (IP) on the latency to complete 5 seconds of drinking in a Lick-Suppression Task. NCS = Noncontingently shocked. *p < 0.05 vs SAL.

The behavioral task used for these experiments was the same one used previously to investigate the effects of the 5-HTergic antagonists on memory (i.e., Lick-Suppression Task). However, instead of using the lower shock level, a higher shock level was used (2.0 mA). The reason for this was that in the previous study we were interested in determining whether interference with 5-HTergic neurotransmission could enhance memory of a weakly learned avoidance habit. By using a low shock level, latencies were normally short, and the facilitative effects of the drugs on behavior could be adequately assessed. However, in the present experiment, we wished to examine the effects of the drugs on the performance of the animals over time. Therefore, the higher shock level was chosen so the habit (i.e., not to drink from a tube that had previously been paired with pain) would, at first, be strongly expressed and then decay over time.

Immediately following training, half of the animals were injected with either saline (SAL), ALAP (60 mg/kg), or pirenperone (PIREN) (1.0 mg/kg) and tested 7, 14, 21, 28, 42, or 56 days later by measuring each animal's latency to complete 5 seconds of drinking. The other half of the animals was trained as described above, injected with SAL immediately after training, and beginning with the 21-day retention test, randomly selected and administered either SAL, ALAP, or PIREN 30 minutes prior to the retention test.

Immediate posttraining injections of ALAP and PIREN resulted in a significant overall increase in the latencies of the drug-injected mice to complete 5 seconds of drinking compared to saline-injected controls. Significant differences were found also in the response of the mice to the drugs over time, indicating that as the training-to-test interval increased, the effects of drugs on behavior correspondingly declined. However, a groups-by-days interaction was not found to be significantly different, indicating that the rate of decay between the drug-injected and nondrug-injected groups was not significantly different. That is, even though both drugs facilitated memory and allowed the memory of the original avoidance habit to be expressed for a longer period of time, the slopes of the forgetting curves were not significantly different from that of the saline-injected controls.

Pretest injections of ALAP and PIREN also resulted in a significant overall increase in response latencies compared to saline-injected controls. However, no significant differences were found in the responsiveness of animals to the drugs over time, indicating that the training-to-test interval was not yet a factor in the animal's responsiveness to the drugs. Finally, the groups-by-days interaction was

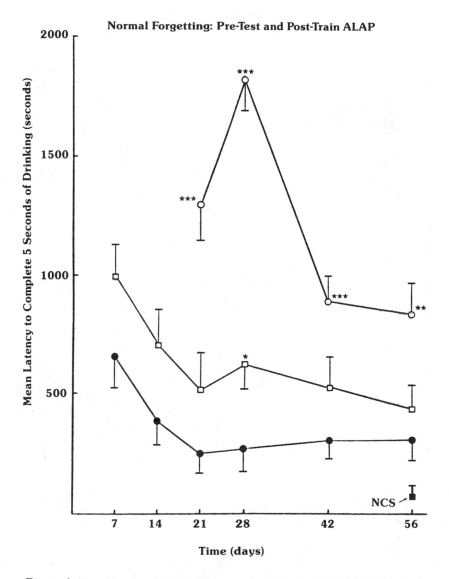

Figure 4. Mean latencies of individual groups of mice injected with ALAP (60 mg/kg), immediately after training (□—□) or 30 minutes prior to the retention test (O—O), compared to saline-injected controls (●—●). NCS = Noncontingently shocked animals that received ALAP prior to testing.
*p < 0.05, **p < 0.01, ***p < 0.001 vs Saline.

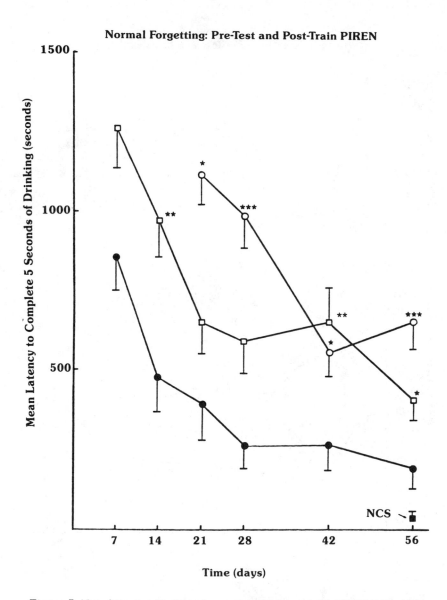

Figure 5. Mean latencies of individual groups of mice injected with PIREN (1.0 mg/kg), immediately after training (□—□) or 30 minutes prior to the retention test (O—O), compared to saline-injected controls (●—●). NCS = Noncontingently shocked animals that received PIREN prior to testing.

*p < 0.05, **p < 0.01, ***p < 0.001 vs Saline.

not significantly different, indicating, as before, that the slopes of the forgetting curves for the different treatment conditions were not significantly different from each other.

The effects of the pretest administration of ALAP and PIREN reconfirmed our earlier observations that these drugs could facilitate memory retrieval. However, within the present experimental framework, the results of this study indicate that these drugs can also restore the memory of habits that are no longer normally accessible to the animal due to a significant decay over time. In addition, the effects of immediate posttraining injections of ALAP and PIREN suggest that these compounds dramatically affect either the formation of the memory trace or its accessibility.

THE EFFECTS OF CYTOTOXIC LESIONS OF THE SEROTONERGIC NERVOUS SYSTEM ON THE PERFORMANCE OF RATS IN A COMPLEX SPATIAL DISCRIMINATION TASK

So far, 5-HT's role in learning and memory has been primarily assessed in aversively motivated tasks (e.g., one-way and two-way active avoidance and passive avoidance). Little information exists regarding 5-HT's involvement in discriminative behavior or in tasks that use food instead of shock as the reinforcer. This latter point is particularly important as 5-HT also plays an important role in nociception (Vasko & Vogt, 1981; Vogt, 1974). In addition, avoidance behavior is only one form of behavior. One would like to know how general 5-HT's involvement in learning and memory extends. The types of behavioral tasks used to assess human intellectual capacities are, in general, of a more complex nature. It would, therefore, be interesting to know whether the animals' performance on comparably taxing paradigms was similarly affected. Therefore, the following experiment was designed to examine the effects of lesions of the 5-HTergic nervous system on the acquisition of a positively reinforced complex spatial discrimination task (Stone 14-unit T-maze) (Altman, Normile, & Ögren, 1985).

The Stone 14-Unit T-Maze is a highly complex spatial discrimination task in which hungry rats run one trial per day, 5 days per week for 5 consecutive weeks for food reward (sweetened condensed milk). The total number of errors each animal makes while traversing the maze each day, as well as the total number of trials it takes each animal to run through the maze on 2 consecutive days with one or less errors, is recorded (trials to criterion).

Lesions were made with the indoleamine neurotoxin, p-chloro-amphetamine (PCA), which has been shown to produce long-lasting reductions in brain 5-HT levels in rats (Fuller, Perry, & Molloy, 1975) with little or no effect on norepinephrine and dopamine (Köhler, Ross, Srebro, & Ögren, 1978; Ögren et al., 1981; Ross, 1976). Since the cytotoxic effects of PCA have been shown to be blocked following 5-HT reuptake inhibition (Ross, 1976), pretreatment with norzimeldine (NZIM), a highly selective 5-HTergic reuptake inhibitor, should make it possible to assess the specificity of the PCA-induced effect. The following treatment conditions were examined: Group 1: SAL-SAL; Group 2: SAL-PCA (10 mg/kg); Group 3: NZIM (20 mg/kg)-PCA (10 mg/kg); and Group 4: NZIM (20 mg/kg)-SAL. All drug treatments were made 8 and 7 days prior to behavioral assessment in the Stone maze. The first injection preceded the second by 60 minutes.

The results of this experiment indicate that lesions of the 5-HTergic nervous system stimulate learning in the Stone maze. Both the mean number of errors per five trial block as seen in Figure 6, and the total number of trials needed to reach criterion, shown in Figure 7, were significantly lower in the PCA-treated group compared to controls. In addition, the enhancement of performance exhibited by the PCA-treated animals was blocked by pretreating the rats with NZIM. Surprisingly, the group treated with NZIM alone also made significantly fewer errors than controls, (Figure 6), although the total number of trials needed to reach criterion failed to reach statistical significance (Figure 7).

The results of this experiment should be viewed with caution as lesions of the 5-HTergic nervous system have been shown to produce variable effects on learning. In general, lesions of the 5-HTergic nervous system appear to stimulate acquisition (Brody, 1970; Lorens, 1978; Lorens & Yunger, 1974; Tenen, 1967). However, a number of studies have observed either no effect (Lorens, 1978; Stevens, Fletcher, & Resnick, 1969) or even an impairment of learning (Köhler & Lorens, 1978). The present study does not, therefore, resolve this issue. Instead, it presents yet another instance in which lesions of the 5-HTergic nervous system stimulate acquisition. In addition, the results of this study suggest that 5-HT's role in learning and memory extends beyond an involvement in avoidance behavior.

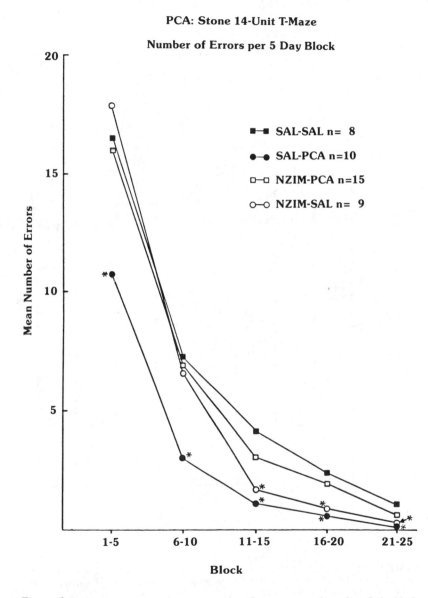

PCA: Stone 14-Unit T-Maze

Number of Errors per 5 Day Block

Figure 6. Each point represents the mean number of errors averaged over five - 5-day blocks for animals trained in the Stone 14-Unit T-Maze. Four drug groups were examined: SAL-SAL; SAL-PCA (10 mg/kg); NZIM (20 mg/kg)-PCA (10 mg/kg); and NZIM (20 mg/kg)-SAL. The first injection preceded the second by 60 minutes.

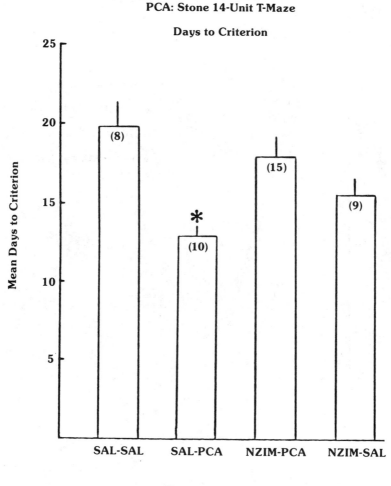

PCA: Stone 14-Unit T-Maze

Figure 7. Each bar represents the mean number of days required to reach criterion in the Stone 14-Unit T-Maze. Criterion = 0 or 1 error on two consecutive trials (days). Treatment groups and doses as described in Figure 6.
*p < 0.01 vs SAL-SAL.

ANALYSIS OF THE COMBINED EFFECTS OF STIMULATION OF THE CHOLINERGIC NERVOUS SYSTEM WITH OXOTREMORINE AND INHIBITION OF SEROTONERGIC REUPTAKE WITH ALAPROCLATE ON MEMORY RETRIEVAL

Clearly, the AChergic nervous system plays a significant role in learning and memory. There is ample reason to suspect that 5-HT plays a role in these processes as well. The purpose of the next experiment was to determine whether memory could be facilitated following combined stimulation of the AChergic nervous system and blockade of 5-HTergic reuptake (Altman, Stone & Ögren, 1985). The drugs used for this study were oxotremorine (OXO), a muscarinic AChergic agonist and ALAP. The behavioral task used was the step-through passive avoidance task. The animals were trained and tested as described previously. However, prior to retention testing (24 hours later), the animals were injected with SAL or with one of several doses of either OXO, ALAP, or a combination of OXO and ALAP. (See Figure 8 for doses).

The results of this study indicate that OXO and ALAP, alone or in combination, facilitate memory retrieval in a dose-dependent fashion, as shown in Figure 8. More importantly, the memory facilitation induced by the combined treatment begins at a dose level below that at which either drug facilitates memory on its own. That is, the dose-response curve for the combined effects of the drugs on memory shifts to the left.

Attempts were made to block the memory enhancement resulting from the different treatments (i.e., ALAP, OXO, or the combination of ALAP+OXO) by pretreating the mice with either scopolamine (a muscarinic cholinergic antagonist) or quipazine. The results of these experiments indicated that: (1) quipazine completely blocked the memory enhancement resulting from ALAP but failed to block either the facilitation of performance induced by OXO or ALAP+OXO, and (2) scopolamine significantly blocked the memory enhancement resulting from OXO as well as that resulting from ALAP+OXO, but failed to alter the enhancement of performance produced by ALAP.

DISCUSSION AND RECOMMENDATIONS

A basic strategy for the development of an effective treatment for the memory loss associated with AD has been to identify those

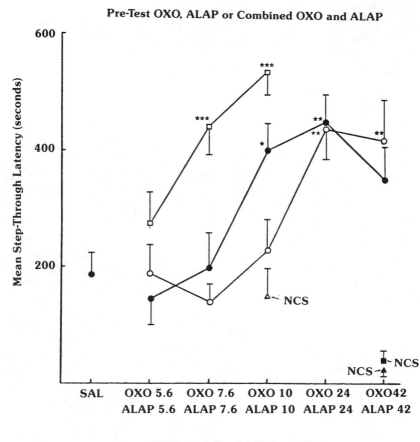

Figure 8. Mean latencies of individual groups of mice injected with one of several doses of OXO (●—●), ALAP (O—O), or a combination of OXO and ALAP (□—□), 30 minutes prior to the retention test. NCS = Noncontingently shocked mice that received OXO (■), ALAP (▲), or a combination of OXO and ALAP (Δ).
*p < 0.05, **p < 0.02, ***p < 0.002 vs Saline.

changes within the brain responsible for the deterioration of memory, pharmacologically reverse these changes, and thus restore function to normal. One of the most commonly reported changes within the brain to be attributed to AD is reduced functioning of the AChergic nervous system (a neurotransmitter system suspected of playing a primary role in learning and memory). Unfortunately, attempts to ameliorate the memory impairments associated with AD by artificially stimulating this system have not been entirely encouraging. An additional problem associated with this approach is that the AChergic nervous system is progressively deteriorating over time. As a result, manipulations that may prove effective initially, may not be effective later. Moreover, there is the likelihood that chronic stimulation of the AChergic nervous system may actually accelerate the memory deterioration as a result of receptor down regulation.

While the AChergic nervous system is surely affected in AD, and likely to be responsible for certain aspects of the cognitive decline, its deterioration is unlikely to be the sole reason for the memory loss. This may partly explain why the results following stimulation of the AChergic nervous system have been so disappointing. However, an effective treatment strategy does not have to be based on the premise that the only way to ameliorate the memory impairments associated with AD is by identifying its cause. The physiological processes underlying learning and memory are the net result of the coordinated actions of several neuronal systems. In addition, a considerable amount of redundancy appears to have been built into the system. It may be possible to take advantage of these features when attempting to develop an effective treatment for AD. An alternate strategy may be to ameliorate the memory deficits associated with AD by manipulating one of the other neurotransmitter systems suspected of playing a role in the processes underlying learning and memory, especially one that is either unaffected or affected to a lesser degree by the disease process. The neurotransmitter system selected would not have to be the one through which the information would normally have traveled, but one that could, under appropriate conditions, be made to carry on a part or all of the function(s) subserved by the original neurotransmitter system.

Recent experimental evidence suggests that 5-HT plays an important role in learning and memory in animals (Altman, 1985; Altman et al., 1984; Archer et al., 1981; Ögren, 1982a,b). However, unlike other neurotransmitter systems such as cholinergic (Bartus, Dean, Beer, & Lippa, 1982; Deutsch, 1973), noradrenergic (Dismukes & Rake, 1972; McGaugh, Liang, Bennett, & Sternberg, 1984; Quartermain, 1982) or dopaminergic (Altman & Quartermain, 1983; Quartermain & Altman, 1982), stimulation of the 5-HTergic nervous system impairs (Archer et al., 1981; Essman, 1973; Fibiger et al., 1978; Joyce & Hurwitz, 1964; Ögren, 1982a), while disruption enhances learning and memory (Brody, 1970; Lorens, 1978; Lorens

& Yunger, 1974; Tenen, 1967). In addition, preliminary results suggest that pretest administration of ALAP enhances memory in aged mice. The evidence suggests, therefore, that manipulations interfering with normal 5-HTergic functioning may be useful in the treatment of AD. This approach may appear inconsistent in light of recent findings suggesting that the functional and structural integrity of the 5-HTergic nervous system may be compromised in AD (Benton et al., 1982; Bowen et al., 1983; Curcio & Kemper, in press; Gottfries et al., 1983; Mann et al., 1984). At present, to what degree this system is affected or how such changes affect brain function and behavior is unknown. Even if greatly affected, such observations do not mitigate the fact that a significant enhancement of learning and/or memory can result from acute and chronic interference with this system in animals.

So far, the results of preliminary trials with ALAP in demented subjects have not been entirely encouraging. In an initial open pharmacokinetic study of ALAP in patients with AD, five of nine patients exhibited a positive effect, but the change in performance was mainly attributed to a change in emotionality (Bergman et al., 1983). In a subsequent double-blind parallel comparison of ALAP and placebo, Dehlin, Hedenrud, Jansson, and Nörgård (1985) found a significantly lower mean score on the Gottfries, Bråne, and Steen (GBS) rating scale for intellectual functioning. However, the clinical relevance of this difference was considered doubtful as it was only statistically significant during one treatment session, and no other differences between ALAP and placebo were seen on any other factor of the GBS scale or the clinical global evaluation (Dehlin et al., 1985). Such results should not, however, discourage future attempts at ameliorating the memory impairments associated with AD via manipulations of the 5-HTergic nervous system, but should serve as an impetus to initiate additional clinical trials with these and other related compounds.

REFERENCES

Altman, H.J. (1985). Mediation of storage and retrieval with two drugs that selectively modulate serotonergic neurotransmission. In D.S. Olton, E. Gamzu, & S. Corkin (Eds.), *Memory dysfunctions: An integration of animal and human research from preclinical and clinical perspectives* (pp. 496-498). New York: New York Academy of Sciences.

Altman, H.J., Nordy, D.A., & Ögren, S.O. (1984). Role of serotonin in memory: Facilitation by alaproclate and zimelidine. *Psychopharmacology, 84,* 496-502.

Altman, H.J., & Normile, H.J. (in press). Enhancement of memory of a previously learned aversive habit following pretest administration of a variety of serotonergic antagonists in mice. *Psychopharmacology.*

Altman, H.J., Normile, H.J., & Ögren, S.O. (1985). Facilitation of discrimination learning in the rat following cytotoxic lesions of the serotonergic nervous system. *Neuroscience Abstracts, 11,* 874.

Altman, H.J., & Quartermain, D. (1983). Facilitation of memory retrieval by centrally administered catecholamine stimulating agents. *Behavioral Brain Research, 7,* 51-63.

Altman, H.J., Stone, W.S., & Ögren, S.O. (1985). Evidence for a functional interaction between serotonergic and cholinergic mechanisms in memory retrieval. (Manuscript submitted for publication.)

Archer, T., Ögren, S.O., & Johensson, C. (1981). The acute effects of p-chloroamphetamine on the retention of fear conditioning in the rat: Evidence for a role of serotonin in memory consolidation. *Neuroscience Letters, 25,* 75-81.

Bartus, R.T., Dean, R.L., Beer, B., & Lippa, A.S. (1982). The cholinergic hypothesis of geriatric memory dysfunction: A critical review. *Science, 217,* 408-417.

Benton, J.S., Bowen, D.M., Allen, S.J., Haan, E.A., Davison, A.N., Neary, D., Murphy, R.P., & Snowdon, J.S. (1982). Alzheimer's disease as a disorder of the isodendritic core. *Lancet, 1,* 456.

Bergman, I., Brane, G., Gottfries, C.G., Jostell, K.-G., Karlsson, I., & Svennerholm, L. (1983). Alaproclate: A pharmacokinetic and biochemical study in patients with dementia of the Alzheimer's type. *Psychopharmacology, 80,* 279-283.

Bowen, D.M., Allen, S.J., Benton, J.S., Goodhardt, M.J., Haan, E.A., Palmer, A.N., Sims, N.R., Smith, C.C.T., Spillane, J.A., Esiri, M.M., Neary, D., Snowdon, J.S., Wilcock, G.K., & Davison, A.N. (1983). Biochemical assessment of serotonergic and cholinergic dysfunction and cerebral atrophy in Alzheimer's disease. *Journal of Neurochemistry, 41,* 266-272.

Bowen, D.M., Davison, A.N., Francis, P.T., Neary, D., & Palmer, A.N. (1984). Alzheimer's disease: Importance of acetylcholine and tangle bearing cortical neurons. In R.J. Wurtman, S.M. Corkin, & J.H.

Growdon (Eds.), *Alzheimer's disease: Advances in basic research and therapies* (pp. 9-28). Cambridge: Center for Brain Sciences and Metabolism Charitable Trust.

Brody, J.F. (1970). Behavioral effects of serotonin depletion by p-chlorophenylalanine (a serotonin depletor) in rats. *Psychopharmacologia, 17,* 14-33.

Curcio, C.A., & Kemper, T. (in press) Nucleus raphe dorsalis in dementia of the Alzheimer's type: Neurofibrillary changes and neuronal packing density. *Journal of Neuropathology and Experimental Neurology.*

Davis, K.L., Mohs, R., Tinklenberg, J.R., Pfefferbaum, A., Hollister, L.E., & Kopell, B.S. (1978). Physostigmine: Improvement of long-term memory processes in normal humans. *Science, 201,* 272-274.

Dehlin, O., Hedenrud, B., Jansson, P., & Nörgård, J. (1985). A double-blind comparison of alaproclate and placebo in the treatment of patients with senile dementia. *Acta Psychiatrica Scandinavica, 71,* 190-196.

Deutsch, J.A. (1973). The cholinergic synapse and the site of memory. In J.A. Deutsch (Ed.), *The physiological basis of memory* (pp. 59-76). New York: Academic Press.

Dismukes, R.K., & Rake, A.V. (1972). Involvement of biogenic amines in memory formation. *Psychopharmacologia, 23,* 17-25.

Drachman, D.A., & Leavitt, J. (1974). Human memory and the cholinergic system. *Archives of Neurology, 30,* 113-121.

Essman, W.B. (1973). Neuromolecular modification of experimentally induced retrograde amnesia. *Confinia Neurology, 35,* 1-22.

Farnebo, L.-O., & Hamberger, B. (1974). Regulation of [3H]5-hydroxytryptamine release from rat brain slices. *Journal of Pharmacy and Pharmacology, 26,* 642-644.

Fibiger, H.C., Lepiane, F.G., & Phillips, A.G. (1978). Disruption of memory produced by stimulation of the dorsal raphe nucleus: Mediation by serotonin. *Brain Research, 155,* 380-386.

Fuller, R.W., Perry, K.W., & Molloy, B.B. (1975). Reversible and irreversible phases of serotonin depletion by p-chloroamphetamine. *European Journal of Pharmacology, 33,* 119-124.

Gottfries, C.G., Adolfsson, R., Aquilonius, S.M., Carsson, A., Eckernäs, S.Å., Nordberg, A., Oreland, L., Svennerholm, L., Wiberg, Å., & Winblad, B. (1983). Biochemical changes in dementia disorders

Alzheimer's type (AD/SDAT). *Neurobiology of Aging, 4,* 261-271.

Joyce, D., & Hurwitz, H.M.B. (1964). Avoidance behavior in the rat after 5-hydroxytryptophan (5-HTP) administration. *Psychopharmacologia, 5,* 424-430.

Köhler, C., & Lorens, S.A. (1978). Open field activity and avoidance behavior following serotonin depletion: A comparison of the effects of parachloraphenylalanine and electrolytic lesions. *Pharmacology, Biochemistry and Behavior, 8,* 223-233.

Köhler, C., Ross, S.B., Srebro, B., & Ögren, S.O. (1978). Long-term biochemical and behavioral effects of p-chloroamphetamine in the rat. In J.H. Jacoby & L.D. Lytle (Eds.), *Serotonin neurotoxins* (pp. 645-663). New York: The New York Academy of Sciences.

Lorens, S.A. (1978). Some behavioral effects of serotonin depletion depend on method: A comparison of 5,7-dihydroxytryptamine, p-chlorophenylalanine, p-chloroamphetamine and electrolytic raphe lesions. *Annals of the New York Academy of Sciences, 305,* 532-555.

Lorens, S.A., & Yunger, L.M. (1974). Morphine analgesia, two-way avoidance and consummatory behavior following lesions in the midbrain raphe nuclei of the rat. *Pharmacology, Biochemistry and Behavior, 2,* 215-221.

Mann, D.M., Yates, P.O., & Marcyniuk, B. (1984). Alzheimer's presenile dementia, senile dementia of the Alzheimer's type and Down's syndrome in middle age form an age related continuum of pathological changes. *Neuropathology and Applied Neurobiology, 10,* 185-207.

Martin, L.L., & Sanders-Bush, E. (1982). The serotonin autoreceptor: Antagonism by quipazine. *Neuropharmacology, 21,* 445-450.

McGaugh, J.L., Liang, K.C., Bennett, C., & Sternberg, D.B. (1984). Adrenergic influences on memory storage: Interaction of peripheral and central systems. In G. Lynch, J.L. McGaugh, & N.M. Weinberger (Eds.), *Neurobiology of learning and memory* (pp. 313-332). New York: Guilford Press.

Normile, H.J., & Altman, H.J. (1985). The effects of serotonergic receptor blockade on learning and memory in mice. *Neuroscience.*

Ögren, S.O. (1982a). Forebrain serotonin and avoidance learning: Behavioral and biochemical studies on the acute effect of p-chloroamphetamine on one-way active avoidance learning in the male rat. *Pharmacology, Biochemistry and Behavior, 16,* 881-895.

Ögren, S.O. (1982b). Central serotonin neurons and learning in the rat. In N.N. Osbourn (Ed.), *Biology of serotonergic transmission* (pp. 317-339). New York: John Wiley & Sons, Ltd.

Ögren, S.O., Fuxe, K., Archer, T., Hall, H., Holm, A.C., & Köhler, C. (1981). Studies on the role of central 5-HT neurons in avoidance learning: A behavioral and biochemical analysis. In B. Haber, S. Gabay, E. Issiderides, & S.G.A. Alivisatos (Eds.), *Serotonin: Current aspects of neurochemistry and function* (pp. 681-705). New York: Plenum Press.

Perry, E.K., & Perry, R.H. (1980). The cholinergic system in Alzheimer's disease. In P.J. Roberts (Ed.), *Biochemistry of dementia* (pp. 135-183). Chichester, Great Britain: John Wiley & Sons, Ltd.

Quartermain, D. (1982). Catecholamine involvement in memory retrieval processes. In A.R. Morrison & P.L. Strick (Eds.), *Changing concepts of the nervous system* (pp. 666-679). New York: Academic Press.

Quartermain, D., & Altman, H.J. (1982). Facilitation of retrieval by d-amphetamine following anisomycin-induced amnesia. *Physiological Psychology, 10,* 283-292.

Ross, S.B. (1976). Antagonism of the acute and long-term biochemical effects of p-chloroamphetamine on the 5HT neurons in the rat brain by inhibitors of 5-hydroxytryptamine uptake. *Acta Pharmacologica et Toxicologica, 39,* 456-467.

Rosser, M.N., Svendsen, C., Hunt, S.P., Mountjoy, C.Q., Roth, M., & Iversen, L.L. (1982). The substantia innominata in Alzheimer's disease: An histochemical and biochemical study of cholinergic marker enzymes. *Neuroscience Letters, 28,* 217-222.

Rylett, R.T., Ball, M.J., & Colhoun, E.H. (1983). Evidence for high affinity choline transport in synaptosomes prepared from hippocampus and neocortex of patients with Alzheimer's disease. *Brain Research, 289,* 169-175.

Schlessinger, K., & Schreiber, R.A. (1968). Effects of p-chlorophenylalanine on conditioned avoidance learning. *Psychonomic Science, 11,* 225-226.

Sims, N.R., Bowen, D.M., Smith, C.C.T., Flock, R.H., Davison, A.N., Snowdon, J.S., & Neary, D. (1980). Glucose metabolism and acetylcholine synthesis in relation to neuronal activity in Alzheimer's disease. *The Lancet, 1,* 333-337.

Sitaram, N., Weingartner, H., & Gillin, J.C. (1978). Human serial learning: Enhancement with arecoline and impairment with scopolamine. *Science, 210,* 274-276.

Srebro, B., & Lorens, S.A. (1975). Behavioral effects of selective raphe lesions in the rat. *Brain Research, 89,* 303-325.

Steranka, L.R., & Barrett, R.J. (1974). Facilitation of avoidance acquisition by lesions of the median raphe nucleus: Evidence for serotonin as a mediator of shock-induced suppression. *Behavioral Biology, 11,* 205-213.

Stevens, D.A., Fletcher, L.D., & Resnick, O. (1969). The effects of *p*-chloroamphetamine, a depletor of brain serotonin on behavior: II. Retardation of passive avoidance learning. *Life Sciences, 8,* 379-385.

Tenen, S.S. (1967). The effects of *p*-chlorophenylalanine, a serotonin depletor, on avoidance acquisition, pain sensitivity and related behavior in the rat. *Psychopharmacologia, 10,* 204-219.

Vasko, M.R., & Vogt, M. (1981). Site of interaction between morphine and 5-hydroxytryptamine-containing neurons in the rat brain. *British Journal of Pharmacology, 73,* 245-246.

Vogt, M. (1974). The effect of lowering the 5-hydroxytryptamine content of the rat spinal cord on analgesia produced by morphine. *Journal of Physiology, 236,* 483-498.

Whitehouse, P.J., Price, D.L., Struble, R.G., Coyle, J.T., & DeLong, M.H. (1982). Alzheimer's disease and senile dementia—Loss of neurons in the basal forebrain. *Science, 215,* 1237-1239.

16

Presynaptic and Postsynaptic Approaches to Enhancing Central Cholinergic Neurotransmission

Fulton T. Crews, PhD, Edwin M. Meyer, PhD, Rueben A. Gonzales, PhD, Cynthia Theiss, Debbie H. Otero, Karin Larsen, Robert Raulli, and Gabriella Calderini, PhD.

Several lines of evidence indicate that dysfunction in cholinergic transmission is related to Alzheimer's disease (AD) and the memory loss associated with senile dementia (see Bartus, Dean, Beer, & Lippak 1982; Coyle, Price, & DeLong, 1983 for review). The symptoms of AD are, in general, an exaggeration of those found during normal aging: Plaques and tangles are found in both cases, EEG changes are similar, and cerebral atrophy occurs in both cases (Drachman, 1983). A major difference appears to be loss of cholinergic neurons in the nucleus basalis of Meynert in patients with AD (Whitehouse et al., 1982). The degeneration of these cholinergic neurons, which innervate the cerebral cortex and hippocampus, is likely to underlie the decrease in choline acetyltransferase (CAT), a marker for cholinergic neurons and nerve terminals found in the frontal cortex and hippocampus of patients with dementia (Bowen, 1980; Perry, E.K., Tomlinson, Blessed, Bergmann, Gibson, & Perry, R.H., 1978; Reisine, Yamamura, Bird, & Enna, 1978). The decrease in CAT activity has been correlated with the decline in mental function in senile dementia (Perry, E.K. et al., 1978). Taken together, these findings suggest that treatments that can enhance cholinergic synaptic transmission in the cerebral cortex and hippocampus may provide a therapeutic and/or curative treatment for patients with AD.

Changes in cholinergic transmission also occur during normal aging. Slight changes in high-affinity choline uptake and acetylcholine (ACh) synthesis have been reported during senescence. However, the most consistent and pronounced presynaptic change in cholinergic function during senescence appears to be a decrease in ACh release (Gibson & Peterson, 1981; Meyer, St. Onge, & Crews, 1984; Pedata, Slavikova, Kotas, & Pepeu, 1983). Decreases in the amount of ACh released per nerve impulse could underlie memory deficits associated with normal aging but which are exaggerated in AD where there is an actual loss of nerve terminals.

Postsynaptic alterations in responsiveness could also contribute to senescent memory dysfunction. Low doses of scopolamine, a muscarinic cholinergic antagonist, have been shown to produce memory and cognitive deficits in young individuals similar to those found to occur naturally in aged subjects given the same tests (Drachman & Leavitt, 1974; Drachman, Noffsinger, Sahakian, & Fleming, 1980). The decreased cholinergic responsiveness observed with cholinergic antagonists may be comparable to changes in cholinergic responsiveness that occur during aging and possibly AD. Microiontophoretic studies show a loss of muscarinic responsiveness in aged hippocampi of Fischer 344 rats. Single-cell recordings of pyramidal cells indicate that aged hippocampal pyramidal cells are significantly less sensitive to ACh but not to glutamate (Lippa et al., 1980). In addition, intracellular recordings of hippocampal CA1 pyramidal cells in slices indicate that both the initial hyperpolarization and the late depolarization due to ACh are markedly reduced in pyramidal cells of old rats (Segal, 1982). This decreased responsiveness to ACh could play a significant role in the pathology of senile dementia and AD, particularly if this change in postsynaptic membrane responsiveness is exaggerated in AD. This report will discuss both presynaptic and postsynaptic approaches to enhancing central cholinergic neurotransmission in AD and normal aging. Decrements in cholinergic neurotransmission are likely to be related to both a presynaptic decrease in the release of ACh and postsynaptic decrease in responsiveness to ACh. In many cases additive and/or synergistic effects may occur during treatment with both presynaptic and postsynaptic therapeutic agents.

Our studies will focus on the cerebral cortex and hippocampus. Hippocampal and cerebral cortical cholinergic innervation is well-defined both chemically and histologically. Both of these regions have cortical architecture dominated by the pyramidal cell. Furthermore, these are the brain regions that appear to be intimately involved in memory function and are innervated by similar forebrain cholinergic nuclei, which are those regions most affected in AD. Differences in other brain regions and peripheral tissues will be mentioned briefly since the differences might provide pharmacological drug selectivity.

MUSCARINIC RECEPTOR SUBTYPES M_1 AND M_2

There appear to be at least two types of muscarinic receptors, M_1 and M_2. Autoradiographic studies using pirenzepine have found M_1 sites to be localized in the cortex, hippocampus, and striatum. M_2 sites are more evenly distributed particularly to the pons, thalamus, and colliculi (Buckley & Burnstock, 1984; Potter et al., 1984). In the cerebral cortex and hippocampus, presynaptic autoreceptors appear to be M_2 receptors, whereas postsynaptic receptors are likely to be M_1 receptors.

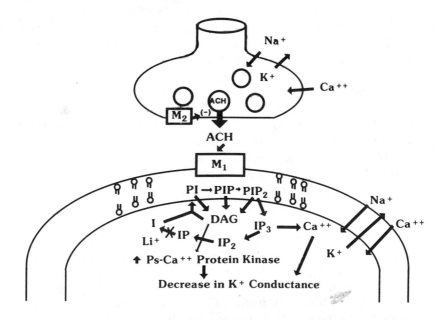

Figure 1. Pre and postsynaptic aspects of cortical cholinergic neurotransmission. Shown is a hypothetical model of cholinergic neurotransmission in both the cerebral cortex and hippocampus. Presynaptic autoreceptors that inhibit ACh release appear to be M_1 and M_2 muscarinic receptors. Postsynaptic receptors appear to be M_1 muscarinic receptors that activate inositol phospholipid metabolism. PI, PIP, and PIP_2 are the lipids phosphatidylinositol, phosphatidylinositol 4-phosphate, and phosphatidylinositol 4,5-bisphosphate, respectively. I, IP, IP_2, and IP_3 are the sugars inositol, inositol phosphate, inositol 1,4-diphosphate, and inositol triphosphate, respectively. DAG is diacylglycerol. Protein kinase C is PS,CA^{++}PK.

Studies separating M_1 and M_2 muscarinic receptor binding sites have found that M_1 receptors contribute approximately 80% of the binding sites in the hippocampus and cerebral cortex with M_2 sites contributing approximately 20% (Potter et al., 1984). Experiments on brains from AD patients indicated that there is an approximately 20% decrease in muscarinic receptor binding in AD patients which is due primarily to the loss of M_2 receptors (Mash, Flynn, & Potter, in press). Losses of M_2 receptors paralleled the losses in CAT activity. Furthermore, lesions of the substantia innominata in rats caused a similar decrease in M_2 receptor sites (Mash et al., in press). These studies suggest that any losses in muscarinic binding sites that do occur in AD are due to the loss of presynaptic M_2 sites.

Functional studies on the presynaptic autoreceptor on rat cholinergic cortical synaptosomes and phosphatidylinositol turnover in rat brain slices also suggest that the autoreceptor is M_2 and the receptor linked to inositol phospholipid turnover is M_1. Oxotremorine is a full agonist as an inhibitor of ACh release; and pirenzepine is a weak antagonist (Meyer & Otero, in press). On the other hand, oxotremorine is a weak partial agonist at stimulating phosphatidylinositol turnover compared to ACh and carbachol as shown in Figure 4. Pirenzepine inhibits phosphoinositide hydrolysis with an ED_{50} of approximately 1 μM (Gonzales & Crews, 1984). Furthermore, septal lesions of the cholinergic input to the hippocampus do not reduce muscarinic stimulation of phosphatidylinositol turnover (Fisher, Boast, & Agranoff, 1980). Taken together with the receptor binding experiments, these studies suggest that cerebral cortical and hippocampal M_2 receptors are primarily presynaptic autoreceptors, and that the predominant M_1 receptors are postsynaptic and coupled to phosphoinositide hydrolysis seen in Figure 1.

Electrophysiological studies on muscarinic receptors have found both excitatory and inhibitory responses. It seems likely that the opposing actions are due to subtypes of muscarinic receptors. The inhibitory response results from an increase in membrane potassium conductance, whereas the excitatory response appears to be due to a decrease in potassium conductance (North & Tokimasa, 1984). Several lines of evidence suggest that the excitatory responses are related to activation of M_1 muscarinic receptors and inhibitory responses are related to M_2 receptors. Excitatory responses are the predominant muscarinic responses in the cerebral cortex and hippocampus, where M_1 binding sites predominate. In contrast, the inhibitory muscarinic receptors in the heart decrease the duration of

TABLE 1

Effects of Pirenzepine on Oxotremorine-Induced Inhibition of ACh Release from Rat Cortical Synaptosomes

Oxotremorine Concentration (μM)	[3H]-ACh Release (dpm/mg Protein)	
	Control	+ Pirenzepine
Cerebral Cortex		
0	1270 ± 40	1360 ± 30
10	870 ± 10	1100 ± 60*
100	840 ± 40	900 ± 30
200	830 ± 30	910 ± 40
Striatum		
0	25,800 ± 900	28,900 ± 200*
10	17,400 ± 1100	26,200 ± 600*
100	17,400 ± 700	23,900 ± 1100*
200	16,200 ± 300	24,900 ± 500*

Rat cortical or striatal synaptosomes were prepared as described previously and incubated for 10 minutes with 1 μM [3H]-choline in Krebs-Ringer buffer at 37° to generate newly synthesized [3H]-ACh. They were washed with cold buffer twice and then incubated with the specified concentration of oxotremorine ±10 μM pirenzepine for 2.5 minutes at 37° in the presence of 50 μM eserine sulfate. The labelled ACh spontaneously released into the medium was separated from choline using a radioenzymatic phosphorylation of choline followed by the ion pair extraction of ACh into hepatone. The [3H]-ACh was then counted by liquid scintillation spectrophotometry. Each value is the mean ± of 4 to 6 determinations involving 2 to 3 separate rat brain preparations. *$p < 0.01$ compared to the same oxotremorine-concentration, pirenzepine-free treated groups (from two-way analysis of variance).

the action potential, increase potassium conductance, and are predominantly M_2 (Potter et al., 1984). These muscarinic receptors appear to inhibit adenylate cyclase. Furthermore, pirenzepine, and stercuronium are much more potent at blocking muscarinic excitation of ganglia, an M_1 rich tissue, than they are at blocking contraction of the ileum, an M_2 rich tissue (Brown, 1984). The segregation of receptor subtypes to presynaptic and postsynaptic locations and their different coupling mechanisms may be exploited to enhance cholinergic neurotransmission.

PRESYNAPTIC ASPECTS

Coupling Between ACh Synthesis and Release

Since AD is due in part to a loss of cholinergic neurons, several attempts have been made to treat the disease by elevating the presynaptic synthesis of this transmitter in the remaining neurons (Drachman, Glosser, Flemming, & Longnecker, 1981; Vroulis, Smith, Brinkman, Schooler, & Gordon, 1981; Wurtman, 1985). It is clear, however, that any treatment that acts presynaptically to increase cholinergic transmission must do more than just elevate transmitter synthesis. ACh release into the synapse must also be increased. Presently, there is little evidence to support the hypothesis that increasing ACh synthesis *per se* augments cholinergic release or transmission but it is well-known that ACh synthesis can be augmented by ACh release (Collier & Ilson, 1977; Marchbanks, 1982; Tucek, 1985). This unidirectional coupling between the release and synthesis of ACh appears to be mediated by the high-affinity choline uptake process, which is found predominately in cholinergic nerve terminals and closely coupled to ACh synthesis (Meyer, Engle, & Cooper, 1982; Tucek, 1985; Yamamura & Snyder, 1973). The affinity of this transporter for choline is high enough in brain cholinergic terminals (K_t between 1 to 3 μM) that circulating choline levels probably saturate it when the nerve is at resting potential. When the nerve terminal is depolarized, transport kinetics are modified in two sequential ways. First, during the depolarization, the affinity for choline decreases so that changes in extracellular choline concentrations can increase ACh release transiently (Meyer et al., 1984). In rat cortical synaptosomes, only choline taken up by the sodium-dependent choline-transporter (not the ubiquitous lower-affinity uptake process associated with phospholipid synthesis) is acetylated even during depolarization (Meyer et al., 1982). Next, as the terminal repolarizes, the affinity for choline returns to normal but the V_{max} for transport increases, apparently in response to the release of ACh and the concomitant reduction of its intracellular levels. Taken together, these characteristics of the high-affinity choline transport system suggest that the cholinergic neuron can homeostatically maintain ACh synthesis after transmitter release in a manner that is insensitive to extracellular choline augmentation, except during prolonged or repeated depolarizations when extracellular choline augmentation may be pharmacologically useful. Therefore it seems likely that the most efficacious treatments for elevating cholinergic transmission presynaptically may involve both an ACh releasing agent as well as extracellular choline augmentation.

Brain ACh Synthesis and Aging

As mentioned above, aging appears to have only slight effects on the parameters associated with ACh synthesis in human and animal brains. For example, using rat cortical synaptosomes or isolated nerve terminals we were unable to demonstrate any age-related decrement in high-affinity choline transport or subsequent choline acetylation in 24-month versus 6-month-old rats (Meyer et al., 1984). This observation suggests that the nondiseased, aged, cholinergic terminal may be able to synthesize enough ACh for functional transmission under normal conditions. It is interesting to note that some peripheral cholinergic neurons are differentially affected by aging. We found that rat atrial high-affinity choline uptake and acetylation were significantly reduced (over 50%) in 24-month-old animals compared to 6-month-old controls (Meyer, Momo, & Baker, in press). Which endogenous or genetic factors make some cholinergic neurons more sensitive than others to aging is not known but may be important for our understanding of how AD affects some brain neurons and not others (e.g., striatal interneurons).

Brain ACh Release and Aging

The release of ACh, like that of other transmitters, is triggered by calcium ions that enter through voltage-sensitive channels (see Cooper & Meyer, 1984, for review). Mobilization of intracellular calcium ions sequestered in mitochondria or endoplasmic reticulum by sodium ion accumulation may also elicit the transmitter's release (Meyer & Cooper, in press; Nicholls & Scott, 1980; Silbergeld, 1977). ACh release is an extremely rapid process (occurring within $100\,\mu sec$ of calcium influx) that preferentially utilizes newly synthesized ACh, perhaps in both vesicular and nonvesicular pools.

After its release ACh can inhibit the further release of ACh via presynaptic muscarinic autoreceptors in a membrane-potential dependent manner (Meyer & Otero, in press; Raiteri, Leardi, & Marchi,

1984). Depolarization reduces the potency of ACh and other agonists for these receptors. As discussed above, these autoreceptors are of the M_2 type in rat cerebral cortices, since they are blocked by atropine and scopolamine at low concentrations, but is relatively insensitive to pirenzepine (Meyer & Otero, in press). Oxotremorine appears to act as a full agonist in this release-modulation system as do carbachol and ACh, while pilocarpine is almost without effect on ACh release. Interestingly, there appears to be some regional variability in the pharmacological sensitivity of this muscarinic receptor-mediated inhibition of ACh release. For example, pirenzepine antagonism of oxotremorine-induced modulation in rat cortical synaptosomes is much less efficacious than in striatal tissue, seen in Table 1. Another difference between these two regions is that carbachol appears to have little effect on the modulation of ACh release in the striatum (Meyer & Otero, 1985, unpublished observation). These results suggest that it may be possible to selectively alter ACh release via autoreceptors in specified brain regions.

It may be important in treating AD to understand how aging affects the release of ACh because this disease is often associated with aging. The aged cholinergic neurons remaining during the disease may be regulated differently from younger cells. Along this line, several laboratories, including ours, have shown that aging reduces the depolarization-induced release of ACh from a variety of preparations, including rat cortical synaptosomes, cortical slices, and mouse brain slices (Gibson & Peterson, 1981; Meyer et al., 1984; Pedata et al., 1983). Conceivably, aging may reduce depolarization-dependent ACh-release by affecting many processes underlying normal transmitter-release, including a variety of plasma membrane ion channels, intracellular calcium levels, coupling between calcium ions and ACh release, presynaptic autoreceptor activity, and intracellular ACh disposition. We discuss results below, suggesting that aging also affects the potency of calcium ions with respect to triggering ACh release, the intracellular mobilization of calcium ions by ouabain and the presynaptic muscarinic modulation of ACh release remain functional during aging, and 4-aminopyridine restores ACh release in old animals to normal levels. Taken together these results suggest that aging affects the coupling between calcium and ACh release but several presynaptic membrane sites remain functional to which agents may be directed to normalize transmission.

Aging and Depolarization-Induced Release of ACh

To study the effects of aging on cortical cholinergic release processes, synaptosomes were used because the released ACh could be diluted rapidly and removed from presynaptic receptors that otherwise inhibit ACh release. As shown in Table 2, the K^+-induced release of newly synthesized [3H]-ACh is significantly reduced in

TABLE 2

Effects of Aging on K^+- and A23187-Induced Release of ACh from Rat Cortical Synaptosomes

Treatment	[3H]-ACh Release (dpm/mg Protein)	
	6 Months	24 Months
1 mM CaCl$_2$		
None	660 ± 20	600 ± 50
35 mM KCl	1060 ± 80	800 ± 50*
2 µg/ml A23187	1020 ± 60 (2)	750 ± 50* (2)
10 µg/ml A23187	1355 ± 90	950 ± 40*
20 µg/ml A23187	1540 ± 709 (2)	1500 ± 100 (2)
Calcium-free Buffer		
None	350 ± 20	340 ± 10
35 mM KCl	190 ± 20	170 ± 10

Cortical synaptosomes from Fischer-344 male rats of the specified age were prepared and loaded with newly synthesized [3H]-Ach as described in Table 1. They were washed and incubated for 2.5 minutes at 37° in the presence of the specified buffer, plus 50 µM eserine sulfate. The labelled ACh released into the medium was separated from the choline and expressed here as means ± SEM of six values/group, except where noted by parentheses.

*$p<0.05$ compared to corresponding treatment, different age-group, according to Student's t-test.

synaptosomes from 24-month old rats compared to 6-month-old animals. No K^+-induced release of [3H]-ACh is observed in calcium-free buffers. As mentioned above, the synthesis of transmitter in this preparation is unaffected by aging, and suggests that similar amounts of transmitter are available for release in each group. While these results corroborate earlier observations that the voltage-dependent, calcium-triggered release of ACh decreases with age, they do not indicate whether the calcium-influx in cholinergic terminals decreases or whether some step subsequent to this ion influx is involved.

Recently, it has been shown that K+ depolarization-induced $^{45}Ca^{2+}$ influx into brain synaptosomes is reduced in 27-month-old rats compared to 6-month-old animals suggesting that this channel-mediated activity becomes hypofunctional during senescense (Peterson & Gibson, 1983). This reduction in calcium-uptake may occur in many neurotransmitter terminals including the cholinergic ones that make up only a small fraction of the total number in that preparation. Alternatively, the age-related reduction in voltage-dependent calcium uptake in synaptosomes may not be attributable to cholinergic neurons. In either case, other changes in the ACh-release process distal to calcium uptake may also be involved in the hypofunctional release associated with senescence.

Aging and the Potency of Calcium Ions to Trigger ACh Release

To determine whether the age-related difference in depolarization-induced ACh release is due solely to a decrement in calcium-influx or involves release processes after this influx, the effects of A23187 on ACh release were studied. A23187 is a calcium ionophore that directly increases calcium influx across plasma membranes bypassing voltage-sensitive channels (Meyer & Cooper, 1981). As shown in Table 2, suboptimal concentrations of A23187 (e.g., 2 and 10 µg/ml) release significantly more [3H]-ACh in 6-month-old rats than in 24-month-old animals, while no difference in release is observed at 20 µg/ml of the ionophore. There is no age-related difference in A23187 (5 µg/ml)-induced $^{45}Ca^{2+}$ influx in rat cortical synaptosomes under these conditions. These results suggest that the age-related decrement in ACh release is due at least in part to the reduced potency of calcium ions at triggering sites but not to the number of release-triggering sites or amount of releasable [3H]-ACh.

TABLE 3

Effects of Aging on Ionophore-Induced $^{45}Ca^{2+}$ Influx into Rat Cortical Synaptosomes

Treatment	$^{45}Ca^{2+}$ Uptake (nmol/mg protein/min)	
	6 Months	24 Months
None	0.21 ± 0.04	0.17 ± 0.03
A23187 (5 µg/ml)	1.54 ± 0.23	1.78 ± 0.21

Rat cortical synaptosomes from each group of rats were prepared and incubated at 37° for 5 minutes with the specified concentration of A23187. $^{45}Ca^{2+}$ was added at the beginning of the incubation as a tracer for the 1 mM buffer concentration of calcium. Synaptosomes were then washed with cold buffer containing 1 mM cobalt ions by vacuum filtration over Millipore filters (0.45 micron diameter) and the $^{45}Ca^{2+}$ taken up by the tissues measured by liquid scintillation spectrophotometry. All values are means ± SEM of at least three determinations.

Aging and Intracellular Mobilization of Calcium Ions by Ouabain

To ascertain whether aging affects the ability of intracellular sodium to mobilize calcium ions in rat cortical cholinergic synaptosomes, we studied the ouabain-induced release of ACh. Ouabain increases the efflux of [3H]-ACh from this preparation in the absense of extracellular calcium ions. Sodium accumulation appears to mobilize intracellular calcium ions, thereby obviating the need for extracellular calcium. Table 4 shows that ouabain increases [3H]-ACh release in 6- and 24-month-old rat synaptosomes to a similar extent in calcium-free buffers suggesting that this Na^+, K^+-ATPase inhibitor is able to mobilize intracellular calcium in both groups of animals. It is interesting to note that the older tissues were able to release as much [3H]-ACh in the presence of ouabain even though they were less sensitive to calcium ions taken up via A23187 treatment. This result suggests that ouabain mobilizes more intracellular calcium in the older tissues to elicit the same amount of ACh release as in the younger tissues. Consistent with this hypothesis is the observation that neuronal intracellular calcium levels appear to increase with age in the rat brain (Landfield & Pitler, 1984).

TABLE 4

Effects of Aging on the Ouabain and 4-Aminopyridine-Induced Release of ACh from Rat Cortical Synaptosomes

Treatment	[³H]-ACh Release (dpm/mg Protein)	
	6 Months	24 Months
1 mM CaCl₂ buffer		
None	660 ± 20	600 ± 50
100 μM Ouabain	1050 ± 60	880 ± 50
10 mM 4-Aminopyridine	1400 ± 70	1410 ± 80
Calcium-free buffer		
None	350 ± 20	340 ± 10
100 μM Ouabain	650 ± 50	540 ± 20

Rat cortical synaptosomes were treated as described in Table 2, except that the drug treatments were altered as specified here. All values are means ± SEM of six values.

Aging and Presynaptic Receptors

To determine whether aging interfered with the muscarinic modulation of ACh release from rat cortical synaptosomes, we examined the effects of various concentrations of the agonist oxotremorine on this process. We found that there was no significant difference in the oxotremorine-induced modulation of spontaneous or K^+-induced [³H]-ACh release in 6-month-old versus 24-month-old rat cortical synaptosomes over an extended dose-response curve for the drug. This result suggests that M_2 muscarinic receptor antagonists may be functional with respect to selectively increasing ACh release in old as well as young cholinergic neurons.

Since muscarinic receptors have been shown to hyperpolarize some cells by activating K^+ channels (North & Tokimasa, 1983), we studied whether these channels may also be involved in the muscarinic modulation of ACh release. We found that the potassium channel blocker, 4-aminopyridine (4-AP), blocked the muscarinic modulation of [³H]-ACh release at a concentration (10mM) that significantly increased transmitter release, while 1 mM 4-AP had no

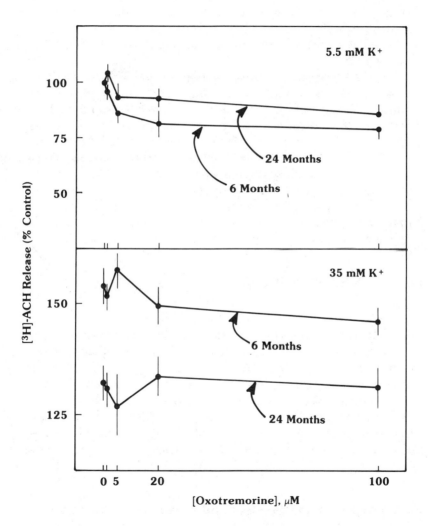

Figure 2. Rat cortical synaptosomes that were preloaded with [³H]-ACh were washed and incubated for 5 minutes in the presence (bottom panel) or absence (top panel) of 35 mM K⁺ and the specified oxotremorine concentration. The [³H]-ACh released into the medium was then measured and expressed as the mean ± SEM of the percent untreated control value (N = 5 animals/group). Control values were 12,400 ± 800 dpm/mg protein for 6-month old animals and 11,700 ± 1,100 dpm/mg protein for 24-month old animals.

effect on either process. 4-Aminopyridine is known to block potassium channels that normally repolarize nerve terminals after firing. This channel blockade may underlie its ability to depolarize terminals and greatly increase transmitter release in a dose-dependent manner. Our finding that 4-AP-induced release-modulation and ACh release occur at similar concentrations is consistent with the hypothesis that a single process, such as the blockade of K^+ channels may underlie both.

Since 4-AP not only increased synaptosomal [3H]-ACh release but also blocked presynaptic muscarinic receptors that normally attenuate ACh release, we examined whether this drug may have differential effects on transmitter release in young versus old tissues. Table 4 shows that there was no significant difference in 4-AP-induced [3H]-ACh release in 6-month-old versus 24-month-old rats. These results are similar to those of Gibson and Peterson (1983) with the more potent analogue 3,4-diaminopyridine. They suggest that 4-AP, which has been used to treat neuromuscular diseases of cholinergic hypofunction such as Eaton-Lambert's Syndrome, may be useful for treating central cholinergic hypofunction as well.

POSTSYNAPTIC ASPECTS

Although there is a 30% to 40% loss of cortical neuronal cell bodies during AD, many studies have found no change in muscarinic receptor binding sites when compared to controls (normal aging is associated with a less severe cortical loss). (See Bartus et al., 1982, for review of binding studies.) Recent studies have suggested that there is a small decrease in muscarinic sites that can be attributed to the loss of presynaptic M_2 autoreceptor sites (Mash et al., in press). Thus, postsynaptic M_1 receptors and the cholinoreceptive structures in the cerebral cortex and hippocampus appear to be present in senescent and AD brains.

Postsynaptic Aspects—Second Messenger Response

Since the cholinergic receptive structures appear to be present in AD, one approach to enhancing cholinergic neurotransmission is to increase or mimic the response to M_1 stimulation. Although the second messenger involved in muscarinic M_1 excitation is not

absolutely clear, our own studies of muscarinic receptor activation
suggest that hydrolysis of inositol phospholipids is an important
second messenger response to M_1 cholinergic stimulation as shown

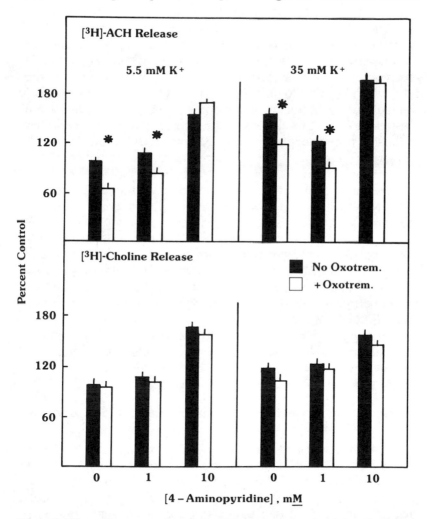

Figure 3. Effects of 4-aminopyridine on the oxotremorine-induced inhibition of spontaneous and K^+-induced release of [^{3}H]-ACh and [^{3}H]-choline. Synaptosomes were loaded with
labelled choline and ACh and then incubated for 2.5 minutes at 37° in the presence or absence of the specified 4-aminopyridine concentration, K^+-concentration, and oxotremorine
(100 μM oxotremorine in 5.5 mM K^+ buffer, 500 μM oxotremorine in 35mM K^+ buffer).
The released [^{3}H]-ACh and [^{3}H]-choline was measured and expressed here as mean $\pm$ SEM
of six values (control = 83,410 dpm/mg protein. *$p < 0.05$ compared to corresponding
oxotremorine-free.

in Figure 1. The regional distribution of M_1 receptor binding sites in brain corresponds with the magnitude of carbachol stimulated inositol lipid hydrolysis (e.g., cortex = hippocampus >hypothalamus = brain stem > cerebellum) (Gonzales & Crews, 1984). In addition, the M_1 selective antagonist, pirenzepine, inhibits carbachol-stimulated inositol lipid hydrolysis with an ED_{50} of approximately 1 μM. Variations in agonist efficacy also support the hypothesis that excitatory M_1 receptors are coupled to inositol phospholipid hydrolysis. Oxotremorine, which appears to be a full agonist at the M_2 receptor, is only weakly effective at shifting M_1 receptor binding sites to agonist conformations and is a weak partial agonist at stimulating the hydrolysis of inositol phospholipids (Fisher, Klinger, & Agranoff, 1983). As shown in Figure 4, carbachol and methacholine are full agonists at activating inositide hydrolysis whereas bethanechol and oxotremorine are partial agonists. Characteristic of other partial agonists, oxotremorine will actually block the ability of carbachol to stimulate inositol lipids hydrolysis above oxotremorine's own maximum response (Gonzales & Crews, 1984). Preliminary studies with the hippocampal slice preparation suggest that oxotremorine is a weak partial agonist compared to carbachol at exciting pyramidal cell neurons. Furthermore, the dose response curves for carbachol-stimulated hippocampal pyramidal cell excitation closely parallel the carbachol dose response curve for inositol lipid hydrolysis. Taken together, these studies suggest that muscarinic M_1 receptors on pyramidal cells stimulate inositol lipid hydrolysis, which results in an excitation of pyramidal cells.

Postsynaptic Aspects—The Phosphoinositide Cascade

The hydrolysis of inositol phospholipids represents the initial event in a cascade that is activated by a wide variety of receptors in a number of tissues. Inositol phospholipids include three phospholipids that differ in the number of phosphate groups on the inositol sugar head group. Phosphatidylinositol is by far the predominate phosphoinositide. The other two phosphoinositides are formed by the sequential phosphorylation of the hydroxyl groups of the 4- and 5-positions of phosphatidylinositol. Studies of nonneuronal tissues have suggested that phosphatidylinositol 4-phosphate, and phosphatidylinositol 4,5-bisphosphate may be broken down first following receptor activation of phospholipase(s) C, (i.e., phosphoinositide phosphodiesterases) which hydrolyze the inositol lipids into diacylglycerol and inositol polyphosphates (Berridge, Dawson, Downes, Heslop, & Irvine, 1983; Putney et al., 1983). Inositol 1,4,5-triphosphate has been shown to mobilize internal stores of calcium in some tissues

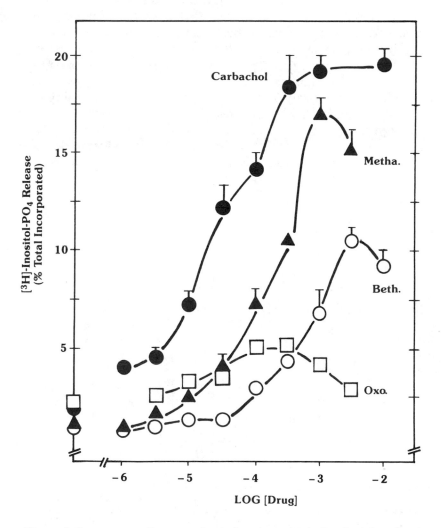

Figure 4. Concentration effect curves for cholinergic agonists for the stimulation of inositide breakdown. The release of [^{3}H]-inositol phosphates after 60 minutes in the presence of agonist was determined as described by Gonzales and Crews (1984). Data are the compilation of five separate experiments (means ± SEM of triplicates).
Metha.=methacholine; Beth.=bethanechol; Oxo.=oxotremorine.

(see Berridge, 1983, for review). Any of the three phosphoinositides can be hydrolyzed to diacylglyerol, which activates a phosphatidyl-serine-calcium dependent protein kinase (PS-Ca kinase) that has extremely high activity in brain tissue (see Figure 1; Hirasawa & Nishizuka, 1985). The activation of protein kinases and/or other events could be linked to the changes in membrane conductance associated with muscarinic receptor activation (see Figure 1). It is not clear how the muscarinic stimulation of phosphoinositide hydrolysis relates to the inhibition of potassium conductance and pyramidal cell excitation in brain.

In addition to muscarinic cholinergic receptors, norepinephrine, histamine, 5-hydroxytryptamine, vasopressin, and several other peptides stimulate phosphoinositide turnover. In brain tissue, norepinephrine and carbachol are the two most active agents at stimulating phosphoinositide breakdown (Gonzales & Crews, 1985). This is in-

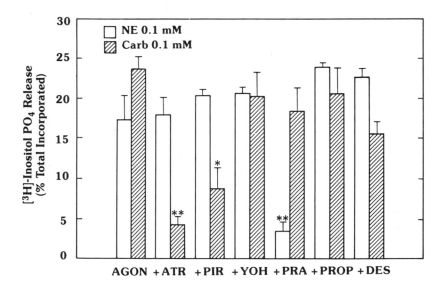

Figure 5. Effects of cholinergic and adrenergic antagonists on carbachol and norepinephrine stimulated inositide breakdown. Cortical slices were prepared and incubated with 0.1 μM [^{3}H]-inositol for 1 hour as described by Gonzales and Crews (1984). After washing out the [^{3}H]-inositol, slices were incubated with the various antagonists and other agents shown (1 μM). After 10 minutes, the slices were exposed to agonists. None of the antagonists by themselves affected the nonstimulated release of inositol phosphates. Release in the absence of carbachol or norepinephrine was subtracted from that in their presence. Results are presented as the mean $\pm$ SEM of triplicates from a single slice preparation. Asterisks represent a significant difference from control (ANOVA, follwed by Newmans-Keuls test; *$p<0.05$, **$p<0.01$).

teresting since morphologic and biochemical data suggest that noradrenergic neurons may be damaged in AD as well as cholinergic neurons. The response to both agonists appears to be primarily neuronal since norepinephrine and carbachol have a several-fold larger response in primary cultures enriched with neurons when compared to cultures enriched with glial cells (Gonzales, Feldstein, Crews, & Raizada, 1986). Norepinephrine stimulates phosphoinositide hydrolysis through the alpha$_1$ receptor. Prazosin, the selective alpha$_1$ antagonist, blocks the response, whereas yohimbine and propranolol, alpha$_2$ and beta antagonists, respectively, do not affect the response to norepinephrine. When norepinephrine and carbachol are added to brain slices together, the hydrolysis of phosphoinositides is increased in an additive manner in the striatum, olfactory bulb, spinal cord, and brain stem (Gonzales & Crews, 1985). However, in the cerebral cortex and particularly in the hippocam-

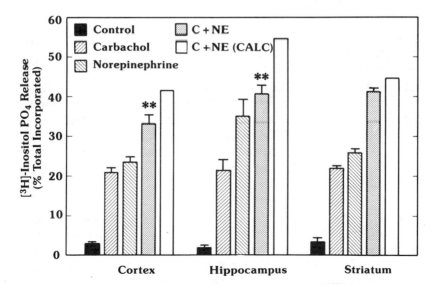

Figure 6. Interaction between carbachol and norepinephrine in cerebral cortex, hippocampus, and striatum. Slices prepared from each region were labelled with [^{3}H]-inositol and then stimulated with 1 mM carbachol, 100 μM norepinephrine, or both for 60 minutes. Values represent the means $\pm$ SEM of 7 determinations with three separate tissue preparations. Each separate slice preparation contained tissue pooled from three rats. The open bars represent the calculated sum of carbachol and norepinephrine alone. An asterisk over the combination of carbachol and norepinephrine indicates that the interaction term in factorial analysis was significantly less than additive ($p < 0.05$).

pus, the effects of norepinephrine and carbachol are much less than additive. One possible explanation for this finding of less than additivity is that the muscarinic and alpha$_1$ receptors are on the same cells and that these two receptors share the same pool of phosphoinositides. If this is the case, activation of alpha$_1$ and muscarinic receptors should produce the same effect on nerve firing. Since the cerebral cortex and hippocampus appear to be the two brain regions where cholinergic transmission is difficient in AD, it is possible that alpha$_1$ agonists may be used to mimic the effects of ACh. Combinations of alpha$_1$ agonists and muscarinic M$_1$ agonists might be effective in the hippocampus and cortex, since in these brain regions they may act on the same nerve cells and are likely to be additive at less than maximal concentrations.

Postsynaptic Aspects—Peptides and Other Modulators

A large number of peptides, including vasopressin and adrenocorticotropin (ACTH), can activate phosphoinositide turnover in brain and other tissues (Berridge, 1983). Almost 20 years ago, deWied first studied these peptides in one-trial avoidance learning situations in rats and found an involvement with learning and memory. These basic findings have been supported by numerous studies in which variations on this theme, by the use of analogues and newly synthesized agonists and antagonists, have been tested supporting the enhancement of learning processes by ACTH and vasopressin (deWied, Witter, & Greven, 1975; Manning & Sawyer, 1984). Although the peptide effect on phosphoinositide hydrolysis in brain is much smaller than that found with cholinergic or adrenergic stimulation, the response to vasopressin in the liver is equal to or greater than the response to norepinephrine as seen in Table 5. The distribution of peptides and their receptors in brain is much more discrete than that of ACh or norepinephrine. It is possible that vasopressin and ACTH may act primarily on pyramidal cells in the cortex and hippocampus while not acting on the large number of other neuronal cell types in slices. Thus, it is possible that peptide stimulation of phosphoinositide hydrolysis in the cerebral cortex is small because only a small fraction of cells is responding. The pyramidal cell in the cortex and hippocampus may be the key site of action, and this restricted distri-

TABLE 5

Effects of Peptides on Inositol Phosphate Hydrolysis

	% of Control	N
Cerebral Cortex		
Control	100 ± 19	8
NE	785 ± 134	3
Carbachol	936 ± 225	6
Somatostatin	255 ± 39	2
ACTH	251 ± 10	3
Substance P	216 ± 44	4
AVP	181 ± 63	2
CCK	70 ± ---	1
Liver		
Control	100 ± 26	5
NE	995 ± 12	2
AVP	1402 ± 343	5

Slices from cerebral cortex or liver were incubated with [^{3}H]inositol for 60 minutes as described by Gonzales and Crews, 1984. Agonists were added for 60 minutes and the accumulation of inositol phosphates determined. Data are presented as % of control for each experiment. The number of separate slice preparations (each a mean ± SEM in triplicate) is shown as N. NE is norepinephrine (100 µM), carbachol is 1 mM. All peptides are 1 µM ACTH=adrenocorticotropin; AVP=arginine vasopressin; CCK=cholecystokinin.

bution could provide selectivity to the action of peptides.

Another potential site of action of peptides is modulation of the response to ACh. Vasoactive intestinal peptide (VIP) has been shown to increase the response to ACh in salivary glands by increasing muscarinic receptor affinity (Lundberg, Hedlund, & Bartfai, 1982). The salivary gland response appears to be mediated by phosphoinositide hydrolysis; however, in a few experiments in brain slices we have not seen an enhanced response to carbachol with VIP. It is possible that other agents will alter muscarinic receptors to enhance responsiveness. ACTH has been reported to enhance the activity of phosphatidylinositol 4-phosphate kinase, the enzyme that synthesizes phosphatidylinositol 4,5-bisphosphate (see van Dongen, Zwiers, Oestreicher, & Gispen, 1985 for review). Since this is suggested to be the phosphoinositide hydrolyzed during agonist activation, ACTH may be able to enhance the response to cholinergic stimulation by increasing the synthesis of this key polyphosphoinositide.

Other methods that might increase the absolute amounts of the polyphosphoinositides also represent an approach to enhancing the response to ACh. Cells seem to contain a relatively small receptor-sensitive pool of inositol lipids, perhaps that located in the plasma membrane and that is separate from the remaining phosphoinositides (Billah & Lapetina, 1982; Fain & Berridge, 1979; Monaco, 1982; Monaco & Woods, 1983; Shukla & Hanahan, 1982). The hormone-sensitive pool amounts to about 8% of membrane phosphoinositides in the insect salivary gland (Fain & Berridge, 1979) and about 17% in rat mammary tumor cells (Monaco, 1982). Depletion of this pool can inactivate the receptor-activated response. A high level of myo-inositol may be important for the maintenance of the response. In endoneurium, a small reduction in the level of myo-inositol results in a large decline in energy utilization, which returns to normal when myo-inositol is restored (Simmons, Winegrad, & Martin, 1982). The function of the alpha$_1$ receptor in regenerating liver is impaired 3 days after hepatectomy. However, this loss in sensitivity can be prevented by adding free inositol (Huerata-Bahena & Garcia-Sainz, 1983). It is possible that large amounts of inositol may be useful in AD patients. The critical factor appears to be to increase the level of polyphosphoinositides in the receptor-sensitive pool. Gonzales and Crews (1985) were able to increase the synthesis of phosphoinositides in brain slices severalfold with manganese. However, the polyphosphoinositides did not increase in content and the muscarinic stimulation of phosphoinositide hydrolysis was not increased. Apparently the receptor-sensitive pool of phosphoinositides was not increased. Thus, peptides and other agents may be used to modulate the muscarinic response by changing the binding site and/or by increasing the receptor sensitive pool of inositol lipids.

Postsynaptic Aspects: Protein Kinase and Membranes

The receptor-activated breakdown of the inositol lipids results in the formation of diacylglycerol as well as the inositol phosphates.

Diacylglycerol activates a phosphatidylserine-calcium dependent protein kinase (PS-Ca kinase) by increasing the affinity for calcium and phosphatidylserine. PS-Ca kinase has very high activity in brain (see Hirasawa & Nishizuka, 1985 for review). The cerebral cortex and hippocampus are two of the highest activity brain regions. Recent studies have shown that phorbol esters or intracellular injection of the activated PS-Ca kinase itself can increase the height of action potentials generated by a negative current in bag cell neurons of Aplysia (DeReimer, Albert, Strong, Greengard, & Kaczmarek, 1984). These studies suggest that activation of this kinase can lead to changes in membrane conductances. Since muscarinic stimulation of phosphoinositide hydrolysis is likely to activate the PS-Ca kinase, agents that either directly activate the kinase or enhance activation may mimic and/or increase muscarinic responses. The phorbol esters represent a group of compounds that are direct activators of PS-Ca kinase. These compounds are tumor promoters likely to be excessively active for therapeutic potential. However, it may be possible to separate the tumor promoting activity from the PS-Ca kinase activity. Phosphatidylserine represents another possibility. The composition of the membrane influences the activity of the PS-Ca kinase and the ability of diacylglycerol to activate the kinase. Phosphatidylserine treatment could increase the content of this lipid in neuronal membranes and thereby enhance the activation of the kinase by diacylglycerol. This would have the advantage of increasing the response to endogenously released ACh and would be additive with any treatments that enhanced the hydrolysis of phosphoinositides.

Postsynaptic Aspects—Electrophysiological Responses

Although the muscarinic M_1 sites appear to be present in the brains of AD patients, there may be changes in the responsiveness of these structures. Golgi preparations on normal senescent brains have found that there is a progressive loss of the dendritic arbor of at least some pyramidal cells (Scheibel, 1979), although some pyramidal cells may still have a complete aborization that is still growing (Buell & Coleman, 1979). In AD patients, the loss of dendritic aborization is exaggerated. In addition to the decreased dendritic aborization, there is progressive loss of dendritic spines in normal aging and a more severe loss in AD (Mehraein, Yamada, & Tarnowska-

Dziduszko, 1975). The dendritic tree and resident dendritic spines appear to be important structures for signal transmission. Cerebral cortical and hippocampal pyramidal cells have many inputs preferentially sited on the distal elements of the dendritic tree (Shepherd, 1979, pp. 362-364). Dendritic spines have been suggested to be subject to modifiability depending on the synaptic input. Thus, deprivation of visual input leads to deformation of dendrites and to losses in dendritic spines (Globus & Scheibel, 1967; Valverde, 1967). The changes in dendritic structure of cortical pyramidal cells may be secondary to decreases in synaptic input and/or changes in membrane structure. Membrane structure and phospholipid metabolism are intimately involved in both secretion and receptor activation (Crews, 1982; Shinitzky, Heron, & Samuel, 1983). Membrane lipid turnover, composition, and bilayer structure change during aging (Crews, Calderini, Battistella, & Toffano, 1984; Rouser, Kritchevsky, Yamamoto, & Baxter, 1972; Shinitzky et al., 1983). One of the most consistent findings is an increased membrane cholesterol. Studies of human, rat, and mouse brain have shown that the content of

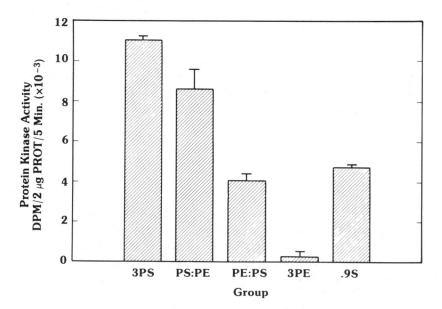

Figure 7. Effect of membrane composition on phosphatidylserine-calcium dependent protein kinase activity. PS, CA^{++} PK was partially purified from rat brain and assayed according to Wise et al. (1982). Shown is the incorporation of ^{32}P into histone H$_2$, which was used as substrate.

cholesterol in membrane increases during aging (see Crews et al., 1982; Rouser et al., 1972; Shinitzky et al., 1983, for review). This change in membrane lipids markedly alters membrane fluidity and a variety of membrane proteins and their functions. Changes in membrane properties that occur during aging could alter ACh release as well as the response to ACh. These changes could stress cholinergic neurons causing them to degenerate in AD patients. Studies on brain membrane changes in AD patients have not been done. An exaggeration of the changes known to occur during senescence would markedly decrease the muscarinic excitatory responses in the hippocampus and cerebral cortex.

The excitatory muscarinic response is due to an inhibition of potassium conductance (Brown, 1984). Muscarinic inhibition of potassium conductance shortens the afterhyperpolarization which permits cells to fire more rapidly. This allows ACh to sensitize cells to other excitatory inputs and promotes multiple bursts of action potentials (North & Tokimasa, 1984). As mentioned above, the stimulatory effects of ACh on hippocampal pyramidal cells is decreased in senescent rats (Lippa et al., 1980). Intracellular studies on hippocampal pyramidal cells indicated that the prolonged depolarization following ACh stimulation was markedly reduced in senescent rats (Segal, 1982). This is consistent with a reduced ability of ACh to inhibit potassium conductance and could be related to changes in membrane lipids that occur during aging. Crews et al. (1982) have shown that slight increases in hippocampal cholesterol can markedly inhibit the response of hippocampal pyramidal cells to carbachol. Since the muscarinic binding site appears to be resistant to changes in membrane cholesterol (Hershkowitz, Heron, Samuel, & Shinitzky, 1982), cholesterol seems to act at a site distal to the agonist-receptor complex. Taken together, these data suggest that changes in membrane properties may uncouple the muscarinic receptor and reduce the response to ACh in senescent pyramidal cells. Recent studies have shown that certain lipid mixtures can reverse the changes in membrane fluidity and cholesterol that occur during aging. Active lipid is a mixture of lipids (e.g., neutral lipids/phosphatidylcholine/phosphatidylethanolamine 7/2/1), which has been shown to decrease the cholesterol content of circulating human lymphocytes and to increase their membrane fluidity and receptor responsiveness (Shinitzky, 1985). In addition, treatment of old mice with an oil fraction from plants, (e.g., membrane modulating lipid that contains 88% to 93% unsaturated fatty acids and has been shown to reverse the increases in brain cholesterol that occur during aging) (Kessler, A.R., Kessler, B., & Shlomo, 1985). Thus, lipid diets that reduce membrane cholesterol may reverse the decline in pyramidal cell muscarinic response that occurs during aging and thereby enhance cholinergic neurotransmission.

Recent studies on hippocampal pyramidal cells have found changes in other electrical properties during aging. The duration of the afterhyperpolarization following bursts of spikes due to an intracellular current pulse is increased in aged rats (Landfield & Pitler, 1984). This afterhyperpolarization is related to calcium-activated potassium conductance that increases as cellular calcium levels increase secondary to depolarization. Elevation of extracellular calcium levels can increase the duration of the afterhyperpolarization in pyramidal cells from young rats. High Mg^{++}:low Ca^{++} medium can shorten the afterhyperpolarizations of senescent pyramidal cells to those of young hippocampal cells. Landfield and Pitler (1984) concluded that the increased duration of the afterhyperpolarization is due to an increase in intracellular calcium. This has an overall inhibitory effect on pyramidal cell firing and could be due to an increased influx and/or a decreased extrusion or buffering of calcium. An increased calcium influx seems unlikely since studies have reported a decreased calcium influx during aging. In contrast, a decrease in calcium pumping has been reported during aging and following *in vitro* increases in membrane cholesterol. Further, increased cholesterol has been shown to decrease the spontaneous activity of Aplysia neurons (Stephens & Shinitzky, 1977). Thus, changes in membrane cholesterol may decrease both the excitatory response to ACh as well as the general excitability of pyramidal cells. The relationship between the reduced response to acetylcholine and the increased afterhyperpolarization is not clear. Both of these phenomena, which would tend to inhibit excitation of pyramidal cells, are related to changes in membrane potassium conductance, and could be secondary to increases in membrane cholesterol. Clearly, one potential approach to AD and age-related memory deficits is the use of membrane-modifying agents like those mentioned above.

SUMMARY AND RECOMMENDATIONS

In this chapter we present a hypothetical model of the hippocampal and cortical cholinergic synapse (see Figure 1). Both presynaptic and postsynaptic decreases in cholinergic neurotransmission appear to occur during aging. The presynaptic deficit and possibly the post-synaptic deficit are exaggerated in patients with AD. Agents that might enhance cholinergic transmission are listed below.

1. Presynaptic M_2 antagonists and postsynaptic M_1 agonists represent one potential approach. As discussed above, the efficacy of muscarinic agonists varies considerably between M_1 and M_2 receptors. It is likely that new compounds will better define receptor subtypes in the future. One possible problem with postsynaptic M_1 agonists could be the tonic stimulation that an agonist would present versus rhythmic sensory-stimulated input that may be important for keying memory in normal cholinergic transmission.

2. Agents that increase the release of ACh would provide for ap-propriate changes in nerve firing. Thus, compounds such as the aminopyridines that enhance release and inactivate M_2 inhibition may be useful in enhancing ACh release. Furthermore, blockade of potassium channels might have beneficial postsynaptic actions by increasing excitability. These treatments could be combined with augmented choline (or lecithin) treatments to maximize ACh syn-thesis and release. As mentioned above, these compounds are cur-rently used clinically for peripheral cholinergic hypofunction.

3. In addition to direct cholinergic agonists, adrenergic alpha$_1$ agonists and certain peptides might be useful in mimicking the cholinergic response and thereby effectively enhancing transmission.

4. Increased sensitivity of the cholinergic response through modu-lation is likely to represent a safe and complete therapy. Peptides appear to have the ability to modulate the ACh response in some tissues. However, which peptides might modulate cortical and hippo-campal responses is not clear. Inositol itself might be useful if it in-creases the phosphoinositides in the receptor-sensitive pool.

5. Lipids and other agents that reverse or modify the membrane changes that occur during aging are likely to benefit AD patients. It is possible that changes in membrane structure underlie both the decrease in ACh release and the decreased responsiveness to ACh that occur during normal aging. If these membrane changes were exaggerated in AD, it could cause excessive excitation of long forebrain cholinergic neurons in an effort to compensate for the loss of synaptic transmission. Excessive excitation might lead to degeneration of these forebrain cholinergic neurons. In any case, it is clear that several aspects of cholinergic transmission, both presynaptic and postsynap-tic, involve changes in membrane lipids. There are several agents

that might be useful for enhancing cholinergic neurotransmission by acting on membranes. Phosphatidylserine may act to enhance the activity of PS-Ca kinase. Active lipid may reverse the fluidity and cholesterol changes that appear to reduce cholinergic responsiveness. Although lipids represent a new class of drugs, they are clearly a potential approach to reversing those effects of aging secondary to changes in membranes.

Thus, there are a variety of agents that may be useful in treating AD. Drugs acting presynaptically should be carefully evaluated for their postsynaptic actions and vice versa. In many cases, both presynaptic and postsynaptic drugs may be given simultaneously for additive therapeutic effects. Thus, muscarinic M_2 antagonists in combination with modulating peptides that enhance ACh responsiveness and lipids that both provide choline for ACh synthesis as well as enhance the response to ACh might provide therapeutic benefits not found with any agent alone. Although the drugs of choice are not currently known, a dedicated effort at enhancing cholinergic neurotransmission is likely to elucidate such drugs in the near future. These compounds should provide therapeutic relief from any of the symptoms of AD similar to the benefits observed in Parkinson's disease with l-dihydroxyphenylalanine (L-DOPA). The benefit these compounds might have on the degeneration of central cholinergic neurons is not known.

REFERENCES

Bartus, R.T., Dean, R.L., Beer, B., & Lippa, A.S. (1982). The cholinergic hypothesis of geriatric memory dysfunction. *Science, 217*, 408-417.

Berridge, M.J. (1983). Rapid accumulation of inositol trisphosphate reveals that agonists hydrolyse polyphosphoinositides instead of phosphatidylinositol. *Biochemistry Journal, 212*, 849-858.

Berridge, M.J., Dawson, R.M.C., Downes, C.P., Heslop, J.P., & Irvine, R.F. (1983). Changes in the levels of inositol phosphates after agonist-dependent hydrolysis of membrane phosphoinositides. *Biochemical Journal, 212,* 473-482.

Billah, M.M., & Lapetina, E.G. (1982). Evidence for multiple metabolic pools of phosphatidylinositol in stimulated platelets. *Journal of Biological Chemistry, 257*(20), 11856-11859.

Bowen, D.M. (1980). Biochemical evidence for nerve cell changes in senile dementia. *Aging of the Brain and Dementia, 13,* 127-138.

Brown, D.A. (1984). Muscarinic excitation of sympathetic and central neurones. *Trends in Pharmacological Sciences,* Supplement (January 1984), 32-34.

Buckley, N., & Burnstock, G. (1984). Autoradiographic localization of peripheral muscarinic receptors. *Trends in Pharmacological Sciences,* Supplement (January 1984), 55-59.

Buell, S.J., & Coleman, P.D. (1979). Dendritic growth in the aged human brain and failure of growth in senile dementia. *Science, 206,* 854-856.

Calderini, G., Bonetti, A.C., Battistella, A., Crews, F.T., & Toffano, G. (1983). Biochemical changes of rat brain membranes with aging. *Neurochemical Research, 8*(4), 483-492.

Collier, B., & Ilson, D. (1977). The effect of preganglionic nerve stimulation on the accumulation of certain analogues of choline by a sympathetic ganglion. *Journal of Physiology, 264,* 489-509.

Cooper, J.R., & Meyer, E.M. (1984). Possible mechanisms involved in the release and modulation of release of neuroactive agents. *Neurochemistry International, 6,* 419-433.

Coyle, J.T., Price, D.L., & DeLong, M.R. (1983). Alzheimer's disease: A disorder of cortical cholinergic innervation. *Science, 219*(4589), 1184-1190.

Crews, F.T. (1982). Rapid changes in phospholipid metabolism during secretion and receptor activation. *International Review of Neurobiology, 23,* 141-163.

Crews, F.T., Calderini, G., Battistella, A., & Toffano, G. (1981). Age dependent changes in the methylation of rat brain phospholipids. *Brain Research, 229,* 256-259.

Crews, F.T., Comacho, A., Phillips, I., Tjeenk Willink, E.C., Calderini, G., Hirata, F., Alexrod, J., McGivney, A., & Siraganian, R. (1982). Effects of membrane fluidity on mast cell and nerve cell function. In L. Horrocks, G.B. Ansell, & G. Porcellati (Eds.), *Phospholipids* in the nervous system (pp. 21-36). New York: Raven Press.

DeReimer, S.A., Albert, K.A., Strong, J.A., Greengard, P., & Kaczmarek, L.K. (1984). Electrophysiological effects of phorbol ester and protein kinase C on the BAC cell neurons of aplysia. Society for Neuroscience Abstracts, 10, 867.

deWied, D., Witter, A., & Greven, H.M. (1975). Behaviorally active ACTH analogues. Biochemical Pharmacology, 24, 1467-1468.

Drachman, D.A. (1983). How normal aging relates to dementia: A critique and classification. In D. Samuel, S. Gershon, S. Algeri, V.E. Grimm, & G. Toffano (Eds.), Aging of the brain (pp. 19-32). New York: Raven Press.

Drachman, D.A., Glosser, G., Flemming, P., & Longnecker, G. (1981). Memory decline in the aged: Treatment with high dose lecithin. Neurology, 31, 101.

Drachman, D.A., & Leavitt, J. (1974). Human memory and the cholinergic system. A relationship to aging? Archives of Neurology, 30, 113-126.

Drachman, D.A., Noffsinger, D., Sahakian, K.S., & Flemming, P. (1980). Aging, memory and the cholinergic system: A study of dichotic listening. Neurobiology of Aging, 1, 39-47.

Fain, J.N., & Berridge, M.J. (1979). Relationship between phosphatidylinositol synthesis and recovery of 5 hydroxytroptamine-responsive Ca^{2+} flux in blowfly salivary glands. Biochemical Journal, 180, 655-661.

Fisher, S.K., Boast, C.A., & Agranoff, B.W. (1980). The muscarinic stimulation of phospholipid labeling in hippocampus is independent of its cholinergic input. Brain Research, 189, 284-288.

Fisher, S.K., Klinger, P.D., & Agranoff, B.W. (1983). Muscarinic agonist binding and phospholipid turnover in brain. Journal of Biological Chemistry, 258(12), 7358-7363.

Gibson, G.E., & Peterson, C. (1981). Aging decreases oxidative metabolism and the release and synthesis of acetylcholine. Journal of Neurochemistry, 37, 978-984.

Gibson, G.E., & Peterson, C. (1983). Amelioration of age-related neurochemical and behavioral deficits with 3,4-diaminopyridine. Neurobiology of Aging, 4, 25-30.

Globus, A., & Scheibel, A.B. (1967). The effect of visual deprivation on cortical neurons: A Golgi study. Experimental Neurology, 19, 331-345.

Gonzales, R.A., & Crews, F.T. (1984). Characterization of the cholinergic stimulation of phosphoinositide hydrolysis in rat brain slices. *Journal of Neuroscience, 4,* 3120-3127.

Gonzales, R.A., & Crews, F.T. (1985). Cholinergic and adrenergic stimulated inositide hydrolysis in brain: Interaction, regional distribution, and coupling mechanisms. *Journal of Neurochemistry, 45,* 1076-1084.

Gonzales, R.A. Feldstein, J.B., Crews, F.T., & Raizada, M.K. (1986). Receptor mediated inositide hydrolysis is a neuronal response: Comparison of primary neuronal and glial cultures. *Brain Research, 345,* 350-355.

Hershkowitz, M., Heron, D., Samuel, D., & Shinitzky, M. (1982). Modulation of protein phosphorylation and receptor binding in brain membranes by changes in lipid microciscosity: Implication for aging. *Progress in Brain Research, 56,* 419.

Hirasawa, K., & Nishizuka, Y. (1985). Autonomic pharmacology. *Annual Review of Pharmacology and Toxicology, 25,* 147-170.

Huerata-Bahena, J., & Garcia-Sainz, J.A. (1983). Inositol administration restores the sensitivity of liver cells formed during liver regeneration to $alpha_1$-adrenergic amines, vasopressin and angiotensin II. *Biochemica et Biophysica Acta, 763,* 125-128.

Kessler, A.R., Kessler, B., & Shlomo, Y. (1985). Changes in the cholesterol level, cholesterol-to-phospholipid mole ratio, and membrane lipid micro-viscosity in rat brain induced by age and a plant oil mixture. *Biochemical Pharmacology, 34*(7), 1121-1124.

Landfield, P.W., & Pitler, T.A. (1984). Prolonged calcium dependent afterhyperpolarizations in hippocampal neurons of aged rats. *Science, 226,* 1089-1092.

Lippa, A.S., Pelham, R.W., Beer, B., Critchett, D.J., Dean, R.L., & Bartus, R.T. (1980). Brain cholinergic dysfunction and memory in aged rats. *Neurobiology of Aging, 1,* 13-19.

Lundberg, J.M., Hedlund, B., & Bartfai, T. (1982). Vasoactive intestinal polypeptide enhances muscarinic ligand binding in cat submandibular salivary gland. *Nature, 295,* 147-179.

Manning, M., & Sawyer, O.W.H. (1984). Design and uses of selective agonists and antagonist analogs of the neuropeptides oxytocin and vasopressin. *Trends in Neurosciences, 7,* 6-9.

Marchbanks, R.M. (1982). Activation of presynaptic choline uptake by acetylcholine release. *Journal of Physiology, 78,* 373-378.

Mash, D.C., Flynn, D.D., & Potter, L.T. (in press). Loss of M_2 muscarine receptors in the cerebral cortex in Alzheimer's disease and with experimental cholinergic denervation. *Science.*

Mehraein, P., Yamada, M., & Tarnowska-Dziduszko, E. (1975). Quantitative study on dendrites and dendritic spines in Alzheimer's disease and senile dementia. In G.W. Kreutzberg (Ed.), *Advances in neurology: Vol. 12. Physiology and pathology of dendrites* (pp. 453-458). New York: Raven Press.

Meyer, E.M., & Cooper, J.R. (1981). Correlations between $Na+$, $K+$-ATPase activity and acetylcholine release in rat cortical synaptosomes. *Journal of Neurochemistry, 36,* 467-475.

Meyer, E.M., & Cooper, J.R. (in press). Role of sodium ions in the ouabain-induced release of acetylcholine in rat cortical synaptosomes. *Biochemical Pharmacology.*

Meyer, E.M., Engle, D.A., & Cooper, J.R. (1982). Acetylation and phosphorylation of choline in synaptosomes: Functional roles for low and high affinity choline uptake. *Neurochemical Research, 17,* 749-759.

Meyer, E.M., Momol, A.E., & Baker, S.P. (in press). Effects of aging on the atrial uptake, acetylation, and release of choline in rats. *Mechanisms of Ageing Research.*

Meyer, E.M., & Otero, D.H. (in press). Pharmacological and ionic characterization of the presynaptic and muscarinic modulation of acetylcholine release. *Journal of Neuroscience.*

Meyer, E.M., St. Onge, E., & Crews, F.T. (1984). Effects of aging on rat cortical presynaptic cholinergic processes. *Neurobiology of Aging, 5,* 315-317.

Monaco, M.E. (1982). The phosphatidylinositol cycle in WRK-1 cells. Evidence for a separate, hormone-sensitive phosphatidylinositol pool. *Journal of Biological Chemistry, 257,* 2137-2139.

Monaco, M.E., & Woods, D. (1983). Characterization of the hormone-sensitive phosphatidylinositol pool in WRK-1 cells. *Journal of Biological Chemistry, 258,* 14125-15129.

Nicholls, D.G., & Scott, I.D. (1980). The regulation of brain mitochondrial calcium-ion transport. The role of ATP in the discrimination between kinetic and membrane-potential-dependent calcium-ion efflux mechanisms. *Biochemistry Journal, 186,* 833-839.

North, R.A., & Tokimasa, T. (1983). Muscarinic activation of

K+-currents. *Journal of Physiology, 342,* 253-266.

North, R.A., & Tokimasa, T. (1984). Muscarinic suppression of calcium-activated potassium conductance. *Trends in Pharmacological Sciences,* Supplement (January 1984), 35-38.

Pedata, F., Slavikova, J., Kotas, A., & Pepeu, G. (1983). Acetylcholine release from rat cortical slices during postnatal development and aging. *Neurobiology of Aging, 4,* 31-35.

Perry, E.K., Tomlinson, B.E., Blessed, G., Bergmann, K., Gibson, P.H., & Perry, R.H. (1978). Correlation of cholinergic abnormalities with senile plaques and mental test scores in senile dementia. *British Medical Journal, 2,* 1457-1459.

Peterson, C., & Gibson, G.E. (1983). Aging and 3,4-diaminopyridine alter synaptosomal calcium uptake. *Journal of Biological Chemistry, 258,* 11482-11486.

Potter, L.T., Flynn, D.D., Hanchett, H.E., Kalinoski, D.L., Luber-Narod, J., & Mash, D.C. (1984). Independent M_1 and M_2 receptors: Ligands, autoradiography, and functions. *Trends in Pharmacological Sciences,* Supplement, (January 1984), 22-31.

Raiteri, M., Leardi, R., & Marchi, M. (1984). Heterogeneity of presynaptic muscarinic receptors regulation neurotransmitter release in the rat brain. *Journal of Pharmacology and Experimental Therapeutics, 228,* 209-214.

Reisine, T.D., Yamamura, H., Bird, E.D., & Enna, S.J. (1978). Pre- and postsynaptic neurochemical alterations in Alzheimer's disease. *Brain Research, 159,* 477-482.

Rouser, G., Kritchevsky, G., Yamanoto, A., & Baxter, D.F. (1972). Lipids in the nervous system of different species as a function of age: Brain, spinal cord peripheral nerve, purified whole cell preparations and subcellular particulates: Regulatory mechanisms and membrane structure. *Advances in Lipid Research, 10,* 261-360.

Scheibel, A.B. (1979). In R. Katzman (Ed.), *Congenital and acquired cognitive disorders research publications: Association for research in nervous and mental disease* (Vol. 57, pp. 107-122). New York: Raven Press.

Schroeder, F. (1984). Role of membrane lipid asymmetry in aging. *Neurobiology of Aging, 5,* 323-333.

Segal, M. (1982). Changes in neurotransmitter actions in the aged rat hippocampus. *Neurobiology of Aging, 3,* 121-124.

Shephard, G.M. (1979). *The synaptic organization of the brain (2nd ed.)*. New York: Oxford University Press.

Shinitzky, M. (1985). Membrane fluidity and cellular functions. In *Physiology of membrane fluidity* (Vol. 1, pp. 1-52). Boca Raton: CRC Press.

Shinitzky, M., Heron, D.S., & Samuel, D. (1983). Restoration of membrane fluidity and serotonin receptors in the aged mouse brain. In D. Samuel, S. Gershon, S. Algeri, V.E. Grimm, & G. Toffano (Eds.), *Aging of the brain* (pp. 329-336). New York: Raven Press.

Shukla, S.D., & Hanahan, D.J. (1982). AGEPC (platelet activating factor) induced stimulation of rabbit platelets: Effects on phosphatidylinositol, di- and tri-phosphoinositides and phosphatidic acid metabolism. *Biochemical and Biophysical Research Communications, 106*, 697-703.

Silbergeld, E.K. (1977). Sodium levels regulate calcium efflux from synaptosomal mitochondria. *Biochemical and Biophysical Research Communications, 77*, 464-469.

Simmons, D.A., Winegrad, A.I., & Martin, D.B. (1982). Significance of tissue myo-inositol concentrations in metabolic regulation of nerve. *Science, 217*, 848-851.

Stephens, C.L., & Shinitzky, M. (1977). Modulation of electrical activity in aplysia neurons by cholesterol. *Nature, 270*, 267-268.

Tucek, S. (1985). Regulation of acetylcholine synthesis in the brain. *Journal of Neurochemistry, 44*, 11-24.

Valverde, F. (1967). Apical dendritic spines of the visual cortex and light deprivation in the mouse. *Experimental Brain Research, 3*, 337-352.

van Dongen, C., Zwiers, H., Oestreicher, A.B., & Gispen, W.H. (1985). ACTH, phosphoprotein B-50 and phosphoinositide metabolism in rat brain membranes phospholipids in the nervous system. *Physiological Roles, 2*, 49-59.

Vroulis, G.A., Smith, R.C., Brinkman, S., Schooler, J., & Gordon, J. (1981). Effects of lecithin on memory in patients with senile dementia of the Alzheimer's type. *Psychopharmacology Bulletin, 17*, 127-128.

Weiss, S.J., McKinney, J.S., & Putney, J.W. (1982). Receptor-mediated net breakdown of phosphatidylinositol 4,5-bisphosphate in parotid acinar glands. *Biochemistry Journal, 206*, 555-560.

Whitehouse, P.J., Price, D.L., Struble, R.G., Clark, A.W., Coyle, J.T., & Delong, M.R. (1982). Alzheimer's disease and senile dementia: Loss of neurons in the basal forebrain. *Science, 215*(5), 1237-1239.

Wise, B.C., Raynor, R.L., & Kuo, J.F. (1982). Phospholipid-sensitive Ca^{2+}-dependent protein kinase from heart. *Journal of Biological Chemistry, 217*(14), 8481-8488.

Wurtman, R.J. (1985). Alzheimer's disease. *Scientific American, 252*(1), 62-74.

Yamamura, H.I., & Snyder, S.H. (1973). High affinity transport of choline into synaptosomes of rat brain. *Journal of Neurochemistry, 21*, 1355-1374.

17

Cholinergic Treatment for Age-Related Memory Disturbances: Dead or Barely Coming of Age?

Raymond T. Bartus, PhD, Reginald L. Dean, MS, and Stephen K. Fisher, PhD

"Perhaps never before in medical science has so much been expected by so many, so quickly, as that which has been asked of the cholinergic hypotheses. . ."
 (Liberal paraphrase of a famous British statesman; ca WW II)

In recent years, widespread scientific and clinical attention has been directed toward the cholinergic hypothesis of geriatric memory loss. This cholinergic hypothesis asserts that:

a. significant, functional disturbances in cholinergic activity occur in the brains of aged and especially demented subjects;

b. these disturbances play an important role in the memory loss and related cognitive problems associated with old age and dementia; and

c. proper enhancement or restoration of cholinergic function may significantly reduce the severity of cognitive loss.

Although considerable evidence supporting an important cholinergic role in age-related cognitive disturbances has accumulated (see recent reviews by Bartus, Dean, Beer, & Lippa, 1982; Bartus, Dean, Pontecorvo, & Flicker, 1985; Coyle, Price, & DeLong, 1983; Davies, 1981), controversy regarding the concept's value as an adequate explanation of the cognitive disturbances continues, while its potential utility for directing an effective treatment remains in doubt. This paper will attempt to focus on some of the more salient issues related to this controversy, particularly as they relate to potential treatment approaches. Furthermore specific suggestions for short-term and long-term research and development activities will be given from the perspective of current treatment goals.

TABLE 1

Major Criticisms of Cholinergic Hypothesis

    a. Philosophical—over simplified
    b. Empirical—lacks exclusivity
    c. Practical—clinical results disappointing

BRIEF HISTORICAL OVERVIEW AND CURRENT SUPPORT

It has been stated that what the cholinergic hypothesis may lack in definitive, quantitative evidence, it seems to enjoy in the diversity and breadth of its support (Bartus et al., 1985). The initial empirical foundation for the cholinergic hypothesis can be traced historically to at least four distinct areas of study: (a) clinical pharmacological observations; (b) animal psychopharmacological studies; (c) basic neuroscience research; and (d) biochemical determinations of human brain tissue, particularly from Alzheimer's patients. Starting from these four somewhat independent areas of investigation, thinking and research directives evolved relatively rapidly, converging into a mutually corroborated network of circumstantial support. Because a detailed description of the historical roots and contemporary evidence for the hypothesis has recently been presented elsewhere (Bartus et al., 1985), only a brief overview will be given here.

Early predescendent clinical records noted that drugs blocking central cholinergic activity produced a dementia-like syndrome with concomitant memory loss (Dundee & Pandit, 1972; Hollister, 1968; Longo, 1966). In fact, this knowledge was employed in the 1950's and 1960's when central anticholinergics were commonly combined with sedative/hypnotics during childbirth to produce an altered state of consciousness in the mother called "twilight sleep." This condition was characterized by an amnesia, involving marked reduction in the ability of the mothers to remember events occurring just prior to and during delivery (Lambrechts & Parkhouse, 1961; Pandit & Dundee, 1970). Interestingly, this phenomenon and therapeutic application was initially described very early in this century (Gauss, 1906) coincidentally close in time to when Alzheimer first published his now-classic case study of the disease which bears his name (Alzheimer, 1907).

In animal psychopharmocological literature, early work in the 1960's, characterizing the behavioral effects of centrally-acting drugs, also began to generate support for an important role of the cholinergic system in mediating learning and memory. Independently, the basic neuroscience research of the same era began to demonstrate that brain regions now known to be rich in cholinergic neuronal elements (e.g., hippocampus, septum, amygdala, and frontal cortex) seemed to play important roles in learning and memory phenomena (Douglas, 1967; Iversen, 1973, 1976; Warren & Akert, 1964). In fact, although it had been speculated very early, on the basis of animal psychopharmacology studies, that disturbances in hippocampal function may mediate the anticholinergic memory deficits, the existence of dense fields of muscarinic receptors in the hippocampus was not actually confirmed biochemically for another decade (Kuhar & Yamamura, 1975; Yamamura & Snyder, 1974; Yamamura, Kuhar & Snyder, 1974; Yamamura, Kuhar, Greenberg & Snyder, 1974).

Finally, attempts to characterize changes in the brains of Alzheimer's patients led to the observation of significantly reduced acetylcholinesterase (AChE) activity by Pope, Hess, and Lewin (1965). However, because of general controversy regarding the specificity of AChE as a reliable cholinergic marker in the brain, and the lack of attention paid by the authors toward the reduced cholinergic activity, this paper remained relatively obscure until recently.

More than 10 years after Pope et al. (1965) first described decreases in AChE activity, Bowen, Smith, White, and Davison (1976) reported their important findings that another cholinergic marker, choline acetyltransferase (CAT) activity, is dramatically reduced in Alzheimer's patients (relative to age-matched controls). They further reported that the reduction in CAT activity is widespread (involving several brain regions) and that some degree of specificity exists (since markers from several other neurotransmitter systems were not similarly reduced). Finally, they suggested that the decrease in CAT activity may be correlated with loss of cognitive function and density of plaques and tangles. Very soon after, similar findings were published by Davies and Maloney (1976) and Perry, E.K., Perry, R.H., Blessed, and Tomlinson (1977). Rightfully so, all three labs are generally credited for independently noting this landmark discovery.

The first formal suggestion that the specific cognitive deficits associated with advanced old age may be similar to those produced by anticholinergic drug treatment (in young subjects) was published by Drachman (1977) and Drachman and Leavitt (1974). Others have since drawn similar parallels between the memory deficits observed in demented Alzheimer's patients and the effects of anticholinergic drugs in young subjects (Davis, Mohs, Davis, Levy, et al., 1981; Smith & Swash, 1978).

Soon after the Drachman study, a series of papers was published showing similarly parallel memory deficits in aged monkeys (Bartus, Fleming, & Johnson, 1978) and scopolamine-treated young monkeys (Bartus & Johnson, 1976). Moreover, some degree of specificity of central muscarinic receptors was demonstrated also, since similar age-mimicking effects on memory were not obtained with a number of other drug treatments, including dopaminergic and beta adrenergic blockers (Bartus, 1978, 1980), several nonspecific and catecholaminergic stimulants (Bartus, 1979a), a nicotinic receptor blocker (Bartus, Dean, & Beer, 1983), and peripheral anticholinergics (Bartus, Dean, & Beer, 1983).

Since the time of these initial studies, considerably more evidence has accumulated, supporting an important cholinergic involvement in the memory loss of aging and dementia. This evidence has been extensively reviewed elsewhere (Bartus et al., 1982, 1985; Coyle et al., 1983) and, therefore, will not be detailed here. A brief survey of the research spanning the last several years, however, reveals that a number of significant neurochemical, electrophysiological, and morphologic changes have been observed in the cholinergic system of aged mammals and demented humans. Moreover, these changes contribute to, or are manifested by, functional deficiencies in central cholinergic activity; these functional deficiencies are correlated with the loss of memory in aged subjects as well as degree of dementia and incidence of neuropathology in demented subjects; similar, artificially-induced cholinergic dysfunctions in young subjects produce cognitive disturbances similar to those found in aged subjects; and, finally, under tightly controlled conditions, reliable (albeit subtle) improvement on objective measures of memory can be obtained in aged and demented subjects by carefully regulating dose and absorption time of certain cholinomimetics. Because this last point is clearly the most pertinent to the overall purpose of this book, and currently the most controversial, a more detailed discussion of it will be reserved for a later section of this paper.

MAJOR CRITICISMS AND ISSUES SURROUNDING THE CHOLINERGIC HYPOTHESIS

Although the cholinergic hypothesis has provided a useful framework for considerable research during the last decade and has enjoyed a certain degree of success and popularity, it is certainly not without critics. Basically, arguments against the cholinergic hypothesis can be organized into three broad types, as depicted in Table 1 and discussed below.

Is the Cholinergic Hypothesis Overly Simplistic?

The first argument can be considered to be primarily philosophical in nature, and relates to our perceptions of how the brain works and how neurological events responsible for complex phenomena such as memory and cognition are commonly presumed to be organized. Critics of the cholinergic hypothesis note that any explanation of age-related cognitive loss that involves only a single neurotransmitter must be grossly oversimplified. Of course, it is difficult to argue with the inherent wisdom of this position. Indeed, few advocates of the cholinergic hypothesis deny that there must certainly be much more to the problem than is currently understood. At the same time, however, proper respect and recognition of the complexities of brain and behavior are not at all inconsistent with the assertions of the cholinergic hypothesis. By suggesting that disturbances in cholinergic neurotransmission play an important role in the loss of memory with old age and dementia, the hypothesis simply attempts to explain much of the currently available data as it relates to what must ultimately prove to be an extremely complicated set of neurochemical events.

Is the Role of the Cholinergic System Exclusive, and if not, What Then?

The second general criticism of the cholinergic hypothesis is related to the first, but is more empirical in nature. It centers on the fact that evidence is accumulating that changes in other (i.e., noncholinergic) neurotransmitter systems also occur with age and dementia, and that noncholinergic variables may, therefore, play a role in the loss of memory associated with aged and demented subjects. For example, changes in noradrenergic (Adolffson, Gottfries, C.G., Oreland, Roos, & Winblad, 1978; Arai, Kosaka, & Iizuka, 1984; Cross et al.,

1981, 1983), dopaminergic (Adolffson et al., 1978; Gottfries, C.G., Gottfries, I., & Roos, 1969; Soininen, MacDonald, ReKonen, & Riekkinen, 1981), serotoninergic (Arai et al., 1984; Bowen et al., 1983) and somatostatin (Davies & Terry, 1981; Davies, Katzman, & Terry, 1980; Emson, Mountjoy, Roth, & Iversen, 1980; Ferrier et al., 1983) markers, as well as degeneration of noradrenaline-containing neurons of the locus coeruleus (Bondareff, Mountjoy, & Roth, 1982; Iversen et al., 1983; Mann, Yates, & Marcyniuk, 1984; Tomlinson, Irving, & Blessed, 1981), have been reported with age and dementia.

Although certain of these observations have been contradicted by negative reports, it is likely that many of the changes will ultimately be substantiated more conclusively. However, a balanced and objective perspective on this issue requires that at least two additional points be considered. The first is that, even accepting the reliability of these observations, the establishment of changes in noncholinergic systems does not mitigate the evidence supporting an important relationship between cholinergic dysfunction and age-related cognitive loss. The other point concerns the nature of the noncholinergic changes. To date, the vast majority of the arguments for the involvement of other systems in the memory loss of Alzheimer's disease (AD) and aging have been based simply on the observation that changes in the markers of these systems occur in the brains of aged or demented subjects (other papers in this volume concerned with noradrenaline by Zornetzer et al. and serotonin by Altman are among the notable exceptions to this statement). Certainly, many functional disorders have been identified with advanced age and especially late-stage AD. It should be clear that simply demonstrating the existence of changes in a neurotransmitter system does not establish a significant relationship to the age-related loss of memory (or any other clinical symptom), nor does it yet provide an effective rationale for potential drug therapy. Once these changes are substantiated, they merely satisfy the first of several multidisciplinary steps required to establish an important functional role in the cognitive disturbances.

In the final analysis, there is little doubt that some of the noncholinergic changes observed, and still others identified in the future, will ultimately be associated more clearly with the loss of cognitive function in aged or demented patients. However, the establishment of such relationships will not likely weaken those involving the cholinergic system. Rather, they will help focus attention more clearly on the relationships presumed to exist between the memory disturbance, changes in cholinergic function, and changes in other non-cholinergic systems.

Have Experimental Treatment Attempts with Cholinomimetics Succeeded or Failed?

The last general criticism of the cholinergic hypothesis is quite practical in nature and revolves around the fact that despite several years of clinical attempts to improve geriatric cognition, no *therapeutically useful* results have been demonstrated with cholinergic agents. Clearly, this criticism is the most important of the three for if it were not true, the others would become moot points. However, careful analysis of the clinical tests performed thus far, and close attention to the details of this criticism, offers a somewhat different perspective on the current state of cholinergic therapy.

Almost from the inception of the cholinergic hypothesis, clinicians were eager to test the idea that cholinomimetics might be effective in the treatment of memory problems associated with AD and aging. These attempts can be classified into one of three approaches: Precursor therapy, anticholinesterase treatment, and muscarinic receptor agonist treatment (for more extensive review, see Bartus et al., 1982, 1985). Because cholinergic precursors have a wide margin of safety, enjoy relatively loose government regulations associated with their use, and were implicated by early *in vitro* data as playing a potentially important, rate-dependent role in acetylcholine (ACh) synthesis, the vast majority of the early clinical studies adopted a precursor therapy approach.

However, scores of clinical trials have now been conducted that fail to demonstrate beneficial cognitive effects with either choline (a major ACh precursor) or lecithin (the major dietary source of choline) in demented or nondemented aged patients (for recent review, see Bartus, Dean, & Beer, 1984). In fact, it had been noted in the past that certain assumptions inherent in this rationale, especially when applied to aged or demented brains, had never been tested and may likely not be true (Bartus & Dean, 1985; Bartus, Dean, Sherman, Friedman, & Beer, 1981; Bartus et al., 1984). The lack of efficacy with precursors, therefore, should not be considered an issue relevant to the viability of the cholinergic hypothesis, for in fact, this effect had been anticipated early in part due to the very cholinergic deficiencies which support the cholinergic hypothesis.

Moreover, these studies with cholinergic precursors and the consistent failure to reverse the memory disturbances in geriatric animals or humans, represent a good example of how significant loss of time and resources might be prevented in future clinical trials. Certainly, the state of the art in this area now seems sufficiently advanced so that scores of clinical trials need no longer be conducted only on the basis of controversial *in vitro* data, derived from tissue preparations from brains of nonaged (i.e., young) rats and mice. Rather, a more rational approach would be to try first to integrate data from relevant neurochemical studies with data obtained from appropriate *in vivo* animal models. Once such a synthesis occurs, the collective results and implications of these animal findings can be more effectively employed to help evaluate new treatment possibilities and direct novel clinical protocols.

In contrast to tests of cholinergic precursors, the testing of cholinergic agonists and cholinesterase inhibitors to improve geriatric memory has not been as extensive, but has been arguably more successful. To date, the most popular cholinomimetic has been the anticholinesterase physostigmine (for review, see Bartus et al., 1984; Corkin, 1981; Johns et al., 1984). Although positive effects have been obtained in both aged humans and nonhuman primates with memory impairments, the effects are quite subtle and require strictly controlled test conditions and special attention to large individual variations in the most effective dose (Bartus, 1979b; Davis, Mohs, & Tinklenberg, 1979; Goodnick & Gershon, 1984). Furthermore, the most consistent effects in humans have been obtained with intravenous injections of the drug (Christie, 1982; Christie, Shering, Ferguson, & Glen, 1981; Davis & Mohs, 1982; Davis et al., 1979; Goodnick & Gershon, 1984). Thus, despite the potential theoretical importance of these data, their direct therapeutic relevance remains in doubt.

The final class of cholinergic agents that have received clinical attention are the direct acting muscarinic agonists. Although very few double-blind trials have been published thus far, early preliminary studies suggest that they may improve geriatric memory (Caine, 1980; Christie et al., 1981) and may offer certain advantages over anticholinesterases (Bartus et al., 1980, 1985).

Whatever the positive results that have been claimed or obtained with cholinergic agents, one must recognize that they are extremely subtle, quite variable, and offer little or no significant therapeutic relief in activities of daily living. Although a tenable explanation for the

TABLE 2

Characteristic Limitations of Available Cholinergics

1. Extremely short half life
2. Lack of specificity to CNS or poor passage through blood-brain barrier
3. High incidence of adverse side effects
4. Extremely narrow therapeutic window

lack of clinically significant effects certainly includes the likelihood that multiple neurochemical factors are involved in the memory problems, other more basic pharmacologic factors may also be involved. Foremost among these is the pharmacokinetic properties of the available cholinergics tested to date. Although any of the shortcomings listed in Table 2 would singularly or collectively be expected to dramatically limit the effectiveness of any pharmaceutical agent intented for almost any central nervous system (CNS) indication, these problems are particularly troublesome in the available cholinomimetics. For example, the half life of physostigmine, arecoline, and most of the other cholinomimetics that have been tested is merely several minutes long (Davis, Mohs, Davis, Rosenberg, et al., 1981; Nutt, Tamminga, Eisler, & Chase, 1979). Further, existing cholinergic agents have little specificity for the intended target organ, the brain. Moreover, many available cholinomimetics have difficulty passing the blood-brain barrier, while the slope of the dose-response curve is very steep and the therapeutic window very narrow. Incidence of adverse side effects is particularly high, in large part because of the undesirable properties of the cholinergics just described. In fact, when one considers the essential characteristics that a drug should possess in order to treat an age-related neurobehavioral disturbance, it is clear that the available cholinergic agents have very few. Thus, until pharmacokinetically suitable cholinergic agents are available, it should not be surprising that clinical efforts remain so disappointing. Recent reports of achieving significant symptomatic improvement when the partial cholinergic agonist, bethanechol, was chronically infused into the ventricles of the brains of Alzheimer's patients (Harbaugh, Roberts, Coombs, Sanders, & Reeder, 1984) offers additional encouragement for this possibility.

At the same time, however, there exist two fundamental issues regarding the cholinergic hypothesis that must be considered within the context of future drug therapy. These are:

1. Can significant improvement in a complex behavioral syndrome (i.e., cognitive loss) be achieved by strengthening one weak line (i.e., the cholinergic) in a hypothetical chain of complicated neurochemical events?; and

2. Can cholinergic agents or methods of enhancing cholinergic activity be developed that offer significant advantages over existing alternatives?

Certainly both of these questions lend themselves to direct empirical test. While a definitive answer to the first question may require some success in the second, there already exists sufficient positive evidence from a number of other equally complex neuropsychiatric disorders to allow one to argue against any *a priori* rejection of the notion. At the same time, although few investigators would expect any cholinergic drug to dramatically and completely reverse the mentally incapacitating symptoms of late-stage AD, it remains an empirical probability that a significant reduction in the earliest cognitive symptoms of dementia and advanced senescence ought to be possible. Certainly, this goal is infinitely more modest than is the search for the etiological factor(s) whose identification might ultimately prevent or cure the disease. Although proper manipulation or elimination of the etiologic factors would represent a more satisfying, lasting solution to this problem, the shorter-term benefits gained by even a modest reduction of the cognitive symptoms could be quite significant in terms of quality of life, cost of care, self-esteem, personal and social trauma, and many other interrelated factors (see Chapter 2).

FUTURE EFFORTS

If one is willing to assume that partial restoration or compensation of age-related cholinergic dysfunction may reduce the severity of the cognitive deficits, and that the discovery or development of newer and different cholinergic drugs is indeed possible, then many exciting treatment possibilities become apparent. These can be grouped into at least four different approaches, as shown in Table 3. Of course, none of these should be considered mutually exclusive of the others.

TABLE 3

Treatment Approaches Based on Cholinergic Hypothesis

1. Improve standard pharmacokinetics of cholinomimetics
2. Develop new cholinergic agents with greater specificity or selectivity
   a. receptor subclasses
   b. brain regions
3. Develop new, nontraditional cholinergic-enhancing agents that circumvent identified cholinergic deficiencies
4. Develop and evaluate more innovative combination therapies

Improve Standard Pharmacokinetics

Perhaps the easiest conceptual approach to developing a more effective cholinergic agent would be to simply find a drug that corrects the serious pharmacokinetic limitations of available cholinergics. From a medicinal chemistry standpoint, this task represents the most straight-forward means of approaching the problem and requires the type of talent and experience typically exemplified in the pharmaceutical industry. With proper attention to physical-chemical variables known (or hypothesized) to affect attributes such as biological half life, passage through blood-brain barrier, etc., in conjunction with cholinergic tests allowing sensitive and sufficiently high volume screening, the goal of developing pharmacokinetically superior cholinergic agents seems quite reasonable. It would then become an extremely interesting (and important) empirical question as to how much more effective such agents might be in the geriatric clinic.

Improve Target Specificity or Selectivity

Another approach to developing more therapeutically effective cholinergic agents involves applying current state of the art knowledge from the neurosciences to find cholinergic agents with far greater specificity and selectivity. For example, a series of studies primarily utilizing pirenzepine (a tricylic muscarinic antagonist) suggests the existence of at least two classes of muscarinic receptors (defined as M_1 and M_2) whose distribution varies between brain regions (Birdsall, Burgen, & Hulme, 1978; Caulfield & Straughan, 1983; Ehlert, Roeske, & Yamamura, 1982; Garvey, Rossor, & Overson, 1984; Hammer, Berrie, Birdsall, Burgen, & Hulme, 1980; Jaup, Stockbrugger, & Dotevall, 1980). The existence of muscarinic receptor heterogeneity provides the potential to develop drugs targeted with greater specificity toward a particular subclass of muscarinic receptors or conformational states. Assuming different functional roles of receptor subclasses, one could expect to achieve far greater selectivity of function and/or anatomical site of action from such drugs, presumably increasing efficacy and potency while reducing side effects. As the accumulation of additional, fundamental information allows further refinements and corrections in the current M_1 vs. M_2) subclassification scheme and as greater characterization of function is achieved, even more powerful means of developing muscarinic agonists with even greater specificity should become available.

Recent evidence suggests that the M_2 subclass of receptors may be preferentially distributed on the presynapter terminal and may functionally modulate the release of ACh (Raiteri, Leardi, & Marchi, 1984). These observations, coupled with more recent evidence of a loss of M_2 receptors in AD, have led to the suggestion that selective M_2 antagonists might be efficacious in treating some of the primary cognitive symptoms of the disease (Mash, Flynn, & Potter, 1985). Although such a possibility is certainly intriguing and worthy of consideration, the need for exercising caution would seem to be particularly important. First, although the M_1 receptor site has a 50-fold greater affinity for pirenzepine than the M_2 site, this difference is not absolute, but one of degree. Thus, it is likely that new agents developed as M_2 antagonists will also antagonize M_1 receptors to some (albeit a lesser) degree. Given the deficient state of the cholinergic system in Alzheimer's patients, any degree of postsynaptic cholinergic antagonism might be contraindicated. Moreover, recent studies suggest that the current classification may be seriously over-simplified, for functionally relevant regional differences between M_1- and M_2-mediated events have been documented which are not revealed by conventional receptor binding techniques (Fisher & Bartus, 1985). Thus, additional basic research may be required to more clearly characterize the receptor subtypes and their regional/functional idiosyncracies before drug development and clinical evaluation may take full advantage of the many intriguing possibilities.

Of course, attempts to develop more specific cholinergic agents need not be limited to muscarinic agonists. Indeed, progress has been made in identifying and developing agents to selectively inhibit acetyl-cholinesterase activity in the CNS. One example is the sulfonyl florides which apparently inhibit CNS acetylcholinesterase, sparing inhibition of butyrylcholinesterase as well as peripheral acetylcholinesterase (Moss et al., 1985). Like many newly developed drugs, the clinical utility of this class awaits future testing.

In addition to the insight gained from conventional enzymatic kinetic techniques and related principles of receptor-ligand binding, newer methods of characterizing cholinergic activity may provide additional means of developing superior cholinergic agents. For example, some of the events within each neuron that are responsible for the transduction and amplification of the initial, cell surface event of receptor occupancy are beginning to be delineated. The muscarinic cholinergic system, for example, utilizes a series of receptor-activated intramembranal and cytoplasmic events, involving a number of biochemical changes (Downes, 1983). One of the most consistent biochemical events initiated by muscarinic receptor activation is an enhanced turnover of phosphatidate and phosphatidylinositol (Abdel-Latif, 1983; Downes, 1983; Fisher, Figueiredo, & Bartus, 1984). Although the precise functional role of this event in cholinergic signal transduction has yet to be established, its active involvement in the post-receptor cascade of events ultimately responsible for the firing of the cholinergic neuron is gaining widespread acceptance (Brown & Masters, 1984; Downes, 1983; Fisher & Agranoff, 1985; Fisher et al., 1984; Nishizuka, 1984). For these reasons, methods of quantifying phospholipid turnover following muscarinic receptor occupancy provide an independent (and perhaps more functionally relevant) means of defining and assessing muscarinic agonists.

Recent studies using these techniques suggest the existence of at least two broad classes of muscarinic agonists (Fisher, Klinger, & Agranoff, 1983; Fisher et al., 1984) — those that stimulate inositol phospholipid turnover two to three times control levels (Class A), versus those that are only partially active, stimulating turnover by only 10 to 15% (Class B). Moreover, Class B agonists actually block the maximal effects of Class A agonists when the two are combined. As shown in Figure 1, these profound differences in classes of muscarinic agonists are not revealed by more conventional methods of receptor-ligand binding systems (Fisher & Bartus, 1985; Fisher et al., 1984). Thus, this information and associated phenomena provide a clear direction and available measurements for developing more unique and specific muscarinic agonists. However, an empirical question of certain importance concerns the physiological effects of increased agonist-induced inositol phospholipid turnover and its relationship to our ultimate therapeutic goals.

We recently provided preliminary evidence suggesting that potential, functional advantages may exist with agonists which have increased effects on inositol phospholipid turnover. Previous work had established that relatively small structural variations in oxotremorine could produce large changes in the enhanced phospholipid turnover in brain tissue (Fisher et al., 1984). From a different perspective, other work had demonstrated that aged rats exhibit a robust deficit in retention of a single trial passive avoidance task (Bartus, Flicker, & Dean, 1983; Gold & McGaugh, 1975; Lippa et al., 1980; Zornetzer, Thompson, & Rogers, 1982), and that muscarinic agonists produce reliable (albeit modest) improvement (Bartus, Dean, & Beer, 1983).

Using aged rats in this task, we recently compared the effects of oxotremorine with two close analogues of oxotremorine (oxotremorine-2 and oxotremorine-M). Both oxotremorine-2 and oxotremorine-M are structurally similar to oxotremorine, but differ in the number of methyl groups attached to the side chain (two and three, respectively). More importantly, the three compounds differ dramatically in their ability to stimulate turnover of phosphatidate, with oxotremorine-M being most effective, oxotremorine-2 being modestly effective, and oxotremorine, only weakly effective. The results of this behavioral comparison are shown in Figure 2 and reveal clearly superior effects of the two analogues. These preliminary data, therefore, raise the possibility that muscarinic agonists that are able to induce larger biochemical signals between the site of the receptor and the eventual physiological response, may be far more efficacious in improving overall cholinergic function and perhaps reducing the cognitive disturbances associates with old age and AD. Furthermore, they suggest that one practical way of accomplishing this might be

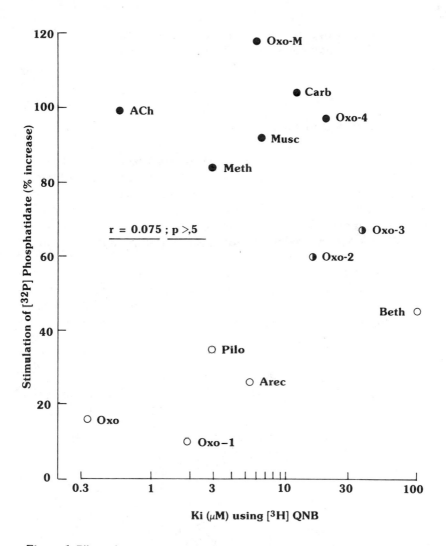

Figure 1. Effects of various muscarinic agonists on ability to stimulate phosphatidate turn-over (plotted along absissa) versus an inverse plot of ability to bind to the muscarinic receptor, measured by displacement of the muscarinic antagonist quinuclidinyl benzilate (QNB). Note that, although wide variation occurs among the agonists in their ability to stimulate phosphatidate, as well as in their affinity for the muscarinic receptor (Ki), no correlation exists between these two variables. However, a relationship does exist in the apparent ability of the agonists to induce a conformational change in the receptor, suggested by their ability to bind to high and low affinity forms of the receptor. This is depicted by the solid circles for full agonists, that bind to both interconvertible forms (and are, therefore, presumed to induce a conformational change) vs. open circles for partial agonists, that bind to a single form of the receptor (and are therefore presumed not to induce change). The results for OXO-2 and OXO-3 yielded mixed data (adapted from Fisher, Figueiredo, & Bartus, 1984).

by increasing the degree to which muscarinic agonists enhance phosphatidylinositol breakdown within the neuronal membrane.

Circumvent Cholinergic Defect

Another potentially useful approach to developing new and more effective cholinergic agents involves trying to circumvent problems in cholinergic transmission with new drugs that enhance the function of cholinergic neurons in nontraditional ways. This approach has particular appeal when age-related cholinergic defects are considered, for certain evidence suggests that the primary functional disturbance in cholinergic neurons may exist within the neuron, beyond the site of the receptor (i.e., downstream in the cascade of events) (Bartus et al., 1982; Lippa & Bartus, 1982). This supposition is based primarily on the observation of robust (i.e., 50 to 60%) decreases in electrophysiological responsiveness of hippocampal neurons of

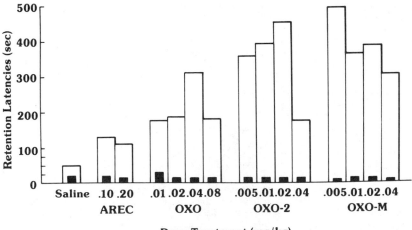

Figure 2. Effects of various doses of the traditional muscarinic agonists, arecoline and oxotremorine vs. two close analogues of oxotremorine (oxotremorine-M and oxotremorine-2) on passive avoidance retention in aged rats (open bars). Note superior efficacy and potency of the two analogues [closed bars representing pre-training, (i.e.,-day one) latencies].

aged rats to iontophoretically applied acetylcholine (Lippa et al., 1980, 1981; Segal, 1982), with only subtle (15 to 20%) (Lippa et al., 1980, 1981) and often inconsistent (Bartus et al., 1982) decreases in muscarinic receptor density.

Although insight into which biochemical event(s) may be primarily responsible for the decreased electrophysiological response is presently lacking, fundamental information related to the cascade of events induced by receptor-activation, nevertheless, provides some direction for testing hypotheses and developing new drug strategies. One such approach revolves around the previously discussed phenomenon of the breakdown of phosphatidyl inositol to inositol phosphates following muscarinic receptor occupancy. A corollary of this reaction is the formation of diacylglycerol (DAG) (Brown & Masters, 1984; Downes, 1983; Nishizuka, 1984). It is believed that DAG acts as a second messenger by activating the important calcium and phospholipid-dependent enzyme, protein kinase C (Brown & Masters, 1984; Downes, 1983; Nishizuka, 1984). Stimulation of the enzyme is believed to be crucial to neuronal firing (Brown & Masters, 1984; Downes, 1983; Nishizuka, 1984). One theoretical possibility that logically presents itself is that the activity of cholinergic neurons may, therefore, be increased by enhancing or mimicking certain of these cytoplasmic biochemical events within the cascade. Phorbol esters provide one possible means of researching this concept. Phorbol esters are lipophilic compounds with inflammatory and tumor-promoting properties that mimick the effects of DAG by stimulating protein kinase C at the same site (Baraban, Gould, Peroutka, & Snyder, 1985; Blumberg et al., 1984).

We recently evaluated the effects of iontophoretically applying acetylcholine (ACh), PMA (a phorbol ester — phorbol-12-myristate-13-acetate) and ACh and PMA simultaneously to hippocampal pyramidal cells in young rats. The results of this experiment demonstrated that, within certain parameters, while ACh modestly stimulated firing rate and the effects of PMA alone were neglibile, when the two were applied simultaneously, a robust increase in firing rate could be achieved (see Figure 3). It should be noted that serious problems of toxicity exist with PMA as a therapeutic drug, and it remains to be seen whether neurons in aged brain would respond similarly. Moreover, the effects of PMA on ACh-stimulated firing rate were not perfectly consistent and apparently depended on the interaction of the various parameters used. Nonetheless, these data provide intriguing evidence that the physiological response of hippocampal

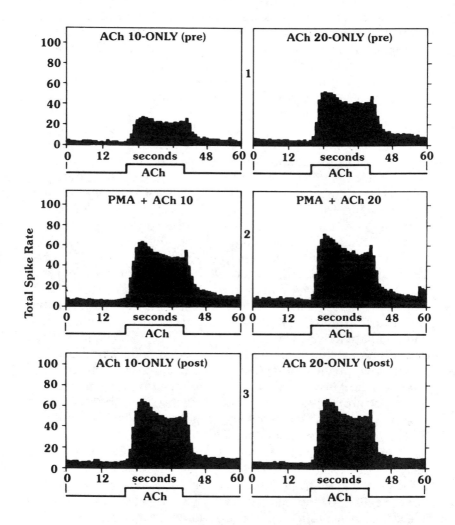

Figure 3. Interaction of iontophoretically applied acetylcholine and phorbol-12-myristate-13-acetate (PMA) on stimulation of hippocampal pyramidal cells in young rats. The left-hand column depicts the effects of 100 nM ACh applied at 10 nA and the right-hand column the effects of 20 nA. The three pairs of graphs illustrate three sequential iontophoretic condltons. The top graphs show baseline activity and the effects of ACh only (raised time line). The middle graphs show the effects of PMA only and ACh applied with PMA; the bottom graphs illustrate the after effects of PMA (post-PMA baseline) and the effects of ACh alone during this time. Note that while PMA exerted no measurable effect alone, it enhanced the effect of ACh when the two were simultaneously applied. Moreover, this effect persisted into the third epoch when PMA was no longer applied, presumably due to a persistence of PMA in the neuronal membrane due to the prior application 1 minute earlier.

neurons to Ach might be modulated by manipulating intracellular biochemical events normally induced by receptor activation. These preliminary findings are, in some ways, consistent with a recent report that PMA can also mimick the contractile action of DAG in isolated smooth muscle (Baraban et al., 1985). This approach, therefore, suggests a potentially novel means of developing drugs to improve cholinergic function that is rich in possibilities and opportunities.

Develop Innovative Combination Therapies

An additional means of improving the therapeutic effects of cholinergic agents would be to develop more innovative combination therapies. As discussed earlier, no authority believes that defects in the cholinergic system are singularly responsible for even the earliest and most basic cognitive disturbances in advanced age or AD. In fact, it has been suggested that to achieve significant improvement of these symptoms, it may be necessary to correct multiple, interactive neurochemical dysfunctions, or more than one aspect of a deficient metabolic pathway (Bartus et al., 1982). Early preliminary data with a piracetam/choline combination in aged rats (Bartus et al., 1981) provided some empirical support for this notion, followed soon after by heuristically encouraging (though therapeutically disappointing) clinical results suggesting superior effects of piracetam/choline and piracetam/lecithin combinations, as well as combinations of divergent cholinergic agents (e.g., precursor with an anticholinesterase; reviewed in Bartus et al., 1984). Given the high probability that other neurochemical disturbances most likely combine with a cholinergic defect to produce the cognitive deficits, a major question becomes which other neurochemical systems may be interactively involved. Although it will be some time before we can expect clear answers to that question, recent circumstantial evidence has begun to suggest that serontonin may also play a role (Bowen et al., 1983; Quirion, Richard, & Dam, 1985; for review, see chapter by Altman, this volume).

In a recent series of tests with young monkeys in the same automated memory paradigm shown to be sensitive to age-related deficits, we evaluated the interaction of the serotonergic and cholinergic systems in mediating recent memory. Low doses of scopolamine were given alone or in combination with the serontonergic antagonists, cinanserin and methysergide. Although only very modest effects of cinanserin and methysergide were obtained when given alone, a robust, interactive deficit in accuracy of memory was obtained when these serotonergic antagonists were combined with scopolamine. These findings suggest that serotonin may play an important role in the specific type of memory most severely impaired by age. More generally, they suggest that although the loss of certain neurotransmitter systems (e.g., serotonin, in this particular case) may not be sufficient by themselves to adequately account for the age-related loss of memory, they may, nevertheless, make an important contribution, particularly when coexistent with a cholinergic deficiency. The implication of these preliminary results is that greater reductions of age-related memory deficits might be achieved if one were to enhance the activity, or restore the proper balance, of both the cholinergic and serotonergic systems. This and similar possibilities lend themselves nicely to evaluation in recently developed animal models of aging (e.g., Bartus & Dean, 1985; Bartus, Flicker, & Dean, 1983). The use of such models offers the opportunity to reduce the otherwise unwieldy number of possibilities to a more practical level for eventual clinical evaluation.

A PARTING PERSPECTIVE

From this discussion it should be clear that, in terms of possible therapeutic approaches, the cholinergic hypothesis has not yet been effectively tested or employed. While one positive role it plays involves the identification of clear directions for drug development activities, it should be apparent that its value extends beyond the important, but short-term treatment of memory-related symptoms. For example, the hypothesis also helps bring into focus a number of more basic issues requiring further research. These include: (a) a more detailed characterization of the nature of the cholinergic defect in brains of aged animals, humans, and Alzheimer's patients, with clearer definitions of the similarities and differences between groups or conditions; (b) the establishment of functional relationships between age-related changes in other neurotransmitter system(s), age-related memory loss, and the cholinergic dysfunctions documented; (c) the development of a more in-depth understanding of the relationship between the primary cholinergic marker of AD (i.e., loss of CAT activity) and the primary neuropathologic markers (plaques and tangles), and the functional consequences of their coexistence.

Information gained from research addressing these issues would not only provide additional insight for understanding the neurochemical variables responsible for the cognitive symptoms and possible means of pharmacologically treating these symptoms, but would also be useful in understanding the nature of the disease and the variables related to its primary neurological targets. Greater knowledge of these latter variables should ultimately help focus attention on the etiologic factors causing the selective, but progressive, loss of neural function and possibly help identify the factors responsible for the neural destruction and effective means of preventing it.

BRIEF SYNOPSIS

To be sure, we are probably a long way from achieving an effective treatment for the symptomatic loss of cognitive function in senescent or demented patients. Presumably, for the time being, complete prevention and cure of AD must be considered even more remote. Yet, in terms of certain medical, social, and economic considerations, much benefit could be gained by simply understanding and treating the early and primary symptoms of the disease, which include recent memory loss and its associated secondary manifestations. The cholinergic hypothesis necessarily suffers from a certain degree of inherent oversimplication and possible myopia. Yet, advantages gained by the research activities it helps stimulate and direct must not be underestimated. It seems clear that the opportunity it provides for increasing our understanding of age-related memory problems and for developing an effective means of reducing the severity of the cognitive symptoms of aged brain and AD, provide adequate testimony for the continued value of the hypothesis as an important heuristic tool.

REFERENCES

Abdel-Latif, A.A. (1983). Metabolism of phosphoinositides. In A. Lajtha (Ed.), *Handbook of neurochemistry* (Vol. 3, pp. 91-131). New York: Plenum Press.

Adolffson, R., Gottfries, C.G., Oreland, L., Roos, B.E., & Winblad,

B. (1978). Reduced levels of catecholamines in the brain and increased activity of monoamine oxidase in platelets in Alzheimer's disease: Therapeutic implications. In R. Katzman, R.D. Terry, & K.L. Bick (Eds.), *Alzheimer's disease: Senile dementia and related disorders* (pp. 441-452). New York: Raven Press.

Alzheimer, A. (1907). Uber eine eigenartige erkrankung der hirnrinde. *Allgemeine Zeitschrift Zur Psychiatrie, 64,* 146-148.

Arai, H., Kosaka, K., & Iizuka, R. (1984). Changes of biogenic amines and their metabolites in postmortem brains from patients with Alzheimer-type dementia. *Journal of Neurochemistry, 43,* 388-393.

Baraban, T.M., Gould, R.J., Perontka, S.J., & Snyder, S.H. (1985). Pharbol ester effects on neurotransmission: Interaction with neurotransmitters and calcium in smooth muscle. *Proceedings of the National Academy of Sciences, USA, 82,* 604-607.

Bartus, R.T. (1978). Short-term memory in the rhesus monkey: Effects of dopamine blockade via acute haloperidol administration. *Pharmacology, Biochemistry and Behavior, 9,* 353-357.

Bartus, R.T. (1979a). Four stimulants of the central nervous system: Effects on short-term memory in young versus aged monkeys. *Journal of the American Geriatric Society, 27,* 289-297.

Bartus, R.T. (1979b). Physostigmine and recent memory: Effects in young and aged nonhuman primates. *Science, 206,* 1087-1089.

Bartus, R.T. (1980). Cholinergic drug effects on memory and cognition in animals. In L.W. Poon (Ed.), *Aging in the 1980's: Psychological issues* (pp. 163-180). Washington, D.C.: American Psychological Association.

Bartus, R.T., & Dean, R.L. (1985). Developing and utilizing animal models in the search for an effective treatment for age-related memory disturbance. In C. Gottfries (Ed.), *Physiological aging and dementia* (pp. 231-267). Basle: S. Karger Press.

Bartus, R.T., Dean, R.L., & Beer, B. (1980). Memory deficits in aged Cebus monkeys and facilitation with central cholinomimetics. *Neurobiology of Aging, 1,* 145-152.

Bartus, R.T., Dean, R.L., & Beer, B. (1983). An evaluation of drugs for improving memory in aged monkeys: Implications for clinical trials in humans. *Psychopharmacology Bulletin, 19,* 168-184.

Bartus, R.T., Dean, R.L., & Beer, B. (1984). Cholinergic precursor therapy for geriatric cognition: Its past, its present and a question of its future. In M.M. Ordy, D. Harman, & R. Alfin-Slater (Eds.), *Nutrition in gerontology* (pp. 191-225). New York: Raven Press.

Bartus, R.T., Dean, R.L., Beer, B., & Lippa, A.S. (1982). The cholinergic hypothesis of geriatric memory dysfunction. *Science, 217,* 408-417.

Bartus, R.T., Dean, R.L., Pontecorvo, M.J., & Flicker, C. (1985). The cholinergic hypothesis: A historical overview, current perspective and future directions. In D. Olton, E. Gamzu, & S. Corkin (Eds.), *Memory dysfunctions: Integration of animal and human research from clinical and preclinical perspectives* (pp. 332-358). New York: New York Academy of Sciences.

Bartus, R.T., Dean, R.L., Sherman, K.A., Friedman, E., & Beer, S. (1981). Profound effects of combining choline and piracetam on memory enhancement and cholinergic function in aged rats. *Neurobiology of Aging, 2,* 105-111.

Bartus, R.T., Fleming, D., & Johnson, H.R. (1978). Aging in the rhesus monkey: Debilitating effects on short-term memory. *Journal of Gerontology, 33,* 858-871.

Bartus, R.T., Flicker, C., & Dean, R.L. (1983). Logical principles for the development of animal models of age-related memory impairments. In T. Crook, S. Ferris, & R.T. Bartus (Eds.), Assessment in geriatric psychopharmacology (pp. 263-299). New Canaan, CT: Mark Powley Associates, Inc.

Bartus, R.T., & Johnson, H.R. (1976). Short-term memory in the rhesus monkey: Disruption from the anticholinergic scopolamine. *Pharmacology, Biochemistry and Behavior, 5,* 39-46.

Birdsall, N.J.M., Burgen, A.S.V., & Hulme, E.C. (1978). The binding of agonists to brain muscarinic receptors. *Molecular Pharmacology, 14,* 723-736.

Blumberg, P.M., Jaken, S., Konig, B., Sharkey, N.A., Leach, K.L., Jeng, A.Y., & Yeh, E. (1984). Mechanism of action of the phorbol ester tumor promoters: Specific receptors for lipophilic ligands. *Biochemical Pharmacology, 33,* 933-940.

Bondareff, W., Mountjoy, C.Q., & Roth, M. (1982). Loss of neurons of origin of the adrenergic projection to cerebral cortex (nucleus locus ceruleus) in senile dementia. *Neurology, 32,* 164-168.

Bowen, D.M., Allen, S.J., Benton, J.S., Goodhardt, M.J., Spillane, J.A., Esiri, M.M., Neary, D., Snowden, J.S., Wilcock, G.K., & Davison, A.N. (1983). Biochemical assessment of serotonergic and cholinergic dysfunction and cerebral atrophy in Alzheimer's disease. *Journal of Neurochemistry, 41,* 266-272.

Bowen, D.M., Smith, C.B., White, P., & Davison, A.N. (1976). Neurotransmitter-related enzymes and indices of hypoxia in senile dementia and other abiotrophies. *Brain, 99,* 459-496.

Brown, J.H., & Masters, S.B. (1984). Does phosphinositide hydrolysis mediate "inhibitory" as well as "excitatory" muscarinic responses? *Trends in Pharmacological Sciences, 5,* 417-419.

Caine, E.D. (1980). Cholinomimetric treatment fails to improve memory disorders. *New England Journal of Medicine, 303,* 585-586.

Caulfield, M., & Straughan, D. (1983). Muscarinic receptors revisited. *Trends in Neurosciences, 6,* 73-75.

Christie, J.E. (1982). Physostigmine and arecholine infusions in Alzheimer's disease. In S. Corkin, K.L. Davis, J.H. Growdon, E. Usdine, & R.J. Wurtman (Eds.), *Alzheimer's disease: A report of progress in research* (pp. 413-422). New York: Raven Press.

Christie, J.E., Shering, A., Ferguson, J., & Glen, A.I.M. (1981). Physostigmine and arecholine: Effects of intravenous infusions in Alzheimer's presenile dementia. *British Journal of Psychiatry, 138,* 46-50.

Corkin, S. (1981). Acetylcholine, aging and Alzheimer's disease: Implications for treatment. *Trends in Neurosciences, 4,* 287-290.

Coyle, J.T., Price, D.L., & DeLong, M.R. (1983). Alzheimer's disease: A disorder of cortical cholinergic innervation. *Science, 219,* 1184-1190.

Cross, A.J., Crow, T.J., Johnson, J.A., Joseph, M.H., Perry, E.K., Perry, R.H., Blessed, G., & Tomlinson, B.E. (1983). Monoamine metabolism in senile dementia of Alzheimer type. *Journal of Neurological Science, 60,* 383-392.

Cross, A.J., Crow, T.J., Perry, E.K., Perry, R.H., Blessed, G., & Tomlinson, B.E. (1981). Reduced dopamine-beta-hydrozylase activity in Alzheimer's disease. *British Medical Journal, 282,* 93-94.

Davies, P. (1981). Theoretical treatment possibilities for dementia of the Alzheimer's type. The cholinergic hypothesis. In T. Crook & S. Gershon (Eds.), *Strategies for the development of an effective treatment for senile dementia* (pp. 19-32). New Canaan, CT: Mark Powley Associates, Inc.

Davies, P., Katzman, R., & Terry, R.D. (1980). Reduced somatostantin-like immunoreactivity in cerebral cortex from cases of Alzheimer's disease and Alzheimer senile dementia. *Nature, 228,* 279-280.

Davies, P., & Maloney, A.J.F. (1976). Selective loss of central cholinergic neurons in Alzheimer's disease [Letter to the editor]. *Lancet, 2,* 1403.

Davies, P., & Terry, R.D. (1981). Cortical somatostantin-like immunoreactivity in cases of Alzheimer's disease and senile dementia of the Alzheimer type. *Neurobiology of Aging, 2,* 9-14.

Davis, K.L., & Mohs, R.C. (1982). Enhancement of memory processes in Alzheimer's disease with multiple-dose intravenous physostigmine. *American Journal of Psychiatry, 139,* 1421-1424.

Davis, K.L., Hollister, L.E., Mohs, R.C., Tinklenberg, J.R., Pfefferbaum, A., & Kopell, B.S. (1978). Physostigmine: Improvement of long-term memory processes in normal humans. *Science, 201,* 272-274.

Davis, K.L., Mohs, R.C., Davis, B.M., Levy, M., Rosenberg, G.S., Horvath, T.B., DeNigris, Y., Ross, A., Decker, P., & Rothpearl, A. (1981). Cholinomimetic agents and human memory: Clinical studies in Alzheimer's disease and scopolamine dementia. In T. Crook & S. Gershon (Eds.), *Strategies for the development of an effective treatment for senile dementia* (pp. 53-70). New Canaan, CT: Mark Powley Associates, Inc.

Davis, K.L., Mohs, R.C., Davis, B.M., Rosenberg, G.S., Horvath, T.B., & DeNigris, Y. (1981). Cholinomimetic agents and human memory: Preliminary observations in Alzheimer's disease. In G. Pepeu & H. Landinsky (Eds.), *Advances in behavioral biology: Vol. 25. Cholinergic mechanisms* (pp. 929-936). New York: Plenum Press.

Davis, K.L., Mohs, R.C., & Tinklenberg, J.R. (1979). Enhancement of memory by physostigmine [Letter to the editor]. *New England Journal of Medicine, 301,* 946.

Douglas, R.J. (1967). The hippocampus and behavior. *Psychological Bulletin, 67,* 416-442.

Downes, C.P. (1983). Inositol phospholipids and neurotransmitter-receptor signalling mechanisms. *Trends in Neurosciences, 6,* 313-316.

Drachman, D.A. (1977). Memory and cognitive function in man: Does the cholinergic system have a specific role? *Neurology, 27,* 783-790.

Drachman, D.A., & Leavitt, J. (1974). Human memory and the cholinergic system: A relationship to aging? *Archives of Neurology, 30,* 113-121.

Dundee, J.W., & Pandit, S.K. (1972). Anterograde amnesic effects of pethidine, hyoscine and diazepam in adults. *British Journal of Pharmacology, 44,* 140-144.

Ehlert, F.J., Roeske, W.R., & Yamamura, H.I. (1982). Muscarinic cholinergic receptor heterogeneity. *Trends in Neurosciences, 5,* 336-339.

Ferrier, I.N., Cross, A.J., Johnson, J.A., Roberts, G.W., Crow, T.J., Corsellis, J.A.N., Lee, Y.C., O'Shaughnessy, D., Adrian, T.E., McGregor, G.P., Baracese-Hamilton, A.J., & Bloom, F.E. (1983). Neuropeptides in Alzheimer type dementia. *Journal of the Neurological Sciences, 62,* 159-170.

Fisher, S.K., & Agranoff, B.W. (1985). The biochemical basis and functional significance of enhanced phosphatidate and phosphoinositide turnover. In J. Eichberg (Ed.), *Phospholipids in the nervous system* (pp. 241-296). New York: John Wiley & Sons.

Fisher, S.K., & Bartus, R.T. (1985). Regional differences in the coupling of muscarinic receptors to inositol phospholipid hydrolysis in guinea pig brain. *Journal of Neurochemistry,* 1085-1095.

Fisher, S.K., Figueiredo, J.C., & Bartus, R.T. (1984). Differential stimulation of inositol phospholipid turnover in brain by analogs of oxotremorine. *Journal of Neurochemistry, 43,* 1171-1179.

Fisher, S.K., Klinger, P.D., & Agranoff, B.W. (1983). Muscarinic agonist binding and phospholipid turnover in brain. *Journal of Biological Chemistry, 258,* 7358-7363.

Garvey, J.M., Rossor, M., & Iverson, L.L. (1984). Evidence for multiple muscarinic receptor subtypes in human brain. *Journal of Neurochemistry, 43,* 299-302.

Gauss, C.J. (1906). Geburten im Kunstlichem Dammerschlaf. *Archieves Gynakologic, 78,* 579-631.

Gold, P.E., & McGaugh, J.L. (1975). Changes in learning and memory during aging. In J.M. Ordy & F.R. Brizzee (Eds.), *Neurobiology of aging* (pp. 53-57). New York: Plenum Press.

Goodnick, P., & Gershon, S. (1984). Chemotherapy of cognitive disorders in geriatric subjects. *Journal of Clinical Psychiatry, 45,* 196-209.

Gottfries, C.G., Gottfries, I., & Roos, B.E. (1969). The investigation of homovanillic acid in the human brain and its correlation to senile dementia. *British Journal of Psychiatry, 115,* 563-574.

Hammer, R., Berries, C.P., Birdsall, N.J., Buren, A.S., & Hulme, E.C. (1980). Pirenzepine distinguishes between different subclasses of muscarinic receptors. *Nature, 283,* 90-92.

Harbaugh, R.E., Roberts, D.W., Coombs, D.W., Sanders, R.L., & Reeder, T.M. (1984). Preliminary report: Intracranial cholinergic drug infusion in patients with Alzheimer's disease. *Neurosurgery, 15,* 514-518.

Hollister, L.E. (1968). *Chemical psychoses.* Springfield, Ill.: Charles C Thomas.

Iversen, S.D. (1973). Brain lesions and memory in animals. In J.A. Deutsch (Ed.), *The physiological basis of memory.* New York: Academic Press.

Iversen, S.D. (1976). Do hippocampal lesions produce amnesia in animals? *International Review of Neurobiology, 19,* 1-49.

Iversen, L.L., Rossor, M.N., Reynolds, G.P., Hills, R., Roth, M., Mountjoy, C.Q., Foote, S.L., Morrison, J.H., & Bloom, F.E. (1983). Loss of pigmented dopamine-B-hydrozylase positive cells from locus coeruleus in senile dementia of Alzheimer's type. *Neuroscience Letters, 39,* 95-100.

Jaup, B.H., Stockbrugger, R.W., & Dotevall, G. (1980). Comparison of action of pirenzepine and 1-hyoscyamine in gastric acid secretion and other muscarinic effects. *Scandinavian Journal of Gastroenterology, 15* (Suppl. 66), 89-94.

Johns, C.A., Haroutunian, V., Davis, B.M., Horvath, T.B., Mohs, R.C., & Davis, K.L. (1984). Acetylcholinesterase inhibitors in Alzheimer's disease and animal models. In R.J. Wurtman, S.H. Corkin, & J.H. Growdon (Eds.), *Alzheimer's disease: Advances in basic research and therapies* (pp. 349-373). Zurich: Center for Brain Sciences and Metabolism Charitable Trust.

Kuhar, M.J., & Yamamura, H.I. (1975). Light autoradiographic localization of cholinergic muscarinic receptors in rat brain by specific binding of a potent antagonist. *Nature, 253,* 560-561.

Lambrechts, W., & Parkhouse, J. (1961). Postoperative amnesia. *British Journal of Anesthesia, 33,* 397-404.

Lippa, A.S., & Bartus, R.T. (1982). Neurobiological aspects of geriatric cognitive dysfunction. In S. Corkin, K.L. Davis, J.H. Growdon, E. Usdin, & R.J. Wurtman (Eds.), *Alzheimer's disease: A report of progress in research* (pp. 223-233). New York: Raven Press.

Lippa, A.S., Critchett, D.J., Ehlert, F., Yamamura, H.I., Enna, S.J., & Bartus, R.T. (1981). Age-related alterations in neurotransmitter receptors: An electrophysiological and biochemical analysis. *Neurobiology of Aging, 2,* 3-8.

Lippa, A.S., Pelham, R.W., Beer, B., Critchett, D.J., Dean, R.L., & Bartus, R.T. (1980). Brain cholinergic dysfunction and memory in aged rats. *Neurobiology of Aging, 1,* 13-19.

Longo, V.G. (1966). Behavioral and electroencephalographic effects of atropine and related compounds. *Pharmacology Review, 18,* 965-996.

Mann, D.M.A., Yates, P.O., & Marcyniuk, B. (1984). A comparison of changes in the nucleus basalis and locus coeruleus in Alzheimer's disease. *Journal of Neurology, Neurosurgery and Psychiatry, 47,* 201-203.

Mash, D.C., Flynn, D.D., & Potter, L.T. (1985). Loss of M_2 muscarinic receptors in the cerebral cortex in Alzheimer's disease and experimental cholinergic denervation. *Science, 228,* 1117-1127.

Moss, D.E., Rodriguez, L.A., Selim, S., Ellett, S.O., Devine, J.V., & Steger, R.W. (1985). The sulfonylfluorides: CNS selective cholinesterase inhibitors with potential value in Alzheimer's disease. In J.T. Hutton & A.D. Kenny (Eds.), *Proceedings of the Fifth Tarbox Parkinson's Disease Symposium: The Norman Rockwell Conference on Alzheimer's Disease* (pp. 337-350). New York: Alan R. Liss.

Nishizuka, Y. (1984). Turnover of inositol phospholipids and signal transduction. *Science, 225,* 1365-1370.

Nutt, J.G., Tamminga, C.A., Eisler, T., & Chase, T.N. (1979). Clinical experience with a cholinergic agonist in hyperkinetic movement disorders. In A. Barbeau, J.H. Growdon, & R.J. Wurtman (Eds.), *Nutrition and the brain: Vol. 5. Choline and lecithin in brain disorders* (pp. 317-324). New York: Raven Press.

Pandit, S.K., & Dundee, J.W. (1970). Preoperative amnesia: The incidence following the intramuscular injection of commonly used premedicants. *Anesthesia, 25,* 493-499.

Perry, E.K., Perry, R.H., Blessed, G., & Tomlinson, B.E. (1977). Necropsy evidence of central cholinergic deficits in senile dementia [Letter to the editor]. *Lancet, 1,* 189.

Pope, A., Hess, H.H., & Lewin, E. (1965). Microchemical pathology of the cerebral cortex in pre-senile dementia. *Transactions of the American Neurology Association, 89,* 15-16.

Quirion, R., Richard, J., & Dam, T.V. (1985). Evidence for the existence of serotonin type-2 receptors on cholinergic terminals in rat cortex. *Brain Research, 333,* 345-349.

Raiteri, M., Leardi, R., & Marchi, M. (1984). Heterogeneity of presynaptic muscarinic receptors regulating neurotransmitter release in the rat brain. *Journal of Pharmacology and Experimental Therapeutics, 228,* 209-214.

Rossor, M.N., Emson, P.C., Mountjoy, C.Q., Roth, M., & Iversen, L.L. (1980). Reduced amounts of immunoreactive somatostatin in the temporal cortex in senile dementia of Alzheimer type. *Neuroscience Letters, 20,* 373-377.

Segal, M. (1982). Changes in neurotransmitter actions in the aged rat hippocampus. *Neurobiology of Aging, 3,* 121-124.

Smith, C.M., & Swash, M. (1978). Possible biochemical basis of memory disorder in Alzheimer's disease. *Annals of Neurology, 3,* 471-473.

Soininen, H., MacDonald, E., Rekonen, M., & Riekkinen, P.J. (1981). Homovanillic acid and 5-Hydrosyindoleacetic acid levels in cerebrospinal fluid of patients with senile dementia of Alzheimer type. *Acta Neurologica Scandinavica, 64,* 101-107.

Tomlinson, B.E., Irving, D., & Blessed, G. (1981). Cell loss in the locus coeruleus in senile dementia of Alzheimer type. *Journal of the Neurological Sciences, 49,* 419-428.

Warren, J.M., & Akert, G.K. (Eds.). (1964). *The frontal granular cortex and behavior.* New York: McGraw Hill Book Co.

Yamamura, H.I., Kuhar, M.J., Greenberg, D., & Snyder, S.H. (1974). Muscarinic cholinergic receptor binding: Regional distribution in monkey brain. *Brain Research, 66,* 541-546.

Yamamura, H.I., Kuhar, M.J., & Snyder, S.H. (1974). In vivo identification of muscarinic cholinergic receptor binding in rat hippocampus. *Brain Research, 80,* 170-176.

Yamamura, H.I., & Snyder, S.H. (1974). Postsynaptic localization of muscarinic cholinergic receptor binding in rat hippocampus. *Brain Research, 78,* 320-326.

Zornetzer, S.F., Thompson, R., & Rogers, J. (1982). Rapid forgetting in aged rats. *Behavioral and Neural Biology, 36,* 49-60.

ACKNOWLEDGEMENT

The authors thank Barbara Hovsepian, Michael Pontecorvo, and Charles Flicker for help in various aspects of preparing this manuscript; Kathy Schill, Ella Margaret Marshall, Karen Clark, Joanne C. Figueiredo, and Donald J. Critchet for technical assistance with some of the experiments described; and Dr. Bernard Beer for encouragement and support.

18

The Functional Status of Central Muscarinic Receptors in Alzheimer's Disease: Assessment and Therapeutic Implications

Nunzio Pomara, MD, and Michael Stanley, PhD

Most current hypotheses on the pathophysiology of cognitive dysfunction in patients with Alzheimer's disease (AD) focus on deficits in various presynaptic components of the cholinergic neurotransmitter system. More specifically, brain samples from patients with AD are distinguished from control samples by the following characteristics:
— extensive reductions in the activity of choline acetyltransferase (CAT) which is both the biosynthetic enzyme for acetylcholine (ACh) and a marker for presynaptic neurons;
— decreases in high-affinity transport for choline; and,
— reductions in the number of cholinergic cell bodies in the subcortical nucleus basalis of Meynert, the major source of extrinsic cholinergic imput to the cortex.
These changes have been extensively reviewed (Bartus, Dean, Beer, & Lippa, 1982; Davies & Maloney, 1976; Rossor, 1982; Whitehouse et al., 1982).

Further evidence implicating a major role for the presynaptic cholinergic deficits in the pathophysiology of cognitive dysfunction in AD has been provided by reports of significant correlations between the density of both plaques and tangles with the severity of dementia before death and decreases in CAT activity in frontal and temporal cortices (Perry et al., 1978). Although reductions in cortical somatostatin content and other noncholinergic elements also have been noted in AD (Greenwald & Davis, 1983; Francis et al., 1985; Morrison, Rogers, Scherr, Benoit, & Bloom, 1985; Rossor, 1982;

Roberts, Crow, & Polak, 1985), these reductions have not yet been related to the cognitive deficits (Bartus et al., 1982; Francis et al., 1985; Rossor, 1982).

Despite these extensive presynaptic deficits, most investigators have reported no significant decrease in the number of muscarinic receptors in AD (Bowen, 1983; Bowen et al., 1979, 1983; Cross et al., 1984; Davies & Verth, 1978; Perry, 1980; Perry, E.K., Perry, Blessed, & Tomlinson, 1977).

The absence of a major change in the number of muscarinic receptors despite extensive losses of presynaptic cholinergic elements in AD has been taken as evidence that alterations in these receptors probably play no significant role in the pathophysiology of this disease. Consequently, most therapeutic strategies based on the cholinergic hypothesis have been directed at correcting presynaptic deficits. These strategies include attempts to increase cholinergic transmission through an enhancement of ACh synthesis with cholinergic precursors, (e.g., choline, lecithin) or by preventing the hydrolysis of ACh at the synapse by means of cholinesterase inhibitors, that is with physostigmine, tetrahydroaminoacridine (THA), or by directly stimulating the muscarinic receptors by means of direct agonists, for example, arecoline and, more recently, RS-86.

The clinical impact of these approaches has not been dramatic. For example, Mohs et al. (1985) demonstrated that oral physostigmine produced a consistent and clinically evident improvement for only about 30% of the patients. This group of investigators also emphasized that physostigmine does not have therapeutic benefits comparable to those seen with L-DOPA in Parkinson's disease or with neuroleptics in schizophrenia. Alzheimer's patients having the most meaningful reduction in symptom severity in response to physostigmine nevertheless remained demented.

Several explanations have been offered for the poor therapeutic outcome using these cholinergic strategies. It has been suggested that:

1. CAT needs two substrates for ACh synthesis (i.e., choline and acetyl coenzyme A). Therefore, if both substrates are depleted in AD, simply increasing choline by means of other cholinergic precursors would not be sufficient to increase ACh synthesis.

2. ACh release is dependent on neuronal activity, and simply increasing choline would not by itself be sufficient to enhance cholinergic transmission.

3. The therapeutic action of physostigmine and other cholinesterase inhibitors might be limited by the failure of enough ACh to be

released presynaptically, by their narrow therapeutic window, by poor penetration into the central nervous system (CNS), and, possibly by their action to cause a "feedback" inhibition of ACh synthesis and release.

4. The use of exogenous direct muscarinic agonists also might have a very narrow therapeutic window, which also may be difficult to overcome.

5. Possible inclusion of patients with other forms of dementia in which the cholinergic system may not necessarily be affected would dilute treatment effects.

6. Deficits in other neurotransmitters (e.g., somatostatin, serotonin, and noradrenaline) also might contribute to the pathophysiology of cognitive dysfunction in patients with AD.

7. The multiple neurotransmitter deficits seen in AD may be secondary to a retrograde degeneration arising from a primary insult to the cortex.

Therefore, therapeutic approaches based solely on cholinergic neuro-transmitter replacement would not be expected to be effective (Morrison et al., 1985; Roberts et al., 1985).

MUSCARINIC RECEPTOR RESPONSIVITY

While all of the foregoing explanations might offer a scientific rationale for the relatively poor therapeutic outcome from completed clinical trials, this review will emphasize some aspects of cholinergic neurotransmission that we feel may not have been adequately explored. Specifically, one of the reasons for the lack of clinically relevant therapeutic response to cholinergic agents in AD may be related to the inability of cholinergic agonists to trigger the appropriate response in the muscarinic receptors that remain in AD.

A tacit but untested assumption of cholinergic therapeutic strategies has been that the remaining muscarinic receptors function normally. This assumption has been allowed to stand because most studies have reported a normal number of muscarinic receptors in brains from patients with AD. Receptor number was measured by quinuclidinyl benzilate (QNB) binding.

Major drawbacks of QNB binding as it has been commonly used in these studies are its failure to differentiate between presynaptic and postsynaptic muscarinic receptors, as well as between low- and high-affinity states.

Thus, in AD there very well could be alterations in the relative proportions of these various subtypes of muscarinic receptors that could have an impact on their functional state which might not be reflected in simple measures of receptor density or affinity as assessed with conventional QNB binding studies.

More recent studies in animals and humans have shown that the number of muscarinic receptors in a given affinity state can be estimated by receptor techniques involving displacement of QNB by various muscarinic agonists having different affinities for the muscarinic receptor. Using these techniques, it may now be possible to estimate changes in high- and low-affinity muscarinic binding sites as well as presynaptic (M_2) and postsynaptic (M_1) receptors in AD. These methods were applied recently in the study of Mash, Flynn, and Potter (1985) in which they compared presynaptic and postsynaptic muscarinic binding sites in brain samples of patients dying with AD and controls. They noted a 23% reduction in the total number of muscarinic receptors in AD as compared to normals. This reduction was due almost entirely to a loss of M_2 receptors, which would be consistent with the reductions in other presynaptic cholinergic markers which also have been observed in AD. Postsynaptic (M_1) muscarinic receptors were unaltered.

On the basis of these findings, Mash et al. (1985) suggested therapeutic trials in early-AD patients using the combination of a cholinesterase inhibitor and an M_2-selective antagonist, which presumably would prevent ACh from inhibiting its own release.

We regard this suggestion as premature and based on the underlying and unproven assumption that the functional state of muscarinic receptors is not altered in AD. It is our contention that one cannot make any definitive statement regarding the functional state of these receptors based solely on static measures of receptor density and affinity. This is illustrated by a number of animal experiments that have attempted to address this question directly.

While some studies report a relation between muscarinic receptor number and response that is in the anticipated direction, this is not always the case. For example, a series of experiments (Lerer, 1985; Lerer, Stanley, Demetriou, & Gershon, 1983; Lerer, Stanley, McIntyre, & Altman, 1984; Stanley & Lerer, 1985) indicated that chronic scopolamine administration in rats was accompanied by an increase in QNB binding, whereas chronic electroconvulsive shock (ECS) administration had an opposite effect; that is, it decreased QNB binding (Figure 1). These changes in receptor num-

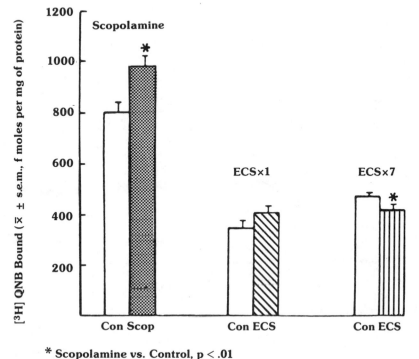

* Scopolamine vs. Control, p < .01

Figure 1. Chronic scopolamine increased, but chronic ECS decreased, the number of muscarinic receptors as measured by QNB binding in rat brain.

ber were associated with parallel changes in the responsivity of the receptors. Thus, the increase in QNB binding with scopolamine was associated with increased sensitivity to the cataleptic effect of pilocarpine (Figure 2), while a decrease in the number of muscarinic receptors with chronic ECS resulted in the expected decrease in sensitivity to the cataleptic effects of pilocarpine (Figure 3).

These findings provide evidence that changes in receptor number may be accompanied by parallel changes in the response to pilocarpine. However, this relationship between functional sensitivity and up or down regulation of corresponding receptors may not always be present. The same group of investigators demonstrated that while a single ECS treatment caused no significant change in the number of QNB binding sites (Figure 1), it nevertheless induced a

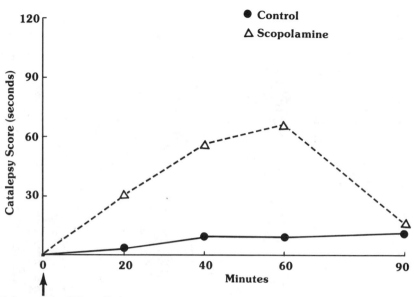

Figure 2. Chronic scopolamine increased pilocarpine induced catalepsy in accord with the increase in the number of muscarinic receptors.

blunted cataleptic response to pilocarpine (Figure 4).

Further examples of dissociations between receptor number and responsivity of the muscarinic receptors are illustrated by the findings of Pedigo, Minor, and Krumrei (1984). They reported significant reductions in muscarinic receptor density in aged rats (Figure 5). However, the administration of oxotremorine was associated with a significantly greater hypothermic response in the oldest group of rats. This response was in the exact opposite direction of what would have been predicted by a decrease in receptor number.

A similar dissociation between receptor changes as measured by QNB binding and responsivity of the muscarinic receptors was shown also in experiments with mice conducted by Marks, O'Connor, Artman, Burch, and Collins (1984). Chronic scopolamine treatment was accompanied by the development of supersensitivity to the hypothermia (Figure 6) and tremor (Figure 7) produced by oxotremorine in the absence of a corresponding increase in the number of muscarinic receptors.

Even in those instances where changes in muscarinic receptor number and responses are in the same direction, the magnitude of the receptor changes need not predict the magnitude of the response. This point is illustrated by the findings of Lippa and colleagues (1980) who reported that pyramidal cells in the hippocampus of aged rats

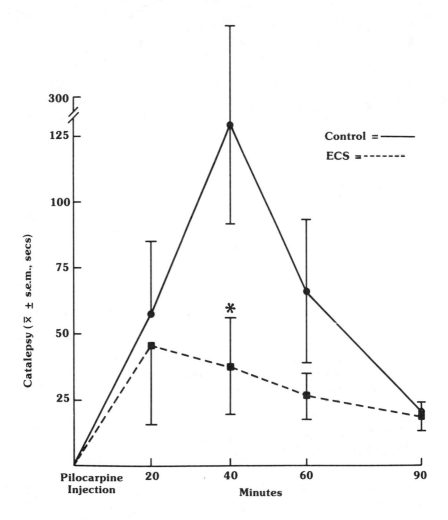

Figure 3. Chronic ECS decreased pilocarpine induced catalepsy in accord with the decrease in the number of muscarinic receptors.

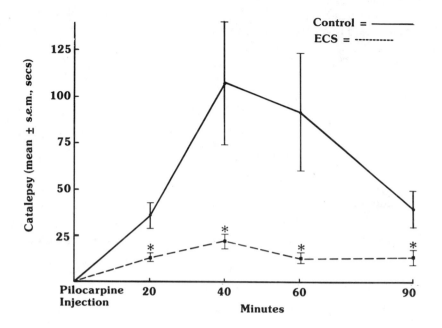

Figure 4. Acute ECS decreased pilocarpine induced catalepsy in rats even though muscarinic receptors, as measured by QNB binding, were not significantly decreased.

exhibited a 50% decrease in the responsivity to iontophoretically applied ACh. However, there was only less than a 20% decline in the number of muscarinic receptors in the same region (Figure 8).

In summary, as can be seen in Table 1, static measures of muscarinic receptor binding cannot always be used as reliable indices of muscarinic functional response.

IMPLICATIONS OF THESE FINDINGS FOR THE TREATMENT OF AD

The cholinergic hypofunction that has been hypothesized to play a role in the memory dysfunction observed in AD patients has been ascribed to a reduction in presynaptic cholinergic input to the cortex. To the extent that cholinergic transmission is equally dependent

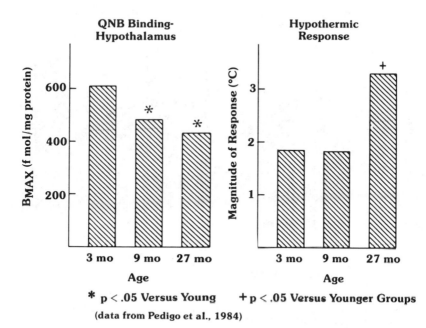

Figure 5. The hypothermic response to oxotremorine was increased in old rats despite a decrease in the number of muscarinic receptors as measured by QNB binding.

on presynaptic and postsynaptic efficiency, it is imperative that the functional responsivity of the remaining muscarinic receptors be determined as well. Although data from a preliminary study by Mash et al. (1985) indicate that postsynaptic M_1 receptors are preserved in AD, the animal data summarized above suggest that the function of these receptors may not remain unchanged.

Changes in the responsivity of muscarinic receptors may occur in the absence of alterations in the total number of receptors. Moreover, an alteration in receptor number is only one of the ways that the responsivity of the receptors can be regulated. Changes in neuronal postsynaptic excitability via resting membrane voltage alterations in the sodium-potassium pump or other ionic channel alterations and other post-receptorial mechanisms are also known to be important regulators of receptor response. Thus, in AD there could be either a hyporesponsivity or hyperresponsivity of the remaining muscarinic receptors that might not be reflected solely in QNB binding

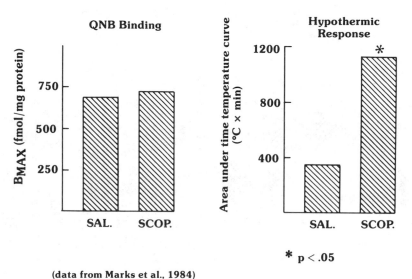

(data from Marks et al., 1984)

Figure 6. The hypothermic response to oxotremorine in mice was increased by chronic scopolamine even though there was no change in the number of muscarinic receptors as measured by QNB binding.

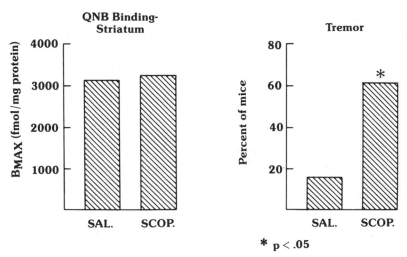

(data from Marks et al., 1984)

Figure 7. The tremor response to oxotremorine in mice was increased by chronic scopolamine even though there was no change in QNB binding.

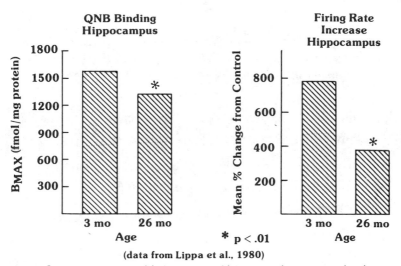

(data from Lippa et al., 1980)

Figure 8. Iontophoretic acetylcholine increased firing rate in hippocampus but the magnitude of the increase was much less than would have been predicted by the decrease in QNB binding for the oldest rats.

studies. Thus, unless one systematically addresses this question *in vivo* or in brain tissue that is still energy dependent, one cannot assume that the responsivity of these receptors remains unchanged in AD.

MEASURES OF MUSCARINIC RECEPTOR FUNCTION

The determination of the functional state of muscarinic receptors is of the utmost importance if we are to design a more rational and potentially more effective therapeutic strategy.

It is obvious that we need to have functional tests for central muscarinic receptors. The reason for wanting to concentrate on this particular system is that the best experimental evidence to date strongly supports a role for ACh in the memory dysfunction seen in AD. Moreover, the only agents that have been shown to have some, albeit limited, therapeutic effect have been those directed at enhancing central cholinergic transmission.

A number of pharmacologically evoked responses that could be used to assess muscarinic receptor function have been developed and are listed in Table 2.

TABLE 1

Summary of Relations Between Receptor Number, as Measured by QNB Binding, and Functional Responsivity of Muscarinic Receptors

1. Changes in QNB binding can be associated with parallel changes in responsivity (Figures 1, 2, and 3).

2. Changes in QNB binding can be associated with opposite changes in functional response (Figure 5).

3. Functional response can change without a change in QNB binding (Figures 6 and 7).

4. Changes in QNB binding and functional response can be in the same direction but of unequal magnitude (Figure 8).

Cholinergic challenges with muscarinic agonists have been shown to induce rapid eye movement (REM) sleep, hypothermia, tremor, and alterations in local cerebral glucose utilization (LCGU). All of these parameters may serve as potentially useful indices of central muscarinic function because of their pharmacological specificities as demonstrated by the stability of the responses and dose-response characteristics.

Rapid Eye Movement (REM) Sleep Induction

The intravenous administration of cholinomimetics (such as phy-sostigmine or arecoline) during the first or second non-REM period of a sleeping subject, has been shown to hasten significantly the on-set of REM sleep (Sitaram & Gillin, 1979; Sitaram, Nurnberger, Gershon, & Gillin, 1980, 1982). This response has been shown to be dose-dependent with higher doses producing cortical arousal in-stead of REM sleep. The induction of REM sleep by muscarinic agonists is blocked by pretreatment with scopolamine, but not meth-

TABLE 2

Muscarinic Responses Following Cholinergic Challenge

Author	Test	Response
Physiological		
Sitaram et al. (1979) Sitaram et al. (1980) Sitaram et al. (1982) Jones et al. (1985)	Arecoline	REM latency
Friedman and Jaffe (1969)	Pilocarpine	Hypothermia
Sitaram et al. (1984)	Arecoline	Hypothermia
Dam et al. (1982)	Oxotremorine	Local cerebral glucose utilization
Behavioral		
Everett (1956)	Tremorine	Tremor
Dam et al. (1982)	Oxotremorine	Tremor
Neurochemical		
George et al. (1970)	Acetylcholine	cyclic GMP
Ferrendelli et al. (1970)	Oxotremorine	cyclic GMP cyclic AMP
Honma et al. (1978)	Cholinomimetics	cyclic AMP cyclic GMP
Ui et al. (1978)	Cholinomimetics	cyclic GMP cyclic AMP
Okada et al. (1982a)	Methacholine	cyclic GMP
Okada et al. (1982b)	Methacholine	cyclic GMP cyclic AMP

scopolamine which does not penetrate the blood-brain barrier. Using the above response as a marker of central muscarinic sensitivity, Sitaram et al. (1980, 1982) found that patients with primary affective disorders had a supersensitive REM induction response both when depressed and when clinically euthymic.

To our knowledge, there are no published studies that have applied this paradigm to the evaluation of muscarinic receptor function in patients with Alzheimer-type dementia. This strategy may prove to be a useful approach in the study of AD, in light of the extensive cholinergic deficits.

Hypothermia

Cholinoceptive neurons have long been known to play a role in the regulation of body temperature.

The studies of Friedman and Jaffe (1969) demonstrated that the systemic administration of pilocarpine, physostigmine, tremorine, and oxotremorine produced a profound fall in temperature, which was antagonized by scopolamine but not by methscopolamine. Furthermore, these investigators also demonstrated that the pilocarpine-induced hypothermia was dose-dependent.

More recent studies by Sitaram, Gillin, and Bunney (1984) also support a role of ACh in the regulation of body temperature in humans. These investigators conducted a series of experiments in which they demonstrated a dose-dependent hypothermic response to intravenous arecoline in humans.

Local Cerebral Glucose Utilization

Another strategy that appears promising in the evaluation of muscarinic receptor function in patients with AD has been suggested by the experiments of Dam, Wamsley, Rapoport, and London (1982). These investigators studied the in vivo effects of the muscarinic agonist, oxotremorine, on LCGU. Systemic treatment with oxotremorine was found to increase LCGU in the cerebral cortex in a dose-related manner. The increase in LCGU induced by oxotremorine was secondary to stimulation of central muscarinic receptors because these effects were blocked completely by scopolamine, but not by methylatropine. Furthermore, the response to oxotremorine coincided with the laminar distribution of cholinergic markers in the cortex.

The technology to measure cerebral glucose utilization using positron emission tomography is currently available. The addition of a cholinergic challenge to this procedure may provide additional information on the status of central muscarinic function in patients with AD.

Tremor

Another cholinergic response described by Dam et al. (1982) that also fulfills the criteria for pharmacological specificity is the induction of tremor in rats after oxotremorine challenge. This group found that all doses of oxotremorine tested produced reliable dose-dependent tremor responses, and as before, scopolamine pretreatment, but not methylatropine, prevented the induction of tremor. Again, this paradigm can be easily adapted to the study of patients with AD.

Cyclic Nucleotides

Other biological parameters that may be useful in the assessment of muscarinic receptor function derive from changes in cyclic nucleotides (cyclic adenosine 3'-5'-monophosphate [AMP] and cyclic guanosine 3'-5'-monophosphate (GMP]) when these are measured in cerebrospinal fluid (CSF) during cholinergic challenge. Palmer (1983) recently reviewed the effects of psychoactive drugs on cyclic nucleotides in the CNS. Heilbronn and Bartfai (1978) reviewed evidence for muscarinic receptor-mediated increases in cyclic GMP levels.

The rationale for such a line of investigation is based on indirect evidence that cyclic nucleotides may be important "second messengers" in muscarinic receptor-mediated neurotransmission (Kebabian, Steiner, & Greengard, 1975).

The evidence for a possible role of cyclic GMP in cholinergic transmission is derived from a number of animal experiments. George, Polson, O'Toole, and Goldberg (1970) demonstrated that perfusion of isolated rat heart resulted in an elevation of cyclic GMP. Subsequently, Ferrendelli, Steiner, McDougal, and Kipnis (1970) administered oxotremorine and reported a 70% increase in cyclic GMP levels in cerebral cortex and cerebellum and a significant decrease in cyclic AMP. Furthermore, they also demonstrated that the peak rise in cyclic GMP following oxotremorine coincided with the maximum tremor activity. Pretreatment with atropine completely prevented the appearance of both tremor and increases in cyclic GMP.

The administration of cholinergic agents to humans also has been known to induce elevations in cyclic GMP in plasma (Honma & Ui, 1978; Okada, Honma, & Ui, 1982a; Okada, Shintomi, Honma, & Ui, 1982b; Ui et al., 1978). To the extent that these pharmacological manipulations can be extended to the study of alterations in cyclic nucleotide levels in the CSF, they may prove useful in the elucidation of muscarinic function in AD. For example, normal controls and patients with AD could show differential response to arecoline challenge as measured by cyclic AMP and cyclic GMP in CSF. These responses could reveal differences in the functional status of the central muscarinic receptors.

Additional strategies for evaluating cholinergic receptor function have been suggested by the studies of Janowsky, Risch, Judd, and Parker (1981) and Nurnberger et al. (1983). These investigators have shown that centrally acting cholinergic agonists produce increases in a number of neuroendocrine parameters (e.g., plasma cortisol, prolactin, growth hormone). However, as pointed out by Lerer and Sitaram (1983), the degree to which these responses, as well as the changes in pulse and blood pressure which also have been observed, are cholinergically mediated is not fully understood. Thus, the utility of these parameters as indices of central cholinergic function may be of limited value at this time.

Obviously the more parameters we can measure from the different categories listed in Table 2 during cholinergic challenges, the more certain we will be about the state of receptor function within this disease and the greater the likelihood of their potential usefulness in the treatment of this disorder. Once the functional responsivity of the remaining muscarinic receptors has been determined (e.g., hyporesponsivity or hyperresponsivity), we will be better able to assess the potential utility that this approach might have in yielding clinically relevant therapeutic agents. Thus, it is clear that if a hyporesponsivity of the postsynaptic, M_1, muscarinic receptors is present in this disorder, simply trying to enhance cholinergic transmission by presynaptic cholinergic manipulations might not be a sufficient therapeutic strategy. In this instance, the coadministration of agents such as thyrotropin-releasing hormone or its analogues, which are known to enhance the sensitivity of these receptors to ACh and to enhance ACh synthesis and release, might be more therapeutic (Yarbrough & Pomara, 1985). Similarly, the determination of a biological measure of muscarinic receptor activation in response to these manipulations might help us to establish the extent to which the limited clinical response to these agents is due to a failure to activate these receptors. In this instance, one is left with the task of searching for other less toxic pharmacological agents that might be given at the dosages that would produce the desired biological and improved clinical response.

On the other hand, a supersensitivity of the remaining muscarinic receptors could contribute by itself to the pathophysiology of AD and dictate different treatment approaches. [It should be noted in this regard that in peripheral smooth muscle tissue, the development of supersensitivity has been shown to be accompanied not only by the expected increased sensitivity to the natural transmitter and / or its chemical derivatives but also by a loss of specificity and increased sensitivity to other agonists (Fleming, McPhillips, & Westfall, 1973).] In the presence of extensive presynaptic cholinergic deficits and reduced acetylcholine synthesis and release, remaining supersensitive muscarinic receptors in AD could be vulnerable to aberrant stimulation by neurotransmitter systems, not necessarily subserving memory functions.

CONCLUSION

The functional status of muscarinic receptors should not be assumed to remain unchanged in AD. Receptor number, as measured by QNB binding, is not a consistent predictor of functional response. Muscarinic receptor responsivity needs to be studied in patients with AD. In the individual patient suffering from AD, findings of hyporesponsivity, hyperresponsivity, or unaltered responsivity may support different therapeutic strategies for the cognitive dysfunction.

REFERENCES

Bartus, R.T., Dean, R.L., Beer, B., & Lippa, A.S. (1982). The cholinergic hypothesis of geriatric memory dysfunction. *Science, 28,* 408-417.

Bowen, D.M. (1983). Biochemical assessment of neurotransmitter and metabolic dysfunction and cerebral atrophy in Alzheimer's disease. In R. Katzman (Ed.), *Banbury report 15. Biological aspects of Alzheimer's disease* (pp. 219-231). Cold Spring Harbor, NY: Cold Spring Harbor Laboratory.

Bowen, D.M., Allen, S.J., Goodhardt, M.J., Haan, E.A., Palmer, A.M., Sims, N.R., Smith, C.C.T., Spillane, J.A., Esiri, M.M., Neary, D., Snowdon, J.S., Wilcock, G.K., & Davison, A.M. (1983). Biochemical assessment of serotonergic and cholinergic dysfunction and cerebral atrophy in Alzheimer's disease. *Journal of Neurochemistry, 41,* 266-272.

Bowen, D.M., White, P., Spillane, J.A., Goodhardt, M.J., Curzon, G., Iwangoff, P., Meier-Ruge, W., & Davison, A.N. (1979). Accelerated aging or selective neuronal loss as an important cause of dementia? *Lancet, I,* 11.

Cross, A.J., Crow, T.J., Johnson, J.A., Perry, E.K., Perry, R.H., Blessed, G., & Tomlinson, B.E. (1984). Studies on neurotransmitter receptor systems in neocortex and hippocampus in senile dementia of the Alzheimer-type. *Journal of the Neurological Sciences, 64,* 109-117.

Dam, M., Wamsley, J.K., Rapoport, S.I., & London, E.D. (1982). Effects of oxotremorine on local glucose utilization in the rat cerebral cortex. *Journal of Neuroscience, 2,* 1072-1078.

Davies, P., & Maloney, A.J.F. (1976). Selective loss of central cholinergic neurons in Alzheimer's disease [Letter to the editor]. *Lancet, 2,* 1403.

Davies, P., & Verth, A. (1978). Regional distribution of muscarinic acetylcholine receptor in normal and Alzheimer's type dementia brains. *Brain Research, 138,* 385-392.

Everett, G.M. (1956). Tremor produced by drugs. *Nature, 177,* 1238.

Ferrendelli, J.A., Steiner, A.L., McDougal, D.B., & Kipnis, D.M. (1970). The effect of oxotremorine and atropine on cGMP and cAMP levels in mouse cerebral cortex and cerebellum. *Biochemical and Biophysical Research Communications, 41,* 1061-1068.

Fleming, W.W., McPhillips, J.J., & Westfall, D.P. (1973). Postjunctional supersensitivity and subsensitivity of excitable tissue to drugs. *Reviews of Physiology, 68,* 55-119.

Francis, P.T., Palmer, A.M., Sims, N.R., Bowen, D.M., Davison, A.N., Esiri, M.M., Neary, D., Snowdon, J.S., & Wilcock, G.K. (1985). Neurochemical studies of early-onset Alzheimer's disease. *New England Journal of Medicine, 313,* 7-11.

Friedman, M.J., & Jaffe, J.H. (1969). A central hypothermic response to pilocarpine in the mouse. *Journal of Pharmacology and Experimental Therapeutics, 167,* 34-44.

George, W.J., Polson, J.B., O'Toole, A.G., & Goldberg, N.D. (1970). Elevation of cyclic GMP in rat heart after perfusion with acetylcholine. *Proceedings of the National Academy of Sciences, USA, 66,* 398.

Greenwald, B.S., & Davis, K.L. (1983). Experimental pharmacology of Alzheimer's disease. In R. Mayeux & W.G. Rosen (Eds.), *The dementias* (pp. 87-102). New York: Raven Press.

Heilbronn, E., & Bartfai, T. (1978). Muscarinic acetylcholine receptor. *Progress in Neurobiology, 11,* 171-188.

Honma, M., & Ui, M. (1978). Plasma cyclic GMP: Response to cholinergic agents. *European Journal of Pharmacology, 47,* 1-10.

Janowsky, D.S., Risch, S.C., Judd, L.L., & Parker, D.C. (1981). Cholinergic supersensitivity in affect disorder patients: Behavioral and neuroendocrine observations. *Psychopharmacology Bulletin, 17,* 129-132.

Jones, D., Kelwala, S., Bell, J., Dube, S., Jackson, E., & Sitaram, N. (1985). Cholinergic REM sleep induction response correlation with endogenous major depressive subtype. *Psychiatry Research, 14,* 99-110.

Kebabian, J.W., Steiner, A.L., & Greengard, P. (1975). Muscarinic cholinergic regulation of cyclic guanosine $3',5'$-monophosphate in autonomic ganglia: Possible role in synaptic transmission. *Journal of Pharmacology and Experimental Therapeutics, 193,* 474-488.

Lerer, B. (1985). Studies on the role of brain cholinergic systems in the therapeutic mechanisms and adverse effects of ECT and lithium. *Biological Psychiatry, 20,* 20-40.

Lerer, B., & Sitaram, N. (1983). Clinical strategies for evaluating ECT mechanisms—Pharmacological, biochemical and psychophysiological approaches. *Progress in Neuropsychopharmacology and Biological Psychiatry, 7,* 309-333.

Lerer, B., Stanley, M., Demetriou, S., & Gershon, S. (1983). Effect of electroconvulsive shock on muscarinic cholinergic receptors in rat cerebral cortex and hippocampus. *Journal of Neurochemistry, 41,* 1680-1683.

Lerer, B., Stanley, M., McIntyre, I., & Altman, H. (1984). Electroconvulsive shock and brain muscarinic receptors: Relationship to anterograde amnesia. *Life Sciences, 35,* 2659-2664.

Lippa, A.S., Pelham, R.W., Beer, B., Critchett, D.J., Dean, R.L., & Bartus, R.T. (1980). Brain cholinergic function and memory in aged rats. *Neurobiology of Aging, 1,* 10-16.

Marks, M.J., O'Connor, M.F., Artman, L.D., Burch, J.B., & Collins, A.C. (1984). Chronic scopolamine treatment and brain cholinergic function. *Pharmacology, Biochemistry and Behavior, 20,* 771-777.

Mash, D.C., Flynn, D.D., & Potter, L.T. (1985). Loss of M_2 muscarine receptors in the cerebral cortex in Alzheimer's disease and experimental cholinergic denervation. *Science, 228,* 1115-1117.

Mohs, R.C., Davis, B.M., Johns, C.A., Mathe, A.A., Greenwald, B.S., Horvath, T.B., & Davis, K.L. (1985). Oral physostigmine treatment of patients with Alzheimer's disease. *American Journal of Psychiatry, 142,* 28-33.

Morrison, J.H., Rogers, J., Scherr, S., Benoit, R., & Bloom, F. (1985). Somatostatin immunoreactivity in neuritic plaques of Alzheimer's patients. *Nature, 314,* 90-92.

Nurnberger, J.J., Jimerson, D.C., Simmons-Alling, S., Tamminga, C., Nadi, N.S., Sitaram, N., Gillin, J.C., & Gershon, E.S. (1983). Behavioral, physiological, and neuroendocrine responses to arecoline in normal twins and "well state" bipolar patients. *Psychiatry Research, 9,* 191-200.

Okada, F., Honma, M., & Ui, M. (1982a). Plasma guanosine $3',5'$-monophosphate response to methacholine and epinephrine in humans. *Journal of Clinical Endocrinology and Metabolism, 54,* 645-647.

Okada, F., Shintomi, Y., Honma, M., & Ui, M. (1982b). Plasma cyclic nucleotide responses to methacholine in patients with Adie's syndrome. *Journal of the Neurological Sciences, 55,* 267-271.

Palmer, G.C. (1983). Effects of psychoactive drugs on cyclic nucleotides in the central nervous system. *Progress in Neurobiology, 21,* 1-133.

Pedigo, N.W., Minor, L.D., & Krumrei, T.N. (1984). Cholinergic drug effects and brain muscarinic receptor binding in aged rats. *Neurobiology of Aging, 5,* 227-333.

Perry, E.K., (1980). The cholinergic system in old age and Alzheimer's disease. *Age/Ageing, 9,* 1-8.

Perry, E.K., Perry, R.H., Blessed, G., & Tomlinson, B.E. (1977). Necropsy evidence of central cholinergic deficits in senile dementia [Letter to the editor]. *Lancet, 2,* 189.

Perry, E.K., Tomlinson, B.E., Blessed, G., Bergmann, K., Gibson, P.H., & Perry, R.H. (1978). Correlation of cholinergic abnormalities with senile plaques and mental test scores in senile dementia. *British Medical Journal, 2,* 1457-1459.

Roberts, G.W., Crow, T.J., & Polak, J.M. (1985). Location of neuronal tangles in somatostatin neurones in Alzheimer's disease. *Nature, 314,* 92-94.

Rossor, M.N. (1982). Neurotransmitters and CNS disease: Dementia. *Lancet, 2,* 1200-1204.

Sitaram, N., & Gillin, J.C. (1979). Acetylcholine: Possible involvement in sleep and analgesia. In K. Davis & P.A. Berger (Eds.), *Brain acetylcholine and neuropsychiatric disease* (pp. 311-343). New York: Plenum Press.

Sitaram, N., Gillin, J.C., & Bunney, W.E. (1984). Cholinergic and catecholaminergic receptor sensitivity in affective illness: Strategy and theory. In R.M. Post & J.C. Ballenger (Eds.), *Neurobiology of mood disorders: Vol. 1. Frontiers of clinical neuroscience* (pp. 629-651). Baltimore: Williams & Wilkins.

Sitaram, N., Nurnberger, J.I., Gershon, E.S., & Gillin, J.C. (1980). Faster REM sleep induction in remitted patients with primary affective illness. *Science, 208,* 200-202.

Sitaram, N., Nurnberger, J.I., Gershon, E.S., & Gillin, J.C. (1982). Cholinergic regulation of mood and REM sleep: Potential model and marker of vulnerability to affective disorder. *American Journal of Psychiatry, 139,* 571-576.

Stanley, M., & Lerer, B. (1985). Electroconvulsive shock and brain cholinergic function: Role of striatal muscarinic receptors. *Convulsive Therapy, 1,* 158-166.

Ui, M., Honma, M., Kunitada, S., Okada, F., Ide, H., Hata, S., & Satoh, T. (1978). Adrenergic and cholinergic modulation of extracellular cyclic nucleotides. In P. Hamet & H. Sands (Eds.), *Advances in cyclic nucleotide research* (Vol. 12, pp. 25-35). New York: Raven Press.

Whitehouse, P.J., Price, D.L., Struble, R.G., Clark, A.W., Coyle, J.T.,

& DeLong, M.R. (1982). Alzheimer's disease and senile dementia: Loss of neurons in the basal forebrain. *Science, 215,* 1237-1239.

Yarbrough, G.G., & Pomara, N. (1985). The therapeutic potential of thyrotropin releasing hormone in Alzheimer's disease. *Progress in Neuropsychopharmacology and Biological Psychiatry, 9,* 285-289.

19

Cholinergic and Somatostatin Deficits in the Alzheimer Brain

Peter Davies, PhD

A pragmatic approach to the development of treatments for Alzheimer's disease (AD) demands that attempts be made to correct observed neurochemical deficiencies: We must try to correct the problems we know exist. By far the most consistent deficits observed are those involving cholinergic and somatostatin neurons. It is now 9 years since the original reports of evidence for deficits in cholinergic transmission in AD (Davies & Maloney, 1976; Perry, E.K., Perry, R.H., Blessed, & Tomlinson, 1977; White et al., 1977), and all reports remain consistent in the demonstration of this problem (Davies, 1983). However, no effective therapeutic measures have resulted from attempts to treat this. Several reports of reduced concentrations of somatostatin in the cerebral cortex of autopsied AD patients have been published (Beal et al., 1985; Davies & Terry, 1981; Davies, Katzman, & Terry, 1980; Rosser, Emson, Mountjoy, Roth, & Iversen, 1980), and some workers have apparently found reduced concentrations of this peptide in the cerebrospinal fluid (CSF) of putative AD patients (Francis & Bowen, 1985). Recently, Francis and Bowen (1985) have reported that potassium-stimulated release of this peptide from samples of biopsy tissue from AD patients is not reduced and question the suggestion of reduced somatostatin transmission in these cases.

The questions to be addressed here are:

1. Does the available evidence really indicate the presence of major abnormalities in one or more neurotransmitter systems?

2. Are the observed deficiencies likely to be a cause of the patient's symptoms?

3. Can we reliably predict which patient has a particular neurotransmitter deficiency?

4. How can observed neurotransmitter deficits be made good?

In addressing these questions the emphasis will be on the cholinergic and somatostatin neurons, as these systems are the most actively studied at present. However, because of speculation concerning the possible roles of the norepinephrine and serotonin systems, the evidence for deficits in these neurotransmitters in AD will also be reviewed.

WHAT DEFICITS ARE WE TRYING TO TREAT?

As detailed in several recent reviews (Davies, 1983; Terry & Katzman, 1983) every presynaptic marker of cholinergic neurons has been reported to be reduced in biopsy or autopsy tissue from patients with AD, and the existence of a cholinergic deficit can no longer be in any doubt. However, few seem to have seriously examined the possible functional significance of this problem. Especially because of the lack of success in attempts to treat AD patients with presumed promoters of cholinergic transmission (Boyd, Graham-White, Blackwood, Glen, & McQueen, 1977; Etienne, Gauthier, Dastoor, Collier, & Ratner, 1978) many have tried to minimize the significance of this deficit and turned to other, generally less well-justified strategies. While this is understandable, it is probably ducking the issue.

It is common knowledge and undeniable that even low doses of specific anticholinergics produce deficits in cognitive function, and especially in tests of short-term memory. Numerous studies and anecdotes have reported that agents with anticholinergic properties can produce confusion, delirium, and, according to certain authors, "Indeed, one of the pressing clinical problems is to differentiate the patient in delirium (which is usually reversible) from the one with dementia (which is usually not)" (Hollister, 1981, p. 8). It seems to this author that it is virtually certain that the cholinergic deficiency in AD patients is one cause of the clinical signs and symptoms of this disease. Thus attempting to treat this problem must be the highest priority. This is not to imply that it is the only treatment needed; however, given the available evidence, a treatment that fails to ameliorate the cholinergic deficit seems likely not to do anything significant for the patient.

A reduced concentration of somatostatin in the cortex (especially temporal cortex) of autopsied AD patients has been found in several studies. Some authors have also found reduced somatostatin concentrations in lumbar spinal fluid from presumed AD patients, although in these studies the nature of the immunoreactive material is somewhat questionable. Other workers have failed to show abnormal levels of somatostatin-like material in CSF (Thal, Fuld, Masur, Sharpless, & Davies, 1983). In the study of biopsy material, Francis and Bowen (1985) reported that normal levels of somatostatin were released on potassium-induced depolarization thereby making it seem unlikely that deficits in somatostatin transmission were present in the brains of living patients. Why, then, do autopsied patients show reductions in the concentration of this peptide, while levels of most neuroactive peptides seem to be normal?

It is possible that reduced steady-state concentrations of somatostatin can occur without reductions in the amount released. It is well known that probably the least reliable measurement of activity in a given neurotransmitter system is the measurement of the concentration of the transmitter itself. In the aminergic system changes in rates of transmitter turnover rarely have predictable effects on steady-state concentrations of amines. This is likely to be true for neuropeptides too, especially because synthesis of precursors and some proteolytic processing must occur in cell bodies that are sometimes some distances from the site of peptide release. Decreased concentrations of somatostatin could result from *increased* somatostatin release if synthesis and release are poorly coupled.

We have little information on the possible clinical significance of a decreased concentration of somatostatin in cortex. Recent studies by our group at Albert Einstein College of Medicine have revealed that a small number of elderly individuals have extremely low levels of somatostatin in the cerebral cortex. Neuropsychological studies seem to demonstrate that these individuals were functioning at a high level within a few months of death and autopsy, and we thus begin to question whether normal steady-state concentrations of peptides are really adequate measures of the possible involvement of these neuronal systems in disease. Apart from the fact that somatostatin concentrations seem to be consistently reduced in the AD cerebral cortex, we have no other grounds to support attempts at treating this presumed problem.

There has been a recent revival of interest in the possible role of norepinephrine and serotonin deficits in AD. The norepinephrine system does sometimes seem to be affected by this disease, as evidenced by severe cell loss from the locus coeruleus (Mann, D.M.A., Lincoln, Yates, Stamp, & Toper, 1980; Tomlinson, Irving, & Blessed, 1981). However, such marked cell loss is by no means a consistent finding and seems to occur with highest frequency in younger female cases. On average, cell loss is less striking, and the 30% to 40% reductions in dopamine beta-hydroxylase activity reported by the Perrys (Perry et al., 1981) are in the same range as reductions in pigmented locus coeruleus cells. Norepinephrine metabolite concentrations seem to be quite consistently elevated in the AD brain, although transmitter concentrations are usually somewhat lower than normal (Gottfries et al., 1983). Such data obtained in animal studies would usually be interpreted to indicate *increased* norepinephrine turnover rather than a noradrenergic deficit. Whether this is the case remains unclear. Biopsy tissue and CSF from AD patients do not show evidence of any major norepinephrine deficit (Bowen et al., 1981; Gottfries & Roos, 1973; Gottfries, Gottfries, & Roos, 1969; Mann, J.J., et al., 1981), and although the small number of younger female patients might have a substantial problem, there does not appear to be a very weighty argument for treatment of noradrenergic deficits in the majority of patients.

The state of the serotonin neurons in the AD brain has been much less well-studied. In autopsy material, only the metabolite, 5-hydroxyindoleacetic acid (5-HIAA) is readily measurable in most patients, and levels tend to be 30% to 40% lower in AD brains as compared to age-matched controls (Gottfries et al., 1983). Some authors have reported smaller deficits in CSF although these have been difficult to observe consistently (Gottfries, Gottfries, & Roos, 1969; Gottfries & Roos, 1973; Mann, J.J., et al., 1981). Biopsy studies support the idea of a limited deficit, the extent of which does not appear to correlate with the degree of dementia (Bowen et al., 1981). Further studies of this system appear to be warranted.

WHO HAS WHAT DEFICIENCY?

As neurochemical and neuropathologic studies of demented individuals expand, it is becoming obvious that dementia is considerably more complex than one would like it to be. Neuropathologic studies reveal that a clinical diagnosis of AD is accurate between 70% and 80% of the time, depending on the diagnostic criteria being used. To a neurochemist this is very distressing because we tend to think that a specific neurotransmitter deficit should produce a unique and identifiable pattern of clinical problems. This may not be true. A recent episode illustrates this point: Two of New York's most experienced neurologists diagnosed AD in a man in his early sixties and were confident of their diagnosis. On autopsy, the man proved to have Pick's disease. In all really classic AD cases, a major cholinergic deficiency has been found. No case of Pick's disease, including the one mentioned above, has been found to have reductions in markers of cholinergic neurons. In our own studies, we have seen several other cases that were thought to have AD but on autopsy proved to have neither the pathologic nor neurochemical features typical of this condition.

My personal viewpoint is that while the cholinergic deficiency is likely to contribute in a fairly major way to the symptomatology of Alzheimer's disease, other disorders and other neurotransmitter deficiencies may produce a very similar pattern of cognitive dysfunction. Selection of patients for inclusion in one or another therapeutic trial thus becomes a major problem. Clinical researchers will have to accept that probably a quarter of the patients to be treated will have been inaccurately diagnosed, and how this will affect the outcome of the studies is difficult to predict. Even if 75% of the patients are correctly identified, it is also possible that neurochemical heterogeneity will be present. Some AD patients do have norepinephrine and/or serotonin deficiencies, and as many as 30% may also have signs of Parkinson's disease (pathologically). There probably is a relatively small subgroup of these generally elderly patients that has a relatively pure cholinergic deficiency. At present we have no reliable way of identifying these individuals.

SPECIFIC TREATMENT STRATEGIES

It should be clear by now that I believe that there are two basic problems preceding those of developing better treatments for the symptoms of AD. The first concerns our failure to properly categorize what percentage of the patient population has a specific neurochemical deficit, and the second concerns our inability to identify patients during life. As more and more demented patients find their way to autopsy, we ought to be able to define what percentage of cases have specific deficits or patterns of neurotransmitter deficiencies. More innovative strategies will be needed to diagnose these deficits during life but these problems are probably solvable. Given our current state of knowledge, there are a few suggestions that can be made to aid the development of new therapeutic agents.

In regard to the cholinergic system, our knowledge is still far from complete regarding regulatory mechanisms at the presynaptic terminal. Presynaptic inhibitory muscarinic autoreceptors clearly exist, but are very difficult to distinguish from postsynaptic sites (Mash & Potter, 1982; McKinney & Coyle, 1982). Specific antagonists for these presynaptic receptors would enhance ACh release without inhibiting its postsynaptic activity. As both ACh release and binding to muscarinic receptors are easy to assay, large numbers of compounds should be screened for relative potency. The relationship between the selectivity of compounds like pirenzepine for M1 and M2 muscarinic receptors and possible selectivity for pre- and postsynaptic sites deserves further attention (Mash & Potter, 1983; Potter et al., 1983), and perhaps would serve as a starting point from which to design even more selective agents.

We still do not know what limits the rate of ACh synthesis *in vivo*. We do know that it is not the activity of choline acetyltransferase: Even the most severe AD case has enough enzyme activity left to support the highest measured rates of ACh turnover. A few agents, like the aminopyridines, seem able to enhance ACh release in some situations (Peterson & Gibson, 1982), but no systematic search for similar activities seems to have been carried out. Despite several writings making the suggestion, no one seems to have tried adding a nicotinic receptor agonist to a muscarinic agonist yet. Perhaps this approach could be attempted using the intraventricular cannula (see Harbaugh, this volume). Some agents have both nicotinic and muscarinic agonist properties (e.g., carbachol), and a short duration of action is perhaps desirable in initial trials.

Whether the somatostatin deficiency is worth trying to treat is not yet clear. Now that stable analogues of the peptide are available (Cutler et al., 1985) these compounds might also be worth adding to the intraventricular cannula pumps. A note concerning the utility of the cannula seems appropriate. While these devices may not prove to be ideal for the majority of demented patients, they offer a very significant research tool in that compounds deemed safe might be tested for acute efficacy prior to the development of analogues that are resistant to degradation and that efficiently cross the blood-brain barrier. The ethics of this proposed usage of the cannula is a matter that will need some further consideration.

If, as some seem to believe, norepinephrine and serotonin deficiencies contribute to the symptoms of AD patients, the vast experience of the pharmaceutical industry in this area ought to be mobilized. It already seems clear that agents that inhibit norepinephrine and / or serotonin reuptake will be inadequate if used alone. However, in patients showing some positive response to physostigmine, the addition of the appropriate agent might prove interesting.

CONCLUSION

The possibility of developing a successful treatment for the symptoms of AD seems to me to be more dependent on the nature of cholinergic neurotransmission than on any other single factor. If the release of ACh really is exquisitely ordered in both space and time, carrying information in a truely staggeringly complex fashion, it is unlikely that any drug treatment will be of much help. If cholinergic terminals are being steadily wiped out by the disease process, as seems likely, no treatment will permit the restoration of information flow. If the cholinergic system is more a tonic system, somewhat like the nigrostriatal dopaminergic neurons, more success should be possible.

If the former scenario proves to be true, attention will have to be directed toward the prevention of the disease. Ironically, this may be easier than treating the symptoms. Like other late-onset neurologic diseases, AD does not appear to influence either brain development or function prior to onset. A significant number of individuals with evidence for autosomal dominant inheritance of AD function at an extremely high level for years prior to disease onset. Thus the brain and / or body has some highly successful means of protection against the genetic defect. Even among sporadic cases, the age-related incidence of the disease argues that most of us have a very effective defense against the expression of the disease. Compared to the fast pace of research aimed at identifying the cause of Huntington's chorea and Parkinson's disease, we are not making as much progress in research to identify the cause, not treatment, of AD.

REFERENCES

Beal, M.F., Mazurek, M.F., Tran, V.T., Chattha, G., Bird, E.D., & Martin, J.B. (1985). Reduced numbers of somatostatin receptors in the cerebral cortex in Alzheimer's disease. *Science, 229,* 289-291.

Bowen, D.M., Sims, N.R., Benton, J.S., Curzon, G., Davison, A.N., Neary, D., & Thomas, D.J. (1981). Treatment of Alzheimer's disease: A cautionary note [Letter to the editor]. *New England Journal of Medicine, 305,* 1016.

Boyd, W.D., Graham-White, J., Blackwood, G., Glen, I., & McQueen, J. (1977). Clinical effects of choline in Alzheimer senile dementia [Letter to the editor]. *Lancet, II,* 711.

Cutler, N.R., Haxby, J.V., Narang, P.K., May, C., Burg, C., & Reines, S.A. (1985). Evaluation of an analogue of somatostatin (L363,586) in Alzheimer's disease [Letter to the editor]. *New England Journal of Medicine, 312,* 725.

Davies, R. (1983). An update on the neurochemistry of Alzheimer's diseases. In R. Mayeux & W.G. Rosen (Eds.), *The dementias* (pp. 75-86). New York: Raven Press.

Davies, P., Katzman, R., & Terry, R.D. (1980). Reduced somatostatin-like immunoreactivity in cerebral cortex from cases of Alzheimer's disease and Alzheimer senile dementia. *Nature, 288,* 279-280.

Davies, P., & Maloney, A.J.R. (1976). Selective loss of central cholinergic neurons in Alzheimer's disease [Letter to the editor]. *Lancet, II,* 1403.

Davies, P., & Terry, R.D. (1981). Cortical somatostatin-like cases of Alzheimer's disease and senile dementia of the Alzheimer type. *Neurobiology of Aging, 2,* 9-14.

Etienne, P., Gauthier, S., Dastoor, D., Collier, B., & Ratner, J. (1978). Lecithin in Alzheimer's disease. *Lancet, II,* 1206.

Francis, P.T., & Bowen, D.M. (1985). Relevance of reduced concentrations of somatostatin in Alzheimer's disease. *Biochemical Society Transactions, 13,* 170-171.

Gottfries, C.G., Adolfsson, R., Aquilonius, S.-M., Carlsson, A., Eckernas, S.-A., Nordberg, A., Oreland, L., Svennerholm, L., Wiberg, A., & Winblad, B. (1983). Biochemical changes in dementia disorders of Alzheimer type. *Neurobiology of Aging, 4,* 261-271.

Gottfries, C.G., Gottfries, I, & Roos, B.E. (1969). Homovanillic acid and 5-hydroxyindoleacetic acid in the cerebrospinal fluid of patients with senile dementia, presenile dementia and Parkinsonism. *Journal of Neurochemistry*, *16*, 1341-1345.

Gottfries, C.G., & Roos, B.E. (1973). Acid monomine metabolism in cerebrospinal fluid from patients with presenile dementia (Alzheimer's disease). *Acta Psychiatrica Scandinavica*, *49*, 257-263.

Hollister, L.E. (1981). An overview of strategies for the development of an effective treatment for senile dementia. In T. Crook & S. Gershon (Eds.), *Strategies for the development of an effective treatment for senile dementia* (pp. 7-18). New Canaan, CT: Mark Powley Associates, Inc.

Mann, D.M.A., Lincoln, J., Yates, P.O., Stamp, J.E., & Toper, S. (1980). Changes in the monoamine containing neurones of the human CNS in senile dementia. *British Journal of Psychiatry*, *136*, 533-541.

Mann, J.J., Stanley, M., Neophytides, A., DeLeon, M.J., Ferris, S.H., & Gershon, S. (1981). Central amine metabolism in Alzheimer's disease: In vivo relationship to cognitive defect. *Neurobiology of Aging*, *2*, 57-60.

Mash, D.C., & Potter, L.T. (1982). Autoradiographic localization of M1 and M2 muscarine receptors in the rat brain. *Society for Neuroscience Abstracts*, *8*, 338.

Mash, D.C., & Potter, L.T. (1983). Changes in M1 and M2 muscarine receptors in Alzheimer's disease and aging, and with lesions of cholinergic neurons in animals. *Society for Neuroscience Abstracts*, *9*, 582.

McKinney, M., & Coyle, J.T. (1982). Regulation of neocortical muscarinic receptors: Effects of drug treatment and lesions. *Journal of Neuroscience*, *2*, 97-105.

Perry, E.K., Perry, R.H., Blessed, G., & Tomlinson, B.E. (1977). Necropsy evidence of central cholinergic deficits in senile dementia [Letter to the editor]. *Lancet, I,* 189.

Perry, E.K., Tomlinson, B.E., Blessed, G., Perry, R.H., Cross, A.J., & Crow, T.J. (1981). Neuropathological and biochemical observations on the noradrenergic system in Alzheimer's disease. *Journal of the Neurological Sciences*, *51*, 279-287.

Peterson, C., & Gibson, G.E. (1982). 3,4-Diaminopyridine alters acetylcholine metabolism and behavior during hypoxia. *Journal of*

Pharmacology and Experimental Therapeutics, 222, 576-582.

Potter, L.T., Flynn, D.D., Hanchett, H.E., Kalinoski, D.L., Luber-Narod, J., & Mash, D.C. (1983). Independent M1 and M2 receptors: Ligands, autradiography and functions. Proceedings of the International Symposium on Subtypes of Muscarinic Receptors (pp. 22-31). Boston, MA: Elsevier Science Publishers.

Rossor, M.N., Emson, P.C., Mountjoy, C.Q., Roth, M., & Iversen, L.L. (1980). Reduced amounts of immunoreactive somatostatin in the temporal cortex in senile dementia of Alzheimer type. *Neuroscience Letters, 20,* 373-377.

Terry, R.D., & Katzman, R. (1983). Senile dementia of the Alzheimer type. *Annals of Neurology, 14,* 497-506.

Thal, L.J., Fuld, P.A., Masur, D.M., Sharpless, N.S., & Davies, P. (1983). Oral physostigmine and lecithin improve memory in Alzheimer's disease. *Psychopharmacology Bulletin, 19,* 454-456.

Tomlinson, B.E., Irving, D., & Blessed, G. (1981). Cell loss in the locus coeruleus in senile dementia of Alzheimer type. *Journal of the Neurological Sciences, 49,* 419-428.

White, P., Goodhardt, M.J., Keet, J.P., Hiley, C.R., Carasco, L.H., Williams, I.E.I., & Bowen, D.M. (1977). Neocortical cholinergic neurons in elderly people. *Lancet, I,* 668-671.

ACKNOWLEDGMENTS

The author is supported by NIH grants MH 38623 and AG 02478. The support of the Commonwealth Fund, the McKnight Foundation, and the Joyce Mertz-Gilmore Foundation is gratefully acknowledged.

20

Development of Neurotransmitter-Specific Therapeutic Approaches in Alzheimer's Disease

Peter J. Whitehouse, MD, PhD

Since the introduction of L-DOPA to treat patients with Parkinson's disease, attempts to develop similar neurotransmitter-specific therapy in Alzheimer's disease (AD) have met with limited success. In this chapter, reasons for this failure are discussed, and a strategy is outlined for the development of new therapies based on a knowledge of changes in specific neuronal systems occurring in AD. Although AD is a multisystem disorder (Price, Whitehouse, & Struble, in press; Whitehouse, Struble, Hedreen, Clark, & Price, 1985d), the primary focus of this review will be on alterations in cholinergic neurons and, particularly, on changes in cholinergic receptors. Dysfunction in the basal forebrain cholinergic system (Whitehouse, Price, Clark, Coyle, & DeLong, 1981; Whitehouse et al., 1982) is the cellular abnormality most closely linked to the clinically apparent cognitive impairments in AD (Blessed, Tomlinson, & Roth, 1968; Perry, E.K., Perry, R.H., Gibson, Blessed, & Tomlinson, 1977; Wilcock, Esiri, Bowen, & Smith, 1982). However, the same approaches to develop drugs active in enhancing cholinergic function can be applied to other neurotransmitter-specific system abnormalities in AD.

Finding new neurotransmitter-specific therapies will require understanding the association between clinical and biological features of AD (i.e., determining which populations of neurons are associated with which cognitive deficits and producing drugs that replace or enhance the function of these affected cell populations). Several facts may explain the limited success of this approach to date. Since AD is a multisystem disorder, it is unclear whether therapy targeted at any one neurotransmitter system will be of major benefit. Our understanding of the roles of neurons affected in AD in normal cognition is limited. In addition, the dynamic functioning of neurons may not be replaceable to any important degree by a program of drug administration. Moreover, in AD, our knowledge concerning alterations in neurotransmitter receptors (the sites at which many drugs act) is rudimentary and, particularly in the case of cholinergic receptors, inconsistent (Whitehouse & Au, in press). Nevertheless, as we learn more about the nature of changes in neurons and associated receptors in AD and improve our ability to develop drugs that are more selective in their actions on those receptors, we should be able to improve currently available neurotransmitter-specific therapies.

Before considering this approach to drug therapy in AD, two general issues relevant to developing any new therapeutic approach will be addressed: problems of defining AD, specifically, the possible existence of subtypes of this condition; and difficulties in selecting the features of the disease to be the target of therapy. A new look at arousal and attentional deficits in AD may be fruitful. Finally, possibilities will be outlined for developing new therapeutic agents based on an understanding of cholinergic receptor alterations that occur in this disorder.

DEFINITION OF THE TARGET DISEASE

Before developing a treatment for any disease, criteria for defining the disease must be clear. Historically, problems in differentiating multi-infarct dementia and other conditions from AD led to the inclusion of a heterogeneous population of patients in early drug trials. Although most recent trials include attempts to differentiate these dementias using clinical rating scales, only at autopsy can a diagnosis of AD be made with assurity. Approximately 10% to 20% of clinically diagnosed cases of AD are not confirmed at postmortem examination. Obviously, it would not be possible to require autopsy confirmation of diagnosis to complete a drug study. Nevertheless, this problem of uncertainty in diagnosis needs to be considered in interpreting the results of drug studies.

In addition, it is unclear whether AD is only one disease or encompasses several disorders. Recent clinical, pathological and neurochemical studies support the view that several subtypes may be included in the term AD. If subtypes exist and are not differentiated in clinical trials, it may be impossible to demonstrate the usefulness of a drug that is only effective for treating a particular subgroup of study participants.

On clinical grounds, several different types of AD have been proposed. Familial AD and sporadic AD can be distinguished, although the relative prevalence of each type is unclear (Folstein & Breitner, 1981). The distinction between AD (a presenile form of dementia occurring before the age of 65) and senile dementia of the Alzheimer's type (SDAT) (occurring after the age of 65) has received renewed attention (Constantinidis, 1978; Seltzer & Sherwin, 1983). We have suggested that the senile form of the condition may represent more closely an accelerated aging process, whereas the presenile form is a more distinct disease entity (Whitehouse, Hedreen, & Price, 1983). Another clinical distinction can be drawn between patients who have a very rapid disease course and those whose rate of progression is slower (Mayeux, Stern, & Spanton, 1985). Moreover, the pattern of cognitive impairment in AD is quite variable. Some patients have prominent early language or praxis problems (Folstein & Breitner, 1981; Foster et al., 1983); others may have major psychiatric symptoms such as psychosis or depression (Fann & Wheless, 1981). Finally, some patients with AD have other associated neurological signs such as seizures, myoclonus, or prominent gait disturbances (Mayeux et al., 1985).

Recent neuropathological studies also demonstrate that considerable variability occurs in AD. For example, neuropathological changes appear to be greater in younger cases than older (Hubbard & Anderson, 1981; Tagliavini & Pilleri, 1983; Whitehouse et al., 1983). In addition, in different cases, the relative density of senile plaques and neurofibrillary tangles varies. Finally, although consistent loss of neurons has been reported in the basal forebrain cholinergic system in AD (Arendt, T., Bigl, Arendt, A., & Tennstedt, 1983; Tagliavini & Pilleri, 1983; Whitehouse et al., 1981, 1982) and in certain regions of telencephalon (Colon, 1973; Herzog & Kemper, 1980; Hooper & Vogel, 1976; Shefer, 1972; Terry, Peck, DeTeresa, Schechter, & Horoupian, 1981), neuronal loss in other areas of brain is more variable. For example, Bondareff and co-workers (Bondareff, Mountjoy, & Roth, 1982) have suggested that two subtypes of AD can be defined by differences in the magnitude of loss of cells in the locus coeruleus.

Neurochemical studies also provide evidence for heterogeneity in AD. Reduction in presynaptic cholinergic markers is a consistent feature of the disease (Bowen, Smith, White, & Davison, 1976; Davies & Maloney, 1976), but alterations in noradrenergic, serotonergic, and dopaminergic markers appear to be more variable (Adolfsson, Carlsson, & Gottfries, 1982; Mann, Lincoln, Yates, Stamp, & Toper, 1980; Perry, E.K. et al., 1981). This heterogeneity in neurochemical alterations is particularly relevant to developing neurotransmitter-specific therapies since different subtypes of patients might respond differently to neurotransmitter-specific agents.

The validity of these proposed subtypes of AD has not been firmly established. Prospective epidemiological studies are needed to examine whether these subtypes are well-defined, consistent entities and to relate clinical heterogeneity to biological variability determined at autopsy.

Positron emission tomography (PET) may also contribute to the definition of subtypes of disease and improve our ability to link clinical and biological features. For example, methyl-spiperone binding sites can be imaged in the brains of living subjects (Wagner et al., 1984). Consistent reductions in cortical serotonin receptors have been reported in AD (Bowen et al., 1983; Cross et al., 1984); spiperone binds primarily to serotonin receptors in cortex (Whitehouse et al., 1985e). Thus, it may be possible to measure the density of serotonin receptors in living patients and to relate receptor changes to clinical symptoms. Neuronal dysfunction occurs in the serotonergic raphe system in AD (Curcio & Kemper, 1984; Mann & Yates, 1983). This system has been implicated as playing a role in sleep disturbance, psychosis, depression, and other symptoms often found in AD (Fischman, 1983). Whether these or other clinical features can be related to alterations in the distribution and density of serotonin or other receptors in the brain as measured by PET remains to be established.

METHODS OF ASSESSMENT

After defining the disease, cognitive impairments to be the targets of therapy need to be defined. Problems still exist in defining the nature of the cognitive impairments in AD and in developing methods for assessing those impairments (Folstein & Whitehouse, in press). Considerable emphasis has been placed on the importance of global assessment devices, such as the Sandoz Clinical Assessment-Geriatric Scale (SCAG) (Salzman, 1983). Although our goal should be improvement of the patient's general capacity for daily living, a more focused assessment approach should be considered in drug development. The mechanism by which drugs are likely to improve the patient's overall behavior is through their effects on specific cognition systems. Therefore, drug studies should include neuropsychological tests that measure (as directly as possible) the effects of the drug on the nervous system.

Based on biological alterations present in AD, attempts to pharmacologically modify arousal and attentional mechanisms might be worth further exploration. Arousal refers to a general state of alertness or activation which determines the subject's readiness to respond to external stimuli. Selective attention is the ability to focus consciousness on a particular set of stimuli pertinent to the task at hand and to ignore irrelevant distractors. Being appropriately aroused and focusing attention on events in the environment are fundamental abilities upon which all other cognition depends. Cholinergic, noradrenergic, and serotonergic abnormalities in AD involve populations of neurons that provide diffuse innervation to telencephalic structures (Price et al., in press; Whitehouse et al., 1985d). The functional importance of these neural groups is unclear, but one reasonable hypothesis is that these neurons are part of the reticular activating system (Whitehouse et al., 1985d). Dysfunction in these cell groups may alter cortical regulatory mechanisms and result in impairments in arousal and selective attention.

New methods of assessing arousal and attention have been developed recently in cognitive psychology (Parasuraman & Davies, 1984). Many of these techniques are based on measuring the time it takes a subject to make a certain response (such as pushing a button) in tasks requiring different types of cognitive processing. This chronometric approach allows assessment of the effect of variables (such as disease or drugs) on these different stages of information processing. AD patients have been shown to be more impaired on reaction-time tasks, which require making choices, than on simple detection tasks (Ferris, Crook, Sathananthan, & Gershon, 1976; Pirozzolo, Christensen, Ogle, Hansch, & Thompson, 1981; Vrtunski, Patterson, Mack, & Hill, 1983). Reaction-time tasks have also been found to be a sensitive measure of cognitive decline, often preceding decrements on standard neuropsychological tests (Vrtunski et al., 1983). Reaction-time measures of attention have also been used to monitor treatment effects. For example, in patients with Parkinson's disease, the effects of motor and mental slowness on psychological tasks were measured and improvement in performance due to L-DOPA was assessed (Rafal, Posner, Walker, & Friedrich, 1984). Although the drug increased the speed of response, no direct effect on cognitive components of reaction time was noted.

Stimulant drugs, such as amphetamines, have well-known effects on arousal in normal subjects. Central mechanisms of action in this class of drugs are not well understood but may involve modification of some of the same neural systems affected in AD. Currently available stimulants play a limited role in the treatment of patients with AD because of side effects, the development of tolerance to their effects, and unclear efficacy (Funkenstein, Hicks, Dysken, & Davis, 1981). However, stimulant drugs might serve as model drugs to study further in AD. Such model drugs could be modified chemically to minimize their undesirable side effects and to promote their therapeutic effects.

NEUROTRANSMITTER RECEPTORS AND DRUG DEVELOPMENT

In AD, knowledge of dysfunction of neurotransmitter-specific systems has led to attempts to develop specific therapies. Most efforts have focused on the cholinergic system (Bartus, Dean, Beer, & Lippa, 1982; Davis & Mohs, 1982; Muramoto, Sugishita, Sugita, & Toyokura, 1979; Peters & Levin, 1979; Thal, Masur, Sharpless, Fuld, & Davies, 1984), since presynaptic cholinergic dysfunction correlates most strongly with the severity of dementia and with the magnitude of senile plaques and neurofibrillary tangles found at autopsy (Blessed et al., 1968; Perry et al., 1977; Wilcock et al., 1982). Moreover, animal experiments have also supported the role of acetylcholine in normal cognitive function (Bartus, Dean, Flicker, & Beer, 1983; Deutsch, 1971; Olton, Walker, & Wolf, 1982). Serotonergic, adrenergic, and peptidergic systems are also involved in normal cognition, and some of these are impaired in AD (Koob & Bloom, 1982; Mann et al., 1980; Price et al., in press; van Dongen, 1981; Whitehouse et al., 1985d). In AD, little clinically useful benefit from modification of these neurotransmitter-specific systems has been realized (Whitehouse, 1985).

As discussed previously, the reasons for this lack of success may be multiple. One reason for these therapeutic failures may be inadequate knowledge of neurotransmitter receptor alterations in AD. For example, the rationale for the use of cholinergic precursors and anticholinesterase inhibitors in AD usually includes the fact that postsynaptic cholinergic receptors are intact in this condition. Although early studies on cholinergic receptors in AD supported this claim

(Bowen et al., 1979; Davies & Verth, 1978), new studies demonstrate that the nature of cholinergic receptor alterations in AD is unclear (Whitehouse & Au, in press). Two groups have provided evidence that a relative increase in density of muscarinic cholinergic receptors occurs in AD (London & Waller, in press; Nordberg, Larsson, Adolfsson, Alafuzoff, & Winblad, 1983), whereas other workers have demonstrated that decreases occur (Reisine, Yamamura, Bird, Spokes, & Enna, 1978; Rinne, J.K., Laakso, Paijarvi, & Rinne, 1984). The existence of subtypes of muscarinic cholinergic receptors has also complicated the analysis of receptor changes in AD. We (Whitehouse et al., 1984; Whitehouse, Kopajtic, Jones, Kuhar, & Price, 1985a) and others (Mash, Flynn, & Potter, 1985) have recently demonstrated that a selective loss of the M2 high-affinity agonist muscarinic cholinergic receptor occurs in AD in areas of brain that receive dense innervation from the basal forebrain cholinergic system. Lesion studies in animals suggest that this M2 high-affinity agonist receptor is located presynaptically on terminals of basal forebrain cholinergic neurons (Mash et al., 1985; McKinney & Coyle, 1982). Precursor loading or anticholinesterase administration might result in stimulation of both M1 excitatory postsynaptic receptors and presynaptic M2 receptors, which may be inhibitory (Mash et al., 1985). The net effect of such strategies on enhancement of cholinergic function might be diminished because of mixed inhibitory and excitatory actions. One novel therapeutic approach would be to develop selective M1 agonists and/or selective M2 antagonists. The selective M1 antagonist, pirenzepine, has been shown to impair memory performance at relatively low doses (Caulfield, Higgins, & Straugham, 1983). Recently, the oxotremorine analogue compound BM-5 (N-methyl-N-[1-methyl-4-pyrrolidino-2-butynyl] acetamide) has been shown to have both presynaptic antagonist and postsynaptic agonist properties (Nordström, Alberts, Westlind, Unden, & Bartfai, 1983). Preliminary studies of the effects of this compound have shown that it increases cortical acetylcholine (ACh) release and may improve maze learning at low doses although a consistent pattern of effects has not emerged (G.L. Wenk, 1985 personal communication). Such compounds may be useful in the treatment of patients with AD.

Another subtype of cholinergic receptor, the nicotinic receptor, has only recently begun to be studied in AD. Although the majority of cholinergic receptors in the central nervous system (CNS) has muscarinic properties, a small percentage demonstrates nicotinic physiological and pharmacological characteristics (Phillis & York, 1968; Segal, 1978). Davies and Feisullin (1981) described a moderate loss of alpha-bungarotoxin binding in temporal cortex in AD. Although this compound binds to nicotinic receptors at the neuromuscular junction, its pharmacology in the CNS is quite different (Morley, Kemp, & Salvaterra, 1979). Using (^{3}H) ACh binding to measure nicotinic receptors, we found a reduction in these receptors in AD that parallels the magnitude and anatomical extent of reductions in presynaptic cholinergic markers (Whitehouse, Martino, Price, & Kellar, 1985c; Whitehouse et al., 1985b). The role of nicotinic receptors in AD needs to be clarified, particularly as it relates to the cognitive dysfunction. Dimethylphenylpiperazinium (DMPP), a drug with nicotinic agonist properties (Romano & Goldstein, 1980), improved memory performance in rats in a T-maze (Flood, Landry, & Jarrik, 1981). Selective nicotinic cholinergic agents might also be worth exploring for use in patients with AD.

Thus, even though the presynaptic cholinergic dysfunction in AD has been described for almost 10 years, the pattern of cholinergic receptor alterations in this condition is still being evaluated. In AD, an improved understanding of cholinergic receptor changes might assist the design of more specific agonist and antagonist drugs to enhance cholinergic function pertinent to cognitive function.

RECOMMENDATIONS

To develop a strategy for treating any disease, one needs to define criteria to diagnose the disease, to develop methods of assessing changes in target symptoms, and to design drugs that enhance function in those biological systems affected by the disease process. In this paper, we suggest one rational approach to developing new drugs for treating patients with AD, based on knowledge of the neuronal dysfunction present in this disorder. The basal forebrain cholinergic system, noradrenergic locus coeruleus, and serotonergic raphe nuclei affected in AD provide diffuse innervation of telencephalon and may be considered rostral extensions of the reticular activating system involved in arousal and attention. Drugs designed to enhance the activity of these cortical regulatory systems could improve the patient's overall functional capacity by improving his or her ability to focus mental efforts.

To evaluate this approach more fully, the existence of subtypes of AD, which may be characterized by abnormalities in different neurotransmitter-specific systems, needs to be considered. Moreover, new efforts should be made to apply recent advances in our understanding of normal arousal and attentional processes to the study of AD. Finally, the development of new drugs should be guided by improved understanding of the neurotransmitter system abnormalities found in AD. Of particular importance are alterations in neurotransmitter receptors. Our recent research on cholinergic receptors in AD has shown that selective reductions occur in the density of high-affinity agonist muscarinic and nicotinic cholinergic receptors. Some drugs are already available; others can be developed whose selective agonist and antagonist actions at subtypes of cholinergic receptors may make them potentially useful in treating patients with AD.

The ideas expressed here are speculative. The ultimate success of neurotransmitter-specific therapies is, of course, uncertain. Nevertheless, the approach to drug development outlined does represent a rational (rather than empirical) way to proceed based on our current knowledge of the disease.

REFERENCES

Arendt, T., Bigl, V., Arendt, A., & Tennstedt, A. (1983). Loss of neurons in the nucleus basalis of Meynert in Alzheimer's disease, paralysis agitans, and Korsakoff's disease. *Acta Neuropathologica, 61,* 101-108.

Bartus, R.T., Dean, R.L., III, Beer, B., & Lippa, A.S. (1982). The cholinergic hypothesis of geriatric memory dysfunction. *Science, 217,* 408-417.

Bartus, R.T., Dean, R.L., III, Flicker, C., & Beer, B. (1983). Behavioral and pharmacological studies using animal models of aging: Implications for studying and treating dementia of Alzheimer's type. Biological aspects of Alzheimer's disease. In R. Katzman (Ed.), *Banbury Report, 15.* Biological aspects of Alzheimer's disease (pp. 207-218). Cold Spring Harbor, N.Y.: Cold Spring Harbor Laboratory.

Blessed, G., Tomlinson, B.E., & Roth, M. (1968). The association between quantitative measures of dementia and of senile change in the cerebral grey matter of elderly subjects. *British Journal of Psychiatry, 114,* 797-811.

Bondareff, W., Mountjoy, C.Q., & Roth, M. (1982). Loss of neurons of origin of the adrenergic projection to cerebral cortex (nucleus locus ceruleus) in senile dementia. *Neurology, 32,* 164-168.

Bowen, D.M., Allen, S.J., Benton, J.S., Goodhardt, M.J., Haan, E.A., Palmer, A.M., Sims, N.R., Smith, C.C.T., Spillane, J.A., Esiri, M.M., Neary, D., Snowdon, J.S., Wilcock, G.K., & Davison, A.N. (1983). Biochemical assessment of serotonergic and cholinergic dysfunction and cerebral atrophy in Alzheimer's disease. *Journal of Neurochemistry, 41,* 266-272.

Bowen, D.M., Smith, C.B., White, P., & Davison, A.N. (1976). Neurotransmitter-related enzymes and indices of hypoxia in senile dementia and other abiotrophies. *Brain, 99,* 459-496.

Bowen, D.M., Spillane, J.A., Curzon, G., Meier-Ruge, W., White, P., Goodhardt, M.J., Iwangoff, P., & Davison, A.N. (1979). Accelerated aging or selective neuronal loss as an important cause of dementia? *Lancet, 1,* 11-14.

Caulfield, M.P., Higgins, G.A., & Straughan, D.W. (1983). Central administration of the muscarinic receptor subtype — selective antagonist pirenzepine selectively impairs passive avoidance learning in the mouse. *Journal of Pharmacy and Pharmacology, 35,* 131-132.

Colon, E.J. (1973). The cerebral cortex in presenile dementia. A quantitative analysis. *Acta Neuropathologica, 23,* 281-290.

Constantinidis, J. (1978). Is Alzheimer's disease a major form of senile dementia? Clinical, anatomical, and genetic data. In R. Katzman, R.D. Terry, & K.L. Bick (Eds.), *Alzheimer's disease: Senile dementia and related disorders* (pp. 15-25). New York: Raven Press.

Cross, A.J., Crow, T.J., Ferrier, I.N., Johnson, J.A., Bloom, S.R., & Corsellis, J.A.N. (1984). Serotonin receptor changes in dementia of the Alzheimer type. *Journal of Neurochemistry, 43,* 1574-1581.

Curcio, C.A., & Kemper, T. (1984). Nucleus raphe dorsalis in dementia of the Alzheimer type: Neurofibrillary changes and neuronal packing density. *Journal of Neuropathology and Experimental Neurology, 43,* 359-368.

Davies, P., & Feisullin, S. (1981). Postmortem stability of alpha-bungarotoxin binding sites in mouse and human brain. *Brain Research, 216,* 449-454.

Davies, P., & Maloney, A.J.F. (1976). Selective loss of central cholinergic neurons in Alzheimer's disease [Letter to the editor]. *Lancet, 2,* 1403.

Davies, P., & Verth, A.H. (1978). Regional distribution of muscarinic acetylcholine receptor in normal and Alzheimer's-type dementia brains. *Brain Research, 138,* 385-392.

Davis, K.L., & Mohs, R.C. (1982). Enhancement of mental processes in Alzheimer's disease with multiple-dose intravenous physostigmine. *American Journal of Psychiatry, 139,* 1421-1424.

Deutsch, J.A. (1971). The cholinergic synapse and the site of memory. *Science, 174,* 788-794.

Fann, W.E., & Wheless, J.C. (1981). Treatment and amelioration of psychopathologic affective states in the dementias of late life. In N.E. Miller & G.D. Cohen (Eds.), *Clinical aspects of Alzheimer's disease and senile dementia* (pp. 161-185). New York: Raven Press.

Ferris, S., Crook, T., Sathananthan, G., & Gershon, S. (1976). Reaction time as a diagnostic measure in senility. *Journal of the American Geriatric Society, 24,* 529-533.

Fischman, L.G. (1983). Dreams, hallucinogenic drug states, and schizophrenia: A psychological and biological comparison. *Schizophrenia Bulletin, 9,* 73-94.

Flood, J.F., Landry, D.W., & Jarvik, M.E. (1981). Cholinergic receptor interactions and their effects on long-term memory processing. *Brain Research, 215,* 177-185.

Folstein, M.F., & Breitner, J.C.S. (1981). Language disorder predicts familial Alzheimer's disease. *Johns Hopkins Medical Journal, 149,* 145-147.

Folstein, M.F., & Whitehouse, P.J. (in press). Cognitive impairment of Alzheimer's disease. *Journal of Neurobehavior Toxicology Teratology.*

Foster, N.L., Chase, T.N., Fedio, P., Patronas, N.J., Brooks, R.A., & DiChiro, G. (1983). Alzheimer's disease: Focal cortical changes shown by positron emission tomography. *Neurology, 33,* 961-965.

Funkenstein, H.H., Hicks, R., Dysken, M.W., & Davis, J.M. (1981). Drug treatment of cognitive impairment in Alzheimer's disease and the late life dementias. In N.E. Miller & G.D. Cohen (Eds.), *Clinical aspects of Alzheimer's disease and senile dementia* (pp. 139-160). New York: Raven Press.

Herzog, A.G., & Kemper, T.L. (1980). Amygdaloid changes in aging and dementia. *Archives of Neurology, 37,* 625-629.

Hooper, M.W., & Vogel, F.S. (1976). The limbic system in Alzheimer's disease. A neuropathologic investigation. *American Journal of Pathology, 85,* 1-20.

Hubbard, B.M., & Anderson, J.M. (1981). A quantitative study of cerebral atrophy in old age and senile dementia. *Journal of the Neurological Sciences, 50,* 135-145.

Koob, G.F., & Bloom, F.E. (1982). Behavioral effects of neuropeptides: Endorphins and vasopressin. *Annual Review of Physiology, 44,* 571-582.

London, E.D., & Waller, S.B. (in press). Relations between choline acetyltransferase and muscarinic binding in aging and Alzheimer's disease. In I. Hanin (Ed.), *Dynamics of cholinergic function* . New York: Plenum Press.

Mann, D.M.A., & Yates, P.O. (1983). Serotonin nerve cells in Alzheimer's disease. *Journal of Neurology, Neurosurgery and Psychiatry, 46,* 96-98.

Mann, D.M.A., Lincoln, J., Yates, P.O., Stamp, J.E., & Toper, S. (1980). Changes in the monoamine containing neurons of the human central nervous system in senile dementia. *British Journal of Psychiatry (London), 136,* 533-541.

Mash, D.C., Flynn, D.D., & Potter, L.T. (1985). Loss of M2 muscarine receptors in the cerebral cortex in Alzheimer's disease and in experimental cholinergic denervation. *Science, 228,* 1115-1117.

Mayeux, R., Stern, Y., & Spanton, S. (1985). Heterogeneity in dementia of the Alzheimer type: Evidence of subgroups. *Neurology, 35,* 453-461.

McKinney, M., & Coyle, J.T. (1982). Regulation of neocortical muscarinic receptors: Effects of drug treatment and lesions. *Journal of Neuroscience, 2,* 97-105.

Morley, B.J., Kemp, G.E., & Salvaterra, P. (1979). Alpha-bungarotoxin binding sites in the CNS. *Life Sciences, 24,* 859-872.

Muramoto, O., Sugishita, M., Sugita, H., & Toyokura, Y. (1979). Effect of physostigmine on constructional and memory tasks in Alzheimer's disease. *Archives of Neurology, 36,* 501-503.

Nordberg, A., Larsson, D., Adolfsson, R., Alafuzoff, I., & Winblad, B. (1983). Muscarinic receptor compensation in hippocampus of Alzheimer patients. *Journal of Neural Transmission, 56,* 13-19.

Nordström, Ö., Alberts, P., Westlind, A., Unden, A., & Bartfai, T. (1983). Presynaptic antagonist-postsynaptic agonist at muscarinic cholinergic synapses. *N*-methyl-*N*-(1-methyl-4-pyrrolidino-2butynyl) acetamide. *Molecular Pharmacology, 24,* 1-5.

Olton, D.S., Walker, J.A., & Wolf, W.A. (1982). A disconnection analysis of hippocampal function. *Brain Research, 233,* 241-253.

Parasuraman, R., & Davies, O.R. (1984). *Varieties of alteration.* New York: Academic Press.

Perry, E.K., Perry, R.H., Gibson, P.H., Blessed, G., & Tomlinson, B.E. (1977). A cholinergic connection between normal aging and senile dementia in the human hippocampus. *Neuroscience Letters, 6,* 85-89.

Perry, E.K., Tomlinson, B.E., Blessed, G., Perry, R.H., Cross, A.J., & Crow, T.J. (1981). Neuropathological and biochemical observations on the noradrenergic system in Alzheimer's disease. *Journal of the Neurological Sciences, 51,* 279-287.

Peters, B.H., & Levin, H.S. (1979). Effects of physostigmine and lecithin on memory in Alzheimer's disease. *Annals of Neurology, 6,* 219-221.

Phillis, J.W., & York, D.H. (1968). Pharmacological studies on a cholinergic inhibition in the cerebral cortex. *Brain Research, 10,* 297-306.

Pirozzolo, F.J., Christensen, K.J., Ogle, K.M., Hansch, E.C., & Thompson, W.G. (1981). Simple and choice reaction time in dementia: Clinical implications. *Neurobiology of Aging, 2,* 113-117.

Price, D.L., Whitehouse, P.J., & Struble, R.G. (in press). Cellular pathology in Alzheimer's and Parkinson's diseases. *Trends in Neurosciences.*

Rafal, R.D., Posner, M.I., Walker, J.A., & Friedrich, F.J. (1984). Cognition and the basal ganglia. Separating mental and motor components of performance in Parkinson's disease. *Brain, 107,* 1083-1094.

Reisine, T.D., Yamamura, H.I., Bird, E.D., Spokes, E., & Enna, S.J. (1978). Pre- and postsynaptic neurochemical alterations in Alzheimer's disease. *Brain Research, 159,* 477-481.

Rinne, J.O., Rinne, J.K., Laakso, K., Paijarvi, L., & Rinne, U.K. (1984). Reduction in muscarinic receptor binding in limbic areas of Alzheimer brain. *Journal of Neurology, Neurosurgery and Psychiatry, 47,* 651-653.

Romano, C., & Goldstein, A. (1980). Stereospecific nicotine receptors on rat brain membranes. *Science, 210,* 647-650.

Salzman, C. (1983). The Sandoz Clinical Assessment-Geriatric Scale.

In T. Crook, S. Ferris, & R. Bartus (Eds.), *Assessment in geriatric psychopharmacology* (pp. 53-58). New Canaan, CT: Mark Powley Associates, Inc.

Segal, M. (1978). General discussion I. In K. Elliott & J. Whelan (Eds.), *Functions of the septo-hippocampal system. Ciba Foundation Symposium 58 (new series)* (pp. 130-137). Amsterdam: Elsevier Science Publishers.

Seltzer, B., & Sherwin, I. (1983). A comparison of clinical features in early- and late-onset primary degenerative dementia. One entity or two? *Archives of Neurology, 40,* 143-146.

Shefer, V.F. (1972). Absolute number of neurons and thickness of the cerebral cortex during aging, senile and vascular dementia, and Pick's and Alzheimer's diseases. *Zhurnal Nevropathologii I Psikhiatrii Imeni S. S. Korsakova, 72,* 1024-1029.

Tagliavini, F., & Pilleri, G. (1983). Neuronal counts in basal nucleus of Meynert in Alzheimer's disease and in simple senile dementia. *Lancet, 1,* 469-470.

Terry, R.D., Peck, A., DeTeresa, R., Schechter, R., & Horoupian, D.S. (1981). Some morphometric aspects of the brain in senile dementia of the Alzheimer type. *Annals of Neurology, 10,* 184-192.

Thal, L.J., Masur, D.M., Sharpless, N.S., Fuld, P.A., & Davies, P. (1984). Acute and chronic effects of oral physostigmine and lecithin in Alzheimer's disease. In R.J. Wurtman, S.H. Corkin, & J.H. Growdon (Eds.), *Alzheimer's disease: Advances in basic research and therapies* (pp. 333-347). Zurich: Center for Brain Sciences and Metabolic Charitable Trust.

van Dongen, P.A.M. (1981). The human locus coeruleus in neurology and psychiatry (Parkinson's Lewy body, Hallervorden-Spatz, Alzheimer's and Korsakoff's disease, (pre)senile dementia, schizophrenia, affective disorders, psychosis). *Progress in Neurobiology, 17,* 97-139.

Vrtunski, P.B., Patterson, M.B., Mack, J.L., & Hill, G.O. (1983). Microbehavioral analysis of the choice reaction time response in senile dementia. *Brain, 106,* 929-947.

Vrtunski, P.B., Patterson, M.B., Woods, D.C., & Hill, G.O. (in press). *Psychomotor decrements in Alzheimer's disease over one year's time.* (Manuscript submitted for publication.)

Wagner, H.N., Jr., Burns, H.D., Dannals, R.F., Wong, D.F., Langstrom, B., Duelfer, T., Frost, J.J., Ravert, H.T., Links, J.M., Rosenbloom, S.B., Lukas, S.E., Kramer, A.V., & Kuhar, M.J. (1984).

Assessment of dopamine receptor densities in the human brain with carbon-11-labeled N-methylspiperone. *Annals of Neurology, 15* (Suppl.), S79-S84.

Whitehouse, P.J. (1985). Treatment of Alzheimer disease. In R.T. Johnson (Ed.), *Current therapy in neurologic disease.* Ontario: B.L. Decker.

Whitehouse, P.J., & Au, K. -S. (in press). Neurotransmitter receptor alterations in Alzheimer's disease. In J. Traber & W.H. Gispen (Eds.), *Senile dementia of Alzheimer type.* Berlin: Springer-Verlag.

Whitehouse, P.J., Hedreen, J.C., & Price, D.L. (1983). Aging and Alzheimer's disease. In W.H. Gispen & J. Traber (Eds.), *Aging of the brain* (pp. 261-274). Amsterdam: Elsevier Science Publishers.

Whitehouse, P.J., Kopajtic, T., Jones, B.E., Kuhar, M.J., & Price, D.L. (1985a). An in vitro receptor autoradiographic study of muscarinic cholinergic receptor subtypes in the amygdala and neocortex of patients with Alzheimer's disease. *Neurology, 35* (Suppl. 1), *217.*

Whitehouse, P.J., Martino, A.M., Antuono, P.G., Coyle, J.T., Price, D.L., & Kellar, K.J. (1985b). Reductions in nicotinic receptors measured using (^{3}H) acetylcholine in Alzheimer's disease. *Society for Neuroscience Abstracts, 11,* 134.

Whitehouse, P.J., Martino, A.M., Price, D.L., & Kellar, K.J. (1985c). Reductions in nicotinic but not muscarinic cholinergic receptors in Alzheimer's disease measured using (^{3}H) acetylcholine. *Annals of Neurology, 18,* 145.

Whitehouse, P.J., Price, D.L., Clark, A.W., Coyle, J.T., & DeLong, M.R. (1981). Alzheimer disease: Evidence for selective loss of cholinergic neurons in the nucleus basalis. *Annals of Neurology, 10,* 122-126.

Whitehouse, P.J., Price, D.L., Struble, R.G., Clark, A.W., Coyle, J.T., & DeLong, M.R., (1982). Alzheimer's disease and senile dementia: Loss of neurons in the basal forebrain. *Science, 215,* 1237-1239.

Whitehouse, P.J., Rajagopalan, R., Kitt, C.A., Jones, B.E., Niehoff, D.L., Kuhar, M.J., & Price, D.L. (1984). Muscarinic cholinergic receptors in the amygdala in Alzheimer's disease. *Neurology, 34* (Suppl. 1), 121.

Whitehouse, P.J., Struble, R.G., Hedreen, J.C., Clark, A.W., & Price, D.L. (1985d). Alzheimer's disease and related dementias: Selective involvement of specific neuronal systems. *CRC Critical Reviews in Clinical Neurobiology, 1,* 319-339.

Whitehouse, P.J., Trifiletti, R.R., Jones, B.E., Folstein, S., Price, D.L., Snyder, S.H., & Kuhar, M.J. (1985e). Neurotransmitter receptor alterations in Huntington's disease: Autoradiographic and homogenate studies with special reference to benzodiazepine receptor complexes. *Annals of Neurology, 18,* 202-210.

Wilcock, G.K., Esiri, M.M., Bowen, D.M., & Smith, C.C.T. (1982). Alzheimer's disease. Correlation of cortical choline acetyltransferase activity with the severity of dementia and histological abnormalities. *Journal of the Neurological Sciences, 57,* 407-417.

Winblad, B., Adolfsson, R., Carlsson, A., & Gottfries, C.G. (1982). Biogenic amines in brains of patients with Alzheimer's disease. In S. Corkin, K.L. Davis, J.H. Growdon, E. Usdin, & R.J. Wurtman (Eds.), *Alzheimer's disease: A report of progress in research* (pp. 25-33). New York: Raven Press.

ACKNOWLEDGMENTS

The author gratefully acknowledges the contributions of the following colleagues to the idea expressed in this paper: Drs. K. Au, M. R. DeLong, B. Gordon, K. J. Kellar, M. J. Kuhar, D. S. Olton, D. L. Price, and G. L. Wenk. The secretarial assistance of Mrs. Colleen Marine is also appreciated.

21

Consideration of Neurotransmitters and Calcium Metabolism in Therapeutic Design

Gary E. Gibson, PhD, and Christine Peterson, PhD

Aging and mild acute hypoxia (low oxygen) impair mental function in humans and animals. Pharmacological reversal of these age- or hypoxic-induced alterations in animals provides one basis for evaluating various therapeutic strategies. Since no entirely adequate animal model of Alzheimer's disease (AD) exists, the effectiveness of this approach for the development of drugs to treat AD is unknown. Hypoxia, aging, and AD share numerous neurotransmitter alterations, which include a major cholinergic deficit. Thus, the alterations due to AD may respond to therapies that effectively treat age- or hypoxic-related disorders.

HYPOXIA

The effects of low oxygen on mental function are well-documented (see Gibson, 1985), but the precise pathophysiological basis for these changes is unknown. Cognitive processes such as critical judgement and the ability to learn complex tasks (Siesjo, 1978), as well as behavior in animals (Gibson, Pelmas, & Peterson, 1983; Gibson, Peterson, & Sansone, 1981a; Saligaut, Moore, Lerclerc, & Boismare, 1981) decline as the oxygen tension is reduced from 20% to 15% or 10%. The most widely investigated explanation for these effects is that hypoxia leads to an energy failure but adenosine triphosphate (ATP) concentrations remain normal during even severe hypoxia (Gurdjian, Stone, & Webster, 1944; Harkonen, Passonneau, & Lowry, 1969). Impaired neurotransmitter function is an attractive mechanism to explain the effects of hypoxia. Neurotransmitters are sensitive to low oxygen, are easily related to neural function, and respond to pharmacological manipulation (Gibson, Pulsinelli, Blass, & Duffy 1981d).

Although multiple neurotransmitters are altered by low oxygen, decreased cholinergic function may play a major role in the production of hypoxic-induced deficits. Glucose metabolism and acetylcholine (ACh) formation are tightly coupled even though less than 1% of the utilized carbohydrate is incorporated into the neurotransmitter (Ksiezak & Gibson, 1981a, 1981b). Oxygen tensions that reduce mental function in humans depress the *in vivo* incorporation of glucose into ACh in rodent brain (Gibson & Duffy, 1981; Gibson et al., 1981b). Serotonin and catecholamine syntheses are also altered by hypoxia. However, the reversal of the impaired catecholamine synthesis by stress makes the physiological significance of this decline questionable (Brown, Davis, & Carlsson, 1974). The formation of the glucose-derived amino acid neurotransmitters is also diminished by low oxygen (Gibson et al., 1981b). In addition, a reduction in arterial oxygen tensions from 100 to 50 mmHg doubles adenosine concentrations, and a further decrease in oxygen tensions to 30 mmHg increases adenosine concentrations sevenfold (Winn, Robio, & Berne, 1981). In general, equivalent degrees of hypoxia decrease ACh synthesis by a greater percentage than they do the other neurotransmitters, but this does not necessarily indicate that the cholinergic deficit is of more pathological significance. Although hypoxia leads to multiple neurotransmitter deficits, the subsequent discussion will concentrate on the pathophysiological role of the cholinergic system.

The decline in ACh metabolism during hypoxia appears to be behaviorally important. Pretreatment with physostigmine delays the onset of death and seizures due to hypoxic-(Scremin & Scremin, 1979) or anemic-(Gibson & Blass, 1976) hypoxia. With milder degrees of hypoxia, the tight rope test is a more sensitive behavioral measure (Gibson et al., 1981b) that can be manipulated pharmacologically (Gibson et al., 1983). Physostigmine, an acetylcholinesterase inhibitor, which acts centrally and peripherally, improves performance on this test whereas neostigmine, which acts only in the periphery, does not. Muscarinic or nicotinic agonists are also beneficial, and their effects are additive when they are administered simultaneously. None of the cholinomimetics tested completely reverse the effects of low oxygen which indicates that other neurotransmitter systems are involved. Thus, both hypoxia and AD lead to central cholinergic and behavioral deficits that partially respond to cholinergic agonists.

Low oxygen decreases neurotransmitter release. The hypoxic-induced decrease in ACh synthesis without a corresponding decline in ACh concentrations implies an impaired release mechanism. This hypothesis was tested directly with brain slices and synaptosomes. Low oxygen depresses the calcium-dependent potassium-stimulated ACh release. Resting release and calcium-independent release are unaltered (Gibson & Peterson, 1982; Peterson & Gibson, 1982). This appears to be a selective effect on the cholinergic system since hypoxic conditions that impair ACh release enhance glutamate release but do not alter norepinephrine, serotonin, or γ-aminobutyric acid release (Hirsch & Gibson, 1984). During hypoxia, ACh formation declines in brain regions, such as the hippocampus, that release ACh, whereas in structures that do not release ACh, such as cell bodies (i.e., septum), synthesis is unaltered (Gibson & Peterson, 1983).

Hypoxia depresses calcium metabolism. The observation that low oxygen decreases only the calcium-dependent ACh release indirectly implies a deficit in calcium homeostasis. The regulation of nerve ending calcium metabolism depends on the interaction of many intracellular organelles and transport processes (see Carvalho, 1982). The main calcium pools of the nerve ending are the calcium attached to the outer surface of the terminal; free cytosolic calcium; that sequestered by organelles, such as mitochondria; and calcium bound to proteins, such as calmodulin. Methods are currently available to estimate calcium-45 fluxes in some of these pools (Scott, Akerman, & Nicholls, 1980). A direct examination of calcium uptake by isolated nerve endings demonstrates a decline of 60% and 82% under 2.5% and 0% oxygen when compared with 100% oxygen, respectively (Peterson & Gibson, 1984). Superficial binding of calcium to the synaptosomal plasma membrane declines from 100% to 29% or 12% when the oxygen tension is reduced from 100% to 2.5% or 0% oxygen, respectively. A reduction in the oxygen tension from 100% to 2.5% decreases mitochondrial calcium uptake (−56%), but increases nonmitochondrial calcium uptake (+50%) (Peterson, Nicholls, & Gibson, 1985a). The deficit in mitochondrial calcium uptake may reduce calcium-dependent acetyl coenzyme — A efflux for cytosolic ACh synthesis (Benjamin & Quastel, 1981). The physiological significance of the increase in cytosolic calcium and whether it is free or bound requires further evaluation. The decline in calcium uptake parallels the hypoxic-induced deficits in the calcium-dependent release of ACh. Thus, altered calcium metabolism may underlie some of the cholinergic deficits that lead to the decline in mental function during hypoxia.

AGING

Several lines of evidence suggest that the sensory and mental impairments that occur in normal subjects under experimental acute hypoxia mimic the behavioral changes that accompany normal aging. This is particularly true of dark adaptation and the ability to perform paired association tasks (McFarland, 1963). Thus, the deficits due to aging and hypoxia may share a common molecular basis, and understanding the mechamism of one, may provide insight into the other. With this concept in mind, the neurochemical variables that are altered by hypoxia were examined during aging.

Aging alters many neurotransmitters, but the cholinergic system appears to be particularly vulnerable and is behaviorally important. Pharmacological interruption of the cholinergic system by scopolamine produces memory deficits in young individuals that resemble those that occur during normal aging (Drachman & Leavitt, 1974; Drachman, Noffsinger, Sahakian, Krudziel, & Fleming, 1980). In aged rodents, a decline in either glucose or choline incorporation into ACh correlates to depressed tight rope test performance (Gibson, Peterson, & Jenden, 1981a), and passive avoidance behavior (Bartus, Dean, Goas, & Lippa, 1980). This age-induced decrease in synthesis occurs without a corresponding reduction in ACh concentrations. The age-related depression in the cholinergic system is not unique since many indicators of other neurotransmitters are also altered by aging (Enna, Samorajski, & Beer, 1981). For example, the monoamine systems (Finch, 1973; Makman et al., 1980), and the synthesis of the amino acid neurotransmitters (Gibson, Peterson, & Sansone, 1981c) decline nearly as much as that of ACh.

Decreased ACh release may underlie the *in vivo* decline in ACh synthesis. Age-related decreases in choline acetyltransferase (McGeer & McGeer, 1975), acetylcholinesterase (Davies & Maloney, 1976) or pyruvate dehydrogenase (Ksiezak-Reding, Peterson, & Gibson, 1984) activities, high affinity choline uptake (Sherman, Kuster, Dean, Bartus, & Friedman, 1981), cholinergic receptor binding (Lippa et al., 1981) or glucose oxidation (Gibson & Peterson, 1981a) are insufficient to account for the large deficits in ACh formation. Unaltered

ACh concentrations, despite the decline in synthesis, suggest that ACh release is impaired. The potassium-stimulated calcium-dependent release of ACh by mouse brain slices declines 40% between 3 and 10 months and another 37% between 10 and 30 months of age. Calcium-independent and resting release are unaffected by aging (Gibson & Peterson, 1981a; Peterson & Gibson, 1983a). This finding has subsequently been extended *in vitro* with synaptosomes (Meyer, Onge, & Crews, 1984), and *in vivo* with cortical electrical stimulation (Pedata, Slavikova, Kotas, & Pepeu, 1983).

Altered calcium metabolism may underlie the age-related deficits in the cholinergic system. This hypothesis is supported by the observation that only the calcium-dependent release of ACh declines during aging. Calcium uptake by isolated nerve terminals from rodent brain decreases from 104% (3 months) to 100% (6 months), 79% (15 months), or 59% (27 months); (Peterson & Gibson, 1983b). However, the superficial binding of calcium to the synaptosomal plasma membrane increases 5% (3 months), 29% (15 months), or 67% (27 months) when compared to 6-month-old rats. More recent studies demonstrate an age-related decline in both the fast and slow components of voltage dependent calcium uptake in synaptosomes (Leslie, Chandler, Barr, & Farrar, 1985). Aging alters both mitochondrial and nonmitochondrial calcium uptake on potassium depolarization (Peterson, Nicholls, & Gibson, 1985b). Under resting conditions, calcium uptake by mitochondria within the synaptosomes decreased (−40%) similarly at 10- and 30-months of age. However, calcium accumulation by the nonmitochondrial compartment increases at 10 months (+19%), and then slightly decreases by 30 months (−12%) when compared to 3 months. Under conditions of potassium depolarization, aging reduces mitochondrial calcium uptake from 100% to 70% or 50% in 3-, 10- and 30-month-old mice, respectively. In isolated brain mitochondria, both ATP-dependent and respiration-linked calcium uptake are markedly reduced (Leslie et al., 1985). Calcium uptake by the nonmitochondrial compartment declines from 100% (3 months) to 60% (10 months), or 39% (30 months) in high-potassium media. These changes in nonmitochondrial calcium may underlie the prolonged calcium-dependent after hyperpolarization that accompanies aging in hippocampal neurons (Landfield & Pitler, 1984). *In vivo,* aging (3-, 10-, and 30-month-old mice, respectively) reduces brain calcium uptake by the cortex (100%, 67%, 56%), hippocampus (100%, 73%, 50%), and striatum (100%, 68%, 49%) when brain calcium-45 is divided by the blood-specific activity (Gibson, Perrino, & Dienel, 1984). This decreased *in vivo* regional calcium uptake parallels the decline in regional ACh synthesis (Gibson & Peterson, 1981b).

The precise molecular basis for the age-related decline in calcium uptake is unknown. Increased brain lactate concentrations during aging (Gibson et al., 1981a, 1981c) may reduce calcium uptake since pH changes influence calcium regulation (Studer & Borle, 1961). The decline is not likely due to altered mitochondrial membrane potentials since they do not appear to be diminished by aging (Peterson, Nicholls, & Gibson, 1985b). Deficits in mitochondrial respiration reduce calcium transport, but the respiratory control ratios of synaptic and nonsynaptic mitochondria are not depressed by aging (Deshmukh, Owen, & Patel, 1979). Since the age-related changes mitochondrial, calcium transport do not appear to be caused by altered substrate oxidation, the deficit may involve the decreased activity of a calcium-transporting protein. In subcellular fractions from normal and aged animals, the activity of the sodium-potassium or the calcium-magnesium ATPases do not vary, but the calcium dependence of the sodium-calcium exchange system indicates a lower maximal ion transport capacity of the aged animals (Michaelis, Johe, & Kitos, 1984). In addition, aging decreases calmodulin concentrations in various brain regions (Teolato, Calderini, Bonetti, & Toffano, 1983).

ALZHEIMER'S DISEASE

Considerable evidence suggests that calcium homeostasis is altered during AD. In the AD brain, tangle-bearing neurons have increased calcium and aluminum concentrations (Perl, Gajdusek, Garruto, Yanagihara, & Gibbs, 1982; Garruto et al., 1984). Altered calcium metabolism may lead to abnormal neurofilament formation (Schlaepfer & Hasler, 1979) and decreased protein degradation during aging (Smith, Perret, & Eng, 1984). Decreased calcium homeostasis due to tissue unresponsiveness to parathyroid hormone leads to dementia (Ettigi & Brown, 1978). Calcium content and uptake decline in platelets from patients with Down's syndrome (McCoy & Sneddon, 1984), a disease in which affected individuals after the age of 35, develop brain pathology similar to that seen in AD. Furthermore, pyruvate dehydrogenase, which may be regulated by mitochondrial calcium homeostasis, is altered in postmortem AD brain (Sorbi, Bird, & Blass, 1983). Decreased calcium uptake by cultered skin fibroblasts directly demonstrates altered calcium metabolism during human aging and AD (Peterson, Gibson, & Blass, 1985). Cultured skin fibroblasts are a convenient model with which to examine human disease because culture conditions eliminate donor drug and nutritional influences. Calcium uptake decreases in fibroblasts from aged donors (−14%) and patients with AD (−43%) when compared to young controls. The observation with tissue culture suggests that the animal experiments are relevant to the study of human aging and AD.

The implications of altered calcium metabolism during aging and AD are largely speculative, but deserve consideration. Many mitochondrial and cytosolic activities are controlled by calcium so disturbances of cell calcium may interfere with many metabolic functions. A decline in the ability of mitochondria to sequester cytoplasmic calcium may have important consequence in denervated hippocampal dendrites (Baudry, Fuch, Kessler, Arst, & Lynch, 1982). Calcium-activated proteolytic enzymes can lead to disruption of the cytoskeleton and neuronal degeneration (Pant & Gainer, 1980; Lasek & Hoffman, 1976), or ceroid formation (Ivy, Schottler, Baudry, & Lynch, 1983). Altered cytoplasmic calcium activates a trans-glutaminase that cross-links proteins, and thus restructures the cell during aging. This may be the underlying mechanism for neurofibrillary tangle formation that is diagnostic of AD (Selkoe, Ihara, & Salazar, 1982). Low calcium concentrations stabilize microtubules but high calcium depolymerize them (Keith, DiPaola, Maxfield, & Shelanski, 1983); a 50% loss in microtubules blocks axonal transport (Ghetti & Ochs, 1978).

The Use of Aminopyridines as Therapeutic Strategies

If diminished calcium metabolism and/or neurotransmitter release are fundamental alterations during hypoxia, aging, or AD, then therapies should be directed toward reversing these neurochemical changes. A wide variety of compounds interact with calcium homeostasis. The calcium antagonists (nimodipine, nitrendipine, verapamil, and nifedipine) are widely used to treat cardiovascular disorders (Rahwan & Witiak, 1982). The calmodulin antagonists, trifluoperazine (Wada, Yanagihara, Izumi, Sakurai, & Kobayashi, 1983), and prenylanine (Karaki, Murakahmi, Nakagawa, Osaki, &

Urakawa, 1982) increase intracellular calcium, but their clinical value is unknown. The calcium ionophore A23187 increases the physiologically active pool of calcium (Akerman & Nicholls, 1981) and stimulates cortical release of ACh (Casamenti, Mantovani, & Pepeu, 1978). The aminopyridines are a class of compounds that enhance neurotransmitter release through an interaction with calcium homeostasis. Our efforts have concentrated on determining the experimental therapeutic effectiveness of the aminopyridines.

The precise molecular mechanism of the aminopyridines is unknown (see Glover, 1982; Thesleff, 1981). At the neuromuscular junction, these drugs stimulate the quantal release of ACh (Molgo, Lemeignan, & Lechat, 1977; Molgo, Lundh, & Thesleff, 1980). The aminopyridines may inhibit repolarization by blocking outwardly directed potassium currents and thereby increase calcium influx (Molgo et al., 1977; Schauf, Colton, Colton, & Davis, 1976). They may also decrease calcium binding to intracellular structures (Lamiable & Millart, 1983), directly activate voltage-sensitive calcium channels to facilitate calcium entry (Lundh & Thesleff, 1977), or excite presynaptic fibers (Lundh, 1978). The aminopyridines have not been examined extensively with central nervous system (CNS) preparations. They stimulate ACh release from non-depolarized brain slices and synaptosomes and are inactive in the absence of calcium (Gibson & Peterson, 1982; Peterson & Gibson, 1982). Detailed structure activity relationships of the aminopyridines have not been performed, but a comparison of the mono-aminopyridines (2-, 3-, or 4-) and diaminopyridines (2,3-, 2,6-, or 3,4-) demonstrates that 3,4-diaminopyridine enhances ACh release most effectively. The response of the major cholinergic brain regions to 3,4-diaminopyridine also varies; striatum is more responsive than hippocampus, which is more responsive than cortex (Schwarz, Spencer, Bernabei, & Pugsley, 1983).

Enhancing neurotransmitter release will be an effective therapy only if synthesis is also elevated. For example, black widow spider venom promotes ACh release but inhibits further synthesis, which ultimately blocks cholinergic function (Baba, Sen, & Cooper, 1977). 4-Aminopyridine stimulates ACh synthesis and release by the hemidiaphragm nerve (Gundersen & Jenden, 1981), synaptosomes, and brain slices (Gibson & Peterson, 1982; Dolezal & Tucek, 1983). 4-Aminopyridine stimulates in vivo cortical ACh release (Corradetti, Mantovani, Loffenholz, & Pepeu, 1982). Thus, if impaired release is pathophysiologically important during hypoxia and aging, the aminopyridines would be attractive candidates to ameliorate the deficits.

Different dosages of the aminopyridines may increase their specificity toward certain neurotransmitter systems. Subconvulsant doses of 4-aminopyridine increase noradrenaline turnover slightly, but do not alter dopamine or 5-hydroxytryptamine (Anden & Leander, 1979). 4-Aminopyridine enhances glutamate and γ-aminobutyric acid releases by rat brain synaptosomes (Tapia & Sitges, 1982) but at much higher concentrations than those required to enhance ACh release (Gibson & Peterson, 1982). Thus, the selectivity of the aminopyridines on ion channels that interact with cholinergic terminals may be enhanced by titrating the dosage.

The aminopyridines partially reverse the effects of hypoxia *in vivo* and *in vitro*. The decline in calcium-dependent ACh release during hypoxia is partially reversed by either 4-aminopyridine (Gibson & Peterson, 1982) or 3,4-diaminopyridine (Peterson & Gibson, 1982). The same concentration of 3,4-diaminopyridine that stimulates ACh release by hypoxic synaptosomes also ameliorates the deficits in calcium homeostasis (Peterson & Gibson, 1984). Thus, the decline in total calcium uptake is reduced from −60% to −31% and −82% to −33% under 2.5% and 0% oxygen, respectively. 3,4-Diaminopyridine also diminishes the hypoxic-induced decrease in superficial binding from −72% to −13% and −88% to −70% with 2.5% and 0% oxygen, respectively, when compared with 100% oxygen. 3,4-Diaminopyridine reduced the mitochondrial calcium deficit (−45% to −8%) but did not influence the nonmitochondrial alterations during hypoxia (Peterson, Nicholls, & Gibson, 1985a). If these *in vitro* changes are pathophysiologically important, then 3,4-diaminopyridine should reverse the *in vivo* effects due to hypoxia, as well. The hypoxic-induced decline in tight rope test performance can be partially diminished by both 4-aminopyridine (from −90% to −40%) (Gibson et al., 1983), and 3,4-diaminopyridine (from −90% to −40%) (Peterson & Gibson, 1982). Electroconvulsant shock-induced amnesia can be reversed by 3,4-diaminopyridine treatment (Davis, R.E., Marriott, Tew, & Voigtman, 1984). The hypoxic-induced decrease in glucose incorporation into ACh in the striatum and hippocampus, but not in the cortex, can be ameliorated by 3,4-diaminopyridine treatment (Peterson & Gibson, 1982). These studies support the hypothesis that deficits in brain function are due to an interaction with calcium homeostasis.

The aminopyridines diminish some of the age-related neurochemical and behavioral deficits *in vivo* and *in vitro*. 3,4-Diaminopyridine partially reverses the age-induced decline in potassium-stimulated calcium uptake by synaptosomes from 3- (+2%), 6- (−6% to +10%), 15- (−36% to −29%), or 27- (−57% to −25%) month-old rats (Peterson & Gibson, 1983). During aging, the increased superficial binding of calcium is reduced from 123% to 109% (15 months) or from 159% to 124% (27 months) by 3,4-diaminopyridine (Peterson & Gibson, 1983b). The age-related alterations in mitochondrial and nonmitochondrial calcium uptake also respond favorably to 3,4-diaminopyridine treatment (Peterson, Nicholls, & Gibson, 1985b). Consistent with the hypothesis that the age-related decline in calcium homeostasis underlies changes in ACh release, 3,4-diaminopyridine enhances the potassium-stimulated, calcium-dependent release of ACh +15% (3 months), +89% (10 months), and +260% (30 months). Finally, 3,4-diaminopyridine also effectively ameliorates age-related deficits in tight rope test performance (Peterson & Gibson, 1983a) and eight-arm maze performance (Davis, H.P., Idowa, & Gibson, 1983).

The therapeutic use of the aminopyridines in humans has been limited. 4-Aminopyridine has been used to treat disorders of neuromuscular transmission: myasthenia gravis (Lundh, Nilsson, & Rosen, 1979), Eaton-Lambert Syndrome (Lundh, Nilsson, & Rosen, 1977), and botulinum toxin poisoning (Ball et al., 1979; Lundh, Leander, & Thesleff, 1977). 4-Aminopyridine improved the cognitive performance of 12 AD patients in a single, double-blind, crossover trial with one dosage (Wesseling et al., 1984). Although the results seem quite tantalizing, they need extension and confirmation. 3,4-Diaminopyridine is a thousand times more potent (Kirsch & Narahashi, 1978) and less toxic (Lemeignan et al., 1982) than 4-aminopyridine. 3,4-diaminopyridine has been used to treat patients with Eaton-Lambert Syndrome with fewer side effects than 4-aminopyridine (Lundh, Nilsson, & Rosen, 1983), but 3,4-diaminopyridine has not been tested for the treatment of hypoxic- or age-related cognitive deficits in humans.

RECOMMENDATION

In summary, the aminopyridines have promise as therapeutic agents for AD. A better understanding of their molecular basis of action may allow development of more effective therapeutic regimens. Combining them with other cholinergic compounds, like physostigmine, may enhance their efficacy. These results also suggest that therapeutic regimens that interact with calcium homeostasis may be beneficial treatments for cognitive disorders.

REFERENCES

Akerman, K.E.O., & Nicholls, D.G. (1981). Calcium transport by intact synaptosomes: Influence of ionophore A23187 on plasma-membrane calcium transport, mitochondrial membrane potential, respiration, cytosolic-free calcium concentration and noradrenalime release. *European Journal of Biochemistry, 115,* 67-73.

Anden, N.E., & Leander, S. (1979). Effects of 4-aminopridine on the turnover of monamines in the central nervous system of the rat. *Journal of Neural Transmission, 44,* 1-12.

Baba, A., Sen, I., & Cooper, J.R. (1977). The action of black widow spider venom on cholinergic mechanisms in synaptosomal preparations of rat brain cortices. *Life Sciences, 20,* 833-842.

Ball, A.P., Hopkinson, R.B., Farrell, I.D., Hutchinson, J.G.P., Paul, R., Watson, R.D.S., Page, A.J.F., Parker, R.G.E., Edwards, C.W., Snow, M., Scott, D.K., Leone-Ganado, A., Hastings, A., Ghosh, A.C., & Gilbert, R.J. (1979). Human botulism caused by clostridium botulinum Type E: The Birmingham outbreak. *Quarterly Journal of Medicine, New Series XLVIII, 191,* 473-491.

Bartus, R.T., Dean, R.L., Goas, J.A., & Lippa, A.S. (1980). Age-related changes in passive avoidance retention and modulation with chronic dietary choline. *Science, 209,* 301-303.

Baudry, M., Fuch, J., Kessler, M., Arst, D., & Lynch, G. (1982). Entorhinal cortex lesions induce a decreased calcium transport in hippocampal mitochondria. *Science, 216,* 411-413.

Benjamin, A.M., & Quastel, J.H. (1981). Acetylcholine synthesis in synaptosomes: Mode of transfer of mitochondrial acetyl coenzyme A. *Science, 213,* 1495-1497.

Brown, R.M., Davis, J.N., & Carlsson, A. (1974). Changes in biogenic amine synthesis and turnover induced by hypoxia and/or foot

Ettigi, P.G., & Brown, G.M. (1978). Brain disorders associated with endocrine dysfunction. *The Psychiatric Clinics of North America*, *1*, 17-36.

Finch, C.E. (1973). Catecholamine metabolism in brain of aging male mice. *Brain Research*, *52*, 261-276.

Garruto, R.M., Fukatsu, R., Yanagihara, R., Gajdusek, D.C., Hook, G., & Fiori, C.E. (1984). Imaging of calciuim and aluminum in neurofibrillary tangle-bearing neurons in parkinsonism-dementia of Guam. *Proceedings of the National Academy of Sciences, USA*, *81*, 1875-1879.

Ghetti, B., & Ochs, S. (1978). On the relation between microtubule density and axoplasmic transport in nerve treated with maytansine *in vitro*. In N. Canal & G. Pozza (Eds.), *Peripheral neuropathies* (pp. 177-186). Amsterdam: Elsevier.

Gibson, G.E. (1985). Hypoxia. In D.W. McCandless (Ed.), *Cerebral energy metabolism and metabolic encephalopathy* (pp. 43-78). New York: Plenum Press.

Gibson, G.E., & Blass, J.P. (1976). Impaired synthesis of acetylcholine in brain accompanying mild hypoxia and hypoglycemia. *Journal of Neurochemistry*, *27*, 37-42.

Gibson, G.E., & Duffy, T.E. (1981). Impaired synthesis of acetylcholine by mild hypoxic hypoxia or nitrous oxide. *Journal of Neurochemistry*, *36*, 28-33.

Gibson, G.E., Pelmas, C.J., & Peterson, C. (1983). Cholinergic drugs and 4-aminopyridine alter hypoxic-induced behavioral deficits. *Pharmacology, Biochemistry and Behavior*, *18*, 909-916.

Gibson, G.E., Perrino, P., & Dienel, G. (1984). Alterations of *in vitro* calcium homeostasis with aging. *Age*, *14*, 62.

Gibson, G.E., & Peterson, C. (1981a). Aging decreases oxidative metabolism and the release and synthesis of acetylcholine. *Journal of Neurochemistry*, *37*, 978-984.

Gibson, G.E., & Peterson, C. (1981b). Aging decreases regional acetylcholine metabolism. *Age*, *4*, 143.

Gibson, G.E., & Peterson, C. (1982). Decreases in the release of acetylcholine with low oxygen *in vitro*. *Biochemical Pharmacology*, *31*, 111-115.

Gibson, G.E., & Peterson, C. (1983). Acetylcholine and oxidative metabolism in septum and hippocampus *in vitro. Journal of Biological Chemistry, 258,* 1142-1145.

Gibson, G.E., Peterson, C., & Jenden, D.J. (1981a). Brain acetylcholine synthesis declines with senescence. *Science, 213,* 674-676.

Gibson, G.E., Peterson, C., & Sansone, J. (1981b). Decreases in amino acid and acetylcholine metabolism during hypoxia. *Journal of Neurochemistry, 37,* 192-201.

Gibson, G.E., Peterson, C., & Sansone, J. (1981c). Neurotransmitter and carbohydrate metabolism during aging and mild hypoxia. *Neurobiology of Aging, 2,* 165-172.

Gibson, G.E., Pulsinelli, W., Blass, J.P., & Duffy, T.E. (1981d). Brain dysfunction in mild to moderate hypoxia. *American Journal of Medicine, 70,* 1247-1254.

Glover, W.E. (1982). The aminopyridines. *General Pharmacology, 13,* 259-282.

Gunderson, C.B., & Jenden, D.J. (1981). Studies of the effects of agents which alter calcium metabolism on acetylcholine turnover in the rat diaphragm preparation. *British Journal of Pharmacology, 72,* 461-470.

Gurdjian, E.S., Stone, W.E., & Webster, J.E. (1944). Cerebral metabolism in hypoxia. *Archives of Neurology and Psychiatry, 51,* 472-477.

Harkonen, M.H.A., Passonneau, J.V., & Lowry, O.H. (1969). Relationships between energy reserves and function in rat superior cervical ganglion. *Journal of Neurochemistry, 16,* 1439-1450.

Hirsch, J.A., & Gibson, G.E. (1984). Selective alteration of neurotransmitter release by low oxygen *in vitro. Neurochemical Research, 9,* 1037-1047.

Ivy, G.O., Schottler, F., Baudry, M., & Lynch, G.S. (1983). Rapid induction of ceroid formation in rat hippocampus by leupeptin. *Neuroscience Abstracts, 9,* 926.

Karaki, H., Murakahmi, K., Nakagawa, K., Osaki, H., & Urakawa, N. (1982). Effects of calmodulin antagonists on tension and cellular calcium content in depolarized vascular and intestinal smooth muscle. *British Journal of Pharmacology, 77,* 661-666.

Keith, C., DiPaola, M., Maxfield, F.R., & Shelanski, M.L. (1983). Microinjection of Ca++-calmodulin causes a localized depolarization of microtubules. *Journal of Cell Biology, 97,* 1918-1924.

Kirsch, G.E., & Narahashi, T. (1978). 3,4-Diaminopyridine. A potent new potassium channel blocker. *Biophysical Journal, 22,* 507-512.

Kziezak, H.J., & Gibson, G.E. (1981a). Acetylcholine synthesis and CO_2 production from variously labeled glucose in rat brain slices and synaptosomes. *Journal of Neurochemistry, 37,* 88-94.

Ksiezak, H.J., & Gibson, G.E. (1981b). Oxygen dependence of glucose and acetylcholine metabolism in slices and synaptosomes from rat brain. *Journal of Neurochemistry, 37,* 305-314.

Ksiezak-Reding, H., Peterson, C., & Gibson, G.E. (1984). The pyruvate dehydrogenase complex during aging. *Mechanisms of Aging and Development, 26,* 67-73.

Lamiable, D., & Millart, H. (1983). High performance liquid chromatographic determination of 4-aminopyridine and 3,4-diaminopyridine in rat cerebrospinal fluid and serum. *Journal of Chromatography, 272,* 221-225.

Landfield, P.W., & Pitler, T.A. (1984). Prolonged Ca2+-dependent afterhypolarizations in hippocampal neurons of aged rats. *Science, 226,* 1089-1092.

Lasek, R.J., & Hoffman, P.N. (1976). The neuronal cytoskeleton, axonal transport and axonal growth. In R. Goldman, T. Pollard, & J. Rosenbloom (Eds.), *Cell motility* (pp. 1021-1049). Cold Spring Harbor, N.Y.: Cold Spring Harbor Laboratory.

Lemeignan, M., Millart, H., Letteron, N., Lamiable, D., Josso, J., Hoisy, H., & Lechat, P. (1982). The ability of 4-aminopyridine and 3,4-diaminopyridine to cross the blood-brain barrier can account for their difference in toxicity. In P. Lechat, S. Thesleff, & W.C. Bowman (Eds.), *Advances in the biosciences* (Vol. 35, pg. 222). New York: Pergamon Press.

Leslie, S.W., Chandler, L.J., Barr, E.M., & Farrar, R.P. (1985). Reduced calcium uptake by rat brain mitochondria and synaptosomes in response to aging. *Brain Research, 329,* 177-183.

Lippa, A.S., Critchett, D.J., Ehlert, F., Yamamura, H.I., Enna, S.J., & Bartus, R.T. (1981). Age-related alterations in neurotransmitter receptors: An electrophysiological and biochemical analysis. *Neurobiology of Aging, 2,* 3-8.

Lundh, H. (1978). Effect of 4-aminopyridine on neuromuscular transmission. *Brain Research, 153,* 307-318.

Lundh, H., Leander, S., & Thesleff, S. (1977). Antagonism of paralysis produced by botulinum toxin in the rat. The effects of tetraethylammonium, guanidine and 4-aminopyridine. *Journal of the Neurological Sciences, 32,* 343-346.

Lundh, H., Nilsson, O., & Rosen, I. (1977). 4-Aminopyridine - A new drug tested in the treatment of Eaton Lambert Syndrome. *Journal of Neurology, Neurosurgery and Psychiatry, 40,* 1109-1112.

Lundh, H., Nilsson, O., & Rosen, I. (1979). Effects of 4-aminopyridine in myasthenia gravis. *Journal of Neurology, Neurosurgery and Psychiatry, 42,* 171-175.

Lundh, H., Nilsson, O., & Rosen, I. (1983). Novel drug of choice in Eaton-Lambert syndrome. *Journal of Neurology, Neurosurgery and Psychiatry, 46,* 684-687.

Lundh, H., & Thesleff, S. (1977). The mode of action of 4-aminopyridine and guanidine on transmitter release from nerve terminals. *European Journal of Pharmacology, 42,* 411-412.

Makman, M.H., Gardner, E.L., Thal, L.J., Hirschhorn, I.D., Seeger, J.F., & Bhargava, G. (1980). Central monoamine receptor systems: Influence of aging, lesion and drug treatment. In R. Alderman, J. Roberts, G.T. Baker, III, S.I. Baskin, & V.J. Cristofalo (Eds.), *Neural regulatory mechanisms during aging* (pp. 91-127). New York: Alan R. Liss.

McCoy, E.E., & Sneddon, J.M. (1984). Decreased calcium content and $^{45}Ca^{2+}$ uptake in Down's syndrome blood platelets. *Pediatric Research, 18,* 914-916.

McFarland, R.A. (1963). Experimental evidence of the relationship between aging and oxygen want in search of a theory of aging. *Ergometrics, 6,* 339-366.

McGeer, E.G., & McGeer, P.L. (1975). Age changes in the human for some enzymes associated with metabolism of catecholamines, GABA and acetylcholine. In J.M. Ordy & J. Brizzee (Eds.), *Behavioral biology* (Vol. 16, pp. 287-295). New York: Plenum Press.

Meyer, E.M., Onge, E.S., & Crews, F.T. (1984). Effects of aging on rat cortical presynaptic cholinergic processes. *Neurobiology of Aging, 5,* 315-317.

Michaelis, M.L., Johe, K., & Kitos, T.E. (1984). Age-dependent alterations in synaptic membrane systems for Ca^{2+} regulation. *Mechanisms of Ageing and Development, 25,* 215-225.

Molgo, J., Lemeignan, M., & Lechat, P. (1977). Effects of 4-aminopyridine at the frog neuromuscular junction. *Journal of Pharmacology and Experimental Therapeutics, 203,* 653-663.

Molgo, J., Lundh, H., & Thesleff, S. (1980). Potency of 3,4-diaminopyridine and 4-aminopyridine on mammalian neuromuscular transmission and the effect of pH on changes. *European Journal of Pharmacology, 61,* 25-34.

Pant, H.C., & Gainer, H. (1980). Properties of a calcium-activated protease in squid axoplasm which selectively degrades neurofilament proteins. *Journal of Neurobiology, 11,* 1-12.

Pedata, F., Slavikova, J., Kotas, A., & Pepeu, G. (1983). Acetylcholine release from rat cortical slices during postnatal development and aging. *Neurobiology of Aging, 4,* 31-35.

Perl, D.P., Gajdusek, D.C., Garruto, P.M., Yanagihara, R.T., & Gibbs, C.J. (1982). Interneuronal aluminum accumulation in amyotropic lateral sclerosis and parkinsonism dementia of Guam. *Science, 217,* 1053-1055.

Peterson, C., & Gibson, G.E. (1983a). Amelioration of age-related neurochemical and behavioral deficit by 3,4-diaminopyridine. *Neurobiology of Aging, 4,* 25-30.

Peterson, C., & Gibson, G.E. (1983b). Aging and 3,4-diaminopyridine alter synaptosomal calcium uptake. *Journal of Biological Chemistry, 258,* 11482-11486.

Peterson, C., & Gibson, G.E. (1984). Synaptosomal calcium metabolism during hypoxia and 3,4-diaminopyridine treatment. *Journal of Neurochemistry, 42,* 248-253.

Peterson, C., Gibson, G.E., & Blass, J.P. (1985). Altered calcium homeostasis in cultured skin fibroblasts from Alzheimer's patients. *New England Journal of Medicine, 312,* 1063-1065.

Peterson, C. & Gibson, G.E. (1982). 3,4-Diaminopyridine alters acetylcholine metabolism and behavior during hypoxia. *Journal of Pharmacology and Experimental Therapeutics, 222,* 576-582.

Peterson, C., Nicholls, D.G., & Gibson, G.E. (1985a). Subsynaptosomal calcium distribution during hypoxia. *Journal of Neurochemistry, 45,* 1779-1790.

Peterson, C., Nicholls, D.G., & Gibson, G.E. (1985b). Subsynaptosomal calcium uptake during aging and 3,4-diaminopyridine treatment. *Neurobiology of Aging, 6,* 297-304.

Rahwan, R.G., & Witiak, D.T. (1981). *Calcium regulation by calcium antagonists*. ACS Symposium Ser. #201, Washington, D.C. American Chemical Society.

Saligaut, C., Moore, N., Lerclerc, J.L., & Biosmare, F. (1981). Hypobaric hypoxia: Central catecholamine levels, cortical PO^2 and avoidance response in rats treated with apomorphine. *Aviation, Space and Environmental Medicine, 52,* 166-170.

Schauf, C.L., Colton, C.A., Colton, J.S., & Davis, F.A. (1976). Aminopyridines and sparteine as inhibitors of membrane potassium conductance: Effects of myxicola giant axons and the lobster neuromuscular junction. *Journal of Pharmacology and Experimental Therapeutics, 197,* 414-425.

Schlaepfer, W.W., & Hasler, M.B. (1979). Characterization of the calcium-induced disruption of neurofilaments in rat peripheral nerve. *Brain Research, 168,* 299-309.

Schwarz, R.D., Spencer, C.J., Bernabei, A.A., & Pugsley, T.A. (1983). The effect of aminopyridines on the release of ^{3}H-acetylcholine from rat brain slices. *Neuroscience Abstracts, 9,* 433.

Scott, I.D., Akerman, K.E.O., & Nicholls, D.G. (1980). Calcium ion transport by intact synaptosomes. *Biochemical Journal, 192, 873-880.*

Scremin, A.M.E., & Scremin, O.U. (1979). Physostigmine-induced cerebral protection against hypoxia. *Stroke, 10,* 142-143.

Selkoe, D.J., Ihara, Y., & Salazar, F.J. (1982). Alzheimer's disease: Insolubility of partially purified paired helical filaments in sodium dodecyl sulfate and urea. *Science, 215,* 1243-1245.

Sherman, K.A., Kuster, J.E., Dean, R.L., Bartus, R.T., & Friedman, E. (1981). Presynaptic cholinergic mechanisms in the brain of aged rats with memory impairments. *Neurobiology of Aging, 2,* 99-104.

Siesjo, B.K. (1978). *Brain energy metabolism.* New York: John Wiley & Sons.

Smith, M.E., Perret, V., & Eng, L.F. (1984). Metabolic studies *in vitro* of the CNS cytoskeletal proteins: Synthesis and degradation. *Neurochemical Research, 9,* 1493-1507.

Sorbi, S., Bird, E.D., & Blass, J.P. (1983). Decreased pyruvate dehydrogenase complex activity in Huntington and Alzheimer brain. *Annals of Neurology, 13,* 72-78.

Studer, R.K., & Borle, A.B. (1961). The effect of hydrogen ion on the kinetics of calcium transport by rat kidney mitochondria. *Annals of Biochemistry and Biophysics, 203,* 707-718.

Aminopyridines and sparteine as inhibitors of membrane potassium conductance: Effects of myxicola giant axons and the lobster neuromuscular junction. *Journal of Pharmacology and Experimental Therapeutics, 197,* 414-425.

Schlaepfer, W.W., & Hasler, M.B. (1979). Characterization of the calcium-induced disruption of neurofilaments in rat peripheral nerve. *Brain Research, 168,* 299-309.

Schwarz, R.D., Spencer, C.J., Bernabei, A.A., & Pugsley, T.A. (1983). The effect of aminopyridines on the release of ^{3}H-acetylcholine from rat brain slices. *Neuroscience Abstracts, 9,* 433.

Scott, I.D., Akerman, K.E.O., & Nicholls, D.G. (1980). Calcium ion transport by intact synaptosomes. *Biochemical Journal, 192, 873-880.*

Scremin, A.M.E., & Scremin, O.U. (1979). Physostigmine-induced cerebral protection against hypoxia. *Stroke, 10,* 142-143.

Selkoe, D.J., Ihara, Y., & Salazar, F.J. (1982). Alzheimer's disease: Insolubility of partially purified paired helical filaments in sodium dodecyl sulfate and urea. *Science, 215,* 1243-1245.

Sherman, K.A., Kuster, J.E., Dean, R.L., Bartus, R.T., & Friedman, E. (1981). Presynaptic cholinergic mechanisms in the brain of aged rats with memory impairments. *Neurobiology of Aging, 2,* 99-104.

Siesjo, B.K. (1978). *Brain energy metabolism.* New York: John Wiley & Sons.

Smith, M.E., Perret, V., & Eng, L.F. (1984). Metabolic studies *in vitro* of the CNS cytoskeletal proteins: Synthesis and degradation. *Neurochemical Research, 9,* 1493-1507.

Sorbi, S., Bird, E.D., & Blass, J.P. (1983). Decreased pyruvate dehydrogenase complex activity in Huntington and Alzheimer brain. *Annals of Neurology, 13,* 72-78.

Studer, R.K., & Borle, A.B. (1961). The effect of hydrogen ion on the kinetics of calcium transport by rat kidney mitochondria. *Annals of Biochemistry and Biophysics, 203,* 707-718.

Tapia, R., & Sitges, M. (1982). Effect of 4-aminopyridine on transmitter release in synaptosomes. *Brain Research, 250,* 291-299.

Teolato, S., Calderini, G., Bonetti, A.C., & Toffano, G. (1983). Calmodulin content in different brain areas of aging rats. *Neuroscience Letters, 38,* 57-60.

Thesleff, S. (1981). Aminopyridine and synaptic transmission. *Neuro-*

Tapia, R., & Sitges, M. (1982). Effect of 4-aminopyridine on transmitter release in synaptosomes. *Brain Research, 250,* 291-299.

Teolato, S., Calderini, G., Bonetti, A.C., & Toffano, G. (1983). Calmodulin content in different brain areas of aging rats. *Neuroscience Letters, 38,* 57-60.

Thesleff, S. (1981). Aminopyridine and synaptic transmission. *Neuroscience, 5,* 1413-1419.

Wada, A., Yanagihara, N., Izumi, F., Sakurai, S., & Kobayashi, H. (1983). Trifluorperazine inhibits $^{45}Ca^{2+}$ uptake and catecholamine secretion and synthesis in adrenal medullary cells. *Journal of Neurochemistry, 40,* 481-486.

Wesseling, H., Agoston, S., Van Dam, G.B.P., Pasma, J., DeWitt, D.J., & Davinga, H. (1984). Effects of 4-aminopyridine in elderly patients with Alzheimer's disease. *New England Journal of Medicine, 310,* 988-989.

Winn, H.R., Rubio, R., & Berne, R.M. (1981). Brain adenosine concentration during hypoxia in rats. *American Journal of Physiology, 241,* H235-H242.

22

Membrane Lipids: Can Modification Reduce Symptoms or Halt Progression in Alzheimer's Disease?

John Rotrosen, MD

This chapter will focus on the possibility that therapeutic advances for Alzheimer's disease (AD) may result from strategies designed to modify, manipulate, or otherwise alter membrane phospholipids. The rationale for these approaches stems from a number of different perspectives, for example, the roles of biomembranes in neurotransmission; neurotransmitter uptake, storage, release, and receptor function; the possible role of membrane phospholipids as sources of neurotransmitter and prostaglandin precursors; the changes occurring in neuronal membranes associated with normal aging; and the (somewhat) more specific degenerative changes seen in AD.

A significant hurdle in the conceptualization, design, and assessment of such strategies is the complexity of membrane structure and function. Neuronal membranes are composed predominantly of phospholipids, other lipids (e.g., cholesterol), and proteins. Phospholipids (phosphatidylethanolamine, PE; phosphatidylcholine, PC; sphingomyelin, SPM; and phosphatidylserine, PS) compose the basic membrane bilayer with their hydrophilic head groups exposed to the extracellular cerebrospinal fluid (CSF) and to the intracellular cytosol; hydrophobic fatty acid tails form the membrane core. The phospholipid bilayer is penetrated to varying degrees by protein receptors, enzymes, and ion channels, which differentially protrude through the membrane or are localized predominantly on the intracellular or extracellular membrane surfaces. Cholesterol, in varying ratios to the membrane phospholipids and proteins, is localized asymmetrically more in the outer layer than the inner, and, with differing ratios in and around certain domains (e.g., there are little or no sterols in the immediate domain of acetylcholine [ACh] receptors). Biomembranes exist in a state of high flux; there is movement both laterally within a monolayer and vertically between bilayers; and myriad metabolic processes affect the lipids themselves, proteins, and smaller molecules. Finally, all of these processes are highly interactive; receptor activated enzymes affect lipid metabolism, and conversely, lipid metabolism affects the microenvironment of protein enzymes, receptors, and ion channels, in turn affecting their exposure, coupling, and activity.

Given this complexity is it even reasonable to attempt to "restore" membrane characteristics, prevent their loss with aging or disease, or to use lipids and phospholipids as "drugs"? Animal data suggest that it is or, at the least, that it is worth trying. Major areas for consideration are (1) Is there lipid change, or other membrane change associated with aging or with AD?; (2) Are there strategies to reverse or prevent alterations in membrane lipids, lipid protein interactions, and lipid metabolism?; (3) Are there disorders or disease models of membrane lipid change (related or not related to AD) that are responsive to therapeutic strategies with lipids?; (4) Will therapeutic trials permit conclusions to be drawn regarding underlying pathology and mechanism of action?; (5) Which strategies are best suited for prevention, which for treatment?; and finally (6) Given the vast quantities of phospholipids and fatty acids that comprise the total membrane pool, can pharmacologic or even nutritional doses of lipids be expected to affect membrane function and metabolism?

THERAPEUTIC GOALS AND POSSIBLE MECHANISMS

This discussion of the use of lipids and other agents to modify membrane function and structure must be viewed in the following context. Until the cause of AD is known, it is unlikely that treatments will be developed that will cure or prevent AD by eliminating or otherwise inactivating a causative agent. Nonetheless, there are extensive data on the development of characteristic pathology associated with AD. It is this pathology—particularly the neuronal degeneration, the loss of cholinergic neurotransmission, the loss of other neurotransmitters, and the reduction of membrane fluidity seen in AD and thought to underly the clinical syndrome—that may in part be susceptible to treatment. The goals of the therapeutic strategies outlined below would then be to (1) arrest the progression of (some of) the degenerative changes that occur throughout the course of AD, and (2) to reduce symptoms associated with already existing levels of pathology. These goals differ from the more ambitious goals of reversing pathology or restoring brain function with techniques, such as neuronal implants. The specific mechanisms by which (some of) the former goals might be achieved can be broken down into three categories:

1. restoring membrane fluidity
2. preventing oxidative and free radical damage to membranes
3. enhancing cholinergic (and other) neurotransmission

Because of the interplay among membrane damage, membrane fluidity, and neurotransmission, some of the agents proposed in the remainder of this chapter may affect all three.

In this context I will briefly review two areas in which we have worked recently. Neither is related specifically to AD, but both may have implications for the development of treatment strategies for AD and may permit speculation on possible mechanisms related to the action of small doses of lipids. The first are studies with PS on cognitive function in aging rodents (Corwin, Dean, Bartus, Rotrosen, & Watkins, 1985; Corwin, Rotrosen, Dean, Bartus, & Watkins, 1983); and these studies will be discussed because of their relevance to the clinical deficits seen in AD. The second are studies with essential fatty acid precursors for prostaglandins (PGs), thromboxanes, and leukotrienes, and with nonsteroidal anti-inflammatory drug (NSAID) inhibitors of PG synthesis and their interactions with alcohol using biochemical, behavioral, and histopathological endpoints (Rotrosen, Mandio, Segarnick, Traficante, & Gershon, 1980; Segarnick, Cooper, & Rotrosen, 1985a; Segarnick, Cordasco, & Rotrosen, 1982a, 1985b; Segarnick, Ryer & Rotrosen, 1985c). This work should be viewed as a distant model relevant in part because some alcohol-induced pathology (including CNS effects) results from membrane changes (Hill & Bangham, 1975; Littleton & John, 1977), because recent evidence suggests that therapeutic strategies with lipids can reverse or prevent some of these changes (Rotrosen et al., 1980; Segarnick et al., 1982, 1985a, 1985b, 1985c; Glen, 1985; Randall et al., 1984), and finally because this work has provided some hints as to how various pools of lipids may differentially contribute to therapy (Segarnick et al., 1985c). I will then attempt to synthesize some of the findings from both areas of research, to discuss these data in the context of the neurotransmitter and membrane fluidity changes occurring in AD, and to propose a spectrum of therapeutic strategies. The editors have encouraged authors to venture beyond the usual focused and limited conclusions and to consider innovative and novel approaches to treatment development.

PROPERTIES OF PHOSPHATIDYLSERINE

PS is unique among the phospholipids comprising biological membranes in that it is acidic, it has a net negative charge, it is localized predominantly on the inner surface of cell membranes, and it contains a high proportion of highly unsaturated fatty acids. In the central nervous system (CNS) PS is important in three separate but related areas:

1. structural—PS comprises 10% to 20% of the total phospholipid in the cell membrane bilayer;
2. metabolic—PS can be formed from, and enzymatically converted to, other biologically active phospholipids;
3. pharmacologic—PS in relatively low doses (mg/kg) elicits a wide variety of neurochemical effects including release and increased turnover of neurotransmitters (particularly acetylcholine [ACh] and dopamine) and increased levels of CNS glucose and cAMP. In vitro, PS affects receptor-enzyme coupling, ion pump activity, and calcium transport.

PS's characteristics in the three areas listed above suggest that it may be an ideal compound to evaluate as a therapeutic agent for the cognitive decline associated with normal aging, and perhaps with AD.

Structural

Rivnay, Globerson, and Shinitzky (1979) and Cimino et al. (1984) have reported that plasma membranes from aged rats have increased rigidity (i.e., decreased fluidity). Since PS contains a much greater proportion of highly unsaturated fatty acids than other phospholipids, it is possible that enrichment of membranes with PS might increase fluidity and therefore be beneficial in aging. It is not clear, however, whether supplementation with PS can actually alter membrane phospholipid content.

Metabolic

Several aspects of PS metabolism and phospholipid methylation are pertinent:

1. Preferential utilization: Although chemically indistinguishable, phospholipids of the same class often function in metabolically differentiable pools. For example, PC formed by N-methylation of PE accounts for less than 1% of total PC but is the source of nearly 100% of the arachidonic acid released by leukocytes in response to chemoattractants (Hirata & Axelrod, 1980). Likewise, in brain, the small amount of PC formed by N-methylation of PE contributes disproportionately large amounts of choline for synthesis of ACh (Blusztajn, Zeisel, & Wurtman, 1979). An analogous situation may exist for PE; that is, PS can be decarboxylated to form a metabolic pool of PE that may be preferentially shunted into the phospholipid methylation pathway.

2. ACh synthesis: The phospholipid methylation pathway may serve as an efficient source of choline for ACh synthesis. Although considerably more PC or choline can be provided through dietary means than by methylation, the exogenous sources may not be able to be efficiently used. Thus the role of phospholipid methylation as a choline synthetic pathway may be physiologically much more significant than would be expected from its rate per se.

3. Membrane fluidity: Associated with the first N-methylation of PE is a rapid and marked decrease in membrane viscosity (increase in fluidity) (Hirata & Axelrod, 1980). Therefore, PS by decarboxylation to PE and subsequent first N-methylation may influence membrane fluidity in a direction favorable in aging.

Pharmacologic

In addition to (or perhaps as a result of) its metabolic and structural properties PS elicits a variety of significant effects *in vivo* when it is administered in low doses. These effects may be considered as "pharmacologic": first, for lack of a better term and second, because of their appearance at low doses (i.e., mg / kg), which may differentiate these effects from the "nutritional" effects sought in precursor loading with (much higher doses) agents, such as lecithin (PC) or choline chloride. The following effects of PS may be relevant to its potential utility in treating age-associated cognitive decline:

PS (150 mg/kg) causes a rapid increase in ACh release from rat cerebral cortex (Casamenti, Mantovani, Amaducci, & Pepeu, 1979). PS (50-100 mg/kg) increases dopamine turnover as measured by increased accumulation of the dopamine metabolite homovanillic acid in rat brain (Calderini 1981; Toffano, Leon, Benvegnu, Boarato, & Azzone, 1976). Moreover, Raese, Patrick, & Barchas (1976) have found that PS (to a much greater extent than any other phospholipid tested) activated a partially purified preparation of tyrosine hydroxylase *in vitro*. PS (12.5-100 mg/kg) also causes a rapid and pronounced increase in norepinephrine turnover as measured by the accumulation of 3-methoxy-4-hydroxyphenylglycol (MHPG) (Toffano & Bruni, 1980).

PS (25-50 mg/kg) causes increases in brain levels of cAMP in the rat. This effect is likely to be mediated by conversion to lyso-PS, since lyso-PS elicits the same effect at lower doses and with a more rapid onset of action (Calderini et al., 1981).

Finally, Drago, Canonico, and Scapagnini (1981), and, more recently, Zanotti, Aporti, Toffano, and Valzelli, (1984) and Corwin et al. (1983, 1985) have reported that PS administered at different doses and over different time courses improves acquisition and retention of a variety of learned behaviors in aged rats. A brief description of our experiments (Corwin et al., 1983, 1985) follows.

BEHAVIORAL EFFECTS OF PHOSPHATIDYLSERINE IN AGED RATS

Passive avoidance behavior was studied with a two-compartment step-through apparatus using the procedure described by Bartus, Dean, Sherman, Friedman, and Beer (1981). Rats were placed into a lighted chamber and permitted to freely explore. When the animal entered the darkened chamber, a trap door was closed, and a 1 mA scrambled footshock applied for 3 seconds. Animals were then returned to their home cages. Twenty-four hours later, animals were placed back into the lighted chamber of the apparatus. The latency to enter the dark chamber was recorded as the dependent measure. Young Fischer 344 rats show long latencies to enter the dark chamber on the retention trial. With aging, retention trial latency declines with a sharp drop-off occurring at around 16 months of age (Lippa et al., 1980).

In our first set of experiments male Fischer 344 rats aged 20 to 24 months were treated ip with sonicated PS (12.5-100 mg/kg) in

Tris buffer (0.05 M pH 7.4) or with vehicle alone, 30 minutes prior to training and again 30 minutes prior to 24-hour retention testing. PS had no effects on latency to enter the dark chamber on the training day. However, on retention testing, marked dose-related enhancement of performance was seen. These effects of PS could not be attributed to changes in shock sensitivity or to changes in psychomotor coordination (Corwin et al., 1983, 1985).

To elucidate the time course of the effect of PS on learning and memory we conducted a second study. PS (50 mg / kg) was administered either 30 minutes prior to training only, 5 minutes post training only, or 30 minutes prior to retention testing only. Improved retention testing was seen in the groups treated prior to training only and immediately after training only, but not in the group treated only before retention testing. These data suggest that PS appears to affect those information processes occuring early in the course of learning (variously described as encoding and/or consolidation).

PS was also found to improve performance of aged rats on an eight-arm radial arm maze apparatus (unpublished, 1984).

ALCOHOL, ESSENTIAL FATTY ACID, PROSTAGLANDIN INTERACTIONS

When administered in vitro or given acutely in vivo, ethanol causes lipid membranes to become more fluid and disordered (Hill & Bangham, 1975; Littleton & John, 1977). This effect probably derives directly from ethanol's ability to become inserted into the membrane lipid matrix. It is likely that it is this biophysical effect on membrane fluidity that mediates many of ethanol's acute actions on enzymatic and receptor-mediated processes. Chronic in vivo exposure to ethanol induces an adaptive reordering of membrane lipid composition (involving increases in cholesterol: phospholipid ratios) and structure, changes in the sensitivity of receptors for dopamine, norepinephrine, serotonin, and histamine, as well as in adenylate cyclase and ATPase activity (in directions opposite that seen with acute administration) (Cicero, 1978; Ellingboe, 1978). When alcohol is withdrawn, this "adaptive; reordering becomes nonadaptive or pathological, and is thought to underly many components of the alcohol withdrawal syndrome.

Ethanol also enhances synthesis of (certain) prostaglandins from their essential fatty acid (EFA) precursors (Manku et al., 1980;

Rotrosen et al., 1980). It is now clear that these effects of EFA metabolism mediate at least some of alcohol's behavioral, physiological, and pathological effects. Thus, pretreatment of animals (mice and rats in most cases) with aspirin and other nonsteroidal anti-inflammatory drugs (NSAIDs) (all of which inhibit prostaglandin synthesis) antagonizes alcohol-induced sedation, prevents alcohol-induced hypothermia and prevents the development of fetal abnormalities associated with animal models of fetal alcohol syndrome (Randall et al., 1984; Segarnick et al., 1982b, 1985b, 1985c). NSAIDs prevent death following administration of massive doses of alcohol (George, Elmer & Collins, 1982; author's unpublished data, 1984).

Relatively small pretreatment doses of EFA precursors markedly potentiate alcohol's sedative effects (Segarnick et al., 1982, 1985b). The withdrawal syndrome seen in mice and rats following prolonged exposure to alcohol is attenuated by similar doses of EFAs administered in a single dose shortly before withdrawal severity is assessed (Anggard, 1983; Segarnick et al., 1983, 1985b). Treatment with EFAs during alcohol administration prevents the development of fatty liver in rats (Segarnick et al., 1985a). In human alcoholics, high levels of long chain EFAs appear to afford protection against the development of hepatic pathology (Wolkin, Segarnick, Siekierski, & Rotrosen, 1985).

DIFFERENTIAL LIPID POOLS

A key question related to these EFA-alcohol interactions, as well as to how lipids might work as "pharmacologic" agents in aging is, "How, in the presence of massive quantities of membrane phopholipid-esterified EFAs, can small doses exert such potent behavioral and physiological effects?" To address this question we have carried out a series of in vitro experiments using human platelets (Segarnick, 1985c). Platelets form prostaglandins and thromboxanes during aggregation induced by such agents as thrombin. It is well-established that the mechanism underlying this is thrombin activation of phospholipase A2 which cleaves the 2-position fatty acid from phospholipids to provide free EFAs which can then be converted to PGs and thromboxanes. Alcohol does not modify PGs formed by this pathway. However, ethanol does enhance conversion of EFAs to PGs when the EFAs are provided in their free form. This suggests that there are at least two discrete metabolic EFA pools, a phospholipid-esterified pool of EFAs that can be stimulated by thrombin and a pool of free EFAs, the use of which can be stimulated by ethanol. Thus, the traditional phospholipid EFA pool is important for PG synthesis when cells are exposed to "catastrophic" conditions; in contrast, homeostatic PG levels may be more regulated by the level of free EFAs. It is this latter pool that may be most affected by acute dietary or pharmacologic manipulations and that most likely is responsible for the observed EFA alcohol interactions.

Crawford (1983) has previously speculated on the existence of two such discrete pools. He points out that the amount of PGs synthesized is so small and that the pool of EFA precursors in cell membranes is so large that it was originally presumed that small changes in EFAs could not affect PG synthesis. However, based on the effects of dietary EFAs and EFA deficiency he suggests that there are "two sources of PG precursor: endogenous synthesis being derived from a metabolic pool, whereas stimulated synthesis (such as in trauma) comes from the cell membrane pool . . . to release free arachidonic acid (AA) from cell membrane phosphoglycerides there is a requirement for a phospholipase attack. Such an attack could be readily visualized if the cell was physically distorted, damaged or cut and would result in immediate and substantial PG production, such as is seen, for example, in stimulated platelets. It seems more likely that cell membranes would routinely be protected from phospholipase attack. This would mean that there could be two levels at which the EFA-PG link operates. In one, the metabolism of dietary linoleic acid results in PG precursor, which immediately becomes available for PG synthesis. The other is the use of membrane AA released by lipase as a direct precursor for PG synthesis . . . The metabolic pathway would be more directly influenced in the short term by the dietary level of EFAs and of other fatty acids, whereas the membrane pool of PG precursor would be expected to be that much more stable and susceptible only to long-term dietary manipulations."

An analogous situation must clearly exist for PS, since the doses of exogenous PS required to elicit effects on behavior and neurotransmitter function are negligible in comparison to the amount of PS already present in cell membranes. Changes resulting from acute low-dose administration must therefore be related to supplementation of a (small) free, metabolically highly-active pool of PS that might be susceptible to enzymatic action specifically because it is not protected in a membrane microenvironment. Metabolic products of PS that might mediate some of its actions include lyso-PS, PE, and free

EFAs. Strong support that lyso-PS is a short-lived intermediate with membrane regulatory properties has been presented by Bruni and Toffano (1982). The actions of PS (or its products) on cognition might be attributable to one or more of the following:
1. increased membrane fluidity,
2. increased synthesis and release of acetylcholine,
3. increased release of other neurotransmitters (e.g., dopamine), and
4. increased PG synthesis.

THERAPEUTIC STRATEGIES

It has earlier been suggested that lipids or agents that modify lipid membranes might reduce symptoms of cognitive impairment and / or halt the progression of CNS degenerative disease via one or more of the following mechanisms:
1. reversing changes in membrane fluidity,
2. preventing oxidative and free radical damage to membranes, and
3. enhancing cholinergic and / or other neurotransmission.
Since some of the agents (or classes of agents) proposed here may affect more than one of these processes, this section will be organized around types of agents rather than mechanisms.

Phosphatidylserine

In the context of these proposed mechanisms, PS is in many ways an ideal candidate for therapeutic trials. Preclinical studies suggest efficacy on a variety of measures of cognitive performance in aged animals. These findings have been replicated in a number of laboratories using different strains of animals, different dosages, different time courses, and different routes of administration (Corwin et al., 1983; Drago et al., 1981; Zanotti et al., 1984). Mechanisms to which PS might owe its efficacy have been elaborated earlier and include possible enhancement of membrane fluidity, increased synthesis and release of ACh and other neurotransmitters, and possibly increased synthesis of PGs (see below). In addition, because of its high proportion of unsaturated fatty acids, it is conceivable that exogenous PS may further act to scavenge free radicals and prevent oxidative damage to membrane phospholipids.

Appropriate human studies assessing the cognitive effects of PS should be carried out: Toxicity does not appear to present immediate concerns. Dosage, route of administration, time course of treatment, and assessment of efficacy (both which measures to use and their temporal relationship to treatment) all need to be worked out.

Key questions that remain, and which would be of greater interest should PS show efficacy in human trials, involve its mechanism of action. Is the entire PS molecule required for efficacy? If not, which moiety is required? Can the same effects be gotten with lyso-PS, phosphatidic acid, serine, phosphoserine, diacylglycerols, EFAs? Are these effects obtainable with PS containing only saturated fatty acids? Given the robustness of the effects on cognitive performance in aged animals, these questions can be answered empirically. While these answers might be important in the conceptualization and design of future strategies, they would be of far more immediate interest should PS show even small effects in clinical trials.

Active Lipid

Active lipid, an egg yolk-derived mixture of neutral lipids, PC and PE in a ratio of 7:2:1, was developed as a pharmacologic tool to modify membrane fluidity (Lyte & Shinitzky, 1983). Active lipid has been reported to reduce symptoms of alcohol withdrawal, to ameliorate opiate withdrawal, to enhance lymphocyte function and rectify immune competence in aging. In addition, active lipid has been reported to reverse changes in membrane fluidity and cholesterol:phospholipid ratios in aged mice, most likely by removing excess cholesterol from membranes. In humans, slight but significant reductions in blood cholesterol and blood pressure have been observed. In addition to its effects on membrane fluidity, active lipid may enhance choline availability and cholinergic neurotransmission.

Safety does not appear to present problems and, therefore, human studies need be conducted before conclusions regarding efficacy in CNS degenerative dementias can be drawn. The same issues regarding dosage, assessment, etc., apply here.

Phosphatidylcholine/Lecithin

This chapter would be incomplete without reference at least to the potential utility of PC as a therapeutic strategy. Presumed mechanisms of action would include both increased membrane fluidity, enhanced availability of choline, enhanced cholinergic neurotransmission, and prevention of the loss of membrane PC (and the proposed membrane degeneration accompanying it) that may occur in AD. Brief therapeutic trials with PC have generally been unsuccessful and have been reviewed in detail previously (Bartus, Dean, Beer, & Lippa, 1982). The possibility that long-term PC treatment will prevent degenerative changes has been addressed by Blusztajn et al. (1984) and is discussed further in the chapter in this volume by Blusztajn and Wurtman.

S-Adenosyl-L-Methionine (SAM)

Another approach toward enhancing membrane fluidity in aging involves administration of SAM as a methyl group donor to activate the phospholipid methylation pathway. Cimino et al. (1984) report that SAM administered to 30-month-old rats restores synaptosomal membrane fluidity to levels seen in 3-month-old controls. Further, they find that this treatment reverses the age-related decline in beta-adrenergic binding sites and partially reverses age-related reductions in dopamine-stimulated adenylate cyclase activity. No behavioral correlates are described in their report that would permit these biochemical changes to be correlated with cognition.

Cimino's findings clearly represent an important avenue for future work since SAM can be safely administered to humans. Again issues of dosage, route of administration, and the type and temporal association of assessment to treatment need be worked out. Several clinical studies with SAM in depression have already been reported and should provide guidelines regarding dosage, etc.

Alcohol

A somewhat paradoxical strategy, although a very direct approach to the issue of membrane fluidity, might involve therapeutic trials with acute low doses of alcohol. The paradox is that conventional wisdom tells that alcohol causes mental deterioration, cognitive decline and, with prolonged use, dementia. Alcohol withdrawal (a state characterized by reduced membrane fluidity) is associated with memory and visuospatial defects (Brandt, Butters, Ryan & Bayog, 1983; Ryan & Butters, 1980), which recover with sobriety. Recently, however, Mann, Cho-Young, and Vogel-Sprott (1984) reported that low doses of alcohol administered to male undergraduates enhanced retrograde memory in free word recall trials. The authors suggest that the improvement may be due to alcohol's effects on brain reward systems. It is possible that this effect is also due to enhanced membrane fluidity and/or to enhanced release of catecholamines. If the effect is related to changes in membrane fluidity, one might expect even more pronounced effects in a population where increased cholesterol:phospholipid ratios and reduced membrane fluidity may contribute to CNS pathology (e.g., aging, alcohol withdrawal).

Again, because of the safety of acute low dose alcohol, such studies could be easily carried out. While such studies would be heuristically useful in addressing the relationship between membrane fluidity and cognitive impairment, it must be cautioned that alcohol is not likely to offer long-term treatment benefits because of the membrane rigidity and tolerance associated with chronic usage. Nonetheless it seems that acute studies are warranted because of their potential implications for designing other agents.

Essential Fatty Acids

Another approach to enhancing membrane fluidity might involve administration of EFAs. These agents are somewhat readily available in vegetable oils (safflower oil contains large amounts of cis-linoleic acid, 18:2 evening primrose oil, 18:2, and gamma linolenic acid, 18:3); longer chain, more highly unsaturated fatty acids are present in high concentrations in fish oils (22:5 and 22:6). Membrane fluidity might be enhanced simply by incorporation of these long chain fatty acids into membrane phospholipids. An alternative, although somewhat more speculative mechanism might involve conversion of EFAs to PGs. Indirect evidence that PGs might affect membrane fluidity is that extremely low concentrations of PG E_1 (on the order of one to two molecules per cell) increase erythrocyte filterability (the rate at which red cells pass through a fixed pore filter). Finally, dietary or other enrichment with these long chain EFAs might reduce or prevent atherosclerotic plaque development because Eskimos who consume high quantities of these EFAs have virtually clean arteries and do not suffer from coronary infarctions or stroke (Gibson & Sinclair, 1981; Sinclair, 1981). While these problems are not considered to be a component of the pathology of AD, the potential importance of such strategies in multi-infarct dementia should not be overlooked.

Although I am not aware of work with EFAs on cognitive function in aging (either clinical or preclinical), Glen (1985) has described limited improvement of cognitive recovery in withdrawing alcoholics treated with evening primrose oil. The potential utility of this approach as well as the known safety of EFA supplementation suggests that both human and animal work with these substances might prove to be worthwhile.

Antioxidants

Schroeder (1985) has reviewed the potential role of membrane peroxidative and cross-linking damage as a contributory factor in the loss of membrane fluidity and membrane lipid asymmetry. He points out that these losses adversely affect numerous aspects of neurotransmission and further that peroxidative damage to membranes increases with aging. A somewhat simplistic, although potentially viable approach to prophylaxis would then be administration of antioxidants such as vitamins E or C or substances currently used as food preservatives such as BHT or EDTA. Other than the known toxicity of high-dose, fat-soluble vitamins, safety does not appear to be a major concern. These ideas are also not new and have been proposed repeatedly in the lay press and through health food advertising. Nonetheless, I am not aware of any properly conducted long-term prospective studies that could either establish or refute the potential efficacy of such approaches in arresting the progression of degenerative CNS dementias. Unfortunately, both preclinical and clinical studies would have to be of long duration, involve large numbers of subjects and therefore be difficult and expensive to conduct.

SUMMARY AND CONCLUSIONS

Given the extent of the degenerative pathology associated with AD, it appears unlikely that pharmacologic or nutritional therapeutic strategies will succeed in significantly ameliorating the symptoms of preexisting disease. Small but measurable improvements in cognitive function may be attainable, such as are seen with physostigmine and cholinergic agonists and, indeed, these studies have made real contributions to our understanding of the pathology and pharmacology of AD. Unfortunately, these approaches do not seem to offer much hope for improving the quality of life for either the victims of AD, their families, or for reducing the costs of this illness. It is in this context that strategies designed to prevent the progression of degenerative dementias are presented. Major issues that must be dealt with in order to assess their efficacy include the lack of early means of detecting and confirming AD, the difficulty and expense of conducting long-term prospective treatment studies, and the absolute lack of animal models or *in vitro* test systems in which potentially active compounds can be screened.

REFERENCES

Anggard, E. (1983). Ethanol, essential fatty acids and prostaglandins. *Pharmacology, Biochemistry and Behavior, 18* (Suppl. 1), 401-407.

Bartus, R.T., Dean, R.L., III, Beer, B., & Lippa, A.S. (1982). The cholinergic hypothesis of geriatric memory dysfunction. *Science, 217,* 408-414.

Bartus, R.T., Dean, R.L., Sherman, K., Friedman, E., & Beer, B. (1981). Profound effects of combining choline and piracetam on memory enhancement and cholinergic function in aged rats. *Neurobiology of Aging, 2,* 105-111.

Blusztajn, J.K., Maire, J.C., Tacconi, M.T., & Wurtman, R.J. (1984). The possible role of neuronal choline metabolism in the pathophysiology of Alzheimer's disease: A hypothesis. In R.J. Wurtman, S.H. Corkin, & J.H. Growdon (Eds.), *Alzheimer's disease: Advances in basic research and therapies.* Zurich: Center for Brain Sciences and Metabolism Charitable Trust.

Blusztajn, J.K., Zeisel, S.H., & Wurtman, R.J. (1979). Synthesis of lecithin (phosphatidylcholine) from phosphatidylethanolamine in bovine brain. *Brain Research, 179,* 319-327.

Brandt, J., Butters, N., Ryan, C., & Bayog, R. (1983). Cognitive loss and recovery in long-term alcohol abusers. *Archives of General Psychiatry, 40,* 435-442.

Bruni, A., & Toffano, G. (1982). Lysophosphatidylserine, a short-lived intermediate with plasma membrane regulatory properties. *Pharmacological Research Communications, 14,* 469-482.

Calderini, G., Teolato, S., Bonnetti, A.C., Battistella, A., & Toffano, G. (1981). Effect of lysophosphatidylserine on rat hypothalamic CAMP in vivo. *Life Sciences, 28,* 2367-2377.

Casamenti, F., Mantovani, P., Amaducci, L., & Pepeu, G. (1979). Effect of phosphatidylserine on acetylcholine output from the cerebral cortex of the rat. *Journal of Neurochemistry, 32,* 529-533.

Cicero, T. (1978). Tolerance to and physical dependence on alcohol: Behavioral and neurobiochemical mechanisms. In M.A. Lipton, A. Dimascio, & K.F. Killam (Eds.), *Psychopharmacology: A generation of progress* (pp. 1603-1615). New York: Raven Press.

Cimino, M., Vantini, G., Algeri, S., Curatola, G., Pezzoli, C., & Stramentinoli, G. (1984). Age-related modification of dopaminergic and beta adrenergic receptor system: Restoration to normal activity by modifying membrane fluidity with S-adenosylmethionine. *Life Sciences, 34,* 2029-2039.

Corwin, J., Dean, R.L., Bartus, R.T., Rotrosen, J., & Watkins, D.L. (1985). Behavioral effects of phosphatidylserine in the aged Fisher 344 rat: Amelioration of passive avoidance deficits without changes in psychomotor task performance. *Neurobiology of Aging, 6,* 11-15.

Corwin, J., Rotrosen, J., Dean, R.L., Bartus, R.T., & Watkins, D.L. (1983, December). *Effects of phosphatidylserine on learning and retention in aged Fisher rats.* Paper presented at the annual meeting of the American College of Neuropsychopharmacology, San Juan, Puerto Rico.

Crawford, M.A. (1983). Background to essential fatty acids and their prostanoid derivatives. *British Medical Bulletin, 39,* 210-213.

Drago, F., Canonico, P.L., & Scapagnini, U. (1981). Behavioral effects of phosphatidylserine in aged rats. *Neurobiology of Aging, 2,* 209-213.

Ellingboe, J. (1978). Effects of alcohol on neurochemical processes.

In M.A. Lipton, A. Dimascio, & K.F. Killam (Eds.), *Psychopharmacology: A generation of progress* (pp. 1603-1615). New York: Raven Press.

George, F.R., Elmer, G.I., & Collins, A.C. (1982). Indomethacin significantly reduces mortality due to acute ethanol exposure. *Substance and Alcohol Actions/Misuse, 3,* 267-274.

Gibson, R.A., & Sinclair, A.J. (1981). Are Eskimos obligate carnivores? [Letter to the editor]. *Lancet, 1,* 1100.

Glen, A.I., Glen, E.M., Macdowell, L.E., & Skinner, F.K. (1985, March). *Essential fatty acids in the management of withdrawal symptoms and tissue damage in alcoholics.* Paper presented at the Second International Congress on Essential Fatty Acids and Prostaglandins, London.

Hill, M., & Bangham, A.D. (1975). General depressant drug therapy: A biophysical aspect. *Advances in Experimental Medicine and Biology, 59,* 1-10.

Hirata, F., & Axelrod, J. (1980). Phospholipid methylation and biological signal transmission. *Science, 209,* 1082-1090.

Lippa, A.S., Pelham, R.W., Beer, B., Critchett, D.J., Dean, R.L., & Bartus, R.T. (1980). Brain cholinergic dysfunction and memory in aged rats. *Neurobiology of Aging, 1,* 13-19.

Littleton, J.M., & John, G. (1977). Synaptosomal membrane lipids of mice during continuous exposure to ethanol. *Journal of Pharmacy and Pharmacology, 29,* 579-580.

Lyte, M., & Shinitzky, M. (1983). Possible reversal of tissue aging by a lipid diet. In R.J. Wurtman, S.H. Corkin, & J.H. Growdon (Eds.), *Alzheimer's disease: Advances in basic research and therapies* (pp. 295-312). Zurich: Center for Brain Sciences and Metabolism Charitable Trust.

Manku, M.S., Oka, M., & Horrobin, D.F. (1979). Differential regulation of the formulation of prostaglandins and related substances from archidonic acid and dihomogammalinolenic acids. I. Effects of ethanol. *Prostaglandins Medicine, 3,* 119-124.

Mann, R.E., Cho-Young, J., & Vogel-Sprott, M. (1984). Retrograde enhancement by alcohol of delayed free recall performance. *Pharmacology, Biochemistry and Behavior, 20,* 639-642.

Raese, J., Patrick, R.L., & Barchas, J.D. (1976). Phospholipid-induced activation of tyrosine hydroxylase from rat brain striatal synaptosomes. *Biochemical Pharmacology, 25,* 2245-2250.

Randall, C.L. (1984, January). Effects of aspirin on ethanol teratogenesis. Paper presented at the Winter Conference on Brain Research, Steamboat Springs, Colo.

Rivnay, B., Globerson, A., & Shinitzky, M. (1979). Viscosity of lymphocyte plasma membrane in aging mice and its possible relationship to serum cholesterol. *Mechanisms of Aging and Development, 10,* 71-79.

Rotrosen, J., Mandio, D., Segarnick, D., Traficante, L.J., & Gershon, S. (1980). Ethanol and prostaglandin E1: Biochemical and behavioral interactions. *Life Sciences, 26,* 1867-1876.

Ryan, C., & Butters, N. (1980). Learning and memory impairment in young and old alcoholics: Evidence for the premature-aging hypothesis. *Alcoholism, 4,* 288-293.

Schroeder, F. (1985). Role of membrane lipid asymmetry in aging. *Neurobiology of Aging, 5* (4), 323-333.

Segarnick, D.J., Cooper, N., & Rotrosen, J. (1985a). Gamma linolenic acid prevents the development of alcohol induced fatty liver in rats. *Prostaglandins, Leukotrienes, and Medicine, 11, 17,* 277-280.

Segarnick, D.J., Cordasco, D.M., & Rotrosen, J. (1982a, December). Prostaglandin and alcohol interactions. Paper presented at the annual meeting of the American College of Neuropsychopharmacology, San Juan, Puerto Rico.

Segarnick, D.J., Cordasco, D.M., and Rotrosen, J. (1985b). Prostanoid modulation of certain behavioral effects of ethanol. *Pharmacology, Biochemistry, and Behavior, 23,* 71-75.

Segarnick, D.J., Rotrosen, J., & Cordasco, D.M. (1982b). Biochemical and behavioral interactions between alcohol and prostaglandin E1. In D.F. Horrobin (Ed.), *Clinical uses of essential fatty acids* (pp. 175-190). Montreal: Eden Press.

Segarnick, D.J., Ryer, H., & Rotrosen, J. (1985c). Precursor- and pool-dependent differential effects of ethanol on human platelet prostanoid synthesis. *Biochemical Pharmacology, 34,* 1343-1346.

Sinclair, H.M. (1981). Are Eskimos obligate carnivores? [Letter to the editor]. *Lancet, 1,* 1217.

Toffano, G., & Bruni, A. (1980). Pharmacological properties of phospholipid liposomes. *Pharmacological Research Communication, 12* (9), 829-845.

Toffano, G., Leon, A., Benvegnu, D., Boarato, E., & Azzore, G.F. (1976). Effect of brain cortex phospholipids on catecholamine content of mouse brain. *Pharmacological Research Communications,* *8,* 581-590.

Wolkin, A., Segarnick, D.J., Siekierski, J., & Rotrosen, J. (1985, March). Clinical and biochemical effects of essential fatty acid supplementation on acute alcohol withdrawal and prolonged abstinence. Paper presented at the Second International Congress on Essential Fatty Acids and Prostaglandins, London.

Zanotti, A., Aporti, F., Toffano, G., & Valzelli, L. (1984). Effects of phosphatidylserine on avoidance relearning in rats (preliminary observations). *Pharmacological Research Communications,* *16,* 485-493.

23

Pathogenesis: Possible Role of Choline Phospholipids

Jan K. Blusztajn, PhD, Pamela G. Holbrook, MS,
Mordechai Liscovitch, PhD, Jean-Claude Maire, PhD,
Charlotte Mauron, BS, U. Ingrid Richardson, PhD,
Mariateresa Tacconi, PhD, and Richard J. Wurtman, MD,

An overwhelming consensus now exists among investigators that a) certain acetylcholine (ACh)-releasing brain neurons, the septal neurons projecting to the hippocampus and basal forebrain neurons innervating the cerebral cortices, are invariably decimated in Alzheimer's disease (AD) (Bowen, Benton, Spillane, Smith, & Allen, 1982; Perry, E.K., Tomlinson, Blessed, Bergman, Gibson & Perry, R.H., 1978; Wilcock, Esiri, Bowen, & Smith, 1982; Wurtman, 1985), b) other neurons (e.g., serotonin-releasing neurons in the raphe nucleus, noradrenergic neurons of the locus coeruleus; cortical somatostatin-releasing neurons) are also often afflicted but to a lesser extent, and, c) many neuronal populations are largely unaffected in the disease. If one or more groups of neurons are invariably damaged in AD, then examination of their biochemical peculiarities may yield insights as to the disease's etiology or to the pathogenetic process that ultimately causes the neurons to die. Moreover, if the deficient neurotransmitter can be implicated in the abnormal behaviors typical of the disease—like ACh in memory loss, norepinephrine in the impaired ability to sustain attention, or serotonin in disturbances of mood or in aggressiveness—then drugs that substitute for the deficient transmitter or that increase its availability in synapses might be useful in treating the disease.

This article focuses on the first of these possibilities that a particular biochemical property unique to cholinergic neurons underlies their special vulnerability in AD. This property has to do with the ways that cholinergic neurons metabolize choline. All cells in the body incorporate free choline into phospholipid molecules [which constitute the majority of all lipids present in neuronal membranes (Ansell,

1973), like phosphatidylcholine, sphingomyelin, and the 1-alkenyl glycerophospholipids]. However, cholinergic cells use choline for additional purposes, that is both as a constituent of membrane phospholipids and as the precursor for ACh, the neurotransmitter that they release into their synapses. When a cholinergic neuron is physiologically active, the rate at which it synthesizes and releases ACh depends upon its choline levels (Blusztajn & Wurtman, 1983). We propose that the need to obtain choline for ACh synthesis may sometimes cause cholinergic neurons to destroy their membranes, particularly when the neurons are firing frequently or when free choline is in relatively short supply. They may cannibalize the choline stored in the phospholipid "reservoir," thus altering membrane composition (and, presumably, function) and even blocking the production of new membranes (Blusztajn & Wurtman, 1983).

Our hypothesis begs the question of the etiology of the AD, focusing instead on why cholinergic neurons are more likely than others to be damaged by the etiologic factor. It applies equally well whether the etiologic factor is present only in diseased cells or is distributed throughout the brain. The factor itself that presumably causes a choline deficiency might be a decrease in choline's production (by de novo synthesis), a decrease in its uptake from the synaptic cleft and extracellular space, or an excessive utilization of choline to form a particular phospholipid. Choline uptake might be impaired if the delivery of oxygen or glucose to the nerve terminals is deficient, perhaps secondary to a diffusion block caused by the perivascular amyloidosis that is characteristic of AD (Mandybur, 1975). Alternatively, the hypothetical choline deficiency might simply result from its overuse for ACh synthesis, as might happen if the firing frequency of vulnerable neurons is persistently enhanced or if the presynaptic storage of ACh is impaired. Once cholinergic terminals begin to deteriorate and release less of the transmitter, it seems likely that surviving, "healthy" terminals might start to release more ACh—because the firing frequencies of their neurons will increase or because release is no longer subject to presynaptic inhibition. Increased ACh synthesis might also be expected to increase the demand for its precursor, choline, within "healthy" terminals, a process that might ultimately lead to "autocannibalism" in these terminals.

The choline obtained by "autocannibalism" could derive from the general metabolic "pool" of choline phospholipids or, perhaps, from a pool specifically mobilized for that purpose. Membrane phospholipids like phosphatidylcholine are compartmented in three ways:

by their subcellular localization (for example, synaptic vesicles vs plasma membranes), by their fatty acid composition, and by their mode of synthesis (methylation of phosphatidylethanolamine vs incorporation of preexisting choline via the CDP-choline or base-exchange pathways). Excessive destruction of membrane phosphatidylcholine might lead to changes in membrane composition (i.e., in the ratios of phosphatidylcholine to other phospholipids or to proteins) or to a loss in total membrane surface. Either alteration could affect the neuron's functional properties and even its viability. Such changes would be most likely to occur in nerve terminals, the neuronal structures that are specialized for neurotransmitter synthesis and release, initially damaging them and only later affecting cell bodies.

The "autocannibalism" hypothesis of the pathogenesis of AD is not presently supported by an overwhelming body of clinical or experimental evidence; but it is consistent with a number of observations:

1. It is the terminals of cholinergic neurons in the cerebral cortex and not the perikarya in the basal forebrain, which apparently degenerate first in AD (Pearson et al., 1983; Perry, R.H., Candy, Perry, E.K., Irving, Blessed, Fairbairn, & Tomlinson, 1985). This is consistent with the fact that most of the neurons' ACh is formed in the presynaptic terminals.

2. Only long-axon cholinergic neurons are affected by the disease process. The short-axon interneurons in the striatum are spared. Perhaps the short-axon neurons can more easily resynthesize their membranes because choline phospholipids are more readily available to them through axoplasmic transport (Abe, Haga, & Kurokawa, 1973; Droz, Brunetti, Di Giambernardino, Koenig, & Porcellati, 1981). This transport would occur over a considerably shorter distance than that separating cholinergic perikarya in the nucleus basalis or septum from terminals in the frontoparietal cortex or hippocampus.

3. Choline is synthesized in brain neurons, de novo, by a multienzymatic pathway. The terminal steps in this pathway are catalyzed by phosphatidylethanolamine N-methyltransferase (PeMT), and involve the stepwise methylation of phosphatidylethanolamine to phosphatidylcholine, using S-adenosylmethionine (SAM) as methyl donor. This newly formed phosphatidylcholine is hydrolyzed to free choline by a number of phospholipases and other hydrolases. We found that free choline constituted 23% of the total phosphatidylcholine synthesized by synaptosomal PeMT (from [^{3}H-methyl]-

SAM) during a 30-minute incubation period. Furthermore, the enrichment of the free choline pool with newly formed [³H]-choline was 50-fold greater than that of the phosphatidylcholine pool by newly formed [³H]-phosphatidylcholine (Blusztajn & Wurtman, 1981). Thus, the relatively small amount of phosphatidylcholine synthesized in nerve terminals *de novo* may have a considerably faster turnover than the bulk of synaptosomal phosphatidylcholine. (One might anticipate that phosphatidylcholine pool that preferentially provided free choline for ACh synthesis would turn over more rapidly than "storage" phosphatidylcholine.) This phosphatidylcholine is also unusual in its very high proportion of polyunsaturated fatty acids (i.e., up to 50-70%) when newly-synthesized by the methylation (Tacconi & Wurtman, 1985) or by the CDP-choline, or the base exchange pathways (Holbrook, Mauron, & Wurtman, 1985) in comparison to the steady state (25%) (Breckenridge, Gombos, & Morgan, 1972).

4. To determine whether an endogenous choline source (perhaps phosphatidylcholine) in brain tissue can support ACh synthesis when exogenous choline is unavailable, we measured ACh release from rat striatal slices superfused with or without choline (Maire & Wurtman, 1985). In the absence of free choline, ACh was released spontaneously at a rate of 7.5 ± 1.3 pmol/mg protein/min (mean $\pm$ S.D.). Electrical field stimulation (15 Hz for 30 min) accelerated this release (25.6 ± 5.9 pmol/mg protein/min). Addition of choline (20 μM) to the superfusate significantly enhanced both the spontaneous (22.7 ± 5.7 pmol/mg protein/min) and the electrically evoked (37.4 ± 6.7 pmol/mg protein/min) release of the transmitter. Although the amount of ACh in the tissue did not depend on extracellular choline concentration (in this range of choline concentrations), choline contents did increase when choline levels in the superfusate were raised.

In the absence of exogenous choline, the combined efflux of *choline + ACh* into the superfusate was 75 pmol/mg protein/min; however, the decrease in *choline + ACh* within the tissue was only 16 pmol/mg protein/min. Thus, an endogenous pool of choline present within a larger molecule must have provided the free choline that sustained ACh synthesis and tissue choline and ACh levels. The only known compounds whose pool sizes would be sufficient for this purpose are the choline-containing phospholipids. Evidence that these compounds are indeed the source of the free choline is provided by the finding that the amount of phosphate in the phos-

pholipids of the slices decreased by 23% when the slices were stimulated (i.e., suggesting that neuronal activity accelerated the metabolic
degradation of phospholipids). Addition of exogenous choline (20
μM) to the superfustate prevented the loss of phospholipid phosphate from stimulated slices (Mauron & Wurtman, 1986). This suggests either that the apparent acceleration in phospholipid
degradation reflected increased need for choline in order to maintain ACh release from cholinergic neurons (i.e., shifting the equilibrium
between ACh, choline, and Ch-PL, towards ACh); or a general increase in phospholipid turnover, related to neuronal firing. In the
former case, the exogenous choline presumably was used to maintain high ACh synthesis, and thus provided sufficient substrate to
allow the rate of Ch-phospholipids synthesis to catch up with their
accelerated degradation.

Apparently, the choline liberated from striatal phospholipids must
first enter the extracellular space and then be transported into cholinergic neurons by the high-affinity choline uptake system before it can
be converted to ACh. Addition of hemicholinium-3 (that blocks this
uptake process) to the superfusate suppresses the release of ACh
by electrical stimulation and decreases striatal ACh levels, even when
these are compared with ACh's release from, and its levels in, tissues incubated without free choline.

Choline efflux from the isolated, perfused chicken heart reportedly is enhanced by cholinesterase inhibitors or by muscarinic
cholinergic agonists, and is blocked by muscarinic antagonists
(Corradetti, Lindmar, & Loffelholz, 1983). This choline apparently
also originates from the hydrolysis of tissue phospholipids, which
apparently is modulated by cholinergic activity.

5. Stimulation of the preganglionic trunk of the cat's superior cervical ganglion for 20 minutes at 20, 4, or even 1 Hz decreased the
number of synaptic vesicles in cholinergic nerve terminals by 75, 54,
or 56%, respectively (Birks, 1974), without altering ganglionic ACh
contents (Birks & MacIntosh, 1961). This finding was interpreted
as suggesting that the choline phospholipids in vesicular membranes
were the source of the choline for ACh synthesis. When, in a similar
experiment, the cat's superior cervical ganglion was stimulated for
a shorter period, phosphatidylcholine levels and the number of synaptic vesicles in presynaptic terminals did not fall. However, if the
ganglion was also exposed to hemicholinium-3, the number of
synaptic vesicles decreased after stimulation to 18% of control, while
ganglionic phosphatidylcholine levels fell to 69% of control (Parducz,

Kiss, & Joo, 1976) (other phospholipids were not affected). These observations indicate that when adequate extracellular choline is not available (e.g., after inhibition of its uptake by hemicholinium-3), vesicular phosphatidylcholine is used to supply choline for ACh synthesis.

6. Patients with Down's Syndrome invariably develop pathological signs (senile plaques and tangles) indistinguishable from those observed in the brains of people with AD (see Epstein, 1983 for a review) as well as a decrease in cortical choline acetyltransferase activity (Yates, Simpson, Maloney, Gordon, & Reid, 1980). Brain phosphatidylethanolamine and phosphatidylserine purified from autopsy specimens of fetuses affected with this genetic disorder exhibit abnormal fatty acid composition (Brooksbank, Martinez, & Balazs, 1985), suggesting that abnormal phospholipid metabolism might also be found in the brains of people with AD. Phosphatidylcholine and phosphatidylethanolamine are metabolized by brain phospholipases and lysophospholipases to form glycerophosphocholine or glycerophosphoethanolamine, respectively. The amounts of glycerophosphocholine in brain autopsy specimens from patients who died with AD reportedly are 3.6-fold higher than those present in samples from normal people (Bárány, Chang, Arús, Rustan, & Frey, 1985). (The amounts of phosphatidylcholine and phosphatidylethanolamine were not found to be changed in that study.) The increase in glycerophosphocholine is suggestive of the increased rates of phosphatidylcholine degradation.

We have studied the relationships between choline-containing phospholipids and ACh levels in a purely cholinergic cell line, the neuroblastoma x glioma hybrid, NG108-15. The synthesis of ACh in these cells was found to vary with extracellular concentrations of choline. When the cells were incubated for one hour in the presence of various concentrations of [3H-methyl]choline, the accumulation of [3H-methyl]ACh exhibited saturable kinetics with an apparent K_m of 193 ± 34 μM, and V_{max} of 268 ± 23 pmol/mg protein/hr. (See Figure 1) At the same time, incorporation of the labeled choline into phosphocholine (an intermediate in phosphatidylcholine synthesis) proceeded at a much higher rate (apparent $V_{max} = 16.8$ nmol/mg protein/hr) and had a lower apparent K_m (14.9 ± 5.4 μM) (Figure 2). Thus, in these cells choline was more likely to be used for phosphatidylcholine than for ACh synthesis (because choline kinase was more likely than choline acetyltransferase to attack the choline). We hypothesized that inhibiting the choline kinase activity might accelerate the cells' ability to form ACh. We observed that addition of ethanolamine to the incubation medium (0.5 mM), which suppressed the phosphocholine and phosphatidylcholine formations (at low choline concentrations), did indeed enhance the labeling of [3H-methyl]ACh (see Figures 3 and 4). These data demonstrate that the dynamic equilibrium among ACh, choline, and phospholipids can be shifted toward ACh when choline's utilization for

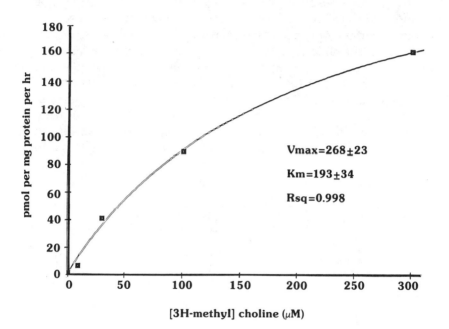

Vmax=268±23

Km=193±34

Rsq=0.998

[3H-methyl] choline (µM)

Figure 1. Effect of [3H-methyl]choline on the accumulation of [3H-methyl]acetylcholine in NG108-15. Acetylcholine synthesis in NG108-15 cells: Dependence on the extracellular choline concentrations. NG108-15 cells (passage 21) were subcultured on 35 mm dishes and allowed to grow for 1 day in the Dulbecco Modified Eagle's Medium containing 5% newborn bovine serum. For the next 2 days, cells were grown in a serum-free medium (N2) (Bottenstein & Sato, 1979) containing 1 mM dibutyryl-cAMP; most cells developed neurites due to the presence of the cAMP. The cells were then incubated for 1 hour in N2 medium containing 7 µCi of choline at various concentrations. Incubations were terminated, after the removal of the media, by the addition of 0.7 ml of methanol, and the cells were then scraped off the dishes. 1.4 ml of chloroform was then added, and the extracts were washed with 0.7 ml of water. Both the organic and aqueous layers were collected and dried under a vacuum. The dry residues of the aqueous extracts were reconstituted in 0.06 ml of water and filtered. 0.02 ml of the filtrates were subjected to high performance liquid chromatography (Liscovitch, Blusztajn, & Wurtman, 1985), the radioactivities in the fractions eluting at the same retention time as authentic acetylcholine were determined, the amounts of [3H-methyl] ACh were calculated assuming that the specific radioactivity of labeled choline was that of the medium. A rectangular hyperbola was fitted to the data. The inset shows the apparent V_{max}, K_m, and the standard errors of their determinations, and a regression coefficient.

phospholipid synthesis is slowed. Related mechanisms might operate in cholinergic neurons of brains of AD patients; that is, increased synthesis of ACh concomitant with decrease production of choline phospholipids — a process that might be beneficial in the short-term (for maintaining cholinergic transmission), but damaging to the neuronal membranes if continued for longer periods.

The hypothesized ability of the choline phospholipids in cholinergic terminals to serve both as a structural component and as a reservoir for an important molecule of lower molecular weight (free choline) is not, of course, unique. Circulating albumin both contributes to the maintenance of colloid osmotic pressure and provides free amino acids when protein consumption is inadequate. Bone is both a structural unit and a vast reservoir for calcium. Protein malnutrition can cause edema when too much albumin is broken down to provide free amino acids; calcium malnutrition can cause osteomalacia and bone breakage when bone is demineralized to provide the blood with

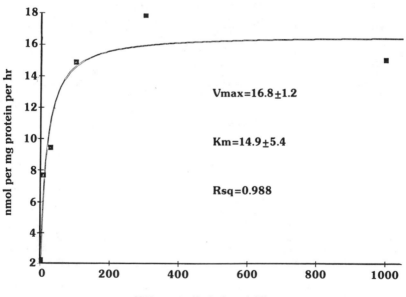

Figure 2. Effect of [3H-methyl]choline on the accumulation of [3H-methyl]phosphocholine in NG108-15. Phosphocholine synthesis in the NG108-15 cells: Dependence on the choline concentrations. The experiments were carried out as described in the legend to Figure 1. Phosphocholine peaks were collected and their radioactivity determined.

free calcium. If our hypothesis concerning the reservoir functions of neuronal choline phospholipids is correct, then consumption of supplemental choline—as such or as dietary phosphatidylcholine (lecithin)—might serve an important nutritional function in patients with AD by providing their diseased cholinergic neurons with some protection against "autocannibalism" of their choline-containing membrane.

RECOMMENDATIONS

Future Research

Available data suggest that an abnormality in the metabolism of choline phospholipids might contribute to the cholinergic deficits observed in AD. More studies are necessary, however, to characterize

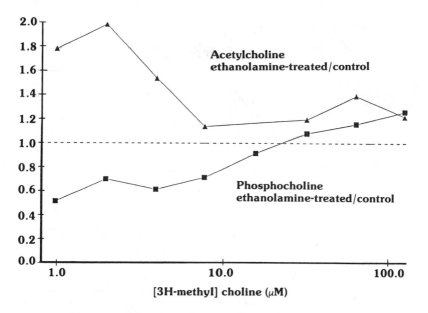

Figure 3. Effect of ethanolamine on the incorporation of [3H-methyl]choline into acetylcholine or phosphocholine in NG108-15 cells. Effect of ethanolamine on the acetylcholine and phosphocholine synthesis in NG108-15 cells. The experiments were carried out as described in the legends to Figures 1 and 2. Ethanolamine (0.5 mM) was added during labeling period only. The results are the ratios of the amounts of labeled acetylcholine or phosphocholine synthesized in the presence or absence of ethanolamine.

this process. Specifically:

1. Measurements should be made in samples of whole brain and of appropriate brain regions taken from AD patients and age-matched controls, of

• amounts of the major phospholipids and their fatty acyl compositions;

• amounts of the intermediates of phospholipid metabolism (i.e., choline, ethanolamine, phosphocholine, phosphoethanolamine, glycerophosphocholine, glycerophosphoethanolamine, serine, inositol, etc.);

• activities of the key enzymes involved in the metabolism of phospholipids (i.e., choline and ethanolamine kinases; choline and

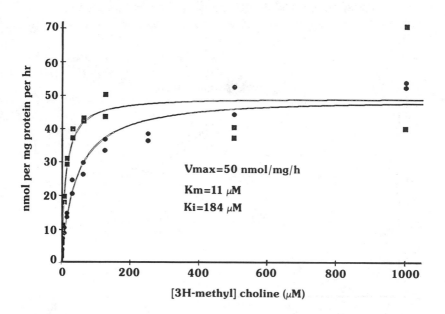

Figure 4. Effect of ethanolamine on the incorporation of [3H-methyl]choline into phosphatidylcholine in NG108-15 cells. Competitive inhibition by ethanolamine of the synthesis of phosphatidylcholine in NG108-15 cells. The experiments were carried out as described in the legends to Figures 1, 2, and 3. The dry residues of organic phases were redissolved in chloroform / methanol 1:1; phosphatidylcholine was purified by thin layer chromatography, its radioactivity determined, and the amounts formed calculated. The graph shows the experimental points (squares for controls; circles for ethanolamine-treated) and the rectangular hyperbolae that are the results of best fits to the experimental points. The inset shows the apparent Vmax and Km for choline, and a Ki for ethanolamine.

ethanolamine cytidylphosphotransferases; diacylglycerol choline and ethanolamine phosphotransferases; base exchange; phosphatidyl-ethanolamine N-methyltransferases; phospholipases A, C, D; glycerophosphocholine and glycerophosphoethanolamine diester-ases; etc.).

2. Measurements of the above compounds in peripheral tissues from AD patients and age-matched controls should also be made. It is possible that an abnormality in phospholipid metabolism exists in AD and is common to many cell types, but it kills only cholinergic neurons early on. If so, one might use this abnormality to develop a diagnostic test for the disease.

3. Using animal models *in vivo* the hypothesis that the choline in phospholipids and ACh are interrelated should be tested.

4. Using cultured cells, synaptosomes and other *in vitro* prepara-tions, the effects of altered choline availability and of prolonged neu-ronal firing on the dynamics of the ACh-choline-phospholipids equilibrium should be determined.

5. The extent to which the fatty acyl composition of particular cho-line phospholipids correlates with their use by cholinergic neurons as a choline source should be determined.

Possible Therapeutic Implications

1. Additional long-term studies are needed to determine whether prolonged supplementation with phosphatidylcholine (which might both enhance ACh release and protect cholinergic terminals against "autocannibalism") can affect the clinical course of AD.

2. Patients receiving various cholinergic drugs that affect the avail-ability of choline or the dynamics of choline phospholipids should be protected against possible "autocannibalism" by giving them sup-plemental phosphatidylcholine.

REFERENCES

Abe, T. Haga, T., & Kurokawa, M. (1973). Rapid transport of phos-phatidylcholine occurring simultaneously with protein transport in the frog sciatic nerve. *Biochemical Journal 136*, 731-740.

Ansell, G.B. (1973). Phospholipids and the nervous system. In G.B. Ansell, J.N. Hawthorne, & R.M.C. Dawson (Eds.), *Form and func-*

tion of phospholipids (pp. 377-422). Amsterdam: Elsevier.

Bárány, M., Chang, Y.-C., Arús, C., Rustan, T., & Frey, W.H., II (1985). Increased glycerol-3-phosphorylcholine in post-mortem Alzheimer's brains [Letter to the editor]. *The Lancet, 1,* 517.

Birks, R.I. (1974). The relationship of transmitter release and storage to the fine structure in a sympathetic ganglion. *Journal of Neurocytology, 3,* 133-160.

Birks, R.I., & MacIntosh, F.C. (1961). Acetylcholine metabolism of a sympathetic ganglion. *Canadian Journal of Biochemistry and Physiology, 39,* 787-827.

Blusztajn, J.K., & Wurtman, R.J. (1981). Choline biosynthesis by a preparation enriched in synaptosomes from rat brain. *Nature, 290,* 417-418.

Blusztajn, J.K., & Wurtman, R.J. (1983). Choline and cholinergic neurons. *Science, 221,* 614-620.

Bottenstein, J.E., & Sato, G.H. (1979). Growth of a rat neuroblastoma cell line in serum-free supplemented medium. *Proceedings of the National Academy of Sciences, USA, 76,* 514-517.

Bowen, D.M., Benton, J.S., Spillane, J.A., Smith, C.C.T., & Allen, S.J. (1982). Choline acetyltransferase activity and histopathology of frontal neocortex biopsies of demented patients. *Journal of the Neurological Sciences, 57,* 191-202.

Breckenridge, W.C., Gombos, C., & Morgan, I.G. (1972). The lipid composition of adult rat brain synaptosomal plasma membranes. *Biochemica et Biophysica Acta, 266,* 695-707.

Brooksbank, B.W.L., Martinez, M., & Balazs, R. (1985). Altered composition of polyunsaturated fatty acyl groups in phosphoglycerides of Down's syndrome fetal brain. *Journal of Neurochemistry, 44,* 869-874.

Corradetti, R., Lindmar, R., & Loffelholz, K. (1983). Mobilization of cellular choline by stimulation of muscarinic receptors in isolated chicken heart and rat cortex *in vivo. Journal of Pharmacology and Experimental Therapeutics, 226,* 826-832.

Droz, B., Brunetti, M., DeGiambernardino, L., Koenig, H.L., & Porcellati, G. (1981). Axonal transport of phosphoglycerides to cholinergic synapses. In G. Pepeu (Ed.), *Cholinergic mechanisms* (pp. 377-386). New York: Plenum Press.

Epstein, C. (1983). Down's syndrome and Alzheimer's disease: Implications and approaches. In R. Katzman (Ed.), *Biological aspects of Alzheimer's disease* (pp. 169-182). Cold Spring Harbor, NY: Cold Spring Harbor Laboratory.

Holbrook, P.G., Mauron, C., & Wurtman, R.J. (1985, May). *Molecular species of phosphatidylcholine formed by base-exchange and phosphocholine transferase in nerve endings.* Paper presented at the satellite meeting of the International Society for Neurochemistry on Phospholipids in the Nervous System, Mantova, Italy.

Liscovitch, M., Freese, A., Blusztajn, J.K., & Wurtman, R.J. (1985). High performance liquid chromatography of water-soluble choline metabolites. *Analytical Biochemistry, 151,* 182-187.

Maire, J.C., & Wurtman, R.J. (1983). Source of choline for the release of choline and acetylcholine from brain slices. *Journal de Physiologic, 80,* 189-195.

Mandybur, T.I. (1975). The incidence of cerebral amyloid angiopathy in Alzheimer's disease. *Neurology, 25,* 120-126.

Mauron, C., & Wurtman, R.J. (1986). *Effects of neuronal firing on phospholipids of rat striatal slices.* (Manuscript in preparation.)

Parducz, A., Kiss, Z., & Joo, F. (1976). Changes of the phosphatidylcholine content and the number of synaptic vesicles in relation to neurohumoral transmission in sympathetic ganglia. *Experientia, 32,* 1520-1521.

Pearson, R.C.A., Sofroniew, M.V., Cuello, A.C., Powell, T.P.S., Eckenstein, S., Esiri, M.M., & Wilcock, G.K. (1983). Persistence of cholinergic neurons in the basal nucleus in a brain with senile dementia of the Alzheimer's type demonstrated by immunohistochemical staining for choline acetyltransferase. *Brain Research, 289,* 375-379.

Perry, R.H., Candy, J.M., Perry, E.K., Irving, D., Blessed, G., Fairbairn, A.F., & Tomlinson, B.E. (1985). Extensive loss of choline acetyltransferase activity is not reflected by neuronal loss in the nucleus of Meynert in Alzheimer's disease. *Neuroscience Letters, 33,* 311-315.

Perry, E.K., Tomlinson, B.E., Blessed, G., Bergman, K., Gibson, P.H., & Perry, R.H. (1978). Correlation of cholinergic abnormalities with senile plaques and mental test scores in senile dementia. *British Journal of Medicine, 2,* 1458-1459.

Tacconi, M.T., & Wurtman, R.J. (1985). Phosphatidylcholine produced in rat synaptosomes by N-methylation is enriched in polyunsaturated fatty acids. *Proceedings of the National Academy of*

Sciences, USA, 82, 4828-4831.

Wilcock, G.K., Esiri, M.M., Bowen, D.M., & Smith, C.C.T. (1982). Alzheimer's disease: Correlation of cortical choline acetyltransferase activity with the severity of dementia and histological abnormalities. *Journal of Neurological Sciences, 57,* 407-417.

Wurtman, R.J. (1985). Alzheimer's disease. *Scientific American, 252,* 62-75.

Yates, C.M., Simpson, J., Maloney, A.J.F., Gordon, A., & Reid, A.H. (1980). Alzheimer-like cholinergic deficiency in Down's syndrome [Letter to the editor]. *The Lancet, 2,* 979.

Drug Delivery to the Brain by Central Infusion: Clinical Application of a Chemical Paradigm of Brain Function

Robert E. Harbaugh, MD

The last 15 years have seen a remarkable increase in our knowledge of the neurochemical aspects of brain function. This information has radically changed our understanding of how the brain works and suggested new treatment approaches for previously hopeless neurologic diseases. Unfortunately, clinical application of such information is plagued by problems of drug delivery to the brain. We have conducted preliminary trials of continuous intracranial drug infusion as a means of overcoming many of these problems.

Presented here is a brief historical outline of the development of a "chemical paradigm" of brain function and its applicability to neurologic disease—particularly Alzheimer's disease (AD). Some problems with drug delivery to the brain will be discussed and our experience with intraventricular infusion systems will be presented. The rationale, benefits, and risks of this therapeutic approach in patients with AD will be reviewed and suggestions for further studies will be made.

A critical aspect of scientific investigation, which is often overlooked, is the choice of a paradigm for any system consideration. Such mental models are used in every step of the scientific method from selection of experiments to interpretation of data. Indeed, it can be argued that scientific progress occurs not so much from new observations as from the rearranging of observations into new paradigms (Kuhn, 1970).

For most of the history of Western thought, a chemical or humoral paradigm of brain function was dominant. It has only been during the last 150 years that emphasis has been placed on an electrical model of central nervous system (CNS) activity (McHenry, 1969).

Recently however, a new understanding of neurotransmitters, neuro-modulators, and neurohormones has rekindled interest in the chem-ical functions of the brain. This "new" way of thinking about brain activity offers great promise for increased understanding and treat-ment of neurologic disease (Axelrod, 1984).

Erasistratus of Chios (c310-250 B.C.) postulated a glandular model of brain function. Vital spirits were carried via the arteries to the brain where they were then changed to animal spirits and distributed to the rest of the body by the hollow nerves (McHenry, 1969). Afflic-tions of the brain were attributed to a relative lack or overabundance of various humors and treatment was aimed at correcting such im-balances. If one reads "neurotransmitter precursors" in the place of "vital spirits" and "neurotransmitters" in the place of "animal spirits," this paradigm of brain function assumes a certain plausibility.

This model of brain function was accepted for 2,000 years, with minor modifications. It was only during the latter part of the 18th century that the first studies of the electrophysiology of the nervous system suggested an alternative paradigm. Luigi Galvani (1737-1798) experimented extensively with animal electricity and first suggested an electrical model of brain function (McHenry, 1969). Over the next 50 years this concept of CNS physiology became firmly entrenched. While cell theory was rapidly accepted for other tissues the CNS, because of this electrical paradigm, was envisioned as a diffuse retic-ular nerve net analogous to a wiring diagram. It was not until the early part of this century that Cajal's meticulous work demonstrated the truth of the neuron doctrine and thus made mandatory the medi-ation of neural transmission by a diffusible substance (Haymaker & Schiller, 1970).

While great strides were being made in understanding the elec-trophysiology of the nervous system, information regarding chemi-cal neurotransmission came rather slowly. Evidence for chemical neurotransmission came from the work of Langley, Elliott, and Dixon around the turn of the century. However, it was not until Loewi demonstrated Vagusstoff in 1921 that chemical transmission in the nervous system became firmly established. Dale greatly expanded this work on cholinergic neurotransmission and Cannon subsequent-ly demonstrated the existence of an adrenergic neurotransmitter (Haymaker & Schiller, 1970).

However, as late as 1970 discussion of neurotransmission was largely limited to acetycholine (ACh), norepinephrine, serotonin, and dopamine and only within the last 15 years has there been a great increase in information regarding neurotransmitter candidates and their potential actions (Snyder, 1984). This interest in the effects of endogenous chemical mediators on brain activity has suggested a chemical paradigm of brain function and new strategies for the treatment of CNS disorders.

Obviously, the electrical and chemical paradigms of brain function are not mutually exclusive and both must be considered in describing normal or pathological neural activity. However, some aspects of CNS activity are best modeled by an electrical paradigm whereas others can be better explained with a chemical model.

The value of any paradigm lies in how well it can be used to describe and explain observations. The electrical paradigm, with its emphasis on anatomically precise hard-wiring of the CNS, is a very attractive model for describing those aspects of brain function characterized by rapid responses of the organism to the environment. For functions such as fine motor control and accurate sensory processing, meticulously organized neuronal connections and rapidly changing on-off responses are mandatory. The electrical model predicts, accurately, that anatomically precise lesions (e.g., division of the optic nerves or corticospinal tracts) produce profound deficits in function.

The chemical paradigm, with its emphasis on the distribution and availability of various neurotransmitters, neuromodulators, and neurohormones, is best used to describe aspects of brain function in which rapid changes in behavior are not necessary. Such CNS activity includes alterations in personality, mood, attention, food intake, motor tone, and reproductive behavior. The dramatic example of narcotic overdose demonstrates the clinical applicability of this chemical paradigm of brain function. As predicted by the model, an anatomically normal nervous system can be rendered nonfunctional by the administration of a neurotransmitter analogue and restoration of function can be achieved by blocking drug effects at the receptor level.

The choice of a functional paradigm will be very important when considering potential treatment for neurologic diseases. If neural dysfunction is secondary to anatomical disruption then neurotransmitter manipulation is unlikely to be effective. Conversely, dysfunction caused by abnormalities in neurochemical distribution or availability may be remedied by neurotransmitter manipulation. For many neurologic diseases both the electrical and chemical paradigms can be invoked. AD may serve as a good example of one of these diseases (Harbaugh, in press-b).

The clinical presentation of patients with AD has been clearly delineated (Reisberg, 1983). In addition to the well-recognized memory dysfunction, these patients also exhibit alterations in attention, language, mood, psychomotor abilities, food intake, and sleep patterns. Before considering the rationality of any drug therapy one should first consider the evidence for both a chemical and an electrical paradigm of brain dysfunction in patients with AD.

Evidence has been accumulating that the short-term memory dysfunction in patients with AD may be due to anatomical disruption of afferent and efferent hippocampal fibers resulting in isolation of the hippocampi from the rest of the brain (A.R. Damasio, personal communication, January 1985). If this proves to be the case, then drug therapy is unlikely to have clinically meaningful effects on short-term memory.

However, there is also substantial evidence to suggest that some symptoms of patients with AD may be secondary to neurochemical abnormalities. Extensive literature on this subject has been reviewed elsewhere (Carlsson, 1983). The well-documented decrease in brain cholinergic activity in such patients has been of particular interest. Evidence for a cholinergic hypothesis of AD and treatment approaches based on this hypothesis have also been extensively reviewed and need not be repeated here (Coyle, Price, & DeLong, 1983). There does, however, seem to be adequate evidence for neurochemical abnormalities to justify treatment approaches that attempt to manipulate neurotransmitter levels in AD patients.

Even if the symptoms of patients with AD can be ameliorated by increasing brain cholinergic activity, there are still substantial difficulties to be overcome in delivering a cholinomimetic substance to the brain (Harbaugh, in press-a). Such difficulties include adverse systemic side effects, peripheral inactivation or metabolism of drugs, inadequate blood-brain barrier penetration, erratic drug absorption, serum protein binding, and poor compliance on the part of the patient. Because of these difficulties, we have been investigating the possibility of delivering a muscarinic agonist to the brain by means of continuous intracranial infusion (Harbaugh, Roberts, Coombs, Saunders, & Reeder, 1984). All clinical trials were approved by the Committee for the Protection of Human Subjects at our institution.

Earlier experience with implantable drug delivery devices (Coombs et al., 1983; Harbaugh, Coombs, Saunders, Gaylor, & Pageau, 1982) had shown that such an approach was technically possible. The potential advantages and risks as well as the rationale of central drug infusion will be briefly discussed. The mechanism of the implantable pump (Intermedic-Infusaid, Norwood, Mass.), which has been previously presented (Harbaugh et al., 1982, 1984), will be reviewed.

The potential advantages of intracranial drug infusion are numerous. Direct infusion of drugs into the cerebral ventricles bypasses the problems of systemic side effects, peripheral drug inactivation, poor drug absorption, serum protein binding, inadequate blood-brain barrier penetration, and poor compliance on the part of the patient. Despite these advantages, intrathecal drug administration has by and large been ineffective (Aird, 1984). Therefore, the first question to be addressed regarding central drug infusion is whether drugs achieve adequate brain penetration from the cerebrospinal fluid (CSF).

In many ways the CSF is an ideal drug delivery medium, with little protein binding and decreased enzymatic activity compared to plasma (Wood, 1980). The subarachnoid space penetrates the brain by means of the Virchow-Robins spaces, and substances in the CSF enter the brain extracellular fluid by diffusion and, with increased CSF pressure, by bulk flow (H. Cserr, personal communication, April, 1985). However, the extent of drug penetration into the brain from the CSF depends not only on the drug being used but also on the method of administration .

Most clinical trials of central drug administration have employed single or intermittent bolus injections into the subarachnoid space or ventricular system. Of all the ways to deliver drugs to the CNS this method is probably the worst. Bolus injections initially result in very high CSF drug concentrations and relatively limited parenchymal penetration (Blasberg, Patlak, & Shapiro, 1977). In addition, a single large bolus of drug is likely to be more toxic and less effective than more frequent, smaller doses (Bleyer, Poplack, & Simon, 1978). However, even with bolus administration drugs will penetrate the parenchyma and, as the CSF is cleared by bulk flow, diffuse back into the subarachnoid space (Blasberg et al., 1977). In situations where high drug concentrations in the CSF or immediately adjacent parenchyma are desired (carcinomatous meningitis, spinal anesthesia / analgesia, chemical rhizotomy), then bolus injections are effective. However, if deeper diffusion into parenchyma is necessary then longer term infusion is preferable.

Intravascular administration of drugs that cross the blood-brain barrier shows a rapid onset of action due to the short circulation time and extensive vascular-CNS interface (Aird, 1984). However, drugs administered into the CSF require much longer for adequate diffusion into the parenchyma (Lee & Olszewski, 1960). As the duration of central drug administration increases, the depth of parenchymal penetration — even of large protein molecules — also increases (Brightman & Reese, 1969). Therefore, to adequately evaluate the effectiveness of central drug administration, infusions must be carried out over a prolonged period.

The site of infusion within the central compartment may also be of significance. Drug penetration into the parenchyma appears to occur more readily through the ependymal than the pial surface (Rall, 1968) and drugs administered into the subarachnoid space may not enter the ventricular system (Bleyer & Poplack, 1978). Therefore, intraventricular drug infusion is a more reasonable approach for achieving diffuse brain penetration than lumbar intrathecal administration. Conversely, if one wishes to confine drug effects to the spinal cord, with minimal effects at higher levels of the neuraxis, then intraspinal infusion may be beneficial (Harbaugh et al., 1982). Thus, some relatively restricted neuropharmacologic effects can be achieved. Theoretically, with stereotactic cannula placement and very low flow rate infusion devices, delivery of minute quantities of drugs to very circumscribed regions of brain parenchyma is possible.

When evaluating the effectiveness of central drug administration, the choice of drug is as important as the method of delivery. The ability of a drug to cross the blood-brain barrier is more likely to be detrimental than beneficial if the drug is given as a continuous central infusion. Drugs that readily cross brain capillaries can be rapidly cleared from the CNS when infused into the CSF (Blasberg, Patlak, & Fenstermacher, 1975). The use of such drugs may be valuable if high local concentrations in tissue adjacent to the subarachnoid space or ependyma is desired. However, if deeper parenchymal penetration is the goal, then lipid insoluble, polar molecules are better candidates for infusion (Blasberg et al., 1975).

When considering drugs for long-term central infusion, chemical and biological stability become important criteria. For continuous infusion via an implantable pump, the infused drug must be stable at body temperature for at least as long as the cycle time of the infusion pump. In addition, if widespread diffusion of an active drug into parenchyma is desired, then the infused drug cannot be rapidly metabolized within the CNS or the CSF. This last consideration may not apply to local intraparenchymal infusion, where a steep concentration gradient of an active drug could be beneficial.

Our clinical experience at Dartmouth (Harbaugh et al., 1984) with implantable infusion devices for central drug administration may serve to illustrate some of the points raised above.

Previous attempts at increasing brain cholinergic activity in patients with AD by administration of ACh precursors, cholinesterase inhibitors, or systemic cholinergic agonists had been attended by the difficulties with drug delivery to the brain that have previously been discussed. Intracranial cholinergic drug infusion was started as a means of testing the validity of the cholinergic hypothesis and as an attempt at therapy for a devastating neurologic disease with no known treatment.

The drug delivery system we used consisted of an Intermedic-Infusaid implantable pump connected to a silastic intracranial catheter. The pump consists of a discoid titanium shell that contains a metal bellows drug chamber and an underlying charging fluid chamber as shown in Figure 1. Vapor pressure, generated by a two-phase fluorocarbon in the charging fluid chamber, compresses the bellows, forcing the drug through an outlet flow restrictor and into the out-

Figure 1

Cross-Sectional Diagram of Infusaid Implantable Pump

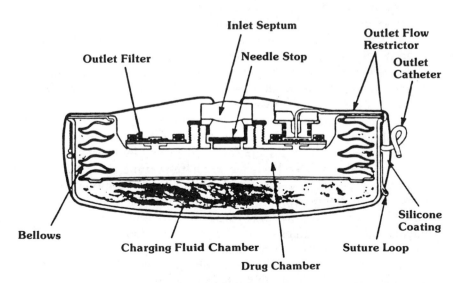

flow catheter. After implantation the drug chamber can be refilled percutaneously via an inlet septum. Each pump has a preset flow rate and the drug dosage is varied by changing the concentration of the infusate.

A stable, water soluble, pure muscarinic agonist, which was not degraded by cholinesterases, was sought for infusion. Bethanechol chloride, an ester of a choline-like compound, has significant muscarinic activity without nicotinic agonist properties; is not hydrolyzed by cholinesterases and is freely soluble and stable in water. The drug is commercially available from Merck, Sharp, & Dohme under the trade name Urecholine. It has no preservatives and a neutral pH.

Following toxicity studies in dogs (Harbaugh et al., 1984), a preliminary clinical trial was approved by the Committee for the Protection of Human Subjects at our institution. All patients had a history of progressive cognitive, memory, and social dysfunction for at least 3 years and demonstrated moderately severe to severe cognitive decline. A thorough clinical, laboratory, and radiologic evaluation was carried out to exclude other causes of progressive dementia. If the patient was then felt to be an acceptable candidate for the study, informed consent was obtained from the patient and the family before proceeding.

Under general anesthesia, patients were positioned and draped as if for ventriculoperitoneal shunt placement. A small frontal craniotomy was done and a cortical biopsy was taken for light and electron microscope documentation of AD and then the intracranial catheter was placed. The pumps were secured in a subcutaneous abdominal pocket and the outflow catheters, tunneled subcutaneously, were connected to the intracranial catheters with straight metal connectors. After connections were secured with nonabsorbable ligatures, the incisions were closed. Pumps were refilled percutaneously, at 3-week intervals, on an outpatient basis.

As discussed, the problems of systemic drug inactivation, serum protein binding, drug absorption, and poor blood-brain barrier penetration are avoided by delivering a muscarinic agonist into the ventricular system. The use of an implantable, continuous infusion pump permits long-term, intracranial infusion of a drug or a placebo on an outpatient basis and avoids any problems of patient compliance. Pump flow rates ranged from 1-2 ml/day, an insignificant amount compared to normal, daily CSF production.

For patients with AD, drug distribution to the hippocampi, locus ceruleus, reticular nucleus of the thalamus and cerebral cortex was desired. Therefore, for the reasons outlined above, a drug was chosen that does not cross the blood-brain barrier when infused into the ventricular system.

The potential advantages of central drug infusion have been discussed. There are, however, some potential disadvantages that require equal consideration. These include the operative risks of catheter placement and pump implantation and the risk of increased neurotoxicity.

As with any neurosurgical procedure, the risks of catheter placement and pump implantation include anesthetic complications, hemorrhage, and infection. Although all of these risks are low, there is probably an irreducible minimum and some complications must be anticipated. Our personal experience with pump implantation now includes about 40 patients who have had pumps implanted for various indications. We have encountered no significant anesthetic complications but we have had one infectious and one hemorrhagic complication.

The risk of neurotoxicity with intracranial drug infusions must also be considered. Certainly, toxicity studies in animals are mandatory before considering intracranial or intraspinal infusion of drugs in human patients. Although such toxicity studies decrease the risk of human neurotoxicity, some unexpected reactions to drug infusions in patients are likely to occur. We have now been infusing bethanechol chloride intracranially in patients with AD for more than 20 months. One patient developed a reversible parkinsonian syndrome of rigidity and bradykinesia and another patient developed a reversible CSF inflammatory response that may or may not have been related to the drug infusion (Harbaugh et al., 1984). Certainly experience with more patients infused for longer periods of time will be necessary before any accurate figures on the risk of neurotoxicity are available. However, to date drug infusions appear to be well-tolerated.

The feasibility of intracranial and intraspinal administrations of neurotransmitter analogues has been demonstrated (Harbaugh et al., 1982, 1984). However, the value of these therapeutic endeavors, over presently available therapy, remains to be proven. We are conducting studies of the effect of intracranial bethanechol infusion on activities of daily living and neuropsychological test scores in a double-blind, placebo-controlled, crossover design. Preliminary studies show family reports of decreased confusion, increased initiative, and improvements in activities of daily living during drug infusion but no subjective improvement in short-term memory was reported. A battery of short-term memory tests has also not shown a statistically significant difference between drug and placebo scores.

Returning to the initial discussion of appropriate paradigms of brain function in AD, our preliminary observations of intracranial cholinergic drug infusion allow for interesting speculation. The patients in our preliminary study (Harbaugh et al., 1984) evidenced moderately severe to severe cognitive decline (Reisberg, Gerris, DeLeon, & Crook, 1982) at the time of entry into the study. If, indeed, the hippocampi become isolated relatively early in the course of AD, then cholinergic replacement therapy would not be expected to have profound effects on short-term memory function in patients at this rather advanced stage of the disease. In other words, this particular symptom of AD could be better explained by an electrical paradigm and would be minimally affected by neurotransmitter manipulation. Interestingly, significant short-term memory improvement was not noted in either subjective family reports or in a brief battery of memory tests (Harbaugh, in press-a).

Conversely, the improvement noted in functions such as mood, initiative, social interactions, and attention might be due to a diffuse alerting effect of muscarinic receptor activation. Both the ability of musarinic agonists to inhibit potassium efflux from neurons thereby increasing the probability of neuronal discharge (Caulfield & Straughan, 1983), and the data from primate studies suggesting that ACh improves the signal-to-noise ratio of excitatory input to cortical neurons during goal-directed behavior (Inoue et al., 1983) fit a hypothesis of a general alerting effect of muscarinic drug infusion.

Clearly, much more work needs to be done to determine if central cholinergic drug infusion has a therapeutic effect in patients with AD, and if so, how this effect is achieved. However, I believe that this technique of drug delivery to the brain will prove to be of greater importance than the outcome of any single clinical trial.

One can anticipate ever increasing information regarding the chemistry of the brain and new fields of inquiry for neuropharmacology and functional neurosurgery. As a founder of neurochemistry, Johann Ludwig Wilhelm Thudichum (1884, pp.259-260) wrote:

> I believe that the great diseases of the brain . . . will be shown
> to be connected with specific chemical changes in neuroplasm
> . . . It is probable that by the aid of chemistry many derangements of the brain and mind, which are at present obscure, will
> become accurately definable and amenable to precise treatment, and what is now an object of anxious empiricism will
> become one for the proud exercise of exact science.

As potentially therapeutic compounds are developed, central drug infusion may prove to be a safe and reliable means of assuring their delivery to the brain.

RECOMMENDATIONS FOR FURTHER RESEARCH

1. Further investigation of intraventricular bethanechol chloride infusion in patients with AD is needed. Double-blind, crossover studies on the effects of drugs on daily activities, neuropsychological test scores, and electrophysiological parameters must all be evaluated for patients in the earlier stages of AD.

2. Other cholinomimetic drugs such as carbachol and arecoline should also be investigated either alone or in combinations like arecoline plus tetrahydroaminoacridine. There are animal models to suggest that combinations of cholinomimetic drugs show supra-additive effects on memory enhancement with only additive toxic effects (A. Cherkin & J.F. Flood, personal communication, December, 1984).

3. Other neurotransmitter system agonists should be investigated. Noradrenergic (Bondareff, Mountjoy, & Roth, 1982) and somatostatin (Davies, Katzman, & Terry, 1980) abnormalities have been documented in patients with AD. The same difficulties with drug delivery that are associated with cholinergic compounds also apply to noradrenergic and somatostatinergic compounds. A recent study, investigating the somatostatin analogue L363,586 in AD patients, failed to show any response to drug administration or to detect any drug in the CSF (Cutler et al., 1985).

REFERENCES

Aird, R.B. (1984). A study of intrathecal, cerebrospinal fluid-to-brain exchange. *Experimental Neurology, 86,* 342-358.

Axelrod, J. (1984). Neuroscience advances. *Science, 225,* 1253.

Blasberg, R.G., Patlak, C.S., & Fenstermacher, J.D. (1975). Intrathecal chemotherapy: Brain tissue profiles after ventriculocisternal perfusion. *Journal of Pharmacology and Experimental Therapeutics, 195,* 73-83.

Blasberg, R.G., Patlak, C.S., & Shapiro, W.R. (1977). Distribution of methotrexate in cerebrospinal fluid and brain after intraventricular administration. *Cancer Treatment Reports, 61,* 633-641.

Bleyer, W.A., & Poplack, D.G. (1978). Clinical studies on the central nervous system pharmacology of methotrexate. In H.M. Pinedo (Ed.), Clinical pharmacology of antineoplastic drugs (pp 115-131). Amsterdam: Elsevier.

Bleyer, W.A., Poplack, D.G., & Simon, R.M. (1978). Concentration x time methotrexate via a subcutaneous reservoir: A less toxic regimen for intraventricular chemotherapy of central nervous system neoplasms. Blood, 51, 835-842.

Bondareff, W., Mountjoy, C.Q., & Roth, M. (1982). Loss of neurons of origin of the adrenergic projection to cerebral cortex (nucleus locus ceruleus) in senile dementia. Neurology, 32, 164-168.

Brightman, M.W., & Reese, R.S., (1969). Junctions between intimately apposed cell membranes in the vertebrate brain. Journal of Cell Biology, 40, 648-677.

Carlsson, A. (1983). Changes in neurotransmitter systems in the aging brain and in Alzheimer's disease. In B. Reisberg (Ed.), Alzheimer's disease. The standard reference (pp 100-106). New York: The Free Press.

Caulfield, M., & Straughan, D. (1983). Muscarinic receptors revisited. Trends in Neurosciences, 6, 73-75.

Coombs, D.W., Saunders, R.L., Gaylor, M.S., Block, A.R., Colton, T., Harbaugh, R.E., Pageau, M.G., & Mroz, W. (1983). Relief of continuous chronic pain by intraspinal narcotics infusion via an implanted reservoir. JAMA, 250, 2336-2339.

Coyle, J.T., Price, D.L., & DeLong, M.R. (1983). Alzheimer's disease: A disorder of cortical cholinergic innervation. Science, 219, 1184-1190.

Cutler, N.R., Haxby, J.V., Narang, P.K., May, C., Burg, C., & Reines, S.A. (1985). Evaluation of an analogue of somatostatin (L363,586) in Alzheimer's disease. New England Journal of Medicine, 312, 725.

Davies, P., Katzman, R., & Terry, R.D. (1980). Reduced somatostatin-like immunoreactivity in cerebral cortex from cases of Alzheimer's disease and Alzheimer senile dementia. Nature, 288, 279-280.

Harbaugh, R.E. (in press-a). Drug delivery to the central nervous system by central infusion. Neuro Views: Trends in Clinical Neurology.

Harbaugh, R.E. (in press-b). Neural transplantation vs. central neurotransmitter augmentation in diseases of the nervous system. Neurobiology of Aging.

Harbaugh, R.E., Coombs, D.W., Saunders, R.L., Gaylor, M., & Pageau, M. (1982). Implanted continuous epidural morphine infusion system: Preliminary report. *Journal of Neurosurgery, 56,* 803-806.

Harbaugh, R.E., Roberts, D.W., Coombs, D.W., Saunders, R.L., & Reeder, T.M. (1984). Preliminary report: Intracranial cholinergic drug infusion in patients with Alzheimer's disease. *Neurosurgery, 15,* 514-518.

Haymaker, W., & Schiller, F. (1970). *The founder of neurology* (2nd ed.). Springfield, IL: Charles C Thomas.

Inoue, M., Oomura, Y., Nishino, H., Aou, S., Sikdar, S.K., Hynes, M., Mizuno, Y., & Katabuchi, T. (1983). Cholinergic role in monkey dorsolateral prefrontal cortex during bar-press feeding behavior. *Brain Research, 278,* 185-194.

Kuhn, T.S. (1970). *The structure of scientific revolutions* (2nd ed.). Chicago: University of Chicago Press.

Lee, J.C., & Olszewski, J. (1960). Penetration of radioactive bovine albumin from cerebrospinal fluid into brain tissue. *Neurology,* 814-822.

McHenry, L.C., Jr. (1969). *Garrison's history of neurology.* Springfield, IL: Charles C Thomas.

Rall, D.P. (1968). Transport through the ependymal linings. *Progress in Brain Research, 29,* 159-167.

Reisberg, B. (1983). Clinical presentation, diagnosis, and symptomatology of age associated cognitive decline and Alzheimer's disease. In B. Reisberg (Ed.), *Alzheimer's disease. The standard reference* (pp 173-187). New York: The Free Press.

Reisberg, B., Ferris, S.H., DeLeon, M.J., & Crook, T. (1982). The global deterioration scale for assessment of primary degenerative dementia. *American Journal of Psychiatry, 139,* 1136-1139.

Snyder, S.H. (1984). Drug and neurotransmitter receptors in the brain. *Science, 224,* 22-31.

Thudichum, J.L.W. (1884). *A treatise on the chemical constitution of the brain — based throughout upon original researches.* London: Bailliere, Tindall & Cox.

Wood, J.H. (1980). Physiology, pharmacology and dynamics of cerebrospinal fluid. In J.H. Wood (Ed.), *Neurobiology of cerebrospinal fluid* (pp 1-16). New York: Plenum Press.

25

Cognitive Dysfunctions and Neural Implants

Don Marshall Gash, PhD, Mary F.D. Notter, PhD, and Jeffrey H. Kordower, PhD

The purpose of the present paper is to review recent advances in the field of neural transplantation and discuss how this new technology may be applied to treating Alzheimer's disease (AD). Since 1979, it has been realized that neurons implanted into a host brain have the capacity to influence behavior and to ameliorate some neural dysfunctions. Experiments employing rodent model systems have demonstrated that a variety of motor, cognitive, and neuroendocrine impairments can be alleviated by neural transplants (for a review, see Gash, Collier, & Sladek, 1985). The ability of neural implants to repopulate damaged areas of the brain and to moderate some deficits in rats, which model deficits seen in human neurodegenerative diseases, has suggested a therapeutic role for neural transplants in treating AD and other neurodegenerative disorders. The data base used to make this suggestion, potential strategies, and recommendations for future directions are presented.

PROPERTIES OF NEURAL TRANSPLANTS

The field of neural transplantation has been the subject of several recent books (Björklund, A., & Stenevi, 1985; Sladek & Gash, 1984) and reviews (Gash, Collier, & Sladek, 1985). Studies from a number of laboratories have demonstrated that fetal central nervous system (CNS) grafts survive transplantation into a host brain and often develop cytoarchitectural features reminiscent of their site of origin in the donor brain (Das, 1974; Stenevi, Björklund, A., & Svendgaard, 1976). The grafted neurons are capable of establishing some afferent and efferent connections with the host brain (Jaeger & Lund, 1980; McLoon & Lund, 1980; Sladek & Gash, 1984a), although the functional significance of these connections is not always clear. In the rodent brain, transplants are capable of relatively long-term survival and function. For example, Freed et al. (1980) examined substantia nigra grafts for periods up to 10 months following transplantation and found that the grafts remained functionally active and showed no histological signs of deterioration.

Several factors have been identified as important for graft survival. Well-vascularized sites within the host brain promote implant survival and rapid vascularization of the implant is probably necessary to prevent graft necrosis (Lindsay & Raisman, 1984; Stenevi et al., 1976). The age of the donor tissue appears to be a critical factor with optimum ages for transplantation varying with regions of the brain and specific neuronal cell types (Boer, Gash, Dick, & Schluter, 1985; Olson, Björklund, H., & Hoffer, 1984; Seiger & Olson, 1977). It also appears that denervated regions in the host brain help promote graft survival and innervation (Nieto-Sampedro et al., 1982; Nieto-Sampedro, Manthrope, Barbin, Varon, & Cotman, 1983; Rosenstein & Brightman, 1984). An example of this latter point comes from studies (Rosenstein & Brightman, 1984) on superior cervical ganglia allografted into the fourth ventricle of neonatal host rats. When grafts were implanted into intact host with care being taken to avoid damage to the host brain, only about 3% of the grafted neurons survived over a 6-month period. However, when the recipient had been bilaterally sympathectomized to denervate pial and choroidal vessels, the grafted ganglia innervated these sites and an average of 20% of the implanted superior cervical ganglia neurons were viable over the 6-month test period.

When the first studies on functional neural transplants were initiated, simple assumptions were made about the conditions that would lead to functional restitution. It was assumed that the grafted neurons would repopulate damaged areas of the host brain and reestablish appropriate connections with host neurons. Several examples of where axonal contacts with appropriate host target tissue are apparently obligatory for functional recovery have been found (Dunnett, Low, Iversen, Stenevi, & Björklund, A., 1982; Gash & Sladek, 1984; Low et al., 1982); but a surprising number of additional avenues have been identified by which grafts can influence regeneration and recovery of function. Examples of some of the ways grafts may contribute to regeneration are shown in diagrammatic form in Figure 1. In the simplest form, the graft acts as a drug generator within the blood-brain barrier and influences host behavior by the chronic basal release of a deficient neurotransmitter, which diffuses into the surrounding host parenchyma and attaches to receptors on host target cells. Adrenal medullary cells grafted into the damaged rat nigrostriatal system appear to ameliorate motor dysfunctions by this mechanism of action (Freed, Hoffer, Olson, & Wyatt, 1984; Freed et al., 1981). A variation of this would be for the graft to produce survival and/or growth promoting factors, which could enhance

Types of Functional Neural Implants

A. Chemical Generator

B. Glial Generator

C. Bridge

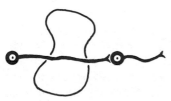

D. Synaptic Contacts

E. Circuitry Restoration

Figure 1. Various ways neural transplants (stippled areas) might promote regeneration and recovery of function are illustrated. A. Neurons in the graft release neurotransmitters, which diffuse and bind to receptors on neurons in the host brain. B. Glial cells from the transplants migrate into the host brain where they can replace deficient host glia. C. Regenerating axons in the host brain grow through the implant to innervate other host neurons. D. Grafted neurons establish contact with host neurons. E. Neuronal afferent and efferent connections are re-established as the neural transplant becomes totally integrated into the host brain.

regeneration in the host CNS. Results from some transplantation experiements are consistent with this suggestion (Björklund, H., Seiger, Hoffer, & Olson, 1983; Labbe, Firl, Mufson, & Stein, 1983; Sabel, Savia, & Stein, 1984).

Glial and endothelial cells are also grafted along with neurons, although their importance in functional recovery has not been well-studied. A recent report by Lindsay and Raisman (1984) elegantly demonstrated the migration of implanted glial cells for distances up to 2 mm into the host parenchyma. Graft oligodendrocytes in mice have been shown to become associated with and myelinate host neuronal processes (Doering & Fedoroff, 1984; Gumpel, Baumann, Raoul, & Jacque, 1983). While the critical studies have not been done, it can be postulated that glial deficiencies, for example in the production of maintenance and growth factors, account for some of the problems observed in regeneration in the aged brain and may play a role in certain neurodegenerative diseases. Under these circumstances, the glial cells in transplants may be as important, or perhaps more important, than grafted neurons for functional recovery.

Kromer, Björklund, A., and Stenevi (1981) have reported that fetal neural grafts may promote functional recovery by serving as a bridge across a lesion site through which regenerating host fibers can grow. Their experiments utilized strips of rat embryonic hippocampus placed in a transplantation cavity that completely transected the septal hippocampal cholinergic pathway. Some adult host septal neurons, as demonstrated by horseradish peroxidase (HRP) retrograde tracing techniques, grew through the embryonic implant and reinnervated the host hippocampus and dentate gyrus. The efficacy of CNS grafts as a "bridge" in regeneration remains uncertain, but Aguayo and his colleagues (Benfey & Aguayo, 1982; Richardson, McGuinness, & Aguayo, 1980) clearly demonstrated a propensity for adult CNS processes to utilize peripheral nervous system (PNS) implants as a bridge to grow to distant target sites.

FUNCTIONAL TRANSPLANTS IN RODENTS WITH COGNITIVE DEFICITS

Both lesion-induced and age-related cognitive dysfunctions have been alleviated by neural implants. Most studies have focused on cholinergic deficits in the hippocampus, where well-defined maze learning deficits follow after disruption of the septal-hippocampal pathway. Crutcher, Kesner, and Novak (1983) have shown that recovery of maze behavior is significantly correlated to the degree of hippocampal acetylcholinesterase depletion. With incomplete cholinergic denervation, radial arm maze performance gradually recovers, perhaps due to sprouting by residual septo-hippocampal fibers. A permanent deficit, however, is seen following complete lesions.

Björklund, Stenevi, and their colleagues have conducted an extensive series of investigations on the extent of reinnervation provided by grafted fetal cholinergic neurons to the septo-hippocampal lesioned hippocampus in adult rats. Fetal septal-diagonal band area grafts implanted into the lesion site innervated the host hippocampus and dentate gyrus in a pattern that closely mimicked the laminar pattern in intact animals (Björklund, A., & Stenevi, 1977). Ingrowing acetylcholinesterase-positive fibers extended for distances of 6 to 8 mm from the grafts and reinnervated the entire dorsal hippocampus formation. Lesioned animals with septal grafts were able to improve acquisition of a simple T-maze rewarded alternation task over levels seen in nongraft recipients and recipients of locus coeruleus transplants (Dunnett et al., 1982). Similar grafts did not improve performance on an eight-arm radial maze task until the recipients were given physostigmine, an acetylcholinesterase inhibitor. Then, grafted animals performed significantly better than lesioned controls (Low et al., 1982).

The partial recovery seen following septal transplantation seems to be mediated by the grafted cells establishing appropriate functional connections with the host hippocampus (Gage, Björklund, A., Stenevi, & Dunnett, 1985). Following transplantation of the cholinergic-rich septal tissue, host hippocampal choline acetyltransferase activity slowly returns to normal levels in the lesioned hippocampus, hippocampal glucose metabolism rates recover as measured by (^{14}C)-2-deoxyglucose utilization, and electrophysiological studies suggest that functional synapses have been established (Gage et al., 1985). Regarding the latter point, in vivo electrophysiological recordings are technically complicated, and it is relevant to note that septal explants in culture, where single cell recordings are more straightforward, establish functional electrophysiological synapses with co-cultured hippocampal neurons (Gahwiler & Brown, 1985).

Using frontal cortex lesions, Stein and his associates have found evidence for a different mechanism that may modulate recovery from some lesion-induced cognitive deficits (Labbe et al., 1983; Stein, Labbe, Firl, & Mufson, 1985). Their experiments involved aspirating out the medial frontal cortex of young adult Sprague-Dawley rats and, 7 days later, grafting frontal cortex tissue from 21- or 22-day rat fetuses. Four days after implantation, the recipients, along with the controls, began testing on a rewarded alternation T-maze task. Frontal cortex recipients, but not the sham-grafted controls nor recipients of fetal cerebellar grafts, exhibited a facilitated recovery of cognitive behavior. While neuronal projections from the graft were found coursing into the host brain, the authors suggested that the rapid recovery observed may have been due to neurotrophic or growth factors produced by the grafts. A subsequent study (Sabel et al., 1984) demonstrated that treatment with a substance known to promote neurite outgrowth, G_{m1} ganglioside, did facilitate behavioral recovery from bilateral lesions of the caudate nucleus.

While old animals probably provide the most relevant rodent model for investigating neurodegenerative disorders, few transplantation studies have been conducted on rats with age-related cognitive deficits. Since aged rodents are expensive and especially susceptible to disease and surgical complications, and only a subset of the population of old rats show learning or memory impairments, studies on aged rats are complicated and should only be undertaken when there is a compelling need. However, the experiments that have been conducted are instructive. Gage, Björklund, A., Stenevi, Dunnett, and Kelly (1984) found that approximately 25 to 30% of female Sprague-Dawley rats in the 21- to 23-month-old age group exhibited spatial learning deficits as measured in a water maze task. Fetal grafts of cholinergic-neuron rich fetal septal tissue into the hippocampus of the aged rats with deficits significantly improved their performance. Histochemical analysis revealed that the grafts provided an extensive acetylcholinesterase-positive innervation of the surrounding host hippocampus. It should be noted that while the graft recipients showed improved performance, they still did not do as well as young and old nonimpaired controls.

Recent studies by our research group (Collier, Gash, Esch, & Sladek, 1985; Collier, Gash, & Sladek, 1985) suggest that transplants can ameliorate noradrenergic deficit-related cognitive disorders in aged rats by pharmacological replacement. Approximately 60% of 22- to 25-month-old Fischer 344 stain rats demonstrated a reduction in brain stem (locus coeruleus) norepinephrine levels, which correlated with passive avoidance performance deficits. Aged rats receiving norepinephrine-rich locus coeruleus region grafts showed significant improvement on a passive avoidance task as compared with unoperated controls and aged animals with fetal cerebellar grafts. Several lines of evidence indicated that the grafts improved host performance through the synthesis and release of norepinephrine into the cerebrospinal fluid. The grafts were implanted into the host third ventricle where they could easily release their contents into the cerebrospinal fluid. In addition, only a moderate innervation of the surrounding host parenchyma was evident. Finally, chronic infusion of norephinephrine into the third ventricle also normalized cognitive performance in these aged rats.

TRANSPLANTS INTO PRIMATES

The success of functional neural transplants in rodents has prompted a number of investigators to begin studies of transplants in primates. One of the first issues that needs to be addressed is the predictive value of rodent studies on the properties of neural transplants in primates. Some class and species variations in graft behavior are to be expected. The question is whether these differences will affect transplantation strategy and what changes will be necessary to conduct safe and effective functional transplants in primates. A systemic analysis and comparison of graft behavior in the rodent and the primate brain would seem to be necessary.

Freed and Wyatt and their colleagues (Morihisa, Nakamura, Freed, Mishkin, & Wyatt, 1984; Wyatt, Morihisa, Nakamura, & Freed, in press) have begun to extend their studies on functional transplants from rodent models of Parkinson's disease to nonhuman primates. Using rhesus monkeys with unilateral 6-hydroxydopamine lesions of the substantia nigra, either fetal rhesus substantia nigra or autografts of adrenal medulla were implanted into the denervated caudate nucleus. When the host brains were examined later by catecholamine fluorescence histochemistry, no evidence of survival of the two substantia nigra grafts was found. A few medullary cells survived in all five recipients. In the best case, 630 fluorescent cells were found 5 months after grafting scattered among four implant sites. Similar to the features found in adrenal medullary transplants in rats (Freed et al., 1984), the grafted rhesus medullary cells remained principally glandular in appearance with few neuritic processes evident and those few remaining within the boundaries of the graft.

Using the rationale that adrenal medullary grafts had effectively ameliorated motor abnormalities in young adult rats with nigrostriatal lesions, Backlund and associates (Backlund, Granberg, Hamberger, Sedvall, Seiger, & Olson, 1985a; Backlund, Granberg, Hamberger, Knutsson, Martensson, Sedvall, Seiger, & Olson, 1985b) have autografted adrenal medullary tissue to the striatum in two patients with Parkinson's disease. In both cases, approximately two-thirds of the left adrenal was removed, minced into small pieces, and stereotaxically implanted into the right caudate nucleus. Both patients have been followed for at least 1 year postgrafting with little change noted in their clinical symptoms. Until more information is available on graft behavior in nonhuman primates and other critical questions are answered (such as the suitability of aged adrenal medullary tissue from long-term parkinsonian patients for transplantation), the justification for proceeding with human investigations is open to question.

Our research group has initiated a series of experiments to compare the properties of cultured neuronal cells implanted into homologous sites in the rodent and nonhuman primate brain. A continuous human cell line labelled IMR-32, which was derived in 1967 from a neuroblastoma growing as an abdominal mass (Tumilowicz, Nichols, Cholon, & Greene, 1970), was chosen for the initial studies because of its properties in culture. IMR-32 cells grow readily under standard culture conditions and have been shown to synthesize a number of neurotransmitters including acetylcholine (ACh), dopamine, norepinephrine, and serotonin (Gupta, Notter, Felten, & Gash, 1985). The cultured cells can be induced to differentiate by a variety of chemical treatments (Bottenstein, 1981; Prasad, 1975). Our experiments employed factors that either irreversibly intercalate with deoxyribonucleic acid (DNA), such as mitomycin C and 5-bromodeoxyuridine (5-BrdU) or elevate AMP (adenosine $3'5'$monophosphate) levels like prostaglandin E_1 and dibutyryl cyclic AMP. Many lines of neuroblastoma cells when induced to differentiate are permanently amitotic (Prasad, 1975) and express characteristics of mature neurons including development of axonal and dendritic processes, continued synthesis and storage of neurotransmitters, the generation of action potentials, and the release of neural transmitters in response to electrical or chemical stimulation (Bottenstein, 1981; Gupta et al., 1985). Mitosis in IMR-32 cells in culture is inhibited and the cells appear to be entering the G_0 state. Differentiated cells show increased acetylcholinesterase staining and send out long processes with beaded varicosities and growth cones (Gupta et al., 1985; also see Figure 2).

A.   B.

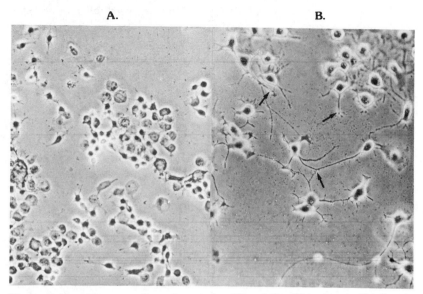

Figure 2. Neuroblastoma cells are shown before (A) and after (B) treatment with mitomy-cin C, and 5-bromodeoxyuridine to induce differentiation. The cells after differentiation (B) resemble mature neurons with elongated neuritic processes coursing from cell to cell and occasional growth cones (arrows). Phase contrast of living cells.

Our routine procedures involve growth of IMR-32 cells in culture and labelling the mitotically active cells with ^{3}H-thymidine just before mitotic arrest. Following 3 days of treatment by differentiating agents (two are often used in combination, such as mitomycin C and 5-BrdU), the cells are trypinized to remove them from the culture dish, washed and pelleted in a centrifuge and resuspended in culture media at a concentration of approximately 20,000 cells / μl. Cells replated after this treatment are viable, attach to the culture dish, and send out new neuritic processes. Two weeks after implantation into the hippocampus of septal-hippocampal lesioned adult rats, the grafted cells are found radiating from the site of infusion for distances up to a millimeter in the host brain. In addition to lodging in sites in the parenchyma, the grafted cells show a propensity for clustering around blood vessels, in the ependyma, and in subarachnoid sites (Kordower, Notter, & Gash, 1984).

We (Gash, Notter, et al., 1985) have used light microscopic auto-radiographic and histochemical procedures to examine the features of IMR-32 cells grafted into the hippocampal region of African green monkeys *(Cercopithecus aethiops)*. Five animals were used, four monkeys that had fimbria-fornix lesions 20 days prior to implantation and one monkey serving as a sham lesion control. Using stereotaxic coordinates from computerized tomographic brain scans, four transplants spaced 3 mm apart and consisting of 80,000 cells each were made into the right hippocampus of each animal. Survival times after transplantation ranged from 51 to 270 days. Grafted cells have been identified in four of the five recipients. An important variable seemed to be the treatment used to differentiate the neuroblastoma cells before transplantation. When a combination of prostaglandin E_1-cyclic AMP had been used, only a few surviving cells could be identified in two hosts and no viable implanted cells were seen in the third monkey. In contrast, long-term implant survival was improved using a mitomycin C-5-BrdU treatment. In both monkeys receiving these grafts (one animal had a fimbria-fornix lesion and the other animal was the lesion control), numerous AChE-positive (acetylcholinesterase) and ^{3}H-thymidine labelled cells were present, often in large numbers, in the needle tracts leading down to the hippocampus. The distribution of grafted cells resembled that seen in the rodent transplants with implanted cells found in the brain parenchyma, around blood vessels, and in the subarachnoid space.

The 270-day survival period of grafted human neuroblastoma cells in the African green monkey brain indicates that long-term survival of grafts without rejection is feasible. The grafted cells demonstrate some of the characteristics desirable in donor cells. They remained nontumorous and sent acetylcholinesterase-positive fibers into the host brain. Their pronounced tendency to aggregate around blood vessels and in subarachnoid spaces may be a reflection of their origin from neural crest cells. However these latter features are not needed, and it may be desirable to attempt to selectively eliminate these characteristics by modifying the cells in culture before transplantation.

RATIONALE FOR USING TRANSPLANTS IN THE TREATMENT OF ALZHEIMER'S DISEASE

How can neural transplants be used to treat AD? At present, neural implants have been successfully employed in moderating deficits resulting from circumscribed cell losses in the rodent brain. Alzheimer's disease involves multiple sites and neurotransmitter systems. In addition to cortical atrophy, significant neuronal losses are found in, among other sites, the nucleus basalis of Meynert, the hippocampus, and often the locus coeruleus and substantia nigra (see chapters by Bartus, and Winblad et al., this volume). Among the neurochemical alterations that have been reported, the three neurotransmitter systems providing global innervation to the cortex (cholinergic, noradrenergic, and serotonergic) show varying degrees of degeneration. Major cholinergic deficits are consistently reported in AD, and there are large subpopulations of patients with noradrenergic and/or serotonergic deficiencies. This points to another complication: A notable heterogeneity exists among AD patients (see Mayeux, Stern, & Spanton, 1985).

Given these data, the difficulties in treatment presented by AD seem insurmountable. In fact, one can speculate that at the end stage of the disease, only mildly palliative measures are possible. The key for any successful treatment probably lies in early intervention. Conceivably, the sequence of events that eventually leads to dementia begins a number of years prior to any clinical symptoms. The precipitating cause(s) gradually destroys neuronal elements critical for normal cortical cognitive functions until the extensive compensatory reserve of the brain is breached. Confusion, dementia, and, eventually, death follow (see Table 1).

Reason suggests that the optimal time for intervention is at the point of crossover from subclinical to clinical symptoms. Any rational course of action depends on a better understanding of the neural correlates of this crossover period. Assuming, for example, that the cholinergic deficits are central to the development of AD, then one would propose to conduct a series of grafts of cholinergic neurons into sites known to be important in learning and memory (e.g., frontal cortex and hippocampus). Other forms of transplant therapy can also be envisioned. For example, the implantation of cells to provide increased titers of important neurotrophic factors might prove to be of reasonable therapeutic value if it was shown that deficiencies in those factors contributed to the disease. The goal of these treatments would be, at a minimum, to arrest the deterioration of intellectual ability and, if possible, promote functional recovery. The ultimate measure would be an improved quality of life for Alzheimer's patients.

TABLE 1

A Theoretical Construct of the Sequence of Events in Alzheimer's Disease

Structural changes	Functional changes	Time course
Gradual neuronal losses	Subclinical cognitive deterioration	10-20 years?
↓	↓	
extensive cell losses in a critical neuronal population	mild cognitive decline	
↓	↓	
	moderate cognitive decline	
	↓	
increasing cascade of involvement of other neural and nonneural systems	early dementia	10 years
↓	↓	
pathologic features of AD	middle dementia	
	↓	
	late dementia	
		death

Note. The function stages are slightly modified from those delineated by Reisberg and his associates (Reisberg et al., 1984; Reisberg, Ferris, deLeon, & Crook, 1985).

RECOMMENDATIONS

The use of neural transplantation therapy in treating AD is in an early stage of evaluation. Studies on rodent models of learning and memory dysfunctions have been promising, and these studies need to be continued to gain a better understanding of the basic principles of neural implants. Preliminary investigations on the properties of neural transplants in nonhuman primates have begun, and an intensified effort in this direction is clearly warranted. As discussed elsewhere (Kordower & Gash, in press), the safety and effectiveness of neural transplants in treating neurodegenerative disorders can only adequately be determined using animals with nervous systems closely resembling humans. Finally, an essential factor for developing a rational transplantation strategy depends on an improved understanding of the brain during the late preclinical and early clinical stages of AD.

REFERENCES

Backlund, E.O., Granberg, P.O., Hamberger, B., Knutsson, E., Martensson, A., Sedvall, G., Seiger, Å., & Olson, L. (1985a). Transplantation of adrenal medullary tissue to striatum in parkinsonism. *Journal of Neurosurgery, 62,* 169-173.

Backlund, E.O., Granberg, P.O., Hamberger, B., Sedvall, G., Seiger, Å., & Olson, L. (1985b). Transplantation of adrenal medullary tissue to striatum in parkinsonism. In A. Björklund & U. Stenevi (Eds.), *Neural grafting in the mammalian CNS* (pp. 551-556). Amsterdam: Elsevier.

Benfey, M., & Aguayo, A.J. (1982). Extensive elongation of axons from rat brain into peripheral nerve grafts. *Nature, 295,* 150-152.

Björklund, H., Seiger, Å., Hoffer, B., & Olson, L. (1983). Trophic effects of brain areas on the developing cerebral cortex: I. Growth and histological organization of intraocular grafts. *Developmental Brain Research, 6,* 131-140.

Björklund, A., & Stenevi, U. (1977). Reformation of the severed septo-hippocampal cholinergic pathway in the adult rat by transplanted septal neurons. *Cell and Tissue Research, 185,* 289-302.

Björklund, A., & Stenevi, U. (Eds.). (1985). *Neural grafting in the mammalian CNS.* Amsterdam: Elsevier.

Boer, G.J., Gash, D.M., Dick, L.B., & Schluter, N. (1985). Vasopressin neuron survival in neonatal Brattleboro rats; Critical factors in graft development and innervation of the host brain. *Neuroscience, 15,* 1087-1109.

Bottenstein, J.E. (1981). Differentiated properties of neuronal cell lines. In G.H. Sato (Ed.), *Functionally differentiated cell lines* (pp. 155-184). New York: Alan R. Liss.

Collier, T.J., Gash, D.M., Esch, V., & Sladek, J.R., Jr. (1985). Impaired regulation of arousal in old age and the consequences for learning and memory: Replacement of brain norepinephrine via neuronal transplants improves memory performance in aged F344 rats. In B. Davis & W. Wood (Eds.), *Homeostatic functions in the elderly* (pp. 99-110). New York: Raven Press.

Collier, T.J., Gash, D.M., & Sladek, J.R., Jr. (1985). *Norepinephrine replacement in aged rats improves performance of a learned task.* (Manuscript submitted for publication.)

Crutcher, K.A., Kesner, R.P., & Novak, J.M. (1983). Medial spetal lesions, radial arm maze performance and sympathetic sprouting: A study of recovery of function. *Brain Research, 262,* 91-98.

Das, G.D. (1974). Transplantation of embryonic neural tissue in the mammalian brain. I. Growth and differentiation of neuroblasts from various regions of the embryonic brain in the cerebellum of neonatal rats. *T.I.T. Journal of Life Science, 4,* 93-124.

Doering, L.C., & Fedoroff, S. (1984). Isolation and transplantation of oligodendrocyte precursor cells. *Journal of Neurological Sciences, 63,* 183-196.

Dunnett, S.B., Low, W.C., Iversen, S.D., Stenevi, U., & Björklund, A. (1982) Septal transplants restore maze learning in rats with fornix-fimbria lesions. *Brain Research, 251,* 335-348.

Freed, W.J., Hoffer, B.J., Olson, L., & Wyatt, R.J. (1984). Transplantation of catecholamine-containing tissues to restore the functional capacity of the damaged nigrostriatal system. In J.R. Sladek, Jr., & D.M. Gash (Eds.), *Neural transplants: Development and function* (pp. 373-406). New York: Plenum Press.

Freed, W.J., Morihisa, J.M., Spoor, E., Hoffer, B.J., Olson, L., Seiger, Å., & Wyatt, R.J. (1981). Transplanted adrenal chromaffin cells in rat brain reduce lesion-induced rotational behavior. *Nature, 292,* 351-352.

Freed, W.J., Perlow, M.J., Karoum, F., Seiger, Å., Olson, L., Hoffer, B.J., & Wyatt, R.J. (1980). Restoration of dopaminergic function by grafting of fetal rat substantia nigra to the caudate nucleus: Long-term behavioral, biochemical and histochemical studies. *Annals of Neurology, 8,* 510-519.

Gage, F.H., Björklund, A., Stenevi, U., & Dunnett, S.B. (1985). Grafting of embryonic CNS tissue to the damaged adult hippocampal formation. In A. Björklund & U. Stenevi (Eds.), *Neural grafting in the mammalian CNS* (pp. 559-573). Amsterdam: Elsevier.

Gage, F.H., Björklund, A., Stenevi, U., Dunnett, S.B., & Kelly, P.A.T. (1984). Intrahippocampal septal grafts ameliorate learning impairments in aged rats. *Science, 225,* 533-536.

Gahwiler, B.H., & Brown, D.A. (1985). Functional innervation of cultured hippocampal neurons by cholinergic afferents from cocultured septal explants. *Nature, 313,* 577-579.

Gash, D.M., Collier, T.J., & Sladek, J.R. (1985). Neural transplantation: A review of recent developments and potential applications to the aged brain. *Neurobiology of Aging, 6,* 131-150.

Gash, D.M., Notter, M.F.D., Dick. L.B., Kraus, A.L., Okawara, S.H., Wechkin, S.W., & Joynt, R.J. (1985). Cholinergic neurons transplanted into the neocortex and hippocampus of primates: Studies on African green monkeys. In A. Björklund & U. Stenevi (Eds.), *Neural grafting in the mammalian CNS* (pp. 595-603). Amsterdam: Elsevier.

Gash, D.M., & Sladek, J.R., Jr. (1984). Functional and non-functional transplants: Studies with grafted hypothalamic and preoptic neurons. *Trends in Neurosciences, 7,* 391-394.

Gumpel, M., Baumann, N., Raoul, M., & Jacque, C. (1983). Survival and differentiation of oligodendrocytes from neural tissue transplanted into newborn mouse brain. *Neuroscience Letters, 37,* 307-311.

Gupta, M., Notter, M.F.D., Felten, S.Y., & Gash, D.M. (1985). Differentiation characteristics of human neuroblastoma cells in the presence of growth modulators and antimitotic drugs. *Developmental Brain Research, 19,* 21-29.

Jaeger, C.B., & Lund, R.D. (1980). Transplantation of embryonic occipital cortex to the tectal region of newborn rats: A light microscopic study of the organization and connectivity of the transplants. *Journal of Comparative Neurology, 194,* 571-597.

Kordower, J., & Gash, D.M. (in press). Animals and experimentation: An evaluation of animal models of Alzheimer's and Parkinson's disease. *Integrative Psychiatry.*

Kordower, J., Notter, M.F.D., & Gash, D.M. (1984). Survival of intrahippocampal transplants of cholinergic neuroblastoma into septal lesioned rats. *Society for Neuroscience Abstracts, 10* (Part 2), 981.

Kromer, L.F., Björklund, A., & Stenevi, U. (1981). Regeneration of the septo-hippocampal pathways in adult rats is promoted by utilizing embryonic hippocampal implants as bridges. *Brain Research, 210,* 173-200.

Labbe, R., Firl, A., Jr., Mufson, E.J. & Stein, D.B. (1983). Fetal rat brain transplants: Reduction of cognitive deficits in rats with frontal cortex lesions. *Science, 221,* 470-472.

Lindsay, R.M., & Raisman, G. (1984). An autoradiographic study of neuronal development, vascularization and glial cell migration from hippocampal transplants labelled in intermediate explant culture. *Neuroscience, 12,* 513-530.

Low, W.C., Lewis, P.R., Bunch, S.T., Dunnett, S.B., Thomas, S.R., Iverson, S.D., Björklund, A., & Stenevi, U. (1982). Functional recovery following neural transplantation of embryonic septal nuclei in adult rats with septo-hippocampal lesions. *Nature, 300,* 260-262.

Mayeux, R., Stern, Y., & Spanton, S. (1985). Heterogeneity in dementia of the Alzheimer type: Evidence of subgroups. *Neurology, 35,* 453-461.

McLoon, S.C., & Lund, R.D. (1980). Specific projections of retina transplanted to rat brain. *Experimental Brain Research, 40,* 273-282.

Morihisa, J.M., Nakamura, R.K., Freed, W.J., Mishkin, M., & Wyatt, R.J. (1984). Adrenal medulla grafts survive and exhibit catecholamine-specific fluorescence in the primate brain. *Experimental Neurology, 84,* 643-653.

Nieto-Sampedro, M., Lewis, E.R., Cotman, C.W., Manthorpe, M., Skaper, S.D., Barbin, G., Longo, F.M., & Varon, S. (1982). Brain injury causes a time-dependent increase in neuronotrophic activity at the lesion site. *Science, 217,* 860-861.

Nieto-Sampedro, M., Manthorpe, M., Barbin, G., Varon, S., & Cotman, C.W. (1983). Injury-induced neuronotrophic activity in adult rat brain: Correlation with survival of delayed implants in the wound cavity. *Journal of Neuroscience, 3,* 2219-2229.

Olson, L., Björklund, H., & Hoffer, B.J. (1984). Camera Bulbi anterior: New vistas on a classic locus for neural tissue transplantation. In J.R. Sladek, Jr. & D.M. Gash (Eds.), *Neural transplants: Development and function* (pp. 125-165). New York: Plenum Press.

Prasad, K.N. (1975). Differentiation of neuroblastoma cells in culture. *Biological Reviews, 50,* 129-165.

Reisberg, B., Ferris, S., Anand, R., De Leon, M., Schneck, M., Buttinger, C., & Borenstein, J. (1984). Functional staging of dementia of the Alzheimer type. *Annals of the New York Academy of Science, 435,* 481-483.

Reisberg, B., Ferris, S., De Leon, M., & Crook, T. (1985). Age-associated cognitive decline and Alzheimer's disease; implications for assessment and treatment. In M. Bergener, M. Ermini, & H.B. Stahelin (Eds.), *Thresholds in aging* (pp. 235-292). London: Academic Press.

Richardson, P.M., McGuinness, U.M., & Aguayo, A.J. (1980). Axons from CNS neurons regenerate into PNS grafts. *Nature, 284,* 264-265.

Rosenstein, J.M., & Brightman, M.W. (1984). Some consequences of grafting autonomic ganglia to brain surfaces. In J.R. Sladek, Jr. & D.M. Gash (Eds.), *Neural transplants: Development and function* (pp. 423-443). New York: Plenum Press.

Sabel, B.A., Slavin, M.D., & Stein, D.G. (1984). G_{M1} ganglioside treatment facilitates behavioral recovery from bilateral brain damage. *Science, 225,* 340-342.

Seiger, Å., & Olson, L. (1977). Quantitation of fiber growth in transplanted central monomine neurons. *Cell and Tissue Research, 179,* 285-316.

Sladek, J.R., Jr., & Gash, D.M. (1984a). Morphological and functional properties of transplanted vasopressin neurons. In J.R. Sladek, Jr. & D.M. Gash (Eds.). *Neural transplants: Development and function* (pp. 243-282). New York: Plenum Press.

Sladek, J.R., Jr., & Gash, D.M. (Eds.). (1984b). *Neural transplants: Development and function.* New York: Plenum Press.

Stein, D.G., Labbe, R., Firl, A., Jr., & Mufson, E.J. (1985). Behavioral recovery following implantation of fetal brain tissue into mature rats with bilateral cortical lesions. In A. Björklund & U. Stenevi (Eds.), *Neural grafting in the mammalian CNS* (pp. 605-614). Amsterdam: Elsevier.

Stenevi, U., Björklund, A., & Svendgaard, N.A. (1976). Transplantation of central and peripheral monoamine neurons to the adult rat brain: Techniques and conditions for survival. *Brain Research, 114,* 1-20.

Tumilowicz, J.J., Nichols, W.W., Cholon, J.J., & Creene, A.E. (1970).

Definition of a continuous human cell line derived from neuroblastoma. *Cancer Research, 30,* 2110-2118.

Wyatt, R.J., Morihisa, J.M., Nakamura, R.K., & Freed, W.J. (in press). Transplanting tissue into the brain for function: Use in a model of Parkinson's disease. *Research Publications of the Association for Research in Nervous and Mental Disease.*

26

Alzheimer's Disease: Strategies for Treatment and Research

Curtis A. Bagne, PhD, Nunzio Pomara, MD,
Thomas Crook, PhD, and Samuel Gershon, MD

Even though Alzheimer's disease (AD) is the most prevalent cause of dementia, no dramatically effective treatments are available at this time. This review of the AD literature will address both substantive issues of treatment and methodologic issues of science and clinical practice. It suggests new treatment strategies as well as methods to improve the productivity of clinical research.

OVERVIEW OF TREATMENT STRATEGIES

Table 1 lists most of the treatment strategies for ameliorating the symptoms of AD that have been clinically tested and reported in the English language literature during the last 20 years. One or more treatments is listed for each strategy. Drugs marketed in the United States are identified with an asterisk. One of the more recent studies is listed for each treatment. These studies focus on but are not limited to AD. Some of the older studies, in particular, come from a time before there was any consistent attempt to distinguish AD from multi-infarct dementia. As we will see later, none of the treatments is clearly effective for most patients and symptoms.

Improve Cerebral Circulation

Abnormal cerebral aging appears to result from both degenerative and vascular mechanisms acting alone or in combination (Dastur, 1985). AD is now recognized as a parenchymal degenerative disease that does not appear to have a vascular pathogenesis (Reisberg,

TABLE 1

Strategies for the Development of an Effective Treatment for AD

Strategy	Treatment	Recent Investigation
Improve cerebral circulation and blood oxygenation		
Blood oxygenation	Hyperbaric oxygen	Raskin et al. (1978)
Vasodilation	Papaverine[a]	Branconnier and Cole (1977, pp. 458-462)
	Cyclandelate[a]	Capote and Parikh (1978)
	Isoxsuprine[a]	Affleck, Treptow, and Herrick (1961)
	Cinnarizine	Bernard and Goffart (1968)
	Betahistine	Rivera et al. (1974)
Anticoagulation	Bishydroxycoumarin[a]	Walsh, A.C., Walsh, B.H., and Melaney (1978)
Reduce blood viscosity	Pentoxifylline[a]	Harwart (1979)
Vasodilation and metabolic activation	Dihydroergotoxine[a]	van Loveren-Huyben et al. (1984)
	Nafronyl (Naftidrofuryl)	Branconnier and Cole (1977b, pp. 186-188)
	Pyritinol	Copper and Magnus (1980)

Metabolic activation

Pyrithioxin	Schefler (1972)
Meclofenoxate	Gedye et al. (1972)
Piracetam	Abuzzahab et al. (1978)
Oxiracetam	Itil et al. (1982)
Pramiracetam	Branconnier et al. (1983)
Aniracetam	Mizuki et al. (1984)
EMD 21657	Noel et al. (1983)

Alter CNS neurotransmitters

"The Cholinergic Hypothesis"

Precursor loading	Choline chloride[a]	Thal et al. (1981)
	Lecithin (acute)[a]	Pomara, Domino, et al. (1983)
	Lecithin (chronic)[a]	Etienne et al. (1981)
	Deanol	Fisman et al. (1981)
Enhance transmitter release	4-Aminopyridine	Wesseling et al. (1984)
Inhibit acetylcholinesterase	Oral physostigmine	Mohs et al. (1985)
	Intravenous physostigmine[a]	Davis and Mohs (1982)
	Pyridostigmine bromide[a]	Agnoli et al. (1983)
	Tetrahydroaminoacridine	Summers et al. (1981)
Receptor stimulation	Arecoline	Christie et al. (1981)
	Bethanechol chloride[a] (continuous intracranial infusion)	Harbaugh et al. (1984)
	Pilocarpine[a]	Caine (1980)

TABLE 1 Continued

Strategy	Treatment	Recent Investigation
Psychostimulation	Methylphenidate[a]	Crook et al. (1977)
	Pentylenetetrazol	Stotsky et al. (1972)
Dopamine precursor loading	Levodopa[a]	Kristensen et al. (1977)
		Jellinger et al. (1980)
Dopamine receptor stimulation	Bromocriptine[a]	Phuapradit et al. (1978)
Opioid antagonism	Naloxone[a]	Reisberg, Ferris, Anand, Mir, Geibel, et al. (1983)
	Naltrexone[a]	Pomara et al. (1985)
Serotonin precursor loading	L-Tryptophan[a]	Smith, Stromgren, et al. (1984)
Inhibit serotonin re-uptake	Alaproclate	Bergman et al. (1983)
Correct monoamine neurotransmitter deficits	Amitriptyline[a]	Reding et al. (1983)
Neuropeptides	ACTH 4-10	Ferris et al. (1976)
	ORG 2766 (ACTH 4-9 analog)	Martin et al. (1983)
	1-Desamino-8-d-arginine vasopressin (DDAVP)[a]	Weingartner et al. (1981)
	Lysine vasopressin	Durso et al. (1982)

Nutritional supplements	Niacin-pentylenetetrazol combination	LaBrecque and Goldberg (1967)
	Vitamin B_{12}[a]	Kral et al. (1970)
	Folate and B_{12}[a]	Shaw et al. (1971)
	B complex and C vitamins[a]	Altman et al. (1973)
	Glutamate-B vitamin-iron[a]	Whitman (1966)
	Dried bakers yeast[a]	Dalderup et al. (1970)
	RNA[a]	Munch-Petersen et al. (1974)
	Zinc sulfate[a]	Czerwinski et al. (1974)
Gerovital H3	Gerovital H3	Zwerling et al. (1975)
Manage secondary symptoms	Antipsychotics[a]	Barnes et al. (1982)

Note. [a]Currently marketed in U.S.

Ferris, & Gershon, 1981). Before it was recognized that AD and multi-infarct dementia were distinct disease processes, it was assumed that most dementias were secondary to progressive cerebral arteriosclerosis and ischemia (Cook & James, 1981). This assumption, since shown to be incorrect, supported frequent use of vasodilators for treatment of dementia.

Some drugs that have been described as cerebral vasodilators do produce mental improvement in patients with dementia. Vasodilators that appear to improve neuronal intermediary metabolism are more effective than those that have only vasodilator action (Yesavage, Tinklenberg, Hollister, & Berger, 1979). Drugs that increase metabolism can indirectly increase cerebral blood flow. Table 1 distinguishes drugs with primary vasodilator action from drugs with mixed vasodilator and metabolic effects (Yesavage et al., 1979). Vasodilator therapy is problematic even in vascular dementias because it can reduce blood flow in ischemic areas (Cook & James, 1981).

Other drugs may have a beneficial effect on vascular dementias through the direct mechanism of increasing cerebral blood flow. Concern about safety has limited long-term anticoagulant therapy for dementia. Pentoxifylline lowers blood viscosity in microcirculation (Schneider, Schmid-Schonbein, & Kiesewetter, 1983) and is currently being tested on demented geriatric patients in a multicenter trial.

Metabolic Activation

Metabolic activation encompasses a host of more specific treatment mechanisms. These include increasing oxidative metabolism, fluidization of cell membranes, and depletion of lipofuscin. A new class of psychotropic agents, the nootropics (Giurgea, 1976), has been included with the metabolic activators (Branconnier, 1983).

Neurotransmitter Strategies

The cholinergic hypothesis (Bartus, Dean, Beer, & Lippa, 1982; Drachman & Glosser, 1981) currently guides more clinical research on AD than any other strategy. It is based on the most clearly established neurochemical and histological changes associated with AD. Furthermore, these changes have been associated with the cognitive impairments that are central to a diagnosis of AD. Any comprehensive treatment strategy for AD will have to address defects in the cholinergic system. Some general strategies for manipulating neurotransmitter systems include precursor loading; alteration of transmitter release, catabolism after release, or reuptake of transmitter fragments; and receptor stimulation. An occasional study has addressed the effects of traditional psychotropics on the primary cognitive symptoms of dementia (Cole, Branconnier, Salomon, & Dessain, 1983).

A major defect, even if confined to one neurotransmitter system, can upset the balance among many neurotransmitter systems. If for no other reason, treatments that alter noncholinergic systems will probably have a place in the treatment of AD. An additional rationale for considering treatments directed at noncholinergic systems is that recent investigations have revealed decreases in somatostatin, dopamine, serotonin, and norepinephrine in AD brains.

Other Treatment Strategies

Peptides play a pervasive role in physiological processes including central nervous system function. Treatment is highly experimental, and the effects of only a few neuropeptides on the symptoms of AD have been evaluated.

Many marketed psychotropic agents have been described as antidementia drugs for managing secondary symptoms (Crook, 1984). For example, neuroleptics are used to treat a broad range of dyssocial and psychotic symptoms that may accompany the disorder; antidepressants are widely used to treat affective symptoms that accompany, and may even mimic, senile dementia; and sedative-hypnotics are used to treat the sleep disorders that predictably occur in dementia patients. These treatments have received little systematic study within the AD population.

Development of Treatment Rationales

Obviously many types of treatments have been tried for AD or age-associated cognitive decline. The introductions to most studies give a rationale for trying the treatment. These rationales often cite some defects in specific brain structures or neurotransmitter and enzymatic systems. They also cite some characteristics of the proposed treatments. An attempt is made to fit treatments to disorders as keys to locks. Success has not been dramatic.

The history of treatments for AD suggests a number of things. Rationales that have been offered are diverse and sometimes inconsistent. They need to be sought, but they seldom work, and should be regarded with caution. Experience with a rational approach continues to support the value of an empirical approach; there is no substitute for data collection and analysis. Perhaps more fundamental to the way we approach the problem, this history raises the question of whether there is any one treatment for the *class* of disorders that has come to be known as AD.

The converse of looking at the variety of treatments for AD is to look at the variety of indications that has been suggested for one of the treatments. Table 2 lists some of the indications that have been suggested in the literature for piracetam. Efficacy has not been clearly established for any of these indications. However, activity profiles for treatments can be almost as broad as the profiles of defects and deficits in multifaceted disorders such as AD.

We have much to learn about both the disorders and the treatments. The process of learning about treatments is illustrated by the history of dihydroergotoxine.

MECHANISMS OF ACTION—EVOLUTION OF UNDERSTANDING

Classification of particular treatments by strategy, as in Table 1, is somewhat tentative and arbitrary because clinical experience in psychopharmacology often precedes understanding of the mechanisms of drug action. This is illustrated by the evolution of our understanding of dihydroergotoxine (Hydergine®) as shown in Table 3. Although this drug has been widely prescribed for 30 years, and was recently the eleventh most widely prescribed drug in the world, much uncertainty still surrounds its use and mechanisms of action (Hollister & Yesavage, 1984). Hydergine® was originally thought to be a vasodilator, but there is little clean-cut evidence that it increases total or regional blood flow (Loew & Weil, 1982). It does appear to correct electroencephalogram (EEG) alterations in models of impaired brain metabolism. Hydergine® binds *in vitro* to receptors specific for dopamine, serotonin, and noradrenaline. Experiments *in vivo* indicate

TABLE 2

Suggested Indications for Piracetam Found in the Literature

Stroke patients
Common symptoms of the elderly
Senile dementia
Dizziness
Memory disturbances
Chronic schizophrenia
Head injuries (mild and severe)
Comatose patients
Chronic and acute alcoholism
Drug dependence
CNS adverse effects of drugs
Cerebral palsy
Language disturbances during development age
Adolescents with poor school results
Neurogenic bladder
Sickle-cell disease

Note. Data are from Spagnoli and Tagnoni (1983).

agonist action of central dopamine and serotonin receptors (Loew & Weil, 1982).

Any treatment that acts through so many mechanisms cannot be expected to benefit all patients with dementia. The response of any one patient would depend on matching a particular profile of defects and deficits with the activity profile of a treatment. Patients vary interindividually and intraindividually. It can be difficult to achieve and maintain a fit between patient and treatment. A few patients purportedly respond to particular treatments. This appears to be the case with Hydergine® and some other candidates for dementia treatments. The combination of multiple mechanisms and limited therapeutic effect, together with patient diversity, provides one explanation of why most proposed treatments for dementia begin with a few positive case reports, only to be lost in the group averages of clinical trials.

If AD patients differ substantially, no small arbitrary sample can be expected to represent the class, and the results from a sample may not represent any individual. As Hollister & Yesavage (1984)

TABLE 3

Evolution in Understanding Mechanisms of Action for Hydergine®

Level of Action / Mechanism of Action	Experimental Findings		References
	Animals	Man	
1. Vascular System			
Central depression of vasomotor nerve activity	CBF ↑		Rothlin (1946/1947)
Peripheral α-adrenoceptor blockade	CBF ↔		Rothlin and Taeschler (1951)
Direct stimulation of smooth muscle		CBF ↑	Geraud et al. (1963)
		CBF ↔	Gottstein (1965)
		CBF,	
		rCBF ↔	McHenry et al. (1971)
		rCBF (iv) ↓ᵃ	Olesen and Skinhoj (1972)
		rCBF (ic) ↔	
2. Metabolism and Neurotransmitters			
Dopamine agonism	Emetic activity ↑ Contralateral rotations, Ungerstedt rats ↑		Wang and Glaviano (1954) Corrodi et al. (1973)

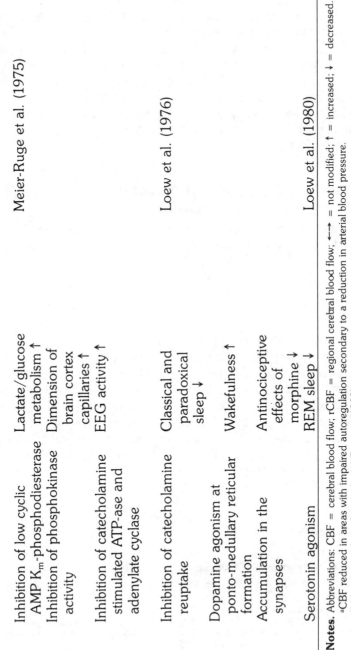

Inhibition of low cyclic AMP K$_m$-phosphodiesterase	Lactate/glucose metabolism ↑	Meier-Ruge et al. (1975)
Inhibition of phosphokinase activity	Dimension of brain cortex capillaries ↑	
Inhibition of catecholamine stimulated ATP-ase and adenylate cyclase	EEG activity ↑	
Inhibition of catecholamine reuptake	Classical and paradoxical sleep ↓	Loew et al. (1976)
Dopamine agonism at ponto-medullary reticular formation	Wakefulness ↑	
Accumulation in the synapses	Antinociceptive effects of morphine ↓	
Serotonin agonism	REM sleep ↓	Loew et al. (1980)

Notes. Abbreviations: CBF = cerebral blood flow; rCBF = regional cerebral blood flow; ←→ = not modified; ↑ = increased; ↓ = decreased.
[a]CBF reduced in areas with impaired autoregulation secondary to a reduction in arterial blood pressure.
Table adapted from Spagnoli and Tognoni (1983).

remind us, "mean levels of improvement are not necessarily indicative of response of individual patients" (p. 896). And Wurtman (1982)
has suggested that progress may depend on the development of a
method "for determining whether or not a proposed treatment
actually works if and when that treatment appears to be effective
in a minority of patients" (p. 496). Before proposing a solution to
this problem, let us consider our achievements in AD treatment.

The best test of a treatment is documented evidence of reproducible clinical benefit. This can be evaluated by considering some
published reports.

SUMMARY OF CLINICAL TRIALS

Some of the treatments shown in Table 1 have been recently
reviewed. A few of these reviews are identified and summarized in
Table 4.

Vasodilators

Yesavage et al. (1979) reviewed 102 studies of eight vasodilators
in senile dementias. Studies were classified according to criteria for
well-controlled trials. Cerebral vasodilators were divided into two
classes: Those with vasodilator action alone and those with mixed
vasodilator and metabolic action.* The drugs with metabolic action
were significantly more effective. Subsequent reviews of vasodilators generally support these same results. According to the U.S. Food
and Drug Administration, there is no body of evidence that supports
the effectiveness of papaverine for any of its claimed indications (Food
and Drug Administration, 1979).

Hydergine®

Dihydroergotoxine (Hydergine®) is probably the most studied and
reviewed drug for senile dementia. Yet, the recent review by Hol-

---

* A vasodilator may be known to have metabolic action because of investigations directed
at explaining an interesting therapeutic effect. Primary vasodilators could affect metabolism
in ways that were never investigated.

TABLE 4

Reviews: Treatments for Dementia

Treatment	Reviewers	Types of Study	Conclusion
Mixed Vasodilators	Yesavage et al. (1979)		
Dihydroergotoxine		33 trials, 22 well-controlled	Best confirmed efficacy of vasodilators.
Nafronyl		8 trials, 7 well-controlled	Promising.
Pyritinol		5 trials, 1 well-controlled	More study needed.
Pentifylline		12 trials, 1 well-controlled	More study needed.
Primary Vasodilators	Yesavage et al. (1979)		
Cyclandelate		18 trials, 7 well-controlled	Results controversial.
Papaverine		13 trials, 9 well-controlled	Little proof of efficacy.
Isoxsuprine		5 trials, 3 well-controlled	Little proof of efficacy.
Cinnarizine		8 trials, 3 well-controlled	Inconclusive.
Vasodilators	Cook and James (1981)	Various	Ergoloid mesylates and nafronyl cautiously recommended for dementia.

TABLE 4 Continued

Treatment	Reviewers	Types of Study	Conclusion
Hydergine®			
	Hollister and Yesavage (1984)	Various	"No alternative drug treatments have been proved better" for senile dementia.
	Loew and Weil (1982)	"Numerous controlled trials in patients with senile mental impairment"	Improvement reported for clinical and psychometric measures and EEG.
	Hughes et al. (1976)	12 similar double-blind, placebo-controlled trials	"Hydergine would seem to be of minor value in dementia therapy."
	McDonald (1979)	26 clinical trials	Generally consistent improvement of symptoms.
Metabolic Enhancers	Branconnier (1983)	Various	
Nafronyl			Marginal therapeutic efficacy.
Centrophenoxine			Little evidence for therapeutic value.
Vincamine			Apparently some therapeutic effect.
Pyrithioxin			Some evidence for efficacy.

Piracetam and piracetam analogues			Little evidence for efficacy, newer analogues may be more efficacious.
Nootropics	Schneck (1983)		"May exert small positive effects on AD."
Choline Salts	Fovall et al. (1983)	Various	A few slight improvements.
Lecithin	Etienne (1983)	Various	No beneficial and reproducible response.
Stimulants	Crook (1979)	Various	Limited benefit, substantial risk.
	Prien (1983)	Various	Do nothing for core symptoms.

lister & Yesavage (1984) raises some of the unanswered questions about the use of Hydergine® for senile dementias. These questions include the indications for use, mechanisms of action, proper dose, optimal duration of treatment, and effectiveness. Although the authors make no attempt to state the definitive answer to any of these questions, they do suggest that a 6-month trial with at least 6 mg/day may be warranted.

Loew & Weil's (1982) review of Hydergine® stresses studies that used the Sandoz Clinical Assessment Geriatric (SCAG) scale. The items in this scale cluster into a number of practical clinical dimensions. These factors are interpersonal relationships, cognitive dysfunction, affect, apathy, somatic functioning, and self-care. Loew reported results of a retrospective analysis of 1,165 patients from 21 Hydergine® studies. Three months of Hydergine® was associated with a statistically significant improvement in all five factors and 14 out of 18 SCAG scale items among patients with "idiopathic-degenerative" dementia. Loew also reviewed evidence that Hydergine® has beneficial effects on psychometric test performance. Effects on EEG power spectra can be interpreted as improvements.

The earlier review of Hydergine® by Hughes, Williams, and Currier (1976) emphasized the differences between statistical and clinical significance of behavioral changes attributed to Hydergine®. They concluded that "Hydergine® is of minor clinical value in the treatment of dementia" (Hughes et al., 1976). McDonald's (1979) review reported that Hydergine® significantly improved 13 of 32 symptoms in at least 50% of six or more double-blind studies. Most clinicians remain skeptical about the beneficial effects of Hydergine® (Hollister, 1984). None of the reviews expresses major concern about adverse effects.

Metabolic Enhancers and Nootropics

Branconnier (1983) has reviewed pharmacologic and clinical studies for a number of metabolic enhancers. Clinical experience and especially rigorous clinical tests, are quite limited for most of these treatments. Most seem to produce some degree of behavioral arousal that does not improve cognitive function as measured by psychometric tests.

Schneck (1983) reviewed the nootropics, but focused on piracetam. Animal studies have identified types of activity that could have important applications in medicine, but there is little evidence for clinical value at this time. Treatment appears to be safe, and more potent nootropics are under development.

Other Treatments

Cholinergic precursor therapy for AD has been studied and reviewed quite thoroughly. Unfortunately there is little evidence for clinical benefit when either choline salts (Fovall, Dysken, & Davis, 1983) or lecithin (Etienne, 1983) is used alone. Lecithin may slow mental deterioration (Etienne, 1983).

Psychostimulants appear to do nothing for the core symptoms of dementia (Prien, 1983). They could benefit a subgroup of under-aroused patients, but this has not been adequately demonstrated. There is substantial risk in using stimulants in demented patients (Crook, 1979). These risks include increased confusion and agitation, induction of paranoid ideation, sudden and precipitous increases in blood pressure and heart rate, and adverse interactions with anti-hypertensive agents (Crook, 1979).

Neuropeptides do have behavioral effects in humans (Jolles, 1983), but clinically significant benefits have not been demonstrated (Ferris, 1983).

Demented patients have behavioral complications that are frequently treated with antipsychotics, particularly when the patients are in long-term care facilities (Helms, 1985). These treatments have not been adequately studied, and the studies seldom focus on AD patients. Results of the studies that have been done are mixed.

Additional Reviews

A number of more comprehensive reviews are relevant to the treatment of AD. Some of these reviews and their perspectives are: Drug treatment of AD by Rosenberg, Greenwald, and Davis (1983); future directions for drug treatment of AD by Pomara, Brinkman, and Gershon (1983); treatment of cognitive decline in the aged by Reisberg et al. (1981) and by Pomara, Reisberg, Ferris, and Gershon (1981); drug treatment for age-related behavioral deficits by Wittenborn (1981); experimental pharmacology of AD by Greenwald and Davis (1983); and cerebroactive drugs by Spagnoli and Tognoni (1983).

Several AD treatments that have received much recent attention have not been extensively reviewed in the literature. These include physostigmine, a rapidly acting acetylcholinesterase inhibitor; direct muscarinic agonists and the opiate receptor antagonists, naloxone and naltrexone.

PHYSOSTIGMINE

Normal Subjects

The effects of physostigmine on cognition and affect for normal subjects were reported by Davis, Hollister, Overall, Johnson, and Train (1976). Physostigmine, given by infusion, was compared to saline in a parallel groups design with 23 subjects. They reported a " 'physostigmine syndrome' consisting of decreased speech, slowed thoughts, mild sedation, expressionless faces, nausea, and decreased spontaneous activity [that] was evident following doses of 1.5 to 2.0 mg of physostigmine" (p. 23). Physostigmine reduced short-term memory, and the groups did not differ in tasks of consolidation from short-term to long-term memory. The doses used in this study were higher than those used subsequently to treat AD.

Another study of the effects of intravenous physostigmine on memory processes of 19 normal young adult male volunteers compared a lower maximum dose (1.0 mg) with saline in a randomized crossover design (Davis et al., 1978). The investigators reported no quantifiable effect on any aspect of short-term memory. Storage into long-term memory was tested with two tasks. The effects of physostigmine on long-term memory in this study are difficult to interpret because of apparent errors of presentation in the text. After these errors are sorted out, the results do appear to support the authors' claim that physostigmine improves storage into long-term memory.

Drachman and Sahakian (1980) compared memory and cognitive function in 13 normal elderly volunteers who received a single subcutaneous injection of 0.8 mg physostigmine with the function of 20 elderly control volunteers who did not receive drugs. They reported that physostigmine produced a statistically nonsignificant trend toward improvement.

Demented Subjects

Some recent studies on the effects of physostigmine used alone in demented patients are presented in Table 5. Christie, Shering, Ferguson, and Glen (1981) used a randomized double-blind design to study the effects of intravenous physostigmine on picture recognition in 11 AD patients. None was severely demented. Compared to saline, 0.375 mg physostigmine, infused over 30 minutes, significantly improved picture recognition at 15 and 30 minutes after the beginning of the infusion. Effects at lower and higher doses were not significant. Performance at 60 minutes tended to be lower than at baseline for most doses and saline. Adverse effects precluded continued testing of some patients and use of some higher planned doses. The authors concluded that memory function remains grossly impaired as compared with normal subjects and that, at the time of the study, physostigmine was not a practical therapy for AD (Christie et al., 1981).

Davis and Mohs (1982) studied 10 moderately demented but cooperative AD patients who were free of psychotropic drugs for at least 2 weeks. The first phase of the study was used to determine the optimal dose of intravenous physostigmine for each patient based on a task that tested storage into long-term memory. This optimal dose was randomized with saline and repeated during the replication phase. Infusions were separated by 2 to 4 days, and probanthine was administered 5 minutes before infusions to block peripheral cholinergic effects. Memory was assessed with three memory tasks: (1) Famous Faces Test, (2) Digit Span Task, and (3) Recognition Memory Test for either 12 words or 12 pictures. Physostigmine had no effect on performance for the Famous Faces Test or the Digit Span Task. During the replication phase, 8 of 10 subjects did better on the Recognition Memory Test when they were on physostigmine compared with saline — the average difference of 7.5% was significant (p<.01).

Muramoto and colleagues provide evidence that physostigmine improves performance on copying geometric figures for some patients with AD. The first of six cases was the subject of a separate report (Muramoto, Sugishita, Sugita, & Toyokura, 1979). Four administrations of physostigmine were randomized with four administrations of saline under double-blind conditions on separate days. Scores based on copying performance of eight geometric figures were remarkably improved on drug. Scores on memory and manual dex-

TABLE 5

Physostigmine for AD			
Investigators, Year, and Reference	Dose and Route	Design	Number of Subjects
Christie et al. (1981)	0.25, 0.375, 0.5, 0.75, or 1 mg intravenous	Double-blind	11
Davis and Mohs (1982)	0.125, 0.25, or 0.5 mg intravenous	Double-blind	10
Muramoto et al. (1984)	1 mg injection 0.3, 0.5, 0.8 mg intravenous 1, 2, 3 mg oral	Double-blind	1 4 1
Smith and Swash (1979)	1 mg injection	Double-blind	1
Ashford et al. (1981)	0.5 mg infusion	Double-blind	6
Delwaide (1980)	1 mg injection	Double-blind	6
Jotkowitz (1983)	10-15 mg/day oral	Single-blind	10
Caltagirone et al. (1982)	1 mg q.i.d., oral	Open	8
Caltagirone et al. (1983)	individualized oral individualized injection	Open	4 4
Mohs et al. (1985)	individualized oral	Double-blind	12

terity tasks were not affected. Of five additional cases repeatedly tested at each of several doses of either intravenous or oral physostigmine, two subjects were reported to show a statistically significant improvement on the figure copying task (Muramoto, Sugishita, & Ando, 1984). None of the beneficial effects lasted more than 3 hours, and two subjects copied figures less accurately at 3 hours than at baseline. The cholinergic system seems to be involved in constructional ability (Muramoto et al., 1984).

Smith and Swash (1979) studied one patient with AD confirmed by biopsy. Injections of physostigmine and saline were given in random order six times over 7 weeks. Physostigmine did not affect the number of correct responses on a number of cognitive tasks, but appeared to specifically reduce the number of intrusion errors.

Six patients with AD did not benefit from 0.5 mg intravenous physostigmine when tested on word learning and visual retention tasks (Ashford, Soldinger, Schaeffer, Cochran, & Jarvik, 1981).

Delwaide, Devoitille, and Ylieff (1980) tested senile dementia patients on a word learning and recall task before, within 4 hours, and within 48 hours after acute physostigmine. They reported no significant variation in performance. Using the same general procedure in the same study, these investigators detected significant beneficial effects with lysine-vasopressin and adverse effects with scopolamine.

Oral Physostigmine

Most subjects in studies reported so far received an acute dose of physostigmine by infusion or injection. Several studies report the effects of longer term oral administration. Jotkowitz (1983) treated 10 patients with mild to severe AD for up to 10 months with 10 to 15 mg oral physostigmine per day, or with placebo according to a single-blind, multiple crossover protocol. No improvement was noted by patients or families who did not know when the patients were on active drug. No improvements were noted in ratings by the neurologist.

Caltagirone, Gainotti, and Masullo (1982) tested eight patients with presenile AD before and after receiving oral physostigmine, 1 mg q.i.d. (4 times a day) for 1 month. This open study reported behavioral improvement in four out of eight patients when this was rated directly by the patients or relatives. No improvement was reported on a battery of tests designed to measure mental deterioration. There was some indication that retest performance was disrupted by arousal induced by physostigmine.

Most studies with physostigmine reveal clinically significant individual differences in response to drug and stress the need to identify the optimal dose for each patient. Another study by Caltagirone, Albanese, Gainotti, & Masullo (1983) used a procedure based on serum cholinesterase activity to determine the optimal dose of physostigmine for each patient. Four patients were evaluated for an optimal oral dose and four other patients for an optimal injected dose. An individual's optimal dose was defined as the dose that reduced plasma cholinesterase activity by at least 15%. The mean optimal dose for oral administration was 3.75 mg ($\pm$0.85) and for subcutaneous administration was 0.75 mg ($\pm$0.05). Cognitive testing was done 45 minutes after oral administration and 25 minutes after injection. These times produced the maximum decrease in serum cholinesterase activity. Although there was some indication that physostigmine induced behavioral arousal, cognitive testing provided almost no evidence of a treatment effect. The authors suggest that one reason for these negative findings may be that physostigmine inhibits both cholinesterase activity and release of acetylcholine (ACh). This suggestion is supported by evidence that physostigmine inhibits ACh release at the peripheral level (Alderdice, 1979).

Another recently reported study on oral physostigmine determined the optimal dose for each patient during a dose-finding phase (Mohs et al., 1985). The Alzheimer's Disease Assessment Scale (ADAS) (Rosen, Mohs, & Davis, 1984), which will be discussed later in this paper, was administered after 3 to 5 days treatment at each of five dose levels. Scale scores were used to select an optimal dose for 10 of 12 patients who responded and did not become delusional. The optimal dose and placebo were given in random order during a replication phase and symptom severity was rated again. Seven of 10 patients improved on physostigmine during the replication phase; three patients became worse. The average improvement from placebo to physostigmine for the 10 patients during the replication phase was 1.3%. Most subjects also participated in a sleep study after both parts of the replication phase. Plasma cortisol levels were monitored every half hour for 12 hours. Data are reported for the seven patients who had an improved score on the ADAS during the replication phase. Two of these subjects had lower average cortisol levels after physostigmine and five had higher levels. Mean percent change in cortisol level was positively and significantly correlated with mean percent change in ADAS scores for this select group of patients.

The overall impression of these studies is, not surprisingly, that physostigmine has some effect on the cholinergic system. There is little evidence that it is a safe and effective treatment for AD.

DIRECT MUSCARINIC AGONISTS

Christie et al. (1981) reported that acute arecoline (2 and 4 mg) generally improved picture recognition within an hour after the start of an infusion. Harbaugh, Roberts, Coombs, Saunders, and Reeder (1984) used an implantable pump to study the effects of chronic administration of bethanechol chloride directly into cerebrospinal fluid (CSF). Family members who were blind to treatment reported encouraging effects on day-to-day activities when the patients were on active drug. Another muscarinic agonist, RS-86, was administered orally over several weeks to both healthy subjects and patients with AD (Spiegel, Azcona, & Wettstein, 1984). RS-86 was well-tolerated, had some beneficial effects on psychometric test performance and clinical measures, and could serve as a tool to test the ACh-deficit hypothesis of AD.

NALOXONE AND NALTREXONE

A number of recent reports address the effects of the opiate antagonist naloxone and its oral analogue, naltrexone, on the cognitive symptoms of AD. Several of these reports are summarized in Table 6.

Reisberg, Ferris, Anand, Mir, De Leon et al. (1983) reported some encouraging clinical results in an open study with five patients. Clinical and psychometric measures were obtained 10 to 15 minutes after acute administration of naloxone. There was no psychometric deterioration following injection. One patient showed a marked clinical improvement; and two others improved modestly. The best responder continued to respond on two additional challenges. This led to a double-blind, multiple-dose, placebo-controlled trial with seven patients with moderate to severe symptoms of AD (Reisberg, Ferris, Anand, Mir, Geibel et al., 1983). The results of this study were published in a letter to the *New England Journal of Medicine*. The effects of single injections were assessed over a period of 6 weeks. Although three dose levels were used, this variable is not reported to have been included in the analysis. Nevertheless, it is reported that naloxone had a statistically significant beneficial effect on the

TABLE 6

Naloxone and Naltrexone for AD

Investigators, Year, and Reference	Dose, Drug and Route	Design	Number of Subjects
Reisberg, Ferris, Anand, Mir, DeLeon, et al. (1983)	1 mg naloxone, iv acute	Open	5
Reisberg, Ferris, Anand, Mir, Geibel, et al. (1983)	1, 5 or 10 mg naloxone, iv, repeated acute	Double-blind, placebo-controlled	7
Panella and Blass (1984)	1.2 mg naloxone, iv	Double-blind, placebo-controlled crossover	12
Steiger et al. (1985)	10 mg naloxone, iv, once, weekly for 4 weeks	Double-blind, placebo-controlled crossover	16
Pomara et al. (1985)	25, 50, 100 mg oral naltrexone	Double-blind, placebo-controlled repeated measures	9

clinical outcome measure and several psychometric measures. This report prompted several other studies.

The results of more recent studies are generally negative with both naloxone (Panella & Blass, 1984; Steiger, Mendelson, Jenkins, Smith, & Gay, 1985) and naltrexone (Pomara, Roberts, Rhiew, Stanley, & Gershon, 1985).

COMBINATION TREATMENTS

Deficits in complex cognitive functions can result from defects in multiple neurotransmitter systems. Effective treatment may require a combination of drugs or even an individualized "cocktail" approach (Carlsson, 1981).

Lecithin and Physostigmine

Table 7 lists some recent studies of combination treatments for AD. Most of these studies combine an ACh precursor with some other drug. Lecithin with physostigmine is the most studied combination. Peters and Levin (1979) titrated doses of physostigmine based on memory enhancement. Outcome was assessed with measures of long-term storage and long-term retrieval based on a list learning task with selective reminding. Although there were five subjects in the study, only three received the lecithin-physostigmine combination. Of these three, lecithin was associated with a significant decrement in both long-term storage and long-term retrieval for two subjects. The addition of physostigmine to lecithin overcame the deficit associated with lecithin in both of these patients, and the combination treatment was better than baseline for one. For the third patient, combination treatment significantly increased performance over levels from both baseline and lecithin alone. No comparisons are reported between lecithin or combination treatment and the placebo condition. The authors conclude that the data are insufficient to warrant use of lecithin plus physostigmine as a clinical regimen. The results did encourage further study.

Peters and Levin (1982) also tested the combination of lecithin and oral physostigmine. The four subjects who received the combination in this study were responders who volunteered from a larger study of subcutaneous physostigmine. The reported dose of lecithin was 7.2 mg per day, which is 0.2% of the dose reported for the previous study. Subjects received a dose of oral physostigmine that was determined individually through a titration procedure. Outcome testing was done during and after a period of oral administration that lasted 10 to 18 months. Outcome measures were similar to those of a previous study, but also included a measure of consistent long-term recall. Memory performance 1 hour after oral physostigmine was compared to performance on lecithin alone. The authors claim

TABLE 7

Combination Treatments for AD

Investigators, Year, and Reference	Combination	Design	Number of Subjects
Peters and Levin (1979)	Oral lecithin & physostigmine injection		3
Peters and Levin (1982)	Lecithin & oral physostigmine		4
Wettstein (1983)	Lecithin & oral physostigmine	Double-blind, crossover	8
Thal et al. (1983)	Lecithin & oral physostigmine	Double-blind, crossover	6
Kaye et al. (1982)	Lecithin & THA	Open	10
Caine (1980)	Lecithin & pilocarpine	Open	2
Friedman et al. (1981)	Choline & piracetam	Open	10
Pomara, Block, et al. (1984)	Lecithin & piracetam	Double-blind, crossover	9
Smith, Vroulis, et al. (1984)	Lecithin & piracetam	Double-blind, crossover	11
Pomara, Block, Abraham, et al. (1983)	Lecithin & Hydergine®	Double-blind, crossover	9

that the beneficial effects of combination treatment over lecithin alone are maintained for 10 to 18 months.

Wettstein (1983) first tested the combination of oral lecithin and injected physostigmine in an open trial before evaluating oral lecithin and physostigmine over a period of 6 weeks in a double-blind, single crossover protocol. No improvement in recent memory or other psychological functions was demonstrated.

Thal, Fuld, Masur, and Sharpless (1983) also conducted a two-phase study of lecithin and physostigmine in combination. This study was well-designed, and the results are clearly presented. It also included biochemical measures that can be used to explore mechanisms of action. The results support the conclusion that the combination of orally-administered physostigmine and lecithin improves memory and can be tolerated by most patients.

Other Combination Treatments

An evaluation of the combination of lecithin and 1,2,3,4-tetrahydro-5-aminoacridine (THA) appeared to produce some benefit in less impaired patients (Kaye et al., 1982). The combination of lecithin and pilocarpine did not produce a beneficial effect (Caine, 1980). A combination of choline and piracetam yielded small, nonsignificant improvements (Friedman et al., 1981). The combination of lecithin and piracetam did not yield any significantly different effects when this treatment was compared with piracetam alone or placebo (Pomara, Block et al., 1984). Another study that involved treatment with the combination of lecithin plus piracetam for several months provided somewhat more evidence for a beneficial effect (Smith, Vroulis, Johnson, & Morgan, 1984).

Pomara, Block, Abraham, Domino, and Gershon (1983) studied the effects of adding lecithin to Hydergine® with a randomized, double-blind, crossover design using both psychometric measures and subjective ratings. Lecithin did not enhance the response to Hydergine®.

Hydergine® alone is a combination treatment consisting of four dihydrogenated peptide alkaloids that have differential effects on dopamine receptors (Markstein, 1983).

Only a few of the possible treatment combinations have been tried under a few conditions. There is no substantial body of evidence for benefit from any of the specific treatment combinations shown in Table 7. The combination of lecithin and physostigmine shows the most established promise for further clinical investigation.

DISCUSSION—TREATMENTS

There is no documented evidence that any treatment for AD provides consistent and substantial benefit. Many studies cite large, individual differences in response, both beneficial and adverse. A number of published reviews prescribe a standard litany of needs for future research. They call for more double-blind studies, use of placebo controls or crossover designs, more objective or more clinically relevant outcome measures, more attention to dose and temporal relations, longer durations of treatment, and larger numbers of more homogeneous subjects. These comments suggest that no treatment for AD has been adequately evaluated. Wurtman (1982) has warned that at "this stage in the development of effective therapies, a false negative—the conclusion that a drug hadn't worked because it improved only a minority of those tested—would be considerably more detrimental than a false positive" (p. 496). This is as true today as it was in 1982.

Current methods for evaluating treatments would be good for identifying treatments that benefit most of the symptoms most of the time for most AD patients. They are not good for detecting small increments of progress. We could probably recognize a "magic bullet" treatment. Short of this, we need better methods for evaluating the treatments that are available and any new treatments that may emerge.

OVERVIEW OF RESEARCH STRATEGIES

Progress in finding safe and effective treatments for AD will depend on:

1. Basic research on the pathogenesis of the disease.
2. Development of new treatment entities.
3. More efficient and effective procedures for evaluating the outcome of treatment.

Most diseases that have been conquered involve a specific bacteria, virus, malignant cell type, or deficiency. In contrast, AD now appears to be a disorder of a very complex system. Basic research will eventually provide a working knowledge of this system. But in the meantime, clinical researchers should be encouraged.

A Clinically-Oriented Empirical Approach

Hollister pointed out at the first of these conferences that a clinically

oriented empirical approach has yielded most of the effective psychotherapeutic drugs. Neither reserpine nor chlorpromazine was originally planned as an antipsychotic drug (Hollister, 1981). The antipsychotic effects of these drugs and the antidepressant effects of
iproniazid, a monoamine oxidase inhibitor, were first discovered by
astute clinicians when these drugs were used for other indications.

A clinically-oriented empirical approach that makes better use of
information and experience can be one of our most rewarding
research strategies. Much more of the information that results from
clinical practice and research can contribute to a cumulative science
of medicine.

Hollister (1981) went on to point out that psychopharmacology
often uses a "bootstrap" method in which drugs are used not only
as treatments, but also as tools to investigate the pathogenesis of
the disorders they treat. Opportunities abound in both clinical practice
and research to use the "bootstrap" method for studying the pathogenesis of AD. As recently as 1985, Reisberg and Ferris pointed out
that "apparently only one study has been published at the present
time investigating the utility of psychopharmacologic agents in the
treatment of the secondary behavioral symptoms of specifically
diagnosed AD patients" (p. 101). This study was reported by Barnes,
Veith, Okimoto, Raskind, and Gumbrecht (1982). Yet, antipsychotics
are widely prescribed to demented patients (Helms, 1985). Information that results from these familiar treatments could be used to
probe to pathogenesis and defects that underlie AD.

Clinical Trials and the Elderly

Demented elderly have been systematically excluded from most
clinical trials with marketed drugs because these people confound
our methods of research. Change in health that occurs between
baseline and endpoint assessments in an elderly sample could be
attributed to many things besides treatment, especially if response
is not fast and dramatic. Standard suggestions for detecting a treatment effect under these conditions are to use larger samples, more
homogeneous subjects, or both. Homogeneous subjects are not
feasible when the things that make people different have accumulated over 6, 7, or more decades and include dementia, and when
the outcome of interest includes sensitive and advanced cognitive
and behavioral functions. Efforts to select homogeneous samples

can even be misdirected because it is difficult to generalize the results of research that depends on a degree of diagnostic accuracy and patient uniformity that is seldom achieved in clinical practice (Sackett & Gent, 1979).

Outcome assessment is the central methodologic problem that has prevented us from making better use of the information that results from clinical practice and has discouraged us from including the elderly in clinical trials. Outcome assessment is a measurement task that can be addressed more effectively. Progress in measuring treatment outcome will enable us to deal more effectively with health problems in the elderly.

OUTCOME ASSESSMENT

Outcome assessment is still the central problem in evaluating treatments for AD, but this problem is being solved.

Two quantitative strategies can be used to assess treatment outcome in clinical research. One is to use the dependent variable, a measure of health, directly as the outcome measure. The book *Assessment in Geriatric Psychopharmacology* (Crook, Ferris, & Bartus, 1983) provides many examples of dependent variables that can be used for evaluating the effects of treatment on AD symptoms. Investigators using a dependent variable as an outcome measure face a very difficult problem in selecting which variable to use. The second strategy is to use a measure of the relation between treatment and health as an outcome measure.

Use of a Dependent Variable as an Outcome Measure

Dependent variables can be specific or comprehensive, subjective or objective. A specific dependent variable uses one dimension of health or function to represent a fundamental aspect or effect of the disease process. This approach is statistically valid in that it provides one measure as required for testing the primary hypothesis. A unidimensional representative outcome measure in commonly used in other fields of medicine, for example, when an antihypertensive is evaluated by measuring systolic blood pressure. An example of a similarly objective and specific measure that has been used to help evaluate AD treatments would be one of the scores obtained from the Buschke Selective Reminding Task (Buschke & Fuld, 1974). No one variable of this sort is used as the primary outcome measure to evaluate treatments for AD because no one dimension of cognition or behavior adequately represents all symptoms of AD.

Comprehensive coverage of AD symptoms can be achieved by using the physician's judgment about global therapeutic effect as an outcome measure. Lehmann (1984) is a strong advocate of this approach, even though these judgments are subjective and very difficult to make because health fluctuates extensively in elderly people who may receive various treatments for multiple disorders, because the AD process has a long and progressive course that affects many aspects of health, and because most AD patients are seldom seen by a physician.

The ADAS by Rosen et al. (1984) represents an approach that is both comprehensive and objective. The version that was used in the recently reported oral physostigmine study "was composed of a total of 40 items and was designed to measure all the symptoms characteristic of patients with Alzheimer's disease" (Mohs et al., 1985, p. 29). Such a scale provides one score for each patient that can be used to test the primary hypothesis. One disadvantage of this rating scale is that it treats diverse items—word recall, ideational praxis, tearfulness, delusions, pacing, tremors—as if they contribute to one or two unitary dimensions of health and function. Conglomerate rating scales that lump symptoms and dimensions sacrifice our ability to distinguish treatments that act through, for example, behavioral activation from those that affect cognitive ability. Information about specific symptoms and health dimensions is needed to develop individualized and rational treatment plans.

Use of the Measured Relation Between Treatment and Health as an Outcome Measure

A second strategy for evaluating outcome in clinical research is to measure the relation between treatment and health *over time* and to use this as an outcome measure. Measurement of this relation builds on all that we know about measuring dependent or health variables. But the dependent variable is not used as the outcome measure. The new outcome measure quantifies the relation between treatment and health over time for each patient. The observed value of this measure is called an effect score. It also could be called a benefit score for which negative values would indicate risk.

The existence of a measure of effect is implied whenever a phychiatrist balances the beneficial antidepressant effects of a drug such as imipramine against its adverse anticholinergic effects. No one assumes that depressed mood and dry mouth form a meaningful unitary dimension. Yet, the risks and benefits of drug are balanced against each other as if they were weights on an old-fashioned scale. Weight is an attribute and effect is a relation, but both can be measured.

The most common procedures for balancing benefit and risk are highly subjective. An objective, operationally defined measure of the relation between treatment and health over time has been developed at Lafayette Clinic. Treatment effects are measured by computation from data for the independent and dependent variables (Bagne, 1985; Bagne & Pomara, 1985).

SOME APPROACHES TO FUTURE CLINICAL RESEARCH

This review of treatment and research strategies suggests a number of things that can be done to make clinical research on AD more productive and cost-efficient. These suggestions will be grouped under four headings: Treatment evaluation, diagnosis, longitudinal studies, and survival studies.

Treatment Evaluation

Treatment evaluation can be more definitive and provide more information about mechanisms of action. Achievement of these objectives depends on the types of data that are collected and the way they are analyzed.

Data should be collected simultaneously on three classes of dependent variables whenever possible. The three classes and their uses are:

1. Variables that measure how well patients function in daily life can be used for evaluating practical, clinical effects. These are exemplified by items on the Sandoz Clinical Adjustment Geriatric Scale (SCAG) (Loew & Weil, 1982). The clinical variables should adequately represent the spectrum of conditions of clinical interest

and would be used to determine whether patients' lives are visibly improved. These variables often can be evaluated from several perspectives — patient self-report in early cases, and the ratings of physicians, family members, and other care givers.
2. Variables that measure basic dimensions of behavior and cognition can be used, for example, to differentiate recall and recognition performance or the effects of behavioral arousal from cognitive ability. These variables are measured with objective psychometric procedures and would serve primarily as dependent variables while exploring mechanisms of action.
3. Variables that measure neuroendocrine and brain activity levels can serve as either independent or dependent variables while exploring mechanisms of action.

All variables would be measured as many times as possible during a period of variable treatment. This maximizes the amount of information for measuring the relation between treatment and health over time. When resources are limited for assessing clinical variables, preference usually would be given to a larger number of simple assessments. Most variables for evaluating clinical response are really quite accessible to raters who have frequent contact with patients because these variables measure how well patients function in the activities of daily living.

Diagnosis

A major research thrust during the next decade is likely to be in the area of developing diagnostic classifications that predict response to treatment. This research will be directed not only at differentiating AD individuals from persons without the disease, but also subtypes of AD patients (Pomara, Brinkman, et al., 1983).

Tomlinson, Blessed, and Roth's findings that differentiated AD from multi-infarct dementia on the basis of pathological changes in the brain at autopsy are now classic (Tomlinson, Blessed, & Roth, 1970). But information about neuritic plaques and neurofibrillary tangles generally is not available before treatment, and changes in these lesions are not used to monitor response to treatment.

Another approach to diagnosis is to measure entities such as endogenous substances in blood, CSF, and other biological materials. These substances generally would be selected to reflect possible neurochemical abnormalities. This strategy can be expected to make important gains during the coming years. A conceptually similar approach is to measure performance on neuropsychological tests at a single point in time (Eslinger, Damasio, Benton, & Allen, 1985).

Still another approach for predicting treatment response is to measure health and function over time in response to test conditions. This approach can be particularly informative for the diagnosis of complex, multifaceted neurologic and psychiatric disorders. It has gained prominence in psychiatry with explorations of the dexamethasone suppression test. This test can be considered an extension of the principle of using a test dose or treatment trial to gain information that can be used for diagnostic purposes. Work represented by Yamaguchi, Meyer, Yamamoto, Sakai, and Shaw (1980) on the differential response of AD and multi-infarct dementia patients to a vasodilator stimulus, carbon dioxide, has had a substantial effect on the development of treatment strategies for dementia. All these approaches measure response to some sort of probe.

The review of treatments indicated that most clinical trials seem to produce a few responders. It may be premature to agree with the conclusion that "predicting improvement in individual patients is impossible" (Hollister & Yesavage, 1984, p. 896) until we measure the relation between treatment and health over time for individual patients and correlate these measures with descriptors of the patients and their conditions. This approach to the development of diagnostic categories designed to predict response to treatment would use the standard statistical procedures of empirical classification.

Progress in diagnosis can be highly rewarding. Even if only a small percentage of patients respond to a given treatment and we can identify those patients, thousands of people with AD would be better off.

Longitudinal Studies

The nervous system of a healthy person can be viewed as an exquisite control system. The parts of this system include neurons, neurotransmitters, receptors, hormones, neuropeptides, and enzymes. This system is severely disrupted in AD. Correlational studies involving various lesions, functions, and endogenous substances have provided some of our most revealing insights into the pathogenesis of AD. Correlational studies are based on assessments made at essentially one point in time for each subject. The results of correlational studies can be used to make predictions based on group membership. Longitudinal studies can provide these results plus information about relations over time. Temporal information from longitudinal studies can help elucidate causality and could provide new insights into the pathogenesis and treatment of AD.

At this point in history we can measure thousands of substances in biological materials. These measures have been used productively in correlational studies and to monitor deviations from normal levels during treatment. The keys to learning more from these measures are to use longitudinal study designs and to measure the relations among variables over time for individuals. These relations can be measured by computation from repeated measures data (see section on outcome assessment). Now that we are learning how to measure these relations, developments in functional pathology and the study of systems can begin catching up with our ability to measure entities.

Survival Studies

Longitudinal studies should also address survival. AD is a chronic disease. As with cancer, it can be fatal. Survival has been a primary outcome measure in evaluating cancer treatments. Small changes in survival have helped identify clinically significant advances in treatment. Patients with AD do not die of memory loss. But if treatment prolongs survival and the length of the survival interval is correlated with a beneficial effect of treatment on cognition and behavior, it could be presumed that treatment is affecting an important pathophysiologic aspect of the disease process. Such a longitudinal study would combine use of life-table methods for survival analysis (Fleiss, Dunner, Stallone, & Fieve, 1976) with procedures for measuring the relation between treatment and health over time.

Many investigators already have advocated studies of treatments that may delay progression of AD. These treatments include Hydergine® and cholinergic precursors.

SOME TOPICS FOR FUTURE CLINICAL RESEARCH

Limitations of the Cholinergic Hypothesis and Potential Problems

Most of the therapeutic strategies utilized in the treatment of memory loss in AD have been directed at a correction of the cholinergic hypofunction believed to play a critical role in the pathophysiology of this disease.

As previously noted, clinical trials with either indirect or direct acting muscarinic agonists (e.g., physostigmine, THA, arecoline, and RS-86) have produced only mildly beneficial effects on some of the psychometric tests used to assess their effects. By and large, these changes have lacked a clinical impact.

It has been said that the poor clinical impact with cholinergic agents might be secondary to the relatively short duration of the clinical trials. Administration of these compounds for longer periods, several months to years, could conceivably result in a better clinical outcome. While this notion needs to be tested, a word of caution is in order. There are numerous experiments in which down regulation of muscarinic receptors or a hyporesponsivity of these receptors has been produced by these manipulations (Ben-Barak, Gazit, Silman, & Dudai, 1981; Pomara, Block, Demetriou, et al., 1983). Thus, these approaches could very well lead to a further compromise in cholinergic transmission.

Another explanation that has been offered for the relatively poor clinical outcome with cholinergic agonists is that these agents may not penetrate the CNS, and consequently, the enhancement of cholinergic transmission, the mechanism by which these agents are to improve memory, might not always be achieved. Thus, in experiments by Mohs et al. (1985), only five of the seven patients who experienced an improvement in AD symptoms during the replication phase had higher cortisol levels after treatment with physostigmine. Increased plasma cortisol was considered to be a sign of central cholinergic activation. But it should be emphasized that even for those patients who benefited from physostigmine, the overall clinical picture of dementia remained unchanged. Thus, it appears that simply increasing cholinergic transmission alone might not be sufficient to have a major clinical impact on this disorder. This is further illustrated by the recent experiments by Harbaugh and colleagues in which the intracranial infusion of bethanehcol chloride, a direct muscarinic agonist, was accompanied by only slight decreases in confusion, increased attention and initiative (Harbaugh et al., 1984). While these results are certainly encouraging and in need of further investigation, they do point out the striking contrast between the dramatic reversal of the scopolamine-induced memory deficits by physostigmine and the limited results of these agents to do the same in AD. These findings raise the possibility of a postsynaptic dysfunction in these patients (Pomara & Stanley, 1986).

The inadequacy of therapeutic strategies solely directed at the cholinergic transmitter system is further illustrated by recent findings that the neuropathology in AD cannot be linked exclusively to cortical cholinergic elements, but may also involve declines in cortical somatostatin and noradrenaline content (Morrison, Rogers, Scherr, Benoit, & Bloom, 1985; Roberts, Crow, & Polak, 1985).

The most significant and therapeutically relevant aspect of these findings is that the reductions in noncholinergic elements in the cortex as well as the degeneration of locus coeruleus neurons that have been observed in AD, cannot simply be ascribed to a primary subcortical degeneration of cholinergic cell bodies in the basal nucleus of Meynert. In rats, lesions in the basal nucleus of Meynert do lead to cholinergic deficits as found in AD, but cortical somatostatin levels remain unchanged. Conversely, lesions of the cortex (which produce somatostatin losses along with losses of other intrinsic neurotransmitter systems in both rats and humans) result in retrograde degeneration of cholinergic cells in the nucleus basalis of Meynert similar to that seen in AD (Probst, Basler, Bron, & Ulrich, 1983; Sofroiew, Pearson, Eckenstein, Cuello, & Powell, 1983).

As recently emphasized by Roberts, Crow, and Polak (1985), these reports and the correlation of cortical pathology (e.g., plaques and tangles), with dementia scores may imply that the cortex, particularly the temporal cortex, may be the main focus of the disease process. If that is the case, then both the cholinergic and noncholinergic deficits may be secondary events to the primary cortical atrophy. Thus, simply attempting to enhance cholinergic transmission would be necessary but not sufficient to reverse the cognitive impairment seen in these patients. Indeed, as emphasized by Dr. Davis and his group, Alzheimer's patients having the best response to physostigmine remained demented, nevertheless.

Therefore, if we accept the converging data that the cortex may be the primary site of pathology in this disorder, it is quite probable that therapeutic strategies directed at delaying or arresting neuronal damage or improving some aspect of neuronal metabolism might be more useful than attempts at improving transmission of isolated neuronal systems.

In this regard, it is worth noting that Hydergine®, a drug that is purported to improve intraneuronal metabolism, is the only drug that has been associated with the greatest, albeit still small, clinical impact in patients with AD.

Prevention and Prophylaxis

Clearly, other agents having a similar profile, such as piracetam and its analogues, need to be tested for longer periods and possibly quite early, perhaps prophylactically, in the population at greater risk of developing a dementia (e.g., the very old and those with a strong family history of AD).

With regard to therapeutic interventions in individuals with advanced dementia, it is clear the cholinergic manipulations alone will not be enough. In this instance, it may prove useful to explore the possibility that other neurotransmitter systems may contribute to the pathophysiology of this disorder.

Noncholinergic Mechanisms of Pathogenesis

There is evidence from our laboratory and others, that the administration of pharmacological agents, such as diazepam, that are believed to increase gamma-aminobutyric acid (GABA)-ergic transmission, can produce memory deficits in normals not qualitatively dissimilar from those found in early AD. As can be seen in Table 8, the administration of a single 10 mg dose of diazepam to normal elderly resulted in memory impairments, as measured by the Buschke task, that have a striking qualitative resemblance to those observed in Alzheimer's patients.

In view of the evidence that diazepam-induced memory impairments may involve GABA-ergic mechanisms, together with the poor therapeutic outcomes generally observed in treating Alzheimer's patients with cholinergic agents, Pomara and colleagues have raised the possibility that a relative increase in GABA-ergic activity that results from extensive reductions in cholinergic and other neurotransmitter function, could be a contributory factor in AD (Pomara, Stanley et

TABLE 8

Comparison of Effects of Diazepam and Dementia

Measure	Effect of Dementia (%)	Effect of 10 mg Diazepam (%)
Consistent long-term retrieval	-94	-55
Consistent long-term storage ratio	-85	-38
Long-term retrieval	-71	-39
Long-term storage	-62	-34
Total recall	-46	-21
Long-term retrieval ratio	-24	-9
Short-term retrieval	+32	+36

Note: Data from Block, DeVoe, Stanley, B., Stanley, M., and Pomara (1985).

al., 1984). Thus, pharmacological agents that could safely decrease central GABA-ergic tone without precipitating convulsions might be worthy of an investigation, particularly in Alzheimer's patients with advanced dementia. The benzodiazepine antagonist (Ro 15-1788) appears a good candidate. This agent has been found to reverse hepatic coma, a condition in which the inhibitory GABA neurotransmitter system is believed to play an important role in the pathogenesis (Bansky et al., 1985; Scollo-Lavizzari & Steinmann, 1985).

It should be noted in this regard that anticholinergic agents have long been used for the treatment of parkinsonism, a disorder which, at least in its early stage, is associated with a selective degeneration of striatal dopaminergic neurons.

Another observation that has been made in AD that should be considered as a possible contributory factor in the memory impairment observed in these patients is the increasing evidence of hypercortisolemia and abnormal dexamethasone suppression test results. Reports by Raskind, Peskind, Rivard, Veith, and Barnes (1982) and Pomara, Oxenkrug et al. (1984) have demonstrated a positive correlation between severity of dementia and postdexamethasone cortisol levels.

To the extent that adrenocortical overactivation in animals has been shown to disrupt the hippocampus (Dekosky, Scheff, & Cotman, 1984; Landfield, Baskin, & Pitler, 1981; Landfield, Waymire, & Lynch, 1978; Sapolsky, Krey, & McEwen, 1983), a brain structure involved in memory, a similar possibility should be considered in AD patients with abnormally high levels of cortisol.

It is quite possible that in these patients a reduction in the hypothalamic-pituitary activity or simply blocking central glucocorticoid receptors might result in an improvement or a slowing down of the deterioration.

SUMMARY

We have reviewed the literature about treatments for AD. That literature is data about the state of our science.

No treatment substantially improves the daily life of most people with AD. Our heritage from decades of use and research with Hydergine® is primarily a series of unanswered questions.

Questions of substance and method are intimately interrelated. "What do we know?" and "How do we know?" are analogous to the sides of a coin. Why don't we know more? Again we must turn to our methods. Much of the unsatisfactory state of knowledge about AD can be traced to inadequate methods for measuring the benefits and risks of treatment and the functional integrity of the body's control systems. New developments emerging in this area can improve the productivity of our research and care for the elderly (Bagne, 1985; Bagne & Pomara, 1985).

Another factor that contributes to the unsatisfactory state of our knowledge is that AD is only just beginning to receive research support in proportion to its contribution to the burden of human suffering. New approaches to AD research wait to be funded and implemented. These include the testing of methods for evaluating the effects of both new and old treatments for groups of patients and for monitoring the responses of individual patients. Diagnostic procedures and classifications can be developed specifically for predicting response to treatment. Longitudinal studies can provide an understanding of functional pathology based on an analysis of the behavior of ordered and disordered systems of individual people. Survival studies can help reveal treatments that modify basic pathophysiological processes in AD.

The cholinergic hypothesis has guided much productive AD research but appears to have important limitations (Pomara & Stanley, 1986a, 1986b). Cholinergic agents may down-regulate muscarinic receptors. The neuropathology of AD is not limited to cholinergic elements. The cortex could be the primary focus of the AD process with retrograde degeneraion of cholinergic cells. One implication of these considerations is that treatment which delays neuronal damage and improves neuronal metabolism may help delay or prevent the most severe manifestations of AD. Prevention needs to be considered more seriously when cure may not be possible.

Patients with advanced dementia may benefit from treatments that decrease central GABA-ergic tone.

We can anticipate a period of substantial progress in relieving the human suffering wrought by AD. This will occur as resources are made available for research, as new treatment entities are developed, and as more efficient and powerful methods of research are applied to old and new hypotheses about the etiology and treatment of AD.

REFERENCES

Abuzzahab, F.S., Merwin, G.E., Zimmerman, R.L., & Sherman, M.C. (1978). A double-blind investigation of piracetam (Nootropil) versus placebo in the memory of geriatric inpatients. *Psychopharmacology Bulletin, 14,* 23-25.

Affleck, D.C., Treptow, K.R., & Herrick, H.D. (1961). The effects of isoxsuprine hydrochloride (Vasodilan) on chronic cerebral arteriosclerosis. *Journal of Nervous and Mental Disease, 132,* 335-338.

Agnoli, A., Martucci, N., Manna, V., Conti, L., & Fioravanti, M. (1983). Effect of cholinergic and anticholinergic drugs on short-term memory in Alzheimer's dementia: A neuropsychological and computerized electroencephalographic study. *Clinical Neuropharmacology, 6,* 311-323.

Alderdice, M.T. (1979). Physostigmine, but not neostigmine, inhibits acetylcholine release. *Brain Research, 178,* 596-599.

Altman, H., Mehta, D., Evenson, R.C., & Sletten, I.W. (1973). Behavioral effects of drug therapy on psychogeriatric inpatients. II. Multivitamin supplement. *Journal of the American Geriatrics Society, 21,* 249-252.

Ashford, J.W., Soldinger, S., Schaeffer, J., Cochran, L., & Jarvik,

L. (1981). Physostigmine and its effect on six patients with dementia. *American Journal of Psychiatry, 138,* 829-830.

Bagne, C.A. (1985). *A measure of treatment effect based on repeated assessments of multiple outcomes: Computational procedures.* (Manuscript submitted for publication.)

Bagne, C.A., & Pomara, N. (1985). *A measure of treatment effect based on repeated assessments of multiple outcomes: A demonstration.* (Manuscript submitted for publication.)

Bansky, G., Meier, P.J., Ziegler, W.H., Walser, H., Schmid, M., & Huber, M. (1985, June). Reversal of hepatic coma by benzodiazepine antagonist (Ro 15-1788) [Letter to the editor]. *Lancet, 1,* 1324-1325.

Barnes, R., Veith, R., Okimoto, J., Raskind, M., & Gumbrecht, G. (1982). Efficacy of antipsychotic medications in behaviorally disturbed dementia patients. *American Journal of Psychiatry, 139,* 1170-1174.

Bartus, R.T., Dean, R.L., Beer, B., & Lippa, A.S. (1982). The cholinergic hypothesis of geriatric memory dysfunction. *Science, 217,* 408-417.

Ben-Barak, J., Gazit, H., Silman, I., & Dudai, Y. (1981). In vivo modulation of the number of muscarinic receptors in rat by cholinergic ligands. *European Journal of Pharmacology, 74,* 73-81.

Bergman, I., Brane, G., Gottfries, C.G., Jostell, K.-G., Karlsson, I., & Svennerholm, L. (1983). Alaproclate: A pharmacokinetic and biochemical study in patients with dementia of Alzheimer type. *Psychopharmacology, 80,* 279-283.

Bernard, A., & Goffart, J.M. (1968). A double-blind cross-over clinical evaluation of cinnarizine. *Clinical Trials Journal, 5,* 945-948.

Block, R.I., DeVoe, M., Stanley, B., Stanley, M., & Pomara, N. (1985). Memory performance in individuals with primary degenerative dementia: Its similarity to diazepam-induced impairments. *Experimental Aging Research, 11,* 151-155.

Branconnier, R.J. (1983). The efficacy of the cerebral metabolic enhancers in the treatment of senile dementia. *Psychopharmacology Bulletin, 19,* 212-219.

Branconnier, R.J., & Cole, J.O. (1977a). Effects of chronic papaverine administration on mild senile organic brain syndrome. *Journal of the American Geriatrics Society, 25,* 458-462.

Branconnier, R.J., & Cole, J.O. (1977b). A memory assessment technique for use in geriatric psychopharmacology: Drug efficacy trial with naftidrofuryl. *Journal of the American Geriatrics Society, 25,* 186-188.

Branconnier, R.J., Cole, J.O., Dessain, E.C., Spera, K.F., Ghazvinian, S., & DeVitt, D. (1983). The therapeutic efficacy of pramiracetam in Alzheimer's disease: Preliminary observations. *Psychopharmacology Bulletin, 19,* 726-730.

Buschke, H., & Fuld, P.A. (1974). Evaluating storage, retention, and retrieval in disordered memory and learning. *Neurology, 24,* 1019-1025.

Caine, E.D. (1980). Cholinomimetic treatment fails to improve memory disorders [Letter to the editor]. *New England Journal of Medicine, 303,* 585-586.

Caltagirone, C., Albanese, A., Gainotti, G., & Masullo, C. (1983). Acute administration of individual optimal dose of physostigmine fails to improve mnesic performances in Alzheimer's presenile dementia. *International Journal of Neuroscience, 18,* 143-148.

Caltagirone, C., Gainotti, G., & Masullo, C. (1982). Oral administration of chronic physostigmine does not improve cognitive or mnesic performances in Alzheimer's presenile dementia. *International Journal of Neuroscience, 16,* 247-249.

Capote, B., & Parikh, N. (1978). Cyclandelate in the treatment of senility: A controlled study. *Journal of the American Geriatrics Society, 26,* 360-362.

Carlsson, A. (1981). Aging and brain neurotransmitters. In T. Crook & S. Gershon (Eds.), *Strageties for the development of an effective treatment for senile dementia* (pp. 93-104). New Canaan, CT: Mark Powley Associates, Inc.

Christie, J.E., Shering, A., Ferguson, J., & Glen, A.I.M. (1981). Physostigmine and areocoline: Effects of intravenous infusions in Alzheimer presenile dementia. *British Journal of Psychiatry, 138,* 46-50.

Cole, J.O., Branconnier, R., Salomon, M., & Dessain, E. (1983). Tricylcic use in the cognitively impaired elderly. *Journal of Clinical Psychiatry, 44* (9, Pt.2), 14-19.

Cook, P., & James, I. (1981). Cerebral vasodilators. *New England Journal of Medicine, 305,* 1508-1513.

Cooper, A.J., & Magnus, R.V. (1980). A placebo-controlled study of pyritinol ('Encephabol') in dementia. *Pharmacotherapeutica, 2,* 317-322.

Corrodi, H., Fuxe, K., Hokfelt, T., Lidbrink, P., & Ungerstedt, U. (1973). Effect of ergot drugs on central catecholamine neurons: Evidence for a stimulation of central dopamine neurons. *Journal of Pharmacy and Pharmacology, 25,* 409-412.

Crook, T. (1979). Central-nervous-system stimulants: Appraisal of use in geropsychiatric patients. *Journal of the American Geriatrics Society, 27,* 476-477.

Crook, T. (1984). *Clinical trials in Alzheimer's disease.* Paper presented at the New York Academy of Sciences, New York.

Crook, T., Ferris, S., & Bartus, R. (Eds.). (1983). *Assessment in geriatric psychopharmacology.* New Canaan, CT: Mark Powley Associates.

Crook, T., Ferris, S., Sathananthan, G., Raskin, A., & Gershon, S. (1977). The effect of methylphenidate on test performance in the cognitively impaired aged. *Psychopharmacology, 52,* 251-255.

Czerwinski, A.W., Clark, M.L., Serafetinides, E.A., Perrier, C., & Huber, W. (1974). Safety and efficacy of zinc sulfate in geriatric patients. *Clinical Pharmacology and Therapeutics, 15,* 436-441.

Dalderup, L.M., van Haard, W.B., Keller, G.H.M., Dalmeier, J.F., Frijda, N.H., & Elshout, J.J. (1970). An attempt to change memory and serum composition in old people by a daily supplement of dried baker's yeast. *Journal of Gerontology, 25,* 320-324.

Dastur, D.K. (1985). Cerebral blood flow and metabolism in normal human aging, pathological aging, and senile dementia. *Journal of Cerebral Blood Flow and Metabolism, 5,* 1-9.

Davis, K.L., Hollister, L.E., Overall, J., Johnson, A., & Train, K. (1976). Physostigmine: Effects on cognition and affect in normal subjects. *Psychopharmacology, 51,* 23-27.

Davis, K.L., & Mohs, R.C. (1982). Enhancement of memory processes in Alzheimer's disease with multiple-dose intravenous physostigmine. *American Journal of Psychiatry, 139,* 1421-1424.

Davis, K.L., Mohs, R.C., Tinklenberg, J.R., Pfefferbaum, A., Hollister, L.E., & Kopell, B.S. (1978). Physostigmine: Improvement of long-term memory processes in normal humans. *Science, 201,* 272-274.

Dekosky, S.T., Scheff, S.W., & Cotman, C.W. (1984). Elevated corticosterone levels. A possible cause of reduced axon sprouting in aged animals. *Neuroendocrinology, 38,* 33-38.

Delwaide, P.J., Devoitille, J.M., & Ylieff, M. (1980). Acute effect of drugs upon memory of patients with senile dementia. *Acta Psychiatrica Belgica, 80,* 748-754.

Drachman, D.A., & Glosser, G. (1981). Pharmacologic strategies in aging and dementia: The cholinergic hypothesis. In T. Crook & S. Gershon (Eds.), *Strategies for the development of an effective treatment for senile dementia* (pp. 35-51). New Canaan, CT: Mark Powley Associates, Inc.

Drachman, D.A., & Sahakian, B.J. (1980). Memory and cognitive function in the elderly: A preliminary trial of physostigmine. *Archives of Neurology, 37,* 674-675.

Durso, R., Fedio, P., Brouwers, P., Cox, C., Martin, A.J., Ruggieri, S.A., Tamminga, C.A., & Chase, T.N. (1982). Lysine vasopressin in Alzheimer disease. *Neurology, 32,* 674-677.

Eslinger, P.J., Damasio, A.R., Benton, A.L., & Allen, M.V. (1985). Neuropsychologic detection of abnormal mental decline in older persons. *Journal of the American Medical Association, 253,* 670-674.

Etienne, P. (1983). Treatment of Alzheimer's disease with lecithin. In B. Reisberg (Ed.), *Alzheimer's disease* (pp. 353-354). New York: Free Press.

Etienne, P., Dastoor, D., Gauthier, S., Ludwick, R., & Collier, B. (1981). Alzheimer disease: Lack of effect of lecithin treatment for 3 months. *Neurology, 31,* 1552-1554.

Ferris, S.H. (1983). Neuropeptides in the treatment of Alzheimer's disease. In B. Reisberg (Ed.), *Alzheimer's disease* (pp. 369-373). New York: Free Press.

Ferris, S.H., Sathananthan, G., Gershon, S., Clark, C., & Moshinsky, J. (1976). Cognitive effects of ACTH 4-10 in the elderly. *Pharmacology, Biochemistry and Behavior, 5* (Suppl. 1), 73-78.

Fisman, M., Mersky, H., & Helmes, E. (1981). Double-blind trial of 2-dimethylaminoethanol in Alzheimer's disease. *American Journal of Psychiatry, 138,* 970-972.

Fleiss, J.L., Dunner, D.L., Stallone, F., & Fieve, R.R. (1976). The life table: A method for analyzing longitudinal studies. *Archives of General Psychiatry, 33,* 107-112.

Food and Drug Administration (1979). Papaverine-ethaverine studies. *FDA Drug Bulletin, 9,* 26.

Fovall, P., Dysken, M.W., & Davis, J.M. (1983). Treatment of Alzheimer's disease with choline salts. In B. Reisberg (Ed.), *Alzheimer's disease* (pp. 346-352). New York: Free Press.

Friedman, E., Sherman, K.A., Ferris, S.H., Reisberg, B., Bartus, R.T., & Schneck, M.K. (1981). Clinical response to choline plus piracetam in senile dementia: Relation to red-cell choline levels [Letter to the editor]. *New England Journal of Medicine, 304,* 1490-1491.

Gedye, J.L., Exton-Smith, A.N., & Wedgewood, J.A. (1972). A method for measuring mental performance in the elderly and its use in a pilot clinical trial of meclofenoxate in organic dementia. *Age/ Ageing, 1,* 74-80.

Geraud, J., Bes, A., Rascol, A., Delpha, M., & Marc-Vergnes, J.P. (1963). Measurement of cerebral blood flow using krypton 85: Some physiopathological and clinical applications. *Revue Neurologique, 108,* 542-557.

Giurgea, C. (1976). Piracetam: Nootropic pharmacology of neurointegrative activity. *Current Developments in Psychopharmacology, 3,* 221-273.

Gottstein, U. (1965). Pharmacological studies of total cerebral blood flow in man with comments on the possibility of improving regional blood flow by drugs. *Acta Neurologica Scandinavica, 41* (Suppl. 14), 136-141.

Greenwald, B.S., & Davis, K.L. (1983). Experimental pharmacology of Alzheimer disease. In R. Mayeux & W.G. Rosen (Eds.), *The dementias* (pp. 87-102). New York: W.G. Rosen.

Harbaugh, R.E., Roberts, D.W., Coombs, D.W., Saunders, R.L., & Reeder, T.M. (1984). Preliminary report: Intracranial cholinergic drug infusion in patients with Alzheimer's disease. *Neurosurgery, 15,* 514-518.

Harwart, D. (1979). The treatment of chronic cerebrovascular insufficiency. A double-blind study with pentoxifylline ('Trental' 400). *Current Medical Research and Opinion, 6,* 73-84.

Helms, P.M. (1985). Efficacy of antipsychotics in the treatment of the behavioral complications of dementia: A review of the literature. *Journal of the American Geriatrics Society, 33,* 206-209.

Hollister, L.E. (1981). An overview of strategies for the development of an effective treatment for senile dementia. In T. Crook & S. Gershon (Eds.), *Strategies for the development of an effective treatment for senile dementia* (pp. 19-32). New Canaan, CT: Mark Powley Associates.

Hollister, L.E. (1984). Drug treatment of memory defects in the elderly. *Psychosomatics, 25* (Suppl), 23-26.

Hollister, L.E., & Yesavage, J. (1984). Ergoloid mesylates for senile dementias: Unanswered questions. *Annals of Internal Medicine, 100,* 894-898.

Hughes, J.R., Williams, J.G., & Currier, R.D. (1976). An ergot alkaloid preparation (Hydergine®) in the treatment of dementia: Critical review of the clinical literature. *Journal of the American Geriatrics Society, 24,* 490-497.

Itil, T.M., Menon, G.N., Bozak, M., & Songar, A. (1982). The effects of oxiracetam (ISF 2522) in patients with organic brain syndrome (a double-blind controlled study with piracetam). *Drug Development Research, 2,* 447-461.

Jellinger, K., Flament, H., Riederer, P., Schmid, H., & Ambrozi, L. (1980). Levodopa in the treatment of (pre) senile dementia. *Mechanisms of Ageing and Development, 14,* 253-264.

Jolles, J. (1983). Vasopressin-like peptides and the treatment of memory disorders in man. *Progress in Brain Research, 60,* 169-182.

Jotkowitz, S. (1983). Lack of clinical efficacy of chronic oral physostigmine in Alzheimer's disease. *Annals of Neurology, 14,* 690-691.

Kaye, W.H., Sitaram, N., Weingartner, H., Ebert, M.H., Smallberg, S., & Gillin, J.C. (1982). Modest facilitation of memory in dementia with combined lecithin and anticholinesterase treatment. *Biological Psychiatry, 17,* 275-280.

Kral, V.A., Solyom, L., Enesco, H., & Ledwidge, B. (1970). Relationship of vitamin B12 and folic acid to memory function. *Biological Psychiatry, 2,* 19-26.

Kristensen, V., Olsen, M., & Theilgaard, A. (1977). Levodopa treatment of presenile dementia. *Acta Psychiatrica Scandinavica, 55,* 41-51.

LaBrecque, D.C., & Goldberg, R.I. (1967). A double-blind study of pentylenetetrazol combined with niacin in senile patients. *Current Therapeutic Research, 9,* 611-617.

Landfield, P.W., Baskin, R.K., & Pitler, T.A. (1981). Brain aging correlates: Retardation by hormonal-pharmacological treatments. *Science, 214,* 581-584.

Landfield, P.W., Waymire, J.C., & Lynch, G. (1978). Hippocampal aging and adrenocorticoids: Quantitative correlations. *Science, 202,* 1098-1102.

Lehmann, E. (1984). Practicable and valid approach to evaluate the efficacy of nootropic drugs by means of rating scales. *Pharmaco-psychiatry, 17,* 71-75.

Loew, D.M., Vigouret, J.M., & Jaton, A.L. (1976). Neuropharmacological investigations with two ergot alkaloids, hydergine and bromocriptine. *Postgraduate Medical Journal, 52*(Suppl. 1), 40-46.

Loew, D.M., Vigouret, J., & Jaton, A. (1980). Neuropharmacology of bromocriptine and dihydroergotoxine (Hydergine®). In M. Goldstein, D. Calne, A. Lieberman, & M. Thorner (Eds.), *Ergot compounds and brain function: Neuroendocrine and neuropsychiatric aspects* (pp. 63-74). New York: Raven Press.

Loew, D.M., & Weil, C. (1982). Hydergine® in senile mental impairment. *Gerontology, 28,* 54-74.

Markstein, R. (1983). Dopamine receptor profile of co-dergocrine (Hydergine®) and its components. *European Journal of Pharmacology, 86,* 145-155.

Martin, J.C., Ballinger, B.R., Cockram, L.L., McPherson, F.M., Pigache, R.M., & Tregaskis, D. (1983). Effect of a synthetic peptide, ORG 2766, on inpatients with severe senile dementia. *Acta Psychiatrica Scandinavica, 67,* 205-207.

McDonald, R.J. (1979). Hydergine®: A review of 26 clinical studies. *Pharmacopsychiatry, 12,* 407-422.

McHenry, L.C., Jaffee, M.E., Kawamura, J., & Goldberg, H.I. (1971). Hydergine® effect on cerebral circulation in cerebrovascular disease. *Journal of the Neurological Sciences, 13,* 475-481.

Meier-Ruge, W., Enz, A., Gygax, P., Hunziker, O., Iwangoff, P., & Reichlmeier, K. (1975). Experimental pathology in basic research of the aging brain. In S. Gershon & A.S. Raskin (Eds.), *Genesis and treatment of psychologic disorders in the elderly* (pp. 55-126). New York: Raven Press.

Mizuki, Y., Yamada, M., Kato, I., Takada, Y., Tsujimaru, S., Inanaga, K., & Tanaka, M. (1984). Effects of aniracetam, a nootropic drug, in senile dementia—A preliminary report. *Kurume Medical Journal, 31,* 135-143.

Mohs, R.C., Davis, B.M., Johns, C.A., Mathe, A.A., Greenwald, B.S., Horvath, T.B., & Davis, K.L. (1985). Oral physostigmine treatment of patients with Alzheimer's disease. *American Journal of Psychiatry, 142,* 28-33.

Morrison, J.H., Rogers, J., Scherr, S., Benoit, R., & Bloom, F.E.

(1985). Somatostatin immunoreactivity in neuritic plaques of Alzheimer's patients. *Nature, 314,* 90-92.

Munch-Petersen, S., Pakkenberg, H., Kornerup, H., Ortmann, J., Ipsen, E., Jacobsen, P., & Simmel-Sgard, H. (1974). RNA treatment of dementia. *Acta Neurologica Scandinavica, 50,* 553-572.

Muramoto, O., Sugishita, M., & Ando, K. (1984). Cholinergic system and constructional praxis: A further study of physostigmine in Alzheimer's disease. *Journal of Neurology, Neurosurgery and Psychiatry, 47,* 485-491.

Muramoto, O., Sugishita, M., Sugita, H., & Toyokura, Y. (1979). Effect of physostigmine on constructional and memory tasks in Alzheimer's disease. *Archives of Neurology, 36,* 501-503.

Noel, G., Jeanmart, M., & Reinhardt, B. (1983). Treatment of the organic brain syndrome in the elderly: A double-blind comparison on the effects of a neurotropic drug and placebo. *Neuropsychobiology, 10,* 90-93.

Oleson, J., & Skinhoj, E. (1972). Effects of ergot alkaloids (Hydergine®) on cerebral haemodynamics in man. *Acta Pharmacologica et Toxicologica, 31,* 75-85.

Panella, J.J., & Blass, J.P. (1984). Lack of clinical benefit from naloxone in a dementia day hospital. *Annals of Neurology, 15,* 308.

Peters, B.H., & Levin, H.S. (1979). Effects of physostigmine and lecithin on memory in Alzheimer disease. *Annals of Neurology, 6,* 219-221.

Peters, B.H., & Levin, H.S. (1982). Chronic oral physostigmine and lecithin administration in memory disorders of aging. In S. Corkin, K. Davis, J. Growdon, E. Usdin, & R. Wurtman (Eds.), *Alzheimer's disease: A report of progress in research* (pp. 421-426). New York: Raven Press.

Phuapradit, P., Phillips, M., Lees, A.J., & Stern, G.M. (1978), Bromocriptine in presenile dementia. *British Medical Journal, 1,* 1052-1053.

Pomara, N., Block, R., Abraham, J., Domino, E.F., & Gershon, S. (1983). Combined cholinergic precursor treatment and dihydroergotoxine mesylate in Alzheimer's disease. *IRCS Medical Science, 11,* 1048-1049.

Pomara, N., Block, R., Demetriou, S., Fucek, F., Stanley, M., & Gershon, S. (1983). Attenuation of pilocarpine-induced hypothermia in response to chronic administration of choline. *Psychopharmacology, 80,* 129-130.

Pomara, N., Block, R., Moore, N., Rhiew, H.P., Berchou, R., Stanley, M., & Gershon, S. (1984). Combined piracetam and cholinergic precursor treatment for primary degenerative dementia. *IRCS Medical Science, 12,* 388-389.

Pomara, N., Brinkman, S., & Gershon, S. (1983). Pharmacologic treatment of Alzheimer's disease: Future directions. In B. Reisberg (Ed.), *Alzheimer's disease. The standard reference* (pp. 387-395). New York: Free Press.

Pomara, N., Domino, E.F., Yoon, H., Brinkman, S., Tamminga, C., & Gershon, S. (1983). Failure of single-dose lecithin to alter aspects of central cholinergic activity in Alzheimer's disease. *Journal of Clinical Psychiatry, 44,* 293-295.

Pomara, N., Oxenkrug, G.F., McIntyre, I.M., Block, R., Stanley, M., & Gershon, S. (1984). Does severity of dementia modulate response to dexamthasone in individuals with primary degenerative dementia? *Biological Psychiatry, 19,* 1481-1487.

Pomara, N., Reisberg, B., Ferris, S.H., & Gershon, S. (1981). Drug treatment of cognitive decline. In F. Pirozzolo & G. Maletta (Eds.), *Behavioral assessment and psychopharmacology* (pp. 107-143). New York: Praeger.

Pomara, N., Roberts, R., Rhiew, H.B., Stanley, M., & Gershon, S. (1985). Multiple, single-dose naltrexone administrations fail to effect overall cognitive functioning and plasma cortisol in individuals with probable Alzheimer's disease. *Neurobiology of Aging, 6,* 233-236.

Pomara, N., & Stanley, M. (1986a). The functional status of central muscarinic receptors in Alzheimer's disease: Assessment and their therapeutic implications. In T. Crook, S. Ferris, R. Bartus, & S. Gershon (Eds.), *Treatment development strategies for Alzheimer's disease (pp. 451-472).* Madison, CT: Mark Powley Associates, Inc.

Pomara, N., & Stanley, M. (1986b). The cholinergic hypothesis of memory dysfunction in Alzheimer's disease—revisited. *Psychopharmacology Bulletin, 22,* 110-118.

Pomara, N., Stanley, B., Block, R., Guido, J., Stanley, M., & Greenblatt, D., Newton, R.E., & Gershon, S. (1984). Diazepam impairs performance in normal elderly subjects. *Psychopharmacology Bulletin, 20,* 137-139.

Prien, R.F. (1983). Psychostimulants in the treatment of senile dementia. In B. Reisberg (Ed.), *Alzheimer's disease* (pp. 381-386). New York: Free Press.

Probst, A., Basler, V. Bron, B., & Ulrich, J. (1983). Neuritic plaques in senile dementia of Alzheimer type: A Golgi analysis in the hippocampal region. *Brain Research, 268,* 249-254.

Raskin, A.S., Gershon, S., Crook, T., Sathananthan, G., & Ferns, S. (1978). The effects of hyperbaric and normobaric oxygen on cognitive impairment in the elderly. *Archives of General Psychiatry, 35,* 50-56.

Raskind, M., Peskind, E., Rivard, M.F., Veith, R., & Barnes, R. (1982). Dexamethasone suppression test and cortisol circadian rhythm in primary degenerative dementia. *American Journal of Psychiatry, 139,* 1468-1471.

Reding, M.J., Young, R., & DiPonte, P. (1983). Amitriptyline in Alzheimer's disease [Letter to the editor]. *Neurology, 33,* 522-523.

Reisberg, B., & Ferris, S.H. (1985). A clinical rating scale for symptoms of psychosis in Alzheimer's disease. *Psychopharmacology Bulletin, 21,* 101-104.

Reisberg, B., Ferris, S.H., Anand, R., Mir, P., De Leon, M.J., & Roberts, E. (1983). Naloxone effects on primary degenerative dementia (PDD). *Psychopharmacology Bulletin, 19,* 45-47.

Reisberg, B., Ferris, S.H., Anand, R., Mir, P., Geibel, V., De Leon, M.J., & Roberts, E. (1983). Effects of naloxone in senile dementia: A double-blind trial [Letter to the editor]. *New England Journal of Medicine, 308,* 721-722.

Reisberg, B., Ferris, S.H., & Gershon, S. (1981). An overview of pharmacologic treatment of cognitive decline in the aged. *American Journal of Psychiatry, 138,* 593-600.

Rivera, V.M., Meyer, J.S., Baer, P.E., Faibish, G.M., Mathew, N.T., & Hartmann, A. (1974). Vertebrobasilar arterial insufficiency with dementia: Controlled trials of treatment with betahistine hydrochloride. *Journal of the American Geriatrics Society, 22,* 397-406.

Roberts, G.W., Crow, T.J., & Polak, J.M. (1985). Location of neuronal tangles in somatostatin neurons in Alzheimer's disease. *Nature, 314,* 92-94.

Rosen, W.G., Mohs, R.C., & Davis, K.L. (1984). A new rating scale for Alzheimer's disease. *American Journal of Psychiatry, 141,* 1356-1364.

Rosenberg, G.S., Greenwald, B., & Davis, K.L. (1983). Pharmacologic treatment of Alzheimer's disease: An overview. In B. Reisberg (Ed.), *Alzheimer's disease* (pp. 329-339). New York: Free Press.

Rothlin, E. (1946/47). The pharmacology of the natural and dihydrogenated alkaloids of ergot. *Schweizerische Akademie der Medizinischen Wissenschaften, 2,* 249-272.

Rothlin, E., & Taeschler, M. (1951). Zur wirkung von adrenalin und hydergin anf die hirndurchblatung. *Helvetica Physiologica et Pharmacologica Acta, 9,* 637-639.

Sackett, D.L., & Gent, M. (1979). Controversy in counting and attributing events in clinical trials. *New England Journal of Medicine, 301,* 1410-1412.

Sapolsky, F.M., Krey, L.C., & McEwen, B.S. (1983). Corticosterone receptors decline in a site-specific manner in the aged rat brain. *Brain Research, 289,* 235-240.

Schefler, S. (1972). Pyritinal on mental stages in geriatrics. *Gaz ed Fr, 79,* 1754-1956.

Schneck, M.K. (1983). Nootropics. In B. Reisberg (Ed.), *Alzheimer's disease* (pp. 362-368). New York: Free Press.

Schneider, R., Schmid-Schonbein, H., & Kiesewetter, H. (1983). The rheological efficiency of parenteral pentoxifylline (Trental) in patients with ischemic brain lesions: Preliminary results. *European Neurology, 22* (Suppl 1), 98-104.

Scollo-Lavizzari, G., & Steinmann, E. (1985). Reversal of hepatic coma by benzodiazepine antagonist (Ro 15-1788) [Letter to the editor]. *Lancet, 1,* 1324.

Shaw, D.M., MacSweeney, D.A., Johnson, A.L., O'Keeffe, R., Naidoo, D., Macleod, D.M., Jog, S., Preece, J.M., & Crowley, J.M. (1971). Folate and amine metabolites in senile dementia: A combined trial and biochemical study. *Psychological Medicine, 1,* 166-171.

Smith, C.M., & Swash, M. (1979, January). Physostigmine in Alzheimer's disease [Letter to the editor]. *Lancet, 1,* 42.

Smith, D.F., Stromgren, E., Petersen, H.N., Williams, D.G., & Sheldon, W. (1984). Lack of effect of tryptophan treatment in demented gerontopsychiatric patients. *Acta Psychiatrica Scandinavica, 70,* 470-477.

Smith, R.C., Vroulis, G., Johnson, R., & Morgan, R. (1984). Comparison of therapeutic response to long-term treatment with lecithin versus piracetam plus lecithin in patients with Alzheimer's disease. *Psychopharmacology Bulletin, 20,* 542-545.

Sofroniew, M.V., Pearson, R.C., Eckenstein, F., Cuello, A.C., & Powell, T.P. (1983). Retrograde changes in cholinergic neurons in the basal forebrain of the rat following cortical damage. *Brain Research, 289,* 370-374.

Spagnoli, A., & Tognoni, G. (1983). 'Cerebroactive' drugs: Clinical pharmacology and therapeutic role in cerebrovascular disorders. *Drugs, 26,* 44-69.

Spiegel, R., Azcona, A., & Wettstein, A. (1984). First results with RS 86, an orally active muscarinic agonist, in healthy subjects and in patients with dementia. In R.J. Wurtman, S.H. Corkin, & J.H. Growdon (Eds.), *Alzheimer's disease: Advances in basic research and therapies* (pp. 391-405). Zurich: Center for Brain Sciences and Metabolism Charitable Trust.

Steiger, W.A., Mendelson, M., Jenkins, T., Smith, M., & Gay, R. (1985). Effects of naloxone in treatment of senile dementia [Letter to the editor]. *Journal of the American Geriatrics Society, 33,* 155.

Stotsky, B.A., Cole, J.O., Lu, L., & Sniffus, C. (1972). A controlled study of the efficacy of pentylenetetrazol (Metrazol) with hard-core hospitalized psychogeriatric patients. *American Journal of Psychiatry, 129,* 387-391.

Summers, W.K., Viesselman, J.O., Marsh, G.M., & Candelora, K. (1981). Use of THA in treatment of Alzheimer-like dementia: Pilot study in twelve patients. *Biological Psychiatry, 16,* 145-153.

Thal, L.J., Fuld, P.A., Masur, D.M., & Sharpless, N.S. (1983). Oral physostigmine and lecithin improve memory in Alzheimer disease. *Annals of Neurology, 13,* 491-496.

Thal, L.J., Rosen, W., Sharpless, N.S., & Crystal, H. (1981). Choline chloride fails to improve cognition in Alzheimer's disease. *Neurobiology of Aging, 2,* 205-208.

Tomlinson, B.E., Blessed, G., & Roth, M. (1970). Observations on the brains of demented old people. *Journal of the Neurological Sciences, 11,* 205-242.

van Loveren-Huyben, C.M., Engelaar, H.F., Hermans, M.B., van der Bom, J.A., Leering, C., & Munnichs, J.M. (1984). Double-blind clinical and psychologic study of ergoloid mesylates (Hydergine®)

in subjects with senile mental deterioration. *Journal of the American Geriatrics Society, 32,* 584-588.

Walsh, A.C., Walsh, B.H., & Melaney, C. (1978). Senile-presenile dementia: Followup on an effective psychotherapy-anticoagulant regimen. *Journal of the American Geriatrics Society, 26,* 467-470.

Wang, S.C., & Glaviano, V.V. (1954). Locus of emetic action of morphine and hydergine in dogs. *Journal of Pharmacology and Experimental Therapeutics, 111,* 329-334.

Weingartner, H., Kaye, W., Gold, P., Smallberg, S., Peterson, R., Gillin, J.C., & Ebert, M. (1981). Vasopressin treatment of cognitive dysfunction in progressive dementia. *Life Sciences, 29,* 2721-2726.

Wesseling, H., Agoston, S., Van Dam, G.B.P., Pasma, J., DeWitt, D.J., & Havinga, H. (1984, April). Effects of 4-aminopyridine in elderly patients with Alzheimer's disease [Letter to the editor]. *New England Journal of Medicine, 310,* 988-989.

Wettstein, A. (1983). No effect from double-blind trial of physostigmine and lecithin in Alzheimer disease. *Annals of Neurology, 13,* 210-212.

Whitman, R.M. (1966). Re-evaluation of a glutamate-vitamin-iron preparation (L-glutavite) in the treatment of geriatric chronic brain syndrome with special reference to research design. *Journal of the American Geriatrics Society, 24,* 859-870.

Wittenborn, J.R. (1981). Pharmacotherapy for age-related behavioral deficiencies. *Journal of Nervous and Mental Disease, 169,* 139-156.

Wurtman, R.J. (1982). Forecast. In S. Corkin, K. Davis, J. Growdon, E. Usdin, & R. Wurtman (Eds.), *Alzheimer's disease: A report of progress in research* (pp. 495-499). New York: Raven Press.

Yamaguchi, F., Meyer, J.S., Yamamoto, M., Sakai, F., & Shaw, T. (1980). Noninvasive regional cerebral blood flow measurements in dementia. *Archives of Neurology, 37,* 410-418.

Yesavage, J.A., Tinklenberg, J.R., Hollister, L.E., & Berger, P.A. (1979). Vasodilators in senile dementias. *Archives of General Psychiatry, 36,* 220-223.

Zwerling, I., Plutchich, R., Hotz, M., Kling, R., Rubin, L., Grossman, J., & Siegel, B. (1975). Effects of a procaine preparation (Gerovital H3) in hospitalized geriatric patients: A double-blind study. *Journal of the American Geriatrics Society, 23,* 355-359.

27

Pharmacologic Treatment — From The Viewpoint of The Clinical Investigator

William M. Petrie, MD

Clinical investigation into the treatment of Alzheimer's disease (AD) has expanded as the pathophysiology of the dementing illness has become better understood. Whereas dementia was formerly an area of therapeutic nihilism, investigators have invested careers in increasing numbers to the understanding and care of dementing illnesses. Despite improvements in the sophistication of research plans and pharmacologic agents used, however, little has been learned to change the outlook for demented patients in the clinic. In psychopharmacologic research, it has been commonplace in the last 5 years to see positive results on a small scale or in open trials followed by negative results in double-blind studies. It is the role of the clinical investigator to convert new data from anatomical, physiologic, and pharmacological studies into treatment regimens helpful in individual patients.

AD remains an illness of unknown etiology and uncertain pathophysiology. Most treatments have not been disease-specific but involve diverse pharmacological actions. The course of AD is incompletely understood and patients at early and late phases of the illness present different problems to the investigator and clinician. Research methods have reached the point where if an effective treatment were found, it could be clearly documented, but logistic and legal problems still complicate potential therapies.

PSYCHOPATHOLOGY

AD is an irreversible, progressive illness beginning with relatively discrete symptomatology and ending in profound failure of many areas of brain function. Many studies have correlated the pathological changes in brain structures, biochemistry, and metabolic function to cognitive symptoms of dementia (Foster et al., 1983; Perry et al., 1978; Tomlinson, Blessed, & Roth, 1970). The distinction between the cognitively normal aged and demented patients is important theoretically and practically if effective treatments are to be found.

Impairment of memory and cognitive function remain the cardinal symptoms of dementia. Change in memory and cognitive response is an extremely complex area as approached in neuropsychological research. From the clinical perspective symptoms are more obvious — patients can no longer learn or solve daily problems of living, they forget recent events to a degree that disrupts and minimizes their effectiveness in the world, and they show an inability to orient themselves spatially and temporally.

So-called malignant memory loss has been described in AD patients and has been related by some to the phenomenon of the intrusion of an inappropriate response from an earlier testing item on a psychometric evaluation. Such intrusion errors have been related to decreased choline acetyltransferase activity and an increased number of senile plaques on autopsy (Fuld, Katzman, Davies, & Terry, 1982). Such findings mesh well with clinical symptoms of patients' incorrect or inappropriate recall of daily events. Other psychological tests put AD patients substantially below normal on tests of memory and learning.

Yet what begins as a disease of memory, more specifically approached from a treatment perspective, later develops into symptoms of visuospatial ability, language, and ultimately gross neurological signs and symptoms. Language problems begin as a loss of spontaneity in speech and develop into symptoms of delayed or inhibited word finding, aphasia, and later mutism. As memory loss progresses, the personality begins to be altered, especially as the continuity of past events and present experience is disrupted. Temporal disorientation further disorganizes the patient's ability to function and exist with environmental support.

Secondary psychiatric symptoms emerge as the personality, impaired by reduced memory, cognitive and coping skills, attempts to adapt to these overwhelming changes. The personality becomes egocentric and little or no emotional energy is available for loved ones or the environment. Intrapsychic changes are misinterpreted as interference from outside and hallucinations and delusions become prominent. Affect is also altered and a mood of apathy and withdrawal develops with worsening disease severity. In fact, patients appear unconcerned with their situation, viewing intervention or attempts at treatment as intrusive or unwanted, or at best to be tolerated. Even routine diagnostic procedures have caused many patients to withdraw from our research studies. It is at this stage of the illness that treatment is most difficult; too many symptoms are present, and changes in one symptom (e.g., mood, memory) may affect others. At this time patients may show bursts of poignant realization of their plight and may discuss issues of death. Here psychotic symptoms may even be adaptive.

As the patient loses the ability for selfcare, even toileting skills are lost, and pathological neurological signs and reflexes are noted.

DIAGNOSIS

Diagnosis is the single most important factor in the study of treatment of dementia. Initial drug studies lumped all demented patients in the category "chronic organic brain syndrome." Effective treatment will ultimately be based on specific syndrome identification, as is true in hypertension where different drugs are used for hypertension of various etiologies. Recent improvements in clinical skills and diagnostic aids have changed the selection process today from studies done 10 years ago. As our understanding of the illness increases, clinicians are able to make finer discrimination among dementia syndromes. Nevertheless, diagnosis is largely a process of excluding other dementia syndromes, which may account for almost 50% of the dementias (Tomlinson et al., 1970). Table 2 summarizes diagnostic studies of patients with the presumptive diagnosis of dementia. Diagnosis cannot be simplified to a standard battery or inventory of questions. Diagnostic assessment may well be different for any two patients and combines information from the patient and family, and the careful investigation of any feasible etiology for the dementing illness.

Diagnostic error continues to be problematic even in research or subspeciality settings.

Diagnosis by exclusion runs the risk of overdiagnoses and the use of more specific, positive criteria has been suggested (Cummings & Benson, 1983). English psychiatrists have documented a 30% error rate in the diagnosis of dementia (Marsden & Harrison, 1972). As patients are referred to subspeciality dementia services, misdiagnoses continue to be significant (Smith & Kiloh, 1981). Even when diagnosis is by specialists with full assessment batteries available, follow-up of patients over time has revealed 20% to 60% with mistaken diagnoses (Kendall, 1974). In dementia, as with any degenerative disease, the longer the illness progresses the easier the diagnosis becomes. Thus, if the clinician waits long enough, he can be much more accurate in diagnosis. If, on the other hand, treatment is initiated early in the illness (as some have suggested is more effective), then diagnostic accuracy is reduced.

Diagnosis in AD

AD has been the target of most efforts in the treatment of dementia. Its onset is insidious, and findings on neurological exam and medical evaluation are nonspecific. Laboratory studies are usually normal, and even computerized tomography (CT) evaluations, as done clinically, cannot identify the illness pathognomonically. Positron emission tomography (PET) has been useful in demonstrating the metabolic changes in AD and in identification of cortical symptoms (Foster et al., 1983). However, unequivocal diagnosis will ultimately rest on autopsy or seldom used biopsy, where the neuropathological findings first described by Alzheimer can be confirmed.

The term primary degenerative dementia has been used in the American Psychiatric Association's Diagnostic and Statistical Manual and takes into account the lack of certainty in diagnosis prior to autopsy. Others have used AD or senile dementia of the Alzheimer's type. Research criteria have been used for AD that include characteristics such as gradual progression, insidious onset, 6 months duration, and diffuse cognitive impairment (Eisdorfer & Cohen, 1980). The exclusion of other conditions is especially important as even subtle changes in endocrine status or medical variables, such as pulmonary or hematologic function, could further impair cognition in demented patients and confound research results.

Efforts have been made to discriminate subgroups within AD. So-called familial AD has been well-documented and contrasted to sporadic AD. Folstein and Breitner (1981) described a pattern of autosomal dominant inheritance, if relatives live long enough. Others (Bondareff, Mountjoy, & Roth, 1981) have suggested that onset prior to 65 connotes a more rapid and malignant course, with the occurrence of motor symptoms earlier in the illness.

Whether possible drug response varies in these two subtypes remains to be seen. Most research studies select AD patients with a relatively certain diagnosis and cut-off scores on certain mental status and psychometric measures to add additional homogeneity to the sample.

Multi-Infarct Dementia

The syndrome of multi-infarct dementia (MID), previously atherosclerotic dementia, is classified by the areas of infarction or the etiology of the vascular disease. MID is much more variable than AD and, though first seen as an exclusionary diagnosis, research has focused specifically on the syndrome in recent years. MID may occur as a lacunar state, in which deep infarcts occur in the basal ganglia, thalamus, and internal capsule; as Binswanger's disease where multiple small infarcts appear in the subcortical white matter; and as cortical infarctions affecting large and medium sized vessels, although these usually lead to motor impairment with or without dementia. An extremely large number of conditions can cause such dementias, although hypertension is the most common.

Clinically, patients show dementia in combination with behavioral and neurological symptoms described by Hachinski et al. (1975). MID has been suggested to account for 15% to 25% of dementias, although more cautious estimates, below 8% (Wells, 1977b), are more in keeping with the overall declining rates of vascular disease. High ischemia scores have correlated highly with CT findings, although CT findings may become less prominent or disappear as vascular lesions resolve.

Efforts at treatment of vascular dementias have included calcium channel blockers, vasodilators, rhealogic agents, and drugs with effects on platelet function. It remains unclear how the brain of vascular dementia patients may react differently from patients with AD. The vasodilating effect of carbon dioxide (CO_2), for instance, was shown to be greater in AD than in patients with vascular dementia (Yamaguchi, Myer, Fumihiko, & Yamaguchi, 1980).

Clinically, such patients have been difficult to locate, and because of fluctuating course and symptomatology are more difficult to study in a systematic fashion. The presence of antihypertensive medications with central effects (e.g., propranolol) and the frequent occurrence of depressive symptoms create more methodologic problems.

Depression

Depression is common in the elderly and, as is well-recognized, may produce a dementia-like picture even with disorientation and neuropsychological impairment (Folstein & McHugh, 1978). It is also true that dementia may be mistaken for depression early in its course (Liston, 1977). It is not clear whether this occurs as a psychological reaction to cognitive losses or if it follows damage to brain areas involved in mood regulation. While depression presenting as dementia clouds diagnosis, depression in dementia may alter the presentation of the illness, especially in psychological responsiveness, spontaneity, and participation in psychometric measures. As the intellectual deficits become more pronounced, depressive symptoms become less prominent. High scores on depression rating scales have been used to exclude certain patients from research, although moderate scores clearly occur in dementia (Miller, 1980). Depression scores have not been used widely to assess the evolution and outcome of depressive ratings on psychomotor performance or activities of daily living. Limited information is available on the response of depression in dementia to drug therapy. It is also conceivable that positive results in a dementia study might be due to antidepressant rather than antidementia effects.

COURSE

Current research efforts are directed at rectifying the paucity of data on the course of the dementias. The course of AD has been classically described as declining gradually and steadily over a period of 5 to 7 years. Remissions have never been reported either naturally or in response to any treatment or intervention. It has been suggested by some that clinical "plateaus" may occur even as cellular degeneration continues (Blass & Barclay, 1985). Others have questioned whether such plateaus exist (Cummings & Benson, 1983).

The concept of the staging of dementia is widely accepted, but, unlike work in neoplastic disease where staging has been used, there has been less consensus in dementia as to where such stages should be demarcated. Because dementia varies so dramatically from the early to the late phases, it is likely that treatments could be designed for one but not for another phase of the illness. For example, in the early stages of AD, memory impairment is prominent and drugs affecting memory function might have their most clear effects.

It has been reported that with dihydroergotoxine, drug treatment is even effective in preventing deterioration in mildly or even unimpaired patients (Kugler, et al., 1978; Speigel, Huber, & Koeberle, 1983). Such a controversial claim, if replicated, would have profound importance for those early in the course of the illness or even for those with a high risk (e.g., familial AD) for the disease. In the later stage of the illness, dysmnesia is less prominent than behavioral disorganization, loss of language skills, and agitation. At this phase of the illness drug effects on memory alone could be obscured and assessed with great difficulty.

While the course of AD has been previously described as 5 to 7 years (Beck, Benson, Spar, Ribenstein, & Scheibal, 1982), there is great variation in this figure. As health facilities and care of demented patients improve, longer survival times have been reported (Blass & Barclay, 1985). Clinical interventions are approached with the least enthusiasm in this lengthening later phase of the illness. Such data are consistent with the fact that AD does not kill patients but leaves them weak enough to be susceptible to aspiration pneumonia, urinary tract infections, and sepsis.

The Global Deterioration Scale (GDS) (Reisberg, Ferris, DeLeon, & Crook, 1982), uses a seven-step progression anchored by discrete points. Deterioration on the GDS has been correlated to findings on computerized tomography (CT) and positron emission tomography (PET) scan (Reisberg, 1983a). A three-stage scheme of forgetfulness, confusion, and dementia has been in clinical use for years. Drug-induced changes from one stage to another would be of great clinical significance.

MID has a more malignant course than primary degenerative dementia (PDD) because of the mortality of the vascular conditions involved. However, if these associated vascular conditions are well-treated, the patient's condition may be stabilized. Nevertheless, survival times of less than 2 to 3 years for MID are not unusual, as they would be for AD.

ASSESSMENT MEASURES

Recent research studies in dementia embody a true team approach to the patient. In addition to psychiatric and medical measures there are neurological assessments, family or significant other assessments, psychometric measures, neurophysiologic tests, and self-rating scales. A complete review of these measures is included in *Assessment in Geriatric Psychopharmacology* (Crook, Ferris, & Bartus, 1983).

There has been some disagreement as to using general versus specific scales for improvement. Studies with dihydroergotoxine produced a modest, yet statistically significant effect on extremely broad measures on the Sandoz Clinical Assessment Geriatric (SCAG) scale (Yesavage, Tinklenberg, Hollister, & Berger, 1979). These measures include mood, confusion, hostility, fatigue, unsociability, bothersomeness, and other symptom areas. Improvement in these general areas was not paralleled by reduction in more concrete areas of mental status exam or psychometric test performance (McDonald, 1982). In contrast to these findings, recent trials using cholinergic agents have produced some change in psychometric ratings but no alteration in more general clinical areas (Christie, Shering, Ferguson, Glen, 1981; Mohs & Davis, 1982).

Where subtle, if any, changes have been the rule in psychopharmacologic trials, what outcomes can be expected to be significant? From a clinical perspective, improvement must have a significant effect on the patient's behavior, manageability, and function. While psychometric assessments and other scales may more clearly define response when it occurs, these must be tied to sensible clinical measures that reflect the mood, function, manageability, and care of the patient. Dementia is not a subtle illness — we must hope for treatments that will affect significant clinical areas of the illness, not abstract or limited functions. If, for example, institutionalization could be prevented for only 10% of dementia admissions annually, $1 billion could be saved (Butler & Lewis, 1973).

ACUTE VERSUS CHRONIC TREATMENT

Trials have involved both acute and chronic treatment schedules. Acute treatment with cholinergic or opiate antagonist drugs has typically followed intravenous injection of the drug with assessments minutes to hours later (Christie, et al., 1981; Mohs & Davis, 1982; Reisberg, 1983). Others have assessed drug effects over 2 to 6 month intervals, reasoning that significant effects will take time to develop. Methodologically, these chronic treatments must be carefully balanced by control groups — and even here may be confused by the little known course of the illness. Acute trials may hope for more optimistic changes than are likely with a degenerative illness.

Therapeutic effects from drugs may take longer than the 3 to 4 months commonly used in trials of these psychopharmacologic agents. With the lengthy course of dementia and the modest effects expected with most agents, trials of a year or more may be necessary. Such effects could be analogous to the effect of aspirin on cardiovascular status — while effects are significant, they are subtle and emerge with long-term treatment. Moreover, the statistician may be in a better position to predict such effects than the clinician.

ADVERSE EFFECTS

A researcher working in development of new anticancer drugs once remarked, "If the drug isn't dangerous, I'm not interested." It is paradoxical that in a disease as devastating as dementia most drugs introduced have been innocuous. With the exception of some cholinergic agents, research subjects risk little in the way of adverse effects. As new treatments emerge, however, safety may become a more important issue, and both acute and chronic toxicity must be understood. In addition, large studies of demented patients will invariably include subjects who die during the protocol. At times the role of a drug in dizziness leading to a fractured hip, leading to a pulmonary embolus, leading to death may be unclear. Large numbers of carefully controlled populations will reduce problems arising from these sources. The fact that demented patients will not remember adverse effects if they occur, makes medical assessment and observation by others more important.

If a drug could reverse symptoms of dementia, even life-threatening side effects could be tolerated, as, for example, high dose steroid therapy used for vasculitis in vascular dementia. As in other areas of medicine, the risk-benefit analysis may have to be approached on a more individual basis rather than with a multicenter clinical trial. It is well to remember that patients over 70 are likely to experience twice as many adverse drug reactions as younger patients (Seidl, Thornton, Smith, & Chuff, 1966).

PRACTICAL ISSUES IN TREATMENT

Patient Population

Because dementia and AD affect so large a portion of the elderly and because the disease varies so greatly from early to late in the course of the illness, how patients are selected for study is extremely important. Whether presenting to a dementia clinic or answering a newspaper ad, it is the family member who brings the patient to research facilities. It is likely that these patients are distinguishable by highly motivated families, access and optimism to treatment possibilities, and other unknown attributes. It is well-known from psychopharmacologic trials in adults that so-called "symptomatic volunteers" differ significantly from clinically encountered populations. This may also be the case with AD patients. For example, in an NYU sample of patients studied early in the forgetfulness stage of dementia, 16 patients showed little or no decline in clinical cognitive assessments or functional assessments over a 2-year follow-up period (Reisberg, et al., 1983). Such a sample, while very interesting, is quite different from others where forgetfulness has been predictive of more grave dementia pathology. Patients also vary considerably as to the nature of the support in their environment, so that in many situations the complexities of a family system may be added to treatment conditions. Placement in nursing homes leads to another type of population of demented patients. Nursing home placement has been more related to social factors than to medical factors (Palmore, 1976), further compounding any treatment variables in this population.

Medical Compliance

Even with nondemented elderly, medication compliance is a serious problem. Reduced vision, small pill size, and difficult-to-open pill containers may seriously reduce effective dosing.

With a forgetful patient, medication compliance will be extremely more difficult, even with diligent family members. Patients will commonly forget dosage when administered on a multiple schedule and may forget taking a dose and repeat it unnecessarily.

One solution may be depot forms of medication. The use of pump delivery systems as employed with insulin, or the delivery system used at Dartmouth Medical Center where the cholinergic drug, bethanechol, was delivered directly to the cerebrospinal fluid may be others.

Informed Consent

The demented patient must consent to participate in research, and modern legal procedures require greater formality in considering the rights of these patients. The process of agreeing to participate in research implies an understanding of the benefits and risks of such procedures and how these would deviate from ordinary treatment. Although family members are routinely consulted for research consents, they cannot "sign for" their relative unless a specific guardianship for medical procedures has been granted. Guardianships are not utilized for most demented patients because of the time and expense involved. Other families have hesitated to declare a relative incompetent because of the effects of that humiliation on the patient. Guardianship for financial affairs is a separate procedure from that for medical procedures (Mills, Winslade, Lyon, & Levine, 1984). Therefore, most severely demented patients will require a probate court guardian to authorize treatment or research. For the lesser demented patient few guidelines exist as to when his or her understanding of the research situation is too impaired by the memory loss and cognitive deficits of the illness to consent. From our experience in a research clinic, more than 50% of patients initially presenting for research projects have little understanding that they suffer from a serious medical illness and often do not see the point of extended research efforts. Third parties are therefore extremely important in guiding, yet allowing, the patient a role in this choice. Researchers are clearly inappropriate for such fiduciary functions as they have a vested interest in the research task.

As treatments become more intrusive and dangerous, issues of informed consent will become more complex.

SPECULATION

In keeping with our current understanding of AD as a degenerative, genetically determined (in part) illness with other unknown etiologic factors, it is difficult to conceptualize curing the disease by any treatment or drug. However, it is reasonable to consider slowing the process of deterioration, especially early in the course of the illness when many personality and cognitive functions are still present to compensate for lost functions. An ideal drug would be given at the earliest signs of malignant memory loss and continued throughout the early and middle phases of the illness. Such a drug would produce an improved clinical state that can be documented further by improvement in psychometric and other assessment instruments. Additional research and development are also urgently needed in the later stages of treatment when personality disorganization, psychosis, agitation, and other secondary symptoms require periodic restraints and sedating drugs under current treatment conditions.

An ideal drug would provide improvement in the earliest phases of the illness without lengthening the later severely regressed stages when both family and patient suffer and costs to society are high. Such a drug would be reasonably safe but probably not without risk.

REFERENCES

Beck, J.C., Benson, D.F., Spar, J.E., Rubenstein, L.Z., & Scheibal, A.B. (1982). Dementia in the elderly: The silent epidemic. *Annals of Internal Medicine, 97,* 231-242.

Blass, J.P., & Barclay, L.L. (1985). New developments in the diagnosis of the dementias. *Drug Development Research, 5,* 39-58.

Bondareff, W., Mountjoy, C.Q., & Roth, M. (1981). Selective loss of neurones of origin of adrenergic projection to cerebral cortex (nucleus locus coeruleus) in senile dementia [Letter to the editor]. *Lancet, 1,* 783-784.

Butler, R., & Lewis, M. (1973). *Aging and mental health.* St. Louis, MO: C.V. Mosby Co.

Christie, J.E., Shering, A., Ferguson, J., & Glen, A.I.M. (1981). Physostigmine and arecoline: Effects of intravenous infusions in Alzheimer presenile dementia. *British Journal of Psychiatry, 138,* 46-50.

Crook, T., Ferris, S., & Bartus, R. (1983). *Assessment in geriatric psychopharmacology.* New Canaan, CT: Mark Powley Associates, Inc.

Cummings, J.L., & Benson, D.F. (1983). *Dementia: A clinical approach.* Boston: Butterworths.

Eisdorfer, C., & Cohen, D. (1980). Diagnostic criteria for primary neuronal degeneration of the Alzheimer's type. *Journal of Family Practice, 11,* 553-557.

Folstein, M., & Breitner, J.C.S. (1981). Language disorder predicts familial Alzheimer's disease. *Johns Hopkins Medical Journal, 149,* 145-147.

Folstein, M.F., & McHugh, P.R. (1978). Dementia syndromes of depression. *Aging, 7,* 87-93.

Foster, N.L., Chase, T.N., Fedio, P., Petronas, N.J., Brooks, R.A., & DiChiro, G. (1983). Alzheimer disease: Focal cortical changes shown by position. *Neurology, 33,* 961-965.

Fuld, P.A., Katzman, R., Davies, P., & Terry, R.D. (1982). Intrusions as a sign of Alzheimer's dementia; chemical and pathological verification. *Annals of Neurology, 11,* 155-159.

Garcia, C.A., Reding, M.J., & Blass, J.P. (1981). Overdiagnosis of dementia. *Journal of the American Geriatrics Society, 29,* 407-410.

Hachinski, V.C., Iliff, L.D., Zilhaki, E., Du Boulay, G.H., McAllister, V.L., Marshall, J., Ross Russell, R.W., & Symon, L. (1975). Cerebral blood flow in dementia. *Archives of Neurology, 32,* 632-637.

Kendall, R.E. (1974). The stability of psychiatric diagnosis. *British Journal of Psychiatry, 124,* 352-356.

Kugler, J., Oswald, W.D., Herzfeld, U., Seud, R., Pingel, J., & Welzel, D. (1978). Long-term treatment of the symptoms of senile cerebral insufficiency: A prospective study of Hydergine. *Dtsch. Med. Woechenschr, 103,* 455-462.

Liston, E., Jr. (1977). Occult presenile dementia. *Journal of Nervous and Mental Disease, 164,* 263-267.

Marsden, C.D., & Harrison, M.J.G. (1972). Outcome of investigation of patients with presenile dementia. *British Medical Journal, 2,* 249-252.

McDonald, R.J. (1982). Drug treatment of senile dementia. In D. Wheatley (Ed.), *Psychopharmacology of old age* (pp. 113-138). London: Oxford University Press.

Miller, N. (1980). The measurement of mood in senile brain disease: Examiner ratings and self-reports. In J.O. Cole & J.E. Barrett (Eds.), *Psychopathology in the aged* (pp. 97-122). New York: Raven Press.

Mills, M.J., Winslade, W.J., Lyon, M.A. & Levine, M.L. (1984).

Clinicolegal aspects of treating dementia patients. *Psychiatric Annals, 14,* 209-211.

Mohs, R.C., & Davis, K.L. (1982). A signal detectability analysis of the effect of physostigmine on memory in patients with Alzheimer's disease. *Neurobiology of Aging, 3,* 105-110.

Nott, P.N., & Fleminger, J.J. (1975). Presenile dementia. The difficulties of early diagnosis. *Acta Psychiatrica Scandinavica, 51,* 210-217.

Palmore, E. (1976). Total chance of institutionalization among the aged. *Gerontologist, 16(6),* 504-507.

Perry, E.K., Tomlinson, B.E., Blessed, G., Bergman, K., Gibson, P.H., & Perry, R.H. (1978). Correlation of cholinergic abnormalities with senile plaques and mental test scores in senile dementia. *British Journal of Medicine, 25,* 1457-1459.

Reisberg, B. (1983a). The Brief Cognitive Rating Scale and Global Deterioration Scale. In T. Crook, S. Ferris, & R. Bartus (Eds.), *Assessment in geriatric psychopharmacology* (pp. 19-35). New Canaan, CT: Mark Powley Associates, Inc.

Reisberg, B. (1983b). Clinical presentation, diagnosis, and symptomatology of age-associated cognitive decline and Alzheimer's disease. In B. Reisberg (Ed.), *Alzheimer's disease. The standard reference* (pp. 173-187). New York: The Free Press.

Reisberg, B., Ferris, S.H., Anand, R., Mir, P., Geibel, V., De Leon, M.J., & Roberts, E. (1983). Effects of naloxone in senile dementia. A double-blind trial [Letter to the editor]. *New England Journal of Medicine, 308(12),* 721-722.

Reisberg, B., Ferris, S.H., De Leon, M.J., & Crook, T. (1982). The Global Deterioration Scale (GDS): An instrument for the assessment of primary degenerative dementia (PDD). *American Journal of Psychiatry, 139,* 1136-1139.

Seidl, L.G., Thornton, F., Smith, J.W., & Chuff, L.E. (1966). Studies on the epidemiology of adverse drug reactions. III. Reactions in patients on a general medical service. *Bulletin of the Johns Hopkins Hospital, 119,* 299-315.

Smith, J.S., & Kiloh, L.G. (1981). The investigation of dementia: Results in 200 consecutive admissions. *Lancet, 1,* 824-827.

Speigel, R., Huber, F., & Koeberle, S.A. (1983). Controlled long-term study with ergoloid mesylates (Hydergine) in healthy, elderly volunteers; results after three years. *Journal of the American Geriatric Society, 31,* 549-555.

Tomlinson, B.E., Blessed, G., & Roth, M. (1970). Observations in the brains of demented old people. *Journal of the Neurological Sciences, 11*, 205-242.

Wells, C.E. (1977a). *Dementia* (2nd ed.). Philadelphia: F.A. Davis Co.

Wells, C.E. (1977b). Diagnostic evaluation and treatment in dementia. In C.E. Wells (Ed.), *Dementia* (2nd ed., pp. 247-276). Philadelphia: F.A. Davis Co.

Yamaguchi, F., Meyer, J.S., Fumihiko, S., & Yamaguchi, F. (1980). Aging and cerebral dilator response to hypercarbia. *Archives of Neurology, 37*, 489-496.

Yesavage, J.A., Tinklenberg, J.R., Hollister, L.E., & Berger, P.A. (1979). Vasodilators in senile dementia: A review of the literature. *Archives of General Psychiatry, 36*, 220-223.

TABLE 1

Symptoms of Dementia

Memory disturbance

Spatial disorientation

Personality change

Temporal disorientation

Loss of spontaneity

Language disturbances

Perseveration

Agraphia

Alexia

Neurological symptoms

TABLE 2

Established Diagnoses in Patients with a Presumptive Diagnosis of Dementia

Atrophy of unknown cause	51%
Creutzfeldt-Jakob disease	1.4%
Dementia from vascular disease	7.7%
Dementia in alcoholics	5.9%
Depression	4.1%
Drug toxicity	3.2%
Huntington's chorea	4.5%
Intracranial masses	5.4%
Normal pressure hydrocephalus	6.3%
Others or uncertain	10%

from Wells (1977a)

TABLE 3

Clinical Features Associated with Multi-Infarct Dementias

Abrupt onset
Stepwise deterioration
Fluctuating course
Relative perservation of personality
Depression
Somatic complaints
Emotional incontinence
History of hypertension
History of strokes
Associated atherosclerosis
Focal neurological signs or symptoms

from Hachinski et al. (1975)

28

A Scientific and Pharmaceutical Industry Perspective

Donald S. Robinson, MD, and Neil M. Kurtz, MD

The pharmaceutical industry will play a central role in developing and testing treatment strategies for Alzheimer's disease (AD). In planning for the next generation of drugs, it is obvious that the diseases associated with the aging process will offer ever expanding market opportunities. As medical advances improve our ability to treat and / or prevent heart disease and cancer, the average life span will increase making AD an increasingly prevalent health problem. There are, however, aspects of AD that will make it a particularly perplexing problem. With AD It is not just the patient who is affected by the sequelae of the illness. While admittedly devastating to the patient, its impact on the family can be equally severe and its toll on society substantial. Cost estimates for providing care to patients with AD are enormous and can only be expected to escalate unless an effective treatment can be found. AD places tremendous financial burdens on the health care system at a time it can ill afford them. These facts coupled with the significant profit motive to the pharmaceutical industry to develop an effective therapy makes finding a treatment for AD a high priority. Because no universally accepted treatment is currently available, the pharmaceutical sponsor of the first truly effective agent will be in an enviable position. Estimates are that a successful drug would have worldwide sales of over one billion dollars per year. This would surpass the H_2 antagonists as the most popular and profitable prescribed drug therapy. One only has to look at the worldwide sales for Hydergine® to appreciate the potential magnitude of the market. Despite controversy over this drug's effectiveness, it currently ranks as the eleventh most commonly prescribed drug in the world.

As if the profit motive and service to society were not ample motivating factors, there exists yet another reason for industry's interest, which perhaps could be the most powerful. The deterioration of higher cognitive processes to the point of a vegetative-like existence is a frightening prospect. The disease has equal predilection for the rich and the poor and can strike senators and corporate executives alike, including those whose decisions determine where research and development monies are spent. Thus, there is a unique personal stake in shaping corporate research strategies. The directors of research are keenly aware that by discovering a treatment for AD they could well be saving either themselves or a member of their own families from a dreaded disease.

Despite many compelling reasons for the pharmaceutical industry to invest in AD research, the cold reality is that it represents a risky venture. Tens of millions of dollars could be invested without any return. Therefore, the prudent sponsor must assess many difficult factors in making a business decision.

It may be informative to provide some insight into the usual drug development process in industry, and how it might be expected to differ in the case of AD. One should imagine a corporate executive who is answerable to the stockholders if unsuccessful. At the onset, the sponsor must decide on the overall direction and goal of a program to discover a therapeutic agent. In essence there are two basic strategies: (1) replacement-oriented therapies, or (2) therapies targeted at the pathogenesis and/or etiology of the illness. The sponsor must be clear which research direction to take because the issues are quite different for each approach, as will be shown. These involve decisions regarding both basic and clinical research strategies.

PRECLINICAL RESEARCH ISSUES

The research process begins with the synthetic chemist who "invents" the molecule which will eventually enter clinical studies. He usually takes some direction from molecules that are known to produce a desired biologic effect, but in the absence of any proved agent, there is no model to use with any certainty. One can make a theoretical case for any one of a number of molecules having potential utility in AD. Let us assume you charge the synthetic chemist to develop a direction, i.e. a likely example would be a specific cholinergic M_1 agonist that has good central nervous system (CNS) penetrability. It is quite likely that a suitable compound could be successfully synthesized. A major problem would then be to assess its biological activity. This involves setting up animal models that would be predictive of clinical effect. Here a major issue has to be confronted. Which animal models should be selected?

ANIMAL MODELS OF AD FOR DRUG DEVELOPMENT

Many, if not most, animal models are developed after a clinically effective drug already exists. These are then employed to define and characterize a drug's biologic and pharmacologic activities more fully. At present, this cannot be done for AD since there is no benchmark drug. This makes the task of defining and interpreting relevant animal models much more difficult. Thus, there are validity questions concerning all existing animal models for AD. For example, one of the more common screening tests currently in use is reversal of electroconvulsive therapy (ECT)-induced amnesia in rats. Single doses of the piracetam class of drugs are known to effectively reverse ECT-induced amnesia, and new agents are often compared to piracetam using this model. Whether this model has any relevance to the treatment of AD is unknown.

The very nature of a disease process that affects primarily higher cognitive functioning in humans brings with it an additional dimension of difficulty. We may be asking an animal model to predict what may be a solely human condition. This combined with the fact that the pharmaceutical industry prefers animal models developed from clinically proved agents or at least based on a knowledge of the basic etiology and pathogenesis of a disease makes for a lessened confidence in the success of this venture.

Therefore, a decision to undertake a preclinical program in this research area must involve a somewhat different mind-set. One cannot launch an industrial research program to treat or cure AD with the same expectations that one could, for example, for developing a new antidepressant. It is important to have realistic expectations, and there must be a willingness to allocate significant resources in the face of greater risk of return on the investments.

PHARMACOLOGY AND TOXICOLOGY ISSUES IN DRUG DEVELOPMENT

Once a lead compound has been identified in preclinical research (based on unproved experimental models), the next step would be to initiate safety evaluations in at least two different animal species to assess the drug's toxicity. Doses of the drug that appear to be acceptably safe and well-tolerated need to be established in the belief that, in terms of safety, the animal toxicology data will be predictive of what can be expected in humans. Although this step is of extreme importance in the evaluation of any compound, its relative importance is even more critical when dealing with a potential agent for AD. The reason for this is as follows: At the forefront of any clinical decision to take a drug into patients with AD will be a requirement for an exceptionally favorable safety profile. Since only modest clinical improvement may be expected or possible, the tenet should be that if you "are not going to do any good, at least make absolutely sure that you do no harm." This implies that before taking a drug into the clinic, one should be convinced that a compound is impressively safe and well-tolerated in the animal testing phase.

Other aspects of AD make the safety issues of paramount importance. It must be understood that an agent will be used in a frail, often debilitated elderly population, which imposes more stringent safety requirements on the drug. The target population presents with age-related alterations in physiology, which may affect pharmacokinetic properties of a drug, thereby influencing its safety profile and tolerability. Those agents that are the safest will be the ones on which it makes the most sense to take a calculated risk. This is one area where academic and industrial perspectives may differ. An academician may find a drug scientifically intriguing, but its safety profile may be unacceptable to a pharmaceutical sponsor because the risk is judged to be too great in clinical practice.

INITIAL CLINICAL TESTING OF A DRUG FOR AD

In designing a clinical testing program for a new agent for the treatment of AD, it should be appreciated that the perspective may be different for a U.S. as opposed to non-American pharmaceutical company. The evidence required to establish safety and efficacy of a new drug by a regulatory agency varies considerably from country to country. What follows is a view of what one might predict would be necessary to convince even the most skeptical of regulatory authorities that a new compound is effective for the treatment of AD.

Initial studies will need to be performed in a healthy population of young-to-middle-aged adults. The primary objective of these studies would be to determine the safety and tolerability of the agent in a healthy human population. The rationale is to understand initially what effects a drug will have under situations where the physiology is presumed normal. Such initial phase I studies should involve both single and multiple doses of the drug. It will be necessary to identify the maximal tolerated single and multiple dose. The results will be extremely important for determining the future of the compound because the agent must be shown to be impressively well-tolerated with little question regarding safety and must support a high therapeutic index in the impaired elderly patient. Pharmacokinetic parameters of absorption, distribution, metabolism, and excretion should be established in the normal young adult initially. The drug should obey linear kinetics without a propensity to accumulate over time.

During the phase I workup of other classes of drugs, attempts are made to identify biological models that can be set up in healthy volunteers to predict clinical activity and / or dosage. This would be very difficult to accomplish for AD. However, in developing a drug for treating symptoms such as memory disturbance, it may be possible to show some evidence of enhanced memory or cognition even in the normal individual. However, this would be difficult to show conclusively and could not be relied on to get a good sense of the therapeutic effects or dosage during initial phase I studies.

Once the studies supporting the safety and tolerability of the compound are completed, the next decision to be faced is whether to repeat these studies in healthy geriatric subjects before proceeding to patients. This is not a straightforward issue, and there can be differences of opinion. It is our opinion that absorption, distribution, metabolism, excretion, and pharmacodynamics should be assessed in normal elderly before proceeding to AD subjects.

PHASE II AND III STUDIES

The initial clinical studies should be designed with a flexible dose-ranging regimen so as to assess safety and tolerability as well as efficacy. It is during these phases where the sponsor attempts to put together a data package that will convince a regulatory agency that its compound is both a safe and effective treatment for the indicated condition. As alluded to above, the sponsor's choice of indication will dictate to a large extent the goal of his program and the design of his studies. There are two broad categories of possible intervention. One involves replacement therapy while the other looks at the pathogenesis and / or etiology of the illness. Each will be discussed under separate headings.

REPLACEMENT THERAPY OF AD

The rationale for this therapy is simple and straightforward: To supply the patient the missing essential substance. If one assumes a deficiency of acetylcholine (ACh) causes the symptoms of AD, a treatment is designed to replace what the brain can no longer provide for itself. The aim of these therapies is solely to produce symptomatic improvement rather than prevention or cure, and the goal is to retard symptom progression.

Various strategies have been explored to increase cholinergic transmission in the CNS. Transplanted brain tissue as described in this text by Dr. Gash is one such approach. Although brain tissue transplantation might ultimately interest the pharmaceutical industry, the more obvious approach is the development of drugs designed to replace ACh. A key feature of such replacement therapy is that it is only a symptomatic treatment. One accepts the fact that the progression of the illness would remain unchecked. One immediate concern for the sponsor planning to embark on a strategy of replacement therapy is an issue raised by Dr. Leber (1983). This comes under the heading of "pseudospecificity." The sponsor must decide whether his agent will treat a symptom related to an illness or only a symptom in general. For example, if memory impairment is selected as a target symptom, the question becomes does your agent treat memory impairment associated with AD, or is it effective in memory impairment of multiple causes, (i.e., normal aging) or for that matter, would it even improve memory in a healthy young adult population. This is an important question, the answer to which would invariably reflect the regulatory viewpoint of that country where the compound is to be approved. Dr. Leber (1983) indicated that a nonspecific symptom such as memory impairment would not constitute an approvable indication. Although this viewpoint may need to be redressed, it is our opinion that it would be quite difficult for a sponsor, given the present regulatory climate, to obtain an approvable indication for a nonspecific symptom such as memory disturbance. The indication would need to be memory impairment associated with a particular pathological process, that is AD.

The next important issue, unique to clinical research involving an agent for AD, is the difficulty of establishing a data base on a homogeneous patient sample. Clinical studies must be designed such that it is clear that one is treating AD rather than only dementia. At present, AD is still a diagnosis of exclusion. Other forms of dementing processes that must be excluded are Pick's disease, multiple-infarct dementia, vitamin deficiencies, Huntington's chorea, Parkinson's disease, various neuroendrocrinopathies, and certain infectious processes. The protocol for clinical trials must clearly specify the diagnostic laboratory tests that will be performed to rule out the possibility that the presenting memory disturbance is due to a process other than AD. The diagnostic criteria for inclusion of patients in the study must be clearly specified. At this point in time, a likely strategy that would be adopted is to employ Diagnostic and Statistical Manual of Mental Disorders of the American Psychiatric Association (DSM-III) criteria. However, if DSM-III criteria are used for defining the patient sample, one may be faced with a situation that is not the most advantageous. Applying strict DSM-III criteria would probably mean that the sample will consist of patients with at least moderate if not predominantly advanced stages of AD. Selecting patients with a more severe form of the illness may subject the drug to an unfair test. There may be little likelihood that an agent can robustly reverse a process that is severe, progressive, and associated with atrophy.

To give an agent the best chance of success, one might wish to select patients with the greatest likelihood of showing clinical improvement. This raises the issue of the importance of early detection of the illness. Present diagnostic techniques do not afford satisfactory early specificity. However, even if this could be done, there are still a number of problems. If one selects patients too early in their illness, one can potentially be subjecting the study to the inclusion of a nonhomogeneous population, as well as one where there may be a significant placebo effect. Therefore, one must design studies with sufficient power and sensitivity to tease out placebo-related effects. This necessitates double-blind placebo-controlled studies of parallel group design. Crossover designs may have a place in the workup of new drugs for AD, but because of carry-over effects and the likelihood that it may take a long time to see any clinically significant changes, crossover designs are probably impractical.

The situation is even more complex if one views AD as a heterogeneous entity with separate forms of the illness: One presenile dementia and the other senile dementia using an arbitrary age cutoff as a chronological definition. There may be some justification for looking at the illness in this way for it appears that the earlier onset form of AD is associated with more diffuse and severe pathology than the later onset forms. It is this so-called presenile form of dementia that shows extensive involvement of other neurotransmitter systems in addition to the cholinergic nervous system. In addition, earlier family studies had indicated a genetic component associated only with the early onset form of AD. However, more recent studies suggest an autosomal dominant form of inheritance for AD irrespective of age of onset (Kokmen, 1984).

In any event, the protocol should specify the form of dementia to be studied or provide for stratification of the sample based on age. Since the "presenile" form of dementia may be characterized by a more rapidly progressive and deteriorating course, it probably makes more sense to study the "senile" form because more stable and homogeneous baseline conditions might be expected on which to base evidence of therapeutic benefit. Finally, the protocol must clearly define both selection criteria and degree of impairment. These criteria will not be used for assessment of treatment effects but rather to assure that each investigator utilizing the clinical program is "talking the same language" and agrees on the manifestations of cognitive impairment associated with the dementias.

Once satisfied that the patient can be adequately defined, one must then address what scales will be used to assess treatment-related effects. The importance of appropriate scales for this purpose cannot be overstated. An ongoing criticism of current studies is that the scales selected to establish efficacy are not designed to show changes of clinical importance. This will be essential in demonstrating to a regulatory agency that a treatment is effective and useful. It must not require an act of faith to believe that the rating scale score changes associated with drug treatment translate into clinical improvement for the AD patient. Scales must be validated to reflect significant improvement in cognition or functioning. It would also behoove the sponsor to keep the scales as simple as possible. Brevity is especially important so that fatigue will not be a factor in patients with limited physical and mental capacities.

A Global Assessment Scale (GAS) completed by a family member caring for the patient may prove to be as valuable as any of the currently available, more complex scales for establishing improved quality of life. In any clinical trial, a number of different scales may be necessary and desirable.

Placebo-control groups are essential in developing a new agent for AD and should be part of the earliest possible phase II trials. Unlike other conditions affecting behavior (i.e., schizophrenia, depression) where there may be ethical considerations about the use of placebo, especially in institutionalized patients, this should not prove to be a restriction in AD since there is no effective therapy. The likelihood of significant nondrug treatment-related ("placebo") effects makes placebo controls mandatory for quantifying any drug effect.

It is quite likely that one of the cardinal symptoms chosen for evaluation will be memory disturbance, a core symptom of the dementing process. Evaluation of memory changes can be a very complicated process in the experience of many investigators. This is because memory function involves a number of different parameters, which may or may not be directly related to the physiology of memory. Associated variables such as motivation, attention, and mood are of extreme importance and will need to be simultaneously evaluated in the course of any study. A criticism of many of the earlier vasodilator studies was the failure to consider these critical covariables. The consensus is that vasodilator drugs do not directly affect the AD process, but they in some way influence these other parameters, secondarily affecting performance on cognitive tests. Thus, while on the surface it may seem that a sponsor who wishes to develop a drug designed to produce only symptomatic improvement may adopt a relatively straightforward approach (i.e., identify symptoms, develop scales to measure those symptoms, and show differences compared to placebo), it is in fact a much more complicated issue. The rigorous review of a regulatory agency will require conduct of studies employing parallel group designs and appropriate negative controls and validated clinically relevant rating scales that assess parameters such as mood, motivation, or attention, as well as cognitive function and intellect. Finally, any drug must be very safe and well-tolerated at therapeutic doses so that a heterogeneous and predominantly physically impaired elderly patient population will not experience undue side effects, excessive drug-drug interactions, or other adverse consequences.

TREATMENT BASED ON PATHOGENESIS OF AD

If a sponsor desires to develop a drug directed at the pathogenesis of AD, one must be prepared to address a totally separate set of questions in designing a clinical development program. It can be argued that it is far too early in our knowledge of AD to be talking about treatment of the underlying cause. However, an equally cogent argument could be made that replacement therapy may never produce the robust effect on AD that will be necessary for a truly meaningful intervention. It may be that it is only by addressing the pathogenesis of the illness that a successful treatment of AD will ever emerge. This is not to belittle a strategy of treating symptoms since there is ample precedence in medicine for symptomatic treatments. However, as medicine becomes more sophisticated, it is becoming increasing evident that trying to treat a progressive degenerative disease with symptomatic treatment frequently produces at best transient, short-lived benefit in a patient population that suffers long-term infirmity — thus the focus on finding curative treatments based on a knowledge of the pathogenesis of an illness. An analogy is the attempt to develop drugs that inhibit cholesterol synthesis so as to prevent atherosclerotic plaque formation and get at the very essence of atherosclerotic heart disease. One would be trying to do much of the same thing with AD. This could lead to either reversing the process or preventing its occurrence. Although admittedly we know relatively nothing about the pathogenesis and/or etiology of AD, keep in mind that the same statement could have been made about atherosclerosis 30 years ago.

Interventions aimed at prevention or cure raise a whole different set of questions from symptomatic treatment of AD. The task of demonstrating prevention or cure is much more difficult in AD. If a drug sponsor felt it possessed such an agent, planning the clinical development program leading to registration would be difficult, complex, and expensive.

The conduct of phase I trials would be much the same. The safety of the drug would be of paramount importance because very long-term treatment strategies would be likely. Problems relating to selecting homogeneous populations in later phase studies are similar. One issue of extreme importance is a need to have some understanding of the natural progression of the illness. In this regard the work of Reisberg, Ferris, DeLeon, and Crook (1982) in staging the illness may be of significant help. Selecting patients currently in stage 4 using Reisberg's classification system should reliably identify a patient sample with unequivocal AD and a moderate degree of dementia. The question that can be put to clinical test is what is the time necessary to progress from stage 4 to stage 5. If it can be shown that compared to a parallel placebo group, a drug prolongs the time from stage 4 to stage 5, a relatively strong case can be made that it retards or reverses the degenerative process. However, what on paper sounds simple in practice will be very difficult to do. Instead of a need for conducting trials of anywhere from 6 weeks to 3 months in length to show efficacy of a symptomatic treatment, clinical trials of several years duration would most likely be necessary. The difficulties of such long-term studies are enormous. There are limited research centers in the world capable of providing the clinical follow-up necessary to obtain meaningful data. The cost of doing this kind of research could be prohibitive to many drug sponsors. However, it might be less expensive than trying to design mortality studies of the type currently used to evaluate preventive treatments of atherosclerotic heart disease.

In line with the rationale outlined above, one could conceptualize the type of study necessary that would be within the resources of a developer of a drug for the prevention of AD. If in fact a clinical trial shows drug-placebo differences over a 2 to 3 year treatment period, a compelling case could be made for the benefit to AD patients, which should be convincing to a regulatory agency.

CHOOSING A RESEARCH DIRECTION IN AD

Clearly selecting and pursuing a treatment strategy for Alzheimer's disease is a difficult and expensive decision. It may be wise to advise the corporate executive to use a historical perspective. Perhaps a look into the past can give a glimpse into the future. In this regard, the potential of serendipity cannot be overlooked when evaluating treatment strategies. Throughout the history of medicine, there are examples of a significant advance coming about as a result of careful clinical monitoring of a drug that was supposed to do something else but had an effect in an unpredicted direction. Iproniazid in tuberculosis patients leading to the new class of monoamine oxidase inhibitors is an outstanding example, as are the tricyclic antidepressants originally developed as antipsychotics. Perhaps there exists a drug available today that when looked at with the proper perspective would shed light on new and effective treatment strategies for AD.

The current direction of many pharmaceutical companies has been aimed toward exploring fully the potential of replacement therapy. One must be skeptical of the potential for replacement therapy. The whole concept, particularly that aimed at ACh treatments, is based largely on histopathological findings. A multitude of factors play a role in producing histopathological findings on autopsy. Some of the changes may be directly related to the pathogenesis of the illness. However, others may be due to factors that play a role in increasing susceptibility to an illness or perhaps maintaining the illness, or for that matter, are merely epiphenomena unrelated to the illness but are produced as a result of the pathologic process. In addition, because something may be deficient does not necessarily mean that replacing it will be of clinical benefit, particularly in a system as complex and redundant as the CNS. Why then has the cholinergic replacement theory become so popular? We believe there exists, with regard to the current cholinergic hypothesis, a situation where there is an important and interesting neurochemical and histopathological finding that lends itself well to the strength of the industrial process (i.e., directed research). The strategy of producing a potent, specific M_1 agonist with good penetrability across the blood-brain barrier is the type of problem the pharmaceutical industry is geared to do and do well. However, potency is a question of dosage, not efficacy. It should be possible to get equally efficacious results with higher doses of existing M_1 agonists. The continuing inability to show this casts doubts on the wisdom of vigorously pursuing a cholinergic replacement therapy. This is not to say that understanding the cholinergic involvement in AD is not important. On the contrary, continued investigation of the cholinergic deficit in AD can lead to important new knowledge. However, there is a difference between a discovery of scientific importance and one that will have eventual applicability as a useful therapeutic adjunct. The two may not go hand and hand. The neuropsychiatric disorder where replacement therapy has proved to be of significant benefit is Parkinson's disease. Although beyond the scope this chapter, there are several reasons to believe that similar success should not be expected with AD. The two conditions are sufficiently different so as to suggest that analogies are not warranted. In addition, replacement therapy in Parkinson's disease has not been without its associated problems (i.e., the so-called "on-off" effect that has been directly attributed to L-DOPA precursor therapy). It is therefore logical to assume, even under the most optimal situation where you could show robust improvement with a replacement-oriented therapy the likelihood of developing a situation similar to the on-off problems of Parkinson's disease, would have to be considered.

Our view is that the treatment development strategies for AD should focus on the degenerating presynaptic neuronal processes. The postsynaptic events have only limited interest or potential in providing a clinically useful therapy. To develop a prevention or cure of AD, it is probably essential to gain an understanding of the mechanism of degeneration and the events leading to neurofibrillary tangles and plaque formation. The advent of a curative therapy rests on discovering why the neuronal systems degenerate in this curious manner, peculiar to AD. These typical pathologic findings are seen in only a few other specific disorders such as Down's syndrome, neurotropic virus infections, and so forth. Although multiple neurotransmitter systems are involved, there seems to be a greater predilection for involvement of the ascending cholinergic pathways, which may be an important clue. It would signify a vulnerability based on nerve cells size, as Professor Davidson points out in a separate chapter, or a unique neurochemical vulnerability to these cholinergic neurons which predisposes them to this insidious pathognomonic degeneration. Neurochemical characterization of these pathologic legions using immunochemical and other techniques may be helpful in finding the composition of plaques and tangles and ultimately their etiologies. It may be that the preponderance of women compared to men affected with AD is related to an endocrine or neurohormonal component to the neuronal degenerative processes. The possibility that hormonal differences may contribute to the risk of developing AD needs to be explored further.

Throughout this discussion there has been no mention of the class of agents referred to as the nootropic drugs. These agents are in fact approved for use in AD in a number of European countries. They have been generally well-received and their sales are impressive. Piracetam has become the benchmark agent. The jury is still out on the question as to whether these drugs can produce clinically significant improvement, and much work needs to be done to further define their actions. A problem in trying to interpret the activity of nootropics is related to the assessment methodology used in most of the early clinical trials. It is quite possible that when the proper methodology is applied to future evaluation of these drugs, robust clinical effects can be demonstrated. It certainly appears that so far this drug class meets the requirements of being very safe and well-tolerated. Therefore, the criteria of not doing any harm is met. This is such an important issue that it would make sense for a sponsor to try to further explore this class of drugs in an effort to determine if they truly hold promise. Since safety may well be a rate-limiting effect with cholinergic treatments (these drugs have a historically low therapeutic index), there may be a distinct advantage for a sponsor wishing to enter this area to pursue the nootropic drug category.

One final statement relating to an industrial perspective on the direction of therapeutic strategies, in reference to the question of patentability: As mentioned above, it is possible that there already exists a treatment that could be proved to be effective in AD. However, and this is where an industry perspective can differ markedly from an academic one, if the drug cannot be patented, then even though it may be effective, its appeal to an industrial sponsor would be greatly diminished.

SUMMARY

More focused and specific treatments await an understanding of the pathogenesis of the illness. Basic research is essential to the development of an effective therapy, and serendipity is likely to play a part in finding a cure for AD.

The situation with AD presents an excellent opportunity for collaboration between academia and industry. There exist some factors which are bringing the two together. AD is an excellent opportunity for relationships to be developed that would suit the purposes of both. The tremendous technological advances in the ability to study the CNS have fostered a high degree of specialization in basic research in the neurosciences, and no pharmaceutical firm is capable of maintaining every experimental model of interest. Hence, considerable collaboration already occurs. The scope of the problem facing science in conquering AD may warrant a formal and concerted effort similar to the development of polio vaccine or analogous to the space program.

AD presents a true challenge for acquiring a more complete understanding of how the brain allows us to perform those higher cognitive functions that set us apart from the rest of the animal kingdom.

REFERENCES

Kokmen, E. (1984). Dementia—Alzheimer's type. *Mayo Clinic Proceedings, 59,* 35-42.

Leber, P. (1983). Establishing the efficacy of drugs with psychogeriatric indications. In T. Crook, S. Ferris, & R. Bartus (Eds.), *Assessment in geriatric psychopharmacology* (pp. 1-12). New Canaan, CT: Mark Powley Associates, Inc.

Reisberg, B., Ferris, S.H., DeLeon, M.J., & Crook, T. (1982). The Global Deterioration Scale for assessment of primary degenerative dementia. *American Journal of Psychiatry, 139* (9), 1136-1139.

29

Summary and Conclusions

Leo E. Hollister, MD

The authors of these chapters were asked to let their imaginations roam, to consider rather unorthodox treatments for Alzheimer's disease (AD). This they did admirably. It is not easy to summarize so many good papers and still find anything new to say.

One can safely say, 80 years after Alzheimer first described the disease that bears his eponym, that we still have very little understanding of it. To paraphrase Winston Churchill's famous statement concerning the Russians, AD is a riddle wrapped in an enigma wrapped in a mystery. This is not to say that we have not learned much about the disease, but rather that our attempts to understand its etiology and to treat it effectively still remain rather primitive.

It is very tempting to draw analogies between AD and Parkinson's disease. Both occur in old age. Both have major neuropathologic lesions affecting nuclei of ascending tracts in the brain. In the case of Parkinson's disease, the ascending tract is a dopaminergic pathway projecting from the substantia nigra to the caudate putamen. In AD, the major tract involved arises in the nucleus basalis of Meynert and provides cholinergic innervation to the hippocampus and cortex. Other tracts may also be involved in AD including those originating from the raphe nucleus and the locus ceruleus. A deficiency of dopamine occurs in Parkinson's disease, and predominantly acetylcholine (ACh) in AD. In the latter, however, decreases in norepinephrine, serotonin, somatostatin are found, as well as other peptides such as substance P, vasopressin, and β-endorphin. Thus, in AD many instruments in the neurochemical orchestra are out of order but we still do not know which causes the most mischief. Finally, attempts at therapy for both diseases have focused on replacing the deficient neurotransmitters. Replacement therapy in Parkinson's disease with levodopa has had moderate success. Replacement therapy attempting to increase cholinergic activity in AD has had little success thus far.

Parkinson's disease may represent the extreme instance of normal brain aging. Recent studies using PET scanning techniques have shown a progressive decline in dopamine synthesis and dopamine receptors over the course of a lifetime. Thus, patients with Parkinson's disease may fall on the extreme portion of a normal distribution curve of declining dopaminergic activity. And any aging person might be at risk if an additional insult were added. Could the same statistical probability of developing AD in old age occur? Could AD also represent an extreme instance of aging brain? It will be interesting to see whether PET scanning studies provide evidence for such a formulation, but some of the neurochemical studies reported at this meeting strongly suggest such a possibility. If so, it will have important implications about the relevance of studies of normal brain aging to the understanding of AD.

Let us now consider some general considerations about treatment. Three possible approaches might be taken. *Replacement therapy* by either giving a precursor of the neurotransmitter deemed to be lacking or by increasing its activity in other ways, can only be considered as a way to add additional years of function. It would not have any effect on the natural history of the disorder. A *curative approach* would presumably attack some fundamental cause. However, our knowledge about fundamental causes of either AD or Parkinson's disease is still sketchy. In fact, it may be a mistake to consider a single cause for either disease. Parkinson's is certainly a syndrome having been reported following infections with the virus of encephalitis lethargica, the entry into the brain of exogenous toxins such as manganese and more recently the fascinating material MTPT, or due to exogenous pharmacological agents such as drugs that block dopamine receptors, or to arteriosclerosis. None of these mechanisms is clearly related to so-called idiopathic Parkinson's disease. Might AD also be a syndrome with multiple possible causes rather than any single one?

A third approach to treatment would be *preventive*. This approach would also imply some knowledge of the pathogenesis of the disease but it could be based on specific hypotheses relating to one or more aspects of the illness.

It is fair to say at this moment that we have no specific treatments for AD, that is, none that is proved. Our greatest reliance is on drugs presumed to increase metabolic activity in the injured brain, so-called metabolic enhancers. The oldest of these are ergoloid mesylates, which have been around for more than three decades, but for which there are still many unanswered questions, such as the proper dose, the proper duration of treatment, the proper route of administration, the goals of treatment, and the mechanism of action. To a lesser extent the same situations may apply with piracetam and its various homologues. These drugs are newer, and their efficacy in AD is still somewhat debatable. We could use much better treatments than those we now have. The most effective present treatment for AD is the judicious use of psychotherapeutic drugs, particularly antipsychotics, to ameliorate the behavioral disturbances.

Virtually all attempts at treatment based on *replacement* of deficient neurotransmitters have been based on the cholinergic deficiency hypothesis. As was pointed out at this meeting, the drugs used so far have not adequately tested this hypothesis and it is by no means sure that they have adequately remedied the deficiency of ACh. New homologues of ACh that pass the blood-brain barrier may be more effective than present approaches with either precursors of ACh, direct cholinergic agonists, or cholinesterase inhibitors. It was also pointed out at this meeting that perhaps we have overlooked carbachol, an old cholinergic agent that has never been adequately tried as a treatment for AD. Finally, many oxotremorine homologues have been synthesized, some of which seem not only to enter the brain readily but to be far more effective than the parent compound itself in increasing cholinergic activity. Any of these approaches might provide a more direct test of the cholinergic hypothesis. The use of an α-1-adrenoreceptor agonist, which in turn might stimulate muscarinic-2-cholinergic receptors, would constitute a somewhat indirect test of the hypothesis. Such a drug would also presumably remedy any deficiency of norepinephrine, a rather constant finding in neurochemical studies of AD. Whether precursor treatment, say with tyrosine, might also be effective in increasing noradrenergic activity is questionable. The dopamine β-hydroxylase step in the biosynthesis of catecholamines from precursors such as tyrosine is rate limiting. To attempt replacement of deficient somatostatin either with homologues that might be more resistant than somatostatin itself to degradation by peptidases or would pass the blood-brain barrier is not presently possible. Replacement therapy by the direct intraventricular administration of drugs such as bethanechol is another exciting but unproved technique. Whether this approach will be more successful than the systemic administration of drugs that have access to the brain remains to be seen. The fascinating new concept of transplanting neural tissue or neural cells into the brain as replacement for missing neurotransmitters is still another exciting prospect. Clearly, many avenues for replacement therapy for AD exist, but we still cannot predict which, if any, may be successful.

It is impossible at present even to consider a *curative* treatment, in the absence of any firm understanding of why selected neurons in the brain die. *Preventive* treatments have postulated that free radical formation or endogenous neurotoxins might be a possible cause for such neuronal death. Commonly used and safe drugs, such as α-tocopherol or ascorbic acid might be reasonable approaches to alleviate the destructive effects of free radicals. The balance between some endogenous neurotoxin and neuronal growth factors might provide another approach to preventing neuronal death. Unfortunately, we do not have neuronal growth factors whose structure is known and whose safety has been demonstrated for human use. The long-term administration of cell membrane constituents might be considered to alleviate the increasing rigidity of cell membranes that occurs with aging. Chronic effects of alcohol, unlike the acute effects of the drug, increase membrane rigidity and accelerate normal brain aging. Membrane constituents such as phosphatidylcholine, phosphatidylserine, or ethanolamine might be considered for such long-term treatment. Attempts to prevent the disease would be extremely difficult to prove in clinical studies unless large numbers of aged persons were followed for long periods of time.

Other possibilities somewhat remote from those we have already discussed might be considered. Another analogy to AD might be Wilson's disease. The discovery that hepatolenticular degeneration was due to deposition of copper in the brain and its alleviation by chelating agents was a major advance. What about reports of excessive amounts of aluminum in the brains of patients with AD? Admittedly, AD does not resemble clinically the dialysis dementia that is definitely associated with aluminum intoxication. Furthermore, aluminum neurotoxicity creates a different kind of helical filament from that observed in AD. Nonetheless, one might consider an empirical trial of various chelating agents. Only a very small number of patients has been treated in this fashion thus far. Another possibility is that AD could be the result of excessive entry of calcium into the cells. A normal brain constituent could become a neurotoxin. It has been suggested that calcium channel blockers including perhaps the very first of these drugs, magnesium, might be tried as a treatment. The notion of giving a precursor such as dihydroepiandrosterone to allow the body to synthesize *in situ* missing sex hormones is a fascinating possibility. By using this precursor one would essentially allow the body to make what it needed. This concept is entrancing but thus far untested.

It is quite fashionable these days to dismiss the use of neurostimulants as a treatment. Older neurostimulants such as pentylenetetrazole have been tested in the past and are now considered to be obsolete. Perhaps a new look should be taken. One might be more inclined to test endogenous neurostimulants such as thyrotropin-releasing hormone (TRH). TRH is small enough being a mere tripeptide to enter the brain readily even when given orally but the half-life of the substance is measured in minutes. Homologues have been made with a longer duration of action, and these might be tested. Whether hormonal treatment is worth resurrecting is somewhat questionable. Past treatments with a variety of sex hormones, thyroid hormones, and adrenal hormones showed a conspicuous lack of success. One hypothesis of AD is that it is an autoimmune disorder. One might be tempted therefore to try to treat the disorder by various immunosuppressants. Such treatment could not be undertaken lightly as most immunosuppressants have dangerous side effects.

AD has been postulated to be the result of infection with a slow neurotropic virus such as that involved in scrapie or Creutzfeldt-Jacob disease. However, increasing numbers of patients infected with human T-cell leukemia virus III have shown evidence of dementia. It will be interesting to see whether the neuropathological consequences of infection with this virus resemble those found in AD. If such resemblances were found, it might spur attempts at treatment of various types with antiviral drugs.

We have not heard very much (at this meeting) about molecular biological techniques for the investigation of AD. An impressive part of the histopathology of AD are the numerous aberrant forms of what had been functioning neurones and nerve fibers. One cannot help thinking that major alterations have occurred in the cytoarchitecture of the neurone and its various components such as tubulin and actin. It should be possible to identify abnormal proteins in the brains of AD patients, to synthesize the gene for these proteins, to clone the gene for the production of such proteins, and to make monoclonal antibodies against them. Such techniques should provide more insight concerning the role of cytoskeletal components in this disorder.

We have many potential treatments that might be tested in AD. However, our resources for such testing are very limited. Clinical studies for testing drugs in mental disorders are at best difficult, tedious, and expensive. Such studies of AD patients are especially difficult because the only definitive diagnosis is based on neuropathologic evidence derived from autopsy. In most series in which the clinical diagnosis of AD has been correlated with the neuropathological findings at postmortem the error rate for the clinical diagnosis is about 15% to 25%. These error rates occur at academic centers and probably underestimate the error rate for clinical diagnosis that occurs elsewhere. Such an error rate could possibly introduce negative bias into controlled trials, so that we might fail to reject the null hypothesis.

In the near future, some investigators may feel constrained to answer some of the unanswered questions about ergoloid mesylates or piracetam homologues. A limited amount of such work might still be worth doing, but it seems unlikely in the long run to lead to much more effective treatments. More energy should be devoted to additional testing of the cholinergic hypothesis. Short of any better leads, this hypothesis is the most logical to test. Even the dopaminergic hypothesis of schizophrenia or the aminergic hypothesis of affective disorders have still not been adequately tested. One must follow any reasonable lead, and this hypothesis is certainly one.

It is tempting to advise patience. The first effective treatment for Parkinson's disease was based on an erroneous premise. Stramonium was used in Charcot's clinic, not to treat the disease but to treat the drooling of saliva. To paraphrase Peter Whitehouse's aphorism that a search for rational treatment might be irrational, one might say about stramonium that an irrational treatment may turn out to be more rational than originally thought. The discovery that stramonium influenced more than the excessive salivation of patients with Parkinson's disease led to the use of antimuscarinic drugs for the next several decades. In the late 1950s, it became possible to measure concentrations of neurotransmitters in brain. With this new technology it became possible to demonstrate a dopamine deficiency consequent to the degeneration of neurons in the substantia nigra observed by neuropathologists many years earlier. This new knowledge then led to replacement therapy for Parkinson's disease, first with L-DOPA and later with dopamine receptor agonists. Such treatment has prevailed for the past 20 years. If the treatment history of Parkinson's disease is any indicator, one should not expect major treatment advances very quickly.

The situation is quite different today. We have entered a new era of biology with many more powerful techniques at our disposal than were known to our predecessors. Furthermore, we have more scientists now than existed during most of the last 100 years. Many of these able people, drawn from a multiplicity of disciplines, are interested in the problems of AD. The roster of participants at this meeting bears this out. Consequently, one should feel optimistic that treatment advances for AD will come more rapidly than those for treatent of Parkinson's disease. With the great interest in AD on the part of neuroscientists, on the part of pharmaceutical houses, on the part of government agencies, and, on the part of the families of the victims of this disastrous disease, one must conclude that we may soon have a better knowledge of the disease and a better treatment for it.

Index

A

Acetylcholine
    actions, 173, 179, 180
    BBB permeability, 253, 673
    brain, 340, 437
    electrical stimulation, 543
    formation, 500
    and memory, 461
    mimicking effects, 404
    potential action, 554
    release, 539, 606-607
        calcium-dependent, 502-504, 507-508
        corticol release, 506
        decrease, 543
        enhancement, 411, 452, 467, 478-479, 549
        increase, 528
        inhibition, 184, 388, 409
    response, 405, 410
    storage, 540
    synthesis, 411, 523, 540, 544, 574
        and aging, 502-503
        enhancement, 412, 467
        increase, 390, 452, 524, 528
        loss of activity, 48
        precursor approach, 427
        and release, 390-398
Acetylcholinesterase, 111, 112, 341, 433
3-Acetylpyridine, 161, 163, 166
ACh (*See* Acetylcholine)
AChE (*See* Acetylcholinesterase)
Acidic amino acid receptors, 112
Acidosis, 163
ACTH
    activity, 247
    age-related changes, 256
    decrease, 246, 279
    elevation, 231, 232
    enhancement, 406
    increase, 155, 239
    regulation, 189
    release, 152
    secretion, 271
    stimulation, 191
    suppression, 200
Active lipid, 529

ADAS (*See* Alzheimer Disease Assessment Scale)
Adenosine triphosphate, 500
Adrenal medullary cells, 569
Adrenocortical axis, 152, 155-157, 163
        hormones, 152
        hyperactivity, 165
        stress response, 152
Adrenocorticotrophic hormone (*See* ACTH)
Afferent fibers, 104
ALAP (*See* Alaproclate)
Alaproclate, 362, 365, 368, 371, 375
Alcohol, 40, 42, 525, 526, 529, 530, 674
Aldosterone, 192
1-Alkenylglycerophospholipids, 540
Alpha-bungarotoxin binding, 490
ALS (*See* Amyotrophic lateral sclerosis)
Altman, Harvey J., 361
Aluminum, 505, 674
Alzheimer's Disease Assessment Scale, 606, 615
Amador, Roberto, 311
Aminopyridine, 506, 508
4-Aminopyridine, 181
Ammon's Horn, 156
Amphetamines, 488
Amygdala, 156, 273, 312, 423
Amyloid deposits, 269
        fibrils, 177
        plaques, 187
        proteins, 187
Amyotrophic lateral sclerosis, 293, 296, 297
Androgen, 192, 199
Androgen-synthetic sites, 189
Androstenedione, 192
Aneuploidy, 275
Anterograde amnesia, 133, 134
Anticholinergics, 474
Antioxidants, 532
Antipsychotic drugs, 613, 665, 673
3-AP (*See* 3-Acetylpyridine)
Aplypsia neurons, 410
Arcuate nucleus, 231
Arecoline
        benefit, 607
        dose-dependent response, 464, 466
        half-life, 429
        inhibition, 206
        investigation, 563
        and REM sleep, 462, 463
        stimulation, 452
Arginine vasopressin, 246-248
Association cortex, 178

Astrocytes, 108, 249
Astroglia, 273
Atherosclerotic heart disease, 643, 645
ATP (*See* Adenosine triphosphate)
Autocannibalism, 540, 549
Autosomal dominant inheritance, 642
AVP (*See* Arginine vasopressin)
Axon(s), 119
    sprouting, 135, 138
    terminals, 137, 140
    transport, 104, 139

B

B cells, 267, 268
Bagne, Curtis A., 585
Banks, William A., 245
Bartus, Raymond T., 15, 421
Basal adrenocortical activity, 166
    flow rate, 251
    ganglia, 178
    metabolic rate, 125, 127
Basal nucleus of Meynert
    atrophy, 52, 274
    cholinergic innervation, 671
    destruction of cholinergic neurons, 187
    loss of cholinergic cell bodies, 67
    loss of neurons, 176
    low ganglioside concentration, 71
    primary lesion in AD, 68
Baudry, Michael, 119
BBB (*See* blood-brain barrier)
Beta-estradiol, 321
Bethanechol
    administration, 607
    delivery, 649
    infusion, 429, 561, 563
    muscarinic activity, 560
    replacement therapy, 673
Binswanger's disease, 643
Biomembranes, 520
Blessed Dementia Scale, 323
Blood-brain barrier
    aging, 245
    alterations, 69, 248-250
    breakdown, 245
    deficiency, 70
    interactions, 251-254, 568
    manipulation, 256
    morphology, 255
    transit, 478
Bolus injections, 557

Botulinum toxin poisoning, 508
Brain
    calpain activity, 130-133
    calpain distribution, 133-135
    cholinergic system
        change of neurons, 338
        innervation, 489, 490, 539
        loss of neurons, 273, 485
        neurobehavioral model, 173
        optimal activity, 179
        receptors, 312
        terminals, 541
    dysfunction, 483
    size, 136
    spectrum, 120, 121
Buschke Selective Reminding Task, 615

C

CA4 cells, 110
Calcium
    activation, 121
    and brain aging, 234
    buffering, 141
    concentrations, 140
    decrease, 505
    dependency, 130
    deterioration, 141
    increase, 185
    release, 501, 504
Calcium-activated proteases, 120
    -dependent proteases, 119, 120, 133
    -dependent proteolysis, 313
    -metabolism, 499, 501, 503, 505-506
    -sensitive protease, 120
Calcium ions, 391
Calmodulin, 120, 151
Calpain
    and brain size, 137
    cellular localization, 121
    concentration, 120, 139
    degeneration, 122
    in brain aging, 134, 135, 142
    lifespan, 130, 131*, 132*
    measurement of activity, 133, 134
    neuron loss, 113
    turnover, 136, 138, 140, 141
Calderini, Gabriella, 385
Calzolari, S., 293
CAT (See Choline acetyltransferase)
Catalytic polypeptide, 120
Catecholaminergic transmitters, 79

Catecholamine metabolism, 278
Catecholamines, 179, 339, 500, 531, 673
Cavagnaro, Joy, 267
Cavicchioli, L., 293
CDP-choline, 541, 542
Central muscarinic receptors, 453
Central drug administration, 558, 559
Central drug infusion, 556, 562
Central nervous system
        actions, 173, 179, 433
        antigenic counterpart, 269
        assessment procedures, 25
        components, 522
        degenerative dementias, 529, 532
        delivery, 557
        denervation, 112
        desynchronization, 182
        development, 113
        effects, 521
        electrical paradigm, 553-555
        embryonic, 271
        functions, 245
        gateway, 181
        immunologic responses, 274
        influence, 267
        infusion, 558
        injury, 101-105, 270, 298, 303
        mechanism, 99
        neuronotrophic factors, 294, 295, 304
        neuropeptide occurrence, 281
        neurotransmitter, 186
        pathology, 531
        penetration, 453, 656
        preparations, 506
        rate of entry, 177
        regeneration, 570
        specificity, 429
        study of, 668
        synapses, 121
        transplantation, 567, 660
Cerebral arteriosclerosis, 590
        blood vessels, 70
        circulation, 585
        cortex, 130, 134, 178, 473
        glucose, 464
Cerebrospinal fluid
        and bethanechol chloride, 607
        extracellular, 519
        investigations, 80
        measurement, 617
        peptides, 281, 473
        production, 249

Ceroid-lipofuscin, 141
p-Chloroamphetamine, 273
Cholesterol, 409, 410, 519, 525
Choline
    and piracetam, 611
    availability, 529
    clinical trials, 67
    concentration, 544
    effects, 68, 69
    metabolization, 539
    phospholipids, 546
    salts, 601
    synthesis, 452, 523
    uptake, 540
Choline acetyltransferase
    activity, 42, 43, 314, 451
    activity reduction, 40, 46, 48, 59, 76, 385
Cholinergic activity
    agents, 430, 432, 625, 646
    agonists, 122, 533, 543
    cells, 133, 134
    deficiency, 79, 222, 440, 673
    dysfunction, 339, 424
    hypothesis, 422, 425, 556, 590, 620, 676
    innervation, 342
    markers, 485
    nervous system, 361, 375, 662
    neurotransmitter system, 451, 453
    precursors, 68, 428
    receptors, 484, 491
    septal input, 111
Cholinergic system
    ability, 605
    activation, 178, 182
    defects, 591
    function, 500-502
    knowledge, 478
    reduction, 253
Cholinergic transmission, 79, 474
    treatment, 255, 421, 429
Cholinesterases, 454, 560
Cholinomimetics
    administration, 501
    effectiveness, 427, 429, 563
    and REM sleep, 462
    usefulness, 293
Cholinoneuronotrophic factor, 273
Cholst, Ina, 311
Choroid plexus, 249
Chromatin, 277
Chromosome aneuploidy, 275
Chronic organic brain syndrome, 641

Ch-PL synthesis, 543
Ciliary ganglion cells, 103
Ciliary ganglion neurons, 105
Cognitive disturbances, 17
Cohen, Gene D., VIII
Commissural-association fibers, 110
Corpus callosum, 103
Corpus striatum, 102
Copper, 674
Cortex, 40, 179, 277, 474, 621
Cortical cholinergic neurons, 67
Corticosterone hypersecretion, 153, 155, 157, 158
Corticotropin-releasing factor, 152, 271
Cortisol, 192
Cortisone-sensitive neurons, 156
Cotman, Carl W., 99
Creutzfeldt-Jacob disease, 36, 38-40, 675
Crews, Fulton T., 385
CRF (See Corticotrophin-releasing factor)
Crook, Thomas, 585
CSF (See Cerebrospinal fluid)
Cushing's syndrome, 167
Cyclic nucleotides, 465
Cyproheptadine, 362, 364

D

Dal Toso, R., 293
Davies, Peter, 473
Dean, Reginald L., 421
Decyberneticization, 176
Dehydroepiandrosterone
        administration, 188-202
        decrease, 173
Dehydroepiandrosterone sulfate
        administration, 188-194, 196-202
        decrease, 173
        effect, 195
Delta sleep-inducing peptide, 251
Dentrites, 119, 139, 185
Dendritic spines, 137
Dentate gyrus, 100, 101, 105
Depression, 644
Depression rating scales, 644
Dexamethasone, 615
DHEA (See Dehydroepiandrosterone)
DHEAS (See Dehydroepiandrosterone sulfate)
Diabetes, 222
Diacylgylcerol, 437, 439
Diaminopyridines, 506
3,4-Diaminopyridine, 499, 506, 507, 509
Diazepam, 622, 623

Differential lipid pools, 526
Digit Span Task, 603
Dihydroergotoxin, 646
5,7-Dihyroxytryptamine, 70
Dimethylphenylpiperazinium, 490
DNA
          cell ratio, 275, 276
          correlation, 174, 574
          fragmentation, 55
          genetic linkage analysis, 74-76
          markers, 74
          recombinant, 75
Dopamine
          change in sensitivity, 525
          decreases, 134, 591, 672
          effects, 297*, 372
          increased turnover, 522, 524
          low turnover, 40
          potential action, 554
          synthesization, 574, 592
Dopamine receptor agonists, 676
Dopaminergic neurons, 151
Dorsal root ganglion cells, 103, 298
Down's syndrome
          calcium content, 505
          pathological signs, 544
          protein CSF levels, 250
          relation to AD, 73, 74
          structural changes, 79
DRG (See Dorsal root ganglion cells)
Drug Product Class Guidelines, 5
DSIP (See Delta sleep-inducing peptide)
Dysmnesia, 645

E

Eaton-Lambert syndrome, 508, 509
Eight-arm maze, 508
Endocrine system, 267
Endorphins, 274
Entorhinal
          ablation, 111
          cell loss, 110, 114
          cortex, 100, 101, 102, 110
          lesions, 105, 110
Ependyma, 574
Ependymal lining, 249
Epinephrine, 271
Ergoloid mesylates, 672
Estradiol, 213, 312, 328, 330
Estradiol therapy, 324
Estradiol valerate, 320

Estrogen
      deficiency, 311, 316
      effectiveness, 311-313, 319, 321
      emotional changes, 315, 318, 322, 325*
      improvement, 320, 323, 324*, 327, 328
      neuronal damage, 159, 330
      psychotropic effects, 317
      ratio, 199, 329
      side effects, 326
      synthesis, 189
Estrogen-synthetic sites, 189
Estrophilic neurons, 313
Ethanol (See Alcohol)
Ethanolamine, 545
Exogenous choline, 543

F

FDA (See Food and Drug Administration)
Famous Faces Test, 603
Fatty acids, 520, 522, 525, 526, 530
Fatty acid precursors, 521
Federal Food, Drug, and Cosmetic Act, 4, 6, 8, 23
Fillit, Howard, 311
Fisher, Stephen K., 421
Fodrin, 120
Follicle-stimulating hormone, 189, 275, 279, 320, 321
Food and Drug Administration, 2, 5, 22, 26
Forebrain cholinergic neurons, 101
Fowler, Christopher J., 67
Frontal cortex, 423, 577
FSH (See Follicle-stimulating hormone)
Fujinami sarcoma virus, 155

G

GABA (See Gamma-aminobutyric acid)
GABA uptake, 297
GABAergic neurons, 181, 182, 625
Gamma-aminobutyric acid, 69, 186, 622, 623
Ganglioside GM, 70
Ganglioside NeuNAc, 70
Gangliosides, 293
GBS (See Gottfries, Bråne, and Steen scale)
Geddes, James W., 99
Gelfoam, 102-105, 107, 108, 110
Genetic component, 74
Genetic defect, 479
Gershon, Samuel, 585
GH (See Growth hormone)
G_1 phase of cell cycle, 277
Glial cells, 107, 108, 136, 159

Glioblastoma, 272
Global Assessment Scale, 662
Global Deterioration Scale, 323, 325, 645
Glucocorticoids
        elevation, 153, 230, 231, 239
        excessive exposure, 155, 167, 168
        inhibitory effects, 157, 163
        loss in hippocampus, 156
        pathways, 199
        toxicity, 161
        vulnerability, 152
Glycerophosphocholine, 544
Glycinergic neurons, 182
Golgi apparatus, 137
Gonadal hormones, 313, 314
Gonzales, Reuben A., 385
Gottfries, Bråne, and Steen scale, 378
Graft-versus-host disease, 270
Granulovascular degeneration, 224, 340
Gray matter disorder, 79
Growth hormone, 275
Guild memory test, 319
GVH (See Graft-versus-host disease)

H

H$_2$ antagonists, 655
Hachinski Ischemic Score, 323
HAE (See Hereditary angioedema)
Haloperidol, 77
Hamilton Depression Scale, 320, 323, 327
Harbaugh, Robert E., 553
Hemicholinium-3, 543
Hereditary angioedema, 197, 198
Hippocampal corticosterone receptors, 157
Hippocampal glia, 156
Hippocampus
        activity, 178
        age-related changes, 248
        brain-aging, 228, 230
        brain response, 506-507, 539
        CAT activity, 40
        cholinergic innervation, 312
        damage, 158, 162-166
        increase, 105
        learning and memory, 269, 423, 562
        lesions, 177, 571
        loss of 5-HT, 41-42
        mechanism, 151, 153
        nerve growth factors, 273
        neuron damage, 159
        neurotoxicity, 161

pyramidal cells, 458
stimulatory effects, 409, 624
rate of aging, 163
sprouting fibers, 110, 111, 313
synaptic plasticity, 99-102
tissue loss, 156-158
topographical pathology, 224
transplantation, 571, 572, 575-577
Hirano bodies, 340
Histocompatibility complex, 198
Histocompatibility antigen system, 268, 270
Holbrook, Pamela G., 539
Hollister, Leo E., 671
Homeostasis, 152
Hormonal therapy, 311
Hormone replacement therapy, 315
Horseradish peroxidase, 570
Hospital Adjustment Scale, 322
5-HT (*See* Serotonin)
Humoral immune response, 278
Huntington's Chorea, 36, 38, 42, 479, 661
Huntington's disease, 42, 72-75
Huntington's genes, 74
Hydergine®
    action, 343
    clinical trials, 598-599*, 600, 622
    efficacy, 23, 76, 624
    and lecithin, 611
    mechanism of action, 592-596
    popularity, 655
    treatment, 619
Hydroxybutyrate, 163
6-Hydroxydopamine lesion, 70, 302
17-Hydroxyprogesterone, 192
5-Hydroxytryptamine, 507
Hyperadrenocorticism, 155, 159, 164, 230
Hyperexcitation, 163
Hyperinnervation, 104
Hypoglycemia, 163
Hypothalamus
    abnormalities, 270
    blood-brain barrier, 281
    inhibitory inputs, 158
    estrogen effect, 312
    mechanism of action, 152, 156
    neuronal damage, 159
    and neuropeptide Y, 275
    release of CRF, 157
    release of LHRH, 190
Hyperthermia; 464, 526
Hypoxia, 163, 499-502, 507

Hypoxia-ischemia, 151, 166
Hypoxia-ischemic injury, 161

I

Implantable infusion devices, 559
Implantable pump, 557, 558, 607
IMR-32 cells, 574, 575
Inositol, 411
Insulin, 649
Interferon production, 270
Intermedi-Infusaid Implantable Pump, 559
Intralimbic vasopressin, 158
Intraventricular infusion system, 553, 558
Iproniazid, 665

K

K+ channels, 173, 182, 201
K+ ions, 177
KA (See Kainic acid)
Kainate sites, 111
Kainic acid, 103, 111, 166
Kostin, Abba J., 245
Kordower, Jeffrey H., 567
Korsakoffs psychosis (See Wernicke-Korsakoffs dementia)
Kurtz, N.M., 655

L

Landfield, Philip W., 221
Larsen, Karen, 385
Larson, John, 119
Layer II stellate neurons, 100
LC (See Locus coeruleus)
L-DOPA, 67, 452, 483, 666, 678
Leber, Paul, 1
Lecithin
        action, 530
        clinical trials, 67-69, 411, 427, 601
        enhancement of ACh synthesis, 452
        nutritional functions, 547
        pharmacologic effects, 523
        precursor loading, 343
Leon, A., 293
Leutinizing hormone, 189, 275, 279, 320
Leutinizing hormone-releasing hormone, 190, 246
LH (See Leutinizing hormone)
LHRH (See Leutinizing hormone-releasing hormone)
Lick-Suppression Task, 365, 368
Life Span Scales, 128
Lipid metabolism, 520
Lipids, 528

Lipofuscin, 142, 167
Liscovitch, Mordechai, 539
Locus coeruleus
    damage, 539, 671
    drug distribution, 560
    innervation, 70, 179, 181, 342, 490
    loss of cells, 327, 340, 475, 476
    neuronal loss, 79, 176-177, 426
    in Parkinson's disease, 52
    stimulation, 345, 346, 348-352
    transplants, 571-573
Luine, Victoria, 311
Lumbar spinal fluid, 474
Lymph nodes, 278
Lymphatic neoplasia, 278
Lymphocyte autoregulation, 274
Lymphocytes, 274-276, 279
Lynch, Gary, 119
Lyso-PS, 524
Lysomomal degradative system, 141
Lysosomes, 139

M

M_1, 387-388, 432, 454
M_1 agonist, 656
M_2, 387-388, 432, 454
Magnesium, 674
Maire, Jean-Claude, 539
Mattis Dementia Rating Scale, 323
Mauron, Charlotte, 539
McEwen, Bruce S., 151, 311
Medial septum, 187
Medulla, 278
Membrane fluidity, 532
    lipid asymmetry, 532
    lipids, 519
    peroxidative damage, 532
Menopausal depression, 319
Metabolic activation, 590
Metabolic enhancers, 672
Metabolic Rate Scales, 126
Met-enkephalin, 69
Methacholine, 463
Methylation, 542
Metyrapone, 166
Meyer, Edwin M., 385
Mg^{2s}, 234
MHC (See Histocompatibility complex)
Microtubule-associated proteins, 120
MID (See Multi-infarct dementia)
Mineralocorticoid, 199

Mini-Mental Status Exam, 323-325
MNNG (*See* N-methyl-N-nitro-N-nitrosoquanidine)
Mono-aminopyridines, 506
Monocyte, 267
Monosialoganglioside, 298
MTPT, 672
Multi-infarct dementia
    cause, 20
    differentiation, 78, 251, 484
    exclusion, 661
    pathology component, 532
    recognition, 590
    survival time, 645
    syndrome, 643
Multiple sclerosis, 36, 122, 270
Muscarinic agonists, 428, 453, 501, 607
Muscarinic antagonists, 543
Muscarinic autoreceptors, 478
Muscarinic receptors
    activation, 433
    and ACh inhibition, 184
    binding, 40, 388, 389
    biochemical confirmation, 423
    distribution, 432
    function, 461, 464
    K^s conductance, 180
    response, 453-458
    stimulation, 452, 673
Myasthenia gravis, 508
Myelin lipids, 79
Myopathy, 159

N

Naloxone, 602, 607
Naltrexone, 602, 607, 608
National Institute on Aging, 18
NDAs (*See* New Drug Applications)
NE (*See* Norepinephrine)
NE-containing locus coeruleus, 343
Neocortical choline acetyltransferase, 76
Neocortex, 224, 273
Neostigmine, 501
Nerve growth factors, 273, 274, 294, 295
Neural implants and transplants, 567, 576, 579
Neural transplantation therapy, 578
Neuritogenesis, 70
Neuroactive peptides, 179
Neurobiological substrate, 338
Neurochemical abnormalities, 556
Neurochemical specificity, 151
Neurodegenerative diseases, 296

Neurodegenerative disorders, 99
Neurofibrillary tangles
    density, 485
    markers, 167
    mechanism, 340, 505, 667
    morphological changes, 78
    pathognomonic findings, 46, 70, 187, 273, 340
    restriction, 119
Neurofilament proteins, 120
Neuronal stability, 119
Neuronotrophic factors, 294-298, 302, 304, 305
Neuropeptide vasopressin, 274
Neuropeptide Y, 274, 275
Neuropeptides
    abundance, 273
    autoregulation, 274
    behavioral effects, 601
    cDNA probes, 75
    clinical studies, 239
    interactions, 281
    local immune function, 272
    reduction, 67
    stimulation, 232
Neurotoxic factors, 104
Neurotransmitter(s)
    alterations, 499
    analogues, 561
    endogenous, 272
    fluidity changes, 522
    information increase, 555
    precursors, 554
    receptors, 488
    release, 528, 569
    specific therapy, 483
    systems, 425
Neurotrophic factors
    activity, 102, 103
    cell implantation, 577
    early prediction, 104
    increase, 101, 102
    production, 108, 113
    transfer, 103
Neurotic plaques, 187, 273
New Drug Applications, 6, 7, 21
NGF (See Nerve growth factor)
Nieto-Sampedro, Manuel, 99
Nigro-striatal system, 569
N-methyl-N-nitro-N-nitrosoquanidine, 276
Noncholinergic mechanisms, 622
Nonsteroidal anti-inflammatory drugs, 521, 526
Nootropics, 590
Noradrenaline, 68, 79, 592

Noradrenergic locus coeruleus, 181, 337
    systems, 273
Noradrenergics, 69, 563
Norepinephrine
    decrease in AD brain, 591
    deficits, 474
    effects, 372, 404, 524
    elevation in AD brain, 476
    grafting, 573
    morphology, 340
    potential actions, 554
    release, 183, 346
    reuptake, 479
    synthesis, 574
Normile, Howard J., 361
Norzimeldine, 372-374
NPY (See Neuropeptide Y)
NSAID (See Nonsteroidal anti-inflammatory drug)
Nucleus basalis, 327, 340
Nucleus basalis magnocellularis, 68, 76
Nucleus locus coeruleus, 341, 352
N-terminal tyrosine, 254
N-tyrosinated peptides, 256

O

ORG 2766, 232, 248, 251
Otero, Debbie H., 385
Oubain, 392, 395, 396
Oxidative metabolism, 590
Oxotremorine
    agonist inhibitors, 388, 392, 400
    agonist properties, 489
    hypothermic response, 456, 459*, 463*-466
    structural variations, 434
    synthesis, 673
Oxytocin, 271

P

P (See Pregnenolone)
Papain, 120
Parathyroid hormone, 505
Parenchyma, 558, 569, 570
Parkinson's disease
    AD analogy, 671
    affected nerve cells, 52
    correlates, 293
    declining dopaminergic activity, 672
    effect of sera, 296, 297
    exclusion, 661
    idiopathic, 45
    intellectual impairment, 46

L-DOPA effectiveness, 452, 483, 487, 666-667
    loss of cells, 42
    loss of dopaminergic neurons, 151
    manifestations, 222
    neurochemistry, 67
    pathological signs, 477
    replacement therapy, 676
    research progress, 479, 677
    reversible syndromes, 561
    selective lesion, 68
    structural changes, 79
    transplants and grafts, 573, 574
Passive Avoidance Test, 68
PC (See Phosphatidylcholine)
PCA (p-Chloroamphetamine), 372, 373*, 374*
PCP (See Phencyclidine)
PDD (See Primary degenerative dementia)
PDGF (See Platelet-derived growth factor)
PE (See Phosphatidylethanolamine)
PeMT, 541
Pentoxifylline, 590
Pentylenetetrazol, 232, 675
Peptides
    abnormalities, 253
    alterations in aging, 246-248
    crossing blood-brain barrier, 251
    effects on behavior, 245
    imbalances, 256
    reduced concentrations in CSF, 473
    site of release, 475
    stable analogues, 478
    treatment strategies, 591
Perikarya, 541
Peripheral nervous system, 104, 271, 274, 570
    neurons, 102
Peterson, Christine, 499
Petrie, William M., 639
PG (See Prostaglandin)
Phagocytic cells, 267
Phencyclidine, 181
Phosphate, 542
Phosphatidate, 433
Phosphatidylcholine, 519, 530, 539, 541, 549
Phosphatidylethanolamine, 519
Phosphatidylserine
    analagous situation, 525
    properties, 522
    treatment strategies, 521
Phosphoinositide hydrolysis, 388
Phospholipid metabolism, 548
Phospholipids, 549

Physostigmine
      clinical trials, 67-68
      cognitive function, 533
      cortisol levels, 620
      efficacy enhancement, 509
      grafting, 571
      and hypothermia, 464
      and lecithin, 609, 610*
      limitations, 620
      and memory, 508, 509, 604*
      oral administration, 605, 606
      and REM sleep, 462
      and seizures, 500
p-Chloroamphetamine, 372
Pick's disease, 250, 477, 661
Pilicarpine
      effect, 392, 455
      response, 456, 463*
      systematic administration, 464
Piperazine estrone sulphate, 319
Piperoxan, 345, 348, 351
Piracetam, 593, 611, 657, 667, 673
Piren (See Pirenperone)
Pirenperone, 365, 368, 371
Pirenzepine, 387-389, 392, 400, 432
Pituitary, 152, 155, 156
Plaques, 33, 79, 224, 451, 667
Platelet-derived growth factor, 302
PMA, 437, 438*
PNS (See Peripheral nervous system)
Polypeptide growth factors, 99
Pomara, Nunzio, 451, 585
Positron emission tomography, 486
Potassium, 185
Potassium channels, 201
      -induced depolarization, 475
      inhibition, 409
Precursor loading, 591
      replacement therapy, 273
Pregnenolone, 189, 192
Premarin, 319
Premenstrual syndrome, 315
Preventive strategies, 223, 225
      therapies, 222, 223, 238, 239
      treatment, 674
Primary degenerative dementia, 645
Progestins, 312
Propranolol, 643
Prostaglandin
      CNS action, 179
      essential fatty acid precursors, 519, 521, 526, 531

        interactions, 525
        synthesis, 278, 528
Proteases, 119
Proton NMR imaging, 72
PS (*See* Phosphatidylserine)
Pseudodementia, 327
Pseudospecificity, 9, 10, 660
Psychostimulants, 601
Psychotropics, 591
PTZ (*See* Pentylenetetrazol)
Pump delivery systems, 648
Purkinje's cells, 134, 169
Pyramidal cells, 100, 182, 386, 458
Pyruvate dehydrogenase, 503, 505

Q

QNB binding (*See* Quinuclidinyl benzylate binding)
Quinolinic acid, 71
Quinuclidinyl benzylate binding
        decrease, 40
        drawback, 453-456, 458*-462*
        inconsistent predictor, 467
Quipazine, 362, 365, 375

R

Randt Memory Test, 323
Raphe neurons, 101
        nuclei, 70, 71, 539, 671
Rapid eye movement, 462
Rauilli, Robert, 385
Reactive synaptogenesis, 105, 110
Recognition Memory Test, 603
Regenerative therapies, 222
Reinforced alteration task, 107
REM (*See* Rapid eye movement)
Replacement therapy
        in brain aging, 222, 223, 238, 660
        potentials, 666, 672, 673
        research strategies, 656, 664
Reserpine, 613
Restriction fragment length polymorphisms, 74, 75
Retardant therapy, 223, 238
RFLP (*See* Restriction fragment length polymorphisms)
Ribonucleic acid, 312
Richardson, U. Ingrid, 539
RNA (*See* Ribonucleic acid)
RNA polymerase, 277
Roberts, Eugene, 173
Robinson, Donald S., 655
Rotrosen, John, 519
RS-86, 607

S

Sabbatsberg Depression Self-Rating Scale, 320
S-adenosyl-1-methionine, 530, 541
SAM (See S-adenosyl-1-methionine)
Sandoz Clinical Assessment Geriatric scale, 1, 486, 616, 646
Sapolsky, Robert M., 151
SCAG (See Sandoz Clinical Assessment Geriatric scale)
Scopolamine
    adverse effects, 605
    memory, 375, 386, 439, 440, 502
    prevention of tremor, 465
    in QNB binding, 454-456
    REM sleep, 462, 464
SDAT (See Senile dementia of the Alzheimer's type)
Senescence
    absence of dementia, 275
    blood-brain barrier changes, 255
    central nervous system changes, 247
    cholinergic changes, 385
    hippocampal damage, 151, 164
    stress, 152
Senile dementia of the Alzheimer's type, 173, 485, 642
Senile plaques
    genesis, 177
    immune system, 269
    marker of AD, 167, 340
    memory loss, 640
    morphological changes, 78
Septal neurons, 101
    system, 111
Septum, 102
Serotonergic antagonists, 365, 440
    nervous system, 361, 371, 372
    neurons, 71
    reuptake inhibition, 362, 479
    transmitter system, 69
Serotonin
    accuracy of memory, 440
    activation of central nervous system, 179
    alterations, 500
    binding to Hydergine®, 592
    change in markers, 474
    deficiencies, 477
    implications for AD, 361, 362
    innervation, 70
    neurons, 476
    neurotransmission, 554
    receptors, 314, 486
    reduction, 39, 68, 591
Serotonin-binding neurons, 539
Serum protein binding, 556

Sex hormone, 188
        steroids, 314
        steroid hormones, 313
SLE (*See* Systemic lupus erythematosus)
Somata, 135
Somatostatin
        drug administration, 563
        reductions in AD, 68, 79, 246, 473
        replacement, 673
Spatial discrimination task, 371
Spectrin, 120
Sphingomyelin, 519, 539
Spiperone, 486
SPM (*See* Sphingomyelin)
Stanley, Michael, 451
Steroid hormone action, 312
Stramonium, 676
Striatal neurons, 101, 104
Striatum, 541
Stone 14-unit F-maze, 371
Subarachnoid sites, 575
Subicular neurons, 101
Substance P, 69
Substantia nigra
        activation, 302
        cell body degeneration reduction, 70
        grafts, 568
        high calpain levels, 134
        implants, 573
        Parkinson's disease, 671
Sulfatides, 79
Synapses, 100, 121, 137, 138, 140
Synaptic loss and replacement, 136
        plasticity, 99, 111, 113
Synaptogenesis, 105
Systemic lupus erythematosus, 195, 202, 270

T

T-cell leukemia virus III, 675
T cells, 268, 269, 271, 272, 277
T-maze, 107, 490, 572
Tacconi, Mariaterese, 539
Tangles, 79, 224, 451, 544
Tanycytes, 250
Tardive dyskinesias, 313
Target cells, 104
Testosterone, 189, 312, 315
1,2,3,4-Tetrahydro-5-aminoacridine, 452, 563, 611, 620
THA (*See* 1,2,3,4-Tetrahydro-5-aminocridine)
Theiss, Cynthia, 385
Thromboxanes, 521, 526, 527

Thymus, 159, 271, 277
Thyrotropin-releasing hormones, 466, 675
Toffano, G., 293
Transplantation, bone marrow, 283
Tremor, 465
Tremorine, 463, 464
Tricyclic antidepressants, 665
Trophic effects, 313
Tyrosine, 673
Tyrosine hydroxylase, 524

U

Urecholine (See Bethanechol)

V

Vasodilators
        critical covariables, 663
        use in dementia, 590, 596, 597, 643
Vasointestinal peptides, 246, 273, 405
Vasopressin, 271, 404, 671
Vasopressin-containing neurons, 313
VIP (See Vasointestinal peptides)
Vitamin C, 532
Vitamin E, 532

W

Wallace, William, 67
Wechsler Adult Intelligence Scale, 323
Weinreb, Herman, 311
Wernicke-Korsakoff dementia, 36[*], 40, 42
Whitehouse, Peter J., 483
Wilson's disease, 674
Winblad, Bengt, 67
Wurtman, Richard J., 539

X

X chromosome, 275

Z

ZIM (See Zimelidine)
Zimelidine 362, 365
Zornetzer, Steven F., 337

THE COMPLETE

POCKET
POSITIVES

Incorporating
Pocket Positives
and
More Pocket Positives

SUMMIT

PRESS

PUBLISHER'S NOTE

The bestselling *Pocket Positives*, compiled by Maggie Pinkney and Barbara Whiter was first published in 1997. Due to its enormous success, a second anthology of inspirational and optimistic quotations, *More Pocket Positives*, was compiled, and published in 1999. Both books are now incorporated here in one volume.

CONTENTS

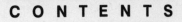

POCKET
POSITIVES

Pages 5 – 335

More
POCKET
POSITIVES

Pages 337 – 672

22 Summit Road, Noble Park
Victoria 3174 Australia
Phone: +61 3 9790 5000
Fax: +61 3 9790 6888

This edition first published 2001

This compilation © Summit Press

Editor: Maggie Pinkney
Cover design and formatting: Peter Bourne

Printed in Australia by Griffin Press

National Library of Australia Cataloguing in Publication data

The complete pocket positives, incorporating Pocket positives and More pocket positives.

ISBN 1 86503 590 4.

1.Quotations. English. 2. Optimism - Quotations, maxims, etc. 3 Success - Quotations, maxims, etc. I. Title: Pocket positives. II. Title: More pocket positives.

POCKET
POSITIVES

Compiled by Maggie Pinkney
and Barbara Whiter

— Introduction —

We all have emotional highs and lows — it's part of being human. The highs aren't a problem, but the lows can take a hold at times, unless we make a conscious effort to get rid of them. This wonderful anthology of 'pocket positives' — small gems of wisdom — provides the key to shaking off the negatives and focusing on life's positive aspects.

These inspirational quotations are a distillation of the benign and healing thoughts of the world's greatest philosophers, poets and mystics, mixed through with the more pithy observations of actors, humorists, novelists, world leaders and exceptional men and women of many other professions. Wherever possible, the dates, nationality and profession of the person quoted is given.

American actress Helen Hayes acknowledged how much we can gain from the reflections of great minds when she wrote:

> We rely upon the poets, the philosophers, and the playwrights to articulate what most of us can only feel, in joy or sorrow. They illuminate the thoughts for which we only grope; they give us the strength and balm we cannot find in ourselves...the wisdom of acceptance and the resilience to push on.

With more than a thousand quotes to choose from, there's something here to suit every occasion — and every mood. It's worth taking a bit of time out every day to dip into and reflect upon these pocket positives — even if you read only one a day. Anyone who takes to heart the wisdom contained in this book will gain a more enlightened, joyful vision of life. As American golfer Walter Hagen so succinctly put it:

> You're only here for a short visit. Don't hurry. Don't worry. And be sure to smell the flowers along the way.

A

— ABILITY —

What lies behind us, and what lies before us are tiny matters, compared to what lies within us.

Ralph Waldo Emerson (1803-1882)
American essayist, poet and philosopher

✳

When you can do the common things of life in an uncommon way, you will command the attention of the world.

Anonymous

✳

God does not ask about your ability.
He asks about your availability.

Anonymous

✳

— ABUNDANCE —

Life is constantly providing us with new funds,
new resources, even when we are reduced to
immobility. In life's ledger there is no such thing
as frozen assets.

Henry Miller (1892-1971)
American author

✦

The world is so full of a number of things,
I'm sure we should all be as happy as kings.

Robert Louis Stevenson (1850-1894)
Scottish novelist, poet and essayist

✦

Develop interest in life as you see it; in people,
things, literature, music — the world is so rich,
simply throbbing with rich treasures, beautiful
souls and interesting people. Forget yourself.

Henry Miller (1891-1980)
American author

✦

— ACCEPTANCE —

God grant me the serenity to accept the things I cannot change, the courage to change the things I can, and the wisdom to distinguish the one from the other.

Reinhold Niebuhr (1892-1971)
American theologian
(Now the prayer of Alcoholics Anonymous)

★

Acceptance of others, their looks, their behaviours, their beliefs, brings you an inner peace and tranquillity — instead of anger and resentment.

Anonymous

★

There is no good in arguing with the inevitable. The only argument available with an east wind is to put on your overcoat.

James Russell Lowell (1819-1891)
American poet and essayist

★

— ACCOMPLISH —

If you have accomplished all that you have
planned for yourself, you have not
planned enough.

Edward Everett Hale (1822-1909)
American minister and writer

✷

To accomplish great things we must not only act,
but also dream; not only plan, but also believe.

Anatole France (1844-1924)
French writer

✷

What three things do you want to accomplish
this year? Write them down and place them on
your refrigerator for inspiration all year long.

Anonymous

✷

He that is over-cautious will accomplish little.

Friedrich Von Schiller (1759-1805)
German historian and poet

✷

— ACHIEVE —

If you can walk
You can dance.
If you can talk
You can sing.

Traditional Zimbabwe

✷

Only those who dare to fail greatly can ever
achieve greatly.

Robert F. Kennedy (1925-1968)
American senator and attorney-general

✷

To achieve great things we must live as though
we were never going to die.

Luc de Clapiers, Marquis de Vauvenargues (1715-1747)
French moralist and writer

✷

Achieving starts with believing.

Anonymous

✷

— ACTION —

Doing is better than saying.

Proverb

✳

There are risks and costs to a programme of action, but they are far less than the long-range risks and costs of comfortable inaction.

John F. Kennedy (1917-1963)
President of the United States, 1960-1963

✳

A good plan violently executed right now is far better than a perfect plan executed next week.

General George Patton (1885-1945)
American army general

✳

Deliberation is the work of many men. Action, of one alone.

Charles de Gaulle (1890-1970)
French statesman

✳

Do the thing and you will have the power.

Ralph Waldo Emerson (1803-1882)
American essayist, poet and philosopher

✶

Suit the action to the word, the word to the
action; with this special observance, that you
o'erstep not the modesty of nature.

William Shakespeare (1564-1616)
English playwright and poet

✶

Keep in mind that, even if you're on the right
track, you can still be left behind if you
just sit there.

Anonymous

✶

After all is said and done, more is said than done.

Anonymous

✶

15

Do what you can with what you have,
where you are.

Theodore Roosevelt (1858-1919)
President of the United States, 1901-1912

✱

Action makes more fortunes than caution.

Luc de Clapiers, Marquis de Vauvenargues (1715-1747)
French moralist and writer

✱

Footprints on the sands of time are not made
by sitting down.

Proverb

✱

Actions speak louder than words.

Proverb

✱

Never confuse activity with action.

F. Scott Fitzgerald (1896-1940)
American novelist

✱

It is vain to say human beings might be satisfied
with tranquillity; they must have action, and they
will make it if they can not find it.

Charlotte Brontë (1816-1855)
English novelist

✶

Those who say a thing cannot be done should not
stand in the way of those who are doing it.

Anonymous

✶

Boast not of what thou would'st have done,
but do
What then thou would'st.

John Milton (1606-1674)
English poet

✶

The great end of life is not knowledge, but action.

Thomas Fuller (1608-1661)
English divine and historian

✶

— ADVERSITY —

There is no education like adversity.

Benjamin Disraeli, (1804-1881)
English statesman and writer

✱

Turn your stumbling blocks into stepping stones.

Anonymous

✱

He knows not his own strength that hath not
met adversity.

Ben Jonson (1573-1637)
English dramatist

✱

The stars are constantly shining, but often we do
not see them until the dark hours.

Anonymous

✱

What does not destroy me makes me strong.

Friedrich Wilhelm Nietzche (1844-1900)
German philosopher and critic

✳

Adversity is the state in which man most easily
becomes acquainted with himself, being
especially free of admirers then.

Samuel Johnson (1709-1784)
English lexicographer, critic and writer

✳

The way I see it, if you want the rainbow, you
gotta put up with the rain.

Dolly Parton (1946-)
American singer and songwriter

✳

Adversity has the same effect on a man that
severe training has on the pugilist — it reduces
him to his fighting weight.

Josh Billings (1818-1885)
American humorist

✳

— ADVICE —

A good scare is worth more than good advice.

Proverb

✱

No-one wants advice — only corroboration.

John Steinbeck (1902~1968)
American novelist

✱

The way of a fool seems right to him, but a wise
man listens to advice.

Proverbs 12:16

✱

Drink nothing without seeing it;
sign nothing without reading it.

Spanish proverb

✱

— AGEING —

Every man desires to live long, but no man would
be old.

Jonathan Swift (1667-1745)
English satirist

✱

Do not go gentle into that good night.
Old age should burn and rage at close of day.

Dylan Thomas (1914-1953)
Welsh poet and writer

✱

He who is of a calm and happy nature will
hardly feel the pressure of age.

Plato (c.427-c.347 BC)
Greek philosopher

✱

Many people realise their hearts' desires late in
life. Continue learning, never stop striving and
keep your curiosity sharp, and you will never
become too old to appreciate life.

Anonymous

✱

None are so old as those who have
outlived enthusiasm.

Henry David Thoreau (1817-1862)
American essayist, poet and mystic

✴

It's sad to grow old, but nice to ripen.

Brigitte Bardot (1934-)
French actress

✴

The years between fifty and seventy are the
hardest. You are always being asked to do things,
and you are not yet decrepit enough to turn
them down.

T.S. Eliot (1888-1965)
American-born poet and dramatist

✴

One of the many things nobody ever tells you
about middle age is that it's such a nice change
from being young.

Dorothy Canfield Fisher (1879-1958)
American novelist

✴

I prefer old age to the alternative.

Maurice Chevalier (1888-1972)
French singer and actor

✱

As a white candle
In a holy place,
So is the beauty
Of an old face.

Joseph Campbell (1879-1944)
Irish poet

✱

I will never be an old man. To me, old age is
always 15 years older than I am.

Bernard Baruch (1870-1965)
American financier and presidential adviser

✱

Ageing seems to be the only available way to live
a long life.

Daniel-Francois-Esprit Auber (1782-1871)
French composer

✱

One wastes so much time, one is so prodigal of life, at twenty! Our days of winter count for double. That is the compensation of the old.

George Sand (Amandine Aurore Lucie Dupin)
(1804-1876)
French novelist

★

Old age is like a plane flying through a storm. Once you're aboard, there's nothing you can do. You can't stop the plane, you can't stop the storm, you can't stop time. So one might as well accept it calmly, wisely.

Golda Meir (1898-1978)
Israeli Prime Minister, 1969-1974

★

Grey hair is great. Ask anyone who's bald.

Lee Trevino (1937-)
American golfer

★

No wise man ever wished to be younger.

Jonathan Swift (1667-1745)
English satirist

★

He who keeps a child in his heart never
grows old.

Anonymous

✱

Old age is like everything else. To make a success
of it, you've got to start young.

Fred Astaire (1899-1987)
American dancer, singer and actor

✱

I look forward to growing old and wise
and audacious.

Glenda Jackson (1937-)
English actor and politician

✱

Youth troubles over eternity, age grasps at a day
and is satisfied to have even the day.

Dame Mary Gilmore (1865-1962)
Australian poet

✱

Age is not important — unless you are a cheese.

Anonymous

✳

On the whole, I take it that middle age is a
happier period than youth.

Alexander Smith (1830-1867)
Scottish poet

✳

To know how to grow old is the master work of
wisdom, and one of the most difficult chapters in
the great art of living.

Henri Frederic Amiel (1821-1881)
Swiss poet and philosopher

✳

The evening of a well-spent life brings its lamps
with it.

Joseph Joubert (1754-1824)
French writer

✳

— AMBITION —

Everybody wants to *be* somebody; nobody wants to *grow*.

Johann Wolfgang von Goethe (1749~1832)
German poet, novelist and playwright

★

Ah, but a man's reach should exceed his grasp,
Or what's a heaven for?

Robert Browning (1812~1889)
English poet

★

If you would hit the mark, you must aim a little above it;
Every arrow that flies feels the attraction of earth.

Henry Wadsworth Longfellow (1807~1882)
American poet

★

No bird soars too high if he soars with his
own wings.

William Blake (1757-1827)
English poet, artist and mystic

When a man is no longer anxious to do better
than well, he is done for.

Benjamin Robert Haydon (1786-1846)
English painter

The rung of a ladder was never meant to rest
upon, but only to hold a man's foot long enough
to enable him to put the other somewhat higher.

Thomas Henry Huxley (1825-1895)
English biologist

— ANGER —

I was angry with my friend;
I told my wrath, my wrath did end.
I was angry with my foe;
I told it not, my wrath did grow.

William Blake (1757-1827)
English poet, artist and mystic

★

Man should forget his anger before he lies down
to sleep.

Thomas de Quincey (1785-1859)
English writer

★

— ANXIETY —

When you don't have any money, the problem is
food. When you have money, it's sex. When you
have both, it's health. If everything is simply jake,
then you're frightened of death.

James Patrick Donleavy (1926-)
Irish-American writer

★

— APPEARANCE —

Clothes and manners do not make the man; but
when he is made, they greatly improve
his appearance.

Henry Ward Beecher (1813-1887)
American clergyman

✳

There are no ugly women, only lazy ones.

Helena Rubenstein (1870-1965)
American cosmetics manufacturer

✳

Look successful, be successful.

Proverb

✳

Good temper is one of the great preservers of
the features.

William Hazlitt (1778-1830)
English essayist

✳

— APPRECIATION —

We are so often caught up in our destination that we forget to appreciate the journey, especially the goodness of the people we meet on the way. Appreciation is a wonderful feeling, don't overlook it.

Anonymous

✶

— ASPIRATIONS —

Our aspirations are our possibilities.

Samuel Johnson (1709-1784)
English lexicographer, critic and writer

✶

We can always redeem the man who aspires and tries.

Johann Wolfgang von Goethe (1749-1832)
German poet

✶

— ATTITUDE —

Attitudes are more important than facts.

Norman Vincent Peale (1898-1993)
American writer and minister

✸

A relaxed attitude lengthens a man's life.

Anonymous

✸

We are all in the gutter, but some of us are looking at the stars.

Oscar Wilde (1854-1900)
Irish poet, wit and dramatist

✸

Nothing is good or bad, but thinking makes it so.

William Shakespeare (1564-1616)
English dramatist and poet

✸

Take the attitude of a student. Never be too big to ask questions. Never know too much to learn something new.

Og Mandino (1923-)
American author

✳

The greatest revolution of our generation is the discovery that human beings, by changing the inner attitudes of their minds, can change the outer aspects of their lives.

William James (1842-1910)
American psychologist and philosopher

✳

If a man does not keep pace with his companions, perhaps it is because he hears a different drummer. Let him step to the music which he hears, however measured or far away.

Henry David Thoreau (1817-1862)
American essayist, poet and mystic

✳

B

— BEAUTY —

People are like stained-glass windows. They sparkle and shine when the sun is out, but when the darkness sets in, their true beauty is revealed only if there is a light from within.

Elisabeth Kubler-Ross (1926-)
Swiss-born American psychiatrist

✦

To look *almost* pretty is an acquisition of higher delight to a girl who has been looking plain for the first fifteen years of her life than a beauty from her cradle can ever receive.

Jane Austen (1775-1817)
English novelist

✦

It is very necessary to have makers of beauty left in a world seemingly bent on making the most evil ugliness.

Vita Sackville-West (1892-1962)
English writer, poet and renowned gardener

✦

Character contributes to beauty. It fortifies a woman as her youth fades. A mode of conduct, a standard of courage, discipline, fortitude and integrity can do a great deal to make a woman beautiful.

Jacqueline Bisset (1946-)
English actress

✶

Though we travel the world over to find the beautiful, we must carry it with us or we find it not.

Ralph Waldo Emerson (1803-1882)
American essayist, poet and philosopher

✶

Things are beautiful if you love them.

Jean Anouilh (1910-1987)
French dramatist

✶

— BEGINNING —

'Tis always morning somewhere in the world.

Richard Henry Horne (1803-1884)
English writer

★

Whatever you can do or dream you can, begin it.
Boldness has genius, power and magic in it.

Johann Wolfgang von Goethe (1749-1832)
German poet, novelist and playwright

★

A journey of a thousand miles must begin with a
single step.

Lao-Tze (c.604 BC)
Chinese philosopher and founder of Taoism

★

All glory comes from daring to begin.

Eugene F. Ware (1841-1911)
American laywyer and verse-writer

★

— BELIEF —

The secret of making something work in your
lives is first of all, the deep desire to make it
work: then the faith and belief that it can work:
then to hold that clear definite vision in your
consciousness and see it working out step by step,
without one thought of doubt or disbelief.

Eileen Caddy
Co-founder of The Findhorn Foundation, Scotland

✶

We are what we believe we are.

Benjamin Nathan Cardozo (1870-1938)
American jurist

✶

The thing always happens that you really believe
in; and the belief in a thing makes it happen.

Frank Lloyd Wright (1869-1959)
American architect

✶

Believe nothing of what you hear, and only half
of what you see.

Proverb

✱

Believe that life is worth living, and your belief
will help create the fact.

William James (1842-1910)
American psychologist and philosopher

✱

Whether you believe you can do a thing or
believe you can't, you are right.

Henry Ford (1863-1947)
American motor car manufacturer

✱

Belief consists in accepting the affirmations of the
soul; unbelief in denying them.

Ralph Waldo Emerson (1803-1882)
American essayist, poet and philosopher

✱

— BEST —

One does not know — cannot know — the best
that is in one.

Friedrich Wilhelm Nietzsche (1844-1900)
German philosopher and critic

✳

It is a funny thing about life; if you refuse to
accept anything but the best, you very often
get it.

W. Somerset Maugham (1874-1965)
English writer

✳

I am easily satisfied with the very best.

Sir Winston Churchill (1874-1965)
English statesman

✳

There is a better way to do it; find it.

Thomas A. Edison (1847-1931)
American inventor

✳

Believe in the best, think your best, study your best, have a goal for your best, never be satisfied with less than your best, try your best, and in the long run things will turn out for the best.

Henry Ford (1863-1947)
American motor car manufacturer

✱

Good, better, best,
May you never rest,
Until your good is better,
And your better best.

Anonymous

✱

Only mediocrity is always at its best.

Max Beerbohm (1872-1956)
English writer and caricaturist

✱

Don't let the best you have done so far be the standard for the rest of your life.

Gustavus F. Swift (1839-1903)
American meat industry magnate

✱

— BIG —

Do not be afraid to take a big step if one is
required. You can't cross a chasm in two
small jumps.

David Lloyd George (1863-1945)
British Prime Minister, 1916-1922

★

Think big.

Anonymous

★

— BIRTHDAYS —

Her birthdays were always important to her, for
being a born lover of life, she would always keep
the day of her entrance into it as a very great
festival indeed.

Elizabeth Goudge (1900-1984)
English author

★

— BLESSED —

'Tis being and doing and having that make
All the pleasures and pains of which
mankind partake;
To be what God pleases, to do a man's best,
And to have a good heart, is the way to be blest.

Lord Byron (1788-1824)
English poet

★

Blest, who can unconcern'dly find
Hours, days, and years, slide soft away
In health of body, peace of mind,
Quiet by day,
Sound sleep by night; study and ease
Together mix'd; sweet recreation,
And innocence, which most does please
With meditation.
Thus let me live, unseen unknown;
Thus unlamented let me die;
Steal from the world, and not a stone
Tell where I lie.

Alexander Pope (1688-1744)
English poet

★

— BLESSING —

May you have food and raiment,
A soft pillow for your head.
May you be half an hour in heaven,
Before the devil knows you're dead.

Traditional Irish

✱

Go, little book, and wish to all
Flowers in the garden, meat in the hall,
A bin of wine, a spice of wit,
A house with lawns enclosing it,
A living river by the door,
A nightingale in the sycamore.

Robert Louis Stevenson (1850-1894)
Scottish novelist, poet and essayist

✱

Now may every living thing, young or old, weak
or strong, living near or far, known or unknown,
living or departed or yet unborn, may every
living thing be full of bliss.

Buddha (5th century BC)
The founder of Buddhism

✱

— BOOKS —

How many a man has dated a new era in his life
from the reading of a book?

Henry David Thoreau (1817~1862)
American essayist, poet and mystic

★

Make books your companions; let your
bookshelves be your gardens: bask in their
beauty, gather their fruit, pluck their roses, take
their spices and myrrh.

Samuel ben Judah ibn Tibbon (1150~1230)
French-Jewish translator and physician

★

A good book is the best of friends, the same today
and forever.

Martin Farquhar Tupper (1810~1889)
English writer

★

It is impossible to mentally or socially enslave a Bible-reading people. The principles of the Bible are the groundwork of human freedom.

Horace Greeley (1811-1872)
American journalist

✸

The New Testament is the very best book that was ever or ever will be known in the world.

Charles Dickens (1812-1870)
English novelist

✸

All that mankind has done, thought, or been is lying in magic preservation in the pages of books.

Thomas Carlyle (1795-1881)
Scottish essayist, historian and philosopher

✸

Books are the quietest and most constant of friends; they are the most accessible and wisest of counsellors, and the most patient of teachers.

Charles W. Eliot (1834-1926)
English educator

✸

We rely upon the poets, the philosophers, and the playwrights to articulate what most of us can only feel, in joy or sorrow. They illuminate the thoughts for which we only grope; they give us the strength and balm we cannot find in ourselves. Whenever I feel my courage wavering I rush to them. They give me the wisdom of acceptance, the will and resilience to push on.

Helen Hayes (1900-1993)
American actress

★

Literature is my Utopia. Here I am not disenfranchised. No barrier of the sense shuts me out from the sweet, gracious discourses of my book friends. They talk to me without embarrassment or awkwardness.

Helen Keller (1880-1966)
Deaf and blind American lecturer, writer and scholar

★

— BRAIN —

The chief purpose of the body is to carry the
brain around.

Thomas A. Edison (1847-1931)
American inventor

★

I not only use all the brains I have, but all
I can borrow.

Woodrow Wilson (1856-1925)
President of the United States, 1913-1921

★

— BRAVERY —

Bravery is being the only one who knows
you're afraid.

Franklin P. Jones (1832-1902)
American capitalist and politician

★

— BRIGHT SIDE —

No one ever hurt their eyesight by looking at the
bright side of life.

Anonymous

If you can't see the bright side, polish the
dull side.

Anonymous

It is worth a thousand pounds a year to have the
habit of looking on the bright side of things.

Samuel Johnson (1709-1784)
English lexicographer, critic and writer

— BUSINESS —

The secret of business is to know something that
nobody else knows.

Aristotle Socrates Onassis (1906-1975)
Greek shipping magnate

✳

Live together like brothers, but do business
like strangers.

Anonymous

✳

Beware of all enterprises that require
new clothes.

Henry David Thoreau (1817-1862)
American essayist, poet and mystic

✳

Customer service is not a business slogan but a
religion unto itself.

Japanese business philosophy

✳

The happiest time in any man's life is when he is in red-hot pursuit of a dollar, with a reasonable prospect of overtaking it.

Josh Billings (1818-1885)
American humorist

✳

It is not the employer who pays wages — he only handles the money. It is the product that pays wages.

Henry Ford (1863-1947)
American motor car manufacturer

✳

Business should be fun. Without fun, people are left wearing emotional raincoats most of their working lives. Building fun into business is vital; it brings life into our daily being. Fun is a powerful motive for most of our activities and should be a direct path of our livelihood. We should not relegate it to something we buy after work with money we earn.

Michael Phillips (1943 -)
American movie producer

✳

C

— CAREERS —

The best careers advice to give to the young is
'Find out what you like doing best and get
someone to pay you for doing it'.

Katharine Whitehorn (1926-)
English newspaper columnist

✶

Never turn a job down because you think it's too
small; you don't know where it could lead.

Julia Morgan (1872-1957)
American architect

✶

Plough deep while sluggards sleep.

Benjamin Franklin (1706-1790)
American statesman and philosopher

✶

— CHANGE —

Things do not change: we change.

Henry David Thoreau (1817-1862)
American essayist and poet

★

You can't step into the same river twice.

Heraclitus (c.535~c.475 BC)
Greek philospher

★

If you don't like it, change it. If you don't want to
change it, it can't be that bad.

Anonymous

★

Change is a part of every life. Resisting is often as
futile as it is frustrating.

Anonymous

★

Everything flows and nothing stays.

Heraclitus (c.535-c.475 BC)
Greek philospher

★

Determination, patience and courage are the
only things needed to improve any situation. And,
if you want a situation changed badly enough,
you will find these three things.

Anonymous

★

We shrink from change; yet is there anything that
can come into being without it? What does
Nature hold dearer, or more proper to herself?
Could you have a hot bath unless the firewood
underwent some change...Is it possible for any
useful thing to be achieved without change? Do
you not see, then, that change in yourself is of the
same order, and no less necessary to Nature?

Marcus Aurelius (121-180 AD)
Roman emperor and philosopher

★

— *CHAOS* —

Chaos often breeds life, when order breeds habit.

Henry Brooks Adams (1838-1918)
American historian, journalist and teacher

✸

I say to you: one must have chaos in oneself in
order to give birth to a dancing star.

Friedrich Wilhelm Nietzsche (1844-1900)
German philosopher and critic

✸

Out of chaos comes order.

Anonymous

✸

A degree of chaos can be liberating to the
creative spirit.

Anonymous

✸

— CHARACTER —

Character consists of what you do on the third
and fourth tries.

James A. Michener (1907-)
American writer

★

Talent develops in quiet places, character in the
full current of human life.

Johann Wolfgang von Goethe (1749-1832)
German poet, novelist and playwright

★

In everyone there is something precious, found in
no-one else; so honour each man for what is
hidden within him — for what he alone has, and
none of his fellows.

Hasidic saying

★

Surely the world we live in is but the world that
lives in us.

Daisy Bates (1836-1915)
Australian social worker

★

The tree which moves some to tears of joy is, in the eye of others, only a green thing which stands in the way. As a man is, so he sees.

William Blake (1757-1827)
English poet, artist and mystic

★

In matters of style, swim with the current; in matters of principle, stand like a rock.

Thomas Jefferson (1743-1826)
President of the United States, 1801-1809

★

A man should endeavour to be as pliant as a reed, yet as hard as cedar wood.

The Talmud

★

— *CHARITY* —

With malice toward none, with charity for all.

Abraham Lincoln (1809-1865)
President of the United States, 1861-1865

★

— CHOICE —

Only she who says
She did not choose, is the loser in the end.

Adrienne Rich (1929-)
American writer

✶

The absence of alternatives clears the
mind marvellously.

Henry Alfred Kissinger (1923-)
German-American statesman and university professor

✶

You can be whatever type of person you choose
to be. Your habits, your behaviours, your
responses, are all your choice.

Anonymous

✶

Happiness or unhappiness is often a matter
of choice.

Anonymous

✶

Only by keeping the past alive in our memories
can we choose what to discard and what to retain
in our present way of life.

Lady (Phyllis Dorothy) Cilento (1894-1987)
Doctor, medical journalist and nutritionist

★

Every tomorrow has two handles. You can take
hold of the handle of anxiety or the handle of
enthusiasm. Upon your choice so will be the day.

Anonymous

★

Two roads diverged into a wood, and I —
I took the one less travelled by,
And that has made all the difference.

Robert Frost (1875-1963)
American poet

★

When you have to make a choice and you don't
make it, that itself is a choice.

William James (1842-1910)
American psychologist and philosopher

★

— COMFORT —

Whenever I have found that I have blundered or
that my work has been imperfect, and when I
have been contemptuously criticised and even
when I have been overpraised, so that I have felt
mortified, it has been my greatest comfort to say
hundreds of times to myself that 'I have worked
as hard and as well as I could, and no man can
do more than this.'

Charles Darwin (1809-1882)
English naturalist

✦

And this for comfort thou must know:
Times that are ill won't still be so;
Clouds will not ever pour down rain;
A sullen day will clear again.

Robert Herrick (1591-1674)
English poet

✦

— COMMITMENT —

We know what happens to people who stay in the middle of the road. They get run over.

Aneurin Bevan (1897-1960)
British Labour politician

✹

In for a penny, in for a pound.

Proverb

✹

I have nothing to offer but blood, toil, tears and sweat.

Sir Winston Churchill (1874-1965)
English statesman

✹

If a job is worth doing, it's worth doing properly.

Proverb

✹

— COMPROMISE —

Better bend than break.

Scottish proverb

✻

You cannot shake hands with a clenched fist.

Indira Gandhi (1917-1984)
Indian stateswoman and Prime Minister

✻

— COMPUNCTION —

The beginning of compunction is the beginning
of a new life.

George Eliot (Mary Ann Evans) (1819-1880)
English novelist

✻

— CONCENTRATION —

Concentration is my motto. First honesty, then industry, then concentration.

Andrew Carnegie (1835-1919)
Scottish-American industrialist and philanthropist

✶

The shortest way to do many things is to do only one thing at once.

Samuel Smiles (1812-1904)
Scottish author and social reformer

✶

— CONFIDENCE —

Confidence is realising that although you aren't the best at something, you still enjoy doing it.

Anonymous

✶

Confidence is the memory of past success.

Anonymous

✶

— CONSCIENCE —

Conscience: something that feels terrible when everything else feels swell.

Anonymous, from *Reader's Digest*, 1949

✱

Conscience is a cur that will let you get past it, but that you cannot stop from barking.

Anonymous

✱

A man's vanity tells him what is honour; a man's conscience what is justice.

Walter Savage Landor (1775-1864)
English poet and writer

✱

— CONSEQUENCES —

In nature there are neither rewards nor punishments — there are consequences.

Robert Green Ingersoll (1833-1899)
American agnostic

✱

— CONSTANCY —

Plus ça change, plus c'est la même chose. (The more things change, the more they stay the same.)

Alphonse Karr (1808-1890)
French writer

✶

— CONTENTMENT —

Contentment is accepting the world as an imperfect place.

Anonymous

✶

Contentment is not an emotion of incredible highs, because incredible highs always guarantee incredible lows. Contentment is satisfaction over a life that's steady, but fulfilling all the same.

Anonymous

✶

— COURAGE —

Come to the edge, he said.
They said: We are afraid.
Come to the edge, he said.
They came.
He pushed them, and they flew...

Guillaume Apollinaire (1880-1918)
French poet

★

There is only one courage and that is the courage
to let go of the past, not to collect it, not to
accumulate it, not to cling to it. We all cling to
the past, and because we cling to the past we
become unavailable to the present.

Bhagwan Shree Rajneesh
Indian spiritual cult leader

★

Courage is what it takes to stand up and speak;
courage is also what it takes to sit down
and listen.

Anonymous

★

Courage is resistance to fear, mastery of fear, not absence of fear.

Mark Twain (1835-1910)
American writer and humorist

★

No one has looked back sadly on a life full of experiences, but many look back wishing they had had the courage to do more.

Anonymous

★

Courage is reckoned the greatest of all virtues, because, unless a man has that virtue, he has no security for preserving any other.

Samuel Johnson (1709-1784)
English lexicographer, critic and writer

★

What the hell — you might be right, you might be wrong — but don't just avoid.

Katharine Hepburn (1909-)
American actor

★

You gain strength, courage and confidence by every experience in which you really stop to look fear in the face...You must do the thing you cannot do.

Eleanor Roosevelt (1884-1962)
First Lady of the United States, 1933-1945

✦

If the creator had a purpose in equipping us with a neck, he surely meant us to stick it out.

Arthur Koestler (1905-1983)
Hungarian-born writer

✦

What a new face courage puts on everything.

Ralph Waldo Emerson (1803-1883)
American essayist, poet and philosopher

✦

A stout heart breaks bad luck.

Miguel de Cervantes (1547-1616)
Spanish writer

✦

Presence of mind and courage in distress,
Are more than brave armies to procure success.

John Dryden (1631-1700)
English poet and dramatist

✱

Any coward can fight a battle when he's sure of winning, but give me the man who has pluck to fight when he's sure of losing.

George Eliot (Mary Ann Evans) (1819-1880)
English novelist

✱

Courage is the price that Life exacts for granting peace.

Amelia Earhart (1898-1937)
American aviator

✱

Man cannot discover new oceans until he has courage to lose sight of the shore.

Anonymous

✱

If one is forever cautious, can one remain a human being?

Alexander Solzhenitsyn (1918-)
Russian writer

✴

— COURTESY —

Civility costs nothing.

Proverb

✴

Good manners are made up of petty sacrifices.

Ralph Waldo Emerson (1803-1882)
American essayist, poet and philosopher

✴

Forget the eliquette books. The whole point of good manners is to put the other person at ease.

Anonymous

✴

— CREATIVITY —

Emptiness is a symptom that you are not living
creatively. You either have no goal that is
important enough to you, or you are not using
your talents and efforts in striving toward an
important goal.

Maxwell Maltz
American motivational writer

✳

Creative minds have always been known to
survive any kind of bad training.

Anna Freud (1895-1982)
Austrian psychoanalyst

✳

When in doubt, make a fool of yourself. There is
a microscopically thin line between being
brilliantly creative and acting like the most
gigantic idiot on earth. So what the hell, leap.

Cynthia Heimel
American feminist writer (from Village Voice, *1983)*

✳

— CRITICISM —

To avoid criticism, do nothing, say nothing,
be nothing.

Elbert Hubbard (1856-1915)
American writer

✦

Great Spirit, grant that I may not criticize my
neighbour until I have walked a mile in
his moccasins.

American Indian prayer

✦

If you judge people, you have no time to
love them.

Mother Teresa of Calcutta (1910-)
Yugoslav-born missionary

✦

A little self-criticism is as beneficial as too much
is harmful.

Anonymous

✦

If you hear that someone is speaking ill of you, instead of trying to defend yourself, you should say: 'He obviously does not know me very well, since there are so many other faults he could have mentioned.'

Epictetus (c.60~110 AD)
Stoic philosopher

★

He has the right to criticise, who has a heart to help.

Abraham Lincoln (1809~1865)
President of United States, 1861~1865

★

— CURIOSITY —

Curiosity is a gift, a capacity of pleasure in knowing, which if you destroy, you make yourselves cold and dull.

John Ruskin (1819~1900)
English author and art critic

✳

A sense of curiosity is nature's original school of education.

Smiley Blanton (1882~1966)
American musician

✳

The important thing is not to stop questioning.

Albert Einstein (1879~1955)
German-born American physicist

✳

Whoever retains the natural curiosity of childhood is never bored or dull.

Anonymous

✳

D

— DEATH —

Death is nothing at all; it does not count. I have only slipped away into the next room.

Canon Henry Scott-Holland (1847-1918)
British cleric

★

Do not stand at my grave and weep;
I am not there. I do not sleep.
I am a thousand winds that blow.
I am the diamond glints on snow.
I am the sunlight on ripened grain.
I am the gentle autumn's rain.
When you awaken in the morning's hush,
I am the swift uplifting rush
Of quiet birds in circled flight.
I am the soft stars that shine at night.
Do not stand at my grave and cry;
I am not there. I did not die.

Anonymous

★

It matters not how a man dies, but how he lives.
The act of dying is not of importance, it lasts so
short a time.

Samuel Johnson (1709-1784)
English lexicographer, critic and writer

✳

It is better to die on your feet than live on
your knees.

Dolores Ibarruri (1895-1989)
Spanish communist leader and orator

✳

Death can show us the way, for when we know
and understand completely that our time on this
earth is limited, and that we have no way of
knowing when it will be over, then we must live
each day as if it were the only one we had.

Elisabeth Kubler-Ross (1926-)
Swiss-born American psychiatrist

✳

To fear death, gentlemen, is nothing other than to think oneself wise when one is not; for it is to think one knows what one does not know. No man knows whether death may not even turn out to be the greatest of blessings for a human being; and yet people fear it as if they knew for certain that it is the greatest of evils.

Socrates (c.469-399 BC)
Greek philosopher

✶

As a goldsmith, taking a piece of gold transforms it into another newer and more beautiful form, even so this self, casting off this body and dissolving its ignorance, makes for itself another newer and more beautiful form.

Brhadaranyaka IV:43-4

✶

Death is but crossing the world, as friends do the seas; they live in one another still.

William Penn (1644-1718)
English Quaker and founder of Pennsylvania, USA

✶

What will survive of us is love.

Philip Larkin (1922-1985)
English poet

✱

Thinking about death...produces love for life.
When we are familiar with death, we accept
each week, each day, as a gift. Only if we are able
thus to accept life — bit by bit — does it
become precious.

Albert Schweitzer (1875-1965)
Alsatian medical missionary

✱

The years seem to rush by now, and I think of
death as a fast approaching end of a journey —
double and treble the reason for loving as well as
working while it is day.

George Eliot (Mary Ann Evans) (1819-1880)
English novelist

✱

Death is the final stage of growth in this life. There is no total death. Only the body dies. The self or spirit, or whatever you may wish to label it, is eternal.

Elisabeth Kubler-Ross (1926-)
Swiss-born American psychiatrist

✶

To die completely, a person must not only forget but be forgotten, and he who is not forgotten is not dead.

Samuel Butler (1835-1902)
English writer and satirist

✶

When we truly love, it is never lost. It is only after death that the depth of the bond is truly felt, and our loved one becomes more a part of us than was possible in life.

Oriental tradition

✶

— DECISIONS —

You don't drown by falling in the water. You
drown by staying there.

Anonymous

✴

No trumpets sound when the important
decisions of our life are made. Destiny is
made known silently.

Agnes de Mille (1908-)
American choreographer

✴

Whenever you see a successful business,
someone once made a courageous decision.

Peter Drucker (1909-)
American management consultant

✴

— DEEDS —

Our grand business in life is not to see what lies dimly at a distance, but to do what lies clearly at hand.

Thomas Carlyle (1795~1881)
Scottish essayist, historian and philosopher

✳

A man can only do what he can do. But if he does that each day he can sleep at night and do it again the next day.

Albert Schweitzer (1875~1965)
Alsatian medical missionary

✳

By his deeds we know a man.

African proverb

✳

What counts in life is not what you say but what you do.

Anonymous

✳

A deed knocks first at Thought
And then — it knocks at Will —
That is the manufacturing spot.

Emily Dickinson (1830-1886)
American poet

✶

Our deeds travel with us from afar, and what we
have been makes us what we are.

George Eliot (Mary Ann Evans) (1819-1880)
English novelist

✶

The shortest answer is doing.

English Proverb

✶

Every thought I have imprisioned in expression I
must free by my deeds.

Kahlil Gibran (1883-1931)
Lebanese writer, artist and mystic

✶

— DEFEAT —

Do not be afraid of defeat. You are never so near victory as when defeated in a good cause.

Henry Ward Beecher (1813-1887)
American clergyman

★

— DELIGHT —

Among the mind's powers is one that comes of itself to many children and artists. It need not be lost, to the end of his days, by anyone who has ever had it. This is the power of taking delight in a thing, or rather in anything, not as a means to some other end, but just because it is what it is. A child in the full health of his mind will put his hand flat on the summer lawn, feel it, and give a little shiver of private glee at the elastic firmness of the globe.

Charles Edward Montague (1867-1928)
English novelist and essayist

★

— DESIRE —

Lord, grant that I may always desire more than I can accomplish.

Michelangelo (1474-1564)
Italian sculptor, painter and poet

✶

Desires are only the lack of something: and those who have the greatest desires are in a worse condition than those who have none, or very slight ones.

Plato (c.427-347 BC)
Greek philosopher

✶

Desire is the very essence of man.

Benedict Spinoza (1632-1677)
Dutch philosopher

✶

— DESPAIR —

Despair doubles our strength.

French proverb

✱

It is always darkest just before the day dawneth.

Thomas Fuller (1608-1661)
English divine and historian

✱

When we are flat on our backs there is no way to look but up.

Roger W. Babson (1875-1967)
American economist

✱

In the midst of winter, I finally learned that there was in me an invincible summer.

Albert Camus (1913-1960)
French writer

✱

— DESTINY —

To live content with small means; to seek
elegance rather than luxury, and refinement
rather than fashion; to be worthy, not
respectable, and wealthy, not rich; to study
hard, think quietly, talk gently, act frankly; to
listen to stars and birds, to babes and sages, with
open heart; to bear all cheerfully, do all bravely,
await occasions, hurry never. In a word to let the
spiritual, unbidden and unconscious, grow up
through the common. This is to be
my symphony.

William Ellery Channing (1780-1842)
American minister

★

If thou follow thy star, thou canst not fail of a
glorious haven.

Dante Alighieri (1265-1321)
Italian poet, statesman and diplomat

★

Destiny: a tyrant's excuse for crime and a fool's excuse for failure.

Ambrose Bierce (1842-1911)
American journalist

✹

Destiny is not a matter of chance, it is a matter of choice.

William Jennings Bryan (1860-1925)
American lawyer and politician

✹

Everything that happens happens as it should, and if you observe carefully, you will find this to be so.

Marcus Aurelius (121-180 AD)
Roman emperor and philosopher

✹

We are not creatures of circumstance; we are creators of circumstance.

Benjamin Disraeli (1804-1881)
English statesman and writer

✹

— DIFFICULTY —

All things are difficult before they are easy.

Thomas Fuller (1608-1661)
English divine and historian

★

The hill, though high, I covet to ascend;
The difficulty will not offend,
For I perceive the way to life lies here.
Come, pluck up heart, let's neither faint nor fear;
Better, though difficult, the right way to go,
Than wrong, though easy,
Where the end is woe.

John Bunyan (1628-1688)
English writer and moralist

★

Keep the faculty of effort alive in you by a little
gratuitous exercise every day. That is be
systematically heroic in little unnecessary points,
do every day or two something for no other
reason than its difficulty.

William James (1842-1910)
American psychologist and philosopher

★

— DIRECTION —

I can't change the direction of the wind. But I can
adjust my sails.

Anonymous

✴

Determine on some course, more than a wild
exposure to each chance.

William Shakespeare (1564-1616)
English playwright and poet

✴

The thing has already taken form in my mind
before I start it. The first attempts are absolutely
unbearable. I say this because I want you to know
that if you see something worthwhile in what I
am doing, it is not by accident but
because of real direction and purpose.

Vincent van Gogh (1853-1890)
Dutch post-impressionist painter

✴

— DISCIPLINE —

Discipline is the soul of an army. It makes small
numbers formidable, procures success to the
weak, and esteem to all.

George Washington (1732-1799)
First President of the United States, 1789-1797

✶

— DISCOVERY —

The real voyage of discovery consists not in
seeking new landscapes but in having new eyes.

Marcel Proust (1871-1922)
French novelist

✶

Discovery consists of seeing what everybody has
seen and thinking what nobody has thought.

Albert Szent-Györgyi (1893-unknown)
Hungarian-born American biochemist

✶

— DREAMS —

Dreams don't have to come true by age 20, 30 or 40: they often occur long past when you thought possible.

Anonymous

★

All big men are dreamers. They see things in the soft haze of a spring day or in the red fire of a long winter's evening. Some of us let great dreams die, but others nourish and protect them, nurse them through bad days till they bring them to the sunshine and light which comes always to those who sincerely hope that their dreams will come true.

Woodrow Wilson (1856-1925)
President of the United States, 1913-1921

★

Some men see things as they are and say 'Why?' I dream things that never were, and say, 'Why not?'

George Bernard Shaw (1856-1950)
Irish dramatist, essayist and critic

★

Go confidently in the direction of your dreams!
Live the life you've imagined.

Henry David Thoreau (1817-1862)
American essayist, poet and mystic

✶

If you have built castles in the air, your work
need not be lost; that is where they should be.
Now put the foundations under them.

Henry David Thoreau (1817-1862)
American essayist, poet and mystic

✶

Take your dream, attach it to a star and never
lose it. If you lose it...you've lost your
enthusiasm; you've settled for something less.
This will never do. Fight like hell for your
dream and get it.

Guru RHH

✶

If there were dreams to sell,
What would you buy?
Some cost a passing-bell;
Some a light sigh.

Thomas Lovell Beddoes (1803-1849)
English poet and physiologist

✱

Those who dream by day are cognizant of many
things which escape those who dream only
by night.

Edgar Allan Poe (1809-1849)
American poet and writer

✱

Dreams are the touchstones of our characters.

Henry David Thoreau (1817-1862)
American essayist, poet and mystic

✱

The future belongs to those who believe in the
beauty of their dreams.

Eleanor Roosevelt (1884-1962)
First Lady of the United States, 1933-1945

✱

Who looks outside dreams; who looks
inside wakes.

Carl Jung (1875-1961)
Swiss psychiatrist

✷

All men dream, but not equally. Those who
dream by night in the dusty recesses of their
minds wake in the day to find that it was vanity:
but the dreamers of the day are dangerous men,
for they may act their dream with open eyes, to
make it possible.

T.E. Lawrence (Lawrence of Arabia) (1888-1935)
English soldier and writer

✷

My dreams were all my own; I accounted for
them to nobody; they were my refuge when
annoyed — my dearest pleasure when free.

Mary Shelley (1797-1851)
English author

✷

Learning to understand our dreams is a matter of learning to understand our heart's language.

Anne Faraday (1935-   )
American psychologist and dream researcher

An uninterpreted dream is like an unopened letter.

Jewish proverb

— *DURABILITY* —

The more I study the world, the more I am convinced of the inability of brute force to create anything durable.

Napoleon Bonaparte I (1769-1821)
French emperor

E

— *EDUCATION* —

Education is simply the soul of a society as it
passes from one generation to another.

G.K. Chesterton (1874-1936)
English writer

✷

If you educate a man you educate a person, but if
you educate a woman you educate a family.

Ruby Manikan (20th century)
Indian church leader

✷

— ENDURANCE —

Nothing happens to any man that he is not
formed by nature to bear.

Marcus Aurelius (121-180 BC)
Roman emperor and philosopher

✦

Endure, and keep yourself for days of happiness

Virgil (70-19 BC)
Roman poet

✦

We could never learn to be brave and patient if
there were only joy in the world.

Helen Keller (1880-1968)
Deaf and blind American lecturer, writer and scholar

✦

No pain, no palm; no thorns, no throne; no gall,
no glory; no cross, no crown.

William Penn (1644-1718)
English Quaker and founder of Pennsylvania, USA

✦

— ENEMIES —

Beware of no man more than yourself; we carry
our worst enemies within us.

Charles Haddon Spurgeon (1834-1892)
English clergyman

★

— ENERGY —

If an unusual necessity forces us onward, a
surprising thing occurs. The fatigue gets worse
up to a certain point, when, gradually or
suddenly, it passes away and we are fresher than
before! We have evidently tapped a new level of
energy. There may be layer after layer of this
experience, a third and fourth wind. We find
amounts of ease and power that we never
dreamed ourselves to own, sources of strength
habitually not taxed, because habitually we never
push through the obstruction of fatigue.

William James (1842-1910)
American psychologist and philosopher

★

— ENJOYMENT —

At the judgement day a man will be called to account for all the good things he might have enjoyed and did not enjoy.

Jewish proverb

He neither drank, smoked, nor rode a bicycle. Living frugally, saving his money, he died early, surrounded by greedy relatives. It was a great lesson to me.

John Barrymore (1882-1942)
American actor

— ENTHUSIASM —

Nothing great was ever achieved
without enthusiasm.

Ralph Waldo Emerson (1803-1882)
American essayist, poet and philosopher

★

None so old as those who have
outlived enthusiasm.

Henry David Thoreau (1817-1862)
American poet, essayist and mystic

★

If you are not getting as much from life as you
want to, then examine the state of
your enthusiasm.

Norman Vincent Peale (1898-1993)
American writer and minister

★

The person who loves always
becomes enthusiastic.

Norman Vincent Peale (1898-1993)
American writer and minister

✦

Act enthusiastic and you become enthusiastic.

Dale Carnegie (1888-1955)
American author and lecturer

✦

You can do anything if you have
enthusiasm...Enthusiasm is at the bottom of all
progress. With it, there is accomplishment.
Without it, there are only alibis.

Henry Ford (1863-1947)
American motor car manufacturer

✦

No man who is enthusiastic about his work has
anything to fear from life.

Samuel Goldwyn (1882-1974)
American film producer

✦

Do not be afraid of enthusiasm. You need it. You can do nothing effectively without it.

Francois Pierre Guillaume Guizot (1787-1874)
French historian and statesman

★

The love of life is necessary to the vigorous prosecution of any undertaking.

Samuel Johnson (1709-1784)
English lexicographer, critic and writer

★

We act as though comfort and luxury were the chief requirements of life, when all that we need to make us really happy is something to be enthusiastic about.

Charles Kingsley (1819-1875)
English writer and clergyman

★

— EXCELLENCE —

Excellence is to do a common thing in an uncommon way.

Booker Taliaferio Washington (1856-1915)
American teacher, writer and speaker

★

— EXCUSES —

He that is good at making excuses is seldom good at anything else.

Benjamin Franklin (1706-1790)
American statesman and philospher

★

The trick is not how much pain you feel — but how much joy you feel. Any idiot can feel pain. Life is full of excuses to feel pain, excuses not to live, excuses, excuses, excuses.

Erica Jong (1942-)
American novelist and poet

★

— EXPERIENCE —

Experience is not what happens to a man. It is what a man does with what happens to him.

Aldous Huxley (1894-1963)
English novelist and essayist

★

Nothing ever becomes real till it is experienced. Even a proverb is no proverb to you till your life has illustrated it.

John Keats (1795-1821)
English poet

★

And other's follies teach us not,
Nor much their wisdom teaches,
And most, of sterling worth, is what
Our own experience teaches.

Alfred, Lord Tennyson (1809-1892)
English poet

★

Experience is the name everyone gives to
their mistakes.

Oscar Wilde (1854-1900)
Irish poet, wit and dramatist

✦

Experience is a hard teacher because she gives
the test first, the lesson afterwards.

Vernon Sanders Law

✦

The art of living is the art of using experience —
your own and other people's.

Herbert Louis Samuel (1870-1963)
British politician and administrator

✦

Experience isn't interesting till it begins to repeat
itself — in fact, till it does that, it hardly
is experience.

Elizabeth Bowen (1899-1973)
Irish novelist

✦

A moment's insight is sometimes worth a life's experience.

Oliver Wendell Holmes (1809-1894)
American writer

Experience is one thing you can't get for nothing.

Oscar Wilde (1854-1900)
Irish poet, wit and dramatist

— *EXTRAORDINARY* —

The difference between ordinary and extraordinary is that little extra.

Anonymous

F

— FAILURE —

When we begin to take our failures
non-seriously, it means we are ceasing to be
afraid of them. It is of immense importance to
learn to laugh at ourselves.

Katherine Mansfield (1888-1923)
New Zealand author

★

If at first you don't succeed you're running
about average.

Margaret H. Alderson *(1959-)*
Journalist

★

A failure is a man who has blundered, but is not
able to cash in on the experience.

Elbert Hubbard (1856-1915)
American writer

★

He who never fails will never grow rich.

Charles Haddon Spurgeon (1834-1892)
English clergyman

✶

We are all of us failures — at least the best of
us are.

J.M. Barrie (1860-1937)
Scottish writer

✶

He's no failure. He's not dead yet.

Gwilym Lloyd George (1894-1967)
Welsh politician

✶

Say not that she did well or ill,
Only 'She did her best'.

Dinah Maria Craik (1826-1887)
English novelist and poet

✶

If men could regard the events of their lives with more open minds they would frequently discover that they did not really desire the things they failed to obtain.

André Maurois (1885-1967)
French writer

★

We learn wisdom from failure much more than success. We often discover what we WILL do, by finding out what we will NOT do.

Samuel Smiles (1812-1904)
Scottish author and social reformer

★

There is only one real failure in life that is possible and that is, not to be true to the best one knows.

Frederic Farrer (1831-1903)
English clergyman and writer

★

— FAITH —

Be still, sad heart! and cease repining;
Behind the clouds is the sun still shining;
Thy fate is the common fate of all,
Into each life some rain must fall.

Henry Wadsworth Longfellow (1807-1882)
American poet

✷

They can because they think they can.

Virgil (70-19 BC)
Roman poet

✷

Without winter, there can be no spring.
Without mistakes, there can be no learning.
Without doubts, there can be no faith.
Without fears, there can be no courage.
My mistakes, my fears and my doubts are my
path to wisdom, faith and courage.

Anonymous

✷

I feel no need for any other faith than my faith in human beings.

Pearl S. Buck (1892-1973)
American novelist

★

In the midst of outer dangers I have felt an inner calm and known resources of strength that only God could give. In many instances I have felt the power of God transforming the fatigue of despair into the buoyancy of hope. I am convinced that the universe is under the control of a loving purpose and that in the struggle for righteousness man has cosmic companionship. Behind the harsh appearances of the world there is a benign power.

Martin Luther King (1929-1968)
American black civil-rights leader

★

Proof is the last thing looked for by a truly religious mind which feels the imaginative fitness of its faith.

George Santayana (1863-1952)
Spanish-American philosopher and poet

★

Dame Edith Sitwell, when asked why she had come to faith, said she had looked at the pattern of a frosted flower on a window-pane, she had studied shells, feathers, petals and grasses, and she knew without doubt there must be a cause...

Quoted in *Christian Poetry*

★

He who sees the Infinite in all things sees God.

William Blake (1757-1827)
English poet, artist and mystic

★

I believe in God and in nature and in the triumph of good over evil.

Johann Wolfgang von Goethe (1749-1832)
German poet, novelist and playwright

★

If you have abandoned one faith, do not abandon all faith. There is always an alternative to the faith we lose. Or could it be the same thing under another mask?

Graham Greene (1904-1991)
English novelist

★

— FATE —

Whatever fate befalls you, do not give way to great rejoicing, or great lamentation...All things are full of change, and your fortunes may turn at any moment.

Arthur Schopenhauer (1788-1860)
Philosopher

✦

Lots of folks confuse bad management with destiny.

Frank McKinney Hubbard (1868-1930)

✦

I do not believe in a fate that falls on men however they act; but I do believe in a fate that falls on them unless they act.

G.K. Chesterton (1874-1936)
English writer

✦

— FAULTS —

When you have faults, do not fear to
abandon them.

Confucius (551~479 BC)
Chinese philosopher

✳

We all have faults. It's important to recognise
your own, but to try and turn a blind eye to the
faults of others.

Anonymous

✳

Love your enemies, for they tell you your faults.

Benjamin Franklin (1706~1790)
American statesman and philosopher

✳

— FEAR —

Fear is never a reason for quitting: it is only
an excuse.

Norman Vincent Peale (1898~1993)
American writer and minister

✴

To fear love is to fear life, and those who fear life
are already three parts dead.

Bertrand Russell (1872~1970)
English philosopher and mathematician

✴

Do the thing you fear and the death of fear
is certain.

Ralph Waldo Emerson (1803~1882)
American essayist, poet and philosopher

✴

There is no fear in love; but perfect love casteth
out fear: because fear hath torment. He that
feareth is not made perfect in love.

1 John 4:18

✴

Nothing in life is to be feared. It is only to
be understood.

Marie Curie (1867-1934)
French physicist

★

Let me assert my firm belief that the only things
we have to fear is fear itself.

Franklin D. Roosevelt (1882-1945)
President of the United States, 1932-1945

★

To conquer fear is the beginning of wisdom, in
the pursuit of truth as in the endeavour after a
worthy manner of life.

Bertrand Russell (1872-1970)
English philosopher and mathematician

★

Considering how dangerous everything is
nothing is really very frightening.

Gertrude Stein (1874-1946)
American author

★

Of all the liars in the world, sometimes the worst are your own fears.

Rudyard Kipling (1865-1936)
English poet and author

★

When I became ill, the years of pain and confusion loomed up like some primitive monster of the deep. I had to face the monster or drown. There were many nights when I thought I was going under for the last time. I lived in fear of dying. The strange paradox is that by confronting my fear of death, I found myself and created a new life.

Lucia Capacchione
American art therapist and pioneer in inner healing

★

Carry your own lantern and you need not fear the dark.

*Leo Rosten's Treasury of Jewish
Quotations*

★

— *FORGIVENESS* —

Forgive your enemies, but never forget
their names.

John F. Kennedy (1917-1963)
President of the United States, 1961-1963

Lift up your eyes and look on one another in
innocence born of complete forgiveness of each
other's illusions.

A Course in Miracles

The forgiving state of mind is a magnetic power
for attracting good. No good thing can be
withheld from the forgiving state of mind.

Catherine Ponder
American motivational writer

To err is human, to forgive, divine.

Alexander Pope (1688-1744)
English poet

✱

The reason to forgive is for your own sake. For our own health Because beyond that point needed for healing, if we hold onto our anger, we stop growing and our souls begin to shrivel.

M. Scott Peck (1936-)
American psychiatrist and writer

✱

One forgives as much as one loves.

Francois, Duc de La Rochefoucauld (1616-1680)
French writer

✱

Sometimes the hardest person to forgive is yourself. But we shouldn't be harder on ourselves than we would be on others.

Anonymous

✱

— FREEDOM —

Once freedom lights its beacon in a man's heart,
the gods are powerless against him.

Jean-Paul Sartre (1905-1980)
French writer

★

I disapprove of what you say, but I will defend to
the death your right to say it.

Voltaire (1694-1778)
French author

★

The moment the slave resolves that he will no
longer be a slave, his fetters fall. He frees himself
and shows the way to others. Freedom and
slavery are mental states.

Mahatma Gandhi (1869-1948)
Indian leader, moral teacher and reformer

★

Freedom is the right to tell people what they do not want to hear.

George Orwell (1903-1950)
English novelist

✳

Man is free at the moment he wishes to be.

Voltaire (1694-1778)
French writer

✳

You only have power over people so long as you don't take everything away from them. But when you've robbed a man of everything he's no longer in your power — he's free again.

Alexander Solzhenitsyn (1918-)
Russian writer

✳

Freedom's just another word for nothing left to lose.

Kris Kristofferson (1936-)
American actor and folk singer

✳

The most beautiful thing in the world is freedom of speech.

Diogenes (412?-323 BC)
Greek philosopher

✦

Liberty, when it begins to take root, is a plant of rapid growth.

George Washington (1732-1799)
First President of the United States, 1789-1797

✦

Liberty means responsibility. That is why most dread it.

George Bernard Shaw (1856-1950)
Irish dramatist, essayist and critic

✦

The love of liberty is the love of others.
The love of power is the love of ourselves.

William Hazlitt (1778-1830)
English essayist

✦

— FRIENDS —

Your friend is the man who knows all about you,
and still likes you.

Elbert Hubbard (1856-1915)
American writer

✱

The only way to have a friend is to be one.

Ralph Waldo Emerson (1803-1882)
American essayist, poet and philosopher

✱

Friendship is always a sweet responsibility, never
an opportunity.

Kahlil Gibran (1883-1931)
Lebanese poet, writer, artist and mystic

✱

So long as we are loved by others I should say
that we are almost indispensable; and no man is
useless while he has a friend.

Robert Louis Stevenson (1850-1894)
Scottish novelist, poet and essayist

✱

Slender at first, they quickly gather force,
Growing in richness as they run their course;
Once started, they do not turn back again:
Rivers, and years, and friendships with good men.

Sanskrit poem

✶

Don't sacrifice your life to work and ideals. The
most important things in life are human
relations. I found that out too late.

Katharine Susannah Prichard (1883-1969)
Australian author

✶

Am I not destroying my enemies when I make
friends of them?

Abraham Lincoln (1809-1865)
President of the United States, 1861-1865

✶

A man who turns his back on his friends soon
finds himself facing a very small audience.

Dick Powell (1904-1963)
American actor

✶

No man is wise enough by himself.

Titus Maccius Plautus (250-184 BC)
Roman poet and comic playwright

✱

Forsake not an old friend; for the new is not comparable to him: a new friend is as new wine; when it is old, thou shalt drink it with pleasure.

Ecclesiastes

✱

Instead of loving your enemies treat your friends a little better.

E.W. Howe (1853-1937)
American novelist

✱

Friendship consists in forgetting what one gives, and remembering what one receives.

Alexandré Dumas (1803-1870)
French novelist

✱

He that is a friend to himself, know; he is a friend to all.

Montaigne (1533-1592)
French essayist

★

Animals are such agreeable friends — they ask no questions, they pass no criticisms.

George Eliot (Mary Ann Evans) 1819-1880
English novelist

★

Be a friend to thyself and others will too.

Thomas Fuller (1608-1661)
English divine and historian

★

What is a friend? A single soul dwelling in two bodies.

Aristotle (384-322 BC)
Greek philosopher

★

The thread of our life would be dark,
Heaven knows!
If it were not with friendship and love
intertwined.

Thomas Moore (1779-1852)
Irish poet

✱

Where there are friends, there is wealth.

Titus Maccius Plautus (250-184 BC)
Roman poet and comic playwright

✱

They are rich who have true friends.

Thomas Fuller (1608-1661)
English divine and historian

✱

Friendship is a sheltering tree.

Samuel Taylor Coleridge (1772-1834)
English poet

✱

Friendship is the gift of the gods, and the most precious boon to man.

Benjamin Disraeli (1804-1881)
English statesman and author

★

You can always tell a real friend: when you've made a fool of yourself he doesn't feel you've done a permanent job.

Laurence J. Peter (1918-)
Canadian writer

★

The light of friendship is like the light of phosphorus, even plainest when all around is dark.

Grace Crowell (1877-1969)
American poet

★

— FULFILMENT —

Fulfilment is deciding what you want out of life,
and working towards it. Fulfilment is not merely
the reaching of a specific destination.

Anonymous

✳

Fulfilment is reaching your own expectations, not
the expectations of others.

Anonymous

✳

It is never too late to be what you might
have been.

George Eliot (Mary Ann Evans)
(1819-1880)
English novelist

✳

— FUTURE —

I am not interested in the past. I am interested in the future, for that is where I expect to spend the rest of my life.

Charles Franklin Kettering (1876-1958)
American engineer and inventor

★

Future — that period of time in which our affairs prosper, our friends are true and our happiness is assured.

Ambrose Bierce (1842-1914)
American writer

★

What are you looking forward to in the next year? The next ten years? Isn't it exciting to imagine all the possibilities the future holds?

Anonymous

★

Never let the future disturb you. You will meet it,
if you have to, with the same weapons of reason
which today arm you against the present.

Marcus Aurelius (121-180 AD)
Roman emperor and philosopher

The best thing about the future is that it comes
only one day at a time.

Abraham Lincoln (1809-1865)
President of United States, (1861-1865)

To most of us the future seems unsure; but then it
always has been, and we who have seen great
changes must have great hopes.

John Masefield (1878-1967)
English poet

G

— GARDENS —

Who loves a garden still his Eden keeps,
Perennial pleasures, plants and wholesome
harvest reaps.

Amos Bronson Alcott (1799-1888)
American teacher and philosopher

★

Yes, in the poor man's garden grow
Far more than herbs and flowers —
Kind thoughts, contentments, peace of mind,
And joy for weary hours.

Mary Howitt (1799-1888)
English author

★

He who has roses in his garden also has roses in
his heart.

Anonymous

★

I scorn the doubts and cares that hurt
The world and all its mockeries,
My only care is now to squirt
The ferns among my rockeries.
In early youth and later life
I've seen an up and seen a down,
And now I have a loving wife
To help me peg verbena down.

...

In peace and quiet pass our days,
With nought to vex our craniums,
Our middle beds are all ablaze
With red and white geraniums.

...

Let him who'd have the peace he needs
Give all his worldly mumming up,
Then dig a garden, plant the seeds,
And watch the product coming up.

George R. Sims (1847-1922)
English poet

✴

One is nearer God's Heart in a garden,
Than anywhere else on earth.

Dorothy Frances Gurney (1858-1932)
English poet

✴

— GENIUS —

Genius is one per cent inspiration and
ninety-nine per cent perspiration.

Thomas A. Edison (1847-1931)
American inventor

✦

One is not born a genius, one becomes a genius.

Simone de Beauvoir (1908-1986)
French writer

✦

Genius is nothing but labour and diligence.

William Hogarth (1697-1764)
English painter and political caricaturist

✦

To believe your own thought, to believe that what
is true for you in your private heart is true for all
men — that is genius.

Ralph Waldo Emerson (1803-1882)
American essayist, poet and philosopher

✦

— GIFTS —

You are surrounded by gifts every living moment
of every day. Let yourself feel appreciation for
their presence in your life and take the time to
acknowledge their splendour.

Lon G. Nungesser
Writer

✱

Earth's crammed with heaven,
And every common bush afire with God.

Elizabeth Barrett Browning (1806-1861)
English poet

✱

O gift of God! a perfect day,
Whereon shall no man work but play,
Whereon it is enough for me
Not to be doing but to be.

Henry Wadsworth Longfellow (1807-1882)
American poet

✱

— GIVING —

You give but little when you give of your possessions. It is when you give of yourself that you truly give.

Kahlil Gibran (1883-1931)
Lebanese poet, writer, artist and mystic

✷

The only gift is a portion of thyself.

Ralph Waldo Emerson (1803-1882)
American essayist, poet and philosopher

✷

The manner of giving is worth more than the gift.

Pierre Corneille (1606-1684)
French dramatist

✷

Every man according as he purposeth in his heart, so let him give; not grudgingly, or out of necessity: for God loveth a cheerful giver.

Corinthians 9:7

✷

— GOALS —

You have to know what you want to get. But when you know that, let it take you. And if it seems to take you off the track, don't hold back, because perhaps that is instinctively where you want to be. And if you hold back and try to be always where you have been before, you will go dry.

Gertrude Stein (1874-1946)
American writer

✱

One can never consent to creep when one feels an impulse to soar.

Helen Keller (1880-1968)
Deaf and blind American lecturer, writer and scholar

✱

Shoot for the moon. Even if you miss it you will land among the stars.

Les (Lester Louis) Brown (1928-)
Journalist

✱

All successful people have a goal. No one can get anywhere unless he knows where he wants to go and what he wants to be or do.

Norman Vincent Peale (1898-1993)
American writer and minister

✶

A man without a purpose is like a ship without a rudder.

Thomas Carlyle (1795-1881)
Scottish essayist, historian and philosopher

✶

The world stands aside for he who knows where he is going.

Proverb

✶

The significance of a man is not in what he attains, but rather in what he longs to attain.

Kahil Gibran (1883-1931)
Lebanese writer, artist and mystic

✶

We're all born under the same sky, but we don't all have the same horizon.

Konrad Adenauer (1876-1967)
German lawyer and statesman

Knowing your destination is half the journey.

Anonymous

Once you say you're going to settle for second, that's what happens to you in life, I find.

John F. Kennedy (1917-1963)
President of United States, 1960-1963

— GOOD —

Do all the good you can,
By all the means you can,
In all the ways you can,
In all the places you can,
At all the times you can,
To all the people you can,
As long as ever you can.

John Wesley (1703–1791)
English evangelist and founder of Methodism

★

Set your sights high, the higher the better. Expect
the most wonderful things to happen, not in the
future but right now. Realise that nothing is too
good. Allow absolutely nothing to hamper you or
hold you up in any way.

Eileen Caddy
Co-founder of The Findhorn Foundation, Scotland

★

What is a weed? A plant whose virtues have not
been discovered.

Ralph Waldo Emerson (1803-1882)
American poet and essayist

★

Goodness does not more certainly make men
happy than happiness makes them good.

Walter Savage Landor (1775-1864)
English poet and writer

★

Nothing can harm a good man, either in life or
after death.

Socrates (469-399 BC)
Greek philosopher

★

What is beautiful is good, and who is good will
soon also be beautiful.

Sappho (died 610 BC)
Greek lyric poet

★

— GREATNESS —

There is a great man, who makes every man feel
small. But the real great man is the man who
makes every man feel great.

G.K. Chesterton (1874~1936)
English author

✶

It's great to be great, but it's greater to
be human.

Will Rogers (1879~1935)
American actor and humorist

✶

For the courage of greatness is adventurous and
knows not withdrawing,
But grasps the nettle danger, with resolute hands,
And ever again
Gathers security from the sting of pain.

Vera Brittain (1893~1970)
English author and poet

✶

Lives of great men all remind us
We can make our lives sublime,
And, departing leave behind us
Footprints on the sands of time.

Henry Wadsworth Longfellow (1807-1882)
American poet

★

We are all worms, but I do believe that I am a
glow-worm.

Sir Winston Churchill (1874-1965)
English statesman

★

One can build the Empire State Building,
discipline the Prussian army, make a state
hierarchy mightier than God, yet fail to overcome
the unaccountable superiority of certain
human beings.

Alexander Solzhenitsyn (1918-)
Russian writer

★

— GROWTH —

The great law of culture is: Let each become all
that he was created capable of being.

Thomas Carlyle (1795-1881)
Scottish essayist, historian and philosopher

★

My business is not to remake myself,
But make the absolute best of what God made.

Robert Browning (1812-1889)
English poet

★

Love not what you are but what you
may become.

Miguel de Cervantes (1547-1616)
Spanish author

★

Moments of guilt, moments of contrition,
moments when we are lacking in self-esteem,
moments when we are bearing the trial of being
displeasing to ourselves, are essential to
our growth.

M. Scott Peck (1936-)
American psychiatrist and writer

✶

Be not afraid of growing slowly. Be afraid of
standing still.

Chinese proverb

✶

Examine myself as I may, I can no longer find the
slightest trace of the anxious, agitated individual
of those years, so discontented with herself, so
out of patience with others.

George Sand (Amandine Aurora Lucie Dupin)
(1804-1876)
French novelist

✶

Large streams from little fountains flow,
Tall oaks from little acorns grow.

David Everett (1770-1813)
English poet and writer

✶

The creation of a thousand forests is
in one acorn.

Ralph Waldo Emerson (1803-1882)
American essayist, poet and philosopher

✶

Real development is not leaving things behind, as
on a road, but drawing life from them,
as on a root.

G.K. Chesterton (1874-1936)
English writer

✶

$\mathcal{H}$

— HABIT —

Habit is a great deadener.

Samuel Beckett (1906-1989)
Irish novelist and dramatist

✶

The chains of habit are too weak to be felt until they are too strong to be broken.

Samuel Johnson (1709-1784)
English lexicographer, critic and writer

✶

Habit is habit, and not to be flung out the window by man, but coaxed downstairs, a step at a time.

Mark Twain (1835-1910)
American writer and humorist

✶

— HAPPINESS —

One joy scatters a hundred griefs.

Chinese proverb

✴

One is happy as a result of one's own efforts,
once one knows the necessary ingredients of
happiness — simple tastes, a certain degree of
courage, self-denial to a point, love of work, and
above all, a clear conscience. Happiness is no
vague dream.

George Sand (Amandine Aurore Lucie Dupin)
(1804-1876)
French novelist

✴

It is impossible for a man to be made happy by
putting him in a happy place, unless he be first in
a happy state.

Benjamin Whichcote (1609-1683)
English philosopher and theologian

✴

The supreme happiness of life is the conviction that we are loved; loved for ourselves, or rather, loved in spite of ourselves.

Victor Hugo (1802-1885)
French poet and author

★

Happiness is as a butterfly which, when pursued, is always beyond our grasp, but which, if you will sit down quietly, may alight upon you.

Nathaniel Hawthorne (1804-1864)
American novelist and short story writer

★

All happiness depends on a leisurely breakfast.

John Gunter (1938-)
English designer

★

We spend so much time yearning for that special item that will finally make us happy, that we don't take the time to look around and discover that we already are.

Anonymous

★

Happiness is a mystery like religion, and should never be rationalised.

G.K. Chesteron (1874-1936)
English author

✸

A lifetime of happiness! No man alive could bear it: it would be hell on earth.

George Bernard Shaw (1856-1950)
Irish dramatist, essayist and critic

✸

Happiness lies in the joy of achievement and the thrill of creative effort.

Franklin D. Roosevelt (1882-1945)
President of the United States, 1933-1945

✸

Action may not always bring happiness, but there is no happiness without action.

Benjamin Disraeli (1804-1881)
English statesman and writer

✸

Knowledge of what is possible is the beginning
of happiness.

George Santayana (1863~1952)
Spanish~American philosopher and poet

Happiness doesn't depend on the actual number
of blessings we manage to scratch from life, only
our attitude towards them.

Alexander Solzhenitsyn (1918~)
Russian writer

When a small child...I thought that success
spelled happiness. I was wrong. Happiness is like
a butterfly which appears and delights us for one
brief moment, but soon flits away.

Anna Pavlova (1881~1931)
Russian ballet dancer

Happiness in this world, when it comes, comes incidentally. Make it the object of pursuit, and it leads us a wild-goose chase, and is never attained.

Nathaniel Hawthorne (1804-1864)
American novelist and short story writer

★

The happiest people seem to be those who are producing something; the bored people are those who are consuming much and producing nothing.

William Inge (1860-1954)
English prelate and author

★

To be without some of the things you want is an indispensable part of happiness.

Bertrand Russell (1872-1970)
English philosopher and mathematician

★

There is no duty we so much underestimate as the duty of being happy. Being happy we sow anonymous benefits upon the world.

Robert Louis Stevenson (1850-1894)
Scottish novelist, poet and essayist

✷

The best way to future happiness is to be as happy as is rightfully possible today.

Charles W. Eliot (1834-1926)
English educator

✷

Most happy is he who is entirely self-reliant, and who centres all his requirements on himself.

Marcus Tullius Cicero (106-43 BC)
Roman orator, statesman and writer

✷

The happiness of life is made up of minute fractions. The little soon forgotten charities of a kiss or smile, a kind look, a hearfelt compliment — countless infinitesimals of pleasurable and genial feelings.

Samuel Taylor Coleridge (1772-1834)
English poet

✷

A man is happy so long as he chooses to
be happy.

Alexander Solzhenitsyn (1918-)
Russian writer

Man's life is happy mainly because he is always
expecting that it will soon be so.

Edgar Allen Poe (1809-1849)
American poet and writer

There is only one happiness in life, to love and to
be loved...

George Sand (Amandine Aurore Lucie Dupin)
(1804-1876)
French novelist

— HATRED —

It's a sign of your own worth sometimes if you
are hated by the right people.

Miles (Stella Maria) Franklin (1879-1954)
Australian writer

✦

Hatred and bitterness can never cure the disease
of fear; only love can do that. Hatred paralyses
life; love harmonises it. Hatred darkens life; love
illumines it.

Martin Luther King (1929-1968)
American black civil-rights leader

✦

Hatred rarely does any harm to its object. It is the
hater who suffers.

Lord Beaverbrook (1879-1964)
Canadian-born newspaper proprietor

✦

— HEALTH —

Health and cheerfulness mutually beget
each other.

Joseph Addison (1672-1719)
English essayist

✴

To wish to be well is a part of becoming well.

Seneca (4 BC-65 AD)
Roman philosopher and statesman

✴

To get the body in tone, get the mind in tune.

Zachary T. Bercovitz (1895-1984)
American doctor and writer

✴

Look to your health; and if you have it, praise
God, and value it next to a good conscience; for
health is the second blessing that we mortals are
capable of; a blessing that money can not buy.

Isaak Walton (1593-1683)
English writer

✴

— HEART —

The heart of the wise, like a mirror, should
reflect all objects, without being sullied by any.

Confucius (551-479 BC)
Chinese philosopher

✳

Keep a green tree in your heart and perhaps a
singing bird will come.

Chinese proverb

✳

The best exercise for the heart is to bend over
backwards for someone else.

Anonymous

✳

I love thee for a heart that's kind.
Not for the knowledge in thy mind.

W.H. Davies (1871-1940)
Welsh poet

✳

— HEAVEN —

Heaven means to be at one with God.

Confucius (551-479 BC)
Chinese philosopher

✶

As much of heaven is visible as we have eyes
to see.

William Winter (1836-1917)
American dramatic critic and poet

✶

The Way of Heaven has no favourites. It is always
with the good man.

Lao-Tze (c.604 BC)
Chinese philosopher and founder of Taoism

✶

Earth has no sorrow that Heaven cannot heal.

Thomas Moore (1779-1852)
Irish poet

✶

— HELP —

If a friend is in trouble, don't annoy him by
asking him if there's anything you can do. Think
of something appropriate and do it.

E.W. Howe (1853-1937)
American writer

✱

No-one is useless in the world who lightens the
burden of it for anyone else.

Charles Dickens (1812-1870)
English author

✱

Many hands make light work.

Proverb

✱

Troubles shared are troubles halved.

Proverb

✱

— HOME —

A man travels the world over in search of what
he needs and returns home to find it.

George Moore (1852-1933)
Irish writer and art critic

★

No place is more delightful than one's
own fireside.

Marcus Tullius Cicero (106-43 BC)
Roman orator, statesman and writer

★

But what on earth is half so dear — so longed for
— as the hearth of home?

Emily Brontë (1818-1848)
English poet and novelist

★

Whom God loves, his house is sweet to him.

Miguel de Cervantes (1547-1616)
Spanish writer

★

A comfortable home is a great source of happiness. It ranks immediately after health and a good conscience.

Sydney Smith (1771-1845)
English essayist, clergyman and writer

★

My kitchen is a mystical place, a kind of temple for me. It is a place where the surfaces seem to have significance, where the sounds and odors carry meaning that transfers from the past and bridges to the future.

Pearl Bailey (1918-1986)
American singer

★

— *HONESTY* —

Being entirely honest with oneself is a good exercise.

Sigmund Freud (1856-1939)
Austrian founder of psychoanalysis

★

— HOPE —

There are no hopeless situations; there are only men who have grown hopeless about them.

Clare Booth Luce (1903-1987)
American playwright

✶

Do not fear to hope...
Each time we smell the autumn's dying scent,
We know that primrose time will come again.

Samuel Taylor Coleridge (1772-1834)
English poet

✶

We should not let our fears hold us back from pursuing our hopes.

John F. Kennedy (1917-1963)
President of the United States, 1960-1963

✶

Great hopes make great men.

Thomas Fuller (1608-1661)
English divine and historian

✶

We must accept finite disappointment, but we must never lose infinite hope.

Martin Luther King (1929-1968)
American black civil-rights leader

★

Hope is itself a species of happiness and, perhaps, the chief happiness which this world affords.

Samuel Johnson (1709-1784)
English lexicographer, critic and writer

★

For what human ill does not dawn seem to be an alleviation?

Thornton Wilder (1897-1975)
American writer

★

Everything that is done in the world is done by hope.

Martin Luther (1483-1546)
German religious reformer

★

— HUMOUR —

Humour is mankind's greatest blessing.

Mark Twain (1835-1910)
American writer and humorist

✳

Total absence of humour renders life impossible.

Colette (1873-1954)
French novelist

✳

Everything is funny, as long as it's happening to
somebody else.

Will Rogers (1879-1935)
American actor and humorist

✳

He deserves paradise who makes his
companions laugh.

The Koran

✳

I

— IDEAS —

Greater than the tread of mighty armies is an idea whose time has come.

Victor Hugo (1802-1885)
French poet and author

★

A crank is a man with a new idea — until it catches on.

Mark Twain (1835-1910)
American writer and humorist

★

What was once thought can never be unthought.

Friedrich Durrenmatt (1921-)
Swiss writer

★

If you don't follow through on your creative ideas, someone else will pick them up and use them. When you get an idea of this sort, you should jump in with both feet, not just stick your toe in the water... Be daring, be fearless, and don't be afraid that somebody is going to criticize you or laugh at you. If your ego is not involved no-one can hurt you.

Guru RHH

✳

A stand can be made against invasion by an army; no stand can be made against invasion by an idea.

Victor Hugo (1802-1885)
French writer

✳

— IGNORANCE —

To be conscious that you are ignorant is a great step to knowledge.

Benjamin Disraeli (1804-1881)
English statesman and writer

✳

— IMAGINATION —

What is now proved was once only imagined.

William Blake (1757-1827)
English poet, artist and mystic

✦

Man's mind, once stretched by a new idea, never regains its original dimension.

Oliver Wendell Holmes (1809-1894)
American writer

✦

Imagination is more important than knowledge.

Albert Einstein (1879-1955)
German-born physicist

✦

This world is but canvas to our imaginations.

Henry David Thoreau (1817-1862)
American essayist, poet and mystic

✦

Imagination is the highest kite one can fly.

Lauren Bacall (1924-)
American actress

Imagination, industry and intelligence — 'the three I's' — are all indispensable to the actress, but of these three the greatest is, without any doubt, imagination.

Ellen Terry (1848-1928)
English actress

There are no rules of architecture for a castle in the clouds.

G.K. Chesterton (1874-1936)
English critic, novelist and poet

— *IMPERFECTION* —

No one should abandon duties because he see defects in them. Every action, every activity, is surrounded by defects as a fire is surrounded by smoke.

Bhagavad Gita

✳

— *IMPRESSION* —

You never get a second chance to make a good first impression.

Anonymous

✳

Every man is a hero and an oracle to somebody, and to that person, whatever he says has an enhanced value.

Ralph Waldo Emerson (1803-1882)
American essayist, poet and philosopher

✳

— INDEPENDENCE —

Depend not on another, but lean instead on
thyself...True happiness is born of self-reliance.

The Laws of Manu, Hindu teachings

✱

It's easy to be independent when you've got
money. But to be independent when you haven't
got a thing — that's the Lord's test.

Mahalia Jackson (1911-1972)
American spirituals singer

✱

The strongest man in the world is he who
stands alone.

Henrik Ibsen (1828-1906)
Norwegian dramatist

✱

Follow your own bent, no matter what
people say.

Karl Marx (1818-1883)
German philosopher

✱

— INDIVIDUALITY —

Conformity is one of the most fundamental
dishonesties of all. When we reject our
specialness, water down our God-given
individuality and uniqueness, we begin to lose
our freedom. The conformist is in no way a free
man. He has to follow the herd.

Norman Vincent Peale (1898-1993)
American writer and minister

✸

Every individual has a place to fill in the world,
and is important, in some respect, whether he
chooses to be or not.

Nathaniel Hawthorne (1804-1864)
American novelist

✸

— INTEGRITY —

If you don't stand for something...you'll fall
for anything.

Anonymous

✱

Integrity without knowledge is weak and useless,
and knowledge without integrity is dangerous
and dreadful.

Samuel Johnson (1709~1784)
British lexicographer, critic and writer

✱

My strength is as the strength of ten,
Because my heart is pure.

Alfred, Lord Tennyson (1809-1892)
English poet

✱

This above all — to thine own self be true,
And it must follow, as night follows day,
Thou canst not then be false to any man.

William Shakespeare (1564-1616)
English playwright and poet

✱

— INTUITION —

Intelligence highly awakened is intuition, which
is the only true guide in life.

Jiddu Krishnamurti (1895-1986)
Indian theosophist

✶

We belittle an intuition, calling it only a hunch,
and therefore not be taken too seriously. I
encourage you to take your hunches and
intuitions very seriously. They contain some of
your highest, most profound insights
and wisdom.

Lucia Capacchione
American art therapist and pioneer in inner healing

✶

Intuition is a truth that arrives in the
mind unbidden.

Anonymous

✶

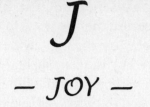

J

– JOY –

May your joys be as deep as the ocean, your sorrows as light as its foam.

Anonymous

✱

The life without festivals is a long road without an inn.

Democritus (c.460 BC)
Greek philosopher

✱

Joy exists only in self-acceptance. Seek perfect acceptance, not a perfect life.

Anonymous

✱

Joy is not in things; it is in us.

Richard Wagner (1813-1883)
German composer

✱

Joy, Lady, is the spirit and the power,
Which wedding nature gives to us in dower,
A new earth and new heaven,
Undreamt of by the sensual and the proud —
Joy is the sweet voice, joy the luminous cloud —
We in ourselves rejoice.

Samuel Taylor Coleridge (1772-1834)
English poet

✴

Joy is one of nature's greatest medicines. Joy is always healthy. A pleasant state of mind tends to bring abnormal conditions back to normal.

Catherine Ponder
American motivational writer

✴

Taking joy in life is a woman's best cosmetic.

Rosalind Russell (1911-1976)
American actress

✴

The more joy we have, the more nearly perfect we are.

Benedict Spinoza (1632-1677)
Dutch philosopher

✴

— JUDGEMENT —

Each person you meet is in a specific stage of their life, a stage you may have passed or not yet reached. Judging them by your standards and experience is therefore not only unfair, but could lead to unnecessary anger and frustration.

Anonymous

★

— JUSTICE —

Though the sword of justice is sharp, it will not slay the innocent.

Chinese proverb

★

Justice is truth in action.

Benjamin Disraeli (1804-1881)
English statesman and writer

★

K

— KINDNESS —

Recompense injury with justice, and recompense kindness with kindness.

Confucius (551-479 BC)
Chinese philosopher

✱

No act of kindness, no matter how small, is ever wasted.

Aesop (c. 550 BC)
Greek fable-maker

✱

My religion is very simple — my religion is kindness.

Dalai Lama (1935-)
Tibetan spiritual leader

✱

Kindness is a language which the blind can see
and the deaf can hear.

Anonymous

✶

Think deeply; speak gently; love much; laugh
often; work hard; give freely; pay promptly;
be kind.

Anonymous

✶

I expect to pass through life but once. If,
therefore, there be any kindness I can show, or
any good thing I can do to any fellow being, let
me do it now, for I shall not pass this way again.

William Penn (1644-1718)
English Quaker and founder of Pennsylvania, USA

✶

Little deeds of kindness,
Little words of love,
Help to make earth happy
Like the heaven above.

Julia Fletcher Carney (1823-1908)
American teacher

★

We cannot always return an act of kindness to
the person who bestowed it, but we can pay back
the debt by helping others.

Anonymous

★

Wise words often fall on barren ground; but a
kind word is never thrown away.

Arthur Helps (1813-1875)
English historian

★

Kindness which is bestowed on the good
is never lost.

Plato (426-c.347 BC)
Greek philosopher

★

The heart benevolent and kind
The most resembles God.

Robert Burns (1759-1796)
Scottish poet

★

The best portion of a good man's life,
His little, nameless, unremembered acts of
kindness and love.

William Wordsworth (1770-1850)
English poet

★

Getting money is not all a man's business: to
cultivate kindness is a valuable part of the
business of life.

Samuel Johnson (1709-1784)
English lexicographer, critic and writer

★

One kind word can warm three winter months.

Japanese saying

★

— KNOWLEDGE —

I thank Thee, Lord, for knowing me better than I
know myself,
And for letting me know myself better than
others know me.
I pray Thee then, make me better than they
suppose,
And forgive me for what they do not know.

Abu Bekr (573-634)
Father-in-law of Mohammed, his follower and successor

✶

We do not know one-millionth of one per cent
about anything.

Thomas A. Edison (1847-1931)
American inventor

✶

I am sufficiently proud of my knowing
something to be modest about my not knowing
everything.

Vladimir Nabokov (1899-1977)
Russian-born American author

✶

A good listener is not only popular everywhere,
but after a while he gets to know something.

Wilson Mizner (1876-1933)
American humorist

★

Knowledge and timber shouldn't be much used
till they are seasoned.

Oliver Wendell Holmes (1809-1894)
American writer and physician

★

Knowledge is the action of the soul.

Ben Jonson (1573-1637)
English dramatist

★

Knowledge advances by steps, and not by leaps.

Thomas Macaulay (1800-1859)
English historian and statesman

★

An investment in knowledge always pays the best interest.

Benjamin Franklin (1706-1790)
American statesman and philosopher

★

What we want is to see the child in pursuit of knowledge, and not knowledge in pursuit of the child.

George Bernard Shaw (1856-1950)
Irish dramatist, essayist and critic

★

It is the greatest nuisance that knowledge can only be acquired by hard work.

W. Somerset Maugham (1874-1965)
English writer

★

Knowledge is power.

Francis Bacon (1561-1626)
English philosopher

★

L

— LAUGHTER —

Laughter is the sensation of feeling good all over, and showing it principally in one place.

Josh Billings (1818~1885)
American humorist

✦

Laughter is sunshine in a house.

William Makepeace Thackeray (1811~1863)
English author

✦

A complete revaluation takes place in your physical and mental being when you've laughed and had some fun.

Catherine Ponder
American motivational writer

✦

Laughter has something in it in common with the ancient winds of faith and inspiration; it unfreezes pride and unwinds secrecy; it makes men forget themselves in the presence of something greater than themselves; something that they cannot resist.

G.K. Chesterton (1874-1936)
English critic, novelist and poet

✶

The most wasted of all days is that on which one has not laughed.

Nicolas Chamfort (1741-94)
French writer

✶

Laugh and the world laughs with you;
Weep, and you weep alone.

Ella Wheeler Wilcox (1850-1919)
American poet

✶

It's impossible to speak highly enough of the virtues, the dangers and the power of shared laughter.

Françoise Sagan (1935-)
French novelist

★

We are all here for a spell. Get all the good laughs you can.

Will Rogers (1879-1935)
American actor and humorist

★

Among those whom I like or admire, I can find no common denominator, but among those I love, I can: all of them make me laugh.

W.H. Auden (1907-1973)
English poet and essayist

★

He who laughs, lasts.

Anonymous

★

— LAZINESS —

For one person who dreams of making fifty
thousand pounds, a hundred people dream of
being left fifty thousand pounds.

A.A. Milne (1882-1956)
English writer

It is the doom of laziness and gluttony to be
inactive without ease, and drowsy
without tranquillity.

Samuel Johnson (1709-1784)
English lexicographer, critic and writer

Indolence is a delightful but distressing state. We
must be doing something to be happy.

William Hazlitt (1778-1830)
English essayist

— LEADERSHIP —

I learned that a great leader is a man who has the
ability to get other people to do what they don't
want to do and like it.

Harry S. Truman (1884-1972)
President of the United States, 1945-1952

✷

Leadership: the art of getting someone else to do
something you want done because he wants to
do it.

Dwight D. Eisenhower (1890-1969)
President of the United States, 1953-1961

✷

The great difference between the real leader and
the pretender is — that the one sees into the
future, while the other regards only the present;
the one lives by the day, and acts upon
expediency; the other acts on enduring
principles and for immortality.

Edmund Burke (1729-1797)
British politician and writer

✷

— LEARNING —

Blessed are those who listen, for they shall learn.

Anonymous

✴

No man e'er found a happy life by chance,
Or yawned it into being with a wish.
An art it is, and must be learnt; and learnt
With unremitting effort, or be lost.

Edward Young (1683-1765)
English poet

✴

Have you learned lessons only of those who
admired you, and were tender with you, and
stood aside for you? Have you not learned great
lessons from those who braced themselves
against you, and disputed the passage with you?

Walt Whitman (1819-1891)
American poet

✴

That is what learning is. You suddenly
understand something you've understood all
your life, but in a new way.

Doris Lessing (1919-)
English novelist

★

What we have to learn to do, we learn by doing.

Aristotle (384-322 BC)
Greek philosopher

★

Natural abilities are like natural plants; they need
pruning by study.

Francis Bacon (1561-1626)
English philosopher

★

Learning makes a man fit company for himself.

Thomas Fuller (1608-1661)
English divine and historian

★

— LIFE —

To live long, live slowly.

Marcus Tullius Cicero (106-43 BC)
Roman orator, statesman and writer

✸

Decide carefully, exactly what you want in life,
then work like mad to make sure you get it!

Hector Crawford (1913-1991)
Australian television program-maker

✸

Life is either a daring adventure or nothing.

Helen Keller (1880-1968)
Deaf and blind American lecturer, writer and scholar.

✸

Live every day as though it's your last. One day
you'll get it right!

Zig Ziglar
American writer and motivational speaker

✸

Life is what happens to you while you're busy making other plans.

John Lennon (1940-1980)
English singer and songwriter

✱

When I hear somebody sigh, 'Life is hard,' I am always tempted to ask, 'Compared to what?'

Sydney J. Harris (1917-)
Newspaper columnist

✱

The greatest use of life is to spend it for something that will outlast it.

William James (1842-1910)
American psychologist and philosopher

✱

Life begets life. Energy creates energy. It is by spending oneself that one becomes rich.

Sarah Bernhardt (1844-1923)
French actress

✱

Each player must accept the cards life deals him. But once they are in hand, he alone must decide how to play the cards in order to win the game.

Voltaire (1694-1778)
French author

★

Life is not the way it's supposed to be. It's the way it is. The way you cope with it is what makes the difference.

Anonymous

★

I have a simple philosophy. Fill what's empty. Empty what's full. And scratch where it itches.

Alice Roosevelt Longworth (1884-1980)
Daughter of American President Theodore Roosevelt

★

The first rule in opera is the first rule in life: see to everything yourself.

Dame Nellie Melba (1865-1931)
Australian opera singer

★

There is no cure for birth and death, save to enjoy the interval.

George Santayana (1863-1952)
Spanish-American philosopher and poet

✴

The main fact of life for me is love or its absence. Whether life is worth living depends on whether there is love in life.

R.D. Laing (1927-)
Scottish psychiatrist

✴

You must understand the whole of life, not just one little part of it. That is why you must read, that is why you must look at the skies, that is why you must sing and dance, and write poems, and suffer; and understand, for all that is life.

Jiddu Krishnamurti (1895-1986)
Indian theosophist

✴

When you were born, you cried and the world rejoiced. Live your life in such a manner that when you die the world cries and you rejoice.

Traditional Indian saying

✱

Life can only be understood backwards; but it must be lived forwards.

Soren Aaby Kierkegaard (1813-1855)
Danish philosopher and theologian

✱

Live all you can; it's a mistake not to. It doesn't so much matter what you do in particular, so long as you have had your life. If you haven't had that, what have you had?

Henry James (1843-1916)
American novelist

✱

These, then, are my last words to you: be not afraid of life. Believe that life is worth living, and your belief will help create the fact.

William James (1842-1910)
American psychologist and philosopher

✱

We love life, not because we are used to living,
but because we are used to loving.

Friedrich Wilhelm Nietzsche (1844-1900)
German philosopher, poet and scholar

✶

The more we live by our intellect, the less we
understand the meaning of life.

Leo Tolstoy (1828-1910)
Russian writer

✶

Children FEEL life. They smell it, roll in it, run
with it, see it all around them. Feel the world
through the eyes of a child.

Anonymous

✶

Life is not made up of great sacrifices and duties
but of little things: in which smiles and kindness
given habitually are what win and preserve the
heart and secure comfort.

Sir Humphry Davy (1778-1829)
English chemist and poet

✶

I want to be thoroughly used up when I die...Life is no brief candle to me. It's a sort of splendid torch which I've got to hold up for the moment and I want to make it burn as brightly as possible before handing it on to future generations.

George Bernard Shaw (1856-1950)
Irish dramatist, essayist and critic

✹

I like life. I have sometimes been wildly, despairingly, acutely miserable, racked with sorrow, but through it all I still know quite certainly that just to be alive is a grand thing.

Agatha Christie (1890-1976)
English mystery writer

✹

Life was meant to be lived. Curiosity must be kept alive...One must never, for whatever reason, turn his back on life.

Eleanor Roosevelt (1884-1962)
First Lady of the United States, 1933-1945

✹

— LONELINESS —

Pray that your loneliness may spur you into
finding something to live for, great enough
to die for.

Dag Hammerskjold (1905-1961)
Swedish diplomat

✦

No man is lonely while eating a bowl
of spaghetti.

Sign in a spaghetti bar

✦

That is part of the beauty of all literature. You
discover that your longings are universal
longings, that you're not lonely and isolated from
anyone. You belong.

F. Scott Fitzgerald (1896-1940)
American novelist

✦

— LOVE —

The rule for us all is perfectly simple. Do not waste time bothering whether you 'love' your neighbour; act as if you did. As soon as we do this we find one of the great secrets. When you are behaving as if you loved someone, you will presently come to love him.

C.S. Lewis (1898-1963)
Irish-born academic, writer and poet

✴

The only thing I know about love is that love is all there is...Love can do all but raise the dead.

Emily Dickinson (1830-1886)
American poet

✴

Let us not be satisfied with just giving money. Money is not enough, money can be got, but they need your hearts to love them. So, spread love everywhere you go: first of all in your own home. Give love to your children, to your wife or husband, to a next-door neighbour.

Mother Teresa of Calcutta (1910-)
Yugoslav-born missionary

✴

To love means never to be afraid of the windstorms of life: should you shield the canyons from the windstorms you would never see the true beauty of their carvings.

Elisabeth Kubler-Ross (1926-)
Swiss-born American psychiatrist

Him that I love, I wish to be free — even from me.

Anne Morrow Lindbergh (1906-)
American writer and aviator

Love is a fruit in season at all times, and within the reach of every hand. Anyone may gather it and no limit is set. Everyone can reach this love through meditation, spirit of prayer, and sacrifice, by an intense inner life.

Mother Teresa of Calcutta (1910-)
Yugoslav-born missionary

Love means to commit oneself without guarantee, to give oneself completely in the hope that our love will produce love in the loved person. Love is an act of faith, and whoever is of little faith is of little love.

Erich Fromm (1900-1980)
German-American psychoanalyst

★

I will greet this day with love in my heart. And how will I do this? Henceforth will I look on all things with love and I will be born again. I will love the sun for it warms my bones; yet I will love the rain for it cleanses my spirit. I will love the light for it shows me the way; yet I will love the darkness for it shows me the stars. I will welcome happiness for it enlarges my heart; yet I will endure sadness for it opens my soul. I will acknowledge rewards for they are my due; yet I will welcome obstacles for they are my challenge.

Og Mandino (1923-)
American author

★

Love seems the swiftest, but it is the slowest of all growths. No man or woman really knows what perfect love is until they have been married for a quarter of a century.

Mark Twain (1835-1910)
American writer and humorist

✳

Love is like quicksilver in the hand.
Leave the fingers open and it stays.
Clutch it, and it darts away.

Dorothy Parker (1893-1967)
American writer and satirist

✳

Love consists in this, that two solitudes protect and touch and greet each other.

Rainer Maria Rilke (1875-1926)
Austrian poet

✳

Love is, above all, the gift of oneself.

Jean Anouilh (1910-1987)
French dramatist

★

Love does not consist in gazing at each other but in looking together in the same direction.

Antoine de Saint-Exupery (1900-1944)
French airman and author

★

By love serve one another.

Galatians 5:13

★

Treasure the love you receive above all. It will survive long after your gold and good health have vanished.

Og Mandino (1923-)
American author

★

Men and women are made to love each other. It's only by loving each other that they can achieve anything.

Christina Stead (1902-1983)
Australian writer

★

I know of only one duty, and that is to love.

Albert Camus (1913-1960)
French writer

★

God doesn't look at how much we do, but with how much love we do it.

Mother Teresa of Calcutta (1910-)
Yugoslav-born missionary

★

Love is the free exercise of choice. Two people love each other only when they are quite capable of living without each other but choose to live with each other.

M. Scott Peck (1936-)
American psychiatrist and writer

★

The heart has reasons which the reason
cannot understand.

Blaise Pascal (1623~1662)
French physicist, theologian and writer

✳

Love gives naught but itself and takes naught but
from itself. Love possesses not nor would it be
possessed; for love is sufficient unto love.

Khalil Gibran (1883~1931)
Lebanese poet, writer, artist and mystic

✳

I define love thus: the will to extend oneself for
the purpose of nurturing one's own or another's
spiritual growth.

M. Scott Peck (1936~)
American psychiatrist and writer

✳

— LUCK —

Anyone who does not know how to make the most of his luck has no right to complain if it passes him by.

Miguel de Cervantes (1547-1616)
Spanish author

✶

I am a great believer in luck, and I find the harder I work the more I have of it.

Stephen Leacock (1869-1944)
English-born Canadian economist and humorist

✶

Luck to me is something else. Hard work — and realising what is opportunity and what isn't.

Lucille Ball (1911-1989)
American actress

✶

M

— MARRIAGE —

A happy marriage has in it all the pleasures of a
friendship, all the enjoyments of sense and
reason, and indeed, all the sweets of life.

Joseph Addison (1672-1719)
English essayist and politician

✱

There is no more lovely, friendly, and charming
relationship, communion, or company than a
good marriage.

Martin Luther (1483-1544)
German religious reformer

✱

Let there be spaces in your togetherness.

Kahlil Gibran (1883-1931)
Lebanese poet, writer, artist and mystic

✱

Chains do not hold a marriage together. It is threads, hundreds of tiny threads which sew people together through the years. That is what makes a marriage last — more than passion or even sex.

Simone Signoret (1921-1985)
French actress

✸

Give your hearts, but not into each
other's keeping,
For only the hand of life can contain your hearts.
And stand together yet not too near together:
For the pillars of the temple stand apart,
And the oak tree and the cypress grow not in
each other's shadow.

Kahlil Gibran (1883-1931)
Lebanese poet, artist and mystic

✸

Two things do prolong thy life.
A quiet heart and a loving wife.

Anonymous

✸

— MIND —

One man who has a mind and knows it can always beat ten men who haven't and don't.

George Bernard Shaw (1856-1950)
Irish dramatist, essayist and critic

✸

Luck favours the mind that is prepared.

Louis Pasteur (1822-1895)
French bacteriologist

✸

When people will not weed their own minds, they are apt to be overrun with nettles.

Horace Walpole (1717-1797)
English writer

✸

The mind of man is capable of anything — because everything is in it, all the past as well as the future.

Joseph Conrad (1857-1924)
English novelist

✸

The greater part of our happiness or misery depends on our dispositions and not on our circumstances. We carry the seeds of the one or the other about with us in our minds wherever we go.

Martha Washington (1731-1802)
First Lady of the United States, 1789-1799

✶

The mind is its own place, and in itself
Can make a heaven of hell, a hell of heaven.

John Milton (1606-1674)
English poet

✶

— MIRACLES —

Miracles happen to those who believe in them.

Bernhard Berenson (1865-1959)
American art critic

✶

The miracle is not to fly in the air, or to walk on
the water; but to walk on the earth.

Chinese proverb

✶

Where there is great love, there are
always miracles.

Willa Cather (1873-1947)
American writer

✶

A miracle is an event which creates faith. Frauds
deceive. An event which creates faith does not
deceive; therefore it is not a fraud, but a miracle.

George Bernard Shaw (1856-1950)
Irish dramatist, playwright and critic

✶

Everything is miraculous. It is a miracle that one does not melt in one's bath.

Pablo Picasso (1881-1973)
Spanish painter

✳

Why, who makes much of a miracle?
As to me I known nothing else but miracles —
To me every hour of night and day is a miracle,
Every cubic inch of space a miracle.

Walt Whitman (1819-1891)
American poet

✳

The miracles of nature are all around us.

Anonymous

✳

— MISERY —

Human misery must somewhere have a stop;
There is no wind that always blows a storm.

Euripides (480-406 BC)
Greek dramatist

✸

The secret of being miserable is to have leisure to
bother about whether you are happy or not.

George Bernard Shaw (1856-1950)
Irish dramatist and critic

✸

One often calms one's grief by recounting it.

Pierre Cornelle (1606-1684)
French dramatist

✸

Who going through the vale of misery use it for a
well; and the pools are filled with water. They go
from strength to strength.

Psalm 84:6-7

✸

— MISTAKES —

I have learned more from my mistakes than from my successes.

Sir Humphry Davy (1778-1829)
English chemist and poet

✱

Nothing would be done at all if a man waited until he could do it so well that no-one could find fault with it.

Cardinal John Henry Newman (1801-1890)
English theologian

✱

The greatest mistake you can make in life is to be continually fearing you will make one.

Elbert Hubbard (1856-1915)
American writer

✱

There's nothing wrong in making a mistake — as long as you don't follow it up with encores.

Anonymous

✱

It is the greatest of all mistakes to do nothing
because you can only do little.

Sydney Smith (1771-1845)
English essayist, clergyman and wit

✶

It has taken me thirty-three years and a bang on
the head to get my values right.

Stirling Moss (1929-)
English racing driver

✶

If you have made mistakes...there is always
another chance for you...you may have a fresh
start any moment you choose, for this thing we
call 'failure' is not the falling down, but the
staying down.

Mary Pickford (1893-1979)
American actress

✶

Some of the best lessons we ever learn, we learn
from our mistakes and failures. The error of the
past is the success and wisdom of the future.

Tyron Edwards (1809-1894)
American theologian

✶

He who never made a mistake never made
a discovery.

Samuel Smiles (1812-1904)
Scottish author and social reformer

✴

The man who makes no mistakes does not
usually make anything.

Edward John Phelps (1822-1900)
American lawyer and diplomat

✴

A man should never be ashamed to own he has
been in the wrong, which is but saying, in other
words, that he is wiser today than he
was yesterday.

Alexander Pope (1688-1744)
English poet

✴

Every great mistake has a halfway moment, a split second when it can be recalled and perhaps remedied.

Pearl S. Buck (1892-1973)
American writer

✱

There are no mistakes, no coincidences; all events are blessings given to us to learn from. There is no need to go to India or anywhere else to find peace. You will find that deep place of silence right in your room, your garden or even your bathtub.

Elisabeth Kubler-Ross (1926-)
Swiss-born American psychiatrist

✱

A life spent making mistakes is not only more honourable but more useful than a life spent doing nothing.

George Bernard Shaw (1856-1950)
Irish dramatist, essayist and critic

✱

— MONEY —

The shortest and best way to make your fortune
is to let people see clearly that it is in their
interests to promote yours.

Jean de la Bruyere (1645-1696)
French satirist

★

Money, it turned out, was exactly like sex: you
thought of nothing else if you didn't have it and
thought of other things if you did.

James Baldwin (1924-1987)
American writer

★

Money is like an arm or leg — use it or lose it.

Henry Ford (1863-1947)
American motor car manufacturer

★

Money can't buy friends, but you can get a better
class of enemy.

Spike Milligan (1918-)
English comedian

★

If money is your hope for independence you will never have it. The only real security that a man can have in this world is a reserve of knowledge, experience and ability.

Henry Ford (1863-1947)
American motor car manufacturer

Money makes money, and the money money makes, makes more money.

Benjamin Franklin (1706-1790)
American statesman and philosopher

Money is like muck, not good except to be spread.

Francis Bacon (1561-1626)
English philosopher

— MUSIC —

I think I should have no other mortal wants, if I could always have plenty of music. It seems to infuse strength into my limbs and ideas into my brain. Life seems to go on without effort, when I am filled with music.

George Eliot (Mary Ann Evans) (1819-1880)
English novelist

★

Music is the medicine of the troubled mind.

Walter Haddon (1516-1537)
English writer

★

He who hears music feels his solitude peopled at once.

Robert Browning (1812-1889)
English poet

★

N

— NATURE —

There can be no very black misery to him who lives in the midst of Nature and has his senses still.

Henry David Thoreau (1817-1862)
American essayist, poet and mystic

★

Every part of this Earth is sacred to my people. Every shining pine needle, every sandy shore, every mist in the dark woods, every clearing and humming insect is holy in the memory and experience of my people

Chief Seathl
From a letter written in 1883 to the President of the United States.

★

— NEGATIVITY —

Every day is irreplaceable, so don't ruin yours by
allowing the negative moods of others to pull you
into their frame of mind.

Anonymous

✳

Try to avoid pessimists — negativity can
be catching.

Anonymous

✳

Don't be too self-critical. Learn to be
on your own side.

Anonymous

✳

— NEGOTIATION —

Let us never negotiate out of fear, but let us never
fear to negotiate.

John F. Kennedy (1917-1963)
President of the United States, 1961-1963

✳

O

— *OCCUPATION* —

When men are rightly occupied, then
amusement grows out of the work as the
colour-petals out of a fruitful flower; when they
are faithfully helpful and compassionate, all their
emotions become steady, deep, perpetual and
vivifying to the soul as the natural
pulse to the body.

John Ruskin (1819-1900)
English author and art critic

✳

Good for the body is the work of the body, good
for the soul is the work of the soul, and good for
either the work of the other.

Henry David Thoreau (1817-1862)
American essayist, poet and mystic

✳

— OPPORTUNITY —

One cannot step twice into the same river.

Heraclitus (c.540–c.480 BC)
Greek philosopher

✱

Problems are only opportunities in work clothes.

Henry John Kaiser (1882–1967)
American industrialist

✱

A wise man will make more opportunities than
he finds.

Francis Bacon (1561–1626)
English philosopher

✱

Do not wait for extraordinary circumstances to
do good; try to use ordinary situations.

Jean Paul Richter (1763–1825)
German novelist and humorist

✱

Failure is only the opportunity to begin again more intelligently.

Henry Ford (1863-1947)
American motor car manufacturer

✱

If heaven drops a date, open your mouth.

Chinese proverb

✱

In the middle of difficulty lies opportunity.

Albert Einstein (1879-1955)
German-born physicist

✱

A diamond is a chunk of coal that made good under pressure.

Anonymous

✱

To improve the golden moment of opportunity,
and catch the good that is within our reach, is the
great art of life.

William James (1842-1910)
American psychologist and philosopher

✳

Opportunities are usually disguised as hard
work, so most people don't recognise them.

Ann Landers (1918-)
American journalist

✳

The people who get on in this world are the
people who get up and look for the
circumstances they want, and, if they can't
find them, make them.

George Bernard Shaw (1856-1950)
Irish dramatist, essayist and critic

✳

— OPTIMISM —

When one door shuts, another opens.

Proverb

★

In the midst of winter, I finally learned there was in me an invincible summer.

Albert Camus (1913-1960)
French writer

★

An optimist is a person who takes action, who moves out ahead of the crowd.

Anonymous

★

The optimist proclaims we live in the best of all possible worlds; and the pessimist fears this is true.

James Cabell (1879-1958)
American novelist and journalist

★

No pessimist ever discovered the secrets of the stars, or sailed to an uncharted land, or opened a new heaven to the horizon of the spirit.

Helen Keller (1880-1968)
Deaf and blind American lecturer, writer and scholar

✶

I count only the sunny hours.

Sundial inscription

✶

As you make your way through life,
Let this ever be your goal,
Keep your eye upon the doughnut
And not upon the hole.

Anonymous

✶

A pessimist sees a glass that's half empty. An optimist sees a glass that's half full.

Anonymous

✶

Over the winter glaciers
I see the summer glow;
And through the wild-piled snowdrift
The warm rosebuds below.

Ralph Waldo Emerson (1803-1882)
American essayist, poet and philosopher

✸

To look up and not down,
To look forward and not back,
To look out and not in —
To lend a hand!

Edward Everett Hale (1882-1909)
American Unitarian clergyman and inspirational writer

✸

An optimist sees an opportunity in every
calamity. A pessimist sees a calamity in
every opportunity.

Anonymous

✸

— ORDER —

Order is the sanity of the mind, the health of the
body, the peace of the city, the serenity
of the state.

Chinese proverb

✸

As the beams to a house, as the bones to the body
— so is order to all things.

Robert Southey (1774-1843)
English poet

✸

Order is heaven's first law.

Alexander Pope (1688-1744)
English poet

✸

A place for everything, and everything in
its place.

Samuel Smiles (1812-1904)
Scottish author and social reformer

✸

— ORGANISATION —

Organisation is always the cornerstone of business success.

Anonymous

✳

A well-spent day brings happy sleep.

Leonardo da Vinci (1452-1519)
Italian painter, sculptor, architect and inventor

✳

I must create a system, or be enslaved by another man's.

William Blake (1757-1827)
English poet

✳

Let all things be done decently and in order.

Corinthians 14:40

✳

— ORIGINALITY —

What is originality? It is being one's self, and
reporting accurately what we see.

Ralph Waldo Emerson (1803-1882)
American essayist, poet and philosopher

★

All good things which exist are the fruits
of originality.

John Stuart Mill (1806-1873)
English philosopher

★

The dogmas of the quiet past are inadequate to
the stormy present. The occasion is piled high
with difficulty, and we must rise to the occasion.
As our case is new, so must we think anew and
act anew.

Abraham Lincoln (1809-1865)
President of the United States, 1860-1863

★

P

— PAIN —

The best way out of emotional pain is through it.

Anonymous

✦

— PARTING —

Moments of kindness and reconciliation are worth having, even if the parting has to come sooner or later.

Alice Munro (1931-)
American writer

✦

Weep if you must,
Parting is here —
But life goes on,
So sing as well.

Joyce Grenfell (1910-1979)
English comedian and writer

✦

— PARENTHOOD —

Who of us is mature enough for offspring before the offspring themselves arrive? The value of marriage is not that adults produce children but that children produce adults.

Peter de Vries (1910-)
American novelist

✴

Children are a bridge to heaven.

Anonymous

✴

A mother is not a person to lean on but a person to make leaning unnecessary.

Dorothy Canfield Fisher (1879-1958)
American writer

✴

One mother teaches more than a hundred teachers.

Jewish proverb

✴

Love children especially, for, like angels, they too
are sinless, and they live to soften and purify our
hearts and, as it were, to guide us.

Feodor Dostoevsky (1821-1881)
Russian writer

✶

Always believe in yourselves as parents. You are
the best your children have.

Anonymous

✶

Anything that parents have not learned from
experience they can now learn from
their children.

Anonymous

✶

Children are likely to live up to what you believe
of them.

Lady Bird Johnson (1912-)
First Lady of the United States, 1963-1969

✶

— PAST —

The past exists only in memory, consequences, effects. It has power over me only as I give it my power. I can let go, release it, move freely, I am not my past.

Anonymous

✳

Even God cannot change the past.

Agathon (c. 446-401 BC)
Greek poet and playwright

✳

Study the past, if you would divine the future.

Confucius (551-479 BC)
Chinese philosopher

✳

— PATIENCE —

With time and patience the mulberry leaf
becomes a silk gown.

Chinese saying

✱

Never cut what you can untie.

Joseph Joubert (1754-1824)
French writer

✱

Patience is a bitter plant, but it has sweet fruit.

Proverb

✱

There is nothing so bitter that a patient mind
cannot find some solace in it.

Lucius Annaeus Seneca (c.55 BC-c.40 AD)
Roman rhetorician

✱

— PEACE —

Deep peace of the running wave to you.
Deep peace of the flowing air to you.
Deep peace of the quiet earth to you.
Deep peace of the shining stars to you.
Deep peace of the Son of Peace to you.

Celtic benediction

✷

Do not be in a hurry to fill up an empty space
with words and embellishments, before it has
been filled with a deep interior peace.

Father Alexander Elchaninov
Russian priest

✷

Do not lose your inward peace for anything
whatsoever, even if your whole world
seems upset.

Saint Francis de Sales (1567-1622)
French Roman Catholic bishop and writer

✷

You will give yourself peace of mind if you perform every act of your life as if it were
your last.

Marcus Aurelius (121-180 AD)
Roman emperor and philosopher

★

Find peace within yourself by accepting not only
what you are, but what you are never
going to be.

Anonymous

★

Under this tree, where light and shade
Speckle the grass like a Thrush's breast,
Here in this green and quiet place
I give myself to peace and rest.
The peace of my contented mind,
That is to me a wealth untold —
When the Moon has no more silver left,
And the Sun's at the end of his gold.

W.H. Davies (1870-1940)
Welsh poet

★

— PERCEPTION —

If the doors of perception were cleansed,
everything would appear to man as it is, infinite.
For man has closed himself up, till he sees all
things through narrow chinks of his cavern.

William Blake (1757-1827)
English poet, artist and mystic

✶

— PERSEVERANCE —

The drops of rain make a hole in the stone not by
violence but by oft falling.

Lucretius (96-55 BC)
Roman poet

✶

God helps those who persevere.

The Koran

✶

But what if I fail of my purpose here?
It is but to keep the nerves at strain,
To dry one's eyes and laugh at a fall,
And, baffled, get up and begin again.

Robert Browning (1812-1889)
English poet

★

Step by step the ladder is ascended.

George Herbert (1593-1633)
English poet

★

Consider the postage stamp; its usefulness
consists in the ability to stick to one thing
till it gets there.

Josh Billings (1818-1885)
American humorist

★

Finish whatever you begin, and experience the
triumph of completion.

Anonymous

★

Nothing in the world can take the place of
persistence. Talent will not; nothing is more
common than unsuccessful men with talent.
Genius will not; unrewarded genius is almost a
proverb. Education will not; the world is full of
educated failures. Persistence and determination
alone are omnipotent.

Calvin Coolidge (1872-1933)
President of the United States 1923-1929

✶

To keep a lamp burning we have to keep putting
oil in it.

Mother Teresa of Calcutta (1910-)
Yugoslav-born missionary

✶

I have learned that success is to be measured not
so much by the position one has reached in life as
by the obstacles which one has overcome while
trying to succeed.

Brooker T. Washington (1856-1915)
American black reformer

✶

— PICK-ME-UPS —

It is almost impossible to remember how tragic a place the world is when one is playing golf.

Robert Lynd (1879-1949)
Irish essayist and journalist

★

There are a few things a hot bath won't cure, but I don't known many of them.

Sylvia Plath (1932-1963)
American poet and writer

★

Noble deeds and hot baths are the best cures for depression.

Dodie Smith (1896-1990)
English Writer

★

Where's the man could ease the heart
Like a satin gown?

Dorothy Parker (1893-1967)
American writer and satirist

★

Thank God for tea. What would the world do without tea?

Sydney Smith (1771~1845)
English clergyman and essayist

✹

Drink tea and forget the world's noises.

Chinese saying

✹

A walk at dawn works wonders for the soul.

Anonymous

✹

A little of what you fancy does you good.

English music hall song

✹

— *PLAN* —

Plan your work and work your plan.

Norman Vincent Peale (1898-1993)
American writer and minister

✳

Plan for the future because that's where you are
going to spend the rest of your life.

Mark Twain (1835-1910)
American writer and humorist

✳

The time to repair the roof is when the sun
is shining.

John F. Kennedy (1917-1963)
President of the United States, 1961-1963

✳

— PLEASURE —

One ought every day at least to hear a little song,
read a good poem, see a fine picture, and, if it
were possible, to speak a few reasonable words.

Johann Wolfgang von Goethe (1749-1832)
German poet, novelist and playwright

★

Life affords no higher pleasure than that of
surmounting difficulties, passing from one step of
success to another, forming new wishes and
seeing them gratified.

Samuel Johnson (1709-1784)
English lexicographer, critic and writer

★

The great pleasure of a dog is that you may make
a fool of yourself with him and not only will he
not scold you, but he will make a fool of
himself too.

Samuel Butler (1835-1902)
English writer

★

Only one hour in the normal day is more pleasurable than the hour spent in bed with a book before going to sleep, and that is the hour spent in bed with a book after being called in the morning.

Rose Macauley (1881-1958)
English novelist and essayist

★

Whenever you are sincerely pleased you are nourished.

Ralph Waldo Emerson (1803-1882)
American essayist, poet and philosopher

★

Pleasure for an hour, a bottle of wine; pleasure for a year, marriage; pleasure for a lifetime, a garden.

Chinese saying

★

— POSSIBILITY —

The only way to discover the limits of the possible is to go beyond them, to the impossible.

Arthur C. Clarke (1917-)
English science fiction writer

✷

All things are possible until they are proved impossible — and even the impossible may only be so, as of now.

Pearl S. Buck (1892-1973)
American novelist

✷

If I were to wish for anything, I should not wish for wealth and power, but for the passionate sense of the potential, for the eye which, ever young and ardent, sees the possible. Pleasure disappoints, possibility never.

Soren Kierkegaard (1813-1855)
Danish philosopher

✷

— POTENTIAL —

Treat people as if they were what they ought to
be and you help them to become what they are
capable of being.

Johann Wolfgang von Goethe (1749-1832)
German poet, novelist and playwright

★

The greater the contrast, the greater the
potential. Great energy only comes from a
correspondingly great tension between opposites.

Carl Jung (1875-1961)
Swiss psychiatrist

★

To be what we are, and to become what we are
capable of becoming is the only end of life.

Robert Louis Stevenson (1850-1894)
Scottish author and poet

★

— POVERTY —

The more you have, the more you are occupied,
the less you give. But the less you have, the more
free you are. Poverty for us is a freedom.

Mother Teresa of Calcutta (1910-)
Yugoslav-born missionary

✱

— POWER —

Knowing others is intelligence; knowing yourself
is true wisdom.
Mastering others is strength; mastering yourself
is true power.

Lao-Tzu (c. 604 BC)
Chinese philosopher and founder of Taoism

✱

I cannot do everything, but I can do something.
One person *can* make a difference.

Anonymous

✱

— PRAISE —

I can live for two months on a good compliment.

Mark Twain (1835-1910)
American writer and humorist

✱

Give credit where it's due.

Proverb

✱

Once in a century a man may be ruined or made insufferable by praise. But surely once a minute something generous dies for want of it.

John Masefield (1878-1967)
English poet.

✱

Some natures are too good to be spoiled
by praise.

Ralph Waldo Emerson (1803-1882)
American essayist, poet and philosopher

✱

— PRAYER —

More things are wrought by prayer than this
world dreams of.

Alfred, Lord Tennyson (1809-1892)
English poet

✳

Ask, and it shall be given to you; seek and ye shall
find; knock and it shall be opened to you.

Matthew 7:7

✳

Teach me to feel another's woe,
To hide the fault I see,
That mercy I to others show,
That mercy show to me.

Alexander Pope (1788-1744)
English poet

✳

When you prayest, rather let thy heart be
without words than thy words without heart.

John Bunyan (1628-1688)
English writer and moralist

✳

You pray in your distress and in your need,
would that you might also pray in the fullness of
your joy and your days of abundance.

Kahlil Gibran (1883-1931)
Lebanese writer, artist and mystic

★

Prayer is not an old woman's idle amusement.
Properly understood and applied it is the most
potential instrument of action.

Mahatma Gandhi (1869-1948)
Indian leader., moral teacher and reformer

★

Oh Lord, help me
To be calm when things go wrong,
To persevere when things are difficult,
To be helpful to those in need,
And to be sympathetic to those whose
hearts are heavy.

Anonymous

★

— PRESENT JOYS —

Gather ye rosebuds while ye may,
Old time is still a-flying:
And this same flower that smiles today
Tomorrow will be dying.

Robert Herrick (1591-1674)
English poet

✱

Ask not what tomorrow may bring, but count as
blessing every day that Fate allows you.

Horace (65-8 BC)
Roman poet

✱

I try to make the here and now as heavenly as
possible, in case there isn't one to ascend into
when we're done. It's a kind of insurance.

Michael Caine (1933-)
English actor

✱

— PROBLEMS —

First ask yourself, is this my problem? If it isn't, leave it alone. If it is my problem, can I tackle it now? Do so. If your problem could be settled by an expert in some field, go quickly to him and take his advice.

Dr Austen Riggs

✹

I'm grateful for all my problems. As each of them was overcome I became stronger and more able to meet those yet to come. I grew on my difficulties.

J.C. Penney (1875-1971)
American retailing magnate

✹

I could do nothing without problems, they toughen my mind. In fact I tell my assistants not to bring me their successes for they weaken me; but rather to bring me their problems, for they strengthen me.

Charles Franklin Kettering (1876-1958)
American engineer and inventor

✹

— PROCRASTINATION —

I have spent my days stringing and unstringing
my instrument, while the song I came to sing
remains unsung.

Rabindranath Tagore (1861-1941)
Indian poet and philosopher

✻

Procrastination is the thief of time.

Edward Young (1683-1765)
English poet

✻

Wasted days can never be recalled.

Anonymous

✻

Q

— QUIET —

When you become quiet, it just dawns on you.

Thomas A. Edison (1847-1931)
American inventor

✷

In the rush and noise of life, as you have intervals, step home within yourselves and be still. Wait upon God, and feel his good presence; this will carry you evenly through your day's business.

William Penn (1644-1718)
English Quaker and founder of Pennsylvania, USA

✷

The good and the wise lead quiet lives.

Euipides (480-406 BC)
Greek dramatist

✷

R

— RECEPTIVENESS —

Let us not therefore go hurrying about and collecting honey, bee-like, buzzing here and there impatiently from a knowledge of what is to be arrived at. But let us open out leaves like a flower, and be passive and receptive: budding patiently under the eye of Apollo and taking hints from every noble insect that favours us with a visit.

John Keats (1795-1821)
English poet

✱

The rain falls on all the fields, but crops grow only in those that have been tilled and sown.

Chinese saying

✱

— REGRET —

To regret one's own experiences is to arrest one's own development. To deny one's own experiences is to put a lie into the lips of one's own life. It is no less than a denial of the soul.

Oscar Wilde (1854-1900)
Irish poet, wit and dramatist

✶

Make the most of your regrets...To regret deeply is to live afresh.

Henry David Thoreau (1817-1862)
American essayist, poet and mystic

✶

What's gone and what's past help
Should be past grief.

William Shakespeare (1564-1616)
English playwright and poet

✶

— RELATIONSHIP —

Only in relationship can you know yourself, not in abstraction, and certainly not in isolation.

Jiddu Krishnamurti (1895-1986)
Indian theosophist

✳

Once the realisation is accepted that even between the closest human beings infinite distances continue to exist, a wonderful living side-by-side can grow up, if they succeed in loving the distance between them, which makes it possible for each to see the other whole against a wide sky.

Rainer Maria Rilke (1875-1926)
Austrian poet

✳

The worst sin towards our fellow creatures is not to hate them, but to be indifferent to them; that's the essence of inhumanity.

George Bernard Shaw (1856-1950)
Irish dramatist, essayist and critic

✳

I do my thing, and you do your thing,
I am not in this world to live up to
your expectations
And you are not in this world to live up to mine.
You are you and I am I,
And if by chance we find each other,
it's beautiful.
If not, it can't be helped.

Frederick (Fritz) Salomon Perls (1893-1970)
German-born American psychologist

✷

Personal relations are the important thing for
ever and ever, and not this outer life of telegrams
and anger.

E.M. Forster (1879-1970)
English novelist

✷

I am a part of all that I have met.

Alfred, Lord Tennyson (1809-1892)
English poet

✷

— RELIGION —

There is only one religion, though there are a hundred versions of it.

George Bernard Shaw (1856-1950)
Irish dramatist, essayist and critic

✳

Be a good human being, a warm-hearted affectionate person. That is my fundamental belief. Having a sense of caring, a feeling of compassion will bring happiness or peace of mind to oneself and automatically create a positive atmosphere.

Dalai Lama (1935-)
Tibetan spiritual leader

✳

Show love to all creatures and thou will be happy; for when thou lovest all things, thou lovest the Lord, for he is all in all.

Tulsi Das Hindu spiritual tradition

✳

He who is filled with love is filled with
God himself.

St Augustine of Hippo (347-430 AD)

★

I consider myself a Hindu, Christian, Moslem,
Jew, Budhist and Confucian.

Mahatma Gandhi (1869-1948)
Indian leader, moral teacher and reformer

★

The worst moment for the atheist is when he is
really thankful, and has nobody to thank.

Dante Gabriel Rossetti (1828-1882)
English poet and painter

★

One man finds religion in his literature and
science; another finds it in his joy and his duty.

Joseph Joubert (1754-1824)
French writer

★

— *REPUTATION* —

The only time you realise you have a reputation
is when you fail to live up to it.

Anonymous

＊

— *RESILIENCE* —

If you fell down yesterday, stand up today.

H.G. Wells (1866~1946)
English author

＊

— *REVOLUTION* —

Revolution is the festival of the oppressed.

Germaine Greer (1939~)
Australian writer and feminist

＊

— *RIGHTEOUSNESS* —

If there be righteousness in the heart, there will
be beauty in the character.
If there be beauty in the character, there will be
harmony in the home.
If there be harmony in the home, there will be
order in the nation.
If there be order in the nation, there will be
peace in the world.

Confucius (551-479 BC)
Chinese philosopher

✶

I must stand with anybody that stands right,
stand with him while he is right, and part with
him when he goes wrong.

Abraham Lincoln (1809-1865)
President of the United States, 1861-1865

✶

Right is might.

Anonymous

✶

— RISK —

And the trouble is, if you don't risk anything, you
risk even more.

Erica Jong (1942-)
American novelist and poet

✱

Don't refuse to go on an occasional wild goose
chase. That's what wild geese are for.

Anonymous

✱

Risk! Risk anything! Care no more for the
opinions of others, for those voices. Do the
hardest thing on earth for you. Act for yourself.
Face the truth.

Katherine Mansfield (1888-1923)
New Zealand author

✱

Risk is what separates the good part of life from
the tedium.

Jimmy Zero
American musician

✱

S

— SAFETY —

The desire for safety stands against every great
and noble enterprise.

Publius Cornelius Tacitus (55-120 AD)
Roman historian

★

It is always safe to learn, even from our enemies;
seldom safe to venture to instruct, even
our friends.

Charles Caleb Colton (1780-1832)
English clergyman and author

★

The only way to be absolutely safe is never to try
anything for the first time.

Magnus Pyke (1908-)
English scientist

★

— SELF-CONFIDENCE —

Self-confidence is the first requisite to great undertakings.

Samuel Johnson (1709~1784)
English lexicographer, critic and writer

★

Self-trust is the first secret of success.

Ralph Waldo Emerson (1803~1882)
American poet and essayist

★

Those who believe they are exclusively in the right are generally those who achieve something.

Aldous Huxley (1894~1963)
English novelist and essayist

★

You can get good fish and chips at the Savoy; and you can put up with fancy people once you understand that you don't have to be like them.

Gracie Fields (1888~1979)
English singer

★

— SELF-CONTROL —

Just as a bicycle chain may be too tight, so may one's carefulness and conscientiousness be so tense as to hinder the running of one's mind.

William James (1842-1910)
American psychologist and philosopher

✳

If your aim is control, it must be self-control first. If your aim is management, it must be self-management first.

Anonymous

✳

Self-command is the main elegance.

Ralph Waldo Emerson (1803-1882)
American essayist, poet and philosopher

✳

— SELF-DISCOVERY —

Learn to get in touch with the silence within yourself and know that everything in this life has a purpose.

Elisabeth Kubler-Ross (1926 ~)
Swiss-born American psychiatrist

✱

Just trust yourself, then you will know how to live.

Johann Wolfgang von Goethe (1749-1832)
German poet, novelist and playwright

✱

Once read thy own breast right,
And thou hast done with fears!
Man gets no other light,
Search he a thousand years.

Matthew Arnold (1822~1888)
English poet and critic

✱

Pearls lie not on the seashore. If thou desirest one
thou must dive for it.

Chinese proverb

✱

In meditation it is possible to dive deeper into the
mind to a place where there is no disturbance
and there is absolute solitude. It is at this point in
the profound stillness that the sound of the mind
can be heard.

A.E.I. Falconar (1926-)
Indian-born philosopher

✱

There is only one journey. Going inside yourself.

Rainer Maria Rilke (1875-1926)
Austrian poet

✱

No one remains quite what he was, once he
recognizes himself.

Thomas Mann (1875-1955)
German novelist

✱

— SELFLESSNESS —

To give and not to count the cost;
To fight and not to heed the wounds;
To toil and not to seek for rest;
To labour and not ask for any reward
Save that of knowing that we do Thy will.

St Ignatius Loyola (1491-1556)
Spanish priest

★

Where self exists, God is not;
Where God exists there is no self.

Sikh morning prayer

★

Inwardness, mildness and self-renouncement do
make for man's happiness.

Matthew Arnold (1822-1888)
English poet and critic

★

— SELF-RESPECT —

Let us not forget that a man can never get away
from himself.

Johann Wolfgang von Goethe (1749-1832)
German poet, novelist and playwright

✷

No-one can make you feel inferior without
your consent.

Eleanor Roosevelt (1884-1962)
First Lady of the United States, 1933-1945

✷

It is difficult to make a man miserable while he
feels he is worthy of himself.

Abraham Lincoln (1809-1865)
President of the United States of America, 1861-1865

✷

If you put a small value upon yourself, rest
assured that the world will not raise it.

Anonymous

✷

A man cannot be comfortable without his
own approval.

Mark Twain (1835-1910)
American writer and humorist

I think somehow we learn who we really are and
then live with that decision.

Eleanor Roosevelt (1884-1961)
First Lady of the United States, 1933-1945

Self-respecting people do not care to peep at
their reflections in unexpected mirrors, or to see
themselves as others see them.

Logan Pearsall Smith (1865-1946)
English writer

— SILENCE —

Well-timed silence hath more eloquence
than speech.

Martin Farquhar Tupper (1810-1889)
English writer

★

— SINCERITY —

What comes from the heart, goes to the heart.

Samuel Taylor Coleridge (1772-1834)
English poet

★

What's a man's first duty? The answer's brief: to
be himself.

Henrik Ibsen (1828-1906)
Norwegian dramatist

★

— SMILE —

It takes seventy-two muscles to frown, but only thirteen to smile.

Anonymous

✳

Smile at each other; smile at your wife, smile at your husband, smile at your children, smile at each other — it doesn't matter who it is — and that will help you to grow up in greater love for each other.

Mother Teresa of Calcutta (1910-)
Yugoslav-born missionary

✳

A smile breaks down most barriers.

Anonymous

✳

— SOLITUDE —

He who does not enjoy solitude will not love
freedom.

Artur Schopenhauer (1788-1860)
German philosopher

✳

I had three chairs in my house; one for solitude,
two for friendship, three for society.

Henry David Thoreau (1817-1862)
American essayist, poet and mystic

✳

Solitude is as needful to the imagination as
society is wholesome for the character.

James Russell Lowell (1819-1891)
American poet, essayist and diplomat

✳

Solitary trees, if they grow at all, grow strong.

Sir Winston Churchill (1874-1965)
English statesman

✳

O Solitude, the soul's best friend,
That man acquainted with himself dost make.

Charles Cotton (1630-1687)
English poet

✸

Go cherish your soul; expel companions; set your
habits to a life of solitude; then will the faculties
rise fair and full within.

Ralph Waldo Emerson (1803-1882)
American essayist, poet and philosopher

✸

Living in solitude till the fullness of time, I still
kept the dew of my youth and the freshness of
my heart.

Nathaniel Hawthorne (1804-1864)
American novelist and short story writer

✸

I never found the companion that was so
companionable as solitude.

Henry David Thoreau (1817-1862)
American essayist, poet and mystic

✸

I am sure of this, that by going much alone, a
man will get more of a noble courage in thought
and word than from all the wisdom that
is in books.

Ralph Waldo Emerson (1803-1882)
American essayist, poet and philosopher

✦

Solitude is the nurse of enthusiasm, and
enthusiasm is the true parent of genius.

Isaac D'Israeli (1766-1848)
English literary critic

✦

— *SOLUTION* —

Every problem contains the seeds of its
own solution.

Anonymous

✦

— SORROW —

Truly, it is in the darkness that one finds the light,
so when we are in sorrow, then this light is
nearest of all to us.

Johannes Eckhart (c.1260-1327)
German mystic

✳

One often calms one's grief by recounting it.

Pierre Corneille (1606-1684)
French dramatist

✳

Pure and complete sorrow is as impossible as
pure and complete joy.

Leo Tolstoy (1828-1910)
Russian novelist

✳

Blessed are they that mourn, for they shall
be comforted.

Matthew 5:4

✳

— STRENGTH —

You must be the anvil or the hammer.

Johann Wolfgang von Goethe (1749-1832)
German poet, novelist and playwright

✸

Be strong and courageous, and do the work.

Chronicles 28:20

✸

The world breaks everyone and afterwards many
are strong at the broken places.

Ernest Hemingway (1899-1961)
American novelist

✸

You who perceive yourself as weak and frail,
with futile hopes and devastated dreams, born
but to die, to weep and suffer pain, hear this: all
power is given unto you in earth and heaven.
There is nothing you cannot do.

A Course in Miracles

✸

— STRUGGLE —

It seems to me that one of the greatest stumbling blocks in life is this constant struggle to reach, to achieve, to acquire.

Jiddu Krishnamurti (1895-1986)
Indian theosophist

★

Better that we should die fighting than be outraged and dishonoured...Better to die than live in slavery.

Emmeline Pankhurst (1858-1928)
Suffragette leader

★

The struggle that is not joyous is the wrong struggle. The joy of the struggle is not hedonism and hilarity, but the sense of purpose, achievement and dignity which is the reflowering of etiolated energy.

Germaine Greer (1939-)
Australian writer and feminist

★

Resistance to tyrants is obedience to God.

Benjamin Franklin (1706-1790)
American statesman and philosopher

✳

Our greatest glory is not in never falling, but in rising every time we fall.

Confucius (551-479 BC)
Chinese philosopher

✳

If a man lives without inner struggle, if everything happens in him without opposition...he will remain such as he is.

G.I. Gurdjieff (1877-1949)
Russian mystic and teacher of the occult

✳

Golf without bunkers and hazards would be lame. So would life.

B.C. Forbes (1880-1954)
American writer

✳

— *SUCCESS* —

Singleness of purpose is one of the chief
essentials for success in life, no matter what
may be one's aim.

John D. Rockefeller, Jr. (1874-1960)
American oil millionaire and philanthropist

✶

I never allow any difficulties. The great secret of
being useful and successful is to admit
no difficulties.

Sir George Gipps (1791-1847)
Governor of New South Wales, 1838-1846

✶

If one advances confidently in the direction of his
dreams, and endeavours to live the life which he
had imagined, he will meet with a success
unexpected in common hours.

Henry David Thoreau (1817-1862)
American essayist, poet and mystic

✶

Success consists of getting up just one more time than you fall.

Anonymous

✷

The only place where success comes before work is a dictionary.

Vidal Sassoon (1928-)
English hair stylist

✷

A lot of successful people are risk-takers. Unless you're willing to do that...to have a go, fail miserably, and have another go, success won't happen.

Phillip Adams (1939-)
Australian author, writer and radio broadcaster

✷

The secret of success is making your vocation your vacation.

Mark Twain (1835-1910)
American writer and humorist

✷

There is only one success — to be able to spend your life in your own way.

Christopher Darlington Morley (1890-1957)
American novelist and essayist

✱

If you want to succeed you should strike out on new paths, rather than travel the worn paths of accepted success.

John D. Rockefeller (1839-1937)
American oil millionaire monopolist and philanthropist

✱

Success is to be measured not so much by the position one has reached in life, as by the obstacles which one has overcome while trying to succeed.

Booker Taliaferro Washington (1856-1915)
American teacher, writer and speaker

✱

There are no gains without pains.

Adlai Stevenson (1900-1965)
American statesman

✶

Do what you love and believe in, and success will
come naturally.

Anonymous

✶

I cannot give you the formula for success, but I
can give you the formula for failure —
which is: try to please everybody.

Herbert Bayard Swope (1882-1958)
American newspaper editor

✶

The toughest thing about success is that you've
got to keep on being a success.

Irving Berlin (1888-1989)
American composer

✶

What's money? A man is a success if he gets up
in the morning and goes to bed at night and in
between does what he wants to do.

Bob Dylan (1941-)
American singer and songwriter

✳

I've never sought success in order to get fame
and money; it's the talent and the passion that
count in success.

Ingrid Bergman (1915-1982)
Swedish-born actress

✳

Getting ahead in a difficult profession requires
avid faith in yourself. You must be able to sustain
yourself against staggering blows and
unfair reversals.

Sophia Loren (1934-)
Italian actress

✳

The door to success has two signs,
Push — and Pull.

Leo Rosten's Treasury of Jewish Quotations

✳

It is no good saying 'we are doing our best.' You have got to succeed in doing what is necessary.

Winston Churchill (1874-1965)
English statesman

★

What is success?
To laugh often and much;
To win the respect of intelligent people and the affection of children;
To earn the appreciation of honest critics and endure the betrayal of false friends;
To appreciate beauty;
To find the best in others;
To leave the world a bit better, whether by a healthy child, a garden patch or a redeemed social condition;
To know even one life has breathed easier because you have lived;
This is to have succeeded.

Ralph Waldo Emerson (1803-1882)
American essayist, poet and philosopher

★

— SUFFERING —

My personal trials have taught me the value of
unmerited suffering. As my sufferings mounted I
soon realised that there were two ways that I
could respond to my situation: either to react
with bitterness or seek to transform the suffering
into a creative force.

Martin Luther King (1929-1968)
American black civil-rights leader

✳

— SUPERIORITY —

There is nothing noble about being superior to
some other man. The true nobility lies in being
superior to your previous self.

Hindu proverb

✳

T

— TALENT —

Everyone has talent. What is rare is the courage
to follow the talent to the dark place where
it leads.

Erica Jong (1942-)
American novelist and poet

✶

All our talents increase in the using, and every
faculty, both good and bad, strengthen
by exercise.

Anne Brontë (1820-1849)
English writer and poet

✶

Conciseness is the sister of talent.

Anton Chekhov (1860-1904)
Russian writer

✶

— TALK —

Who is there that can make muddy water clear?
But if allowed to remain still, it will gradually
become clear of itself...Be sparing of speech, and
things will come right of themselves.

Lao-Tzu (c. 604 BC)
Chinese philosopher and founder of Taoism

✶

I don't care how much a man talks, if he only
says it in a few words.

Josh Billings (1818-1885)
American humorist

✶

Talking and eloquence are not the same: to
speak, and to speak well, are two things.

Ben Jonson (1573-1637)
English dramatist

✶

When you have nothing to say, say nothing.

Charles Caleb Colton (1780-1832)
English clergyman, sportsman, gambler and author

★

To talk is our chief business in this world, and talk is by far the most accessible pleasure. It costs nothing in money; it is all profit, it completes education, founds and fosters friendships, and can be enjoyed at any age and in almost any state of health.

Robert Louis Stevenson (1850-1894)
Scottish novelist, poet and essayist

★

The fact that people are born with two eyes and two ears but only one tongue suggests that they ought to look and listen twice as much as they speak.

Anonymous

★

— TEACHING —

It is the supreme art of the teacher to awaken joy
in creative expression and knowledge.

Albert Einstein (1879-1955)
German-born physicist

✻

— TEARS —

The soul would have no rainbow
Had the eyes no tears.

John Vance Cheney (1848-1922)
American poet

✻

The liquid drops of tears that you have shed
Shall come again, transform'd to orient pearl,
Advantaging their loan with interest
Of ten times double gain of happiness.

William Shakespeare (1564-1616)
English playwright and poet

✻

— *THANKS* —

When you arise in the morning
Give thanks for the morning light.
Give thanks for your life and strength.
Give thanks for your food
And give thanks for the joy of living.
And if perchance you see no reason for
giving thanks,
Rest assured the fault is in yourself.

American Indian saying

★

Myself in constant good health, and in a
handsome and thriving condition. Blessed be
Almighty God for it.

Samuel Pepys (1633-1703)
English diarist

★

— THOUGHTS —

You may believe that you are responsible for what you do, but not for what you think. The truth is that you are responsible for what you think, because it is only at this level that you can exercise choice. What you do comes from what you think.

A Course in Miracles

✴

A man is what he thinks about all day long.

Ralph Waldo Emerson (1803-1882)
American essayist, poet and philosopher

✴

Every thought you have makes up some segment of the world you see. It is with your thoughts, then, that we must work, if your perception of the world is to be changed.

A Course in Miracles

✴

The most immutable barrier in nature is between one man's thoughts and another's.

William James (1842-1910)
American psychologist and philosopher

★

Thinking is the hardest work there is, which is probably why so few engage in it.

Henry Ford (1863-1947)
American motor car manufacturer

★

Mind is everything; we become what we think.

Buddha (5th century BC)
Founder of Buddhism

★

The mind is never right but when it is at peace within itself.

Seneca (4 BC-65 AD)
Roman philosopher and statesman

★

A great many people think they are thinking
when they are merely rearranging
their prejudices.

William James (1842-1910)
American psychologist and philosopher

★

Every revolution was first a thought in one
man's mind.

Ralph Waldo Emerson (1803-1882)
American essayist, poet and philosopher

★

Life does not consist mainly — or even largely —
of facts and happenings. It consists mainly of the
storm of thoughts that are forever blowing
through one's mind.

Mark Twain (1835-1910)
American writer and humorist

★

— TIME —

Don't serve time, make time serve you.

Willie Sutton (1860-1928)
American educationist

✶

Dost thou love life? Then do not squander time;
for that's the stuff life is made of.

Benjamin Franklin (1706-1790)
American statesman and philosopher

✶

Your time may be limited, but your imagination
is not.

Anonymous

✶

These trying times are the good old days we'll be
longing for in a few years.

José Ferrer (1909-1992)
American actor

✶

There is a time to be born, and a time to die, says
Solomon, and it is a memento of a truly wise
man; but there is an interval of infinte
importance between these two times.

Leigh Richmond (1772-1827)
English writer

✳

Take time to think...it is the source of power.
Take time to play...it is the secret of
perpetual youth.
Take time to read...it is the fountain of wisdom.
Take time to pray...it is the greatest power
on earth.
Take time to laugh...it is the music of the soul.
Take time to give...it is too short a day to
be selfish.

Anonymous

✳

It is familiarity with life that makes time speed quickly. When every day is a step into the unknown, as for children, the days are long with the gathering of experience.

George Robert Gissing (1857-1903)
English novelist

✶

Lose an hour in the morning and you will be all day hunting for it.

Richard Whately (1787-1863)
English Archbishop of Dublin

✶

You have to live on this twenty-four hours of daily time. Out of it you have to spin health, pleasure, money, content, respect and the evolution of your immortal soul. Its right use, its most effective use, is a matter of the highest urgency and of the most thrilling actuality. All depends on that. We shall never have any more time.

Arnold Bennett (1867-1931)
English novelist

✶

Time goes, you say? Ah no! Alas,
Time stays, *we* go.

Henry Austin Dobson (1840-1921)
English poet

★

Let us spend one day as deliberately as nature,
and not be thrown off the track by every nutshell
and mosquito's wing that falls on the rails. Let us
rise early and fast, or break fast, gently and
without perturbation; let company come and let
company go, let the bells ring and the children
cry — determined to make a day of it. If the
engine whistles, let it whistle till it is hoarse for
its pains. If the bell rings, why should we run?
Time is but the stream I go a-fishing in.

Henry David Thoreau (1817-1862)
American essayist and poet

★

Time is what we want most, but what, alas, we
use worst.

William Penn (1644-1718)
English Quaker and founder of Pennsylvania, USA

★

An inch of gold will not buy an inch of time.

Chinese proverb

★

If only I could stand on a street corner with my hat in my hand, and get people to throw their wasted time into it!

Bernard Berenson (1865-1959)
American art critic

★

The future is something which everyone reaches at the rate of sixty minutes an hour, whatever he does, whoever he is.

C.S. Lewis (1898-1963)
Irish-born academic, writer and poet

★

We have to make the most of every secondo.

David Helfgott (1947-)
Australian concert pianist

★

Time is
Too slow for those who wait,
Too swift for those who fear,
Too long for those who grieve,
Too short for those who rejoice,
But for those who love, time is
Eternity. Hours fly, flowers die,
New days, new ways, pass by.
Love stays.

Sundial inscription

✳

The busier you are, the more you find time to do
— and vice versa.

Anonymous

✳

Our todays and yesterdays are the blocks with
which we build.

Henry Wadsworth Longfellow (1807-1882)
American poet

✳

— TODAY & TOMORROW —

Look to this day...In it lies all the realities and
verities of existence, the bliss of growth, the
splendour of action, the glory of power. For
yesterday is but a dream and tomorrow is only a
vision. But today, well-lived, makes every
yesterday a dream of happiness and every
tomorrow a vision of hope.

Sanskrit proverb

✸

Happy the man, and happy he alone,
He who can call today his own:
He who, secure within, can say
Tomorrow do thy worst, for I have lived today.

John Dryden (1631-1700)
English poet

✸

Don't start living tomorrow — tomorrow never
arrives. Start working on your dreams and
ambitions today.

Anonymous

✸

The bud of a rose is just as beautiful as the full bloom. Appreciate what you have at the moment.

Anonymous

✷

Carpe diem. (Seize the day.)

Horace (65-8 BC)
Roman poet

✷

It's only when we truly know and understand that we have a limited time on earth — and that we have no way of knowing when our time is up — that we will begin to live each day to the fullest, as if it was the only one we had.

Elisabeth Kubler-Ross (1926-)
Swiss-born American psychiatrist

✷

What's lost today may be won tomorrow.

Miguel de Cervantes (1547-1616)
Spanish writer

✷

After all, tomorrow is another day.

Margaret Mitchell (1900-1949)
American novelist

✦

There is left for myself but one day in the week
— today. Any man can fight the battles of
today...It isn't the experiences of today that drives
men mad. It is the remorse for something that
happened yesterday, and the dread of what
tomorrow may disclose.

Robert J. Burdette (1844-1914)
American humorist

✦

One today is worth two tomorrows; never leave
that till tomorrow which you can do today.

Benjamin Franklin (1706-1790)
American statesman and philosopher

✦

— TOLERANCE —

Tolerance not only saves others from your prejudices and fears, but frees your soul to explore and accept the world that has been given to you.

Anonymous

✶

Give to every other human being every right that you claim for yourself.

Robert G. Ingersoll (1833-1899)
American lawyer and orator

✶

— TRANSFORMATION —

The meeting of two personalities is like the contact of two chemical substances: if there is any reaction, both are transformed.

Carl Jung (1875-1961)
Swiss psychiatrist

✶

— TRAVEL —

Travel is fatal to prejudice, bigotry, and
narrow-mindedness.

Mark Twain (1835-1910)
American writer and humorist

★

Travel and change of place impart new vigour
to the mind.

Seneca (4 BC-65 AD)
Roman philosopher

★

Everyone's travels through life end the same way,
so you might as well enjoy the journey.

Anonymous

★

The soul of a journey is liberty, perfect liberty, to
think, feel, do just as one pleases.

William Hazlitt (1778-1830)
English essayist

★

— TRUTH —

The truth hurts like a thorn at first; but in the
end it blossoms like a rose.

Samuel Ha-Nagid (c. 900)
Jewish scholar

✳

Men stumble over the truth from time to time,
but most pick themselves up and hurry off as if
nothing happened.

Sir Winston Churchill (1874-1965)
English statesman

✳

It takes two to speak the truth — one to speak,
and another to hear.

Henry David Thoreau (1817-1862)
American essayist, poet and mystic

✳

Nothing gives us rest but the sincere search for
truth.

Blaise Pascal (1623-1662)
French physicist, theologian and writer

✳

Rather than love, than money, than fame,
give me truth.

Henry David Thoreau (1817-1862)
American essayist, poet and mystic

✱

If you do not tell the truth about yourself you
cannot tell it about other people.

Virginia Woolf (1882-1941)
English writer

✱

Truth is within ourselves; it takes no rise
From outward things, whate'er you may believe.
There is an inmost centre in us all,
Where truth abides in fullness.

Robert Browning (1812-1889)
English poet

✱

The man who speaks the truth is always at ease.

Persian proverb

✱

The truth is cruel, but it can be loved and it makes free those who love it.

George Santayana (1863~1952)
Spanish philosopher, poet and novelist

It is good to know the truth and speak it, but it is better to talk of palm trees.

Chinese proverb

— *TRYING* —

Until you try, you don't know what you can't do.

Henry James (1843~1916)
American novelist

U

— UNDERSTANDING —

A single moment of understanding can flood a
whole life with meaning.

Anonymous

✻

If one is master of one thing and understands one
thing well, one has at the same time insight into
and understanding of many things.

Vincent Van Gogh (1853~1890)
Dutch post-impressionist painter

✻

— UNIQUE —

All cases are unique, and very similar to others.

T.S. Eliot (1888~1965)
American-born poet and dramatist

✻

V

— VICTORY —

He...got the better of himself, and that's the best kind of victory one can wish for.

Miguel de Cervantes (1547-1616)
Spanish author

＊

— VIRTUE —

Virtue is never left to stand alone. He who has it will have neighbours.

Confucius (551-479 BC)
Chinese philosopher

＊

W

— WEALTH —

Lazy men are soon poor.

Proverb

✳

Wealth is a good servant, but a bad master.

Anonymous

✳

Be not penny-wise; riches have wings and
sometimes they fly away of themselves;
sometimes they must be sent flying to bring
in more.

Francis Bacon (1561-1626)
English philosopher

✳

— WINNING —

An integral part of being a star is having the will
to win. All the champions have it.

Betty Cuthbert (1938-)
Australian Olympic gold-medal sprinter

✴

Only a loser finds it impossible to accept a
temporary set-back. A winner asks why.

Ita Buttrose (1942-)
Media personality

✴

You have to make more noise than anyone else,
you have to make yourself more obtrusive than
anyone else, you have to fill all the papers more
than anyone else, in fact you have to be there all
the time...if you are really going to get your
reform realised.

Emmeline Pankhurst (1858-1928)
Suffragette leader

✴

— WISDOM —

Be wiser than other people if you can, but do not tell them so.

Earl of Chesterfield (1694~1773)
English statesman

✷

True wisdom consists in knowing one's duty exactly. True piety in acting what one knows. To aim at more than this, is to run into endless mistakes.

Bishop Thomas Wilson (1663~1755)
English churchman

✷

In seeking wisdom, the first step is silence, the second listening, the third remembering, the fourth practising, the fifth — teaching others.

Ibn Gabirol (Avicebron) (1020~c.1070)
Jewish poet and philosopher

✷

Knowledge comes, but wisdom lingers.

Alfred, Lord Tennyson (1809-1892)
English poet

✱

I don't think much of a man who is not wiser
today than he was yesterday.

Abraham Lincoln (1809-1865)
President of the United States, 1861-1865

✱

A wise man hears one word and
understands two.

Jewish proverb

✱

The foolish man wonders at the unusual, but the
wise man at the usual.

Ralph Waldo Emerson (1803-1882)
American essayist, poet and philosopher

✱

Be with wise men and become wise.

Proverbs 13:20

✱

The wisdom of the wise, and the experience of the ages, may be preserved by quotations.

Isaac D'Israeli (1766-1848)
English literary critic

✱

He who knows others is learned; he who knows himself is wise.

Lao-Tze (c. 604 BC)
Chinese philosopher and founder of Taoism

✱

It is the province of knowledge to speak and it is the privilege of wisdom to listen.

Oliver Wendell Holmes (1809-1894)
American writer

✱

Every man is a damn fool for at least five minutes
every day; wisdom consists in not exceeding
the limit.

Elbert Hubbard (1856-1915)
American writer

✱

The price of wisdom is above rubies.

Job 28:18

✱

Nine-tenths of wisdom is being wise in time

Theodore Roosevelt (1858-1919)
President of the United States, 1901-1912

✱

It is characteristic of wisdom not to do
desperate things.

Henry David Thoreau (1817-1862)
American essayist, poet and mystic

✱

— WORDS —

Try to say the very thing you really mean, the whole of it, nothing more or less or other than what you really mean. That is the whole art and joy of words.

C.S. Lewis (1898~1963)
Irish~born academic, writer and poet.

✳

Man does not live by words alone, despite the fact that sometimes he has to eat them.

Broderick Crawford (1911~)
American actor

✳

— WORK —

To my mind the best investment a young man starting out in business could possibly make is to give all his time, all his energies to work, just plain, hard work.

Charles M. Schwab (1862-1939)
American industrialist

✳

The glory of a workman, still more of a master-workman, that he does his work well, ought to be his most precious possession; like the 'honour of a soldier', dearer to him than life.

Thomas Carlyle (1795-1881)
Scottish essayist, historian and philosopher

✳

It is impossible to enjoy idling thoroughly unless one has plenty of work to do.

Jerome K. Jerome (1859-1927)
English playwright and humorist

✳

Choose a job you love, and you will never have to work a day in your life.

Anonymous

✦

What's really important in life? Sitting on the beach? Looking at television eight hours a day? I think we have to appreciate that we're alive for only a limited period of time, and we'll spend most of our lives working. That being the case, I believe one of the most important priorities is to do whatever we do as well as we can. We should take pride in that.

Victor Kermit Kiam (1926-)
American corporate executive

✦

The force, the mass of character, mind, heart or soul that a man can put into any work, is the most important factor in that work.

A.P. Peabody (1811-1893)
American writer

✦

The highest reward for man's toil is not what he gets for it but what he becomes by it.

John Ruskin (1819-1900)
English writer and art critic

★

Whatsoever thy hand findeth to do, do it with thy might.

Ecclesiastes

★

Work is love made visible.

Kahlil Gibran (1883-1931)
Lebanese poet, author, artist and mystic

★

Nothing is really work unless you would rather be doing something else.

J.M. Barrie (1860-1937)
Scottish novelist

★

In order that people may be happy in their work, these three things are needed: They must be fit for it. They must not do too much of it. And they must have a sense of success in it.

John Ruskin (1819-1900)
English writer and art critic

✶

Well begun is half done.

Proverb

✶

The more one works, the more willing one is to work.

Lord Chesterfield (1694-1773)
English statesman and author

✶

It is work that gives flavour to life.

Henri-Frederic Amiel (1828-1881)
Swiss philosopher and critic

✶

There is no substitute for hard work.

Thomas A. Edison (1847-1931)
American inventor

To generous souls, every task is noble.

Euripides (480-406 BC)
Greek dramatist

No race can prosper till it learns that there is as
much dignity in tilling a field as in writing
a poem.

Booker Taliaferro Washington (1856-1915)
American teacher; writer and speaker

— WORRY —

I've found that worry and irritation vanish into
thin air the moment I open my mind to the many
blessings I possess.

Dale Carnegie (1888-1955)
American author and lecturer

✳

As a cure for worrying, work is better
than whisky.

Thomas A. Edison (1845-1931)
American inventor

✳

I have spent most of my life worrying about
things that have never happened.

Mark Twain (1835-1910)
American writer and humorist

✳

I am an old man and have had many troubles,
but most of them never happened.

Anonymous

✳

You're only here for a short visit. Don't hurry. Don't worry. And be sure to smell the flowers along the way.

Walter C. Hagen (1892-1969)
American golfer

✴

Worry is interest paid on trouble before it falls due.

William Inge (1860-1954)
English prelate and author

✴

Worries go down better with soup than without.

Jewish proverb

✴

Y

— YES —

Where we are free to act, we are free to refrain
from acting, and where we are able to say no, we
are also able to say yes.

Aristotle (384-322 BC)
Greek philosopher

✱

Say yes to life.

Anonymous

✱

For what has been — thanks!
For what shall be — yes!

Dag Hammarskjold (1905-1961)
Swedish diplomat

✱

— YOU —

Always be a first-rate version of yourself, instead
of a second-rate version of somebody else.

Judy Garland (1922-1969)
American singer

✴

You have to live with yourself, so it's important
that you are fit for yourself to know.

Anonymous

✴

Don't compromise yourself. You are all
you've got.

Janis Joplin (1943-1970)
American singer and songwriter

✴

If I try to be like him, who will be like me?

Jewish proverb

✴

One person's definition of success is another's
first step. Only you can rate your
accomplishments, and find peace within yourself.

Anonymous

✦

To be nobody but yourself — in a world which is
doing its best, night and day, to make you
everybody else — means to fight the hardest
battle which any human being can fight, and
never stop fighting.

e.e. cummings (1894-1962)
English poet

✦

— YOUTH —

Youth is a disease that must be borne with
patiently! Time, indeed, will cure it.

R.H. Benson (1871-1914)
English novelist

✦

Z

— ZEAL —

Zeal without knowledge is fire without light.

Thomas Fuller (1608~1661)
English divine and historian

★

— Subject Index —

Ability, 9
Abundance, 10
Acceptance, 11
Accomplish, 12
Achieve, 13
Action, 14
Adversity, 18
Advice, 20
Ageing, 21
Ambition, 27
Anger, 29
Anxiety, 29
Appearance, 30
Appreciation, 31
Aspirations, 31
Attitude, 32

Beauty, 34
Beginning, 36
Belief, 37
Best, 39
Big, 41
Birthdays, 41
Blessed, 42
Blessing, 43
Books, 44
Brain, 47
Bravery, 47
Bright Side, 48
Business, 49

Careers, 51
Change, 52
Chaos, 54
Character, 55
Charity, 56
Choice, 57
Comfort, 59
Commitment, 60

Compromise, 61
Compunction, 61
Concentration, 62
Confidence, 62
Conscience, 63
Consequences, 63
Constancy, 64
Contentment, 64
Courage, 65
Courtesy, 69
Creativity, 70
Criticism, 71
Curiosity, 73

Death, 74
Decisions, 79
Deeds, 80
Defeat, 82
Delight, 82
Desire, 83
Despair, 84
Destiny, 85
Difficulty, 87
Direction, 88
Discipline, 89
Discovery, 89
Dreams, 90
Durability, 94

Education, 95
Endurance, 96
Enemies, 97
Energy, 97
Enjoyment, 98
Enthusiasm, 99
Excellence, 102
Excuses, 102
Experience, 103
Extraordinary, 105

Failure, 106
Faith, 109
Fate, 112
Faults, 113
Fear, 114
Forgiveness, 117
Freedom, 119
Friends, 122
Fulfilment, 128
Future, 129

Gardens, 131
Genius, 133
Gifts, 134
Giving, 135
Goals, 136
Good, 139
Greatness, 141
Growth, 143

Habit, 146
Happiness, 147
Hatred, 154
Health, 155
Heart, 156
Heaven, 157
Help, 158
Home, 159
Honesty, 160
Hope, 161
Humour, 163

Ideas, 164
Ignorance, 165
Imagination, 166
Imperfection, 168
Impression, 168
Independence, 169
Individuality, 170
Integrity, 171
Intuition, 172

Joy, 173
Judgement, 175
Justice, 175

Kindness, 176
Knowledge, 180

Laughter, 183
Laziness, 186
Leadership, 187
Learning, 188
Life, 190
Loneliness, 197
Love, 198
Luck, 205

Marriage, 206
Mind, 208
Miracles, 210
Misery, 212
Mistakes, 213
Money, 217
Music, 219

Nature, 220
Negativity, 221
Negotiation, 221

Occupation, 222
Opportunity, 223
Optimism, 226
Order, 229
Organisation, 230
Originality, 231

Pain, 232
Parting, 232
Parenthood, 233
Past, 235
Patience, 236
Peace, 237

Perception, 239
Perseverance, 239
Pick-me-ups, 242
Plan, 244
Pleasure, 245
Possibility, 247
Potential, 248
Poverty, 249
Power, 249
Praise, 250
Prayer, 251
Present Joys, 253
Problems, 254
Procrastination, 255

Quiet, 256

Receptiveness, 257
Regret, 258
Relationship, 259
Religion, 261
Reputation, 263
Resilience, 263
Revolution, 263
Righteousness, 264
Risk, 265

Safety, 266
Self-confidence, 267
Self-control, 268
Self-discovery, 269
Selflessness, 271
Self-respect, 272
Silence, 274
Sincerity, 274
Smile, 275
Solitude, 276
Solution, 278
Sorrow, 279
Strength, 280

Struggle, 281
Success, 283
Suffering, 289
Superiority, 289

Talent, 290
Talk, 291
Teaching, 293
Tears, 293
Thanks, 294
Thoughts, 295
Time, 298
Today & Tomorrow, 304
Tolerance, 307
Transformation, 307
Travel, 308
Truth, 309
Trying, 311

Understanding, 312
Unique, 312

Victory, 313
Virtue, 313

Wealth, 314
Winning, 315
Wisdom, 316
Words, 320
Work, 321
Worry, 326

Yes, 328
You, 329
Youth, 330

Zeal, 331

POCKET
POSITIVES

Compiled by Maggie Pinkney

Contents

Introduction   340

Ability – Authority   343

Balance – Boredom   370

Challenges – Curiosity   383

Death – Dreams   419

Education – Experience   427

Failure – Friendship   445

Gardens & Gardening – Guilt   472

Habit – Humour   494

Ideals & Idealism – Invention   515

Joy – Justice   527

Kindness – Knowledge   531

Laughter – Luck   535

Marriage – Music   554

Nature   563

Obstacles – Originality   567

Parting – Problems   575

Regret – Risk   591

Self-acceptance – Sympathy   601

Tact – Truth   624

Understanding – Unity   635

Victory – Vocation   636

Walking – Worth   639

Yesterday, Today & Tomorrow – Youth   653

Zeal   660

Subject Index   661

Write down your own Pocket Positives   665

Introduction

Mankind would lose half its wisdom built up over centuries if it lost its great sayings. They contain the best parts of the best books.

Thomas Jefferson (1743-1826)

The resounding success of *Pocket Positives* has inspired us to assemble this new anthology of benign and healing thoughts to provide you with encouragement and inspiration. Again, these quotations are drawn from a wide range of sources — including the world's greatest philosophers, religious leaders, poets, novelists and humorists, as well as people from many other walks of life.

What all these men and women — from the distant past to the present — have in common is the ability to inspire us in some way, whether it is with their love, enthusiasm, compassion, courage, wisdom, success or pure zest for life. It's not that they are superhuman. Many quotations reveal that their authors are deeply acquainted with sorrows, failures and fears. But they have managed to keep sight of the larger picture, and to fight back. In fact, one of the most comforting aspects of this anthology is that it shows us that whatever our problems are, we are not alone. Someone else, somewhere, has felt as we do, and has experienced what we are going through. This is in itself a consolation, and certainly helps one to gain an all-important sense of perspective.

In this selection, many themes occur again and again — each time expressed in a fresh new way. For example, Austrian psychiatrist Alfred Adler wrote, 'We can be cured of depression in only fourteen days if every day we will try to think of how we can be helpful to others.' Mark Twain reached the same conclusion: 'The best way to cheer yourself up is to cheer someone else up,' he advised. A similar sentiment is expressed yet again — and with great elegance — by Ralph Waldo Emerson: 'It is one of the most beautiful compensations of this life that no man can sincerely try to help another without helping himself.'

Some of the famous men and women who share their thoughts with us in these 'pocket positives' give us a sense of understanding and acceptance. Others, such as Martin Luther King, Winston Churchill, Aung San Suu Kyi and Helen Keller, inspire us by their example as much as by their words.

Quotations are arranged under subject heads for easy reference, and an index of sources is also included. Keep this companionable anthology by your bedside and read it regularly. It will help you to enjoy a more fulfilling and meaningful life. Simply open it at any page until you find a quote that 'speaks' to you in your present frame of mind. As Albert Einstein said, 'There are two ways to live your life. One is as though nothing is a miracle. The other is as though everything is a miracle.'

Welcome to *More Pocket Positives*!

A

Ability

One of the greatest of all principles is that men can do what they think they can do.

Norman Vincent Peale, 1898-1993
American writer and minister

★

It is better to have a little ability and use it well than to have much ability and make poor use of it.

Anonymous

★

They are able who think they are able.

Virgil, 70-19 BC
Roman poet

★

Achievement

It was a golden year beyond my dreams. I proved you're never too old to achieve what you really want to do.

Heather Turland, b. 1960
Australian women's marathon gold medallist,
Commonwealth Games, 1998

✦

Achievement is largely the product of steadily raising one's level of aspiration and expectation.

Jack Nicklaus, b. 1940
American golfer

✦

All the things we achieve are things we have first of all imagined and then made happen.

David Malouf, b. 1934
Australian writer

✦

Action

To will is to select a goal, determine a course of action that will bring one to that goal, and then hold to that action till the goal is reached. The key is action.

Michael Hanson, 1863-1908
American mathematician

☆

Action is the antidote to despair.

Joan Baez, b. 1941
American folk singer

☆

Well done is better than well said.

Benjamin Franklin, 1706-1790
American statesman and scientist

☆

A little knowledge that *acts* is worth infinitely more than knowledge that is idle.

Kahlil Gibran, 1882-1931
Lebanese poet, artist and mystic

☆

In our era the road to holiness necessarily passes through the world of action.

Dag Hammarskjold, 1905-1961
Swedish statesman and humanitarian

★

Just go out there and do what you've got to do.

Martina Navratilova, b. 1956
Czechoslovakian-born American tennis champion

★

Don't wait for a light to appear at the end of the tunnel, stride down there . . . and light the bloody thing yourself.

Sara Henderson, b. 1936
Australian outback station manager and writer

★

As life is action and passion, it is required of man that he should share the passion and action of his time, at peril of being judged not to have lived.

Oliver Wendell Holmes, 1809-1894
American writer and physician

★

All mankind is divided into three classes: those that are immovable, those that are movable, and those that move.

Benjamin Franklin, 1706-1790
American statesman and scientist

☆

The shortest answer is doing.

English proverb

☆

A good deed, no matter how small, is worth more than all the good intentions in the world.

Anonymous

☆

You can't build a reputation on what you're going to do.

Henry Ford, 1863-1946
American car manufacturer

☆

Knowledge without Action is useless.
Action without Knowledge is foolishness.

Sai Baba
Indian spiritual master

☆

However brilliant an action may be it should not be esteemed great unless the result of a great motive.

Duc de La Rochefoucauld 1613-1680
French writer

★

Action may not always bring happiness, but there is no happiness without action.

Benjamin Disraeli, 1804-1881
British Prime Minister and writer

★

How may a man gain self-knowledge? By contemplation? Certainly not; but by action. Try to do your duty and you will find what you are fit for. But what is your duty? The demand of the hour.

Johann von Goethe, 1749-1832
German writer, dramatist and scientist

★

Our grand business in life is not to see what lies dimly at a distance, but to do what clearly lies at hand.

Thomas Carlyle, 1795-1881
Scottish historian, essayist and critic

★

Sometimes the only way for me to find out
what it is I want to do is go ahead and do
something. Then the moment I start to act, my
feelings become clear.

Hugh Prather, b. 1938
American writer

The man who does things makes many
mistakes, but he never makes the biggest
mistake of all — doing nothing.

Benjamin Franklin, 1706-1790
American statesman and scientist

Adventurousness

Not all those that wander are lost.

J. R. R. Tolkien, 1892-1973
English author

Adversity

A man of character finds a special attractiveness in difficulty, since it is only by coming to grips with difficulty that he can realise his potentialities.

Charles de Gaulle, 1890-1970
French statesman and general

☆

A woman is like a teabag — you can't tell how strong she is until you put her in hot water.

Nancy Reagan, b. 1923
First Lady of the United States of America

☆

Adversity introduces a man to himself.

Anonymous

☆

When you're up to your ears in trouble, try using the part that isn't submerged.

Anonymous

☆

Advice

If I were asked to give what I consider the single most useful piece of advice for all humanity it would be this: Expect trouble as an inevitable part of life, and when it comes, hold your head high, look it squarely in the eye and say, 'I will be bigger than you. You cannot defeat me.' Then repeat to yourself the most comforting words of all, 'This too will pass.'

Ann Landers, b. 1918
American advice columnist

★

Seek ye counsel of the aged, for their eyes have looked on the faces of the years and their ears have hearkened to the voices of Life. Even if their counsel is displeasing to you, pay heed to them.

Kahlil Gibran, 1883-1931
Lebanese poet, artist and mystic

★

When you can, always advise people to
do what you see they really want to do, so
long as what they want to do isn't dangerously
unlawful, stupidly unsocial or obviously
imposssible. Doing what they want to do,
they may succeed; doing what they don't
want to do, they won't.

James Gould Cozzens, 1903-1978
American writer

★

Do a little more than you're paid to;
Give a little more than you have to;
Try a little harder than you want to;
Aim a little higher than you think possible;
And give a lot of thanks to God for health,
family and friends.

Art Linkletter
American television personality

★

Consult your friend on all things, especially on
those which concern yourself. His counsel may
then be useful where your own self-love may
impair your judgement.

Seneca, c. 4 BC - 65 AD
Roman philosopher, dramatist, poet and statesman

★

Whenever you are asked if you can do a job, tell 'em, 'Certainly I can!' — and get busy and find out how to do it.

Theodore Roosevelt, 1858-1919
President of the United States of America

✦

We have to steer our true life's course. Whatever your calling is in life! The whole purpose of being here is to figure out what that is as soon as possible, so you go about the business of being on track, of not being owned by what your mother said, what society said, whatever people think a woman is supposed to be . . . when you can exceed other people's expectations and be defined by your own!

Oprah Winfrey, b. 1954
American television personality

✦

Generosity gives assistance rather than advice.

Marquis de Vauvenargues, 1715-1745
French soldier and writer

✦

Ageing

Old age is not an illness, it is a timeless ascent. As power diminishes, we grow toward the light.

May Sarton, 1912-1995
American writer and poet

★

One should never count the years — one should count one's interests. I have kept young trying never to lose my childhood sense of wonderment. I am glad I still have a vivid curiosity about the world I live in.

Helen Keller, 1880-1968
Blind and deaf American writer and scholar

★

Wrinkles should merely indicate where smiles have been.

Mark Twain, 1835-1910
American humorist and writer

★

Ageing is a life-spanning process of growth and development from birth to death. Old age is an integral part of the whole, bringing fulfilment and self-actualisation. I regard ageing as a triumph, a result of strength and survivorship.

Margaret Kuhn, b. 1905
American civil rights activist

★

I have no romantic feelings about age. Either you are interesting at any age or you are not. There is nothing particularly interesting about being old — or being young, for that matter.

Katharine Hepburn, b. 1907
American actress

★

There is nothing more liberating than age.

Liz Carpenter, b. 1920
American feminist writer

★

I am delighted to be with you. In fact, at my age, I am delighted to be anywhere.

Ronald Reagan, b. 1911
President of the United States of America

★

Thank God I have the seeing eye, that is to say, as I lie in bed I can walk step by step on the fells and rough land seeing every stone and flower and patch of bog and cotton pass where my old legs will never take me again.

Beatrix Potter, 1866-1943
British children's writer and illustrator

☆

The wiser mind
Mourns less for what age takes away
Than what it leaves behind.

William Wordsworth, 1770-1850
English poet

☆

It is quite wrong to think of old age as a downward slope. On the contrary, one climbs higher and higher with the advancing years, and that, too, with surprising strides. Brain-work comes as easily to the old as physical exertion to the child. One is moving, it is true, towards the end of life, but that end is now a goal, and not a reef in which the vessel may be dashed.

George Sand (Amandine Dupin) 1804-1876
French novelist

☆

By the bye, as I must leave off being young, I find many Douceurs in being a sort of Chaper-one for I am put on the Sofa near the fire and can drink as much wine as I like.

Jane Austen, 1775-1816
English novelist
From a letter to her sister Cassandra

☆

I prefer to forget both pairs of glasses and spend my declining years saluting strange women and grandfather clocks.

Ogden Nash, 1902-1971
American humorous poet

☆

Perhaps middle age is, or should be, a period of shedding shells: the shell of ambition, the shell of material accumulations and possessions, the shell of ego.

Anne Morrow Lindbergh, b. 1906
American writer

☆

I am still not ready to accept completely grey hair. I try to keep fit — eat vegetarian meals, walk, swim and practise yoga. Mostly I accept my body as a record of my life.

Margaret Henry, b. 1934
Australian writer

★

I am 65 and I guess that puts me in with the geriatrics. But if there were 15 months in every year, I'd only be 48. That's the trouble with us. We number everything. Take women, for example, I think they deserve to have more than 12 years between the ages of 28 and 40.

James Thurber, 1894-1961
American writer and cartoonist

★

Our hearts are young 'neath wrinkled rind: life's more interesting than we thought.

Andrew Lang, 1844-1912
Scottish poet

★

When I passed the seventieth milestone ten
months ago I instantly realised that I had
entered a new country and a new atmosphere...
I now believe that the best of life begins at
seventy, for then your work is done; you know
that you have done your best, let the quality
of the work be what it may; that you have
earned your holiday...and that henceforth
to the setting of the sun nothing will
break it, nothing interrupt it.

Mark Twain, 1835-1910
American humorist and writer

⭐

I gave my youth and beauty to men. I am going
to give my wisdom and experience to animals.

Brigitte Bardot, b. 1934
French actress and animal rights campaigner

⭐

One of the signs of passing youth is the birth of
a sense of fellowship with other human beings
as we take our place among them.

Virginia Woolf, 1882-1941
English novelist

⭐

Becoming a grandmother is more often
a middle-age than an old-age event. For
many women today this is a time when, free
of immediate family responsibilities, they
discover new skills and at last are able to do
what they want to do. The idea of old age is
also changing. Women in their sixties and
seventies do not get old. Instead we enter an
active and satisfying 'third age', and after that,
at eighty, a happy and contented 'fourth age'.

Sheila Kitzinger, b. 1929
Obstetrician and writer

✯

Life has got to be lived — that's all there
is to it. At seventy, I would say the advantage
is that you take life more calmly. You know
that 'this too will pass!'

Eleanor Roosevelt, 1884-1962
*First Lady of the United States of America, writer and
diplomat*

✯

Grow old along with me!
The best is yet to be.

Robert Browning, 1812-1889
English poet

✯

The process of maturing is an art to be learned, an effort to be sustained. By the age of fifty you have made yourself what you are and, if it is good, it is better than your youth.

Marya Mannes, b. 1904
American journalist

☆

Age puzzles me. I thought it was a quiet time. My seventies were interesting and fairly serene, but my eighties are passionate. I grow more intense as I age.

Florida Scott-Maxwell, 1883-1979
American-born English writer and psychologist

☆

Age only matters when one is ageing. Now that I have arrived at a great age, I might as well be twenty.

Pablo Picasso, 1881-1973
Spanish painter and sculptor

☆

Ambition

Ambition never gets anywhere until it forms a partnership with work.

Anonymous

☆

If you wish in this world to advance
Your merits you're bound to enhance,
You must stir it and stump it,
And blow your own trumpet
Or, trust me, you haven't a chance!

W. S. Gilbert, 1836-1911
English dramatist and librettist

☆

The fellow who has an abundance of push gets along very well without pull.

Anonymous

☆

Anger

Anybody can become angry. That is not difficult; but to be angry with the right person and to the right degree, and at the right time, and for the right purpose, and in the right way: that is not within everybody's capability and it is not easy.

Aristotle, 384-322 BC
Greek philosopher

✯

For every minute you remain angry you give up sixty seconds of peace of mind.

Ralph Waldo Emerson, 1803-1882
American essayist, poet and philosopher

✯

Anger is short-lived in a good man.

Thomas Fuller, 1608-1661
English clergyman and writer

✯

Animals

Love the animals: God has given them the
rudiments of thought and joy untroubled.

Feodor Dostoevsky, 1821-1881
Russian writer

★

All animals except man know that the
ultimate of life is to enjoy it.

Samuel Butler, 1835-1902
English writer

★

God made all the animals and gave
them our love and our fear,
To give sign, we and they are his children,
one family here.

Robert Browning, 1812-1889
English poet

★

Heaven goes by favour. If it went by merit, you
would stay out and your dog would go in.

Mark Twain, 1835-1910
American humorist and writer

★

I think I could turn and live with animals,
they're so placid and self-contained. I stand
and look at them long and long.

Walt Whitman, 1819-1892
American poet and writer

★

Our perfect companions never have
fewer than four feet.

Colette, 1873-1954
French writer

★

I really don't think I could consent to
go to Heaven if I thought there were to
be no animals there.

George Bernard Shaw, 1856-1950
Irish writer, dramatist and critic

★

Apology

A man should never be ashamed to own
he has been in the wrong, which is but saying,
in other words, that he is wiser today
than he was yesterday.

Alexander Pope, 1688-1744
English poet

★

A true apology is more than just
acknowledgement of a mistake. It is
recognition that something you have said or
done has damaged a relationship and that you
care enough about the relationship to want it
repaired and restored.

Norman Vincent Peale, 1898-1993
American writer and minister

★

A sincere apology takes courage and humility.

Anonymous

★

Attitude

I've never been poor, only broke. Being poor
is a frame of mind. Being broke is only
a temporary setback.

Mike Todd, 1903-1958
American film producer

★

The greater part of our happiness or
misery depends on our dispositions and
not our circumstances.

Martha Washington, 1732-1802
First Lady of the United States of America

★

There is nothing either good or bad, but
thinking makes it so.

William Shakespeare, 1564-1616
English poet and playwright

★

I don't sing because I'm happy;
I'm happy because I sing.

William James, 1842-1910
American psychologist and philosopher

★

If, from time to time, we look at the blessings
in our lives, at the warmth and care and love
so many people respond with when there is a
tragedy, at the fact that we can walk and talk,
eat and breathe, then maybe we would re-
evaluate our bad moods and become aware
that all negative thoughts bring with them
more negativity, but all love shared
returns a thousandfold.
'As a man thinketh' perhaps best describes how
we are the creators of our own worlds.

Elisabeth Kübler-Ross, b. 1926
Swiss-born American psychiatrist

★

I always prefer to believe the best of
everybody; it saves so much trouble.

Rudyard Kipling, 1865-1936
Indian-born British poet and writer

★

Life appears to me too short to be spent in nursing animosity or registering wrong.

Charlotte Brontë, 1816-1855
British novelist

☆

It is our attitude at the beginning of a difficult undertaking which, more than anything else, will determine its successful outcome.

William James, 1842-1910
American psychologist and philosopher

☆

Nothing can hurt you unless you give it the power to do so.

A Course in Miracles

☆

Authority

When you make peace with authority, you become authority.

Jim Morrison, 1943-1971
American rock singer

☆

B

Balance

There are as many nights as days, and the one
is just as long as the other in the year's course.
Even a happy life cannot be without a measure
of darkness, and the word 'happy' would lose
its meaning if it were not balanced by sadness.
It is far better to take things as they come
along with patience and equanimity.

Carl Jung, 1875-1961
Swiss psychiatrist

✰

Everyone is a moon and has a dark side which
he never shows to anybody.

Mark Twain, 1835-1910
American humorist and writer

✰

To be a woman is to have interests and duties, raying out in all directions from the central mother-core, like spokes from the hub of a wheel . . . We must be open to all points of the compass; husband, children, friends, home, community; stretched out, exposed, like a spider's web to each breeze that blows, to each call that comes. How difficult for us, then, to achieve a balance in the midst of these contra-dictory tensions, and yet how necessary for the proper functioning of our lives.

Anne Morrow Lindbergh, b. 1906
American writer

★

Beauty

Beauty is the gift of God.

Aristotle, 384-322 BC
Greek philosopher

★

Cheerfulness and contentment are great beautifiers and are famous preservers of youthful good looks.

Charles Dickens, 1812-1870
English writer

★

Everything has its beauty but not
everyone sees it.

Confucius, c. 550-c. 478 BC
Chinese philosopher

★

Beauty is God's handwriting,
Welcome it
in every fair face,
every fair day,
every fair flower.

Charles Kingsley, 1819-1875
English writer, poet and clergyman

★

Beauty is no quality in things themselves;
it exists merely in the mind which
contemplates them; and each mind
perceives a different beauty.

David Hume, 1711-1776
Scottish philosopher and historian

★

Beginning

The distance doesn't matter; it is only
the first step that is difficult.

Marquise de Deffand, 1697-1780
French noblewoman

☆

There is an old saying 'well begun is half done'
. . . I would use instead — Not begun at
all until half done.

John Keats, 1795-1821
English poet

☆

The right moment for starting on your next job
is not tomorrow or next week; it is *instanter*,
or in the American idiom, right now.

Arnold Toynbee, 1899-1975
English historian

☆

Belief

Believe you can, and you can. Belief is one of the most powerful of all problem dissolvers. When you believe that a difficulty can be overcome, you are more than halfway to victory over it already.

Norman Vincent Peale, 1898-1993
American writer and minister

★

I believe in one God and no more, and I hope for happiness beyond this life. I believe in the equality of man; and I believe that religious duties consist in doing justice, loving mercy and in endeavouring to make our fellow creatures happy.

Thomas Paine, 1737-1809
English-born American revolutionary philosopher and writer

★

No one of you is a believer until he desires for his brother that which he desires for himself.

Islamic spirituality

★

Best

I do the very best I know how — the very best I can; and I mean to keep on doing it until the end.

Abraham Lincoln, 1809-1865
American statesman and President

★

When we do the best we can, we never know what miracle is wrought in our life, or the life of another.

Helen Keller, 1880-1968
Blind and deaf American writer and scholar

★

I have tried simply to write the best I can; sometimes I have good luck and write better than I can.

Ernest Hemingway, 1898-1961
American writer

★

Blessings

Let there be many windows in your soul,
That all the glories of the universe
May beautify it.

Ralph Waldo Trine, 1866-1958
American poet and writer

Bless the four corners of this little house
And be the lintel blessed;
And bless the hearth, and bless the board
And bless each place of rest.

Anonymous

Reflect on your present blessings, of
which every man has many, not on your past
misfortunes, of which all men have some.

Charles Dickens, 1812-1870
English writer

Books

No entertainment is so cheap as reading,
nor any pleasure so lasting.

Lady Mary Wortley Montague, 1689-1762
English poet and writer

✯

Then I thought of reading — the nice and
subtle happiness of reading . . . this joy not
dulled by age, this polite and unpunishable
vice, this selfish, serene, lifelong intoxication.

Logan Pearsall Smith, 1865-1946
American essayist

✯

A good book is the precious lifeblood of a
master spirit, embalmed and treasured up on
purpose to a life beyond life.

John Milton, 1608-1674
English poet

✯

A library is thought in cold storage.

Herbert Samuel, 1870-1963
British statesman

✯

For books are more than books,
they are the life
The very heart and core of ages past,
The reason why men lived and
worked and died,
The essence and quintessence of their lives.

Amy Lowell, 1874-1925
American poet and writer

★

Study has been for me the sovereign remedy
against all the disappointments of life. I have
never known any trouble that an hour's
reading would not dissipate.

Charles Louis de Montesquieu, 1689-1755
French political philosopher

★

Books are the legacies that a great genius leaves
to mankind, which are delivered down from
generation to generation as presents to the
posterity of those who are not yet born.

Joseph Addison, 1672-1719
English essayist

★

The books read in childhood . . . create in one's mind a sort of false map of the world, a series of fabulous countries into which one can retreat at odd moments throughout the rest of life, and which in some cases can even survive a visit to the real countries which they are supposed to represent.

George Orwell, 1903-1950
English novelist and essayist

★

Books, books, books. It was not that I read so much. I read and re-read the same ones. But all of them were necessary to me. Their presence, their smell, the letters of their titles, and the texture of their leather bindings.

Colette, 1873-1954
French writer

★

We read books to find out who we are. What other people, real or imaginary, do and think and feel is an essential guide to our understanding of what we ourselves are and may become.

Ursula LeGuin, b. 1929
American science fiction writer

★

The best effect of any book is that it excites the reader to self activity.

Thomas Carlyle, 1875-1881
Scottish historian, essayist and critic

★

My early and invincible love of reading I would not exchange for all the riches of India.

Edward Gibbon, 1737-1794
British historian

★

You may have tangible wealth untold,
Caskets of jewels and coffers of gold.
Richer than I you can never be —
I had a mother who read to me.

Strickland Gillilan, 1869-1954
Writer and poet

★

Mankind would lose half its wisdom built up over the centuries if it lost its great sayings. They contain the best parts of the best books.

Thomas Jefferson, 1743-1826
President of the United States of America

★

No furniture so charming as books, even if you never open them, or read a single word.

Sydney Smith, 1771-1845
English clergyman, essayist and wit

☆

. . . books, because of their weight and texture, and because of their sweetly token resistance to manipulation, involve our hands and eyes, and then our minds and souls, in a spiritual adventure I would be very sorry for my grandchildren not to know about.

Kurt Vonnegut, b. 1922
American novelist

☆

When I am attacked by gloomy thoughts, nothing helps me so much as running to my books. They quickly absorb me and banish the clouds from my mind.

Michel de Montaigne, 1533-1592
French essayist

☆

Boredom

Life is so full of exciting things to do and see
that we should never be bored. Watch the
sunrise from a hot-air balloon, go swimming
with dolphins, take up bushwalking, join a
book club, learn a foreign language. Try out at
least one new and interesting thing each year.

Anonymous

☆

There is no such thing as an uninteresting
subject; the only thing that can exist is an
uninterested person.

G. K. Chesterton, 1874-1936
English writer and critic

☆

Is not life a hundred times too short for
us to bore ourselves?

Friedrich Nietzsche, 1844-1900
German philosopher

☆

C

Challenges

If you continuously face challenges,
one of two things can happen:
You either collapse under the strain, lose
confidence in your ability and walk away
defeated — perhaps to fight again later or to
just drift into a life of non-challenge. Or you
win a few impossibles and are then encouraged
to have a go at the next impossible. So that
before long, you find the impossibles have
become possible.

Sara Henderson, B. 1936
Australian outback station manager and writer

☆

There are no problems — only challenges.

Anonymous

☆

Change

Keep in mind in how many things you yourself have already seen change. The universe is change. Life is understanding.

Marcus Aurelius, 121-180 AD
Roman emperor and philosopher

⭐

Life is change. Growth is optional. Choose wisely.

Karen Kaiser Clark, b. 1938
American legislator and feminist

⭐

We must always change, renew, rejuvenate ourselves; otherwise we harden.

Johann von Goethe, 1749-1832
German writer, dramatist and scientist

⭐

Learn to adapt, adjust and accommodate.

Sai Baba
Indian spiritual master

⭐

If you don't like the way the world is, you change it. You have an obligation to change it. You just do it one step at a time.

Marian Wright Edelman, b. 1937
American attorney and civil rights activist

✮

The foolish and the dead alone never change their opinions.

James Russell Lowell, 1819-1891
American poet and diplomat

✮

To live is to change, and to be perfect is to have changed often.

Cardinal John Henry Newman, 1801-1890
English theologian and writer

✮

There is no sin punished more implacably by nature than the sin of resistance to change.

Anne Morrow Lindbergh, b. 1906
American writer

✮

Only the wisest and stupidest of men
never change.

Confucius, c. 550-c. 478 BC
Chinese philosopher

☆

If you are not happy with yourself, make a
conscious effort to change whatever it is you
don't like. It is never too late to become a
better, more caring person.

Anonymous

☆

Let us never confuse stability with stagnation.

Mary Jean LeTendre, b. 1948
American educator

☆

Progress is impossible without change; and
those who cannot change their minds cannot
change anything.

George Bernard Shaw, 1856-1950
Irish dramatist, writer and critic

☆

Character

I desire so to conduct the affairs of this
administration that if at the end, when I
come to lay down the reins of power, I have
lost every other friend on earth, I shall at least
have one friend left, and that friend shall
be down inside of me.

Abraham Lincoln, 1809-1865
American statesman and President

★

The strongest man in the world is the
man who stands alone.

Henrik Ibsen, 1828-1906
Norwegian writer, dramatist and poet

★

Character-building begins in our infancy
and continues until death.

Eleanor Roosevelt, 1884-1962
*First Lady of the United States of America,
writer and diplomat*

★

Character cannot be developed in ease and quiet. Only through experience of trial and suffering can the soul be strengthened, vision cleared, ambition inspired and success achieved.

Helen Keller, 1880-1968
Blind and deaf American writer and scholar

The best index to a person's character is how he treats people who can't do him any good, and how he treats people who can't fight back.

Abigail Van Buren, b. 1918
American advice columnist

It is easy in the world to live after the world's opinions. It is easy in solitude to live after our own; but the great man is he who, in the midst of the crowd, keeps with perfect sweetness the independence of solitude.

Ralph Waldo Emerson, 1803-1882
American essayist, poet and philosopher

Children & Parents

Of all the joys that brighten suffering earth,
What joy is welcom'd like a newborn child!

Caroline Norton, 1808-1877
Irish writer and reformer

★

Every child born into the world is a
new thought of God, an ever fresh and
radiant possibility.

Kate Douglas Wiggin, 1856-1923
American writer and educator

★

Children are an affirmation of life itself. They
have shown me how much fun it is to simply
enjoy nature; the sea even when the water is
freezing, the stars which twinkle and hint at
life beyound ourselves, the earth which
squishes and squelches in my hands,
these are things I enjoy again.

Susan Bourke
Australian writer

★

God sent childen for another purpose than merely to keep up the race — to enlarge our hearts; and to make us unselfish and full of kindly sympathies and affections; to give our souls higher aims; to call out all our faculties to extended enterprise and exertion; and to bring round our firesides bright faces, happy smiles and loving, tender hearts.

Mary Botham Howitt, 1799-1888
English author

★

The soul is healed by being with children.

Feodor Dostoevsky, 1821-1881
Russian writer

★

To talk to a child, to fascinate him, is much more difficult than to win an electoral victory. But it is more rewarding.

Colette, 1873-1954
French writer

★

It's always been my feeling that God lends you
your children until they're about eighteen
years old. If you haven't made your points
with them by then, it's too late.

Betty Ford, b. 1918
First Lady of the United States of America

★

We should say to each of them: Do you
know what you are? You are a marvel. You
are unique . . . You may become a
Shakespeare, a Michelangelo, a Beethoven.
You have the capacity for anything . . .

Pablo Casals, 1876-1973
Spanish cellist, conductor and composer

★

What good mothers and fathers instinctively
feel like doing for their babies is
usually best after all.

Benjamin Spock, 1903-1998
American paediatrician

★

You are the bows from which your
   children as living arrows are sent forth.
The Archer sees the mark upon the path
   of the infinite,
And He bends you with His might that
   His arrows may go swift and far.
Let your bending in the Archer's
   hand be for gladness;
For even as He loves the arrow that flies,
   so He loves the bow that is stable.

Kahlil Gibran, 1883-1931
Lebanese poet, artist and mystic

★

I think it must be written somewhere that
the virtues of the mother shall be
visited on the children.

Charles Dickens, 1812-1870
English novelist

★

My mother was the making of me. She was
so true, so sure of me, and I felt that
I had someone to live for; someone
I must not disappoint.

Thomas Edison, 1847-1931
American inventor

★

All that I am or hope to be,
I owe to my mother.

Abraham Lincoln, 1809-1865
American statesman and President

★

My mother had a great deal of trouble with
me, but I think she enjoyed it.

Mark Twain, 1835-1910
American humorist and writer

★

Mother is the name for God in the lips and
hearts of little children.

William Makepeace Thackeray, 1811-1863
English writer

★

The mother's heart is the child's school room.

Henry Beecher Ward, 1818-1887
American clergyman and writer

★

To bring up a child in the way he should go,
travel that way yourself once in a while.

Josh Billings, 1818-1885
American humorist

★

If a child lives with approval,
He learns to like himself.

Dorothy Law Nolte
American poet

★

There are two lasting legacies we can
hope to give to our children. One of
these is roots; the other, wings.

Anonymous

★

When I was a boy of fourteen, my father was
so ignorant I could hardly stand to have the old
man around. But when I got to be twenty-one,
I was astonished at how much he had learned
in seven years.

Mark Twain, 1835-1910
American humorist and writer

★

I'm doing this for my father. I'm quite happy
that they see me as my father's daughter. My
only concern is that I prove worthy of him.

Aung San Suu Kyi, b. 1945
*Burma's democratically elected leader,
winner of Nobel Peace Prize and daughter of
Burma's hero Aung San*

★

Choice

You don't get to choose how you're going
to die. Or when. You can decide how
you're going to live now.

Joan Baez, b. 1941
American folksinger

☆

Choice, not chance, determines destiny.

Anonymous

☆

Few people make a deliberate choice between
good and evil; the choice is between what we
want to do and what we ought to do.

Anonymous

☆

In any moment of decision, the best thing
you can do is the right thing, the next best
thing is the wrong thing, and the worst
thing is to do nothing.

Theodore Roosevelt, 1858-1919
President of the United States of America

☆

He who deliberates at length before taking a single step will spend his whole life on one leg.

Chinese proverb

✦

Civility

A drop of honey catches more flies than a gallon of gall.

Abraham Lincoln, 1809-1865
American statesman and President

✦

Civility costs nothing and buys everything.

Lady Mary Wortley Montague, 1689-1762
British poet and writer

✦

If a man is gracious and courteous to strangers, it shows he is a citizen of the world.

Francis Bacon, 1561-1626
British philosopher, essayist and courtier

✦

The great secret, Eliza, is not having bad
manners or good manners, or any particular
sort of manners, but having the same
manner for all human souls . . .

George Bernard Shaw, 1856-1950
Irish dramatist, writer and critic

[Pygmalion]

★

They say courtesy is contagious.
So why not start an epidemic?

Anonymous

★

Punctuality is the politeness of kings.

Louis XV111, 1755-1824
King of France

★

Comforting Words

Master, what is the best way to
meet the loss of someone we love?
By knowing that when we truly love, it is never
lost. It is only after death that the depth of the
bond is truly felt, and our loved one becomes
more a part of us than was possible in life.

Oriental tradition

☆

Do but consider, however, if we live apart, as
we must, it is much the same whether I am
hundreds or thousands of miles distant from
you. The same Providence will watch over us
there as here. The sun that shines on you will
also afford me the benefit of its cheering rays.

Elizabeth Macarthur, 1767-1850
English-born wife of John Macarthur, founder of
the Australian wool industry, in a letter to her
mother in England

☆

And remember, we all stumble,
every one of us. That's why it's a
comfort to go hand in hand.

E. K. Brough
American writer

✯

For the winter is past,
the rain is over and gone.
The flowers are springing up and the time
of the singing of the birds has come.
Yes, spring is here.

Song of Solomon 2: 11-12

✯

Communication

Starting with self-communication in
private, you can then develop your ability
to communicate with others. Being clear
with yourself opens the way for being
more clear with others about how you
feel and think, enriching your relationships
and social interactions.

Lucia Capacchione
American art therapist and pioneer in inner healing

✯

Use what language you will, you can never say anything to others but what you are.

Ralph Waldo Emerson, 1803-1882
American essayist, poet and philosopher

☆

Only connect!

E. M. Forster, 1879-1970
English novelist

☆

How wonderful it is to say the right thing at the right time. A good man thinks before he speaks; the evil man pours out his evil words without a thought.

Proverbs 15:23, 28

☆

Give every man thy ear, but few thy voice.

William Shakespeare, 1564-1616
English playwright and poet

☆

Speaking without thinking is like shooting without taking aim.

Spanish proverb

☆

Compassion

Compassion is not a sloppy, sentimental feeling for people who are underprivileged or sick . . . it is an absolutely practical belief that, regardless of a person's background, ability or ability to pay, he should be provided with the best that society has to offer.

Neil Kinnock. b. 1942
Welsh politician

✩

When a man has pity on all living creatures then only is he noble.

Buddha, c. 563-483 BC
Indian religious leader and founder of Buddhism

✩

By compassion we make others' misery our own, and so, by relieving them, we relieve ourselves also.

Thomas Browne, 1605-1682
English author and physician

✩

Conscience

The one thing that doesn't abide by majority rule is a person's conscience.

Harper Lee, b. 1926
American novelist

✫

A good conscience is a soft pillow.

German proverb

✫

Keep pace with the drummer you hear, however measured or far away.

Henry David Thoreau, 1817-1862
American essayist, poet and mystic

✫

The voice of conscience is so delicate that it is easy to stifle it: but it is also so clear that it is impossible to mistake it.

Mme Anne de Staël, 1766-1817
Swiss-born French writer

✫

Better to stand ten thousand sneers than
one abiding pang, such as time could
not abolish, of bitter self-reproach.

Thomas de Quincey, 1785-1859
English essayist

★

Some good must come by clinging to the
right. Conscience is a man's compass, and
though the needle sometimes deviates,
though one perceives irregularities in
directing one's course by it, still one
must try to follow its direction.

Vincent Van Gogh, 1853-1890
Dutch post-impressionist painter

★

He that loses his conscience has nothing left
that is worth keeping.

Isaak Walton, 1593-1683
English writer

★

A peace above all earthly dignities,
A still and quiet conscience.

William Shakespeare, 1564-1616
English playwright and poet

★

Contentment

To be content, look backward on those who possess less than yourself, not forward on those who possess more.

Benjamin Franklin, 1706-1790
American statesman and scientist

✭

A person who is not disturbed by the incessant flow of desires can alone achieve peace, and not the man who strives to satisfy such desires.

Bhagavad Gita

✭

Health is the greatest gift, contentment the greatest wealth, faithfulness the best relationship.

Buddha. c. 563-483 BC
Indian religious leader, founder of Buddhism

✭

He is richest who is content with the least, for content is the wealth of nature.

Socrates, 468-399 BC
Greek philosopher

✭

Conversation

Conversation. What is it? A mystery! It's the art of never seeming bored, of touching everything with interest, of pleasing with trifles, of being fascinating with nothing at all. How do we define this lively darting about with words, of hitting them back and forth, this short brief smile of ideas which should be conversation?

Guy de Maupassant, 1850-1893
French writer

★

Ideal conversation must be an exchange of thought, and not, as many of those who worry most about their shortcomings believe, an eloquent exhibition of wit or oratory.

Emily Post, 1873-1960
American etiquette writer

★

Good nature is more agreeable in conversation than wit and gives a certain air to the countenance which is more amiable than beauty.

Joseph Addison, 1672-1719
English essayist

★

Conversation has a kind of charm about it, an insinuating and insidious something that elicits secrets from us just like love or liquor.

Seneca, c. 4 BC-65 AD
Roman philosopher, dramatist, poet and statesman

☆

For one word a man is often declared to be wise, and for one word he can be judged to be foolish. We should be careful indeed what we say.

Confucius, c. 550-c. 478 BC
Chinese philosopher

☆

That is the happiest conversation where there is no competition, no vanity, but a calm quiet interchange of sentiments.

Samuel Johnson, 1709-1784
English lexicographer, essayist and wit

☆

Courage

I am not afraid of storms for I am
learning to sail my ship.

Louisa May Alcott, 1832-1888
American novelist

★

Life shrinks or expands in proportion
to one's courage.

Anaïs Nin, 1903-1977
French novelist

★

Fearlessness may be a gift, but perhaps
more precious is the courage acquired through
endeavour, courage that come from cultivating
the habit of refusing to let fear dictate one's
actions, courage that could be described as
'grace under pressure' — grace which is
renewed repeatedly in the face of harsh,
unremitting pressure.

Aung San Suu Kyi, b. 1945
*Burma's democratically elected leader and winner of
Nobel Peace Prize*

★

Courage is the price that life
  extracts for granting peace.
The soul that knows it not, knows
  no release
From little things,
Knows not the livid loneliness of fear
Nor mountain heights where
  bitter joy can hear
The sound of wings.

Amelia Earhart, 1898-1937
American aviator

☆

A light supper, a good night's sleep, and
a fine morning have sometimes made a hero
of the same man who, by an indigestion, a
restless night and a rainy morning, would
have proved a coward.

Lord Chesterfield, 1694-1773
English statesman

☆

Never bend your head, always hold it high.
Look the world in the face.

Helen Keller, 1880-1968
Blind and deaf American writer and scholar

☆

I wanted you to see what real courage is, instead of getting the idea that courage is a man with a gun in his hand. It's when you know you're licked before you begin but you begin anyway and you see it through no matter what.

Harper Lee, b. 1926
American novelist

My message to you is:
Be courageous!
Be as brave as your fathers before you.
Have faith!
Go forward.

Thomas Edison, 1847-1931
American inventor

Facing it, always facing it, that's the way to get through. Face it.

Joseph Conrad, 1856-1924
Polish-born British writer

Courage faces fear and thereby masters it.
Cowardice represses fear and is thereby
mastered by it.

Martin Luther King, Jr, 1929-1968
American civil rights leader and minister

★

It's better to be a lion for a day than
a sheep all your life.

Sister Elizabeth Kenny, 1866-1952
Australian nurse and pioneer in polio treatment

★

I hate a fellow whom pride, or cowardice, or
laziness drives into a corner, and who does
nothing when he is there but sit and growl;
let him come out as I do, and bark.

Samuel Johnson, 1709-1784
English lexicographer, essayist and wit

★

The bravest thing you can do when you are not
brave is to profess courage and act accordingly.

Corra May White Harris, 1869-1935
American writer

★

No coward soul is mine,
No trembler in the world's
   storm-troubled sphere;
I see Heaven's glory shine,
And faith shines equal, arming
   me from fear.

Emily Brontë,1818-1848
British novelist and poet

Strength alone knows courage. Weakness is
below even defeat, and is born vanquished.

Anne Sophie Swetchine, 1782-1857
Russian writer

I count he braver who overcomes his desires
than he who overcomes his enemies.

Aristotle, 384-322 BC
Greek philosopher

Creativity

No matter how old you get, if you can keep the desire to be creative, you're keeping the man-child alive.

John Cassavetes
American film director

★

In every real man a child is hidden who wants to play.

Friedrich Nietzche, 1844-1900
German philosopher

★

Art is an essential reminder of what it is in life that lasts, of why one lives. Art communicates, celebrates, mourns and remembers. What else in our lives can do this?

Bella Lewitzky, b. 1916
American ballet dancer

★

Poetry ennobles the heart and the eyes,
and unveils the meaning of all things upon
which the heart and the eyes dwell. It discovers
the secret rays of the universe, and restores
us to forgotten paradises.

Dame Edith Sitwell, 1887-1964
English poet

✴

Masterpieces are not single and solitary births;
they are the outcome of many years of thinking
in common, of thinking by the body of
the people, so that the experience of the
mass is behind the single voice.

Virginia Woolf, 1882-1941
English novelist

✴

Creativity is so delicate a flower that praise
tends to make it bloom, while discouragement
often nips it in the bud. Any of us will put
out more and better ideas if our efforts
are appreciated.

Alex F. Osborn, 1888-1966
American advertising director and writer

✴

Crisis

The English word 'crisis' is translated by the Chinese by two little characters; one means 'danger' and the other means 'opportunity'.

Anonymous

Granted that we face a world crisis which often leaves us standing amid the surging murmur of life's restless sea. But every crisis has both its dangers and its opportunities. Each can spell either salvation or doom. In a dark, confused world the spirit of God may yet reign supreme.

Martin Luther King, Jr, 1929-1968
American civil rights leader and minister

Criticism

A true critic ought to dwell upon excellencies
rather than imperfections.

Joseph Addison, 1672-1719
English essayist

★

There is nothing as easy as denouncing. It don't
take much to see that something is wrong, but
it does take some eyesight to see what will put
it right again.

Will Rogers, 1879-1935
American humorist and writer

★

Don't find fault. Find a remedy.

Henry Ford, 1863-1947
American car manufacturer

★

Deal with the faults of others as gently
as your own.

Chinese proverb

★

Crying

I have always felt sorry for people afraid of feeling, of sentimentality, who are unable to weep with their whole heart. Because those who do not know how to weep do not know how to laugh either.

Golda Meir, 1898-1978
Prime Minister of Israel

✮

We need never be ashamed of our tears.

Charles Dickens, 1812-1870
English writer

✮

'It opens the lungs, washes the countenance, exercises the eyes, and softens down the temper,' said Mr Bumble. 'So cry away.'

Charles Dickens, 1812-1870
[Oliver Twist]

✮

Curiosity

Curiosity will conquer fear even more than bravery will.

James Stephens, 1882-1950
Irish novelist

★

Curiosity is the key to creativity.

Akio Morita
Japanese businessman

★

Curiosity has its own reason for existing . . . Never lose a holy curiosity.

Albert Einstein, 1877-1955
German-born American physicist

★

Disinterested intellectual curiosity is the life blood of real civilisation.

George Macaulay Trevelyan, 1876-1962
British historian

★

A generous and elevated mind is distinguished by nothing more certainly than an eminent degree of curiosity.

Samuel Johnson, 1709-1784
English lexicographer, essayist and wit

Curiosity is nothing more than freewheeling intelligence.

Anonymous

Those with a lively sense of curiosity learn something new every day of their lives.

Anonymous

D

Death

I think of death as some delightful journey
That I shall take when my tasks are done.

Ella Wheeler Wilcox, 1850-1919
American writer and poet

✪

We sometimes congratulate ourselves at the
moment of waking from a troubled dream; it
may be so the moment after death.

Nathaniel Hawthorne, 1804-1864
American writer

✪

Life is a great surprise. I do not see why death
should not be an even greater one.

Vladimir Nabokov, 1899-1977
Russian-born American novelist

✪

The dead don't die. They look on and help.

D. H. Lawrence, 1855-1930
English writer and poet

★

Life does not cease to be funny when people die any more than it ceases to be serious when people laugh.

George Bernard Shaw, 1856-1950
Irish dramatist, writer and critic

★

There is no need to be afraid of death. It is not the end of the physical body that should worry us. Rather, our concern must be to live while we're alive — to release our inner selves from the spiritual death that comes from living behind a facade designed to conform to external definitions of who and what we are.

Elisabeth Kübler-Ross, b. 1926
Swiss-born American psychiatrist and writer

★

The world is the land of the dying; the next is the land of the living.

Tyron Edwards, 1809-1894
American theologian

★

You would know the secret of death.
But how shall you find it unless you seek
it in the heart of life?
The owl whose night-bound eyes are blind unto
the day cannot unveil the mystery of light.
If you would indeed behold the spirit of death,
open your heart wide unto the body of life.
For life and death are one,
even as river and sea are one.

Kahlil Gibran, 1883-1931
Lebanese poet, artist and mystic

✯

The gods conceal from men the happiness of
death, that they may endure life.

Lucan, 39-65 AD
Roman poet

✯

Depression

We can be cured of depression in only fourteen days if every day we will try to think of how we can be helpful to others.

Alfred Adler, 1870-1937
Austrian psychiatrist

★

The best way to cheer yourself up is to cheer someone else up.

Mark Twain, 1835-1910
American humorist and writer

★

Never give way to melancholy; resist it steadily, for the habit will encroach.

Sydney Smith, 1771-1845
English clergyman essayist and wit

★

Difficulties

Nothing is easy to the unwilling.

Thomas Fuller, 1608-1661
English clergyman and writer

☆

The difficulties of life are meant to make us
better, not bitter.

Anonymous

☆

Tackle any difficulty at first sight because the
longer you leave it the larger it grows.

Anonymous

☆

Do what is easy as if it were difficult,
and what is difficult as if it were easy.

Baltasar Gracian, 1601-1658
Spanish writer and priest

☆

Disappointment

Disappointment should be cremated, not embalmed.

Henry S. Haskins
American writer

☆

Disappointment is often the salt of life.

Theodore Parker, 1810-1860
American Unitarian minister

☆

Wisdom comes by disillusionment.

George Santayana, 1863-1952
Spanish philosopher and writer

☆

Nothing worthwhile is achieved without patience, labour and disappointment.

Anonymous

☆

Doubt

If a man will begin with certainties, he shall end in doubts. But if he will be content to begin with doubts, he shall end in certainties.

Francis Bacon, 1561-1626
British philosopher, essayist and courtier

☆

Doubt is often the beginning of wisdom.

M. Scott Peck, b. 1936
American psychiatrist and writer

☆

Doubt is an incitation to think.

Anonymous

☆

Dreams

Always live your life with one more dream to fulfil. No matter how many of your dreams you have realised in the past, always have a dream to go. Because when you stop dreaming, life becomes a mundane existence.

Sara Henderson, b. 1936
Australian outback station manager and writer

✭

It seems to me we can never give up longing and wishing while we are thoroughly alive. There are certain things we feel to be beautiful and good, and we must hunger after them.

George Eliot (Mary Ann Evans), 1819-1880
English novelist

✭

I like the dreams of the future better than the history of the past.

Thomas Jefferson, 1743-1826
President of the United States of America

✭

E

Education

Learning . . . should be a joy and full of excitement. It is life's greatest adventure; it is an illustrated excursion into the minds of noble and learned men, not a conducted tour through a jail.

Taylor Caldwell, 1900-1985
American writer

✫

The roots of education are bitter, but the fruit is sweet.

Aristotle, 384-322 BC
Greek philosopher

✫

Give a man a fish and you feed him for a day. Teach a man to fish and you feed him for a lifetime.

Chinese proverb

✫

Learning is the only wealth tyrants cannot despoil. Only death can dim the lamp of knowledge that is within you. The true wealth of a nation lies not in its gold or silver but in its learning, wisdom and in the uprightness of its sons.

Kahlil Gibran, 1883-1931
Lebanese poet, artist and mystic

☆

If a man empties his purse into his head, no one can take it from him.

Benjamin Franklin, 1706-1790
American statesman and scientist

☆

For as the old saying is,
When house and land are gone and spent
Then learning is most excellent.

Samuel Foote, 1720-1777
English actor, dramatist and wit

☆

Train a child in the way he should go, and when he is old he will not depart from it.

Proverbs, 12:4

☆

The primary purpose of a liberal education is to make one's mind a pleasant place in which to spend one's leisure.

Sydney J. Harris, b. 1911
American journalist

☆

The supreme end of education is expert discernment in all things — the power to tell the good from the bad, the genuine from the counterfeit, and to prefer the good and genuine to the bad and counterfeit.

Samuel Johnson, 1709-1784
English lexicographer, essayist and wit

☆

What you teach your children is what you *really* believe in.

Cathy Warner Weatherford, b. 1951
American educator

☆

Education should be gentle and stern, not cold and lax.

Joseph Joubert, 1754-1824
French writer and moralist

☆

Effort

I loathe drudgery as much as any man, but I have learned that the only way to conquer drudgery is to get through it as neatly, as efficiently, as one can. You know perfectly well that a dull job slackly done becomes twice as dull; whereas a dull job which you try to do just as well as you can becomes half as dull. Here again, effort appears to me the main art of living.

Harold Nicolson, 1886-1968
Diplomat, politician, writer and diarist

✯

It takes less time to do a thing right than it does to explain why you did it wrong.

Henry Wadsworth Longfellow, 1807-1882
American poet and writer

✯

Whatever is worth doing is worth doing well.

Lord Chesterfield, 1694-1773
English statesman

✯

Empowerment

My will shall shape my future. Whether I fail
or succeed shall be no man's doing but my
own. I am the force. I can clear any obstacle
before me or I can be lost in the maze. My
choice; my responsibility; win or lose, only I
hold the key to my destiny.

Elaine Maxwell
American writer

★

It isn't until you come to a spiritual understanding of who you are — not necessarily a
religious feeling, but deep down, the spirit
within — that you can begin to take control.

Oprah Winfrey, b. 1954
American television personality

★

Most powerful is he who has
control over himself.

Seneca, 4 BC- AD 65
Roman philosopher, dramatist, poet and statesman

★

Never doubt that a small group of thoughtful committed citizens can change the world. Indeed, it is the only thing that ever has.

Margaret Mead, 1901-1978
American anthropologist and writer

★

One oral utterance, which boldly states how you want your life to be, is worth more than a dozen books read or lectures attended. Spoken words describing the good you want, help you to claim it and release it into your own life quickly.

Catherine Ponder
American motivational writer

★

I am only one; but still I am one. I cannot do everything, but still I can do something; I will not refuse to do the something I can do.

Helen Keller, 1880-1968
Blind and deaf American writer and scholar

★

Encouragement

Correction does much but encouragement
does more.

Johann von Goethe, 1749-1832
German writer, dramatist and scientist

★

It must be tempting to succumb to what I call
the FUD factor. I know because I've been
there. The Fear, Uncertainty and Doubt is only
put there by the detractors and critics who
don't know you anyway. You are there because
you are the best and they are not, remember
that. I know you will ignore the distractions.
FOCUS on the job at hand, and
CONCENTRATE on yours and the team's
GOALS (in that order). You will succeed
because you have what it takes . . .

Kieren Perkins, b. 1973
Australian Olympic swimming gold medallist
*From a fax in June 1997 to Mark Taylor, Australian
cricket captain 1994-1999*

★

I don't blame the system for my mistakes, I blame myself . . . Right now I'm being offered six potentially wonderful pictures. I think I'm a good example for anyone who thinks their situation is hopeless. Keep putting one foot in front of the other, keep showing up, and you can turn it around.

John Frankenheimer
American film director

⭐

Encouragement is like premium gasoline. It helps to take the knock out of living.

Anonymous

⭐

A few words of encouragement can sometimes tip the scales between another's failure or success.

Anonymous

⭐

Enjoyment

Our wealth lies not in what we have
but in what we enjoy.

Anonymous

★

True enjoyment comes from activity of
the mind and exercise of the body; the two
are ever united.

Alexander von Humboldt, 1769-1859
German statesman, naturalist and writer

★

Why not learn to enjoy the little things?
There are so many of them.

Anonymous

★

I spent most of my money on wine, women
and fast cars – and wasted the rest.

Josh Gaspero
American publisher

★

Enthusiasm

Every great and commanding movement in the
annals of the world is a triumph of enthusiasm.

Ralph Waldo Emerson. 1803-1882
American essayist, poet and philosopher

★

You must learn day by day, year by year, to
broaden your horizon. The more things you
love, the more you are interested in, the more
you enjoy, the more you are indignant about,
the more you have left when anything happens.

Ethel Barrymore, 1879-1959
American actress

★

If it were as easy to arouse enthusiasm as
it is suspicion, just think what could be
accomplished.

Anonymous

★

You can do anything if you have enthusiasm. Enthusiasm is the yeast that makes your hopes rise to the stars. Enthusiasm is the spark in your eye, the swing in your gait, the grip of your hand, the irresistible surge of your will and your energy to execute your ideas. Enthusiasts are fighters, they have fortitude, they have staying qualities. Enthusiasm is at the bottom of all progress! With it, there is accomplishment. Without it, there are only alibis.

Henry Ford, 1863-1947
American car manufacturer

★

We could hardly wait to get up in the morning!

Wilbur Wright, 1867-1912 and
Orville Wright , 1871-1948
American inventors

★

Just don't give up trying what you really want to do. Where there is love and inspiration, I don't think you can go wrong.

Ella Fitzgerald, 1918-1996
American singer

★

Let your enthusiasm radiate in your voice, your actions, your facial expressions, your personality, the words you use, and the thoughts you think! Nothing great was ever achieved without enthusiasm.

Ralph Waldo Emerson, 1803-1882
American essayist, poet and philosopher

★

Love the moment, and the energy of that moment will spread beyond all boundaries.

Corita Kent, b. 1918
American graphic artist

★

Nothing is so contagious as enthusiasm . . . It is the genius of sincerity and truth accomplishes no victories without it.

Edward Bulwer-Lytton, 1803-1873
British novelist and politician

★

Epitaphs

She would rather light a candle than curse the darkness, and her glow has warmed the earth.

Adlai Stevenson, 1900-1965
American lawyer, statesman and
United Nations ambassador

[Written on the death of Eleanor Roosevelt]

☆

The friend of man, the friend of truth;
The friend of age, the guide of youth;
If there's another world, he lives in bliss;
If there is none, he made the best of this.

Robert Burns, 1759-1796
Scottish poet

[Epistle to the Rev. John McMath]

☆

You could write a list of epitaphs which describe a perfect life. They describe Peter's [Peter Cook's] perfectly.

1. He added to the sum of human happiness.
2. He never harmed anyone but himself.
3. He left the world a better place than he found it.
4. He never achieved anything at the expense of anyone else.
5. He made innumerable friends, but not one enemy.
6. He never complained.
7. He was never mean, boastful, envious or vain.
8. He never told anyone else how to behave.
9. He never betrayed a confidence.
10. He made people laugh.

God bless him.

Stephen Fry, b. 1947
English actor, comedian and writer

[Peter Cook Remembered]

Error

Truth emerges more readily from error than from confusion.

Francis Bacon, 1561-1626
British philosopher, essayist and courtier

☆

Things could be worse. Suppose your errors were counted and published every day like those of a baseball player.

Anonymous

☆

Great services are not cancelled by one act or by one single errror.

Benjamin Disraeli, 1804-1881
British Prime Minister and writer

☆

An error doesn't become a mistake until you refuse to correct it.

Anonymous

☆

Excellence

The secret of joy in work is contained in
one word — excellence. To know how to do
something well is to enjoy it.

Pearl S. Buck, 1892-1972
American writer and missionary

☆

Excuses

Excuses fool no one but the person
who makes them.

Anonymous

☆

The man who really wants to do something
finds a way; the other man makes an excuse.

Anonymous

☆

Experience

The best advice you'll get is from someone who
has made the same mistake himself.

Anonymous

★

Experience is the child of Thought, and
Thought is the child of Action.

Benjamin Disraeli, 1804-1881
British Prime Minister and writer

★

There are many truths of which the full
meaning cannot be realised until personal
experience has brought it home.

John Stuart Mill, 1806-1873
English philosopher, reformer and politician

★

Experience is the wisdom that enables
us to recognise the folly that we have
already embraced.

Ambrose Bierce, 1842-1914
American journalist

★

We should be careful to get out of experience only the wisdom that is in it — and stop there; lest we be like the cat that sits down on the stove-lid. She will never sit down on a hot stove-lid again — and that is well; but also she will never sit down on a cold one anymore.

Mark Twain, 1835-1910
American humorist and writer

☆

Experience is a good teacher, but she sends in terrific bills.

Minna Antrim, 1861-1950
American writer

☆

The least expensive education is to learn from the mistakes of others.

Anonymous

☆

F

Failure

The difference between failure and success
is doing a thing nearly right and doing
a thing exactly right.

Anonymous

✯

Our greatest glory is not in never falling, but in
rising every time we fall.

Confucius, c. 550-478 BC
Chinese philosopher

✯

We have forty million reasons for failure, but
not a single excuse.

Rudyard Kipling, 1865-1936
Indian-born British poet and writer

✯

Failure is the line of least persistence.

Anonymous

✯

Only those who dare to fail greatly can ever achieve greatly.

Robert F. Kennedy, 1925-1968
American lawyer and politician

★

Nothing is ever entirely wrong. Even a broken clock is right twice a day.

Anonymous

★

Good people are good because they've come to wisdom through failure.

William Saroyan, 1908-1981
American writer and dramatist

★

My downfall raises me to great heights.

Napoleon Bonaparte, 1769-1821
French emperor and general

★

There is no failure except in not trying.

Elbert Hubbard, 1856-1915
American writer

★

Faith

I believe that God is in me as the sun is in the
colour and fragrance of a flower — the light in
my darkness, the voice in my silence.

Helen Keller, 1880-1968
Blind and deaf American writer and scholar

✫

Let nothing disturb you. Let nothing frighten
you. Everything passes away except God.

St Theresa, 1515-1582
Spanish nun

✫

The reason why birds can fly and we can't is
simply that they have perfect faith, for to have
faith is to have wings.

J. M. Barrie, 1860-1937
Scottish writer and dramatist

✫

Faith is the subtle chain
Which binds us to the infinite; the voice
Of deep life within, that will remain
Until we crowd it thence.

Elizabeth Oakes Smith, 1806-1893
American writer

✫

Blessed are they they that have not seen, and
yet have believed.

John 20:29

★

I pray hard, work hard and leave
the rest to God.

Florence Griffith Joyner, b. 1953
American track athlete

★

I am positive I have a soul; nor can all the
books with which the materialists have
pestered the world ever convince me of
the contrary.

Laurence Sterne, 1713-1768
Irish-born British writer

★

Yes, I have doubted. I have wandered off the
path. I have been lost. But I always returned. It
is beyond the logic I seek. It is intuitive — an
intrinsic, built-in sense of direction. I seem to
find my way home. My faith has wavered but
has saved me.

Helen Hayes, 1900-1993
American actress

★

We live in a scary horrible world now, with murder, war, poverty, hunger. I think people need to be reassured there is a higher meaning to all this chaos.

Nina Sodowski
American film producer

☆

Faith is the bird that feels the light when the dawn is dark.

Rabindranath Tagore, 1861-1941
Indian poet and philosopher

☆

The suffering and agonising moments through which I have passed over the last few years have also drawn me closer to God. More than ever before I am convinced of the reality of a personal God.

Martin Luther King, Jr, 1929-1968
American civil rights leader and minister

☆

Reason is itself a matter of faith. It is an act
of faith to assert that our thoughts have any
relation to reality at all.

G. K. Chesterton, 1874-1936
English writer and critic

Faith builds a bridge across the gulf of death,
To break the shock blind nature cannot shun,
And lands thought smoothly on the
farther shore.

Edward Young, 1683-1765
English poet, dramatist and clergyman

With faith, man can achieve anything.
Faith is the foundation for the realisation
of God.

Sai Baba
Indian spiritual master

Faults

The greatest fault is to be conscious of none.

Thomas Carlyle, 1795-1881
Scottish historian, essayist and critic

☆

We must touch his weaknesses with a delicate hand. There are some faults so nearly allied to excellence, that we can scarce weed out the fault without eradicating the virtue.

Oliver Goldsmith, 1728-1774
British writer

☆

A man's faults are the faults of his time, while his virtues are his own.

Johann von Goethe, 1749-1832
German writer, dramatist and scientist

☆

Always acknowledge a fault frankly. This will throw those in authority off their guard and give you opportunity to commit more.

Mark Twain, 1835-1910
American humorist and writer

☆

Fear

I have not ceased being fearful, but I have ceased to let fear control me. I have accepted fear as a part of life — specifically the fear of change, the fear of the unknown; and I have gone ahead despite the pounding in my heart that says: turn back, you'll die if you venture too far.

Erica Jong, b. 1942
American author

✭

Fear: the best way out is through.

Helen Keller, 1880-1968
Blind and deaf American writer and scholar

✭

I believe anyone can conquer fear by doing the things he fears to do, provided he keeps doing them until he gets a record of successful experiences behind him.

Eleanor Roosevelt, 1884-1962
*First Lady of the United States of America,
writer and diplomat*

✭

Fear is an emotion indispensable for survival.

Hannah Arendt, 1906-1975
German-born American political philosopher

☆

Fear is a question. What are you afraid of and why? Our fears are a treasure house of self knowledge if we explore them.

Marilyn French, b. 1929
American novelist

☆

Within a system which denies the existence of basic human rights, fear tends to be the order of the day. Fear of imprisonment, fear of torture, fear of death, fear of losing friends, family, property or means of livelihood, fear of poverty, fear of isolation, fear of failure . . . Yet even under the most crushing state machinery, courage rises up again and again, for fear is not the natural state of civilised man.

Aung San Suu Kyi, b. 1945
Burma's democratically elected leader and Nobel Peace Prize winner

☆

Avoiding danger is no safer in the long run than outright exposure. The fearful are caught as often as the bold.

Helen Keller, 1880-1968
Blind and deaf American writer and scholar

★

It is not death that a man should fear, but he should fear never beginning to live.

Marcus Aurelius, 121-180 AD
Roman emperor and philosopher

★

Fools & Foolishness

The greatest lesson in life is to know that even fools are right sometimes.

Winston Churchill, 1874-1965
British statesman and Prime Minister

★

Each day, and the living of it, has to be a conscious creation in which discipline and order are relieved with some play and pure foolishness.

May Sarton, 1912-1995
American writer

★

Mix a little foolishness with your serious plans;
it's wonderful to be silly at the right moment.

Horace, 65-8 BC
Roman poet

If people didn't sometimes do silly things,
nothing intelligent would ever get done.

Ludwig Wittgenstein, 1889-1952
Austrian-born English philosopher

A little nonsense now and then
Is relished by the best of men.

Anonymous

Let us be grateful for the fools. But for them
the rest of us could not succeed.

Mark Twain, 1835-1910
American humorist and writer

Forgiveness

Good, to forgive,
Best, to forget!
Living, we fret;
Dying, we live.

Robert Browning, 1812-1889
English poet

★

Forgiveness is the key to action and freedom.

Hannah Arendt, 1906-1975
German-born American political philosopher

★

A quarrel between friends, when made up,
adds a new tie to friendship, as experience
shows that the callosity formed round a broken
bone makes it stronger than before.

St Francis de Sales, 1567-1622
French theologian

★

For my part I believe in the forgiveness of sins
and the redemption of ignorance.

Adlai Stevenson, 1900-1965
American lawyer, statesman and
United Nations representative

★

Forgive us our trespasses as we forgive them
that trespass against us.

The Lord's Prayer

✯

The man who opts for revenge should
dig two graves.

Chinese proverb

✯

He that cannot forgive others breaks the bridge
over which he must pass himself; for every
man has need to be forgiven.

Thomas Fuller, 1608-1661
English clergyman and writer

✯

It is very easy to forgive others their mistakes;
it takes more grit and gumption to forgive
them for having witnessed your own.

Jessamyn West, 1907-1984
American writer

✯

Forgiveness is not an occasional act, it is a
permanent attitude.

Martin Luther King, Jr, 1929-1968
American civil rights leader and minister

✯

Freedom

In the future days, which we seek to make secure, we look forward to a world founded upon four essential freedoms. The first is freedom of speech and expression — everywhere in the world. The second is freedom of every person to worship God in his own way — everywhere in the world. The third is freedom from want . . . The fourth is freedom from fear.

Franklin D. Roosevelt, 1882-1945
President of the United States of America

★

To be free is to have achieved your life.

Tennessee Williams, 19ll-1983
American dramatist

★

Where the spirit of the Lord is, there is liberty.

2 Corinthians, 3:17

★

They that can give up essential liberty to obtain a little temporary safety deserve neither liberty nor safety.

Benjamin Franklin, 1706-1790
American statesman and scientist

★

Free choice is the greatest gift God gives to his children.

Elisabeth Kübler-Ross, b. 1926
Swiss-born American psychiatrist

★

I wish that every human life might be pure transparent freedom.

Simone de Beauvoir, 1908-1986
French writer

★

To move freely you must be deeply rooted.

Bella Lewitzky, b. 1916
American ballet dancer

★

Every human being has the liberty to do that which is good, just and honest.

Anonymous

★

Freedom ends when it begins to deprive
another of his freedom.

Anonymous

✯

Liberty is not a means to a higher political end.
It is itself the highest political end.

Lord Acton, 1834-1902

British political philosopher and historian

✯

The hope of the world is still in dedicated
minorities. The trail-blazers in human,
academic, scientific and religious freedom
have always been in the minority.

Martin Luther King, Jr, 1929-1968
American civil rights leader and minister

✯

Friendship

We are all travellers in the wilderness of this world, and the best we can find in our travels is an honest friend.

Robert Louis Stevenson, 1850-1894
Scottish writer and poet

✵

True happiness consists not in the multitude of friends but in the worth and choice.

Ben Jonson, c. 1573-1637
English dramatist and poet

✵

Friendship is a divine elixir that draws you towards people and allows you to spread yourself further.

Deborah Forster
Australian journalist

✵

A real friend will tell you when you have spinach stuck in your teeth.

Anonymous

✵

I have learned that to have a good friend is the purest of all God's gifts, for it is a love that has no exchange or payment.

Frances Farmer, 1910-1970
American actress and writer

✫

I want someone to laugh with me, someone to be grave with me, someone to please me and help my discrimination with his or her own remark, and at times, no doubt, to admire my acuteness and penetration.

Robert Burns, 1759-1796
Scottish poet

✫

The antidote for fifty enemies is one friend.

Aristotle, 384-322 BC
Greek philosopher

✫

A real friend is one who walks in when the rest of the world walks out.

Walter Winchell, 1879-1972
American journalist

✫

Friendship improves happiness and abates misery by doubling our joy and dividing our grief.

Joseph Addison, 1672-1719
English essayist

★

It is one of the blessings of friends that you can afford to be stupid with them.

Ralph Waldo Emerson, 1803-1882
American essayist, poet and philosopher

★

Fame is the scentless sunflower, with gaudy crown of gold;
But friendship is the breathing rose, with sweets in every fold.

Oliver Wendell Holmes, 1809-1894
American writer and physician

★

You can make more friends in two months by becoming interested in other people than you can in two years by trying to get other people interested in you.

Dale Carnegie, 1888-1955
American writer and lecturer

★

Friendship with oneself is all-important
because without it one cannot be friends
with anyone else in the world.

Eleanor Roosevelt, 1884-1962
*First Lady of the United States of America, writer and
diplomat*

✭

For whoever knows how to return a kindness
he has received must be a friend above price.

Sophocles, 496-406 BC
Greek tragedian

✭

The best mirror is an old friend.

English proverb

✭

Anyone can sympathise with the sufferings of a
friend, but it takes a fine nature to sympathise
with a friend's success.

Oscar Wilde, 1854-1900
Irish playright, novelist and wit

✭

If you have a friend worth loving
Love him. Yes, and let him know
That you love him, ere life's evening
Tinge his brow with sunset's glow;
Why should good words ne'er be said
Of a friend until he is dead?

Daniel W. Hoyt
Poet

☆

I always felt that the great high privilege, relief and comfort of friendship was that one had to explain nothing.

Katherine Mansfield, 1888-1923
New Zealand short story writer

☆

Under the magnetism of friendship the modest man becomes bold; the shy, confident; the lazy, active; or the impetuous, prudent and peaceful.

William Makepeace Thackeray, 1811-1863
English writer

☆

465

True friendship is a plant of slow growth and must undergo and withstand the shocks of adversity before it is entitled to the appellation.

George Washington, 1732-1799
President of the United States of America

★

A friendship counting nearly forty years is the finest kind of shade-tree I know.

James Russell Lowell, 1819-1891
American poet and diplomat

★

Oh, the inexpressible comfort of feeling safe with a person; having neither to weigh thoughts nor measure words, but pour them all out, as they are, chaff and grain together, knowing that a faithful hand will take and sift them, keep what is worth keeping, and then, with the breath of kindness, blow the rest away.

Geoge Eliot (Mary Ann Evans), 1819-1880
English novelist

★

The truth is friendship is every bit as sacred and eternal as marriage.

Katherine Mansfield, 1888-1923
New Zealand short story writer

★

Old books, old wine, old Nankin blue,
All things, in short, to which belong
The charm, the grace, that Time makes
   strong — All these I prize, but
   (entre nous)
Old friends are best!

Henry Austin Dobson, 1840-1921l
English poet

✦

Life is nothing without friendship.

Cicero, 106-43 BC
Roman orator

✦

To know someone here or there with whom
   you feel there is understanding in spite of
distances or thoughts unexpressed — that can
   make of this earth a garden.

Johann von Goethe, 1749-1832
German writer, dramatist and scientist

✦

Think where man's glory most begins
   and ends,
And say that my glory was I had such
   friends.

W. B. Yeats, 1865-1939
Irish poet, dramatist and writer

✦

We take care of our health, we lay up money, we make our room tight, and our clothing sufficient; but who provides wisely that he shall not be wanting in the best property of all — friends?

Ralph Waldo Emerson, 1803-1882
American essayist, poet and philosopher

☆

If a man does not make new acquaintance as he advances through life, he will soon find himself alone. A man, sir, should keep his friendship in constant repair.

Samuel Johnson, 1709-1784
English lexicographer, essayist and wit

☆

A friend is a present which you give yourself.

Robert Louis Stevenson, 1850-1894
Scottish writer and poet

☆

One's friends are that part of the human race with which one can be human.

George Santayana, 1863-1952
Spanish philosopher and writer

☆

It is the friends that you can call
at 4 a.m. that matter.

Marlene Dietrich, 1901-1992
German actress and singer

✪

A friend is someone with whom I may be
sincere. Before him I may think aloud.

Ralph Waldo Emerson, 1803-1882
American essayist, poet and philosopher

✪

Friendship gilds prosperity and lessens adversity
by dividing and sharing it.

Cicero, 106-43 BC
Roman orator

✪

The most I can do for my friend is simply to
be his friend. I have not wealth to bestow
on him. If he knows that I am happy in
loving him, he will want no other reward.
Is not friendship divine in this?

Henry David Thoreau, 1817-1862
American essayist, poet and mystic

✪

Let there be no purpose in friendship save
the deepening of the spirit.
For love that seeks aught but the disclosure
of its own mystery is not love but a
net cast forth, and only the unprofitable
is caught . . .
And in the sweetness of friendship
let there be laughter, and sharing of
pleasures.
For in the dew of little things the heart
finds its morning and is refreshed.

Kahlil Gibran, 1883-1931
Lebanese poet, artist and mystic

★

A companion loves some agreeable qualities
which a man may possess, but a friend loves
the man himself.

James Boswell, 1740-1795
Scottish lawyer and diarist

★

When befriended, remember it; when you
befriend, forget it.

Benjamin Franklin, 1706-1790
American statesman and scientist

★

Love is like the wild rose-briar;
Friendship like the holly tree.
The holly is dark when the rose-briar
  blooms,
But which one blooms most constantly?

Emily Brontë, 1818-1848
English novelist and poet

☆

Life is to be fortified by many friendships.
To love and be loved is the greatest
happiness of existence.

Sydney Smith, 1771-1845
English clergyman, essayist and wit

☆

The glory of friendship is not the outstretched
hand, nor the kindly smile, nor the joy of
companionship; it is the spiritual inspiration
that comes to one when he discovers
that someone else believes in him
and is willing to trust him.

Ralph Waldo Emerson, 1803-1882
American essayist, poet and philosopher

☆

G

Gardens & Gardening

He who plants a garden plants happiness.

Chinese proverb

✧

What makes a garden,
And why do gardens grow?
Love lives in gardens
God and lovers know.

Carolyn Giltinam, early 19th century
English poet

✧

Every time I talk to a savant I feel quite sure
that happiness is no longer a possibility. Yet
when I talk to my gardener, I'm convinced of
the opposite.

Bertrand Russell, 1872-1970
English philosopher, mathematician and writer

✧

How to be happy when you are miserable.
Plant Japanese poppies with cornflowers and
mignonette, and bed out the petunias among
the sweet-peas so they shall scent each other.
See the sweet-peas coming up.

Rumer Godden, b. 1907
English writer

✯

God Almighty first planted a garden. And indeed it is the purest of human pleasures.

Francis Bacon, 1561-1626
English philosopher and courtier

✯

Proceed my Friend, pursue thy healthful
    toil.
Dispose thy ground and meliorate thy soil;
Range thy young plants in walks,
    or clumps, or bow'rs,
Diffuse o'er sunny banks thy fragrant
    flow'rs:
And, while the new creation round
    thee springs,
Enjoy unchecked the guiltless bliss it brings.

John Scott, 1730-1793
British poet

✯

A man has at least made a start in discovering the meaning of human life when he plants shade trees under which he knows full well he will never sit.

D. Elton Trueblood, b. 1900
American Quaker scholar

★

The planting of trees is the least self-centred of all that we can do. It is a purer act of faith than the procreation of children.

Thornton Wilder, 1897-1975
American writer

★

There is no unbelief:
Whoever plants a seed beneath the sod
And waits to see it push away the clod,
He trusts in God.

Elizabeth York Case, 1840-1911
American writer

★

Gardening is an act of grace.

May Sarton, 1912-1995
American writer and poet

★

Genius

A genius! For thirty-seven years I've practised fourteen hours a day, and now they call me a genius!

Pablo Sarasate, 1844-1908
Spanish violinist and composer

★

The secret of genius is to carry the spirit of the child into old age, which means never losing your enthusiasm.

Aldous Huxley, 1894-1963
English writer

★

Genius is nothing more than inflamed enthusiasm.

Anonymous

★

Every production of genius must be the production of enthusiasm.

Benjamin Disraeli, 1804-1881
English statesman and writer

★

Men give me credit for some genius. All the genius I have is this: When I have a subject in mind, I study it profoundly. Day and night it is before me. My mind becomes pervaded with it ...the effort which I have made is what people are pleased to call the fruit of genius. It is the fruit of labour and thought.

Alexander Hamilton, 1755-1804
American statesman

✮

Often genius is just another way of spelling perseverance.

Anonymous

✮

True genius resides in the capacity for evaluation of uncertain, hazardous and conflicting information.

Winston Churchill, 1874-1965
British statesman and Prime Minister

✮

Everyone is a genius at least once a year; a real genius has his original ideas closer together.

George Lichtenberg, 1742-1799
German physicist, satirist and writer

✮

The highest intellects, like the
tops of mountains, are the first to
reflect the dawn.

Lord Macaulay, 1800-1859
English historian, statesman, essayist and poet

★

Good sense travels on well-worn paths;
genius never.

Cesar Lombroso, 1836-1909
Italian founder of criminology

★

If people knew how hard I work to gain my
mastery, it would not seem so wonderful at all.

Michelangelo, 1475-1564
Italian painter and sculptor

★

Gifts

In all ranks of life the human heart yearns for the beautiful; and the beautiful things that God makes are his gift to all alike.

Harriet Beecher Stowe, 1811-1896
American author and social reformer

★

When you arise in the morning, think of what a precious privilege it is to be alive — to breathe, to think, to enjoy, to love.

Marcus Aurelius, 121-180 AD
Roman emperor and philosopher

★

God's gifts put man's best dreams to shame.

Elizabeth Barrett Browning, 1806-1861
English poet

★

Giving

A bit of fragrance always clings to the hand
that gives you roses.

Chinese proverb

✫

Giving whether it be time, labour, affection,
advice, gifts, or whatever, is one of life's
greatest pleasures.

Rebecca Russell, b. 1905
American writer

✫

You find true joy and happiness in life when
you give and give and go on giving.

Eileen Caddy
Co-founder of the Findhorn Foundation, Scotland

✫

We make a living by what we get, but we make
a life by what we give.

Winston Churchill, 1874-1965
British statesman and Prime Minister

✫

It is well to give when asked, but it is better to give unasked, through understanding.

Kahlil Gibran, 1883-1931
Lebanese poet, artist and mystic

✯

It is more blessed to give than to receive.

Acts of the Apostles, 20:35

✯

Not what we give, but what we share,
For the gift without the giver is bare.

James Russell Lowell, 1819-1891
American poet and diplomat

✯

The love we give away is the only
love we keep.

Elbert Hubbard, 1856-1915
American writer

✯

If there be any truer measure of a man than by what he does, it must be by what he gives.

Robert South, 1634-1716
English Church of England theologian

✯

It is possible to give away and become richer. It is also possible to hold on too tightly and lose everything. Yes, the liberal man shall be rich. By watering others, he waters himself.

Proverbs 11:24, 25

★

A cheerful giver does not count the cost of what he gives. His heart is set on pleasing and cheering him to whom the gift is given.

Julian of Norwich
Revelations of Divine Love

★

The wise man does not lay up treasure. The more he gives to others, the more he has for his own.

Lao-Tze, c. 600 BC
Chinese philosopher and founder of Taoism

★

The heart of the giver makes the gift dear and precious.

Martin Luther, 1483-1546
German protestant reformer

★

He that gives should never remember; he that receives should never forget.

The Talmud

★

Generosity consists less of giving a great deal than in gifts well timed.

Jean de La Bruyere
French writer

★

The hand that gives, gathers.

English proverb

★

Goals

I knew I was going to be a comedian when I was about six. You get what you believe you'll get. You have to really want it and you'll get it.

Billy Connolly, b. 1942
Scottish comedian

★

No bird soars too high if he soars with his own wings.

William Blake, 1757-1827
English poet and artist

★

Far away there in the sunshine are my highest aspirations. I may not reach them but I can look up and see their beauty, believe in them and try to follow.

Louisa May Alcott, 1832-1888
American novelist

★

Awake, arise and stop not 'til the goal is reached.

Sai Baba
Indian spiritual leader

★

When goals go, meaning goes. When meaning goes, purpose goes. When purpose goes, life goes dead on our hands.

Carl Jung, 1875-1961
Swiss psychiatrist

★

Efforts and courage are not enough without purpose and direction.

John F. Kennedy, 1917-1963
President of the United States of America

★

The difference between a dream and a goal is a plan.

Anonymous

★

If you aspire to the highest place, it is no disgrace to stop at the second or even the third place.

Cicero, 106-43 BC
Roman orator, statesman and essayist

★

Aim at the sun, and you may not reach it; but your arrow will fly far higher than if you aimed at an object on a level with yourself.

Judy Hawes, b. 1913
American children's author

☆

Set your sights high, the higher the better.
Expect the most wonderful things to
    happen, not in the future but right now.
Realise that nothing is too good.
Allow absolutely nothing to hamper you or
    hold you up in any way.

Eileen Caddy
Co-founder of the Findhorn Foundation, Scotland

☆

Never look down to test the ground before taking your next step; only he who keeps his eye fixed on the far horizon will find his right road.

Dag Hammarskjold, 1905-1961
Swedish statesman and humanitarian

☆

Good Points

Think of someone you admire very much.
Write down a list of the things you admire
most about this person. You have just listed
your own good points!
Read them through carefully, and give yourself
credit for having these fine qualities.

Anonymous

★

A man generally has the good or ill qualities he
attributes to mankind.

William Shenstone, 1714-1763
English poet

★

Goodness

The greatest pleasure I know is to do a good action by stealth, and to have it found out by accident.

Charles Lamb, 1775-1834
British essayist

✫

Waste no more time arguing
what a good man should be. Be one.

Marcus Aurelius, 121-180 AD
Roman emperor and philosopher

✫

True goodness springs from a man's heart. All men are born good.

Confucius, c. 550-c. 478 BC
Chinese philosopher

✫

Good, the more communicated, the more abundant grows.

John Milton, 1608-1674
English poet

✫

It was only when I lay there on rotting prison straw that I sensed within myself the first stirrings of the good. Gradually it was disclosed to me that the line separating good and evil passes, not through states, not between classes, not between political parties either, but right through every human heart and through all human hearts.

Alexander Solzhenitsyn, b. 1918
Russian writer

★

For the good are always merry,
Save by an evil chance,
And the merry love the fiddle,
And the merry love to dance.

W. B. Yeats, 1865-1939
Irish poet, dramatist and writer

★

Good is itself, what ever comes.
It grows, and makes, and bravely
Persuades, beyond all tilt of wrong;
Stronger than anger, wiser than strategy,
Enough to subdue cities and men
If we believe it with a long courage
of truth.

Christopher Fry, b. 1909
English verse dramatist

★

Greatness

Great men are the guide-posts and landmarks
in the state.

Edmund Burke, 1729-1797
British statesman and philosopher

★

No great man lives in vain. The history of the
world is but the biography of great men.

Thomas Carlyle, 1795-1881
Scottish historian, essayist and critic

★

Keep away from people who try to belittle
your ambitions. Small people always do that,
but the really great make you feel that you,
too, can become great.

Mark Twain, 1835-1910
American humorist and writer

★

Greatness lies not only in being strong, but in
the right use of strength.

Henry Ward Beecher, 1813-1887
American clergyman

★

I studied the lives of great men and famous women, and I found that the men and women who got to the top were those who did the jobs they had in hand, with everything they had of energy and enthusiasm and hard work.

Harry S. Truman, 1884-1972
President of the United States of America

☆

The heights by great men reached
   and kept
Were not attained by sudden flight,
But they, while their companions slept,
Were toiling upward in the night.

Henry Wadsworth Longfellow, 1807-1882
American poet and writer

☆

The measure of a truly great man is the courtesy with which he treats lesser men.

Anonymous

☆

Great lives never go out. They go on.

Benjamin Harrison, 1833-1901
President of the United States of America

☆

Growth

Growth, in some curious way, I suspect, depends on being always in motion just a little bit, one way or another.

Norman Mailer, b. 1932
American writer

★

No one remains quite what he was when he recognises himself.

Thomas Mann, 1875-1955
German writer

★

You must learn day by day, year by year, to broaden your horizons. The more things you love, the more you are interested in, the more you enjoy, the more your are indignant about — the more you have left when anything happens.

Ethel Barrymore, 1879-1959
American actress

★

Women are always being tested . . . but ultimately, each of us has to define who we are individually and then do the very best job we can to grow into that.

Hillary Clinton
First Lady of the United States of America and lawyer

★

We learn from experiences, both good and bad, and with that knowledge comes change . . . and growth.

Anonymous

★

Growing up is, after all, only the understanding that one unique and incredible experience is what everyone shares.

Doris Lessing, b. 1919
British writer

★

Life is a lively process of becoming.

General Douglas MacArthur, 1880-1964
American military leader

★

Who is not satisfied with himself will grow.

Hebrew proverb

★

Guilt

There's no point in being crippled by guilt.
Simply acknowledge to yourself that you have
done something wrong, learn by it, and get on
with the rest of your life.

Anonymous

☆

Should we all confess our sins to one another
we would all laugh at one another for our lack
of originality.

Kahlil Gibran, 1883-1931
Lebanese poet, artist and mystic

☆

We all feel guilty about something. The
only positive thing about such feelings is that
they help one to change and to behave better
in the future.

Anonymous

☆

H

Habit

Dull habit can rob you of life's rich variety. Make a point of doing things differently sometimes. Meet some friends for breakfast, get up early and go for an early morning walk and, in summer, have a picnic dinner on the beach. Life will take on a new glow.

Anonymous

★

Cultivate only the habits that you are willing should master you.

Elbert Hubbard, 1856-1915
American writer

★

We must make automatic and habitual, as early as possible, as many useful actions as we can.

William James, 1842-1910
American psychologist and philosopher

★

Happiness

Happiness must be cultivated. It is like character. It is not a thing to be safely let alone for a moment, or it will run to weeds.

Elizabeth Stuart Phelps, 1815-1852
American novelist

★

I don't know what your destiny will be; but one thing I know: the only ones among you who will be really happy are those who will have sought and found how to serve.

Albert Schweitzer, 1875-1965
French medical missionary

★

The great essentials to happiness in this life are something to do, something to love and something to hope for.

Joseph Addison, 1672-1719
English essayist

★

Whether happiness may come or not,
one should try and prepare one's self to
do without it.

George Eliot (Mary Ann Evans) 1819-1880
English novelist

✭

Most people are about as happy as they make
up their minds to be.

Abraham Lincoln, 1809-1865
American statesman and President

✭

Cherish all your happy moments: they make a
fine cushion for old age.

Booth Tarkington, 1869-1946
American writer and dramatist

✭

Anything you're good at contributes
to happiness.

Bertrand Russell, 1872-1970
English philosopher, mathematician and writer

✭

If only we'd stop trying to be happy, we could have a pretty good time.

Edith Wharton, 1862-1937
American novelist

✯

Many persons have a wrong idea of what constitutes true happiness. It is not attained through self-gratification but through fidelity to a worthy cause.

Helen Keller, 1880-1968
Blind and deaf American writer and scholar

✯

If you want to understand the meaning of happiness, you must see it as a reward and not as a goal.

Antoine de Saint-Exupery, 1900-1944
French writer and aviator

✯

All who would win joy, must share it; happiness was born to be a twin.

Lord Byron, 1788-1824
English poet

✯

When we cannot find contentment in ourselves, it is useless to seek it elsewhere.

Duc de la Rochefoucauld, 1613-1680
French writer

★

Happiness arises in the first place from the enjoyment of one's self, and, in the next, from the friendship and conversations of a few select companions.

Joseph Addison, 1672-1719
English essayist

★

We have no more right to consume happiness without producing it than to consume wealth without producing it.

George Bernard Shaw, 1856-1950
Irish dramatist, writer and critic

★

There are eight requisites for contented
  living:
health enough to make work a pleasure,
wealth enough to support your needs,
strength to battle with difficulties and
  overcome them,
grace enough to confess your sins and
  forsake them,
patience enough to toil until some good is
  accomplished,
charity enough to see some good in your
  neighbour,
faith enough to make real the things of God,
hope enough to remove all anxious fear
  regarding the future.

Johann von Goethe, 1749-1832
German writer, dramatist and scientist

☆

Happiness is like coke — something you
get as a by-product in the process of making
something else.

Aldous Huxley, 1894-1964
British novelist

☆

The secret of happiness is not in doing what one likes, but in liking what one has to do.

J. M. Barrie, 1860-1937
Scottish writer and dramatist

★

Happiness is not best achieved by those who seek it directly.

Bertrand Russell, 1872-1970
British philosopher, mathematician and writer

★

It is neither wealth, nor splendour but tranquillity and occupation which give happiness.

Thomas Jefferson, 1743-1826
President of the United States of America

★

Knowledge of what is possible is the beginning of happiness.

George Santayana, 1863-1952
Spanish philosopher and writer

★

Hate

Hatred rarely does any harm to its object. It is the hater who suffers. His soul is warped and his life poisoned by dwelling on past injuries or projecting schemes of revenge. Rancour in the bosom is the foe of personal happiness.

Lord Beaverbrook, 1879-1964
Canadian-born British newspaper owner and writer

★

Hate is like acid. It can damage the vessel in which it is stored as well as destroy the object on which it is poured.

Ann Landers, b. 1918
American advice columnist

★

I have decided to stick with love. Hate is too great a burden to bear.

Martin Luther King, Jr, 1929-1968
American civil rights leader and minister

★

If you hate a person, you hate something in him that is part of yourself. What isn't part of ourselves doesn't disturb us.

Herman Hesse, 1877-1962
German novelist and poet

☆

Always remember that others may hate you but those who hate you don't win unless you hate them. And then you destroy yourself.

Richard M. Nixon, 1913-1994
President of the United States of America

☆

Rather perish than hate and fear, and twice rather die than make oneself hated and feared — this must some day become the highest maxim for every single commonwealth.

Friedrich Nietzsche, 1844-1900
German philosopher

☆

I shall never permit myself to sink so low as to hate any man.

Booker T. Washington, 1856-1915
American educator and writer

☆

Health

I am convinced digestion is the great secret of life.

Sydney Smith, 1771-1845
English clergyman, essayist and wit

★

The Mind is the Key to Health and Happiness.

Sai Baba
Indian spiritual master

★

Cheerfulness is the best promoter of health and is as friendly to the mind as to the body.

Joseph Addison, 1672-1719
English essayist

★

O health! health is the blessing of the rich! the riches of the poor! who can buy thee at too dear a rate, since there is no enjoying this world without thee?

Ben Jonson, 1573-1637
English dramatist and poet

★

One swears by wholemeal bread, one by
sour milk; vegetarianism is the only road to
salvation of some, others insist not only on
vegetables alone, but on eating those raw . . .
The scientific truth may be put quite briefly:
eat moderately, having an ordinary
mixed diet, and don't worry.

Robert Hutchison, 1871-1960
British medical writer

☆

The preservation of health is a duty.
Few seem conscious that there is such
a thing as physical morality.

Herbert Spencer, 1820-1903
English philosopher and journalist

☆

Health is Wealth.
Look after it.

Sai Baba
Indian spiritual master

☆

Heart

If a good face is a letter of recommendation, a good heart is a letter of credit.

Edward Bulwer-Lytton, 1803-1873
English novelist, dramatist and politician

★

The heart's affections are divided like the branches of the cedar tree; if the tree loses one strong branch, it will suffer but it does not die. It will pour all its vitality into the next branch so that it will grow and fill the empty space.

Kahlil Gibran, 1883-1931
Lebanese poet, artist and mystic

★

There is no better exercise for the heart than reaching down and lifting people up.

Anonymous

★

To put the world in order we must first put
the nation in order;

to put the nation in order, we must first put
the family in order;

to put the family in order, we must cultivate
our personal life;

and to cultivate our personal life, we must
set our hearts right.

Confucius, c. 550- c. 478 BC
Chinese philosopher

And now here is my secret, a very simple
secret; it is only with the heart that one
can see properly; what is essential is
invisible to the eye.

Antoine de Saint-Exupery, 1900-1944
French novelist and aviator

Heaven

My idea of heaven is eating foie gras to the
sound of trumpets.

Sydney Smith, 1771-1845
English clergyman, essayist and wit

★

Grant me paradise in this world; I'm not so
sure I'll reach it in the next.

Tintoretto, 1518-1594
Venetian painter

★

The loves that meet in Paradise shall
cast out fear,
And Paradise hath room for you and
me and all.

Christina Rossetti, 1830-1894
English poet

★

All we know
Of what they do above,
Is that they happy are, and that they love.

Edmund Waller, 1606-1687
English poet and politician

★

Helping

It is one of the most beautiful compensations of this life that no man can sincerely try to help another without helping himself.

Ralph Waldo Emerson, 1803-1882
American essayist, poet and philosopher

★

Doing nothing for others is the undoing of one's self. We must be purposely kind and generous or we miss the best part of life's existence. The heart that goes out of itself gets large and full of joy. This is the great secret of the inner life. We do ourselves most good by doing something for others.

Horace Mann, 1796-1859
American educationalist, writer and politician

★

If someone listens, or stretches out a hand, or whispers a word of encouragement, or attempts to understand a lonely person, extraordinary things begin to happen.

Loretta Girzatis, b. 1920
American educator and writer

★

Hands that help are holier than lips that pray.

Sai Baba
Indian spiritual master

✯

When you tell your trouble to your neighbour you present him with a part of your heart. If he possesses a great soul, he thanks you; if he possesses a small one, he belittles you.

Kahlil Gibran, 1883-1931
Lebanese poet, artist and mystic

✯

Do something for somebody every day for which you do not get paid.

Albert Schweitzer, 1875-1965
French medical missionary

✯

No man can live happily who regards himself alone, who turns everything to his own advantage. Thou must live for another, if thou wishest to live for thyself.

Seneca, c. 4 BC - 65 AD
Roman philosopher, dramatist, poet and statesman

✯

He who does not live in some degree for others, hardly lives for himself.

Michel de Montaigne, 1533-1592
French essayist

★

Only a life lived in the service of others is worth living.

Albert Einstein, 1879-1955
German-born American physicist

★

Home

He is happiest, be he king or peasant, who finds peace in his home.

Johann von Goethe, 1749-1832
German writer, dramatist and scientist

★

The ornament of a house is the friends who frequent it.

Ralph Waldo Emerson, 1803-1882
American essayist, poet and philosopher

★

The ideal of happiness has always taken
material form in the house, whether cottage
or castle; it stands for permanence and
separation from the world.

Simone de Beauvoir, 1908-1986
French novelist

★

Seek home for rest,
For home is best.

Thomas Tusser, 1524-1580
English farmer

★

If you want a golden rule that will fit
everybody, this is it. Have nothing in your
houses that you do not know to be useful
or believe to be beautiful.

William Morris, 1834-1896
English designer and craftsman

★

'Home' is any four walls that enclose
the right person.

Helen Rowland, 1875-1950
American writer

★

Mid pleasures and palaces we may roam,
Be it ever so humble, there's no place
like home.

J. H. Payne, 1791-1852
American dramatist, poet and actor

★

The strength of a nation is derived from the
integrity of its homes.

Confucius, c. 551- c. 478 BC
Chinese philosopher

★

Hope

The frailest hope is better than despair.

Maria Brooks, 1795-1845
American poet

★

Of all the forces that make for a better world,
none is so indispensable, none so powerful as
hope. Without hope man is only half alive.

Charles Sawyer, 1887-1979
Writer

★

We judge of man's wisdom by his hope.

Ralph Waldo Emerson, 1803-1882
American essayist, poet and philosopher

✬

Hope for the best, but prepare for the worst.

Proverb

✬

Hope! of all ills that men endure
The only cheap and universal cure.

Abraham Cowley, 1618-1667
English poet and dramatist

✬

He who has health has hope. And he who has
hope has everything.

Arabian proverb

✬

Humour

Imagination was given to man to compensate
for what he is not, and a sense of humour to
console him for what he is.

Anonymous

☆

A sense of humour is a sense of proportion.

Kahlil Gibran, 1883-1931
Lebanese poet, artist and mystic

☆

The best sense of humour belongs to the man
who can laugh at himself.

Anonymous

☆

Our five senses are incomplete without the
sixth — a sense of humour.

Anonymous

☆

I

Ideals & Idealism

What is the use of living if it not be to strive for noble causes and to make this muddled world a better place for those who will live in it after we are gone?

Winston Churchill, 1874-1965
British statesman and Prime Minister

★

The ideals that have lighted my way and, time after time, have given me new courage to face life cheerfully have been Kindness, Beauty and Truth.

Albert Einstein, 1879-1955
German-born American physicist

★

Each time a man stands up for an ideal, or acts to improve the lot of others, or strikes out against injustice, he sends forth a tiny ripple of hope . . . and crossing each other from a million different centres of energy and daring those ripples build a current that can sweep down the mightiest walls of oppression and resistance.

Robert F. Kennedy, 1925-1968
American lawyer and politician

☆

What do we live for, if it is not to make life less difficult for each other?

George Eliot (Mary Ann Evans), 1819-1880
English novelist

☆

An ideal is often but a flaming vision of reality.

Joseph Conrad, 1857-1924
Polish-born English writer

☆

Ideas

The ideas I stand for are not mine. I borrowed them from Socrates. I swiped them from Chesterfield. I stole them from Jesus. And I put them in a book. If you don't like their rules, whose would you use?

Dale Carnegie, 1888-1955
American writer and lecturer

★

Ideas shape the course of history.

John Maynard Keynes, 1883-1946
English economist

★

There's an element of truth in every idea that lasts long enough to be called corny.

Irving Berlin, 1888-1998
American composer

★

There is nothing in the world more powerful than an idea. No weapon can destroy it; no power can conquer it, except the power of another idea.

Anonymous

★

If you are possessed of an idea, you find it expressed everywhere, you even smell it.

Thomas Mann, 1875-1955
German writer

✩

A belief is not merely an idea the mind possesses, it is an idea that possesses the mind.

Robert Bolton
English film director

✩

Imagination

Knowledge is limited. Imagination encircles the whole world.

Albert Einstein, 1879-1955
German-born American physicist

✩

Imagination is the beginning of creation. You imagine what you desire, you will what you imagine and at last you create what you will.

George Bernard Shaw, 1856-1950
Irish dramatist, writer and critic

✩

Imagination finds a road to the realm of the gods, and there man can glimpse that which is to be after the soul's liberation from the world of substance.

Kahlil Gibran, 1883-1931
Lebanese poet, artist and mystic

★

When I examine myself and my methods of thought, I come to the conclusion that the gift of fantasy has meant more to me than my talent for absorbing positive knowledge.

Albert Einstein, 1879-1955
German-born American physicist

★

Imagination is the eye of the soul.

Joseph Joubert, 1754-1824
French writer and moralist

★

Imperfection

All things are literally better, lovelier and more beloved for the imperfections which have been divinely appointed, that the law of human life may be Effort, and the law of human judgement — Mercy.

John Ruskin, 1819-1900
English author and art critic

✬

Independence

The greatest thing in the world is to know how to be self-sufficient.

Michel de Montaigne, 1533-1592
French essayist

✬

Individuality & Conformity

Every individual human being born on this
earth has the capacity to become a unique and
special person, unlike any who has ever existed
before or will ever exist again.

Elisabeth Kübler-Ross, b. 1926
American psychiatrist and writer

✦

Never be afraid to tread the path alone.
Know which is your path and follow it
wherever it may lead you; do not feel you
have to follow in someone else's footsteps.

Eileen Caddy
Co-founder of the Findhorn Foundation, Scotland

✦

Remember always that you have not only
the right to be an individual, you have an
obligation to be one. You cannot make any
useful contribution in life unless you do this.

Eleanor Roosevelt, 1884-1962
*First Lady of the United States of America,
writer and diplomat*

✦

When she stopped conforming to the conventional picture of femininity she finally began to enjoy being a woman.

Betty Friedan, b. 1921
American feminist writer

★

It is a blessed thing that in every age someone has had the individuality enough and the courage enough to stand by his own convictions.

Robert G. Ingersoll, 1833-1899
American lawyer, politician and writer

★

Don't surrender your individuality, which is your greatest agent of power, to the customs and conventionalities that have got their life from the great mass . . . Do you want to be a power in the world? Then be yourself.

Ralph Waldo Trine, 1866-1958
American poet and writer

★

The best things and best people rise out of their separateness; I'm against a homogenised society because I want the cream to rise.

Robert Frost, 1874-1963
American poet

★

Once conform, once do what other people do because they do it, and a lethargy steals over all the finer nerves and faculties of the soul. She becomes all outer show and inner emptiness: dull, callous and indifferent.

Virginia Woolf, 1882-1941
English novelist

★

I am still puzzled as to how far the individual counts; a lot, I fancy, if he pushes the right way.

T. E. Lawrence (Lawrence of Arabia) 1888-1935
British soldier, archaeologist and author

★

What's a man's first duty?
The answer's brief: to be himself.

Henrik Ibsen, 1828-1906
Norwegian writer, dramatist and poet

★

I didn't belong as a kid, and that always bothered me. If only I'd known that one day my differentness would be an asset, then my early life would have been much easier.

Bette Midler, b. 1945
American singer and comedian

★

What is right for one soul may not be right for another. It may mean having to stand on your own and do something strange in the eyes of others. But do not be daunted. Do whatever it is because you know within it is right for you.

Eileen Caddy
Co-founder of the Findhorn Foundation, Scotland

☆

At bottom every man knows well enough that he is a unique human being, only once on this earth: and by no extraordinary chance will such a marvellously picturesque piece of diversity in unity as he is, ever be put together a second time.

Friedrich Nietzsche, 1844-1900
German philosopher

☆

Insight

A moment's insight is sometimes worth a life's experience.

Oliver Wendell Holmes, 1809-1894
American writer and physician

★

Ideas often flit across our minds more complete than we could make them after much labour.

Duc de la Rochefoucauld, 1613-1680
French writer

★

In luminous flashes of sudden vision, we may discover jewels of wisdom hidden within ourselves. These flashes might come in words (a powerful phrase or poem) or in a glowing visual image or both. When these insights reveal themselves to us, it is as if a veil of mist simply dropped away. Universal and timeless truths seem to emerge from the shadows and stand bathed in the light of deep understanding.

Lucia Capacchione
American art therapist

★

Intuition

Because of their age-long training in human relations — for that is what feminine intuition really is — women have a special contribution to make to any group enterprise . . .

Margaret Mead, 1901-1978
American anthropologist and writer

★

Invention

To invent, you need a good imagination and a pile of junk.

Thomas Edison, 1847-1931
American inventor

★

Invention is a combination of brains and materials. The more brains you use, the less materials you need.

Charles F. Kettering, 1876-1958
American engineer and inventor

★

J

Joy

Great joy, especially after a sudden change of circumstances, is apt to be silent, and dwells rather in the heart than on the tongue.

Henry Fielding, 1707-1754
English dramatist and writer

★

To get the full value of joy you must have someone to divide it with.

Mark Twain, 1835-1910
American humorist and writer

★

Joy seems to me a step beyond happiness — happiness is a sort of atmosphere you can live in sometimes when you're lucky. Joy is a light that fills you with hope and faith and love.

Adela Rogers St John, 1894-1988
American journalist

★

'On with the dance! Let joy be unconfined' is my motto, whether there's any dance to dance or joy to unconfine.

Mark Twain, 1835-1910
American humorist and writer

★

Man only likes to count his troubles, but he does not count his joys.

Feodor Dostoevsky, 1821-1881
Russian writer

★

There is no such thing as the pursuit of happiness, there is only the discovery of joy.

Joyce Grenfell, 1910-1979
English actress and writer

★

Judgement

There is so much good in the worst of us,
And so much bad in the best of us,
That it hardly becomes any of us
To talk about the rest of us.

Anonymous

☆

Judge a tree from its fruit: not from the leaves.

Euripides, c. 484-406 BC
Greek dramatist and poet

☆

Why beholdest thou the mote that is in thy
brother's eye, but considerest not the beam
that is in thy own eye?

Matthew, 7:3

☆

No man can justly censure or condemn
another, because indeed no man truly
knows another.

Thomas Browne, 1605-1682
English physician and writer

☆

Justice

Live and let live is the rule of common justice.

Sir Roger L'Estrange, 1616-1704
French writer

★

Injustice anywhere is a threat to
justice everywhere.

Martin Luther King, Jr, 1929-1968
American civil rights leader and minister

★

The probability that we may fail in the struggle
ought not to deter us from the support of a
cause we believe to be just.

Abraham Lincoln, 1809-1865
American statesman and President

★

K

Kindness

Guard within yourself that treasure, kindness.
Know how to give without hesitation, how to
lose without regret, how to acquire without
meanness . . . Know how to replace in your
heart, by the happiness of those you love, the
happiness that may be wanting in yourself.

George Sand (Amandine Dupin) 1804-1876
French novelist

★

Perfect kindness acts without
thinking of kindness.

Lao-Tze, c. 600 BC
Chinese philosopher and founder of Taoism

★

Your own soul is nourished when you are kind;
it is destroyed when you are cruel.

Proverbs 11: 17

★

Wise sayings often fall on barren ground; but a kind word is never thrown away.

Arthur Helps, 1813-1875
English historian

☆

When you are kind to someone in trouble, you hope they'll remember and be kind to someone else. And it'll become like a wildfire.

Whoopi Goldberg, b. 1955
American actress

☆

So many gods, so many creeds,
So many paths that wind and wind
While just the art of being kind
Is all the sad world needs.

Ella Wheeler Wilcox, 1850-1919
American writer and poet

☆

A good deed is never lost. He who sows courtesy reaps friendship, and he who plants kindness gathers love.

Anonymous

☆

Knowledge

Knowledge is power itself.

Francis Bacon, 1561-1626
British philosopher, essayist and courtier

★

Knowledge is of two kinds. We know a subject ourselves, or we know where we can find information upon it.

Samuel Johnson, 1709-1784
English lexicographer, essayist and wit

★

Knowledge and understanding are life's faithful companions who will never be untrue to you. For knowledge is your crown, and understanding your staff; and when they are with you, you can possess no greater treasures.

Kahlil Gibran, 1883-1931
Lebanese poet, artist and mystic

★

If we value the pursuit of knowledge we must be free to follow wherever that search may lead us.

Adlai Stevenson, 1900-1965
American lawyer, statesman and
United Nations representative

★

A man's merit lies in his knowledge and deeds, not in his colour, faith, race or descent. For remember, my friend, the son of a shepherd who possesses knowledge is of greater worth to a nation than the heir to the throne, if he be ignorant. Knowledge is your true patent of nobility, no matter who your father or what your race may be.

Kahlil Gibran, 1883-1931
Lebanese poet, artist and mystic

★

The desire of knowledge, like the thirst of riches, increases ever with the acquisition of it.

Laurence Sterne, 1713-1768
British writer and clergyman

★

L

Laughter

Let there be more joy and laughter
in your living.

Eileen Caddy
Co-founder of the Findhorn Foundation, Scotland

☆

You grow up the day you have your first real
laugh at yourself.

Ethel Barrymore, 1879-1959
American actress

☆

Laughter gives us distance. It allows us
to step back from an event, deal with
it, and then move on.

Bob Newhart
American comedian

☆

Laughter is a property in man
essential to his reason.

Lewis Carroll, 1832-1898
English writer, mathematician and clergyman

★

It is a splendid habit to laugh inwardly at
yourself. It is the best way of regaining your
good humour and of finding God without
further anxiety.

Abbé de Tourville, 1842-1903
French priest

★

The two best physicians of them all —
Dr Laughter and Dr Sleep.

Gregory Dean, 1907-1979
British physician

★

Laughter can relieve tension, soothe the pain of
disappointment, and strengthen the spirit for
the formidable tasks that always lie ahead.

Dwight D. Eisenhower, 1890-1969
American statesman and President

★

If you like a man's laugh before you know anything of him, you may say with confidence that he is a good man.

Feodor Dostoevsky, 1821-1881
Russian writer

★

When you know how to laugh and when to look upon things as too absurd to take seriously, the other person is ashamed to carry through even if he was serious about it.

Eleanor Roosevelt, 1884-1962
First Lady of the United States of America, writer and diplomat

★

A man isn't really poor if he can still laugh.

Anonymous

★

Leadership

Setting an example is not the main means of influencing another, it is the only means.

Albert Einstein, 1879-1955
German-born American physicist

★

The question, 'Who ought to be boss?' is like asking 'Who ought to be the tenor in the quartet?' Obviously, the man who can sing tenor.

Henry Ford, 1863-1947
American car manufacturer

★

Treat people as if they were what they ought to be, and you help them become what they are capable of becoming.

Johann von Goethe, 1749-1832
German writer, dramatist and scientist

★

Our chief want is someone who will inspire us to be what we know we could be.

Ralph Waldo Emerson, 1803-1882
American essayist, poet and philosopher

★

Leisure

Work is not always required . . . there is such a thing as sacred idleness, the cultivation of which is now fearfully neglected.

George MacDonald, 1824-1905
British poet and novelist

★

It is impossible to enjoy idling thoroughly unless one has plenty of work to do.

Jerome K. Jerome, 1859-1927
English humorous writer and novelist

★

To be able to fill leisure intelligently is the last product of civilisation.

Bertrand Russell, 1872-1970
English philosopher, mathematician and writer

★

A perpetual holiday is a good working definition of hell.

George Bernard Shaw, 1856-1950
Irish dramatist, writer and critic

★

Life

As long as you live, keep learning how to live.

Seneca, c. 4 BC-65 AD
Roman dramatist, poet and statesman

★

Is it so small a thing
To have enjoy'd the sun,
To have liv'd light
In the spring,
To have lov'd, to have thought, to have done?

Matthew Arnold, 1822-1888
English poet, essayist and educationalist

★

I could not, at any age, be content to take my place in a corner by the fireside and simply look on. Life was meant to be lived. Curiosity must be kept alive. The fatal thing is the rejection. One must never, for whatever reason, turn his back on life.

Eleanor Roosevelt, 1884-1962
First Lady of the United States of America, writer and diplomat

★

Life is a single short sentence — but I want my life to read like a beautiful sentence, one that nobody wants to end.

Neil Diamond
American singer/songwriter

✯

Do not take life too seriously. You will never get out of it alive.

Elbert Hubbard, 1856-1915
American writer

✯

My feeling about life is a curious kind of triumphant sensation about seeing it bleak, knowing it so, and walking into it fearlessly because one has no choice.

Georgia O'Keefe, 1887-1986
American artist

✯

Try as much as possible to be wholly alive, with all your might, and when you laugh, laugh like hell, and when you get angry, get good and angry. Try to be alive because you will be dead soon enough.

William Saroyan, 1908-1981
American writer and dramatist

✯

There is no cure for birth and death, save to enjoy the interval.

George Santayana, 1863-1952
Spanish philosopher and writer

★

It's not how things turn out — it's the joy of doing it!

Barbra Streisand, b. 1942
American singer and actress

★

Let your life lightly dance on the edges of Time like dew on the tip of a leaf.

Rabindranath Tagore, 1861-1941
Indian poet and philosopher

★

Life is good only when it is magical and musical, a perfect timing and consent, and when we do not anatomise it. You must treat the days respectfully . . . You must hear the bird's song without attempting to render it into nouns and verbs.

Ralph Waldo Emerson, 1803-1882
American essayist, poet and philosopher

★

The love of life is necessary to the vigorous prosecution of any undertaking.

Samuel Johnson, 1709-1784
English lexicographer, essayist and wit

The purpose of life is to matter — to count, to stand for something, to have it make some difference that we lived at all.

Leo Rosten, b. 1908
Polish-born American writer and humorist

There are two things to aim for in life: first to get what you want; and, after that, to enjoy it. Only the wisest of mankind achieve the second.

Logan Pearsall Smith, 1865-1946
American-born British wit, writer and critic

Life is a traveller on a Holy journey.

Sai Baba
Indian spiritual master

The bread of life is love, the salt of love is work, the sweetness of life is poetry, and the water of life is faith.

Anna Jameson, 1794-1860
English writer

★

Life is no brief candle to me, it is a sort of splendid torch which I've got hold of for the moment and I want to make it burn as bright as possible before handing it on to a future generation.

George Bernard Shaw, 1856-1950
Irish dramatist, writer and critic

★

At the end of your life, you will never regret not having passed one more test, not winning one more verdict or not closing one more deal. You will regret time not spent with a husband, a friend, a child or parent.

Barbara Bush, b. 1925
First Lady of the United States of America

★

I have never given very deep thought to a philosophy of life, though I have a few ideas that I think are very useful to me:

Do whatever comes your way to do as well as you can.
Think as little as possible about yourself.
Think as much as possible about other people.
Dwell on things that are interesting.
Since you get more joy out of giving joy to others you should put a good deal of thought into the happiness that you are able to give.

Eleanor Roosevelt, 1884-1962
First Lady of the United States of America, writer and diplomat

★

The most fruitful of all the arts is the art of living well.

Cicero, 106-43 BC
Roman orator

★

Loneliness

Always remember that you are not the only one who has ever felt rejected, unloved and lonely at some time. Reach out and help someone else in trouble, and you could be amazed at the changes in yourself — and your life!

Anonymous

☆

If you want people to be glad to meet you, you must be glad to meet them — and show it.

Johann von Goethe, 1749-1832
German writer, dramatist and scientist

☆

Loneliness is a state of mind.

Anonymous

☆

Love

Great is the power of might and mind,
But only love can make us kind,
And all we are or hope to be
Is empty pride and vanity —
If love is not a part of all
The greatest man is very small.

Helen Steiner Rice, 1900-1981
American poet

✪

The story of love is not important —
what is important is that one is capable of love.
It is perhaps the only glimpse we are permitted
of eternity.

Helen Hayes, 1900-1993
American actress

✪

If we make our goal to live a life of
compassion and unconditional love, then the
world will indeed become a garden where all
kinds of flowers can bloom and grow.

Elisabeth Kübler-Ross, b. 1926
Swiss-born American psychiatrist and writer

✪

Love is patient, love is kind. It does not envy, it does not boast, it is not proud. It is not rude, it is not self-seeking, it is not easily angered, it keeps no records of wrongs . . .

1 Corinthians 13: 4-5

☆

Ego wants to get and forget,
Love want to give and forgive.

Sai Baba
Indian spiritual master

☆

Above all, love each other deeply, because love covers over a multitude of sins.

1 Peter 4:8

☆

There is a land of the living and a land of the dead, and the bridge is love.

Thornton Wilder, 1897-1975
American author and dramatist

☆

Love begins when a person feels another person's need to be as important as his own.

Anonymous

☆

Love makes all hard hearts gentle.

George Herbert, 1593-1633
English poet

☆

Love is the only force capable of transforming
an enemy into a friend.

Martin Luther King, Jr, 1929-1968
American civil rights leader and minister

☆

In our life there is a single colour, as on an
artist's palette, which provides the meaning of
life and art. It is the colour of love.

Marc Chagall, 1887-1985
French artist

☆

Immature love says: 'I love you
because I need you.'
Mature love says: 'I need you
because I love you.'

Erich Fromm, 1900-1980
American psychoanalyst

☆

One word frees us of all the weight and pain of life; that word is love.

Sophocles, 496-406 BC
Greek tragedian

★

All love is sweet,
Given or returned
Common as light is love,
And its familiar voice wearies not ever.

Percy Bysshe Shelley, 1792-1822
English poet

★

A loving heart is the truest wisdom.

Charles Dickens, 1812-1870
English writer

★

Love will teach us all things: but we must learn how to win love; it is got with difficulty: it is a possession dearly bought with much labour and a long time; for one must love not sometimes only, for a passing moment, but always. And let not men's sin dishearten thee: love a man even in his sin, for that love is a likeness of the divine love, and is the summit of love on earth.

Feodor Dostoevsky, 1821-1881
Russian novelist

★

Love is a fruit in season at all times, and within reach of every hand.

Mother Teresa of Calcutta, 1910-1997
Albanian-born missionary

★

To love another person is to help them love God.

Soren Kierkegaard, 1813-1855
Danish philosopher and theologian

★

Love comforteth like sunshine after rain.

William Shakespeare, 1564-1616
English playwright and poet

★

The root of the matter is a very simple and old-fashioned thing, a thing so simple that I am almost ashamed to mention it for fear of the derisive smile with which wise cynics will greet my words. The thing I mean — please forgive me for mentioning it — is love, or compassion. If you feel this, you have a motive for existence, a guide in action, a reason for courage, an imperative necessity for intellectual honesty.

Bertrand Russell, 1872-1970
English philosopher, mathematician and writer

★

Luck

The harder you work, the luckier you get.

Gary Player, b. 1935
South African golfer

★

Luck is being ready for the chance.

Anonymous

★

I never knew an early-rising, hard-working, prudent man, careful of his earnings, and strictly honest, who complained of bad luck.

Joseph Addison, 1672-1719
English essayist and politician

★

Luck is infatuated with the efficient.

Persian proverb

★

Good luck often has the odour of perspiration about it.

Anonymous

★

Shallow men believe in luck. Strong men believe in cause and effect.

Ralph Waldo Emerson, 1803-1882
American essayist, poet and philosopher

☆

Luck is good planning, carefully executed.

Anonymous

☆

Good luck is what a lazy man calls a hard-working man's success.

Anonymous

☆

M

Marriage

A marriage makes of two fractional lines a whole; it give to two purposeless lives a work, and doubles the strength of each to perform it; it gives to two questioning natures a reason for living and something to live for.

Mark Twain, 1835-1910
American humorist and writer

★

The most important things to do in this world are to get something to eat, something to drink and somebody to love you.

Brendan Behan, 1923-1964
Irish writer

★

Love one another, but make not a bond
of love;

Let it rather be a moving sea between the
shores of your souls.
Fill each other's cup but drink not from the
one cup.
Give one another of your bread but eat not
from the same loaf.
Sing and dance together and be joyous, but
let each one of you be alone.
Even as the strings of a lute are alone
though they quiver with the same music.

Kahlil Gibran, 1883-1931
Lebanese poet, artist and mystic

★

A good marriage is like Dr Who's Tardis, small
and banal from the outside but spacious and
interesting from within.

Katharine Whitehorn, b. 1938
English essayist and politician

★

Well, what is a relationship? It's about two people having tremendous weaknesses and vulnerabilities, like we all do, and one person being able to strengthen the other in their areas of vulnerability. And vice versa. You need each other. You complete each other, passion and romance aside.

Jane Fonda, b. 1937
American actor and political activist

★

Love thy wife as thyself; honour her more than thyself. He who lives unmarried lives without joy . . . The children of a man who marries for money will prove a curse to him. All the blessings of a household come through the wife, therefore should her husband honour her.

The Talmud

★

Partnership, not dependence, is the real romance in marriage.

Muriel Fox, b. 1928
American business executive

★

She who dwells with me,
Whom I loved with such communion,
That no place on earth
Can ever be a solitude to me.

William Blake, 1710-1850
English poet

★

Men and women are made to love each other.
It's only by loving each other that they can
achieve anything.

Christina Stead, 1902-1983
Australian novelist

★

Let not the marriage of true minds
Admit impediments. Love is not love
Which alters when it alterations finds,
Or bends with the remover to remove.

William Shakespeare, 1564-1616
English dramatist and poet

★

How do I love thee? Let me count the ways.
I love thee to the depth and breadth and
height my soul can reach.

Elizabeth Barrett Browning, 1806-1861
English poet

★

Mind

The mind is an iceberg — it floats with only one-seventh of its bulk above water.

Sigmund Freud, 1856-1939
Austrian founder of psychoanalysis

The true, strong and sound mind is the mind that can embrace equally great things and small.

Samuel Johnson, 1709-1784
English lexicographer, essayist and wit

The mind ought sometimes to be amused, that it may the better return to thought and to itself.

Phaedrus, c. 15 BC-50 AD
Translator of Aesop's fables into Latin

Miracles

Miracles are instantaneous; they cannot be summoned but they come of themselves, usually at unlikely moments and to those who least expect them.

Katherine A. Porter, 1890-1980
American author

☆

Miracles happen only to those who believe in them. Otherwise why does not the Virgin Mary appear to Lamaists, Mohammedans or Hindus, who have never heard of her?

Bernard Berenson, 1865-1959
American art critic

☆

There are two ways to live your life. One is as though nothing is a miracle. The other is as though everything is a miracle.

Albert Einstein, 1879-1955
German-born American physicist

☆

Mistakes

You know, by the time you've reached my age, you've made plenty of mistakes if you've lived your life properly.

Ronald Reagan, b. 1911
President of the United States of America

✯

Anyone who has never made a mistake has never tried anything new.

Albert Einstein, 1879-1955
German-born American physicist

✯

Nobody makes a greater mistake than he who does nothing because he could do so litttle.

Edmund Burke, 1729-1797
British politician

✯

Even a mistake may turn out to be the one thing necessary to a worthwhile achievement.

Henry Ford, 1863-1947
American car manufacturer

✯

Morality

What is moral is what you feel good after, and what is immoral is what you feel bad after.

Ernest Hemingway, 1899-1964
American novelist

★

If your morals make you dreary, depend upon it, they are wrong.

Robert Louis Stevenson, 1850-1894
Scottish writer

★

Music

Music produces a kind of pleasure which human nature cannot do without.

Confucius, c. 550-c. 478BC
Chinese philosopher

★

Music has charms to soothe a savage breast.

William Congreve, 1670-1729
British dramatist

★

After silence, that which comes closer to
expressing the inexpressible is music.

Aldous Huxley, 1894-1963
English writer

★

Music religious hearts inspires;
It wakes the soul, and lifts it high,
And wings it with sublime desires,
And fits it to bespeak the Deity.

Joseph Addison, 1672-1719
English essayist

★

Mozart's music gives us permission to live.

John Updike, b. 1932
American novelist and poet

★

N

Nature

Come forth into the light of things,
Let Nature be your teacher.

William Wordsworth, 1770-1850
British poet

✯

After you have exhausted what there is in
business, politics, conviviality, and so on —
have found that none of these finally satisfy,
or permanently wear — what remains?
Nature remains.

Walt Whitman, 1819-1892
American poet

✯

Nature never did betray
The heart that loved her.

William Wordsworth, 1770-1850
British poet

✯

Tune your ear
To all the wordless music of the stars
And to the voice of nature, and your heart
Shall turn to truth and goodness as the plant
Turns to the sun . . .

Ralph Waldo Trine, 1866- 1958
American poet and writer

Love all God's creation, both the whole and
every grain of sand. Love every leaf, every ray
of light. Love the animals, love the plants, love
each separate thing. If thou love each thing
thou wilt perceive the mystery of God in all;
and when once thou perceive this, thou wilt
thenceforth grow every day to a fuller
understanding of it: until thou come at last to
love the whole world with a love that will then
be all-embracing and universal.

Feodor Dostoevsky, 1821-1881
Russian novelist

There is a pleasure in the pathless woods,
There is a rapture on the lonely shore,
There is society, where none intrudes,
By the deep Sea, and music in its roar:
I love not Man the less, but Nature more.

Lord Byron, 1788-1824
English poet

☆

To see a world in a Grain of Sand,
And a Heaven in a Wild Flower,
Hold Infinity in the palm of your hand,
And Eternity in an hour.

William Blake, 1757-1827
English poet and artist

☆

Those undescribed, ambrosial mornings when a
thousand birds were heard gently twittering
and ushering in the light, like the argument to
a new canto of an epic and heroic poem. The
serenity, the infinite promise of such a morning
...Then there was something divine and
immortal in our life.

Henry David Thoreau, 1817-1862
American essayist, poet and mystic

☆

Pity the eye that sees no more in the sun than a stove to keep it warm and a torch to light its way between the home and business office. That is a blind eye, even if capable of seeing a fly a mile away.

Kahlil Gibran, 1883-1931
Lebanese poet, artist and mystic

★

All through my life, the new sights of Nature made me rejoice like a child.

Marie Curie, 1867-1934
Polish-born chemist

★

Every morning was a cheerful invitation to make my life of equal simplicity, and I may say innocence, with Nature herself.

Henry David Thoreau, 1817-1862
American essayist, poet and mystic

★

O

Obstacles

Obstacles are those frightful things you see
when you take your eyes off your goal.

Henry Ford, 1863-1947
American car manufacturer

☆

Opportunity

All of us do not have equal talent, but all of us
should have an equal opportunity to develop
our talents.

John F. Kennedy, 1917-1963
President of the United States of America

☆

There is no security on this earth; there is only
opportunity.

General Douglas MacArthur, 1880-1964
American military leader

☆

God helps those that help themselves.

Benjamin Franklin, 1706-1790
American statesman and scientist

★

Grab a chance and you won't be sorry for a might-have-been.

Arthur Ransome, 1844-1967
British novelist

★

There is a tide in the affairs of men
Which, taken at the flood, leads on to
  fortune;
Omitted, all the voyage of their life
Is bound in shallows and in miseries.
On such a full sea are we now afloat,
And we must take the current when it
  serves,
Or lose our ventures.

William Shakespeare, 1564-1616
English poet and playwright

★

When one door closes, another opens; but often we look so long at the closed door that we do not see the one that has opened.

Anonymous

★

Next to knowing when to seize an opportunity, the most important thing in life is to know when to forgo an advantage.

Benjamin Disraeli, 1804-1881
British Prime Minister and writer

✦

Great opportunities come to men who make the most of small ones.

Anonymous

✦

Optimism

I am an optimist. It does not seem too much use being anything else.

Winston Churchill, 1874-1965
British statesman, Prime Minister and writer

✦

One of the things I learned the hard way was that it doesn't pay to get discouraged. Keeping busy and making optimism a way of life can restore your faith in yourself.

Lucille Ball, 1911-1989
American actress

✦

It's easy to become disheartened by the constant stream of tragedy and violence that is beamed into our living rooms, but never lose sight of the fact that many dedicated individuals and organisations are working constantly to ameliorate suffering. So next time it all seems too much to bear, focus on all the good being done by these good people.

Anonymous

★

All things are possible until they are proved impossible — even the impossible may only be so, as of now.

Pearl S. Buck, 1892-1972
American writer and missionary

★

Make the most of the best and the least of the worst.

Robert Louis Stevenson, 1850-1894
Scottish writer and poet

★

There is not enough darkness in the whole world to extinguish the light of one small candle.

Spanish proverb

★

I am an optimist, unrepentant and militant.
After all, in order not to be a fool an optimist
must know how sad a place the world
can be. It is only the pessimist who finds
this out anew every day.

Peter Ustinov b. 1921
English writer, actor and dramatist

★

A positive thinker does not refuse to *recognise*
the negative, he refuses to *dwell* on it. Positive
thinking is a form of thought which habitually
looks for the best results from the worst
conditions. It is possible to look for something
to build on; it is possible to expect the best for
yourself even though things look bad. And the
remarkable fact is that when you seek good,
you are very likely to find it.

Norman Vincent Peale, 1898-1993
American writer and minister

★

The optimist is wrong as often as is the
pessimist. But he has a lot more fun.

Anonymous

★

Inside my head I construct an airtight box. I keep inside it what I want to think about and everything else stays beyond the walls. . . Inside is love and friends and optimism. Outside is negativity, can't do-ism, any criticism of me and mine. Most of the time the box is as strong as steel.

Virginia Kelley
Mother of President Clinton

★

However much I am at the mercy of the world, I never let myself get lost by brooding over its misery. I hold firmly to the thought that each one of us can do a little to bring some portion of that misery to an end.

Albert Schweitzer, 1875-1965
French medical missionary

★

'Tis easy enough to be pleasant,
When life flows along like a song;
But the man worthwhile is the one
    who will smile
When everything goes dead wrong.

Ella Wheeler Wilcox, 1850-1919
American writer and poet

★

Two men look out between the same bars:
One sees mud, and one the stars.

Frederick Langbridge, 1849-1923
Irish religious writer

☆

A good business manager hires optimists for
the sales department and pessimists for the
accounts department.

Anonymous

☆

The world is changing and it is my optimistic
belief that gradually, patchily, maybe with one
step back for every two steps forward, it is
changing for the better.

Pamela Bone
Australian journalist

☆

Originality

Every human being is intended to have a character of his own; to be what no others are, and to do what no other can do.

William Ellery Channing, 1780-1842
American clergyman

✫

The merit of originality is not novelty; it is sincerity. The believing man is the original man; whatsoever he believes, he believes it for himself, not for another.

Thomas Carlyle, 1795-1881
Scottish historian, essayist and critic

✫

Originality exists in every individual because each of us differs from the others. We are all primary numbers divisible only by ourselves.

Jean Guitton
French writer

✫

P

Parting

When you part from your friend, you grieve
not; for that which you love most in him may
be clearer in his absence, as the mountain to
the climber is clearer from the plain.

Kahlil Gibran, 1883-1931
Lebanese poet, artist and mystic

☆

Adieu, adieu, kind friends, adieu, adieu, adieu,
I can no longer stay with you, stay with you.
I'll hang my harp on a weeping willow-tree,
And may the world go well with thee.

Unknown

☆

Peace

The world will never have lasting peace so long as men reserve for war the finest human qualities. Peace, no less than war, requires idealism and self-sacrifice and a righteous and dynamic faith.

John Foster Dulles, 1888-1959
American Secretary of State

✪

I am a man of peace. I believe in peace. But I do not want peace at any price. I do not want the peace that you find in stone; I do not want the peace that you find in the grave; but I do want the peace which you find embedded in the human breast, which is exposed to the arrows of the world, but which is protected from all harm by the power of Almighty God.

Gandhi, 1869-1948
Indian political leader

✪

576

Peace is a daily, a weekly, a monthly process, gradually changing opinions, slowly eroding old barriers, quietly building new structures. And however undramatic the pursuit of peace, the pursuit must go on.

John F. Kennedy, 1917-1963
President of the United States of America

✰

The peace of God, the peace of men,
Be upon each window, each door,
Upon each hole that lets in light,
Upon the four corners of my house,
Upon the four corners of my bed.

Gaelic blessing

✰

Peace is not an absence of war, it is a virtue, a state of mind, a disposition for benevolence, confidence, justice.

Benedict Spinoza, 1632-1677
Dutch philosopher

✰

Perseverance

When you get into a tight place and everything goes against you, till it seems as though you could not hang on a minute longer, never give up then, for that is just the place and time that the tide will turn.

Harriet Beecher Stowe, 1811- 1896
American author and social reformer

★

When I was a young man, I observed that nine out of ten things I did were failures. I didn't want to be a failure, so I did ten times more work.

George Bernard Shaw, 1856-1950
Irish dramatist, writer and critic

★

Winners never quit — and quitters never win.

Anonymous

★

By perseverance the snail reached the ark.

Charles Haddon Spurgeon, 1834-1892
British Baptist preacher

★

I'm extraordinarily patient, provided I get my own way in the end.

Margaret Thatcher, b. 1925
British Prime Minister

★

We haven't failed. We now know a thousand things that won't work, so we're that much closer to finding what will.

Thomas Edison, 1847-1931
American inventor

★

Never give in! Never give in! Never, never never — in nothing great or small, large or petty — never give in except to convictions of honour and good sense.

Winston Churhill, 1874-1965
British statesman and Prime Minister

★

Great works are performed not by strength but by perseverance.

Samuel Johnson, 1709-1784
English lexicographer, essayist and wit

★

If at first you don't succeed,
Try, try again.

William Edward Hickson, 1803-1870
British educationalist

★

Too many people let others stand in their way
and don't go back for one more try.

Rosabeth Moss Kanter, b. 1943
American writer and educator

★

Austere perseverance, harsh and continuous,
may be employed by the smallest of us and
rarely fails its purpose, for its silent power
grows irresistibly greater with time.

Johann von Goethe, 1749-1832
German writer, dramatist and scientist

★

Pleasure

Pleasure is very seldom found where it is sought; our brightest blazes of gladness are commonly kindled by unexpected sparks.

Samuel Johnson, 1709-1784
English lexicographer, essayist and wit

☆

Give me books, fruit, French wine and fine weather and a little music out of doors, played by someone I don't know.

John Keats, 1795-1821
British poet

☆

A book of verses underneath the Bough,
A jug of Wine, a Loaf of Bread — and Thou
Beside me singing in the Wilderness;
O! Wilderness were Paradise enow!

Omar Khayyam, 1048-1131 AD
Persian poet

☆

Potential

If we did all the things we are capable of doing
we would truly astound ourselves.

Thomas Edison, 1847-1931
American inventor

★

Compared to what we ought to be we are
only half awake. We are making use of only a
small part of our physical and mental
resources. Stating the thing broadly, the human
individual thus lives far within his limits.
He possesses the power of various sorts which
he habitually fails to use.

William James, 1842-1910
American psychologist and philosopher

★

No matter what your level of ability, you have
more potential than you can ever develop in a
lifetime.

Anonymous

★

Power

The sole advantage of power is that you can do more good.

Seneca c. 4 BC-65 AD
Roman philosopher, dramatist, poet and statesman

★

No extraordinary power should be lodged in any one individual.

Thomas Paine, 1737-1809
English-born American revolutionary, philosopher and writer

★

I have never been able to conceive how any rational being could propose happiness to himself from the exercise of power over others.

Thomas Jefferson, 1743-1826
President of the United States of America

★

Praise

If you don't like what I do, tell me. If you like what I do, tell my boss.

Sign on department store counter

★

There is no such whetstone, to sharpen a good wit and encourage a will to learning, as is praise.

Roger Ascham, 1515-1568
English scholar and educationalist

★

It is a sure sign of mediocrity to be niggardly with praise.

Marquis de Vauvenargues, 1715-1747
French soldier and moralist

★

Praise is the best diet for us, after all.

Sydney Smith, 1771-1845
English clergyman, essayist and wit

★

Man lives more by affirmation than by bread.

Victor Hugo, 1802-1885
French poet and writer

☆

The advantage of doing one's praising for oneself is that one can lay it on so thick and exactly in the right places.

Samuel Butler, 1835-1902
English writer

☆

The test of any man's character is how he takes praise.

Anonymous

☆

Prayer

Teach us to delight in simple things,
And mirth that has no bitter springs;
Forgiveness free of evil done,
And love to all men 'neath the sun.

Rudyard Kipling, 1865-1936
Indian-born British writer and poet

★

Who rises from Prayer a better man,
his prayer is answered.

George Meredith, 1831-1891
English poet and statesman

★

Prayer is the song of the heart. It reaches the
ear of God even if it is mingled with the cry
and tumult of a thousand men.

Kahlil Gibran, 1883-1931
Lebanese poet, artist and mystic

★

Let me be a little kinder,
Let me be a little blinder
To the faults of those around me.

Edgar A. Guest, 1881-1959
English-born American journalist, poet and author

★

Prejudice

Prejudices, it is well known, are most difficult to eradicate from the heart whose soil has never been loosened or fertilised by education; they grow there, firm as weeds among rocks.

Charlotte Brontë, 1816-1855
British novelist

✯

It is never too late to give up your prejudices.

Henry David Thoreau, 1817-1862
American essayist, poet and mystic

✯

What white people have to do is to find out in their own hearts why it is necessary to have a nigger in the first place. I'm not a nigger, I am a man, but if you think I'm a nigger, it means you need to.

James Baldwin, 1924-1987
American writer, poet and civil rights activist

✯

Most prejudice is based upon fear of the unknown.

Anonymous

✯

Problems

If there was nothing wrong in the world, there wouldn't be anything for us to to do.

George Bernard Shaw, 1856-1950
Irish dramatist, writer and critic

★

Problems are a major part of life.
Don't whinge about why you always have problems. Rest assured, no matter what, throughout your life you will always have to deal with problems. So don't waste time. Get on with the solving. Take it from someone who has been there — the solving gets easier as you go along.

Sara Henderson, b. 1936
Australian outback station manager and writer

★

A problem well stated is a problem half solved.

Charles Franklin Kettering, 1876-1958
American engineer and inventor

★

It is in the whole process of meeting and solving problems that life has meaning. Problems are the cutting edge that distinguishes between success and failure. Problems call forth our courage and our wisdom; indeed, they create our courage and our wisdom. It is only because of problems that we grow mentally and spiritually. It is through the pain of confronting and resolving problems that we learn.

M. Scott Peck, b. 1936
American psychiatrist and writer

✩

I think these difficult times have helped me to understand better than before how infinitely rich and beautiful life is in every way and that so many things that one goes around worrying about are of no importance whatsoever.

Isak Dinesen (Karen Blixen) 1885-1962
Danish writer

✩

Those things that hurt, instruct.

Benjamin Franklin, 1706-1790
American statesman and scientist

✩

The marvellous richness of human experience would lose something of rewarding joy if there were no limitations to overcome. The hilltop hour would not be half so wonderful if there were no dark valleys to traverse.

Helen Keller, 1880-1968
Blind and deaf American writer and scholar

☆

Remember, without that uncomfortable bit of grit, the oyster would not produce those priceless pearls.

Anonymous

☆

When it is dark enough, you can see the stars.

Ralph Waldo Emerson, 1803-1882
American essayist, poet and philosopher

☆

R

Regret

I don't regret anything I've ever done, so long
as I enjoyed doing it at the time.

Katharine Hepburn, b. 1909
American actress

☆

Make it a rule of life never to regret and never
look back. We all live in suspense, from day to
day, from hour to hour; in other words, we are
the hero of our own story.

Mary McCarthy, 1912-1989
American author and critic

☆

Regret is an appalling waste of energy;
you can't build on it; it is good only for
wallowing in.

Katherine Mansfield, 1888-1923
New Zealand short story writer

☆

Be not like him who sits by his fireside and watches the fire go out, then blows vainly upon the dead ashes. Do not give up hope or yield to despair because of that which is past, for to bewail the irretrievable is the worst of human frailties.

Kahlil Gibran, 1883-1931
Lebanese poet, artist and mystic

★

I have no regrets. I wouldn't have lived my life the way I did if I was going to worry about what people were going to say.

Ingrid Bergman, 1915-1982
Swedish-born American actress

★

There's no point dwelling on what might or could have been. You just have to go forward.

Jack Nicholson, b. 1937
American actor

★

You can't have rosy views about the future if your mind is full of the blues about the past.

Anonymous

★

Relationships

You haven't learned life's lesson very well if you haven't noticed that you can give the tone or colour, or decide the reaction you want of people in advance. It's unbelievably simple.

If you want them to take an interest in you, take an interest in them first.

If you want to make them nervous, become nervous yourself.

If you want them to shout and raise their voices, raise yours and shout.

If you want them to strike you, strike first.

It's as simple as that. People will treat you as you treat them. It's no secret. Look about you. You can prove it with the next person you meet.

Winston Churchill, 1874-1965
British statesman and Prime Minister

★

The world is a looking glass, and gives back to every man the reflection of his own face.

William Makepeace Thackeray, 1811-1863
British writer

★

A man's feeling of good-will towards others is the strongest magnet for drawing good-will towards himself.

Lord Chesterfield, 1694-1773
English statesman

★

We can't choose our relatives or workmates. But if you find yourself forced to put up with the company of someone who really rubs you up the wrong way, try to find something about them that you like. Then focus on that quality. You'll feel better, and the other person may even respond to your more accepting attitude.

Anonymous

★

People is all everything is, all it has ever been, all it can ever be.

William Saroyan, 1908-1981
American writer and dramatist

★

Relaxation

Treat yourself to a massage, hire a favourite video, have a hot bath and an early night, or read a book in the sun — make a point of doing something really relaxing as often as you can. It will do you no end of good physically and mentally, and will re-charge your batteries so you can face up to life's everyday challenges.

Anonymous

✩

Religion

I love you, my brother, whoever you are — whether you worship in your church, kneel in your temple, or pray in your mosque. You and I are all children of one faith, for the diverse paths of religion are fingers of the loving hand of one Supreme Being, a hand extended to all, offering completeness of spirit to all, eager to receive all.

Kahlil Gibran, 1881-1931
Lebanese poet, artist and mystic

✩

One's religion is whatever one is most interested in.

J. M. Barrie, 1860-1937
Scottish writer and dramatist

☆

I am a deeply religious unbeliever.

Albert Einstein, 1879-1955
German-born American physicist

☆

It makes all the difference in the world to your life whether you arrive at a philosophy and a religion or not. It makes the difference between living in a world which is merely a constant changing mass of phenomena and living in a significant, ordered universe.

Mary Ellen Chase, 1887-1973
American educator and author

☆

In my religion there would be no exclusive doctrine; all would be love, poetry and doubt.

Cyril Connolly, 1903-1974
English writer, critic and literary editor

☆

Every religion is a Lamp that illumines
the Path of Truth.

Sai Baba
Indian spiritual master

✦

The cosmic religious experience is the
strongest and noblest driving force behind
scientific research.

Albert Einstein, 1879-1955
German-born American physicist

✦

Responsibility

The willingness to accept responsibilty for
one's own life is the source from which self-
respect springs.

Joan Didion, b. 1935
American writer and journalist

✦

None of us is responsible for all the things that
happen to us, but we are responsible for the
way we react to them.

Anonymous

✦

Restrictions

Every man takes the limits of his own vision
for the limits of the world.

Arthur Schopenhauer, 1788-1860
German philosopher

★

I think the very restrictions which were put
on woman, which made her emphasise the
personal world, caused something very good
to be born. Whereas men dealt in terms of
nations, in terms of statistics, abstract ideology,
woman, because her world was restricted to
the personal, was more human. Now that she
is beginning to step beyond her confines, I
hope she can bring to the world the sense of
personal value of human beings, some
empathy and some sympathy.

Anaïs Nin, 1909-1977
French writer

★

Right

We should always do right, because it will
gratify some people and astonish the rest.

Mark Twain, 1835-1910
American humorist and writer

★

Risk

Take calculated risks. This is quite different
from being rash.

George S. Patton, 1885-1945
American military leader

★

Being myself includes taking risks with myself,
taking risks on new behaviour, trying new ways
of 'being myself', so that I can see how it is I
want to be.

Hugh Prather, b. 1938
American writer

★

To gain that which is worth having, it may be necessary to lose everything.

Bernadette Devlin, b. 1947
Irish politician

☆

No man is worth his salt who is not ready at all times to risk his body, to risk his well-being, to risk his life in a great cause.

Theodore Roosevelt, 1858-1919
President of the United States of America

☆

Courageous risks are life-giving. They help you grow, make you brave and better than you think you are.

Joan L. Curcio
American educator

☆

S

Self-acceptance

I was raised to sense what someone wanted me to be and to be that kind of person. It took me a long time not to judge myself through someone else's eyes.

Sally Field, b. 1946
American actor

★

I was born a jackdaw; why should I be an owl?

Ogden Nash, 1902-1971
American humorous poet

★

There are big dogs and little dogs, but the little dogs should not be disheartened by the existence of the big dogs. All must bark, and bark with the voice God gave them.

Anton Chekhov, 1860-1904
Russian dramatist and short story writer

★

One has just to be oneself.
That's my basic message.
The moment you accept yourself as you are,
all burdens, all mountainous burdens,
simply disappear.
Then life is a sheer joy, a festival of lights.

Bhagwan Shree Rajneesh
Indian spiritual leader

✹

Self-confidence

I'm trying to be myself more and more. The more confidence you have in yourself, which I think only comes with experience and age, the more you realise this is you and life isn't long. So get on with it!

Kylie Minogue, b. 1968
Australian singer and actor

✹

The important thing is not what they think of me, it is what I think of them.

Queen Victoria, 1819-1901
British Monarch and Empress of India

✹

Self-discipline

Some people regard discipline as a chore. For me, it is a kind of order that sets me free to fly.

Julie Andrews, b. 1934
British singer and actress

★

People who are unable to motivate themselves must be content with mediocrity, no matter how impressive their other talents.

Andrew Carnegie, 1835-1919
Scottish/American industrialist and philanthropist

★

Self-improvement

I know of no more encouraging fact than the unquestioned ability of a man to elevate his life by conscious endeavour.

Henry David Thoreau, 1817-1862
American essayist, poet and mystic

★

There's only one corner of the universe you can be certain of improving, and that's your own self.

Aldous Huxley, 1894-1963
English writer

✸

Every man has to seek in his own way to make his own self more noble and to realise his own true worth.

Albert Schweitzer, 1875-1965
French medical missionary

✸

I tell you that as long as I can conceive something better than myself I cannot be easy unless I am striving to bring it into existence or clearing the way for it.

George Bernard Shaw, 1856-1950
Irish dramatist, writer and critic

✸

Self-knowledge

Your vision will become clear only when you can look into your heart. Who looks outside, dreams. Who looks inside, awakes.

Carl Jung, 1875-1961
Swiss psychiatrist

⭐

Your goal is to find out who you are.

A Course in Miracles

⭐

Reason is your light and your beacon of Truth. Reason is the source of Life. God has given you Knowledge, so that by its light you may not only worship him, but also see yourself in your weakness and strength.

Kahlil Gibran, 1883-1931
Lebanese poet, artist and mystic

⭐

Who in the world am I? Ah, that's the puzzle.

Lewis Carroll, 1832-1898
English mathematician and author

⭐

Resolve to be thyself; and know that he
Who finds himself, loses his misery.

Matthew Arnold, 1822-1888
British writer

★

To know oneself one should assert himself.

Albert Camus, 1913-1960
Algerian-born French writer

★

Self-respect

If you put a small value upon yourself you
can be sure that the world will not raise
your price.

Anonymous

★

Great God, I ask thee for no meaner pelf
Than that I may not disappoint myself.

Henry David Thoreau, 1817-1862
American essayist, poet and philosopher

★

To have the sense of one's own intrinsic worth, which constitutes self-respect, is potentially to have everything: the ability to discriminate, to love and to remain indifferent. To lack it is to be locked within oneself, paradoxically incapable of either love or indifference.

Joan Didion, b. 1935
American author and journalist

★

And above all things, never think that you're not good enough yourself. A man should never think that. My belief is that in life people will take you at your own reckoning.

Anthony Trollope, 1815-1882
British novelist

★

I have to live with myself, and so
I want to be fit for myself to know,
I want to be able as days go by,
Always to look myself straight in the eye.

Edgar A. Guest, 1881-1959
English-born American journalist, poet and author

★

Simplicity

Remember that very little is needed to
make a happy life.

Marcus Aurelius, 121-180 AD
Roman emperor and philosopher

★

A truly great man never puts away the
simplicity of a child.

Chinese proverb

★

The ability to simplify means to eliminate the
unnecessary so that the necessary may speak.

Hans Hofmann, 1880-1966
German-born American painter

★

Our life is frittered away by detail . . .
Simplify, simplify.

Henry David Thoreau, 1817-1862
American essayist, poet and mystic

★

Possessions, outward success, publicity, luxury — to me these have always been contemptible. I assume that a simple and unassuming manner of life is best for everyone, best for both the body and the mind.

Albert Einstein, 1879-1955
German-born physicist

★

Sisters

Sisters stand between one and life's circumstances.

Nancy Mitford, 1904-1973
English writer

★

Sisters, when they do get on, can be closer than anyone else; closer than parents who are apt to leave the stage halfway through the play, closer than husbands or lovers who never knew Act One. Friends can change and brothers marry. Sisters tend to stick around.

Jane Gardam, b. 1928
English novelist

★

I have lost such a treasure, such a sister, such a friend as never can have been surpassed. She was the sun of my life, the gilder of every pleasure, the soother of every sorrow. I had not a thought concealed from her; and it is as if I had lost a part of myself.

Cassandra Austen
From a letter written on the death of her sister, novelist Jane Austen, in 1817

★

For there is no friend like a sister
In calm and stormy weather;
To cheer one on the tedious way,
To fetch one if one goes astray,
To lift one if one totters down,
To strengthen while one stands.

Christina Rossetti, 1830-1894
English poet

★

Solitude

Loneliness is the poverty of self; solitude is the richness of self.

May Sarton, 1912-1995
American writer and poet

✭

I was never less alone than when by myself.

Edward Gibbon, 1737-1794
English historian and politician

✭

In solitude we give passionate attention to our lives, to our memories, to the details around us.

Virginia Woolf, 1882-1941
English novelist

✭

Arranging a bowl of flowers in the morning can give a sense of quiet in a crowded day — like writing a poem or saying a prayer. What matters is that one be for a time inwardly attentive.

Anne Morrow Lindbergh, b. 1906
American writer

✭

The best thinking has been done in solitude.
The worst has been done in turmoil.

Thomas Edison, 1847-1931
American inventor

★

The more powerful and original a mind, the
more it will incline to the religion of solitude.

Aldous Huxley, 1894-1963
English writer

★

Sorrow

The deeper the sorrow that carves into your
being, the more joy you can contain. Joy and
sorrow are inseparable.

Kahlil Gibran, 1883-1931
Lebanese poet, artist and mystic

★

Sorrows are our best educators. A man
can see further through a tear than through
a telescope.

Anonymous

★

Happiness is beneficial for the body, but it is grief that develops the powers of the mind.

Marcel Proust, 1871-1922
French writer

☆

Where there is sorrow there is holy ground.

Oscar Wilde, 1854-1900
Irish dramatist, novelist and wit

☆

The groundwork of life is sorrow. But that once established one can start to build. And until that is established one can build nothing: no life of any sort.

D. H. Lawrence, 1855-1930
British writer, poet and critic

☆

Have courage for the greatest sorrows of life and patience for the small ones, and when you have laboriously accomplished your daily tasks, go to sleep in peace. God is awake.

Victor Hugo, 1802-1885
French poet and writer

☆

Strength

If we are strong, our strength will
speak for itself.
If we are weak, words will be no help.

John F. Kennedy, 1917-1963
President of the United States of America

☆

Our strength lies, not alone in our proving
grounds and our stockpiles, but in our ideals,
our goals and their universal appeal to all men
who are struggling to breathe free.

Adlai Stevenson, 1900-1965
*American statesman, lawyer and United Nations
representative*

☆

Decision is one of the duties of strength.

H. G. Wells, 1866-1946
English writer

☆

Success

Success is all about the quiet accumulation
of small triumphs.

J. P. Donleavy, b. 1926
Irish-born American writer and dramatist

⭐

There are two kinds of success. One is the very
rare kind that comes to the man who has the
power to do what no one else has the power to
do. That is genius. But the average man who
wins what we call success is not a genius. He is
a man who has merely the ordinary qualities
that he shares with his fellows, but who has
developed those ordinary qualities to a more
than ordinary degree.

Theodore Roosevelt, 1858-1919
President of the United States of America

⭐

We are prone to judge success by the index of
our salaries or the size of our automobiles,
rather than by the quality of our service and
our relationship to humanity.

Martin Luther King, Jr, 1929-1968
American civil rights leader and minister

⭐

A minute's success pays the failure of years.

Robert Browning, 1812-1889
English poet

★

I hope I have convinced you — the only
thing that separates successful people from
the ones who aren't is the willingness to work
very, very hard.

Helen Gurley Brown, b. 1922
American publisher and author

★

Success is not about money and power. Real
success is about relationships. There's no point
in making $50 million a year if your teenager
thinks you're a jerk and you spend no time
with your wife.

Christopher Reeve, b. 1952
American screen actor

★

The secret of success is constance to purpose.

Benjamin Disraeli, 1804-1881
British Prime Minister and writer

★

Self-trust is the first secret of success.

Ralph Waldo Emerson, 1803-1882
American essayist, poet and philosopher

☆

Eighty percent of success is showing up.

Woody Allen, b. 1935
American film director, writer and comedian

☆

The difference between failure and success is doing a thing nearly right and doing a thing exactly right.

Anonymous

☆

My formula for success? Rise early, work late, strike oil.

John Paul Getty, 1892-1976
American oil magnate

☆

The men I have seen succeed have always been cheerful and hopeful, who went about their business with a smile on their faces, and took all the changes and chances to this mortal life like men.

Charles Kingsley, 1819-1875
English writer, poet and clergyman

✮

Success is a state of mind. If you want success, start thinking of yourself as a success.

Anonymous

✮

You must never conclude, even though everything goes wrong, that you cannot succeed. Even at the worst there is a way out, a hidden secret that can turn failure into success and despair into happiness. No situation is so dark that there is not a ray of light.

Norman Vincent Peale, 1898-1993
American writer and minister

✮

Half the things that people do not succeed in, are through the fear of making the attempt.

James Northcote, 1746-1831
English painter

✮

The secret of success is to do the common things uncommonly well.

John D. Rockefeller, 1839-1937
American oil magnate and philanthropist

⭐

To succeed in the world we must do all we can to appear successful.

Duc de La Rochefoucauld, 1613-1680
French writer

⭐

One only gets to the top rung on the ladder by steadily climbing up one at a time, and suddenly all sorts of powers, all sorts of abilities which you thought never belonged to you — suddenly become within your own possibility and you think, 'Well, I'll have a go, too.'

Margaret Thatcher, b. 1925
British Prime Minister

⭐

As is the case in all branches of the arts, success depends in a very large measure upon individual initiative and exertion, and cannot be achieved except by dint of hard work.

Anna Pavlova, 1881-1931
Russian ballet dancer

⭐

Do your work with your whole heart and you will succeed — there is so little competition.

Elbert Hubbard, 1856-1915
American writer

★

There are many paths to the top of the mountain, but the view is always the same.

Chinese proverb

★

It's Up To You!

If you think you're a winner you'll win.
If you dare to step out you'll succeed.
Believe in your heart, have a purpose to start.
Aim to help fellow man in his need.
Thoughts of faith must replace every doubt.
Words of courage and you cannot fail.
If you stumble and fall, rise and stand ten feet tall,
You determine the course that you sail.

Anonymous

★

Suffering

A man who fears suffering is already suffering
from what he fears.

Michel de Montaigne, 1533-1592
French essayist and moralist

★

Recognising the necessity for suffering I have
tried to make of it a virtue. If only to save
myself from bitterness, I have attempted to see
my personal ordeals as an opportunity to transform myself and heal the people involved in
the tragic situation which now obtains. I have
lived these past few years with the conviction
that unearned suffering is redemptive.

Martin Luther King, Jr, 1929-1968
American civil rights leader and minister

★

Although the world is very full of suffering, it
is also full of the overcoming of it.

Helen Keller, 1880-1968
Blind and deaf American writer and scholar

★

Never to suffer would have been never to have been blessed.

Edgar Allan Poe, 1809-1849
American poet and writer

☆

Strength is born in the deep silence of long-suffering hearts; not amid joy.

Felicia Hemans, 1793-1835
British poet

☆

Who will tell whether one happy moment of love, or the joy of breathing or walking on a bright morning and smelling the fresh air, is not worth all the suffering and effort which life implies?

Erich Fromm, 1900-1980
American psychoanalyst

☆

Sympathy

Sympathy is the golden key that unlocks the
hearts of others.

Anonymous

⭐

Pity may represent no more than the
impersonal concern which prompts the
mailing of a cheque, but true sympathy is
the personal concern which demands the
giving of one's soul.

Martin Luther King, Jr, 1929-1968
American civil rights leader and minister

⭐

Sympathy is thinking with your heart.

Anonymous

⭐

T

Tact

Silence is not always tact, and it is tact that is golden, not silence.

Samuel Butler, 1835-1902
English writer

☆

Tact is the ability to describe others as they see themselves.

Abraham Lincoln, 1809-1865
American statesman and President

☆

In the battle of existence, talent is the punch; tact is the clever footwork.

Wilson Mizner, 1876-1933
American writer, wit and dramatist

☆

Thought

Few people think more than two or three times a year. I have made an international reputation for myself by thinking once or twice a week.

George Bernard Shaw, 1856-1950
Irish dramatist, writer and critic

✪

Great thoughts come from the heart.

Marquis de Vauvenargues, 1715-1747
French soldier and writer

✪

As soon as man does not take his existence for granted, but beholds it as something unfathomably mysterious, thought begins.

Albert Schweitzer, 1875-1965
French medical missionary

✪

All that we are is the result of what we have thought; it is founded on our thoughts, it is made up of our thoughts. If a man speaks or acts with a pure thought, happiness follows him, like a shadow that never leaves him.

Buddha, 563-483 BC
Indian religious teacher and founder of Buddhism

✪

Thinking is the talking of the soul with itself.

Plato, c. 429-347 BC
Greek philosopher

★

It is not best that we should all think alike; it is difference of opinion which makes horse races.

Mark Twain, 1835-1910
American humorist and writer

★

Time

The moment passed is no longer; the future may never be; the present is all of which man is master.

Jean-Jacques Rousseau, 1712-1778
Swiss-born French philosopher and essayist

★

Oh, be swift to love! Make haste to be kind. Do not delay; the golden moments fly!

Henry Wadsworth Longfellow, 1807-1882
American poet and writer

★

A man who dares waste one hour of time has
not discovered the value of life.

Charles Darwin, 1809-1882
English naturalist

★

In reality, killing time
Is only the name for another
of the multifarious ways
By which time kills us.

Sir Osbert Sitwell, 1892-1969
English poet and writer

★

Enjoy the present hour,
Be thankful for the past,
And neither fear nor wish
Th' approaches of the last.

Abraham Cowley, 1618-1667
English poet and dramatist

★

Tolerance

All human beings are born free and equal
in dignity and rights.

Universal Declaration of Human Rights

✯

Understanding everything makes one
very tolerant.

Mme Anne de Staël, 1766-1817
Swiss-born French writer

✯

If you cannot mould yourself as you would
wish, how can you expect other people to be
entirely to your liking?

Thomas à Kempis, c. 1380-1471
German monk

✯

No man can justly censure or condemn
another, indeed no man truly knows another.

Sir Thomas Browne, 1605-1682
English physician and writer

✯

You have no idea of the tremendous release and deep peace that comes from meeting yourself and your brothers totally without judgement.

A Course in Miracles

★

We must respect the other fellow's religion, but only in the sense and to the extent that we respect his theory that his wife is beautiful and his children smart.

H. L Mencken, 1880-1956
American writer, critic and satirist

★

O God, help us not to despise or oppose what we do not understand.

William Penn, 1644-1718
English Quaker and founder of Pennsylvania

★

One ought to examine himself for a very long time before thinking of condemning others.

Molière, 1622-1673
French dramatist and actor

★

Travel

Travelling and freedom are perfect
partners and offer an opportunity to grow
in new dimensions.

Donna Goldfein, b. 1933
American writer

✫

Keep things on your trip in perspective, and
you'll be amazed at the perspective you gain on
things back home while you're away . . . One's
little world is put into perspective by the
bigger world out there.

Gail Rubin Bereny, b. 1942
American writer

✫

Give me the clear blue sky over my head, and
the green turf beneath my feet, a winding road
before me, and a three hours' march to dinner.

William Hazlitt, 1778-1830
British essayist

✫

The wise man travels to discover himself.

James Russell Lowell, 1819-1891
American poet and diplomat

☆

For my part, I travel not to go anywhere, but to go. I travel for travel's sake. The great affair is to move.

Robert Louis Stevenson, 1850-1894
Scottish writer and poet

☆

A traveller. I love his title. A traveller is to be reverenced as such. His profession is the best symbol of our life. Going from — toward; it is the history of every one of us.

Henry David Thoreau, 1817-1862
American essayist, poet and mystic

☆

One of the pleasantest things in the world is going on a journey; but I like to go by myself.

William Hazlitt, 1778-1830
British essayist

☆

Truth

Truth never damages a cause that is just.

Gandhi, 1869-1948
Indian political leader

★

The pursuit of truth shall set you free — even
if you never catch up with it.

Clarence Darrow, 1857-1938
American lawyer, writer and reformer

★

Half the misery in the world comes of want of
courage to speak and to hear the truth plainly,
and in a spirit of love.

Harriet Beecher Stowe, 1811-1896
American author and social reformer

★

Ethical axioms are found and tested not very
differently from the axioms of science. Truth is
what stands the test of experience.

Albert Einstein, 1879-1955
German-born American physicist

★

The best test of truth is the power of the thought to get itself accepted in the competition of the market.

Oliver Wendell Holmes, 1809-1894
American writer and physician

⭐

If you tell the truth you don't have to remember anything.

Mark Twain, 1835-1910
American humorist and writer

⭐

I never give them hell. I just tell the truth and they think it's hell.

Harry S. Truman, 1884-1972
American statesman and President

⭐

God offers to every mind its choice between truth and repose.

Ralph Waldo Emerson, 1803-1882
American essayist, poet and philosopher

⭐

There are no new truths, but only truths that have been recognised by those who have perceived them without noticing.

Mary McCarthy, 1912-1989
American writer

☆

It is the calling of great men, not so much to preach new truths, as to rescue from oblivion those old truths which it is our wisdom to remember and our weakness to forget.

Sydney Smith, 1771-1845
English essayist, clergyman and wit

☆

U

Understanding

Everything that I understand, I understand only
because I love.

Leo Tolstoy, 1828-1910
Russian writer

★

I have striven not to laugh at human actions,
not to weep at them, nor to hate them, but to
understand them.

Benedict Spinoza, 1632-1677
Dutch philosopher

★

Unity

United we stand, divided we fall.

English proverb

★

V

Victory

Victory — a matter of staying power.

Elbert Hubbard, 1856-1915
American writer

✩

Victory at all costs, victory in spite of terror,
victory no matter how long and hard the
road may be; for without victory there is
no survival.

Winston Churchill, 1874-1965
British statesman and Prime Minister

✩

In war there is no substitute for victory.

General Douglas MacArthur, 1880-1964
American military leader

✩

Virtue

A virtue to be serviceable must, like gold, be alloyed with some commoner but more durable metal.

Samuel Butler, 1835-1902
English writer

✯

Virtue is its own reward.

John Dryden, 1631-1700
English poet, satirist and dramatist

✯

No one gossips about other people's secret virtues.

Bertrand Russell, 1872-1970
English philosopher, mathematician and writer

✯

Virtue, perhaps, is nothing more than politeness of the soul.

Honoré de Balzac, 1799-1850
French writer

✯

Vocation

Each honest calling, each walk of life, has its own elite, its own aristocracy based upon excellence of performance.

James Bryant Conant
Writer

☆

Every calling is great when greatly pursued.

Oliver Wendell Holmes, 1809-1894
American writer and physician

☆

It is well for a man to respect his own vocation whatever it is and to think himself bound to uphold it and to claim for it the respect it deserves.

Charles Dickens, 1812-1870
English writer

☆

W

Walking

Walking is man's best medicine.

Hippocrates, c. 460-c. 377 BC
Greek physician

★

Walking not only strengthens the muscles and bones and is good for the heart and digestion, it also relaxes the mind and soothes the spirit. And it doesn't cost a thing. All you need is a pair of comfortable shoes (essential) and a dog (optional). So what are you waiting for? Take at least three long walks a week, and you'll soon be hooked.

Anonymous

★

Walking is the best possible exercise. Habituate yourself to walk very far.

Thomas Jefferson, 1743-1826
President of the United States of America

★

Wealth

Riches are for spending.

Francis Bacon, 1561-1626
British philosopher, essayist and courtier

✦

I've been rich and I've been poor;
rich is better.

Sophie Tucker, 1884-1966
American singer

✦

Few rich men own their own property. The
property owns them.

Robert G. Ingersoll, 1833-1899
American lawyer, orator and writer

✦

Increase of material comforts, it may be
generally laid down, does not in any way
whatsoever conduce to moral growth.

Gandhi, 1869-1948
Indian political leader

✦

Unto whomsoever much is given, of him shall
be much required.

St Luke 12:48

✫

Money can't buy happiness, but it
can buy freedom.

Anonymous

✫

Riches are chiefly good because they
give us time.

Charles Lamb, 1775-1834
English essayist

✫

Wealth may be an excellent thing, for it means
power, it means leisure, it means liberty.

James Russell Lowell, 1819-1891
American poet and diplomat

✫

One can never really be too thin or too rich.

Wallis Simpson, Duchess of Windsor, 1896-1986
American socialite and wife of the Duke of Windsor

✫

Riches do not consist in the possession of treasures but in the use of them.

Napoleon Bonaparte, 1769-1821
French emperor and general

Life's greatest riches have nothing to
do with money.

Anonymous

The day, water, sun, moon, night — I do not
have to purchase these things with money.

Titus Maccius Plautus, c. 254-184 BC
Roman dramatist

Wisdom

Wisdom is to live in the present, plan for the
future and profit from the past.

Anonymous

★

Wisdom is the right use of knowledge. To know
is not to be wise. Many men know a great deal,
and are all the greater fools for it. There is no
fool so great as the knowing fool. But to know
how to use knowledge is to have wisdom.

Charles Haddon Spurgeon, 1834-1892
British Baptist preacher

★

Blessed is the man who finds wisdom,
the man who gains understanding, for he
is more profitable than silver and yields
better returns than gold.

Proverbs 3:13-15

★

Keep me away from the wisdom which does not cry, the philosophy which does not laugh and the greatness which does not bow before children.

Kahlil Gibran, 1883-1931
Lebanese poet, artist and mystic

✯

By three methods may we learn wisdom: first, by reflection, which is noblest; second, by imitation, which is easiest; and third, by experience, which is the bitterest.

Confucius, c.550-478 BC
Chinese philosopher

✯

The growth of wisdom may be gauged exactly by the diminution of ill-temper.

Friedrich Nietzsche, 1844-1900
German philosopher

✯

The most manifest sign of wisdom is a continual cheerfulness; a state like that in the regions above the moon, always clear and calm.

Michel de Montaigne, 1533-1592
French essayist

✯

Wonder

For a man who cannot wonder is but a pair of spectacles behind which there are no eyes.

Thomas Carlyle, 1795-1881
Scottish historian, essayist and critic

★

If I had influence with the good fairy who is supposed to preside over the christening of all children, I should ask that her gift to each child in the world be a sense of wonder so indestructible that it would last throughout life.

Rachel Carson, 1907-1964
American writer and biologist

★

Tyger! Tyger! burning bright
In the forests of the night,
What immortal hand or eye
Could frame thy fearful symmetry?

William Blake, 1757-1827
English poet and artist

★

The world will never starve for want of wonders; but only for want of wonder.

G.K. Chesterton, 1874-1936
English writer, poet and critic

✩

It is a wholesome and necessary thing for us to turn again to the earth and in the contemplation of her beauties to know the sense of wonder and humility.

Rachel Carson, 1907-1964
American writer and biologist

✩

I am so absorbed in the wonder of earth and the life upon it that I cannot think of heaven and the angels. I have enough for this life.

Pearl S. Buck, 1892-1972
American writer and missionary

✩

Work

Thank God — every morning when you get
up — that you have something to do which
must be done, whether you like it or not. Being
forced to work, and forced to do your best,
will breed in you a hundred virtues which the
idle will never know.

Charles Kingsley, 1819-1875
English writer, poet and clergyman

★

Who said you should be happy? Do your work.

Colette, 1873-1954
French writer

★

Each morning sees some task begun,
Each evening sees its close.
Something attempted, something done,
Has earned a night's repose.

Henry Wadsworth Longfellow, 1807-1882
American poet and writer

★

Laziness may appear attractive, but work gives satisfaction.

Anne Frank, 1929-1945
Dutch schoolgirl diarist and victim of the Nazis

★

Work saves us from three great evils: boredom, vice and need.

Voltaire, 1694-1778
French writer, poet and philosopher

★

If you can't get the job you want, accept any work you can get and do your very best. You could be surprised where it leads.

Anonymous

★

What is the use of health, or of life, if not to do some work therewith?

Thomas Carlyle, 1795-1881
Scottish historian, essayist and critic

★

Work is much more fun than fun.

Noel Coward, 1899-1973
English dramatist, actor and composer

★

My grandfather once told me there were two kinds of people: those who do the work and those who take the credit. He told me to try to be in the first group — there was much less competition.

Indira Gandhi, 1917-1984
Prime Minister of India

✩

Hire yourself out to work that is beneath you rather than become dependent on others.

The Talmud

✩

I long to accomplish a great and noble task, but it is my chief duty to accomplish small tasks as if they were great tasks.

Helen Keller, 1850-1968
Blind, deaf American writer and scholar

✩

Career is too pompous a word. It was a job, and I have always felt privileged to be paid for what I love doing.

Barbara Stanwyck, 1907-1990
American screen actress

✩

There is no point in work unless it absorbs you like an absorbing game. It if doesn't absorb you, if it's never any fun, don't do it.

D. H. Lawrence, 1885-1930
British writer, poet and critic

★

My father taught me to work, but not to love it. I never did like to work, and I don't deny it. I'd rather read, tell stories, crack jokes, talk, laugh — anything but work.

Abraham Lincoln, 1809-1865
American statesman and President

★

Work is the grand cure of all the maladies and miseries that ever beset mankind.

Thomas Carlyle, 1795-1881
Scottish historian and essayist

★

Without work all life goes rotten.

Albert Camus, 1913-1960
Algerian-born French writer

★

No man needs sympathy because he has to work . . . Far and away the best prize that life offers is the chance to work hard at work worth doing.

Theodore Roosevelt, 1858-1919
President of the United States of America

★

Worry

What's the use of worrying?
It never was worthwhile,
So, pack up your troubles in your old kit-bag,
And smile, smile, smile.

George Asaf, 1880-1951
American songwriter

★

The reason why worry kills more people than work is that more people worry than work.

Robert Frost, 1874-1963
American poet

★

When I look back on all these worries I remember the story of the old man who said on his deathbed that he had had a lot of trouble in his life, most of which never happened.

Winston Churchill, 1874-1965
British statesman and Prime Minister

★

There are no troubles in my life except the troubles inseparable from being a spirit living in the flesh.

George Santayana, 1863-1952
Spanish philosopher and writer

★

Worth

A man passes for what he is worth. What he is engraves itself on his face in letters of light.

Ralph Waldo Emerson, 1803-1882
American essayist, poet and philosopher

★

Y

Yesterday, Today & Tomorrow

Today is yesterday's pupil.

Thomas Fuller, 1608-1661
English clergyman and writer

★

I've shut the door on yesterday
And thrown the key away —
Tomorrow has no fears for me,
Since I have found today.

Vivian Y. Laramore
American poet

★

Light tomorrow with today.

Elizabeth Barrett Browning, 1806-1861
English poet

★

Finish every day and be done with it. You have done what you could. Some blunders and absurdities no doubt crept in; forget them as soon as you can. Tomorrow is a new day; begin it well and serenely and with too high a spirit to be cumbered with your old nonsense. This day is all that is good and fair. It is too dear, with its hopes and invitations, to waste a moment on yesterdays.

Ralph Waldo Emerson, 1803-1882
American essayist, poet and philosopher

★

Yesterday is a cancelled cheque.
Tomorrow is a promissory note.
Today is ready cash. Use it!

Anonymous

★

Out of Eternity the new Day is born;
Into Eternity at night will return.

Thomas Carlyle, 1795-1851
Scottish historian, essayist and critic

★

Do not ask what tomorrow may bring, and count as profit every day that Fate allows.

Horace 65-8 BC
Roman poet

✪

Write in your heart that every day is the best day of the year.

Ralph Waldo Emerson, 1803-1882
American essayist, poet and philosopher

✪

Redeem thy misspent time that's past;
Live this day as if 'twere thy last.

Thomas Ken, 1637-1711
English bishop

✪

As yesterday is history and tomorrow may never come, I have resolved from this day on, I will do all the business I can honestly, have all the fun I can reasonably, do all the good I can do willingly, and save my digestion by thinking pleasantly.

Robert Louis Stevenson, 1850-1894
Scottish writer and poet

✪

Tomorrow is the most important thing in life. Comes into us at midnight very clean. It's perfect when it arrives and it puts itself in our hands. It hopes we've learned something from yesterday.

John Wayne, 1907-1979
American screen actor

★

The only limit to our realisation of tomorrow will be our doubts of today. Let us move forward with strong and active faith.

Franklin D. Roosevelt, 1882-1945
President of the United States of America

★

You

Start treating yourself as if you are the
most important asset you'll ever have.
After all, aren't you?

Anonymous

☆

Be yourself. Nobody is better qualified.

Anonymous

☆

Our problem is that we make the mistake of
comparing ourselves with other people.
You are not inferior or superior to any human
being . . . You do not determine your success by
comparing yourself to others, rather you
determine your success by comparing your
accomplishments to your capabilities. You are
'number one' when you do the best you can
with what you have, every day.

Zig Siglar
American motivational writer

☆

Youth

Youth is the time to go flashing from one end of the world to the other . . . to try the manners of different nations; to hear the chimes at midnight; to see the sunrise in town and country; to be converted at a revival; to circumnavigate metaphysics; write halting verses; run a mile to see a fire, and wait all day long in the theatre to applaud *Hernani*.

Robert Louis Stevenson, 1850-1894
Scottish writer and poet

✯

Youth is happy because it has the ability to see beauty. Anyone who keeps the ability to see beauty never grows old.

Franz Kafka, 1883-1924
Austrian novelist

✯

On with the dance! Let joy be unconfined;
No sleep till morn when Youth and Pleasure meet
To chase the glowing Hours with flying feet.

Lord Byron, 1788-1821
English poet

✯

In case you're worried about what's going to become of the younger generation, it's going to grow up and start worrying about the younger generation.

Anonymous

★

It takes a lifetime to become young.

Pablo Picasso, 1881-1973
Spanish artist

★

The real lost souls don't wear their hair long and play guitars. They have crew cuts, trained minds, sign on for research on biological warfare, and don't give their parents a moment's worry.

J. B. Priestley, 1894-1984
English writer and dramatist

★

Z

Zeal

Through zeal, knowledge is gained, through lack of zeal, knowledge is lost. Let a man who knows this double path of gain and loss thus place himself that knowledge may grow.

Buddha, 563-483 BC
Indian religious teacher and founder of Buddhism

Subject Index

Ability, 343
Achievement, 344
Action, 345
Adventurousness, 349
Adversity, 350
Advice, 351
Ageing, 354
Ambition, 362
Anger, 363
Animals, 364
Apology, 366
Attitude, 367
Authority, 369

Balance, 370
Beauty, 371
Beginning, 373
Belief, 374
Best, 375
Blessings, 376
Books, 377
Boredom, 382

Challenges, 383
Change, 384
Character, 387
Children & Parents, 389
Choice, 395
Civility, 396
Comforting Words, 398
Communication, 399
Compassion, 401
Conscience, 402
Contentment, 404

Conversation, 405
Courage, 407
Creativity, 412
Criticism, 415
Crying, 416
Curiosity, 417

Death, 419
Depression, 422
Difficulties, 423
Disappointment, 424
Doubt, 425
Dreams, 426

Education, 427
Effort, 430
Empowerment, 431
Encouragement, 433
Enjoyment, 435
Enthusiasm, 436
Epitaphs, 439
Error, 441
Excellence, 442
Excuses, 442
Experience, 443

Failure, 445
Faith, 447
Faults, 451
Fear, 452
Fools & Foolishness, 454
Forgiveness, 456
Freedom, 458
Friendship, 461

Gardens & Gardening, 472
Genius, 475
Gifts, 478
Giving, 479
Goals, 483
Goodness, 487
Greatness, 489
Growth, 491
Guilt, 493

Habit, 494
Happiness, 495
Hate, 501
Health, 503
Heart, 505
Heaven, 507
Helping, 508
Home, 510
Hope, 512
Humour, 514

Ideals & Idealism, 515
Ideas, 517
Imagination, 518
Imperfection, 520
Independence, 520
Individuality & Conformity,
521
Insight, 525
Intuition, 526
Invention, 526

Joy, 527
Judgement, 529
Justice, 530

Kindness, 531
Knowledge, 533

Laughter, 535
Leadership, 538
Leisure, 539
Life, 540
Loneliness, 546
Love, 547
Luck, 552

Marriage, 554
Mind, 558
Miracles, 559
Mistakes, 560
Morality, 561
Music, 561

Nature, 563

Obstacles, 567
Opportunity, 567
Optimism, 569
Originality, 574

Parting, 575
Peace, 576
Perseverance, 578
Pleasure, 581
Potential, 582
Power, 583
Praise, 584
Prayer, 586
Prejudice, 587
Problems, 588

Regret, 591
Relationships, 593
Relaxation, 595
Religion, 595
Responsibility, 597

Restrictions, 598
Right, 599
Risk, 599

Self-acceptance, 601
Self-confidence, 602
Self-discipline, 603
Self-improvement, 603
Self-knowledge, 605
Self-respect, 606
Simplicity, 608
Sisters, 609
Solitude, 611
Sorrow, 612
Strength, 614
Success, 615
Suffering, 621
Sympathy, 623

Tact, 624
Thought, 625
Time, 626
Tolerance, 628
Travel, 630
Truth, 632

Understanding, 635
Unity, 635

Victory, 636
Virtue, 637
Vocation, 638

Walking, 639
Wealth, 640
Wisdom, 643
Wonder, 645
Work, 647
Worry, 651
Worth, 652

Yesterday, Today &
   Tomorrow, 653
You, 657
Youth, 658

Zeal, 660

Write down your own Pocket Positives

Write down your own
Pocket Positives

Write down your own
Pocket Positives

Write down your own
Pocket Positives

Write down your own
Pocket Positives

Write down your own
Pocket Positives

Write down your own
Pocket Positives

Write down your own
Pocket Positives